W9-BGL-589

Don't Hire a Crook!

How to Avoid Common Hiring (and Firing) Mistakes

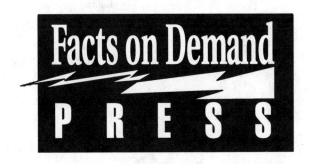

©1999 By Facts on Demand Press
4653 South Lakeshore Drive, Suite 3
Tempe, AZ 85282
(800) 929-3811
www.brbpub.com

Don't Hire a Crook!

How to Avoid Common Hiring (and Firing) Mistakes

©1999 By Facts on Demand Press
4653 South Lakeshore Drive, Suite 3
Tempe, AZ 85282
(800) 929-3811

ISBN 1-889150-09-6
Edited by: Michael Sankey & James R. Flowers Jr.
Cover Design by Robin Fox & Associates

Cataloging-in-Publication Data

025.5 DEM	DeMey, Dennis L. Don't hire a crook : how to avoid common hiring (and firing) mistakes / Dennis L. DeMey, James R. Flowers, Jr. – 1st ed.

   480 p. ; 7 x 10 in.

    Includes bibliographical references and index.

    Summary: Details proper hiring procedures, discusses employment issues, teaches pre-employment screening techniques and provides hiring policies and forms. Also includes tools and contact information for verifying applicant claims.

    ISBN 1-889150-09-6

    1. Employee selection. 2. Employee screening I. Flowers, Jr., James Robert, 1973- II. Title

HF5549.4.S38D46 1999   658.3'112
                                       QBI98-1549

This book is dedicated to Kathy and Adam
for their inspiration, support and tolerance.

Acknowledgments

A special note of thanks is due Michael Berzansky of Ocean Township, NJ, a State and Federal Labor Arbitrator and a long time friend whose invaluable assistance and encouragement aided in completion of this project.

I would not have been able to continue to develop techniques and realize their success if not for the many clients who took the time to listen, test my theories and implement the new techniques. Although I am unable to list all of them here, there is one organization that bears mention. The executives and management of the Jersey Shore Medical Center in Neptune, New Jersey have given me their most enthusiastic support. The progressive leadership of this facility fortified my confidence to endure the indifference of those who resist change.

Dennis L. DeMey

Contents

Forward..7

Before You Start...8

A Few Words About . . . Recruitment.......................................10
    Why Sound Recruitment is Important.................................. 10
    Before Looking at Candidates... 11
    Using Classified Ads... 11
    Using Community & Colleges Sources................................. 12
    How Does Microsoft Recruit Employees?............................ 13
    The Bottom Line 13

SECTION ONE: THE 3 STAGES OF THE HIRING PROCESS.............14

STAGE ONE: GATHERING INFORMATION 15

Documentation..16
    Establish Paperwork Policies & Stick to Them 17
    Require that All Forms Be Completed 18

The Basic Application Form..21
    The Purpose of the Application 21
        Include a Place for the Social Security Number.................. 21
        Importance of the Signature Line 22
        Ample Space vs. Additional Forms...................................... 23
        Subject Areas To Avoid 23

Other Critical Pre-Hiring Forms..25
    Applicant Waiver.. 25
        A closer look at the Applicant Waiver 26
    Employment Eligibility Verification (I-9)............................. 27
        A closer look at the I-9 Form 28
    Other Release Forms 29
        A closer look at the General Release Form 30
        Sample Specific Release: Criminal Release Form 31
    Applicant/Resume Evaluation Form.................................... 33
        A closer look at the Applicant/Resume Evaluation Form 33

STAGE TWO: VERIFYING THE INFORMATION 35

Pre-Employment Screening..37
    Develop a Company Screening Policy 38
    Components of a Pre-Employment Background Check 39
        1) Which Screening Options are Applicable 39
        2) What are the Geographic Boundaries of the Search?....... 40
        3) Who Will Screen?... 40

Before you go on —Beware of Fake Ids 42

How to Do a Proper Background Check 44
Document, Document, Document 44
Social Security Number Verification 46
What to Look for in the Results 47
Credit History Checks 51
The Bureaus 51
Consumer Reports vs. Credit Reports 52
Employment History Verification 53
Verifying Employment by Phone 53
A closer look at the Pre-Employment Check by Phone 55
Verifying Employment by Mail 56
Problems With Verifying Prior Employment 57
What About Personal References? 58
Criminal History Checks 59
How to Perform a Criminal History Search 61
A Few Comments on Negative Findings 63
Local Police Record Request 65
A closer look at the Local Police Record Request 66
Verification of Educational Background 67
Obtaining the Information Necessary 68
A closer look at the Request For Educational Verification ... 69
Confirmations of Professional Licenses & Registrations 70
The Privacy Question 71
What Information May Be Available 71
Licensing Agency Search Fees 72
Types of Licensing, Registration & Certification 72
Other Means of Licensing & Registration 73
Military Service Records Check 74
Request For Military Records form (Front) 75
Request For Military Records Form (Reverse) 76
Motor Vehicle Reports 77
How to Obtain a Driving Record 77
Sample Driving Record Abstract 78
What to Look for on the Record Abstract 80
Civil Record Searches 82
Civil Court Searches 82
Lien and Judgment Searches 83
What to Look For in Civil Records 84
Type of Case 85
Record Location 85

Testing Methods 86
Psychological Testing 86
Reid Psychological Systems 86
The Abbreviated Reid Report 87
Drug Testing 89
Is Drug Testing Important to Business Today? 89
Establish a Drug Testing Policy 90
When Drug Testing May Be Administered 91
Technologies Used for Drug Testing 91
The Other Side 92
Keep In Mind 92
Web Sites Related to Drugs & the Workplace 93

Other Methods of Testing 94
    Handwriting Analysis 94
    Skills & Aptitude Testing 94
    Lie Detector Tests 94
    Untested Applicant Results 94

The Interview **96**
Before The Interview 96
    Working in Groups 96
    Computer-Assisted Interviewing 97
    Computer-Assisted Employment Contracts 97
    A Guide to Proper Questioning 99
    What You Should Ask 102
    Give the Applicant Time to Ask Questions 103
    Questions After the Interview 103

STAGE THREE: MAKING AN OFFER OF EMPLOYMENT **105**

After The Decision **107**
Rejecting Candidates 108
    Rejection Letter Sample 108
    Before Hiring 109
Hiring a Candidate 109
Orientation 110
Probationary Employment 112
Job Descriptions 113
    Duties & Responsibilities 113
    Specifications & Requirements 115
    Ready-Made Job Descriptions 116

Proper Forms **117**
New Employee Record Chart 117
    A closer look at the New Employee Record Chart 117
Employee Data Sheet 118
    A closer look at the Employee Data Sheet 119
Induction Form 120
    A closer look at the Induction Form 120
Confidentiality & Non-Compete Agreements 121
    A closer look at the Confidentiality Agreement 122
    A closer look at the Non-Compete Agreement 123
New Hire Reporting Requirements 124
    New Hire Reporting Offices 125
    A closer look at the New Hire Reporting Form 126
Other Areas to Consider 127
    Hours of Employment 127
    Pay Rate 127
    Benefits 127
    Sick Leave 127
    Holidays 127
    Vacation 127
Retention Efforts 129
    A Few Words About Dress Codes 130

Summary of the Three Stages 131
        Stage 1 – Gathering Information 131
        Stage 2 – Pre-Employment Screening 132
        Stage 3 – Making an Offer of Employment 133
    Sample Company Hiring Policy 138

SECTION TWO: IF PROBLEMS DEVELOP 139

Unsatisfactory Performance 140
    Reasons for Unsatisfactory Performance 140
    Performance Reviews 142
        Designing a Performance Review Form 142
        Sample Performance Review Form 146
    What to Do If You Find a Discrepancy 148
        Corrective Interviews 148
        How to Conduct Corrective Interviews 149
        A Motivational Approach to Discipline 150
    How to Handle a Grievance 152

Termination 153
        Legitimate Reasons for Dismissal 153
        Employment At-Will 153
        Restrictions On The Right To Terminate At-Will 154
        Common Law Limitations 155
    Exit Interviews 156
        Exit Interview Report 157

SECTION THREE: ABIDING BY THE LAW 158

Legal Issues Explained 159
    Important Federal Discrimination Laws 159
    Other Major Statutes 169
        Industry Specific Requirements 171
        Advisories 172
    Legal Issues Affecting Employees 174
        Record Retention Requirements 174
        Inspections 174
        Employee Searches 174
        Hours of Employment 176
        AIDS 176
        Surveillance 177
    FCRA Explained 177
        Who is Affected? 177
        What, Exactly, is a Consumer Report? 177
        The Three FCRA Notices 178
        The Process 179

Workers' Compensation Issues 182
    Tips on Reducing Workers' Compensation Fraud 182
        Which Employees Commit Fraud the Most? 182
        Signs of Potential Fraud 183
        Proactive Suggestions 183
    Complying with Workers' Compensation Laws 184
        The Dilemma 184

History 185
Remedies for Consideration 187
    First Report 187
    Report Content 187
    Medical Providers 188
    Lost Time Claims 188
    Home Visits 189
    Anticipated Results 189
    Health Care Benefits 190

SECTION FOUR: TOOLS FOR VERIFICATION 192

Forms 193
    Applicant/Resume Evaluation 195
    Applicant Waiver 196
    Basic Application 197-199
    Confidentiality Agreement 200
    Criminal Background Check Release 201
    Employee Data Sheet 202
    Employee Eligibility Verification (I-9) 203
    Exit Interview 204-205
    General Release Form 206
    Induction Form 207
    Local Police Information Request 208
    Military Records Request 209-210
    New Employee Record Chart 211
    New Hire Reporting 212
    Non-Compete Agreement 213
    Performance Review 214-215
    Pre-Employment Check by Phone 216
    Rejection Letter Sample 217
    Request For Education Verification 218
    Request For Information 219
    Substance Abuse Screening Test Consent 220
    Workers' Compensation Release 221

Social Security Number Allocations 223

Using A Pre-Employment Screening Company 231
    Profiles of 134 Screening Companies 233

State Criminal Record Agencies 265

State Motor Vehicle Record Agencies 273

Accredited Educational Institutions 285

Credit Report Designations 453

State Public Record Restrictions Table 457

Recommended Resources 459

Forward

As this book was being prepared, other books on the subject were examined. It seems that the "old standard" of merely reading resumes and conducting interviews is the only method of hiring that is being written about in contemporary books. In fact, one of the foremost human resource trade associations has scheduled whole seminars on hiring that focus entirely on reading resumes and interviewing.

If you think this book is only about how to interview, think again. *Don't Hire a Crook!* examines the nuts and bolts of "how to hire" and more!

Before You Start . . .

Read This

It's no secret that good people are hard to find. Most businesses have long recognized that their success depends on the quality and competence of their employees. Of all the variables that contribute to the success and viability of a business, probably none is more important than the quality of the people involved. Thus, it is not surprising that companies are eager to attract, hire and retain a productive, satisfied and well-motivated staff.

Throughout the US, employers of all types and sizes are becoming increasingly frustrated with inadequate hiring processes. Furthermore, civil litigation based on wrongful discharge claims and negligent hiring practices has risen sharply. Increasingly, employers have found themselves on the losing end of the legal battle.

Two factors have been largely responsible for these losses.

♦ Some juries accept the idea that the "employer could have or should have known."

♦ A frequent lack of documentation usually leaves the court little recourse but to find in the plaintiff's favor.

Companies can avoid these problems by establishing formal, functional, effective hiring procedures.

Finding the perfect candidate is never easy. People are complex. There seems to be no clear-cut method of appraising them. Success in recruiting qualified individuals takes time, effort and careful attention to the pre-employment process. Since the chances of discovering the major problems employees bring with them to the workplace are slim, there is a clear need to rely on simple, inexpensive methods of testing the accuracy and honesty of the applicant's statements and claims.

Much has been written about how to train and develop employees effectively. Though these activities are important, **remember — if the wrong employee is selected initially, no training program or motivational techniques will compensate for the hiring error.**

In addition, many organizations are filling vacancies from within and promoting their current employees. In order to do so, these companies must make sure that new-hires are promotable. Thus, it becomes even more important to carefully scrutinize applicants.

Quite frankly, the hiring techniques used by most businesses do not and have not worked for many years. Most personnel departments and department managers spend much of the pre-employment process simply reviewing applications and conducting interviews. These actions are insufficient. Anyone can look good on paper and devise impressive answers to questions about his or her strengths and weaknesses.

If you don't believe it, consider these findings about job applicants:

18.7%	Lied about their criminal record [1]
14.8%	Lied about the Workers' Compensation claims [1]
29.6%	Misrepresented their education history [1]
25%	Misrepresented their prior employment history [1]
23%	Have used other names [2]
29%	Had lived at addresses not listed on their applications [2]
16%	Had serious motor vehicle violations – Drugs, Alcohol, Revoked License [2]
6%	Supplied false Social Security Numbers [2]

Though frustrated with the results, many executives and company bureaucracies continue to employ faulty hiring methods. Unfortunately, there has been little effort to present any substantial relief . . . until now.

This book breaks down the pre- and post-hiring processes into stages that are easy-to-understand and implement. Additionally, sample forms and tables are included to assist the reader in implementing the processes proposed in this book.

All forms used in this book are freely available for use. You can download them from www.brbpub.com/crook.htm.

The techniques presented herein have proven to be effective. *Don't Hire a Crook!* provides a simple, sequential system for selecting only the best applicants and maintaining employee quality. Above all, the techniques of *Don't Hire a Crook!* are **fair**, comprehensive and adaptable to any organization. You now have a consultant-on-a-shelf!

---

[1] From CIC, a nationwide pre-employment record checking company offering criminal, credit, driving, workers compensation and prior employment reports. CIC headquarters are in Tampa Bay, FL, with local representation nationwide. Further information may be obtained from CIC by calling 800-321-4473.

[2] From ADAM Safeguard, Inc.

A Few Words About . . .

Recruitment

Before learning the methods described in this book, it is important to understand the need for change. Perhaps the most important reason to evaluate your procedures is to make employment with your company cost effective.

Why Sound Recruitment is Important

In recent years, the cost of hiring employees has risen substantially. Few companies understand and have calculated the actual costs, many of which are *hidden*. According to Michael Berzanksy, a federal and state labor arbitrator, the average cost to replace a clerk is about $5,000, and the normal cost to replace a middle management employee is between $25,000 and $30,000. However, these turnover costs typically only include severance pay plus the expense of searching for a replacement.

Yet there are many other costs that are not as easily identified. For instance, those responsible for hiring must take into consideration the fact that new employees must be trained before becoming productive on the job. The decrease in productivity, though temporary, can cost money.

The costs that are most commonly ignored are those that are incurred *before* termination. Consider how much time and money is spent on the following prior to termination:

- Progressive discipline.

- Theft and/or fraudulent workers' compensation claims.

- A decrease in the quality of the employee's work, especially if he or she suspects that termination is imminent.

- Disruption and chaos caused in the interim between the onset of problems and the termination.

- Repairing customer ill will that is generated by problem employees.

Likewise, a vacant position can lead to the following costs, some of which may occur on a company-wide level, depending on the position:

- Lost production.

- A decrease in efficiency.

- Potential loss of valuable accounts.

These costs, combined with the standard expenses of placing advertisements, screening and interviewing, add up. Some companies must also consider the cost of outplacement services and unemployment insurance. A well-developed hiring process can eliminate and/or diminish these costs significantly. Examining and adjusting your company's hiring policies is ultimately more cost effective than maintaining the status quo. The policy adjustment process begins with recruiting . . .

Before Looking for Candidates

Before advertising a vacancy, carefully reexamine the position. If ever there is a time to restructure, eliminate and/or enhance a position, it is prior to filling it.

Ask the following questions, before announcing the vacancy:

♦ Is the position a necessary one? Is it redundant, integral or in-between?

♦ Is the position in the right department?

♦ How does the position relate to the other jobs within the company? Is it closely related to other positions or is it one that is pretty much a stand-alone job?

♦ How frequently has this position been vacant? If the answer is "often," try to address why. Reducing turnover saves time and money.

♦ Is the position supervisory in nature? Should it be?

♦ Should the position be split into one or more jobs?

♦ Should more than one person be hired with the same title?

♦ Does the job description need updating?

Taking the time to examine the position prior to seeking applicants can reduce turnover and confusion that results from making changes *after* hiring someone.

Using Classified Ads

Here are some tips for using classified ads to advertise job openings:

Don't rely solely on the local paper.

Consider trade magazines and/or newspapers that might better reach applicants in your industry.

Beware of politically incorrect language.

Don't write, "salesman needed." Use "salesperson" instead. Otherwise, a bias may be implied and discrimination alleged.

Don't exaggerate benefits and/or the position itself.

When the position is exaggerated, applicants may either start the application process without completing it (thereby wasting your time and theirs) or they will get the job and be disappointed.

Do include schedule requirements.

Doing so will prevent people who are incapable of meeting these requirements from applying.

Do specify the job duties.

If there are any tasks that may be unpleasant and must be performed frequently, be sure to include those as well. If you don't include that the person must be able to answer 16 phone lines, applicants who can't may discontinue the application process, having wasted your time.

When listing duties, don't be vague. It is important that the applicant understand what is involved. Also, don't list the obvious, i.e. in an ad for a "hair stylist" do not list "styling hair" as a job requirement. Listing the redundant costs money since the fees for most advertisements are based on the number of words or lines.

Consider Whether to Include the Company's Name

Do you work for a well-known company? If so, including the name may attract candidates who are only interested in the prestige and/or security that comes from working for a well-known organization. Plus, if the position is related to research and development, inclusion of the company's name can give your competition a clue as to what new products are being developed and/or the direction the company is taking.

Ask Laypersons to Read a Preliminary Copy of the Job Ad

Ask family members, friends or even strangers to read the job ad and give an interpretation of it. These people are likely to point out items that have been neglected or areas that are unclear, such as abbreviations or vague statements. In addition, it is important to understand the perception that the ad conveys, and asking for the assistance of a layperson can help.

Using Community & College Sources

Don't underestimate your community's potential. Contact local high schools and vocational schools, and establish a relationship with them. These institutions are excellent places from which to recruit employees. Many students appreciate the opportunity to gain experience while completing their education. In some cases, students can attend school for a portion of the day and then work for the remainder.

Twenty years ago, these students might have only been capable of filing tasks. Now, they are capable of much more, especially when it comes to operating computers.

It is important to know that these services are very popular because of their success rate. As such, businesses that are interested should contact their local board of education, and be prepared to wait as long as a year. The board will also have more specifics on the programs available.

In addition, there are many cooperative and internship programs available on the college level. These programs are available for many industries. Typically, the students work for a business for a semester, and at the end, the employer and the assigned professor determine the student's grade. Students in these programs are highly motivated given that the opportunity provides work experience and affects their grades. The benefits of these programs are mutual. The students get experience and possibly college credit whereas the businesses get qualified help.

Employees from these sources may not be the best choice for full-time positions. However, they can be an excellent source for augmenting your staff, especially with part-time employees and interns.

Companies must inquire about these opportunities in advance and become familiar with the institution's rules. Once your company has established a relationship with educational facilities, you can use the connection as an ongoing resource. In fact, you may develop a reputation within the university or school that makes their best and brightest want to work for you.

How Does Microsoft Recruit Employees?

According to Ron Lieber, writer of "Wired for Hiring: Microsoft's Slick Recruiting Machine" in the February 6, 1996 issue of *Fortune*, recruiters "should attend meetings of units for which they hire. It helps them keep tabs on hiring needs." In other words, prior to devising a recruitment strategy for a particular position, it is important to understand the functions and needs of the department within which the position exists.

Also, in the article, David Pritchard, Microsoft's Director of Recruiting, admits "We get about 12,000 resumes a month, and every one gets logged into a computer with information on when it arrived, what people thought of it, and when we sent a response." The article also indicates that computers weed out the resumes by looking for keywords. While such a strategy might be too costly for smaller companies, any company can follow Microsoft's lead by logging the information manually. Regardless, larger companies should consider using computers to expedite, document and track their recruiting process.

The Bottom Line

Without applicants, one cannot hire an employee. However, one can have a lot of applicants with no real candidates. Recruiting applicants properly can make the rest of the process go much smoother. If you are an employer, take time out to examine your recruitment policies and then move on to the three stages of the hiring process.

<u>Section One</u>
The 3 Stages of the Hiring Process

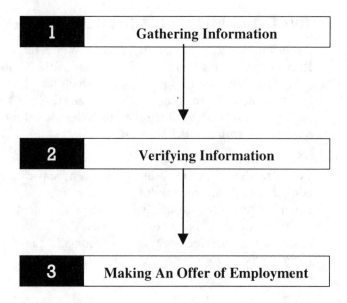

Stage One:

Gathering Information

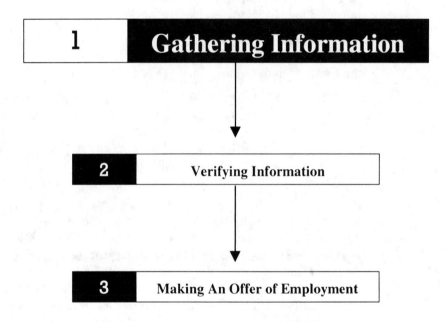

Documentation

The Foundation of Proper Employment

One of the business trends that began in the late sixties and eventually took root was the desire to minimize paperwork. Everyone seemed to be in a hurry; paperwork only slowed things down. The results of this trend have negatively impacted the hiring process and the workplace.

Many companies have reduced personnel paperwork to a bare minimum. Yet, the information absent from an employee's personnel file may cost him or her thousands of dollars during the term of employment.

> **EXAMPLE:** When a new employee fills out his or her W-4 form, the supervisor often only asks for the name, address and Social Security Number. However, if specific dependent deductions are incorrect, an employee's wages may be over or under deducted, ultimately costing him or her money at tax time.

Likewise, these missing documents can cost the employer an even larger amount. If an employer fails to be specific when identifying employee dependents, necessary benefits coverage may be lost. Judges and arbitrators have ruled against employers who are not able to produce proof to support their actions. Lack of paperwork has impacted litigation based on equal pay, civil rights, workers' compensation and more. Hundreds of thousand of dollars have been awarded because vital information was missing or not obtained prior to employing an individual. A common instance occurs when an employer is not careful in verifying the Social Security Number provided during the payroll process, an employee's benefits are assigned to someone with a similar number.

In any legal action that involves wage and hourly claims, discrimination or class action suits, government agencies and the courts can compel an employer to produce related personnel records, by subpoena if necessary.

Discrimination laws exist at both the Federal and State government levels. These laws lead to class action suits that originate from groups of current employees, former employees and applicants. The ever-present possibility of such suits makes it imperative that employers document their actions from the time of hire to the time of termination.

HOT
TIP

In contemporary employee selection, paperwork is your foundation for success and may be your best defense against challenges.

In reviewing their company's personnel practices, employers should always keep in mind the goal of protecting against judicial imposition. However, defensive personnel policies alone will not prevent unfair discharge litigation or union grievances. Still, if the employer focuses on maintaining good internal relations with employees, he or she can help eliminate many of the major sources of potential problems.

If you are an employer and haven't taken time to formally examine and design the employment paperwork used by your company, it is imperative that you make time to do so right away. There may be questions on the forms that are illegal, essential items may be missing, or something simple, like more room to write, may be necessary.

Establish Paperwork Policies & Stick to Them

Employers should establish firm policies regarding what paperwork and procedures they will use during the recruiting process, through the application and hiring process, and beyond. Policies must be written and maintained to be effective and avoid ambiguity. Once established, these policies should be strictly enforced. Consider the psychological effect. If a company makes a greater effort to be consistent about following its policies, then shouldn't it follow that its employees and the members of its community, mindful of that example, will reciprocate by a show of greater respect for following rules and policies?

> **EXAMPLE:** Suppose ABC Company's policies state that "any applicant who is caught omitting a past employer on his or her application must be rejected." Mr. Horvath, ABC Company's personnel manager, interviews a promising candidate named Mr. Rosetto. However, Mr. Horvath learns during the screening process that Mr. Rosetto excluded a past employer from his application. Adhering to company policy, Mr. Horvath decides not to hire Mr. Rosetto and follows it up with detailed documentation. Mr. Rosetto is upset and complains to people he knows. The word spreads that ABC Company is "not to be fooled with," which attracts good applicants and discourages the bad ones.

In the above example, Mr. Horvath performs several actions that are beneficial to ABC Company. First of all, he sticks to company policy, helping to establish positive expectations within the community and the workforce. Secondly, Mr. Horvath protects ABC Company by documenting his actions. Were Mr. Rosetto to pursue litigation, Mr. Horvath would *not* have to rely on his memory to recount the steps he took. In other words, the case would not boil down to the word of Mr. Horvath versus the word of Mr. Rosetto. Mr. Horvath would have evidence to support his claims.

Require that All Forms Be Completed

Insist that all blanks on the forms be completed. At the top of the forms, include some text to explain that applications not completed in full will not be accepted. For example,

> "All blanks on this form must be filled in completely or it will not be processed. If an item does not pertain to you, write 'N/A' in the blank provided. Additional or explanatory information may be included on the reverse or on separate sheets."

Have a person, designated as an "intake person," review the application for completeness. Any blank items should be marked with ink and returned to the applicant for completion.

Items that are often left blank include the names of former supervisors, as well as the addresses and telephone numbers of past employers. These pieces of information are important to the verification process, and, if the applicant does not provide them, it costs additional time and money to complete the process.

There is really no logical reason for the information to be neglected. Applicants surely know the names of their former supervisors given that, with the exception of entrepreneurs, most employees have a supervisor of some kind. They should know the phone numbers of their past employers since they used them to call in sick, report from the field or find out the latest on a project. If they want the job bad enough, they will and should supply this information. If they don't, then they probably weren't right for the job anyway.

In fact, an incomplete application may be an indicator of the applicant's worthiness. Perhaps the applicant is careless or does not pay enough attention to detail. Likewise, he or she may be trying to hide something, something that may cost your company severely.

If the subject "forgets" to provide his or her signature, doubt should be raised. The absence of a signature makes the documents worthless, and therefore may be a deliberate attempt to deny responsibility for questionable actions he or she might commit in the future.

If the company requires that all portions of the application be complete, a surprising number of applicants will find a reason to leave without having finished the paperwork. Depending on the text of the forms they are asked to sign, they might realize that the employer is going to do a criminal history check or verify their educational background. If an applicant leaves at this point in the process, it may not be clear what the "problem" was, but rest assured that one just went away.

Consistently require the same set of forms for every applicant. Failure to do so could be viewed as negligence or even discrimination.

Also, include *all* the forms that will be required in the *initial* application packet. Why? Chances are, if the applicant has a reason for not wanting to submit to a criminal check, education verification, drug test or some other procedure, he or she will not return with the completed paperwork. Thus, the employer has saved the time and the $25-150 involved in the verification process, simply by demonstrating how extensive it is from day one

EXAMPLE: Lies —Where There's One, There May Be More

Sally fills out an application for employment, but chooses not to include a local bank as one of her previous employers. Her prospective employer discovers her deception and requests an employment verification from the bank. The bank reports that Sally only worked there for three months and had poor attendance during that time. In fact, eventually she never returned to work.

When confronted with this information during a second interview, Sally admits that she's been untruthful. She explains that at the time of her employment at the bank, she was going through a divorce. She had two children, one of which was pre-school age, and since her family was not in the area, she had a great deal of difficulty with childcare. The stress and demands of being a single mother made it impossible to work full time, and she had been unable to find a part-time position. Thus, she took the job at the bank and performed poorly. Ultimately, she moved closer to her family, hoping to reorganize her life. She was embarrassed about the situation and remains so.

There is an emotional appeal to Sally's story. One can understand the difficulty of raising children alone and making ends meet. However, what if what Sally said was yet another attempt at deception?

Perhaps Sally, in concert with others, actually defrauded the bank through a phony loan scheme. In the end, she agreed to resignation and repayment and therefore wasn't prosecuted. In this version of the scenario, the bank might be contractually obligated to keep Sally's actions under wraps, and a criminal history check might not reveal this information.

Excusing Sally's deception based on the emotions her confession elicited could cost the company in the long run. If you find yourself in this situation, think logically. Don't feel sorry for someone to the extent that you let that person get away with something he or she shouldn't. If you are about to hire someone and you've already had a situation where you've had to give him or her a second chance, the person is not a logical choice. Applicants know that they have very little opportunity to make a good impression, and that everything said or done during the application process can be a "strike" against them. Chances are, if Sally were rejected after the deception had been revealed, she would know why.

EXAMPLE: Cross Check the Details

> Everything about Jack's application checks out, except the address on his driver's license is in a different county than the one in which he has claimed that he has lived for the past five years. During a discussion about the discovery, Jack explains that he is single and has often moved about, so he uses his parents' address for his license and registration rather than notify the DMV every time he moves.

Satisfactory? Maybe.

What if a Motor Vehicle Report (MVR) on Jack disclosed that his driving privileges had been suspended for numerous violations, including a conviction for Driving While Intoxicated (DWI)? Later, a closer look at a copy of his driver's license shows that his date of birth is off by 25 years. It turns out that the driver's license number given is actually that of his father, Jack Sr.

Without sound and effective hiring procedures in place, neither of these examples would have not been brought to the attention of the employer.

The point is that a well-documented consistently applied pre-employment application process will go a long way in eliminating poor hiring decisions and/or future litigation. The bottom line? Proper paperwork policies can lead to a more effective, efficient organization that is staffed with the best possible candidates.

The Basic Application Form

Its Importance & How to Make it Work for You

The best way to insure that the hiring process is successful is to develop and fine-tune every phase of hiring and employment. No stage should be neglected. However, if there is one part of the process that deserves special attention, it is the design and use of the Basic Application Form. Why? The application is the first and most important step in establishing an honest and productive working relationship.

If an applicant is willing to deceive a prospective employer on the application itself, imagine what he or she will lie about later. Take the time to close the loopholes and catch those crooks!

The Purpose of the Application

Since the Basic Application provides the opportunity to stop problems before they start, prior to making any modifications to the application (as well as other forms), it is important to examine its functions. The purposes of the application are:

♦ To obtain information required by law and essential to government reporting.

♦ To secure the information necessary to participate in employee benefit programs.

♦ To provide the employer with contact information for regular communication and emergency situations.

♦ To supply information, such as a Social Security Number, that will enable verification of the applicant's statements and credentials.

♦ To furnish information that will assist in choosing the right candidate for the job.

If you are an employer, ask yourself, "Does my company's application(s) meet these objectives?"

Include a Place for the Social Security Number

Social Security Numbers dramatically enhance your capability to evaluate potential employees. Always include a spot for them on your application, and make sure that its position on the form is prominent and that there is sufficient space to provide it legibly.

Much of the information on typical applications can be verified by running a Social Security Number search (see page 46) or by requesting a credit report (see page 51) on the applicant. Crucial employment information such as the name, address and Social Security Number can and should be verified in this manner.

Also, running an applicant's Social Security Number through a credit bureau's verification system reveals a great deal. Statistics compiled from 500 recent background investigations performed by ADAM Safeguard revealed that 23% of the applicants used additional names not shown on the application. 29% had an address other than the one they listed. In addition, 4.9% supplied Social Security Numbers which were not theirs! Some of the numbers belonged to deceased individuals!

Yet, in the same group of applicants, prior employers were identified and easily contacted in 72% in of the cases. In many cases, the employers contacted were exactly those listed on the application.

There are many pre-employment companies that can authenticate this information for you. Shop around. Find out how extensive their verifications are and, if applicable, check for volume discounts. For more about using a vendor, see pages 231.

Importance of the Signature Line

Of course, an application should always include the applicant's signature and the date signed.

Immediately above where the signature is recorded, there should be some wording that indicates that all information provided must be true and that any attempt to deceive is reason for denial or dismissal. Here is a sample statement that may be used:

> "I agree that any omission, falsification, or misrepresentation is cause for immediate termination at any time during my employment."

Additional wording should release from liability those who provide information about the applicant:

> "I hereby authorize investigation of all statements at this time with no liability arising therefrom."

Also, many employers neglect to have the signature witnessed. Do not make this mistake. Should litigation arise, the witnessing of the signature and date or lack thereof could impact the case.

Ample Space vs. Additional Forms

Space on the Basic Application is precious. Before an application is put into use, fill out a sample application for yourself and see if there is truly enough room.

All applicants should be encouraged to list all previous employers and former places of residence (i.e. past addresses). How many years to go back is the up to the employer, but fifteen to twenty years is reasonable. As such, ample room for such information must be made available. If the current application is not adequate, one option is to use supplemental forms to record this information. If additional forms and/or sheets are used, make sure that each page is identified with the applicant's name *and* firmly attached to the application.

Subject Areas to Avoid

In recent years, the advent of both state and federal EEOC legislation has outlawed and/or restricted topics that were included in most applications. At the same time, these government agencies have not established a standard format or prescribed list of questions for an application form.

Title VII of the Civil Rights Act of 1964 prohibits discrimination on the basis of race, color, age, sex and national origin. Questions pertaining to these areas are hazardous because they can lead to unlawful use (e.g. discrimination). However, the areas covered by the Civil Rights Act of 1964 are not the only ones that should be avoided.

The Basic Application should *not* include questions related to:

- date of birth
- arrests
- height or weight
- home or auto ownership
- gender
- marital status
- number and ages of children
- race, national origin or religious affiliation

Avoidance of these topics is also essential during the interview process. Refer to page 99 for some interview "no-nos."

Of course, the date of birth is an essential identifier. Although an employer cannot ask for the date of birth on the application, it is required on the I-9 Form (see stage two). Likewise, finding out if the applicant has a criminal record is a must. Even though one cannot ask an applicant if he or she has been arrested, one can ask, "Have you been *convicted* of a crime?"

All of the above topics have been challenged at one time or another by various government agencies or court rulings. There are exceptions, however. For example, the date of birth is essential to some positions. Truck drivers, bartenders and certain law enforcement officials must meet a minimum age requirement, and their age must be verified prior to employment.

Given that there are restraints on the questions which may be asked, it is essential to gather on the application form as much detailed work history and job-related information on candidates for use in the selection process.

This information can be having the applicant fill out:

1.   A release form, which includes required identifiers for background screening.

2.   An I-9 form, which also includes the required identifiers.

Shrewd employers require the I-9 to be completed along with the rest of the initial paperwork. Doing so, provides a great deal of information that is necessary to the verification process.

Other Critical Pre-Hiring Forms

In addition to the Basic Application Form, there are a number of other forms that should be used during the pre-employment process. The purpose of this chapter is to examine these forms and their uses. However, it is important to note there are additional forms that should be used *after* hiring. These forms are discussed later in the book.

Applicant Waiver

As mentioned previously, it can be very difficult to obtain information from previous employers. Anti-discrimination regulations and the drastic increase of labor-related litigation have made employers uncertain as to what can be revealed about past employees. Almost everyone is afraid of being sued, and so it seems safer to say little or nothing at all. One way to address this problem is to use the Applicant Waiver form.

Keep in mind, many former employers will not release any information on a current or past employee without a signed release from that employee.

The Applicant Waiver is a *release* to check references, employment history and verify other information obtained from the applicant. A signed copy of the waiver should be sent with any written inquires to these reference points. To eliminate any doubt as to the validity of the request as well as to expedite it, employers should include the following with any request

♦ A notarized copy of the request. (Although not required, it is recommended that the waiver be notarized. Notarization increases the response rate.)

♦ Include the signature of a company executive.

♦ Enclose a business card. (Use of letterhead is also advised.)

♦ Include a self-addressed, stamped envelope.

From the applicant's perspective, experience indicates that falsification, distortion and error are reduced if the applicant knows that the data he or she gives in the interview and on the application will be checked for accuracy. Using the Applicant Waiver form is an easy way to make the intention to verify information clear from the start.

A closer look at the Applicant Waiver

<u>**Applicant Waiver Form**</u>

(To be signed by all job applicants along with application form.)

1. I agree and understand that all the information and statements on my application are correct and no attempt has been made to conceal or withhold pertinent information. I agree that any omission, falsification, or misrepresentation is cause for my immediate termination at any time during my employment.

2. In connection with this request, I authorize all corporations, companies, credit agencies, persons, educational institutions, law enforcement agencies and former employers to release information they may have about me, and release them from any liability and responsibility from doing so; further, I authorize the procurement of an investigative consumer report and understand that such report may contain information as to my background, mode of living, character and personal reputation. This authorization, in original and copy form, shall be valid for this and any future reports that may be requested. Further information may be made available upon written request from _____

3. I hereby authorize investigation of all statements at this time with no liability arising therefrom.

_____   _____
Signature   Date

_____   _____
Signature of Company Representative   Date

. . .

STATE of:_____ This Instrument was acknowledged before me this _____ day of

COUNTY of:_____ _____, 19 ____, by _____

My commission will expire: _____ AS WITNESS
_____

_____
Notary Public   No.

This statement reiterates the policy that all information provided must be true, and that deception is cause for denial or termination.

This paragraph authorizes the prospective employer to verify the information.

A full size version of the form is available on page 196.

Employment Eligibility Verification (I-9)

The Immigration Reform and Control Act (IRCA) of 1986 obligates every employer to verify, within three days of hire, the identity and employment authorization of every employee hired. To adhere to the directives of this act, employers must use the Employment Eligibility Verification Form, more commonly known as the I-9 Form.

Although the I-9 Form is not required to be complete until the applicant has been hired, it is an excellent tool to use as part of the pre-employment procedure. To complete this form, employers need to see proper identification from the applicant.

Obtaining copies of applicant identity documents is a benefit, since the documents will help immediately in the verification process. If the applicant refuses to disclose proper ID, then there is no reason to continue considering him or her for employment.

The purposes of the IRCA are to prohibit employment of illegal aliens, offer amnesty to qualified illegal aliens and expand the scope of federal anti-discrimination laws. Per the ICRA, employers of four or more employees are forbidden from discriminating on the basis of national origin, citizenship or "intending citizenship" (i.e. whether someone has the intention of becoming a citizen). However, the act does not exclude the preference of a citizen over an equally-qualified, legal alien.

According to the November 1998 issue of *You and the Law*, "the appeals court held that [Section 1981 of the Civil Rights Act of 1991] does prohibit discrimination based on citizenship. *You and the Law* also advises that you not "use citizenship to disqualify anyone from a position at your company, except in those very narrow circumstances where . . . citizenship is a bona fide occupational qualification" such as "positions involving national security."

In addition to the mandatory use of the I-9 form, employers are required to *maintain* proof of the applicant's identity. In other words, the employer must retain copies of the items presented for verification. Passports, drivers' licenses, Social Security cards, birth certificates and alien registration cards are some of the documents typically used to comply with the ICRA.

Also, retention of these documents can be very important after hiring.

> **EXAMPLE:** John was hired for a management position. He was foreign born and had allegedly immigrated to the US some time ago. While preparing the information necessary to ensure that John received his company benefits, a clerk noticed that the date of birth on his application did not match that of his alien registration card. John was informed and a copy of his birth certificate was requested but never produced. John's supervisor gave him time to comply, but suspicions grew further when it was discovered that the date of birth on his

driver's license did not match either of the other documents. Confronted with these inconsistencies, John abruptly left the building without explanation and never returned. A report along with copies of the documents was given to the local immigration office.

In the above example, the documents should have been shown to be inconsistent prior to hiring. Nonetheless, the maintenance of them allowed for the situation to be rectified. reestablishing the company's compliance with the ICRA.

A closer look at the I-9 Form

A full size version of the form is available on page 203.

This section must be completed by the *employee* upon being hired, but should be completed during the application process.

The signature is critical if someone other than the applicant completes the form.

The *employer* must complete this section, and include date and signature.

EMPLOYMENT ELIGIBILITY VERIFICATION (I-9)

SECTION I. EMPLOYEE INFORMATION AND VERIFICATION: (To be completed and signed by employee)

NAME:_____
            Last   First   Middle   Maiden

ADDRESS:_____
            Street number and name   City   State   Zip

DATE OF BIRTH: _____   SOCIAL SECURITY NUMBER: _____

I attest, under penalty of perjury, that I am (check one):
_____ A citizen or national of the United States
_____ An alien lawfully admitted for permanent residence (Alien #A_____).
_____ An alien authorized by the Immigration and Naturalization Service to work in the U.S.(Alien #A_____).
            or Admission Number _____. Expiration of employment authorization, if any _____).

I attest, under penalty of perjury, the documents that I have presented as evidence of identity and employment eligibility are genuine and relate to me. I am aware that federal law provides for imprisonment and/or fine for any false statement or use of false documents in connection with this certificate.

SIGNATURE: _____ DATE: _____

PREPARER/TRANSLATOR CERTIFICATION (if prepared by other than the individual). I attest, under penalty of perjury, that the above was prepared by me at the request of the named individual and is based on all information of which I have any knowledge.

SIGNATURE: _____ NAME (print or type):_____
ADDRESS:_____
            Street number and name   City   State   Zip
****

SECTION II. EMPLOYER REVIEW AND VERIFICATION: (To be completed and signed by employer)
Examine one document from those in List A and check the correct box, *or* examine one document from List B *and* one from List C and check the correct boxes. Provide the *Document Identification Number* and *Expiration Date*, for the document checked in that column.

List A	List B	List C
Identity and Employment Eligibility Eligibility	Identity	and Employment
____ United States Passport	____ A State issued drivers license	____Original Social Security Number
____ Certificate of U.S. Citizenship	or I.D. card with a photograph,	Card (other than a card stating
____ Certificate of Naturalization	or information, including name,	it is not valid for employment)
____ Unexpired foreign passport with	sex, date of birth, height, weight,	____ A birth certificate issued by
attached Employment Authorization	and color of eyes.	State, county, or municipal
____Alien registration Card with photograph	____ U.S. Military Card	authority bearing a seal or other
	____ Other (Specify document and	certification
	issuing authority)	____ Unexpired INS Employment
		Authorization. Specify form.
Document I.D.# _____	Document I.D.# _____	Document I.D.# _____
Exp. Date _____	Exp. Date _____	Exp. Date _____

CERTIFICATION: I attest, under penalty of perjury, that I have examined the documents presented by the above individual, that they appear to be genuine, relate to the individual named, and that the individual, to the best of my knowledge, is authorized to work in the United States.

SIGNATURE: _____ NAME (print of type):_____ TITLE: _____

EMPLOYER:_____
            Name   Address   Date

Other Release Forms

Either a General Release Form or a series of subject-specific release forms should be incorporated into the application and screening process. While the General Release Form may be sufficient for many types of job hiring, in more-complex hiring scenarios a selection of the various subject-specific release forms should be used. These subject-specific release forms focus on all of the items an employer intends to verify for the records they will be obtaining. In some states a signed release may be *required* prior to conducting a criminal background check or a driving record request.

As in the sample General Release Form, there should be wording to exonerate all persons, agents, employees or third party vendors supplying information.

If obtaining a credit report, driving record and criminal history is intended, then that should be specifically identified in the release, which would make it a sample release. A sample of a Criminal History Release follows on page 31.

Requesting Driving Records is more complex because many states have their own forms which requestors must use. Although rules vary from state to state, as a general rule, employers *can* access these records. The key is that the states *require* verification and signature(s) from the employer. Consult the State Motor Vehicle Record Agencies Section starting on page 273 for individual states' requirements for acquiring driving records.

A closer look at The General Release Form

While one may utilize specific release forms for education and credit, the all-encompassing General Release Form will be of great benefit to supply information to employers and anyone else who may have knowledge about the applicant. Check the State Motor Vehicle Record Agencies and State Criminal Record Agencies Sections to find out if your state requires a signed release.

Here is a sample General Release Form:

General Release Form

In connection with my application for employment (including contract for service) with you, I understand that investigative inquiries are to be made on me including consumer credit, criminal convictions, motor vehicle, and other reports. These reports will include information as to my character, work, habits, performance and experience along with reasons for termination of past employment from previous employers. Further, I understand that you will be requesting information from various Federal, State, and other agencies that maintain records concerning my past activities relating to my driving, credit, criminal, civil, education, and other experiences.

I authorize without reservation any party or agency contacted by this employer to furnish the above-mentioned information.

I hereby consent to your obtaining the above information from _____ and/or any of their licensed agents. I understand to aid in the proper identification of my file or records, the following personal identifiers, as well as other information, is necessary.

Print Name _____

Social Security Number _____-____-_____

Date of Birth _____ Sex _____ Race_____

Current Address _____

City/State/Zip Code+4_____

Former Address _____

Applicant Signature _____ Date_____

Prospective Employer _____

A full size version of the form is available on page 206.

This is a sample of a criminal release form. It is useful if an applicant has resided in a state with which the employer is unfamiliar. In other words, many states require a notarized release, but don't require a specific release form to be used — in which case, this form will suffice.

Sample Specific Release: Criminal Release Form

Criminal Background Check
Release Form

NAME_____
　　　　　Last　　　　　　　　First　　　　　　　Middle　　　　Maiden

ADDRESS_____
　　　　　Street　　　　　　　　　　　City　　　　　　　　State

ALIASES OR OTHER NAMES USED _____

DATE OF BIRTH _____ AGE____ RACE_____ SEX____

SOCIAL SECURITY #_____

DRIVER'S LICENSE #_____ STATE_____

* * *

I hereby authorize _____ of _____
　　　　　　　　　　　　　　Name　　　　　　　　　Name of Company

_____
　　　　　　　Company Address/City/State/Zip

to conduct a criminal background check on myself through the

_____
　　　　　　Name of State and Police Agency

X_____
　　Applicant Signature

* * *

STATE of_____ This Instrument was acknowledged before me this _____ day of

COUNTY of_____ _____, 19 ____, by _____

My commission will expire:　_____ AS WITNESS

_____

　　　　　　　　　　　　_____
　　　　　　　　　　　　Notary Public　　　　No.

A full size version of the form is available on page 201.

Substance Abuse Test Consent

Government agencies have increased emphasis on health, safety and accident prevention in the workplace. This fact, coupled with the spiraling costs of fringe benefits, has made drug screening a common component of Stage Two (i.e. Verifying the Information). However, the act of presenting a Drug Abuse Test Consent form for completion during Stage One, regardless of whether a test will actually be conducted, can act as a deterrent.

Many applicants look good on paper, pass the typical test and make a great impression during the interview. Then, when the Drug Abuse Test Consent is presented, suddenly the job they so badly wanted, wasn't what they thought. An excuse is given and they leave without filling out the form. The time and money for the actual test have been saved.

Government sources have indicated that alcohol and drug abuse cost businesses billions of dollars in additional healthcare coverage, accident coverage, and loss of productivity. In the workplace, substance abuse can lead to a high degree of employee absenteeism, higher medical costs and an increase in on-the-job accidents. Thus, it is simply cost effective and liability conscious to institute and adhere to substance abuse testing procedures.

If an employee is found to be sick or "handicapped" due to alcohol and/or drug addiction(s), the mere existence of that addiction cannot be the grounds for dismissal.

Under the Rehabilitation Act of 1973, current employees with drug or alcohol problems are considered handicapped and must be treated like those who suffer from other disabilities.

A normal, acceptable procedure is to have the employee examined by a doctor regardless of whether drug and/or alcohol testing is performed. The employer of an addict may want to offer him or her the opportunity to enter drug or alcohol rehabilitation, which might be comprised of a 30, 60 or 90 day hospitalization. However, entrance into such a program must be voluntary and the employer generally pays for the treatment if there is no healthcare insurance.

If an employee repeatedly demonstrates problems as the result of an addiction and also does not take the steps necessary to correct these problems, he or she then becomes "unemployable" and is eligible for termination.

A Substance Abuse Test Consent Form is presented on page 220.

Applicant/Resume Evaluation Form

It's bad enough that employees are taking frivolous legal actions, but a new wave of litigation stems from those that are *not* hired. An evaluation form that clearly indicates the reasons why the applicant was not employed should always accompany the company copy of a rejected application. If the reason for rejection was based on an established company policy, the documentation will be further supported by the existence of such policies. The rejection and acceptance of candidates is a step that should be recorded. As such, the Applicant Evaluation Form is a handy tool for documenting the review of applications. A full size version of the form is available on page 195.

A closer look at Applicant/Resume Evaluation Form

APPLICANT/RESUME EVALUATION

Completion of this form assists compliance with non-discrimination guidelines and ensures the basis for hire and reject decisions are documented and job related.

Name of Applicant: _____

Date Application/Resume Received: _____

Position Available: _____

Will Applicant be Interviewed: _____ Yes   Date of Interview: _____

                                   _____ No   Reason for Rejection: _____
                                                              Code Number(s)

Will Job be extended: _____ Yes Title: _____   Salary: _____

                          _____ No

Job-Related Reason Applicant is Best Qualified: _____

_____

If No, Reason for Rejection: _____
                            Code Number(s)

_____

Signature Interviewer/Evaluator   Position/Department   Date

You have the right to hire qualified individuals and to reject unqualified individuals. Selection and rejection decisions must be based on valid job-related criteria that are consistently applied to all applicants. The following are acceptable reasons for rejection provided the same statement could not be applied to the selected candidate. If numbers 1-8 do not apply, please complete 9 with a job-related reason.

1. *Does not meet minimum job requirements*
2. *Meets minimum requirements but not best qualified*
3. *Cannot work required hours/schedule*
4. *Cannot perform physical requirements of job*
5. *Prior experience unrelated*
6. *Less related experience than person selected*
7. *Less related education/training than person selected*
8. *Lower skill level than person selected*
9. *Other (specify)_____*

These codes allow for very specific descriptions as to why an applicant was rejected. Combined with a copy of the submitted application and/or resume, this information can be crucial to winning a court case.

This form complies with non-discrimination guidelines and ensures that the basis for hire or rejection are documented and job-related. An employer should not rely on memory to recall the specifics, which may be questioned later. Many of the suits filed against an employer are not filed by current employees, but by applicants who were rejected. These cases present a circumstance where there is very limited knowledge available about the plaintiff. It is not always easy to understand the motivations or background of an applicant given that the company's relationship with him or her is typically short-lived.

Stage Two:
Verifying Information

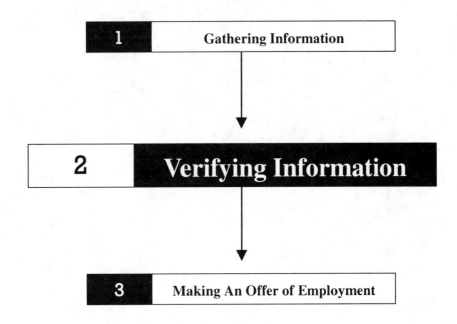

Pre-Employment Screening

So now the applicant has filled out all the requisite paperwork. The information he or she provided checks out. Basically, everything looks good. The applicant is willing to start now and help is needed. What is next? Hiring or screening?

Unsure? Consider this true story:

> **EXAMPLE:** On October 8, 1997, a local gas station reported to police that on his first day of employment, an employee walked away with a large amount of cash that belonged to the station. A police check of his application yielded several fictitious names, addresses and personal identifiers. The guy walked in, looked good, filled out the application and was put to work immediately. After working most of the day, he walked away with what amounted to several weeks pay.

It is obvious in the above example that even a basic background check would have uncovered the crook before he got the cash. The employer in this example went directly from the application process to hiring without verifying any information.

In the above example, an important step was skipped. That step is screening.

Over 25% of all applications contain misrepresentations!

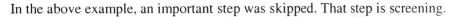

Once you have an application and resume from the applicant, it is important to verify the contents of the documents. In other words, you must screen your applicants. This process of verification is generally known as a "Pre-Employment Check" or "Background Investigation." The purpose of a pre-employment check is to develop a picture of the background and character of an applicant. Essentially, the results of an effective check should provide an accurate assessment of the applicant's reputation, reliability, truthfulness and qualifications.

Traditionally, the sources of background information are prior employers and character references. Even though traditional means might seem comprehensive, they are flawed and inadequate.

Many companies also obtain credit reports, verify education and in some cases even request a criminal history search and driving record check. The type of position, policies of the company and availability of the information usually determine the extent of the check.

Develop a Company Screening Policy

As with all other aspects of the pre- and ongoing employment process, employers should establish and adhere to strict policies regarding background screening. Regardless of the details of such polices, there should be a specified minimum amount of screening that is accomplished for each applicant without fail. Failure to follow the policy in every case can be the basis for litigation and can result in the hiring of unqualified or troublesome employees.

When pre-employment paperwork and screening are handled haphazardly, the risk of discrimination charges increases. Even if an applicant is a friend's relative or long acquaintance, the same rules should apply.

> **EXAMPLE:** Several applicants for a position complete the required paperwork, and screening confirms that each is telling the truth. Then, Mr. Whalen, fresh from college and a relative of a current employee, expresses an interest in the position. The employer likes Mr. Whalen and hires him on the spot. Ultimately, one applicant inquiries as to why she did not get the job. Feeling slighted, she files a complaint under the Americans with Disabilities Act via the Equal Employment Opportunity Commission (EEOC). One of these agencies investigates the matter and determines that though all of the applicants were put through screening, the one hired was not. In this case, discrimination can be assumed.

As an employer, do not expose your company to this type of litigation. It is imperative to stick to a regimented company policy, regardless of who is being considered for employment.

Components of a Pre-Employment Background Check

There are three components that must be considered when developing a company screening policy.

1.) Which Screening Options are Applicable?

The table below lists screening options every employer should consider, assuming that the proper release forms have been signed by the individual that is to undergo screening.

Of course, not every option applies to every screening applicant, as the table indicates. For example, if the position does not require special skills, verification of college or professional licensing credentials may not be necessary. The type of position, policies of the company and availability of the information usually determine the extent of the check.

Screening Options Table	All Applicants	Management	Whenever Claimed or Required	Forms Located
Social Security Number Verification	•	•		N/A
Credit History Checks		•		N/A
Employment History Verification	•	•		216, 219
Criminal History Checks	•	•		201
Verification of Educational Background		•	•	218
Confirmation of Professional Licenses & Registrations			•	N/A
Military Service Records Checks			•	209-210
Motor Vehicle Reports	•	•		N/A
Civil Record Searches		•		N/A

2.) What are the Geographic Boundaries of the Search?

It is important to know what geographic area is covered by a particular government agency. If the information you need is available from your local courthouse, great. Check to see if statewide screening may be done from a local court or DMV licensing office in your home state, but do not assume this is the case in another state or county. If you require a statewide criminal record search, but the applicant is from a state that has no such search available (CA, NC, TN, UT and VT), be prepared to do searching at the county court level. Budget permitting, a criminal search in the applicant's home county and all counties within a 50-mile radius of a listed residence on the application may suffice.

3.) Who Will Screen?

Now that we have discussed what needs to be screened, it is important to address the following question: who will do the screening?

Readers who want to do their own screening will find the proper techniques within these pages. All the forms and tools to provide complete verifications are contained between the two covers of this book.

For many businesses, time is a premium. For a relatively small expense, employers can hire a pre-employment screening company to handle the task. These companies can be found in telephone directories, advertisements or by calling the local police department for a recommendation. Business groups and trade associations may also offer contacts that have good reputations. Many private investigation firms offer pre-employment screening as a service. The Internet is also a good resource for finding screening companies. Using a search engine, type "pre-employment," "background info" or "screening" and the results will be more than sufficient.

Visit www.publicrecordsources.com **to find profiles of over 200 of the nation's leading screening agencies.**

Remember that regardless of whether the employer does the screening or if a vendor is hired to do so, the proper forms and waivers must be filled out and signed by the prospective employee. Nonetheless, familiarity with the issues discussed in these pages will enhance the effectiveness and interpretation of the results.

Once employers are aware of current screening methods, they can make the decision to do screening in-house or to hire a company. By understanding the process one has to go through to get the answers required, one can more easily decide who should perform that process. Many companies would rather leave it to the "experts." However, understanding the possibilities allows a company to request specific types of searches and investigations from these "experts."

To know more about how to choose the right vendor, go to Using a Pre-Employment Screening Company on page 231, which includes profiles of over 150 quality screening firms.

___ Before you go on . . .
Beware of Fake IDs

An alarming problem for employers has been the increasing number of job applicants providing phony identification and documents. This trend has gone far beyond embellishing a resume or covering suspicious gaps of employment. The reasons why vary from being an illegal alien to hiding a criminal background. Among this group are debtors trying to evade collection. For whatever reason, employers are responsible and subject to fines and some penalties if they fail to properly identify an employee.

It is a good idea to have the "intake person" make copies of the identifying documents presented and not permit an applicant to simply fill in a Social Security Number or drivers' license number without adequate proof. These extra steps eliminate the potential for an applicant to claim that an "error" must have been made in transcribing his or her identification numbers. Plus, the employer will have proof on file that the numbers on the application match those on the supporting documents.

To further complicate the identity problem, there are now many sources that supply false identification for a price. In fact, a number of books have been written just for this purpose. One, entitled *ID For Sale in the Mail*, covers everything from birth certificates to college diplomas. But, one doesn't even have to go to the library or a bookstore. A quick search of the Internet for "fake ID" provides everything you can imagine without leaving home. Not only will the Internet supply you with books for sale, you can also download samples of fake identification from anywhere in the world. There are vendors offering fake identification packages, including software that will teach you how to make your own fake IDs at home. Some sources even include stick-on holograms and complete lamination kits for as low as $49.00.

With false drivers' licenses, Social Security cards, marriage certificates, military records and union identification cards obtained easily or made in one's home, the issue of fake document availability impacts every facet of pre-employment screening.

While Social Security Numbers or drivers' license numbers may be within proper limits; checking the numbers is only the first step toward identity verification. The next step is to obtain the reports that fully document the ownership of a number (see Social Security Number Allocations starting page 223).

The identification verification sections in this book will help you discover fraudulent details before you perform a background check. When the information appears to be within the proper criteria, then a background check can begin. But remember — just because the information conforms to the charts, a match doesn't prove that it belongs to the applicant.

The use, possession and manufacture of fake or counterfeit documents is illegal. Law enforcement agencies on all levels work jointly to discover and dismantle counterfeiting operations. The US Secret Service is the lead agency involved in the investigation and prosecution of those who are caught participating in such activities. Sophisticated manufacturing facilities have been found in homes, offices, hotel rooms and even vehicles. Anyone who encounters counterfeit forms of identification should contact the local Secret Service office. They will notify the appropriate agency in the area. Do not be afraid to alert the government – private sector cooperation is essential in combating this form of illegal activity.

A person who provides counterfeit information may be trying to deceive you or may even be one of **America's Most Wanted**.

How to Do a Proper Background Check

Screening Options Table	All Applicants	Management	Whenever Claimed or Required	Forms Located
Social Security Number Verification	•	•		N/A
Credit History Checks		•		N/A
Employment History Verification	•	•		216, 219
Criminal History Checks	•	•		201
Verification of Educational Background		•	•	218
Confirmation of Professional Licenses & Registrations			•	N/A
Military Service Records Checks			•	209-210
Motor Vehicle Reports	•	•		N/A
Civil Record Searches		•		N/A

There are many aspects to a proper and professional background check. Not all of them apply to every applicant. The goal of this section is to help determine which screening options are needed and how to implement them.

Document, Document, Document

There should be a separate file devoted specifically to each applicant, containing documentation of each verification attempt. You should include the date, the name of the person/organization with whom you spoke and some general notes about the outcome. Even if you are unable to reach a particular employer or reference, document the attempt. It is important to document your efforts to practice quality hiring procedures. Detailed documentation can jog your memory and win lawsuits.

The employer should keep track of every request that is made. Sometimes multiple police departments are contacted, in which case copies of all of these communications should be kept in the personnel file. Copies of the letters should be maintained as well as a recording of the details as to when and to whom the request was mailed. In some cases, the employer may not receive a response at all or may be told to check another source. Thus, retention of copies of the original request serve as proof that an attempt has been made.

Social Security Number Verification

	All Applicants	Management	Whenever Claimed or Required	Forms Located
Social Security Number Verification	•	•		N/A

Social Security Number verification is the most important means of screening. More than any other item, the Social Security Number acts as a personal identifier. If an applicant is not who he or she claims, they shouldn't be hired. Social Security Number verification is the best means by which to ensure that those who are hired are, indeed, who they say they are.

What if an applicant gave the Social Security Number of Barbara Walters, Jay Leno's date of birth and the name John Smith? Sounds easy to spot, doesn't it? The fact is, if this information were included as part of a criminal history search without fingerprints, no record would be found, making it seem as though the applicant had no criminal past. On the other hand, a Social Security Number check would instantly reveal the attempt at deception. In other words, identity can be easily falsified and remain undetected, unless a Social Security Number Verification is performed.

> **EXAMPLE:** Ms. Reisen worked for an employer who did not perform a Social Security Number verification as part of the hiring process. One day, she went to the personnel department to report a recent marriage. During the discussion, Ms. Reisen indicated that she need to change her name to Mrs. Sharneck, and stated that she also had a new Social Security Number. Perplexed, the personnel department decided to have the matter investigated.
>
> The original number had never been issued. The new one was a recent issue that belonged to someone else on the other side of country. When confronted with these discrepancies, Ms. Reisen admitted that she had supplied a fake Social Security Card twice, but refused to say why. The discussion was witnessed and therefore Ms. Reisen was terminated for providing false information.

The real tragedy is that Ms. Reisen had been employed there for five years! During that time, she may have committed many other forms of deception.

Conducting a Social Security Number verification is accomplished through the utilization of credit bureaus, such as Trans Union, Equifax and Experian.

The data that comprises the results of a Social Security Number verification is known as "header information." It can contain any or all of the following:

♦ The state of and approximate year of issue of the Social Security Number.

♦ Status as an invalid, non-issued or misused Social Security Number.

♦ Status as a Social Security Number that has been used to file a death claim.

♦ Address(es) of the Social Security Number user.

♦ Employer(s) of the user.

♦ The year of birth or age of the user.

♦ Additional or multiple users of the number.

When an individual applies for credit, he or she must provide the header information to the potential credit lender. Lenders work in conjunction with the bureaus when deciding whether to extend credit. Thus, the information obtained by the lenders is used to upgrade the records of the credit bureaus.

Each time, the information he or she provides is provided to the credit agencies. The information is logged into the report by date. Every time an individual applies for credit, the exact spelling and format on the application is reported to the credit bureau, hence the credit or the credit header will report all name variations and addresses that applicants use. Updated information is also obtained through collection activity. If collection agencies receive any new information on a subject, they report it through the credit bureau's system.

Keep in mind that there may be mistakes. Also, different credit bureaus can have different information. One credit bureau may have extensive information on the subject whereas another may have very little. Lenders do not necessarily utilize and/or communicate with every bureau. Consequently, one bureau may be more up-to-date than another in a specific region. In instances where such a search is crucial, it is wise to verify using more than one bureau.

What to Look for in the Results

Does the Social Security Number provided match the subject?

If not, verify that the number provided was entered correctly by the credit bureau as well as the company staff.

Also, ask the applicant to provide proof of the Social Security Number.

Does the name in the results match that of the subject?

The middle name/initial is important for proper identification, especially if the subject has a relatively common name. Also, be sure to obtain the suffix, if one is used.

The subject may have the same name as a relative, with only a suffix to distinguish between them, i.e. Jr. (junior), Sr. (senior) or I (the first), II (the second), etc.

An individual's proper name may be George David Smith, but the subject prefers to go by the name David Smith. He or she may also have used a shortened version of his or her name as a matter of convenience and that will show here.

Have additional names been revealed?

Perhaps a maiden name has been identified that was not provided. If the subject is recently married, most of that person's information may appear under the maiden name, suggesting an additional search to that effect.

Also, the subject may have divorced and resumed the use of the maiden name. The subject may have even had another name from a previous marriage.

Regardless, it is important to determine why variations of the name exist to enable proper identification and facilitate subsequent searches.

Has the number been issued by the Social Security Administration?

When faking an identity, people frequently use numbers that have not even been issued by the Social Security Administration. To see if a number has been truly issued, check the Social Security Number Allocations Section beginning on page 223.

If the results of the verification indicate that the number has not been issued, ask the applicant to provide proof of his or her Social Security Number.

Was the number used to file a death claim?

Numbers used to file a death claim are also utilized in the falsifying of an identity. If the results indicate that this is the case, ask for proof that the applicant is truly entitled to the use of the number.

Be aware that it may appear that someone is using the Social Security Number of a deceased person, when in reality he or she has only collected Social Security benefits as a relative of the deceased person.

In what state was the number issued?

It is entirely possible that the number was issued in a state other than the state in which the applicant now resides, and is not, in itself, cause for alarm.

However, such information can indicate other areas of the application that should be reviewed. Perhaps it hasn't been that long since the applicant moved from the state of origin, in which case he or she should have listed the previous address(es) from that state.

In what year was the number issued?

First of all, compare the year of issue to the applicant's date of birth.

Around 1984, it became mandatory to obtain a Social Security Number for a child at birth. Prior to this, there was no time limitation. However, most individuals acquired a Social Security Number at a fairly early age, generally no later than the time they entered the work force.

Immigrants should obtain a Social Security Number upon accepting employment in the US.

Do the addresses (and the corresponding time frames) provided by subject concur with those obtained from the verification?

If the information does not match or addresses other than those provided appear, the employer should question the applicant about these findings. The omission of addresses may be intentional, and therefore, further investigation may be warranted.

However, the absence of an address may merely be an oversight. The subject may have resided at the location for only a short time or may have used the address of a friend or relative while between residences. Many individuals, particularly those who are single, will use a parent's address as their permanent address rather than their actual place of residence, which is more likely to fluctuate.

Do the past employers (and the corresponding time frames) given by the subject coincide with those revealed by the SSN verification?

If additional employers are identified, they should be contacted to verify the validity of previous employment. At the same time, if the Request for Information (see page 57) is used, a review of the applicant's performance can be obtained. Regardless of the response(s) received, the applicant should be questioned about the omission of the previous employer(s).

Does the date/year of birth and/or age match that provided by the subject?

In some instances, the age or year of birth may be off by a year or two. Sometimes this is due to a computer or typographical error.

If there is a great difference, the subject should be asked for proof of birth, preferably a birth certificate.

Is the subject using and/or associated with more than one Social Security Number?

All additional Social Security Numbers should be investigated. However, the extra numbers may actually be very similar to that of the subject and potentially the result of a typographical error. The number may belong to a spouse, relative or friend who applied for credit jointly with the subject.

Are additional individuals using the same Social Security Number?

Doing a record header search may reveal more than one individual is using the same SSN. All additional individuals could be investigated because there are several legitimate reasons for the existence of these individuals.

The additional individual may be a friend or relative who has applied for joint credit with the applicant.

Also, there may have been a typographical error if the additional individual happens to have a Social Security Number that is very similar to that of the applicant.

If the applicant has or claims to have no knowledge of the additional individuals, he or she should be advised to contact the credit bureau from which the information was obtained. It may be necessary for the applicant to have his or her credit report corrected to eliminate any future problems.

It is possible that the applicant is entirely unaware of the additional individual. He or she may be the victim of someone who is using his or her SSN for dubious purposes. Do not assume that the applicant is up to something. However, there is *no* legal reason to change one's Social Security Number. If a person is identified as using more than one number and states that he or she "changed it," he or she is not to be trusted.

Credit History Checks

	All Applicants	Management	Whenever Claimed or Required	Forms Located
Credit History Checks		•		N/A

Similar to the verification of Social Security Numbers, credit reports can validate some of the information contained in the Basic Application. Credit reports can also reveal an applicant's outstanding debts, liens, judgments and bankruptcies as well as addresses and employer information. These reports are most often obtained for management positions and for those who will have access to money on the job.

The Bureaus

There are three major credit bureaus. The following is a list of these companies as well as their web addresses and phone numbers, which can be used to order reports and/or dispute them:

Equifax

www.equifax.com

800-685-1111

Experian (formerly TRW)

www.experian.com   Confirmation # 1506857608

800-682-7654   1888-Experian

             397-3742 (new #)

Trans Union

www.transunion.com

800-916-8800

These bureaus obtain information on a daily basis from private enterprises and government agencies. The private sources are principally credit grantors, such as banks, department stores and credit card companies. The bureaus also collect data on judgments, liens and records from all levels of government for the purpose of updating their credit reports and the corresponding header information.

The three bureaus have more than 2,000 affiliated local bureaus across the country. Some are franchises while others are independent affiliates.

In addition, there are numerous agencies who may enter information into the credit system as they check credit for legitimate business purposes. Each entry, including the applicant's address, is required. Every time a consumer fills out a credit application for any purpose (credit card, store credit, mortgages, auto purchase, apartment rentals, etc.) the information supplied by the consumer is provided to the "Big Three" credit bureaus.

Consumer Reports vs. Credit Reports

It is important to note that there is a difference between a consumer credit report and a credit report used for pre-employment purposes. Credit reports for employment uses are more expensive, and the credit reporting agency must be *authorized* to obtain reports for pre-employment purposes. Furthermore, when a credit report is obtained on an applicant and derogatory information is present, the credit bureau notifies the applicant. The notification includes the identity of the agency/organization that requested the report.

Under an amendment to the Fair Credit Reporting Act (FCRA), dated September 30, 1997, additional requirements have been imposed on employers. Prior to obtaining such a report, the employee must be informed in writing of the company's intention to do so, and a signature from the applicant agreeing to allow access to the information must be obtained. Further, a summary of the applicant's rights must be given to the candidate prior to taking any adverse action as a result of the credit check.

If a friendly merchant offers to provide a credit report as a favor or for very little money and an employer accepts the offer, both are in serious violation of the FCRA. It is imperative that companies adhere to the FCRA. For more information on the act, see page 177.

Employment History Verification

	All Applicants	Management	Whenever Claimed or Required	Forms Located
Employment History Verification	•	•		216, 219

There are two ways to verify previous employment — by phone and by mail.

Verifying by phone is generally the best method to learn the truth. Information that would not be committed to in writing is often revealed in a phone conversation. Perhaps the applicant was slow, lazy or argumentative in the workplace. Such characteristics are not easy to prove, and as such, the previous employer may not have any documentation to support these claims. Nonetheless, he or she might mention such traits during a verification by phone.

Verifying information can be helpful in obtaining written documentation of one's efforts. However, only basic information, such as the dates of employment, is usually provided by mail.

In some cases, the person providing the information may have had a personality conflict with the applicant, and therefore provides false information in order to bring harm to the applicant.

Ⅼ⟶ Be careful not to accept implicitly what is reported

Verifying Employment by Phone

If, as an employer, you are lucky enough to make contact with a prior employer via phone, ask to speak with the applicant's immediate supervisor. The former supervisor is more likely to provide in-depth and personal knowledge about the candidate whereas the human resources department is most often limited to merely verifying dates of employment and payroll information. However, even the most cooperative representative of the previous employer may only relate information that is documented in personnel files.

As mentioned previously, in some cases a person will discuss an issue over the phone that he or she would not commit to in response to a written request. Sometimes a prior employer will tell of problems or suspicions in confidence.

If this happens, return the courtesy by keeping it that way. Sometimes the person you speak with will accidentally blurt out something relevant. Use the information provided as an off-the-record comment, but do not acknowledge the source. In other words, treat the previous employer as you would like to be treated yourself.

On the other hand, if someone provides written material that is derogatory or states that proof will be made available, feel free to use the information and refer to its source. However, in all cases, only provide the applicant with information that is totally necessary and only if it is the basis for rejection.

Making a decision based on an undocumented discussion by phone is extremely risky. A rejection that is based on a phone conversation that does not have supporting documentation is unlikely to hold up in a court of law.

The extent of the documentation of phone verifications varies depending on the person making the call. Some take copious notes while others merely jot down key words. Regardless, the Pre-Employment Check by Phone is designed to maximize the results of a phone verification. The questions on the form are designed to relate the information obtained to specific requirements of the job.

A closer look at the Pre-Employment Check by Phone

A full size version of the form is available on page 216.

Pre-Employment Check by Phone

Name of Applicant: _____

Name of Company Contacted:_____

Name and Title of Reference: _____ Telephone: _____

• •

INSTRUCTIONS:
Contact the reference, preferably the applicant's immediate supervisor. Identify yourself and state that you are "calling to verify some of the information given to_____
by _____ who we are considering for a position."

• •

What were the dates of his/her employment with you? From _____ To _____

What was the nature of his/her job? _____

What did you think of his/her work? _____

How would you describe his/her performance in comparison with other people? _____
_____

What job progress did he/she make? _____

What were his/her earnings? _____ Bonus? _____

Why did he/she leave your Company? _____

Would you re-employ? _____

What are his/her strong points? _____

What are his/her limitations? _____

How did he/she get along with other people? _____

Could you comment on his/her:
(a) attendance   _____
(b) dependability   _____
(c) ability to take on responsibility   _____
(d) potential for advancement   _____
(e) degree of supervision needed   _____
(f) overall attitude_____

Did he/she have any personal difficulties that interfered with his/her work?_____
_____

Is there anything else of significance that we should know? _____
_____

SIGNATURE: _____ DATE: _____

Start with a check of the dates of tenure – though approximate, compare this with what is represented on the application.

Compare the information here with the applicant's representation of his or her previous earnings.

Verifying Employment by Mail

When a former employer is reluctant or unavailable to provide information about a previous employee over the phone, a request should be mailed.

Always make your request official. Use company letterhead, an officer's signature and/or a raised corporate seal so that there can be no doubt as to the validity of your request. One way to control the information you receive is to use the Request for Information form.

Also, be sure to enclose a self-addressed stamped envelope to expedite the response. Over all, do whatever you can to make your written request appealing and easy to respond to.

Along with the Request for Information a copy of the signed Applicant Waiver form (see page 25) should be mailed to that company. Both of these forms have proven to be effective at maximizing the responses received and providing useful information.

Other commonly used letters and forms ask for a *detailed* evaluation. These efforts are normally fruitless. The more detailed the request is, the more likely it will be ignored.

If the information supplied by the applicant is correct, all that is required of the previous employer is to signify the accuracy with a single check mark, sign and return the request.

Employers may want to produce the Request for Information in duplicate so that the former employer may maintain a record of the request. Doing so, will give them the opportunity to protect themselves, should it become necessary to have documented proof of their actions regarding the matter. The inclusion of a copy of the signed Applicant Waiver should alleviate any liability concerns that the previous employer may have about providing the information that is needed.

In some cases, it is not practical to wait for the results of the employment history verification prior to hiring the applicant. If this is the case, simply indicate on the request that your company has already employed the applicant.

Although verifying past employment can be frustrating because it is often difficult to get a response, it is crucial that the attempt be made and documented. If a jury were to become involved, there is a possibility that a jury member might think, "You didn't even contact his/her last employer before hiring him/her?"

It is not absolutely necessary that a response is received, but it is important to make an effort and support it with documentation.

Request for Information (Past Employment)

DATE _____

REQUEST FOR INFORMATION

To Whom It May Concern:

Mr./Ms. _____ has applied for a position as a
_____ and states that he/she was employed by you as a
_____ from _____ to _____.

Will you kindly reply to this inquiry and return this sheet in the enclosed self-addressed envelope. Your reply will be held in strict confidence and will in no way involve you in any responsibility.

Sincerely,

Signature: _____

Name (print/type): _____ Title: _____

Company: _____ Telephone: _____

****

Is employment record correct as stated above?   Yes _____ No _____
What were this employee's duties? _____
Did he/she have custody of money or valuables?   Yes _____ No _____
Were his accounts properly kept?   Yes _____ No _____
Was his/her conduct satisfactory?   Yes _____ No _____
Do you recommend him/her for rehire?   Yes _____ No _____

He/she was: Discharged _____ Laid Off _____ Resigned _____

Please list any Workers Compensation Claims: _____

	EXCELLENT	GOOD	FAIR	POOR
Quality of work	_____	_____	_____	_____
Cooperation	_____	_____	_____	_____
Safety Habits	_____	_____	_____	_____
Personal Habits	_____	_____	_____	_____
Attendance	_____	_____	_____	_____

REMARKS: _____

_____

Company Name: _____

Person Completing Form: _____ Title: _____

Date: _____

A full size version of the form is available on page 219.

Problems with Verifying Prior Employment

When you fill out an application or prepare your resume, do you include every single past employer? More than likely, you don't. Therefore, it is safe to assume that most applicants selectively record the details of their previous employment.

Applicants leave out information concerning employers with whom they have had a bad work experience. Likewise, employers do not always reveal the truth about former employees.

Short of a full-scale investigation, there is little hope of uncovering the names of employers that the applicant chooses not to list. As such, problematic work history and other key information crucial to employment decisions may go undiscovered.

The employers that the applicant *does* include may be a source of trouble as well. There are few laws that *require* a former employer to respond to a pre-employment inquiry, and if they do respond, there is no guarantee that they are going to be truthful. In some cases, employers will "rewrite" history to simply get rid of a problem employee.

Even if the employer wants to tell the truth, he or she may choose not to because of liability concerns. The number of US lawsuits filed against former employers has been steadily increasing for the past ten years. Even if a past employer tells the truth, he or she might be sued.

> **EXAMPLE:** Suppose an employer named Mr. Hulse suspected his assistant, Miss Miller of theft. Later, Hulse fired Miller due to her inability to meet deadlines. Then Hulse observed that the theft ceased at the same time Miller was terminated. Hulse might believe that the culprit was Miller, but can't prove it. Without proof and with a high degree of liability involved, Mr. Hulse does not reveal his suspicions to those seeking details of Miller's past employment. If he were to do so, he would certainly be putting himself and the company at risk for a lawsuit.

With the time and financial costs involved in such litigation, companies have become wary of giving detailed information about a past employee's performance. In fact, many companies provide only a minimal response or none at all. Almost all former employers require a written request and then respond with only basic information about the applicant. With or without the proper paperwork, the prior employer may still not disclose that the applicant is a source of friction (i.e. "the office troublemaker") or practices poor hygiene, resulting in the loss of customers.

Applicants are aware of what is likely to be revealed by former employers. Some are even savvy enough to have friends call pretending to be a prospective employer so that they can find out precisely what will be said.

Those applicants that have gotten into trouble are not likely to admit it, and many know that their past employers will not discuss it either because of liability issues. Given that past bad behavior is not likely to be revealed by previous employers, applicants have virtually nothing to lose. Moving from job to job, they repeat their transgressions, costing companies dearly.

So what can be done? Employers must abide by the law as well as institute and follow proper procedures. Essentially, employers must do the best that they can to verify all the details about the applicant.

What about Personal References?

We've discussed the unreliability of past employers, but what about personal references? Once again, the applicant selects whom to list. Applicants purposefully choose individuals whom they believe will provide a good reference. Often those listed are best friends, close neighbors or other casual acquaintances. They are people who are going to say "good things."

If you do check references, listen for specifics. Take your time and ask questions. Think about the following:

♦ Does the person referenced seem professional?

♦ What is the reference's relationship (i.e. former employer, co-worker, etc.) to the applicant?

♦ Does he or she provide details about the applicant?

♦ If the reference says that the applicant "is hard-working," ask for an example. If he or she can't provide one, it may be an indication that the person is not being truthful.

A friend or acquaintance probably won't say that the applicant is the funniest person he or she knows, gets half drunk every night and keeps losing jobs because the alcohol and late hours affects attendance and performance. The fact that an applicant is a great worker but only works long enough to collect unemployment or has a side business so he won't be staying long is probably not going to be revealed.

Criminal History Checks

	All Applicants	Management	Whenever Claimed or Required	Forms Located
Criminal History Checks	•	•		201

Every employee is entrusted with some form of responsibility, be it large or small. Whether someone is a government official, a business professional or in-home caretaker, he or she is given responsibilities. As such, it is important to feel confident that one's employees will not take advantage of their responsibilities and commit crimes on the job. One way to achieve such confidence is to have criminal background checks performed for prospective employees.

Yet, investigation into the criminal history of an applicant has become a controversial subject. Many questions have been raised.

♦ How far should employers go to protect themselves from hiring the wrong person?

♦ What justifies the need for a criminal background check?

♦ Who should be allowed to conduct such a search?

The news media is constantly reporting on employees who commit serious crimes. These reports have no real common denominator. Perpetrators range from high-level figures to local volunteers, and the crimes run the gamut from theft to sexual assault, even murder.

> **EXAMPLE:** In 1997, a Stafford Township, NJ karate instructor admitted to committing sexual acts with seven pre-teen boys and one five-year-old girl. The subject was on parole from the State of Texas for similar charges. The resulting investigation uncovered that the subject used several other names and was a suspect for similar crimes in four additional states.

A criminal history background check combined with a Social Security Number verification would have prevented the subject from obtaining a position that facilitated the commission of his crimes.

The end result of such crimes is often the ruination of many lives, careers and even businesses. When it is revealed that the perpetrator had a history of

negligent hiring

violence, drug abuse and/or mental illness, it is clear that the employer is in trouble. The company will certainly lose business, will suffer severe damage to their reputation and, most likely, will be sued. People believe, and perhaps justifiably so, that the company should have known what kind of employee they had hired.

Business owners need to consider the possibility that one of their employees may commit a serious crime, and that the company itself will be liable. Employers should ask these questions:

♦ Can the company withstand the negative publicity that would result from such an unfortunate incident?

♦ Are such incidents covered by the company's current insurance policies?

♦ From where would the funds to pay the legal bills originate?

♦ Are personal assets protected by the corporate structure?

♦ How much business is likely to be lost?

Thankfully, federal and state legislatures have been responding to these issues by passing new laws that require criminal background checks. In 1998, New Jersey lawmakers proposed new laws that require criminal history checks for real estate appraisers, those who work with the institutionalized elderly, healthcare workers, childcare workers and sports volunteers. Similarly, in August 1998, the State of New York approved a law allowing parents to investigate nannies and au pairs.

How to Perform a Criminal History Search

For some industries, lawful employment actually requires that a full, national criminal history be conducted. Industries affected by the mandate include power plants and related field governed by the Nuclear Regulatory Commission. No employee can be hired and have access to a nuclear power plant in the US without first having passed the required, national criminal history search. Other than the industries affected by this mandate, there is *no* method for obtaining a national criminal history.

Criminal record searching is perhaps the most complicated and inconclusive part of the screening process.

First, there is no national database available to employers or the general public. All states but one (MS) have a central state agency that collects criminal record information from state police and the court system. Five states deny access. Of the remaining 45 states, 17 states have severely restrictive policies and require extensive forms or the use of fingerprints. Thus, an extended delay is often experienced.

In addition, there are many stories of records not making it from the courthouse to the record center. Also, there is no consistency in record keeping regarding people who have been arrested for a crime, but the trial has dragged out as much as a year. The reality is, the applicant who looks good on paper, may be awaiting disposition on a major felony that occurred 11 months ago.

So, in those states where records are unavailable, checking criminal records at the county level is a must. This can get costly if multiple counties are searched, but may still be worth the expense. If an applicant lives in close proximity to the border of another county and an employer does not check the records from both counties, there is a chance a criminal record will go unnoticed.

Commercial vendors of criminal records or pre-employment screening firms offer a strong alternative to accessing the records yourself. They are professionals and know the ins and outs of working with state agencies and county courts.

However, beware of the vendors promising to look up a record in their "national database." There is no such database in existence that is available to the public.

There are several states and a handful of courts willing to sell their criminal record database to vendors, but the vast majority of records must still be searched through the government agencies.

What levels should be checked?

Criminal history checks should be done statewide in those states that provide for such a search. When statewide searches are not available, at a minimum the county of residence should be checked. It is not a bad idea to check the surrounding counties also, especially if a large city is nearby. If the applicant has lived in four different counties, or lived in one county but worked in another, those counties should be checked individually.

Federal searches are not part of typical screening procedures. However, certain positions, such as that of a worker in a nuclear facility, require a search via the National Crime Information Center (NCIC). If such a search is mandated, fingerprints and cooperation with the FBI is required.

What is needed from the applicant?

Most states and all counties do *not* require fingerprints for a statewide search. Normally, state agencies require the name, date of birth, Social Security Number, range of years to check and any additional names that are used by the subject of the search. County checks are by name, date of birth and Social Security Number. County courts are more apt to charge for additional name searches. Many jurisdictions require signed release forms. In some states, the applicant's signature must be notarized.

What are the typical costs and turnaround times for the searches?

Purchasing criminal checks directly from the courts normally costs between $5.00 and $10.00 at the county level and range from $10.00 to $25.00 at the state level. State searches take anywhere from three to forty-five days to be processed and returned, and the typical turnaround time at the county level is three to thirty days. When accompanied by a fingerprint card, the fee is typically $25.00 and receiving the results takes considerably longer. Using a screening vendor will increase your costs but will reduce your turnaround time.

Statewide criminal history searches range in cost from $10.00 to $25.00 depending upon the venue. The turnaround time can be as short as three days in states such as Florida and New Jersey or as long as thirty days in states like Pennsylvania and Washington.

What information will be found in the report?

The information received normally provides details on convictions and pending cases. In New Jersey, the State Police provide all convictions and all cases that appear to be open without disposition. They do not provide any case where there has been acquittal or "not guilty" verdict.

A Few Comments on Negative Findings

The presence of a criminal history should not always result in automatic rejection, especially if the applicant has admitted that he or she has a criminal record. Federal and state human resource personnel are required to consider the following factors in determining whether a criminal record is reason for rejection:

♦ The nature and seriousness of the crime

♦ The circumstances under which the crime occurred

♦ The date of the crime and the age of the applicant when the crime was committed

♦ Whether the crime was an isolated event

♦ Evidence of rehabilitation

There are also specific rules regarding disqualification. For example, a person may be denied examination, eligibility or appointment when he or she has made a false statement of any material fact or attempted any deception or fraud in any part of the selection or appointment process.

In short, any applicant who lies during the application process can't even take the required tests, much less get the job.

Local Police Record Request

Depending on the requirements of the position, it may be necessary to conduct a criminal background check. Normally this background check is conducted at a central state agency and/or local courthouses. Sometimes the check may include a search of the records held by local law enforcement agencies.

It is not always easy to obtain police records and information. There is no requirement for local law enforcement agencies to perform a records check. However, most local departments throughout the US do respond to written requests.

The response to such requests is varied. Some police departments include criminal data and others provide only general character information. Nevertheless, the results of these requests have often been the lynchpin to making a decision or identifying a potential problem.

To facilitate the need to obtain police record information, this book includes a letter that has proven effective. The letter, referred to as the Local Police Record Request, is straightforward, requires very little customization and takes only a minute to read. To make the letter even more effective, have it printed on company letterhead, and include a raised seal by a Notary Public and an original signature (i.e. not one that has been stamped on the page). Following these techniques will remove questions of authenticity so that the police department may begin processing the request without further delay.

The results of a Police Record Request can reveal surprising and important information.

> **EXAMPLE:** Mr. Hill applies for a job working for a pharmacy. The employer initiates the verification process and at first, everything appears normal. However, there seems to be a severe absence of any credit information, an expired driver's license and a several year gap in employment. His resume explains these discrepancies. Supposedly, Mr. Hill had spent his time "participating in social work with the poor in Afghanistan." Then, the results of a Police Record Request arrive. Although the local police department had no contact with Mr. Hill, they did receive an international police agency memo that indicated he had been recently released from prison in Afghanistan. Apparently, he had attempted to smuggle cocaine into the United States.

Mr. Hill is certainly not someone one would want working in a pharmacy! As in this example, a Police Record Request can answer lingering questions and make the hiring decision clear-cut.

A closer look at the Local Police Record Request

Using the example below, recreate this letter on your company's stationary. Replace all information contained within parenthesis with the appropriate information for your company.

A full size version of the form is available on page 208.

TO BE PRINTED ON YOUR LETTERHEAD

(DATE)

(NAME OF POLICE DEPARTMENT)
Att: Records
(STREET ADDRESS)
CITY, STATE, ZIP)

Re: (NAME OF EMPLOYEE)

Dear Sir/Madam:

Our medical facility is conducting a background check on the above-captioned prospective employee. I am writing to obtain local criminal history and/or character information from your Department. Enclosed please find a consent form with original signature, which has been notarized, authorizing the release of this information. Please indicate on the form the results of your record check, or lack thereof, and return it to us in the self-addressed stamped envelope provided.

Please advise us if there are any additional requirements, fees, etc. necessary to obtain this information.

Thank you for your assistance in this matter.

Sincerely,

(NAME - TYPED)
(TITLE - TYPED)

Verification of Educational Background

	All Applicants	Management	Whenever Claimed or Required	Forms Located
Verification of Educational Background		•	•	218

Educational background encompasses high school diplomas, GEDs, college/university degrees, trade school completion and extension courses. Unfortunately, such accomplishments are often overstated or fraudulently reported. Applicants claim successful completion of a degree or program without actually having earned it.

The educational accomplishments of an applicant tend to enhance his or her status as a viable candidate for a position. Therefore, there is a temptation to falsify one's educational background in order to appear more qualified.

Unfortunately, employers do not always confirm education claims because they don't know how. As with many areas of pre-employment, the "how" seems to be a mystery! The truth is that many facts about education claims can be verified using the Accredited Educational Institutions Section starting on page 285 of this book. The actual existence of the institution, its location, level and the types of degrees offered can be verified within these pages.

Fortunately, educational claims are very easy to verify. Attendance and completion can often be confirmed with a single phone call. If an employer requires a transcript or written verification, the process takes longer and usually involves obtaining the signature of the subject.

> **EXAMPLE:** An applicant mentions on his application that he received a "BA degree from Remington College in Lafayette, Louisiana." A quick look in the Accredited Educational Institutions Section reveals that Remington *only* grants an Associate Degree. In this case, the applicant is caught in a lie without the prospective employer having to place a single phone call.

Keep in mind, many professional and trade schools go out of business every year, and frequently, the records of their graduates are no longer available.

29% of applicants in a recent study misrepresented their educational background.

Obtaining the Information Necessary

The Request for Education Verification (see next page) places the burden of information gathering on the applicant. He or she must provide the details of education accomplishments in the spaces provided. The Request for Education Verification shows the employer's intent to verify educational background, and the applicant's signature confirms the applicant's awareness of this fact. Copies of this statement and signature may be sent to any educational institution that requires a written request for verification.

More important is the idea that with these statements clearly present on the Basic Application, applicants will be wary of making false education claims. If the applicant has prepared a glowing resume laced with phony or overstated achievements, he or she will quickly become aware that the deception has a good chance at being discovered.

Keep in mind that people say, "What's the big deal if someone 'gussies-up' their resume?" Think about it. If applicants "gussy-up" their resumes, maybe they will "gussy-up" their expense account reports.

Educational claims should always be verified, *even* if the degree listed is not one that is required for the position.

Be sure to utilize the Accredited Educational Institutions in Section 4. All the information necessary to verify someone's educational background is contained within these pages. **Take advantage of it**.

A closer look at the Request For Education Verification Form

This is the form that should be used to confirm higher education issues – whether or not they attended a college or university and earned a degree there. Have the applicant sign it early as part of the application process. This will weed out applicants who would otherwise falsify their education background.

A full size version of the form is available on page 218.

Date_____

REQUEST FOR EDUCATION VERIFICATION

Registrar's Office:

The applicant identified below has applied for a position with our organization. He/she has claimed attendance, credits and/or degree as denoted herein. Would you kindly verify this information and return this form in the enclosed self addressed stamped envelope. Please note, the applicant has signed for the release of this request.

NAME OF FACILITY

ADDRESS　　　　CITY　　　　　STATE　　ZIP

ATTENDANCE:　　FROM_____ TO _____
　　　　　　　　　　　MO.　YR.　　　MO.　YR.

CREDITS
RECEIVED: _____　GRADUATE: YES　NO　_____
　　　　TOTAL　　　　　　　　　　AWARDS-LEVEL

DEGREE: YES　NO _____ DATE _____
　　　　　　DEGREE RECEIVED

I hearby authorize the release to certify my records as stated above.

Signature　_____

Name(print)　_____

Address　_____

City/State/Zip　_____

Date of Birth　_____

SS# _____

Pay close attention to verifying the dates attended.

Check degree claimed against types of degrees granted by the school.

Confirmation of Professional Licenses & Registrations

	All Applicants	Management	Whenever Claimed or Required	Forms Located
Confirmation of Professional Licenses & Registrations			•	N/A

Depending on the profession or industry, both businesses and individuals must have a license, possess a permit and/or be registered to legally practice and/or operate.

There are clear distinctions between these methods of certification. Licensing requires that the subject have proved a level of professional competence, such as passing the Certified Public Accountant (CPA) examination. In contrast, registration is usually just signing up and posting a bond.

Unlike licensing, registration is *not* an indication of competency.

Nonetheless, verification of an applicant's claims of certification is important.

> **EXAMPLE:** XYZ Company believed that their screening policies were effective, but management decided to confirm this opinion by contracting an third party to investigate. Apparently, XYZ Company employed over a hundred employees who claimed to be certified emergency medical technicians (EMTs). When XYZ was questioned as to whether these certifications had ever been verified, the response was, "You can do that?" Thus, the verification process was initiated.
>
> After only a few phone calls to state agencies, it was uncovered that one of the licenses had never been issued and several had not been renewed. In the end, one liar was terminated and several employees were transferred, pending renewal of their certifications. Best of all, the only cost involved was the phone calls.

Generally, a particular board handles one or several types of professional and/or business certifications. As such, certification information is relatively easy to verify.

Agencies and registries maintain a wealth of information about licensees or registrants in their files. If you're an employer, you'll want to know if the applicant has a license or certification. They may deliberately omit it if it had been previously suspended.

The Privacy Question

While some agencies consider this information private and confidential to one extent or another, most agencies freely release at least some basic data over the phone or by mail.

Research indicates that many agencies appear to make their own judgments regarding what is considered private and confidential in their files. For example, according to BRB Publications' *Sourcebook of State Public Records*, although most agencies will not release a Social Security Number, 8% do. On the other hand, 45% of the agencies indicate that they will disclose adverse information about a registrant, and many of those will only disclose selected portions of the information.

In any event, the basic rule to follow when you contact a licensing agency is to **ask what specific kinds of information are available.**

What Information *May* Be Available

An agency may be willing to release part or all of the following—

- Field of Certification
- Status of License/Certificate
- Date License/Certificate Issued
- Date License/Certificate Expires
- Current or Most Recent Employer
- Social Security Number
- Address of Subject
- Complaints, Violations or Disciplinary Actions

Licensing Agency Search Fees

Several trends are common when verifying search fees of the various licensing agencies. They are as follows:

♦ There is no charge to verify if a particular person is licensed and this can usually be done over the phone.

♦ The fee for copies or faxes ranges from $0.25 to $2.00.

♦ A fee of $5 to $20 usually applies to written requests. This is due to the fact that the written certification releases more information than a verbal inquiry, i.e. disciplinary action or exam scores.

♦ A fee that is $25 or more is usually for a list of licensed professionals. For example, a hospital that needs a roster of registered nurses in a certain geographic area.

Types of Licensing, Registration & Certification

Private Licensing and Certification—requires a proven level of minimum competence before license is granted. These professional licenses separate the true "professions" from the third category below. In many of these professions, the certification body, such as the American Institute of Certified Public Accountants, is a private association whereas the licensing body, such as the New York State Education Department, is the licensing agency. Also, many professions may provide additional certifications in specialty areas.

State Licensing and Certification—requires certification through an examination and/or other requirements supervised directly by the state rather than by a private association.

Individual Registration—required if an individual intends to offer specified products or services in the designated area, but does not require certification that the person has met minimum requirements. An everyday example would be registering a handgun in a state that does not require passing a gun safety course.

Business Registration—required if a business intends to do business or offer specified products or services in a designated area, such as registering a liquor license. Some business license agencies require testing or a background check. Others merely charge a fee after a cursory review of the application.

Special Permits—give the grantee specific permission to do something, whether it is to sell hot-dogs on the corner or to put up a three story sign. Permits are usually granted at the local rather than state level of government.

Other Means of Licensing and Registration

Although much of the licensing and registration occurs at the state level, you should be aware of other places you may want to search.

Local government agencies at both the county and municipal levels require a myriad of business registrations and permits in order to do business (construction, signage, etc.) within their borders. Even where you think a business or person, such as a remodeling contractor, should have local registrations you want to check out, it is still best to start at the state level.

County Recorder's Office and City Hall. If you decide to check on local registrations and permits, call the offices at both the county—try the county recorder—and municipal level—try city hall—to find out what type of registrations may be required for the person or business you are checking out.

Just as on the state level, you should expect that basic information will be just a phone call away and that you will not be charged for obtaining a status summary.

Professional Associations. As mentioned above, many professional licenses are based on completion of the requirements of professional associations. In addition, there are many professional designations from such associations that are not recognized as official licenses by government. Other designations are basic certifications in fields that are so specialized that they are not of interest to the states, but rather only to the professionals within an industry. For example, if your company needs to hire an investigator to check out a potential fraud against you, you might want to hire a CFE—Certified Fraud Examiner—who has met the minimum requirements for that title from the Association of Certified Fraud Examiners.

Military Service Records Check

	All Applicants	Management	Whenever Claimed or Required	Forms Located
Military Service Records Check			•	209-210

Military records are accessible to the public under the Freedom of Information Act (FOIA), and are available for free by mail. In order to achieve maximum results, Standard Form 180 should be used. The form includes the specific locations to address inquiries, which are determined based on the branch in which the applicant served.

This form, known in its various updates as Form 180, is produced by the Federal Government and can be obtained from the National Personnel Records Center in St. Louis, Missouri. The current version is online at www.nara.gov/regional/mprsf180.html.

A full size version of the form is available on pages 209-210.

Request For Military Records Form (Front)

Standard Form 180 (Rev. 4-96) (EG)
Prescribed by NARA (36 CFR 1228.162(a))

NSN 7540-00-142-9360

OMB No. 3095-0029 Expires 9/30/98

REQUEST PERTAINING TO MILITARY RECORDS

To ensure the best possible service, please thoroughly review the instructions at the bottom before filling out this form. Please print clearly or type. If you need more space, use plain paper.

SECTION I - INFORMATION NEEDED TO LOCATE RECORDS (Furnish as much as possible.)

1. NAME USED DURING SERVICE (Last, first, and middle)	2. SOCIAL SECURITY NO.	3. DATE OF BIRTH	4. PLACE OF BIRTH

5. SERVICE, PAST AND PRESENT   (For an effective records search, it is important that ALL service be shown below.)

BRANCH OF SERVICE	DATES OF SERVICE		CHECK ONE		SERVICE NUMBER DURING THIS PERIOD (If unknown, please write "unknown.")
	DATE ENTERED	DATE RELEASED	OFFICER	ENLISTED	
a. ACTIVE SERVICE					
b. RESERVE SERVICE					
c. NATIONAL GUARD					

6. IS THIS PERSON DECEASED?   If "YES" enter the date of death.   ☐ NO   ☐ YES _____

7. IS (WAS) THIS PERSON RETIRED FROM MILITARY SERVICE?   ☐ YES   ☐ NO

SECTION II - INFORMATION AND/OR DOCUMENTS REQUESTED

1. REPORT OF SEPARATION (DD Form 214 or equivalent). This contains information normally needed to verify military service. It may be furnished to the veteran, the deceased veteran/s next of kin, or other persons or organizations if authorized in Section III, below. NOTE: If more than one period of service was performed, even in the same branch, there may be more than one Report of Separation. Be sure to show EACH year for which you need a copy.

☐ An UNDELETED Report of Separation is requested for the year(s) _____ . This normally will be a copy of the full separation document including such sensitive items as the character of separation, authority for separation, reason for separation, reenlistment eligibility code, separation (SPD/SPN) code, and dates of time lost. An undeleted version is ordinarily required to determine eligibility for benefits.

☐ A DELETED Report of Separation is requested for the year(s) _____ . The following information will be deleted from the copy sent: authority for separation, reason for separation, reenlistment eligibility code, separation (SPD/SPN) code, and for separations after June 30, 1979, character of separation and dates of time lost.

2. OTHER INFORMATION AND/OR DOCUMENTS REQUESTED _____

3. PURPOSE (OPTIONAL - An explanation of the purpose of the request is strictly voluntary. Such information may help the agency answering this request to provide the best possible response and will in no way be used to make a decision to deny the request.) _____

SECTION III - RETURN ADDRESS AND SIGNATURE

1. REQUESTER IS

☐ Military service member or veteran identified in Section I, above

☐ Next of kin of deceased veteran _____ (relation)

☐ Legal guardian (must submit copy of court appointment)

☐ Other (specify) _____

2. SEND INFORMATION/DOCUMENTS TO (Please print or type. See instruction 3, below.)

Name _____

Street _____ Apt. _____

City _____ State _____ ZIP Code _____

3. AUTHORIZATION SIGNATURE REQUIRED (See instruction 2, below.) I declare (or certify, verify, or state) under penalty of perjury under the laws of the United States of America that the information in this Section III is true and correct.

Signature of Requester (Please do not print.) _____

Date of this request _____ Daytime phone ( ) _____

Request for Military Records Form (Reverse)

STANDARD FORM 180 BACK (Rev. 4-96)

LOCATION OF MILITARY RECORDS

The various categories of military service records are described in the chart below. For each category there is a code number which indicates the address at the bottom of the page to which this request should be sent.

1. Health and personnel records. In most cases involving individuals no longer on active duty, the personnel record, the health record, or both can be obtained from the same location, as shown on the chart. However, some health records are available from the Department of Veterans Affairs (VA) Records Management Center (Code 11). A request for a copy of the health record should be sent to Code 11 if the person was discharged, retired, or released from active duty (separated) on or after the following dates: ARMY-- October 16, 1992; NAVY--January 31, 1994; AIR FORCE and MARINE CORPS--May 1, 1994. Health records of persons on active duty are generally kept at the local servicing clinic, and usually are available from Code 11 a week or two after the last day of active duty.

2. Records at the National Personnel Records Center. Note that it takes at least three months, and often six or seven, for the file to reach the National Personnel Records Center (Code 14) in St. Louis after the military obligation has ended (such as by discharge). If only a short time has passed, please send the inquiry to the address shown for active or current reserve members. Also, if the person has only been released from active duty but is still in a reserve status, the personnel record will stay at the location specified for reservists. A person can retain a reserve obligation for several years, even without attending meetings or receiving annual training.

3. Definitions and abbreviations. DISCHARGED--the individual has no current military status; HEALTH--Records of physical examinations, dental treatment, and outpatient medical treatment received while in a duty status (does not include records of treatment while hospitalized); TDRL--Temporary Disability Retired List.

4. Service completed before World War I (before 1929 for Coast Guard officers). The oldest military service records are at the National Archives (Code 6). Send the request there if service was completed before the following dates: ARMY--enlisted, 11/1/1912, officer, 7/1/1917; NAVY--enlisted, 1/1/1886, officer, 1/1/1903; MARINE CORPS--1/1/1905; COAST GUARD--enlisted, 1/1/1915, officer, 1/1/1929.

BRANCH   CURRENT STATUS OF SERVICE MEMBER   WHERE TO WRITE ADDRESS CODE

BRANCH	CURRENT STATUS OF SERVICE MEMBER	WHERE TO WRITE ADDRESS CODE
AIR FORCE	Discharged, deceased, or retired with pay (See paragraph 1, above, if requesting health record.)	14
	Active (including National Guard on active duty in the Air Force), TDRL, or general officers retired with pay	1
	Reserve, retired reserve in nonpay status, current National Guard officers not on active duty in the Air Force, or National Guard released from active duty in the Air Force	2
	Current National Guard enlisted not on active duty in the Air Force	13
COAST GUARD	Discharged, deceased, or retired (See paragraph 1, above, if requesting health record.)	14
	Active, reserve, or TDRL	3
MARINE CORPS	Discharged, deceased, or retired (See paragraph 1, above, if requesting health record.)	14
	Individual Ready Reserve or Fleet Marine Corps Reserve	5
	Active, Selected Marine Corps Reserve, or TDRL	4
ARMY	Discharged, deceased, or retired (See paragraph 1, above, if requesting health record.)	14
	Reserve; or active duty records of current National Guard members who performed service in the U.S. Army before 7/1/72	7
	Active enlisted (including National Guard on active duty in the U.S. Army) or TDRL enlisted	9
	Active officers (including National Guard on active duty in the U.S. Army) or TDRL officers	8
	Current National Guard enlisted not on active duty in Army (including records of Army active duty performed after 6/30/72)	13
	Current National Guard officers not on active duty in Army (including records of Army active duty performed after 6/30/72)	12
NAVY	Discharged, deceased, or retired (See paragraph 1, above, if requesting health record.)	14
	Active, reserve, or TDRL	10

ADDRESS LIST OF CUSTODIANS (BY CODE NUMBERS SHOWN ABOVE) - where to write / send this form

1 Air Force Personnel Center HQ AFPC/DPSRP 550 C Street West, Suite 19 Randolph AFB, TX 78150-4721	**5** Marine Corps Reserve Support Command (Code MMI) 15303 Andrews Road Kansas City, MO 64147-1207	**8** U.S. Total Army Personnel Command 200 Stovall Street Alexandria, VA 22332-0400
		12 Army National Guard Readiness Center NGB-ARP 111 S. George Mason Dr. Arlington, VA 22204-1382
2 Air Reserve Personnel Center/DSMR 6760 E. Irvington Pl. #4600 Denver, CO 80280-4600	**6** Archives I Textual Reference Branch (NNR1), Room 13W National Archives and Records Administration	**9** Commander USAEREC Attn: PCRE-F 8899 E. 56th St. Indianapolis, IN 46249-5301
		13 The Adjutant General (of the appropriate state, DC, or Puerto Rico)
3 Commander CGPC-Adm-3 U.S. Coast Guard 2100 2nd Street, SW. Washington, DC 20593-0001	**7** Commander U.S. Army Reserve Personnel Center ATTN: ARPC-VS 9700 Page Avenue St. Louis, MO 63132-5200	**10** Bureau of Naval Personnel Pers-313D 2 Navy Annex Washington, DC 20370-3130
		14 National Personnel Records Center (Military Personnel Records) 9700 Page Avenue St. Louis, MO 63132-5100
4 Headquarters U.S. Marine Corps Personnel Management Support Branch (MMSB-10) 2008 Elliot Road Quantico, VA 22134-5030		**11** Department of Veterans Affairs Records Management Center P.O. Box 5020 St. Louis, MO 63115-5020

Specific answers from the veteran greatly assist the processing of requests by the National Personnel Records Center. In addition, while some information can be obtained without the veteran's signature, it is most effective to include his or her signature. The results of the request will appear on a form that is known as "32 CFR 286, 32 CFR 310."

Confirmation of one's military background can be important, especially if the applicant has claimed to be the recipient of special training and/or experience as a result of service in the military. Such skills, should they prove to have been earned, might make a particular candidate a clear finalist for the position.

Motor Vehicle Reports

	All Applicants	Management	Whenever Claimed or Required	Forms Located
Motor Vehicle Reports	•	•		N/A

Reports on drivers are commonly known as driving records or MVRs (Motor Vehicle Reports). Some employers believe that MVR checks should only be required for employees whose positions require the operation of a motor vehicle. It is true that an employee who operates a motor vehicle on behalf of the employer can be a serious liability. However, an applicant's driver report provides insight into his or her background and character regardless of the position for which he or she is applying.

Specifically, the report can be used to verify the driver's license number, address, date of birth and identity.

Recorded on MVRs are the driving activities of the driver, such as moving violations, motor vehicle accidents, driving with a revoked license and driving while impaired. Obtaining and reviewing this information can enhance the assessment of an applicant. In some cases it may make the decision easy. For instance, if Mr. Brady's MVR shows that he has been caught several times for driving while impaired, chances are he will not make an excellent bus driver or machine operator.

Some applicants are required to drive 30 to 60 miles to the prospective job site. If an MVR report is part of screening procedures, it may be discovered that some of the applicants drove to the location to drop off their applications, they were driving with a revoked license. Clearly, these applicants are already breaking the rules, and if hired, they may break those of the company as well.

How to Obtain a Driving Record

Driving record information is retrievable from individual state motor vehicle departments. There is no national database, but the states communicate regarding out-of-state violations. With the advent of the federally mandated Commercial Driver's License System (CDL) drivers may no longer carry valid licenses in more than one state. Thus, all commercial license history information is maintained by the home state of the licensed driver.

Many states restrict access to driving records or to personal information (addresses, height, weight, etc.) to the general public. However, employers or their agents are entitled to the full information. States will typically require a signed affidavit form the requester, attesting to the fact that the information is being used for employment purposes. Providing a signed copy of the General Release Form may also prove helpful in making the request seem official enough to be processed.

The Driver License Number

At this time, there is not a national numbering system. Each state determines its own system of assigned driver license numbers. States use the Social Security Number as an identifier and many use the SSN as the actual driver license number. Some states, such as New Jersey, New York and Washington, have concocted a code from the name and date of birth to form a unique license number. The table on page 280 gives the format for each state. This is a good source to use when verifying if a license number is valid.

Fees and Turnaround Times

If the local DMV is right around the corner and you have the time or manpower to visit and pull a record, great! Otherwise, you will need to mail your request or use the services of a professional vendor to access a driving record. The state fee varies anywhere from a $1.00 to $16.00 (Rhode Island charges the most money). Typically, if you send a request by mail to the DMV, expect a one to four week wait. The hidden costs of doing the record search yourself include employee's time, postage and the inherent cost of waiting for the results. For a few dollars more, it may be worth hiring a vendor to access the record and deliver it to you. Vendors can usually process such requests within 1 to 48 hours, depending on the state.

The pre-employment screening companies found on pages 231-263 provide a driving record access services for employers.

The State Motor Vehicle Record Agencies Section, found on pages 273-280, provides detailed information on each state DMV and how to obtain records from them.

Sample Driving Record Abstract

The printed driving record is also known as an abstract. It contains a wealth of information about the licensee.

In the sample driving record abstract that follows, note that this license was suspended effective November 9, 1997, but the driver, one Kermit Dee Frogg, was allowed restricted driving privileges as of May 19, 1998. (We wonder if Miss Piggy knows how bad a driver "Kermie" is?)

ABC Driving Records Company, Inc.   PO Box 160147, Sacramento, CA 95816
California Driver Record — B5036   Order Date: 11/6/1998   Seq #: 1

Name:	Frogg, Kermit Dee	As of:	11/11/98
Address:	1234 Sesame St.	Misc.:	Ordered by your company
City,St,Zip:	Sacramento, CA 95831	License #:	Q2398456

Sex:	Male	Weight:	35lbs	DOB:	11/11/1968	Age: 22
Eyes:	Black	Height	1' 08"	Issue Date:	11/11/1995	
Hair:	Black			Exp. Date:	11/11/1999	

Year License First Issued: 1995   STATUS: VALID

Violations/Convictions — Failures To Appear — Accidents

Type	Viol.	Conv.	ACD	V/C	Description	Location	Docket	License	PT
ABS	10/01/1996	01/08/1997	S94	22350	prima facie spd viol–too fast cond	Encino	2541341	123456	1
FTA	04/14/1997	—	F04	2733D	Seat belt not used as req	Encino	2540554		
FTA			D45	4050A	FTA for trial/court appearance				
ABS	06/01/1997	04/30/1997	A11	23140a	DUI BAC at or over __ (DTL req.)	San Diego	2465154	123445	3
ABS	05/20/1998	08/19/1998	F04	2731D	Seat Belt not used as req.	Encino	4561514	1234567	0

Suspensions — Revocations

Actions	Ord/Date	Eff/Date	End/Date	Code	Description
Suspended	10/10/1997	11/9/1997		16070	fail to maintain req. liability ins.
Priv Rein	05/19/1998			16072	restricted driving privilege

** Verbal Notice Document on File

Miscellaneous State Data

Restriction:	Rest 01 – Must wear corrective lenses when driving
Restriction:	Rest 52 – Restricted to driving to/from/during course of employment per CVC 16072

AKA   Kermie D Frogg

Driver Class: C Any housecare and 2 axle vehicles <26,001 GVWR

End of Report for Frogg, Kermit Dee

(Thank you to American Driving Records, Inc. for help preparing this sample driving record abstract. For more information on American Driving Records, call 800-766-6877.)

What to Look for on the Record Abstract

Does the name on the abstract match that on the job application?

Every state motor vehicle agency requires that the name on one's driver's license match that of one's birth certificate. However, if one has married or divorced, the name may differ. Also, keep in mind that the name written on the application is not necessarily a fake one, it may be a preferred name or nickname.

Is the driver's license number provided valid, and does it match the subject?

If the results read "Driver Not Found" or the results have a different individual's name/address on it, confirm that the number used to search is indeed the number supplied by the applicant. If the number was recorded correctly, ask the subject to present his or her license, and verify the number.

Keep in mind that each state has its own format for driver's license numbers. In some states, a person's Social Security Number is also used as his or her driver's license number. In other states, the license number is coded to verify the driver.

> **EXAMPLE:** In New Jersey, the driver's license format is 1 alpha character followed by 14 numeric characters. The initial letter is equivalent to the first initial of the driver's last name. The first 9 numbers are coded to the driver's last name, first name and middle initial. The following 4 numbers are coded using the driver's month and year of birth. The last number is coded to the driver's eye color.

Does the address on the abstract match the address(es) provided?

Drivers' licenses are generally issued for a four to five-year period. Some people choose not to report address changes to the DMV until it is time to renew their licenses.

Nonetheless, the presence of addresses on the driver's abstract that are *not* present on the application should be questioned further.

Does the date of birth match?

The date of birth on the application should match the one listed on the driver's license abstract.

A mother and daughter or father and son may have the same name and/or address. However, comparing the two dates of birth should confirm the subject's identity. MVRs provide yet another means by which to obtain a verifiable birth date.

What is the status of the license? Valid, expired, suspended or revoked?

If a license has been expired for a long period of time, the possibility exists that the subject may be holding a license in another state. If so, an additional abstract request should be made from that state, if it is identified.

Also, if the applicant's license has been suspended or revoked, the reasons should be noted as they may impact the hiring decision. Past suspensions, though no longer in effect, will usually appear on an MVR if they are less than 39 months old.

Examine violations, accidents and points

The presence or absence of violations, accidents and points can be useful in assessing the character of the applicant.

Civil Record Searches

	All Applicants	Management	Whenever Claimed or Required	Forms Located
Civil Record Searches		•		N/A

Civil records encompass a wide range of records from numerous types of government agencies. Records can be found at local courthouses, recorder's offices, Secretary of State offices, US District Courts and US Bankruptcy Courts. Most county courts are actually part of a state court system. Also, there may be multiple courts in the same county with different jurisdictions, either geographic or by type of case.

Searching civil records can provide valuable insight into an applicant's character and financial background. These searches can uncover important and previously unknown information about the candidate, including additional names, addresses, former employer(s) and medical treatment/injuries as well as the existence of judgments, liens, bankruptcies and pending litigation.

Because the cost for these searches is relatively low, many companies are including them as part of their standard screening procedures. In some cases, searches are not performed for all applicants, but rather for promotional consideration as well as filling supervisory, management and other high-level positions.

Civil Court Searches

Civil court searches produce abstracts that identify the applicant as a plaintiff in civil cases and can identify the existence of open and closed litigation where the applicant is a defendant. The information obtained includes the following case information: type of action, location, docket number, date filed and identity of the defendant(s).

Court searches are often conducted separately for plaintiffs and defendants. To maximize results, make sure to search for both.

Court searches should be conducted for each locality wherein the applicant has resided and/or worked. In those areas where entire regions or states are accessible, employers should conduct the most extensive search possible.

Typical fees range from free to $5.00 per document plus copy and certification fees. Records at the US District courts are normally $15.00 each. You can generally search records with a full name and SSN; however, some court indices may only permit searching within a certain number or range of years without incurring additional fees. Again, court records indicate not only completed cases, but also when there is a pending or open case.

Many jurisdictions will not do searches. If this is the case, employers must perform these searches in person or arrange to have them done by a third party.

Many courts offer free public access terminals that permit requesters to view an index or list of cases within a general timeframe. If the requester wishes to view the document or order a copy, the terminal gives the index or docket number. It may take one to three weeks to receive a response by mail, so it is recommended to go directly to the court or find someone to go for you.

Lien & Judgment Searches

Liens, judgments and real estate transactions are normally usually found at county recorder's offices. This type of search indicates fines, payments, restitution and other levies the applicant owes to. Depending on the state, federal tax liens, state tax liens and Uniform Commercial Code filings are recorded at county recorder offices, Secretary of State offices or both.

The fees and response times for recorder office searching are very similar to those at the courts. Secretary of State offices are a different story. Many of these agencies offer free searching over the phone or on the Internet. Check www.brbpub.com for an updated list of state (and county) sites offering free access via the Internet.

Bankruptcy proceedings are a jurisdiction of the federal government and records are found at one of the 190 US Bankruptcy Courts. Each court has assigned counties, and there is at least one US Bankruptcy Court in each state. Fees are generally $15.00 per record.

On many occasions, the results of lien and judgment searches have surprised employers. Candidates for executive positions have been discovered to have bankruptcies and excessive tax liens. These searches have also uncovered lawsuits filed by former employers. In some cases, the applicant mentioned the lawsuit but neglected to include that is was filed because he or she apparently failed to return company property upon termination. One suit in particular involved the failure to return a company-leased vehicle. In fact, the applicant drove the car to the interview!

What to Look For in Civil Records

Variations of Names or Aliases

All names and variations of them, regardless of when they were discovered, should be searched for separately. Whether searches are conducted through a database or in person, the exact name provided is the name that the court searches, without variation. In other words, the court will not search using variations of the name unless the employer specifically provides a list of each name to be searched. Sometimes these names will not be uncovered until the results of the first search are received, in which case subsequent searches should be conducted.

Keep in mind, cases may be located under a shortened version of the proper name, under a maiden name or even a married name.

Additional Parties or Paper Trails

Suppose the driver's license abstract for an applicant is devoid of any problems. However, a court search reveals that the applicant was involved in an auto accident and related litigation. Some accidents are not reported to the police, and if the person were only a passenger in one of the vehicles, no indication would appear on his or her license abstract.

Reviewing litigation may reveal a connection between the applicant and a particular business. Whether it is a business he or she owns or used to work for, both options provide additional avenues for research.

Personal Identifiers

As mentioned previously, everyone has personal identifiers. Personal identifiers are pieces of information that serve to identify a person. Typical identifiers include a Social Security Number, a date of birth, a driver's license number and even addresses.

Employers should compare the identifiers contained in the results of any search with those provided by the applicant. Doing so will reveal new information, confirm existing information and verify that both sets of the documents refer to the same individual.

Identifiers are crucial in verifying that someone is truly involved in a court case, especially if he or she has a common name.

Dates of the Case

If a search uncovers a case involving a previous employer, the date(s) of the case should be compared to the period of employment as it appears on the application/resume. Do the dates match? If not, the applicant may not have reported his or her employment history accurately.

Sometimes applicants will admit that they were involved in litigation with a previous employer, but they will "alter" the dates during which this occurred to make their position seem more justifiable.

The Statute of Limitations in most states is two years, and it is not uncommon to file a suit just before the statute runs out. Thus, the matter that provoked the lawsuit may have occurred up to two years prior to the actual filing of the suit.

Type of Case

Medical Malpractice/Tort/Auto

These are all personal injury cases. All suits and judgments in these categories should be thoroughly investigated. For protection, businesses should know about any prior injury(ies) or medical treatment(s) the applicant may have had.

Bankruptcy

If a bankruptcy is indicated, obtain a copy of the petition and list of creditors. These documents may provide information regarding employment, income, insurance, medical treatment, assets and business affiliations as well as other valuable data.

Tax Lien/State Lien/Foreclosure

These cases can involve federal and/or state income taxes, property taxes, unemployment and disability, motor vehicle fines, alimony and child support. These kinds of cases also give insight into the applicant's character and/or financial situation.

Record Location

As with other types of public records, search all venues where the applicant may have had activity (i.e. lived, worked and/or visited for long periods of time). Know the location of the applicant's residence, past employers, etc. Does the applicant make frequent visits to another area for recreational purposes, commute long distances or frequently visit family?

Do *not* assume that because an applicant lives in a particular area, all cases involving him or her are filed in the same area. If an incident occurred somewhere else, it is possible that litigation arising from the incident was filed in that location instead. When in doubt, check it out!

Testing Methods

Rather than relying solely on public records and information requests, many employers are verifying the claims of applicants using various means of testing. The most common types are psychological and drug testing.

Psychological Testing

The use of psychological testing as a screening method has been in use for a long time. Commonly known as "the pencil and paper test," the initial use was to identify applicants who are prone to theft. Over time, the creators of these tests developed surveys designed to provide employers with more tools. Now, tests can be used to determine characteristics such as loyalty, attendance, work ethic, drug avoidance and congeniality. Some of the tests identify candidates who learn quickly, while others rate an applicant's verbal skills and specific job expertise.

The results appear to provide qualities and traits that employers cannot detect during interviews. Today such testing can even be accomplished by computer or telephone, depending on the provider used. Based on the test and method selected, the cost may be lower than $2.00 per applicant.

It has been argued that psychological testing screens out people who have mental disabilities, and is therefore a violation of the Americans with Disabilities Act (ADA). However, the issue has not been fully resolved in the legal arena. As such, a company's best bet is to establish a logical need for such tests, i.e. the employee will be carrying firearms on the job or working with small children.

Reid Psychological Systems

In Chicago, researchers at Reid Psychological Systems, a national leader in the development of pre-employment screening programs for almost 50 years, found that over 95% of college students surveyed were willing to make at least one false statement to get a job, and 41% have already done so.

In conducting this survey, Reid researchers found ten areas in which participating students most frequently misrepresented themselves when trying to get a job. The ten false statements include:

♦ Exaggerating involvement in school activities

- Exaggerating interpersonal skills

- Exaggerating the title of past business positions

- Exaggerating personal knowledge or impressions of prospective employer's corporate culture and history

- Exaggerating demeanor

- Exaggerating problem-solving skills

- Exaggerating computer experience

- Claiming untruthfully that one was well respected by past employers

- Minimizing moodiness

- Exaggerating future goals

The results of the study revealed that participants were more likely to make false statements about qualities that employers could not readily prove. Qualities such as personality, hobbies and competence were the areas most often misrepresented. In general, people conceal or minimize undesirable acts and qualities while exaggerating desirable behaviors and traits.

The Abbreviated Reid Report[3]

According to Stephen Coffman, president of Reid Psychological Systems, the "competitive nature of today's job market forces some people to devise strategies, such as misrepresenting their background, to acquire employment." However, Coffman admits, "not all college graduates make false statements to get a job." Nonetheless, he feels that it is "difficult to distinguish between individuals who do and do not misrepresent their qualifications." Therefore, he says that the "Abbreviated Reid Report is one method that many employers are using to identify quality applicants and to reduce hiring errors."

The Abbreviated Reid Report, which is a 23-item measurement scale, measures attitudes toward possible behavior. Applicants who performed well on the test were considered least likely to mislead a potential employer.

The study demonstrates the need for employment screening methods, such as pre-employment tests, employment background checks, and structured interviews. Reid has found that comprehensive and objective screening criteria can be an employer's "safety net" against hiring those who are prone to counter productive behavior.

---

[3] For more information about The Reid System and other Reid services, contact Gary W. Koeb at Reid Psychological Systems (800-922-7343), www.reidsystems.com.

The Abbreviated Reid Report is just one component of The Reid System – a unique collection of employment screening services that includes assessment and selection tests as well as background information services and telephone-based interview programs.

According to Reid Psychological Systems' press releases, the following are true:

- 95% of surveyed college students were willing to tell at least one false statement to get a job.

- 35.6% of applicants admit to shouting matches at work.

- 14.7% of applicants admit to theft of merchandise from an employer.

- 4.4% of applicants admit to theft of cash from an employer.

- 29% of applicants admit to missing paid work time without permission.

- 37.6% admit to a history of criminal acts.

- 35% of business professionals admitted to misrepresenting the truth to their clients, customers, and fellow employees.

- 20% admitted they had padded their business expense account for personal gain.

- 35% of employees admitted to late arrivals, early departures, excessive socializing and unauthorized work breaks at least monthly.

Drug Testing

The contents of this section are presented for general awareness. The information provided is not to be considered complete or as a recommendation. As with many employer options, legal input from professionals is recommended.

In the public sector, pre-employment and random drug testing have been legal for many years. A number of employees in safety-sensitive positions have caused accidents and been found to be impaired by alcohol or drugs. Railroad accidents, airline crashes, and the Exxon Valdez Oil Spill were drug or alcohol-related. The demand to protect the population and environment has compelled government agencies to develop policies and procedures designed to prevent such catastrophes. The policy of drug testing has expanded to include pre-employment, random, and post-accident. In fact, the first thought after an accident is, "Were they tested?" It has become standard practice across North America to test any involved party for drugs or alcohol after an "accident." Operators involved in auto, construction or job-related accidents very often have blood samples taken at hospitals or doctors' offices, and are routinely tested for drugs or alcohol. In some cases, law enforcement personnel make the request, while in other cases the presence, or absence, of foreign substances can influence medical treatment so a test is conducted.

In either event, the results can impact the involved parties. If an employee is found to have an illegal substance, a traffic or criminal charge may follow. If the employee is the only one injured, then an employer's insurance rates are sure to increase. On the other hand, when third parties are injured, the employer's liability increases automatically and litigation is sure to follow.

The following brief segments are provided as an overview for employers' examination.

Is Drug Testing Important to Business Today?

The United States Department of Labor estimates that 75% of drug users are employed. Employment of drug abusers has been shown to increase health care costs as well as create a loss in productivity. The National Institute of Drug Abuse reports that nearly one in four employed Americans, between the ages of eighteen and thirty-four, used drugs in the past year, and that 3.1 million employed Americans, between the same ages, used cocaine in the past year.

According to Psychemedics Corporation, government studies reveal that one out of six workers has a drug problem, and show that drug abusers, on average:

- Cost an employer $7,000 to $10,000 annually (National Institute of Health Statistics)[4]

- Cost companies 300% more in medical costs and benefits[4]

- Are absent up to 16 times more often[4]

- Are 1/3 less productive[4]

In surveys of drug abusers themselves:

- 44% admitted selling drugs to co-workers[4]

- 18% admitted stealing from employers[4]

While the statistics vary, it is a given by all companies comparing their operations before and after implementing drug testing, that the following occur:

- Substance abusers have many more on-the-job accidents than non-abusers.

- They use up to 6 times more sick leave.

- Have 3 times as many injuries and their utilization of workers' compensation claims can be as high as 5 times that of the non-abuser.

The issue of drug testing should become part of risk management and has notoriously resulted in the form of higher insurance premiums, litigation costs, and certainly effected the bottom line of many companies. According to the American Management Association, 87% of major US firms now test employees, job applicants, or both for drug use. While many of the known statistics come from larger companies, it stands to reason that all companies, no matter what their size, should compare the additional costs of hiring a drug abuser versus the cost of drug testing.

Establish a Drug Testing Policy

All stages of pre-, ongoing and post-employment procedures should be established in writing. Drug testing is no exception. According to "Drug Testing: This cup's for you," an article by Walter Lambeth, Jr. and Douglas H. Duerr in the October 1998 issue of *You and the Law*, drug policies should include the following information:

- Which substances are prohibited.

- Conditions under which testing will be required.

---

[4] For more information on Psychemedics Corporation, visit
www.westgaard.com:8080/Invite/christoph.html.

♦ What will happen if an employee tests positive or refuses to submit to testing.

When Drug Testing May Be Administered

Pre-Employment:

These tests are performed during the employment process, and before an applicant performs a covered function. They can also be administered when an employee is being transferred.

Post-Accident:

Chemical tests may be performed after an accident.

Random:

Testing of employees by random selection and in a manner that provides that all employees have an equal chance of being selected.

For Cause:

Testing of any employee who, because of their behavior or performance, can be reasonably suspected of having a drug or alcohol in their system.

Technologies Used for Drug Testing

Urine testing is the most common way to test for most drugs, and this method appears to be the least expensive.

Urine testing will only detect drug usage within the past two or three days.

Saliva specimens are easy to collect and don't pose the troubles of privacy and intrusion that urine testing does. This type test is relatively new, and the full potential is not yet completely understood.

Adhesive **sweat patches** that can collect drugs and metabolites present in sweat. They can be worn for a long period before being removed.

Hair testing is not invasive and currently provides the longest window for the detection of drug abuse, estimated at 90 days. Psychemedics Corporation has the only patent for hair testing.

The April 7, 1998 SmithKline Beecham drug testing index disclosed that 5% of the nearly 5 million workplace drug tests, performed by the company's clinical laboratories in 1997, were positive for illegal substances. That release indicated that there was a continued shift in the drugs that were detected most frequently, indicating that marijuana was detected in 60% of all positive test results as compared to 54% in 1996. Additionally, the positive test results for cocaine declined from nearly 23% in 1996 to just over 16% in 1997. Those who they tested fell into one of two categories; workers in safety-sensitive positions and all others.

While there are various methods for drug testing, and the statistics are noteworthy, the final consideration may well be the financial impact.

The Other Side

It is evident that increasing numbers of employers, both large and small, throughout North America have adopted drug testing. However, there is always another side at work.

As employers have spent time and money to make the workplace a safer environment, other factors have been busy too. It's just like "cops and robbers," every time cops come up with a way to catch crooks, the crooks eventually figure out a way to counteract those methods. Once again, books can be found that are written on the subject of drug testing and how to beat it. Not only do they define ways, from the simple to the elaborate, to try to beat a drug test, these books also specify the detection times for each drug and how long it stays in one's system. Details of how to substitute another's urine for your own, where to get the containers, and what to put in them are spelled out. They even provide specific brand names, 900 telephone numbers and opinions on which products work the best. As with Fake IDs, one only needs to go to the Internet, type in "drug testing," and everything necessary can be obtained in minutes. The Internet even offers a product called *Clean'n Clear*. It comes with a double-your-money-back guarantee and guarantees passing of drug tests. The advertiser boasts that this product is undetectable, confidential, and has free same-day shipping — all for just $19.95.

No business should institute a drug testing program without first establishing a comprehensive policy and set of procedures.

Many of the companies that provide drug testing services can assist employers by furnishing basic policies, which can then be adjusted to an individual company's needs.

Keep In Mind

Jane Esater Bahls article, "Dealing With Drugs: Keep it Legal" in the March 1998 issue of *HR Magazine*, recommends that one "[b]ase employment decisions on the person's performance or violation of company rules, and don't assume that every abuser is an addict."

Web Sites Related to Drugs & the Workplace

Institute for a Drug-Free Workplace
www.drugfreeworkplace.org

> The site includes the following mission statement on the main page: "The Institute for a Drug-Free Workplace is an independent, self-sustaining coalition of businesses, business organizations and individuals dedicated to preserving the rights of employers and employees in drug-abuse prevention programs and to positively influencing the national debate of these issues."

Making Your Workplace Drug Free: A Kit for Employers
www.health.org/wpkit

> This site is geared towards helping employees establish a drug free work environment. Both employee and employer fact sheets are included.

Other Methods of Testing

Handwriting Analysis

Investigators and psychologists have long used handwriting analysis as a means by which to understand another person. Now, employers are also using handwriting analysis as a tool to screen applicants.

The analysis involves a close examination of the shape and direction of letters in a sample piece of handwriting from the applicant.

Handwriting analysis is less expensive than full-blown psychological testing. Shop around to obtain the best price.

Skills & Aptitudes Testing

Some companies utilize written examinations that test an individual's knowledge of a subject or his or her intelligence level.

These tests can also come involve demonstrations of one's ability to handle physical labor (i.e. lifting objects that will be lifted often on the job). Sometimes these tests involve taking dictation, writing a letter and/or filing.

Basing a hiring decision on the results of a skills and/or aptitudes test can result in charges of discrimination. Consult your state's laws regarding such testing.

Lie Detector Tests

Most employers are prohibited from administering lie detector tests as a condition of employment under the federal Employee Polygraph Protection Act. The exceptions to this act include occupations that involve pharmaceuticals, national security, private security and/or defense.

The most common type of lie detector test measures stress when pertinent questions are intermixed with non-pertinent questions. History has shown that these tests can be manipulated or beaten with muscle control.

Untested Applicant Results

A study of 20,000 protective services job applicants, report in the March 1997 issue of *Security Magazine*, underscores the risk in employing untested applicants. Here are some of the statistics on the applicants who were surveyed:

♦ 33% admitted to being tempted to steal from an employer.

♦ 7% of the applicants had a criminal record.

- 30% misrepresented their employment records.

- 47% had one or more accidents or moving violations on their driving records.

- 10% had four or more moving violations, two or more accidents, a DUI or DWI, or had a suspended drivers' license.

- 21% had records of previous workers' compensation claims.

On February 23, 1996, *USA Today* reported on the results of a three-year survey of 11,000 high schoolers, college students and adults. The Josephson Institute of Ethics, a group devoted to character education, conducted the study, which resulted in the following statistics:

- 37% of high schoolers say they stole from a store in the past 12 months, up 33% from 1993.

- 65% cheated on an exam, up from 61%.

- 17% of collegiate respondents say they stole in the past year, up from 16% in 1993.

- 24% of college respondents said they would lie to get or keep a job, up from 21%.

- 47% of adult respondents said they would accept and auto body repairman's offer to include unrelated damages in an insurance claim.

The Interview

Before the Interview . . .

. . . give the Applicant a Task

When you call an applicant to schedule an interview, give him or her an assignment as well. The task might be to visit your company's web site, retail location or that of competitor. Ask him or her to make observations and develop suggestions.

During the course of the interview, ask the applicant about his or her experience performing the task. Some candidates, recognizing that the assignment is an opportunity to prove themselves, will go so far as to provide multi-page reports. Regardless, the assignment will illustrate how well an applicant can handle direction and execute a task. At a minimum, the assignment will make each interview worthwhile given that at the very least some feedback about the company will be received.

Working in Groups . . .

. . . before interviewing

As the saying goes, "Two heads are better than one." If possible, have more than one person read resumes and applications. Different perspectives will emerge, and the process of elimination will be expedited. One reviewer might notice discrepancies in a particular resume that slipped by the other person who read it. Also, if two people each have a stack of resumes, and each removes from his or her stack all those lacking adequate experience, the selection process will move much faster.

. . . during interviews

In addition, interviewing in teams can be beneficial. When two people interview a candidate, the memory of the event is shared. In other words, the ability to recall the events of the interview no longer depends upon a single person from your company. Likewise, if the interview becomes significant to a legal proceeding, the number of witnesses will be larger.

Likewise, one interviewer might focus on phrasing questions properly, ensuring that all questions are asked and making sure that pertinent topics are covered whereas the other interviewer might be more of an observer, who studies the responses as well as attempts to recall and record them clearly.

Restrict notes made during the interview to comments that relate to the job. Do not record comments on the appearance or other superficial characteristics of the candidate. Such notes can be seen as discriminatory if used as evidence in a trial.

Computer-Assisted Interviewing

The use of computers is infiltrating almost every facet of life. Therefore, it is no surprise that computers have also become involved in the interviewing process.

Everything from completing interactive applications on screen to Interactive Voice Response (IVR) telephone interviews are being used by major corporations. Of course, the expense of these technologies can make them cost-prohibitive. Nonetheless, these technologies have saved companies time and significantly reduced their turnover rates.

An article entitled "Computer-Assisted Interviewing Shortens Hiring Cycle" was published in the February 1998 issue of *HR Magazine*. According to the article, Nike is one company using these technologies. In fact, the article also reports that when a new Nike store opened, "6,000 people responded to ads for workers needed to fill 250 positions. Nike used IVR technology to make the first cut. Applicants responded to eight questions over the telephone; 3,500 applicants were screened out because they weren't available when needed or didn't have retail experience. The rest had a computer-assisted interview at the store, followed by a personal interview."

There are some who argue that using computers makes the interview process too impersonal and may result in the rejection of candidates who are truly worthy. One thing is for sure, computers cannot be accused of discrimination.

Computer-Assisted Employment Contacts

The following companies provide computer-assisted employment products and services:

Personnel Systems & Technologies Corporation (PSTC)
www.pstc.com

SHL Aspen Tree Software

www.aspentree.com

  800-899-7451
  marketing@aspentree.com

TelServe

www.telserve.com

Wonderlic

www.wonderlic.com

▬▬ A Guide to Proper Questioning

There are so many restrictions as to what employers can ask applicants that they often feel handcuffed. Some questions *definitely* cannot be asked without serious liability issues being raised.

There are some topics that should never be the source of questions in an interview. The following topics and consequently, the sample questions are never acceptable:

ECONOMIC STATUS
Do you own your own home?
Have you ever had your wages garnished?
Have you ever filed bankruptcy?

NATIONAL ORIGIN
Where were you born?
What country are you from?
Where are your ancestors from?

RELIGION
What is your religion?
Are you religious?

UNION MEMBERSHIP
Do you belong to any unions?

In addition to questions that can never be asked, there are those that must be phrased carefully. What follows are some topics that are commonly troublesome questioning areas. Both acceptable and unacceptable examples have been included.

AGE	
Possible Discrimination	How old are you? What is your date of birth?
Acceptable	Do you meet the state minimum age requirement for employment?

AVAILABILITY	
Possible Discrimination	Can you work Saturdays and Sundays?

Acceptable	Our hours of work are _____. At times, our work requires overtime — can you work such a schedule? Do you have any obligations that would prevent work-related travel?

CITIZENSHIP

Possible Discrimination	Where were you born?
Acceptable	Are you legally authorized to work in the US?

CRIMINAL HISTORY

Possible Discrimination	Have you ever been arrested?
Acceptable	Have you ever been convicted of a crime?

DISABILITIES

Possible Discrimination	Do you have any disabilities? Do you have any health problems? Have you ever filed for workers' compensation?
Acceptable	Can you perform the essential functions of the job you are applying for with or without reasonable accommodations?

MEMBERSHIPS

Possible Discrimination	To what organizations do you belong?
Acceptable	Do you want to provide any additional information that relates to your ability to perform this job?

MILITARY HISTORY

Possible Discrimination	Have you ever served in the armed forces of another country? What type of discharge did you receive?

Acceptable	Are you a US veteran?

NAME	
Possible Discrimination	Have you ever had your name changed?
Acceptable	Is there any additional information we need, about your name, to verify your employment and educational background?

RELATIONSHIPS	
Possible Discrimination	Who is the next of kin we should notify in the event of an emergency?
Acceptable	Is there someone we should notify in case of an emergency?

As mentioned in the preceding section, it is considered discriminatory to ask for vital information such as an individual's date of birth, and this would not be the time to ask for the Social Security Number or driver's license number. However, in order to conduct an appropriate screening of an applicant, specific personal identifiers and prior names are required. Some of these questions will be contained in the application and other portions may be contained in the I-9 form. The simplest way to avoid the appearance of discrimination while obtaining the necessary information is to include a line in the pre-employment inquiry release, which identifies the need for that information. The bottom line is that an employer can obtain the appropriate information using a proper form while not asking for this information in an interview, which could be considered discriminatory.

While a face to face interview is a very good tool in the selection process, it has its limitations. There is an assumption by some that little quirks exhibited during an interview will be magnified during employment. It is important to keep in mind, that though this may be true, these characteristics might remain little quirks. Nervous applicants might pull their ears, rub their foreheads, wring their hands or fidget in their seats. Other quirks include speaking rapidly or cracking of the voice. Likewise, an interview that is flawless does not necessarily mean that the person's employment will be problem free as well.

If you are truly unsure, consider a second interview. Almost everyone is at least a little nervous during an initial meeting. Often a person is much more comfortable the second time around.

Also, a lot of the same questions are used for interviews throughout the job market. Consider developing questions that you've never been asked — ones that will give you a chance to get to know even the most seasoned applicant. Develop specific scenarios that might arise were he or she to fill the position and ask for a sample response. Don't think of it as trying to catch someone off guard. Rather, consider it an opportunity for the applicant to demonstrate his or her capabilities.

What You Should Ask

The following questions are ones that are "safe." In other words, they won't be cause for discrimination claims and just about everyone should be able to answer them given the opportunity. In fact, starting with these types of questions can help the applicant relax. He or she will not feel as though you are simply getting down to business.

Where did you hear about the opening?

Ask this question of *every* applicant, and keep track of the responses regardless of whether the applicant becomes a finalist. Why? It is important to track the source of your applicants. Don't assume that the ad in the local paper is the source. It might be word-of-mouth, the Internet or something else entirely. Tracking this information need not be elaborate, it can be as simple as a tally sheet. Also, if you are not the person responsible for advertising vacancies, be sure to share your findings with that person.

What do you know about our company?

This question gives you the opportunity to find out how your company is perceived, as well as how prepared the applicant is. He or she may have taken the time to research the company, and this will give him or her the opportunity to showcase the ability to be prepared.

What motivates you?

Asking this question allows the interviewer to find out ways in which to motivate the person if he or she is hired. Perhaps, the employee likes to hear words of encouragement. If this is the case, once hired, the supervisor can make sure to encourage that employee.

What are your interests?

This question should be easy to answer and may make the applicant more comfortable given that the applicant will be speaking about things about which he or she is passionate. In addition, if hired, the employer will know what kinds of rewards (other than raises) to implement. In other words, if the applicant responds to this question by saying, "I'm a big fan of the Phoenix Suns." Then the employer might reward good performance by purchasing tickets for him or her.

What do/don't you like to do the most on a job?

The answer to these questions can be expedite the process of elimination. For instance, if the applicant says, "I don't like having to deal with customers," then the interviewer would realize that he or she is not the right person to answer the 800 line. Also, if there are multiple positions available, the answers to these questions can determine how to proceed, i.e. the position which best suits the applicant might become clear.

Can you give an example of a work experience of which you are proud?

Anyone can say, "I am a hard-worker." Asking for examples of previous employment, can enhance the assessment of the applicant. Perhaps the example provided is very similar to something that he or she would be doing for your company. If so, the example might indicate whether he or she would handle things to your satisfaction.

Give the Applicant Time to Ask Questions

Encourage all applicants to ask questions during the interview. Perhaps some applicants will not be interested in the position once they find out they have to work weekends. Also, an applicant that asks questions as well as answering them is typically well prepared.

Questions *After* the Interview

If you are the interviewer, give yourself at least five minutes between interviews during which you may compose yourself and mentally review the previous interview.

Ask yourself the following questions:

Did the applicant arrive on time?

If not, consider giving a second interview, to see if he or she will arrive on time, especially if punctuality is very important to the position.

Did the person seem enthusiastic about the position?

Those who do the best work are those you love their jobs. Even though applicants aren't really qualified at this stage in the process to "love" their job, he or she may be passionate about the industry or eager to learn. Overall, an upbeat person might perform really well if the position is customer service oriented.

Keep in mind, nerves, road rage or a bad day might make someone seem nonchalant. Use your best judgment, but a second interview might be a good idea.

Did the applicant understand your questions?

If the position is technical in nature, the applicant should not ask for a definition of all the terms used during the interview. The applicant should already be familiar with the majority of them if he or she is truly qualified.

Also, did you have to explain most of your questions? If so the person may not be capable of handling the responsibilities of the position and/or your questions may need to be reexamined. As a test, try a few of them differently during the next interview, or ask fellow employees and/or laypersons to interpret the questions to determine if your meaning is clear.

Did the person respond promptly to most questions?

A great deal of hesitancy may indicate someone who is unprepared and/or overstating his or her qualifications. Likewise, someone who answers too quickly to every question may not be taking the time to listen and/or is not thinking things through.

Stage Three:

Making an Offer of Employment

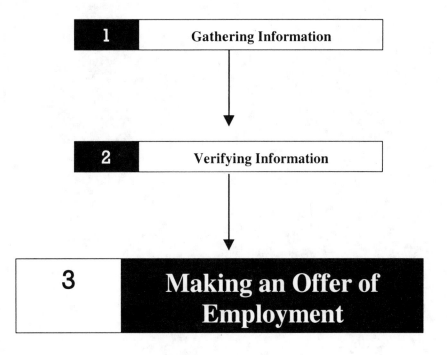

After the Decision

After the application process, after the screening and after the interviews, a decision has to be made. Only you and your company can decide which candidate best suits your needs. However, this section will show you how to act on your decision.

Rejecting Candidates

It is rare that only one person will apply for a job and also happen to be the perfect candidate. Thus, it is important to examine methods for the rejection of candidates who have been interviewed. The following options come to mind:

♦ Do nothing to notify the rejected candidate.

♦ Notify the applicant *only* if he or she contacts you.

♦ Notify the rejected applicant by phone.

♦ Notify the rejected candidate by mail.

The first two options are simply rude. Consider the fact that if someone really wants to work for your company, the applicant may postpone any further job seeking until he or she hears from you. Thus, avoiding the inevitable will only delay the applicant's search for work, which may be financially damaging to him or her. In other words, follow *The Golden Rule* – "Do unto others as you would have them do to you."

Option 3 is acceptable. However, it has its flaws. For instance, giving notice of rejection by phone does not create a "paper trail," i.e. it does not result in documentation that may be important in the future. Furthermore, rejection by phone can be awkward and uncomfortable for both parties.

Option 4 is the preferred method. Designing and implementing a form letter is the best way to handle a rejection. Rejection letters provide documentation and negate the need for an uncomfortable phone conversation.

Send rejection letters promptly to avoid awkward phone calls and/or visits from the rejected applicants. Also, maintain a copy of all rejection letters within a file devoted exclusively to the applicant.

Rejection Letter Sample

A full size version of this form is available on page 217.

(To be produced on your company letterhead)

(Insert date)

Dear *(insert name)*:

Thank you for your interest in working for our organization. Many talented and qualified people applied for this position, including you. After much consideration, we have hired another applicant.

Thank you for your time, and good luck in your job search.

Sincerely,

(Insert your name and signature here)

Before Hiring . . .

Check to make sure that the applicant will not be in violation of non-compete agreements he or she signed at other companies. Also, if the applicant works for a competitor, do not hire him or her until his or her employment for the other company has ended. Furthermore, once hired, do not allow the new employee to solicit past clients from his or her previous job.

Hiring a Candidate

At this point, the applicants have been processed, screened and interviewed. All those rejected have been sent letters signifying that someone else has been chosen. It's time to make an offer of employment to the most impressive candidate.

Make the moment a positive and memorable one by doing the following:

♦ Congratulate the applicant chosen.

♦ Explain the importance and value of the company's hiring policy.

♦ Indicate that hiring efforts are aimed at finding the best employees and providing a truly safe working environment.

♦ Acknowledge that the hiring process is a complicated one and that he or she "passed the test."

♦ Let them know that the company is proud to extend an offer of employment, and wants him or her to be a part of the team.

Have a welcome package prepared to give to the applicant that is hired. This packet should include his or her job description, a brief history of the company, appropriate policies, mission/vision statement, and a schedule that includes the date of orientation.

Above all, make a serious attempt to establish a friendly relationship from day one. Let the new hire go home excited, happy and ready to start work.

If a group is used to reject or accept candidates, be sure that the body is composed of diverse individuals. If the group consists of people from only one gender and/or ethnic background, a rejected applicant may allege discrimination.

Orientation

One of the goals of every company should be to build an efficient and stable workforce. The recruiting and selection process is only the initial stage of building a world-class organization. Development of the workforce must be continuous if the full potential of the employees is to be realized.

An effective orientation program should provide new employees with an understanding of the organization and how their performance contributes to the success of the organization as a whole. A successful program includes the following:

- The history of the company

- The company's structure and organization (e.g. names, titles and key staff)

- A copy of the company/department organizational chart

- A presentation on company benefits that includes supplemental literature

- A tour of the facility

Keep in mind that for most new employees, the first few days on the job are anxious and uncertain ones. Studies have shown that a lack of well-developed orientation programs can intensify this anxiety. The resulting stress can interfere with the progress of training and acclimation. Thus, it is recommended that at least one day be designated solely for orientation and basic tasks.

What follows is a list of procedures that, where applicable, should be included in every orientation program:

1. A welcome to the company

2. Locations of locker and wash room facilities

3. Locations of cafeteria and break facilities

4. Review of security regulations

5. Locations of work areas

6. Review of pay rate, hours, breaks and time keeping procedures

7. Summary of work group's accomplishments and duties

8. Introduction to fellow workers

9. Practice on the job, including:

    Preparation for work

    Sample tasks

Follow-up

10. Review of safety rules and the required safety equipment

11. Reminder to ask questions and seek assistance

Near the end of the first day on the job, do the following:

♦ Review pay procedure

♦ Discuss parking and car pooling

♦ Explain dispensary facilities

♦ Review safety rules

♦ Explain the work of the department and how the employee's job ties in

♦ Check on progress and questions before quitting time

During the first two weeks on the job, the following should be accomplished:

♦ Review of benefit plans

♦ Check on safety habits

♦ Follow up on progress and performance

♦ Review any items about which the employee has questions

Probationary Employment

Establish probation policies in writing and provide copies to all probationary employees.

Probationary employees may be terminated without explanation so long as that fact is made clear in the policies.

In addition, consider the details of the probationary period. Do you refer to it as a "60-day probation"? If so, employees might think that they are guaranteed the opportunity to work for the full 60 days, unless you make it clear in your policies. Also, consider using the term "working days" to extend the probationary period.

Job Descriptions

Job descriptions define the duties and requirements for a particular position, and as such, they can eliminate a host of problems. When an employee is provided with a clearly written job description, he or she can't deny knowledge of his or her position's responsibilities. Furthermore, how can someone live up to the expectations of his or her position, if they haven't been explained?

To prepare a job description, the first step is to gather all the pertinent information that is available regarding the position. The object of the job description is to create a realistic portrait of the job's scope and requirements. The single most important feature of this portrait is a comprehensive statement that relates the exact duties of the job.

If you are an employer, use the following lists of questions to establish the two parts of a job description: "Duties & Responsibilities" and "Specifications & Requirements."

Duties & Responsibilities

Physical Environment & Working Conditions

♦ Will the job be performed in an office, warehouse, factory or outdoors?

♦ What are the working conditions?

♦ Will it be hot or cold?

♦ Will there be dust, fumes or other hazards?

♦ Are there any unusual physical or environmental factors associated with the job?

Equipment, Machinery & Tools

♦ What equipment, machinery and tools will the employee be working with?

♦ Will the employee be using any special devices, instruments or gauges?

Extent of Authority & Responsibility

♦ How difficult is the job? Is it fairly simple? Or is it complex and very difficult?

♦ What is the intent and nature of the responsibility inherent in the position?

♦ How much authority will the employee be expected to exercise?

Contact With Others

♦ What is the nature and type of contact the person will have with other employees?

♦ Will there be contact with the general public and/or government officials?

♦ Will there be contact with customers or clients?

♦ If there will be contact, what will be the extent of that contact, and what are the possible ramifications of it?

Access to Information

♦ Will the employee be working with confidential and/or competitive information?

♦ What is the degree of discretion the person will be expected to exercise with regard to privileged information?

Independent Judgment, Initiative & Supervision

♦ Are the duties of the employee standardized and routine?

♦ To what degree will the person be supervised on the job?

♦ Will the person be expected to make decisions on his/her own? If so, how often, and what will the nature of those decisions be?

Job Structure

♦ Is the job fairly structured with little variability?

♦ Is there a high degree of uncertainty involved so much so that one cannot always rely on precedent or company policy for guidance?

♦ What is the nature and extent of the pressure and stress related to the job?

Terms of Employment

♦ What is the amount and manner of compensation?

♦ What are the hours of work?

♦ Is there shift work, work on weekends and/or work at night?

♦ Is there travel involved or even possible relocation?

Special Features

♦ Are there any special aspects or features of the job that would be important for an accurate and complete job description?

♦ Who are the new employee's supervisors, subordinates and peers?

Specifications & Requirements

Level of Education

♦ How much education is really necessary for this position?

♦ Will a high school education suffice or is a college degree essential?

♦ Is post-graduate work crucial? How much education is desirable?

♦ In what field or course of study should the person have specialized? Is a specific major preferred or required?

♦ Is any level of certification required and/or desired?

Prior Work Experience

♦ What type of work experience should the employee possess?

♦ How much experience is required? Years?

♦ What level of managerial or supervisory experience should the employee possess?

Specialized Skills

♦ Should the employee have specialized or technical skills?

♦ Must the employee be computer literate and/or able to type?

♦ What software should the employee be familiar with?

♦ Are there any legal or statutory requirements the employee must meet (e.g. being a licensed nurse)?

♦ What level of speaking, writing and reading are required?

Personality Traits

♦ Are certain personality traits desirable or undesirable for the position (e.g. an outgoing personality being an excellent trait for a receptionist)?

> **EXAMPLE:** Ms. Beardsley could make any computer program hum. Face to face with her supervisor, she was exuberant.

The only problem was that she could not answer the telephone properly. She forgot the company name and became terribly perplexed when asked a simple question. Ultimately, her supervisor learned that she was a "back-room" employee and not a "front-room" employee. In other words, a review of her work experience revealed that Ms. Beardsley had always worked with computers in a closed environment and had never experienced the front-end of any business.

Readymade Job Descriptions

The National Academy of Sciences, Committee on Occupational Classification and Analysis has created the *Dictionary of Occupational Titles* (DOT). Job Descriptions for everything from an abalone diver to a wrong-address clerk are included. Thankfully, the full text of the DOT is available on the Web. By visiting www.wave.net/upg/immigration/dot_index.html, one can access the full-text of the dictionary at no cost and download a searchable version.

Proper Forms

New Employee Record Chart

It is extremely important that a detailed report be kept of all employee data. The New Employee Records Chart lists the forms that must be filled out when hired and beyond. The form provides recruiters and personnel departments alike with the ability to ensure that the company's post-hiring paperwork requirements are met. A full size version of the form is available on page 211.

A closer look at the New Employee Record Chart

New Employee Record Chart

Employee _____   Position _____

Department _____   Date Employed _____

The above new employee must have checked item(s) in file.

Document	Required	Completed
Employment Application	_____	_____
Employee Data Sheet	_____	_____
W-4	_____	_____
I-9	_____	_____
Induction Form	_____	_____
Applicant Waiver Release	_____	_____
Substance Abuse Test Consent	_____	_____
Non-Compete Agreement	_____	_____
Confidentiality Agreement	_____	_____

_____

_____

_____
Supervisor

_____
Date

You may want the employee to initial receipt and completion of all these documents.

Employee Data Sheet

The Employee Data Sheet (see next page) should be completed as soon as possible after an applicant has accepted a position. The Sheet provides information which may not be asked at the time of application, but which is necessary for internal record keeping and administration. Personal information, such as date of birth and Social Security Number, is required for any death benefits and health insurance that is provided. Additionally, the same information may be required on a spouse and children in order to declare them as beneficiaries. The data on the form should be updated every year. Keeping abreast of employee status in areas such as marriage, dependents, addresses and telephone numbers.

Changes in marital status may affect a benefit program or provide insight into an employee's change in performance. If an employee's new address signifies that he or she has moved further away, an increase in travel time might explain a recent increase in tardiness. Overall, being aware of personal developments can help an employer understand and deal with changes in an employee's demeanor.

Always compare the information on the Employee Data Sheet with the documents completed during the application process. Taking this extra step can catch a liar before he or she enters your workplace!

A closer look at the Employee Data Sheet

A full size version of the form is available on page 203.

EMPLOYEE DATA SHEET

> **THE FOLLOWING INFORMATION IS NECESSARY TO MAINTAIN COMPANY RECORDS ON ALL OUR EMPLOYEES**

EMPLOYEE #:_____ DEPARTMENT:_____ DATE OF HIRE: _____

NAME: _____

ADDRESS:_____

HOME TELEPHONE NUMBER: _____

SOCIAL SECURITY #: _____ DATE OF BIRTH: _____

RACE (PLEASE CIRCLE):

WHITE   BLACK   HISPANIC   ASIAN   AMERICAN INDIAN   OTHER _____

ARE YOU A CITIZEN OF THE UNITED STATES?   _____ YES   _____NO

ALIEN REGISTRATION #: _____

MARITAL STATUS: ____ SINGLE   ____ MARRIED   ____ DIVORCED

                    ____ LEGALLY SEPARATED   ____ WIDOWED

DATE OF MARRIAGE: _____   SPOUSE'S NAME: _____

SPOUSE'S SS#: _____   SPOUSE'S DATE OF BIRTH: _____

CHILDREN:

NAME	DATE OF BIRTH	AGE	SEX
NAME	DATE OF BIRTH	AGE	SEX
NAME	DATE OF BIRTH	AGE	SEX
NAME	DATE OF BIRTH	AGE	SEX

WHO WOULD YOU LIKE US TO NOTIFY IN CASE OF EMERGENCY?

NAME: _____   RELATIONSHIP: _____

ADDRESS: _____

TELEPHONE NUMBER: _____

This information is necessary for benefits and deductions. It is best to update this information annually.

Induction Form

It is a good practice to notify all employees, at the time of hire, the terms and conditions of their employment. Even though the company may have an employee booklet or handbook, use of the Induction Form provides a concise and memorable synopsis of key rules and benefits.

There are several advantages to using the Induction Form. For instance, it eliminates confusion. When a supervisor "goes over" work hours, time keeping, holidays, vacations and other policies, the new employee often feels overwhelmed. Sometimes he or she is required to absorb so much information at once that not all of it is remembered correctly later. Misunderstandings develop, and then the employer must deal with a disgruntled employee. The Induction Form covers areas of great concern to employees and provides them with a clear, concise way to refer back to this information.

A copy of the completed Induction Form should be given to the employee and one should be retained in the employer's personnel file. Keeping a copy on file should provide the proof necessary to resolve any misunderstandings that may arise. A full size version of the form is available on page 207.

A closer look at the Induction Form

INDUCTION FORM

NAME: _____ SS#: _____

CLOCK #: _____ STARTING DATE: _____

JOB TITLE: _____

DEPT: _____ SUPERVISOR: _____

COMPANY BENEFITS AND RULES

1. HOURS: _____ AM/PM until _____ AM/PM a _____ lunch, and two _____ minute rest breaks, one at _____ and one at _____. The regular work week is _____ to _____.

2. TIME RECORDS: Punch only your own time card and in case of a mistake, take your card IMMEDIATELY to the office. After seven minutes, employees are docked 15 minutes for being late and repeated lateness is cause for discipline. If you are unable to come to work, call (___)___-___ before the start of your shift.

3. HOLIDAYS: New Years Day, Good Friday, Memorial Day, 4th of July, Labor Day, Thanksgiving, Friday after Thanksgiving, and Christmas Day.

4. VACATIONS: You will earn _____ of vacation for each _____ of employment prior to _____ up to a maximum of _____ days. _____ weeks after_____ years of service and _____ weeks after _____ years.

5. INSURANCE: The company provides _____ insurance for all employees after _____ of service. If you wish coverage for your eligible dependents, this can be arranged through payroll deduction. After _____ months, the company provide $_____ of life insurance and a weekly sick and accident insurance program that pays a maximum of $_____ for 26 weeks after the first day of an accident and after the eighth day of illness.

If you have any questions at any time regarding your pay, benefits or job assignment, please discuss it with your supervisor.
I have read and understand the information above.

_____   _____
DATE   EMPLOYEE'S SIGNATURE

Witness:
_____   _____
Date   Signature

Confidentiality & Non-Compete Agreements

In every industry, employees have access to information that should be considered confidential. With regard to confidentiality, new employees are often overlooked. Entry-level recruits initially have minimal responsibilities, perhaps only handling mundane tasks, such as answering phones, typing and/or posting bills. They seem to present no threat to a business. Yet, while performing their duties, they get to know the business very well.

Employees come to know almost everything, much of which should remain in confidence. They learn about customer lists, product costs, profit formulas, supply sources, trade secrets, business methods and/or confidential personnel information. The potential for disaster on a company-wide level grows, unless adequate precautions are taken to ensure that confidentiality is maintained.

Yet, before a company can begin to monitor confidentiality, it must address exactly what is and/or needs to be confidential. When examining a particular subject, employers should ask:

♦ What if this information became public?

♦ What if this information was given to competitors?

♦ What effect would public/competitor knowledge have on the company?

The answers to these questions should provide a clear idea as to whether some of form of confidentiality protection should be implemented. Typically, this is accomplished through the use of an agreement. Two such agreements have been provided within these pages.

A confidentiality agreement indicates that an employee has been notified of has agreed to keep private and/or secret the information that has been outlined in the pages that accompany the agreement.

A non-compete agreement is used to prevent an employee from working for a company that is in the same business for a prescribed period of time. Typical time frames range from one to five years. Non-compete agreements often include a specific area, region or number of miles from the employer.

Enforcing these agreements can be expensive and problematic depending upon the nature of the business and the terms of the agreement. Regardless, the use of such agreements represents a documented attempt to notify employees of company policy and to protect the integrity of the organization.

A business attorney can tailor these agreements to meet a particular company's needs. Regulations governing the use and enforceability of such agreements vary. Nonetheless, signed copies of these agreements should be maintained for each employee. Likewise, the agreements should be updated yearly by having the employee initial and date the original.

Without the presence and proper use of these agreements, employees can justifiably claim that they did nothing wrong when they merely "passed on" information to someone else. They can also deny any verbal notifications of confidentiality. In other words, employers should not assume that every employee automatically agrees on what is confidential and what is not. Rather, the employer should make it exceedingly clear what is public and what is private. These agreements are simply the proof that such efforts have been taken.

A closer look at the Confidentiality Agreement

CONFIDENTIALITY AGREEMENT

In consideration of being employed by _____ (Company), the undersigned hereby agrees and acknowledges:

1. That during the course of my employ there may be disclosed to me certain trade secrets of the Company; said trade secrets consisting of:

    a) Technical information: Methods, processes, formulae, compositions, inventions, machines, computer programs, and research projects.

    b) Business information: Customer lists, pricing data, sources of supply, and marketing, production, or merchandising systems or plans.

2. I shall not during, or at any time after the termination of my employment with the Company, use for myself or others, or disclose or divulge to others any trade secrets, confidential information, or any other data of the Company in violation of this agreement.

3. That upon the termination of my employ from the Company:

    a) I shall return to the Company all documents relating to the Company, including but not necessarily limited to: drawings, blueprints, reports, manuals, correspondence, consumer lists, computer programs, and all other materials and all copies thereof relating in any way to the Company's business, or in any way obtained by me during the course of my employ. I further agree that I shall not retain any copies of the forgoing.

    b) The Company may notify any future or prospective employer of the existence of this agreement.

    c) This agreement shall be binding upon me and my personal representatives and successors in interest, and shall inure to the benefit of the Company, its successors, and assigns.

    d) The enforceability of any provision to this agreement shall not impair or affect any other provision.

    e) In the event of any breach of this agreement, the Company shall have full rights to injunctive relief, in addition to any other existing rights, without requirement of posting bond.

_____   _____
SIGNATURE   DATE

A full size version of the form is available on page 200.

A closer look at a Non-Compete Agreement

GENERAL NON-COMPETE AGREEMENT

For good consideration and as an inducement for _____ (Company), to employ _____ (Employee), the undersigned employee hereby agrees not to directly or indirectly compete with the business of the Company during the period of _____ years following termination of employment and notwithstanding the cause of reason for termination.

The term "not to compete" as used herein shall mean that the Employee shall not own, operate, consult to, or be employed by any firm in a business substantially similar to or competitive with the present business of the Company or such business activity in which the Company may engage during the term of employment.

The Employee acknowledges that the Company shall or may in reliance of this agreement provide Employee access to trade secrets, customers, and other confidential data and that the provisions of this agreement are reasonably necessary to protect the Company.

This agreement shall be binding upon and inure to the benefit of the parties, their successors, assigns, and personal representatives.

Signed under seal this _____ day of _____, 19 _____.

_____
Company

_____
Employee

A full size version of the form is available on page 213.

New Hire Reporting Requirements

A new-hire reporting requirement was hidden in the Personal Responsibility and Work Opportunity Action of 1996. This statute requires all employers to report specific information on all new hires to a state agency without exception. Each state then provides the information to the US Department of Health and Human Services (DHHS) for inclusion in a national database. The main purpose of these provisions is to aid in the collection of child support monies that are owed by deadbeat parents. The information can also be used to identify workers' compensation and employment insurance fraud.

Since each state is mandated to establish its own reporting system, as an employer you should contact your state government if you have not received a notice. The DHHS web site at <u>www.acf.dhhs.gov/programs/cse</u> provides state agency contact phone numbers, frequently asked questions and policy requirements.

Essentially, the information about your company and the new-hire that is normally found on a W-4 form is the same information that is required by this statute. The minimum time frame for reports is within 20 days of hire, but states can impose a shorter duration. As with other employer requirements, it is clear that the employers are subject to fines for failure to comply.

No one escapes this requirement. Do not let new-hire reports slip through the cracks.

The forms to use for new hire reporting vary by state. To determine the requirements for a particular state, contact that state's responsible agency directly (see the following page for a list of phone numbers) or through the Internet. Typically, the agency responsible is that state's department of wages or taxation. In New Jersey, the information is sent to the Department of Labor, Division of Wage and Hour. However, New Jersey has also established a New-Hire Operations Center with toll free numbers. Also, if the company uses a payroll service, that service may provide the necessary forms.

Since this is a relatively new mandate, we have included a generic new hire reporting form. Your state may have its own form.

New Hire Reporting Offices

Alabama	334-353-8491	Montana	888-866-0327
Alaska	907-269-6685	Nebraska	402-691-9957
Arizona	602-252-4045	Nevada	888-639-7241
Arkansas	800-259-2095	New Hampshire	603-228-4033
California	916-657-0529	New Jersey	888-624-6339
Colorado	303-297-2849	New Mexico	888-878-1607
Connecticut	860-424-5044	New York	800-972-1233
Delaware	302-369-2160	North Carolina	888-514-4568
District of Columbia	888-689-6088	North Dakota	701-328-3582
Florida	850-413-9102	Ohio	800-208-8887
Georgia	888-541-0469	Oklahoma	800-317-3785
Guam	671-475-3360	Oregon	503-986-6053
Hawaii	808-587-3739	Pennsylvania	888-724-4737
Idaho	800-627-3880	Puerto Rico	787-767-1500
Illinois	800-327-4473	Rhode Island	888-870-6461
Indiana	800-437-9136	South Carolina	800-768-5858
Iowa	515-281-5331	South Dakota	888-827-6078
Kansas	888-219-7801	Tennessee	888-715-2280
Kentucky	800-817-2262	Texas	888-839-4473
Louisiana	888-223-1461	Utah	801-526-4361
Maine	207-287-2886	Vermont	802-244-7308
Maryland	888-634-4737	Virgin Islands	340-776-3700
Massachusetts	617-577-7200 X30488	Virginia	800-979-9014
Michigan	800-524-9846	Washington	800-562-0479
Minnesota	800-672-4473	West Virginia	800-835-4683
Mississippi	800-241-1330	Wisconsin	888-300-4473
Missouri	800-585-9234	Wyoming	800-970-9258

A closer look at the New Hire Reporting Form

New Hire Reporting Form

Send Completed Form to:_____

_____

_____
<small>Name & Address of New Hire State Contact</small>

Fax form to: _____
<small>Agency fax</small>

or   _____

For info, call:_____
<small>Agency phone</small>

—EMPLOYER INFORMATION —

Federal Employer
Identification Number   _____

Employer Name _____

Address   _____
<small>(Please indicate the address Income Witholding Order will be sent)</small>

City/State/Zip+4_____

—EMPLOYEE INFORMATION —

Social Security Number   _____-____-_____

Employee Name   _____

Employee Address   _____

City/State/Zip Code+4   _____

A full size version of the form is available on page 212.

Other Areas to Consider

The following areas are subjects that must be addressed for each position within a company. These topics may be covered with informational hand-outs, fill-in-the-blank forms or verbal discussions. However, some form of written communication is preferable. Employee handbooks are an excellent method of dispensing information, which should be kept current.

Hours of Employment

- What are the days of the work week?
- What are the hours of work?
- What are the start and stop times?
- What is the pay period?
- What is the policy for breaks and lunches?
- What are overtime rules and compensatory time rules?

Pay Rate

- Is the employee exempt or non-exempt?
- Per diem or contract?
- Conditions for gaining special pay – bonuses, incentives, etc.

Benefits

- What benefits are provided?
- Who is eligible for benefits?
- What family members are covered, if any?
- What is the cost to employee?

Sick Leave

- What is the method of accrual?
- What are the limitations?
- What is the notification policy?

Holidays

- ♦ Which holidays are paid holidays?
- ♦ What makes an employee eligible for holiday pay?

Vacation

- ♦ What is the method or accrual?
- ♦ How long before the length of vacation time increases?
- ♦ What are the increments of use; by the hour, half-day, full-day?

Retention Efforts

Throughout the United States, companies of all types and sizes have placed a great deal of effort on employee retention. Some programs include childcare centers (24 hours), flexible work schedules, work at home days, telecommuting, and other incentives.

In addition, many companies have begun to offer signing bonuses.

If you are an employer, offer employees a bonus for referring qualified applicants. They know the company's structure and can probably determine if someone they know is a good candidate.

There are other types of bonuses as well. Large, established companies can provide pensions, stock options or contributing investment plans to ongoing employees. New or smaller businesses don't usually have those options, but any business can offer profit-sharing when business is good. Without having a fixed program, the employer could announce something along these lines: "We had a good quarter, so here is a $200 bonus."

When someone puts in a forty-hour work week and does an excellent job, but is rarely told so, he or she can develop resentment. He or she might think, "No one around here cares how hard I work." If this is the case, the employee might not work so hard. He or she might feel like there is "no point if no one says anything about it one way or the other."

The reality is that everybody wants to feel important and be recognized. Everyone likes to be treated nicely. Employers of all sizes need to step back and look at their work force regardless of whether it is comprised of two people or two hundred. Employers should define what can be done to keep employees happy and to let them know they are important. It may sound "hokey," but it works. A few words of encouragement or a nice gesture can go a long way toward boosting morale and cultivating loyalty.

When a raise is given, it's forever. Periodic gestures can be just as effective at increasing employee satisfaction. An extra day off, a free tank of gas or a gift certificate with a note for a "job well done" are inexpensive, personal means by which to express your satisfaction with an employee's efforts. Tickets for an amusement park, sporting event or a concert have become popular as well. Clothing such as caps, shirts and sweatshirts with the company logo on them last for a long time, generate good will and are effective as advertising.

Some businesses buy their employees lunch every Friday. They have pizza, Chinese food, sub sandwiches or whatever the employees decide upon. The help is happy, and they brag about it. Five pizzas and soft drinks for twenty people is not very expensive.

Be creative and do what works for the employees, not just for the clients.

A few words about Dress Codes

Establishing a dress code can be difficult if only words are used. If you are in charge of establishing and/or implementing a dress code policy, take the time to make the policy a visual one. Gather some contemporary magazines, clip pictures that represent "do's and don'ts" and then post them in plain sight. If your company is large, make several copies and distribute them in more than one spot.

Also, be sure to provide a transitional period. Some employees may need to make purchases in order to conform to the new policy. Furthermore, consider making one day of the week a "casual" or "dress-down" day. Doing so will make the new policy easier to swallow, and increase morale by lowering dry cleaning costs. You might even consider allowing costumes on Halloween and other holidays, provided that safety is maintained of course.

Summary of the Three Stages

Let's look back and review the main points of the hiring process.

Stage 1 - Gathering Information

Basic Application Form

Remember this is a must. Without it, nothing else can be accomplished correctly.

I-9 Form

This is a requirement and an excellent way to verify the applicant's identity. Don't wait. Require every applicant to complete an I-9 at the outset.

General Release Form

This should be an all encompassing release detailing every potential provider for background proposed including credit reports, criminal histories, motor vehicle, prior employers and a screening firm if they are to be used. If an applicant doesn't sign this form don't go any further.

Specific Release Form

Remember, a separate release is required for pre-employment credit reports and criminal checks. It doesn't matter whether the work is done in-house or by a vendor, it's the law.

Confidentiality Form

Employees who can become aware of a companies private matters or personal/medical information are candidates for this form. Proof of notice may be required to defend a company in a future liability matter.

Substance Abuse Consent Form

Whether or not a drug test will actually be given, it can be valuable to see if a candidate is agreeable.

━━ Stage 2 - Pre-Employment Screening

Examine the Application

Check to make sure it is complete and signed. Then verify the information by comparing the entries with the charts in Section 4 of this book.

Call or Mail Prior Employers

Contact past employers to verify the information provided. Pay close attention to the dates of employment with an eye for gaps or deceptions.

Verify the Social Security Number

Verify the Social Security Number through the credit bureaus.

Equifax
www.equifax.com

800-685-1111

Experian
www.experian.com

800-682-7654

Trans Union
www.transunion.com

800-916-8800

This simple and inexpensive search can tell a story all by itself.

Obtain a criminal history search

Even when employees do not have contact with public, violence in the work place has been on the increase. The need to protect employees is real.

Motor Vehicle Reports

Motor vehicle reports should be obtained for anyone who may drive on company business — even if they only occasionally pick-up the mail or drop off a package. This is also a good tool for assessing overall character.

Verify those credentials - required or claimed.

Credentials include professional license and higher education degrees or accomplishments. Before giving any weight to these claims for final selection, make sure they are true. Not only do we want to eliminate the liar, but there is a need to be fair to all applicants.

Conduct the Interview

If an interview is scheduled then an applicant is being considered for employment. Set a pleasant and positive atmosphere.

Be prepared. List the questions to be asked and the topics to be covered ahead of time.

Be consistent. Ask every applicant the same questions. A simple list will keep you on target and also become a document for the personnel file.

Always have an evaluation form at hand. Don't entrust the details to memory. Plus, it's a document.

Applicants may inquire about pay rate, hours of work, raises, vacations, benefits and the like. Have a checklist to refer to or to supply to the candidate.

Any employer can do these simple things. It promotes organization, consistency and a professional atmosphere. Often times, businesses learn about themselves by preparing for this process.

Stage 3 - Making an Offer of Employment

At this point, the chosen candidate has completed the application forms appropriately, passed the screening stage and had a successful interview. Now is the time to welcome the new employee and congratulate them. It's a good idea to express pride in the organization and be enthusiastic about the candidates selection.

This is also the time to gently set the rules by making company policies clear. When introducing the induction papers, the focus should be on the positive aspects for the new employee. This is where one can go over the company benefits, whatever they are. Using the Induction Form, the work hours, lunch and break periods as well as paid holidays can be set forth. It is good to set positives before the negative, i.e. discuss company paid holidays followed by sick time policies.

W-4 Payroll Form

Be sure to verify social security number and number of dependants claimed by the employee.

New Hire Requirement Form

New Hire forms should be completed by the employer at this stage. Use the phone numbers on page 125 to obtain the forms for your state.

New Employee Data Sheet

Fill out the new employee data sheet with all the personal information such as spouse and children and their personal identifiers that will be required at the minimum for notifying someone in the case of emergency. This information is also required for any medical benefits, life insurance policies or other such items that may be ultimately offered to an employee.

Verify, Verify, Verify

This is also the time for your final check by verifying this information against the information provided in the application and used for the screening process.

Even in a small company it is a good idea to introduce the new employee to fellow workers, also the supervisors and other key personnel. Give a brief tour of the facility or shop, no matter what the size. Then an orientation program should be scheduled as the employee enters the workplace.

The flow charts that follow are useful in visualizing the three stages of the hiring process.

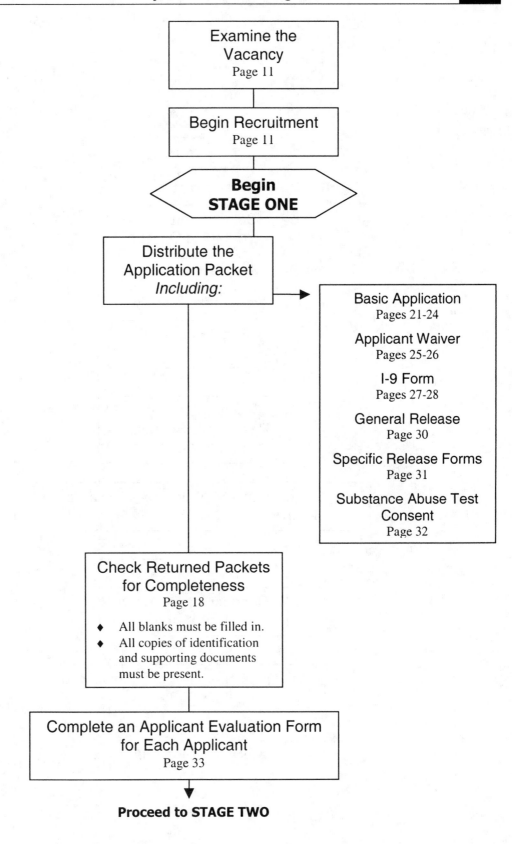

Examine the
Vacancy
Page 11

Begin Recruitment
Page 11

**Begin
STAGE ONE**

Distribute the
Application Packet
Including:

Basic Application
Pages 21-24

Applicant Waiver
Pages 25-26

I-9 Form
Pages 27-28

General Release
Page 30

Specific Release Forms
Page 31

Substance Abuse Test
Consent
Page 32

Check Returned Packets
for Completeness
Page 18

♦ All blanks must be filled in.
♦ All copies of identification
   and supporting documents
   must be present.

Complete an Applicant Evaluation Form
for Each Applicant
Page 33

Proceed to STAGE TWO

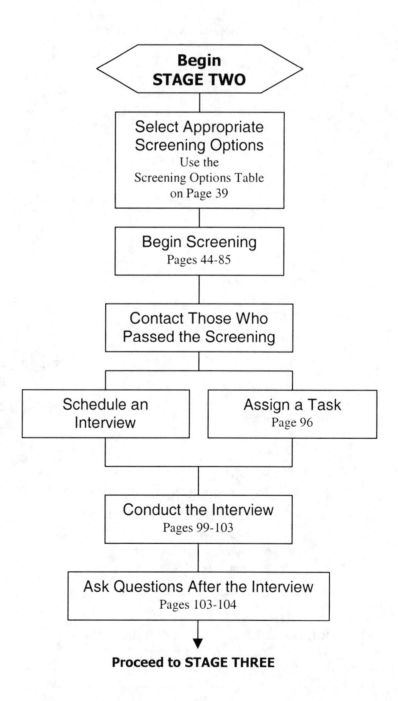

Begin
STAGE TWO

Select Appropriate
Screening Options
Use the
Screening Options Table
on Page 39

Begin Screening
Pages 44-85

Contact Those Who
Passed the Screening

Schedule an
Interview

Assign a Task
Page 96

Conduct the Interview
Pages 99-103

Ask Questions After the Interview
Pages 103-104

Proceed to STAGE THREE

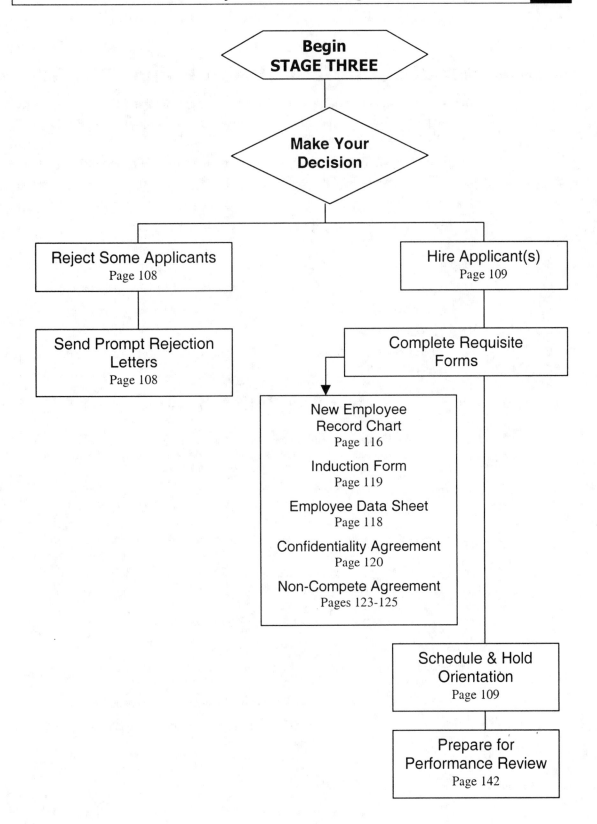

Begin STAGE THREE

Make Your Decision

Reject Some Applicants
Page 108

Hire Applicant(s)
Page 109

Send Prompt Rejection Letters
Page 108

Complete Requisite Forms

New Employee Record Chart
Page 116

Induction Form
Page 119

Employee Data Sheet
Page 118

Confidentiality Agreement
Page 120

Non-Compete Agreement
Pages 123-125

Schedule & Hold Orientation
Page 109

Prepare for Performance Review
Page 142

▬ Sample Company Hiring Policy

Finally, take all the tools, forms and advice found in this book and use it to establish your full, company policy on hiring. Put this policy in writing. An example policy for a company with twenty employees is provided below.

> **NOTE:** This sample policy assumes that all paperwork has been completed, signed and examined.

X Y Z C o m p a n y

20 Employees Total

4 Supervisors	2 Bookkeepers/Billing
3 Secretarial/Clerical	1 Bookkeeper/Accounts Payable
2 Administrators	3 Drivers/Delivery
1 Personnel/Benefits/Mail	7 Laborers

S c r e e n i n g P o l i c y M e t h o d s

Supervisors: Social Security Number verification, pre-employment credit report, criminal history, MVR, prior employment verification, civil record search, confidentiality agreement, education verification.[1]

Secretary: Social Security Number verification, criminal history, MVR, prior employment verification, confidentiality agreement. Benefits person – MVR.[2]

Bookkeepers: Social Security Number verification, pre-employment credit report, criminal history, prior employer verification, confidentiality agreement.

Drivers: Social Security Number verification, MVR[3], criminal history, prior employment verification.

Laborers: Social Security Number verification, criminal history, prior employment verification.

* * *

[1] Education verification on level of accomplishment claimed. This company has no requirement for a degree.

[2] This person uses his or her own vehicle to pick up mail and on the way home from work.

[3] These drivers' MVRs are run every six months so that the employer can be aware of any suspensions or any other serious violations.

Section Two
If Problems Develop

Unsatisfactory Performance

Every organization needs to decide what it considers to be unsatisfactory performance. Once this has been determined, managers, supervisors and entry-level employees need to be informed as to what is considered unsatisfactory.

— Reasons for Unsatisfactory Performance

The following are reasons for unsatisfactory performance. Depending on the circumstances, the reasons may be understandable, but still must be dealt with by the employer. Regardless, this list will help employers gain insight into the point-of-view of those whom they must discipline.

♦ Perhaps the employee was not informed of the company's policies. If employees are ignorant of the rules, they cannot be expected to abide by them. Communication is key.

♦ Maybe the employee was never informed as to what constitutes *acceptable* behavior or job performance.

♦ The employee may not understand his or her importance to the company as a whole. Maybe the employee feels powerless or unimportant. All employees should feel empowered.

♦ The employee may have personal problems. If this is the case, never respond by saying, "You are paid to do a job and you should leave your personal problems at home!" The reality is that everyone has personal problems, and they are not always left at the door when a person comes to work.

♦ Perhaps the employee lacks incentive. The rewards for good performance may have not been made clear.

♦ The employee's training may have been inadequate or incomplete. In this case, retraining is an option that should be explored.

♦ Perhaps when hired, there was no consideration given to whether the employee is an introvert or an extrovert. Sometimes an introvert may be asked to perform the duties of a receptionist, which can create havoc. In other words, perhaps the wrong type of person

If you are an employer, take the time to listen to your employees when problems develop. The problem may have resulted from a lack of communication, a loophole in a policy, not following proper procedures or something else entirely. However, taking the time to listen will give you the opportunity to prevent future problems. Perhaps, a policy will need to be made more clear or a new one will need to be established. Essentially, taking the time to listen may provide the solutions necessary.

Performance Reviews

Performance reviews are an excellent way to maintain quality employment. As mentioned earlier, the job description informs the employee of the company's expectations of him or her. The performance review is the follow-up.

Performance reviews give employers the opportunity to examine employee performance and let them know areas where they need to improve. Oftentimes, a performance evaluation is conducted in conjunction with a salary review, and therefore is used to determine if a pay increase should be given, and if so, how much.

There are many times when a review may be conducted. Here are a few reasons:

♦ The employee has reached the end of his or her probationary period.

♦ The employee is being considered for promotion.

♦ The employee has exhibited unsatisfactory performance.

♦ Company policy requires that a review be conducted annually.

♦ The employee has performed exceptionally well.

If the review was triggered by exceptional performance, retention efforts, such as giving him or her concert tickets, can be made.

Performance reviews are yet another means of good communication between employee and employer. Likewise, it is a step that should be documented.

By documenting performance reviews, two goals are accomplished:

♦ The employee has a written copy of areas that need improvement, and therefore may refer back to it.

♦ The employer has a document that can be used to illustrate a history of problems, if that is the case.

Designing a Performance Review Form

Given that job descriptions vary widely, as do each company's needs, employers should develop their own form. However, here some items that should be at the top.

♦ A place for the employee's name and job title.

♦ A place for the name of the supervisor conducting the review.

♦ A place for the date of the review.

The following areas should be given three or four blank lines each as well as a place for a letter grade or indication of "fair, poor, needs improvement, excellent, above average, decreased performance, satisfactory":

Availability

♦ Has the employee been punctual, tardy or a combination thereof?

♦ What about breaks? Has the employee used break and lunch times properly?

Job Awareness

♦ Does the employee seem to be aware of his or her responsibilities?

♦ Is he or she living up to the expectations of the job?

♦ Does the employee understand the relationship between his or her job and the company as a whole?

♦ Does the employee follow the chain of command when seeking assistance or making grievances?

Behavior

♦ Is the employee polite?

♦ Is he or she well mannered, especially with customers?

♦ Does he or she use good judgment?

Compliance with Policy

♦ Does the employee follow the rules?

♦ To what lengths does he or she go to adhere to policies and procedures?

♦ Has the employee neglected or ignored any of the rules?

♦ Does he or she follow safety rules?

Dependability

♦ Can the employee be counted on to perform assigned tasks?

♦ Does he or she seem willing to help others?

Initiative

♦ Does the employee raise issues that need to be addressed?

- Does he or she develop solutions?
- Does the employee identify tasks that need to be accomplished and then performs them without be asked to do so?
- Does he or she provide ideas to better the company and/or its products?
- Is the employee self-motivated?

Interaction With Others

- Does the person get along well with other employees?
- Does he or she communicate and cooperate with them?
- What about with customers?
- How does he or she handle suggestions and constructive criticism?

Independence

- Does the employee need constant supervision?
- Is the employee capable of tracking his or her assignments, or does he or she need to be reminded frequently?
- Does the employee arrive to work and begin accomplishing tasks, or does he or she always need direction?

Quality

- How accurate are the results of the employee's work?
- What do customers and/or co-workers think of the employee's work?
- How frequently are errors made?
- Does the employee take action to correct errors?

Productivity

- Over-all, how much does the employee contribute?
- Does the employee end the work week with a significant amount of tasks accomplished?
- Does the time the employee spends on tasks seem reasonable?

Summaries of Performance

After the portion of the form dealing with the above specifics, there should be some space for over-all evaluation areas. The following should be included:

♦ New and/or noteworthy accomplishments since the last evaluation.

♦ Areas which are in need of improvement.

♦ Recommendations for improvement.

♦ An over-all letter grade or designation, such as "Excellent, Above Average, Average, Below Average, Unsatisfactory, Not Rated."

There should also be additional room for comments from the employee, a date for the next review, and a place for the signatures of both the reviewer(s) and the employee reviewed.

As with all employee documents, the employee should be given a copy of the performance review and a copy should be maintained in his or her personnel file.

Sample Performance Review Form

A full size version of the form is available on pages 214-215.

Performance Review

Employee Name _____   Reviewer Name _____

Job Title _____   Date of Review _____

	Circle One	*Reviewer Notes*
Availability	Excellent	_____
Punctuality/Absence	Satisfactory	_____
Time Awareness	Needs Improvement	_____
Job Awareness	Excellent	_____
Accountabilities	Satisfactory	_____
Sets Goals	Needs Improvement	_____
Behavior	Excellent	_____
Interaction w/ Others	Satisfactory	_____
Manners/Neatness	Needs Improvement	_____
Complies w/ Policies	Excellent	_____
Follows Procedures	Satisfactory	_____
Safety Rules	Needs Improvement	_____
Dependability	Excellent	_____
Performs assignments	Satisfactory	_____
	Needs Improvement	_____
Initiative	Excellent	_____
Develops Solutions	Satisfactory	_____
Provides Ideas	Needs Improvement	_____
Independence	Excellent	_____
Tracks Assignments	Satisfactory	_____
Needs Supervision	Needs Improvement	_____
Productivity	Excellent	_____
Quality/Accuracy	Satisfactory	_____
Corrects Errors	Needs Improvement	_____

Continued

Sample Performance Review Form (page 2)

Performance Review – Page 2

_____
Employee Name
New and/or noteworthy accomplishments since last evaluation

_____
_____
_____
_____

Areas in need of improvement

_____
_____
_____
_____

Recommendations

_____
_____
_____
_____

Overall Performance Summary   **Excellent**
  (Circle one)   Satisfactory
                                       Needs Improvement

Employee Comments

_____
_____
_____
_____

_____   _____
Employee Signature   Reviewer Signature

_____   _____
Date   Date of Next Review

What to Do If You Find a Discrepancy

When verifying an application (either before or during employment), one may uncover "minor" discrepancies that do not warrant severe disciplinary action, such as an address that is not current or an old phone number. Ask yourself, does this seem to be a mistake or an attempt at deception? Spotting and acknowledging discrepancies may provide opportunities to decrease deception on a company-wide level.

When a situation along these lines occurs, keep things low key, yet notify the employee or applicant of your discovery. Calmly talk with him or her about what you've uncovered. See how he or she responds. Not only will you learn more about your employee (or potential employee), but also you will establish a communicative, working environment that is based on honesty.

Unless your discovery is in error, the employee will recognize that he or she has been "caught." Yet, he or she will be relieved that no disciplinary action will be taken. The employee may even feel better about the company given that you have been reasonable and understanding.

You and your company's capacity for uncovering deception will grow in the employee's eyes, making him or her less likely to take advantage of the company in the future. He or she will think twice about abusing sick days or filing fraudulent workers' compensation claims for fear of being caught again. In addition, if the person talks about the experience with fellow employees, others will learn that misrepresentation does not go undiscovered at your company. Reports of the incident may even reach other members of the community who are potential applicants. With time, your company will develop a reputation for taking hiring seriously.

Corrective Interviews

Many managers and supervisors shy away from conducting corrective interviews because they view them as distasteful, and they feel certain that such interviews will create a caustic environment that will leave both the employee and the manager unhappy. There's no doubt that corrective interviews can be agonizing ordeals for a manager who has not be trained on how to conduct them.

Remember, many times poor job performance is the result of the abdication of responsibility by former or current managers. It is easier to "turn your head" than to practice fair but firm managerial behavior. In addition, frequently managers do not take the time to spell out, in measurable terms, the employee's job requirements.

How to Conduct Corrective Interviews

The following guidelines will assist in conducting corrective interviews, making them a pleasant experience for both the employer and employees:

Conduct all corrective interviews in private. Many supervisors witness a violation of a work or safety rule and feel that they must act immediately to correct the employee. Consequently, the supervisor disciplines the employee in front of his or her peers, negatively impacting the employee's self-esteem.

Set aside time. Provide enough time so that the session will not be rushed. Eliminate the possibility of interruptions. Also, do not schedule the meeting just before the employee's break or lunch period.

Remain calm. Avoid anger and irritation. It is not "get-even" time. Plan the interview so that you may open the dialogue in a relaxed manner. Remember to think objectively.

Prepare for the interview beforehand. Do the following:

♦ Get the facts.

♦ Identify the reason for the poor performance and/or conduct.

♦ Consider the employee's entire performance, not just the areas of unsatisfactory behavior. When possible, point out positive aspects of employee's performance.

Stick to the topic. Do not discuss salary in relation to performance.

Do not place blame. Allow the employee the opportunity to maintain self-esteem. Do not put the employee in a remorseful position. The object is to improve performance, not punish.

Start slowly. Begin the interview with a "small talk." Don't talk about the employee's unsatisfactory performance right away. Ease into it. However, there are situations where getting directly to the problem may be the most effective.

Be up front. Inform the employee of the purpose for the meeting. For example, "The reason for this meeting is to discuss your job and how I can help you overcome some of the difficulties you may be experiencing."

Review the employee's job description. Be prepared to discuss all of the employee's responsibilities. Do not give the impression that the interview is structured by having the job description or a list of the responsibilities in front of you.

Start with the good news. Discuss the parts of the employee's job that he or she is doing best. Start by asking how the employee feels he or she is doing in the areas. The employee will probably respond that he or she feels "good" about them. Since it is true, respond that his or her performance in these areas is "better than good." Review of these positive aspects will make the employee realize that the meeting is not a "witch hunt" and should alleviate suspicions and defensiveness.

Progress from the good to the bad. Continue the list of job responsibilities until reaching the area of poor performance. Ask him or her to rate performance in these areas as well. You might even have the employee choose from "excellent, good, fair or poor."

Be specific regarding the poor performance. Point out an area in which the employee can improve. Give an example and add that you will do all that you can to help the employee better his or her performance. Broad statements only result in confusion, resistance and defensiveness. Determine the examples *before* holding the meeting.

Give equal time to the employee. He or she should be allowed to present his or her side of the story. Don't interrupt and never show displeasure or disagreement. You may find that you did not have all the facts.

End on a positive note. Tell the employee that the interview was a valuable tool, and that you hope the employee also found it to be of value.

Follow-up. Don't say you're going to check on the employee's progress and then fail to do so. However, don't crowd the employee by constantly looking over his or her shoulder. Continue to provide coaching as needed, and as performance improves, use your best judgment to decrease your coaching on the issue.

When an employee's performance improves it is important to acknowledge that that is the case. Without recognition of a job well done, the employee may not realize that there are certain behaviors he or she should not change.

A Motivational Approach to Discipline

When disciplining an employee, be sure to make statements centered on the behavior rather than on the person. Also, make sure that the statements originate from you by including the phrase "I feel." For example, don't say, "You have an attitude when you answer the phone" or "You are a very neat person." Instead, say, "*When you* answer the phone, *I feel* as though you have an attitude sometimes" or "*When you* write illegibly, *I feel* frustrated when trying to process your reports."

In other words, follow this basic model:

> "When you (fill-in-the-blank with a description of the
>   unacceptable behavior), I feel (mention your reaction and/or
>   conflict here)."

Here are some more examples:

> "*When you* arrive late, *I feel* overwhelmed trying to handle the customers."

> "*When you* miss your deadline, *I feel* pressured to take up the slack."

By focusing on the behavior of the employee, you will not risk injuring his or her self-esteem, which can lower the employee's productivity and make him or her resent you. Also, by including "I feel" statements, you are expressing your opinion clearly, and acknowledging that it is only *your* opinion, not necessarily that of everyone else.

Oftentimes supervisors who use this approach will say, "When you (blank), I feel disappointed." Then, the supervisor will follow-up with some positive statements, indicating that he or she believes in the capabilities of the employee (e.g. "I know you can do better. I saw the excellent job you did on the [blank] project."). These types of statements usually result in the employee feeling that the supervisor cares about what he or she does. In fact, he or she will know that the supervisor is disappointed with poor performance and expects better from him or her. If such statements are used, employees may leave disciplinary meetings resolved to do better and feeling confident that someone actually cares about their performance.

Give the employee an opportunity to provide a solution. Ask him or her, "What do you think you might do differently next time?" People are less resistant to their own suggestions. Plus, when a solution is provided directly from the person being disciplined, it feels less like a punishment.

How to Handle a Grievance

Handling grievances is a tricky task. These tips may make your handling of the grievance process easier:

- If an employee thinks he or she has a grievance, whether real or imaginary, it is a grievance in any case and deserves fair, open-minded, patient and considerate treatment.

- The person who is the immediate supervisor of the employee should be the first person to whom the grievance is presented.

- Grievance procedures must allow for employees to appeal and/or take their grievances to a higher level, if the original complaint is ignored, neglected, unfairly handled or if the immediate supervisor refused to acknowledge the grievance.

- Every supervisor should be informed that it is an essential part of the job to properly handle the grievances of his or her employees, and that the organization holds him or her responsible for doing so.

- Every employee should know that he or she has the right to make a grievance, and that the organization and its procedures ensure this right.

- Whether the grievance is justified or not, the employee should receive a timely decision and explanation for the basis of the decision.

- When dealing with an employee's complaint or grievance, the supervisor should discuss it in a friendly manner. The supervisor should not be augmentative, antagonistic or defensive. He or she should avoid any inference or threat of retaliation against the employee.

- When employees have complaints or grievances, the supervisor should listen fully to the employee's viewpoint, reserve judgment, discuss the grievance in private and take prompt action on the problem, if possible.

- If the supervisor or organization is at fault, the mistake should be openly admitted and prompt action should be taken to correct it.

- Don't pass the buck in accepting a grievance, in acting on a grievance, in explaining the decision on the grievance or rejecting a grievance. Only if the supervisor lacks the authority to handle the grievance, should he or she turn the matter over to someone in authority.

Termination

Legitimate Reasons for Dismissal

The following are typical and acceptable reasons for termination:

- Dishonesty.
- Failure to accomplish assigned duties.
- Committing illegal acts while on the job and/or job site.
- Endangering others.
- Violation of company policies.
- Non-compliance with company policies.
- Disclosing confidential information.
- Habitual tardiness.
- Excessive absences.
- Abusing benefits.
- Insubordination.
- Poor performance.
- Theft.
- Fraud.
- Misrepresentation.

Employment At-Will

The rule of the common law doctrine of employment at-will is created when an employee agrees to work for an employer, and there is no specification as to how long the parties expect the employment relationship to last. Under this century-old common law rule, employment relationships can, in general, be terminated at the discretion of either party.

This means that at any time, and without notice, at-will employees may quit work or be dismissed by the employer "for good cause, for no cause, or even for cause morally wrong." However, though the employee may quit for any reason, there are many restrictions on the employer's right to terminate.

In the United States, employment is considered to be of vital importance to the quality of a worker's life. However, the jobs of two out of every three workers depend almost entirely on the continued good will of their employers. The legal system, in general, presumes that the jobs of at-will employees may be terminated at the will of their employers. They also recognize that employees have a similar right to leave their jobs at any time.

Restrictions on the Right to Terminate At-Will

Congress and state legislatures have passed laws that restrict the authority of employers to exercise uncontrolled discretion in terminating employees. These laws have slowly eroded the right of employers to terminate employees for any reason or for no apparent reason. The prohibitions are reasonably definite and apply only to actions taken after their passage. Therefore, an employer can anticipate, catalog and implement the legislative exceptions with more certainty than is the case with exceptions created by the courts.

The following is a listing of the major federal statutes that place limits on the discretionary termination of at-will employees by employers:

1) Prohibitions Against Dismissals in Retaliation for Behavior Worthy of Public Protection

   a) Protected Labor Relations Activity

      i) Railway Labor Act (1962)

      ii) National Labor Relations Act (1935)

   b) Protected Activity in Support of Health and Safety Laws

      i) Energy Reorganization Act of 1974

      ii) Federal Water Pollution Control Act (1948)

      iii) Air Pollution Prevention and Control Act (1977 amend.)

      iv) Occupational Safety and Health Act (1970)

      v) Coal Mine Health and Safety Act (1969)

      vi) Railroad Safety Act (1975)

   c) Miscellaneous Activities Worthy of Public Protection

      i) Jury System Improvement Act of 1978

2) Prohibitions Against Dismissals of Employees Who are Members of Protected Groups

　　a) Members of Groups that Have Been Victims of Past Discrimination

　　　　i) Title VII of the Civil Rights Act of 1964

　　　　ii) Age Discrimination in Employment Act (1967)

　　b) Members of Groups Requiring Protection Against Economic Disadvantage

　　　　i) Fair Labor Standards Act (1938)

　　　　ii) Veteran's Employment Act (1976)

　　　　iii) Employee Retirement Income Security Act (1974)

　　　　iv) Consumer Credit Protection Act (1968)

　　c) Members of Groups Requiring Protection Against Political Discrimination

　　　　i) Civil Service Act (1978)

These federal statutes prevent employers from taking action against an employee for exercising a right under the various laws. An employee that files a complaint, gives testimony or otherwise participates in a proceeding provided by these laws, cannot be discharged for his or her actions. Many states also have statutes protecting employees from retaliation for filing claims or participating in proceedings under workers' compensation, disability laws, unemployment insurance laws, etc. Additionally, more and more judges are finding "whistle blower's" exceptions to employment at-will based upon employee conduct that is not the subject of a specific anti-retaliation statute.

If you choose to terminate an employee, make sure that your decision is consistent with company policy, does not violate any contracts with the employee and that there is documentation of efforts to warn the employee. Pretend that you will have to explain your reasoning to a jury, complete with evidence. If you feel that your argument is weak, reconsider the termination until a later time.

Common Law Limitations

The legislative exceptions to the doctrine of employment at-will have created a lot of business for the court system. The courts in turn have performed their traditional role by enforcing these statutory rules in the cases brought before them.

Some judges have gone beyond the words of these statutes and have created an additional set of exceptions. Many of the exceptions are "judge-made" or common law exceptions based on public policies that the judge believes are embodied in a state statute.

There are also times when common law exceptions have nothing to do with statutes or public policy, but are based on traditional rules of contract law that the judge believes obligate an employer.

Common law exceptions can be categorized into two very traditional areas of the common law: contract law and tort law.

Contract law   regulates the manner in which agreements between parties are interpreted and enforced.

Tort law   regulates relationships between parties who may have no agreement or contract with respect to the matter at issue.

Anyone having doubts or questions about a legal issue should contact an attorney with the appropriate expertise. Guesswork or depending on general theory obtained from some third party could result in embarrassment and be very costly.

Exit Interviews

One of the best ways to learn the real reason for a resignation is to hold an exit interview. It is imperative that any allegations made by the employee during the interview be kept confidential, if he or she so desires.

Exit interviews can indicate trouble spots or point out areas where improvements can and should be made.

> **EXAMPLE:** Mrs. Citta had to terminate Mrs. Emmets, who had continually violated company rules. Citta scheduled an exit interview with Emmets. She was very upset about being terminated and began to tell Citta, including name and dates, what employees were punching each other time cards, who was sleeping on the job, leaving early, stealing fuel from company vehicles and more. She was adamant about her allegations, and when Citta wrote them down, Emmets agreed to sign her name to indicate the veracity of her statements. Mrs. Citta had the allegations investigated, and about 90% of them were true.

Exit Interview Report

An exit interviews report form is included on pages 204-205.

<u>Section Three</u>
Abiding by the Law

Legal Issues Explained

Since there are so many laws governing employment practices, it is difficult to keep up with them. What affects one employer may not affect another, whereas some laws govern everyone. This section provides an overview of the many legal issues and how they apply.

Important Federal Discrimination Laws

In general, it is illegal to discriminate on the basis of race, color, religion, sex, age or national origin in all employment practices, which include hiring, discharging, promotion, compensation, and all other terms, privileges, and conditions of employment.

The table on the following page indicates laws that might affect your company. Following this table, are summaries of each of the laws, including contacts for more information.

Name of Law:	Affects . . .
ALL EMPLOYERS	
Civil Rights Act of 1866, 1871 & the Equal Protection Clause of the 14th Amendment (Page 161)	Discrimination based on race & sex
Equal Pay Act of 1963 (Page 162)	Discrimination based on sex
Immigration Reform & Control Act of 1986 (Page 164)	Discrimination based on citizenship
National Labor Relations Act & Related Laws (Page 162)	Interstate commerce, discrimination based on race, national origin, religion, sex, religion & union activity/affiliation
Title IX, Education Amendments Act of 1972 (Page 162)	Employers of students, discrimination based on sex
Personal Responsibility & Work Opportunity Reconciliation Act of 1996 (Page 165)	New hire procedures
EMPLOYERS WITH 15 OR MORE EMPLOYEES	
Title VII, Civil Rights Act of 1964 as amended by the Equal Employment Opportunity Act of 1972 (Page 160)	Discrimination based on race, color, religion, sex & national origin
Americans with Disabilities Act (Page 165)	Discrimination against the disabled
EMPLOYERS WITH 20 OR MORE EMPLOYEES	
Age Discrimination in Employment Act of 1967 (Page 160)	Discrimination against age
Age Discrimination in Employment Act of 1975 (Page 160)	Discrimination against age
EMPLOYERS WITH 50 OR MORE EMPLOYEES	
Executive Orders 11246, 11375 & Revised Orders 4 & 14 (Page 161)	Discrimination against race & sex
Rehabilitation Act of 1973 (Page 163)	Discrimination against disabled
Pregnancy Discrimination Act of 1978 (Page 164)	Discrimination against pregnant women

Age Discrimination in Employment Act of 1967

Who it Affects: Employers of 20 or more persons.

Details: Prohibits discriminating against persons between the ages of 40 and 70. Certain apprenticeship programs, retirement or benefit systems are exempted from these prohibitions. Forty-four states also have age laws, some of which have no age 40 to 70 limitation; therefore, all ages are protected.

For More Info: US Equal Employment Opportunity Commission
202-663-4900
www.eocc.gov

Act found at www.eeoc.gov/laws/adea.html

Age Discrimination in Employment Act of 1975

Who it Affects: Employers of 20 or more persons.

Details: This is an amendment to the 1967 Act mentioned above. It prohibits discrimination on the basis of age against all persons 40 or older by employers receiving federal funds.

For More Info: US Equal Employment Opportunity Commission
202-663-4900
www.eocc.gov

Act found at www.eeoc.gov/laws/adea.html

Title VII, Civil Rights Act of 1964 as amended by Equal Employment Opportunity Act of 1972

Who it Affects:
- All private employers of 15 or more persons.
- All educational institutions, both public and private.
- State and local governments.
- Public and private employment agencies.
- Labor unions with 15 or more members.
- Joint labor-management committees for apprenticeship and training.

Details: Prohibits discrimination on the basis of race, color, religion, sex, or national origin. It also prohibits practices caused by statistically determined adverse impact, as well as intentional, unequal treatment.

For More Info: US Equal Employment Opportunity Commission
202-663-4900
www.eocc.gov

Act found at www.eeoc.gov/laws/vii.html

Civil Rights Act of 1866, 1871 & the Equal Protection Clause of the 14th Amendment

Who it Affects: All persons within the United States.

Details: The Civil Rights Act of 1866 prohibits discrimination on the basis of race in the contract and property rights. The Civil Rights Act of 1871 prohibits public officials from violating any constitutional rights of persons, including discrimination against race, sex, etc. The Equal Protection Clause of the 14th Amendment provides equal protection under the law for all persons within the United States.

For More Info: US Equal Employment Opportunity Commission
202-663-4900
www.eeoc.gov

Executive Orders 11246, 11375 & Revised Orders 4 & 14

Who it Affects: All organizations that hold government contracts. The orders apply specifically to contractors and subcontractors who have government contracts in excess of $50,000 or who employ 50 or more people.

Details: These are Presidential orders rather than laws. These orders prohibit discrimination in employment and require Affirmative Action Plans by all federal contractors and subcontractors. Revised Order 4 covers under-utilization of females and minorities. Rule 401:2741 covers payment of dues in private clubs that discriminate on the basis of race, sex, etc.

For More Info: Office of Federal Contract Compliance
Department of Labor

Act found at www.dol.gov/dco/esa/pbulic/reqs/compliance/ofccp/fs11246.htm

Equal Pay Act of 1963

Who it Affects: All employers in the US. Subject to the Fair Labor Standards Act.

Details: Requires equal pay for men and women performing work substantially similar in skill, effort, responsibility, and working conditions unless wage differentials are due to bona fide systems of seniority, merit, output or some business factor other than sex.

For More Info: US Equal Employment Opportunity Commission
202-663-4900
www.eocc.gov

Act found at www.eeoc.gov/laws/epa.html

National Labor Relations Act & Related Laws

Who it Affects: Employers involved in interstate commerce.

Details: Governs employers involved in interstate commerce and prohibits discrimination on the basis of race, national, origin, sex, religion and union activity/affiliation.

For More Info: National Labor Relations Board
www.nlrb.gov

Title IX, Education Amendments Act of 1972

Who it Affects: Employees of students of any educational institution receiving federal financial aid.

Details: Extends coverage of the Equal Pay Act and prohibits discrimination on the basis of sex against employers of students.

For More Info: US Equal Employment Opportunity Commission
202-663-4900
www.eocc.gov

Rehabilitation Act of 1973

Who it Affects: Companies, holding government contracts of $10,000.

Details: The Act requires to take affirmative action to employ and advance qualified, handicapped individuals who meet reasonable standards for employment, that are job related and consistent with business necessity and safe performance of the job. As part of a company's affirmative action plan, reasonable accommodations must be made to the physical and mental limitations of an employee or applicant, unless it can be demonstrated that such an accommodation would impose an undue hardship on the conduct of the company's business.

For More Info: US Equal Employment Opportunity Commission
202-663-4900
`www.eocc.gov`

Act found at
`www.doc.gov/public/search/schall.htm`

Vietnam Era Veteran's Readjustment Assistance Act

Who it Affects: All organization holding a government contract in excess of $10,000.

Details: Section 402 of this act requires taking affirmative action to employ and advance qualified disabled veterans, generally from the Vietnam era, disabled and non-disabled, specifically. The Act also requires contractors to list all of their job openings with the appropriate local state employment services.

For More Info: The Office of Veterans' Reemployment Rights
Department of Labor
`www.dol.gov`

Freedom of Information Act (FOIA) & Privacy Act Of 1974 (PA)

Who it Affects: All employees.

Also, all US citizens with regard to access to information on public officials and information compiled by the CIA and FBI.

Details: The FOIA is an information access law, whereas the PA is
                      an information protection law with limited access provisions.
                      Anyone may submit a FOIA request for any type of record,
                      but a PA request may only be made by the individual (or
                      their legally authorized representative) covered by the
                      requested records. The Privacy Act provides employees
                      access to all information maintained and used in the hiring
                      process, as well as to grant salary increases and promotions
                      (i.e. performance appraisals), and allows for such
                      information to be contested or rebutted in a written
                      document; that must be maintained in the same file.

For More Info: www.usdoj.gov/foia/att_a.htm

Pregnancy Discrimination Act of 1978

Who it Affects: All employers and female employees.

Details: Prohibits discrimination in employment practices on the
                      basis of pregnancy, and requires that medical coverage and
                      leave policies for pregnancy be the same as other medical
                      coverage and/or disability policies.

For More Info: US Equal Employment Opportunity Commission
                      202-663-4900
                      www.eocc.gov

Immigration Reform & Control Act Of 1986 (IRCA)

Who it Affects: All employers and employees.

Details: Prohibits employers from hiring illegal aliens. This means
                      that employers are required to verify that employees hired
                      after November 6, 1986 are legally entitled to work in this
                      country. Employees must provide employers with documents
                      that show eligibility to work, and identity. Employers must
                      complete an Employment Eligibility Verification Form,
                      known as Form I-9 and provided in this book, attesting under
                      penalty of perjury that they are either US nationals or aliens
                      authorized to work in the United States.

For More Info: Department of Justice
                      US Immigration & Naturalization Service
                      202-514-2000
                      www.ins.usdoj.gov/index.htm

Personal Responsibility & Work Opportunity Reconciliation Act of 1996 (PRWORA)

Who it Affects: All employers and employees.

Details: Also known as the *New Hire Reporting Program*. New Hire reporting is a process by which an employer must report information on newly-hired employees to a designated State agency shortly after the date of hire. States will match New Hire reports against child support records to locate parents, establish an order or enforce an existing order for child support. Once these matches are done, the State New Hire agency transmits new hire reports to the National Directory of new hires (NDNH).

For More Info: Federal Office of Child Support Enforcement
(210) 401-9267
Department of Health and Human Services
www.acf.dhhs.gov

Americans with Disabilities Act (ADA)

Who it Affects: Employers with 15 or more employees.

Details: Prohibits from using job applications that include questions about an applicant's health, or about the nature or severity of a disability. This Act also limits an employer's use of physical examinations, and there are different sets of requirements depending on whether the examination involves an applicant or an employee. Pre-employment physical examinations may not be given under this Act before a job offer has been made. However, once an offer has been made, the rules change. After an offer has been made and before an applicant begins work, an employer may require a medical exam, and condition the job offer on the exam results, providing the following conditions are met:

♦ The medical exam must be given to all new employees in the same job category, regardless of any disabilities.

♦ Information gathered during the exam must be maintained on separate forms and in separate files for each employee.

The information must be kept confidential, except for the

fact that when appropriate, supervisors and managers may receive information about necessary work restrictions and accommodations.

For More Info: US Equal Employment Opportunity Commission
202-663-4900
www.eocc.gov

Act found at www.eeoc.gov/laws/ada.html

Fair Credit Reporting Act (FCRA)

Who it Affects: All employers, screening firms, credit card companies and any entity involved in providing "consumer reports."

Details: The purpose of the Act is to benefit consumers by strengthening privacy provisions and defining more clearly (maybe) the responsibilities and liabilities of business that provide information to access and data from credit and consumer information reporting agencies.

This Act is one of the most influential laws to impact not only employers and employees, but also all Americans. Refer to page 177 for a more detailed explanation.

For More Info: The Consumer Response Center
Federal Trade Commission
Washington, DC 20580
(202) 326-2222
www.ftc.gov

Consumer Reporting Employment Clarification Act of 1998 (Amendment to FCRA)

Who it Affects: All employers, screening firms, credit card companies and any entity involved in providing "consumer reports."

Details: This Act, which is retroactive to October 1, 1997, clarifies criminal record convictions and driving records on commercial drivers.

The Act removes the time limitation on the use of criminal records of older than 7 years within consumer reports. Previously, the FCRA stated that unless an applicant was applying for a position that paid $75,000 or more per year, criminal record information older than 7 years could not be reported by a consumer reporting agency. However, criminal *arrest* information, without conviction, still has a limitation of 7 years.

For More Info: The Consumer Response Center
Federal Trade Commission
Washington, DC 20580
(202) 326-2222
www.ftc.gov

Other Major Statutes

This section was taken directly from the US Department of Labor's web site at `www.dol.gov/dol/opa/pbulic/aboutdol/lawsprog.htm`.

The US Department of Labor administers and enforces more than 180 federal laws. These mandates and the regulations that implement them cover many workplace activities for about ten million employers and 125 million workers.

Following is a brief description of the principal statutes most commonly applicable to businesses. The intent is to acquaint you with the major labor laws and not to offer a detailed exposition of laws and regulations enforced by the Department of Labor.

Wages & Hours

The Fair Labor Standards Act prescribes standards for wages and overtime pay, which affect most private and public employment. The Wage and Hour Division of the Employment Standards Administration administers the act. It requires employers to pay covered employees the federal minimum wage and overtime of one-and-one-half-times the regular wage. It prohibits certain types of work in an employee's home. It restricts the hours that children under 16 can work and forbids their employment in certain jobs deemed too dangerous. Wage and Hour Division also enforces the workplace provisions of the Immigration and Nationality Act that apply to aliens authorized to work in the US.

Workplace Safety & Health

The Occupational Safety And Health Act (OSHA) is administered by the Occupational Safety and Health Administration (OSHA). Safety and health conditions in most private industries are regulated by OSHA or OSHA-approved state systems. Employers must identify and eliminate unhealthful or hazardous conditions; employees must comply with all rules and regulations that apply to their own workplace conduct. Covered employers are required to maintain safe and healthful work environments in keeping with requirements of the law. Effective OSHA safety and health regulations supersede others originally issued under these other laws: the Walsh-Healey Act, the Services Contract Act, the Contract Work Hours and Safety Standards Act, the Arts and Humanities Act and the Longshore and Harbor Workers' Compensation Act.

Pensions & Welfare Benefits

The Employee Retirement Income Security Act (ERISA) regulates employers who offer pension or welfare benefit plans for their employees. It preempts many similar state laws and is administered by the Pension and Welfare

Benefits Administration (PWBA). Under the statute, employers must fund an insurance system to protect certain kinds of retirement benefits, with premium payments to the federal government's Pension Benefit Guaranty Corp. Pension plans must meet a wide range of fiduciary, disclosure and reporting requirements. Employee welfare plans must meet similar requirements. PWBA also administers reporting requirements for continuation of health-care provisions, required under the Comprehensive Omnibus Budget Reconciliation Act of 1985 (COBRA).

Unions & Their Members

The Labor-Management Reporting and Disclosure Act (also known as the Landrum-Griffin Act) deals with the relationship between a union and its members. It safeguards union funds, requires reports on certain financial transactions and administrative practices of union officials, labor consultants, etc. The act is administered by the Office of Labor-Management Standards, which is part of the Employment Standards Administration.

Employee Protection

Most labor and public-safety laws and many environmental laws mandate whistleblower protections for employees who complain about employers. Remedies can include job reinstatement and payment of back wages. Enforcement is usually by the agency most concerned; e.g., OSHA enforces protections afforded by the Occupational Safety and Health Act.

Veteran's Reemployment Rights Act

Certain persons who serve in our armed forces have a right to reemployment with the employer they were with when they entered service. This includes those called up from the reserves or National Guard. These rights are administered by the Office of the Assistant Secretary for Veterans' Employment and Training.

Plant Closings & Layoffs

Such occurrences may be subject to the Worker Adjustment and Retraining Notifications Act (WARN). WARN offers employees early warning of impending layoffs or plant closings. It is administered by the Employment and Training Administration.

Garnishment of Wages

Garnishment of employee wages by employers is regulated under the Consumer Credit and Protection Act and administered by the Wage and Hour Division of ESA.

The Family & Medical Leave Act

Administered by the Wage and Hour Division of ESA, the law requires employers of 50 or more employees to give up to 12 weeks of unpaid, job-related leave to eligible employees for the birth or adoption of a child or for the serious illness of the employee or a family member.

Government Contracts, Grants or Financial Aid

Recipients of government contracts, grants or financial aid are subject to wage, hour, benefits and safety and health standards under:

♦ The Davis-Bacon Act, which mandates payment of prevailing wages and benefits to employees of contractors engaged in US government construction projects;

♦ The McNamara-O'Hara Service Contract Act, which set wage rates and other labor standards for employees of contractors furnishing services to the US government;

♦ The Walsh-Healey Public Contracts Act, which requires the Department of Labor to settle disputes of awards to manufacturers supplying products to the US government.

Administration and enforcement are by ESA's Wage and Hour Division. Non-discrimination and affirmative action requirements in other statutes are regulated by ESA's Office of Federal Contract Compliance Programs.

Industry-Specific Requirements

Agriculture

The Migrant and Seasonal Agricultural Worker Protection Act regulates the hiring and employment activities of agricultural employers, contractors and associations using migrant and seasonal workers. The Fair Labor Standards Act has special child-labor regulations that apply to agricultural employment, except for family farms that do not hire outside workers. Administration is by ESA's Wage and Hour Division.

The Immigration and Nationality Act requires employers who want to use foreign temporary workers to get a certificate from the Employment and Training Administration certifying that there are insufficient available and qualified Americans to do the work. The Immigration Reform and Control Act requires all employers of such workers to furnish reports on them to the government.

Mining Safety & Health

The Federal Mine Safety and Health Act of 1977 covers all people who work on mine property. Administration is by the Mine Safety and Health Administration (MSHA).

The Act ensures employer responsibility for the health and safety of miners; mandates regular inspections of underground and surface mines; establishes miners' training requirements; enables dangerous mines to be closed and prescribes penalties for health and safety violations. MSHA enforces safety and health regulations at more than 4,600 underground and surface coal mines and 11,000 non-coal mines. Health and safety regulations cover numerous hazards, including respirable dust, airborne contaminants and noise; design and maintenance requirements for equipment; roof falls; flammable and explosive gases, dust and smoke; electrical equipment; fires; storage, transport and use of explosives and access to mine entrances and exits.

Construction

Several agencies administer programs related solely to the construction industry. OSHA has special occupational safety and health standards for construction; ESA's Wage and Hour Division, under Davis-Bacon and related acts, requires payment of prevailing wages and benefits; ESA's Office of Federal Contract Compliance Programs has special regulations on non-discrimination and affirmative action hiring; the anti-kickback section of the Copeland Act precludes a federal contractor from inducing any employee to sacrifice any part of the compensation required.

Transportation

Most laws with labor provisions regulating the transportation industry are administered by agencies outside the Department of Labor. However, longshoring and maritime industry safety and health standards are issued and enforced by OSHA. The Longshoring and Harbor Workers' Compensation Act, administered by ESA, requires employers to assure that workers' compensation is funded and available to eligible employees.

Advisories

For more detail and guidance on laws and regulations covered in this fact sheet, call the appropriate Department of Labor agency listed in your phone book under US Government.

Other federal agencies besides the Department of Labor enforce laws and regulations that affect employers. The Equal Employment Opportunity Commission generally enforces statutes that ensure non-discrimination in employment. The Taft-Hartley Act regulates a wide range of employer-employee conduct and is administered by the National Labor Relations Board. For more information on these laws, consult these agencies; they are listed in your phone book under US Government.

Legal Issues Affecting Employees

Record Retention Requirements

Under the Civil Rights and Age Discrimination Acts, all applications must be retained for specific periods, but not less than three years. However, most companies keep the personnel records of former employees much longer to answer reference checks and other inquiries involving insurance.

At a minimum, all personnel records should be retained for a period of three years. Other employee support information, such as times cards or time sheets and work tickets, needs to be kept only for two years. Microfilm copies are generally acceptable.

Inspections

In attempt to discourage theft, consider a policy that requires employees, upon request, to open briefcases, lunch boxes, desks, lockers, toolboxes, packages and personal automobiles on company property for inspection. If an employer plans to implement such a spot-check program, the following should be considered:

♦ Provide ample advance notice of the employer's rights and intention to implement the program. Have new-hires sign an acknowledgement that permits a search of personal property at the employer's discretion.

♦ Insure that the inspections or searches are not discriminatory, nor aimed at a protected class of employees.

♦ Be sure to have reasonable cause for conducting the search. The US Supreme Court has ruled that, in the public sector, employers may search employer property such as employee offices, desks, and files, without a warrant or probable cause, as long as the search is "reasonable." Apply the inspection uniformly; avoid the appearance of being "out to get" an individual or group of individuals.

Employee Searches

Employee theft is a major problem that involves privacy rights in the workplace. An employer can begin to control employee theft by implementing a consistent policy that makes the following clear to all employees:

♦ Company supplies, products or manufactured items of any type may not be removed from their normal locations, (e.g., concealed in an employee's person, toolbox, or locker) nor removed from company property.

- Company supplies, products, or manufactured items shall not be given to an employee as a gift, reward or token, except by personnel specifically authorized to do so. Such authorization must be in writing and a removal pass must accompany the item.

- No employee may remove discarded, rejected, or scrap items; specific authorization must be obtained in advance.

Hours of Employment

The Fair Labor Standards Act, which is commonly referred to as the Wages and Hour Act, contains provisions and standards concerning minimum wages, equal pay, maximum hours and overtime pay, record keeping and child labor. The requirements apply to employees in certain enterprises. However, the law provides exemptions from its standards for employees in certain other types of employment.

The amount of money an employee should receive under the minimum wage and overtime provisions cannot be determined without knowing the number of hours he or she has worked. The FLSA does not specifically define "hours of work." The Wage and Hour Division of the US Department of Labor has issued regulations on the subject (29 Code of Federal Regulations, Sec. 785.1-785.50), which is summarized below.

"Suffered Or Permitted" To Work:

In general, all of the time an employee is required to be on duty, on the employer's premises, or at a prescribed workplace and all time during which he is "suffered or permitted" to work for the employer. Even if the employer has not requested the employee to perform the work, the employee may only desire to finish a task, correct errors, prepare time or production reports, the reason is immaterial and the time must be counted as hours worked if the employer "knows or has reason to believe" that the employee is continuing to work. This basic rule also applies to work performed away from the employer's premises, job site or even at home. It is the duty of management to exercise its control and to see that work is not performed if it does not want it to be performed.

Preparatory and Concluding Activities:

Hours worked include all the time the employee spends engaged in the principal activities that he or she has been employed to perform. Work time does not include activities that are "preliminary or postliminary" to work unless there is a contract or custom providing for payment of wages for this time. For example, normal commuting from home is not ordinarily considered work time. However; time spent walking from the time clock to the workstation is a matter of custom and generally counted as work time. Time spent changing clothes on the employer's premises is usually not considered work time unless the employee is required to wear certain clothes to perform the job.

AIDS

Individuals who have been exposed to the AIDS virus pose another major privacy issue. AIDS, like any other workplace privacy issue, requires discretion, education and confidentiality.

A recent US Supreme Court decision (Bragdon v. Abbott 1998) ruled that a person's HIV infection is a disability under the ADA (Americans with Disabilities Act). The ADA prohibits disability discrimination in employment and requires that employers offer accommodations for the disabled.

Surveillance

There are no specific federal requirements that restrict the private-sector employer's right to monitor employee activities at work. However, some states restrict electronic monitoring of the employee work, rest, and recreation areas. A few state legislators are proposing legislation that would limit computer monitoring of employees' work habits.

There are numerous bills pending on state and federal levels on this issue, and they periodically receive media attention. Be sure to check the appropriate region's status, so as not to end up on the wrong side of the law.

FCRA Explained

The Fair Credit Reporting Act (FCRA), first enacted in 1970, was meant to eliminate abuses such as using credit information against the best interests of the individual by defining what consumer credit reports may include, by identifying who may assemble them and by declaring the permissible purposes for these reports. Intended to guarantee that the information supplied by Consumer Reporting Agencies (CRAs) is as accurate as possible, the original 1970 FCRA had many drawbacks and loopholes. Foremost among complaints were consumers' frustrations about CRAs unwillingness to quickly correct erroneous information. The FCRA was amended effective September 30, 1997, to correct some problems. It remains the law of the land.

Who is affected?

The FCRA applies to many types of transactions involving individuals, including:

- Obtaining credit
- Obtaining employment
- Obtaining insurance, and
- Certain other personal business transactions

The focus of this section is on the FCRA's effect on employment. The applicability of the FCRA is much more pervasive than most people realize. For example, every employer using a consumer report to determine the worthiness of employees and potential employees has to be especially diligent to avoid serious legal problems if the FCRA rules are not followed.

The amended FCRA states that an employer who wishes to utilize a consumer report must make the individual — whether they are a job applicant or a current employee — aware that a consumer report may be obtained, and the individual must agree to such use. Additionally, the individual must be notified promptly if information in a consumer report *may* result in a negative employment decision.

What, exactly, is a consumer report?

A consumer report contains information about a person's credit characteristics, and may include information about his or her character, general reputation and lifestyle. Any such report is prepared by a consumer reporting agency — a business that assembles such reports for other businesses or individuals and subjects the user to the FCRA.

A fundamental principle of the FCRA is that only entities with a permissible purpose may obtain consumer reports. In other words, the use of personal credit and related information about an individual for purposes other than those enumerated in the act is not allowed, not for politics, not for newspaper reports, not for fun. This provides everyone with a degree of personal financial privacy.

On the other hand, no one is subject to the FCRA when backgrounding an individual in connection with a real business purpose, such as developing competitive intelligence on the individual's company, rental of a business office, extension of business credit, or purchase of a company owned by the individual.

Also, if an employer wishes to investigate someone's background using company employees as investigators, that employer would not have to worry about some aspects of the FCRA. However, like so many businesses nowadays, an employer may not have the time or resources to conduct the investigation in-house, and it becomes beneficial to hire a CRA to do the work, even though that imposes some extra requirements.

For sensitive positions, it is not unusual for employers to order *investigative* consumer reports, ones that include interviews with an applicant's or employee's friends, neighbors, and associates. These are often listed on the application as references. Whether certain portions of the FCRA cover verifying references depends on who does the verification. Acquiring an employee's driving record from a CRA is another type of consumer report, as is a criminal history, credit payment records or other background information.

If an employer fails to get an applicant's permission before requesting a consumer report, or an employer fails to provide pre-adverse action disclosures and adverse action notices to unsuccessful job applicants, the FCRA allows the victims to sue employers for damages in federal court. Additionally, the Federal Trade Commission allows for fines that can be placed on the CRA for non-compliance, up to $2,500 per violation.

The Three Notices

The Federal Trade Commission prescribes three notices that CRAs and consumer report users must provide:

1. A summary of FCRA rights must be provided to consumers with every credit report.

2. A notice must be sent with *every* consumer report to users or purchasers of information from CRAs regarding their responsibilities under the law.

3. A notice must be sent to furnishers of information (creditors) regarding their responsibilities.

If you are an employer and you wish to conduct business with a CRA, which may be any outside investigator, they should have these forms (1 and 2) for you. If not, it may be wise to ask them why they don't, since their use of the forms would serve as an indication of their compliance with the FCRA.

The Process

Employers must notify an individual applicant or employee in writing – in a document consisting solely of this notice – that a report may be obtained.

Employers must acquire the person's written authorization before asking a CRA for a report.

If the consumer report includes any adverse information that causes the employer to take "adverse action" against an employee or potential employee, such as denying a job application or reassigning, terminating, denying a promotion, then the individual must be given a pre-adverse action disclosure before the employer can legally take the adverse action. Additionally, the pre-adverse action disclosure must include a copy of the consumer report and a copy of "A Summary of Your Rights Under the Fair Credit Reporting Act" (Form 2, described above) – which is prescribed by the Federal Trade Commission and made available to the employer by the CRA. This Summary of Consumer Rights should be gladly furnished to employers by the CRA – a CRA is required to by law.

Then, after an employer has taken an adverse action, the employer must give the individual notice – orally, in writing, or electronically - that the action has been taken. This is defined as an adverse action notice, which must include:

♦   The name, address and phone number of the CRA that supplied the report

♦   A statement that the CRA who supplied the report did not make the decision to take the adverse action and cannot give specific reasons for it

♦   A notice of the individual's right to dispute the accuracy or completeness of any information the agency furnished, and his or her right to an additional free consumer report from the agency upon request within 60 days.

Though the FCRA rules sound somewhat harsh on the CRAs, the CRA protects itself by requiring that employers or investigators certify that they are in compliance with the FCRA, and that the information will not be misused. Misuse is construed as a violation of federal or state equal employment opportunity laws or regulations. Nonetheless, there are number of reasons why an employer would want to run a credit check.

EXAMPLE: After advertising a vacancy for a job where money is handled, the employer wants credit reports on each applicant, hoping to eliminate those with poor credit histories.

Under the FCRA, the employer can get credit reports – one type of consumer report – if each applicant is notified properly in writing that a credit report may be requested, and the applicant has given written consent. Before the employer rejects *any* applicant based on credit report information, the employer must make a pre-adverse action disclosure to the applicant. The disclosure must include a copy of the credit report and summary of consumer rights under the FCRA. Once an applicant is rejected, the employer must provide an adverse action notice if the credit report information affected the decision.

An employer wants to draw consumer reports on long-term employees who are vying for one major promotion. The employer can legally obtain consumer reports after the employees have been notified of the intent to obtain reports, and they give their written permission. This permission must be granted on a "separate document" – using a release document from employees' personnel files won't do. The employer must notify the employees and have their permission before the employer receives the reports.

If any information in a consumer report influences an adverse decision, the applicant or employee is entitled to the notices, even when the information itself isn't negative.

Do the FCRA rules sound burdensome on the employer and the CRA? Not as burdensome as having the FTC come after you and having employee lawsuits pending, all because you skirted these laws that protect the rights of the individual.

EXAMPLE: An employer finds that amounts of money are missing. The employer suspects that an employee is taking the money. In order to determine whom the guilty individual may be, the employer decides to ask a private investigator to draw up reports on the suspects. Can the employer do this?

No, the employer cannot without the prior, written permission of the individual. Because of this, an employer should have all employees sign the disclosure form during the application process so that is available for future use.

The bottom line: in the accepting of applications, an employer should have applicant's read and agree to, then sign, a separate consent form allowing the employer to draw a consumer report. The employer needs to follow the rules regarding adverse information, and so inform the applicants of any problems in a pre-adverse action disclosure, and later, an adverse action notice. These can be standard form letters that are accompanied by the individual's "rights information," which should be provided to the employer by the CRA.

How is an employer to determine if the information they're asking someone else to find constitutes a consumer report? What if the investigator doesn't inform the employer about FCRA obligations, or if the investigator is unaware of the FCRA rules? The employer is responsible for knowing FCRA rules. Legitimate CRAs and investigators are responsible for knowing FCRA as well, but in the event the employer is not told by the investigator that the report is subject to the FCRA, the employer is still responsible and liable for damages to the individual harmed if the FCRA applies.

The best advice to employers is: never risk requesting a consumer credit report without first obtaining written authorization from the subject. When deciding a request a credit report, the employer should consider whether the disclosure and authorization requirements may be more burdensome than the benefits of attaining the report.

To view the full text of the FCRA and notices of rights, visit www.ftc.gov/ftc/formal.htm.

Workers' Compensation Issues

___ Tips for Reducing Workers' Compensation Fraud

A number of organizations have instituted safety committees who, monthly or quarterly, review all incidents and injuries in an effort to examine causes and to implement programs where applicable. Still others have reports generated by the department heads that maintain their reports, comments, and in some cases, investigation narratives and statements at their location.

In many businesses, public and private, there are accident and injury reporting methods in place. Some companies have safety committees that review all injuries on a monthly basis. For each injury, major or minor, some investigation and documentation usually takes place. Often tremendous information has been gathered and strong efforts have been made in order to document the incident. However, companies often make the mistake of maintaining these records in a single location under the supervision of an individual. Copies of these files must be transmitted to those who are ultimately responsible for processing the claims. Furthermore, allowing a single individual to maintain the records can create a situation wherein records are "misplaced" or "altered."

Which Employees Commit Fraud the Most?

If the employee…

…has been problematic,

…is facing a layoff or termination and knows his or her employment will end,

…is new on the job,

or

….has a history of short-term employment,

then he or she may be more likely to commit workers' compensation fraud.

Signs of Potential Fraud

The following are signs that a claim may be fraudulent:

♦ The employee was off for a period of time just prior to claiming the injury.

♦ The injury occurs late on the last day of the work week or immediately upon return to work.

♦ The injury was not witnessed.

♦ The injury was not properly reported or was reported late.

♦ The description of the injury is vague or changes.

♦ The recovery is taking longer than the injury should warrant.

♦ Internal rumors suggest that the injury was faked.

♦ You hear that the employee is working somewhere else, is self-employed or is performing activities that he or she claims to be unable to do.

♦ After the incident, the employee is never at home or a member of the household states that he or she "just stepped out" when a call is made.

Proactive Suggestions

Employers can reduce chances of workers' compensation fraud. If you are an employer, consider the following proactive suggestions:

♦ Use sound screening practices.

♦ Show your employees that you care about them.

♦ Train all employees on your company's method of reporting accidents and document the process.

♦ Have employees document the injury at first report. Their explanations may change over time.

♦ Establish a mechanism whereby employees can notify the company of fraudulent activities.

♦ Get involved in the investigation and prosecution of fraudulent claims.

♦ Notify employees that the company and the insurer will work together to investigate and prosecute those who file fraudulent claims.

♦ Educate employees as to what fraud is and what the rules are if they are found guilty.

♦   Be aware of employees who are seasonal, facing a layoff or have been problematic in the workplace. These are the types of employees commonly associated with the filing of fraudulent claims.

Complying with Workers' Compensation Laws

Workers' Compensation is America's oldest social insurance program. For more than 80 years, most states have required all employers to maintain this insurance. The system is designed to cover the employer's medical expenses and lost wages for employees who are injured on the job. If you, as the business operator, fail to provide coverage, then you may be in violation of your state's laws, leaving you open to fines and penalties.

It gets a whole lot worse if an employee is injured and the employer is not covered. Who will pay the medical bills and lost wages? Even if the company can afford it, the chances of escaping serious problems are slim. In today's litigious society, even a minor injury prompts a worker to contact an attorney. In fact, many employees deliberately look for an opportunity to file a compensation claim. Unfortunately, many workers view compensation as a benefit, i.e. time off with pay. Just as applicants are schooled in application tricks, some have a degree in abusing the workers' compensation system.

Under the American's With Disability Act, employers are not allowed to run a search for prior workers' compensation claims until they have made an offer of employment. See page 221 for a sample release form.

The consequences of noncompliance with workers' compensation laws vary in each state, but they are usually severe. Often the state becomes financially responsible for medical, wage and disability payments. Ultimately, the company will assume responsibility for all the payments, plus horrendous fines, penalties and interest far beyond estimation. Some states suspend the employer's business license or revoke the corporate charter. If you cannot pay, the state can sue you, seize your assets and shut the company down. Essentially, you can lose everything. All of this is true, even if the compensation claim proves fraudulent. So, to protect your assets, check your state's requirements and adhere to the rules.

The Dilemma

Workers' Compensation presents a complex issue, riddled with hard to solve problems. While there is not any single solution, modifications to standard practices can be beneficial. Before addressing some potential remedies, we need to look at the evolution of the problem.

History

During the 1950s and 1960s, the typical on-the-job injury was handled differently than it is today. Since then, two to three generations of the working population have emerged in a different environment. Our parents and grandparents not only had a different work ethic and values, but were also subject to different rules concerning employee injury.

In that time frame, an insurance company's adjuster controlled the medical treatment, records, and payment. The adjuster investigated the injury, its cause and circumstances, obtained reports, and conducted interviews in person. He or she would visit the scene, take photographs, and make diagrams where applicable. The adjuster determined if the injury was work-related and justified compensation. He or she was responsible for examining, adjusting and charting medical treatment, and paying the providers. The adjuster would often visit and make payment to the injured employee, again, in person. Many of the adjusters would see the claimant on a weekly or biweekly basis to update his or her paperwork, report on progress and issue payment.

The worker knew the adjuster was coming and had to be home or he or she wouldn't get paid. The company, through the adjuster's report, could monitor payments, progress, treatment, and prognosis. The adjusters were involved on a personal basis and had control over the claims process. They also developed their own network of people, from all backgrounds, who would confide in them of suspected abuse and irregularities. Those adjusters could spot malingerers and would follow up on any information provided to them. After all, within their territory, adjusters were known in those communities and everyone knew they would be around. In actuality, as part of their jobs they were the fraud unit.

The system wasn't perfect. Personal visits usually took place by schedule on a specific day of the week and at an approximate time of day. The employee had to be home or risk a delay in getting paid. If the employee wasn't home, he or she had to have an excuse and knew they would be questioned as to the reason for their absence.

Of course, there was a cost factor involved. The adjusters were paid their salary and they had the expense of an automobile. Some had company cars while others were reimbursed for their own. Regardless, the cost of the insurance, operation, and maintenance all added up. There was also the cost of cameras, film, developing, forms, photocopying, supervision, medical benefits, and pension.

Over time, the claims departments were viewed as expense factors. They were not income producers. Further reasoning indicated that the same results could be obtained by telephone contact and that the required reports could be obtained by mail. Eventually, this philosophy was adopted and through attrition and the reassigning of personnel, the street adjuster began to disappear.

This pattern became a trend and soon only major cases received any personal attention. As time passed, new adjusters were trained to handle claims by phone and mail. The experienced adjusters who remained were assigned to major cases for investigation.

A hard look at the growing troubles in workers' compensation claims indicates the methods of the last twenty years or so are not and have not been working for a long time. The cost of workers' compensation has soared by more than 40 billion dollars over the last ten to fifteen years.

All of this means that now is the time to re-examine the elements of the claims process, from first report to medical treatment, and implement programs that can help prevent abuse of workers' compensation by claimants and providers alike.

The following are examples of remedies that can be tailored for integration with current policies and procedures. They are designed to aid in controlling the cost of claims and support the litigation process.

Remedies for Consideration

First Report

The initial injury report can be the most critical document in a file. Yet it is often considered a nuisance, and therefore minimal information is recorded. Lack of detail allows an injured employee to exaggerate the claim as time goes by. Sometimes employees include, as part of their claims, pre-existing injuries, or injuries incurred subsequent to the initial loss.

To curtail such faulty records, better reporting methods must be established. Standards should be set and forms provided for utilization. By providing precise forms, with instructions to those designated to take reports, minimal training would be required for implementation. Once in place, a business will have established the primary requirement necessary to gain control over the claim. Regardless, every injury should be documented as soon as possible — in detail.

Report Content

In addition to the basic who, where and when, a descriptive narrative should be mandatory. The narrative should include exactly how the injury occurred, what parts of the anatomy were affected, and what the employee was doing when it happened. All witnesses should be interviewed in the same manner.

If a finger is cut by a box cutter and requires two sutures, it may be a relatively simple matter. However, if the injury resulted from a slip and fall, an exact description should be obtained:

Here are some questions that are examples of getting specific.

◆ "Which foot or leg went out from under you?"

◆ "Did it go backward, to the front, or to a side?"

◆ "What hit the ground (hand, elbow, arm, shoulder, head)?"

◆ "Was any other part of your body injured (cut, bruised, strained)?"

◆ "What caused you to fall (slippery surface, water, oil, object)?"

If any witnesses were present, there should be documentation as to what they saw, heard, and the contents of any conversation they had with the injured worker, as well as their perceptions as to any cause of the injury. If other workers were present, but deny any knowledge, the employer should document that as well. If they didn't see it, ask, "What were you doing at the time, exactly?"

There are two primary benefits from taking the time to describe injuries in detail. First, a well-documented injury report protects an honest worker from future misunderstandings that arise when details are unknown. It also assists the adjuster in total assessment. At the same time, it limits the malingerer's ability to include other injuries, which could not possibly have been physically related to the incident. Second, the initial report can be supplied to the medical provider for comparison to future reports from the same individual.

Medical Providers

It is no longer prudent to simply select a provider and contract for treatment of on-the-job injuries. To control total cost of workers' compensation these contracts must be specific. The agreement should require that the injury and the treatment be causally related to the incident, as detailed by the worker and his or her supervisor. If any other symptoms are present or claimed in the future, and are not a result of the loss, then the claimant can be advised, "Yes, you have that condition, but it was not caused by this incident" and referred to his or her health provider. The details obtained at the first notice can limit the scope and duration of the claim.

Often times, an apparent minor injury becomes severe somewhere between the time of injury at the work place and the doctor's office. Usually, the physician only knows what he or she is told by the employee, and without supporting documentation has little choice but to accept the employee's word as the truth. However, if discrepancies are noted early, they can be instrumental in spotting malingerers and curtailing fraud. In order to do so, physicians need direction and support.

The next measure is to provide the treating physicians with the required forms to be completed at their office upon first treatment or as soon as possible. The first portion of this form should be exactly the same as the initial report, except, in this case, the injured worker answers the questions with a medical professional present. The second half of the medical form should include a detailed, prior medical history. This process allows for a comparison with past and future reports, and any drastic differences would be obvious and questionable. Additionally, use of this form provides the employer, and hence the adjuster, with the identity of the family physician and potentially relevant prior medical treatment.

Lost Time Claims

These types of claims require still further attention and controls. Remember the adjuster who used to visit the injured worker? Some of that story needs to be taken and put to work again. Those values, ethics, and morals of old can't be instilled in employees for the future, but the employer can attempt to change their perception by being more proactive. The criteria for implementing the following program can vary depending upon each organization's policies, structure, and claims experience.

Home Visits

During the recuperation period, a personal visit to an injured worker's residence can provide valuable information for total claim evaluation. The first portion of the visit should be part of a wellness program; with questions designed to document medical treatment, past and future, including progress and projected recovery periods. Emphasis should be placed on caring about the worker's condition, ensuring satisfaction with medical treatment, and determining if any needs are not being addressed. The course of treatment and potential "return to work" date, as they understand it, can be correlated to the medical reports being received.

An honest employee will be happy that the adjuster, and therefore, the employer, cares enough to visit and ask of his or her needs and opinions. There is little doubt that morale plays a major role in both employee performance and recovery.

A review of medical treatment billings, including dates and scopes of services, should be conducted with the injured worker during the visit.

While the interviewer is present, he or she is in a position to observe the physical condition of the worker as well as other circumstances, which may be relevant. The interviewer should be trained to observe and detail anything that may indicate activity not consistent with the claimant's limitations. The range of details could include vehicles or equipment indicative of a side business to the wearing of apparel which would be difficult to put on when considering the claim.

In some instances, due to the sheer volume of claims, coupled with staffing shortages, the ability to incorporate the program may be limited. In other cases, the success of the program can generate a desire to monitor even lesser claims. In any event, a patient interview and survey of medical treatment can be undertaken by telephone. Although nothing can replace in-person contact, it is better to have a partial program than none at all.

Anticipated Results

Having such a program sends a message to all claimants that someone will check up on them, and, that they can't just go home and do whatever they want. The implementation of this program should focus on suspected malingerers with file histories containing obvious red flags or discrepancies. Identifying the fraudulent activity, prosecuting the subject and publicizing the results can achieve the short-term goal, which is to control workers' compensation claim costs.   Ultimately, employees who even consider stretching the truth will have second thoughts.

Interview results may provide patterns of questionable practices of providers. Further scrutinizing of these practices could demonstrate inappropriate treatment, billing or other actions. These issues should be dealt with as soon as they are discovered rather than allowing them to continue undetected.

> **EXAMPLE:** Mrs. Cummings, an injured worker, tells the interviewer that she told her physician that she felt able to return to work, and yet the doctor told her to take a couple more weeks off "to be on the safe side." In scenarios like this one, a closer look at that practitioner's files would be in order. The physician probably will have scheduled Mrs. Cummings for follow up visits. Hence, the company may be paying for unwarranted treatment and lost time.

The interviewer needs to let the injured worker know that he or she is coming and let the providers know that their services are being monitored.

By reviewing treatment invoices or schedules with the worker, the interviewer may find that heat treatment and physical therapy billed for were part of a standard routine, but all of the TENS unit or ultrasound treatments billed for were not administered. A similar examination of equipment providers should be part of the program. The fact is, a simple and well-orchestrated visit/interview can go a long way toward controlling many aspects of the claim cost.

Health Care Benefits

Some questionable claims can be refused based on an examination of the claimant's past health insurance utilization. A number of "new" injuries have been documented as pre-existing or not work-related because of prior treatment by the employee's family physician or emergency care facilities. When these types of cases are identified they can easily be supported by documents, not only of treatment, but also by details of how, when and where an injury really occurred.

> **EXAMPLE:** At a marina, Mr. Leone suffered a fall on the deck of a boat, and fractured several of his ribs. In pain, he was taken to a nearby hospital for examination, and x-rays provided the diagnosis. The prescribed treatment was some pain medication, a chest wrap and plenty of rest. Lost time was projected to be six to eight weeks.

Mr. Leone worked on a loading dock in the trucking industry. He had exhausted most of his sick time and didn't want to lose his income. So, he went to the loading dock the morning after his fall and placed himself on the ground. When another worker showed up, Leone alleged that he fell off the dock and hurt his ribs. He was taken to the local hospital for treatment under workers' compensation. He thought he would be able to get some time to rest, recover *and* get paid. However, his act of fraud was discovered, by accident, when a change in health care providers produced a past treatment audit.

Another claimant alleged respiratory distress due to workplace environmental conditions. The medical history taken by the workers' compensation providers denied any prior illness or treatment, and indicated the worker as a non-smoker. Yet, personal medical history obtained from the health insurance provider of a prior employer detailed a long history of respiratory ailments, including treatment, and that the worker had been a 2-1/2 pack-a-day smoker for many years.

Section Four
Tools for Verification

Forms

Feel free to use these forms as templates for your company's own custom forms. Not all of the forms included in this book will be useful to every business. A few alterations might make the forms work even better. However, be careful not to add questions that expose the company to discrimination claims.

Not all positions within a company perform the same function. Rather, one company may have a varied work force, ranging from drivers to clerks to professionals. As such, one generic application for all positions is typically insufficient and is not recommended. Employers should consider using applications that are tailored to individual positions or "job families." The extra effort and minor expense of producing tailor-made applications is more than offset by the long-range savings of time and money.

The table on the following page lists the forms in this section, the page in which they are discussed within *Don't Hire A Crook!* and the page they are located in this section. The stage during which they are used is also indicated.

All forms used in this book are freely available for use. You can download them from www.brbpub.com/crook.htm**.**

Alphabetical List of Forms & Their Locations

Name of Form	Page Number In Text	Page Number In Forms	Stage Number
Applicant/Resume Evaluation	33	195	1
Applicant Waiver	25-26	196	1
Basic Application, page 1	21	197	1
Basic Application, page 2	21	198	1
Basic Application, page 3	21	199	1
Confidentiality Agreement	121-2	200	3
Criminal Background Check Release	31	201	1
Employee Data Sheet	118	202	3
Employment Eligibility Verification (I-9)	27-28	203	1
Exit Interview Report, page 1	157	204	N/A
Exit Interview Report, page 2	157	205	N/A
General Release Form	30	206	1
Induction Form	120	207	3
Local Police Information Request	65	208	2
Military Records Request, front	75	209	2
Military Records Request, reverse	76	210	2
New Employee Record Chart	117	211	3
New Hire Reporting Form	126	212	3
Non-Compete Agreement	123	213	3
Performance Review, page 1	146	214	N/A
Performance Review, page 2	147	215	N/A
Pre-Employment Check by Phone	55	216	2
Rejection Letter Sample	108	217	3
Request For Education Verification	69	218	2
Request For Information	57	219	2
Substance Abuse Screening Test Consent	32	220	1
Workers' Compensation Release	182	221	N/A

Applicant/Resume Evaluation

APPLICANT/RESUME EVALUATION

Completion of this form assists compliance with non-discrimination guidelines and ensures the basis for hire and reject decisions are documented and job related.

Name of Applicant: _____

Date Application/Resume Received: _____

Position Available: _____

Will Applicant be Interviewed: _____ Yes   Date of Interview: _____

_____ No   Reason for Rejection: _____
Code Number(s)

Will Job be extended: _____ Yes Title: _____ Salary: _____

_____ No

Job-Related Reason Applicant is Best Qualified: _____

_____

If No, Reason for Rejection: _____
Code Number(s)

_____
Signature Interviewer/Evaluator   Position/Department   Date

You have the right to hire qualified individuals and to reject unqualified individuals. Selection and rejection decisions must be based on valid job-related criteria that are consistently applied to all applicants. The following are acceptable reasons for rejection provided the same statement could not be applied to the selected candidate. If numbers 1-8 do not apply, please complete 9 with a job-related reason.

1. *Does not meet minimum job requirements*
2. *Meets minimum requirements but not best qualified*
3. *Cannot work required hours/schedule*
4. *Cannot perform physical requirements of job*
5. *Prior experience unrelated*
6. *Less related experience than person selected*
7. *Less related education/training than person selected*
8. *Lower skill level than person selected*
9. *Other (specify)* _____

Applicant Waiver

Applicant Waiver Form

(To be signed by all job applicants along with application form.)

1. I agree and understand that all the information and statements on my application are correct and no attempt has been made to conceal or withhold pertinent information. I agree that any omission, falsification, or misrepresentation is cause for my immediate termination at any time during my employment.

2. In connection with this request, I authorize all corporations, companies, credit agencies, persons, educational institutions, law enforcement agencies and former employers to release information they may have about me, and release them from any liability and responsibility from doing so; further, I authorize the procurement of an investigative consumer report and understand that such report may contain information as to my background, mode of living, character and personal reputation. This authorization, in original and copy form, shall be valid for this and any future reports that may be requested. Further information may be made available upon written request from _____

3. I hereby authorize investigation of all statements at this time with no liability arising therefrom.

_____   _____
Signature   Date

_____   _____
Signature of Company Representative Date

                    *   *   *

STATE of:_____   This Instrument was acknowledged before me this _____ day of

COUNTY of:_____   _____, 19 _____, by _____

My commission will expire: _____ AS WITNESS.

_____

                    _____   _____
                    Notary Public   No.

Basic Application (page 1)

Application must be filled in completely or it will not be processed. If a box does not pertain to you, indicate with **N/A** in that space

_____ is an equal opportunity employer whose policy is to select the most qualified candidates without regard to race, religion, color, sex, age, marital or military status, history of disability or national origin.

Date_____   Social Security # [ ][ ][ ] [ ][ ][ ] [ ][ ][ ][ ]

Drivers License #_____ State_____
    (only if you will be operating a company vehicle)

Last Name _____   First Name _____   Initial _____

Street Address _____   City _____   State _____   Zip _____

Home Phone #_____   Work Phone #_____

Have you ever worked or attended school under another name?   ( ) yes   ( ) no
    If yes, state dates: _____

Position applying for: 1._____   2. _____ Salary desired_____

How did you contact _____
    ( ) Newspaper   ( ) Employee Referral   ( ) Employment Agency   ( ) Other
Please specify: _____

Have you ever worked for _____   ( ) yes   ( ) no
    When? _____   Where? _____

Do you have any relatives employed by _____   ( ) yes   ( ) no
    If yes, Name:_____   Where? _____

Are you a citizen of the USA. or a lawfully admitted resident alien? ( ) yes ( ) no If yes, Alien Reg. #_____

Have you ever been convicted of a crime or offense other than for minor traffic violations?   ( ) yes   ( ) no

If "Yes," explain _____
Conviction of a crime is not an automatic disqualification for employment. All factors will be considered.

Have you ever served in the Armed Forces? ( ) yes ( ) no Military occupation _____

Date of duty, from _____ to _____ Branch _____ Serial #_____
    Month Day Year   Month Day Year

EDUCATION	NAME & ADDRESS	No. YEARS ATTENDED	COURSE, MAJOR or DEGREE
High School			
College			
Post Graduate			
Business or Trade			
Other			

Basic Application (page 2)

PRIOR WORK HISTORY (list in order, present employer first)

DATES		Name & Address of Employer	Rate of Pay		Supervisor's Name & Title	Phone No.
From	To		Start	Finish		

Briefly describe what you did; include job title:

Reason for leaving

DATES		Name & Address of Employer	Rate of Pay		Supervisor's Name & Title	Phone No.
From	To		Start	Finish		

Briefly describe what you did; include job title:

Reason for leaving

DATES		Name & Address of Employer	Rate of Pay		Supervisor's Name & Title	Phone No.
From	To		Start	Finish		

Briefly describe what you did; include job title:

Reason for leaving

DATES		Name & Address of Employer	Rate of Pay		Supervisor's Name & Title	Phone No.
From	To		Start	Finish		

Briefly describe what you did; include job title:

Reason for leaving

Basic Application (page 3)

Other experience(s) skills you would like to mention: _____

_____

_____

_____

_____

At least (2) two Personal References:

Name: _____ Phone #: _____

Address:_____ Years Known: _____

Name: _____ Phone #: _____

Address:_____ Years Known: _____

In case of emergency notify:_____

Phone numbers:_____

Address:_____

Relationship:_____

Print Name_____ S.S. #_____

I AGREE AND UNDERSTAND THAT ALL THE STATEMENTS AND INFORMATION ON MY APPLICATION ARE CORRECT AND NO ATTEMPT HAS BEEN MADE TO CONCEAL OR WITHHOLD PERTINENT INFORMATION. I AGREE THAT ANY OMISSION, FALSIFICATION, OR MISREPRESENTATION IS CAUSE FOR IMMEDIATE TERMINATION AT ANY TIME DURING MY EMPLOYMENT.

I HEREBY AUTHORIZE INVESTIGATION OF ALL STATEMENTS AT THIS TIME WITH NO LIABILITY ARISING THEREFROM _____.

I WILL ABIDE BY ALL RULES, REGULATIONS AND POLICIES OF _____

AT THE OPTION OF THE COMPANY, I AGREE TO PHYSICAL EXAMINATION BY A PHYSICIAN CHOSEN BY _____ WITH THE UNDERSTANDING THAT MY EMPLOYMENT AT _____ DEPENDS UPON MY PASSING THE PHYSICAL.

I UNDERSTAND THAT A 90 WORKING PROBATIONARY PERIOD WILL BE IN EFFECT IN THE EVENT EMPLOYMENT IS OFFERED.

DATE_____SIGNATURE_____

Confidentiality Agreement

CONFIDENTIALITY AGREEMENT

In consideration of being employed by _____ (Company), the undersigned hereby agrees and acknowledges:

1.   That during the course of my employ there may be disclosed to me certain trade secrets of the Company; said trade secrets consisting of:

    a)   Technical information: Methods, processes, formulae, compositions, inventions, machines, computer programs, and research projects.

    b)   Business information: Customer lists, pricing data, sources of supply, and marketing, production, or merchandising systems or plans.

2.   I shall not during, or at any time after the termination of my employment with the Company, use for myself or others, or disclose or divulge to others any trade secrets, confidential information, or any other data of the Company in violation of this agreement.

3.   That upon the termination of my employ from the Company:

    a)   I shall return to the Company all documents relating to the Company, including but not necessarily limited to: drawings, blueprints, reports, manuals, correspondence, consumer lists, computer programs, and all other materials and all copies thereof relating in any way to the Company's business, or in any way obtained by me during the course of my employ. I further agree that I shall not retain any copies of the forgoing.

    b)   The Company may notify any future or prospective employer of the existence of this agreement.

    c)   This agreement shall be binding upon me and my personal representatives and successors in interest, and shall inure to the benefit of the Company, its successors, and assigns.

    d)   The enforceability of any provision to this agreement shall not impair or affect any other provision.

    e)   In the event of any breach of this agreement, the Company shall have full rights to injunctive relief, in addition to any other existing rights, without requirement of posting bond.

_____   _____
SIGNATURE   DATE

Criminal Background Check Release

Criminal Background Check
Release Form

NAME_____

         Last   First   Middle   Maiden

ADDRESS_____

         Street   City   State

ALIASES OR OTHER NAMES USED _____

DATE OF BIRTH _____ AGE____ RACE_____ SEX____

SOCIAL SECURITY #_____

DRIVER'S LICENSE #_____ STATE_____

* * *

I hereby authorize _____ of _____

                Name   Name of Company

_____

Company Address/City/State/Zip

to conduct a criminal background check on myself through the

_____ .

Name of State and Police Agency

X_____

Applicant Signature

* * *

STATE of:_____   This Instrument was acknowledged before me this _____ day of

COUNTY of:_____   _____, 19 ____, by _____

My commission will expire: _____ AS WITNESS.

_____

_____

                Notary Public   No.

Employee Data Sheet

EMPLOYEE DATA SHEET

THE FOLLOWING INFORMATION IS NECESSARY TO MAINTAIN COMPANY RECORDS ON ALL OUR EMPLOYEES

EMPLOYEE #:_____ DEPARTMENT:_____ DATE OF HIRE: _____

NAME: _____

ADDRESS:_____

HOME TELEPHONE NUMBER: _____

SOCIAL SECURITY #: _____ DATE OF BIRTH: _____

RACE (PLEASE CIRCLE):

WHITE   BLACK   HISPANIC   ASIAN   AMERICAN INDIAN   OTHER _____

ARE YOU A CITIZEN OF THE UNITED STATES?   _____ YES   _____NO

ALIEN REGISTRATION #: _____

MARITAL STATUS: _____ SINGLE   _____ MARRIED   _____ DIVORCED

              _____ LEGALLY SEPARATED   _____ WIDOWED

DATE OF MARRIAGE: _____ SPOUSE'S NAME: _____

SPOUSE'S SS#: _____ SPOUSE'S DATE OF BIRTH: _____

CHILDREN:

NAME	DATE OF BIRTH	AGE	SEX
NAME	DATE OF BIRTH	AGE	SEX
NAME	DATE OF BIRTH	AGE	SEX
NAME	DATE OF BIRTH	AGE	SEX

WHO WOULD YOU LIKE US TO NOTIFY IN CASE OF EMERGENCY?

NAME: _____ RELATIONSHIP: _____

ADDRESS: _____

TELEPHONE NUMBER: _____

Employment Eligibility Verification (I-9)

EMPLOYMENT ELIGIBILITY VERIFICATION (I-9)

SECTION I. EMPLOYEE INFORMATION AND VERIFICATION: (To be completed and signed by employee)

NAME:_____

       Last   First   Middle   Maiden

ADDRESS:_____

      Street number and name   City   State   Zip

DATE OF BIRTH: _____ SOCIAL SECURITY NUMBER: _____

I attest, under penalty of perjury, that I am (check one):
_____ A citizen or national of the United States
_____ An alien lawfully admitted for permanent residence (Alien #A_____).
_____ An alien authorized by the Immigration and Naturalization Service to work in the U.S.(Alien #A_____).
      or Admission Number _____. Expiration of employment authorization, if any _____).

I attest, under penalty of perjury, the documents that I have presented as evidence of identity and employment eligibility are genuine and relate to me. I am aware that federal law provides for imprisonment and/or fine for any false statement or use of false documents in connection with this certificate.

SIGNATURE: _____ DATE: _____

PREPARER/TRANSLATOR CERTIFICATION (if prepared by other than the individual). I attest, under penalty of perjury, that the above was prepared by me at the request of the named individual and is based on all information of which I have any knowledge.

SIGNATURE: _____ NAME (print or type):_____
ADDRESS:_____
      Street number and name   City   State   Zip
****

SECTION II. EMPLOYER REVIEW AND VERIFICATION: (To be completed and signed by employer)
Examine one document from those in List A and check the correct box, *or* examine one document from List B *and* one from List C and check the correct boxes. Provide the *Document Identification Number* and *Expiration Date*, for the document checked in that column.

List A Identity and Employment Eligibility Eligibility	List B Identity	List C and Employment

____ United States Passport
____ Certificate of U.S. Citizenship
____ Certificate of Naturalization
____ Unexpired foreign passport with
    attached Employment Authorization
____Alien registration Card with photograph
	____ A State issued drivers license
	    or I.D. card with a photograph,
	    or information, including name,
	    sex, date of birth, height, weight,
	    and color of eyes.
	____ U.S. Military Card
	____ Other (Specify document and
	    issuing authority)
		____Original Social Security Number
		    Card (other than a card stating
		    it is not valid for employment)
		____ A birth certificate issued by
		    State, county, or municipal
		    authority bearing a seal or other
		    certification
		____ Unexpired INS Employment
		    Authorization. Specify form.

Document I.D.# _____ Exp. Date _____	Document I.D.# _____ Exp. Date _____	Document I.D.# _____ Exp. Date _____

CERTIFICATION: I attest, under penalty of perjury, that I have examined the documents presented by the above individual, that they appear to be genuine, relate to the individual named, and that the individual, to the best of my knowledge, is authorized to work in the United States.

SIGNATURE: _____ NAME (print of type):_____ TITLE: _____

EMPLOYER:_____
      Name   Address   Date

Exit Interview Report (page 1)

EXIT INTERVIEW REPORT

ALL ANSWERS ARE HELD STRICTLY CONFIDENTIAL

Employee's Name: _____   Employee #: _____

Department: _____   Position: _____

Dates of Employment: From _____   To _____

Supervisor: _____

Reason for leaving Company: _____

Return of:

_____ keys   _____ company documents   _____ uniform

_____ I.D. card   _____ safety equipment   _____ tools

_____ credit card   _____ other company property   _____ company auto

Employee informed of restriction on:

_____ trade secrets   _____ employment with competitor (if applicable)

_____ patents   _____ removing company documents

_____ other data   _____ other _____

Employee exit questions:

1.   Did management adequately recognize employee contributions? _____
_____

2.   Do you feel that you have had the support of management on the job? _____
_____

3.   Were you adequately trained for your job? _____
_____

4.   Did you find your work rewarding? _____
_____

(Continued)

Exit Interview Report (page 2)

EXIT INTERVIEW REPORT   PAGE 2

5.   Do you feel you were fairly treated by the company? _____
_____

6.   Were you paid an adequate salary for the work you did? _____
_____

7.   Were you content with your working conditions? _____
_____

8.   Do you feel your supervision was adequate? _____
_____

9.   Did you understand company policies and the reasons for them? _____
_____

10.   Have you observed incidences of theft of company property? _____
_____

11.   How can the company improve security? _____
_____

12.   How can the company improve working conditions? _____
_____

13.   What are the company's strengths? _____
_____

14.   What are the company's weaknesses? _____
_____

15.   Other comments: _____
_____
_____
_____

USE ADDITIONAL SHEETS FOR FURTHER COMMENTS

General Release Form

General Release Form

In connection with my application for employment (including contract for service) with you, I understand that investigative inquiries are to be made on myself including consumer credit, criminal convictions, motor vehicle, and other reports. These reports will include information as to my character, work, habits, performance and experience along with reasons for termination of past employment from previous employers. Further, I understand that you will be requesting information from various Federal, State, and other agencies that maintain records concerning my past activities relating to my driving, credit, criminal, civil, education, and other experiences.

I authorize without reservation any party or agency contacted by this employer to furnish the above-mentioned information.

I hereby consent to your obtaining the above information from _____ _____ and/or any of their licensed agents. I understand to aid in the proper identification of my file or records, the following personal identifiers, as well as other information, is necessary.

Print Name _____

Social Security Number ____-__-_____

Date of Birth _____ Sex _____ Race_____

Current Address _____

City/State/Zip Code+4_____

Former Address _____

Applicant Signature _____ Date_____

Prospective Employer _____

Induction Form

INDUCTION FORM

NAME: _____SS#: _____

CLOCK #: _____   STARTING DATE: _____

JOB TITLE: _____

DEPT: _____   SUPERVISOR: _____

COMPANY BENEFITS AND RULES

1. HOURS: _____AM/PM until _____AM/PM a_____ lunch, and
   two_____ minute rest breaks, one at _____ and one at _____. The regular
   work week is _____ to _____.

2. TIME RECORDS: Punch only your own time card and in case of a mistake, take your card
   IMMEDIATELY to the office. After seven minutes, employees are docked 15 minutes for
   being late and repeated lateness is cause for discipline. If you are unable to come to work, call
   (___)____-_____ before the start of your shift.

3. HOLIDAYS: New Years Day, Good Friday, Memorial Day, 4th of July,
   Labor Day, Thanksgiving, Friday after Thanksgiving, and Christmas Day.

4. VACATIONS: You will earn _____ of vacation for each _____ of employment
   prior to _____ up to a maximum of _____ days. _____ weeks after_____
   years of service and _____ weeks after _____ years.

5. INSURANCE: The company provides_____ insurance for all employees after _____ of service. If you wish coverage for your eligible dependents, this
   can be arranged through payroll deduction. After _____ months, the company provide $_____ of life insurance and a weekly sick and accident insurance pro-
   gram that pays a maximum of $_____ for 26 weeks after the first day of an acci-
   dent and after the eighth day of illness.

   If you have any questions at any time regarding your pay, benefits or job assignment,
   please discuss it with your supervisor.
   I have read and understand the information above.

_____   _____
DATE   EMPLOYEE'S SIGNATURE

Witness:

_____   _____
Date   Signature

Local Police Information Request

TO BE PRINTED ON YOUR LETTERHEAD

(DATE)

(NAME OF POLICE DEPARTMENT)
Att: Records
(STREET ADDRESS)
CITY, STATE, ZIP)

Re: (NAME OF EMPLOYEE)

Dear Sir/Madam:

Our medical facility is conducting a background check on the above-captioned prospective employee. I am writing to obtain local criminal history and/or character information from your Department. Enclosed please find a consent form with original signature, which has been notarized, authorizing the release of this information. Please indicate on the form the results of your record check, or lack thereof, and return it to us in the self-addressed stamped envelope provided.

Please advise us if there are any additional requirements, fees, etc. necessary to obtain this information.

Thank you for your assistance in this matter.

Sincerely,

(NAME - TYPED)
(TITLE - TYPED)

Military Records Request (front)

Also available online at: www.nara.gov/regional/mprsf180.html

---

Standard Form 180 (Rev. 4-96) (EG)
Prescribed by NARA (36 CFR 1228.162(a))

NSN 7540-00-142-9360

OMB No. 3095-0029 Expires 9/30/98

REQUEST PERTAINING TO MILITARY RECORDS

To ensure the best possible service, please thoroughly review the instructions at the bottom before filling out this form. Please print clearly or type. If you need more space, use plain paper.

SECTION I - INFORMATION NEEDED TO LOCATE RECORDS (Furnish as much as possible.)

1. NAME USED DURING SERVICE (Last, first, and middle)	2. SOCIAL SECURITY NO.	3. DATE OF BIRTH	4. PLACE OF BIRTH

5. SERVICE, PAST AND PRESENT (For an effective records search, it is important that ALL service be shown below.)

	BRANCH OF SERVICE	DATES OF SERVICE		CHECK ONE		SERVICE NUMBER DURING THIS PERIOD (If unknown, please write "unknown.")
		DATE ENTERED	DATE RELEASED	OFFICER	ENLISTED	
a. ACTIVE SERVICE						
b. RESERVE SERVICE						
c. NATIONAL GUARD						

6. IS THIS PERSON DECEASED? If "YES" enter the date of death. ☐ NO ☐ YES _____

7. IS (WAS) THIS PERSON RETIRED FROM MILITARY SERVICE? ☐ YES ☐ NO

SECTION II - INFORMATION AND/OR DOCUMENTS REQUESTED

1. **REPORT OF SEPARATION** (DD Form 214 or equivalent). This contains information normally needed to verify military service. It may be furnished to the veteran, the deceased veteran/s next of kin, or other persons or organizations if authorized in Section III, below. NOTE: If more than one period of service was performed, even in the same branch, there may be more than one Report of Separation. Be sure to show EACH year for which you need a copy.

☐ An UNDELETED Report of Separation is requested for the year(s) _____ . This normally will be a copy of the full separation document including such sensitive items as the character of separation, authority for separation, reason for separation, reenlistment eligibility code, separation (SPD/SPN) code, and dates of time lost. An undeleted version is ordinarily required to determine eligibility for benefits.

☐ A DELETED Report of Separation is requested for the year(s) _____ . The following information will be deleted from the copy sent: authority for separation, reason for separation, reenlistment eligibility code, separation (SPD/SPN) code, and for separations after June 30, 1979, character of separation and dates of time lost.

2. **OTHER INFORMATION AND/OR DOCUMENTS REQUESTED** _____

3. **PURPOSE** (OPTIONAL - An explanation of the purpose of the request is strictly voluntary. Such information may help the agency answering this request to provide the best possible response and will in no way be used to make a decision to deny the request.) _____

SECTION III - RETURN ADDRESS AND SIGNATURE

1. REQUESTER IS

☐ Military service member or veteran identified in Section I, above

☐ Next of kin of deceased veteran _____ (relation)

☐ Legal guardian (must submit copy of court appointment)

☐ Other (specify) _____

2. SEND INFORMATION/DOCUMENTS TO (Please print or type. See instruction 3, below.)

Name _____

Street _____ Apt. _____

City _____ State _____ ZIP Code _____

3. AUTHORIZATION SIGNATURE REQUIRED (See instruction 2, below.) I declare (or certify, verify, or state) under penalty of perjury under the laws of the United States of America that the information in this Section III is true and correct.

Signature of Requester (Please do not print.) _____

Date of this request _____ (____) _____ Daytime phone

Military Records Request (reverse)

Also available online at: www.nara.gov/regional/mprsf180.html

STANDARD FORM 180 BACK (Rev. 4-96)

LOCATION OF MILITARY RECORDS

The various categories of military service records are described in the chart below. For each category there is a code number which indicates the address at the bottom of the page to which this request should be sent.

1. **Health and personnel records.** In most cases involving individuals no longer on active duty, the personnel record, the health record, or both can be obtained from the same location, as shown on the chart. However, some health records are available from the Department of Veterans Affairs (VA) Records Management Center (Code 11). A request for a copy of the health record should be sent to Code 11 if the person was discharged, retired, or released from active duty (separated) on or after the following dates: ARMY-- October 16, 1992; NAVY--January 31, 1994; AIR FORCE and MARINE CORPS--May 1, 1994. Health records of persons on active duty are generally kept at the local servicing clinic, and usually are available from Code 11 a week or two after the last day of active duty.

2. **Records at the National Personnel Records Center.** Note that it takes at least three months, and often six or seven, for the file to reach the National Personnel Records Center (Code 14) in St. Louis after the military obligation has ended (such as by discharge). If only a short time has passed, please send the inquiry to the address shown for active or current reserve members. Also, if the person has only been released from active duty but is still in a reserve status, the personnel record will stay at the location specified for reservists. A person can retain a reserve obligation for several years, even without attending meetings or receiving annual training.

3. **Definitions and abbreviations**. DISCHARGED--the individual has no current military status; HEALTH--Records of physical examinations, dental treatment, and outpatient medical treatment received while in a duty status (does not include records of treatment while hospitalized); TDRL--Temporary Disability Retired List

4. **Service completed before World War I (before 1929 for Coast Guard officers)**. The oldest military service records are at the National Archives (Code 6). Send the request there if service was completed before the following dates: ARMY--enlisted, 11/1/1912, officer, 7/1/1917; NAVY--enlisted, 1/1/1886, officer, 1/1/1903; MARINE CORPS--1/1/1905; COAST GUARD--enlisted, 1/1/1915, officer, 1/1/1929.

BRANCH	CURRENT STATUS OF SERVICE MEMBER	WHERE TO WRITE ADDRESS CODE
AIR FORCE	Discharged, deceased, or retired with pay (See paragraph 1, above, if requesting health record.)	14
	Active (including National Guard on active duty in the Air Force), TDRL, or general officers retired with pay	1
	Reserve, retired reserve in nonpay status, current National Guard officers not on active duty in the Air Force, or National Guard released from active duty in the Air Force	2
	Current National Guard enlisted not on active duty in the Air Force	13
COAST GUARD	Discharged, deceased, or retired (See paragraph 1, above, if requesting health record.)	14
	Active, reserve, or TDRL	3
MARINE CORPS	Discharged, deceased, or retired (See paragraph 1, above, if requesting health record.)	14
	Individual Ready Reserve or Fleet Marine Corps Reserve	5
	Active, Selected Marine Corps Reserve, or TDRL	4
ARMY	Discharged, deceased, or retired (See paragraph 1, above, if requesting health record.)	14
	Reserve; or active duty records of current National Guard members who performed service in the U.S. Army before 7/1/72	7
	Active enlisted (including National Guard on active duty in the U.S. Army) or TDRL enlisted	9
	Active officers (including National Guard on active duty in the U.S. Army) or TDRL officers	8
	Current National Guard enlisted not on active duty in Army (including records of Army active duty performed after 6/30/72)	13
	Current National Guard officers not on active duty in Army (including records of Army active duty performed after 6/30/72)	12
NAVY	Discharged, deceased, or retired (See paragraph 1, above, if requesting health record.)	14
	Active, reserve, or TDRL	10

ADDRESS LIST OF CUSTODIANS (BY CODE NUMBERS SHOWN ABOVE) - where to write / send this form

1	Air Force Personnel Center HQ AFPC/DPSRP 550 C Street West, Suite 19 Randolph AFB, TX 78150-4721	5	Marine Corps Reserve Support Command (Code MMI) 15303 Andrews Road Kansas City, MO 64147-1207	8	U.S. Total Army Personnel Command 200 Stoval Street Alexandria, VA 22332-0400	12	Army National Guard Readiness Center NGB-ARP 111 S. George Mason Dr. Arlington, VA 22204-1382
2	Air Reserve Personnel Center/DSMR 6760 E. Irvington Pl. #4600 Denver, CO 80280-4600	6	Archives I Textual Reference Branch (NNR1), Room 13W National Archives and Records Administration	9	Commander USAEREC Attn: PCRE-F 8899 E. 56th St. Indianapolis, IN 46249-5301	13	The Adjutant General (of the appropriate state, DC, or Puerto Rico)
3	Commander CGPC-Adm-3 U.S. Coast Guard 2100 2nd Street, SW. Washington, DC 20593-0001	7	Commander U.S. Army Reserve Personnel Center ATTN: ARPC-VS 9700 Page Avenue St. Louis, MO 63130-5200	10	Bureau of Naval Personnel Pers-313D 2 Navy Annex Washington, DC 20370-3130	14	National Personnel Records Center (Military Personnel Records) 9700 Page Avenue St. Louis, MO 63132-5100
4	Headquarters U.S. Marine Corps Personnel Management Support Branch (MMSB-10) 2008 Elliot Road Quantico, VA 22134-5030			11	Department of Veterans Affairs Records Management Center P.O. Box 5020 St. Louis, MO 63115-5020		

New Employee Record Chart

New Employee Record Chart

Employee _____   Position _____

Department _____   Date Employed _____

The above new employee must have checked item(s) in file.

Document	Required	Completed
Employment Application	_____	_____
Employee Data Sheet	_____	_____
W-4	_____	_____
I-9	_____	_____
Induction Form	_____	_____
New Hire Report	_____	_____
Applicant Waiver Releases	_____	_____
Substance Abuse Test Consent	_____	_____
Non-Compete Agreement	_____	_____
Confidentiality Agreement	_____	_____

_____

_____

_____
Supervisor

_____
Date

New Hire Reporting

New Hire Reporting Form

Send Completed Form to:_____   Fax form to: _____

                                                 Agency fax

_____   or   _____

_____   For info, call:_____

    Name & Address of New Hire State Contact   Agency phone

—EMPLOYER INFORMATION —

Federal Employer
Identification Number   _____

Employer Name   _____

Address   _____
           (Please indicate the address where Income Witholding Order will be sent)

City/State/Zip+4_____

—EMPLOYEE INFORMATION—

Social Security Number   _____-____-_____

Employee Name   _____

Employee Address _____

City/State/Zip Code+4_____

—EMPLOYEE INFORMATION—

Social Security Number   _____-____-_____

Employee Name   _____

Employee Address _____

City/State/Zip Code+4_____

Non-Compete Agreement

GENERAL NON-COMPETE AGREEMENT

For good consideration and as an inducement for _____ (Company), to employ _____ (Employee), the undersigned employee hereby agrees not to directly or indirectly compete with the business of the Company during the period of _____ years following termination of employment and notwithstanding the cause of reason for termination.

The term "not to compete" as used herein shall mean that the Employee shall not own, operate, consult to, or be employed by any firm in a business substantially similar to or competitive with the present business of the Company or such business activity in which the Company may engage during the term of employment.

The Employee acknowledges that the Company shall or may in reliance of this agreement provide Employee access to trade secrets, customers, and other confidential data and that the provisions of this agreement are reasonably necessary to protect the Company.

This agreement shall be binding upon and inure to the benefit of the parties, their successors, assigns, and personal representatives.

Signed under seal this _____ day of _____, 19 _____.

_____
Company

_____
Employee

Performance Review (page 1)

Performance Review

Employee Name   Reviewer Name

Job Title   Date of Review

	Circle One	*Reviewer Notes*
Availability Punctuality/Absence Time Awareness	Excellent Satisfactory Needs Improvement	
Job Awareness Accountabilities Sets Goals	Excellent Satisfactory Needs Improvement	
Behavior Interaction w/ others Manners/Neatness	Excellent Satisfactory Needs Improvement	
Complies w/ Policy Follows Procedures Safety Rules	Excellent Satisfactory Needs Improvement	
Dependability Performs assignments	Excellent Satisfactory Needs Improvement	
Initiative Develops Solutions Provides Ideas	Excellent Satisfactory Needs Improvement	
Independence Tracks Assignments Needs Supervision	Excellent Satisfactory Needs Improvement	
Productivity Quality / Accuracy Corrects Errors	Excellent Satisfactory Needs Improvement	

Continued

Performance Review (page 2)

Performance Review – Page 2

_____
Employee Name

New and/or noteworthy accomplishments since last evaluation

_____
_____
_____
_____

Areas in need of improvement

_____
_____
_____
_____

Recommendations

_____
_____
_____
_____

Overall Performance Summary: Excellent
(Circle one)   Satisfactory
                                          Needs Improvement

Employee Comments

_____
_____
_____
_____

_____   _____
Employee Signature   Reviewer Signature

_____   _____
Date   Date of Next Review

Pre-Employment Check by Phone

Pre-Employment Check by Phone

Name of Applicant: _____

Name of Company Contacted: _____

Name and Title of Reference: _____ Telephone: _____

* *

INSTRUCTIONS:
Contact the reference, preferably the applicant's immediate supervisor. Identify yourself and state that you are "calling to verify some of the information given to_____
by _____ who we are considering for a position."
* *

What were the dates of his/her employment with you? From _____ To _____

What was the nature of his/her job? _____

What did you think of his/her work? _____

How would you describe his/her performance in comparison with other people? _____
_____

What job progress did he/she make? _____

What were his/her earnings? _____ Bonus? _____

Why did he/she leave your Company? _____

Would you re-employ? _____

What are his/her strong points? _____

What are his/her limitations? _____

How did he/she get along with other people? _____

Could you comment on his/her:
(a) attendance   _____
(b) dependability   _____
(c) ability to take on responsibility _____
(d) potential for advancement _____
(e) degree of supervision needed _____
(f) overall attitude_____

Did he/she have any personal difficulties that interfered with his/her work?_____
_____

Is there anything else of significance that we should know? _____
_____

SIGNATURE: _____ DATE: _____

Rejection Letter Sample

(To be produced on your company letterhead)

(Insert date)

Dear *(insert name)*:

Thank you for your interest in working for our organization. Many talented and qualified people applied for this position, including you. After much consideration, we have hired another applicant.

Thank you for your time, and good luck in your job search.

Sincerely,

(Insert your signature and name here)

Request For Education Verification

Date_____

REQUEST FOR EDUCATION VERIFICATION

Registrar's Office:

    The applicant identified below has applied for a position with our organization. He/she has claimed attendance, credits and/or degree as denoted herein. Would you kindly verify this information and return this form in the enclosed self addressed stamped envelope. Please note, the applicant has signed for the release of this request.

NAME OF FACILITY

ADDRESS   CITY   STATE   ZIP

ATTENDANCE: FROM_____ TO _____
                         MO.   YR.   MO.   YR.

CREDITS
RECEIVED: _____   GRADUATE: YES   NO   _____
         TOTAL   AWARDS-LEVEL

DEGREE: YES NO _____ DATE _____
              DEGREE RECEIVED

    I hearby authorize the release to certify my records as stated above.

Signature   _____

Name(print)   _____

Address   _____

City/State/Zip _____

Date of Birth   _____

SS# _____

Request For Information

DATE _____

REQUEST FOR INFORMATION

To Whom It May Concern:

Mr./Ms. _____ has applied for a position as a
_____ and states that he/she was employed by you as a
_____ from _____ to _____.

Will you kindly reply to this inquiry and return this sheet in the enclosed self-addressed envelope. Your reply will be held in strict confidence and will in no way involve you in any responsibility.

Sincerely,

Signature: _____

Name (print/type): _____   Title: _____

Company: _____   Telephone: _____

****

Is employment record correct as stated above?	Yes _____	No _____

What were this employee's duties? _____

Did he/she have custody of money or valuables?	Yes _____	No _____
Were his accounts properly kept?	Yes _____	No _____
Was his/her conduct satisfactory?	Yes _____	No _____
Do you recommend him/her for rehire?	Yes _____	No _____

He/she was: Discharged _____   Laid Off _____   Resigned _____

Please list any Workers Compensation Claims: _____

	EXCELLENT	GOOD	FAIR	POOR
Quality of work	_____	_____	_____	_____
Cooperation	_____	_____	_____	_____
Safety Habits	_____	_____	_____	_____
Personal Habits	_____	_____	_____	_____
Attendance	_____	_____	_____	_____

REMARKS: _____
_____
_____

Company Name: _____

Person Completing Form: _____   Title: _____

Date: _____

Substance Abuse Screening Test – Applicant Consent

SUBSTANCE ABUSE SCREENING TEST

APPLICANT CONSENT FORM

I, _____, understand and agree that the medical examination I am
      (Name)
about to receive includes a:

(   ) Blood test for substance (drug/alcohol) abuse or chemical dependency.
(   ) Urine test for substance (drug/alcohol) abuse or chemical dependency.

I understand that if I decline to sign this consent and thereby decline to take the test, the medical examination will not be completed. The Employee Relations Department will be so notified and my application for employment will be rejected.

I understand that if the test is confirmed as positive, the results will be reported to the Employee Relations Department. An exception will be made for the use of legally prescribed medications taken under the directions of a physician.

I have taken the following drugs or substances within the last 96 hours:

Identify Name and Amount

(   ) Sleeping Pills_____
(   ) Diet Pills   _____
(   ) Pain Relief Medication_____
(   ) Cold Medication_____
(   ) Anti-Malarial Drugs_____
(   ) Any Other Medication or Substance_____

I hereby (   ) consent (   ) refuse to consent to the medical examination including the test(s) for substance (drug/alcohol) abuse and for the release of the test results to:

_____
(Name of Employer)

I hereby release_____
             (Name of Medical Facility)

the physicians, technicians, or employees of and the agents of all of the above-named parties, from any and all claims or causes of action resulting from this analysis and the release of the information regarding the results thereof.

_____
      Signature of Applicant

      Date:_____

Witness:

_____
    Signature   Date

Workers' Compensation Release

Workers' Compensation Release Form

From: Employer _____ Re: Employee _____

Address _____ Address _____

_____ Social Security # _____

--- EMPLOYEE AUTHORIZATION ---

I, _____, do hereby authorize certify that I received an offer
Employee Name

of employment from _____
Employer Name and Address

on _____ and authorize the _____
Date Name of State & Workers' Compensation Agency

_____ to release all information from Bureau files.
Workers' Compensation Agency

I affirm the information I have provided herein is true. I understand that if I make any false statements which I do not believe to be true and thereby mislead the public servant to whom this request is directed in performing his/her official function, I may be subject to State Criminal Codes where provided.

_____ X_____
Date Employee Signature

--- EMPLOYER CERTIFICATION ---

I _____, _____, an employee of
Name Title with Employer

and acting as agent for _____ do hereby certify that
Employer

_____ has extended an offer of employment to
Employer

_____ on _____ and I agree that information
Employee Date

requested from the_____
State Workers' Compensation Agency

With regard to _____ will be used by _____
Employee Employer

in conformance with both the Americans With Disabilities Act and _____
State and its Laws regarding Workers' Compensation

I affirm the information I have provided herein is true. I understand that if I make any false statements which I do not believe to be true and thereby mislead the public servant to whom this request is directed in performing his/her official function, I may be subject to State Criminal Codes where provided.

_____ X_____
Date Signature

_____
Title

Social Security Number Allocations

The Social Security Administration holds information about an individual as confidential, and, by law, cannot disclose it except in very restricted cases where regulations allow release of personal information. However, for verifying the authenticity of a card, Social Security Numbers are very revealing, especially when the numeric codes used for the assignment of the nine digit numbers are known. Those codes are given here.

Social Security Number Chart 1

A Social Security Number's first three digits, known as the area number, are determined by (but do not necessarily match) the Zip Code of the mailing address shown on the application for a Social Security Number. In using Social Security Number Chart 1, keep in mind these rules about the Numbers :

♦ Any Social Security Number beginning with 000 is not valid.

♦ An asterisk (*) indicates new areas where Social Security Numbers will be allocated, but are not yet issued. If a job applicant would present a card that begins with one of these numbers, it would not be a valid card (as of July 1, 1998).

♦ (**) 700-728 - Once issued to railroad employees, the practice was discontinued as of July 1, 1963.

♦ While at first it would seem that if a person's Social Security Number did not match their primary state of residence or birth state, then the card would be suspect. That is not always the case as there are certain three digit numbers that have been transferred from one state to another. Or, in some cases, an area has been divided for use among certain geographic locations. These exceptions are given in the following chart. Numbers designed as "not yet issued" are intended for use later for the state above it.

Social Security Number Chart 1

This is a numerical listing of Social Security Number "area" codes. Includes US Territories and locations where United States Social Security Numbers have been issued. Italicized items (each accompanied by an asterix) are card numbers not yet issued as of July 1, 1998.

Numbers Inclusive	Location	Numbers Inclusive	Location	Numbers Inclusive	Location
001 – 003	New Hampshire	362 – 386	Michigan	520	Wyoming
004 – 007	Maine	387 – 399	Wisconsin	521 – 524	Colorado
008 – 009	Vermont	400 – 407	Kentucky	650 – 653	not yet issued
010 – 034	Massachusetts	408 – 415	Tennessee	525	New Mexico
035 – 039	Rhode Island	756 – 763*	not yet issued	585	New Mexico
040 – 049	Connecticut	416 – 424	Alabama	648 – 649	not yet issued
050 – 134	New York	425 – 428	Mississippi	526 – 527	Arizona
135 – 158	New Jersey	587	Mississippi	600 – 601	Arizona
159 – 211	Pennsylvania	588*	not yet issued	528 – 529	Utah
212 – 220	Maryland	752 – 755*	not yet issued	646 – 647	not yet issued
221 – 222	Delaware	429 – 432	Arkansas	530	Nevada
223 – 231	Virginia	676 – 679*	not yet issued	680*	not yet issued
691 – 699*	not yet issued	433 – 439	Louisiana	531 – 539	Washington
232 – 236	West Virginia	659 – 665*	not yet issued	540 – 544	Oregon
232	North Carolina	440 – 448	Oklahoma	545 – 573	California
237 – 246	North Carolina	449 – 467	Texas	602 – 626	California
681 – 690*	not yet issued	627 – 645	Texas	574	Alaska
247 – 251	South Carolina	468 – 477	Minnesota	575 – 576	Hawaii
654 – 658*	not yet issued	478 – 485	Iowa	750 – 751*	not yet issued
252 – 260	Georgia	486 – 500	Missouri	577 – 579	Dist. of Columbia
667 – 675	not yet issued	501 – 502	North Dakota	580	Virgin Islands
261 – 267	Florida	503 – 504	South Dakota	580 – 584	Puerto Rico
589 – 595	Florida	505 – 508	Nebraska	596 – 599	Puerto Rico
268 – 302	Ohio	509 – 515	Kansas	586	Guam
303 – 317	Indiana	516 – 517	Montana	586	American Samoa
318 – 361	Illinois	518 – 519	Idaho	586	Philippine Islands

Social Security Number Chart 2

This is an alphabetical listing by state or territory name, including all locations where United States Social Security Numbers have been issued.

Location	Numbers Inclusive	Location	Numbers Inclusive	Location	Numbers Inclusive
Alabama	416 - 424	Kentucky	400 - 407	Oklahoma	440 - 448
Alaska	574	Louisiana	433 - 439	Oregon	540 - 544
American Samoa	586	Maine	004 - 007	Pennsylvania	159 - 211
Arizona	526 - 527, 600 - 601	Maryland	212 - 220	Philippine Islands	586
		Massachusetts	010 - 034	Puerto Rico	580 - 584 596 - 599
Arkansas	429 - 432	Michigan	362 - 386		
California	545 - 573, 602 - 626	Minnesota	468 - 477	Rhode Island	035 - 039
		Mississippi	425 - 428, 587	South Carolina	247 - 251
Colorado	521 - 524			South Dakota	503 - 504
Connecticut	040 - 049	Missouri	486 - 500	Tennessee	408 - 415
Delaware	221 - 222	Montana	516 - 517	Texas	449 - 467, 627 - 645
Dist. Of Columbia	577 - 579	Nebraska	505 - 508		
Florida	261 - 267, 589 - 595	Nevada	530	Utah	528 - 529
		New Hampshire	001 - 003	Vermont	008 - 009
Georgia	252 - 260	New Jersey	135 - 138	Virgin Islands	580
Guam	586	New Mexico	525, 585	Virginia	223 - 231
Hawaii	575 - 576			Washington	531 - 539
Idaho	518 - 519	New York	050 - 134	West Virginia	232 - 236
Illinois	318 - 361	North Carolina	232, 237 - 246	Wisconsin	387 - 399
Indiana	303 - 317			Wyoming	520
Iowa	478 - 485	North Dakota	501 - 502		
Kansas	509 - 519	Ohio	268 - 302		

Social Security Number Chart 3

While the first three digits of every nine digit Social Security Number denote the *area* or state where the application for an original Social Security Number was submitted, the middle two digits (digit four and five, which are known as the *group numbers*) are also numerically coded. Lastly, within each nine digit Social Security Number, are the *serial numbers*, which comprise the last four digits. These four serial numbers run consecutively from 0001 through 9999. Once serial number 9999 is assigned, the next *group number* (the two middle digits) is assigned, and serial number 0001 would be the first assigned with it.

These fourth and fifth digits range from 01 to 99 but they are not assigned in consecutive order. For administrative purposes, the first two-digit group numbers consist of the ODD numbers from 01 through 09. Later, the EVEN numbers from 10 through 98 are issued.

After all the numbers in group 98 of a particular area are issued, then the EVEN groups 02 through 08 (02, 04, 06, 08) are used, followed by the ODD groups, 11 through 99.

Thus, the order of issuance of the two middle digit numbers are:

        1st: ODD - 01, 03, 05, 07, 09 2nd: EVEN – 10 to 98

        3rd: EVEN – 02, 04, 06, 08 4th *and finally:* ODD – 11 to 99

By examining the latest monthly Highest Group Issued Table for the *latest* SSN area ranges to date, and invalid number can spotted when it greater than the number the Social Administration has issued.

For example, if presented with an Social Security Card with the number 606-39-0001, check the latest Highest Group Issued Table (Social Security Chart 3 below is effective as of July, 1998). Finding that the latest 606 number issue was 606 06, number 606 39 could *not* have been issued, therefore it is not legitimate. However, a card with 606 03 would be a number that had been issued.

Consider this: if the card read 606-03-0001, it could be a valid card, although it would probably have to belong to someone quite young, as 606 03 is quite close to the latest number issued, 606 06.

Social Security Chart 3 – Highest Group Issued Table shows the Social Security Number area (first three) numbers and group (middle two) numbers that are in the process of being issued as of July 1, 1998.

Social Security Chart 3 – Highest Group Issued Table as of July 1, 1998

Area #s	Group #s	Area #s	Group #s	Area #s	Group #s	Area #s	Group #s	Area #s	Group #s
001	92	012	82	023	80	034	80	045	96
002	90	013	82	024	80	035	66	046	96
003	90	014	82	025	80	036	66	047	96
004	98	015	82*	026	80	037	66*	048	96
005	98	016	80	027	80	038	64	049	96
006	96	017	80	028	80	039	64	050	88
007	96	018	80	029	80	040	98	051	88
008	82	019	80	030	80	041	98	052	88
009	82	020	80	031	80	042	98*	053	88
010	82	021	80	032	80	043	96	054	88
011	82	022	80	033	80	044	96	055	88

An asterisk (*) indicates a change that became effective 7/01/98.

Continued Next Page

Social Security Chart 3 *Continued* – Highest Group Issued Table as of July 1, 1998

Area #s	Group #s	Area #s	Group #s	Area #s	Group #s	Area #s	Group #s	Area #s	Group #s
056	88	120	86	186	76	250	99	314	19
057	88	121	86	187	76	251	99	315	19
058	88*	122	86	188	76	252	99	316	19
059	88*	123	86	189	76	253	99	317	19*
060	88*	124	86	190	76	254	99	318	94
061	88*	125	86	191	76	255	99	319	94
062	86	126	86	192	76	256	99	320	94
063	86	127	86	193	76	257	99	321	94
064	86	128	86	194	76	258	99	322	94
065	86	129	86	195	76	259	99	323	94
066	86	130	86	196	76	260	99	324	94
067	86	131	86	197	76	261	99	325	94
068	86	132	86	198	76	262	99	326	94
069	86	133	86	199	76	263	99	327	94
070	86	134	86	200	76	264	99	328	94
071	86	135	04	201	76	265	99	329	94
072	86	136	04	202	76	266	99	330	94
073	86	137	04	203	76	267	99	331	94
074	86	138	04	204	76	268	02	332	94
075	86	139	04	205	76	269	02	333	94
076	86	140	04	206	76	270	02	334	94
077	86	141	04	207	76	271	02	335	94
078	86	142	04	208	76	272	02	336	94
079	86	143	04*	209	76	273	02	337	94
080	86	144	04*	210	76	274	02	338	94
081	86	145	02	211	76	275	02	339	94
082	86	146	02	212	53*	276	02	340	94
083	86	147	02	213	51	277	02	341	94
084	86	150	02	214	51	278	02	342	94
085	86	151	02	215	51	279	02	343	94
086	86	152	02	216	51	280	02	344	94
087	86	153	02	217	51	281	02	345	94
088	86	154	02	218	51	282	02	346	94*
089	86	155	02	219	51	283	02	347	94*
090	86	156	02	220	51	284	02	348	94*
091	86	157	02	221	90	285	02	349	92
092	86	158	02	222	88	286	02	350	92
093	86	159	78	223	81	287	02	351	92
094	86	160	78	224	81	288	02	352	92
095	86	161	78	225	81	289	02	353	92
096	86	162	78	226	81	290	02	354	92
097	86	163	78	227	81	291	02	355	92
098	86	164	78	228	79	292	02	356	92
099	86	165	78	229	79	293	02	357	92
100	86	166	78	230	79	294	02	358	92
101	86	167	78	231	79	295	02	359	92
102	86	168	78	232	45	296	02	360	92
103	86	169	78	233	45	297	02	361	92
104	86	170	78	234	45	298	02	362	23
105	86	171	78*	235	45	299	02*	363	23
106	86	172	78*	236	43	300	98	364	23
107	86	173	76	237	89*	301	98	365	23*
108	86	174	76	238	87	302	98	366	21
109	86	175	76	239	87	303	19	367	21
110	86	176	76	240	87	304	19	368	21
111	86	177	76	241	87	305	19	369	21
112	86	178	76	242	87	306	19	370	21
113	86	179	76	243	87	307	19	371	21
114	86	180	76	244	87	308	19	372	21
115	86	181	76	245	87	309	19	373	21
116	86	182	76	246	87*	310	19	374	21
117	86	183	76	247	99	311	19	375	21
118	86	184	76	248	99	312	19	376	21
119	86	185	76	249	99	313	19	377	21

Social Security Chart 3 *Continued* – Highest Group Issued Table as of July 1, 1998

Area #s	Group #s	Area #s	Group #s	Area #s	Group #s	Area #s	Group #s	Area #s	Group #s
378	21	442	11	506	39	570	99	635	62*
379	21	443	11	507	37	571	99	636	60
380	21	444	11	508	37	572	99	637	0
381	21	445	11	509	15	573	99	638	60
382	21	446	11	510	15	574	25	639	60
383	21	447	08	511	15	575	81	640	60
384	21	448	08	512	15	576	81	641	60
385	21	449	99	513	15	577	29	642	60
386	21	450	99	514	15	578	29	643	60
387	17	451	9	515	13	579	29	644	60
388	17	452	99	516	33*	580	31	645	60
389	17	453	99	517	31	581	99	646	42
390	17	454	99	518	55*	582	99	647	40
391	17	455	99	519	53	583	99	648	14
392	17	456	99	520	39	584	99	649	14
393	17	457	99	521	99	585	99	650	07
394	17	458	99	522	99	586	37	651	07
395	17	459	99	523	99	587	83	652	07*
396	17	460	99	524	99	589	75	653	05
397	15	461	99	525	99	590	75	654	03
398	15	462	99	526	99	591	75	655	03
399	15	463	99	527	99	592	75	656	03
400	53	464	99	528	99	593	75*	657	03
401	53	465	99	529	99	594	75*	658	01
402	53	466	99	530	99	595	73	667	03*
403	51	467	99	531	41*	596	58	668	01
404	51	468	35	532	39	597	58*	669	01
405	51	469	35*	533	39	598	56	670	01
406	51	470	33	534	39	599	56	671	01
407	51	471	33	535	39	600	79	672	01
408	85*	472	33	536	39	601	79	673	01
409	83	473	33	537	39	602	06	674	01
410	83	474	33	538	39	603	06	675	01
411	83	475	33	539	39	604	06	680	09*
412	83	476	33	540	53	605	06	700	18
413	83	477	33	541	53	606	06	701	18
414	83	478	27	542	53	607	06	702	18
415	83	479	27	543	51	608	06	703	18
416	49*	480	27	544	51	609	06	704	18
417	47	481	27	545	99	610	06	705	18
418	47	482	27	546	99	611	06*	706	18
419	47	483	27*	547	99	612	06*	707	18
420	47	484	25	548	99	613	06*	708	18
421	47	485	25	549	99	614	06*	709	18
422	47	486	15	550	99	615	06*	710	18
423	47	487	15	551	99	616	06*	711	18
424	47	488	15*	552	99	617	06*	712	18
425	85*	489	13	553	99	618	04	713	18
426	83	490	13	554	99	619	04	714	18
427	83	491	13	555	99	620	04	715	18
428	83	492	13	556	99	621	04	716	18
429	95	493	13	557	99	622	04	717	18
430	93	494	13	558	99	623	04	718	18
431	93	495	13	559	99	624	04	719	18
432	93	496	13	560	99	625	04	720	18
433	97	497	13	561	99	626	04	721	18
434	97	498	13	562	99	627	62	722	18
435	97	499	13	563	99	628	62	723	18
436	97*	500	13	564	99	629	62	724	28
437	95	501	25	565	99	630	62	725	18
438	95	502	23	566	99	631	62	726	10
439	95	503	29	567	99	632	62	728	14
440	11	504	27	568	99	633	62*		
441	11	505	39	569	99	634	62*		

Sample Social Security Activity Report

```
NAME:                          MARY SMITH
SOCIAL SECURITY NUMBER:        111-11-1111
STATE OF ISSUE:                PENNSYLVANIA
YEAR OF ISSUE:                 1960


SOCIAL SECURITY NUMBER VERIFICATION:

03-94:  MARY A. SMITH, 1 MAIN ST., PATERSON, NJ 07513

12-93:  MARY B. SMITH, 1 MAIN ST., PATERSON, NJ 07513

01-93:  MARY SMITH, 2 FIRST ST., GARFIELD, NJ 07026

09-92:  MARY A. JONES, 3 MAPLE ST., GARFIELD, NJ 07026

03-91:  MARY A. SMITH, 3 MAPLE ST., GARFIELD, NJ 07026

03-91:  C. SMITH, 3 MAPLE ST., GARFIELD, NJ  07026

09-90:  MARY JONES, 4 CEDAR ST., PASSAIC, NJ 07055

03-90:  MARY JONES, 5 PALM COURT, BOCA RATON, FL

08-89:  MARY JONES, 6 OCEAN VIEW WAY, FT. LAUDERDALE, FL


AKA LISTED AS:  MARY JONES
EMPLOYER LISTED IN 01-93:  ABC COMPANY, NJ
EMPLOYER LISTED IN 03-90:  DEF COMPANY, FLORIDA
YEAR OF BIRTH LISTED AS:  1945
AGE LISTED AS:  49
MIDDLE INITIAL LISTED AS:  A and B
SPOUSE INITIAL LISTED AS:  C

SUBJECT'S NUMBER WAS ALSO USED ONCE IN 03-91 BY A C. SMITH.
INVESTIGATION REVEALS THAT THIS APPEARS TO BE THE SUBJECT'S
SPOUSE.

SUBJECT IS ALSO LISTED AS USING SOCIAL SECURITY NUMBER
222-22-2222.  INVESTIGATION REVEALS THAT THIS NUMBER APPEARS TO
BELONG TO HER SPOUSE, C. SMITH.

SUBJECT IS ALSO LISTED AS USING SOCIAL SECURITY NUMBER
333-33-3333 IN 03-90 AND 09-90.  THE ONLY INFORMATION FOUND IN
CONNECTION WITH THIS NUMBER INVOLVES THIS SUBJECT.  INFORMATION
FOLLOWS:

09-90:  MARY JONES, 4 CEDAR ST., PASSAIC, NJ 07055

03-90:  MARY JONES, 5 PALM COURT, BOCA RATON, FL
```

Social Security Number - Cross-checking with resume, application, and other sources Required!

Check Against Date of Birth on Application and Resume

How to Verify Social Security Numbers Free Through the Social Security Administration

The Social Security Administration (SSA) Enumeration Verification Services (EVS) is a free service that permits employers to match names and SSNs before submitting W-2 Forms (Wage and Tax Statements). This service is also available to third-party submitters (accountants, service bureaus, etc.).

This form of Social Security Number verification through the Social Security Administration can only be done after an employee is hired.

Making sure names and SSNs entered on the W-2 match Social Security's records is important because unmatched records can result in additional processing costs for the employer and uncredited earnings for employees. Uncredited earnings can affect future eligibility to (and amounts paid under) Social Security's retirement, disability and survivors program.

How to Use EVS

EVS is easy to use. Employers must complete the registration form, sign the appropriate privacy act statement and mail or fax the forms to SSA. Soon after, SSA issues a requester identification code to the employee who can then submit a data file or paper listing for verification.

EVS is ideal to verify an entire payroll database or hire more than 50 workers at a time. Requests for verification can be submitted year around and generally take 30 days or less to process.

Employers with less than 50 Requests

To verify less than 50 names and SSNs, you do not need to use Social Security's EVS or register ahead of time. By calling the toll-free number for employers, 1-800-772-6270, or SSA's general toll-free number, 1-800-772-1213, employers receive verification for up to 5 names/SSNs over the telephone. Include first name, last name, middle initial, date of birth, sex, and SSN. Both telephone numbers are open for service weekdays from 7:00 AM to 7:00 PM Eastern Time.

To verify 6 to 50 names and SSNs contact a local Social Security office (there are over 1,300 local offices).

Registration Instructions for Employers and Third-Party Submitters

For more information, visit the SSA's home page at www.ssa.gov.

Using a Pre-Employment Screening Company

There are many reasons to hire a professional firm to perform all or part of your pre-employment screening tasks. These firms are experts in public record information; they understand the legal issues and limits, and may even be able to help you with your company screening policies. A screening firm does not necessarily need to be located in your city or state. Most professional pre-employment screening firms are national in scope and have the ability to provide quality background checks for all sizes of companies.

Although, just like some applicants, all business that look good are not necessarily so. The two aspects of screening companies that can be used to determine which one to choose are cost and response time. However, most important is the quality of the information.

How to Select a Screening Vendor

There are many ways to find screening vendors. Selecting the right vendor from several prospective companies is more complicated. However, by using the following tips, your selection can be simplified:

Obtain price quotes and response time estimates

The cheapest service isn't always best. The vendor should clearly explain what services and searches are being performed, and from what government agencies. Be sure to compare "apples to apples." A price quote that includes both a county and statewide criminal record search (which is advisable) will cost more than a mere county search.

If you know that it takes 48 hours to obtain a criminal record in your county, but the vendor claims 24 hour response time, ask why. The average turnaround time to do a quality pre-employment screen varies from 24 to 72 hours, depending on the government agencies involved. A criminal record check involving fingerprints may actually take several weeks.

Ask for References and Contact Them

Of course, they are not going to offer references from dissatisfied customers, but calling references offers the opportunity to verify their response time claims and ask about customer service issues. Find out if the vendor is a member of any national or state professional organizations. Also, check with the local Better

Business Bureau. Ask about the extent of the vendor's staff and years of experience.

Be Leery of National Database Search Claims

There is a big distinction between doing a "national search" and "being able to search nationally." While many vendors claim that they are be able to perform a criminal record or driving record search from any state, there is no such thing as a national database for either of these types of records. If you want a "national search" on a criminal record history, you will have to check every state and, in certain instances, every county in a state. Such an extensive search costs hundreds of dollars.

Is the company openly concerned about full compliance with state and federal laws?

Most reputable vendors will state that they understand and comply with the Fair Credit Reporting Act (FCRA - see page 177). Ask how long the vendor maintains copies of the results they provide (if not for at least three years, there is a problem). Ask how the vendor stays current on federal and state laws. A vendor should be knowledgeable about the access requirements and restrictions to criminal and driving records from all states.

What type and quality of customer service is available from the vendor?

Is the vendor willing to help train your staff? Is the vendor willing to help with the company's policies and forms designed to comply with FCRA and state laws? If they are in a different time zone, be sure to find out their hours of operation for customer support.

Once you have the answers . . .

Does the vendor's performance match its claims? There is nothing wrong with asking a vendor to give you a free trial period or to perform a test. Give several vendors the same applicant name and compare the results.

If your company does not have dedicated personnel or time to devote to searching, by all means consider hiring a professional to perform all or portions of the search. Regardless, by understanding all the components of the screening process, one can more easily decide which vendor to select.

Pre-Employment Screening Company Profiles

4th Corner Network Inc
215 Flora St
Bellingham, WA 98225
Telephone: **Fax:**
800-321-2455   800-321-2455
360-671-2455   360-734-1286
www.4thcorner.com
Founded: 1978
Special Services: Credit Reports, Former
Employer Interviews, Workers' Compensation
History, Local Document Retrieval
Online Databases: SCOMIS
Memberships: NAPPS, ION, PRRN
Statement of Capabilities:
The 4th Corner Network is adept at locating
computer-based information and obtaining the
paper originals. Turnaround times are usually the
same or next business day. Their fees are
structured to allow clients maximum flexibility.

AAA Truth Verification Laboratories Inc
500 Executive Blvd #303
Ossining, NY 10562-2535
Telephone: **Fax:**
800-727-8846   914-271-5562
914-271-0000
www.drugd-tech.com
Founded: 1955
Special Services: Credit Reports, Profile/Aptitude
Testing, Former Employer Interviews, Workers'
Compensation History, Local Document Retrieval,
Drug Testing - In house, Drug Testing - Outsourced
Online Databases: AT&T Infomaster
Memberships: ASIS, NASA, NAIS
Statement of Capabilities:
Providing a full complement of pre-employment
screening services, AAA Truth Verification Labs
(TVL) provides a Windows-based online system
for ordering employee background checks called
TVL CIC Backtrak. TVL also provides forensic
analysis services including voice analysis of
audio recordings. In addition to computer access,
information can be obtained from TVL via
telephone, fax, or mail.

Accu-Screen Inc
PO Box 20767
Tampa, FL 33622-0767
Telephone: **Fax:**
800-689-2228   813-831-1839
813-837-1920
www.accuscreen.com
Founded: 1994
Special Services: Drug Testing - In house, Drug
Testing - Outsourced, Profile/Aptitude Testing,
Former Employer Interviews, Workers'
Compensation History, Local Document Retrieval,
Credit Reports
Memberships: SHRM, ASIS, NAIS
Statement of Capabilities:
Accu-Screen is a nationwide information service
that provides pre-employment screening and drug
testing services. Clients include some of the
nation's largest corporations. They employ a
large staff of field agents across the US,
retrieving information from every county and
federal court. They specialize in county criminal
searches.

Accufax
PO Box 35563
Tulsa, OK 74153
Telephone: **Fax:**
800-256-8898   918-622-9453
918-627-2226
www.Accufax-us.com
Founded: 1983
Special Services: Credit Reports, Profile/Aptitude
Testing, Workers' Compensation History, Local
Document Retrieval
Memberships: NAA, NASA, NFIB, ACB
Statement of Capabilities:
Accufax provides pre-employment background
checks nationwide with 48-72 hour turnaround
time on criminal, Dept. of Correction, MVR,
workmen's compensation, known sex offenders,
and wanted fugitive records. They also do
personality profiles using the Hogan Personality
Inventory.

Accurate Screening & Credit Reporting Inc

2315-10 North Pearl #137
Tacoma, WA 98409
Telephone: **Fax:**
  800-431-5962   258-474-3831
  258-472-2426
  www.accuratescreening.com
Founded: 1989
Special Services: Credit Reports, Former Employer Interviews, Local Document Retrieval
Online Databases: Trans Union, JIS Link, Eviction Link
Memberships: NARPM
Statement of Capabilities:

Associated Credit Bureau certified, Accurate Screening & Credit Reporting, provides clients with accurate pictures of applicants. Timely, in-depth reports are of highest quality and scope due to superior quality control, never compromising principles or standards of excellent. With 9 years experience, they pride themselves on their an excellent reputation within the industry.

AccuScreen Systems

1038 Main St
Baton Rouge, LA 70802
Telephone: **Fax:**
  800-383-6476   504-383-6445
  504-343-8378
Founded: 1974
Special Services: Drug Testing - In house, Credit Reports, Profile/Aptitude Testing, Workers' Compensation History, Former Employer Interviews, Local Document Retrieval, Drug Testing - Outsourced
Online Databases: US Datalink
Memberships: ASIS
Statement of Capabilities:

AccuScreen Systems is a full service pre-employment screening agency with experience to manage drug testing programs throughout the US. They assist in establishing drug testing policies, administer random drug tests, and file reports on behalf of clients. AccuScreen is licensed in Louisiana to provide services to the gaming industry. Their parent, Investigations Unlimited, provides investigative services, specializing in internal theft of products or trade secrets and civil matters, including sexual harassment cases.

ACQUIRE

2009 Vine Ave
McAllen, TX 78501
Telephone: **Fax:**
  512-443-0771   512-443-0771
  www.barronwebs.com/acquire
Founded: 1997
Special Services: Drug Testing - In house, Drug Testing - Outsourced, Profile/Aptitude Testing, Former Employer Interviews, Local Document Retrieval
Online Databases: IRSC
Statement of Capabilities:

ACQUIRE sells drug-testing kits in cases of 15 for on-site testing, and they also offer MRO certified lab testing of "positives." They offer INS (Immigration Naturalization Services) searches for Texas. They specialize in pre-employment screening. Normal turnaround time is 24 hours.

ADAM Safeguard

PO Box 1210
Toms River, NJ 08754
Telephone: **Fax:**
  800-722-2326   732-286-9201
  732-286-0800
  www.adamsafeguard.com
Founded: 1973
Special Services: Credit Reports, Drug Testing - Outsourced, Workers' Compensation History
Online Databases: Experian, Trans Union, Equifax, iiX, Superior Online, NJ Courts & DMV
Memberships: IALEIA, IACP
Statement of Capabilities:

ADAM Safeguard is the only company to provide a "How-to" book to all registed clients. The owner of ADAM Safeguard is co-author of *Don't Hire a Crook!* ADAM Safeguard conducts pre-employment background checks for all types of businesses. Ordering is processed by fax, phone and mail as well as HireCheck software for direct access via modem.

ADREM Profiles Inc

5461 W Waters Ave #900
Tampa, FL 33634
Telephone: **Fax:**
  800-281-1250   888-522-3736
  813-890-0334
  www.adpro.com
Founded: 1992
Special Services: Drug Testing - Outsourced, Credit Reports, Workers' Compensation History, Local Document Retrieval

Memberships: SHRM
Statement of Capabilities:

ADREM Profiles is an international, full service public records research and retrieval company. Their comprehensive retrieval network allows access to information repositories within the 3,347 counties and independent cities throughout the United States. They offer cost-plus pricing, a private label delivery system, compliance and technical support plus ADREM Advantage, their 24 hour Internet ordering and retrieval system. Their products and services are all designed to help achieve business objectives.

Advance Credit Reports Inc

PO Box 724
Matleson, IL 60443

Telephone:	Fax:
800-806-9803	800-796-8601
708-720-4000	708-720-4053

http://members.aol.com/
imsworks

Founded: 1992
Special Services: Credit Reports, Former Employer Interviews, Workers' Compensation History
Online Databases: Experian, Equifax, Avert
Statement of Capabilities:

Advance Credit Reports' primary service entails providing credit information on perspective tenants for landlords and businesses. Services also include pre-employment and criminal history reports. Normal turnaround time is same day on most reports.

Advanced Data Research Inc

HC 3 Box 406
Lampe, MO 65681

Telephone:	Fax:
800-238-3607	417-779-3710
417-779-3715	

www.adrinform.com

Founded: 1995
Special Services: Credit Reports, Former Employer Interviews, Workers' Compensation History, Local Document Retrieval
Online Databases: Equifax, Experian/First American, DAC, DBT Online, Courtlink, Ink
Memberships: AIIP, NAFE, INA
Statement of Capabilities:

Specializing in employment background screening , they can also assist clients in establishing suitable screening programs. Various packages are compiled of reports ranging from credit reports and criminal, court, work, driving records, Workers' compensation claims, work and personal reference checks, credentials confirmation, and Social Security validations.

Advantage Services Inc

PO Box 818
Duluth, GA 30096

Telephone:	Fax:
800-486-4432	800-969-1377
770-623-4321	770-623-3377

Founded: 1990
Special Services: Drug Testing - Outsourced, Credit Reports, Former Employer Interviews, Local Document Retrieval
Online Databases: Experian
Memberships: SHRM
Statement of Capabilities:

Since 1990, Advantage Services Inc (ASI) has specialized in verifications, references, criminal history, financial history, driving records, professional licensures and more. Clients select only those options that apply to their recruiting needs. No enrollment fees. ASI does not require minimum orders. Turnaround time is 1-4 days, depending upon the services requested. Their staff prides itself on providing excellent customer service and thorough and accurate reports.

Alliant Inc

5300 W Sahara #151
Las Vegas, NV 89102

Telephone:	Fax:
800-731-1321	800-731-1321

Founded: 1996
Special Services: Drug Testing - Outsourced, Credit Reports, Profile/Aptitude Testing, Former Employer Interviews, Workers' Compensation History, Local Document Retrieval
Online Databases: DIALOG, Dun & Bradstreet, LEXIS-NEXIS, CDB Infotek
Memberships: SHRM, SCIP, AIIP, ASIS, NAIS
Statement of Capabilities:

Alliant provides a wide range of nationwide services, including employment screening, background investigation, forensic toxology services and business information reports to high technology and general business companies including the Fortune 500, government agencies, and supporting organizations. They utilize a network of over 3000 court record researchers. Investigations are based on real time searches, eliminating possible errors due to outdated or incomplete record information. They provide no-charge customized Windows-based software allowing customers to order products and track in-process work status.

Allington International
20160 Center Ridge Rd
Cleveland, OH 44116
Telephone: **Fax:**
800-747-5202   440-333-0506
440-333-0505
Special Services: Drug Testing - Outsourced, Credit Reports, Former Employer Interviews, Workers' Compensation History, Local Document Retrieval
Online Databases: PACER
Memberships: ASIS, NAPSI, NPRRA, PRRN
Statement of Capabilities:
  Allington Researchers has performed nuclear power plant background screens under Atomic Energy Department guidelines. They offer a variety of background services with excellent turnaround time pricing. Allington is a full service, licensed and insured investigation agency.

Allstate Legal Court Service
PO Box 485
Granger, IA 50109
Telephone: **Fax:**
888-260-2816   515-999-9267
515-999-2757
Founded: 1994
Special Services: Local Document Retrieval
Memberships: ABW, PRRN
Statement of Capabilities:
  Allstate Legal Court Services provides general and specialized research and document retrieval in Iowa, also tenant and pre-employment screening services. Parent company is Allstate Legal Court Research.

Amherst Group Inc
4804 Arlington Ave
Riverside, CA 92504
Telephone: **Fax:**
800-521-0237   909-785-5888
909-785-5777
www.amherst-group.com
Founded: 1982
Special Services: Credit Reports, Former Employer Interviews, Workers' Compensation History, Local Document Retrieval
Online Databases: Trans Union, Equifax, iiX
Memberships: APA, ASIS, NALI, NAPI
Statement of Capabilities:

Founded in 1982, The Amerst Group, a national company with clients throughout the US, specializes in commercial investigations and information services. They assist hundreds of organizations with their information needs. Their national network provides fast, accurate and reliable information. Placing orders for service may be accomplished by telephone, facsimile or the Internet. Tracking each order, their turnaround time is 24-72 hours with the majority being completed within 48 hours.

AMS Pre-Employment Services
174 Main St
Eatontown, NJ 07724
Telephone: **Fax:**
732-460-2505   732-460-2508
www.amsnj.com
Founded:
Special Services: Drug Testing - In house, Drug Testing - Outsourced, Credit Reports, Profile/Aptitude Testing, Former Employer Interviews, Workers' Compensation History, Local Document Retrieval
Statement of Capabilities:
  AMS Pre-Employment Services can provide a variety of services, customized to client's specific needs. A goal is to allow clients to successfully screen future applicants and help protect the most important resource of any company, its employees. AMS utilizes a vast network of databases coupled with an experienced investigative unit.

Androcles Inc
2827 ALT 19 N
Palm Harbor, FL 34683
Telephone: **Fax:**
800-245-2318   800-813-4336
813-781-1807   813-781-0687
www.infolion.com
Founded: 1994
Special Services: Credit Reports, Former Employer Interviews, Workers' Compensation History, Local Document Retrieval
Memberships: ABA, ASIS, IACP
Statement of Capabilities:
  Androcles Inc, a full service employment screening company, executes nationwide searches in 24-48 hours. While specializing in criminal history searches, the Androcles research team delivers standard and customized employment screening packages, accessed from federal, state and county repositories. The President of Androcles has over 20 years

experience in the information industry and is a member of the labor and employment section of the Florida Bar. The Vice President has over 30 years law enforcement experience, has consulted internationally and has degrees in Marketing and Public Administration.

Applicant Insight Ltd

PO Box 458
New Port Richey, FL 34656
Telephone: **Fax:**
727-841-7616 727-841-0918
Founded: 1990
Special Services: Former Employer Interviews
Online Databases: Judicial Information System, Pinellas County, PACER, State Police, LEXIS/NEXIS, ERIN, NAIC
Memberships: SILA
Statement of Capabilities:

Applicant Insight prepares in-depth background verification reports for the insurance and health care industries. The core of each report is information developed from past supervisors and other business references. These interviews are complemented by public record searches to develop a profile of each applicant. They also publish educational materials including "Background Report Requirements for the Insurance Industry" and "Negligent Hiring--A Manager's Guide," and a Fair Credit Reporting Act Compliance Kit.

Applicant Research Corp

195 Clarksville Rd
Lawrencevill, NJ 08648-5303
Telephone: **Fax:**
800-929-0654 800-321-2943
609-716-3000 609-716-3062
Founded: 1994
Special Services: Credit Reports, Former Employer Interviews, Local Document Retrieval
Memberships: SHRM
Statement of Capabilities:

Applicant Research Corporation emphasizes a close working relationship with employers. The company gathers background information about job applicants and personnel. Workport is a unique product available from Applicant Research. It lists prior employment research records exchanged among participating employers.

Applicant Screening & Processing (ASAP)

3592 Aloma Ave #11
Winter Park, FL 32792
Telephone: **Fax:**
800-330-3793 800-482-4611
407-702-0974 407-702-0981
Founded: 1993
Special Services: Drug Testing - In house, Credit Reports, Workers' Compensation History
Online Databases: Experian
Memberships: NAA, NACRA
Statement of Capabilities:

ASAP specializes in eviction and criminal information updated weekly for screening prospective residents. They also offer credit reports and complete application processing by experienced staff. Most services are available via fax or using their free computer software.

Application Researchers

PO Box 11
Chattanooga, TN 37401
Telephone: **Fax:**
800-865-5272 423-265-6235
423-265-6035
www.cdc.net/appres
Founded: 1994
Special Services: Drug Testing - Outsourced, Credit Reports, Former Employer Interviews, Workers' Compensation History, Local Document Retrieval
Memberships: NAWBO, SHRM
Statement of Capabilities:

With relevant hands-on skills and experience in the field, Application Researchers staff has human resources backgrounds with knowledge of processes, and federal and state law relative to employment.

APSCREEN Inc

2043 Westcliff Dr #300
Newport Beach, CA 92660
Telephone: **Fax:**
800-327-8732 714-646-5160
714-646-4003
Founded: 1980
Special Services:
Online Databases: Experian
Memberships: NPRRA, SHRM, ACFE, WAD, CII, ASIS
Statement of Capabilities:

APSCREEN is one of the oldest employment screening firms in the United States. They are a broker of credit data and a certified fraud examiner. They specialize in bank searches and asset reports. They also provide international expert testimony regarding improper employment screening, white collar fraud and assets research.

AR Employment Screening Inc

6948 Indianapolis Blvd
Hammond, IN 46324
Telephone: **Fax:**
888-311-1630   219-989-3056
219-989-3050
Founded:
Special Services: Credit Reports, Former Employer Interviews, Workers' Compensation History, Local Document Retrieval
Statement of Capabilities:
AR Employment Screening is a provider of pre-employment screening services offering hand searches of individual courthouses, nationwide, to ensure a complete and up-to-date report. Although criminal history checks are the specialty, they also provide civil, federal, motor vehicle, employer and education verification and credit history reports. Friendly customer support staff is available and no inconvenient electronic voice systems are used. Turnaround times average 2-3 business days.

ATT Loss Prevention Inc

PO Box 1681
Torrington, CT 06790
Telephone: **Fax:**
800-733-4405   860-482-0377
860-496-1472
www.attloss.com
Founded:
Special Services: Drug Testing - In house, Drug Testing - Outsourced, Workers' Compensation History
Online Databases: Experian, Equifax, Dun & Bradstreet
Memberships: WAD
Statement of Capabilities:
Att Loss prevention is an information company that provides its services to businesses only. Att is known for hard to get information. Att also offers capabilities to retrieve reports for pre-employment background screening, workers compensation, SSNs, education, criminal histories in the US and out of country. A main specialty is CNSs on old numbers and locates. They offer services with no monthly fee or minimums.

Avert Inc

301 Remington St
Fort Collins, CO 80524
Telephone: **Fax:**
800-367-5933   800-237-4011
www.avert.com
Founded: 1986
Special Services: Credit Reports, Former Employer Interviews, Workers' Compensation History
Statement of Capabilities:
Avert helps employers minimize risk and hire safe, honest and competent employees. Use Avert's on-line ordering system, OrderXpert, and retrieve reports to your desktop. Avert offers services such as KnowledgeLink Help Desk for building a compliant pre-employment screening program to fit the need. Legal and fair to all parties, Avert is a good outsource for pre-employment screening as well as providing a proactive approach to reducing fraud, theft, turnover, and violence in the workplace.

Avian Corporate Records Research Notary

PO Box 161232
Austin, TX 78716
Telephone: **Fax:**
512-326-2638   512-326-3354
Founded: 1997
Special Services: Former Employer Interviews, Workers' Compensation History, Local Document Retrieval
Statement of Capabilities:
Avian specializes in on-site court records searching and document retrieval. Their services include filing and processes services, tenant screening, employment screening/verification, real estate owner searches, driver records, judgment/lien searches, and evictions.

Background America Inc

1900 Church St #400
Nashville, TN 37203
Telephone: **Fax:**
800-697-7189   615-321-9585
615-320-9800
www.background-us.com
Founded: 1983
Special Services: Local Document Retrieval
Memberships: ASIS, SHRM
Statement of Capabilities:
Background America is an information technology company that specializes in

employment screening services. BAI offers professional background checks to over 3500 clients nationwide in healthcare, insurance, retail, manufacturing, and other markets. BAI has developed a unique, Internet-based production system that enables registered users to order and retrieve background reports online from a web page.

Background Bureau Inc

880 Alexandraia Pike
Fort Thomas, KY 41075
Telephone: **Fax:**
800-854-3990 606-781-5888
606-781-3400
Founded: 1982
Special Services: Profile/Aptitude Testing, Former Employer Interviews, Workers' Compensation History, Credit Reports
Online Databases: Trans Union, DAC, AMS
Statement of Capabilities:
Background Bureau (BBI) specializes in 2-day turnaround of applicant information, providing hard-searched courthouse records. BBI features an aptitude/ability paper & pencil procedure known as "Predictive Profile." BBI also wholesales reports to other background screening companies. Provides service to 48 states and in Canada.

Backgrounds Express LLC

100 N Main #402
Memphis, TN 38103
Telephone: **Fax:**
888-811-4667 888-811-4668
901-578-3287 901-578-7889
www.process-service.com
Founded: 1991
Special Services: Credit Reports, Former Employer Interviews, Workers' Compensation History, Local Document Retrieval
Online Databases: Equifax, Equifax, Experian
Memberships: NAPPS
Statement of Capabilities:
Backgrounds Express offers same day service on requests received by 2PM M-F. They also own and update daily a database of all forcible detainers filed in Shelby County, TN since January 1, 1996 (over 40,000 suits). They also have 14 private process servers and offer same day delivery of court documents.

Background Research Services

PO Box 3
Willow Creek, CA 95573
Telephone: **Fax:**
800-707-1671 800-707-8849
530-629-2929 530-629-1199
Founded: 1997
Special Services: Credit Reports, Former Employer Interviews, Workers' Compensation History, Local Document Retrieval
Online Databases: Social Security Administration, Experian
Statement of Capabilities:
BRS will provide some information within the first 24 hours, and fax a written report within 1-2 working days after all information is gathered. Hard copies mailed within the week. They access many sources of information to be sure clients have everything needed for informed decisions. BRS is affiliated with a PI to help BRS access and retrieve a wide range of information. A BRS partner is a past credit collector with a wide range of knowledge in information gathering. We try to provide our clients with personalized service and courtesy service.

Backtrack Inc

8200-A Tyler Blvd
Mentor, OH 44060
Telephone: **Fax:**
440-205-8280 440-205-8355
www.backtrackinc.com
Founded: 1993
Special Services: Credit Reports, Former Employer Interviews, Workers' Compensation History, Local Document Retrieval
Online Databases: Experian, iiX
Memberships: SHRM, NPRRA
Statement of Capabilities:
Backtrack provides employment screening services, criminal records, employment and education verification, driving records, credit history, Social Security trace, workers' compensation claims, military records. 48-72 hour turnaround available.

Business Directions Inc

3355 Lenox Rd #660
Atlanta, GA 30326
Telephone: **Fax:**
800-280-3282 800-946-9111
404-266-2999 404-266-0282
www.Business-Directions.com
Founded: 1984

Special Services: Drug Testing - Outsourced, Credit Reports, Former Employer Interviews, Workers' Compensation History, Local Document Retrieval
Online Databases: Equifax
Statement of Capabilities:

Business Directions can provide a criminal history report in all counties of the US. Their maximum turnaround time is 72 hours; 86% of all requests are completed with 48. They provide online access to download and upload data via the Internet or they can provide free software.

California Consulting & Research

PO Box 5238
Playa Del Rey, CA 90296
Telephone: **Fax:**
310-670-1256   310-670-3130
Special Services: Credit Reports, Former Employer Interviews, Workers' Compensation History, Local Document Retrieval

Candidate Confirmation

314 Lake St
Libertyville, IL 60048
Telephone: **Fax:**
847-362-0007   847-367-8984
Founded: 1990
Special Services: Credit Reports, Former Employer Interviews, Workers' Compensation History, Local Document Retrieval
Online Databases: Online Searches
Memberships: ASIS
Statement of Capabilities:

Candidate Confirmation provides its services for human resource departments, employers, and landlords. Candidate Confirmation combines 25 years of investigative experience with the most recent computer database information to develop a clear profiles. Checks are conducted in accordance with the FCRA and required legal guidelines. Reports are timely, accurate and uniformly conducted. No sign up fee, no minimum requirements; volume discounts are available. The client faxes a release to Candidiate Confirmation and a written report is returned within 3 days.

CARCO Automated Products

PO Box 9600
St. James, NY 11787
Telephone: **Fax:**
516-862-9300   516-584-7094
Founded: 1977
Special Services: Credit Reports, Workers' Compensation History
Online Databases: Trans Union
Memberships: SHRM, ASIS
Statement of Capabilities:

CARCO provides automated online support of employee screening to businesses through its new Zipcrim technology. Zipcrim allows CARCO clients to request screening data on criminal and employment histories, credit information, and other public record information. Providing services nationwide, CARCO continues to develop automated products for accessing other categories of risk mitigation information for business purposes.

CBC Employment Screening Services

5555 Airport Hwy #205
Toledo, OH 43615-7331
Telephone: **Fax:**
800-772-0130   800-772-0440
419-861-7555   419-861-7565
Founded: 1988
Special Services: Drug Testing - Outsourced, Credit Reports, Profile/Aptitude Testing, Former Employer Interviews, Workers' Compensation History, Local Document Retrieval
Online Databases: Professional Alternatives
Memberships: SHRM
Statement of Capabilities:

CBC Employment Screening Services provides individualized attention to their clients. Each client is assigned a specialist. They have developed a software package that allows customers to request and obtain reports directly from a PC. They assist clients in complying wit the FCRA and other laws that affect background screening. They will customize employment questions and reports at no extra charge. They also offer volume discounting.

Central Valley Records Service

2101 Ottawa Ct
Modesto, CA 95356

Telephone: **Fax:**
209-524-3849 209-525-8786

Founded: 1996

Special Services: Local Document Retrieval

Statement of Capabilities:

Central Valley Records Service specializes in pre-employment background checks and provides criminal and civil searches in Stanislaus, San Joaquin and Merced counties. 24-48 hour turnaround time is standard. Over 20 years experience with onsite, up-to-date searches performed. Reasonable pricing and convenient monthly billing.

ChoicePoint Inc

1000 Alderman Dr
Alphretta, GA 30005

Telephone: **Fax:**
770-752-6000 770-752-6005
www.choicepointinc.com

Founded:

Special Services: Drug Testing - Outsourced, Credit Reports, Former Employer Interviews, Local Document Retrieval, Profile/Aptitude Testing

Statement of Capabilities:

ChoicePoint, a Equifax Company, is a leading provider of intelligence information to help businesses, governments, and individuals to better understand with whom they do business. ChoicePoint services the risk management information needs of the property and casualty insurance market, the life and health insurance market, and business and government, including asset-based lenders and professional service providers. Offers a variety of useful online products.

CIC Applicant Background Checks

12505 Starkey Rd #K
Largo, FL 33773

Telephone: **Fax:**
800-321-4473 727-524-8881
727-535-4473
www.hirecheck.com

Founded: 1988

Special Services: Drug Testing - In-house, Credit Reports, Profile/Aptitude Testing, Former Employer Interviews, Workers' Compensation History, Local Document Retrieval

Online Databases: Equifax, Trans Union

Memberships: SHRM, IAHSS, ASIS, NHRA, AMA, NAPEO

Statement of Capabilities:

CIC provides pre-employment background checks to companies of all sizes. Ordering is by phone, fax, e-mail, or Internet, connected to their proprietary software, HireCheck. CIC complies with the Fair Credit Reporting Act and specializes in criminal record searches, driving records, credit reports for employment, workers' compensation, and verifications. As the winner of the best product award in 1995 from Human Resources Executive Magazine, the windows-based HireCheck system allows clients to enter orders, customize searches, and track projects.

CMS Insight

PO Box 100029
Roswell, GA 30077

Telephone: **Fax:**
800-714-5534 770-992-7162
770-992-9077
www.CMSINSIGHT.com

Founded: 1985

Special Services: Credit Reports, Local Document Retrieval

Memberships: SHRM

Statement of Capabilities:

CMS Insight compiles independent analytical assessments of employees and prospective employees from public record background search information. The detail depends on customer needs. They also provide credit risk analysis of businesses fir credit departments.

Compass Solutions

PO Box 2826
Seattle, WA 98111

Telephone: **Fax:**
800-814-8213 800-257-8893
206-505-8213 206-505-7480

Founded: 1989

Online Databases: Equifax

Memberships: NACM, SHRM

Statement of Capabilities:

Compass Solutions specializes in full-service hiring directions, and they focus on pre-employment background investigations, performing statewide checks for criminal records, driver/vehicle records, etc. Compass has a strong presence in Washington, Oregon and Utah. Client services available seven days a week.

Compu-Fact Research
615 Mosport
St Charles, MO 63304
Telephone: **Fax:**
314-291-3308   314-291-3308
Founded: 1993
Special Services: Credit Reports, Former
Employer Interviews, Workers' Compensation
History, Local Document Retrieval
Online Databases: Equifax, Equifax, Trans Union

Corporate Information Services
PO Box 1717
Lilburn, GA 30048
Telephone: **Fax:**
770-931-3101   770-381-5977
www.opsecintl.com
Founded:
Special Services: Drug Testing - Outsourced,
Credit Reports, Profile/Aptitude Testing, Local
Document Retrieval
Memberships: ASIS

Corporate Intelligence Consultants
PO Box 444
Perryville, OH 43552-0444
Telephone: **Fax:**
419-874-2201   419-874-5591
www.corpintel.com
Founded: 1977
Special Services: Credit Reports, Former
Employer Interviews, Workers' Compensation
History, Local Document Retrieval
Memberships: ASIS, NCISS, WAD, AICPA,
AFSAIRS, INOA
Statement of Capabilities:
Corporate Intelligence's staff has more than 300
years of investigative and security consulting
experience.

Corporate Screening Services Inc
PO Box 36129
Cleveland, OH 44136
Telephone: **Fax:**
800-229-8606   888-815-4567
440-816-0500   440-243-4204
www.corporate-screening.com
Founded:
Special Services: Credit Reports
Memberships: NCISS, SHRM, ASIS, AIIP
Statement of Capabilities:
Corporate Screening utilizes a national network
of resources for public record search and retrieval

services. They offer complete pre-employment
and business background investigative packages;
can customize to fit needs. Complies with FCRA.
Their applicant Screening Engine (CSS EASE)
allows registered users to access complete
investigative results and updates over the
Internet. This has recently expanded to include
online public record search ordering, free and
easy to use.

Corporate Solutions Inc
1691 Georgetown Rd
Hudson, OH 44236
Telephone: **Fax:**
800-528-0130   800-528-0140
330-650-5211   330-650-5214
www.corpsolutionsinc.com
Founded: 1991
Special Services: Credit Reports, Former
Employer Interviews, Workers' Compensation
History, Local Document Retrieval
Online Databases: DAC Services
Memberships: ASIS, SHRM
Statement of Capabilities:
Corporate Solutions provides employment
background screening services to businesses and
government agencies nationwide. Clients request
information via fax with easy to use order forms.
An online system will soon be in place. They
provide clients with customized employment
applications, instructions on how to read and
understand credit reports and driving records,
interpretation reference profiles of candidates,
total customer support. Average turnaround time:
24-48 hours. Their sister company - CSI
Management Systems Inc - provides training and
development to Human Resource Managers and
other staff involved in the hiring process.

Credential Check
30833 Northwestern Hwy, #118
Farmington Hills, MI 48334
Telephone: **Fax:**
800-824-3251   248-626-2374
248-626-2277
www.credentialcheck.com
/quality
Founded: 1984
Special Services: Credit Reports, Former
Employer Interviews, Workers' Compensation
History
Statement of Capabilities:
Specializes in pre-employment profile reports
only, features of Credential Check include: 24
hour turnaround time, full references obtained

detailing performance, with no contract, minimal order or membership required. Employees are highly educated and several have more than 1 degree. They are very knowledgeable of laws pertaining to consumer reporting agencies. Licensed private investigating agency that has appeared in national publications. Criminal record search includes all places applicant lived and worked in last 7 years.

Credit Information Corporation

3550 McKelvey Rd #210
Bridgeton, MO 63044
Telephone: **Fax:**
800-899-6396 888-242-5242
314-344-0084 314-344-2998
Founded: 1989
Special Services: Drug Testing - Outsourced, Credit Reports, Former Employer Interviews, Workers' Compensation History, Local Document Retrieval
Online Databases: Equifax
Memberships: NAA, IREM
Statement of Capabilities:
Credit Information Corporation's management team has 60 years experience in risk management. Their forte is the blending of technologically acquired information with manually obtained data so that landlords and employers will have the necessary facts on which good decisions can be made.

CRIS Information Services

17177 N Laural Park Dr, #416
Livonia, MI 48152
Telephone: **Fax:**
800-343-2747 888-770-6651
734-462-4015 734-462-0314
Founded:
Special Services: Drug Testing - Outsourced, Credit Reports, Former Employer Interviews, Workers' Compensation History, Local Document Retrieval
Statement of Capabilities:
CRIS Information Services provide pre-employment screening programs designed to provide only the information required. They utilize a program built around the client's needs, saving time and money. Requests for unique and specialized reports are met. At-a-glance report structure; no trying to decipher penal codes or court records. All reports completed within 3-4 business days.

CSI Industries

319 N Main St
Burlington, IA 52601
Telephone: **Fax:**
800-615-2850 319-753-5268
319-753-0223
Memberships: SHRM
Statement of Capabilities:
CSI Industries performs criminal and background checks using court records at local county courthouses. They also can serve as "the neutral third party" needed for compliance with the recent changes in the Iowa Drug Testing/Screening laws.

Data Research Inc

PO Box 267
Sylvania, OH 43560-0267
Telephone: **Fax:**
888-328-2882 419-824-0068
419-882-2327
www.dataresearch.com
Special Services: Credit Reports, Former Employer Interviews, Workers' Compensation History, Local Document Retrieval
Online Databases: OPEN
Memberships: ASIS, ACFE, NAIS, ION, USPSA
Statement of Capabilities:
Data Research Inc guarantees a 72-hour turnaround on pre-employment screening investigations.

Data Screen Inc

6239 Oakmont Blvd #398
Ft Worth, TX 76132
Telephone: **Fax:**
817-294-7671 817-294-0773
Founded: 1991
Statement of Capabilities:
Data Screen is a licensed investigations company specializing in criminal background checks in Texas. Reports from major counties are available in 24 hours or less. Most other counties are available in 24-48 hours. MVR reports are also available.

Data-Trac Network Inc

784 Franklin Ave
Garden City, NY 11530
Telephone: **Fax:**
516-335-0982 516-878-4022
www.DATA-TRAC.com
Founded: 1990

Special Services: Credit Reports, Former Employer Interviews, Workers' Compensation History
Memberships: ION
Statement of Capabilities:
Data-Trac is an online investigative network providing instant access to public records. They also offer customized pre-employment services and records searches. They maintain a database and are a public record manufacturer.

Deception Control Inc
1885 W Commercial Blvd #125
Ft Lauderdale, FL 33309
Telephone: **Fax:**
800-776-1660 954-776-7687
954-771-6900
www.Deception.com
Founded: 1975
Special Services: Drug Testing - In house, Drug Testing - Outsourced, Credit Reports, Former Employer Interviews, Profile/Aptitude Testing, Workers' Compensation History, Compensation History
Online Databases: FDLE
Memberships: NALI, ASIS, APA
Statement of Capabilities:
Deception Control has an easy to use remote dial up system that can be accessed nationwide. Searches can be tailored to clients' needs, including nationwide searches using extensive online capabilities. They specialize in criminal records, civil litigation, insurance investigation and background searches. Drug testing programs are also available nationwide.

Eagle Communications
6204 Westerham Rd
Cleveland, OH 44124
Telephone: **Fax:**
216-646-9179 216-446-9181
Founded: 1989
Special Services: Drug Testing - Outsourced, Credit Reports, Former Employer Interviews, Workers' Compensation History, Local Document Retrieval
Online Databases: iiX, Public Credit Service
Memberships: PRRN, NPRRA
Statement of Capabilities:
Eagle Communications is an information brokerage firm whose owners have more the 25 years experience in legal assistance and more than 18 years of investigative and public record research experience. They provide clients with the professional, prompt service. In clear, concise

formats, reports are interpreted to clients to assure understanding.

Edge Information Management Inc
1901 S Harbor City Blvd #401
Melbourne, FL 32901
Telephone: **Fax:**
800-725-3343 800-780-3299
407-722-3343
www.edgeinformation.com
Founded: 1991
Special Services: Credit Reports, Former Employer Interviews
Online Databases: Trans Union
Statement of Capabilities:
Edge Information Management provides medium to large businesses with the opportunity of requesting and retrieving public record information through various access methods including proprietary DOS and Windows software programs, toll-free fax lines, and their Message Acquisition Center (MAC). Edge clients have the flexibility to decide how individual locations will make requests, determine the information the locations receive, select the communication method, and create customized reports from the screening data.

Edith Wiggins/Marvin Singer
1725 Taylor 1A
San Francisco, CA 94133
Telephone: **Fax:**
415-771-9369 415-441-8519
Founded: 1994
Special Services: Local Document Retrieval
Memberships: NALA
Statement of Capabilities:
Edith Wiggins/Marvin Singer provide public record research in San Francisco and San Mateo counties CA. Normal turnaround time is 1 day or less. They specialize in pre-employment criminal checks. Over 13 years experience in public record research.

Employers Reference Source
PO Box 310178
Newington, CT 06131
Telephone: **Fax:**
888-512-2525 888-520-2110
860-666-1418 860-666-1471
Founded: 1990
Special Services: Drug Testing - In house, Drug Testing - Outsourced, Credit Reports, Former

Employer Interviews, Workers' Compensation History, Local Document Retrieval
Online Databases: Experian
Memberships: SHRM
Statement of Capabilities:
Employers Reference Source provides a turnaround time of 3 days for a complete comprehensive report.

Employers Resource

PO Box 215
Collingswood, NJ 08108
Telephone: **Fax:**
800-818-3938   800-532-8679
609-858-3960   609-858-4699
Founded: 1970
Special Services: Drug Testing - Outsourced, Credit Reports, Former Employer Interviews
Online Databases:

Employment Research Services of Central California

11750 Dublin Blvd, #201C
Dublin, CA 94568
Telephone: **Fax:**
800-315-8606   925-551-8228
925-551-7750
Founded: 1992
Special Services: Drug Testing - In house, Drug Testing - Outsourced, Credit Reports, Profile/Aptitude Testing, Former Employer Interviews, Workers' Compensation History, Local Document Retrieval
Memberships: ASIS, SHRM
Statement of Capabilities:
Part of a 10 office national chain providing full service screening and testing, Employment Research Services is known for consistent 3 day or less turnaround, full narrative reports with in-depth analysis, and no up-charges on quoted rates. Corollary information found during research is provided Free. Local management has 30+ years HR experience and comprehensive regional industry knowledge. Their extensive behavioral testing system supports client hiring and operations capabilities. Service is available by the report or it can be installed in-house with full training. Proprietary computer system available to volume clients. Screening provided worldwide in addition to all states.

EMPRESERV of Dallas

2340 Trinity Hills, 3220
Carrollton, TX 75006
Telephone: **Fax:**
800-808-1173   972-418-1435
972-416-9670
Founded: 1991
Special Services: Credit Reports, Former Employer Interviews
Online Databases: DATEQ
Statement of Capabilities:
Offering comprehensive report in 3-4 days, all Employment Research Services of Dallas employees are licensed private investigators. Backgrounds of partners include computer technologies and a previous paralegal with a criminal justice degree.

Employment Research Services (ERS)

PO Box 1206
Gretna, LA 70054
Telephone: **Fax:**
800-948-0015   800-948-0016
504-366-5060   504-366-0073
Founded: 1993
Special Services: Credit Reports, Former Employer Interviews, Workers' Compensation History, Drug Testing - In-house, Drug Testing - Outsourced
Online Databases: Equifax, PACER, AMS
Memberships: SHRM
Statement of Capabilities:
Employment Research Services pays special attention to individual client needs. ERS reports are designed to help develop subject profiles, and not just fill-in-the-blank type reports. Some branches listed here, others listed under separate titles. Branches not listed are in Glenside PA, Spring TX, Albuquerque NM. Affiliated with others in Los Angeles, San Francisco, Jackson MS, Houston, and Seattle.

Employment Screening Resources

25 Mitchell Blvd #4
San Rafael, CA 94903
Telephone: **Fax:**
888-999-4474   888-999-4387
415-472-7788   415-472-2147
www.ESRcheck.com
Founded: 1996
Special Services: Drug Testing - Outsourced, Credit Reports, Former Employer Interviews, Workers' Compensation History

Online Databases: IRSC
Memberships: SHRM, ION
Statement of Capabilities:
Employment Screening Resources (ESR) combines investigative, legal and human resources experience to assist human resources and security departments in conducting screening. ESR specializes in California employers and provides services nationally. In compliance with the Fair Credit Reporting Act. ESR reports highlight and summarize important information, not merely providing raw data or computer printouts. ESR offers unlimited support, training and consultation. All background consultants have college degrees and experience in investigations or human resources. ESR offers a performance guarantee. All reports are done in four business days or less, or there is no charge.

Employment Screening Service
207 E Bay St #306
Charleston, SC 29401
Telephone: **Fax:**
803-853-7243   803-853-7246
Founded: 1991
Special Services: Drug Testing - Outsourced, Credit Reports, Former Employer Interviews, Local Document Retrieval
Online Databases: AMCS
Statement of Capabilities:
Employment Screening Service specializes in pre-employment background checks that provide clients with an accurate analysis of whether a candidate will truly perform on the job.

Employment Screening Services
2700 Highway 280 E #60
Birmingham, AL 35223
Telephone: **Fax:**
800-780-7830   205-802-7824
205-802-7862
Founded: 1994
Special Services: Drug Testing - In house, Drug Testing - Outsourced, Credit Reports, Profile/Aptitude Testing, Former Employer Interviews, Workers' Compensation History, Local Document Retrieval
Online Databases: AMS
Memberships: ABA, ALTA, NAHB, ICA, PRRN
Statement of Capabilities:
Employment Screening Services provides 48-hour turnaround time on their reports. They have two full-time attorneys on staff. Their customer service department has over 25 years experience

in investigations for criminal and credit reports. Their database is indexed is by Social Security Number.

Employment Screening Services Inc
9 S Washington St #601
Spokane, WA 99201
Telephone: **Fax:**
800-473-7778   800-321-2905
509-624-3851   509-624-2905
www.employscreen.com
Founded: 1986
Special Services: Drug Testing - Outsourced, Credit Reports, Former Employer Interviews, Workers' Compensation History, Profile/Aptitude Testing, Local Document Retrieval, Local Document Retrieval
Memberships: SHRM
Statement of Capabilities:
Employment Screening Services (ESS) reports pay special attention to discrepancies between information uncovered by ESS and the information listed on a job applicant's application. ESS offers consultation on how to interpret findings and how they relate to the hiring process. A quarterly newsletter provides tips on employment screening techniques and keeps clients up-to-date on industry developments.

Employment Verification Services
2120 Grand Ave
Des Moines, IA 50312-5304
Telephone: **Fax:**
515-244-1101   515-244-5119
Founded: 1991
Special Services: Credit Reports, Profile/Aptitude Testing, Former Employer Interviews, Local Document Retrieval
Statement of Capabilities:
Employment Verification Services is a member of the National Association of Personnel Services.

Factual Business Information
8300 Executive Center Dr #204
Miami, FL 33166
Telephone: **Fax:**
305-592-7600   305-592-7131
Founded: 1965
Special Services: Credit Reports, Former Employer Interviews, Workers' Compensation History

Memberships: SHRM
Statement of Capabilities:

Factual Business Information provides employment screening services. Through a nationwide network of sources and databases, they furnish background searches that include criminal court records on the federal, state or county level, workers' compensation history, motor vehicle reports, employment and scholastic verifications, personal credit histories, business information services, tag checks, Social Security traces and license verifications. All finalized reports are provided in computer-generated format. Billing is monthly and may be broken down either by applicant or search-type for convenience. Their clients are companies with a minimum of 100 employees.

Fidelity Search Inc

1468 Bellemeade Ave
Evansville, TN 47714
Telephone: **Fax:**
812-479-8704   812-479-8706
Founded: 1976
Special Services: Drug Testing - In house, Drug Testing - Outsourced, Credit Reports, Profile/Aptitude Testing, Former Employer Interviews, Workers' Compensation History, Local Document Retrieval
Online Databases: Trans Union
Statement of Capabilities:

Fidelity Search is a full service pre-employment screening firm, specializing in drug testing for DOT and non-DOT programs. They also have more than 50 years experience in polygraph testing and general investigations.

First Check

15058 Beltway Ste 119
Dallas, TX 75244
Telephone: **Fax:**
972-980-9987
www.firstcheck.com
Founded: 1985
Special Services: Drug Testing - Outsourced, Credit Reports, Profile/Aptitude Testing

GA Public Record Services Inc

8035 ERL Thornton Fwy #415
Dallas, TX 75228
Telephone: **Fax:**
214-320-9836   214-320-2992
www.gaprs.com
Founded: 1989
Memberships: ASIS, SHRM, NPRRA

Statement of Capabilities:

GA Public Record Services, a licensed investigation company, specializes in on-site criminal and civil background searches. They have a national network of experienced research professionals, whom they screen and audit on a regular basis to ensure that quality standards are met. They provide free software to allow for efficient and secure exchange of information.

GiS (General Information Services Inc)

PO Box 749032
Dallas, TX 75374-9032
Telephone: **Fax:**
800-447-0798   800-528-7836
214-265-8817   214-265-7572
www.genifno.com
Founded:
Special Services: Credit Reports, Former Employer Interviews, Workers' Compensation History, Local Document Retrieval
Online Databases: iiX
Memberships: ASIS, SHRM, NAPEO, SILA
Statement of Capabilities:

GiS understands that being unique in the pre-employment investigation industry means having outstanding turnaround time and the support of great automation. As the information gathered about an applicant is generally the same no matter which company you choose, the difference is in the delivery. GiS offers service, quality, competitive pricing and automation along with a comprehensive product line.

Global Projects Ltd

520 Washington Blvd #500
Marina del Rey, CA 90292
Telephone: **Fax:**
310-314-8760   310-392-0797
Founded: 1912
Special Services: Drug Testing - In house, Credit Reports, Profile/Aptitude Testing, Former Employer Interviews, Workers' Compensation History, Local Document Retrieval
Online Databases: CDB Infotek, Experian
Memberships: ABA, APA (2), ATLA, NALI, ION, WAD
Statement of Capabilities:

For 22 years Global Projects has been active in the US and abroad conducting investigative research for attorneys, corporations, government agencies and financial institutions. Their extensive experience is used in intelligence gathering, litigation, and other business needs.

Their staff is composed of experienced professionals from a variety of fields including legal, law enforcement, electronics, finance, intelligence and human resources.

Hart & Associates Inc
1200 Country Club Ln #A
Ft Worth, TX 76112
Telephone: **Fax:**
800-429-4240   817-446-3775
817-429-4044
www.hartassociates.com
Founded: 1996
Special Services: Drug Testing - In house, Drug Testing - Outsourced, Credit Reports, Profile/Aptitude Testing, Former Employer Interviews, Workers' Compensation History, Local Document Retrieval
Online Databases: AccuSearch
Memberships: ASIS, SHRM
Statement of Capabilities:
Hart & Associates has flexible office hours to accommodate client's early morning or late evening needs. Personal interviews and evaluations are conducted in person or via an 800 service. Free consultations concerning physical security, safety and risk management are available to customers. Various means of drug testing are available, including random testing and reasonable suspicion testing. They also offer psychological testing, academic credential verification, credit and financial history checks, driving history reports and fingerprinting.

Hire Expectation
PO Box 846
National City, CA 91951-0846
Telephone: **Fax:**
619-474-7667   619-474-7467
Founded: 1994
Special Services: Credit Reports, Former Employer Interviews, Local Document Retrieval, Education/Credential verifications
Online Databases: iiX
Memberships: PRRN
Statement of Capabilities:
Hire Expectation, formerly Hiring Information, offers a full range of employee screening and research services. They specialize in criminal record research and retrieval. They also provide the same types of searches for other purposes such as tenant screening. Their growing network of over 250 correspondents provide onsite document retrieval and research. Hire

Expectation offers affordable employment background screening packages.

HR Services
PO Box 1155
Lima, OH 45802
Telephone: **Fax:**
800-939-2462   419-221-2687
419-224-2462
www.hrservicesinc.com
Founded: 1993
Special Services: Credit Reports, Profile/Aptitude Testing, Former Employer Interviews
Memberships: SHRM
Statement of Capabilities:
HR Services provides all the information necessary to make informed decisions. They are committed to providing clients with daily reports and customized solutions to their background checking needs. They offer telephone pre-screening through their proprietary system ("Dial App") helping employers streamline the hiring process.

Human Factor, The
1046 Washington St
Raleigh, NC 27605
Telephone: **Fax:**
800-967-5675   919-839-8391
919-839-8390
www.team-building.com
Founded: 1978
Special Services: Profile/Aptitude Testing
Memberships: APA, NHRMA, SHRM
Statement of Capabilities:
The Human Factor specializes in integrated datasets of human resource skills, competencies, aptitudes, preferences, and interests for management development, including competitive compensation, hiring/recruiting, and training. They keep industry benchmarks and comparative HR data. They validate and design special in-house assessment instruments for selection and training.

Human Resource Profile Inc
8506 Beechmont Ave
Cincinnati, OH 45255-4708
Telephone: **Fax:**
800-969-4300   513-388-4320
513-388-4300
www.hrprofile.com
Founded: 1991
Special Services:
Online Databases: Equifax, Experian

Memberships: SHRM, ASIS

Statement of Capabilities:

Specializes in employment screening and focuses on clients with high turnover and constant need for background checks. These clients are best served by HRP's commitment to industry-leading in-house technology development, quality and client support. HRP's proprietary software packages (PRISM and SuperCATS) help HR and risk management departments with criminal background checks and loss prevention. Both programs are available in DOS or Windows. The HRP objective is to catch the liars, not the honest ones.

Indepth Profiles Inc

8321 E 61st #104

Tulsa, OK 74133

Telephone: **Fax:**

800-364-8319   800-416-9504

918-610-0192   918-610-1183

www.idprofiles.com

Founded: 1985

Special Services: Credit Reports, Former Employer Interviews, Workers' Compensation History, Local Document Retrieval

Online Databases: Ink

Memberships: NAWBO, NFPA, SHRM, PRRN, NATSS

Statement of Capabilities:

Indepth Profiles specializes in pre-employment background investigations, national criminal record retrieval, motor vehicle records, credit reports, references, professional licensing verification and various other services. They offer 24-hour service on Arkansas and Oklahoma records.

Industrial Foundation of America

16420 Park Ten Pl #520

Houston, TX 77084

Telephone: **Fax:**

800-592-1433   800-628-2397

281-398-0082

Founded: 1960

Special Services: Workers' Compensation History

Statement of Capabilities:

The Industrial Foundation is made up of a variety of businesses throughout the US. The information provided is the compilation of data from thousands of public court records, loss runs from insurance companies, and accident reporting from their most important resource -- their members. They specialize in accurate and inexpensive employment data, including motor vehicle records, criminal reports and educational verifications.

Info Net Inc

750 S Lincoln #104-223

Corona, CA 91720

Telephone: **Fax:**

800-707-4636   909-371-2050

909-278-1573

Founded: 1992

Special Services: Credit Reports, Former Employer Interviews, Workers' Compensation History, Local Document Retrieval

Statement of Capabilities:

Info Net specializes in applicant background checks with an emphasis on customer service and quick turnaround times. Specializes in the Los Angeles area including access to the complex area court systems.

Info Quest Inc

PO Box 15521

Surfside Beach, SC 29575

Telephone: **Fax:**

800-507-9628   800-588-1152

843-215-3463   843-215-4065

www.sconthegreen.com/infoquest

Founded: 1995

Special Services: Credit Reports, Profile/Aptitude Testing, Former Employer Interviews, Workers' Compensation History, Local Document Retrieval

Online Databases: iiX

Memberships: AIIP, NPRRA, PRRN

Statement of Capabilities:

Info Quest Inc specializes in pre-employment screening. Their focus is on excellent customer service, fast and accurate turnaround as well as the flexibility to work with small or large clients. You can fax a request for a free sample report or call for a list of current clients and references.

Information Management Systems Inc

PO Box 2924

New Britain, CT 06050-2924

Telephone: **Fax:**

860-229-1119   860-225-5524

www.imswebb.com

Founded: 1989

Special Services:

Online Databases: Experian, Trans Union, PACER

Memberships: ION, PRRN

Infotrax Screening & Research Inc

4211 Rex Rd
Friendswood, TX 77546
Telephone: **Fax:**
888-221-3461   888-221-3462
281-992-0199   281-992-0288
Founded: 1995
Special Services: Credit Reports, Local Document Retrieval
Online Databases: iiX, iiX, CSC Credit Bureaus

Inquisitive Research Corporation

167 Main Street
Metuchen, NJ 08840-2744
Telephone: **Fax:**
800-906-2006   908-756-9849
908-756-9847
www.iqresearch.com
Founded: 1944
Special Services: Credit Reports, Workers' Compensation History, Local Document Retrieval
Online Databases: Equifax
Statement of Capabilities:
Inquisitive Research Corporation specializes in pre-employment screening. They focus on one-on-one service and get to know you as a person, not just an account number. There are no membership fees, no monthly minimums and no start up costs when using their services. Customized screening programs and volume discount plans are available.

InSearch Investigations

PO Box 10215
Glendale, AZ 85318
Telephone: **Fax:**
888-306-0404   602-699-1860
602-669-0805
www.InSearch.net
Founded: 1995
Special Services: Credit Reports
Online Databases: Credit Data Southwest
Statement of Capabilities:
InSearch Investigations specializes in criminal records, and they offer civil and federal background information. They offer 48-72 hour turnaround times. They can also provide criminal information for Puerto Rico, the Virgin Islands, the United Kingdom, and Canada.

Intellenet Inc

22 South pack Square
Ashville, NC 28801
Telephone: **Fax:**
800-280-9898   828-251-0665
828-251-9898
Founded: 1988
Special Services: Credit Reports, Former Employer Interviews, Local Document Retrieval
Statement of Capabilities:
Intellenet offers nationwide pre-employment research services, including criminal record checks, driving records, verification of previous employment, etc.

International Research Bureau

1331 E Lafayette St #A & B
Tallahassee, FL 32301
Telephone: **Fax:**
800-447-2112   800-814-7714
850-942-2500
www.irb-online.com
Founded: 1986
Statement of Capabilities:
International Research Bureau (IRB) has been successfully providing fast and accurate nationwide employment and tenant backgrounds, asset searches, locates and other specialized public record services for over 12 years. Being conveniently headquartered in Florida's capital also enables them to obtain original documentation daily on an expedited basis from this state.

International Research Bureau Inc (IRB)

1331 E Lafayette St #A-B
Tallahassee, FL 32301
Telephone: **Fax:**
800-447-2112   800-814-7714
850-942-2500
www.IRB-ONLINE.com
Founded: 1986
Statement of Capabilities:
IRB has provided fast and accurate nationwide employment and tenant backgrounds, asset searches, locates and other specialized public record services for over 12 years. Being conveniently headquartered in Florida's capital enables IRB to obtain original documentation daily on an expedited basis.

Interstate Reporting Co Inc

5317 N 118th Ct
Milwaukee, WI 53225

Telephone:	**Fax:**
800-837-6635	414-527-1198
414-438-2260	

Founded: 1984
Special Services: Credit Reports, Former Employer Interviews, Local Document Retrieval
Memberships: NAIS
Statement of Capabilities:

Interstate Reporting Co (IRC) utilizes database sources, gateways and personal interviews to obtain information. Specific information is obtained upon request. IRC has provided medical profession background reports for ten years.

Investigative & Background Solutions Inc

4155 E Jewell Ave
Denver, CO 80222

Telephone:	**Fax:**
800-580-0474	303-692-8511
303-692-8050	

www.ibs-denver.com
Founded: 1993
Special Services: Drug Testing - Outsourced, Credit Reports, Former Employer Interviews, Workers' Compensation History
Online Databases: Trans Union
Memberships: ION

Justifacts Credential Verification Inc

98 Devonshire Dr, PO Box 357
Delmont, PA 15626

Telephone:	**Fax:**
800-356-6885	412-468-4289
412-468-5935	

www.justifacts.com
Founded: 1982
Special Services: Credit Reports, Former Employer Interviews, Workers' Compensation History, Local Document Retrieval
Memberships: SHRM, PRRN
Statement of Capabilities:

Justifacts is a nationwide information service that provides comprehensive pre-employment screening services, verifications and record searches for some of the nation's largest corporations. They employ experienced researchers who conduct interviews with past supervisors and other references. Services can be accessed by e-mail or by fax.

KeySearch Inc

PO Box 380123
Birmingham, AL 35238-0123

Telephone:	**Fax:**
205-408-0065	888-408-0071
	205-408-0071

www.keysearchinc.com
Founded: 1997
Special Services: Drug Testing - In house, Drug Testing - Outsourced, Credit Reports, Former Employer Interviews, Workers' Compensation History
Statement of Capabilities:

KeySearch Inc assists companies nationwide with their employment screening needs, enabling clients to utilize previous employment data and education confirmations. Their services included many types of searches, including: criminal records, federal, outstanding warrants, motor vehicle, credit reports, workers' compensation, civil, professional licenses and bankruptcy. They provide reference checks and assistance with drug policies.

LABORCHEX

3900 Lakeland Dr #300
Jackson, MS 39208

Telephone:	**Fax:**
800-880-0366	800-844-2722
601-664-6760	601-664-6580

www.LABORCHEX.com
Founded: 1991
Statement of Capabilities:

LABORCHEX specializes in previous employment verification and job performance reviews including highly-detailed screenings for DOT commercial drivers. Also available are criminal and MVR checks, workers' compensation records (post-hire only), credit reports, national address searches, transcripts, and professional licensing validation. Combining computer-access to national databases with a hands-on approach in generating reports, they personally contact clients with screening details via their Red Flag service. Their Confidential Security Line (CSL) allows workers to anonymously report workplace incidents such as theft, drug use, violence through a toll free number.

Major Legal Services Inc

The Park Plaza
1111 Chester Ave #510
Cleveland, OH 44114
Telephone: **Fax:**
216-579-7982   216-579-1662
www.LAWPLACEMENT.com
Founded: 1989
Special Services: Profile/Aptitude Testing, Former Employer Interviews
Memberships: EMA, NAPPS, NALV, NALSC
Statement of Capabilities:
Major Legal Services specializes in recruiting and employment screening services involving attorneys, paralegals, legal secretaries and other law firm personnel.

Merola Services

PO Box 12216
Albany, NY 12212
Telephone: **Fax:**
518-869-8002   518-869-7755
Founded: 1988
Online Databases: Superior Information Services, Superior Information Services, Dun & Bradstreet, Equifax, DMVs
Statement of Capabilities:
Merola Services is certified to provide New York State DMV records, police reports, MV 104s, abstracts, and vehicle information, with instant access to New York DMV and New Jersey driver/vehicle information, and Florida DMV. On a nationwide basis, Merola Services secure police reports, driver/vehicle and insurance information where available. Services include: locate missing witnesses to accidents, skip tracing, phone number ownership, surname scan by city, state and nationwide. Also, criminal records and real property records by county, asset searches, and pre-employment screening.

Metropolitan Tenant Information Services Inc

8950 Gross Point Rd #H-130
Skokie, IL 60077
Telephone: **Fax:**
847-470-2524   847-470-3523
Founded: 1995
Special Services: Credit Reports, Former Employer Interviews
Online Databases: Experian
Statement of Capabilities:
Metropolitan Tenant Information Services' basic report includes court filing information from 8 counties for a more comprehensive check; a history of any action taken by a landlord to get his rent or his property regardless of whether it goes to court; and add'l 30 day follow-up searches of court data for new filings to alert clients to potential problems (included at no extra cost).

Myers Research & Consulting Inc

PO Box 1395
Stow, OH 44224
Telephone: **Fax:**
330-688-3004   330-688-3419
www.myersresearchconsult.com
Founded: 1988
Special Services: Former Employer Interviews, Workers' Compensation History, Credit Reports
Online Databases: PACER, PACER, iiX, Avert
Statement of Capabilities:
The founder and president of Myers Research & Consulting has an extensive human resources background and has acquired a staff of other human resource professionals, giving a unique perspective to the pre-employment screening business. Myers screens databases for accuracy before using them on behalf of clients.

National Applicant Screening Inc

9431 Wesport Rd #340
Louisville, KY 40241
Telephone: **Fax:**
502-426-8100   502-425-6924
Founded: 1996
Special Services: Credit Reports, Former Employer Interviews, Workers' Compensation History, Local Document Retrieval
Online Databases: DAC
Memberships: APA, ASIS, SFSA
Statement of Capabilities:
National Applicant Screening (NAS) specializes in sensitive position applicant screening (computer, human resource, law department, accounting/audit personnel, supervisors, managers and executives). They customize a package of background checks appropriate for the position being filled. To search and review public records, they have over 100 contractors nationwide, mostly former FBI agents and professional investigators. Every report is personally reviewed (looking for attempts by the applicant to conceal derogatory information) by a trained investigator before being released.

National Background Reports Inc
243 Adams Ave
Memphis, TN 38103
Telephone: **Fax:**
   800-526-4654   901-526-4753
   901-526-4654
   www.nbri.com
Founded:
Special Services:
Memberships: PRRN, NPRRA, AIIP
Statement of Capabilities:
   NBRI is a licensed professional, full service public record research company, specializing in searches requiring adherence to the Fair Credit Reporting Act, such as criminal background reports on prospective employees and tenants.

National Information Access Bureau
1142 Auahi St #1524
Honolulu, HI 96814
Telephone: **Fax:**
   800-787-6422   808-394-0849
   808-394-0904
Founded: 1995
Special Services: Drug Testing - Outsourced, Credit Reports, Profile/Aptitude Testing, Workers' Compensation History
Online Databases: Equifax, Trans Union, CDB Infotek, DAC Services
Statement of Capabilities:
   National Information Access Bureau specializes in nationwide public record searches, pre-employment background screening and asset/lien searches. Nationwide criminal and civil background searches for individuals are also available.

National Research Company
750 Old Main St
Rocky Hill, CT 06067
Telephone: **Fax:**
   800-334-1551   860-529-4375
   860-529-3006
Founded: 1982
Special Services: Credit Reports, Former Employer Interviews, Workers' Compensation History, Local Document Retrieval
Statement of Capabilities:
   National Research Company can complete a criminal conviction record search is 2-3 business days in all 50 states.

Online Screening Services Inc
PO Box 728
Safety Harbor, FL 34695
Telephone: **Fax:**
   800-358-5383   800-952-6477
   813-724-2963   813-724-0184
   www.onlinescreening.com
Founded: 1995
Special Services: Credit Reports, Former Employer Interviews, Workers' Compensation History
Online Databases: Trans Union
Memberships: NAPPS, NAFE
Statement of Capabilities:
   Online Screening Services has over 20 years of experience in the investigative industry. Highly sensitive work is handled correctly and according to the law. Each specialized customer service representatives works in a specific field of expertise, allowing fast and accurate responses to questions. They accept requests via fax, mail or modem. They always provide a report within 2 working days. Reports are easy to order, easy to understand and sources are clearly identified. No up-front or hidden frees; there are no minimums or service contracts required.

Orion Research Services
3864 Commander Dr
Atlanta, GA 30341
Telephone: **Fax:**
   888-526-7466   770-451-7944
   770-457-4776
   www.orionresearch.com
Founded: 1997
Special Services: Credit Reports, Former Employer Interviews, Workers' Compensation History, Local Document Retrieval
Online Databases: Trans Union
Memberships: PRRN
Statement of Capabilities:
   Orion Research Services offers same day service on all products. In fact, they can retrieve Georgia State criminal records within as little as one hour for a rush fee.

Pauline & Duke
1188 Bishop St #1603
Honolulu, HI 96813
Telephone: **Fax:**
   800-665-6955   800-472-6280
   808-533-2031   808-536-3492
Founded: 1994

Special Services: Credit Reports, Former Employer Interviews, Workers' Compensation History, Local Document Retrieval
Online Databases: PACER
Statement of Capabilities:

Pauline & Duke is located in the heart of downtown Honolulu, and is close to all city, state and federal courts. They specialize in background screening, real property asset search and business/people locating. Other popular services include Process of Service, civil investigation and document retrieval. Orders can be sent via fax with most turnaround times of 24 hours or less.

Personal Background Investigations Inc

945 Tacoma Ave S #F
Tacoma, WA 98402
Telephone: **Fax:**
800-949-9982   206-272-9482
206-233-1948
Founded: 1992
Special Services:
Online Databases: DISCIS
Memberships: NPRRA, PRRN, NASE
Statement of Capabilities:

Personal Background Investigations (PBI) is a research reporting agency specializing in background information. PBI offers a full range of background information including adult felony and misdemeanor records, juvenile felony and misdemeanor, credit record history, driving record history and employment/education history verifications. National searches and individual locating is available.

Peter Levine Associates, Inc

PO Box 2552
Framingham, MA 01701
Telephone: **Fax:**
800-370-1943   508-390-4266
508-370-4233
www.levinereferencecheck.com
Founded: 1977
Special Services: Credit Reports, Former Employer Interviews, Workers' Compensation History
Memberships: ION
Statement of Capabilities:

Peter Levine Associates has over 20 year experience providing comprehensive reference checking, pre-employment, reference auditing, credential verification, merger & acquisitions referencing. Services include criminal-felony searches, drivers records, workers compensation,

civil and credit reports. National and international capabilities. The principle has over 25 years experience.

Phoenix Research Corp

PO Box 579
Commack, NY 11787
Telephone: **Fax:**
800-944-5692   800-430-3232
516-361-7272   516-361-7118
Founded: 1982
Special Services: Credit Reports, Former Employer Interviews, Workers' Compensation History, Local Document Retrieval
Online Databases: Trans Union, Superior Online, Nexis-Lexis, Ready Real Estate, NJ & NY DMVS
Memberships: ASIS, CII, W.A.D.
Statement of Capabilities:

Phoenix Research provides employment screening services to large and small corporations through a variety of sources and data banks. Licensed in New York, New Jersey, Conneticut, & Florida, they offer investigative services to supplement research. Experienced in conducting background investigations for the New York Banking Department relative to licensing. They also perform more complicated due diligence investigations. Affidavits of due diligence are available for court services. Credit reports & litigation searches are available for insurance providers and landlords. Credit cards accepted.

Pre-Employment Drug Screening Services

5932 Pine Grove Tr #102
Chattanooga, TN 37421
Telephone: **Fax:**
423-892-6451   423-892-8517
Founded: 1995
Special Services: Drug Testing - In house, Drug Testing - Outsourced, Credit Reports, Workers' Compensation History, Local Document Retrieval

Pre-Employment Screening

9700 Mackenzie #222
St Louis, MO 63123
Telephone: **Fax:**
800-298-8344   314-638-3999
314-638-3600
www.preemploymentscreening.com
Founded: 1995
Special Services: Drug Testing - Outsourced, Credit Reports, Former Employer Interviews,

Workers' Compensation History, Local Document Retrieval
Online Databases: Ink
Statement of Capabilities:

Founders has over 40 years of employer services experience. They specialize in providing Missouri statewide criminal and worker's comp records in 24-48 hours. There is no minimums, start-up fees, or contracts, and volume discounts are available. They allow prospective customers a free trial search and offer customized reports for clients' specific needs. Competitively priced and endorsed by many associations.

Pre-Employment Solutions

8700 Crownhill #703
San Antonio, TX 78209
Telephone: **Fax:**
800-735-9555   210-829-5556
210-829-5505
www.pre-employment.com
Founded: 1993
Special Services: Drug Testing - Outsourced, Credit Reports, Former Employer Interviews
Online Databases: iiX
Memberships: PRRN
Statement of Capabilities:

Pre-Employment Solutions' (Texas) is committed to rapid response; most reports and completed in less than 48 hours with many in less than 24. They have developed proven interviewing techniques, encouraging open-expression elicit performance assessments in over 60% of previous employment verifications.

Pre-Employment Solutions Inc

7 Piedmont Ctr #300
Atlanta, GA 30305
Telephone: **Fax:**
404-364-1829   404-816-0032
Founded: 1992
Special Services: Credit Reports, Former Employer Interviews, Local Document Retrieval
Memberships: SHRM
Statement of Capabilities:

Pre-Employment Solutions (Georgia) has a 24-72 hour turnaround time. Their clients include; financial services, temporary services, property management, hotels, hospitals, auto/truck dealers, manufacturers, consultants, nursing homes and restaurant chains. They do offer volume discounts.

Precision Screening Inc

601 W 18th St
Austin, TX 78701
Telephone: **Fax:**
888-875-9799   512-320-5486
512-236-1917
www.precisescreen.com
Special Services: Drug Testing - Outsourced, Former Employer Interviews, Local Document Retrieval
Online Databases: PACER
Statement of Capabilities:

Precision Screening is a full service, pre-employment screening firm offering criminal searches, verifications and driver histories. They report to both wholesale companies and retail clients nationwide. They also offer Internet retrieval which allows clients to access previously ordered information instantly. Turnaround time is 1-72 hours.

PREMIER Insurance

1285 Coventry Ct
Roselle, IL 60172
Telephone: **Fax:**
888-440-1800   888-353-1801
Founded: 1991
Special Services: Drug Testing - Outsourced, Credit Reports, Former Employer Interviews, Workers' Compensation History, Local Document Retrieval
Online Databases: Crime Search
Memberships: ASIS, SHRM
Statement of Capabilities:

PREMIER InfoSource is a nationwide provider of drug testing and pre-employment reports. All reports are tailored to the client's needs and are completed within 48-72 hours from time of request. Pre-employment reports can include employment verifications, criminal history, credential verification to name a few. PREMIER provides pre-employment and random drug testing nationwide by representing the largest national NIDA/SAMHSA Certified Testing Laboratories in the country. PREMIER InfoSource provides a complete and comprehensive service into one easy-to-read report.

Presearch Background Services
PO Box 50134
Colorado Springs, CO 80949-0134
Telephone: **Fax:**
800-562-8077   800-562-8071
719-533-1880   719-260-7172
Founded: 1995
Special Services: Workers' Compensation
History, Local Document Retrieval
Online Databases: PACER
Statement of Capabilities:
PreSearch specializes in serving the healthcare industry, providing criminal information as a Colorado Board of Nursing Approved Agency. PreSearch also specializes in criminal history retrieval services in Colorado courts, with access to online sources as well as manual searching.

Professional Research Services Inc
7151 Metro Blvd #210
Minneapolis, MN 55439
Telephone: **Fax:**
612-941-9040   612-941-9041
Founded: 1990
Special Services:
Online Databases: Trans Union
Statement of Capabilities:
Professional Research Services (PRS) is a national company offering comprehensive background screening that includes verbal responses within 24-48 hours followed by documented hard copy. Client anonymity is maintained throughout the investigative process.

Professional Services Bureau
315 S College #245
Lafayette, LA 70503
Telephone: **Fax:**
800-960-2214   318-235-5318
318-234-9933
Founded: 1989
Special Services: Credit Reports, Former Employer Interviews, Workers' Compensation History, Local Document Retrieval
Online Databases: Trans Union, Equifax, NCI Network, Dun & Bradstreet, State DMV, Rhino Services, CDB Infotek, PACER
Memberships: ION, NAIS, NAPPS, PRRN, ACA, ICA
Statement of Capabilities:
Professional Services Bureau is a full service investigation agency covering Louisiana and Mississippi. They offer background, criminal, employment, insurance, financial, activity checks, fraud, and missing person investigations, also surveillance and process service. They perform courthouse research, document filing and retrieval at all municipal, state and federal courts. Other services are title abstracting, notary services and claims adjusting. Their firm has proprietary sources of background information in South Louisiana. All 64 Louisiana parishes can be researched in about 48 hours; about 72 hours for Mississippi.

Profiles Plus Inc
29296 US 19 #205
Clearwater, FL 33761
Telephone: **Fax:**
727-786-4000   727-786-4698
Founded: 1985
Special Services: Drug Testing - Outsourced, Former Employer Interviews, Workers' Compensation History, Local Document Retrieval
Memberships: ASIS
Statement of Capabilities:
Profiles Plus is a background verification company specializing in pre-employment verification for a wide range of employers nationwide. They assign an individual researcher to each client. Forty-eight hour verbal rush service available. Profiles Plus was founded by a former special agent for the states of Illinois and Florida.

Property Owners' Exchange Inc
6630 Baltimore National Pike #208
Baltimore, MD 21228
Telephone: **Fax:**
800-869-3200   800-869-7675
410-719-0100   410-719-6715
www.poeknows.com
Founded: 1973
Special Services: Credit Reports, Former Employer Interviews, Workers' Compensation History, Local Document Retrieval
Online Databases: Experian
Memberships: NAHB, NAA
Statement of Capabilities:
Property Owners' Exchange recognizes that property managers need to look beyond property-related court and credit records to character-related issues, such as convictions for drug-related offenses and other crimes of violence. They make recommendations based upon the subjective review of subject history.

Quest & Associates

PO Box 79022
Pittsburgh, PA 15222
Telephone: **Fax:**
412-563-1007 412-563-6869
Founded: 1990
Special Services: Credit Reports, Local Document Retrieval
Memberships: PRRN
Statement of Capabilities:

Quest & Associates, a Pennsylvania-based corporation, specializes in the processing and retrieval of public records. They have researchers available throughout Pennsylvania, enabling them to respond to record requests promptly. The scope of information available to them includes, but is not limited to, county federal and state conviction histories, civil records, bankruptcy information and specific Department Motor Vehicle information.

Quick Search

2639 Walnut Hill #109
Dallas, TX 75229
Telephone: **Fax:**
214-358-2840 214-358-6057
Founded: 1991
Special Services: Drug Testing - Outsourced, Local Document Retrieval, Credit Reports
Memberships: SHRM, PRRN
Statement of Capabilities:

Quick Search has correspondent relationships in jurisdictions outside of Texas, including Maryland, Colorado, New Mexico, and Louisiana as well as nationwide access generally. Their normal turnaround time is 2-3 business days for criminal and 2-3 business days for civil records. Projects are generally billed once a month by the number of names searched.

Records Search Inc

6365 Taft St #200
Hollywood, FL 33024
Telephone: **Fax:**
800-881-5993 888-800-8547
954-989-9965 954-894-1068
www.rsi-alertnet.com
Founded: 1988
Special Services: Drug Testing - In house, Drug Testing - Outsourced, Credit Reports, Profile/Aptitude Testing, Workers' Compensation History, Local Document Retrieval
Online Databases: Choicepoint
Memberships: ASIS, ACFE, INTELNET, SHRM, WAD

Statement of Capabilities:

Records Search (RSI) provides pre-employment background screening, employee attitude surveys, drug testing and business information services. Their screening specifically includes an applicant's previous employment verification, SSN verification, character references, any tendency toward excessive workers' compensation claims, verification of driving records as well as credit, education and criminal history. RSI operates in full compliance with the FCRA. They conduct courthouse research at county, state and federal levels. They produce customized reports to meet client's needs.

Records Search LLC

PO Box 0571
Los Gatos, CA 95030
Telephone: **Fax:**
800-600-9924 408-399-4750
408-399-4747
www.recordssearch.com
Founded: 1994
Special Services: Drug Testing - In house, Credit Reports, Workers' Compensation History, Local Document Retrieval
Online Databases: Experian
Memberships: PRRN
Statement of Capabilities:

Records Search LLC is are a nationwide pre-employment screening firm. They provide a convenient online ordering system to clients.

Redi-Info Information Services

PO Box 12145
Oklahoma City, OK 73157
Telephone: **Fax:**
800-349-7334 800-410-3299
www.REDI-INFO.com
Founded: 1992
Special Services:
Online Databases: Equifax, Equifax, Trans Union, MetroNet, Dun & Bradstreet, iiX
Memberships: ACFE, ACA
Statement of Capabilities:

Redi-Info maintains an extensive list of online resources for nationwide record retrieval. Reports may be ordered by fax or online via the Internet. They accumulate search results in an in-house database for the purpose of developing reports and locating persons or businesses in the future.

RefCheck

320 S Walnut St
Clearwater, MN 55320
Telephone: **Fax:**
320-558-2435   320-558-2329
Founded: 1988
Special Services: Credit Reports, Former
Employer Interviews
Online Databases: Online Searches
Statement of Capabilities:
RefCheck provides employers with information
required in the hiring process, thereby assisting
the business community in acquiring the best
employees for available positions.

RefCheck Information Services

3962 Brown Park Dr #1
Hilliard, OH 43026
Telephone: **Fax:**
614-777-8844   614-777-8876
www.refcheck.com
Founded: 1986
Special Services:
Online Databases: Experian
Memberships: SHRM
Statement of Capabilities:
Founded and operated by human resource
professionals, RefCheck Information Services
specializes in providing human resource-based
pre-employment screening checks. They offer a
wide range of services from questionnaires for
entry-level positions to in-depth interviews. They
also do background checks, criminal and driver
history checks, and other related services. Their
goal is to assist clients with designs that product
the most appropriate reference package.

Rental Research Services Inc

11300 Minnetonka Mills Rd
Minnetonka, MN 55305-5151
Telephone: **Fax:**
800-328-0333   800-642-5226
612-935-5700   612-935-9212
www.RENTAL RESEARCH.com
Founded: 1970
Special Services: Credit Reports, Former
Employer Interviews, Local Document Retrieval,
Workers' Compensation History
Online Databases: Experian
Memberships: NASA
Statement of Capabilities:
Rental Research provides tenant and employment
screening services and conducts criminal,
driving, and MV record searches statewide.
Credit reports are available on a national level.

They maintain a proprietary statewide unlawful
detainer database taken from all Minnesota
county court records, plus Cass County (Fargo)
North Dakota and nearby WS counties. They also
maintain a problem renter database, and a
statewide felony and gross misdemeanor
conviction database acquired through Minnesota
Bureau of Criminal Apprehension.

Research Data Service

9030 W Sahara Ave #270
The Lakes, NV 89117
Telephone: **Fax:**
702-733-4990   702-733-1646
http://vegasmart.com/research
Founded: 1980
Special Services: Credit Reports, Workers'
Compensation History, Local Document Retrieval
Online Databases: Trans Union
Memberships: SHRM
Statement of Capabilities:
RDS offers over a hundred different types of
searches, including: credit reports, pre-
employment and tenant rental screening, SSN
traces, address updates, public and court records,
driver records, criminal histories, worker's
compensation, real property, Secretary of State.
They offer special individual comprehensive
reports and corporate comprehensive reports.

Research Specialists

PO Box 540488
Grand Prairie, TX 75054-0488
Telephone: **Fax:**
800-771-7547   888-522-3600
972-263-0500   972-263-1992
Founded: 1983
Special Services: Drug Testing - Outsourced,
Credit Reports, Former Employer Interviews,
Workers' Compensation History, Local Document
Retrieval
Online Databases: DBT, KnowX, Trans Union,
Information America, Experian, PACER
Statement of Capabilities:
Research Specialists is a full service
investigations company with associates
worldwide. They have provided investigation
services to hundreds of clients. They dedicate
themselves to the single goal of providing their
clients with the "service they deserve with the
results they demand." All of their results are
guaranteed.

Safehire

1372 Marsh Rd
Eureka, CA 95501
Telephone: **Fax:**
  707-443-5798   707-443-5798
Founded: 1009
Special Services: Local Document Retrieval
Statement of Capabilities:
  With a turnaround time of 24-48 hours, Safehire covers Ventura and Riverside counties in California; Lane and Marion in Oregon; and Pierce, King and Snohomish in Washington.

Security Information Service Inc

8585 N Stemmons Fwy #M28
Dallas, TX 75247
Telephone: **Fax:**
  800-525-5747   214-637-1443
  214-637-4055
  www.ticnet.com/sis
Founded: 1967
Special Services: Credit Reports, Former Employer Interviews, Workers' Compensation History, Local Document Retrieval
Online Databases: Accu-Source
Memberships: ASIS, WAD, ACFE
Statement of Capabilities:
  Security Information Service provides a unique online system, SIS Online Services, as well as maintaining a nationwide network of former FBI agents to conduct any kind of investigation or security services worldwide.

Security Research Consultants

PO Box 18852
St Louis, MO 63118
Telephone: **Fax:**
  800-464-2158   314-464-3050
  314-464-3999
Founded: 1996
Special Services:
Online Databases: iiX, TCI Credit Retriever, MO Dept of Revenue, MO Workers' Compensation Div, CDB Infotek, IQ Data, IRB, AFR
Memberships: AIIP, NAPI, NAWBO, SHRM
Statement of Capabilities:
  Security Research Consultants is a licensed and insured private investigations firm. They specialize in background investigations of any type--from retrieving one record to a comprehensive investigation. Services are customized to fit the client's specific needs. Volume and package pricing are available. They have a network of record retrievers across the nation and have accounts with government

agencies. Turnaround time for retrieval of most records is from same day to 3 days. Findings are compiled in a report that is typed in a professional, easy to read format.

SingleSource Services Corp

2320 S Third St #7
Jacksonville Beach, FL 32250
Telephone: **Fax:**
  800-713-3412   877-835-5787
  904-241-1821   904-241-0601
  www.SingleSourceServices.com
Founded: 1995
Special Services: Credit Reports, Drug Testing - Outsourced, Former Employer Interviews, Local Document Retrieval, Profile/Aptitude Testing, Workers' Compensation History, Employee Hotlines
Online Databases: FDLE, FDLE, DBT/Autotrack
Memberships: ACFE, NPRRA, PRRN
Statement of Capabilities:
  SingleSource Services provide full pre-employment screening nationwide, specializing in the SE states. They offer daily service to all Florida State Records in Tallahassee, Florida including Leon County and Duval County. On all other locations, they offer two business day service.

Sound Services Inc

PO Box 111088
Tacoma, WA 98411-1088
Telephone: **Fax:**
  253-472-7336   253-472-3150
Founded: 1992
Special Services: Local Document Retrieval, Credit Reports
Online Databases: Equifax
Memberships: NASA, NAA
Statement of Capabilities:
  Sound Services, formerly Puget Sound Credit Reporting, utilizes online records from both Washington and Oregon as well as court record retrievers in California to review subject histories. They specialize in tenant and pre-employment screening reports.

Southern Research Company Inc

PO Box 1590
Shreveport, LA 71165-1590
Telephone: **Fax:**
  888-772-6952   318-424-1801
  318-227-9700
Founded: 1956

Special Services: Credit Reports, Former Employer Interviews, Workers' Compensation History, Local Document Retrieval
Online Databases: Clerk of Court, MVRs, PACER
Memberships: ASIS, PRRN
Statement of Capabilities:

Southern Research gathers background information concerning individuals and businesses, helping and assisting clients in the decision-making process. These background investigations are customized, and tailored to a specific need depending on the amount of information requested.

Spyglass Pre-employment Specialists Inc

3721 W 61st Pl
Chicago, IL 60629
Telephone: **Fax:**
733-581-0180   773-581-0181
http://yp.ameritech.net/spyglass
Founded: 1990
Special Services: Former Employer Interviews, Workers' Compensation History
Memberships: PRRN
Statement of Capabilities:

Spyglass is a minority owned business that specializes in retrieving public records, especially criminal court cases.

St Ives of California

1124 2nd St
Old Sacramento, CA 95814
Telephone: **Fax:**
800-995-9443   916-446-7459
916-446-5900
www.McBRIDE1.com
Founded: 1991
Special Services: Credit Reports, Former Employer Interviews, Workers' Compensation History, Local Document Retrieval
Online Databases: AT&T Infomaster
Memberships: ASIS, SHRM, ACFE, ABA, NAFE
Statement of Capabilities:

St Ives of California maintains a proprietary database of businesses and individuals that they have processed through their offices by name, SIC or SSN, DOB, AKA, zip code, requestor and case type. This data has proved useful for new employment screening projects. They do not offer online service; all requests are processed by fax. They have excellent sources for most informational needs in Hawaii, the Philippines, Puerto Rico, and Jamaica.

Staftrack Inc

PO Box 1133
Largo, fl 33779
Telephone: **Fax:**
800-275-2966   727-581-3725
727-581-3603
www.STAFTRACK.com
Special Services: Credit Reports, Former Employer Interviews, Workers' Compensation History, Local Document Retrieval
Online Databases: Experian
Statement of Capabilities:

Florida-based Staftrack is a leader in databased and computerized access to information vital to pre-employment screening. They offer a wide range of information to meet client's screening needs, including driver records, workers comp claims, credit info, SS searches, fraud prevention and their standard Credit Profile. Offers instant access to the Staftrack Termination and Verified Work History database. Other screening reports include work records, criminal histories, educational verifications and occupational license checks.

Strategic Information Resource Center

5705 Nevilla Place
El Paso, TX 79932
Telephone: **Fax:**
915-833-6510   915-833-8015
Founded: 1997
Special Services: Credit Reports, Former Employer Interviews, Workers' Compensation History
Online Databases: PACER
Memberships: AIIP
Statement of Capabilities:

Strategic Information Resource Center specialize in professional background for manufacturing environments and trade feasibility studies. They offer online request capability.

Suburban Record Research

12 Main St
Dover, MA 02030
Telephone: **Fax:**
617-536-3486   508-785-2852
Founded: 1982
Special Services: Local Document Retrieval, Workers' Compensation History

Memberships: ABA, NALI, NPRRA
Statement of Capabilities:
Suburban Record Research provides reliable, 24-hour turnaround time in most instances. Accessing Massachusetts Secretary of State, Superior Court, Land Court, Registry of Deeds (including recorded land), they provide UCC at local level detail reports, rundowns, "bring downs" and most all other public record retrieval/information services for financial, legal, general business operations.

TABB Inc
530 Main St, PO Box 10
Chester, NJ 07930
Telephone: **Fax:**
800-887-8222　　908-879-8675
908-879-2323
Founded: 1986
Memberships: ASIS, SHRM
Statement of Capabilities:
TABB Inc, a licensed private investigation company, specializes in pre-employment background investigations and screening. A variety of reports are available to meet the specific needs of the customer. Reports include 48-hour criminal record searches, motor vehicle records, credit history, education, professional license and earnings verification. Reports may be ordered by online computer, fax, phone or by mail. Most reports are available in 48 hours. Statewide criminal records in Florida are available in 48 hours.

Tenant Check Inc
7432 Oak Ridge Hwy
Knoxville, TN 37931
Telephone: **Fax:**
423-769-5553　　423-769-9271
Founded: 1980
Special Services: Credit Reports, Former Employer Interviews, Local Document Retrieval
Memberships: ACA, NAR, NAA
Statement of Capabilities:
Tenant Check specializes in both pre-employment and tenant screening. They are capable of 4-6 hour turnaround times. They can perform criminal history checks, complete landlord history checks and verification of account (date opened, funds and NSF). They also perform past employer interviews and education verifications.

Tenant Infobureau Services
251 W lafayette Frontage Rd
St Paul, MN 55107
Telephone: **Fax:**
800-222-8362　　651-293-3909
651-293-1234
Founded: 1982
Special Services: Drug Testing - Outsourced, Credit Reports, Local Document Retrieval
Online Databases: iiX
Memberships: MBAA, NAA

Tenant Verification Service
54 Mark Dr #104
San Rafael, CA 94903
Telephone: **Fax:**
800-366-6659　　415-479-2019
415-479-2810
Founded: 1985
Special Services: Credit Reports, Former Employer Interviews
Online Databases: Experian
Statement of Capabilities:
Within a day of the request, Tenant Verification can provide screenings. Services include credit reports, current and former landlords, employer and bank reference checks and verifications.

The Cole Group
5225 Katy Fwy #305
Houston, TX 77007
Telephone: **Fax:**
713-880-9494
Founded: 1973
Special Services: Profile/Aptitude Testing, Local Document Retrieval, Local Document Retrieval, Drug Testing - In house, Drug Testing - Outsourced
Memberships: ACFE
Statement of Capabilities:
The Cole Group is an applicant screening company. They have over 24 years of experience in furnishing applicant screening. Services include records research, urinalysis drug screening, driving histories, Social Security verification, administration of psychological profile examinations and in-depth, one-on-one personal interviews with job candidates.

The Pre-Check Company
14701 Detroit Ave #LL70
Cleveland, OH 44107-4109
Telephone: **Fax:**
800-268-2435　　216-226-0777
216-226-7700

www.pre-check.com
Founded: 1991
Special Services: Drug Testing - In house, Drug Testing - Outsourced, Credit Reports, Profile/Aptitude Testing, Former Employer Interviews, Workers' Compensation History, Local Document Retrieval
Statement of Capabilities:
The Pre-Check Company specializes in pre-employment screening. They provide national coverage with 3-4 day turnaround time. They offer hair testing for drug abuse, which is more than twice as effective as urine testing because hair cannot be adulterated like urine tests can.

Tyler-McLennon Inc
707 W 7th St
Austin, TX 78701
Telephone: **Fax:**
512-482-0808 512-482-8727
www.tyler-mclennon.com
Founded: 1988
Special Services: Workers' Compensation History, Local Document Retrieval
Online Databases: PACER
Memberships: ABA, NAFE, NPRRA, PRRN, Texas Association of Legal Investigators, Texas Association of Business
Statement of Capabilities:
Tyler-McLennon specializes in public records searches in Texas both at the county and federal level. Located in Austin, they have access to all state offices. They perform court record searches, real estate, property ownership, bankruptcies, asset/lien, UCC searches, also motor vehicle ownership and driving record searches. They utilize database hook-ups with Texas counties and physically does the searches in many. They have employees in Dallas/Ft. Worth, Houston, Austin, Corpus Christi and Tyler, and representatives elsewhere. Larger clients may choose to order and receive records online.

Validata In
3020 Mercer University Blvd #200
Atlanta, GA 30341
Telephone: **Fax:**
770-458-9810 770-458-2322
Founded: 1990
Special Services: Drug Testing - Outsourced, Profile/Aptitude Testing, Credit Reports, Workers' Compensation History, Local Document Retrieval
Statement of Capabilities:
Validata provides a menu of services that allows clients to choose the reports that fit the job

functions of applicants. Reports are available by phone, fax, mail, or secure fax box. Validata personnel are always available to assist in interpreting results.

Vericon Resources Inc
238 Perimeter Park Dr #370
Atlanta, GA 30341
Telephone: **Fax:**
800-795-3784 800-915-1020
770-457-9922 770-457-5006
www.vericon.com
Founded: 1988
Special Services: Credit Reports, Drug Testing - Outsourced, Profile/Aptitude Testing, Former Employer Interviews, Workers' Compensation History
Memberships: SHRM, ASIS
Statement of Capabilities:
Vericon Resources is a background investigation business specializing in employment screening. In the US and abroad, they conduct customized employment investigations for medium to Fortune 500 companies. Developed exclusively for clients, FACTSTRACK Online provides quick easy access to all services. Vericon has been profiled in a variety of publications including the Wall Street Journal, Entrepreneur, Security Management, Executive Woman, and Atlanta area news journals.

Verifacts Inc
7326 27th St W #C
University Place, WA 98466-4637
Telephone: **Fax:**
800-568-5665 800-799-5885
253-565-9109 253-566-1231
www.verifacts.com
Founded:
Special Services: Credit Reports, Former Employer Interviews, Workers' Compensation History, Local Document Retrieval
Memberships: NACM, NASA
Statement of Capabilities:
Verifacts has a variety of service options including credit and social searches, statewide criminal searches over the Internet, and online software with national tenant history and eviction data. Full employment screening services include credit, social searches, criminal reports, employment verification, DMV, worker's compensation and more.

Verified Credentials Inc

20890 Kenbridge Ct
Lakeville, MN 55044

Telephone: **Fax:**
800-473-4934   612-985-7200
612-985-7212

Founded: 1984

Special Services: Former Employer Interviews

Online Databases: Equifax

Statement of Capabilities:

Verified Credentials Inc (VCI) assigns each client to an account manager specializing in the client's field. Employment screening has been VCI's only business for more than 15 years. They have an in-house criminal department dedicated solely to locating and auditing court searchers on a continuous basis. Orders may be placed by phone, fax, mail or by using "VCI-Net," an online direct data transfer system that allows clients to submit and retrieve requests using a modem. VCI provides criminal record searches in the twin cities metro area.

Veritas - Truth in Capabilities

3133 Middleton Dr
Troy, MI 48024-1224

Telephone: **Fax:**
248-647-3234   248-647-3235

Founded: 1963

Special Services: Drug Testing - Outsourced, Former Employer Interviews

Statement of Capabilities:

Veritas' staff has over 35 years of executive search experience for closely-held companies. They understand the importance of background investigation.

Western Reporting Corporation

141 E 5600 S #300
Salt Lake City, UT 84107

Telephone: **Fax:**
800-466-1996   800-351-4558
801-281-2000   801-291-2005
www.WesternReporting.com

Founded: 1994

Special Services: Credit Reports, Former Employer Interviews, Workers' Compensation History, Local Document Retrieval

State Criminal Record Agencies

Every state except Mississippi[5] has a central repository of major misdemeanor, felony arrest records and convictions. **Not all states open their criminal records to the public**. Of those states that *will* release records to the public, many require fingerprints or signed release forms. The information that *could be* disclosed on the report includes the arrest record, criminal charges, fines, sentencing and incarceration information. Some states will disclose arrests without dispositions.

If you are searching for records in a state where records are closed to the public, then the best places to search for criminal record activity is at the city or county level with the county or district court clerk. Many of these searches can be done with a phone call.

---

[5] Mississippi is currently working on a statewide database, but no completion date has been set.

Alabama

Alabama Department of Public Safety,
A.B.I., Identification Unit, PO Box 1511,
Montgomery, AL 36192; (Courier:
502 Washington St, Montgomery, AL 36104);
334-242-4244, 334-242-4270 (Fax), 8AM-5PM.

Access by: mail, visit, online.

Tips: Must have notarized release form from recorded person. The request must be on a state form (call to have copy sent).

Online search: The State Court Administration has an online system (SJIS) containing criminal records from all 75 Alabama county courts There are fees. Call (800) 392-8077 for more information

Alaska

Department of Public Safety,
Records and Identification, 5700 E Tudor Rd,
Anchorage, AK 99507;
907-269-5765, 907-269-5091 (Fax),
8AM-4:30PM.

Access by: mail, visit.

Tips: "Interested Party" reports are processed for employment purposes. "Any Person" reports can be processed for those who have a proper letter of explanation (and fingerprints). "Full Criminal History Report" is only available for criminal justice agencies. Requester must provide verification of status as an "interested party." Interested party is defined a person who employs, appoints or permits the subject with or without compensation with supervisory power over others. If authorized, a requester may also request a national check by the FBI for an add'l $24.00.

Arizona

Department of Public Safety, Criminal History
Records Unit, PO Box 6638, Phoenix, AZ 85005-
6638; (Courier: 2102 W Encanto, Phoenix, AZ
85005); 602-223-2223, 8AM-5PM.

Access by: mail only.

Tips: Record access is limited to agencies that have specific authorization by law including Arizona employers or pre-employment search firms.

Arkansas

Arkansas State Police, Identification Bureau,
#1 State Police Plaza Dr, Little Rock, AR 72209;
501-618-8500, 501-618-8404 (Fax), 8AM-5PM.

Access by: mail, visit.

Tips: Must have signed release form from person of record. Include the following in your request-name, date of birth, sex, Social Security Number, driver's license number.

California

Department of Justice, PO Box 903417,
Sacramento, CA 94203-4170; (Courier:
4949 Broadway, Sacramento, CA 95820);
916-227-3460, 8AM-5PM.

— **Restricted access** —

The person of record can get his/her information. The CA Penal Code does authorize certain categories of businesses (childcare, elderly, handicapped workers, etc.) to receive limited criminal background information. Call to determine if your request is authorized and they will send request form.

Colorado

Bureau of Investigation, State Repository,
Identification Unit, 690 Kipling St,
Suite 3000, Denver, CO 80215;
303-239-4230, 303-239-0865 (Fax), 8AM-5PM.

Access by: mail, visit, online

Tips: Must have a request disclaimer stating "This record shall not be used for the direct solicitation of business or pecuniary gain" signed by requester. Include the following in your request-full name, date of birth, sex, race. The following data is not available-sealed records or juvenile records.

Online search: Electronic Clearance System (ECS). This is an overnight batch system, open M-F from 7AM to 4PM. Requesters must register. For information, call (303) 239-4230

Connecticut

Department of Public Safety,
Bureau of Identification, PO Box 2794,
Middleton, CT 06759-9294; (Courier:
1111 Country Club Rd, Middleton, CT 06457);
860-685-8480, 860-685-8361 (Fax), 8:30AM-
4:30PM.
www.state.ct.us/dps

Access by: mail only.

Tips: Records are open to the public. There are no restrictions; however, only conviction information is released. The following data is not available: pending cases, dismissals, or juvenile records.

Delaware

Delaware State Police Headquarters, Criminal Records Section, PO Box 430, Dover, DE 19903-0430; (Courier: 1407 N Dupont Highway, Dover, DE 19930); 302-739-5880, 302-739-5888 (Fax), 8AM-4PM.

Access by: mail, visit.

Tips: This agency will only release records with dispositions for pre-employment requesters. Must have a signed release form for the fingerprint search and release of information.

District of Columbia

Metropolitan Police Department, Identification and Records Section, 300 Indiana Ave NW, Rm 3055, Washington, DC 20001; 202-727-4302 (Police), 202-879-1373 (Superior Court), 8AM-5PM.

Access by: mail, visit.

Tips: Must have release form from person of record. The following data is not available: convictions or pending cases. The Superior Court, Criminal Division, is located at 500 Indiana NW, same zip.

Florida

Florida Department of Law Enforcement, User Services Bureau, PO Box 1489, Tallahassee, FL 32302; (Courier: 2331 Phillip Rd, Tallahassee, FL 32308); 850-488-6236, 850-488-1413 (Fax), 8AM-5PM.

Access by: mail, visit, online.

Online search: Access is available for pre-approved, pre-paid accounts. All criminal history records are available. For more information, call Julie Boland at (850) 488-6236.

Georgia

Georgia Bureau of Investigations, Attn: GCIC, PO Box 370748, Decatur, GA 30037-0748; (Courier: 3121 Panthersville Rd, Decatur, GA 30037); 404-244-2601, 404-244-2878 (Fax), 8AM-4PM.

Access by: mail, visit

Tips: You must first contact the Bureau to receive an "Awareness Package." An OAC# is then assigned. This must be done before a search request is honored. Certain law enforcement agencies, who are online, retrieve records for investigative/ background purposes. Juvenile records, traffic ticket information, out-of-state or federal charges and certain misdemeanors and local ordinance violations may not be available on this system.

Hawaii

Hawaii Criminal Justice Data Center (HCJDC), Liane Moriyama, Administrator, 465 S King St, Room 101, Honolulu, HI 96813; 808-587-3106, 8AM-4PM.

Access by: mail, visit.

Tips: They will release only convictions. Arrests without dispositions are not released. Public Access (in person) printouts are available only in Hawaii at the HCJDC and main police stations.

Idaho

State Repository, Bureau of Criminal Identification, PO Box 700, Meridian, ID 83680-0700; (Courier: 700 S Stratford Dr, Meridian, ID 83642); 208-884-7130, 208-884-7193 (Fax), 8AM-5PM.

Access by: mail, visit.

Tips: Must have a signed release form from person of record. They will release the full arrest record without dispositions.

Illinois

Illinois State Police, Bureau of Identification, 260 N Chicago St, Joliet, IL 60432-4075; 815-740-5164, 815-740-5193 (Fax), 8AM-4PM M-F
www.state.IL.us/isp/isphpage. htm

Access by: mail, visit, online

Tip: No records are released without a disposition of conviction. Requester must use the state's Uniform Conviction Information Form signed by person of record.

Online search: UCIA - Uniform Conviction Information Act. Online access for a fee. Upon signing an interagency agreement with ISP and establishing an account, users can submit inquiries over modem. Replies are sent via U.S. mail. Users must utilize LAPLINK for windows, version 6.0 or later.

Indiana

Indiana State Police, Central Records, IGCN-100 N Senate Ave Room 302, Indianapolis, IN 46204-2259; 317-232-8266, 8AM-4:30PM.

Access by: mail, visit.

Tips: Only employers or the subject can request records using State Form 8053. The record will show all activity, including arrests, dismissals, and convictions.

Iowa

Division of Criminal Investigations, Bureau of Identification, Wallace State Office Bldg, Des Moines, IA 50319; 515-281-5138, 515-281-7996 (Alternate Telephone), 515-242-6297 (Fax), www.state.IA.us/government/dps/dci/crimhist.htm 8AM-4:30PM.

Access by: mail, fax, visit

Tips: A signed release or waiver is not required, but if not included the reports will not show any arrest over 18 months old without a disposition. Request Form A is required for each surname. This form can be obtained from the web site, by fax, mail, or in person. Iowa law requires employers to pay the fee for potential employees' record checks. Fax search: Only those requesters who have opened a pre-paid account may fax.

Kansas

Kansas Bureau of Investigation, Criminal Justice Records Division, 1620 SW Tyler, Attn: NCJRC, Topeka, KS 66612-1837; 785-296-8200, 785-296-6781 (Fax), 8AM-5PM.
www.kbi.state.us

Access by: mail, fax

Tips: Non-criminal justice agencies, organizations, individuals and commercial companies are entitled to receive recorded conviction information. Each request must be on a separate "Records Check Request Form." First time requesters must complete a user's agreement. The following data is not available-expunged records, non-conviction information or juvenile records.

Kentucky

Kentucky State Police, Records Section, 1250 Louisville Rd, Frankfort, KY 40601; 502-227-8713, 502-227-8734 (Fax), 8AM-4PM.

Access by: mail, visit

Tips: Requests accepted for employment purposes, nursing homes and adoptive/foster parent background searches. A signed release is also required. Kentucky courts at the local level will not do criminal searches and refer all requesters to the Administrative Office of Courts in Frankfurt (502-573-2350).

Louisiana

State Police, Bureau of Criminal Identification, 265 S Foster, Baton Rouge, LA 70806; 225-925-6095, 225-925-7005 (Fax), 8AM-4:30PM.

Access by: mail, visit.

Tips: Records are not available to the public. Records are available for employment screening purposes only if the employment (such as child care or schools) falls under a state statute requiring a criminal record check.

Maine

Maine State Police, State Bureau of Identification, 36 Hospital St, Augusta, ME 04330; 207-624-7009, 8AM-5PM.

Access by: mail, visit.

Tips: Requests must be in writing. Include purpose of the inquiry and name and address of requester.

Maryland

*Criminal Justice Information System,
Public Safety & Correctional Records,
PO Box 5743, Pikeville, MD 21282-5743;
(Courier: 6776 Reisterstown Rd, Rm 200,
Pikeville, MD 21208);
410-764-4501, 888-795-0011 (Alternate
Telephone), 410-974-2169 (Fax), 8AM-3:30PM.*

Access by: mail, online.

Tips: Include the following in your request-signed release and set of fingerprints. Requesters must also submit a copy of their photo ID. All private parties must first write to this office and receive a "petition package" and then apply for a petition number. Employers and investigative firms are eligible to apply for this petition number.

Online search: The State Court Administrator's office has online access to criminal records. Land records may also be accessed from this system. Call (410) 260-1031 for a sign-up package

Massachusetts

*Criminal History Systems Board, 200 Arlington
Street, #2200, Chelsea, MA 02150;
617-660-4600, 617-660-4613 (Fax), 9AM-5PM.*

Access by: mail only.

Tips: Must use their Personnel Record Request Form. Third party request forms are available.

Michigan

*Michigan State Police, Ident. Section,
Central Records Division, 7150 Harris Dr,
Lansing, MI 48913;
517-322-5531, 517-322-0635 (Fax), 8AM-5PM.*

Access by: mail, fax.

Tips: Non-profit organizations may submit a copy of Federal Form 501C3 in lieu of payment for a name search. Fax search: the state will permit ongoing requesters to set up a pre-paid account and submit requests by fax.

Minnesota

*Bureau of Criminal Apprehension, Records &
Identification, 1246 University Ave, St Paul, MN
55104; 651-642-0670, 8:15AM-4PM.*

Access by: mail, visit

Tips: For most requesters, to obtain the entire adult history, including all arrests, you must have a notarized release form signed by person of record, but to get a 15 year record of convictions only, a consent form is not required. Other access: a tape available of the 15 year record for the news media and other approved users.

Mississippi

— Records not available from state agency —

Mississippi does not have a central state repository of criminal records. They suggest that you obtain information at the county level by a county court search.

Missouri

*Missouri State Highway Patrol, Criminal Record
& Identification Division, PO Box 568, Jefferson
City, MO 65102-0568; (Courier: 1510 E Elm St,
Jefferson City, MO 65102);
573-526-6153, 573-751-9382 (Fax), 8AM-5PM.*

Access by: mail, visit.

Tip: Only convictions are reported.

Montana

*Department of Justice, Criminal History Records
Program, 303 N Roberts, Room 374, Helena, MT
59620-1418;
406-444-3625, 406-444-0689 (Fax), 8AM-5PM.*

Access by: mail, fax, visit

Nebraska

*Nebraska Highway Patrol, CID, PO Box 94907,
Lincoln, NE 68509-4907; (Courier: 1500
Nebraska Highway 2, Lincoln, NE 68502);
402-479-4924, 402-479-4978 (Alternate
Telephone), 402-471-4545 (switchboard),
8AM-4PM.*

Access by: mail, visit.

Tip: State keeps record of requesters and will inform the person of record if asked.

Nevada

Nevada Highway Patrol, Record & ID Services, 555 Wright Way, Carson City, NV 89711-0585; 775-687-5713, 775-687-3978 (Fax), 8AM-5PM.

Access by: mail, visit.

Tip: Will not release an arrest record without a disposition, unless a waiver is submitted.

New Hampshire

State Police Headquarters, Criminal Records, James H. Hayes Bldg, 10 Hazen Dr, Concord, NH 03305; 603-271-2538, 8:15AM-4:15PM.

Access by: mail, visit.

Tips: Requester must have "authorization in writing, duly signed and notarized, explicitly allowing the requester to receive such information." Also specify exactly what information is needed.

New Jersey

Division of State Police, Records and Identification Section, PO Box 7068, West Trenton, NJ 08628-0068; 609-882-2000 2878, 609-530-5780 (Fax), 9AM-5PM.

Tips: While criminal records are not open to the public, records can be obtained by employers, investigators, and attorney firms. Either a name check ($15.00 fee) or a fingerprint check ($25.00 fee) is available. A cover letter from the subject is required. The record is returned only to the subject.

New Mexico

Department of Public Safety, Records Bureau, PO Box 1628, Santa Fe, NM 87504-1628; (Courier: 4491 Serrillos Rd, Santa Fe, NM 87504); 505-827-9181, 505-827-3396 (Fax), 8AM-5PM.

Access by: mail, visit. Must have a notarized signed release from person of record authorizing the State of New Mexico to release records to requester. Except for law enforcement officials, specify which records you want. Juvenile records are not released.

New York

Division of Criminal Justice Services, 4 Tower Place, Albany, NY 12203; 518-457-6043, 518-457-6550 (Fax), 8AM-5PM.

— Restricted access —

Tips: Records are released by court order, subpoena or to person of record only. The public must search at the county level. Thirteen counties in New York can be searched from the Unified Court System in New York City. Call Rene Elias at 212-428-2810 for more information.

North Carolina

State Bureau of Investigation, Identification Section, 407 N Blount St, Raleigh, NC 27601-1009; 919-662-4500 300, 919-662-4380 (Fax), 7:30AM-5PM.

— Restricted access —

Record access is limited to criminal justice and other government agencies authorized by law.

North Dakota

Bureau of Criminal Investigation, PO Box 1054, Bismarck, ND 58502-1054; (Courier: 4205 N State St, Bismarck, ND 58501); 701-328-5500, 701-328-5510 (Fax), 8AM-5PM.
www.state.nd.us/ndag

Access by: mail, visit.

Tips: Must have a signed release form from person of record or a current address. Subject will be notified of the request. Only convictions will be released.

Ohio

Ohio Bureau of Investigation, Identification Division, PO Box 365, London, OH 43140; (Courier: 1580 St. Rte 56, London, OH 43140); 614-466-8204, 614-852-2556 (Alternate Telephone), 614-852-4453 (Fax), 8AM-5:45PM.

Access by: mail only.

Tips: Must have a signed, witnessed release form from person of record. Must also have a full set of fingerprints with the release form.

Oklahoma

State Bureau of Investigation, Criminal History Reporting, 6600 N Harvey, Bldg 6, #300, Oklahoma City, OK 73116; 405-848-6724, 8AM-5PM.

Access by: mail, visit.

Tip: Computer searches include arrests without dispositions.

Oregon

Oregon State Police, Identification Services Section, PO Box 430034, Salem, OR 97208; (Courier: 3772 Portland Rd NE, Salem, OR 97303); 503-378-3070, 503-378-2121 (Fax), 8AM-5PM.

Access by: mail, online.

Tip: If record exists, person of record will be notified of the request and the record will not be released for 14 additional days.

Online search: Bulletin board service used for requesting and receiving criminal history reports. Results are posted as "No Record" or "In Process" the latter means a record will be mailed in 14 days. Users must complete an application and will be billed. Call (503) 373-1808, ext 230 to receive the application.

Pennsylvania

State Police Central Repository, 1800 Elmerton Ave, Harrisburg, PA 17110-9758 717-783-9973, 717-772-3681 (Fax), 8:15AM-4:15PM.

Access by: mail, visit.

Tips: Must make request on Request Form #SP4-164 or the request will be returned. Information will include felony and misdemeanor convictions and open cases less than 3 years old.

Rhode Island

Department of Attorney General, Bureau of Criminal Identification, 150 S Main Street, Providence, RI 02903; 401-421-5268, 8AM-5PM.

Access by: mail, visit.

Tips: Criminal records are only released to law enforcement agencies or with a signed notarized authorization from the subject. Required is a picture ID of the requester. The Notary on the authorization will be called for verification. Or, you may also obtain records at the county level.

South Carolina

South Carolina Law Enforcement Division (SLED), Criminal Records Section, PO Box 21398, Columbia, SC 29221; (Courier: 440 Broad River Rd, Columbia, SC 29210); 803-737-9000, 803-737-4205 (Alternate Telephone), 803-896-7022 (Fax), 8:30AM-5PM.

Access by: mail, visit.

Tip: Criminal records are open without restrictions.

South Dakota

Division of Criminal Investigation, Office of Attorney General, 500 E Capitol, Pierre, SD 57501-5070; 605-773-3331, 605-773-4629 (Fax), 8AM-5PM.

Access by: mail only.

Tips: Each request (other than criminal justice agencies) must include a signed authorization using the state form and a fingerprint card. The form requires identifying information: color of hair and eyes, height, weight, date of birth, Social Security Number. The following data is not available-juvenile records, minor traffic violations or out-of-state or federal charges.

Tennessee

Tennessee Bureau of Investigation, Records and Identification Unit, 1144 Foster Ave, Menzler-Nix Bldg, Nashville, TN 37210; 615-741-0430, 8AM-5PM.

— Restricted access —

Record access is limited to agencies that have specific authorization by law. Database cannot be accessed by the public or by private employers.

Texas

Crime Records Service, Correspondence Section, PO Box 15999, Austin, TX 78761-5999; (Courier: 5805 N Lamar, Austin, TX 78752); 512-424-2079, 8AM-5PM.
txdps.state.TX.us

Access by: mail, visit, online

Tips: To obtain ALL arrest information (conviction and non-conviction), must have a signed release form from the person of record and full set of fingerprints of person of record. To obtain conviction data only, submit full name, sex, race, and DOB. No letter of authorization is needed for the conviction only report.

Online search: Records can be pulled from the web site. Requesters must establish an account and have a pre-paid bank to work from.

Utah

*Bureau of Criminal Identification,
4501 S 2700 W-Box 148280, Salt Lake City, UT
84114-8280; (Courier: 4501 S 2700 W, Salt Lake
City, UT 84119);
801-965-4561, 801-965-4749 (Fax), 8AM-5PM.*

— Restricted access —

Record access is limited to agencies that have specific authorization by law or by subpoena. You can obtain information at the county level. A subject may obtain his/her own record for $10.00, call (801) 965-4445.

Vermont

*State Repository, Vermont Criminal Information
Center, 103 S. Main St., Waterbury, VT 05671-
2101; 802-244-8727, 802-244-1106 (Fax), 8AM-
4:30PM.*

— Restricted access —

Record access is restricted to law enforcement officials, judiciaries and those permitted by statute. You may obtain information at the county level.

Virginia

*Virginia State Police, CCRE, PO Box C-85076,
Richmond, VA 23261-5076; (Courier: 7700
Midlothian Turnpike, Richmond, VA 23235);
804-674-2084, 804-674-2277 (Fax), 8AM-5PM.*

Access by: mail, online.

Tips: Must have a signed release form from person of record, including notarized signatures for both subject and requester. Must use form "SP-167."

Online search: Certain entities, including screening companies, are entitled to online access. The system is ONLY available to IN-STATE accounts. Software package purchase required. The system is windows oriented, but won't handle networks. The PC user must be a stand-alone system. Minimum usage requirement: 25 requests per month.

Washington

*Washington State Patrol, Identification Section,
PO Box 42633, Olympia, WA 98504-2633;
(Courier: 321 Cleveland Ave, #A, Tumwater, WA
98501);
360-705-5100, 360-664-9461 (Fax), 8AM-5PM.*
watch.wsp.WA.gov

Access by: mail, online.

Online search: This agency offers access through a system called WATCH, which can be accessed from their web site. To set up a WATCH account, call (360) 705-5100 or e-mail to criminhis@wsp.gov

Tips: The State Court Administrator's office maintains a database of criminal records in their JIS-Link. Records do not include arrests unless case is filed. There is a set-up fee and a per hour access charge. Call 360-705-5277 for packet.

West Virginia

*State Police, Criminal Identification Bureau,
Records Section, 725 Jefferson Rd,
South Charleston, WV 25309;
304-746-2277, 304-746-2402 (Fax), 8AM-5PM.*

Access by: mail only.

Tips: Requestors must use their "39A Card." Search can be initiated in person, results mailed. The state will also sell an "incident report" of a specific criminal action for $15.00, call (304) 746-2178.

Wisconsin

*Wisconsin Department of Justice, Crime
Information Bureau, Record Check Unit, PO Box
2688, Madison, WI 53701-2688; (Courier: 123 W
Washington Ave, Madison, WI 53703); 608-266-
5764; 8AM-4:30PM.*

Access by: mail, fax, visit.

Tips: Fax search: Incoming fax permitted only for customers with accounts. There must be a supply of return envelopes on hand.

Wyoming

*Division of Criminal Investigation, Criminal
Record Section, 316 W 22nd St,
Cheyenne, WY 82002;
307-777-7523, 307-777-7252 (Fax),
8:30-10:30AM; 1:30-3:30PM.*

Access by: mail, visit.

Tips: Must have a notarized, signed release form from the person of record. Must also have a standard 8" x 8" orange fingerprint card (that you must get from this office) with properly rolled fingerprints of person and notarized signature of applicant. Must also fill out waiver from their office that is on the back of the fingerprint card.

State Motor Vehicle Record Agencies

The record retrieval industry often refers to driving records as "MVRs." Typical information on an MVR might include full name, address, Social Security Number, physical description and date of birth as well as the actual driving history. Also, the license type, restrictions and/or endorsements can provide background data on an individual.

Employers and their agents are considered permissible users of driving records, and in recent years there have been major changes regarding the release of motor vehicle data to the public. This is the result of the Driver's Privacy Protection Act (DPPA). Thus, some states differentiate between casual requesters and permissible users; some states only release to permissible users. If a driver has "opted-out" in a state that allows for such a thing, that driver's personal information will not be released to a casual requester. In some states, personal information is never released, even if the requester is classified as permissible.

Following the list of State MVR Agencies is the State Drivers' License Identifier Table. Use the State Drivers' License Identifier Table as a help in determining the authenticity of a Drivers' License.

Alabama

*Department of Public Safety, Central Records,
PO Box 1471, Montgomery, AL 36102-1471;
(Courier: 500 Dexter Ave, Montgomery, AL
36104); 334-242-4400, 334-242-4639 (Fax),
8AM-5PM.*

Access by: mail, visit, online. Fee is $5.75 per record for all access modes.

Alaska

*Division of Motor Vehicles, Driver's Records,
PO Box 20020, Juneau, AK 99802-0020;
(Courier: 450 Whitter St, Room 105, Juneau, AK
99802); 907-465-4335 (Motor Vehicle Reports
Desk), 907-463-5860 (Fax), 8AM-5PM.*

Access by: mail, visit, online. Search costs $5.00 per record. A private company or individual must have a signed release from the licensee or a subpoena.

Arizona

*Motor Vehicle Division, Record Services Section,
PO Box 2100, Mail Drop 539M, Phoenix, AZ
85001; (Courier: Customer Records Services,
1801 W Jefferson, LobbyRoom 345, Phoenix, AZ
85007);
602-255-8357, 8AM-5PM.*

Access by: mail, visit, online. Current fees are $3 for 39 month records and $5 for certified 5 year records. All non-exempt requests must be signed and notarized.

Arkansas

*Department of Driver Services, Driving Records
Division, PO Box 1272, Room 127, Little Rock,
AR 72203; (Courier: 7th & Wolfe Sts, Ledbetter
Bldg, Room 127, Little Rock, AR 72202);
501-682-7207, 501-682-2075 (Fax),
8AM-4:30PM*
www.state.ar.us

Access by: mail, visit, online. Fees are $7.00 for insurance record and $10.00 for CDL's. Full charge for a "no record found." Signed authorization by the driver needed.

California

*Department of Motor Vehicles,
Information Services, PO Box 944247, Mail
Station G199, Sacramento, CA 94244-2470;
(Courier: Bldg East – 1st FL, 2415 First Ave,
Sacramento, CA 95818); 916-657-8098, 916-657-
5564 (Alternate Telephone), 8AM-5PM.*

Access by: mail, phone, visit, online. Searches-driver record by name and license number - $5.00; guarantor's signature-$20.00; license status only $1.00. Requests are held for 10 days while the state notifies the licensee. Addresses not released unless requester pre-approved and posts $50,000 surety bond.

Colorado

*Motor Vehicle Division, Driver Services, Denver,
CO 80261-0016; (Courier:
1881 Pierce Street, Lakewood, CO 80261);
303-205-5600, 303-205-5990 (Fax), 8AM-5PM.*

Access by: mail, visit. Fee is $2.20 per record.

Connecticut

*Department of Motor Vehicles,
Copy Records Section, 60 State St,
Room 305, Wethersfield, CT 06109-1896;
860-263-5154, 8:30AM-4:30PM T,W,F; 8:30AM-
7:30PM Th; 8:30AM-12:30 S.*

Access by: mail, visit, online. Fee for walk-in or mail-in driving records is $10.00 per record. A license status check is $5.50. Requesters must complete From J-235.

Delaware

*Division of Motor Vehicles, Driver Services,
PO Box 698, Dover, DE 19903; (Courier:
303 Transportation Circle, Dover, DE 19901);
302-739-4343, 302-739-2602 (Fax),
8AM-4:30PM M-T-Th-F; 12:00PM-8PM W.*

Access by: mail, visit, online. Fee for all search modes is $4.00 per request. Mail requesters must use DMV Form MV703. Walk-in requesters may obtain records from centers in Wilmington, New Castle, Dover, and Georgetown.

District of Columbia

Department of Motor Vehicles,
Driver Records Division, 301 "C" St, NW,
Washington, DC 20001; 202-727-6761,
8:15AM-4PM M-T-Th-F; 8:15AM-7:00PM W.

Access by: mail, visit, online. Fee for a driving record is $5.00.

Florida

Department of Highway Safety & Motor Vehicles,
Division of Drivers Licenses, PO Box 5775,
Tallahassee, FL 32314-5775;
(Courier: 2900 Apalachee Pky, Rm B-239,
Neil Kirkman Bldg, Tallahassee, FL 32399);
850-488-0250, 850-487-7080 (Fax),
8AM-4:30PM.
www.hsmv.state.fl.us

Access by: mail, visit, online. Fee is $3.10 for a certified three or seven year record. There is a full charge for a "no record found."

Georgia

Department of Motor Vehicles, Driver's License
Section, MVR Unit, PO Box 1456, Atlanta, GA
30371-2303; (Courier: 959 E Confederate Ave,
Atlanta, GA 30316);
404-624-7478, 8AM-3:30PM.

Access by: mail, visit. Fees: $5.00 for a 3 year period; $7.00 for a 7 year period. The driver's notarized signature is needed (except for court subpoena). Walk-in requests are also available from the State Patrol Posts.

Hawaii

Traffic Violations Bureau, Abstract Section, 1111
Alakea St, Honolulu, HI 96813;
808-538-5530, 7:45AM-9:00PM.

Access by: mail, visit. Fee is $7.00 per request. There is a full charge even if no record is found. Walk-in requests can be at any District Traffic Court or Traffic Violations Bureau Office.

Idaho

Idaho Transportation Department, Driver's
Services, PO Box 34, Boise, ID 83731-0034;
(Courier: 3311 W State, Boise, ID 83703);
208-334-8736, 208-334-8739 (Fax),
8:30AM-5PM
www.state.id.us/itd/dmv.html

Access: mail, fax, visit, online. $4.00 per record fee.

Illinois

Abstract Information Unit, Drivers Services
Department, 2701 S Dirksen Prky,
Springfield, IL 62723;
217-782-2720, 8AM-4:30PM.

Access by: mail, visit. Fee is $5.00 per record; includes certification. There is a full charge for a "no record found." The person of record will be informed. Requests can be made at any Driver Services Facility statewide.

Indiana

Bureau of Motor Vehicles, Driver Records,
Indiana Government Center North,
100 N Senate Room N405
Indianapolis, IN 46204;
317-232-2894, 8:15AM-4:30PM.

Access by: mail, visit, online. Fee is $4.00 per record, except for online requests ($5.00). Fee is $8.00 for a certified record, and $12.00 for certified complete history. Walk-in requests use the Customer Service Center, 402 W. Washington St, Indianapolis, Room W160.

Iowa

Department of Transportation, Driver Service
Records Section, PO Box 9204, Des Moines, IA
50306-9204; (Courier: Park Fair Mall, 100
Euclid, Des Moines, IA 50313);
515-244-9124, 515-237-3152 (Fax),
8AM-4:30PM.

Access by: mail, visit. Fee for certified mail-in or walk-in is $5.00 per record. There is no charge for a no record found. DOT "Super Stations" in Cedar Rapids, Council Bluff, Davenport, and Sioux City offer a public access terminals to view driving records. The fee is $1.00 per record.

Kansas

Department of Revenue, Driver Control Bureau,
PO Box 12021, Topeka, KS 66612-2021;
(Courier: Docking State Office Building, 915
Harrison, 1st Floor, Topeka, KS 66612);
785-296-3671, 785-296-6851 (Fax),
8AM-4:45PM.

Access by: mail, visit, online. Fee is $5.00 ($3.50 for your own) for a walk-in or mail-in request. An accident report is available for $3.50 per page.

Kentucky

Division of Driver Licensing, State Office Bldg, MVRS, 501 High Street, 2nd Floor, Frankfort, KY 40622; 502-564-6800 2250, 502-564-5787 (Fax), 8AM-4:30PM.

Access by: mail, visit, online. Fee is $3.00 per record. Request records in person at the address listed above or any of 11 Kentucky field offices.

Louisiana

Dept of Public Safety and Corrections, Office of Motor Vehicles, PO Box 64886, Baton Rouge, LA 70896; (Courier: 109 S Foster, Baton Rouge, LA 70806); 225-925-6009, 225-922-2814 (Alternate Telephone), 504-925-6915 (Fax), 8AM-4:30PM M-F.

Access by: mail, visit, online. Fee for mail-in or walk-in requests is $15.00 per name. Fee for online or tape requests is $6.00. Walk-in requesters may "view" a record for no charge. A fee applied for a hard copy. Records can be requested from MV offices in New Orleans, Lake Charles, Monroe, Baton Rouge, Shreveport, Alexandria.

Maine

Bureau of Motor Vehicles, Driver License & Control, 29 State House Station, Augusta, ME 04333-0029; 207-287-9005, 207-287-2592 (Fax), 8AM-5PM. www.state.me.us/sos/bmv/dlc/dlchmpg.htm

Access by: mail, fax, visit, online. Fee is $5.00 for a non-certified record and $6.00 for certified. A "no record found" incurs a full charge, except for walk-in requesters.

Maryland

MVA, Driver Records Unit, 6601 Ritchie Hwy, NE, Glen Burnie, MD 21062; 410-787-7758, 8:15AM-4:30PM. mva.state.md.us

Access by: mail, visit, online. Fee for a driving record is $5.00. Another $5.00 to have it certified. MVA offices statewide will accept mail-in requests for records. In-person inquires may be processed at over 25 MVA offices in Maryland.

Massachusetts

Registry of Motor Vehicles, Driver Control Unit, Box 199150, Boston, MA 02119-9150; 617-351-9213, 617-351-9219 (Fax), 8AM-4:30PM M-T-W-F; 8AM-7PM Th. www.state.MA.us/rmv

Access by: mail, phone, visit. Fee is $10.00 per record. The Registry offers a phone-in request line at (617) 351-4500. Orders can be paid with a credit card; results are mailed. You may request a record from any field office.

Michigan

Department of State Police, Record Look-up Unit, 7064 Crowner Dr, Lansing, MI 48918; 517-322-1624, 517-322-1181 (Fax), 8AM-4:45PM.

Access by: mail, phone, fax, visit, online. Fee for obtaining a record is $6.55 per search. Certification is an additional $1.00. For actual drivers, the record is immediately available by phone.

Minnesota

Driver & Vehicle Services, Records Section, 445 Minnesota St, #180, St Paul, MN 55101; 651-296-6911, 8AM-4:30PM. www.dps.state.mn.us/dvs

Access by: mail, visit, online. Fees: $5.50 per certified record; $4.50 per non-certified record.

Mississippi

Department of Public Safety, Driver Records, PO Box 958, Jackson, MS 39205; (Courier: 1900 E Woodrow Wilson, Jackson, MS 39216); 601-987-1274, 8AM-5PM.

Access by: mail, visit. Fee is $7.00 per request.

Missouri

Department of Revenue, Driver License Bureau, PO Box 200, Jefferson City, MO 65105-0200; (Courier: Harry S Truman Bldg, 301 W High St, Room 470, Jefferson City, MO 65105); 573-751-4300, 573-526-4769 (Fax), 7:45AM-4:45PM.

Access by: mail, phone, fax, visit, online. Fee is $1.50 per record for walk-in or mail-in requests. Telephone search costs $1.50 per page. Phone-in and fax-in (add an add'l $.75) service is available for pre-approved, established accounts.

Montana

Motor Vehicle Division, Driver's Services, PO Box 201430, Helena, MT 59620-1430; (Courier: Records Unit, 303 N Roberts, Room 262, Helena, MT 59620);
406-444-4590, 406-444-1631 (Fax), 8AM-5PM.
www.mt.gov

Access by: mail, phone, fax, visit. Fees are $4.00 per 3-year record history and $10.00 for certified. In general; employment, insurance, and news organizations are able to access records. Mail search: state purpose and use letterhead. Established pre-paid accounts may fax requests and receive results for an add'l $2.00 per record. 16 MV stations in the state provide driving records. ID must be provided.

Nebraska

Department of Motor Vehicles, Driver Records Division, PO Box 94789, Lincoln, NE 68509-4789; (Courier: 301 Centennial Mall, S, Lincoln, NE 68509); 402-471-4343, 8AM-5PM
www.nol.org/home/dmv/driverec.htm

Access by: mail, visit, online. Fee is $3.00 per record. Drivers can view records in person for no fee.

Nevada

Department of Motor Vehicles and Public Safety, Records Section, 555 Wright Way, Carson City, NV 89711-0250;
775-687-5505, 775-687-3693 (Fax), 8AM-5PM.

Access by: mail, phone, visit. Fee is $5.00 per record. A mail request must be on department approved forms. Phone-in requesters must be pre-approved; call 702-687-5505 for information. In-state toll free line at 800-992-7945.

New Hampshire

Department of Motor Vehicles, Driving Records, 10 Hazen Dr, Concord, NH 03305;
603-271-2322, 8:15AM-4:15PM.

Access by: mail, visit. Records are $7.00. A certified records is $10.00. Unless written, notarized authorization by subject is received, only specific business entities may receive records with personal information.

New Jersey

Motor Vehicle Services, Driver's Abstract Section, CN142, Trenton, NJ 08666;
609-292-6500, 888-486-3339 (In-state only), 609-292-6500 (Suspensions), 8AM-5PM.

Access by: mail, visit, online. Fee is $10.00 for mail-in or walk-in requests. Driving records can obtained at any of the four Regional Service Centers Deptford, Wayne, Eatontown, or Trenton.

New Mexico

Motor Vehicle Division, Driver Services Bureau, PO Box 1028, Santa Fe, NM 87504-1028;
(Courier: Joseph M. Montoya Bldg, 1100 S St. Francis Dr, 2nd Floor, Santa Fe, NM 87504);
505-827-2234, 505-827-2267 (Fax), 8AM-5PM.

Access by: mail, visit, online. No fee for mail or walk-in requests. The law lists 9 permissible user groups and permits release of records with written consent.

New York

Department of Motor Vehicles, Data Preparation & Control, Empire State Plaza, Albany, NY 12228-0430;
518-474-0642, 518-473-5595 (Alternate Telephone), 8AM-5PM.

Access by: mail, phone, visit, online, Fee is $5.00 per record search, $4.00 if online or by tape. Only drivers wishing to obtain their own record may call. There is an additional $5.00 fee. In person search costs $5.00 per search. Records can be ordered from most any county-operated motor vehicle office.

North Carolina

Division of Motor Vehicles, Driver's License Section, 1100 New Bern Ave, Raleigh, NC 27697;
919-715-7000, 8AM-5PM.

Access by: mail, visit, online. Fee is $5.00 per record. Certified records are $7.00.

North Dakota

Department of Transportation, Driver License & Traffic Safety Division, 608 E Boulevard Ave, Bismarck, ND 58505-0700; 701-328-2603, 701-328-2435 (Fax), 8AM-5PM.

Access by: mail, fax, visit. Fee is $3.00 per record. Copy of the abstract is sent to the driver whose record was requested, identifying the requester. Pre-approved accounts must use a credit card for fax requests.

Ohio

Department of Public Safety, Bureau of Motor Vehicles, 1970 W Broad St, Columbus, OH 43223-1102; 614-752-7600, 8AM-5:30PM M-T-W; 8AM-4:30PM Th-F.
www.ohio.gov/odps

Access by: mail, phone, visit, online. Fee is $2.00 per record for non-CDL (commercial drivers) and $3.00 per record for CDL. A license status record is $2.00.

Oklahoma

MVR Desk, Drivers Record Services, PO Box 11415, Oklahoma City, OK 73136; (Courier: 3600 Martin Luther King Blvd, Oklahoma City, OK 73111); 405-425-2262, 8AM-4:45PM.

Access by: mail, visit. Fee is $10.00 per driving record. A full fee is charged for a "no record found," except for walk-in requesters. Many MV offices across the state will sell records.

Oregon

Driver and Motor Vehicle Services, Record Services, 1905 Lana Ave, NE, Salem, OR 97314; 503-945-5000, 8AM-5PM.

Access by: mail, phone. Fees: $1.50 for a 3 year non-employment driving record; $2.00 for a 3 year employment driving record; $3.00 for 5 year combination of both records; $1.50 per record for a driver license information report. There is a charge of $1.50 for no record found.

Pennsylvania

Department of Transportation, Driver Record Services, PO Box 68695, Harrisburg, PA 17106-8695; (Courier: 1101-1125 Front Street, Harrisburg, PA 17104); 717-391-6190, 800-932-4600 (In-state only), 7:30AM-4:30PM.

Access by: mail, visit. Fee is $5.00 for each record. A 10 year employment record for commercial drivers is available. Casual requesters must have a signed, notarized release from the driver on Form DL-503. Walk-ins: state processes one record request while you wait.

Rhode Island

Division of Motor Vehicles, Driving Record Clerk, Operator Control, 345 Harris Ave, Providence, RI 02909; 401-222-2994, 401-222-6120 (Fax), 8:30AM-4:30PM.

Access by: mail, visit. Fee is $16 per record request, highest fee in the nation. In-person request results are picked up the next day or mailed back.

South Carolina

Division of Motor Vehicles, Driver Records Section, PO Box 100178, Columbia, SC 29202-3178; (Courier: 955 Park St, Columbia, SC 29201); 803-737-2940, 803-737-1077 (Fax), 8:30AM-5PM.

Access by: mail, visit, online. Fee is $2.00 per record request. Most DMV Branch offices in the state will process records while you wait.

South Dakota

Dept of Commerce & Regulation, Office of Driver Licensing, 118 W Capitol, Pierre, SD 57501; 605-773-6883, 605-773-3018 (Fax), 8AM-5PM.

Access by: mail, phone, visit, online. Fee is $4.00 per record. Pre-approved accounts may order via the telephone. Requesters must certify for what reason they are obtaining the information.

Tennessee

Dept. of Safety, Financial Responsibility Section, Attn: Driving Records, 1150 Foster Ave, Nashville, TN 37249-4000; 615-741-3954, 8AM-4:30PM.

Access by: mail, visit. Fee is $5.00 per record. In person search at offices in Memphis, Knoxville, Chattanooga, Kingsport, Jackson, Lawrenceburg, Fall Branch, and Cookeville

Texas

Department of Public Safety, Driver Records Section, PO Box 15999, Austin, TX 78761-5999; (Courier: 5805 N Lamar Blvd, Austin, TX 78752); 512-424-2032, 8AM-5PM.

Access by: mail, visit. Fees are $6.00 for 3 year driving record, $10.00 if certified. A license status including latest address is $4.00 per report. There is a full charge for a "no record found."

Casual requesters should use Form DR-1.

Utah

Department of Public Safety, Driver's License & Driving Records Section, PO Box 30560, Salt Lake City, UT 84130-0560; (Courier: 4501 South 2700 West, 3rd Floor South, Salt Lake City, UT 84119); 801-965-4437, 801-965-4496 (Fax), 8AM-5PM.

Access by: mail, visit. Fee is $4.25 per record. Records can be obtained at any one of 17 branch offices throughout the state

Vermont

Department of Motor Vehicles, DI-Records Unit, 120 State St, Montpelier, VT 05603; 802-828-2050, 802-828-2098 (Fax), 7:45AM-4:30PM. This office is closed on Wednesday mornings.

Access by: mail, visit, online. $4.00 for 3 year record; $8.00 for 8 year record. There is a full charge for a "no record found."

Virginia

Department of Motor Vehicles, Motorist Records Services, PO Box 27412, Richmond, VA 23269; 804-367-0538, 8:30AM-5:30PM M-F; 8:30AM-12:30PM S.

Access by: mail, visit, online. Fee is $5.00 for mail or walk-in requests. Casual requesters cannot obtain records without consent. Mail request must be on a DMV form or letterhead. 72 MV field offices answer record requests.

Washington

Department of Licensing, Driver Services Division, PO Box 9030, Olympia, WA 98507-9030; (Courier: 1125 Washington Street SE, Olympia, WA 98504); 360-902-3921, 360-902-3900 (General Information), 360-586-9044 (Fax), 8AM-4:30PM.

Access by: mail, visit. Fee is $4.50 per record. There is no charge for a no record found. All mail or walk-in requests require a signed authorization from the subject.

West Virginia

Division of Motor Vehicles, Driver Improvement Unit, Building 3, State Capitol Complex, Charleston, WV 25317; 304-558-0238, 304-558-0037 (Fax), 8:30AM-4:30PM. www.state.wv.us/dmv

Access by: mail, visit, online. Fee is $5.00 per record including no record founds. Branch offices in 9 cities can issue instant records.

Wisconsin

Division of Motor Vehicles, Records & Licensing Section, PO Box 7995, Madison, WI 53707-7995; (Courier: 4802 Sheboygan Ave, Room 301, Madison, WI 53707); 608-266-2353, 608-267-3636 (Fax), 7:30AM-4:30PM.

Access by: mail, phone, visit. Fee is $3.00 per driving record. Pre-approved accounts may order driving records by phone. Fee is $4.00 if a human operator reads back the record, $3.00 for a digitized computer readback.

Wyoming

Wyoming Department of Transportation, Driver Services, PO Box 1708, Cheyenne, WY 82003-1708; (Courier: 5300 Bishop Blvd, Cheyenne, WY 82002); 307-777-4800, 307-777-4773 (Fax), 8AM-5PM.

Access by: mail, visit. Fee is $5.00 per record, $3.00 by tape. Companies requesting records must identify themselves and certify the purpose for the

report. Individual licensees may request a copy of
their own record at any field office.

State Drivers' License Identifier Table

State	License Format
Alabama	Seven numbers; there is no code or sequential arrangement which determines the characters making the license number.
Alaska	One to seven numbers. There is no code for license format; numbers are assigned by computer in numerical order.
Arizona	Social Security Number or one letter plus eight numbers. Current military licenses remain valid until out of service, some duplicates are issued without photo.
Arkansas	Social Security Number or nine numbers. If the number is not the social security number, the first digit is "9," the next seven are sequential, and the last is a check digit.
California	Current License Format: One letter followed by seven numbers. Computer generated—but not in sequential order. Old License Format: One letter followed by four to seven numbers. After the February 1986 automation, all license numbers were "converted" to seven numbers by adding zeros (i.e, old number B34512 converted to B-0034512). Some licenses without the zeros may still exist.
Colorado	Beginning January 30, 1994, all driver licenses have a permanent nine-digit numeric number for each driver.
Connecticut	Nine numbers. The first two digits are the driver's month of birth and the seven additional numbers are the next available sequential numbers.
Delaware	One to seven numbers; computer generated, there is no coding.
District of Columbia	Driver's Social Security Number or seven numbers (permit). There is no numerical code sequence to the permit numbers.
Florida	One letter followed by twelve numbers (effective February 13, 1989). The old license format is one letter followed by eleven numbers. The letter corresponds to the first letter of the last name, and the numbers reflect a code representing the name, date of birth, and sex. Florida has indicated that this code is classified, and not released to the public.
Georgia	Seven to nine numbers or Social Security Number. There is no code or sequential arrangement which determines the characters making the license number.

State	License Format
Hawaii	Social Security Number or nine digit number (at licensee request). There is no "code" for the nine digit users.
Idaho	Since 05/01/93, nine character—2 alpha, 6 numeric, 1 alpha.
Illinois	One letter and eleven numbers. This is coded; however, coding "translation" is not available to the public.
Indiana	Ten numbers. Other than the fact the first 3 digits denote the License Branch where issued on applications since July 1988, Indiana reports that no codes or sequential arrangements are used to determine license number.
Iowa	Nine digits (Social Security Number) or nine alpha-numeric characters (fourth and fifth are alpha characters).
Kansas	Social Security number, or assigned number consisting of the letter "K" plus eight numbers. This format has been in use since 5/13/91. The older format was six alternating alpha-numeric characters (i.e., A1B2C3).
Kentucky	Social Security Number or a 1 alpha and 8 numeric combination. The alpha corresponds to the first initial of last name. The state is phasing out use of the Social Security Number.
Louisiana	Seven digits preceded by two zeros (e.g., 001234567). Louisiana reports there is no code or sequential arrangement which determines the characters making the license number other than the double zeros at the beginning.
Maine	Seven numbers; if under 21 the license is seven numbers and an "X." Maine reports there is no code or sequential arrangement which determines the characters of the license number.
Maryland	1 letter and 12 numbers. The letter represents the first letter of the driver's last name. The twelve numbers are coded in groups of three, creating a unique total number: the first three digits are coded to the last name; the second three to the first name; third group to the middle name; and the last group is coded to the month and day of birth.
Massachusetts	A computer generated number of one letter and eight numbers is automatically issued. At the driver's request, the Social Security Number can be used. (Previously, it was the other way around.)
Michigan	A soundex system using one letter followed by twelve numbers. The numbers are coded as follows: three numbers for the last name, three numbers for the first name, three numbers for the middle name, and three numbers for the birth month and day. Because a small number of drivers' names and birth dates have the same number, MI is using the first initial of the last name with the code 726 or 727 to assign drivers a unique driver license number.
Minnesota	One letter followed by twelve numbers. The letter represents the first letter of the last name; the numbers represent a coding of the last name, the first name, the middle name and date of birth.
Mississippi	The Social Security Number.
Missouri	Social Security Number or an assigned number consisting of one alpha

State	License Format
	and five to nine numerics or nine numerics only.
Montana	Since 07/01/94, Social Security Number or nine numbers (*made-up number**). ID cards, since 07/01/94, are 9 digits—the first initial of the last name followed by 8 randomly generated numbers.
Nebraska	One letter (A, B, C, E, G, H, or V) and up to eight digits.
Nevada	Effective 1/1/98, Nevada began issuing a ten digit number which is not based on the individual's SSN. Prior to 1/1/98, the license had twelve numbers and was computer-generated based on the individual's SSN and was coded. If applicant had never been issued a SSN, then the letter "X" plus eight digits was issued. However, effective 1/1/98, the X number followed by eight digits is no longer used.
New Hampshire	Two numbers, three letters, and five numbers. The license number is coded as follows: birth month (two digits); the first letter of the last name; the last letter of the last name; the first letter of the first name; the year of birth (two digits); day of month (two digits); and a computer "twin" number (usually one, never a zero).
New Jersey	First letter of last name and fourteen numbers. **EXAMPLE**: Driver License Number "S5778-40771-01024" is interpreted as follows: S - first initial of last name of the driver (i.e., Smith) 5778 - coded next four letters of last name (i.e., mith) 407 - coded first name (John) 71 - coded middle initial (J.) 01 - coded birth month for males (January) 02 - year of birth (1902) 4 - coded eye color (blue) In another example, if the driver was a female, Christine J. Smith, with the same date and year of birth and eye color, the driver license number would be "S5778-12471-51024" and would be interpreted as follows: S - first initial of last name of the driver (i.e., Smith) 5778 - coded next four letters of last name (i.e., mith) 124 - coded first name (Chris) 71 - coded middle initial (J.) 51 - coded birth month for females (January) 02 - year of birth (1902) 4 - coded eye color (blue)
New Mexico	Nine numbers. New Mexico reports there is no code or sequential arrangement determining the numbers in the license.

State	License Format
New York	In the third quarter of 1992, New York began assigning nine-digit numeric "Client Identification Numbers" to its drivers.
North Carolina	One to eight numbers. North Carolina indicates there is no code or sequential arrangement which determines the digits making-up the license number.
North Dakota	Social Security Number; non-CDL driver may request an assigned number (nine digits beginning with 9).
Ohio	Two letters and six numbers. Ohio operator license two-character alpha prefixes were assigned in the following manner: "QA" through "QG" Series Issued November 1, 1990 through September 10, 1992. "RA" through "RR" Series Issued September 10, 1992 to date.
Oklahoma	Social Security Number or an assigned nine-digit number.
Oregon	One to seven numbers. License numbers are computer-generated in numeric order. All newly issued numbers are seven digits. Numbers are not recycled upon surrender of license.
Pennsylvania	Eight numbers. Pennsylvania reports that there is no code or sequential arrangement which determines the actual digits making the license number.
Rhode Island	Seven numbers ("V" and six numbers for disabled veterans). The first two numbers represent the year of issuance, the third digit represents the location of license issue, and the last four digits are sequential numbers.
South Carolina	Nine numbers. South Carolina license numbers are computer-generated on a sequential basis.
South Dakota	Social Security Number or eight digit computer-generated number.
Tennessee	Seven or Eight numbers. Tennessee indicates the eighth digit is a check-digit based upon a confidential algorithmic formula.
Texas	Eight numbers, beginning with "0" or "1." License numbers are sequential and computer-generated.
Utah	Can be four to ten numbers, but currently only nine digit numbers are being issued. In the future ten digit numbers will be utilized. Utah reports there is no code or sequential arrangement which determines the characters making the license number.
Virginia	Social Security Number; or "T" followed by eight numbers. Licenses issued prior to December of 1991 may reflect an "R" instead of a "T."
Vermont	Eight digits; the last digit is a check-digit which may be numeric or alpha "A." Vermont reports there is no code or sequential arrangement that determines the characters making the license number—other than numeric order from the computer.
Washington	First five letters of last name, first initial, middle initial, three numbers, and two letters or numbers (i.e., WASHI G E 222 O3). Coding of the last five characters is "not released due to security reasons;" however, this code is widely-known among professional MVR providers and insurance

State	License Format
	industry personnel.
West Virginia	A seven digit alpha/numeric series, with no correlation to type of license issued, is used as follows—
	A000001 - A999999 E000001 - E999999
	S000001 - S999999 B000001 - B999999
	1X00001 - 1X99999 H000001 - H999999
	C000001 - C999999 XX00001 - XX99999
	D000001 - D999999 0000001 - 0999999
Wisconsin	One letter followed by thirteen numbers. The coding of driver license numbers is as follows: License Number "A5364683945805"
	A = First letter of last name
	536 = Coded from last name
	468 = Coded from first name and middle initial
	3-9 = Birth year
	458 = Coded month and day of birth, sex
	05 = Tie-breaker, check-digit
Wyoming	Ten Numbers or nine numbers (six numbers, hyphen, three numbers; i.e., 101565-142). Numbers are computer-generated with a "check digit."

Accredited Educational Institutions

US Colleges & Universities

College & University Tools

Employers, human resource professionals and pre-employment screening firms recognize the importance of credentials and education. However, too many times a business will hire a new employee without verifying what is represented on the employment application. *Don't Hire A Crook!* has been compiled with the express purpose of allowing you to quickly confirm and/or access student attendance records at accredited colleges, universities and post-secondary institutions.

The Accredited Educational Institutions profile college and universities that are recognized as accredited by a specific accrediting body which, in turn, are approved by the *Commission on Recognition of Postsecondary Accreditation (COPRA)*. Please note that the accreditation process is an ongoing process and may be determined or changed on an annual basis. For further information regarding the accreditation process, we suggest you contact *COPRA* at 2100 Martin Luther King Ave SE, Washington, DC 20020-5732, 202-727-3699.

There are a total of almost 4000 accredited institutions profiled in this publication. A CD-ROM version, which is available from BRB Publications, 800-929-3811, also contains these and an additional 1,700 accredited non-degree granting institutions.

Basic Information

Institutions are listed in alphabetical order within each state and by city name within multiple campus institutions. The address and telephone number given is the location of the Registrar, usually where student records are located. Office hours, fax numbers, types (levels) of degrees granted, and an indication of how many years back records are maintained are included when possible.

Internet addresses are given for nearly 3,000 institutions. These sites are an excellent source of information about the school.

Branch campuses are listed, and it is indicated when records are maintained at a central location.

Alumni Association Records

Profiles may include an alumni association address and phone number. However, some schools have no such organization since they are very technically oriented or narrow in their fields of study. Note: an alumni association is a good place to a find a current address or a maiden name.

How to Read the College Profiles

In addition to its directory information, the descriptive format for each institutional profile contains three categories:

♦ Attendance Confirmation

♦ Degree Information

♦ Copies of Transcripts

Permissible Access Modes

The types of requests accepted (i.e. by phone, fax, mail, etc.) are noted. For example, Auburn University's access information states that its Registrar will allow you to request attendance and degree information by phone, fax, or by mail, but for copies of transcripts, only written (mail) requests will be processed. Increasingly, colleges and universities prefer requests for attendance and degree information be made via the telephone when the information is computerized, conveniently allowing most questions to be quickly answered.

Also In the Profiles

Watch for limitations on the use of information and access to it. In many entries, special programs, certifications and their telephone numbers are listed.

For almost all colleges and universities listed, the types of degrees they grant is given, i.e. associates, masters, bachelors, etc. This is a quick way of checking a job applicant's claim of having earned a degree there.

Performing the Verification

It is always best to have as much information (identifiers such as date of birth, years attended, maiden name, etc.) about a subject before performing a search. Remember, too, that in 93% of schools a signed release is necessary from the subject before transcript information can be released.

Identifying Information

Although it is obvious that you must give the name of the student or graduate in order to obtain information about him or her, you should not overlook the possibility that the person went by another name or name variation while in school. **Be prepared to search by the name at the time of attendance.** A clear example of this is a married woman, but there is also the possibility that someone who today goes by the moniker C. Alexander Ernst, was just plain Carl A. Ernst when he was in school.

Always Try the Phone

Even when a college or university indicates that it does not take telephone calls for information about students and former students, **most of these institutions will accept a phone call to confirm or deny information** that you already have in your possession. Try this if you have the following kinds of questions—

- Did Robert Ogden graduate with a BS in Biology in 1990? (yes or no response.)
- Did Joanna Nichols receive a degree from your school? (looking for a yes-no answer, not the details.)

Other questions that should be answered

Does the school require a self-addressed stamped envelope (**SASE**) with your requests, or are credit cards accepted for payment, and are there any other restrictions or requirements to pass along?

Proper Identification

When you call with this kind of request, regardless of the purpose, be sure to identify yourself up front as someone with an obvious proper need to know. For example—

- I'm a reporter doing a story on Hunter Storm.
- I'm considering hiring a former student named Fernando Gomez.
- Andrea Downs applied for a loan from our bank.
- I'm about to sign a large contract with Santiago Venezuela.

Verifying by Mail

Always include in your letter or request, a note stating that the registrar should feel free to call you collect or at your free 800 number if there are any questions about your request.

Just as with a telephone call, include in your cover note a proper, valid reason for your request, and indicate the urgency of your request as well.

Even if not requested, we advise always to include a prepaid return envelope (SASE) for the results. This, again, is a matter of courtesy that is likely to get you a better than average level of service.

Again, be aware that the overwhelming majority of schools **require a signed release and a fee to obtain a transcript**. You will find the Request for Education Verification on page 218. When you are requesting a transcript (and have a signed release from the graduate), make certain that you have all the information the registrar will need to complete your request in a timely manner. This information might include the address and telephone number of the graduate in case the school wants to verify the request directly with the graduate. Also, if the college has an internal student identification number system, include that number as well if available. Since there will be a fee, we recommend sending a blank check with a limited dollar amount, (i.e. not more than $25.00).

Key Things to Keep in Mind

Here are some additional **searching tips—**

♦ At larger universities, it will help if you know the student's degree or major. This is especially true if you are trying to obtain information by telephone.

♦ Older records are usually archived. Whether they are on microfiche or stored in a box in the basement, count on it taking longer for the school to complete your search.

♦ Branch campuses generally do not maintain official transcript files; however, many, when asked by a requester with a legitimate purpose, will confirm attendance or a degree.

♦ Some schools allow students to block or restrict access to their records. If this happens to you, a signed release is advised. On the other hand some schools, which are otherwise restrictive, will permit the student to leave a release in his/her file to facilitate a verification. It wouldn't hurt to ask if a school indicates they have such a policy.

♦ Many schools who accept fax requests, ask that a written request follow in the mail. Most schools consider any information faxed back to a requester to be unofficial or uncertified.

♦ Always remember: if a subject or an employee claims to have a four-year (or higher) degree from an institution that offers only a two-year associate's degree, you have an immediate indication of that person's character or memory.

Other Information Sources About Colleges

The *Public Record Research System*, available from BRB Publications, gives entire information on fees, accessibility requirements and other useful data on college and university records.

If you are looking for a good overall general description of curriculum, degrees offered, number of students, etc., we suggest several publications. The Accredited Institutions of Post Secondary Education is distributed annually by *The Oryx Press,* (800) 279-6799, for the American Council On Education and offers extensive details on academics and accreditation. The folks at Peterson's, (800) 338-3282, offer several excellent titles including *Peterson's Guide to Four-Year Colleges* and *Peterson's Guide to Two-year Colleges.*

Accredited Educational Institutions

Alabama

Alabama Agricultural and Mechanical University Registrar, PO Box 908, Normal, AL 35762, 205-851-5254 (Fax: 205-851-5253) 8AM - 5PM. www.asnaam.aamu.edu. Enrollment: 4800. Records go back to 1875. Alumni records are maintained here. Degrees granted: Bachelors; Masters; Doctorate. Attendance and degree information available by phone, fax, mail. Transcripts available by fax, mail.

Alabama Aviation and Technical College Registrar, Route 6, Box 62, Dothan, AL 36303-9234, www.maf.mobile.al.us/~aatc 334-774-5113, 800-624-3468 (Fax: 334-774-6399) 7.45AM-4:30PM M-Th; 7:45AM-3:15PM F. Enrollment: 300. Records go back to 1960. Alumni records are maintained. Degrees granted: Associate. Attendance and degree information available by fax, mail. Transcripts available by fax, mail.

Alabama Christian College
(See Faulkner University)

Alabama Southern Community College Registrar, PO Box 2000, Monroeville, AL 36461, 334-575-3156 X252 (Fax: 334-575-5356) www.ascc.edu. 7:30AM-4:30PM. Enrollment: 1800. Records go back to 1965. Degrees granted: Associate. Special programs- Forestry, 334-575-3156 X237. Attendance and degree information available by phone, fax, mail. Transcripts available by fax, mail.

Alabama Southern Community College (Thomasville Campus), Registrar, Hwy 43 S, Thomasville, AL 36784, 334-575-3156 X252 (Fax: 334-575-5356) www.ascc.edu. Records are located at Alabama Southern Community College, Monroeville.

Alabama State University Registrar, 915 S Jackson St, Montgomery, AL 36101-0271, 334-229-4243 (Fax: 334-834-0336) www.alasu.edu. 8AM-6PM M-Th, 8AM-5PM F. Enrollment: 5400. Records go back to 1874. Alumni records maintained here; call 334-229-4280. Degrees granted: Associate; Bachelors; Masters. Attendance and degree information available by phone, fax, mail. Transcripts available by fax, mail.

Alabama Technical College
(See Gadsden State Community College)

Alexander City State Junior College
(See Central Alabama Com. College)

Athens State College, Records Office, 300 N Beaty St, Athens, AL 35611, 205-233-8165, 205-233-8167 (Fax: 205-233-6565) 8AM-4:30PM. iquest.com/~athens. Enrollment: 2600. Records go back to 1823. Alumni records maintained here; call 205-233-8275. Degrees granted: Bachelors. Attendance and degree information available by phone, fax, mail. Transcripts available by fax, mail.

Auburn University Registrar, 100 Mary Martin Hall, Auburn, AL 36849-5146, 334-844-4770 (Fax: 334-844-6436) 7:45AM-4:45PM. www.auburn.edu. Enrollment: 19780. Records go back to 1960. Alumni records maintained here; call 334-844-2586. Degrees granted: Bachelors; Masters; Doctorate. Attendance and degree

information available by phone, fax, mail. Transcripts available by mail.

Auburn University at Montgomery Registrar, 7300 University Dr, Montgomery, AL 36117-3596, 334-244-3614 (Fax: 334-244-3795) www.aum.edu. 8AM - 5PM. Enrollment: 5882. Records go back to 1976. Alumni records maintained here; call 334-244-3356. Degrees granted: Bachelors; Masters. Attendance and degree information available by phone, mail. Transcripts available by mail.

Baker Gains Central Campus Registrar, 1365 Martin L King Ave, Mobile, AL 36603-5362,. Records are located at Bishop State Community College, Mobile.

Bessemer State Technical College Registrar, PO Box 308, Bessemer, AL 35021, 205-428-6391 (Fax: 205-424-5119) 8AM-4PM. www.bham.net/bscc. Enrollment: 5121. Records go back to 1965. Degrees granted: Associate. Attendance and degree information available by phone, fax, mail. Transcripts available by fax, mail.

Bevill State Community College (Brewer), Registrar, 2631 Temple Ave N, Fayette, AL 35555, 205-932-3221. School will not confirm attendance or degree information. Transcripts available by fax, mail.

Bevill State Community College, Registrar, Box 800, Sumiton, AL 35148, 205-648-3271 X5432, 205-932-3221 (Fax: 205-648-2288). 8AM-4:30PM. Enrollment: 5000. Records go back to 1969. Alumni records maintained here; call 205-648-3271 X5409. Degrees granted: Associate. Attendance and degree information available by phone, fax, mail. Transcripts available by fax, mail.

Birmingham-Southern College Registrar, 900 Arkadelphia Rd, PO Box 549018, Birmingham, AL 35254, 205-226-4698, 205-226-4697 (Fax: 205-226-3064) www.bsc.edu. 8:15AM-4:45PM. Enrollment: 1565. Records go back to 1856. Alumni records maintained here; call 205-226-4609. Degrees granted: Bachelors; Masters. Special programs- Adult Study. Attendance and degree information available by phone, fax, mail. Transcripts available by mail.

Bishop State Community College Registrar, 351 N Broad St, Mobile, AL 36603-5898, 334-690-6421 (Registrar), 334-690-6801 (switchboard) (Fax: 334-438-5403). 8AM-4:30PM. Enrollment: 4640. Records go back to 1960. Degrees granted: Associate; Certificates. Attendance and degree information available by phone, fax, mail. Transcripts available by fax, mail.

Bishop State Community College (Carver), Registrar, 414 Stanton St, Mobile, AL 36617, 334-473-8692 (Fax: 334-471-5961). 8AM-4:30PM. Degrees granted: Associate. Attendance degree and transcript information available by fax, mail.

Bishop State Community College (Southwest), Registrar, 925 Dauphin Island Pkwy, Mobile, AL 36605-3299, 334-479-7476 (Fax: 334-473-2049). 8AM-7PM M-Th; 8AM-4:30PM F. Records go back to 1955. Alumni records maintained here; call 334-

690-6808. Degrees granted: Associate. Attendance and degree information available by phone, fax, mail. Transcripts available by fax, mail.

Brewer State Junior College
(See Bevill State Com. College)

Central Alabama Community College, Registrar, 908 Cherokee Rd, PO Box 699, Alexander City, AL 35010, 205-234-6346 (Fax: 205-234-0384) www.viper.net/~cacc. 7:30AM-4:30PM. Enrollment: 2500. Records go back to 1965. Degrees granted: Associate. Special programs- Tech Records prior 1989 merger, 205-378-5576 X6420. Attendance and degree information available by phone, fax, mail. Transcripts available by fax, mail.

Chattahoochee Valley State Community College Director of Admissions, 2602 College Dr, Phenix City, AL 36869, 334-291-4928 (Fax: 334-291-4994). 8AM-5PM. Enrollment: 1900. Records go back to 1974. Alumni records maintained here also. Call 334-291-4941. Degrees granted: Associate. Attendance, degree and transcript information available by fax, mail.

Community College of the Air Force/RRR Registrar, Simler Hall Ste 128, 130 W Maxwell Blvd, Maxwell Air Force Base, AL 36112-6613, 334-953-6436, 334-953-6438 (Fax: 334-953-5231). 7AM-5PM. Records go back to 1976. Degrees granted: Associate. Attendance and degree information available by phone, mail. Transcripts available by mail.

Concordia College Registrar, 1804 Green St, PO Box 1329, Selma, AL 36701, 334-874-5700 (Fax: 334-874-5755). 8AM-4PM. Enrollment: 500. Records go back to 1940's. Alumni records are maintained. Degrees granted: Associate; Bachelors. Attendance and degree information available by phone, fax, mail. Transcripts available by fax, mail.

Douglas MacArthur State Technical College, Registrar, 1708 N Main St, Opp, AL 36467, 334-493-3573 X233 (Fax: 334-493-7003). 7:30AM-4:30PM. Enrollment: 550. Records go back to 1965. Degrees granted: Associate. Attendance, degree and transcript information available by phone, fax, mail.

Draughons Junior College
(See South College)

Enterprise State Junior College Registrar, 600 Plaza Dr, PO Box 1300, Enterprise, AL 36331, 334-347-2623 X233 (Fax: 334-347-2623 X324) www.esjc.cc.al.us. 7:45AM-4:30PM. Enrollment: 1900. Records go back to 1965. Degrees granted: Associate. Attendance and degree information available by phone, fax, mail. Transcripts available by fax, mail.

Faulkner University Registrar, 5345 Atlanta Hwy, Montgomery, AL 36109-3398, 334-260-6241 (Fax: 334-260-6201) www.Faulkner.edu. 8AM-5PM. Enrollment: 2090. Records go back to 1942. Alumni records maintained here; call 334-260-6136. Degrees granted: Associate; Bachelors; Masters; JD. Attendance and degree information available by phone, fax, mail. Transcripts available by mail.

Gadsden State Community College Registrar, PO Box 227, Gadsden, AL 35902-0227, 205-549-8261 (Fax: 205-549-8444) 7:30AM-4PM. www.gadsdenst.cc.al.us. Enrollment: 6200. Records go back to 1925. Alumni records maintained here; call 205-549-8224. Degrees granted: Associate. Attendance and degree information available by phone, fax, mail. Transcripts available by fax, mail.

George C. Wallace State Community College Registrar, Route 6, Box 62, Dothan, AL 36303, 334-983-3521 X301 (Fax: 334-983-6066) www.wallace.edu. 7:45AM-4:30PM M-Th; 7:45AM-3:15PM F. Enrollment: 3000. Records go back to 1949. Alumni records maintained here; call 334-983-3521 X426. Degrees granted: Associate. Attendance and degree information available by phone, fax, mail. Transcripts available by fax, mail.

George Corley Wallace State Community College Registrar, PO Drawer 1049, 3000 Range Line Rd, Selma, AL 36702-1049, 334-876-9227 (Fax: 334-876-9300). 7:30AM-4:30PM M-Th, 7:30AM-3PM F. Enrollment: 1700. Records go back to 1965. Alumni records are maintained. Degrees granted: Associate. Attendance and degree information available by phone, fax, mail. Transcripts available by fax, mail.

Harry M. Ayers State Technical College Registrar, PO Box 1647, Anniston, AL 36202-1647, 205-835-5400 (Fax: 205-835-5474) www.ayers.cc.al.us. 7:30AM - 4:30PM. Enrollment: 600. Records go back to 1965. Alumni records are maintained here. Degrees granted: Associate. Attendance and degree information available by phone, fax, mail. Transcripts available by mail.

Herzing College of Business and Technology Registrar, 280 W Valley Ave, Birmingham, AL 35209, 205-916-2800 (Fax: 205-916-2807) www.herzing.edu. 8:30AM-4:30 PM. Records go back to 1971. Alumni records are maintained here. Degrees granted: Associate. Attendance and degree information available by phone, mail. Transcripts available by mail.

Hobson State Technical College (See Alabama Southern Com. College)

Huntingdon College Registrar, 1500 E Fairview Ave, Montgomery, AL 36106-2148, 334-833-4430, 334-833-4431 (Fax: 334-833-4502) www.huntingdon.edu. 8AM-5PM Sep-May, 7:30AM-4PM Jun-Aug. Enrollment: 650. Records go back to 1900. Alumni records maintained here; call 334-833-4504. Degrees granted: Associate; Bachelors. Attendance and degree information available by phone, fax, mail. Transcripts available by fax, mail.

International Bible College Registrar, 3625 Helton Dr, PO Box IBC, Florence, AL 35630, 205-766-6610 (Fax: 205-760-0981) www.ibc.edu. 8AM-4:30PM. Enrollment: 155. Records go back to 1971. Alumni Records: 1912 Wilson Ave, Russelville, AL 35653. Degrees granted: Associate; Bachelors. Special programs- Bible. Attendance and degree information available by phone, fax, mail. Transcripts available by fax, mail.

J. F. Drake State Technical College Registrar, 3421 Meridian St, Huntsville, AL 35811, 205-539-8161 X110 (Fax: 205-539-6439) 7:30AM-4:30PM. Enrollment: 575. Records go back to 1961. Alumni records

maintained here; call 205-539-8161. Degrees granted: Associate. Attendance and degree information available by phone, fax, mail. Transcripts available by fax, mail.

J.F. Ingraham State Technical College Registrar, 5375 Ingraham Rd, PO Box 209, Deatsville, AL 36022, 334-285-5177 (Fax: 334-285-5328) 8AM - 5PM. Enrollment: 1140. Records go back to 1977. Degrees granted: Associate. Attendance and degree information available by phone, mail. Transcripts available by mail.

Jacksonville State University Registrar, 700 N Pelham Rd, Jacksonville, AL 36265-1602, 205-782-5400 (Fax: 205-782-5121) www.jsu.edu. 8AM-4:30PM. Enrollment: 7700. Records go back to 1900. Alumni records maintained here; call 205-782-5404. Degrees granted: Bachelors; Masters; Educational Specialists. Attendance and degree information available by phone, fax, mail. Transcripts available by fax, mail.

James H. Faulkner State Community College Registrar, 1900 Hwy 31 S, Bay Minette, AL 36507, 334-937-9581 X2134 (Fax: 334-580-2253). 8AM-5PM. Enrollment: 3418. Records go back to 1965. Degrees granted: Associate. Attendance and degree information available by phone, mail. Transcripts available by fax, mail.

Jefferson Davis Community College Registrar's Office, 220 Alco Dr, PO Box 958, Brewton, AL 36427-0958, 334-867-4832, 334-809-1590 (Fax: 334-867-7399) 7:30AM-4:30PM. www.jeffdavis.cc.al.us. Enrollment: 1630. Records go back to 1965. Degrees granted: Associate. Attendance and degree information available by phone, fax, mail. Transcripts available by fax, mail.

Jefferson State Community College Registrar, 2601 Carson Rd, Birmingham, AL 35215-3098, www.quicklink.net/bhma/jscc. 205-853-1200 X7704, 205-856-7705 (Fax: 205-853-0340) 8AM-4:30PM. Enrollment: 5000. Records go back to 1965. Alumni records maintained here; call 205-254-2564. Degrees granted: Associate. Attendance, degree and transcript information available by fax, mail.

John C. Calhoun State Community College Registrar, PO Box 23216, Decatur, AL 35609-2216, 205-306-2601, 205-306-2593 www.calhoun.cc.al.us (Fax: 205-306-2885) 8AM-8PM M-Th; 8AM-4PM F. Enrollment: 7800. Records go back to 1950. Alumni records are maintained. Degrees granted: Associate. Attendance and degree information available by phone, fax, mail. Transcripts available by mail.

John M. Patterson State Technical College Registrar, 3920 Troy Hwy, Montgomery, AL 36116, 334-288-1080 X274 (Fax: 334-284-9357). 8AM-6:30PM M-Th, 8AM-4PM F. Enrollment: 1100. Records go back to 1962. Degrees granted: Associate. Attendance and degree information available by phone, fax, mail. Transcripts available by fax, mail.

Judson College Registrar, PO Box 120, Marion, AL 36756, 334-683-5129, 334-683-5112 (Fax: 334-683-5147) www.judson-il.edu. 8AM-5PM. Enrollment: 400. Records go back to 1838. Alumni records maintained here; call 334-683-5167. Degrees granted: Bachelors. Certification: Teacher. Special programs - Adult Studies, 334-683-5125; Degree Completion, 334-683-5169. Attendance and degree information available by phone, fax, mail. Transcripts available by fax, mail.

Lawson State Community College Registrar, 3060 Wilson Rd SW, Birmingham, AL 35221, 205-929-6309, 205-925-2515 X205 (Fax: 205-929-6316). 8AM-5PM. Enrollment: 2042. Records go back to 1968. Alumni records are maintained. Degrees granted: Associate. Attendance and degree information available by phone, fax, mail. Transcripts available by mail.

Lurleen B. Wallace State Junior College Registrar, PO Box 1418, Andalusia, AL 36420, 334-222-6591 X273 (Fax: 334-222-6567). 8AM-5PM. Enrollment: 995. Records go back to 1969. Degrees granted: Associate. Attendance and degree information available by phone, mail. Transcripts available by written request only.

Marion Military Institute Registrar, 1101 Washington St, Marion, AL 36756, 334-683-2304 (Fax: 334-683-2380). 8AM-4PM. Enrollment: 340. Records go back to 1920. Alumni records maintained here; call 334-683-2350. Degrees granted: Associate. Attendance and degree information available by phone, fax, mail. Transcripts available by written request only.

Miles College Registrar, PO Box 3800, Birmingham, AL 35208, 205-929-1423 (Fax: 205-929-1418). 8AM-5PM. Enrollment: 1300. Records go back to 1905. Alumni records maintained here; call 205-923-2771 X291. Degrees granted: Bachelors. Attendance and degree information available by phone, fax, mail. Transcripts available by fax, mail.

Mobile College (See University of Mobile)

N F Nunnelly State Technical College (See Central Alabama Community College)

Northeast Alabama Community College Registrar, PO Box 159, Hwy 35, Rainsville, AL 35986, 205-638-4418 X238 (Fax: 205-228-6861) 8AM-4:30PM. Enrollment: 1530. Records go back to 1965. Alumni records maintained here; call 205-638-4418 X246. Degrees granted: Associate. Attendance and degree information available by phone, fax, mail. Transcripts available by fax, mail.

Northwest Alabama Community College (See Bevill State Community College)

Northwest Shoals Community College Registrar, PO Box 2545, George Wallace Blvd, Muscle Shoals, AL 35662, 205-331-5200 (Fax: 205-331-5366). 7:30AM-4PM. Enrollment: 2530. Records go back to 1963. Degrees granted: Associate. Attendance and degree information available by phone, fax, mail. Transcripts available by mail.

Oakwood College Registrar, Oakwood Rd NW, Huntsville, AL 35896, 205-726-7346, 205-726-7352 (Fax: 205-726-7199) 9AM-4PM M-Th, 9AM-Noon F. www.oakwood.edu. Enrollment: 1756. Records go back to 1896. Alumni records maintained here; call 205-726-7039. Degrees granted: Associate; Bachelors. Attendance and degree information available by phone, fax, mail. Transcripts available by fax, mail.

Patrick Henry State Junior College (See Alabama Southern Com. College)

Prince Institute of Professional Studies Registrar, 7735 Atlanta Hwy, Montgomery, AL 36117, 334-271-1670 (Fax: 334-271-1671) 8AM-5PM. Records go back to 1976. Degrees granted: Associate. Attendance and degree information available by phone, mail. Transcripts available by mail.

Reid State Technical College Registrar, I-65 at Hwy 83, PO Box 588, Evergreen, AL 36401, 334-578-1313 (Fax: 334-578-5355). 7AM-4PM. Enrollment: 860. Records go back to 1963. Alumni records are maintained here. Degrees granted: Associate. Attendance and degree information available by phone, fax, mail. Transcripts available by fax, mail.

Samford University Registrar, 800 Lakeshore Dr, Birmingham, AL 35229, 205-870-2732, 205-870-2911 (Fax: 205-870-2908) www.samford.edu. 8AM-4PM. Enrollment: 4445. Records go back to 1887. Alumni records are maintained. Degrees granted: Associate; Bachelors; Masters; Doctorate. Attendance and degree information available by phone, fax, mail. Transcripts available by fax, mail.

Sanford Dixon Bishop State Junior Col.
(See Bishop State Community College)

Selma University Admissions & Records, Director, 1501 Lapsley St, Selma, AL 36701, 334-872-2533 (Fax: 334-872-7746). 8:30AM-4PM. Enrollment: 200. Records go back to 1892. Degrees granted: Associate; Bachelors. Attendance and degree information available by phone, fax, mail. Transcripts by mail.

Shelton State Community College Registrar, 9500 Old Greensboro Rd, Tuscaloosa, AL 35405, 205-391-2214 (Fax: 205-391-3910). 8AM-5PM. Enrollment: 6120. Records go back to 1950. Alumni records maintained here; call 205-391-2221. Degrees granted: Associate. Attendance and degree information available by phone, fax, mail. Transcripts available by fax, mail.

Snead State Community College Registrar, PO Drawer D, 220 N Walnut St, Boaz, AL 35957, 205-593-5120 X207, 205-593-5120 X209 (Fax: 205-593-7180). 7:30AM-4PM. Enrollment: 1668. Records go back to 1934. Alumni records are maintained here also. Call 205-593-5120. Degrees granted: Associate. Special programs-Veterinary Technology, 205-593-5120 X249. Attendance and degree information available by phone, fax, mail. Transcripts available by mail.

Southeastern Bible College Registrar, 3001 Hwy 280 E, Birmingham, AL 35243, 205-970-9208 (Fax: 205-970-9207). 8AM-4:30PM. Enrollment: 160. Records go back to 1940. Degrees granted: Associate; Bachelors. Attendance and degree information available by phone, fax, mail. Transcripts by mail.

Southern Christian University Registrar, 1200 Taylor Rd, Montgomery, AL 36117-3553, 334-277-2277 (Fax: 334-271-0002) 9AM-5PM. www.southern christian.edu. Enrollment: 180. Alumni records are maintained here. Degrees granted: Bachelors; Masters; Doctorate. Attendance and degree information available by phone, fax, mail. Transcripts available by mail.

Southern Union State Community College Registrar, PO Box 1000, Wadley, AL 36276, 205-395-2211 (Fax: 205-395-2215) www.suscc.cc.al.us. 7:30AM -4:30PM. Enrollment: 4000. Records go back to 1922. Alumni records maintained here; call 205-745-6437. Degrees granted: Associate. Attendance and degree information available by phone, fax, mail. Transcripts by mail.

Southwest State Technical College
(See Bishop State Community College)

Sparks State Technical College Registrar, PO Drawer 580, Hwy 432 S, Eufaula, AL 36072-0580, 334-687-3543 (Fax: 334-687-0255). 8AM-5PM. Enrollment: 780.

Records go back to 1963. Degrees granted: Associate. Attendance and degree information available by phone, mail. Transcripts available by mail.

Spring Hill College, Registrar, 4000 Dauphin St, Mobile, AL 36608, 334-380-2240 (Fax: 334-460-2192) www.shc.edu. 8AM-5PM. Enrollment: 1500. Records go back to 1830. Alumni records maintained here; call 334-380-2280. Degrees granted: Associate; Bachelors. Attendance and degree information available by phone, fax, mail. Transcripts available by mail.

Stillman College Registrar, PO Drawer 1430, Tuscaloosa, AL 35403, 205-366-8816, 205-366-8815 (Fax: 205-366-8996) www.stillman.edu. 8AM-5PM. Enrollment: 1000. Records go back to 1955. Alumni records maintained here; call 205-366-8885. Degrees granted: Bachelors. Attendance and degree information available by phone, fax, mail. Transcripts available by mail.

Talladega College Registrar, 627 W Battle St, Talladega, AL 35160, 205-761-6219, 205-761-6341 (Fax: 205-362-2268 & 205-761-6440). 9AM-5PM. Enrollment: 786. Records go back to 1867. Alumni records maintained here; call 205-761-6203. Degrees granted: Bachelors. Attendance and degree information available by phone, fax, mail. Transcripts available by mail.

Trenholm State Technical College Registrar, 1225 Air Base Blvd, Montgomery, AL 36108, 334-832-9000, 334-240-9631 (Fax: 334-832-9777). 8AM-5PM. Enrollment: 680. Records go back to 1966. Alumni records are maintained. Degrees granted: Associate. Attendance information available by phone, mail. Degree and transcript information available by mail.

Troy State University (Dothan), Registrar, PO Box 8368, 3601 US Hwy 231 N, Dothan, AL 36304-0368, 334-983-6556 X229 (Fax: 334-983-6322) www.tsud.edu. 7:45AM-5:30PM M-Th; 8AM-Noon F. Enrollment: 2300. Records go back to 1981. Alumni records are maintained here. Degrees granted: Associate; Bachelors; Masters. Special programs- Tech Mgmt, 334-983-6556 X264; Edu Leadership, 334-983-6556. Attendance and degree information available by phone, fax, mail. Transcripts available by mail.

Troy State University, University Records, University Ave, Troy, AL 36082, 334-670-3170 (Fax: 334-670-3538). 8AM-5PM. Enrollment: 9200. Records go back to 1887. Alumni records are maintained. Degrees granted: Associate; Bachelors; Masters. Attendance and degree information available by phone, fax, mail. Transcripts by fax.

Troy State University Montgomery, Registrar's Office, 231 Montgomery, PO Drawer 4419, Montgomery, AL 36103-4419, 334-241-9511 (Fax: 334-241-9714) www.tsum.edu. 8AM-5:30PM. Enrollment: 3300. Records go back to 1972. Alumni records maintained here; call 334-241-9523. Degrees granted: Associate; Bachelors; Masters; ED.S. Special programs - External Degree, 334-241-9553. Attendance and degree information available by phone, fax, mail. Transcripts available by fax, mail.

Tuskegee University Office of the Registrar, Tuskegee, AL 36088, 334-727-8507. 8AM-4:30PM. Enrollment: 3140. Records go back to 1881. Alumni records maintained here; call 334-727-8342. Degrees granted: Associate; Bachelors; Masters; Doctorate. Attendance and degree information available by phone, mail. Transcripts available by mail.

U.S. Sports Academy Registrar, 1 Academy Dr, Daphne, AL 36526, www.sport.ussa.edu 334-626-3303 (Fax: 334-626-1149) Enrollment: 213. Records go back to 1972. Alumni records are maintained. Degrees granted: Masters; Doctorate. Attendance and degree information available by phone, mail. Transcripts available by mail.

United States Sports Academy Registrar, One Academy Dr, Daphne, AL 36526, 334-626-3303 (Fax: 334-626-1149) www.sport.ussa.edu. 8AM-5PM. Enrollment: 211. Records go back to 1974. Degrees granted: Masters; Doctorate. Attendance and degree information available by phone, fax, mail. Transcripts available by fax, mail.

University of Alabama Records Office, PO Box 870134, Tuscaloosa, AL 35487-0134, 205-348-4886 (Fax: 205-348-8187) www.ua.edu. 8AM-4:45PM. Enrollment: 19000. Alumni Records: Alumni Hall, The University of Alabama, PO Box 1928, Tuscaloosa, AL 35486. Degrees granted: Bachelors; Masters; Doctorate. Attendance and degree information available by phone, fax, mail. Transcripts available by fax, mail.

University of Alabama Birmingham Registrar, Hill University Center, 1400 University Blvd, Birmingham, AL 35294, 205-934-8222 (Fax: 205-975-6168) www.uab.edu. 8AM-6PM M-Th; 8AM-5PM F. Enrollment: 15000. Records go back to 1967. Alumni records maintained here; call 205-934-3555. Degrees granted: Bachelors; Masters; Doctorate. Attendance and degree information available by phone, fax, mail. Transcripts available by fax, mail.

University of Alabama at Birmingham-Walker College Registrar, 1411 Indiana Ave, Jasper, AL 35501, 205-387-0511 (Fax: 205-387-5175) www.uab.edu. 8AM-5PM. Enrollment: 1000. Records go back to 1938. Alumni records are maintained. Degrees granted: Associate. Attendance and degree information available by phone, fax, mail. Transcripts available by fax, mail.

University of Alabama in Huntsville Office of Records, University Center #116, Huntsville, AL 35899, 256-890-6753 (Registrar), 256-890-6120 (switchboard) (Fax: 256-895-6073) info.uah.edu/. 8:15AM-5PM. Enrollment: 6460. Records go back to 1968. Alumni records maintained here; call 256-890-6085. Degrees granted: Bachelors; Masters; Doctorate. Attendance and degree information available by phone, fax, mail. Transcripts available by fax, mail.

University of Mobile Dean, Graduate & Special Programs, PO Box 13220, Mobile, AL 36663-0220, 334-675-5990 (Fax: 334-675-9816). 8AM-4:30PM. Enrollment: 1782. Records go back to 1963. Formerly **Mobile College**. Alumni records maintained here; call 334-675-5990 X224. Degrees granted: Associate; Bachelors; Masters. Attendance and degree information available by phone, fax, mail. Transcripts available by fax, mail.

University of Montevallo Registrar, Station 6040, Montevallo, AL 35115-6001, 205-665-6040, 205-665-6039 (Fax: 205-665-6042) 8AM-5PM. www.montevallo.edu. Enrollment: 3000. Records go back to 1896. Alumni Records: Station 6215, Montevallo, AL 35115-6001. Degrees granted: Bachelors; Masters; Educational Specialist. Attendance and degree information available by phone, fax, mail. Transcripts available by fax, mail.

University of North Alabama Registrar, Box 5044, Florence, AL 35632-0001, 205-765-4316 (Fax: 205-765-4349) 8AM-4:30PM. www.unaalpha.edu. Enrollment:

5200. Records go back to 1850. Alumni Records: Box 5047, Florence, AL 35632-0001. Degrees granted: Bachelors; Masters. Attendance and degree information available by phone, fax, mail. Transcripts by mail.

University of South Alabama University Registrar, AD 165, Mobile, AL 36688-0002, 334-460-6251 (Fax: 334-460-7738) www.usouthal.edu. 8AM-5PM. Enrollment: 12000. Records go back to 1963. Alumni Records: Plantation Creole House, Mobile, AL 36688. Degrees granted: Bachelors; Masters; Doctorate. Attendance and transcript information available by mail. Degree information available by phone, mail.

University of West Alabama Registrar, 205 N Washington St, Livingston, AL 35470, 205-652-3400 (Fax: 205-652-4065) www.westal.edu. 8AM-5PM. Records go back to 1913. Formerly **Livingston**

University. Alumni records are maintained. Degrees granted: Associate; Bachelors; Masters. Attendance and degree information available by phone, fax, mail. Transcripts available by mail.

Virginia College at Birmingham Registrar, 65 Bagby Dr, Homewood, AL 35209, 205-802-1200 (Fax: 205-802-7045) www.vc.edu. 9AM-6PM M-Th, 9AM-4PM F. Enrollment: 400. Records go back to 1993. Degrees granted: Associate. Attendance and degree information available by phone, fax, mail. Transcripts available by fax, mail.

Virginia College — Huntsville Registrar, 2800-A Bob Wallace Ave, Huntsville, AL 35805, 205-533-7387 (Fax: 205-533-7785). 8AM-5PM. Enrollment: 300. Records go back to 1993. Degrees granted: Associate. Attendance, degree and transcript information available by mail.

Walker College
  (See University of Alabama Birmingham-Walker College)

Walker State Technical College
  (See Bevill State Community College)

Wallace State Community College Registrar, PO Box 2000, Hanceville, AL 35077, 205-352-8128, 205-352-8142 (Fax: 205-352-8228). 7:30AM-4PM. Enrollment: 5550. Records go back to 1966. Alumni records maintained here; call 205-352-8161. Degrees granted: Associate. Special programs- Allied Health, 205-352-8348. Attendance and degree information available by phone, fax, mail. Transcripts by mail.

Alaska

Alaska Bible College, Registrar, Box 289, Glennallen, AK 99588, 907-822-3201 (Fax: 907-822-5027). 8AM-Noon, 1-5PM. Enrollment: 54. Records go back to 1970. Degrees granted: Associate; Bachelors. Attendance and degree information available by phone, fax, mail. Transcripts by fax, mail.

Alaska Pacific University, Registrar, 4101 University Dr, Anchorage, AK 99508, 8AM-5PM. 907-564-8210 (Fax: 907-563-9640) www.corecom.net/apu. Enrollment: 550. Records go back to 1960. Alumni records are maintained here also. Call 907-564-8256. Degrees granted: Associate; Bachelors; Masters. Attendance and degree information available by phone, fax, mail. Transcripts available by fax, mail.

Alaska Vocational-Technical Center, Registrar, 889 Second Ave, Seward, AK 99664, 907-224-3322 (Fax: 907-224-3380) 8AM-5PM. www.educ.state.ak.us/avtec/home Records go back to 1958. Alumni records are maintained here. Degrees granted: Associate. Attendance and degree information available by phone, mail. Transcripts available by mail.

Anchorage Community College
  (See University of Alaska Anchorage)

Charter College, Registrar, 2221 E Northern Lights Blvd, Suite 120, Anchorage, AK 99508, www.chartercollege.org. 907-277-1000 (Fax: 907-274-3342) Enrollment: 850. Records go back to 1986. Alumni records are maintained here. Degrees granted: Associate. Attendance and degree information available by phone, mail. Transcripts available by mail.

Islands Community College
  (See Univ. of Alaska SE Sitka Campus)

Kenai Peninsula College, Registrar, 34820 College Dr, Soldotna, AK 99669, 907-262-0300 (Fax: 907-262-9280). Records located at University of Alaska Anchorage.

Kodiak College, Registrar, 117 Benny Benson Dr, Kodiak, AK 99615, 907-486-1235 (Fax: 907-486-1264) 9AM-6PM. www.kodiak.alaska.edu. Enrollment: 1200. Records go back to 1970. Degrees granted: Associate. Attendance and degree information available by phone, fax, mail. Transcripts available by fax, mail.

Kuskokwim College
  (See University of Alaska Fairbank)

Mananuska-Susitna College, Registrar, PO Box 2889, Palmer, AK 99645, 907-745-9712 (Fax: 907-745-9747) 8AM-8:30PM M-

Th; 8AM-5PM F. www.uaa.alaska.edu Enrollment: 1300. Records go back to 1958. Alumni records are maintained. Degrees granted: Associate; Certificates. Attendance and degree information available by phone, fax, mail. Transcripts available by fax, mail.

Prince William Sound Community College, Registrar, PO Box 97, Valdez, AK 99686, www.uaa.alaska.edu/pwscc/home 907-834-1632, 907-834-1600 (Fax: 907-834-1627) 8:30AM-5:30PM. Enrollment: 1900. Records go back to 1980. Alumni records are maintained here. Degrees granted: Associate. Special programs- Rural Alaska Teacher Education, 907-834-1631. Attendance and degree information available by phone, fax, mail. Transcripts available by fax, mail.

Sheldon Jackson College, Registrar, 801 Lincoln, Sitka, AK 99835, 907-747-5216, 907-747-5220 www.sj-alaska.edu (Fax: 907-747-2588) 8AM-Noon, 1-5PM. Enrollment: 300. Records go back to 1898. Alumni records maintained here; call 907-747-2589. Degrees granted: Associate; Bachelors. Attendance and degree information available by phone, fax, mail. Transcripts available by fax, mail.

Tanana Valley Community College
  (See University of Alaska Fairbanks)

University of Alaska (Kuskokwim), Registrar, PO Box 368, Bethel, AK 99559, 907-543-4562 (Fax: 907-543-4527) www.alaska.edu. Records are located at University of Alaska Fairbanks.

University of Alaska (Northwest), Registrar, Pouch 400, Nome, AK 99762, 907-443-2201 (Fax: 907-474-5379) www.alaska.edu. Records located at University of Alaska Fairbanks.

University of Alaska Anchorage, Enrollment Services, 3211 Providence Dr, Anchorage, AK 99508-8038, 907-786-1480 http://orion.alaska.edu/www/cwis.html. (Fax: 907-786-4888) 8AM - 4:30PM. Enrollment: 18100. Records go back to 1950's. Alumni records maintained here; call 907-786-1942. Degrees granted: Associate; Bachelors; Masters; Certificates. Attendance and degree information available by phone, fax, mail. Transcripts available by fax, mail. Transcripts are only provided upon written request from student.

University of Alaska Anchorage (Matanuska-Susitna College), Registrar, PO Box 2889, Palma, AK 99645, 907-745-9774 (Fax: 907-745-9747) Enrollment: 1100.

www.uaa.alaska.edu/matsu/msc Records go back to 1974. Alumni records are maintained here. Attendance and degree information available by phone, mail. For official transcript, go to Anchorage campus.

University of Alaska Fairbanks, Office of the Registrar, PO Box 757495, Fairbanks, AK 99775-7495, 907-474-6300, 907-474-6244 (Fax: 907-474-7097) 8AM - PM. http://zorba.uafadm.alaska.edu Enrollment: 7000. Records go back to 1922. Alumni records maintained here; call 907-474-7081. Degrees granted: Associate; Bachelors; Masters; Doctorate. Special programs-Mineral & Petroleum Engineering, 907-474-7366; Wildlife Biology, 907-474-7671. Attendance and degree information available by phone, fax, mail. Transcripts available by fax, mail.

University of Alaska Fairbanks (Chukchi Branch), Registrar, PO Box 297, Kotzebue, AK 99752, www.uad.edu. 907-442-3400 (Fax: 907-474-5379) Records are located at University of Alaska Fairbanks.

University of Alaska Southeast, Registrar, 11120 Glacier Hwy, Juneau, AK 99801, 907-465-6458 (Fax: 907-465-6365). 9AM-5PM. Enrollment: 5177. Records go back to 1970's. Alumni records maintained here; call 907-465-6457. Degrees granted: Bachelors; Masters. Attendance and degree information available by phone, fax, mail. Transcripts available by fax, mail.

University of Alaska Southeast (Ketchikan Campus), Registrar, Ketchikan, AK 99901, 907-225-6177 (Fax: 907-225-3624) www.uase.ketch.alaska.edu. 8AM-5PM. Enrollment: 800. Records go back to 1980. Alumni records are maintained here at the same phone number. Degrees granted: Associate. Certifications: Welding, Tourism, Accounting, Business Information. Attendance and degree information available by fax, mail. Transcripts available by fax, mail.

University of Alaska Southeast (Sitka Campus), Registrar, 1332 Seward Ave, Sitka, AK 99835, 907-465-6268 (Fax: 907-465-6365). 8AM-5PM. Enrollment: 1500. Records go back to 1982. Degrees granted: Associate. Attendance and degree information available by mail. For transcript information, go to the Juneau campus.

Arizona

Academy of Business College, Registrar, 2525 W Beryl Ave, Phoenix, AZ 85021, 602-942-4141 www.primenet.com/~/aob. (Fax: 602-943-0960) 7:45AM-8PM M-Th, 7:45AM-5PM F. Enrollment: 200. Records go back to 1982. Degrees granted: Associate. Special programs- Accounting: Business: Legal Assistant: PC Technician. Attendance and degree information available by phone, fax, mail. Transcripts available by fax, mail.

Al Collins Graphic Design School, Registrar, 1140 S Priest Dr, Tempe, AZ 85281, 602-966-3000 X142 (Fax: 602-902-0663) www.alcollins.com. 8AM-5PM. Enrollment: 1000. Records go back to 1978. Alumni records are maintained. Degrees granted: Associate; Bachelors. Attendance and degree information available by phone, fax, mail. Transcripts available by fax, mail.

American Graduate School of International Management (Thunderbird Campus), Registrar, 15249 N 59 Ave, Glendale, AZ 85306, 602-978-7980 (Fax: 602-439-5432) www.t-bird.edu. 9AM-4:30PM. Enrollment: 1450. Records go back to 1947. Alumni records maintained here; call 602-978-7135. Degrees granted: Masters. Attendance and degree information available by phone, fax, mail. Transcripts available by mail.

American Indian Bible College
(See American Indian College of the Assemblies of God)

American Indian College of the Assemblies of God, Registrar, 10020 N 15th Ave, Phoenix, AZ 85021, 602-944-3335 X236, 602-944-3335 X15 (Fax: 602-943-8299). Enrollment: 120. Formerly **American Indian Bible College**. Alumni records are maintained here. Degrees granted: Associate; Bachelors. Attendance and degree information available by fax, mail. Transcripts available by mail. Student ID number needed.

American Institute, Registrar, 3343 N Central Ave, Phoenix, AZ 85012, 602-252-4986 (Fax: 602-252-8130). 8AM-6PM. Enrollment: 300. Records go back to 1980. Degrees granted: Associate. Attendance and degree information available by phone, fax, mail. Transcripts available by written request only.

Apollo College Phoenix, Inc, Registrar, 8503 N 27th Ave, Phoenix, AZ 85051, 602-864-1571 (Fax: 602-864-8207) 8AM-5PM. www.apollocollege.com. Enrollment: 350. Records go back to 1967. Degrees granted: Associate. Attendance and degree information available by phone, mail. Transcripts available by mail.

Apollo College- Tri-City, Inc, Registrar, 630 W Southern Ave, Mesa, AZ 85210-5004, 602-831-6585 (Fax: 602-827-0022) www.apollocollege.com. 8AM-5PM. Enrollment: 200. Records go back to 1975. Degrees granted: Associate. Attendance and degree information available by phone, mail. Transcripts available by mail.

Arizona Automotive Institute
(See National Education Center Arizona Automotive Institute)

Arizona Bible College, Registrar, 1718 W Maryland Ave, Phoenix, AZ 85015, 602-242-6400 (Fax: 602-242-1992). 7:30AM-4:30PM. Enrollment: 150. Records go back to 1971.

Alumni records are maintained here. Degrees granted: Associate; Bachelors. Certification: One Year Bible. Attendance and degree information available by phone, fax. Transcripts available by fax, mail.

Arizona Institute of Business & Technology, Registrar, 6049 N 43rd Ave, Phoenix, AZ 85019, 602-242-6265 X214 (Fax: 602-973-2572) www.aibt.edu. 8AM-5PM. Degrees granted: Associate. Attendance and degree information available by phone, mail. Transcripts available by mail.

Arizona Institute of Business & Technology (Tucson Campus), Registrar, 1844 South Albernom Way, Tucson, AZ 85711, 520-748-9799 (Fax: 520-748-9355) www.aibt.edu. 8AM-5PM. Enrollment: 500. Records go back to 1996. Alumni records are maintained here. Degrees granted: Associate. Attendance and degree information available by phone, mail. Transcripts available by mail.

Arizona Institute of Business and Technology (Branch), Registrar, 925 S Gilbert Rd Ste 201, Mesa, AZ 85204, 602-545-8755, 602-545-8755 (Fax: 602-926-1371) www.aibt.edu. 7:30AM-8PM M-Th, 8AM-4:30PM F. Enrollment: 300. Records go back to 1983. Degrees granted: Associate. Attendance, degree and transcript information available by fax, mail.

Arizona Institute of Business and Technology, Registrar, 4136 N 75th Ave, Phoenix, AZ 85033, 602-849-8208 (Fax: 602-849-0110). 8AM-10PM M-Th, 8AM-5PM F. Enrollment: 198. Records go back to 1980. Alumni Records: Suite 104, Phoenix, AZ 85033. Degrees granted: Associate. Attendance, degree and transcript information available by fax, mail. Transcript request must be in writing from student.

Arizona State University (East), Registrar, 6001 S Power Rd, Bldg 314, Mesa, AZ 85206-0903, 602-727-3278 www.asu.edu. 8AM-5PM. Records go back to 1996. Degrees granted: Bachelors; Masters; Doctorate. Attendance and degree information available by phone, mail. Get transcripts from main campus in Tempe.

Arizona State University, Registrar, Tempe, AZ 85287-0312, 602-965-3124, 602-965-7302 (Fax: 602-965-2295) www.asu.edu. 8AM-5PM. Enrollment: 45000. Records go back to 1885. Alumni Records: Alumni Center, Arizona State University, Box 871004, Tempe, AZ 85287-1004. Degrees granted: Bachelors; Masters; Doctorate. Attendance and degree information available by phone, fax, mail. Transcripts available by mail.

Arizona State University West, Registrar, 4701 W Thunderbird Rd, PO Box 37100, Phoenix, AZ 85069-7100, 602-543-8123, 602-543-8111 (Fax: 602-543-8312) www.asu.west.edu. 8AM-6PM M-Th, 8AM-4PM F. Enrollment: 4800. Records go back to 1980. Alumni Records: Alumni Center, Arizona State University, Box 871004, Tempe, AZ 85287-1004. Degrees granted: Bachelors; Masters. Attendance and degree information available by phone, mail. Transcripts available by mail.

Arizona Western College, Registrar, PO Box 929, Yuma, AZ 85366, 520-317-6000, 520-726-1000 (Fax: 520-344-7543) www.awc.cc.az.us. 7AM-5PM M-Th. Enrollment: 8000. Records go back to 1962.

Degrees granted: Associate. Attendance, degree and transcript information available by fax, mail. Will confirm attendance only by phone, with student's permission.

Central Arizona College, Registrar, 8470 N Overfield Rd, Coolidge, AZ 85228, 520-426-4444, 520-426-4260 (Fax: 520-426-4234) 8AM-4:30PM. www.cac.cc.az.us. Enrollment: 5000. Records go back to 1969. Degrees granted: Associate. Attendance and degree information available by phone, fax, mail. Transcripts available by fax, mail.

Chandler-Gilbert Community College, Registrar, 2626 E Pecos Rd, Chandler, AZ 85225-2479, 602-732-7308, 602-732-7000 (Fax: 602-732-7099) 140.198.129.30. 8:30AM-7PM. Enrollment: 3500. Records go back to 1987. Degrees granted: Associate. Special programs - Aviation, 602-732-7054. Attendance and degree information available by phone, fax, mail. Transcripts available by fax, mail.

Chaparral College, Registrar, 4585 E Speedway Blvd Ste 204, Tucson, AZ 85712, 520-327-6866 (Fax: 520-325-0108) www.chap.col.com/imdes.html. 7:30AM-10:05PM. Enrollment: 450. Records go back to 1973. Formerly **Chaparral Career College**. Degrees granted: Associate. Attendance and degree information available by phone, fax, mail. Transcripts available by fax, mail.

Cochise College, Registrar, 4190 Hwy 80, Douglas, AZ 85607-9724, 520-364-0241 (Fax: 520-364-0236) www.cochise.cc.az.us. 8AM-4:30PM. Enrollment: 4500. Records go back to 1965. Degrees granted: Associate. Special programs- Aviation, 520-364-0314. Attendance and degree information available by phone, fax, mail. Transcripts available by mail.

DeVry Institute of Technology, Phoenix, Registrar, 2149 W Dunlap Ave, Phoenix, AZ 85021, 602-870-9222 (Fax: 602-870-1209) www.devry-phx.edu. 8AM-5PM. Enrollment: 3200. Records go back to 1967. Alumni Records: Alumni Assoc., One Oakbrook Tower Ste 100, Oak Brook, IL 60181-4624. Degrees granted: Associate; Bachelors. Attendance and degree information available by phone, fax, mail. Transcripts available by fax, mail.

Denver Business College (Branch), Registrar, 1457 W Southern Ave #8, Mesa, AZ 85202, 602-834-1000 (Fax: 602-491-2970) www.commonwealth.edu. 8AM-7PM. Enrollment: 144. Records go back to 1987. Alumni records are maintained here. Degrees granted: Associate. Special programs - Criminal Justice: Business: Accounting. Attendance and transcript information available by fax, mail. Degree information available by phone, fax, mail.

Dine College, Records/Admissions Officer, Tsaile, AZ 86556, 520-724-6630, 520-724-6633 (Fax: 520-724-3349) 9AM-4PM. www.crystal.ncc.mus. Enrollment: 2017. Records go back to 1991. Degrees granted: Associate. Attendance and degree information available by fax, mail. Transcripts available by fax.

Eastern Arizona College, Records Office, Thatcher, AZ 85552-0769, 520-428-8250, 520-428-8270 (Fax: 520-428-8462) www.eac.cc.az.us. 9AM-4PM. Enrollment: 5000. Records go back to 1895. Alumni records maintained here; call 520-428-8295.

Degrees granted: Associate. Attendance and degree information available by phone, fax, mail. Transcripts available by fax, mail.

Embry-Riddle Aeronautical University (Branch), Registrar, 3200 Willow Creek Rd, Prescott, AZ 86301, 520-708-3803, 520-776-3805 (Fax: 520-708-3806) www.pr.erau.edu. 8AM-5PM. Enrollment: 1550. Records go back to 1978. Alumni records maintained here; call 520-708-6692. Degrees granted: Associate; Bachelors; Masters. Attendance and degree information available by phone, fax, mail. Transcripts available by fax, mail.

Estrella Mountain Community College, Registrar, 3000 N Dysart Rd, Phoenix, AZ 85323, 602-935-8000 (Fax: 602-935-8870) www.emc.maricopa.edu. 8AM-5PM. Enrollment: 4771. Records go back to 1992. Degrees granted: Associate. Attendance and degree information available by phone, mail. Transcripts available by mail.

Estrella Mountain Community College, Registrar, 3000 North Dysart Rd, Avondale, AZ 85323, 602-935-8000 (Fax: 602-935-8870) www.emc.edu. 8AM-5PM. Enrollment: 3000. Records go back to 1992. Degrees granted: Associate. Attendance and degree information available by phone, mail. Transcripts available by mail.

Frank Lloyd Wright School of Architecture, Registrar, Taliesin West, Scottsdale, AZ 85261, 602-860-2700 (Fax: 602-391-4009). 9AM-4:30PM. Enrollment: 35. Records go back to 1945. Alumni records are maintained here. Degrees granted: Bachelors; Masters. Attendance and degree information available by phone, fax, mail. Transcripts available by fax, mail.

Gateway Community College, Registrar, 108 N 40th St, Phoenix, AZ 85034, 602-392-5189, 602-392-5194 (Fax: 602-392-5209) www.gwc.maricopa.edu/. 8AM-7PM M-Th; 8AM-5PM F. Enrollment: 7000. Records go back to 1968. Degrees granted: Associate. Attendance and degree information available by phone, fax, mail. Transcripts available by fax, mail.

Glendale Community College, Registrar, 600 W Olive Ave, Glendale, AZ 85302, 602-435-3319 (Fax: 602-435-3303) www.gc.maricopa.edu. 8AM-7:30PM M-Th, 9AM-4PM F. Enrollment: 18000. Records go back to 1965. Alumni records maintained here; call 602-435-3014. Degrees granted: Associate. Attendance and degree information available by phone, fax, mail. Transcripts available by mail.

Golf Academy (Chandler Campus), Registrar, 1 San Marcos Pl, Chandler, AZ 85224, 602-786-4692. Alumni records are maintained. Degrees granted: Associate. Attendance and degree information available by phone, mail. Transcripts available by mail.

Grand Canyon University, Registrar, 3300 W Camelback Rd, PO Box 11097, Phoenix, AZ 85061, 602-589-2850, 602-589-2500 (Fax: 602-589-2594) www.grand-canyon.edu. 8AM-5PM M-Th; 9AM-4PM F. Enrollment: 1878. Records go back to 1949. Alumni records maintained here; call 602-249-3300. Degrees granted: Bachelors; Masters. Special programs- College of Continuing Education. Attendance and degree information available by phone, fax, mail. Transcripts by fax, mail.

High-Tech Institute, Registrar, 1515 E Indian School Rd, Phoenix, AZ 85014-4901, 602-279-9700 (Fax: 602-279-2999) www.high-techinstitute.com. 8AM-5PM. Enrollment: 750. Records go back to 1981. Degrees granted: Associate. Attendance and

degree information available by phone, mail. Transcripts available by mail.

ITT Technical Institute, Registrar, 4837 E McDowell Rd, **Phoenix**, AZ 85008-4292, 602-252-2331, 602-231-0871 (Fax: 602-267-8727). 7AM-7PM M-Th; 8AM-5PM F. Enrollment: 400. Records go back to 1968. Alumni Records: Alumni Assoc., 5975 Castle Creek Pkwy N Dr, Indianapolis, IN 46250. Degrees granted: Associate; Bachelors. Attendance and degree information available by phone, fax, mail. Transcripts available by mail.

ITT Technical Institute, Registrar, 1840 E Benson Hwy, **Tucson**, AZ 85714-1770, 520-294-2944. 8AM-10PM. Records go back to 1980. Degrees granted: Associate. Attendance and degree information available by phone, fax, mail. Transcripts available by mail.

Judson Baptist College
(See Southwest Conservative Baptist Bible College)

Keller Graduate School of Management (East Valley Center), Registrar, 1201 S Alma School Rd Ste 5450, Mesa, AZ 85210, 602-827-1511 (Fax: 602-827-2552) www.keller.edu. They are not housed here. They are located at Keller Graduate School of Management, (Phoenix/Northwest Center).

Keller Graduate School of Management (Phoenix/Northwest Center), Registrar, 2149 W Dunlap Ave, Phoenix, AZ 85021, 602-870-0117, 800-528-0250 X430 (Fax: 602-870-0022) www.keller.edu. 8:30AM-8PM M-Th, 8:30AM-5PM, Sat by appointment. Enrollment: 500. Records go back to 1973. Alumni records maintained here; call 602-870-0117. Degrees granted: Masters. Special programs- Project Management: Human Resources: Business Administration. Attendance and degree information available by phone, fax, mail. Transcripts available by mail.

Lamson Junior College, Registrar, 1980 W Main St, Suite 250, Mesa, AZ 85201, 602-898-7000 (Fax: 602-967-6645) www.lamson.edu. 8AM-5PM. Enrollment: 200. Degrees granted: Associate. Attendance and degree information available by phone, mail. Transcripts available by mail.

Mesa Community College, Registrar, 1833 W Southern Ave, Mesa, AZ 85202, 602-461-7478, 602-461-7477 (Fax: 602-461-7805) www.mc.maricopa.edu. 8AM-8PM M-Th. Enrollment: 23500. Records go back to 1965. Alumni records maintained here; call 602-461-7501. Degrees granted: Associate. Attendance, degree and transcript information available by fax, mail.

Miller Institute
(See ITT Technical Institute)

Mohave Community College, Registrar, 1971 Jagerson Ave, Kingman, AZ 86401, 520-757-0847 (Fax: 520-757-0808) 8AM-5PM. www.mohave.cc.az.us. Enrollment: 5800. Records go back to 1971. Degrees granted: Associate. Attendance and degree information available by phone, fax, mail. Transcripts available by mail.

National Education Center-Arizona Automotive Institute, Director of Graduate Placement, 6829 N 46th Ave, Glendale, AZ 85301, 602-934-7273 (Fax: 602-937-5000). Enrollment: 500. Records go back to 1993. Formerly **Arizona Automotive Institute**. Attendance and degree information available by phone, mail. Transcripts available by mail.

Navajo Community College
(See Dine College)

Navajo Community College, Registrar, PO Box 126, Tsaile, AZ 86556, 520-724-6669 (Fax: 520-724-6664) www.navajo.edu. 8AM-5PM. Enrollment: 1276. Records go back to 1967. Degrees granted: Associate. Attendance and degree information available by phone, mail. Transcripts available by mail.

Northern Arizona University, Registrar, Box 4103, Flagstaff, AZ 86011-4092, 520-523-2100, 520-523-2109 (Fax: 520-523-1414) www.nau.edu/~regis. 8AM-5PM Fall/Spring; 7:30AM-4:30PM Summer. Enrollment: 13931. Records go back to 1900. Alumni Records: PO Box 6034, Flagstaff, AZ 86011. Degrees granted: Bachelors; Masters; Doctorate. Attendance and degree information available by phone, mail. Transcripts available by mail.

Northland Pioneer College, Registrar, 103 First Ave at Hopi Dr, PO Box 610, Holbrook, AZ 86025, 520-524-1993, 520-524-6111 (Fax: 520-524-1997) www.northland.cc.az.us. 8AM-5PM. Enrollment: 4500. Records go back to 1974. Degrees granted: Associate. Certification: CAS. Special programs-Nursing: Legal Assistant, 520-537-2976. Attendance and degree information available by phone, fax, mail. Transcripts available by fax, mail.

Occupational Training Center, Registrar, 4136 North 75th St, Suite 200, Phoenix, AZ 85033, 602-849-0308 (Fax: 602-849-2135) www.otc.tec.az.us. 8AM-5PM. Enrollment: 800. Records go back to 1990. Degrees granted: Associate. Attendance and degree information available by phone, mail. Transcripts available by mail.

Paradise Valley Community College, Registrar, 18401 N 32nd St, Phoenix, AZ 85032, 602-493-2610 (Fax: 602-493-2983) www.pvc.maricopa.edu. 8AM-7PM M-Th; 8AM-5PM F. Enrollment: 5235. Records go back to 1987. Degrees granted: Associate. Attendance and degree information available by fax. Transcripts available by fax, mail.

Paralegal Institute, Inc., Registrar, 2933 W Indian School, Phoenix, AZ 85017, 602-212-0501 (Fax: 602-212-0502). 8AM-5PM. Records go back to 1975. Degrees granted: Associate. Special programs- Home Study Program. Attendance and degree information available by phone, fax, mail. Transcripts available by fax, mail. Student ID number needed.

Parks College (Branch Campus), Registrar, 6992 E Broadway, Tucson, AZ 85710, 520-886-7979 (Fax: 520-886-2395). 8AM-5PM M-Th; 8AM-3PM F. Records go back to 1987. Degrees granted: Associate. Attendance, degree and transcript information available by fax, mail.

Phoenix College, Registrar, 1202 W Thomas Rd, Phoenix, AZ 85013, 602-285-7502 www.pc.maricopa.edu (Fax: 602-285-7813) 7:30AM-7:30PM M-Th; 7:30AM-4:30PM F. Enrollment: 12000. Records go back to 1920. Alumni records are maintained here. Degrees granted: Associate. Certification: Fire Science. Attendance and degree information available by phone, fax, mail. Transcripts available by fax, mail.

Pima County Community College District, Registrar, 4907 E Broadway Blvd, Tucson, AZ 85709-1120, 520-206-6060 www.pima.edu. 8:15AM-4:45PM. Enrollment: 27950. Records go back to 1969. Alumni Records: Alumni Assoc., Pima County CC, 4905 E Broadway Blvd, Tucson, AZ 85709. Degrees granted: Associate; Basic; Advanced & Technical. Special programs-Associate, 520-748-4903; Advanced &

Technical, 520-478-4961. Attendance and degree information available by phone, fax, mail. Transcripts available by mail.

Pima Medical Institute (Branch), Registrar, 957 S Dobson Rd, Mesa, AZ 85202, 602-345-7777 (Fax: 602-649-3249). 8AM-10PM. Records go back to 1970. Degrees granted: Associate. School will not confirm attendance information. Degree information available by phone, mail. Transcripts available by mail.

Pima Medical Institute, Registrar, 3350 E Grant Rd, Tucson, AZ 85716, 520-326-1600 (Fax: 520-795-3463). 7:15AM-8:30PM M-Th, 8AM-5PM F. Records go back to 1972. Alumni records maintained here; call 520-326-1600. Degrees granted: Associate. Adverse incident record source- Student Services. Attendance and degree information available by phone, fax, mail. Transcripts available by mail.

Prescott College, Registrar, 220 Grove Ave, Prescott, AZ 86301, 520-776-5164 (registrar), 520-776-5176 (office) (Fax: 520-776-5175) http://92tec.asu.edu/prescott.col/. 8AM-5PM M-F; Summer 8AM-5PM M-Th. Enrollment: 870. Records go back to 1966. Alumni records maintained here; call 520-776-5223. Degrees granted: Bachelors; Masters. Attendance and degree information available by phone, mail. Transcripts available by written request only. Transcript Clerk, 520-776-5162.

Rio Salado College, Registrar, 2323 W 14th St, Tempe, AZ 85281, 602-517-8150 (Fax: 602-517-8199) www.rio.maricopa.edu. 8:15AM-5:45PM M-Th; 8:15AM-4:45PM F. Enrollment: 20000. Records go back to 1978. Alumni records maintained here; call 602-517-8000. Degrees granted: Associate. Special programs - Chemical Dependency. Attendance and degree information available by phone, fax, mail. Transcripts by fax, mail.

Scottsdale Community College, Registrar, 9000 E Chaparral Rd, Scottsdale, AZ 85250, 602-423-6000, 602-423-6100 (Fax: 602-423-6200) www.sc.maricopa.edu. 8AM-7PM M-Th, 8AM-4PM F. Enrollment: 10000. Records go back to 1976. Alumni records are maintained here. Degrees granted: Associate. Attendance and degree information available by phone, fax, mail. Transcripts available by fax, mail.

Scottsdale Culinary Institute, Registrar, 8100 E Camelback Rd, Scottsdale, AZ 85251-3940, 602-990-3773 (Fax: 602-990-0351) www.chef.com/culinary/. 8AM-5PM. Enrollment: 120. Records go back to 1989. Degrees granted: Associate. Attendance and degree information available by phone, mail. Transcripts available by mail.

South Mountain Community College, Admissions & Records, 7050 S 24th St, Phoenix, AZ 85040, 602-243-8000, 602-243-8153 (Fax: 602-243-8199) Enrollment: 2500. www.smc.maricopa.edu. Records go back to 1980. Alumni records are maintained. Degrees granted: Associate. Attendance and

degree information available by phone, fax, mail. Transcripts available by fax, mail;

Southwestern College, Registrar, 2625 E Cactus Rd, Phoenix, AZ 85032, 602-992-6101 (Fax: 602-404-2159) 8:30AM-4:30PM. www.netwrx.netswc. Enrollment: 200. Records go back to 1960. Degrees granted: Associate; Bachelors. Special programs - Elementary Education: Christian Ministries w/ Minor in Youth Counseling or Business: Biblical Studies: Secondary Education. Attendance and degree information available by phone, fax, mail. Transcripts by mail.

The Art Institute of Phoenix, Registrar, 2233 W Dunlop, Phoenix, AZ 85021, 602-678-4300 (Fax: 602-216-0439) www.aii.edu. 8AM-5PM. Enrollment: 600. Records go back to 1996. Degrees granted: Associate. Special programs - Culinary Arts: Liberal Arts. Attendance and degree information available by phone, mail. Transcripts available by mail.

The Bryman School, Registrar, 4343 N 16th St, Phoenix, AZ 85016-5338, 602-274-4300 (Fax: 602-248-9087) www.bryman.edu. 8AM-5PM. Records go back to 1989. Degrees granted: Associate. Attendance and degree information available by phone, mail. Transcripts available by mail.

The Refrigeration School, Registrar, 4210 E Washington St, Phoenix, AZ 85034-1894, 602-275-7133 www.refrigerationschool.com. 8AM-5PM. Enrollment: 119. Records go back to 1973. Degrees granted: Associate. Attendance and degree information available by phone, mail. Transcripts available by mail.

Universal Technical Institute, Registrar, 3121 W Weldon Ave, Phoenix, AZ 85017-4599, 602-264-4164 (Fax: 602-274-6993) www.uti.edu.com. 8AM-5PM. Enrollment: 320. Records go back to 1968. Degrees granted: Associate. Attendance and degree information available by phone, mail. Transcripts available by mail.

University of Advancing Computer Technology, Registrar, 2625 W Baseline Rd, Tempe, AZ 85283, 602-437-0405 (Fax: 602-383-8222) www.uact.edu. 8AM-5PM. Enrollment: 850. Records go back to 1993. Alumni records are maintained here. Degrees granted: Associate; Bachelors. Special programs - Science: Mechanical Design. Attendance and degree information available by phone, mail. Transcripts available by mail.

University of Arizona, Registrar, Tucson, AZ 85721, 520-621-2211 (Fax: 520-621-8944) www.arizona.edu. 8AM-5PM. Enrollment: 34000. Records go back to 1885. Alumni records are maintained here. Degrees granted: Bachelors; Masters; Doctorate. Attendance and degree information available by phone, mail. Transcripts available by mail.

University of Arizona (International), Registrar, 9000 South Rita Rd, Tucson, AZ 85747, 520-574-6300 (Fax: 520-574-6494) www.azintl.edu. 8AM-5PM. Enrollment: 106.

Records go back to 1996. Degrees granted: Associate. Attendance and degree information available by phone, mail. Transcripts available by mail.

University of Phoenix, Registrar, 4615 E Elwood St 3rd Flr, Phoenix, AZ 85072-2069, 602-966-9577, 602-966-5050 (Fax: 602-894-1758) www.uophx.edu. 8AM-6PM. Enrollment: 31000. Records go back to 1979. Alumni records are maintained. Degrees granted: Associate; Bachelors; Masters. Attendance and degree information available by phone, fax, mail. Transcripts by fax, mail.

University of Phoenix (Phoenix Main), Registrar, 4605 E Elwood St, PO Box 52076, Phoenix, AZ 85072-2076, 602-804-7600 www.uophx.edu. Records are located at University of Phoenix, (Phoenix Main), Phoenix, AZ.

University of Phoenix, Registrar, PO Box 52069, Phoenix, AZ 85072, 602-921-8014, 602-966-7400 (Fax: 602-894-1758) www.uophx.edu. 8AM-6PM. Enrollment: 36000. Records go back to 1980. Alumni records are maintained here. Degrees granted: Bachelors; Masters; Nursing. Attendance, degree and transcript information available by fax, mail.

University of Phoenix (Tucson Main), Registrar, 5099 E. Grant Rd, Suite 120, Tucson, AZ 85712, 520-881-6512 (Fax: 520-795-6177) www.uophx.edu. Attendance and degree information available by phone, fax, mail. Transcript records are housed at Univ. of Phoenix, Registrar, Phoenix, AZ.

Western International University, Registrar, 9215 N Black Canyon Hwy, Phoenix, AZ 85021, 602-943-2311 (Fax: 602-371-8637) www.wintu.edu. 8AM-5PM. Enrollment: 1499. Records go back to 1984. Alumni records are maintained. Degrees granted: Associate; Bachelors; Masters. Attendance and degree information available by phone, mail. Transcripts available by written request only.

Yavapai College, Registrar, 1100 E Sheldon St, Prescott, AZ 86301, 520-776-2150, 800-922-6787 (Fax: 520-776-2151) www.yavapai.cc.az.us. 9AM-5:30PM. Enrollment: 7000. Records go back to 1994. Degrees granted: Associate. Attendance and degree information available by phone, fax, mail. Transcripts available by fax, mail.

Arkansas

Arkansas Baptist College, Registrar, 1600 Bishop St, Little Rock, AR 72202, 501-374-7856 (Fax: 501-372-0321). 10AM-5PM. Enrollment: 315. Records go back to 1884. Alumni records are maintained here. Degrees granted: Bachelors. Attendance, degree and transcript information available by mail.

Arkansas State University (Beebe Branch), Registrar, Drawer H, Beebe, AR 72012, 501-882-8260, 501-882-8280 (Fax: 501-882-8370) www.asub.ark.net.edu. 8AM-5PM. Enrollment: 2000. Records go back to 1927. Alumni records maintained here; call 501-882-6452. Degrees granted: Associate. Attendance and degree information available by phone, fax, mail. Transcripts available by mail.

Arkansas State University (Newport Branch), Registrar, PO Box 1120, Newport, AR 72112, 870-512-7826 (Fax: 870-512-7807). Records are located at Arkansas State University, (Beebe Branch), Registrar, Beebe, AR.

Arkansas State University, Registrar, PO Box 1570, State University, AR 72467, 870-972-2031 (Fax: 870-972-3843) www.astate.edu. 8AM-5PM. Records go back to 1909. Alumni Records: PO Box 1990, State University, AR 72467. Degrees granted: Associate; Bachelors; Masters; Doctorate; Specialist. Attendance and degree information available by phone, fax, mail. Transcripts available by fax, mail.

Arkansas Tech University, Registrar, Russellville, AR 72801, 501-968-0272 (Fax: 501-968-0683) www.atu.edu. 8AM-5PM. Enrollment: 4000. Records go back to 1909. Alumni records maintained here; call 501-968-0242. Degrees granted: Associate; Bachelors; Masters. Certification: Medical Transcription. Attendance and degree information available by phone, fax, mail. Transcripts available by mail. Attendance confirmed only for students currently enrolled.

Black River Technical College, Registrar, Hwy 304 E, PO Box 468, Pocahontas, AR 72455, 870-892-4565 (Fax: 870-892-3546). 8AM-4:30PM. Enrollment: 3031. Records go back to 1991. Degrees granted: Associate. Attendance, degree and transcript information available by mail.

Central Baptist College, Registrar, 1501 College Ave, Conway, AR 72032, 501-329-6872 (Fax: 501-329-2941) www.cbc.edu. 8AM-4:30PM. Enrollment: 300. Records go back to 1952. Alumni records are maintained here. Degrees granted: Associate; Bachelors. Attendance and degree information available by phone, fax, mail. Transcripts available by fax, mail.

Crowley's Ridge College, Registrar, 100 College Dr, Paragould, AR 72450, 870-236-6901, 800-264-1096 (Fax: 870-236-7748) 8AM-5PM. www.pioneer.crc.paragould.ar.us. Enrollment: 200. Records go back to 1964. Alumni records are maintained here. Degrees granted: Associate. Special programs- Liberal Arts. Attendance and degree information available by phone, fax, mail. Transcripts available by mail.

East Arkansas Community College, Registrar, 1700 Newcastle Rd, Forrest City, AR 72335-9598, 870-633-4480 X219 (Fax: 870-633-7222) 8AM-8PM M-Th; 8AM-4:30PM F. Enrollment: 1900. Records go back to 1974. Degrees granted: Associate. Attendance and degree information available by phone, fax, mail. Transcripts available by fax, mail.

Garland County Community College, Registrar, 101 College Dr, Hot Springs, AR 71913-9174, 501-760-4222, 501-760-4210 (Fax: 501-760-4100) www.gccc.cc.ar.us. 8AM-6PM. Enrollment: 2000. Records go back to 1973. Degrees granted: Associate. Attendance and degree information available by phone, fax, mail. Transcripts available by fax, mail.

Harding University, Registrar, Box 10776, 900 E Center Ave, Searcy, AR 72149-0001, 501-279-4403, 501-279-4404 (Fax: 501-279-4388) www.harding.edu. 8AM-5PM. Enrollment: 4000. Records go back to 1924. Alumni Records: Box 768, Searcy, AR 72149-0001. Degrees granted: Associate; Bachelors; Masters. Attendance and degree information available by phone, fax, mail. Transcripts available by fax, mail.

Henderson State University, Registrar, 1100 Henderson St, Arkadelphia, AR 71999-0001, 870-230-5135, 870-230-5028 (Fax: 870-230-5144) www.hsu.edu. 8AM-5PM. Enrollment: 3614. Records go back to 1890. Alumni records maintained here; call 870-230-5401. Degrees granted: Associate; Bachelors. Special programs- Masters

Aviation Program. Attendance and degree information available by phone, fax, mail. Transcripts available by fax, mail.

Hendrix College, Registrar, 1600 Washington Ave, Conway, AR 72032-3080, 501-329-6811, 501-450-1226 (Fax: 501-450-1200) 192.131.98.11. 8AM-5PM. Enrollment: 1000. Records go back to 1886. Alumni records maintained here; call 501-450-1223. Degrees granted: Bachelors. Attendance, degree and transcript information available by fax, mail.

John Brown University, Registrar, Siloam Springs, AR 72761, 501-524-7103, 501-524-7138 (Fax: 501-524-9548) www.jbu.edu. 7:30AM-5PM. Enrollment: 1400. Records go back to 1919. Alumni records maintained here; call 501-524-7330. Degrees granted: Associate; Bachelors; Masters. Special programs- Adult Ed (Advance Program), 501-524-7259. Attendance and degree information available by phone, fax, mail. Transcripts available by fax, mail.

Lyon College, Office of the Registrar, PO Box 2317, 2300 Highland Rd, Batesville, AR 72503, 870-698-4204, 870-698-4203 (Fax: 870-698-4622) www.lyon.edu. 8AM-5PM. Enrollment: 521. Records go back to 1872. Formerly **Arkansas College**. Alumni records maintained here; call 870-698-4238. Degrees granted: Bachelors. Special programs- National Testing Information, 870-698-4327. Attendance and degree information available by phone, fax, mail. Transcripts available by mail with signature of student.

County Community College, Registrar, PO Drawer 1109, Blytheville, AR 72316, 871-762-1020 (Fax: 870-763-3704). 8AM-4:30PM. Enrollment: 1800. Records go back to 1975. Degrees granted: Associate. Attendance information available by phone, fax, mail. Degree and transcript information available by fax, mail.

Mountain Home Technical College, Registrar, 213 East 6th St, Mountain Home, AR 72653, 870-425-3949 (Fax: 870-425-4031). Enrollment: 650. Degrees granted: Associate. Attendance and degree information available by phone, fax, mail. Transcripts available by fax, mail.

North Arkansas College, Registrar, 1515 Pioneer Dr, Harrison, AR 72601, 870-743-3000, 870-391-3241 (Fax: 870-391-3339) 8AM-5PM. http://pioneer.northark.cc.ar.us. Enrollment: 1802. Records go back to 1974. Alumni records are maintained here. Degrees granted: Associate. Attendance and degree information available by phone, fax, mail. Transcripts available by fax, mail.

Northwest Arkansas Community College, Registrar, One College Dr, Bentonville, AR 72712, 501-636-9222 (Fax: 501-619-4116). 8AM-6PM M-Th; 8AM-4PM F. Enrollment: 3000. Records go back to 1990. Alumni records maintained here; call 501-619-4184. Degrees granted: Associate. Special programs- Nursing, 501-619-4257 Attendance, degree and transcript information available by fax, mail.

Ouachita Baptist University, Registrar, OBU Box 3757, Arkadelphia, AR 71998-0001, 870-245-5578 (Fax: 870-245-5500) www.obu.edu. 8AM-5PM. Enrollment: 1600. Records go back to 1940's. Alumni Records: Box 3762, Arkadelphia, AR 71998-0001. Degrees granted: Bachelors. Attendance and degree information available by phone, fax, mail. Transcripts available by fax, mail.

Petite Jean Technical College, Registrar, 1 Bruce St, Morrelton, AR 72110, 501-354-

2465 (Fax: 501-354-9948). 8:30AM-4:30PM. Enrollment: 925. Records go back to 1961. Alumni records are maintained here. Degrees granted: Associate. Attendance and degree information available by phone, mail. Transcripts available by mail.

Philander Smith College, Registrar, 812 W 13th St, Little Rock, AR 72202, 501-370-5220, 501-370-5221 (Fax: 501-370-5225). 8:30AM-5PM. Enrollment: 956. Records go back to 1989. Alumni records maintained here; call 501-370-5392. Degrees granted: Bachelors. Special programs- Degree Completion Program, 501-370-5283. Attendance and degree information available by phone, fax, mail. Transcripts available by fax, mail.

Phillips Community College (University of Arkansas), Registrar, 1000 Campus Dr, PO Box 785, Helena, AR 72342, 870-338-6474 (Fax: 870-338-7542) www.tccc.ccc.ar.us. 8AM-4:30PM. Enrollment: 2400. Records go back to 1965. Formerly **Phillips County Community College**. Degrees granted: Associate. Special programs- Nursing Program: Medical Lab Tech. Attendance and degree information available by phone, fax, mail. Transcripts available by fax, mail.

Pulaski Technical College, Registrar, 3000 W Scenic Dr, North Little Rock, AR 72118-3399, 501-771-1000, 501-812-2221 www.scenic.ptc.tec.ar.us. (Fax: 501-812-2316) 8AM-4:30PM. Enrollment: 3000. Records go back to 1945. Degrees granted: Associate. Attendance and degree information available by phone, fax, mail. Transcripts available by fax, mail.

Remington College, Registrar, 7601 Scott Hamilton Dr, Little Rock, AR 72229, 501-565-7000 www.remington.edu. Records go back to 1967. Degrees granted: Associate. Attendance and degree information available by phone, mail. Transcripts available by mail.

Rich Mountain Community College, Registrar, 1100 College Drive, Mena, AR 71953, www.rmcc.cc.ar.us. 501-394-7622 X1410 (Fax: 501-394-2760) 8AM-4:30PM. Enrollment: 765. Records go back to 1980. Alumni records maintained here; call 501-394-7622 X1220. Degrees granted: Associate. Attendance, degree and transcript information available by fax, mail.

Shorter College, Registrar, 604 Locust St, North Little Rock, AR 72114, 501-374-6305, www.shorter.edu. 501-374-6305 X214 (Fax: 501-374-9333) 8:30AM - 5pm. Enrollment: 200. Records go back to 1995. Alumni records are maintained here. Degrees granted: Associate. Attendance information available by phone, fax, mail. Degree and transcript information available by mail.

South Arkansas Community College, Registrar, PO Box 7010, El Dorado, AR 71731-7010, 870-862-8131 (Fax: 870-864-7122) 8AM-5PM. Enrollment: 1200. www.seminole.saccw.cc.ar.us. Records go back to 1975. Alumni records maintained here; call 870-862-8131. Degrees granted: Associate. Attendance and degree information available by phone, fax, mail. Transcripts available by fax, mail.

Southern Arkansas University, Registrar, SAU Box 1404, Magnolia, AR 71753, 870-235-4031 (Fax: 870-235-4931) www.saumag.edu. 8AM-5PM. Enrollment: 2745. Records go back to 1920. Alumni Records: SAU Box 1416, Magnolia, AR 71753. Degrees granted: Associate; Bachelors; Masters. Attendance and degree information available by phone, mail.

Transcripts available by mail. Will fax transcripts to other universities only.

Southern Arkansas University Tech, Registrar, SAU Tech Station, Camden, AR 71701, 870-574-4500, 870-574-4493 (Fax: 870-574-4520). 8AM-5:30PM. Enrollment: 900. Records go back to 1979. Alumni records are maintained here. Degrees granted: Associate. Attendance information available by phone, fax, mail. Degree and transcript information available by mail.

Southern Arkansas University, El Dorado Branch
(See South Arkansas Com. College)

Southern Baptist College
(See Williams Baptist College)

University of Arkansas, Registrar, Silas Hunt Hall, Fayetteville, AR 72701, 501-575-5451, 800-377-8632 (Fax: 501-575-4651) 8AM-4:30PM. www.uark.edu. Enrollment: 14900. Records go back to 1870. Formerly **University of Arkansas, Fayetteville**. Alumni records are maintained here. Degrees granted: Bachelors; Masters; Doctorate. Attendance and degree information available by phone, fax, mail. Transcripts available by fax, mail. Will fax results for verification but not for transcripts.

University of Arkansas Community College at Hope, Registrar, Highway 29 South, Hope, AR 71801, 870-777-5722 (Fax: 870-777-5957) www.uacch.cc.ar.us. 8AM-5PM. Enrollment: 1200. Records go back to 1965. Alumni records are maintained here. Degrees granted: Associate. Attendance and degree information available by phone, mail. Transcripts available by mail.

University of Arkansas at Little Rock, Registrar, 2801 S University Ave, Little Rock, AR 72204, 501-569-3110, 501-569-3127 (Fax: 501-569-8956) www.ualr.edu. 8AM-5PM. Enrollment: 10000. Records go back to 1950. Alumni records maintained

here; call 501-569-3194. Degrees granted: Associate; Bachelors; Masters; Doctorate Attendance, degree and transcript information available by fax, mail.

University of Arkansas at Monticello, Registrar, Monticello, AR 71656, 870-460-1035 (Fax: 870-460-1935) cotton.uamont.edu. 8AM-4:30PM. Enrollment: 2300. Records go back to 1950. Alumni records maintained here; call 870-460-1027. Degrees granted: Bachelors. Attendance, degree and transcript information available by fax, mail.

University of Arkansas at Pine Bluff, Registrar, 1200 N University Dr, Pine Bluff, AR 71611, 870-543-8486, 870-543-8494 (Fax: 870-543-8014) www.uapd.edu. 8AM-5PM. Enrollment: 3000. Records go back to 1923. Alumni records maintained here; call 870-543-8499. Degrees granted: Associate; Bachelors; Masters. Special programs- Fish Biology. Attendance and degree information available by phone, fax, mail. Transcripts available by fax, mail.

University of Arkansas for Medical Sciences, Registrar, 4301 W Markham St, Little Rock, AR 72205, 501-686-5000 (Fax: 501-686-8160) www.ums.edu. 8AM-4:30PM. Enrollment: 750. Records go back to 1876. Alumni records maintained here; call 501-686-6685. Degrees granted: Associate; Bachelors; Masters; Doctorate; PhD, MD, Pharm. Special programs- Nursing, 501-686-5224: Health Professions, 501-686-5730: Graduate School, 501-686-5454: College of Pharmacy, 501-686-6499. Attendance and degree information available by phone, fax, mail. Transcripts available by mail.

University of Central Arkansas, Registrar, 201 Donaghey Ave, Conway, AR 72035-0001, 501-450-5200 (Fax: 501-450-5734) www.uca.edu/registrar. 8AM-4:45PM. Enrollment: 9000. Records go back to 1908. Alumni records maintained here; call 501-450-3114. Degrees granted: Associate;

Bachelors; Masters; Ed. S. Adverse incident record source- Dean of Students, 501-450-3416. Attendance and degree information available by phone, fax, mail. Transcripts available by fax, mail.

University of the Ozarks, Registrar, 415 N College Ave, Clarksville, AR 72830, 501-979-1215, 501-979-1212 (Fax: 501-979-1355) www.ozarks.edu. 8AM-Noon,1-4:30PM. Enrollment: 563. Records go back to 1915. Alumni records maintained here; call 501-979-1237. Degrees granted: Associate; Bachelors; Masters. Attendance and degree information available by phone, fax, mail. Transcripts available by fax, mail.

Westark College, Registrar, PO Box 3649, Fort Smith, AR 72913, 501-788-7230, 501-788-7231 (Fax: 501-788-7402) www.westark.edu. 8AM-7PM M-Th, 8AM-4:30PM F. Enrollment: 5200. Records go back to 1929. Alumni records maintained here; call 501-788-7022. Degrees granted: Associate. Attendance, degree and transcript information available by mail. Will not fax out transcripts.

Williams Baptist College, Registrar, Box 3663, Walnut Ridge, AR 72476, www.wbc2.wbcoll.edu. 870-886-6741 X104 (Fax: 870-886-3924) 8AM-4:30PM Winter, 9AM-4PM Summer. Enrollment: 600. Records go back to 1941. Alumni records maintained here; call 870-886-6741. Degrees granted: Bachelors. Attendance and degree information available by phone, fax, mail. Transcripts available by mail. Will fax to confirm attendance and degree.

California

Academy of Art College, Registrar, 79 New Montgomery, San Francisco, CA 94105, 415-274-2251. 9AM-5PM. Enrollment: 4500. Records go back to 1930. Degrees granted: Bachelors. Attendance and degree information available by phone, mail. Transcripts available by mail.

Academy of Chinese Culture and Health Sciences, Registrar, 1601 Clay St, Oakland, CA 94612, 510-763-7787 (Fax: 510-834-8646) www.acchs.edu. 9AM-5PM. Enrollment: 140. Records go back to 1984. Degrees granted: Masters. Special programs- Chinese Medicine. Attendance, degree and transcript information available by fax, mail. Search requires signed release.

Allan Hancock College, Registrar, 800 S College Dr, Santa Maria, CA 93454-6399, 805-922-6966 X3248 (Fax: 805-922-3477). 8AM-6PM M-F. Enrollment: 10000. Records go back to 1954. Degrees granted: Associate. Attendance and degree information available by phone, fax, mail. Transcripts available by fax, mail.

American Academy of Dramatic Arts West, Registrar, 2550 Paloma St, Pasadena, CA 91107, 626-798-0777 (Fax: 626-798-5047) www.aada.edu. 8:30AM-5PM. Enrollment: 300. Records go back to 1975. Degrees granted: Associate. Attendance and degree information available by phone. Transcripts available by written request only.

American Baptist Seminary of the West, Registrar, 2606 Dwight Way, Berkeley, CA 94704-3029, 510-841-1905 (Fax: 510-841-2446) www.adsw.edu. 8AM-4PM. Enrollment: 81. Degrees granted: Masters. Attendance and degree information available by phone, fax, mail. Transcripts available by fax, mail.

American College of Traditional Chinese Medicine, Registrar, 455 Arkansas St, San Francisco, CA 94107, 415-282-7600 (Fax: 415-287-0856) www.actcm.org. 9AM-5PM. Enrollment: 198. Records go back to 1980. Alumni records are maintained here. Degrees granted: Masters. Certification: TCM. Special programs- Acupuncture. Attendance information available by written request only. Degree information available by fax, mail. Transcripts available by fax, mail.

American Conservatory Theater, Registrar, 30 Grant Ave, San Francisco, CA 94108, 415-834-3350 (Fax: 415-834-3300) www.act-sfbay.org. 9AM-6PM M-Th; 9AM-5PM F. Enrollment: 120. Records go back to 1972. Alumni records are maintained here. Degrees granted: Masters. Attendance and degree information available by phone, fax, mail. Transcripts available by mail.

American Film Institute Center for Advanced Film/TV Studies, Registrar, 2021 N Western Ave, Los Angeles, CA

90027, 213-856-7714, 213-856-7698 (Fax: 213-856-7720) www.afionline.org. 9AM-5:30PM. Enrollment: 288. Records go back to 1914. Alumni records maintained here; call 213-886-7680. Degrees granted: Masters. Special programs- Master of Fine Arts. . Attendance, degree and transcript information available by written request only.

American Institute of Health Sciences, Registrar, 3711 Long Beach Blvd, Suite 200, Long Beach, CA 90807, 562-988-2278 (Fax: 562-988-1791) www.aihs.edu. 8AM-5PM. Enrollment: 88. Records go back to 1994. Alumni records are maintained. Degrees granted: Associate; Bachelors. Attendance and degree information available by phone, mail. Transcripts available by mail.

American Intercontinental University (Branch), Registrar, 1651 Westwood Blvd, Los Angeles, CA 90024, 310-470-2000, 800-333-2652 (Fax: 310-477-8640). 9AM-5PM. Enrollment: 575. Records go back to 1984. Formerly **American College for the Applied Arts**. Alumni records are maintained. Degrees granted: Associate; Bachelors. Special programs- Business Administration: Visual Communications: Fashion Design: Fashion Marketing: Interior Design. Attendance and degree information available by phone, mail. Transcripts available by mail.

American River College, Registrar, 4700 College Oak Dr, Sacramento, CA 95841, 916-484-8261 www.arc.losrios.cc.ca.us. (Fax:

916-484-8864) 7:30AM-8PM M-Th, 7:30AM-5PM F. Enrollment: 20000. Records go back to 1955. Alumni records maintained here; call 916-568-3100 X8990. Degrees granted: Associate. Attendance information available by phone, fax, mail. Degree and transcript information available by fax, mail. Phone and fax inquiry limited to Enrollment.

Antelope Valley College, Registrar, 3041 W Ave K, Lancaster, CA 93536, 805-722-6332 (Fax: 805-722-6351). 8AM-4:30PM. Enrollment: 9578. Records go back to 1929. Alumni records are maintained. Degrees granted: Associate. Attendance, degree and transcript information available by mail.

Antioch University (Southern California (Los Angeles)), Registrar, 13274 Fiji Way, Marina Del Rey, CA 90292, 310-578-1080 (Fax: 310-822-4824) www.antiochla.edu. 9:30AM-7PM M-Th; 9AM-1PM F. Enrollment: 525. Records go back to 1972. Records prior to 7/85 at Administrative Headquarters; Yellow Springs, OH. Alumni records maintained here; call 310-578-1080 X115. Degrees granted: Bachelors; Masters. Special programs- Liberal Arts: Psychology: Organizational Management: Creative Writing. Attendance and degree information available by fax, mail. Transcripts available by mail. Signed student release must be faxed with inquiry.

Antioch University (Southern California), Registrar, 801 Garden St, Santa Barbara, CA 93101, 805-962-8179 (Fax: 805-962-4786) www.antiochsb.edu. 8AM-5PM M-Th; 8AM-1PM F. Enrollment: 285. Records go back to 1985. Pre-1985 records are housed at Antioch University, 795 Livermore St, Yellow Springs, OH 45387, 513-767-6401. Alumni records maintained here; call 805-962-8179 X314. Degrees granted: Bachelors; Masters. Special programs- Liberal Arts. Attendance and degree information available by phone, fax, mail. Transcripts available by mail.

Armstrong University, Registrar, 2222 Harold Way, **Berkeley**, CA 94704, 510-848-2500 (Fax: 510-835-8935) Enrollment: 250. www.armstrong.edu. Records go back to 1918. Degrees granted: Associate; Bachelors; Masters. Attendance and degree information available by phone, mail. Transcripts available by mail.

Armstrong University, Registrar, 1608 Webster St, **Oakland**, CA 94612, 510-835-7900 (Fax: 510-835-8935) 8:30AM-5:30PM.

:30PM. Enrollment: 3112. Records go back to 1913. Alumni records maintained here; call 562-903-4728. Degrees granted: Bachelors; Masters; Doctorate. Attendance and degree information available by phone, mail. Transcripts available by mail.

Brooks College, Registrar, 4825 E Pacific Coast Hwy, Long Beach, CA 90804, 562-597-6611, 562-498-2441 (Fax: 562-597-7412) 8AM-5PM. www.brookscollege.edu. Enrollment: 1041. Records go back to 1970. Alumni records are maintained here. Degrees granted: Associate. Special programs- Interior Design: Graphic Design: Fashion Design: Fashion Merchandising. Attendance, degree and transcript information available by phone, fax, mail.

Brooks Institute of Photography, Registrar, 801 Alston Rd, Santa Barbara, CA 93108, 805-966-3888 X233, 805-966-3888 X229 (Fax: 805-564-1475) www.brooks.edu. 8AM-5PM. Enrollment: 320. Records go back to 1947. Alumni records are maintained here. Degrees granted: Bachelors; Masters; Diploma; Certificates. Attendance and degree

www.armstrong.edu Enrollment: 180. Records go back to 1920. Alumni records are maintained here. Degrees granted: Associate; Bachelors; Masters. Attendance information available by phone, fax, mail. Transcripts available by mail.

Art Center College of Design, Registrar, 1700 Lida St, PO Box 7197, Pasadena, CA 91109, 626-396-2316, 626-396-2314 www.artcenter.edu (Fax: 626-568-0258 or 626-396-2209) 8:30AM-4:30PM M-Th; 8:30AM-4PM F. Enrollment: 1200. Records go back to 1930. Alumni records maintained here; call 626-396-2305. Degrees granted: Bachelors; Masters. Attendance and degree information available by phone, fax, mail. Transcripts available by mail.

Art Institute of Southern California, Registrar, 2222 Laguna Canyon Rd, Laguna Beach, CA 92651, 714-376-6000 (Fax: 714-376-6009). 8AM-5PM. Enrollment: 129. Records go back to 1979. Alumni records are maintained here. Degrees granted: Bachelors. Special programs- Call 714-376-6000 X233. Attendance and degree information available by mail. Transcripts available by mail.

Arts Institute International, Registrar, 101 Jessie St, San Francisco, CA 94105-3593, 415-974-6666 (Fax: 415-982-0113). 9AM-5PM. Enrollment: 100. Records go back to 1939. Formerly **Louise Salinger Academy of Fashion**. Degrees granted: Associate; Bachelors. Special programs- Fashion Design and Merchandising. Attendance and degree information available by phone, fax, mail. Transcripts available by fax, mail.

Azusa Pacific University, Registrar, 901 E Alosta, Azusa, CA 91702-7000, 626-969-3434 X3013 (Fax: 626-812-3011) www.apu.edu. 8:30AM-5PM M-Th; 8:30AM-4:30PM F; Closed 9:30-10:30AM M,W,F. Enrollment: 5000. Records go back to 1880. Alumni records maintained here; call 818-812-3026. Degrees granted: Bachelors; Masters; Doctorate. Attendance and degree information available by phone, fax, mail. Transcripts available by mail.

Bakersfield College, Registrar, 1801 Panorama Dr, Bakersfield, CA 93305, 805-395-4011 (Fax: 805-395-4230) www.bc.kern.cc.ca.us. 8AM-7PM M-Th, 8AM-4:30PM F. Enrollment: 12510. Records go back to 1913. Alumni records are maintained here. Degrees granted: Associate.

information available by phone, fax, mail. Transcripts available by fax, mail.

Brooks Institute of Technology
   (See Brooks Institute of Photography)

Bryman College, Registrar, 3208 Rosemeade Blvd, El Monte, CA 91731, 626-573-5470 X171 (Fax: 626-280-4011). 9AM-5PM. Enrollment: 500. Records go back to 1970. Formerly **National Education Center (Bryman)**. Alumni records are maintained. Degrees granted. Certification: Medical, Dental, Business. Attendance, degree and transcript information available by fax, mail.

Butte College, Registrar, 3536 Butte Campus Dr, Oroville, CA 95965, 530-895-2361 (Admissions & Records), 530-895-2511 (Fax: 530-895-2411). 8:30AM-4PM. Enrollment: 12000. Records go back to 1974. Degrees granted: Associate. Attendance, degree and transcript information available by fax, mail.

Cabrillo College, Director, Admissions & Records, 6500 Soquel Dr, Aptos, CA 95003, www.cabrillo.cc.ca.us. 408-479-6201 (Fax: 408-479-5782) 8AM-7:30PM M-Th, 8AM-

Attendance, degree and transcript information available by mail.

Barstow College, Registrar, 2700 Barstow Rd, Barstow, CA 92311, 760-252-2411 (Fax: 760-252-1875) www.barstow.cc.ca.us. 8AM-5PM. Enrollment: 1709. Records go back to 1964. Degrees granted: Associate. Attendance and degree information available by fax, mail. Transcripts available by mail.

Bethany College of the Assemblies of God, Registrar, 800 Bethany Dr, Scotts Valley, CA 95066, 408-438-3800 X1444 (Fax: 408-438-1621) www.bethany.edu. 8AM-5PM. Enrollment: 550. Records go back to 1919. Alumni records maintained here; call 408-438-3800 X1470. Degrees granted: Associate; Bachelors; Masters. Special programs- Teacher Education, 408-438-3800 X1503: Cert Program in Addiction Counseling, 408-438-3800X1521. Attendance information available by phone, fax, mail. Degree information available by phone, fax, mail. Transcripts available by fax, mail.

Bethel Seminary — San Diego, Registrar, 6116 Arosa St, San Diego, CA 92115, 619-582-8188, 800-238-4352 (Fax: 619-265-1714) www.bethel.edu. 8AM-5PM. Enrollment: 150. Records go back to 1977. Alumni Records: Alumni Assoc., 3900 Bethel Dr, St Paul, MN 55112. Degrees granted: Masters; Doctorate. Attendance and degree information available by phone, mail. Transcripts available by mail.

Bethesda Christian University, Registrar, 730 North Euclid St, Anaheim, CA 92805, 714-517-1945 (Fax: 714-517-1948) 8:30AM-4:30PM. Enrollment: 200. Records go back to 1976. Alumni records are maintained here. Degrees granted: Associate. Attendance and degree information available by phone, mail. Transcripts available by mail.

Biola University, Registrar, 13800 Biola Ave, La Mirada, CA 90639, 562-903-4720 (Fax: 562-903-4748) www.biola.edu. 8AM-4

5PM F. Enrollment: 13500. Records go back to 1959. Alumni records are maintained here also. Call 408-479-6100. Degrees granted: Associate. Attendance, degree and transcript information available by fax, mail. Signed release required if student does not want directory information released.

California Baptist College, Registrar, 8432 Magnolia Ave, Riverside, CA 92504, 909-689-5771 X222, 909-343-4222 (Fax: 909-343-4539). 8AM-5PM. Enrollment: 2000. Alumni records maintained here; call 909-343-4226. Degrees granted: Bachelors; Masters. Certification: Athletic Training, Church Business, Church Growth, Church Music, Computer (Bus. Applications, Programming), Public Administration. Attendance information available by phone, fax, mail. Transcripts available by fax, mail. Signed release for 3rd party only.

California College for Health Sciences, Registrar, 222 W 24th St, National City, CA 91950-9998, 619-477-4800 X320, 619-477-4800 X355 (Fax: 619-477-4360) www.cchs.edu. 8AM-5PM. Enrollment: 9000. Records go back to 1978. Degrees granted: Associate; Bachelors; Masters. Attendance and degree information available by phone, fax, mail. Transcripts available by fax, mail.

California College of Arts and Crafts, Registrar, 5212 Broadway, Oakland, CA 94618, 510-594-3600, 510-594-3641 (Registrar) (Fax: 510-594-1941). 8AM-4:30PM. Enrollment: 1120. Records go back to 1907. Alumni records maintained here; call 415-703-9540. Attendance and degree information available by phone, fax, mail. Transcripts available by fax, mail.

California College of Podiatric Medicine, Registrar, 1210 Scott St, San Francisco, CA 94115, 415-292-0414, www.ccpm.edu 415-292-0562 (Fax: 415-292-0439) 9AM-5:30PM. Enrollment: 414. Records go back to 1916. Alumni records maintained here; call 415-292-0484. Degrees granted: Doctorate; DPM. Attendance information available by phone, fax, mail. Degree and transcript information available by fax, mail.

California Culinary Academy, Registrar, 625 Polk St, San Francisco, CA 94102-3368, 415-771-3536 (Fax: 415-771-2194) www.baychef.com. Enrollment: 700. Records go back to 1982. Degrees granted: Associate. Attendance and degree information available by phone, fax, mail. Transcripts available by fax, mail.

California Design College, Registrar, 3440 Wilshire Blvd, Los Angeles, CA 90010, 213-251-3636 (Fax: 213-385-3545) Enrollment: 300. Records go back to 1991. Degrees granted: Associate. Attendance and degree information available by phone, fax. Transcripts available by fax, mail.

California Institute of Integral Studies, Registrar, 9 Peter Yorke Way, San Francisco, CA 94109, 415-674-5500 X207, 415-674-5500 X209 www.ciis.edu. 10AM-5PM. Alumni records maintained here; call 415-674-5500 X227. Degrees granted: Bachelors; Masters; Doctorate. Certification: ODT, EXA. Attendance and degree information available by phone, fax, mail. Transcripts available by mail.

California Institute of Technology, Registrar, 1200 E California Blvd, Pasadena, CA 91125, 626-395-6354 (Fax: 626-577-4215) www.caltech.edu. 8AM-Noon, 1:00-5PM. Enrollment: 2000. Records go back to 1940. Alumni Records: 345 S Hill Ave, Pasadena, CA 91125. Degrees granted: Bachelors; Masters; Doctorate. Attendance and degree information available by phone, fax, mail. Transcripts available by mail.

California Institute of the Arts, Registrar, 24700 McBean Pkwy, Valencia, CA 91355, 805-253-7843 (Fax: 805-254-8352) www.calarts.edu. 8:30AM-4PM. Enrollment: 1030. Records go back to 1930. Alumni records maintained here; call 805-255-1050 X2749. Degrees granted: Bachelors; Masters. Attendance and degree information available by phone, fax, mail. Transcripts available by fax, mail.

California Lutheran University, Registrar, 60 W Olsen Rd, Thousand Oaks, CA 91360, 805-493-3105 (Fax: 805-493-3104) www.clunet.edu. 8:15AM-7PM M; 8:15AM-5PM T-F. Enrollment: 3000. Records go back to 1959. Alumni records maintained here; call 805-493-3170. Degrees granted: Bachelors; Masters. Attendance and degree information available by phone, mail. Transcripts available by mail.

California Maritime Academy, Registrar, 200 Maritime Academy Dr, PO Box 1392, Vallejo, CA 94590-0644, 707-648-4262,

707-649-3603 (Fax: 707-649-4773) www.csum.edu. 9AM-4:30PM. Enrollment: 400. Records go back to 1920. Alumni records maintained here; call 707-648-5386. Degrees granted: Bachelors. Attendance and degree information available by phone, fax, mail, Transcripts available by mail.

California Polytechnic State University, San Luis Obispo, Academic Records, San Luis Obispo, CA 93407, 805-756-2531 www.ess.calpoly.edu/_records/ (Fax: 805-756-7237) 10AM-4PM. Enrollment: 16500. Records go back to 1901. Alumni records maintained here; call 805-756-2586. Degrees granted: Associate; Bachelors; Masters. Attendance and degree information available by phone, mail. Transcripts available by mail. Mail request requires signed release.

California School of Professional Psychology, Alameda, Registrar, 1005 Atlantic Ave, Alameda, CA 94501, 510-523-2300 (Fax: 510-521-0728) www.cspp.edu/. 9AM-5PM. Enrollment: 800. Records go back to 1970. Degrees granted: Masters; Doctorate. Attendance, degree and transcript information available by fax, mail.

California School of Professional Psychology, Fresno, Registrar, 5130 E Clinton Way, Fresno, CA 93727, 209-456-2777 X2157 (Fax: 209-253-2267) www.cspp.edu. 9AM-4:30PM. Enrollment: 400. Records go back to 1973. Alumni Records: 1000 S Fremont, Alhambra, CA 91803-1360. Degrees granted: Masters; Doctorate. Special programs- Clinical Psychology: Forensic Psychology: Organizational Behavior. Attendance and degree information available by fax, mail. Transcripts available by mail.

California School of Professional Psychology, Los Angeles, Registrar, 1000 S Fremont Ave, Alhambra, CA 91803-1360, 626-284-2777 (Fax: 626-284-0550). 8:30AM-4PM. Enrollment: 740. Records go back to 1969. Alumni records are maintained. Degrees granted: Doctorate. Attendance and degree information available by phone, fax, mail. Transcripts available by mail.

California School of Professional Psychology, San Diego, Registrar, 6160 Cornerstone Ct E, San Diego, CA 92121-3725, 619-623-2777 (Fax: 619-552-1974). 8:30AM-5:00PM. Enrollment: 630. Records go back to 1971. Alumni records are maintained here. Degrees granted: Masters; Doctorate. Certification: Doctoral Respecialization. Attendance and degree information available by fax, mail. Transcripts available by mail. Requests must be accompanied by "release of info" form.

California State Polytechnic University, Pomona, Registrar, 3801 W Temple Ave, Pomona, CA 91768, 909-869-7659 (Fax: 909-869-6828) www.csupomona.edu. 8AM-5PM. Alumni records maintained here; call 909-869-2963. Degrees granted: Bachelors; Masters. Attendance and degree information available by phone, fax, mail. Transcripts available by mail.

California State University, Bakersfield, Registrar, 9001 Stockdale Hwy, Bakersfield, CA 93311-1099, 805-664-2147, 805-664-3405 (Fax: 805-664-3389) www.csubak.edu. 8AM-5PM. Enrollment: 5300. Records go back to 1970. Alumni records maintained here; call 805-664-3211. Degrees granted: Bachelors; Masters. Attendance and degree information available by fax, mail. Transcripts available by written request only, requested by the student.

California State University, Chico, Admissions & Records, 180 - Meriam Library, Chico, CA 95929-0220, 530-898-5143 www.csuchico.edu (Fax: 530-898-4359) 8AM-5PM Office; 9AM-4PM Phone. Enrollment: 12625. Records go back to 1927. Alumni records maintained here; call 530-898-6472. Degrees granted: Bachelors; Masters. Attendance and degree information available by phone, mail. Transcripts available by mail.

California State University, Dominguez Hills, Registrar, 1000 E Victoria St, Carson, CA 90747, 310-243-3300, 310-243-2052 (records) www.csudh.edu (Fax: 310-516-4573) 8AM-6PM M-Th; 8AM-Noon F. Enrollment: 13000. Records go back to 1960. Alumni Records: Alumni Relations, 1000 E Victoria St, ERCG-521, Carson, CA 90747. Degrees granted: Bachelors; Masters. Attendance and degree information available by phone, fax, mail. Transcripts available by mail.

California State University, Fresno, Registrar, 5150 N Maple Ave, M/S 57, Fresno, CA 93740-8026, 209-278-2191, 209-278-6067 www.csufresno.edu (Fax: 209-278-4812) 8AM-5PM. Enrollment: 17500. Records go back to 1911. Alumni Records: Alumni Assoc., Keats Bldg, Rm 113 M/S 124, Fresno, CA 93740-8023 (Fax: 209-278-6790). Degrees granted: Bachelors; Masters; Doctorate. Attendance information available by fax, mail. Attendance, degree and transcript information available by fax, mail.

California State University, Fullerton, Registrar, PO Box 6900, Fullerton, CA 92834-6900, 714-278-2011, 714-278-2300 (Admissions & Records) 8AM-5PM. admrec.fullerton.edu. Enrollment: 4205. Alumni records maintained here; call 714-278-2586. Degrees granted: Bachelors; Masters. Attendance and degree information available by phone, fax, mail. Transcripts available by mail.

California State University, Hayward, Registrar, 25800 Carlos Bee Blvd, Hayward, CA 94542, 510-885-3075 (Fax: 510-885-3816) www.csuhayward.edu. 8AM-5PM. Enrollment: 10650. Records go back to 1960. Alumni records maintained here; call 510-885-3724. Degrees granted: Bachelors; Masters. Attendance and degree information available by phone, fax, mail. Transcripts available by mail.

California State University, Long Beach, Records Transcripts, 1250 Bellflower Blvd, Long Beach, CA 90840, 562-985-5487, 562-985-5471 (Fax: 562-985-4973) www.csulb.edu. Enrollment: 25205. Records go back to 1949. Alumni records maintained here; call 562-985-5299. Degrees granted: Bachelors; Masters. Attendance and degree information available by phone, fax, mail. Transcripts available by mail.

California State University, Los Angeles, Registrar, 5151 State University Dr, Los Angeles, CA 90032, 213-343-3940, 213-343-3853 (Fax: 213-343-3840) www.calstatela.edu. 10AM-5PM M-Th; 10AM-Noon F. Records go back to 1965. Degrees granted: Bachelors; Masters; Doctorate. Attendance and degree information available by phone, mail. Transcripts available by mail.

California State University, Northridge, Admissions & Records, 18111 Nordhoff St, Northridge, CA 91330, www.csun.edu. 818-677-3700, 818-677-3000 (Fax: 818-677-3766) 8AM-5PM M & Th; 10AM-7PM T&W; 8AM-4PM F; Phone 7AM-5PM.

Enrollment: 26000. Records go back to 1957. Alumni Records: Alumni Assoc., 9528 Etiwanda, Northridge, CA 91330. Degrees granted: Bachelors; Masters. Attendance and degree information available by fax, mail. Transcripts available by mail. Release may be required if student requested confidentiality.

California State University, Sacramento, Admissions & Records, 6000 J St, Sacramento, CA 95819-6048, 916-278-7111 (undergraduate), 916-278-6011 (Fax: 916-278-5603) www.csus.edu. 8AM-5PM. Enrollment: 23000. Records go back to 1949. Alumni Records: 7750 College Town Dr #203, Sacramento, CA 95826. Degrees granted: Bachelors; Masters. Attendance and degree information available by phone, fax, mail. Transcripts available by mail.

California State University, San Bernardino, Registrar, 5500 State University Pkwy, San Bernardino, CA 92407-2397, 909-880-5200 (Fax: 909-880-7021) www.csusb.edu. 8AM-6PM M-Th; 8AM-5PM F. Records go back to 1970's. Alumni records maintained here; call 909-880-5008. Degrees granted: Bachelors; Masters. Attendance and degree information available by phone, fax, mail. Transcripts available by fax, mail. Transcript request requires a special form.

California State University, San Marcos, Registration & Records, San Marcos, CA 92096-0001, 760-750-4814 (Fax: 760-750-3700) www.csusm.edu. 9AM-5PM. Enrollment: 4500. Records go back to 1990. Alumni records maintained here; call 760-750-4409. Degrees granted: Bachelors; Masters; Teaching Credential. Attendance and degree information available by phone, fax, mail. Transcripts available by mail.

California State University, Stanislaus, Registrar, 801 W Monte Vista Ave, Turlock, CA 95382, 209-667-3264 (Fax: 209-667-3788) lead.csustan.edu. 8AM-5PM. Enrollment: 6100. Records go back to 1960. Alumni records maintained here; call 209-667-3131. Degrees granted: Bachelors; Masters. Special programs- Call 209-667-3264. Attendance and degree information available by phone, fax, mail. Transcripts available by mail.

California Western School of Law, Registrar's Office, 225 Cedar St, San Diego, CA 92101, 619-525-1414 (Fax: 619-525-7092) www.cwsl.edu. 8AM-5PM. Records go back to 1962. Alumni records maintained here; call 619-239-0391 X7644. Attendance and degree information available by phone, fax, mail. Transcripts available by fax, mail. Signed release may be necessary.

Canada College, Dottie Shiloh, 4200 Farm Hill Blvd, Redwood City, CA 94061, www.smcccd.cc.ca.us/smcccd/canada/canada.htm. 650-306-3124 (Fax: 650-306-3475) 8AM-8:15PM M-Th; 8AM-4:30PM F. Enrollment: 5710. Records go back to 1968. Degrees granted: Associate. Attendance and degree information available by phone, fax, mail. Transcripts available by fax, mail.

Cerritos College, Registrar, 11110 Alondra Blvd, Norwalk, CA 90650, 562-860-2451 X2118 www.cerritos.edu (Fax: 562-467-5005) 8AM-9PM M-Th, 8AM-4:30PM F. Records go back to 1955. Alumni records maintained here; call 562-860-2451. Degrees granted: Associate. Attendance and degree information available by phone, mail. Transcripts available by mail.

Cerro Coso Community College, Registrar, 3000 College Heights Blvd, Ridgecrest, CA 93555-7777, 760-384-6357,

760-384-6358 (Fax: 760-375-4776) wwwcc.ca.us. 8AM-7PM M-Th; 8AM-4PM F. Enrollment: 6000. Records go back to 1973. Alumni records maintained here; call 760-384-6230. Degrees granted: Associate. Attendance and degree information available by phone, fax, mail. Transcripts available by fax, mail.

Chabot College, Registrar, 25555 Hesperian Blvd, Hayward, CA 94545, 510-786-6703, 510-786-6605 (Fax: 510-732-0212) www.clpccdca.us. 8AM-8PM M-Th, 8AM-1PM F. Enrollment: 13500. Records go back to 1960. Alumni records maintained here; call 510-786-6600; 485-5214 (alumni foundation). Degrees granted: Associate. Attendance and degree information available by phone, fax, mail. Transcripts available by mail.

Chaffey College, 5885 Haven Ave, Rancho Cucamonga, CA 91737, 909-941-2483, 909-941-2483 X2645 (Records) www.chaffeyca.us. 8AM-7PM M-Th; 8AM-4PM F. Enrollment: 13500. Records go back to 1950. Alumni records maintained here; call 909-987-2152. Degrees granted: Associate. Attendance, degree and transcript information available by mail.

Chapman University, Registrar, 333 N Glassell St, Orange, CA 92866, 714-997-6701 (Fax: 714-997-6986) www.chapman.edu. 8AM-4:30PM. Enrollment: 5600. Records go back to 1958. Alumni records are maintained here also. Call 714-997-6783. Degrees granted: Associate; Bachelors; Masters; Teaching Credential. Attendance and degree information available by phone, mail. Transcripts available by mail.

Charles R. Drew University of Medicine and Science, Registrar, 1731 E 120th St, Los Angeles, CA 90059, 213-563-9326 (Registrar), 213-563-4800 (Main) (Fax: 213-569-0597) www.cdrewu.edu. 8AM-5PM. Enrollment: 625. Records go back to 1966. Alumni records are maintained. Degrees granted: Doctorate. Attendance information available by phone, fax, mail. Degree and transcript information available by fax, mail.

Christ College Irvine
(See Concordia University (Irvine))

Christian Heritage College, Registrar, 2100 Greenfield Dr, El Cajon, CA 92019, 619-590-1784, 619-441-2200 (Fax: 619-440-0209). 8:30AM-3PM. Enrollment: 575. Records go back to 1977. Alumni records maintained here; call 619-590-1750. Degrees granted: Bachelors. Special programs- CLIMB (Adult Degree Completion), 619-590-1719. Attendance and degree information available by phone, fax, mail. Transcripts available by mail.

Church Divinity School of the Pacific, Registrar, 2451 Ridge Rd, Berkeley, CA 94709-1211, 510-204-0715 (Fax: 510-644-0712) http://cdsp.edu. 8AM-4PM. Enrollment: 110. Records go back to 1920's. Alumni records maintained here; call 510-204-0745. Degrees granted: Masters. Attendance and degree information available by fax, mail. Transcripts available by mail.

Citrus College, Registrar, 1000 W Foothill Blvd, Glendora, CA 91741-1899, 626-914-8511 (Fax: 626-914-8823) www.citrusca.us. 8AM-8PM M-Th, 8AM-4PM F. Enrollment: 11000. Records go back to 1915. Alumni records maintained here; call 626-963-0323. Degrees granted: Associate. Attendance and degree information available by phone, fax, mail. Transcripts available by mail.

City College of San Francisco, Registrar, 50 Phelan Ave, San Francisco, CA 94112, 415-239-3838 (Fax: 415-239-3936) www.ccsfca.us. 8AM-7:30PM M-Th; 8AM-4PM F. Enrollment: 75000. Records go back to 1935. Degrees granted: Associate. Attendance, degree and transcript information available by fax, mail. Information may be requested by the student or a legal representative with student's signed release.

Claremont Graduate University, Registrar's Office, 170 E 10th St, Claremont, CA 91711, 909-621-8285, 909-607-3370 (Fax: 909-607-7285) www.cgu.edu. 8:30AM-5PM. Enrollment: 200. Records go back to 1925. Alumni records maintained here; call 909-621-8204. Degrees granted: Masters; Doctorate. Attendance and degree information available by phone, fax, mail. Transcripts available by written request only.

Claremont McKenna College (Bauer Center), Registrar, 500 E 9th St, Claremont, CA 91711-6400, 909-621-8101 (Fax: 909-607-6015) www.mckenna.edu. 8AM-5PM. Enrollment: 950. Records go back to 1946. Alumni Records: Alumni Assoc., 850 Columbia Ave, Claremont, CA 91711-6400. Degrees granted: Bachelors. Attendance and degree information available by phone, fax, mail. Transcripts available by mail.

Claremont School of Theology, Registrar, 1325 N College Ave, Claremont, CA 91711-3199, 909-626-3521 (Fax: 909-626-7062) www.cst.edu. 8:30AM-Noon, 1-5PM. Enrollment: 430. Records go back to 1965. Alumni records are maintained. Degrees granted: Masters; Doctorate. Attendance and degree information available by phone, fax, mail. Transcripts available by fax, mail.

Cleveland Chiropractic College, Registrar, 590 N Vermont Ave, Los Angeles, CA 90004, 213-660-6166 X58 (Fax: 213-660-3190) www.cccla.edu. 7AM-3:30PM. Enrollment: 531. Records go back to 1908. Alumni records are maintained. Degrees granted: Bachelors; Doctorate; Doctor of Chiropractic. Attendance and degree information available by fax, mail. Transcripts available by written request only.

Coastline Community College, Registrar, 11460 Warner Ave, Fountain Valley, CA 92708, 714-241-6168 (Fax: 714-241-6288) http://coastline.cccd.edu. 8AM-6:30PM M-Th, 8AM-2PM F. Records go back to 1976. Degrees granted: Associate. Attendance and degree information available by phone, fax, mail. Transcripts available by fax, mail.

Cogswell Polytechnical College, Registrar, 1175 Bordeaux Dr, Sunnyvale, CA 94089-1299, 408-541-0100 X110 (Fax: 408-747-0764) www.cogswell.edu. 9AM-5:45PM. Enrollment: 500. Records go back to 1956. Formerly **Cogswell College**. Alumni records are maintained here. Degrees granted: Bachelors. Attendance and degree information available by phone, fax, mail. Transcripts available by fax, mail; information available to employers only.

Coleman College, Registrar, 7380 Parkway Dr, La Mesa, CA 91942-1500, 619-476-3990 (Fax: 619-463-0162) www.coleman.edu. 9AM-8PM M-Th. Enrollment: 1100. Records go back to 1963. Alumni records are maintained here. Degrees granted: Associate; Bachelors; Masters; Certificates. Attendance and degree information available by phone, fax, mail. Transcripts available by fax, mail.

College of Alameda, Registrar, 555 Atlantic Ave, Alameda, CA 94501, 510-748-2228 (Fax: 510-769-6019) www.peraltdca.us.

9AM-7 M,T; 8AM-4:30PM W-F. Enrollment: 5595. Records go back to 1974. Alumni records maintained here; call 510-522-7221. Degrees granted: Associate. Attendance information available by phone, fax, mail. Degree information available by fax, mail. Transcripts available by mail. Phone requests accepted if signed release is faxed or on file.

College of Marin, Registrar, 835 College Ave, Kentfield, CA 94904, 415-457-8811 8AM-5PM. www.marin.cc.ca.us. Enrollment: 8847. Records go back to 1952. Alumni records are maintained here. Degrees granted: Associate. Special programs- Dental Assisting: Nursing. Attendance and degree information available by phone, mail. Transcripts available by mail.

College of Marin, Admissions, 1800 Ignacio Blvd, Novato, CA 94949, 415-883-2211, 415-485-9417 www.marin.cc.ca.us. 9AM-3PM M-Th; 9AM-Noon F. Enrollment: 8500. Records go back to 1926. Alumni records are maintained here. Degrees granted: Associate. Attendance and degree information available by mail. Transcripts available by written request only.

College of Notre Dame, Registrar's Office, 1500 Ralston Ave, Belmont, CA 94002, 415-508-3521 (Fax: 415-508-3736) www.cnd.edu. 8:30AM-7PM M-Th; 8:30AM-4PM F. Enrollment: 1725. Records go back to 1851. Alumni records maintained here; call 415-508-3510. Degrees granted: Associate; Bachelors; Masters. Attendance and degree information available by phone, fax, mail. Transcripts available by mail.

College of Oceaneering, Registrar, Los Angeles Harbor, 272 S Fries Ave, Wilmington, CA 90744, 310-834-2501 (Fax: 310-834-7132). 7:30AM-4:30PM. Enrollment: 400. Records go back to 1976. Alumni records are maintained here. Degrees granted: Associate. Attendance and degree information available by fax, mail. Transcripts available by mail.

College of Osteopathic Medicine of the Pacific
(See Western Univ. of Health Sciences)

College of San Mateo, Registrar, 1700 W Hillsdale Blvd, San Mateo, CA 94402, www.smccd.cc.ca.us/csm/csm. 650-574-6165 (Fax: 650-574-6506) 8AM-10PM M-Th; 8AM-4:30PM F. Records go back to 1922. Alumni records maintained here; call 650-574-6141. Degrees granted: Associate. Attendance and degree information available by phone, fax, mail. Transcripts available by mail.

College of the Canyons, Admissions and Records Office, 26455 N Rockwell Canyon Rd, Santa Clarita, CA 91355, 805-259-7900 (Fax: 805-259-8302) www.coc.cc.ca.us. 9AM-7PM M-Th. Enrollment: 7272. Records go back to 1969. Alumni records are maintained. Degrees granted: Associate. Attendance and degree information available by phone, fax, mail. Transcripts available by mail.

College of the Desert, Registrar, 43-500 Monterey Ave, Palm Desert, CA 92260, 760-773-2518 (Fax: 760-776-0136) www.desert.cc.ca.us. 8:30AM-7PM M-Th; 8:30AM-3PM F. Enrollment: 10000. Records go back to 1963. Alumni records maintained here; call 760-773-2567. Degrees granted: Associate. Attendance information available by written request only. Degree information available by phone, fax, mail. Transcripts available by mail.

College of the Redwoods, Dir, Admissions & Records, Attn: Transcripts, 7351 Tompkins Hill Rd, Eureka, CA 95501, 707-445-6711, 707-445-6700 (Fax: 707-445-6990) 8:30AM-7PM M-Th; 8:30AM-4PM F. www.redwoods.cc.ca.us. Enrollment: 7000. Records go back to 1965. Alumni records maintained here; call 707-445-6992. Degrees granted: Associate. Attendance, degree and transcript information available by fax, mail. With signed release attendance and degree information may be faxed.

College of the Sequoias, Student Records Ofc, 915 S Mooney Blvd, Visalia, CA 93277, 209-730-3775 (Fax: 209-730-3894). 8:30AM-4PM. Enrollment: 9000. Records go back to 1922. Alumni records maintained here; call 209-730-3861. Degrees granted: Associate. Attendance and degree information available by phone, fax, mail. Transcripts available by fax, mail. Will not fax transcripts.

College of the Siskiyous, Registrar, 800 College Ave, Weed, CA 96094, 916-938-5215 (Fax: 916-938-5367) 9AM-3PM. www.siskiyous.edu Enrollment: 2774. Records go back to 1957. Alumni records maintained here; call 916-938-5373. Degrees granted: Associate. Attendance, degree and transcript information available by fax, mail.

Columbia College, Admissions and Records, 11600 Columbia College Dr, Sonora, CA 95370-8582, 209-588-5231, 209-588-5233 www.yosemite.cc.ca.us/columbia (Fax: 209-588-5330) 8AM-6:30PM M-Th; 8AM-4:30PM F. Enrollment: 3000. Records go back to 1968. Degrees granted: Associate. Certification: Vocational. Attendance, degree and transcript information available by fax, mail.

Columbia College Hollywood, Registrar, 18618 Oxnard St, Tarzana, CA 91356-1411, 818-345-8414 (Fax: 818-345-9053) 8AM-4:30PM. www.columbiacollege.edu Enrollment: 210. Records go back to 1952. Degrees granted: Associate. Attendance, degree and transcript information available by phone, fax, mail. Transcript information released by phone to student only.

Compton Community College, Admissions and Records Coordinator, 1111 E Artesia Blvd, Compton, CA 90221, 310-900-1600 www.compton.cc.ca.us (Fax: 310-900-1695) 8AM-7PM M-W; 8AM-4:30PM Th-F. Enrollment: 5000. Records go back to 1929. Alumni records are maintained. Degrees granted: Associate. Attendance and degree information available by phone, fax, mail. Transcripts available by mail.

Computer Learning Center, Registrar, 222 S Harbour Blvd, Anaheim, CA 92805, 714-956-8060 (Fax: 714-776-2102) www.clcx.com. Enrollment: 500. Records go back to 1990. Degrees granted: Associate. Attendance and degree information available by phone, mail. Transcripts available by mail.

Computer Learning Center, Registrar, 3130 Wilshire Blvd, Los Angeles, CA 90010, 213-386-6311 (Fax: 213-384-9744) www.clcx.com. Enrollment: 450. Records go back to 1990. Degrees granted: Associate. Attendance and degree information available by phone, mail. Transcripts available by mail.

Concorde Career Institute, Registrar, 1717 S Brookhurst St, Anaheim, CA 92804-6461, 714-635-3450 (Fax: 714-535-3168) 8AM-5PM. Enrollment: 550. Records go back to 1968. Degrees granted: Associate. Special programs- Medical Assistant. Attendance and degree information available by phone, mail. Transcripts available by mail.

Concorde Career Institute, Registrar, 4150 Lanhershim Blvd, North Hollywood, CA 91602-2896, 818-766-8151 (Fax: 818-766-1587) 8AM-5PM. Enrollment: 600. Records go back to 1973. Degrees granted: Associate. Special programs- Respiratory Therapy Surgical. Attendance and degree information available by phone, mail. Transcripts available by mail.

Concorde Career Institute, Registrar, 570 W Fourth St, Suite 107, San Bernardino, CA 92416, 909-884-8891 (Fax: 909-384-1768) 8AM-5PM. Enrollment: 850. Records go back to 1968. Degrees granted: Associate. Attendance and degree information available by phone, mail. Transcripts available by mail.

Concordia University, Registrar, 1530 Concordia W, Irvine, CA 92715-3299, 714-854-8002 (Fax: 714-854-6854). 8AM-4:30PM. Enrollment: 1500. Records go back to 1978. Formerly **Christ College**. Alumni records are maintained here. Degrees granted: Associate; Bachelors; Masters. Certification: Lutheran Teaching; Director of Christian Education. Attendance, degree and transcript information available by fax, mail.

Consortium of California State University
(See California State University-Statewide Nursing Program)

Contra Costa College, Registrar, 2600 Mission Bell Dr, San Pablo, CA 94806, www.contracosta.cc.ca.us. 510-235-7800 X382 (Fax: 510-236-6768) 8AM-4:30PM M-F; 5:30-8:30PM M-Th. Enrollment: 8500. Records go back to 1950. Alumni records are maintained here. Degrees granted: Associate. Attendance and degree information available by phone, mail. Transcripts available by mail. Transcript request form in A&R office.

Cosumnes River College, Admissions & Records, 8401 Center Pkwy, Sacramento, CA 95823, 916-688-7410 (Fax: 916-688-7467) www.crc.losrios.cc.ca.us. 8AM-8PM M-Th; 8AM-5PM F. Enrollment: 12000. Records go back to 1970. Alumni records are maintained here. Degrees granted: Associate. Attendance, degree and transcript information available by fax, mail.

Crafton Hills College, Registrar, 11711 Sand Canyon Rd, Yucaipa, CA 92399, 909-389-3372 (Fax: 909-389-9141). 8AM-8PM M-Th; 8AM-4:30PM F. Enrollment: 5200. Records go back to 1972. Alumni records maintained here; call 909-389-3300. Degrees granted: Associate. Attendance and degree information available by phone, fax, mail. Transcripts available by fax, mail.

Cuesta College, Records Office Rm 3110, Hwy 1, San Luis Obispo, CA 93403, 805-546-3139, 805-546-3100 X2253 (Fax: 805-546-3904) www.Bass.CuestaCA.US. 9AM-4PM M-Th; 9AM-3PM F. Enrollment: 8000. Records go back to 1965. Alumni records are maintained here also. Call 805-546-3915. Degrees granted: Associate. Attendance and degree information available by phone, fax, mail. Transcripts available by fax, mail.

Cuyamaca College, Associate Dean of Admissions and Records, 900 Rancho San Diego Parkway, El Cajon, CA 92019, 619-670-1980 www.gcccd.cc.ca.us/cuyamaca. (Fax: 619-660-4399) 8AM-7PM M-Th; 8AM-4:30PM F; 9AM-1PM S. Enrollment: 6050. Records go back to 1978. Alumni records maintained here; call 619-670-1980. Degrees granted: Associate. Special programs- Weekend College, 619-735-4351: Telecourse 619-660-4444. Attendance, degree and transcript information available by mail.

Cypress College, Registrar, 9200 Valley View St, Cypress, CA 90630, 714-826-2220 (Fax: 714-826-4224) 198.120.22.12. 8AM-7PM M-Th; 8AM-1PM F. Enrollment: 14600. Records go back to 1966. Degrees granted: Associate. Attendance and degree information available by phone, mail. Transcripts available by written request only.

D-Q University, Registrar, PO Box 409, Davis, CA 95617-0409, 530-758-0470 (Fax: 530-758-4891) www.wheel.dcn.davis.ca.us/go/dquaaa/. 8AM-5PM. Enrollment: 535. Records go back to 1971. Alumni records are maintained here. Degrees granted: Associate. Attendance and degree information available by phone, fax, mail. Transcripts available by fax, mail.

De Anza College, Registrar, 21250 Stevens Creek Blvd, Cupertino, CA 95014-5793, www.deanza.fhda.edu 408-864-5300 (Fax: 408-864-8329) 8AM-7:30PM M-Th; 8AM-3PM F (Summer: closed Fri.). Enrollment: 25000. Records go back to 1967. Degrees granted: Associate. Attendance, degree and transcript information available by mail.

DeVry Institute of Technology, Registrar's Office, 901 Corporate Center Dr, Pomona, CA 91768, 909-622-9800, 800-243-3660 (Fax: 909-622-8346) www.devry.edu. 8:30AM-8PM M-Th; 8:30AM-4:30PM F; 9AM-1PM Sat. Enrollment: 3300. Records go back to 1983. Alumni records maintained here; call 800-243-3660 X601. Degrees granted: Associate; Bachelors. Special programs- 800-243-3660 X317. Attendance and degree information available by phone, fax, mail. Transcripts available by fax, mail. Phone confirmation is given only if release on file.

Design Institute of San Diego, Registrar, 8555 Commerce Ave, San Diego, CA 92121, 619-566-1200 (Fax: 619-566-2711). 8:30AM-4:30PM. Enrollment: 240. Records go back to 1977. Alumni records maintained here; call 619-566-1200. Degrees granted: Bachelors. Attendance and degree information available by phone, fax, mail. Transcripts available by fax, mail.

Diablo Valley College, Registrar, 321 Golf Club Rd, Pleasant Hill, CA 94523, 925-685-1230 X327 (Fax: 925-609-8085) www.dvc.edu. 8AM-8PM M-Th; 8AM-4:30PM F. Enrollment: 20000. Records go back to 1949. Degrees granted: Associate. Attendance and degree information available by phone, fax, mail. Transcripts available by fax, mail.

Dominican College of San Rafael, Registrar, 50 Acacia Ave, San Rafael, CA 94901-2298, 415-457-4440, 415-485-3221 (Fax: 415-458-3730) www.dominican.edu. 9AM-7PM M-Th; 9AM-5PM F. Enrollment: 1500. Records go back to 1890. Alumni records are maintained here. Degrees granted: Bachelors; Masters. Attendance and degree information available by phone, fax, mail. Transcripts available by fax, mail.

Dominican School of Philosophy and Theology, Registrar, 2401 Ridge Rd, Berkeley, CA 94709, 510-849-2030 (Fax: 510-849-1372) 9AM-4:30PM M-Th; 9AM-3PM. Enrollment: 70. Degrees granted: Bachelors; Masters. Certification: Theology Attendance, degree and transcript information available by fax, mail.

Don Bosco Technical Institute, Registrar, 1151 San Gabriel Blvd, Rosemead, CA 91770-4299, 626-307-6522, 626-307-6500 (Fax: 626-280-9316). 8AM-3:30PM. Enrollment: 200. Records go back to 1968. Alumni records maintained here; call 626-

307-6528. Degrees granted: Associate. Attendance and degree information available by phone, fax, mail. Transcripts available by mail.

East Los Angeles College, Registrar, 1301 Avenida Cesar Chavez, Monterey Park, CA 91754, www.lafn.org/education/elac. 213-265-8650 (Fax: 213-265-8688) 8AM-7PM M-Th; 8AM-1PM F. Enrollment: 17000. Records go back to 1956. Alumni records maintained here; call 213-265-8650. Degrees granted: Associate. Attendance, degree and transcript information available by mail.

El Camino College, Registrar, Admissions, 16007 Crenshaw Blvd, Torrance, CA 90506, 310-660-3418, 310-660-6526 (Records). 8AM-7:30PM. Records go back to 1945. Alumni records are maintained here also. Call 310-660-3500. Degrees granted: Associate. Attendance and degree information available by phone, fax, mail. Transcripts available by fax, mail.

Emmanuel Bible College (Branch Campus of Nazarene Bible College), Registrar, 1605 E Elizabeth St, Pasadena, CA 91104, 818-791-2575 www.xicom.com/edu/emmaus. (Fax: 818-398-2424) 8AM-5PM. Records go back to 1983. Alumni records are maintained. Degrees granted: Associate; Bachelors Attendance, degree and transcript information available by fax, mail.

Emperor's College of Traditional Oriental Medicine, Registrar, 1807-B Wilshire Blvd, Santa Monica, CA 90403, 310-453-8300 (Fax: 310-829-3838) www.emperors.com. 9AM-6PM. Enrollment: 400. Records go back to 1982. Alumni records are maintained here. Degrees granted: Masters. Attendance, degree and transcript information available by mail.

Empire College, Registrar, 3033 Cleveland Ave Ste 102, Santa Rosa, CA 95403, 707-546-4000 (Fax: 707-546-4058) 8AM-5PM. Enrollment: 450. Degrees granted: Associate; JD. Attendance and degree information available by phone, fax, mail. Transcripts available by fax, mail.

Evergreen Valley College, Director of Admissions & Records, 3095 Yerba Buena Rd, San Jose, CA 95135, 408-270-6441 (Fax: 408-223-9351). 8AM - 5PM. Enrollment: 10000. Records go back to 1975. Degrees granted: Associate. Attendance information available by phone, mail. Degree information available by phone, fax, mail. Transcripts available by mail.

Fashion Career of California, Registrar, 1923 Morena Blvd, San Diego, CA 92110, www.fashioncollege.com. 619-275-4700 (Fax: 619-275-0635) Enrollment: 120. Records go back to 1983. Degrees granted: Associate. Attendance and degree information available by phone, fax, mail. Transcripts available by fax, mail.

Fashion Institute of Design and Merchandising (Branch), Registrar, 3420 S Bristol St, Suite 400, Costa Mesa, CA 92626, 714-546-0930 (Fax: 714-540-8118). Records are not housed here. They are located at Fashion Institute of Design and Merchandising, Registrar, 919 S Grand Ave, Los Angeles, CA 90015.

Fashion Institute of Design and Merchandising, Registrar, 919 S Grand Ave, Los Angeles, CA 90015, 213-624-1200 (Fax: 213-624-4777). 8AM-5PM. Enrollment: 2600. Records go back to 1970. Alumni records are maintained here. Degrees granted: Associate. Attendance and degree information

available by phone, fax, mail. Transcripts available by fax, mail.

Fashion Institute of Design and Merchandising (Branch), Registrar, 1010 Second Ave Ste 200, San Diego, CA 92101, 619-235-4515 (Fax: 619-232-4322). Records are not housed here. They are located at Fashion Institute of Design and Merchandising, Registrar, 919 S Grand Ave, Los Angeles, CA 90015.

Fashion Institute of Design and Merchandising (Branch), Registrar, 55 Stockton St, San Francisco, CA 94108, 415-433-6691 (Fax: 415-296-7299) www.fidm.com. 8AM-Noon, 1-3:30PM M; 8AM-Noon, 1-5:30PM T-Th; 8AM-Noon, 1-5PM F. Enrollment: 675. Records go back to 1980. Alumni records are maintained here. Degrees granted: Associate. Attendance and degree information available by phone, fax, mail. Transcripts available by fax, mail.

Feather River College, Registrar, 570 Golden Eagle Ave, Quincy, CA 95971, 530-283-0202 X285 (Fax: 530-283-3757) 8AM-5PM. www.frcc.cc.ca.us. Enrollment: 1434. Records go back to 1988. Alumni records are maintained here. Degrees granted: Associate. Attendance and degree information available by fax, mail. Transcripts available by fax, mail.

Fielding Institute, 2112 Santa Barbara St, Santa Barbara, CA 93105, 805-687-1099 (Ext. 3119) (Fax: 805-687-9793) www.fielding.edu. 9AM-5PM. Enrollment: 1350. Records go back to 1975. Alumni records are maintained here. Degrees granted: Masters; Doctorate. Certification: Neuro-behavioral Certificate Program. Special programs- CE - Group Psychotherapy, 805-687-1099. Attendance and degree information available by phone, fax, mail. Transcripts available by fax, mail. Will e-mail if registered with Fielding.

Foothill College, Registrar, 12345 El Monte Rd, Los Altos Hills, CA 94022, 650-949-7325 www.foothill.fhda.edu (Fax: 650-949-7048) 8:30AM-7:30PM M-Th, 8:30AM-Noon F. Enrollment: 15000. Records go back to 1958. Degrees granted: Associate. Attendance and degree information available by phone, fax, mail. Transcripts available by fax, mail.

Foundation College, Registrar, 3478 Buskirk Ave, Suite 100, Pleasant Hills, CA 94523, www.foundation.edu. 510-256-4231 (Fax: 510-256-4237) Enrollment: 392. Records go back to 1995. Alumni records are maintained here. Degrees granted: Associate. Attendance and degree information available by phone, mail. Transcripts available by mail.

Franciscan School of Theology, Registrar, 1712 Euclid Ave, Berkeley, CA 94709, 510-848-5232 (Fax: 510-549-9466) 8:30AM-12:30PM, 1:30-4:30pm. Enrollment: 100. Records go back to 1968. Alumni records are maintained here. Degrees granted: Masters. Attendance, degree and transcript information available by written request only.

Fresno City College, Registrar, 1101 E University Ave, Fresno, CA 93741, 209-442-4600, www.sccd.cc.ca.us. 209-442-8240 (Fax: 209-237-4232) 8AM-6:45PM M-Th; 8AM-5PM F; 7AM-6PM Summer. Enrollment: 18546. Records go back to 1948. Alumni Records: 1525 E Weldon Ave, Fresno, CA 93704. Degrees granted: Associate. Attendance information available by mail. Degree and transcript information available by fax, mail.

Fresno Pacific University, Registrar, 1717 S Chestnut Ave, Fresno, CA 93702, 209-453-

2037, 209-453-2000 (Fax: 209-453-3676) www.fresno.edu. 9AM-5:30PM; Phone 8AM-5:30PM. Enrollment: 1070. Records go back to 1965. Alumni records are maintained here also. Call 209-453-2058. Degrees granted: Associate; Bachelors; Masters; Teaching Credential. Special programs- Graduate Office, 209-453-2016: Center/Degree Completion, 209-453-2280. Attendance and degree information available by phone, fax, mail. Transcripts available by fax, mail.

Fuller Theological Seminary, Registrar, 135 N Oakland Ave, Pasadena, CA 91182, 626-584-5408 (Fax: 626-584-5449) www.fuller.edu. 9AM-Noon, 1-5PM M-Th; 1-5PM F. Records go back to 1947. Alumni records maintained here; call 626-584-5498. Degrees granted: Associate; Bachelors; Masters; Doctorate. Attendance and degree information available by phone, fax, mail. Transcripts available by mail.

Fullerton College, Admissions and Records, 321 E Chapman Ave, Fullerton, CA 92634-2095, 714-992-7568 (Fax: 714-870-7751) 8AM-7PM M-Th; 8AM-1PM F. www.fullcoll.edu. Enrollment: 18700. Records go back to 1913. Alumni records are maintained here. Degrees granted: Associate. Attendance and degree information available by phone, mail. Transcripts available by mail.

Gavilan College, Admissions Office, 5055 Santa Teresa Blvd, Gilroy, CA 95020, 408-848-4735 (Fax: 408-848-4801) 8AM-5PM. www.gavilan.gilroy.cc.ca.us. Enrollment: 4555. Records go back to 1919. Degrees granted: Associate. Attendance and degree information available by phone, fax, mail. Transcripts available by mail.

Glendale Community College, Office of Admissions & Records, 1500 N Verdugo Rd, Glendale, CA 91208, 818-240-1000 (Fax: 818-551-5255) www.glendale.cc.ca.us. 8AM-8PM M-Th, 9AM-Noon F. Enrollment: 14149. Records go back to 1927. Alumni records maintained here; call 818-240-1000 X5126. Degrees granted: Associate. Attendance and degree information available by fax, mail. Transcripts available by mail.

Golden Gate Baptist Theological Seminary, Registrar, 201 Seminary Dr, Mill Valley, CA 94941-3197, 415-380-1648, 415-380-1640 (Fax: 415-380-1642) 8:30AM-4:30PM. www.ggbts.edu. Enrollment: 1200. Records go back to 1944. Alumni records are maintained here also. Call 415-380-1494. Degrees granted: Masters; Doctorate. Special programs- Ethnic Leadership Development, 415-380-1630: Continuing Education, 415-380-1450. Attendance and degree information available by phone, fax, mail. Transcripts available by fax, mail.

Golden Gate University, Records Office, 536 Mission St, San Francisco, CA 94105-2968, 415-442-7211, 415-442-7200 (Fax: 415-442-7807) www.ggu.edu. 9AM-6:30PM M-Th; 9AM-5:30PM F. Enrollment: 4172. Records go back to 1900. Alumni Records: 562 Mission St, San Francisco, CA 94105-2968. Degrees granted: Associate; Bachelors; Masters; Doctorate. Special programs- LLB, J.D., 415-442-6600. Attendance and degree information available by phone, fax, mail. Transcripts available by fax, mail.

Golden West College, Registrar, 15744 Golden West St, PO Box 2710, Huntington Beach, CA 92647, 714-895-8128, 714-892-7711 X55026 (Fax: 714-895-8960) www.gwc.cccd.edu. 8AM-7PM M-Th; 8AM-3PM F. Enrollment: 13094. Records go back to 1966. Alumni records are maintained here also. Call 714-895-8315. Degrees granted: Associate. Special programs- Office of

Instruction, 714-895-8134. Attendance and degree information available by phone, fax, mail. Transcripts available by fax, mail.

Golf Academy of San Diego, Registrar, 2022 University Dr, Vista, CA 92083, 760-414-1501 (Fax: 760-414-9269) Records go back to 1982. Alumni records are maintained. Degrees granted: Associate. Attendance and degree information available by phone, mail. Transcripts available by mail.

Graduate Theological Union, Registrar, 2400 Ridge Rd, Berkeley, CA 94709, 510-649-2462, 510-649-2400 (Fax: 510-649-1730) www.gtu.edu. 9AM-5PM. Enrollment: 450. Records go back to 1962. Alumni records are maintained here. Degrees granted: Masters; Doctorate. Attendance and degree information available by phone, fax, mail. Transcripts available by fax, mail.

Grossmont College, Registrar, 8800 Grossmont College Dr, El Cajon, CA 92020, www.gcccd.cc.ca.us/grossmont. 619-465-1700 (Fax: 619-644-7933) 8AM-7PM M-Th; 8AM-3PM F. Enrollment: 15000. Records go back to 1935. Alumni records maintained here; call 619-465-1700 X169. Degrees granted: Associate. Attendance and degree information available by mail. Transcripts available by fax, mail.

Hartnell College, Registrar, 156 Homestead Ave, Salinas, CA 93901, 408-755-6711 (Fax: 408-759-6014). 8AM-7PM M-Th; 8AM-5PM F. Enrollment: 7550. Records go back to 1920. Alumni records maintained here; call 408-755-6810. Degrees granted: Associate. Attendance information available by written request only. Degree information available by phone, fax, mail. Transcripts available by fax, mail.

Harvey Mudd College, Registrar, 301 E 12th St, Claremont, CA 91711, 909-621-8090, 909-621-8125 (Fax: 909-621-8494) www.hmc.edu. 8AM-Noon, 1-5PM. Enrollment: 670. Records go back to 1955. Transcripts available since founding; other records for past 10 years. Alumni records maintained here; call 909-607-3162. Degrees granted: Bachelors; Masters. Attendance and degree information available by phone, fax, mail. Transcripts available by fax, mail.

Heald Business College — Concord, Dean of Instruction, 2150 John Glenn Dr, Ste 100, Concord, CA 94520, 925-827-1300 (Fax: 925-827-1486) www.heald.edu. 9AM-5PM. Enrollment: 500. Records go back to 1863. Degrees granted: Associate. Special programs- Arts: Science. Attendance and degree information available by phone, fax, mail. Transcripts available by mail.

Heald Business College — Fresno, Registrar, 255 W Bullard Ave, Fresno, CA 93704, 209-438-4222 (Fax: 209-438-6368) 8AM-7PM. www.heald.edu. Degrees granted: Associate. Attendance and degree information available by phone, fax, mail. Transcripts available by fax, mail.

Heald Business College — Hayward, Registrar, 777 Southland Dr, Suite 210, Hayward, CA 94545, 510-784-7001 (Fax: 510-784-7050) www.heald.edu. 8AM-5PM. Records go back to 1863. Degrees granted: Associate. Attendance and degree information available by phone, fax, mail. Transcripts available by fax, mail.

Heald Business College - Sacramento, Registrar, 2910 Prospect Park Dr, Rancho Cordova, CA 95670, 916-638-1616 (Fax: 916-853-8282) www.heald.edu. 7:30AM-8PM. Enrollment: 580. Records go back to 1917. Degrees granted: Associate. Attendance

and degree information available by phone, fax, mail. Transcripts available by fax, mail.

Heald Business College — Salinas, Dean of Students, 1450 N Main St, Salinas, CA 93906, 408-443-1700, 408-657-2400 (Fax: 408-443-1050) www.heald.edu. 8AM-5PM. Enrollment: 500. Records go back to 1992. Alumni records maintained here. Degrees granted: Associate. Attendance and degree information available by phone, fax, mail. Transcripts available by fax, mail.

Heald Business College — San Francisco, Registrar, 1453 Mission St, San Francisco, CA 94103, 415-673-5500 (Fax: 415-626-3260). 8AM-5PM. Enrollment: 303. Records go back to 1965. Degrees granted: Associate. Special programs- Hospitality & Tourism. Attendance and degree information available by fax, mail.

Heald Business College - San Jose, Registrar, 2665 N First St Ste 110, San Jose, CA 95134, 408-955-9555 (Fax: 408-955-9580) www.heald.edu. 8AM-5PM. Enrollment: 300. Records go back to 1970. Degrees granted: Associate. Attendance and degree information available by phone, fax, mail. Transcripts available by fax, mail.

Heald Business College - Santa Rosa, Registrar, 2425 Mendocino Ave, Santa Rosa, CA 95403, 707-525-1300 (Fax: 707-527-0251) www.heald.edu/campus_srb.htm. 9AM-4:30PM. Records go back to 1986. Alumni records are maintained here. Degrees granted: Associate. Attendance, degree and transcript information available by fax, mail.

Heald Business College — Stockton, Registrar, 1605 E March Ln, Stockton, CA 95210, www.heald.edu. 209-477-1114 (Fax: 209-477-2739) 7:30AM-7PM. Enrollment: 400. Records go back to 1863. Degrees granted: Associate. Attendance and degree information available by phone, fax, mail. Transcripts available by fax, mail.

Heald College School of Business - Oakland, Registrar, 1000 Broadway, Ste 290, Oakland, CA 94607, 510-444-0201 (Fax: 510-839-2084) www.heald.edu. 8AM-6PM. Enrollment: 350. Records go back to 1975. Degrees granted: Associate. Attendance, degree and transcript information available by fax, mail.

Heald College School of Technology - Hayward, Registrar, 24301 Southland Dr Ste 500, Hayward, CA 94545, 510-783-2100 (Fax: 510-783-3287) www.heald.edu. 8AM-6PM. Enrollment: 400. Records go back to 1920. Degrees granted: Associate. Attendance and degree information available by phone, fax, mail. Transcripts available by fax, mail.

Heald College of Technology — San Francisco, Registrar, 250 Executive Park Blvd, Suite 100, San Francisco, CA 94134, 415-822-2900 (Fax: 415-822-2401) www.heald.edu. 8AM-5PM. Records go back to 1863. Degrees granted: Associate. Attendance and degree information available by phone, fax, mail. Transcripts available by fax, mail.

Heald College, School of Business & Technology, Office of the Dean of Instruction, 341 Great Mall Pkwy, Milpitas, CA 95035, 408-295-8000 (Fax: 408-934-7777) www.heald.edu. Enrollment: 600. Records go back to 1863. Degrees granted: Associate. Attendance, degree and transcript information available by fax, mail.

Heald College — Santa Clara
(See Heald Institute of Technology)

Heald Institute of Technology — Martinez, Registrar, 2860 Howe Rd, Martinez, CA 94553, 925-228-9000 (Fax: 925-229-3792) www.heald.edu. 8AM-5PM. Enrollment: 700. Records go back to 1985. Alumni records are maintained. Degrees granted: Associate. Attendance and degree information available by phone, fax, mail. Transcripts available by fax, mail.

Heald Institute of Technology — Milpitas, Registrar, 341-A Great Mall Pkwy, Milpitas, CA 95035-8008, 408-295-8000 (Fax: 408-934-7777) www.heald.edu. Records go back to 1983. Degrees granted: Associate. Attendance and degree information available by phone, mail. Transcripts available by mail.

Heald Institute of Technology — Sacramento, Registrar, 3737 Marconi Ave, Sacramento, CA 95821, 916-972-0999 X22,24 (Fax: 916-972-1288). 8AM-5PM. Enrollment: 600. Records go back to 1868. Degrees granted: Associate. Attendance and degree information available by phone, fax, mail. Transcripts available by fax, mail.

Heald Institute of Technology - San Francisco, Registrar, 250 Executive Park Blvd, Suite 1000, San Francisco, CA 94134, 415-822-2900 (Fax: 415-822-2401) www.heald.edu. 8:30AM-4:30PM. Records go back to 1983. Degrees granted: Associate. Attendance and degree information available by phone, mail. Transcripts available by mail.

Heald Institute of Technology - San Jose, Registrar, 341 Great Mall Pkwy, Milpitas, CA 95035, 408-934-4900 (Fax: 408-934-1006). 8AM-5PM. Enrollment: 400. Records go back to 1863. Degrees granted: Associate. Attendance, degree and transcript information available by fax, mail.

Hebrew Union College — Jewish Institute of Religion, Registrar, 3077 University Ave, Los Angeles, CA 90007, 213-749-3424 (Fax: 213-747-6128). 9AM-5PM. Enrollment: 68. Records go back to 1972. Alumni records maintained here; call 213-749-3424. Degrees granted: Bachelors; Masters; Doctorate. Special programs- U of S CA Judaic Studies Dept, 213-749-3424. Attendance and degree information available by phone, fax, mail. Transcripts available by mail.

Holy Names College, Registrar, 3500 Mountain Blvd, Oakland, CA 94619-9989, 510-436-1133, 510-436-1134 (Fax: 510-436-1137) www.hnc.edu. 9:30AM-3:30PM. Enrollment: 900. Records go back to 1868. Alumni records maintained here; call 510-436-1240. Degrees granted: Bachelors; Masters. Attendance and degree information available by phone, fax, mail. Transcripts available by mail.

Hope International University, Registrar, 2500 E Nutwood Ave, Fullerton, CA 92831, 714-879-3901 X256 (Fax: 714-992-0274) 8AM-5PM. www.hiu.edu. Enrollment: 1000. Records go back to 1928. Alumni records are maintained here. Degrees granted: Associate; Bachelors; Masters. Special programs- Traditional Undergrad, 714-879-3901: Excel-Degree Completion, 714-879-3901 X600: Spanish Certificate, 714-879-3901 X269: Center for International Education, 714-879-3901: Graduate Program, 714-879-3901 X604. Attendance and degree information available by phone, fax, mail. Transcripts available by mail.

Humboldt State University, Registrar, Arcata, CA 95521, 707-826-4402, 707-826-6196 (Fax: 707-826-6194 or 707-826-6186)

8:30AM-4:30PM. www.humboldt.edu. Enrollment: 7600. Records go back to 1922. Alumni records maintained here; call 707-826-3132. Degrees granted: Bachelors; Masters. Attendance and degree information available by phone, fax, mail. Transcripts available by fax, mail.

Humphrey College, Registrar, 6650 Inglewood St, Stockton, CA 95207, 209-478-0800 (Fax: 209-478-8721) 8AM-7PM. Enrollment: 660. Records go back to 1896. Alumni records are maintained here. Degrees granted: Associate; Bachelors; JD. Attendance and degree information available by phone, fax, mail.. Transcripts available by fax, mail.

ITT Technical Institute, Registrar, 525 Muller, **Anaheim**, CA 92801, 714-535-3700 (Fax: 714-535-1802) www.itt.com. 8AM-5PM. Enrollment: 560. Records go back to 1983. Alumni Records: ITT Technical Institute, 9511 Angola Ct, Indianapolis, IN 46268. Degrees granted: Associate. Attendance and degree information available by phone, fax, mail. Transcripts available by fax, mail.

ITT Technical Institute, Registrar, 10863 Gold Center Dr, **Rancho Cordova**, CA 95670, 916-851-3900 (Fax: 916-851-9225) 8AM-5PM. Enrollment: 500. Records go back to 1984. Degrees granted: Associate; Bachelors Attendance, degree and transcript information available by phone, fax, mail.

ITT Technical Institute, Registrar, 630 E Brier Dr Ste 150, **San Bernardino**, CA 92408-2800, 909-889-3800 (Fax: 909-888-6970) 8AM-5PM. Enrollment: 550. Records go back to 1984. Alumni Records: ITT Technical Institute, 9511 Angola Ct, Indianapolis, IN 46268. Degrees granted: Associate; Bachelors. Attendance, degree and transcript information available by fax, mail.

ITT Technical Institute, Registrar, 9680 Granite Ridge Dr, **San Diego**, CA 92123-2662, 619-571-8500 (Fax: 619-571-1277). 7AM-6PM. Records go back to 1980. Alumni Records: ITT Technical Institute, 9511 Angola Ct, Indianapolis, IN 46268. Degrees granted: Associate; Bachelors. Attendance, degree and transcript information available by fax, mail.

ITT Technical Institute, Registrar, 5104 Old Ironsides Dr, Ste 113, **Santa Clara**, CA 95054, 408-496-0655 www.itt.com. Records go back to 1983. Degrees granted: Associate; Bachelors. Attendance and degree information available by phone, mail. Transcripts available by mail.

ITT Technical Institute, Registrar, 12669 Encinitas Ave, **Sylmar**, CA 91342-3664, 818-364-5151 (Fax: 818-364-5150) 8AM-5PM. Enrollment: 600. Records go back to 1985. Alumni Records: ITT Technical Institute, 9511 Angola Ct, Indianapolis, IN 46268. Degrees granted: Associate. Attendance, degree and transcript information available by phone, fax, mail.

ITT Technical Institute, Registrar, 20050 S Vermond, **Torrance**, CA 90502, 310-380-1555 (Fax: 310-380-1557) www.ittesi.com. 8AM-5PM M-W,F; 11AM-8PM Th. Enrollment: 500. Records go back to 1989. Alumni Records: ITT Technical Institute, 9511 Angola Ct, Indianapolis, IN 46268. Degrees granted: Associate. Attendance and degree information available by phone, fax, mail. Transcripts available by fax, mail. Phone inquiry available to students only.

ITT Technical Institute, Registrar, 6723 Van Nuys Blvd, **Van Nuys**, CA 91405-4620,

818-989-1177 (Fax: 818-364-5150) Records go back to 1984. Alumni records are maintained. Degrees granted: Associate. Attendance and degree information available by phone, mail. Transcripts available by mail.

ITT Technical Institute, Registrar, 1530 W Cameron Ave, **West Covina**, CA 91790-2767, 626-960-8681 (Fax: 626-337-5271). 8AM-5PM. Enrollment: 650. Records go back to 1982. Alumni Records: ITT Technical Institute, 9511 Angola Ct, Indianapolis, IN 46268. Degrees granted: Associate; Bachelors. Attendance and degree information available by phone, fax, mail. Transcripts available by fax, mail. Phone inquiry available to students only.

Imperial Valley College, Registrar, PO Box 158, Imperial, CA 92251, 760-352-8320 (Fax: 760-355-2663) www.imperial.cc.ca.us. Enrollment: 6000. Records go back to 1924. Alumni records are maintained here. Degrees granted: Associate. Attendance and degree information available by phone, mail. Transcripts available by mail.

Indian Valley College
(See College of Miran)

Institute of Computer Technology, Registrar, 3200 Wilshire Blvd, #400, Los Angeles, CA 90010-1308, 213-381-3333 (Fax: 213-736-5203) www.ictcollege.edu. 8AM-5PM. Enrollment: 700. Records go back to 1985. Degrees granted: Associate; Bachelors. Attendance and degree information available by phone, mail. Transcripts available by mail.

Institute of Transpersonal Psychology, Registrar, 744 San Antonio Rd, Palo Alto, CA 94303, 650-493-4430 X14 (Fax: 650-493-6835) www.tmn.com/itp/index.htm/. Enrollment: 325. Records go back to 1975. Alumni records are maintained here. Degrees granted: Masters; Doctorate. Attendance and degree information available by phone, fax, mail. Transcripts available by mail.

Interior Designers Institute, Registrar, 1061 Camelback Rd, Newport Beach, CA 92660, 949-675-4451 (Fax: 949-759-0667) 8AM-5PM M-Th; 9AM-4PM F. Enrollment: 400. Records go back to 1961. Degrees granted: Associate; Bachelors. Attendance, degree and transcript information available by fax, mail.

International School of Theology, Registrar, 24600 Arrowhead Springs, San Bernardino, CA 92414-0001, 909-886-7876 (Fax: 909-882-8458) www.leaderu.com/isot/. Enrollment: 63. Records go back to 1991. Degrees granted: Masters. Attendance and degree information available by phone, mail. Transcripts available by mail.

Irvine Valley College, Admissions & Records, Transcript Unit, 5500 Irvine Center Dr, Irvine, CA 92620, www.ivc.cc.ca.us. 714-451-5461, 714-451-5220 (Fax: 714-451-5443) 9AM-7PM M-Th; 9AM-3PM F. Enrollment: 11300. Records go back to 1969. Alumni records maintained here; call 714-451-5272. Degrees granted: Associate. Certification: Occupational. Special programs- Call 714-451-5100. Attendance, degree and transcript information available by fax, mail.

Jesuit School of Theology at Berkeley, Registrar, 1735 LeRoy Ave, Berkeley, CA 94709-1193, 510-841-8804, 510-649-2462 (Fax: 510-649-1730). 8:30AM-5PM. Enrollment: 190. Records go back to 1969. Degrees granted: Masters; Doctorate. Attendance and degree information available

by phone, fax, mail. Transcripts available by fax, mail.

John F. Kennedy University, Registrar, 12 Altarinda Rd, Orinda, CA 94563, 925-254-0200 (Fax: 925-254-6949). 10AM-6PM. Records go back to 1964. Alumni records are maintained here. Degrees granted: Bachelors; Masters. Attendance and degree information available by phone, fax, mail. Transcripts available by mail.

Kelsey - Jenney College, Registrar, 201 "A" St, San Diego, CA 92101, 619-233-7418 (Fax: 619-544-9610). 7:30AM-9:40PM. Enrollment: 950. Records go back to 1950. Degrees granted: Associate Attendance, degree and transcript information available by fax, mail, transcript by student only.

Kelsey - Jenney College, Registrar, 7310 Miramar Rd, Suite 300, San Diego, CA 92126, 619-549-5070 (Fax: 619-693-5784). 7:30AM-9:40PM. Enrollment: 950. Records go back to 1950. Degrees granted: Associate. Attendance, degree and transcript information available by fax, mail. Tanscript by student only.

Kings River Community College, Admissions & Records Office, 995 N Reed Ave, Reedley, CA 93654, 209-638-3641 (Fax: 209-638-5040). 8AM-7PM. Records go back to 1926. Degrees granted: Associate. Special programs- Agriculture: Mechanical Agriculture: Aeronautics: Dental Assisting: Forestry. Attendance and degree information available by phone, fax, mail. Transcripts available by mail.

L.I.F.E Bible College, Registrar, 1100 Covina Blvd, San Dimas, CA 91773, 909-599-5433 X306, 909-599-8999 (Fax: 909-599-6690) www.lifebible.edu. 8AM-5PM. Enrollment: 425. Records go back to 1930. Alumni records maintained here; call 909-599-5433 X220. Degrees granted: Associate; Bachelors. Attendance and degree information available by phone, fax, mail. Transcripts available by mail.

La Sierra University, Registrar, 4700 Pierce St, Riverside, CA 92515, 909-785-2006 (Fax: 909-785-2447). 8:30AM-4:30PM M-Th; 8:30AM-Noon F. Enrollment: 1500. Records go back to 1922. Alumni records are maintained. Degrees granted: Associate; Bachelors; Masters; Doctorate; Specialist. Attendance, degree and transcript information available by fax, mail.

Lake Tahoe Community College, Director of Admissions & Records, One College Dr, South Lake Tahoe, CA 96150-4524, 530-541-4660 X211, 530-541-4660 X217 (Fax: 530-541-7852) 8AM-5PM. www.ltcc.cc.ca.us Enrollment: 2800. Records go back to 1976. Alumni records maintained here; call 530-541-4660. Degrees granted: Associate. Special programs-Intensive Spanish Summer Institute, 530-541-4660 X252. Attendance and degree information available by phone, fax, mail. Transcripts available by fax, mail. Confirmation given if release on file.

Laney College, Registrar, 900 Fallon St, Oakland, CA 94607, 510-464-3122 (Fax: 510-466-7394) www.peralta.cc.ca.us. 8AM-7PM M-T, 8AM-4:30PM W-F. Enrollment: 10000. Records go back to 1940. Alumni records maintained here; call 510-464-3162. Degrees granted: Associate. Attendance and degree information available by fax, mail. Transcripts available by mail.

Las Positas College, Admissions & Records, 3033 Collier Canyon Rd, Livermore, CA 94550, 925-373-5815 (Fax: 925-606-

6437) http://registrar.colorado.edu. 9AM-7:30PM M-Th, 9AM-5PM F. Enrollment: 6700. Records go back to 1960. Alumni records maintained here; call 925-373-4942. Degrees granted: Associate. Attendance, degree and transcript information available by fax, mail.

Lassen College, Registrar, PO Box 3000, Susanville, CA 96130, 530-257-6181 (Fax: 530-251-8802) www.lassenca.us/. 8AM-4:30PM. Enrollment: 800. Records go back to 1927. Degrees granted: Associate. Attendance and degree information available by phone, fax, mail. Transcripts available by fax, mail. Degree verification phone: 530-251-8842. Attendance verification: 530-251-8808.

Lee College, Registrar, 1360 South Anaheim Blvd, Anaheim, CA 92805, 714-758-1500 (Fax: 714-758-1220) 8AM-5PM. Enrollment: 300. Records go back to 1989. Alumni records are maintained here. Attendance and degree information available by phone, mail. Transcripts available by mail.

Life Chiropractic College — West, Registrar, 2005 Via Barrett, San Lorenzo, CA 94580, 510-276-9013, 510-276-1436 (Fax: 510-276-4893) www.lifewest.edu. 8AM-5PM. Records go back to 1979. Alumni records are maintained here. Degrees granted: Doctorate. Attendance, degree and transcript information available by fax, mail.

Lincoln University, Registrar, 281 Masonic Ave, San Francisco, CA 94118, 415-221-1212 (Fax: 415-387-9730) 9AM-5PM. www.lincolnuc.edu. Records go back to 1926. Degrees granted: Bachelors; Masters. Attendance and degree information available by phone, fax, mail. Transcripts available by mail.

Loma Linda University, Office of University Records, Loma Linda, CA 92350, 909-558-4508 (Fax: 909-558-4879) www.llu.edu. 8:30AM-4PM M,T; 9AM-4PM W; 9AM-6PM Th; 8:30AM-2PM F. Enrollment: 3000. Records go back to 1905. Alumni records are maintained here. Degrees granted: Associate; Bachelors; Masters; Doctorate Attendance, degree and transcript information available by fax, mail.

Long Beach City College, Registrar, 4901 E Carson St, Long Beach, CA 90808, 562-420-4139, 562-938-4144 (Verifications) (Fax: 562-420-4118) www.lbccca.us. 8AM-6:30PM M-Th, 8AM-4PM F. Enrollment: 23000. Records go back to 1927. Alumni records maintained here; call 310-420-4203. Degrees granted: Associate. Attendance and degree information available by phone, mail. Transcripts available by mail.

Los Angeles City College, Registrar, 855 N Vermont Ave, Los Angeles, CA 90029, 213-953-4448, 213-953-4382 (Fax: 213-953-4536) www.laccd.edu/. 9AM-7PM. Enrollment: 15000. Records go back to 1990. Alumni records maintained here; call 213-953-4415. Degrees granted: Associate. Special programs- Cinema, 213-953-4000: Dental Technology, 213-953-4000: Human Services, 213-953-4000: Radiological Technology, 213-953-4000. Attendance, degree and transcript information available by fax, mail.

Los Angeles College of Chiropractic, Registrar, 16200 E Amber Valley Dr, Whittier, CA 90604, 562-902-3380, 562-947-8755 X380 (Fax: 562-947-5724). 8AM-5PM. Enrollment: 800. Records go back to 1911. Alumni records maintained here; call 562-947-8755. Degrees granted: Doctorate; Chiropractic. Attendance, degree and transcript information available by mail.

Los Angeles Harbor College, Registrar, 1111 Figueroa Pl, Wilmington, CA 90744, 310-522-8216 (Fax: 310-834-1882) www.edwab.adsu.edu/ 9AM-7PM M-Th; 9AM-3PM F. Enrollment: 8000. Records go back to 1949. Degrees granted: Associate. Attendance and degree information available by fax, mail. Transcripts available by mail.

Los Angeles Masters College
(See Masters College)

Los Angeles Mission College, Registrar, 13356 Eldridge Ave, Sylmar, CA 91342-3245, 818-364-7663, 818-364-7865 (Fax: 818-364-7755). 9AM-7PM M & Th; 9AM-4PM T,W,F. Records go back to 1975. Alumni records maintained here; call 818-364-7795. Degrees granted: Associate. Attendance, degree and transcript information available by mail.

Los Angeles Pierce College, Registrar, 6201 Winnetka Ave, Woodland Hills, CA 91371, 818-719-6401. 8:30AM-8:30PM M-Th, 8:30AM-4PM F. Records go back to 1940. Alumni records are maintained. Degrees granted: Associate. Attendance and degree information available by phone, fax, mail. Transcripts available by mail.

Los Angeles Southwest College, Admission Office, 1600 W Imperial Hwy, Los Angeles, CA 90047, 213-241-5320 (Fax: 213-241-5464). 8:30AM-8PM M-Th; 9AM-1PM F. Enrollment: 5000. Records go back to 1967. Alumni records maintained here; call 213-241-5381. Degrees granted: Associate. Attendance and degree information available by fax, mail. Transcripts available by mail.

Los Angeles Trade-Technical College, Registrar, 400 W Washington Blvd, Los Angeles, CA 90015, 213-744-9420 (Fax: 213-744-9425) www.lattc.laccd.cc.ca.us. 8:30AM-8PM M-Th; 8:30AM-4PM F. Enrollment: 13000. Records go back to 1928. Alumni records maintained here; call 213-744-9003. Degrees granted: Associate. Attendance and degree information available by fax, mail. Transcripts available by mail.

Los Angeles Valley College, Registrar, 5800 Fulton Ave, Van Nuys, CA 91401, www.lavc.cc.ca.us. 818-781-1200 X255 (Fax: 818-781-4672) 8:30AM-8:30PM M-Th, 8:30AM-4PM F. Records go back to 1940. Degrees granted: Associate. Attendance information available by mail. Degree and transcript information available by fax, mail.

Los Medanos College, Registrar, 2700 E Leland Rd, Pittsburg, CA 94565, 925-439-2181, 625-439-2181 X251 & 254 (Verifications) (Fax: 925-427-1599 (Attn: Admissions)) 9AM-8PM M-Th; 9AM-3PM F. www.losmedanos.net. Enrollment: 8500. Records go back to 1974. Degrees granted: Associate. Attendance and degree information available by phone, fax, mail. Transcripts available by fax, mail.

Loyola Marymount University, Registrar, Loyola Blvd at W 80th St, Los Angeles, CA 90045, 310-338-2740 (Fax: 310-338-4466) www.lmu.edu. 8AM-5PM. Alumni records are maintained here also. Call 310-338-3067. Degrees granted: Bachelors; Masters. Attendance and degree information available by phone, fax, mail. Transcripts available by fax, mail.

MTI Western Business College, Registrar, 5221 Madison Ave, Sacramento, CA 95841, 916-339-1500 (Fax: 916-339-0305) www.mticollege.com. Records go back to 1975. Degrees granted: Associate. Attendance and degree information available by phone, mail. Transcripts available by mail.

Maric College of Medical Careers, Registrar, 3666 Kearney Villa Rd, San Diego, CA 92123, 619-279-4500 (Fax: 619-279-4885) www.edmd.com. Enrollment: 3000. Records go back to 1982. Alumni records are maintained here. Degrees granted: Associate. Attendance and degree information available by phone, mail. Transcripts available by mail.

Marin Community College (Indian Valley), Admissions and Records Office, 1800 Ignacia Blvd, Navato, CA 94949, 415-883-2211 www.marin.cc.ca.us. 9AM-3PM M-Th; 9AM-Noon F. Enrollment: 8300. Records go back to 1926. Alumni records are maintained here. Degrees granted: Associate. Attendance, degree and transcript information available by mail.

Marymount College, Registrar, 30800 Palos Verdes Dr E, Rancho Palos Verdes, CA 90274-6299, 310-377-5501 X214 (Fax: 310-377-6223) www.marymountpv.edu. 8:30AM-5PM. Enrollment: 900. Records go back to 1972. Alumni records are maintained. Degrees granted: Associate. Attendance and degree information available by phone, fax, mail. Transcripts available by fax, mail.

Master's College (The), Registrar's Office #42, 21726 Placerita Canyon Rd, Santa Clarita, CA 91321-1200, 805-259-3540 X317, 805-259-3540 X311 (Fax: 805-254-7609) 8:30AM-5PM. www.masters.edu. Enrollment: 850. Records go back to 1927. Alumni records are maintained here. Degrees granted: Bachelors; Masters. Attendance and degree information available by phone, fax, mail. Transcripts available by fax, mail.

Masters College (The), Registrar, PO Box 221450, Newhall, CA 91322, 805-259-3540 X317 (Fax: 805-254-7609) www.masters.edu. Enrollment: 800. Records go back to 1927. Formerly **Los Angeles Baptist College.** Alumni records are maintained here. Degrees granted: Bachelors; Masters. Special programs- Master's Institute, 805-259-3540. Attendance and degree information available by phone, mail. Transcripts available by mail.

Masters Institute, Registrar, 50 Airport Pkwy, Suite 8, San Jose, CA 95110-1011, 408-441-1800 www.mastersi.edu (Fax: 408-441-1826) 8AM-4:30PM. Enrollment: 250. Records go back to 1984. Degrees granted: Associate. Attendance and degree information available by phone, mail. Transcripts available by mail.

Mendocino College, Registrar, PO Box 3000, Ukiah, CA 95482, 707-468-3103, 707-468-3101 (Fax: 707-468-3120) 9AM-5PM. www.mendocino.cc.ca.us. Enrollment: 4500. Records go back to 1973. Degrees granted: Associate. Attendance and degree information available by phone, fax, mail. Transcripts available by fax, mail.

Menlo College, Office of the Registrar, 1000 El Camino Real, Atherton, CA 94027-4185, 650-688-3764 (Fax: 650-324-2347) www.menlo.edu. 9AM-5PM. Enrollment: 500. Records go back to 1930. Alumni Records: c/o External Relations, 1000 El Camino Real, Atherton, CA 94027-4185. Degrees granted: Associate; Bachelors. Attendance and degree information available by phone, fax, mail. Transcripts available by fax, mail.

Mennonite Brethren Biblical Seminary, Registrar, 4824 E Butler Ave, Fresno, CA 93727-5097, 209-452-1723 (Fax: 209-251-7212) www.fresno.edu/mbseminary. 8AM-5PM. Enrollment: 175. Records go back to 1955. Alumni records are maintained here. Degrees granted: Masters. Special programs-MFCC, 209-452-1718. Attendance and

degree information available by phone, fax, mail. Transcripts available by fax, mail.

Merced College, Registrar, 3600 M St, Merced, CA 95340, 209-384-6000, 209-384-6188 www.merced.cc.ca.us (Fax: 209-384-6338) 8AM-4PM M,T,Th,F; 8AM-7PM W. Enrollment: 7445. Records go back to 1965. Degrees granted: Associate. Special programs- 209-384-6187. Attendance and degree information available by phone, fax, mail. Transcripts available by mail.

Merritt College, Registrar, 12500 Campus Dr, Oakland, CA 94619, 510-531-4911, 510-466-7377 (Verifications) (Fax: 510-436-2512) 8AM-4:30PM. www.peralta.cc.ca.us. Enrollment: 5387. Records go back to 1953. Alumni Records: Alumni Assoc., 333 E Eighth St, Oakland, CA 94606. Degrees granted: Associate. Attendance, degree and transcript information available by fax, mail.

Mills College, Registrar, 5000 MacArthur Blvd, Oakland, CA 94613, 510-430-2083 (Fax: 510-430-3314) www.mills.edu/. 9AM-4PM. Enrollment: 1165. Records go back to 1871. Alumni records maintained here; call 510-430-2110. Degrees granted: Bachelors; Masters. Attendance and degree information available by phone, fax, mail. Transcripts available by fax, mail.

Mira Costa College, Admissions & Records, One Barnard Dr, Oceanside, CA 92056, 760-757-2121, 760-795-6620 (Fax: 760-795-6626) www.miracosta.cc.ca.us. 8AM-7PM M-Th; 8AM-4:30PM F. Enrollment: 8500. Records go back to 1937. Alumni records maintained here; call 760-757-2121 X6613. Degrees granted: Associate. Special programs- Licensed Vocational Nursing, 760-795-6842; International Student Program, 760-795-6896. Attendance, degree and transcript information available by fax, mail.

Mission College, Registrar, 3000 Mission College Blvd, Santa Clara, CA 95054, www.wvmccd.cc.ca.us/mc. 408-748-2700 (Fax: 408-980-8980) 9:30AM-7PM M-Th, 9:30AM-2PM F. Enrollment: 10000. Degrees granted: Associate. Attendance and degree information available by phone, fax, mail. Transcripts available by mail.

Modesto Junior College, Registrar, 435 College Ave, Modesto, CA 95350, 209-575-6470, 209-575-6853 (Admissions) (Fax: 209-575-6666; 575-6723 (records)) www.ccc-infonet.edu/mjccat/ welcome.html. 8AM-5PM; Admissions: 8AM-6:45PM M-Th; 8-4:30PM F; Summer: 7:30-5:30 M-Th. Enrollment: 14000. Records go back to 1921. Alumni records maintained here; call 209-575-6308. Degrees granted: Associate. Attendance and degree information available by phone, mail. Transcripts available by fax, mail.

Monterey Institute of International Studies, Registrar, 425 Van Buren, Monterey, CA 93940, 408-647-4121 (Fax: 408-647-4199) www.miis.edu. 9AM-4PM. Enrollment: 750. Records go back to 1959. Alumni records maintained here; call 408-647-4105. Degrees granted: Bachelors; Masters. Attendance and degree information available by phone, fax, mail. Transcripts available by fax, mail.

Monterey Peninsula College, Admissions & Records, 980 Fremont St, Monterey, CA 93940, 408-646-4002, 408-646-4007 (Fax: 408-655-4015) www.mpc.edu. 8AM-6:30PM M-Th; 8AM-2:30PM F. Enrollment: 12000. Records go back to 1947. Degrees granted: Associate. Attendance information available by fax, mail. Degree information available by

phone, fax, mail. Transcripts available by mail.

Moorpark College, Registrar, 7075 Campus Rd, Moorpark, CA 93021, 805-378-1429, 805-378-1400 www.vcccd.cc.ca.us (Fax: 805-378-1583) 7AM-7PM M-Th; 7AM-5PM F. Enrollment: 11700. Records go back to 1967. Degrees granted: Associate. Special programs- Exotic Animal Training, 805-378-1441. Attendance and degree information available by fax, mail. Transcripts available by mail.

Morally College of Health Sciences, Registrar, 1499 N State St, Bldg 1450, San Jacinto, CA 92583, 909-487-0763 (Fax: 909-654-0876) 8AM-5PM. Enrollment: 200. Records go back to 1996. Degrees granted: Associate. Attendance and degree information available by phone, mail. Transcripts available by mail.

Mount San Jacinto College, Registrar, 1499 N State St, San Jacinto, CA 92583, 909-487-6752 (Fax: 909-654-6738) www.msjc.cc.ca.us. 8AM-7PM M-Th, 8AM-4:30PM F. Enrollment: 8000. Records go back to 1963. Degrees granted: Associate. Attendance, degree and transcript information available by mail.

Mount St. Mary's College, Registrar, 12001 Chalon Rd, Los Angeles, CA 90049, 310-954-4020, 310-954-4021 (Fax: 310-471-4029) www.msmc.la.edu. 8:30AM-4:30PM. Enrollment: 2000. Records go back to 1925. Alumni records maintained here; call 310-954-4082. Degrees granted: Associate; Bachelors; Masters. Attendance and degree information available by phone, fax, mail. Transcripts available by fax, mail.

Mount St. Mary's College (Doheny), Registrar, 10 Chester Pl, Los Angeles, CA 90007, 213-477-2520,2251,2252 (Fax: 213-477-2519) www.msmc.la.edu. 9:30AM-6PM M-Th; 8:30AM-4PM F. Enrollment: 2000. Records go back to 1949. Alumni Records: 12001 Chalon, Los Angeles, CA 90049. Degrees granted: Associate; Bachelors; Masters. Attendance and degree information available by phone, fax, mail. Transcripts available by fax, mail. Fax inquiry accepted only with prior authorization.

Mt. San Antonio College, Director, Admissions & Records, 1100 N Grand Ave, Walnut, CA 91789, 909-594-5611 X4419, 909-594-5611 X4415 (Verifications) (Fax: 909-468-3932) www.mtsac.ed. 8AM-8PM M-Th, 8AM-4:30PM F. Enrollment: 22330. Records go back to 1947. Alumni records are maintained here. Degrees granted: Associate. Attendance and transcript information available by mail. Degree information available by phone, mail.

Napa Valley College, Admissions & Records, 2277 Napa-Vallejo Hwy, Napa, CA 94558, 707-253-3000 (Fax: 707-253-3064) www.nvc.cc.ca.us/nvc/. 7:30AM-8PM M-Th; 7:30AM-5PM F. Enrollment: 8000. Records go back to 1942. Alumni records are maintained here. Degrees granted: Associate; Associate of Arts, Associate of Science. Attendance, degree and transcript information available by fax, mail.

National Hispanic University, Registrar, 14271 Story Rd, San Jose, CA 95127-3823, 408-254-6900 (Fax: 408-254-6903) Records go back to 1993. Degrees granted: Associate; Bachelors; Masters. Attendance and degree information available by phone, mail. Transcripts available by mail.

National University, Registrar, 11255 N Torrey Pines Rd, La Jolla, CA 92037, 619-

California

642-8260 (Fax: 619-642-8718) www.nu.edu. 8AM-5PM. Enrollment: 9000. Records go back to 1971. Alumni records are maintained here. Degrees granted: Associate; Bachelors; Masters. Attendance and degree information available by phone, fax, mail. Transcripts available by fax, mail.

Naval Postgraduate School, Registration & Scheduling, Code 01B1, 589 Dyer Rd, Monterey, CA 93943-5133, 408-656-2591 (Fax: 408-656-2891) www.nps.navy.mil. 8AM-4:30PM. Enrollment: 1326. Records go back to 1948. Alumni records maintained here; call 408-656-4011. Degrees granted: Masters; Doctorate. Certification: Aviation Safety. Attendance and degree information available by phone, fax, mail. Transcripts available by fax, mail.

New College of California, Registrar, 50 Fell St, San Francisco, CA 94102, 415-437-3486, 415-241-1351 (Law School Registrar) (Fax: 415-626-5541) www.newcollege.edu. 8AM-4:30PM. Records go back to 1972. Alumni records are maintained here. Degrees granted: Bachelors; Masters. Attendance and degree information available by phone, fax, mail. Transcripts available by fax, mail.

New School of Architecture, Registrar, 1249 F Street, San Diego, CA 92101, www.newschoolarch.edu. 619-235-4100 (Fax: 619-235-4651) Records go back to 1994. Degrees granted: Bachelors; Masters. Attendance and degree information available by phone, mail. Transcripts available by mail.

Northwestern Polytechnic University, Registrar, 117 Fourier Ave, Freemont, CA 94539, 510-657-5911 (Fax: 510-657-8975) www.npu.edu. 8AM-5PM. Enrollment: 450. Records go back to 1985. Alumni records are maintained here. Degrees granted: Bachelors; Masters. Attendance and degree information available by phone, fax, mail. Transcripts available by fax, mail.

Occidental College, Registrar, 1600 Campus Rd, Los Angeles, CA 90041-3314, 213-259-2686 (Fax: 213-341-4886) www.oxy.edu. 8AM-Noon, 1-5PM M,W,F; 8AM-5PM T & Th. Records go back to 1887. Alumni records are maintained here. Degrees granted: Bachelors; Masters. Attendance and degree information available by phone, fax, mail. Transcripts available by mail.

Ohlone College, Admissions & Records, 43600 Mission Blvd, Fremont, CA 94539, 510-659-6100 (Fax: 510-659-7321) 9AM-3:50PM, 5-7:50PM M-Th; 9AM-4PM F. www.ohlone.cc.ca.us. Enrollment: 8500. Records go back to 1970. Degrees granted: Associate. Attendance and degree information available by fax, mail. Transcripts available by mail.

Orange Coast College, Student Records, 2701 Fairview Rd, PO Box 5005, Costa Mesa, CA 92628, 714-432-5072 www.occ.cccd.edu. 8:00AM-7PM M-Th; 8AM-3PM F. Enrollment: 24500. Records go back to 1949. Alumni records maintained here; call 714-432-5645. Degrees granted: Associate. Attendance and degree information available by phone, mail. Transcripts available by mail.

Otis College of Art and Design, Office of Registration & Records, 9045 Lincoln Blvd, Los Angeles, CA 90045, 310-665-6800, 310-665-6950 (Fax: 310-665-6805) 8:30AM-5PM. www.primenet\~otisart. Enrollment: 750. Records go back to 1950. Alumni records maintained here; call 310-665-6859. Degrees granted: Bachelors; Masters. Attendance and degree information available by phone, mail. Transcripts available by mail.

Oxnard College, Registrar, 4000 S Rose Ave, Oxnard, CA 93033-6699, 805-986-5810 (Fax: 805-986-5806) www.oxnard.cc.ca.us. 8AM-5PM. Enrollment: 2250. Records go back to 1975. Alumni records maintained here; call 805-986-5808. Degrees granted: Associate. Attendance and degree information available by phone, fax, mail. Transcripts available by fax, mail.

Pacific Christian College
(See Hope International University)

Pacific College of Oriental Medicine, Registrar, 7445 Mission Valley Rd Ste 105, San Diego, CA 92108-4407, 619-574-6909 (Fax: 619-574-6641) www.ormed.edu. 9AM-5PM. Enrollment: 310. Records go back to 1986. Degrees granted: Masters. Special programs- Oriental Body Therapy, 619-574-6909: Holistic Health Practitioner, 619-574-6909 Attendance, degree and transcript information available by mail.

Pacific Graduate School of Psychology, Registrar, 935 E Meadow Dr, Palo Alto, CA 94303, 650-843-3524 (Registrar), 800-818-6136 (Admissions) (Fax: 650-856-6734) www.pgsp.edu. 9:30AM-5:30PM. Enrollment: 300. Records go back to 1975. Alumni records maintained here; call 650-843-3403. Degrees granted: Doctorate. Attendance and degree information available by phone, fax, mail. Transcripts available by fax, mail.

Pacific Lutheran Theological Seminary Registrar, 2700 Marin Ave, Berkeley, CA 94708-5264, 510-524-5264. 8AM-4:30PM. Records go back to 1950. Alumni records are maintained here. Degrees granted: Masters. Attendance, degree and transcript information available by mail.

Pacific Oaks College, Registrar, 5 Westmoreland Pl, Pasadena, CA 91103, 626-397-1342, 800-303-1342 (Fax: 626-685-2531) www.pacificoaks.edu. 8:30AM-6PM M-Th; 8:30AM-4:30PM F. Enrollment: 600. Records go back to 1959. Alumni records maintained here; call 626-397-1314. Degrees granted: Bachelors; Masters. Certification: Post-Graduate. Special programs- Extension Division, 626-397-1375. Attendance and degree information available by phone, fax, mail. Transcripts available by mail. Fax requests for transcripts in emergency situations only.

Pacific School of Religion, Registrar, 1798 Scenic Ave, Berkeley, CA 94709, 510-849-8200, 510-849-0528 (Fax: 510-845-8948). 8:30AM-5PM. Enrollment: 200. Records go back to 1866. Alumni records are maintained here. Degrees granted: Masters; Doctorate. Attendance and degree information available by phone, fax, mail. Transcripts available by fax, mail.

Pacific States University, Registrar, 1516 S Western Ave, Los Angeles, CA 90006, 213-731-2383 (Fax: 213-731-7276) www.psuca.edu. 8AM-5PM. Records go back to 1996. Degrees granted: Associate; Bachelors. Attendance and degree information available by phone, mail. Transcripts available by mail.

Pacific Union College, Records Office, Angwin, CA 94508-9707, 707-965-6673 (Fax: 707-965-6432) www.puc.edu. 8:30AM-4:30PM M-Th; 8:30AM-1PM F. Enrollment: 1500. Records go back to 1887. Alumni records maintained here; call 707-965-6306. Degrees granted: Associate; Bachelors; Masters. Attendance and degree information available by phone, fax, mail. Transcripts available by fax, mail.

Palmer College of Chiropractic-West, Registrar, 90 E Tasman Dr, San Jose, CA 95134, 408-944-6099 (Fax: 408-944-6196) 8AM-4:30PM. www.palmer.edu. Enrollment: 745. Records go back to 1981. Alumni records maintained here; call 408-944-6043. Degrees granted: Doctorate. Attendance and degree information available by fax, mail. Transcripts available by mail.

Palo Verde College, Registrar, 811 W Chanslorway, Blythe, CA 92225, 760-922-6168 (Fax: 760-922-0230) www.paloverde.cc.ca.us. 8AM-5PM M-Th; 8AM-4:30PM F. Enrollment: 2300. Records go back to 1955. Degrees granted: Associate. Special programs- LVN Program, 760-921-5346. Attendance and degree information available by phone, fax, mail. Transcripts available by fax, mail.

Palomar College, Registrar, 1140 W Mission Rd, San Marcos, CA 92069, 619-744-1150 X2169, 619-744-1150 X2633 (Fax: 619-744-2932) www.palomar.edu. 7:30AM-7PM M-Th; 7:30AM-2PM F. Enrollment: 24437. Records go back to 1946. Degrees granted: Associate. Attendance and degree information available by phone, fax, mail. Transcripts available by fax, mail.

Pasadena City College, Records Office, 1570 E Colorado Blvd, Pasadena, CA 91106, 626-585-7475, 626-585-7396 www.paccd.cc.ca.us. 8AM-7:30PM M-Th; 8AM-4:30PM F. Enrollment: 2700. Records go back to 1945. Alumni records are maintained. Degrees granted: Associate. Special programs- Financial Aid, 626-585-7401. Attendance and degree information available by phone, fax, mail. Transcripts available by fax, mail. Verification Phone: 626-585-7294; Fax: 626-585-7915.

Patten College, Registrar, 2433 Coolidge Ave, Oakland, CA 94601, 510-533-8300 X220 (Fax: 510-534-8969). 9AM-5:30PM. Records go back to 1989. Alumni records maintained here; call 510-533-8300 X255. Degrees granted: Bachelors. Attendance and degree information available by fax, mail. Transcripts available by mail.

Pepperdine University, Registrar, 24255 Pacific Coast Hwy, Malibu, CA 90263, 310-456-4542, 310-456-4382 (Fax: 310-456-4358) www.pepperdine.edu. 8AM-5PM. Enrollment: 7800. Records go back to 1937. Alumni records maintained here; call 310-456-4248. Degrees granted: Bachelors; Masters; Doctorate. Attendance and degree information available by phone, fax, mail. Transcripts available by fax, mail. Transcript may be requested by phone on emergency basis.

Phillips Graduate Institute, Registrar, 5445 Balboa Blvd, Encino, CA 91316-1509, 818-386-5600 X638, 818-509-5959 X252 (Fax: 818-386-5699) www.pgi.edu. 8AM-5PM. Enrollment: 300. Records go back to 1983. Formerly **California Family Study Center.** Alumni records maintained here; call 818-386-5600. Degrees granted: Masters. Attendance and degree information available by phone, fax, mail. Transcripts available by fax, mail.

Phillips Junior College, Registrar, 15400 Sherman Way, Suite 250, Van Nuys, CA 91406, 818-895-2220 Records go back to 1984. Degrees granted: Associate. Attendance and degree information available by phone, mail. Transcripts available by mail.

Pitzer College, Registrar, 1050 N Mills Ave, Claremont, CA 91711-6101, 909-607-3036 (Fax: 909-607-7161) www.pitzer.edu. 8AM-5PM. Enrollment: 750. Records go back to 1963. Alumni records maintained here; call 909-621-8000 X8130. Degrees granted: Bachelors. Attendance and degree information available by phone, fax, mail. Transcripts available by mail.

Platt College, Registrar, 7470 N Figueroa St, Los Angeles, CA 90041-1717, 213-258-8050 (Fax: 213-258-8532) 8AM-5PM. www.plattcollege.edu. Records go back to 1987. Degrees granted: Associate. Attendance and degree information available by phone, mail. Transcripts available by mail.

Platt College, Registrar, 3901 MacArthur Blvd, Newport Beach, CA 92600, 714-833-2300 (Fax: 714-833-0269) 8AM-5PM. www.plattdesign.com. Enrollment: 180. Records go back to 1985. Degrees granted: Associate. Attendance and degree information available by phone, mail. Transcripts available by mail.

Platt College, Registrar, 9521 Business Center Dr, Bldg #9, Rancho Circamanga, CA 91730, 909-989-1187 (Fax: 909-941-9660) 8AM-5PM. www.plattdesign.com. Records go back to 1987. Degrees granted: Associate. Attendance and degree information available by phone, mail. Transcripts available by mail.

Point Loma Nazarene University, Registrar, 3900 Lomaland Dr, San Diego, CA 92106, 619-849-2286, 619-849-2287 (Fax: 619-849-2289) www.ptloma.edu. 8AM-4:30PM. Enrollment: 2459. Records go back to 1902. Alumni records maintained here; call 619-849-2586. Degrees granted: Bachelors; Masters; EDS. Attendance and degree information available by fax, mail. Transcripts available by mail.

Pomona College, Registrar, 550 N College Ave, Claremont, CA 91711, 909-621-8147 (Fax: 909-621-8671) www.pomona.edu. 8AM-5PM. Enrollment: 1500. Records go back to 1887. Alumni records maintained here; call 909-621-8110. Degrees granted: Bachelors. Special programs- Liberal Arts. Attendance and degree information available by phone, fax, mail. Transcripts available by mail.

Porterville College, Registrar, 100 E College Ave, Porterville, CA 93257, 209-791-2220 (Fax: 209-791-2349) www.pc.cc.ca.us. 8AM-7PM M-Th; 8AM-4:30PM F. Enrollment: 3400. Records go back to 1927. Alumni records maintained here; call 209-791-2270. Degrees granted: Associate. Attendance information available by phone, fax, mail. Degree and transcript information available by fax, mail.

Queen of the Holy Rosary College, Registrar, PO Box 3908, Mission San Jose, CA 94539, 510-657-2468 (Fax: 510-657-1734). 8AM-4PM. Enrollment: 224. Records go back to 1930. Degrees granted: Associate. Attendance, degree and transcript information available by fax, mail.

Rand Graduate School of Policy Studies, Registrar, 1700 Main St, PO Box 2138, Santa Monica, CA 90407-2138, 310-393-0411 X6419, 310-393-0411 X7690 (Fax: 310-451-6978). 8AM-5PM. Enrollment: 58. Records go back to 1948. Alumni records are maintained here. Degrees granted: Doctorate. Attendance and degree information available by phone, fax, mail. Transcripts available by mail.

Rio Hondo College, Registrar, 3600 Workman Mill Rd, Whittier, CA 90601-1699, 562-692-0921, 562-908-3415 (Admissions & Records) (Fax: 562-692-8318) 8AM-8PM M-Th, 8AM-4PM F. www.rh.cc.ca.us. Enrollment: 12000. Records go back to 1963.

Alumni records maintained here; call 562-692-0921 X3445. Degrees granted: Associate. Attendance and degree information available by phone, fax, mail. Transcripts available by mail. Verifications Phone: 562-692-8318

Riverside Community College, Registrar, 4800 Magnolia Ave, Riverside, CA 92506-1299, 909-222-8603 (Fax: 909-222-8028 (Attn: Transcript Office)) 8AM-6PM M-Th; 8AM-4PM F. www.rccd.cc.ca.us. Enrollment: 18000. Degrees granted: Associate. Attendance information available by fax, mail. Degree information available by phone, fax, mail. Transcripts available by mail.

Sacramento City College, Registrar, 3835 Freeport Blvd, Sacramento, CA 95822, www.losrios.cc.ca.us 916-558-2351 (Fax: 916-558-2190) 7:30AM-8PM M-Th; 7:30AM-4:30PM F. Enrollment: 18000. Records go back to 1916. Degrees granted: Associate. Attendance information available by phone, fax, mail. Degree and transcript information available by fax, mail.

Saddleback College, Office of Admissions and Records, 28000 Marguerite Pkwy, Mission Viejo, CA 92692, 714-582-4555 www.saddleback.cc.ca.us (Fax: 714-347-8315) 8AM-8PM M-Th; 8AM-4:30PM F. Enrollment: 23000. Records go back to 1968. Degrees granted: Associate. Attendance, degree and transcript information available by fax, mail. Will confirm degree and attendance over the phone.

Saint Mary's College of California, Office of the Registrar, PO Box 4748, Moraga, CA 94575-4748, 925-631-4214 (Fax: 925-376-8339) www.stmarys-ca.edu. 8:30AM-4:30PM. Enrollment: 4875. Records go back to 1875. Alumni Records: Alumni Assoc., Saint Mary's College of California, PO Box 3400, Moraga, CA 94575-3400. Degrees granted: Associate; Bachelors; Masters. Attendance and degree information available by phone, fax, mail. Transcripts available by fax, mail.

Salvation Army School for Officers' Training, Registrar, 30840 Hawthorne Blvd, Rancho Palos Verdes, CA 90275, 310-544-6467 (Fax: 310-265-6514). 8:15AM-4:15PM. Enrollment: 83. Records go back to 1900's. Degrees granted: Associate. Attendance and degree information available by phone, fax, mail. Transcripts available by mail.

Samra University of Oriental Medicine, Registrar, 3000 South Robertson Blvd, 4th Flr, Los Angeles, CA 90034, 310-202-6444 (Fax: 310-202-6007) www.samra.edu. 10:30AM-6:30PM. Enrollment: 350. Records go back to 1982. Degrees granted: Masters. Attendance and degree information available by fax, mail. Transcripts available by mail.

Samuel Merritt College, Registrar, 370 Hawthorne Ave, Oakland, CA 94609, 510-869-6130, 510-867-6511 (Fax: 510-869-6525). 8AM-5PM. Enrollment: 600. Records go back to 1909. Alumni records maintained here; call 510-869-6614. Degrees granted: Bachelors; Masters. Attendance and degree information available by phone, fax, mail. Transcripts available by fax, mail.

San Bernardino Valley College, Registrar, 701 S Mt Vernon Ave, San Bernardino, CA 92410, 909-888-6511 X1651 (Fax: 909-889-4988). 8AM-7PM. Records go back to 1926. Alumni records are maintained here. Degrees granted: Associate. Attendance information available by written request only. Degree information available by phone, fax, mail. Transcripts available by fax, mail.

San Diego City College, Registrar, 1313 Twelfth Ave, San Diego, CA 92101, 619-584-6925 (Fax: 619-230-2135). 8AM-7:30PM. Records go back to 1950. Alumni records maintained here; call 619-230-2453. Degrees granted: Associate. Attendance, degree and transcript information available by fax, mail.

San Diego Mesa College, Registrar, 7250 Mesa College Dr, San Diego, CA 92111, 619-627-2682 (Fax: 619-627-2960) 8AM-7PM M-Th, 8AM-3:30PM F. www.sdmesa.sdccdca.us. Enrollment: 24101. Records go back to 1964. Degrees granted: Associate Attendance, degree and transcript information available by fax, mail.

San Diego Miramar College, Registrar, 10440 Black Mountain Rd, San Diego, CA 92126, 619-536-7844 (Records), 619-584-6931 (District) (Fax: 619-693-1899) www.sdccdca.us. 8AM-5PM M-Th; 8AM-3PM F. Enrollment: 9773. Records go back to 1946. Degrees granted: Associate. Special programs- Continuing Education, 619-527-5280: Law Enforcement Academy, 619-536-7320. Attendance, degree and transcript information available by fax, mail.

San Diego State University, Registrar, 5500 Campanile Dr, San Diego, CA 92182-7455, www.sdsu.edu. 619-594-7800 (Fax: 619-594-4902) 8AM-4:30PM. Enrollment: 29000. Records go back to 1890. Alumni records maintained here; call 619-594-ALUM. Degrees granted: Bachelors; Masters; Doctorate. Special programs- College of Extended Studies, 619-594-5821. Attendance and degree information available by phone, fax, mail. Transcripts available by mail.

San Francisco Art Institute, Registrar, 800 Chestnut St, San Francisco, CA 94133, 415-749-4535 (Fax: 415-749-4579). 9AM-5PM. Enrollment: 700. Records go back to 1930's. Alumni records maintained here; call 415-749-5842. Degrees granted: Bachelors; Masters. Attendance and degree information available by phone, fax, mail. Transcripts available by mail.

San Francisco College of Mortuary Science, Registrar, 1598 Dolores St, San Francisco, CA 94110, 415-824-1313 (Fax: 415-824-1390) www.sfcms.org. 8AM-4:30PM. Enrollment: 75. Records go back to 1965. Alumni records are maintained. Degrees granted: Associate. Attendance and degree information available by phone, fax, mail. Transcripts available by fax, mail.

San Francisco Conservatory of Music, Registrar, 1201 Ortega St, San Francisco, CA 94122, 415-759-3422 (Fax: 415-759-3499) www.sfcm.edu. 9AM-5PM. Enrollment: 255. Records go back to 1956. Alumni records maintained here; call 415-759-3428. Degrees granted: Bachelors; Masters. Attendance and degree information available by phone, fax, mail. Transcripts available by fax, mail.

San Francisco State University, Registrar, 1600 Holloway Ave, San Francisco, CA 94132, 415-338-2350, 415-338-2077 (Fax: 415-338-0588) www.sfsu.edu. 8:30AM-5PM. Enrollment: 27500. Records go back to 1909. Alumni records maintained here; call 415-338-2217. Degrees granted: Bachelors; Masters; Doctorate. Special programs- 415-338-2350. Attendance and degree information available by phone, fax, mail. Transcripts available by mail.

San Francisco Theological Seminary, Registrar, 2 Kensington Rd, San Anselmo, CA 94960, 415-258-6553, 415-258-6500 (Fax: 415-454-2493) www.sfts.edu. 8:30AM-

5PM. Enrollment: 700. Records go back to 1900. Alumni records are maintained here. Degrees granted: Bachelors; Masters; Doctorate. Certification: Spir. Direction. Attendance and degree information available by phone, fax, mail. Transcripts available by fax, mail.

San Joaquin College of Law, Registrar, 901 5th St, Clovis, CA 93612, 209-323-2100 (Fax: 209-323-5566) www.sjcl.org. 9AM-5PM. Enrollment: 235. Records go back to 1974. Alumni records are maintained here. Degrees granted: Masters; Doctorate; Juris. Attendance information available by phone, fax, mail. Degree and transcript information available by fax, mail.

San Joaquin Delta College, Registrar, 5151 Pacific Ave, Stockton, CA 95207, 209-954-5635, 209-954-5625 (Fax: 209-954-5600) www.sjdccd.cc.ca.us. 8AM-8:30PM M-Th; 8AM-5PM F. Enrollment: 16000. Records go back to 1963. Degrees granted: Associate. Attendance information available by fax, mail. Degree information available by phone, fax, mail. Transcripts available by mail.

San Joaquin Valley College, Registrar, 8400 W Mineral King Ave, Visalia, CA 93291-9283, 209-651-2500 (Fax: 209-651-0574) www.sjvc.edu. Enrollment: 1400. Records go back to 1994. Degrees granted: Associate. Attendance and degree information available by phone, mail. Transcripts available by mail.

San Jose Christian College, Registrar, PO Box 1090, 790 S 12th St, San Jose, CA 95112, 408-293-9058, 800-355-5300 (Fax: 408-293-7352) www.sjchristiancol.edu. 8AM-4:30PM. Enrollment: 350. Records go back to 1939. Degrees granted: Associate; Bachelors. Certification: Bible Counseling, Family Ministry, Children's Ministry, Missions, Pastoral Ministry, Sports Ministry, Music, Worship. Attendance and degree information available by phone, fax, mail. Transcripts available by fax, mail.

San Jose City College, Registrar, 2100 Moorpark Ave, San Jose, CA, 95128, 408-298-2181, 408-288-3700 (Fax: 408-298-1935) www.sjcc.cc.ca.us. 8AM-7PM M-Th; 9AM-5PM F. Enrollment: 11000. Records go back to 1955. Alumni records are maintained here. Degrees granted: Associate. Attendance and degree information available by phone, fax, mail. Transcripts available by written request only.

San Jose State University, Registrar, One Washington Square, San Jose, CA 95192, 408-283-7500, 408-924-2059 (Fax: 408-924-2050) www.sjsu.edu. 8AM-5PM. Records go back to 1917. Alumni records maintained here; call 408-924-6515. Degrees granted: Bachelors. Attendance and degree information available by phone, fax, mail. Transcripts available by mail.

San Mateo Count Community College, District Office, Admissions Office, 1700 W Hillsdale Blvd, San Mateo, CA 94402, www.smcccd.cc.ca.us/sncccd/csn/csn. 650-574-6165 (Fax: 650-574-6506) 8AM-10PM M-Th; 8AM-4:30PM F. Enrollment: 12000. Records go back to 1922. Alumni records are maintained here. Degrees granted: Associate. Attendance and degree information available by phone, fax, mail. Transcripts available by mail.

Santa Ana College
(See Rancho Santiago College)

Santa Ana Community College, Registrar, 1530 W 17th St, Santa Ana, CA

92706, 714-564-6000, 714-564-6005 (Fax: 714-564-6379) www.rancho.cc.ca.us. 8AM-9PM M-Th; 8AM-5PM F. Enrollment: 2500. Records go back to 1930. Degrees granted: Associate. Attendance and degree information available by phone, fax, mail. Transcripts available by fax, mail.

Santa Barbara City College, Registrar, 721 Cliff Dr, Santa Barbara, CA 93109, 805-965-0581 (Fax: 805-963-7222) www.sbcc.net. 8AM-7:30PM M-Th; 8AM-4:15PM F. Enrollment: 11500. Records go back to 1958. Alumni records are maintained here. Degrees granted: Associate. Attendance and transcript information available by fax, mail. Degree information available by phone, fax, mail.

Santa Clara University, Registrar, Santa Clara, CA 95053, 408-554-4331 (Fax: 408-554-6926) www.scu.edu. 8AM-5PM. Enrollment: 7451. Records go back to 1800's. Alumni records maintained here; call 408-554-6800. Degrees granted: Bachelors; Masters; Doctorate. Attendance and degree information available by phone, fax, mail. Transcripts available by fax, mail.

Santa Monica College, Admissions & Records, 1900 Pico Blvd, Santa Monica, CA 90405, 310-450-5150, 310-450-5150 (Ext. 9880) (Fax: 310-399-1730) www.smc.edu. 8AM-8PM M-Th; 8AM-4PM F. Enrollment: 26000. Records go back to 1920. Degrees granted: Associate. Attendance, degree and transcript information available by mail.

Santa Rosa Junior College, Admissions & Records, Transcripts, 1501 Mendocino Ave, Santa Rosa, CA 95401, 707-527-4514 (Fax: 707-527-4798) www.santarosa.edu. 8AM-5PM. Enrollment: 32000. Records go back to 1917. Alumni records maintained here; call 707-527-4733. Degrees granted: Associate. Attendance and degree information available by fax, mail. Transcripts available by mail.

Saybrook Institute Graduate School & Research Center, Registrar, 450 Pacific Ave 3rd Flr, San Francisco, CA 94133, 415-433-9200 X116 (Fax: 415-433-9271) www.saybrook.org. 8:30AM-4:30PM. Enrollment: 350. Records go back to 1971. Alumni records are maintained here. Degrees granted: Masters; Doctorate. Attendance and transcript information available by fax, mail. Degree information available by phone, fax, mail.

School of Nursing, Registrar, 1200 N State St, Muir Hall Rm 114, Los Angeles, CA 90033-1084, 213-226-4911 (Fax: 213-226-6427). Enrollment: 241. Records go back to 1898. Degrees granted: Associate Attendance, degree and transcript information available by phone, mail.

Scripps College, Registrar, 1030 N Columbia Ave, Claremont, CA 91711, www.scrippscol.edu. 909-621-8273, 909-607-2981 (Fax: 909-621-8323) 8AM-5PM, 1-4PM. Enrollment: 700. Records go back to 1926. Alumni records maintained here; call 909-621-8054. Degrees granted: Bachelors. Certification: Post-Bac, Pre-Med. Special programs- Post Baccalaureate Pre-Med, 909-621-8764. Attendance and degree information available by phone, fax, mail. Transcripts available by fax, mail.

Scripps Research Institute (The), Graduate Office, 10550 N Torrey Pines Rd, TPC 19, La Jolla, CA 92037, 619-784-8469 (Fax: 619-784-2802) www.scripps.edu. 8:30AM-5PM. Enrollment: 100. Records go back to 1989. Degrees granted: Doctorate; PhD. Attendance and degree information

available by phone, fax, mail. Transcripts available by fax, mail.

Sequoia Institute, Registrar, 420 Whitney Pl, Fremont, CA 94539-7663, 510-490-6900 (Fax: 510-490-8599) www.seq.edu.com. Records go back to 1977. Degrees granted: Associate. Attendance and degree information available by phone, mail. Transcripts available by mail.

Shasta College, Registrar, PO Box 496006, Redding, CA 96049, 916-225-4841 (Fax: 916-225-4995) dlj.shasta.cc.ca.us/. 8AM-7PM M-Th, 8AM-4PM F Summer: 8AM-7PM M-Th, 8AM-4PM F. Enrollment: 11595. Records go back to 1950's. Alumni records are maintained here. Degrees granted: Associate. Attendance, degree and transcript information available by fax, mail.

Sierra College, Assistant Dean, 5000 Rocklin Rd, Rocklin, CA 95677, 916-781-0430 www.sierra.cc.ca.us (Fax: 916-781-0403) 7:45AM-7:45PM M-Th; 7:45AM-4:45PM F; Business Office closes at 5PM. Enrollment: 17000. Records go back to 1937. Alumni records maintained here; call 916-773-5659. Degrees granted: Associate. Attendance, degree and transcript information available by fax, mail.

Silicon Valley College, Registrar, 41350 Christy St, Fremont, CA 94538, www.svcollege.com 510-623-9966 (Fax: 510-623-9822) 8AM-9PM M-Th; 8AM-5PM F. Records go back to 1991. Degrees granted: Associate. Attendance and degree information available by phone, mail. Transcripts available by mail.

Simpson College, Registrar, 2211 College View Dr, Redding, CA 96003, 916-224-5600 X2111 (Fax: 916-224-5608) 8AM-6PM. www.simpsonca.edu. Enrollment: 1200. Records go back to 1921. Alumni records maintained here; call 916-224-5600 X2503. Degrees granted: Associate; Bachelors; Masters. Attendance and degree information available by phone, fax, mail. Transcripts available by fax, mail.

Skyline College, Admissions/Records Of., 3300 College Dr, San Bruno, CA 94066, www.smcccd.cc.ca.us/smcccd/skyline/skyline 650-738-4252, 650-738-4251 7:30AM-10PM M-Th, 7:30AM-4:30PM F, 8AM-Noon Sat. Records go back to 1969. Degrees granted: Associate. Special programs- Auto, 650-738-4371; Cosmetology, 650-738-4165; Respiratory Therapy, 650-738-4382. Attendance, degree and transcript information available by mail.

Solano Community College, Admissions & Records, 4000 Suisun Valley Rd, Suisun, CA 94585, 707-864-7171, 707-864-7000 (Fax: 707-864-7175) www.solano.cc.ca.us. 8AM-8PM M-Th; 8AM-3PM F. Enrollment: 10000. Records go back to 1945. Degrees granted: Associate. Attendance, degree and transcript information available by fax, mail, signature required.

Sonoma State University, Registrar, 1801 E Cotati Ave, Rohnert Park, CA 94928, www.admrec.sonoma.educ/. 707-664-2778 (Fax: 707-664-2060) 8AM-4:30PM. Records go back to 1960. Alumni records maintained here; call 707-664-2426. Degrees granted: Bachelors. Attendance and degree information available by phone, fax, mail. Transcripts available by mail.

South Baylo University, Registrar, 1126 N Brookhurst St, Anaheim, CA 92801, 714-533-1495 (Fax: 714-533-1640). 10AM-6PM. Enrollment: 235. Records go back to 1982. Degrees granted: Masters. Attendance and degree information available by mail. Transcripts available by fax, mail.

South Baylo University (Branch), Registrar, 2727 W 6th St, Los Angeles, CA 90057, 213-738-1974. Records are located at South Baylo University, Registrar, 1126 N Brookhurst St, Anaheim, CA 92801.

Southern California College, Registrar, 55 Fair Dr, Costa Mesa, CA 92626, 714-556-3610 (Fax: 714-966-5471) www.sccu.edu. 8AM-4:30PM. Enrollment: 1200. Records go back to 1920. Alumni records are maintained here. Degrees granted: Bachelors; Masters. Attendance and degree information available by phone, fax, mail. Transcripts available by fax, mail.

Southern California College of Optometry, Registrar, 2575 Yorba Linda Blvd, Fullerton, CA 92831-1699, 714-449-7445 (Fax: 714-992-7878) www.scco.edu. 8AM-5PM. Enrollment: 382. Records go back to 1904. Alumni records maintained here; call 714-449-7461. Degrees granted: Doctorate. Attendance information available by phone, fax, mail. Degree and transcript information available by mail.

Southern California Institute of Architecture, Registrar, 5454 Beethoven St, Los Angeles, CA 90066, 310-574-1123 (Fax: 310-574-3801) www.sciarc.edu. Enrollment: 440. Records go back to 1972. Alumni records are maintained here. Degrees granted: Bachelors; Masters. Special programs- 310-574-1123 X321. Attendance and degree information available by phone, fax, mail. Transcripts available by written request only.

Southern California School of Culinary Art, Registrar, 1420 El Centro St, South Pasadena, CA 91030, 626-403-8490 (Fax: 626-403-8494) www.scscs.com. 8AM-5PM. Enrollment: 140. Records go back to 1994. Alumni records are maintained here. Degrees granted: Associate. Attendance and degree information available by phone, mail. Transcripts available by mail.

Southwestern College, Admissions Center, 900 Otay Lakes Rd, Chula Vista, CA 91910, 619-482-6550 (Fax: 619-482-6489) www.swc.cc.ca.us. 7:30AM-8PM M-Th; 7:30AM-3PM F. Enrollment: 18000. Records go back to 1800. Degrees granted: Associate. Attendance, degree and transcript information available by fax, mail.

Southwestern University School of Law, Registrar, 675 S Westmoreland Ave, Los Angeles, CA 90005, 213-738-6734, 213-738-6733 (Fax: 213-383-1688). Enrollment: 1200. Records go back to 1913. Alumni records maintained here; call 213-738-6814. Degrees granted: Doctorate; JD. Attendance, degree and transcript information available by mail.

St. John's Seminary, Registrar, 5012 Seminary Rd, Camarillo, CA 93012-2598, 805-482-2755 (Fax: 805-482-3470). 8AM-4:30PM. Enrollment: 110. Records go back to 1939. Alumni records are maintained here. Degrees granted: Masters. Attendance and degree information available by phone, fax, mail. Transcripts available by mail.

St. John's Seminary College, Registrar, 5118 E Seminary Rd, Camarillo, CA 93012-2599, 805-482-2755 X202 (Fax: 805-987-5097). 8AM-4PM. Enrollment: 71. Records go back to 1940. Alumni Records: Rev Bill Piletic, 5118 Seminary Rd, Camarillo, CA 93012. Degrees granted: Bachelors. Attendance, degree and transcript information available by mail.

St. Patrick's Seminary, Registrar, 320 Middlefield Rd, Menlo Park, CA 94025, 650-325-5621 (Fax: 650-322-0997). 9AM-Noon, 1-4PM. Enrollment: 68. Records go back to 1896. Alumni records are maintained here. Degrees granted: Masters. Attendance and degree information available by phone, fax, mail. Transcripts available by mail. Will fax non-transcript information only.

Stanford University, Transcripts & Registration, Old Union Bldg, Stanford, CA 94305, www.stanford.edu. 650-723-2086 (transcripts), 650-723-5790 (verifications) (Fax: 650-725-7248) 8AM-5PM. Records go back to 1891. Alumni records maintained here; call 650-723-2021. Degrees granted: Bachelors; Masters; Doctorate. Attendance and degree information available by phone, fax, mail. Transcripts available by mail.

Starr King School for the Ministry, Registrar, 2441 LeConte Ave, Berkeley, CA 94709, 510-845-6232 (Fax: 510-845-6273). 9AM-5PM. Enrollment: 70. Records go back to 1900's. Alumni records are maintained here. Degrees granted: Masters. Attendance, degree and transcript information available by phone, fax, mail.

State Center Community College, Registrar, 1101 E University Ave, Fresno, CA 93741, 209-442-4600 (Fax: 209-485-7304). 8AM-7PM M-Th; 1-5PM F. Enrollment: 19000. Records go back to 1910. Degrees granted: Associate. Special programs- Liberal Arts: Business. Attendance and degree information available by phone, fax, mail. Transcripts available by mail.

Taft College, Registrar, 29 Emmons Park Dr, Taft, CA 93268, 805-763-7700 (Fax: 805-763-7705) www.taft.cc.ca.us/. 8AM-5PM. Enrollment: 1400. Records go back to 1922. Degrees granted: Associate. Special programs- Dental Hygiene, 805-765-4384. Attendance and degree information available by phone, fax, mail. Transcripts available by fax, mail.

Thomas Aquinas College, Registrar, 10000 N Ojai Rd, Santa Paula, CA 93060, 805-525-4417 X402 (Fax: 805-525-0620) 8:30AM-5PM. www.thomasaquinas.edu. Enrollment: 220. Records go back to 1971. Alumni records maintained here; call 805-525-4417. Degrees granted: Bachelors. Attendance and degree information available by fax, mail. Transcripts available by mail.

Thomas Jefferson School of Law, Registrar, 2121 San Diego Ave, San Diego, CA 92110, 619-297-9700 (Fax: 619-294-4713) www.jeffersonlaw.edu. 8AM-6PM. Enrollment: 600. Records go back to 1969. Formerly **Western State University College of Law of San Diego**. Alumni records maintained here. Attendance, degree and transcript information available by mail.

U.S. International University, Registrar, 10455 Pomerado Rd, San Diego, CA 92131, 619-271-4300 (Fax: 619-635-4739) www.usiu.edu. 8AM-5PM. Enrollment: 1951. Records go back to 1956. Degrees granted: Associate; Bachelors; Masters; Doctorate. Attendance and degree information available by phone, mail. Transcripts available by mail.

United States International University, Registrar, 10455 Pomerado Rd, San Diego, CA 92131, 619-635-4580, 619-635-4581 (Fax: 619-693-8562) www.usiu.edu. 8AM-5:30PM. Enrollment: 1300. Records go back to 1950. Alumni records are maintained here. Degrees granted: Associate; Bachelors; Masters; Doctorate. Certification: Education. Attendance and degree information available by phone, fax, mail. Transcripts available by

mail. Transcript requires signed release by student.

University of California, Berkeley, Registrar, 128 Sproul Hall, Berkeley, CA 94720-5404, 510-642-4814, 510-642-1883 (Fax: 510-643-8050) 9AM-Noon, 1-4PM. www.registrar.berkeley.edu Enrollment: 33000. Records go back to 1902. Alumni records maintained here; call 510-642-7026. Degrees granted: Bachelors; Masters; Doctorate. Certification: Teaching Credentials Attendance, degree and transcript information available by fax, mail.

University of California, Davis, Office of the Registrar, One Shields Ave, Mrak Hall, Davis, CA 95616, 530-752-3639, 530-752-3639 (Fax: 530-752-6906) 8AM-5PM. www.registrar.ucdavis.edu. Enrollment: 25000. Records go back to 1920's. Alumni records maintained here; call 530-752-1128. Degrees granted: Bachelors; Masters; Doctorate. Attendance and degree information available by phone, fax, mail. Transcripts available by mail.

University of California, Hastings College of the Law, Registrar, 200 McAllister St, San Francisco, CA 94102, 415-565-4613 (Records Office) (Fax: 415-565-4863) www.uchastings.edu. 9AM-3:30PM. Enrollment: 1250. Records go back to 1975. Alumni records maintained here; call 415-565-4615. Attendance and degree information available by phone, fax, mail. Transcripts available by mail.

University of California, Irvine, Registrar, Irvine, CA 92717-4975, 949-824-6124, 949-824-5418 (Fax: 949-824-7896) www.uci.edu. 8AM-5PM. Enrollment: 17000. Records go back to 1965. Alumni Records: Phineas Banning Alumni House, UCI, Irvine, CA 92697-1225. Degrees granted: Associate; Bachelors; Masters; Doctorate. Attendance and degree information available by phone, mail. Transcripts available by mail.

University of California, Los Angeles, Office of the Registrar, Transcripts, 1105 Murphy Hall, Box 951429, Los Angeles, CA 90095-1429, 310-825-3801, 310-206-0482 (Verification Desk) (Fax: 310-825-6235) www.ucla.edu/. 9AM-5PM. Enrollment: 36000. Records go back to 1898. Alumni Records: 405 Hilgard Ave-James West Center, Los Angeles, CA 90095. Degrees granted: Bachelors; Masters; Doctorate. Attendance and degree information available by phone, fax, mail. Transcripts available by fax, mail. Phone number required.

University of California, Riverside, Registrar, Riverside, CA 92521, 909-787-7284, 909-787-3401 (Fax: 909-787-7368) www.ucr.edu. 8AM-5PM. Enrollment: 9063. Alumni Records: Alumni Assoc., 3127 Hinderaker Hall, Riverside, CA 92521. Degrees granted: Bachelors; Masters; Doctorate. Certification: EDUC. Special programs- Extension Office, 909-787-7105. Attendance and degree information available by phone, fax, mail. Transcripts available by mail.

University of California, San Diego, Office of the Registrar, 9500 Gilman Dr, La Jolla, CA 92093-0021, 619-534-3150 (Fax: 619-534-5723) www.reg.ucsd.edu/. 8AM-4:30PM. Enrollment: 18000. Records go back to 1960. Alumni records are maintained here. Degrees granted: Bachelors; Masters; Doctorate; MD. Attendance and degree information available by phone, mail. Transcripts available by fax, mail.

University of California, San Francisco (Health Science), Registrar, 500 Parnassus

Ave, MV 200 West, San Francisco, CA 94143, 415-476-4527, 415-476-8280 8AM-5PM. www.ucsf.edu. Records go back to 1920. Alumni records maintained here; call 415-476-1471. Degrees granted: Masters; Doctorate; Professional Degree. Attendance, degree and transcript information available by mail.

University of California, Santa Barbara,
Registrar, Santa Barbara, CA 93106, 805-893-3135, 805-893-4215 (Fax: 805-893-2985) www.registrar.ucsb.edu. 8AM-Noon, 1-5PM. Enrollment: 18200. Records go back to 1900's. Alumni Records: 6550 Hollister Ave, Goleta, CA 93117. Degrees granted: Bachelors; Masters; PhD. Attendance and degree information available by phone, fax, mail. Transcripts available by fax, mail.

University of California, Santa Cruz,
Registrar, 190 Hahn Student Services, Santa Cruz, CA 95064, 408-459-4412 (Fax: 408-459-5051) www.ucsc.edu. 8AM-5PM. Enrollment: 10000. Records go back to 1966. Phone number for transcripts is 408-459-2902. Alumni Records: Carriage House, Santa Cruz, CA 95064 (Fax: 408-459-3412). Degrees granted: Bachelors; Masters; Doctorate. Certification: Post-Bac. Special programs- University Extension,740 Front St, Santa Cruz, CA 95060. Attendance and degree information available by phone, fax, mail. Transcripts available by mail.

University of Judaism, Registrar, 15600
Mulholland Dr, Los Angeles, CA 90077, 310-476-9777 (Fax: 310-471-3657) www.uj.edu. 9AM-5PM. Enrollment: 200. Records go back to 1947. Alumni records are maintained here. Degrees granted: Bachelors; Masters. Attendance and degree information available by phone, fax, mail. Transcripts available by written request only.

University of La Verne, Registrar, 1950
Third St, La Verne, CA 91750, 909-593-3511 X4000 (Fax: 909-392-2703) 8AM-5PM M,W,F; 8AM-7PM T,Th. www.ulaverne.edu Enrollment: 6000. Records go back to 1891. Alumni records maintained here; call 909-593-3511 X4680. Degrees granted: Associate; Bachelors; Masters; Doctorate Attendance, degree and transcript information available by fax, mail.

University of Phoenix (San Diego
Campus), Registrar, 3890 Murphy Canyon Rd Ste 200, San Diego, CA 92123, 619-576-7469 (Fax: 619-576-0032) www.UOPHX.EDU. 8AM-6PM. Enrollment: 3000. Records go back to 1976. Degrees granted: Bachelors. Special programs- Business Management: Nursing. Attendance and degree information available by mail. Transcript records are housed at University of Phoenix, Registrar, PO Box 52069, Phoenix, AZ 85072, 602-929-4141. A written request may be required.

University of Phoenix (Online), Registrar,
100 Spear St #110, San Francisco, CA 94105, www.uophx.edu/online. 415-541-0141 (Fax: 415-541-0761) Enrollment: 3145. Records go back to 1976. Alumni Records: Alumni Assoc., 4615 E Elwood ST, Phoenix, AZ 85072. Degrees granted: Bachelors; Masters. Attendance and degree information available by phone, fax, mail. Transcript records are housed at University of Phoenix, Registrar, PO Box 52069, Phoenix, AZ 85072. 602-929-4141. A written request may be required.

University of Phoenix (San Jose Main),
Registrar, 3590 N 1st St, San Jose, CA 95134-1805, 408-435-8500 (Fax: 408-435-8250) www.uophx.edu/northcal. Alumni records are maintained here. Degrees granted: Bachelors; Masters. Attendance and degree information available by written request only.

Transcript records are housed at University of Phoenix, Registrar, PO Box 52069, Phoenix, AZ 85072, 602-929-4141. A written request may be required.

University of Redlands, Registrar, 1200 E
Colton Ave, Redlands, CA 92373-0999, 909-793-2121 (Fax: 909-335-5515) www.redlands.edu. 8AM-5PM. Enrollment: 3723. Records go back to 1903. Alumni records are maintained here. Degrees granted: Bachelors; Masters. Special programs-Masters Communicative Disorders: Masters Music. Attendance and degree information available by phone, fax, mail. Transcripts available by mail.

University of San Diego, Registrar, 5998
Alcala Park, San Diego, CA 92110-2492, 619-260-4557 (Fax: 619-260-4649) www.acusd.edu. 8:30AM-5PM. Enrollment: 6600. Records go back to 1949. Alumni records maintained here; call 619-260-4819. Degrees granted: Bachelors; Masters. Attendance and degree information available by phone, fax, mail. Transcripts available by mail.

University of San Fernando Valley-College of Law
(See University of LaVerne, College of Law)

University of San Francisco, Registrar,
2130 Fulton St, San Francisco, CA 94117-1080, 415-422-6316, 415-422-2781 (Fax: 415-422-6321) www.usfca.edu/. 8:30AM-6:30PM M-Th, 8:30AM-5PM F. Enrollment: 8000. Records go back to 1986. Alumni records maintained here; call 415-422-6431. Degrees granted: Bachelors; Masters; Doctorate. Attendance and degree information available by phone, mail. Transcripts available by fax, mail.

University of Santa Clara
(See Santa Clara University)

University of Southern California, Registrar,
Los Angeles, CA 90089-0912, 213-740-7445, 213-740-9230 (Fax: 213-740-8710) www.usc.edu. 8:30AM-5PM. Enrollment: 28000. Records go back to 1880. Alumni records maintained here; call 213-740-1234. Degrees granted: Bachelors; Masters; Doctorate. Special programs-Contact Ruth Johnson, 213-740-8500. Attendance and degree information available by phone, fax, mail. Transcripts available by fax, mail. Request by phone for years after 1979 only. Call 212-743-1516. Transcript request for years after 1980 call 800-613-3741, also online through www.gettranscripts.com.

University of West Los Angeles,
Registrar, 1155 W Arbor Vitae St, Inglewood, CA 90301-2902, 310-342-5200, 310-342-5250 (Fax: 310-342-5295). 8:30AM-6:30PM. Enrollment: 595. Records go back to 1966. Alumni records maintained here; call 310-342-5200. Degrees granted: Bachelors; Doctorate; Para-Legal. Request attendance, degree and transcript information available by fax, mail. Only attendance and degree information available via fax.

University of West Los Angeles - Law School, Registrar, 1155 W Arbor Vitae St,
Inglewood, CA 90301, 310-342-5200, 310-215-3339 (Fax: 310-342-5295) 8:30AM-6:30PM. Enrollment: 550. Records go back to 1966. Alumni records are maintained here. Degrees granted: Bachelors; Doctorate. Attendance and degree information available by fax, mail. Transcripts available by mail.

University of the Pacific, Registrar, 3601
Pacific Ave, Stockton, CA 95211, 209-946-2135 (Fax: 209-946-2596). 8AM-5PM. Enrollment: 5850. Records go back to 1900. Alumni records maintained here; call 209-946-2391. Degrees granted: Bachelors; Masters; Doctorate. Attendance and degree information available by phone, fax, mail. Transcripts available by fax, mail.

Ventura College, Registrar, 4667 Telegraph
Rd, Ventura, CA 93003, 805-654-6457 (Fax: 805-654-6466) www.ventura.cc.ca.us. 8AM-7:30PM M-Th, 8AM-5PM F. Enrollment: 10500. Records go back to 1945. Alumni records maintained here; call 805-648-8927. Degrees granted: Associate. Attendance and degree information available by phone, mail. Transcripts available by mail.

Victor Valley College, Admissions &
Records Dept, 18422 Bear Valley Rd, Victorville, CA 92392, 619-245-4271 (Fax: 619-245-9745). 8:30AM-5PM. Enrollment: 8329. Records go back to 1961. Alumni records are maintained here. Degrees granted: Associate. Certification: Occupation. Attendance information available by phone, fax, mail. Degree and transcript information available by fax, mail.

Vista College, Registrar, 2020 Milvia St,
Berkeley, CA 94704, 510-841-8860 X245 (Fax: 510-841-7333) www.peralta.cc.ca.us. 8AM-7PM M,T; 8AM-4:30PM W-F. Enrollment: 3500. Records go back to 1960. Alumni records maintained here; call 510-841-8431 X267. Degrees granted: Associate. Attendance and degree information available by fax, mail. Transcripts available by mail.

Waterman Training Institute, Registrar,
126 Second Ave, San Mateo, CA 94401, 650-344-7652 (Fax: 650-344-7653) 8AM-5PM. Enrollment: 26. Records go back to 1994. Attendance and degree information available by phone, mail. Transcripts available by mail.

West Coast University Orange County Center, Registrar, 440 Shatto Pl, Los
Angeles, CA 90020, (Fax: 213-380-4362). Enrollment: 600. Records go back to 1909. Alumni records are maintained here. Degrees granted: Associate; Bachelors. Special programs- Computer Engineering: Business. Attendance and degree information available by phone, mail. Transcripts available by mail.

West Hills Community College,
Registrar, 300 Cherry Lane, Coalinga, CA 93210, www.westhills.cc.ca.us/. 209-935-0801 (Fax: 209-935-3788) 8AM-5PM. Enrollment: 3800. Records go back to 1932. Alumni records maintained here; call 209-935-0801 X3224. Degrees granted: Associate. Attendance and degree information available by phone, fax, mail. Transcripts available by fax, mail.

West Los Angeles College, Attn:
Admissions, 4800 Freshman Dr, Culver City, CA 90230, 310-287-4329 (Fax: 310-841-0396). 9AM-8PM M-Th; 9AM-3:30PM F. Alumni records are maintained here. Degrees granted: Associate. Attendance, degree and transcript information available by mail.

West Valley College, Registrar, 14000
Fruitvale Ave, Saratoga, CA 95070, 408-867-2200, 408-741-2001 (Fax: 408-867-5033) www.wvmccd.cc.ca.us/wvc. 9AM-7PM M-Th; 9AM-4PM F. Enrollment: 11000. Records go back to 1964. Degrees granted: Associate. Attendance, degree and transcript information available by written request only.

Western Institute, Registrar, 120 Avram St,
Suite 102-A, Rohnert Park, CA 94928, 707-664-9267 (Fax: 707-664-9237) www.sonic.net/wish. 8AM-5PM. Enrollment: 52. Records go back to 1995. Degrees

granted: Associate. Attendance and degree information available by phone, mail. Transcripts available by mail.

Western State University College of Law of Orange County, Registrar, 1111 N State College Blvd, Fullerton, CA 92631, 714-738-1000 (Fax: 714-879-3882) www.wsulaw.edu. 9AM-8:30PM. Enrollment: 814. Records go back to 1966. Alumni records are maintained here. Degrees granted: Doctorate; Juris Doctor. Attendance information available by fax, mail. Degree information available by phone, fax, mail. Transcripts available by mail.

Western University of Health Sciences, Student Affairs Office, 309 E Second St, College Plaza, Pomona, CA 91766-1854, 909-469-5340, 909-623-6116 (Fax: 909-623-9623) www.westernu.edu. 8:30AM-5PM. Enrollment: 1200. Records go back to 1978. Alumni records maintained here; call 909-469-5275. Degrees granted: Masters; Doctorate. Certification: P.A.. Special programs- Rotations, 909-469-5260: Academic Affairs, 909-469-5251: Allied Health, 909-469-5378: Pharmacy, 909-469-5599. Attendance, degree and transcript information available by fax, mail.

Westminster Theological Seminary in California, Registrar, 1725 Bear Valley Pkwy, Escondido, CA 92027, 760-480-8474 (Fax: 760-480-0252) www.wtscal.edu. 8AM-4:30PM. Enrollment: 243. Records go back to 1991. Alumni records are maintained here. Degrees granted: Masters; Doctorate. Attendance and degree information available

by phone, fax, mail. Transcripts available by mail.

Westmont College, Registrar, 955 La Paz Rd, Santa Barbara, CA 93108-1089, 805-565-6060 (Fax: 805-565-6234) 8AM-4:30PM. www.westmont.edu. Enrollment: 1250. Records go back to 1940. Alumni records maintained here; call 805-565-6056. Degrees granted: Bachelors. Attendance and degree information available by phone, fax, mail. Transcripts available by fax, mail.

Whittier College, Office of the Registrar, 13406 E Philadelphia St, Whittier, CA 90601, 562-907-4241 (Fax: 562-698-4067) www.whittier.edu. 8AM-5PM. Enrollment: 1300. Records go back to 1902. Alumni records are maintained here. Degrees granted: Bachelors; Masters. Attendance and degree information available by phone, fax, mail. Transcripts available by mail.

Woodbury University, Registrar's Office, PO Box 7846, Burbank, CA 91510-7846, 818-767-0888 X270 (Fax: 818-768-8628) 8AM-8PM M-Th; 8AM-5PM F. www.woodbury.edu. Enrollment: 1072. Records go back to 1930. Alumni records maintained here. Degrees granted: Bachelors; Masters. Attendance and degree information available by phone, fax, mail. Transcripts available by mail.

Wright Institute, Registrar, 2728 Durant Ave, Berkeley, CA 94704, 510-841-9230. Enrollment: 242. Records go back to 1969. Alumni records are maintained here. Degrees granted: Doctorate. Attendance and degree

information available by phone, mail. Transcripts available by mail.

Yeshiva Ohr Elchonon – Chabad / West Coast Talmudic Seminary, Registrar, 7215 Waring Ave, Los Angeles, CA 90046, 213-937-3763 (Fax: 213-937-9456). 8:30AM-4PM. Enrollment: 35. Records go back to 1956. Alumni records are maintained here. Degrees granted: Bachelors. Attendance and degree information available by phone, fax, mail. Transcripts available by mail.

Yo San University of Traditional Chinese Medicine, Registrar, 1314 Second St, Santa Monica, CA 90401, 310-917-2202 (Fax: 310-917-2203) www.yosan.edu. 9AM-6PM. Enrollment: 160. Alumni records maintained here; call 310-917-2202. Degrees granted: Masters. Attendance and degree information available by phone, fax, mail. Transcripts available by fax, mail.

Yuba College, Records Office, 2088 N Beale Rd, Marysville, CA 95901, www.yuba.cc.ca.us 530-741-6871 (Fax: 530-741-6872) 8AM-6PM M-Th; 8AM-5PM F. Enrollment: 11250. Records go back to 1926. Degrees granted: Associate. Attendance, and degree information available by mail. School does not provide transcripts.

Colorado

Adams State College, Registrar, 208 Edgemont Blvd, Alamosa, CO 81102, 719-587-7321, 719-587-7327 (Fax: 719-587-7522) www.adams.edu. 8AM-4:45PM. Enrollment: 2140. Records go back to 1925. Alumni records maintained here; call 719-587-7121. Degrees granted: Associate; Bachelors; Masters. Attendance and degree information available by phone, fax, mail. Transcripts available by fax, mail.

Aims Community College, Registrar, PO Box 69, Greeley, CO 80632, 970-330-8008 (Ext. 6440) (Fax: 970-339-6669) www.aims.edu. 8AM-5PM Summers closed Friday.. Enrollment: 7000. Records go back to 1967. Degrees granted: Associate. Attendance and degree information available by phone, fax, mail. Transcripts available by fax, mail.

Arapahoe Community College, Registrar, 2500 W College Dr, PO Box 9002, Littleton, CO 80160-9002, 303-797-5621 (Fax: 303-797-5970) www.arapahoe.edu. 8AM-5PM. Enrollment: 7500. Records go back to 1966. Degrees granted: Associate. Attendance and degree information available by phone, fax, mail. Transcripts available by fax, mail.

Bel-Rea Institute of Animal Technology Registrar, 1681 S Dayton St, Denver, CO 80231-3048, 303-751-8700, 800-950-8001 (Fax: 303-751-9969) www.bel:rea.com. 8AM-5PM. Enrollment: 375. Records go back to 1970. Degrees granted: Associate. Attendance and degree information available by phone, fax, mail. Transcripts available by mail.

Beth-El College of Nursing (University of Colorado at Colorado Springs), Registrar, 2790 N Academy Blvd Ste 200, PO Box 7150, Colorado Springs, CO 80933-7150, 719-262-3361 (Registrar), 719-262-3383

(Admissions & Records) (Fax: 719-262-3116). 9AM-5PM. Enrollment: 450. Records go back to 1907. Alumni records are maintained here. Degrees granted: Bachelors; Masters. Certification: NNP, Forensics, Post Masters Certificate, Nurse Practitioner. Special programs- Nursing, 719-262-4422. Attendance and degree information available by phone, fax, mail. Transcripts available by fax, mail.

Blair College, Registrar, 828 Wooten Rd, Colorado Springs, CO 80915, 719-574-1082 (Fax: 719-574-4493) Not Available. 7:30AM-7PM. Enrollment: 350. Records go back to 1900. Degrees granted: Associate. Attendance and degree information available by phone, fax, mail. Transcripts available by fax, mail.

Cambridge College, Registrar, 11059 E Bethany Dr, Suite 110, Aurora, CO, 303-338-9700 (Fax: 303-338-9701) 8AM-5PM. www.cambridge.edu. Enrollment: 211. Records go back to 1994. Degrees granted: Associate. Attendance and degree information available by phone, mail. Transcripts available by mail.

College for Financial Planning, Registrar, 4695 S Monaco, Denver, CO 80237-3403, 303-220-1200 8AM-5PM. Enrollment: 839. Records go back to 1995. Degrees granted: Masters. Attendance and degree information available by phone, mail. Transcripts available by mail.

Colorado Aero Technology, Registrar, 10851 W 120th Ave, Broomfield, CO 80021-3465, 303-466-1714, 303-466-7383 (Fax: 303-469-3797) www.coloradoaerotech.com. 9AM-5PM. Enrollment: 425. Records go back to 1972. Alumni records are maintained here. Degrees granted: Associate. Attendance and degree information available by phone, mail. Transcripts available by mail.

Colorado Christian University, Registrar, 180 S Garrison St, Lakewood, CO 80226, 303-238-5386 X140 (Fax: 303-274-7560) 8AM-5PM. www.ccu.edu. Enrollment: 1700. Records go back to 1915. Alumni records maintained here; call 303-238-5386 X521. Degrees granted: Associate; Bachelors; Masters. Certification: Education, LPC, Comp, OM. Attendance and degree information available by phone, fax, mail. Transcripts available by fax, mail.

Colorado College, Registrar, 14 E Cache la Pourde St, Colorado Springs, CO 80903, 719-389-6610, 719-389-6611 (Fax: 719-389-6931) www.cc.colorado.edu. 8:30AM-5PM. Enrollment: 1963. Records go back to 1895. Alumni records maintained here; call 719-389-6000. Degrees granted: Bachelors; Masters. Attendance and degree information available by phone, fax, mail. Transcripts requestable by fax, mail.

Colorado Institute of Art, Registrar, 200 E Ninth Ave, Denver, CO 80203-9947, 303-837-0825 (Fax: 303-860-8520). 7:30AM-5PM. Enrollment: 1500. Records go back to 1960's. Alumni records are maintained here. Degrees granted: Associate; Bachelors. Special programs- Culinary Arts, 303-837-0825. Attendance and degree information available by phone, fax, mail. Transcripts available by fax, mail.

Colorado Mountain College (Roaring Fork), Registrar, 3000 County Rd 114, Glenwood Springs, CO 81601, 970-947-8000, 970-945-7456 (Fax: 970-945-7841) www.coloradomtn.edu. Records are located at Colorado Mountain College, Registrar, Glenwood Springs, CO.

Colorado Mountain College, Registrar, Box 10001, 831 Grand Ave, Glenwood

Springs, CO 81602, 800-621-8559, 970-945-8691 (Fax: 970-947-8387) 8AM-5PM. www.coloradomnt.edu. Enrollment: 20000. Records go back to 1967. Alumni records are maintained here. Degrees granted: Associate. Special programs- Call 970-945-8691. Attendance, degree and transcript information available by fax, mail. Need student's authorization to education records.

Colorado Mountain College (Timberline), Registrar, 901 S Hwy 24, Leadville, CO 80461, 719-486-2015 (Fax: 719-486-3212). Records are located at Colorado Mountain College, Registrar, Glenwood Springs, CO.

Colorado Mountain College (Alpine), Registrar, 1370 Bob Adams Dr, Steamboat Springs, CO 80477, 970-870-4444 (Fax: 970-870-0845). Records are located at Colorado Mountain College, Registrar, Glenwood Springs, CO.

Colorado Northwestern Community College, Registrar, 500 Kennedy Dr, Rangely, CO 81648, 970-675-3218, 970-675-3217 (Fax: 970-675-3343) www.cnc.cc.co.us. 8AM-5PM. Enrollment: 1800. Records go back to 1960. Alumni records are maintained. Call 970-675-3346. Degrees granted: Associate. Special programs- Dental Hygiene: Aviation. Attendance and degree information available by phone, fax, mail. Transcripts available by fax, mail. Will not send transcripts to anyone except student.

Colorado School of Mines, Registrar, 1500 Illinois St, Golden, CO 80401, 303-273-3200, 303-273-3208 (Fax: 303-273-3278) 8AM-5PM. gn.mines.colorado.edu. Enrollment: 3000. Records go back to 1876. Alumni records maintained here; call 303-273-3295. Degrees granted: Bachelors; Masters; PhD; Professional. Special programs- Office of Special Programs & Continuing Ed, 303-273-3200 X3321. Attendance and degree information available by phone, fax, mail. Transcripts available by fax, mail.

Colorado State University, Records & Registration, Rm 100 Admin Annex, Fort Collins, CO 80523-8021, 970-491-7148 (Fax: 970-491-2283) www.colostate.edu. 7:45AM-4:45PM Winter; 7:30AM-4:30PM Summer. Enrollment: 21000. Records go back to 1875. Alumni Records: 645 S Shields St, Fort Collins, CO 80521. Degrees granted: Bachelors; Masters; Doctorate. Attendance and degree information available by phone, fax, mail. Transcripts available by mail.

Colorado Technical University, Records, 4435 N Chestnut St, Colorado Springs, CO 80907, 719-598-0200, 719-598-6769 (Registrar) (Fax: 719-598-3740) www.colotechu.edu. 8AM-6PM. Enrollment: 1600. Records go back to 1926. Formerly **Colorado Technical College**. Degrees granted: Associate; Bachelors; Masters; Doctorate. Attendance, degree and transcript information available by mail. Phone and fax verification for employment purposes only.

Commonwealth International University Registrar, 7350 N Broadway, Denver, CO 80221, 303-426-1000 (Fax: 303-426-0641) 8AM-8PM. Enrollment: 400. Records go back to 1958. Degrees granted: Associate; Bachelors; Masters. Attendance and degree information available by fax, mail. Transcripts available by mail.

Community College of Aurora, Registrar, 16000 E Centretech Pkwy, Aurora, CO 80011, www.cca.ccc.oes.edu. 303-361-7411 (Fax: 303-361-7432) 9AM-6PM M-Th, 8AM-5PM F. Enrollment: 4600. Records go back to 1983. Alumni records maintained here; call

303-360-4797. Degrees granted: Associate. Attendance and degree information available by phone, fax, mail. Transcripts available by fax, mail.

Community College of Denver, Registrar, PO Box 173363, Denver, CO 80217-3363, 303-556-2430, 303-556-6325 (Fax: 303-556-8555) 8:30AM-5PM M,Th,F; 8:30AM-6PM T; 10:30AM-6PM W. Records go back to 1969. Alumni Records: 1068 9th St, Denver, CO 80204. Degrees granted: Associate. Attendance and degree information available by phone, fax, mail. Transcripts available by mail. Student signature required.

Denver Academy of Court Reporting, Registrar, 7290 Samuel Dr, Suite 200, Denver, CO 80221, 303-427-5292 www.dac.edu. 8AM-5PM. Enrollment: 350. Records go back to 1982. Degrees granted: Associate. Attendance and degree information available by phone, mail. Transcripts available by mail.

Denver Automotive & Diesel College, Registrar, 460 S Lipan St, Denver, CO 80223-9960, www.denverautomotivediesel.com. Tele: 303-722-5727 7AM-6PM. Enrollment: 135. Records go back to 1968. Degrees granted: Associate. Attendance and degree information available by phone, mail. Transcripts available by mail.

Denver Business College
(See Commonwealth International University)

Denver Conservative Baptist Seminary Registrar, PO Box 10000, Denver, CO 80250-0100, 303-761-2482 X221 (Fax: 303-761-8060). 8AM-4:30PM. Enrollment: 625. Records go back to 1950. Alumni records are maintained here. Degrees granted: Masters; Doctorate. Attendance and degree information available by phone, fax, mail. Transcripts available by fax, mail.

Denver Institute of Technology
(See Westwood College of Technology)

Denver Institute of Technology (Health Careers Division), Registrar, 7350 N Broadway Annex HCD, Denver, CO 80221-3653, 303-650-5050 (Fax: 303-426-1832). Degrees granted: Associate. Attendance, degree and transcript information available by written request only.

Denver Technical College, Registrar, 925 S Niagara St, Denver, CO 80224-1658, 303-329-3340 X228 (Fax: 303-322-0386) www.dtc.edu. 7AM-5PM. Enrollment: 1200. Records go back to 1986. Alumni records are maintained here. Degrees granted: Associate; Bachelors; Masters. Attendance and degree information available by phone, fax, mail. Transcripts available by fax, mail.

Denver Technical College at Colorado Springs, Registrar, 225 S Union Blvd, Colorado Springs, CO 80910-3138, 719-632-3000 (Ext. 102) (Fax: 719-632-1909) www.DTC.EDU. 8AM-6PM M-Th, 8AM-Noon. Records go back to 1985. Alumni records are maintained here. Degrees granted: Associate; Bachelors. Attendance and degree information available by phone, fax, mail. Transcripts available by fax, mail.

Fort Lewis College, Records Office, 108MSC, 1000 Rim Dr, Durango, CO 81301, 970-247-7350 (Fax: 970-247-7598) 9AM-Noon, 1-4PM. www.fortlewis.edu. Enrollment: 4430. Records go back to 1925. Alumni records maintained here; call 970-247-7427. Degrees granted: Associate; Bachelors. Attendance and degree

information available by phone, fax, mail. Transcripts available by fax, mail.

Front Range Community College, Registrar, 3645 W 112th Ave, Westminster, CO 80030, 303-404-5322 (Registrar), 303-466-8811 (switchboard) (Fax: 303-439-2614) 9AM-5PM M,Th; 9AM-7PM T,W; 9AM-4PM F. www.frcc.cc.co.us/. Enrollment: 13000. Records go back to 1970. Alumni records maintained here; call 303-404-5373. Degrees granted: Associate. Attendance, degree and transcript information available by fax, mail.

ITT Technical Institute, Registrar, 500 E 84th Ave, Thornton, CO 80229-5338, 303-695-1913, 303-288-4488 (Fax: 303-751-5603). 8AM-5PM. Enrollment: 250. Records go back to 1989. Alumni Records: Alumni Assoc., 5975 Castle Creek Pkwy N, Indianapolis, IN 46250-0466. Degrees granted: Associate; Bachelors. Attendance and degree information available by phone, fax, mail. Transcripts available by fax, mail.

Iliff School of Theology, Registrar, 2201 S University Blvd, Denver, CO 80210, 303-744-1287 X227, 303-765-3127 (Fax: 303-777-3387) www.iliff.edu. 8AM-4:30PM. Enrollment: 350. Records go back to 1892. Alumni records maintained here; call 303-744-127 X285. Degrees granted: Masters. Attendance and degree information available by phone, fax, mail. Transcripts available by mail.

Johnson & Wales University (Branch Campus), Registrar, 616 W Lionshead Cir, Vail, CO 81657, 970-476-2993 (Fax: 970-476-2994) www.jwu.edu. 8AM-4PM. Enrollment: 40. Records go back to 1993. Alumni Records: 8 Abbott Park Pl, Providence, RI 02903. Degrees granted: Associate. Special programs- Culinary. Attendance and degree information available by phone, mail. Transcript requests should go to the Norfolk, VA location.

Lamar Community College, Registrar, 2401 S Main St, Lamar, CO 81052, 719-336-2248 X125, 719-336-2248 X140 (Fax: 719-336-2448). 8AM-5PM. Enrollment: 1000. Records go back to 1937. Alumni Records: Alumni Assoc., 2401 S Main St, Lamar, CO 81052. Degrees granted: Associate. Attendance and degree information available by phone, fax, mail. Transcripts available by fax, mail. Phone requests only for records since 1987.

Loretto Heights College
(See Regis University)

Mesa College
(See Mesa State College)

Mesa State College, Admissions & Records Office, PO Box 2647, Grand Junction, CO 81502, 970-248-1698 (Fax: 970-248-1131) 8AM-5PM. www.mesastate.edu. Enrollment: 4700. Records go back to 1928. Alumni Records: 1041 Mesa Ave, Grand Junction, CO 81501. Degrees granted: Associate; Bachelors; Masters. Attendance and degree information available by phone, fax, mail. Transcripts available by fax, mail. Need copy of driver's license with Fax requests.

Metropolitan State College of Denver, Registrar, Campus Box 84, PO Box 173362, Denver, CO 80217-3362, 303-556-3991 (Fax: 303-556-3999) www.mscd.edu. 8AM-5:30PM Summer; 7:30AM-6:30PM M-Th, 8AM-5PM F Fall. Enrollment: 17550. Records go back to 1963. Alumni records maintained here; call 303-556-8320. Degrees granted: Associate; Bachelors; Masters;

Doctorate. Special programs- Recreation and Leisure Services. Attendance, degree and transcript information available by fax, mail.

Morgan Community College, Registrar, 17800 Rd 20, Fort Morgan, CO 80701, 970-867-3081 (Fax: 970-867-6608). 8AM-5PM. Enrollment: 1200. Records go back to 1971. Alumni records are maintained here. Degrees granted: Associate. Attendance, degree and transcript information available by mail.

Naropa Institute, Registrar, 2130 Arapahoe Ave, Boulder, CO 80302, 303-546-3500, 303-546-5289 (Fax: 303-546-3536). 9AM-3PM M-Th. Records go back to 1974. Alumni records maintained here; call 303-546-3595. Degrees granted: Bachelors; Masters. Special programs- Continuing Education, 303-546-5289. Attendance and degree information available by phone, fax, mail. Transcripts available by fax, mail.

National Technological University, Registrar, 700 Centre Ave, Fort Collins, CO 80526, 970-495-6408, 970-495-6433 (Fax: 970-498-0601) www.ntu.edu. 8AM-5PM. Enrollment: 1500. Records go back to 1984. Alumni records are maintained here. Degrees granted: Masters. Special programs- Call 970-495-6405. Attendance, degree and transcript information available by fax, mail.

National Theatre Conservatory, Registrar, 1050 13th St, Denver, CO 80204, 303-446-4855 (Fax: 303-821-2117). 9AM-5PM. Enrollment: 24. Records go back to 1985. Degrees granted: Masters; Graduate Certificates. Special programs- Acting, 303-446-4855. Attendance, degree and transcript information available by fax, mail.

Nazarene Bible College, Registrar, 1111 Academy PK Loop, Colorado Springs, CO 80910-3717, 719-596-5110 (Fax: 719-550-9437) www.nbc.edu. 8AM-4:30PM. Enrollment: 350. Records go back to 1968. Alumni records are maintained here. Degrees granted: Associate; Bachelors. Attendance and degree information available by phone, fax, mail. Transcripts available by fax, mail.

Northeastern Junior College, NJC Records Office, 100 College Dr, Sterling, CO 80751, 970-521-6700 X658, 970-521-6659 (Fax: 970-522-4664) www.gonjc.edu. 8AM-4:30PM. Enrollment: 3500. Records go back to 1989. Alumni records maintained here; call 970-521-6690. Degrees granted: Associate. Attendance, degree and transcript information available by fax, mail.

Otero Junior College, Registrar, 1802 Colorado Ave, La Junta, CO 81050, 719-384-6833 (Fax: 719-384-6933) 7:30AM-8:30PM M-Th, 7:30AM-5PM F. www.ojc.cccoes.edu Enrollment: 1000. Records go back to 1942. Degrees granted: Associate. Attendance and degree information available by phone, fax, mail. Transcripts available by fax, mail.

Parks Junior College (Branch), Registrar, 6 Abilene St, Aurora, CO 80011, 303-367-2757 (Fax: 303-361-9706). 7AM-6PM. Enrollment: 300. Records go back to 1989. Degrees granted: Associate. Attendance, degree and transcript information available by fax, mail.

Parks Junior College, Registrar, 9065 Grant St, Denver, CO 80229, 303-457-2757 (Fax: 303-457-4030). 10:30AM-7:30PM. Records go back to 1970. Degrees granted: Associate. Attendance information available by phone, fax, mail. Degree and transcript information available by mail.

Pikes Peak Community College, Records Office, Box 8, 5675 S Academy Blvd, Colorado Springs, CO 80906-5498, 719-540-7158 (Fax: 719-540-7190) 8AM-8PM M,T; 8AM-5PM W-F. www.ppcc.cccoes.edu Enrollment: 7000. Records go back to 1969. Alumni records maintained here; call 719-540-7614. Degrees granted: Associate. Attendance and degree information available by phone, fax, mail. Transcripts available by mail.

Pima Medical Institute (Branch), Registrar, 1701 W 72nd Ave #130, Denver, CO 80221, 303-426-1800 (Fax: 303-430-4048) 7:30AM-6:30PM M-Th; 8AM-5PM F. Enrollment: 350. Records go back to 1989. Degrees granted: Associate. Attendance and degree information available by phone, fax, mail. Transcripts available by fax, mail.

Pueblo College of Business and Technology, Registrar, 1955 N Union Blvd, Colorado Springs, CO 80909-2229, 719-545-3100 (Fax: 719-545-4530). 7:30AM-4:30PM. Enrollment: 180. Records go back to 1983. Degrees granted: Associate. Attendance and degree information available by phone, mail. Transcripts available by mail.

Pueblo Community College, Registrar, 900 W Orman Ave, Pueblo, CO 81004, www.pcc.cccoes.edu. 719-549-3016, 719-549-3010 (Fax: 719-543-7566) Records located at Pueblo Community College, Registrar, Pueblo, CO.

Red Rocks Community College, Registrar, 13300 W Sixth Ave, Lakewood, CO 80228-1255, 303-988-6160, 303-914-6360 (Fax: 303-989-6919) 8AM-7PM M-Th, 9AM-5PM F. www.rrcc.cccoes.edu Enrollment: 6832. Records go back to 1969. Degrees granted: Associate. Attendance and degree information available by phone, fax, mail. Transcripts available by fax, mail.

Regis University, Associate Registrar, 3333 Regis Blvd, Denver, CO 80221-1099, 303-458-4114, 303-458-4100 (Main Operator) (Fax: 303-964-5536) www.regis.edu. 8:30AM-5PM. Enrollment: 9648. Records go back to 1877. Alumni records maintained here; call 303-458-3535. Degrees granted: Bachelors; Masters. Special programs- Regis College, 303-458-4900: School for Health Care Professionals: Graduate Program, 303-458-4349: School for Professional Studies-Undergraduate, 303-458-1662: School for Professional Studies-Graduate, 303-458-4080. Attendance and degree information available by phone, fax, mail. Transcripts available by fax, mail.

Rockmont College
(See Colorado Christian University)

Rocky Mountain College of Art and Design, Registrar, 6875 E Evans Ave, Denver, CO 80224-2359, 303-753-6046 X113 (Fax: 303-759-4970) www.rmcad.edu. 8AM-10PM. Enrollment: 400. Records go back to 1963. Alumni records maintained here; call 800-888-2787. Degrees granted: Bachelors. Attendance and degree information available by phone, fax, mail. Transcripts available by mail.

Technical Trades Institute, Registrar, 772 Horizon Dr, Grand Junction, CO 81501-9977, 970-245-8101 (Fax: 970-243-8074) 7:30AM-7PM M-Th; 8AM-5PM F. Enrollment: 178. Records go back to 1986. Degrees granted: Associate. Attendance and degree information available by phone, mail. Transcripts available by mail.

Technical Trades Institute & Emery Aviation, Registrar, 2315 E Pikes Peak, Colorado Springs, CO 80909, 719-632-7626 (Fax: 719-632-7451) Enrollment: 260. Records go back to 1965. Degrees granted:

Associate. Attendance and degree information available by phone, fax, mail. Transcripts available by fax, mail.

Teikyo Loretto Heights University, Registrar, 3001 S Federal Blvd, Denver, CO 80236, 303-937-4200 8AM - 5PM. Records go back to 1995. Degrees granted: Bachelors. Attendance and degree information available by phone, mail. Transcripts available by mail.

Trinidad State Junior College, Registrar, 600 Prospect St, Trinidad, CO 81082, 719-846-5621, 800-621-T622 (Fax: 719-846-5667) www.tsjc.cccoes.edu. 8AM-5PM. Enrollment: 1500. Records go back to 1940. Alumni records maintained here; call 719-846-5649. Degrees granted: Associate. Special programs- Gunsmithing: Recreation Vehicle Service Technician: Aqua Farm, 719-846-5621. Attendance and degree information available by phone, fax, mail. Transcripts available by fax, mail.

United States Air Force Academy (Department of the Air Force), HQ USAFA/DFRR, 2354 Fairchild Dr Ste 6D106, USAF Academy, CO 80840-6210, 719-333-3970 (Fax: 719-333-6650) www.usafa.af.mil. 7AM-4:30PM. Enrollment: 4000. Records go back to 1959. Alumni Records: Alumni Assoc., 3116 Academy Dr Ste 100, USAF Academy, CO 80840-4425. Degrees granted: Bachelors. Attendance and degree information available by phone, fax, mail. Transcripts available by fax, mail. Active duty military may Fax requests. Will not fax transcripts.

University of Colorado Health Sciences Center, Admissions & Records, 4200 E 9th Ave, Box A054, Denver, CO 80262, 303-399-1211, 303-315-7676 (Fax: 303-315-3358) www.uchsc.edu. 8AM-4:30PM. Enrollment: 2300. Records go back to 1988. Alumni Records: Alumni Development, Box A065, Denver, CO 80262. Degrees granted: Bachelors; Masters; Doctorate; MD, DDS, Pharm D, ND. Attendance and degree information available by phone, fax, mail. Transcripts available by mail.

University of Colorado at Boulder, Office of the Registrar, Campus Box 68, Boulder, CO 80309, 303-492-6970, 303-492-4911 (Fax: 303-492-4884) www.registrar.colorado.edu. 9AM-5PM. Enrollment: 25000. Records go back to 1896. Alumni Records: Campus Box 459, Boulder, CO 80309. Degrees granted: Bachelors; Masters; Doctorate. Certification: Teacher. Attendance and degree information available by phone, fax, mail. Transcripts available by fax, mail. Phone requests are taken for transcripts if student is requesting transcript in person.

University of Colorado at Colorado Springs, Registrar, PO Box 7150, Colorado Springs, CO 80933-7150, 719-262-3361, 719-262-3376 (Fax: 719-262-3116) www.uccs.edu. 8AM-7PM M, 8AM-5PM T-F. Enrollment: 6500. Records go back to 1970. Alumni records maintained here; call 719-262-3046. Degrees granted: Bachelors; Masters; Doctorate. Attendance and transcript information available by fax, mail. Degree information available by phone, fax, mail.

University of Colorado at Denver, Transcript Office, Campus Box 167, PO Box 173364, Denver, CO 80217-3364, 303-556-3415, 303-556-2389 (Fax: 303-556-4829) 8AM-5PM. www.cudenver.edu. Enrollment: 11000. Records go back to 1960. Alumni records maintained here; call 303-556-2549. Degrees granted: Bachelors; Masters; Doctorate. Attendance and degree

information available by phone, fax, mail. Transcripts available by fax, mail.

University of Denver, Registrar, 2199 S University Blvd, Denver, CO 80208, 303-871-2284 (Fax: 303-871-4300) www.du.edu. 8AM-4:30PM. Enrollment: 8492. Records go back to 1882. Alumni records maintained here; call 303-871-2103. Degrees granted: Bachelors; Masters; Doctorate. Attendance and degree information available by phone, fax, mail. Transcripts available by fax, mail.

University of Denver, College of Law, Registrar, 7039 E 18th St, Denver, CO 80220, 303-871-6132, 800-525-2787 (Fax: 303-871-6915) www.law.du.edu. 8AM-5PM. Enrollment: 10000. Records go back to 1864. Alumni records are maintained here. Degrees granted: Doctorate. Attendance and degree information available by phone, fax, mail. Transcripts available by mail.

University of Northern Colorado, Registrar's Office, Carter Hall 3002, Greeley, CO 80639, 970-351-2231 (Fax: 970-351-1870) www.univnorthco.edu. 8AM-5PM. Enrollment: 10450. Records go back to 1890. Alumni Records: Alumni Assoc, University of Northern Colorado, Faculty Apartments, Greeley, CO 80639. Degrees granted: Bachelors; Masters; Doctorate. Certification: Teacher. Attendance and degree information

available by phone, fax, mail. Transcripts available by fax, mail.

University of Phoenix (Denver Main), Registrar, 7800 E Dorado Pl, Englewood, CO 80111, 303-755-9090 (Fax: 303-694-6084) www.uophx.edu. Enrollment: 3000. Records go back to 1976. Alumni Records: Alumni Assoc, PO Box 52069, Phoenix, AZ 85072. Degrees granted: Bachelors; Masters. Attendance and degree information available by phone, fax, mail. Transcript records are housed at University of Phoenix, Registrar, Phoenix, AZ.

University of Southern Colorado, Registrar, 2200 Bonforte Blvd, Pueblo, CO 81001, 719-549-2261 (Fax: 719-549-2419) 8AM-5PM. www.uscolo.edu. Enrollment: 4800. Records go back to 1933. Alumni records maintained here; call 719-549-2114. Degrees granted: Bachelors; .Masters. Attendance and degree information available by phone, fax, mail. Transcripts available by fax, mail.

Western Bible College
(See Colorado Christian University)

Western State College of Colorado, Registrar, Gunnison, CO 81231, 970-943-2047 (Fax: 970-943-2212) www.western.edu. 8AM-5PM. Enrollment: 2514. Records go

back to 1911. Alumni records maintained here; call 970-943-2090. Degrees granted: Bachelors. Attendance and degree information available by phone, fax, mail. Transcripts available by mail.

Westwood College of Technology, Registrar, 7350 N Broadway, Denver, CO 80221-3653, 303-650-5050 (Fax: 303-426-1832) www.info.westwood.edu. 7AM-10PM M-Th; 7AM-5PM F; 8AM-1PM Sat. Enrollment: 975. Records go back to 1953. Alumni records are maintained here. Degrees granted: Associate; Bachelors. Attendance and degree information available by phone, fax, mail. Transcripts available by fax, mail.

Yeshiva Toras Chaim Talmudic Seminary, Registrar, 1555 Stuart St, PO Box 40067, Denver, CO 80204, 303-629-8200 (Fax: 303-623-5949). 8AM-5PM. Enrollment: 18. Records go back to 1967. Degrees granted: Masters; 1st Professional Degree. Attendance, degree and transcript information available by phone, fax, mail.

Connecticut

Albertus Magnus College, Registrar, New Haven, CT 06511-1189, 203-773-8514 (Fax: 203-773-3117). 8:30AM-4:30PM. Enrollment: 1000. Records go back to 1925. Alumni records maintained here; call 203-773-8502. Degrees granted: Associate; Bachelors; Masters. Attendance information available by phone, fax, mail. Degree information available by phone, mail. Transcripts available by mail.

Asnuntuck Community — Technical College, Director of Records, 170 Elm St, Enfield, CT 06082, 860-253-3015 (Fax: 860-253-3016) 8:30AM-5PM. Enrollment: 2000. www.qvctc.commnet.edu/asctc/index Records go back to 1973. Alumni records maintained here; call 860-253-3019. Degrees granted: Associate; Certificates. Attendance and degree information available by phone, fax, mail. Transcripts available by mail.

Bais Binyomin Academy, Registrar, 132 Prospect St, Stamford, CT 06901, 203-325-4351 (Fax: 203-325-4352) 9AM-5PM. Enrollment: 100. Records go back to 1976. Alumni records are maintained here. Degrees granted: Bachelors. Special programs-Rabbinical College. Attendance and degree information available by phone, fax, mail. Transcripts available by mail.

Briarwood College, Registrar, 2279 Mt Vernon Rd, Southington, CT 06489, www.briarwood.edu 860-628-4751 (Fax: 860-628-6444) Enrollment: 540. Records go back to 1968. Alumni records are maintained here also. Call 860-628-4751. Degrees granted: Associate. Attendance and degree information available by phone, fax, mail. Transcripts available by fax, mail.

Bridgeport Engineering Institute
(See Fairfield University)

Capital Community Technical College, Registrar, 61 Woodland St, Hartford, CT 06105, 860-520-7898 (520-7800 switch board), 860-520-7899 (Fax: 860-520-7906) webster.commnet.edu. 8:30AM-5PM. Enrollment: 3000. Records go back to 1947.

Alumni records maintained here; call 860-520-7819. Degrees granted: Associate. Attendance and degree information available by phone, fax, mail. Transcripts available by fax, mail.

Capital Community-Technical College (Flatbush), Registrar, 61 Woodland St, Hartford, CT 06105, 860-520-7941 (Fax: 860-520-7906) webster.commnet.edu. 8:30AM-4:30PM. Enrollment: 1648. Records go back to 1967. Alumni Records: Capital Community-Technical College Woodland, 61 Woodland CT, Hartford, CT 06105. Degrees granted: Associate. Attendance and degree information available by phone, fax, mail. Transcripts available by fax, mail.

Central Connecticut State University, Registrar's Office, 1615 Stanley St, New Britain, CT 06050, 860-832-2236, 860-832-2235 (Fax: 860-832-2522) 8AM-5PM. www.ccsu.ctstateu.edu. Enrollment: 11500. Records go back to 1902. Degrees granted: Bachelors; Masters. Attendance and degree information available by phone, mail. Transcripts available by mail.

Charter Oak State College, Registrar, 66 Cedar St #301, Newington, CT 06111-2646, 860-666-4595 (Fax: 860-666-4852) www.cosc.edu. 8:30AM-5PM. Enrollment: 1300. Records go back to 1974. Alumni records maintained here; call 860-666-4595 X25. Degrees granted: Associate; Bachelors. Attendance and degree information available by phone, fax, mail. Transcripts available by mail.

Connecticut College, Registrar, 270 Mohegin Ave, New London, CT 06320, 860-439-2068 (Fax: 860-439-5421) www.concol.edu. 8:30AM-5PM. Enrollment: 1780. Records go back to 1920. Alumni records maintained here; call 860-439-2300. Degrees granted: Bachelors. Attendance and degree information available by phone. Transcripts available by fax, mail.

Eastern Connecticut State University, Registrar's Office, 83 Windham St, Willimantic, CT 06226-2295, 860-465-5224

(Fax: 860-465-4382). 8:15AM-5PM. Enrollment: 4600. Records go back to 1889. Alumni records maintained here; call 860-465-5238. Degrees granted: Associate; Bachelors; Masters. Attendance and degree information available by phone, fax, mail. Transcripts available by fax, mail.

Fairfield University, Registrar, Fairfield, CT 06430, 203-254-4000, 203-254-4288 (Fax: 203-254-4109) www.fairfield.edu/. Enrollment: 5000. Records go back to 1951. Alumni records maintained here; call 203-254-4280. Degrees granted: Associate; Bachelors; Masters; Masters in Nursing, Business, Education. Special programs-Foreign Campuses, 203-254-4220. Attendance and degree information available by phone, fax, mail. Transcripts available by fax, mail.

Gateway Community — Technical College, Registrar, 60 Sargent Dr, New Haven, CT 06511, 203-789-7041 (Fax: 203-777-8415) www.commnet.edu/gwctc. 8:30AM-4:30 PM. Enrollment: 4843. Records go back to 1968. Student records are at 60 Sargent Dr, New Haven, CT, 06511, 203-789-7041 & 203-234-3325. Alumni records are maintained here. Degrees granted: Associate. Special programs- Auto Tech: Alternative Fuel Certification: Dietetic Tech: Graphic Communications Tec: Postal Service Management: Pharmacy. Attendance and degree information available by phone, fax, mail. Transcripts available by mail.

Gateway Community — Technical College (North Haven), Registrar, 88 Bassett Rd, North Haven, CT 06473, 203-234-3300 (Fax: 203-867-6098). 8:30AM-4:30PM. commnet.edu/gwctc/index.html Enrollment: 5000. Records go back to 1966. Alumni records maintained here; call 203-234-3342. Degrees granted: Associate. Attendance and degree information available by phone, fax, mail. Transcripts available by mail.

Greater Hartford Community College
(See Capital Com. Technical College)

Greater New Haven State Technical College
(See Gateway Com. Technical College)

Hartford College for Women, Registrar, 1265 Asylum Ave, Hartford, CT 06105, 860-768-5600, 860-768-5644 (Fax: 860-768-5693). Enrollment: 250. Records go back to 1932. Alumni records are maintained here. Degrees granted: Associate; Bachelors. Attendance and degree information available by phone, mail. Transcripts available by mail.

Hartford Graduate Center
(See Rennselaer at Hartford)

Hartford Graduate Center, Registrar, 275 Windsor St, Hartford, CT 06120-2991, 860-548-2400 (Fax: 860-548-7823) www.hgc.edu. 8AM-5PM. Enrollment: 776. Records go back to 1966. Degrees granted: Masters. Attendance and degree information available by phone, mail. Transcripts available by mail.

Hartford Seminary, Registrar, 77 Sherman St, Hartford, CT 06105, 860-509-9500 (Fax: 860-509-9509). 9AM - 5PM. Enrollment: 400. Records go back to 1945. Alumni records are maintained here. Degrees granted: Masters; Doctorate. Attendance and degree information available by phone, fax, mail. Transcripts available by mail.

Hartford State Technical College
(See Capital Com. Technical College)

Holy Apostles College and Seminary, Registrar, Cromwell, CT 06416, 860-632-3000, 860-632-3033 (Fax: 860-632-3075) www.novavista.com/holyapostles. 9AM-4PM. Enrollment: 133. Records go back to 1956. Alumni records maintained here; call 860-632-3077. Degrees granted: Associate; Bachelors; Masters; M. Div. Attendance and degree information available by phone, fax, mail. Transcripts available by mail.

Housatonic Community - Technical College, Registrar, 900 Lafayette Blvd, Bridgeport, CT 06604, 203-332-5088, 203-332-6479 (Fax: 203-332-5251). 8AM-4:30PM. Enrollment: 3300. Records go back to 1966. Alumni records are maintained here. Degrees granted: Associate. Attendance and degree information available by phone, fax, mail. Transcripts available by fax, mail.

Katharine Gibbs School, Registrar, 142 East Ave, Norwalk, CT 06851, 203-838-4173, 800-845-5333 (Fax: 203-899-0788). 7:30AM-5PM. Alumni records are maintained here. Degrees granted: Associate. Attendance and degree information available by phone, fax, mail. Transcripts available by fax.

Manchester Community - Technical College, Registrar, PO Box 1046, Manchester, CT 06045-1046, 860-647-6147 (Fax: 860-647-6328) 8AM-4:30PM. www.mctc.commnet.edu. Enrollment: 6000. Records go back to 1963. Alumni records maintained here; call 860-647-6137. Degrees granted: Associate. Attendance and degree information available by phone, fax, mail. Transcripts available by mail.

Mattatuck Community College
(See Naugatuck Valley Community Technical College)

Middlesex Community - Technical College, Registrar, 100 Training Hill Rd, Middletown, CT 06457, 860-343-5720, 860-343-5724 (Fax: 860-344-7488). 8:30AM-4:30PM. Enrollment: 2200. Records go back to 1966. Alumni records maintained here; call 860-343-5744. Degrees granted: Associate. Special programs- Environmental Science-

BioTechnology, 860-343-4880: Broadcast Communications, 860-343-5896: Ophthalmic Design & Dispensing, 860-343-5845. Attendance and degree information available by phone, fax, mail. Transcripts available by mail.

Mitchell College, Registrar, New London, CT 06320, 860-701-5000, 860-701-5186 (Fax: 860-437-0632). 8:30AM-4:30PM. Enrollment: 600. Records go back to 1939. Alumni records are maintained here. Degrees granted: Associate. Attendance, degree and transcript information available by fax, mail.

Mohegan Community College
(See Three Rivers Com./Tech College)

Naugatuck Valley Community - Technical College, Registrar, 750 Chase Pkwy, Waterbury, CT 06708, 203-575-8040, 203-575-8011 (Fax: 203-575-8085) 8:30AM-4:30PM. www.nvctc.commnet.edu. Enrollment: 5000. Records go back to 1967. Alumni records maintained here; call 203-596-8757. Degrees granted: Associate. Special programs- Nursing: Physical Therapy: Automotive Tech: Respiratory Care: Manufacturing Engineer: Computer Drafting Design. Attendance and degree information available by phone, fax, mail. Transcripts available by fax, mail.

Northwestern Connecticut Community - Technical College, Registrar, Park Place E, Winsted, CT 06098, 860-738-6314 (Fax: 860-379-4465) www.commnet.edu/nwctc. 8:30AM-4:30PM. Enrollment: 2000. Records go back to 1965. Degrees granted: Associate. Certification: Career. Attendance and degree information available by phone. Transcripts available by fax, mail.

Norwalk Community - Technical College, Registrar, 188 Richards Ave, Norwalk, CT 06854, 203-857-7035, 203-857-7287 (Fax: 203-857-7012). 9AM-6:30PM M-Th; 9AM-4PM F. Enrollment: 5300. Records go back to 1961. Alumni records maintained here; call 203-857-7270. Degrees granted: Associate. Special programs- Nursing: EMT: Architectural Engineering. Attendance and degree information available by fax, mail. Transcripts available by mail.

Paier College of Art, Registrar, 20 Gorham Ave, Hamden, CT 06514, 203-287-3032 (Fax: 203-287-3021) www.paier.art. 9AM-4PM. Enrollment: 250. Records go back to 1950. Alumni records maintained here; call 203-287-3036. Degrees granted: Associate; Bachelors; Diplomas & Certificates. Attendance and degree information available by phone, fax, mail. Transcripts available by mail.

Quinebaug Valley Community-Technical College, Records Office, 742 Upper Maple St, Danielson, CT 06239, 860-774-1130 (Fax: 860-774-7768) www.comnet.edu. 8:30AM-4:30PM. Enrollment: 1230. Records go back to 1972. Alumni records maintained here. Degrees granted: Associate. Attendance information available by phone, fax, mail. Transcripts available by written request only. Will confirm degree only with student permission. Will confirm date of graduation but not degree earned.

Quinnipiac College, Registrar, 275 Mount Carmel Ave, Hamden, CT 06518, 203-281-8695 www.quinnipiac.edu (Fax: 203-281-8749) 8AM-5PM M-Th, 8AM-4PM F. Enrollment: 5000. Records go back to 1929. Alumni records maintained here; call 203-281-8667. Degrees granted: Bachelors; Masters. Attendance and degree information

available by phone, fax, mail. Transcripts available by mail.

Rensselaer at Hartford, Registrar, 275 Windsor St, Hartford, CT 06120, 860-548-2425, 860-548-2423 (Fax: 860-548-7823) www.hgc.edu. 9AM-6PM M-Th; 9AM-5PM F. Enrollment: 1903. Records go back to 1980. Formerly **Hartford Graduate Center**. Alumni records maintained here; call 860-548-2482. Degrees granted: Masters. Attendance and degree information available by phone, fax, mail. Official transcripts may only be obtained from Rennselaer Polytechic Institute in Troy, NY.

Sacred Heart University, Registrar, 5151 Park Ave, Fairfield, CT 06432, 203-371-7890, 203-371-7893 (Fax: 203-365-7509) 8AM-8PM M-Th, 8AM-4PM F. www.sacredheart.edu. Enrollment: 5600. Records go back to 1963. Alumni records maintained here; call 203-371-7861. Degrees granted: Associate; Bachelors; Masters. Attendance and degree information available by phone, fax, mail. Transcripts available by written request only.

Saint Basil's College, Registrar, 195 Glenbrook Rd, Stamford, CT 06902, 203-324-4578 (Fax: 203-357-7681) 9AM-4PM. Enrollment: 65. Records go back to 1939. Degrees granted: Bachelors. Attendance and degree information available by fax, mail. Transcripts available by mail.

Saint Joseph College, Registrar, 1678 Asylum Ave, West Hartford, CT 06117, 860-232-4571 X489 (Fax: 860-231-8396) www.sjc.edu. 8:30AM-4:30PM. Enrollment: 2000. Records go back to 1933. Alumni records are maintained here. Degrees granted: Bachelors; Masters. Certification: Six year. Attendance and degree information available by phone, fax, mail. Transcripts available by mail. Signed release required to verify grades or status.

South Central Community College
(See Gateway Com. Technical College)

Southern Connecticut State University, Registrar, New Haven, CT 06505-0901, 203-392-5300, 203-392-5301 (Fax: 203-392-5320) www.scsu.ctstateu.edu. 8:30AM-4:45PM. Enrollment: 12500. Records go back to 1893. Alumni Records: 501 Crescent St, New Haven, CT 06515. Degrees granted: Associate; Bachelors; Masters. Attendance, degree and transcript information available by fax, mail.

St. Vincent's College, Registrar, 2800 Main St, Bridgeport, CT 06606, 203-576-5578 (Fax: 203-576-5318) 8AM-5PM. www.stvincent.edu Enrollment: 163. Records go back to 1992. Degrees granted: Associate. Attendance and degree information available by phone, mail. Transcripts available by mail.

Teikyo Post University, Registrar, 800 Country Club Rd, Waterbury, CT 06708, 203-596-4619, 203-596-4616 (Fax: 203-596-4699) www.teikyopost.edu. 8AM-5PM. Enrollment: 1598. Records go back to 1950's. Alumni records are maintained here. Degrees granted: Associate; Bachelors. Special programs- 203-596-4622. Attendance and degree information available by phone, fax, mail. Transcripts available by mail.

Thames Valley State Technical College
(See Three Rivers Com. Technical College)

Three Rivers Community—Technical College, Registrar, PO Box 629, Mahan Dr, Norwich, CT 06360, 860-823-2850, 860-885-2301 (Fax: 860-886-0691). 8:30AM-4:30PM. Enrollment: 3400. Records go back to 1963.

Alumni records maintained here; call 860-823-2943. Degrees granted: Associate. Attendance, degree and transcript information available by fax, mail.

Three Rivers Community - Technical College (Thames), Registrar, 574 New London Tpke, Norwich, CT 06360, 860-885-2301, 860-885-2606 (Fax: 860-886-4960). 8AM-4PM. Enrollment: 4100. Records go back to 1966. Alumni Records: Mahan Drive, Norwich, CT 06360. Degrees granted: Associate. Attendance information available by fax, mail. Degree information available by phone, fax, mail. Transcripts available by mail.

Trinity College, Registrar, 300 Summit St, Hartford, CT 06106, 860-297-2118 www.trincoll.edu/admin/registrar/ (Fax: 860-297-5179) 10AM-Noon, 1-3PM. Enrollment: 1939. Records go back to 1910. Alumni records maintained here; call 860-297-2400. Degrees granted: Bachelors; Masters. Attendance and degree information available by phone, fax, mail. Transcripts available by fax, mail.

Tunxis Community-Technical College, Registrar, 271 Scott Swamp Rd, Farmington, CT 06032, 860-679-9511, 860-679-9543 (Fax: 860-676-8906) www.tunxis.cc.ct.us. 8:30AM-7PM. Enrollment: 3500. Records go back to 1971. Alumni records are maintained here. Degrees granted: Associate. Special programs- Dental Hygiene, 860-679-9521: Drug & Alcohol Rehab Counselor: Physical Therapist Assistant. Attendance and degree information available by fax, mail. Transcripts available by mail.

United States Coast Guard Academy, Registrar, 15 Mohegan Ave, New London, CT 06320-4195, 860-444-8214 (Fax: 860-444-8216). 7:30AM-4:30PM. Enrollment: 930. Records go back to 1930. Alumni records maintained here; call 861-444-8238. Degrees granted: Bachelors. Attendance and degree information available by phone, fax, mail. Transcripts available by mail.

University of Bridgeport, Registrar, 380 University Ave, Bridgeport, CT 06601, 203-576-4636, 203-576-4634 (Fax: 203-576-4633) www.bridgeport.edu. 8:30AM-4:30PM. Records go back to 1927. Alumni records maintained here; call 203-576-4508. Degrees granted: Associate; Bachelors; Masters; Doctorate. Certification: Six year certificate. Attendance and degree information available by phone, fax, mail. Transcripts available by fax, mail.

University of Connecticut, Office of the Registrar, Certifications Office, U-77E, 233 Glenbrook Rd, Wilbur Cross Bldg RM 144, Storrs, CT 06269-4077, 860-486-3331, 860-486-6180 (Fax: 860-486-0062) 8AM-5PM.

Enrollment: 22936. www.uconn.edu. or www.regis.uconnvm.uconn.edu Records go back to 1900. Alumni Records: Alumni Assoc., U-53, 2384 Alumni Dr, Storrs, CT 06269-3053. Degrees granted: Associate; Bachelors; Masters; Doctorate. Special programs- School of Law, 860-570-5136: School of Social Work, 860-570-9135: School of Medicine, 860-679-2153: School of Dentistry, 860-679-2207. Attendance and degree information available by phone, fax, mail. Transcripts available by fax, mail.

University of Connecticut Health Center, Registrar, 263 Farmington Ave, Farmington, CT 06032, 860-679-2000 (Fax: 860-679-7699). 8AM-5PM. Enrollment: 507. Records go back to 1931. Degrees granted: Bachelors. Attendance and degree information available by phone, mail. Transcripts available by mail.

University of Connecticut School of Medicine, Registrar, UCONN School of Medicine, Farmington, CT 06030-1905, 860-679-2990, 860-679-3125 (Fax: 860-679-1902) www.uchc.edu. 8AM - 5PM. Enrollment: 350. Records go back to 1968. Alumni records maintained here; call 860-679-2153. Degrees granted: Doctorate. Attendance and degree information available by phone, fax, mail. Transcripts available by fax, mail.

University of Hartford, Registrar, 200 Bloomfield Ave, West Hartford, CT 06117, 860-768-5589 (Fax: 860-768-4593) www.hartford.edu. 8:30AM-7:30PM M-Th, 8:30AM-4:30PM F. Enrollment: 5630. Records go back to 1950; there may be records as old as the 1800's. Alumni Records: Alumni Relations, 312 Bloomfield Ave, West Hartford, CT 06117. Degrees granted: Associate; Bachelors; Masters; Doctorate; Engineering. Attendance and degree information available by phone, fax, mail. Transcripts available by fax, mail.

University of New Haven, Registrar, 300 Orange Ave, West Haven, CT 06516, 203-932-7301, 203-932-7302 (Fax: 203-932-6096) www.newhaven.edu. 8:30AM - 4:30PM. Enrollment: 5200. Records go back to 1920. Alumni records maintained here; call 203-932-7268. Degrees granted: Associate; Bachelors; Masters; Doctorate. Attendance and degree information available by phone, fax, mail. Transcripts available by fax, mail.

Weselyan University, Registrar, Middletown, CT 06459, 860-685-2748, 860-685-2810 (Fax: 860-685-2601) 8:30AM - 5PM. www.weselyan.edu/registrar/home.ntml. Enrollment: 3000. Records go back to 1800's. Alumni records maintained here; call 860-685-2200. Degrees granted: Bachelors; Masters; Ph.D. Special programs- Studies

Abroad. Attendance and degree information available by phone, fax, mail. Transcripts available by fax, mail.

Western Connecticut State University, Registrar, Danbury, CT 06810, 203-837-9200 (Fax: 203-837-9049) www.wcsu.ctstateu.edu. 8AM-4:30PM. Enrollment: 5600. Records go back to 1904. Alumni records maintained here; call 203-837-8290. Degrees granted: Associate; Bachelors; Masters. Attendance and degree information available by phone, fax, mail. School does not provide transcripts. Transcript requires student request.

Wilcox College of Nursing, Registrar, 28 Crescent St, Middletown, CT 06547, 860-344-6719, 860-344-6261 (Fax: 860-344-6999). 8AM-4:30PM. Enrollment: 100. Records go back to 1911. This school has been closed. Contact Ann Marie Yodh, Director of Education, Middlesex Hospital, 860-344-6480. Alumni records maintained here; call 860-344-6401. Degrees granted: Associate. Attendance and degree information available by phone, fax, mail. Transcripts available by fax, mail.

Yale Divinity School, Registrar, 409 Prospect St, New Haven, CT 06511, 203-432-5312 (Fax: 203-432-5356) 9AM - 5PM. www.ywc.edu/divinity. Enrollment: 300. Records go back to 1800's. Alumni records maintained here; call 203-432-5033. Degrees granted: Masters. Special programs- Admissions Office, 203-432-5360. Attendance and degree information available by phone, fax, mail. Transcripts available by fax, mail. Students or former students only may make requests.

Yale University, Registrar, PO Box 208321, New Haven, CT 06520-8321, 203-432-2331, 203-432-2330 (Fax: 203-432-2334) www.yale.edu. 8AM-4:30PM. Enrollment: 11132. Records go back to 1700's. Alumni records maintained here; call 203-432-1100. Degrees granted: Bachelors; Masters; Doctorate. Special programs- Call 203-432-4771. Attendance and degree information available by phone, fax, mail. Transcripts available by fax, mail. Only students may receive their transcripts.

Delaware

Brandywine College of Widener University
(See Widener University of Law)

Delaware Law School of Widener University (The)
(See Widener University School of Law)

Delaware State University, Records Department, 1200 N Dupont Hwy, Dover, DE 19901-2277, 302-739-4917, 302-739-4914 (Fax: 302-739-2856) www.dsc.edu. 8:30AM-4:30PM. Enrollment: 3175. Records go back to 1891. Alumni Records: Alumni Assoc, Thomasson Bldg, 1200 N DuPont Hwy, Dover, DE 19901. Degrees granted:

Bachelors; Masters. Attendance and degree information available by phone, fax, mail. Transcripts available by fax, mail.

Delaware Technical & Community College (Terry), Registrar, 1832 N Dupont Pkwy, Dover, DE 19901, 302-741-2718 (Fax: 302-741-2778) www.dtcc.edu. 8:30AM-7:30PM M-Th, 8:30AM-4PM F. Enrollment: 1700. Records go back to 1975. Alumni records maintained here; call 302-741-2782. Degrees granted: Associate. Attendance and degree information available by phone, fax, mail. Transcripts available by mail.

Delaware Technical & Community College (Owens Campus), Registrar, PO Box 610, Georgetown, DE 19947, 302-856-5400 (Fax: 302-856-5392) www.dtcu.edu. Records are located at Delaware Technical & Community College, Registrar, Dover, DE.

Delaware Technical & Community College (Stanton/Willington), Registrar, 400 Stanton Christiana Rd, Newark, DE 19713, 302-454-3959 (Fax: 302-454-3184) www.dtcc.edu/. 8:30AM-8PM M-Th; 8:30AM-4:30PM F. Enrollment: 6422. Records go back to 1968. Alumni Records: Alumni Assoc., 333 Shipley St, Wilmington,

DE 19801. Degrees granted: Associate. Attendance and degree information available by phone, fax, mail. Transcripts available by mail.

Delaware Technical Community College Southern, Registrar, 333 Shipley St, Wilmington, DE 19801, 302-571-5317 (Fax: 302-577-6432) www.hopi.dtcc.edu. Enrollment: 3000. Records go back to 1973. Alumni records are maintained here. Degrees granted: Associate. Attendance, degree and transcript information available by fax, mail.

Goldey-Beacom College, Registrar, 4701 Limestone Rd, Wilmington, DE 19808, 302-998-8814 (Fax: 302-998-8631) www.lancassn.gbc.edu. 8AM-5PM. Enrollment: 1700. Records go back to 1886. Alumni records maintained here; call 302-998-8814. Degrees granted: Associate; Bachelors; Masters. Attendance, degree and transcript information available by fax, mail.

University of Delaware, Office of the Registrar, Student Services Bldg, Newark, DE 19716-6220, 302-831-2131 (Fax: 302-831-3005) www.udel.edu. 8AM-5PM. Enrollment: 21280. Alumni records maintained here; call 302-831-8741. Degrees granted: Associate; Bachelors; Masters; PhD. Attendance and degree information available by phone, fax, mail. Transcripts available by fax, mail.

Wesley College, Registrar, 120 N State St, Dover, DE 19901, 302-736-2439, 302-736-2434 (Fax: 302-736-2301) www.wesley.edu. 8:30AM-4:30PM. Enrollment: 1399. Records go back to 1946. Alumni records maintained here; call 302-736-2355. Degrees granted: Associate; Bachelors; Masters. Attendance and degree information available by phone, fax, mail. Transcripts available by mail.

Widener University (School of Law), Registrar, 4601 Concord Pike, PO Box 7474,

Wilmington, DE 19803-0474, 302-477-2170, 302-477-2009 (Fax: 302-477-2258). 9AM-5PM. Enrollment: 2000. Records go back to 1971. Alumni records are maintained here. Degrees granted: Masters; Juris Doctor. Special programs- Legal Education Institute (Paralegal) prior 1989, 610-499-4000. Attendance and degree information available by phone, fax, mail. Transcripts available by mail.

Wilmington College, Registrar, 320 Dupont Hwy, New Castle, DE 19720, 302-328-9401 X110 (Fax: 302-328-7918) www.willcoll.edu. 8:30AM-6PM M-Th, 8:30AM-4:30PM F. Enrollment: 5000. Records go back to 1968. Alumni records maintained here; call 302-328-9401 X101. Degrees granted: Associate; Bachelors; Masters. Attendance and degree information available by fax, mail. Transcripts available by mail.

District of Columbia

American University, Registrar, 4400 Massachusetts Ave NW, Washington, DC 20016, 202-885-2200 (Fax: 202-885-1046) 9AM-6PM M-Th, 9AM-5PM F. www.american.edu. Records go back to 1973. Alumni Records: Penley Campus, 140 Constitution Hall, Washington, DC 20016. Degrees granted: Bachelors; Masters; Doctorate. Attendance and degree information available by phone, fax, mail. Transcripts available by fax, mail.

Benjamin Franklin University
(See George Washington University)

Catholic University of America, Registrar, 620 Michigan Ave NE, Cardinal Station, Washington, DC 20064, 202-319-5311, 202-319-5300 (Fax: 202-319-5831) www.cua.edu. 9AM-5PM. Enrollment: 6000. Records go back to 1887. Alumni records maintained here; call 202-319-5608. Degrees granted: Bachelors; Masters; Doctorate; Licentiate. Attendance and degree information available by phone, fax, mail. Transcripts available by fax, mail. Will fax to confirm attendance and degree not transcripts.

Corcoran School of Art, Registrar, 500 17th St NW, Washington, DC 20006-4899, 202-639-1835, 202-628-9484 (Fax: 202-639-1821). 9AM-5PM. Enrollment: 1400. Records go back to 1965. Alumni records maintained here; call 202-639-1809. Degrees granted: Bachelors. Special programs- Certificate Program, 202-639-1820. Attendance and degree information available by phone, fax, mail. Transcripts available by fax, mail. Will confirm attendance only with "yes" or "no."

Defense Intelligence College
(See Joint Military Intelligence College)

Dominican House of Studies, Registrar, 487 Michigan Ave NE, Washington, DC 20017, 202-529-5300 (Fax: 202-636-4460) . 9AM-4PM. Enrollment: 66. Records go back to 1945. Degrees granted: Masters; M. Div, S.T.L. Attendance, degree and transcript information available by written request only.

Gallaudet University, Registrar, 800 Florida Ave NE, Washington, DC 20002, 202-651-5393, 202-651-2000 (Fax: 202-651-5182) 8:30AM-4:30PM. www.gallaudet.edu. Enrollment: 2130. Records go back to 1856. Alumni records maintained here; call 202-651-5060. Degrees granted: Bachelors; Masters; Doctorate. Special programs- Study of Deafness. Attendance, degree and transcript information available by fax, mail.

George Washington University, Registrar, 2121 I St NW Ste 101, Washington, DC 20052, 202-994-4909 (Fax: 202-994-4448) www.gwu.edu/. 8AM-5PM. Enrollment: 19000. Records go back to 1820. Alumni records maintained here; call 202-994-6435. Degrees granted: Associate; Bachelors; Masters; Doctorate. Attendance and degree information available by fax, mail. Transcripts available by mail.

Georgetown University, Registrar, 37th and O Sts NW, Wash., DC 20057, 202-687-4020 www.guweb.georgetown.edu/registrar. (Fax: 202-687-3608) 9AM-5PM. Enrollment: 12618. Records go back to 1977. Alumni records maintained here; call 202-687-1789. Degrees granted: Bachelors; Masters; Doctorate. Attendance and degree information available by phone, fax, mail. Transcripts available by fax, mail.

Howard University, Registrar, 2400 Sixth St NW, Washington, DC 20059, 202-806-2712, 202-806-2710 (Fax: 202-806-4466) www.howard.edu. 8AM-5PM. Enrollment: 10952. Records go back to 1867. Alumni records maintained here; call 202-806-8010. Degrees granted: Bachelors; Masters; Doctorate. Attendance and degree information available by phone, fax, mail. Transcripts available by mail.

Johns Hopkins University (School of Advanced International Studies), Registrar, 1740 Massachusetts Ave NW, Washington, DC 20036, 202-663-5708, 202-663-5709 (Fax: 202-663-5615) www.jhu.edu. 9AM-4:45PM. Enrollment: 450. Records go back to 1943. Alumni records are maintained here. Degrees granted: Masters; Doctorate. Attendance and degree information available by phone, fax, mail. Transcripts available by fax, mail.

Joint Military Intelligence College, Registrar, Defense Intelligence Analysis Center, Washington, DC 20340-5100, 202-231-3344. Enrollment: 435. Degrees granted: Masters. Attendance and degree information available by phone, fax, mail. Transcripts available by mail.

Mount Vernon College, Registrar, 2100 Foxhall Rd NW, Washington, DC 20007, 202-625-4527 (Fax: 202-625-6735) www.mvc.edu. 9AM-5:30PM. Enrollment: 600. Alumni records maintained here; call 202-625-4685. Degrees granted: Associate; Bachelors; Masters. Attendance and degree

information available by phone, fax, mail. Transcripts available by fax, mail.

Oblate College, Registrar, 391 Michigan Ave NE, Washington, DC 20017-1587, 202-529-6544, 202-529-5244. 9AM-3PM. Enrollment: 25. Records go back to 1950. Degrees granted: Bachelors; Masters. Attendance and degree information available by phone, mail. Transcripts available by mail.

Potomac College, Registrar, 5005 MacArthur Blvd, Washington, DC 20016, 202-686-0876 (Fax: 202-686-0818) www.potomac.edu. 8AM-5PM. Records go back to 1994. Degrees granted: Associate. Attendance and degree information available by phone, mail. Transcripts available by mail.

Southeastern University, Registrar, 501 Eye St SW, Washington, DC 20024, 202-488-8162 X264 (Fax: 202-488-8093). 10AM-7PM M-F; 10AM-2PM Sat. Enrollment: 458. Records go back to 1990. Alumni records maintained here; call 202-488-8162 X251. Degrees granted: Associate; Bachelors; Masters. Attendance and degree information available by phone, fax, mail. Transcripts available by fax, mail.

Strayer College, Registrar, 1025 15th St NW, Washington, DC 20005, 202-408-2400 (Fax: 202-289-1831). 8AM-5PM. Enrollment: 7419. Records go back to 1981. Degrees granted: Associate; Bachelors; Masters. Attendance and degree information available by phone, mail. Transcripts available by mail.

Trinity College, Registrar, 125 Michigan Ave NE, Washington, DC 20017, 202-884-9200 (Fax: 202-884-9229) 9AM-5PM. www.consortium.org/~trinity. Enrollment: 1400. Records go back to 1902. Alumni records are maintained here. Degrees granted: Bachelors; Masters. Attendance and transcript information available by fax, mail. Will fax to confirm attendance and degree.

University of the District of Columbia (Georgia/Harvard Street), 11th and Harvard Sts NW, Washington, DC 20009, 202-274-5000. Records are located at University of the District of Columbia, Registrar, Connecticut Ave, Washington, DC.

University of the District of Columbia, Registrar, 4200 Connecticut Ave NW, Washington, DC 20008, 202-274-6072 (Fax: 202-274-6073) www.udc.com.. 8:30AM-5PM. Enrollment: 9660. Records go back to 1851. Alumni Records: Alumni Affairs, 4250 Connecticut Ave, Washington, DC 20008

(Fax: 202-274-5305). Degrees granted: Masters. Attendance, degree and transcript information available by mail.

University of the District of Columbia School of Law, Registrar, 4200 Connecticut Ave NW, Washington, DC 20008, 202-274-7348, 202-274-7340 (Fax: 202-274-5583) www.udc.edu. 9AM-5:30PM. Enrollment: 172. Records go back to 1991. Alumni records maintained here; call 202-274-7349. Degrees granted: Doctorate. Attendance and degree information available by phone, fax, mail. Transcripts available by mail.

Washington Theological Union, Registrar, 6896 Laurel St. NW, Washington, DC 20012, 202-541-5211, 800-334-9922 (Fax: 202-726-1716). 8AM-5PM. Enrollment: 250. Records go back to 1970. Alumni records are maintained here. Degrees granted: Masters. Attendance and degree information available by phone, fax, mail. Transcripts available by written request only.

Wesley Theological Seminary, Registrar, 4500 Massachusetts Ave NW, Washington, DC 20016, 202-885-8650, 202-885-8600 (Fax: 202-885-8605) www.wesleysem.org. 9AM-4PM. Enrollment: 670. Records go back to 1884. Alumni records are maintained here. Degrees granted: Masters; Doctorate. Attendance and degree information available by phone, fax, mail. Transcripts available by mail. Search requires name plus signed release. Other helpful information: social security number, approximate years of attendance. Fee is $5.00

Florida

American Trade Institute, Registrar, 1395 NW 167th St, Ste 200, Miami, FL 33169, 305-628-1000 (Fax: 305-628-1461). 9AM-5PM. Enrollment: 250. Records go back to 1976. Formerly **Flagler Career Institute**. Degrees granted: Associate. Attendance and degree information available by phone, fax, mail. Transcripts available by fax, mail.

Art Institute of Fort Lauderdale, Registrar, 1799 SE 17th St, Fort Lauderdale, FL 33316-3000, 954-463-3000 X451, 800-275-7603 (Fax: 954-523-7676). 8AM-5PM. Enrollment: 2300. Records go back to 1968. Degrees granted: Associate; Bachelors. Attendance and transcript information available by fax, mail. Degree information available by phone, fax, mail.

Atlantic Coast Institute, Registrar, 5225 W Broward Blvd, Fort Lauderdale, FL 33317, 954-581-2223, 800-581-8292 (Fax: 954-583-9458). 8AM-5PM. Enrollment: 208. Records go back to 1975. Degrees granted: Associate. Attendance, degree and transcript information available by mail.

Baptist Bible Institute
(See Florida Baptist Theological College)

Barry University, Registrar, 11300 NE Second Ave, Miami Shores, FL 33161-6695, 305-899-3948, 305-899-3860 (Fax: 305-899-3946) www.barry.edu. 8:30AM-5PM. Enrollment: 7048. Records go back to 1940. Alumni records maintained here; call 305-899-3175. Degrees granted: Bachelors; Masters; Doctorate. Attendance and degree information available by phone, fax, mail. Transcripts available by mail.

Bethune-Cookman College, Registrar, 640 Dr Mary McLeod Bethune Blvd, Daytona Beach, FL 32114-3099, 904-255-1401 X363 (Fax: 904-257-5338) 8:30AM-5PM. www.bethune.cookman.edu. Enrollment: 2400. Records go back to 1904. Alumni records maintained here; call 904-255-1401. Degrees granted: Bachelors. Attendance information available by fax, mail. Degree information available by phone, fax, mail. Transcripts available by mail.

Brevard Community College, Enrollment Services, 1519 Clearlake Rd, Cocoa, FL 32922, 407-632-1111 X3701 (Fax: 407-634-3752) www.brevard.cc.fl.us/. 8AM-7PM M,Th; 8AM-5PM T,W,F. Enrollment: 12500. Records go back to 1962. Alumni records are maintained here. Degrees granted: Associate. Attendance and degree information available by phone, mail. Transcripts available by mail (form).

Broward Community College, Registrar, 225 E Las Olas Blvd, Fort Lauderdale, FL 33301, 954-761-7465 (Fax: 954-761-7466) 8AM-4PM. www.broward.cc.fl.us. Enrollment: 77122. Records go back to 1951. Alumni records maintained here; call 954-761-7414. Degrees granted: Associate. Attendance and degree information available by phone, fax, mail. Transcripts available by mail.

Caribbean Center for Advanced Studies (Miami Institute of Psychology), Registrar, 8180 NW 36th St 2nd Fl, Miami, FL 33166-6653, 305-593-1223 (Fax: 305-592-7930) www.MIP.EDU. 9AM - 6PM. Enrollment: 675. Records go back to 1980. Degrees granted: Bachelors; Masters; Doctorate. Attendance, degree and transcript information available by fax, mail.

Central Florida Community College, Registrar, PO Box 1388, Ocala, FL 34478, 352-237-2111, 352-854-2322 (Fax: 352-873-5882) www.CFCCFL.US. 8AM-7PM M-Th, 8AM-4:30PM F. Enrollment: 6000. Records go back to 1958. Alumni records are maintained here. Degrees granted: Associate. Attendance and degree information available by fax, mail. Transcripts available by mail.

Chipola Junior College, Registrar, 3094 Indian Circle, Marianna, FL 32446-2053, 850-526-2761 (Fax: 850-718-2344) www.firnedu/chipola/. 7:30AM-4:30PM. Enrollment: 2500. Records go back to 1947. Alumni records are maintained here. Degrees granted: Associate. Attendance and degree information available by phone, mail. Transcripts available by mail.

City College (Branch), Registrar, 2400 SW 13th St, Gainesville, FL 32608, 352-335-4000 (Fax: 352-335-4303). 8AM-8PM. Enrollment: 330. Records go back to 1989. Formerly **Career College** (Branch). Degrees granted: Associate. Special programs- Specialized Phlebotomy Lab. Attendance information available by phone, fax, mail. Degree and transcript information available by mail.

Clearwater Christian College, Registrar, 3400 Gulf-to-Bay Blvd, Clearwater, FL 33759-4595, 813-726-1153 (Fax: 813-726-8597) www.clearwater.edu. 8AM - 4:30PM. Enrollment: 530. Records go back to 1966. Alumni records are maintained here. Degrees granted: Associate; Bachelors. Attendance information available by phone, fax, mail. Degree and transcript information available by fax, mail.

College of Boca Raton
(See Lynn University)

Cooper Career Institute, Registrar, 2247 Palm Beach Lakes Blvd, West Palm Beach, FL 33409, 561-640-6999 (Fax: 561-686-8778). 8:30AM-5:30PM. Enrollment: 200. Records go back to 1900's. Formerly **Cooper Academy of Court Reporting**. Alumni records are maintained here. Degrees granted: Associate. Special programs- Court Reporting: Medical Stenoscription. Attendance, degree and transcript information available by fax, mail.

Daytona Beach Community College, Records Office, PO Box 2811, Daytona Beach, FL 32120-2811, 904-255-8131 (Fax: 904-254-4489) www.dbcc.cc.fl.us. 8AM-7PM M-Th; 8AM-4:30PM F. Enrollment: 12400. Records go back to 1958. Alumni records maintained here; call 904-255-8131 X4436. Degrees granted: Associate. Attendance information available by fax, mail. Degree information available by phone, fax, mail. Transcripts available by mail.

Eckerd College, Registrar, 4200 54th Ave S, St Petersburg, FL 33711, 813-864-8217 (Fax: 813-864-8060) www.eckerd.edu. 8:30AM-5PM. Enrollment: 1380. Records go back to 1960. Alumni records maintained here; call 813-864-8219. Degrees granted: Bachelors. Attendance and degree information available by phone, fax, mail. Transcripts available by fax, mail.

Edison Community College, Registrar, 8099 College Pkwy SW, PO Box 60210, Fort Myers, FL 33906-6210, 941-489-9317 (Fax: 941-489-9094). 8:30AM-7PM M & T; 8:30AM-4:30PM W-F. Enrollment: 10000. Records go back to 1950's. Alumni records are maintained here. Degrees granted: Associate. Attendance information available by mail. Degree information available by phone, fax, mail. Transcripts available by fax, mail. Fax and mail requests require signed student permission.

Education America, Registrar, 2410 E Busch Blvd, Tampa, FL 33612, 813-935-5700 (Fax: 813-935-7415) 8-11AM, 4-8PM M-Th; 8-5PM F. www.webcoast.com/TampaTech. Enrollment: 1250. Records go back to 1948. Also known as National Education Center - Tampa Technical Institute. Degrees granted: Bachelors. Attendance, degree and transcript information available by fax, mail. Must use school's form to request transcript.

Edward Waters College, Registrar, 1658 Kings Rd, Jacksonville, FL 32209, 904-366-2717 (Fax: 904-366-2760). 8AM-5PM. Enrollment: 515. Records go back to 1866. Alumni records are maintained here. Degrees granted: Bachelors. Attendance and degree information available by fax, mail. Transcripts available by mail.

Embry-Riddle Aeronautical University, Registrar, 600 S Clyde Morris Blvd, Daytona Beach, FL 32114-3900, 904-226-6030 (Fax: 904-226-7070) www.db.erau.edu. 8AM-4PM. Enrollment: 4135. Records go back to 1945. Alumni records maintained here; call 904-226-6160. Degrees granted: Associate; Bachelors; Masters. Special programs-Aviation Maintenance Technology 904-226-6779: Extended Campus, active records, 904-226-6910: Extended Campus, inactive records, 904-226-6920. Attendance and degree information available by phone, fax, mail. Transcripts available by fax, mail.

Flagler College, Registrar, PO Box 1027, 74 King St, St Augustine, FL 32085-1027, 904-829-6481 (Fax: 904-826-0094) www.flagler.edu. 8AM-Noon, 1-5PM. Enrollment: 1600. Records go back to 1968. Alumni records are maintained here. Degrees granted: Bachelors. Attendance and degree information available by phone, fax, mail. Transcripts available by mail.

Florida Agricultural and Mechanical University, Registrar's Office, Foote Hilyer Admin Ctr #112, Tallahassee, FL 32307-3200, 850-599-3115 (Fax: 850-561-2428) 8AM-5PM. www.famu.edu. Enrollment: 11018. Records go back to 1887. Alumni records maintained here; call 850-599-3861. Degrees granted: Associate; Bachelors; Masters; Doctorate. Attendance and degree information available by phone, fax, mail. Transcripts available by mail. Will Fax to confirm attendance and degree.

Florida Atlantic University, Registrar, 777 Glades Rd, PO Box 3091, Boca Raton, FL 33431-0991, 561-297-2711 (Fax: 561-297-2756) www.fau.edu. 8AM-6PM M-Th, 8AM-5PM F. Enrollment: 19000. Records go back to 1965. Alumni records maintained here; call 561-297-3010. Degrees granted: Associate; Bachelors; Masters; Doctorate. Attendance and degree information available by phone, fax, mail. Transcripts available by fax, mail.

Florida Baptist Theological College, Registrar, PO Box 1306, Graceville, FL 32440, 850-263-3261 (Fax: 850-263-7506) www.fbtc.edu. 8AM-4:30PM. Enrollment: 501. Records go back to 1947. Alumni records maintained here; call 850-263-3261 X485. Degrees granted: Associate; Bachelors. Special programs- Theology: Christian Education: Elementary Educ.: Music. Attendance and degree information available by phone, fax, mail. Transcripts available by written request only.

Florida Christian College, Registrar, 1011 Bill Beck Blvd, Kissimmee, FL 34744, 407-847-8966 (Fax: 407-847-3925). 8:30AM-4:30PM. Enrollment: 175. Records go back to 1976. Alumni records maintained here; call 407-847-8966 X313. Degrees granted: Associate; Bachelors. Attendance information available by phone, fax, mail. Degree information available by fax. Transcripts available by mail.

Florida College, Registrar, 119 Glen Arven Ave, Temple Terrace, FL 33617, 813-988-5131, 813-899-6706 (Fax: 813-899-6772) 8AM-5PM. www.flcoll.edu. Enrollment: 400. Records go back to 1945. Alumni records are maintained here. Degrees granted: Associate; Bachelors. Special programs- Biblical Studies. Attendance information available by phone, fax, mail. Degree and transcript information available by fax, mail.

Florida Community College at Jacksonville, Registrar, 501 W State St, Jacksonville, FL 32202, 904-632-3100 (Fax: 904-632-5105) www.fccj.cc.fl.us. Enrollment: 19000. Records go back to 1966. Degrees granted: Associate. Special programs- Nursing Program: Vocational & Adult Studies. Attendance and degree information available by phone, fax, mail. Transcripts available by written request only.

Florida Computer & Business School, Registrar, 1321 SW 107th Ave, Suite 201B, Miami, FL 33174, 305-553-6065 (Fax: 305-225-0128) 9AM-8PM. Enrollment: 300. www.floridacomputer&businessschool.com. Records go back 5 years in-house; remainder off-site. Degrees granted: Associate; Diploma, Specialized Associate Degree. Attendance, degree and transcript information available by fax, mail.

Florida Institute of Technology, Registrar, 150 W University Blvd, Melbourne, FL 32901-6988, 407-674-8115, 407-674-8117 (Fax: 407-727-2419) www.fit.edu. 8AM-5PM. Enrollment: 4500. Records go back to 1958. Alumni records maintained here; call 407-674-7190. Degrees granted: Associate; Bachelors; Masters; Doctorate. Attendance and degree information available by phone, fax, mail. Transcripts available by fax, mail.

Florida International University, Registrar, University Park, Miami, FL 33199, 305-348-2383 (Fax: 305-348-2941) www.fiu.edu. 8AM-5PM M,Th,F; 8AM-7PM T,W. Enrollment: 28000. Records go back to 1973. Alumni records are maintained here. Degrees granted: Bachelors; Masters; Doctorate. Special programs- School of Hospitality Management, 305-948-4500: School of Journalism & Mass Communications, 305-940-5625: School of Nursing, 305-940-5915: School of Policy Management, 305-940-5890: School of Social Work, 305-940-5880: Continuing Education (non-credit), 305-940-5669: College of Business Administration, 305-348-2751. Attendance and degree information available by phone, mail. Transcripts available by mail.

Florida Keys Community College, Registrar, 5901 W College Rd, Key West, FL 33040, 305-296-9081 (Fax: 305-292-5155) www.firn.edu/fkcc. 8:30AM-4PM. Enrollment: 3800. Records go back to 1965. Degrees granted: Associate. Attendance and degree information available by phone, fax, mail. Transcripts available by mail.

Florida Memorial College, Registrar, 15800 NW 42nd Ave, Miami, FL 33054, 305-626-3750, 305-626-3754 (Fax: 305-626-3755) www.fmc.edu. 8AM-5PM. Enrollment: 1600. Records go back to 1879. Alumni records maintained here; call 305-626-3657. Degrees granted: Bachelors. Attendance and degree information available by phone, fax, mail. Transcripts available by mail.

Florida Metropolitan University (Tampa College, Pinellas Campus), Registrar, 2471 N McMullen Booth Rd, Clearwater, FL 34619-1354, 813-725-2688 (Fax: 813-796-3722). 8AM-8PM. Enrollment: 800. Records go back to 1989. Formerly **Tampa College.** Alumni records are maintained here. Degrees granted: Associate; Bachelors; Masters. Attendance and degree information available by phone, fax, mail. Transcripts available by mail.

Florida Metropolitan University, Registrar, 995 E Memorial Blvd, Lakeland, FL 33801, 941-686-1444 (Fax: 941-682-1077). 10AM-7:30PM. Enrollment: 500. Records go back to 1970. Degrees granted: Associate; Bachelors; Masters. Attendance and transcript information available by fax, mail. Degree information available by phone, fax, mail.

Florida Metropolitan University, Registrar, 3319 W Hillsborough Ave, Tampa, FL 33614, 813-879-6000 (Fax: 813-871-2483). 8AM-8PM. Enrollment: 850. Records go back to 1950. Degrees granted: Associate; Bachelors; Masters. Attendance and degree information available by fax, mail. Transcripts available by mail.

Florida National College, Registrar, 4206 West 12th Ave, Hialeah, FL 33012, 305-821-3333 (Fax: 305-362-0595) 8AM-5PM. www.florida/national.com. Enrollment: 1000. Records go back to 1982. Alumni records are maintained here. Degrees granted: Associate. Attendance and degree information available by phone, mail. Transcripts available by mail.

Florida Southern College, Registrar, 111 Lake Hollingsworth Dr, Lakeland, FL 33801, 941-680-4127 (Fax: 941-680-4565) 8AM-5PM. www.flsouthern.edu. Enrollment: 1600. Records go back to 1915. Alumni records maintained here; call 941-680-4110. Degrees granted: Bachelors; Masters. Special programs- Orlando Program, 407-855-1302: Charlotte-DeSoto Program, 941-494-7373. Attendance and degree information available by phone, fax, mail. Transcripts available by written request only.

Florida State University, Registrar, A3900 University Center, Tallahassee, FL 32306-2480, 850-644-1050, 850-644-5887 (Fax: 850-644-1597) www.fsu.edu. 8AM-5PM. Enrollment: 30000. Records go back to 1857. Records go back to 1857 as the Seminary West of Suwannee; to 1909 as the FL State College for Women; to 1947 as the FL State University. Alumni Records: Alumni Office, Florida State University, C550 UCC, Tallahassee, FL 32306-2610. Degrees granted: Associate; Bachelors; Masters; Doctorate. Attendance and degree information available by phone, fax, mail. Transcripts available by fax, mail.

Florida Technical College, Registrar, 8711 Lone Star Rd, Jacksonville, FL 32211, 904-724-2229 (Fax: 904-720-0920) 8AM-6PM. Enrollment: 100. Records go back to 1984. Degrees granted: Associate. Special programs: CAD/ BMT/ Ctt/ Java/ Electronics. Attendance and degree information available by fax, mail. Transcripts available by mail.

Fort Lauderdale College, Registrar, 1040 Bayview Dr, Fort Lauderdale, FL 33304, 954-568-1600 (Fax: 954-568-2008) www.flc.edu. 8AM-8PM M-Th; 9AM-1PM F. Enrollment: 450. Records go back to 1940. Degrees granted: Associate; Bachelors; Masters. Attendance information available by fax, mail. Degree information available by phone, fax, mail. Transcripts available by mail.

Golf Academy of the South, Registrar, 307 Daneswood Way, Casselberry, FL 32707, 407-699-1990. Degrees granted: Associate. Attendance and degree information available by phone, mail. Transcripts available by mail.

Gulf Coast Community College, Admissions & Records, 5230 W US Hwy 98, Panama City, FL 32401, 850-872-3892 (Fax: 850-913-3308) www.gc.cc.fl.us. 7:30AM-6PM M-Th; 7:30AM-4PM F. Enrollment: 8000. Records go back to 1960. Degrees granted: Associate; PSAV Certification. Attendance and degree information available by phone, fax, mail. Transcripts available by fax, mail.

Hillsborough Community College, HCC Admissions Office, PO Box 31127, Tampa, FL 33631-3127, 813-253-7004 (Fax: 813-253-7578) www.hcc.cc.fl.us. 8AM-4:30PM. Enrollment: 9870. Records go back to 1970. Alumni Records: Alumni Assoc., PO Box 31127, Tampa, FL 33631. Degrees granted: Associate. Attendance and degree information available by phone, fax, mail. Transcripts available by mail. Order transcripts: HCC Admissions Office, Hillsborough CC, PO Box 5096, Tampa FL, 33675-5096.

Hobe Sound Bible College, Registrar, PO Box 1065, 11298 SE Gomez Ave, Hobe Sound, FL 33455, 561-546-5534, 561-545-1405 (Ext. 117) (Fax: 561-545-1422) www.hws.edu. 8AM-5PM. Enrollment: 144. Records go back to 1960. Alumni records maintained here; call 561-545-1458. Degrees granted: Associate; Bachelors. Attendance, degree and transcript information available by phone, fax, mail.

ITT Career Institute-Jacksonville
(See Flagler Career Institute in Jacksonville, FL)

ITT Career Institute-Miami
(See Flagler Career Institute in Miami, FL)

ITT Technical Institute (Branch of Fort Wayne, IN), Registrar, 3401 S University Dr, **Fort Lauderdale**, FL 33328, 954-476-9300, 800-488-7797 (Fax: 954-476-6889) www.ittesi.com. 8AM-5PM. Enrollment: 450. Records go back to 1991. Alumni records are maintained here. Degrees granted: Associate. Special programs- Electrical Engineering. Attendance information available by phone, fax, mail. Degree and transcript information available by fax, mail.

ITT Technical Institute (Branch of Tampa, FL), Registrar, 6600 Youngerman Circle, #10, **Jacksonville**, FL 32244, 904-573-9100, 800-318-1264 (Fax: 904-573-0512) www.ittesi.com. 8AM-5PM. Enrollment: 450. Records go back to 1991. Alumni Records: Alumni Assoc., 5975 Castle Creek Pkwy N, Indianapolis, IN 46250. Degrees granted: Associate; Bachelors in Electronics. Attendance and degree information available by phone, mail. Transcripts available by mail.

ITT Technical Institute, Registrar, 2600 Lake Lucien Dr, **Maitland**, FL 32751-9754, 407-660-2900 (Fax: 407-660-2566) www.ittesi.edu. 9AM-8PM. Enrollment: 450. Records go back to 1990. Alumni records are maintained here. Degrees granted: Associate; Bachelors. Attendance, degree and transcript information available by fax, mail. Requests must have student's signature.

ITT Technical Institute, Registrar, 4809 Memorial Hwy, **Tampa**, FL 33634-7350, 813-885-2244 (Fax: 813-888-6078) www.ittesi.com. 8AM-5PM. Enrollment: 600. Records go back to 1984. Alumni records are maintained here. Degrees granted: Associate; Bachelors. Special programs- Electronics Engineering. Attendance and degree information available by phone, fax, mail. Transcripts available by fax, mail.

Indian River Community College, Registrar, 3209 Virginia Ave, Fort Pierce, FL 34981-5596, 561-462-4766 (Fax: 561-462-4699) www.ircc.cc.fl.us. 8AM-5PM. Enrollment: 4370. Records go back to 1960. Alumni records maintained here; call 561-462-4786. Degrees granted: Associate. Special programs- Educational Services Dept, 561-462-4740. Attendance, degree and transcript information available by mail.

International Academy of Merchandising and Design, Registrar, 5225 Memorial Hwy, Tampa, FL 33634-7350, 813-881-0007 X235 (Fax: 813-881-0008). 8AM-6:30PM. Records go back to 1985. Degrees granted: Associate. Attendance and degree information available by phone, fax, mail. Transcripts available by mail.

International College (Branch), Registrar, 8695 College Pkwy Ste 217, Fort Myers, FL 33919, 941-482-0019 (Fax: 941-482-1714) www.internationalcollege.edu. 9:30AM-6:30PM. Enrollment: 610. Records go back to 1989. Alumni records are maintained here. Attendance and degree information available by phone, fax, mail. Transcripts available by fax, mail.

International College, Registrar, 2654 E Tamiami Trail, Naples, FL 34112-5707, 941-774-4700 (Fax: 941-774-4593) 9AM-6:30PM. www.internationalcollege.edu. Enrollment: 500. Records go back to 1990. Alumni records are maintained here. Degrees granted: Associate; Bachelors. Attendance information available by written request only. Degree information available by phone, fax, mail. Transcripts available by fax, mail.

International Fine Arts College, Registrar, 1737 N Bayshore Dr, Miami, FL 33132, 305-373-4684, 305-999-5000 (Fax: 305-374-7946) www.ifac.edu. 7AM-6PM. Enrollment: 700. Records go back to 1971. Alumni records are maintained. Degrees granted: Associate. Special programs- Film Animation: Visual Arts. Attendance and degree information available by phone, fax, mail. Transcripts available by fax, mail. Need signed release on special form provided by college.

Jacksonville University, Registrar, 2800 University Blvd N, Jacksonville, FL 32211, 904-745-7090 (Fax: 904-745-7086) 8:30AM-5PM. www.junix.ju.edu. Enrollment: 2416. Records go back to 1934. Alumni records maintained here; call 904-745-7201. Degrees granted: Bachelors; Masters. Special programs- Marine Science, 904-745-7301. Attendance and degree information available by phone, fax, mail. Transcripts available by mail.

Johnson & Wales University (Branch Campus), Registrar, 1701 NE 127th St, North Miami, FL 33181, 305-892-7038 (Fax: 305-892-7019) www.jwu.edu. 8:30AM-4:30PM. Enrollment: 1250. Records go back to 1991. Alumni records maintained here; call 401-598-1854. Degrees granted: Associate; Bachelors. Attendance and degree information available by phone, fax, mail. Transcripts available by mail.

Jones College, Registrar, 5353 Arlington Expy, Jacksonville, FL 32211-5588, 904-743-1122 (Fax: 904-743-4446) www.jones.edu. 8AM-5PM. Enrollment: 850. Records go back to 1940's. Alumni records are maintained here. Degrees granted: Associate; Bachelors. Attendance, degree and transcript information available by fax, mail.

Jones College (Branch), Registrar, 5975 Sunset Dr Ste 302, South Miami, FL 33143, 904-743-1122, 904-669-9606 (Fax: 904-669-9504). Records are located at Jones College, Registrar, Jacksonville, FL.

Keiser College (Branch), Registrar, 1800 W International Speedway Blvd #3, **Daytona Beach**, FL 32114, 904-255-1707 (Fax: 904-239-0995) www.keisercollege.cc.fl.us. 7:30AM-8PM M-Th; 7:30AM-4PM F. Records go back to 1993. Degrees granted: Associate Attendance, degree and transcript information available by fax, mail.

Keiser College, Registrar, 1500 NW 49th St, Fort Lauderdale, FL 33309-3779, www.keisercollege.cc.fl.us. 954-776-4456 (Fax: 954-771-4894) 8AM-5PM M-Th, 8AM-Noon F. Enrollment: 950. Records go back to 1979. Alumni records are maintained here. Degrees granted: Associate. Attendance, degree and transcript information available by mail.

Keiser College (Branch), Registrar, 701 S Babcock St, **Melbourne**, FL 32901-1461, 407-255-2255 (Fax: 407-725-3766) 9AM-6:30PM. www.keisercollege.cc.fl.us. Records go back to 1977. Degrees granted: Associate. Attendance and degree information available by fax, mail. Transcripts available by mail.

Keiser College (Branch), Registrar, 1700 Halstead Blvd, **Tallahassee**, FL 32308-3489, 850-942-9494 www.keisercollege.cc.fl.us. (Fax: 850-942-9497) 8AM-10:30PM M-F; 8AM-3:30PM S. Enrollment: 350. Records go back to 1992. Alumni records are maintained here. Degrees granted: Associate. Special programs- Computer Graphics & Design. Attendance, degree and transcript information available by fax, mail.

Lake City Community College, Registrar, Rte 19 Box 1030, Lake City, FL 32025, 904-752-1822 (Fax: 904-755-1521) 8AM-4:30PM. www.firn.edu/lccc. Enrollment: 2139. Records go back to 1964. Degrees granted: Associate. Attendance information available by phone, mail. Degree and transcript information available by mail.

Lake-Sumter Community College, Registrar, 9501 US Hwy 441, Leesburg, FL 34788-8751, 352-365-3572 (Fax: 352-365-3553) www.lscc.cc.fl.us. 8AM-9PM M-Th, 8AM-4:30PM F. Enrollment: 2650. Records go back to 1962. Alumni records maintained here; call 352-787-3747. Degrees granted: Associate. Attendance and degree information available by phone, mail. Transcripts available by mail.

Lakeland College of Business
(See Tampa College of Lakeland)

Lynn University, Registrar, 3601 N Military Tr, Boca Raton, FL 33431, 561-994-0770 X177, 561-994-0770 X233 (Fax: 561-994-1674) www.lynn.edu. 9AM-6PM M-Th; 9AM-5PM F. Enrollment: 1500. Records go back to 1966. Alumni records maintained here; call 561-994-0770 X236. Degrees granted: Associate; Bachelors; Masters. Attendance and degree information available by phone, fax, mail. Transcripts available by fax, mail.

Manatee Community College, Registrar, 5840 26th St W, Bradenton, FL 34207, 941-755-1511 X4231 (Fax: 941-755-1511 X4714) www.sol.sarasota.fl.us/mcc.html. 8AM-4:30PM. Enrollment: 8000. Records go back to 1958. Alumni records maintained here; call 941-755-1511 X4389. Degrees granted: Associate. Attendance and degree information available by phone, fax, mail. Transcripts available by fax, mail.

Miami—Dade Community College, Registrar, 300 NE Second Ave, Miami, FL 33132, 305-237-3336 (Fax: 305-237-7025) 8AM-7PM M-Th; 8AM-4:30PM F. www.mdcc.com. Records go back to 1959. Alumni records maintained here; call 305-237-3240. Degrees granted: Associate. Attendance and degree information available by fax, mail. Transcripts available by mail.

Miami—Dade Community College — Kendall Campus, Registrar, 11011 S W 104 St, Miami, FL 33176, 305-237-2222 (Fax: 305-237-2964) www.kendall.mdcc.edu. Enrollment: 19000. Records go back to 1960. Formerly **Miami-Dade Community College-South Campus.** Alumni records are maintained here. Degrees granted: Associate. Attendance and degree information available by phone, fax, mail. Transcripts available by fax, mail.

National School of Technology, Registrar, 9020 SW 137th Ave, Miami, FL 33186, 305-386-9900 (Fax: 305-388-1740) www.national-school-tech.edu. 8AM-6PM. Enrollment: 500. Records go back to 1981. Degrees granted: Associate; SAD. Attendance information available by phone, fax, mail. Degree and transcript information available by fax, mail.

North Florida Community College, Registrar, 100 Turner Davis Dr, Madison, FL 32340, 850-973-1622, 850-973-1605 (Fax: 850-973-1697) www.firn.edu/webfile/cc/nfcc. 8AM-4:30PM. Enrollment: 1073. Records go back to 1958. Formerly **North Florida Junior College.** Alumni records are maintained here. Degrees granted: Associate. Special programs- AS Interpreter Training, 850-973-1612. Attendance and degree information available by phone, fax, mail. Transcripts available by fax, mail.

Northwood University (Branch), Registrar, 2600 N Military Trail, West Palm Beach, FL 33409, 561-478-5500 (Fax: 561-640-3328) www.northwood.edu. 9AM-5PM. Enrollment: 1200. Records go back to 1986. Alumni records are maintained here. Degrees granted: Associate; Bachelors. Attendance and degree information available by phone, mail. Transcripts available by mail.

Nova Southeastern University, Registrar, 3301 College Ave, Fort Lauderdale, FL 33314, 954-262-7200, 954-262-7400 (Fax: 954-262-7265) www.nova.edu. 8:30AM-7PM M-Th; 8:30AM-6PM F, 9AM-Noon S. Enrollment: 15500. Records go back to 1967. Formerly **Nova U or Southeastern University of the Health Sciences.** Alumni records maintained here; call 954-262-7418. Degrees granted: Bachelors; Masters; Doctorate; Physician Asst., Occupational Therapy Cert. Attendance and degree information available by phone, fax, mail. Transcripts available by fax, mail.

Nova University
(See Nova Southeastern University)

Okaloosa-Walton Community College, Registrar, 100 College Blvd, Niceville, FL 32578, 850-678-5111, 850-729-5373 (Fax: 850-729-5323) www.owcc.cc.fl.us. Enrollment: 16000. Records go back to 1968. Alumni records maintained here; call 850-729-5357. Degrees granted: Associate. Special programs- Call 850-729-5373. Attendance, degree and transcript information available by mail.

Orlando College, Registrar, 5421 Diplomat Cir, Orlando, FL 32810, 407-628-5870 (Fax: 407-628-1344). 10AM-7PM M-W; 8:30AM-7PM Th; 8:30AM-5PM F. Records go back to 1956. Degrees granted: Associate; Bachelors; Masters. Attendance and degree information available by phone, fax, mail. Transcripts available by fax, mail.

Orlando College (Branch), Registrar, 2411 Sand Lake Rd, Orlando, FL 32809, 407-851-2525 (Fax: 407-851-1477). 9AM-7:30PM M-Th; 9AM-5PM F. Enrollment: 850. Records go back to 1991. Degrees granted: Associate; Bachelors; Masters. Special programs- Medical Assistant. Attendance and degree information available by phone, mail. Transcripts available by written request only.

Palm Beach Atlantic College, Registrar, 901 S Flagler Dr, PO Box 24708, West Palm Beach, FL 33416-4708, 561-803-2075 (Fax: 561-803-2081) www.pbac.edu. 8AM-7PM M-Th, 8MA-5PM F, 9AM-1PM Sat. Enrollment: 2000. Records go back to 1968. Alumni records maintained here; call 561-803-2016. Degrees granted: Bachelors; Masters. Attendance and degree information available by phone, fax, mail. Transcripts available by fax, mail.

Palm Beach Community College, Registrar, 4200 Congress Ave, Lake Worth, FL 33461-4796, 561-439-8106, 561-439-8102 (Fax: 561-439-8383) www.pbcc.cc.fl.us. 8AM-7PM M-Th; 8AM-4PM F. Enrollment: 18000. Records go back to 1933. Alumni records are maintained here also. Call 561-439-8072. Degrees granted: Associate. Special programs- Nursing: Criminal Justice Degree. Attendance and degree information available by phone, fax, mail. Transcripts available by fax, mail.

Pasco-Hernando Community College, Registrar, 36727 Blanton Rd, Dade City, FL 33525-7599, 813-847-2727 (Fax: 813-816-3300). 8AM-4:30PM. Enrollment: 7200. Records go back to 1972. Degrees granted: Associate. Attendance and degree information available by phone, fax, mail. Transcripts available by fax, mail.

Pensacola Junior College, Registrar, 1000 College Blvd, Pensacola, FL 32504-8998, 850-484-1600 (Fax: 850-484-1689) www.pjc.cc.fl.us. 7:30AM-4PM. Enrollment: 17341. Records go back to 1948. Alumni records are maintained here. Degrees granted: Associate. Attendance and degree information available by phone, fax, mail. Transcripts available by fax, mail.

Polk Community College, Registrar, 999 Ave H NE, Winter Haven, FL 33881-4299, 941-297-1000 (Fax: 941-297-1023). 8AM-5PM. Enrollment: 6000. Records go back to 1966. Alumni records are maintained here. Degrees granted: Associate. Certification: EMT & Paramedic. Attendance, degree and transcript information available by fax, mail.

Prospect Hall School of Business, Registrar, 2620 Hollywood Blvd, Hollywood, FL 33020, 954-923-8100. 8AM-8PM. Enrollment: 200. Records go back to 1973. Degrees granted: Associate. Special programs- All computer-oriented courses. Attendance, degree and transcript information available by written request only.

Ringling School of Art and Design, Registrar, 2700 N Tamiami Tr, Sarasota, FL 34234, 941-351-5100, 941-359-7529 (Fax: 941-359-7517) www.rsad.edu. 8:30AM-4:30PM. Enrollment: 825. Records go back to 1931. Alumni records are maintained here. Degrees granted: Bachelors. Certification: BFA. Attendance, degree and transcript information available by fax, mail.

Rollins College, Office of Student Records, 1000 Holt Ave, Winter Park, FL 32789-4499, 407-646-2144 (Fax: 407-646-1576) www.rollins.edu. 8:30AM-5PM. Enrollment: 3500. Records go back to 1895. Alumni records maintained here; call 407-646-2266. Degrees granted: Associate; Bachelors; Masters. Attendance, degree and transcript information available by fax, mail.

Saint Leo College, Registrar, MC 2278, PO Box 6665, Saint Leo, FL 33574, 352-588-8235 (Fax: 352-588-8390) www.saintleo.edu. 8AM-5PM. Enrollment: 6500. Records go back to 1920. Alumni Records: Alumni/Parent Relations, PO Box 6665 MC 2244, Saint Leo, FL 33574. Degrees granted: Bachelors; Masters. Special programs-Restaurant/Hotel Management. Attendance and degree information available by phone, fax, mail. Transcripts available by fax, mail. Confidentiality restrictions apply.

Santa Fe Community College, Registrar, 3000 NW 83rd St, Gainesville, FL 32606, 352-395-5443 (Fax: 352-395-5922) 8AM-4:30PM. www.santafe.cc.fl.us. Enrollment: 12500. Records go back to 1966. Degrees granted: Associate; Bachelors. Attendance and degree information available by phone, fax, mail. Transcripts available by fax, mail.

Seminole Community College, Registrar, 100 Weldon Blvd, Sanford, FL 32773-6199, 407-328-2025, 407-328-2028 (Fax: 407-328-2029) www.seminole.cc.fl.us. 8:30AM-7:30PM M-Th; 8:30AM-4PM F. Enrollment: 7500. Records go back to 1966. Alumni records are maintained here. Degrees granted: Associate. Attendance and degree information available by phone, fax, mail. Transcripts available by fax, mail.

South College, Registrar, 1760 N Congress Ave, West Palm Beach, FL 33409, 561-697-9200 (Fax: 561-697-9944) www.southcollege.edu. 8AM-7PM M-Th; 8AM-5PM F; 9AM-Noon S. Enrollment: 400. Records go back to 1986. Degrees granted: Associate; Bachelors. Special programs-Physical Therapy Assistants Program. Attendance, degree and transcript information available by mail. Fax available to confirm attendance and degree.

South Florida Community College, Registrar, 600 W College Dr, Avon Park, FL 33825, 941-453-6661 (Fax: 941-453-2365) www.sfcc.cc.fl.us. Enrollment: 13000. Degrees granted: Associate. Attendance, degree and transcript information available by fax, mail.

Southeastern Academy, Inc., Registrar, 233 Academy Dr, PO Box 421768, Kissimmee, FL 32742, 407-847-4444 (Fax: 407-847-8793). 8:30AM-5PM. Enrollment: 400. Records go back to 1975. Attendance and degree information available by phone, fax, mail. Transcripts available by fax, mail.

Southeastern College of Osteopathic Medicine
(See Nova Southeastern College)

Southeastern College of the Assemblies of God, Registrar, 1000 Longfellow Blvd, Lakeland, FL 33801, 941-667-5000, 941-667-5011 (Fax: 941-667-5200) www.secollege.edu. 8AM-4:30PM. Enrollment: 1200. Records go back to 1935. Alumni records maintained here; call 941-667-5072. Degrees granted: Bachelors. Attendance and degree information available by phone, fax, mail. Transcripts available by fax, mail.

Southern College, Registrar, 5600 Lake Underhill Rd, Orlando, FL 32807, 407-273-1000 (Fax: 407-273-0492). 8AM-5PM. Enrollment: 450. Records go back to 1968. Degrees granted: Associate. Attendance and transcript information available by fax, mail. Degree information available by phone, fax, mail.

Southwest Florida College of Business, Registrar, 1685 Medical Lane Ste 200, Fort Myers, FL 33907, 941-939-4766 (Fax: 941-936-4040). 8AM-7PM. Enrollment: 250. Records go back to 1983. Degrees granted: Associate. Attendance and degree information available by phone, fax, mail. Transcripts available by mail.

Spurgeon Baptist Bible Collge, Registrar, 4440 Spurgeon Dr, Mulberry, FL 33860, 941-425-3429, 941-425-3338 (Fax: 941-425-3861) www.spurgeon.edu. Enrollment: 40. Records go back to 1970. Alumni records are maintained here. Degrees granted: Associate; Bachelors. Attendance and degree information available by phone, fax, mail. Transcripts available by fax, mail.

St. John Vianney College Seminary, Registrar, 2900 SW 87th Ave, Miami, FL 33165, 305-223-4561, 305-223-4562 (Fax: 305-223-0650) 8:30AM-4:30PM. Enrollment: 40. Records go back to 1959. Alumni records are maintained here. Degrees granted: Bachelors. Attendance information available by phone, fax, mail. Degree and transcripts available by mail.

St. Johns River Community College, Registrar, 5001 St Johns Ave, Palatka, FL 32177-3897, 904-312-4200 (Fax: 904-312-4292) www.firn.edu/sjcc/. 8AM-5PM. Records go back to 1958. Degrees granted: Associate. Attendance, degree and transcript information available by mail.

St. Petersburg Junior College, Registrar, PO Box 13489, St Petersburg, FL 33733-3489, 813-341-3600, 813-341-3170 (Fax: 813-341-3150) www.spjc.cc.fl.us. 8AM-4PM. Enrollment: 19000. Records go back to 1928. Alumni records maintained here; call 813-341-3600. Degrees granted: Associate. Attendance and degree information available by phone, fax, mail. Transcripts available by fax, mail.

St. Thomas University, Registrar, 16400 NW 32nd Ave, Miami, FL 33054, 305-628-6537 (Fax: 305-628-6551) www.stu.edu. 9AM-5PM M,Th,F; 9AM-6:30PM T,W. Enrollment: 2200. Records go back to 1961. Alumni records maintained here; call 305-628-6641. Degrees granted: Bachelors; Masters. Special programs- Sports Administration Programs. Attendance and degree information available by phone, fax, mail. Transcripts available by mail.

St. Vincent de Paul Regional Seminary, Registrar, 10701 S Military Tr, Boynton Beach, FL 33436-4899, 561-732-4424 (Fax: 561-737-2205). 9AM-4PM. Enrollment: 72. Records go back to 1963. Degrees granted: Masters. Attendance and degree information available by phone, fax, mail. Transcripts available by mail.

Stetson University, Registrar, 421 N Woodland Blvd, Deland, FL 32720, 904-822-7140 (Fax: 904-822-7146) www.stetson.edu. 8AM-4:30PM. Enrollment: 2000. Alumni records maintained here; call 904-822-7480. Degrees granted: Bachelors; Masters; EDS. Attendance and degree information available by phone, mail. Transcripts available by mail.

Tallahassee Community College, Registrar, 444 Appleyard Dr, Tallahassee, FL 32304-2895, 850-921-2269 (Fax: 850-921-0563) www.tallahassee.cc.fl.us. 8AM-7PM M-Th; 8AM-5PM F. Enrollment: 10000. Records go back to 1966. Degrees granted: Associate. Attendance and degree information available by phone, fax, mail. Transcripts available by fax, mail.

Talmudic College of Florida, Registrar, 1910 Alton Rd, Miami Beach, FL 33139-1507, 305-534-7050 (Fax: 305-534-8444) 9AM-5:30PM. www.talmudicu.edu. Enrollment: 40. Records go back to 1974. Alumni records are maintained here. Degrees granted: Bachelors; Masters; Doctorate; 1st Talmudic Degree. Attendance and degree information available by phone, fax, mail. Transcripts available by fax, mail.

Tampa College
(See Florida Metropolitan University)

Tampa College (Branch), Registrar, Sabal Business Ctr, 3924 Coconut Palm Dr, Tampa, FL 33619, 813-621-0041 (Fax: 813-621-6283). 8:30AM-8PM. Enrollment: 600. Records go back to 1990. Degrees granted: Associate; Bachelors; Masters. Attendance and degree information available by phone, fax, mail. Transcripts available by mail.

Trinity International University, Registrar, 500 NE First Ave, Miami, FL 33132, 305-577-4600 X131 (Fax: 305-577-4612) 8:30AM - 4PM. Enrollment: 400. Records go back to 1939. Alumni records are maintained here. Degrees granted: Bachelors; Masters. Attendance and degree information available by phone, fax, mail. Transcripts available by fax, mail.

United Electronics Institute of Florida, Registrar, 3924 Coconut Palm Dr, Tampa, FL 33619, 813-626-2999 (Fax: 813-623-5769). Enrollment: 250. Records go back to 1890. School is out of business. Degrees granted: Associate. Attendance and degree information available by phone, mail. Transcripts available by mail.

University of Central Florida, Registrar, 4000 Central Florida Blvd, PO Box 160114, Orlando, FL 32816-0114, 407-823-3100, 407-823-5148 (Fax: 407-823-5652) www.ucf.mail.edu. 8AM-7PM M & Th; 8AM-5PM T,W,F. Enrollment: 27000. Records go back to 1965. Alumni records maintained here; call 407-823-2556. Degrees granted: Bachelors; Masters; Doctorate. Attendance and degree information available by phone, fax, mail. Transcripts available by mail.

University of Florida, Office of the Registrar, PO Box 114000, Gainesville, FL 32611-4000, 352-392-1374 (Fax: 352-392-3987) www.reg.ufl.edu. 8AM-5PM. Enrollment: 39951. Records go back to 1800's. Alumni Records: 2012 W University Ave, Gainesville, FL 32611. Degrees granted: Associate; Bachelors; Masters; Doctorate; Specialist, Engineer, Professional Degrees. Attendance and degree information available by phone, fax, mail. Transcripts available by mail. Use official form to request transcript.

University of Miami, Office of the Registrar, PO Box 248026, Coral Gables, FL 33124-4627, 305-284-5455 www.miami.edu. (Fax: 305-284-3144) 8:30AM-5PM. Enrollment: 12496. Records go back to 1926. Alumni Records: 1550 Bresia Ave, Coral Gables, FL 33124-3410. Degrees granted: Bachelors; Masters; Doctorate. Certification: Continuing Studies, 305-284-4000. Attendance and degree information available by phone, fax, mail. Transcripts available by fax, mail.

University of North Florida, Registrar, 4567 St Johns Bluff Rd S, Jacksonville, FL 32224-2645, 904-620-2620 (Fax: 904-620-2403) www.unf.edu. 8AM - 6PM. Enrollment: 10700. Records go back to 1972. Alumni records maintained here; call 904-620-4723. Degrees granted: Bachelors; Masters; Doctorate. Attendance and degree information available by fax, mail. Transcripts available by mail.

University of Sarasota, Registrar, 5250 17th St, Sarasota, FL 34235, 941-379-0404, 800-331-5995 (Fax: 941-379-9464) 10AM - 4PM. Enrollment: 1500. Records go back to 1969. Alumni records are maintained here also. Call 941-379-0404. Degrees granted: Bachelors; Masters; Doctorate. Attendance and degree information available by phone, fax, mail. Transcripts available by mail.

University of South Florida, Registrar's Office, SVC 1034, 4202 E Fowler Ave, Tampa, FL 33620-6100, 813-974-2000 (Fax: 813-974-5271) www.usf.edu/. 8AM-5PM. Enrollment: 36000. Records go back to 1956. Alumni records maintained here; call 813-974-9127. Degrees granted: Associate; Bachelors; Masters; Doctorate. Special programs- Marine Science: Medical. Attendance and degree information available by phone, fax, mail. Transcripts available by fax, mail.

University of Tampa, Registrar, 401 W Kennedy Blvd, Tampa, FL 33606-1490, 813-253-6251 (Fax: 813-258-7238). 8:30AM-5PM. Enrollment: 2800. Records go back to 1933. Alumni records are maintained here. Degrees granted: Associate; Bachelors; Masters. Attendance and degree information available by phone, fax, mail. Transcripts available by mail.

University of West Florida, Registrar, 11000 University Pkwy, Pensacola, FL 32514-5750, 850-474-2244, 850-474-2117 (Fax: 850-474-3360) www.uwf.edu. 8AM-5PM. Enrollment: 8000. Records go back to 1967. Alumni records maintained here; call 850-474-2758. Degrees granted: Associate; Bachelors; Masters; Doctorate; Specialist. Special programs- Marine Biology: Accounting: Education. Attendance and degree information available by phone, fax, mail. Transcripts available by fax, mail.

Valencia Community College (West), Registrar, PO Box 3028, 1800 S Kirkman Rd, Orlando, FL 32811, 407-299-5000 X1506 www.gate.net/~valencia. (Fax: 407-299-1832) 7:30AM-9PM M-Th, 7:30AM-5PM F. Enrollment: 14301. Records go back to 1971. Alumni Records: Alumni Assoc., 190 N Orange Ave, Orlando, FL 32801. Degrees granted: Associate. Attendance, degree and transcript information available by mail.

Ward Stone College
(See National School of Technology)

Warner Southern College, Registrar, 5301 US Hwy 27 S, Lake Wales, FL 33853-8725, 941-638-7204, 941-638-1426 (Fax: 941-638-1472) www.warner.edu. Enrollment: 616. Records go back to 1969. Alumni records are maintained here. Degrees granted: Associate; Bachelors. Attendance and degree information available by phone, fax, mail. Transcripts available by fax, mail.

Webber College, Registrar, PO Box 96, Babson Park, FL 33827, 941-638-2929, 941-638-1431 www.webber.edu. (Fax: 941-638-2919; 941-638-1317 (Registrar)) 8AM-5PM. Enrollment: 460. Records go back to 1927. Alumni records maintained here; call 941-638-2941. Degrees granted: Bachelors; Masters. Attendance and degree information available by phone, fax, mail. Transcripts available by fax, mail.

Webster College (Branch Campus), Registrar, 2127 Grand Blvd, Holiday, FL 34690, 813-942-0069 (Fax: 813-938-5709) 8AM-10PM. Enrollment: 168. Records go back to 1984. Degrees granted: Associate. Attendance and degree information available by phone, mail. Transcripts available by mail.

Webster College (Branch Campus), Registrar, 1530 SW Third Ave, Ocala, FL 34474, 352-629-1941 (Fax: 352-629-0926). 8AM-9:30PM. Enrollment: 210. Records go back to 1984. Degrees granted: Associate. Attendance and degree information available by phone, fax, mail. Transcripts available by fax, mail.

Georgia

Abraham Baldwin Agricultural College, Registrar's Office, ABAC 3, 2802 Moore Hwy, Tifton, GA 31794-2601, 912-386-3236 www.abac.peachnet.edu. (Fax: 912-386-3913) 8AM-5PM. Enrollment: 2300. Records go back to 1930's. Alumni records maintained here; call 912-386-3265. Degrees granted: Associate. Attendance, degree and transcript information available by fax, mail.

Agnes Scott College, Registrar, 141 E College Ave, Decatur, GA 30030, 404-638-6137, 404-638-6306 (Fax: 404-638-5255) 8:30AM-4:30PM. www.scottlan.edu. Enrollment: 750. Records go back to 1889. Alumni records maintained here; call 404-638-6323. Degrees granted: Bachelors; Masters. Attendance and degree information available by phone, fax, mail. Transcripts available by fax, mail.

Albany Junior College
(See Darton College)

Albany State University, Registrar, 504 College Dr, Albany, GA 31705-2794, 912-430-4638, 912-430-4639 (Fax: 912-430-2953) www.lsnet.peachnet.edu OR www.asurams.edu. 8AM-5PM. Enrollment: 3200. Records go back to 1903. Alumni records maintained here; call 912-430-4658. Degrees granted: Bachelors; Masters; 6 year Education Major Degree. Attendance and degree information available by phone, fax, mail. Transcripts available by fax, mail.

American College, Registrar, 3330 Peachtree Rd NE, Atlanta, GA 30326, 404-812-4113 (Fax: 404-812-4479). 8AM-4:30PM. Enrollment: 2000. Records go back to 1971. Alumni records are maintained here. Degrees granted: Associate; Bachelors. Attendance and degree information available by phone, fax, mail. Transcripts available by fax, mail.

American Schools of Professional Psychology (Georgia School of Professional Psychology), Registrar, 990 Hammond Dr NE, 11th Flr, Bldg One, Atlanta, GA 30328, 770-671-1200 (Fax: 770-671-0476). 8:30AM-5:30PM. Enrollment: 450. Records go back to 1990. Degrees granted: Masters; Doctorate. Special programs- Clinical Psychology. Attendance and degree information available by phone, fax, mail. Transcripts available by fax, mail.

Andrew College, Registrar, 413 College St, Cuthbert, GA 31740-1395, 912-732-2171 www.andrewco.sowega.net. (Fax: 912-732-2176) 8:30AM-Noon, 1-4:30PM. Enrollment: 350. Records go back to 1883. Alumni records are maintained here. Degrees granted: Associate. Attendance and degree information available by phone, fax, mail. Transcripts available by fax, mail.

Armstrong Atlantic State University, Registrar, 11935 Abercorn Ext, Savannah, GA 31419-1997, 912-927-5278, 912-927-5275 (Fax: 912-921-5462). 8:15AM-7PM M-Th; 8:15AM-5PM. Enrollment: 5700. Records go back to 1935. Alumni records maintained here; call 912-927-5263. Degrees granted: Associate; Bachelors; Masters. Attendance information available by phone, fax, mail. Degree information available by phone, mail. Transcripts available by mail.

Art Institute of Atlanta, Registrar, 3376 Peachtree Rd NE, Atlanta, GA 30326, 404-266-1341 X369, 800-275-4242 (Fax: 404-266-1383) www.aii.edu. 7:30AM - 7PM. Enrollment: 1420. Records go back to 1975. Art Institute records available since 1975; formerly **Massey Junior College** 1949-1975. Alumni records maintained here; call 404-266-1341 X314. Degrees granted: Associate; Bachelors. Attendance and degree information available by phone, fax, mail. Transcripts available by mail.

Athens Area Technical Institute, Registrar, 800 Hwy 29 N, Athens, GA 30601-1500, 706-355-5012, 706-355-5000 (Fax: 706-369-5753) admin1.athens.tec.ga.us/home.html. 8AM-5PM M-Th, 8AM-4PM F. Enrollment: 7000. Records go back to 1967. Alumni records are maintained here. Degrees granted: Associate. Certification: Applied Technology. Attendance and degree information available by phone, fax, mail. Transcripts available by fax, mail.

Atlanta Christian College, Registrar, 2605 Ben Hill Rd, East Point, GA 30344, 404-761-8861, 404-669-2095 (Fax: 404-669-2024). 8:30AM - 4:30PM. Enrollment: 325. Records go back to 1937. Alumni records maintained here; call 404-669-2091. Degrees granted: Associate; Bachelors. Attendance and degree information available by phone, fax, mail. Transcripts available by fax, mail.

Atlanta College of Art, Registrar, 1280 Peachtree St NE, Atlanta, GA 30309, 404-733-5001 (Fax: 404-733-5201). 8AM-5PM M-Th, 8:45AM-3:30PM F. Enrollment: 420. Records go back to 1950. Alumni records maintained here; call 404-733-5001. Degrees granted: Bachelors. Attendance and degree information available by phone, mail. Transcripts available by mail.

Atlanta Junior College
(See Atlanta Metropolitan College)

Atlanta Metropolitan College, Registrar, 1630 Metropolitan Pkwy SW, Atlanta, GA 30310, 404-756-4001 (Fax: 404-756-5686). 8:30AM-5PM. Enrollment: 2000. Records go back to 1974. Degrees granted: Associate. Attendance and degree information available by phone, fax, mail. Transcripts available by fax, mail.

Atlanta University
(See Clark Atlanta University)

Augusta State University, Registrar, 2500 Walton Way, Augusta, GA 30904-2200, 706-737-1408 (Fax: 706-737-1777) www.aug.edu. Enrollment: 5700. Records go back to 1957. Formerly **Augusta College**. Alumni records maintained here; call 706-737-1759. Degrees granted: Associate; Bachelors; Masters; Education Specialist. Attendance and degree information available by phone, fax, mail. Transcripts available by fax, mail.

Augusta Technical Institute, Registrar, 3116 Deans Bridge Rd, Augusta, GA 30906, 706-771-4035, 706-771-4037 (Fax: 706-771-4034) http://augusta.tec.ga.us. 8AM - 4:30PM. Enrollment: 2325. Records go back to 1961. Alumni records are maintained here. Degrees granted: Associate. Attendance and degree information available by phone, fax, mail. Transcripts available by fax, mail. Student signature required on all fax requests. Written requests only accepted for records older than 1985.

Bainbridge College, Registrar, Hwy 84 E, Bainbridge, GA 31717, 912-248-2504 (Fax: 912-248-2525) www.bbc.peachnet.edu. 8AM-6PM M,T; 8AM-5PM W,Th,F. Enrollment: 1180. Records go back to 1973. Alumni records maintained here; call 912-248-2506. Degrees granted: Associate. Certification: Technical Studies. Attendance, degree and transcript information available by fax, mail.

Bainbridge Junior College
(See Bainbridge College)

Bauder College, Registrar, Phipps Plaza, 3500 Peachtree Rd NE, Atlanta, GA 30326-9975, 404-237-7573 (Fax: 404-237-1642) 8AM-4PM. www.bauder.edu. Enrollment: 410. Records go back to 1970. Degrees granted: Associate. Attendance and degree information available by phone, fax, mail. Transcripts available by fax, mail.

Berry College, Registrar, Box 49400, Mt Berry, GA 30149-0400, 706-236-2282 (Fax: 706-290-2179) www.berry.edu. 8AM-5PM. Enrollment: 1756. Records go back to 1902. Alumni records maintained here; call 706-236-2256. Degrees granted: Bachelors; Masters; Ed.S. Attendance and degree information available by phone, fax, mail. Transcripts available by fax, mail.

Brenau University, Registrar, One Centennial Cir, Gainesville, GA 30501, 770-534-6203, 770-534-6204 (Fax: 770-538-4790) www.brenau.edu. 8:30AM-5PM. Enrollment: 2400. Records go back to 1800's. Alumni records maintained here; call 770-534-6164. Degrees granted: Bachelors; Masters; Education Specialist. Attendance and degree information available by phone, fax, mail. Transcripts available by fax, mail.

Brewton Parker College, Registrar, Hwy 280, Mount Vernon, GA 30445, 912-583-2241 (Fax: 912-583-4498) www.bpc.edu. 8AM-5PM. Enrollment: 1660. Records go back to 1904. Alumni records are maintained here. Degrees granted: Associate; Bachelors. Attendance and degree information available by phone, fax, mail. Transcripts available by fax, mail.

Chattahochee Technical Institute, Registrar, 980 S Cobb Dr, Marietta, GA 30060, 770-528-4545 (Fax: 770-528-4578) www.chat-tec.com. 8AM-7:30PM M-Th; 8AM-4PM F. Enrollment: 2500. Records go back to 1966. Degrees granted: Associate. Attendance and degree information available by phone, fax, mail. Transcripts available by written request only.

Clark Atlanta University, Registrar, James P Brawley Dr at Fair St SW, Atlanta, GA 30314, 404-880-8759 (Fax: 404-880-6083) 9AM-5PM. galaxy.cau.edu/cau/ctsps.html. Enrollment: 5300. Records go back to 1988. Alumni records maintained here; call 404-880-8022. Degrees granted: Bachelors; Masters; Doctorate; Specialist. Attendance and degree information available by phone, fax, mail. Transcripts available by fax, mail.

Clayton College & State University, Registrar, PO Box 285, Morrow, GA 30260, 770-960-5110, 770-961-3504 (Fax: 770-961-3752) www.clayton.edu. 8AM-6PM M-Th; 9AM-5PM F; 8AM-Noon Sat. Enrollment: 5000. Records go back to 1969. Alumni records maintained here; call 770-961-3580. Degrees granted: Associate; Bachelors Attendance, degree and transcript information available by fax, mail.

Clayton Junior College
(See Clayton State College)

Coastal Georgia Community College, Registrar, 3700 Altama Ave, Brunswick, GA 31520-3644, www.131.144.99.196/college. 912-264-7235, 912-262-3075 (Fax: 912-262-3072) 8AM - 5PM. Enrollment: 1920. Records go back to 1969. Formerly **Brunswick College**. Alumni records maintained here; call 912-262-3303. Degrees granted: Associate. Attendance and degree information available by phone, fax, mail. Transcripts available by fax, mail.

Columbia Theological Seminary, Registrar, PO Box 520, 701 Columbia Dr, Decatur, GA 30031, 404-378-8821 (Fax: 404-377-9696) www.ctsnet.edu. 8:30AM-4:30PM. Enrollment: 650. Records go back to 1930. Alumni records are maintained here. Degrees granted: Masters; Doctorate; M.Div, TH.M, MATS, D.Min, TH.D. Special programs- Lay Institute, 404-378-8821: Continuing Education Program, 404-378-8821: Spirituality program, 404-378-8821 X404. Attendance and transcript information available by fax, mail. Degree information available by phone, fax, mail.

Columbus State University, Registrar, 4225 University Ave, Columbus, GA 31907-5645, 706-568-2237, 706-568-2238 (Fax: 706-568-2462) www.colstate.edu. 8AM - 6PM M-Th; 8AM - 5PM F. Enrollment: 5500. Records go back to 1957. Formerly **Columbus College**. Alumni records maintained here; call 706-568-2280. Degrees granted: Associate; Bachelors; Masters. Certification: Comp Sci, Criminal Justice. E.D.S. Special programs- COMPASS, 706-568-2410. Attendance and degree information available by phone, fax, mail. Transcripts available by fax, mail.

Columbus Technical Institute
(See Columbus State Community College)

Covenant College, Registrar, 14049 Scenic Hwy, Lookout Mountain, GA 30750, 706-820-1560 X1134 (Fax: 706-820-2820) 8AM-4:30PM. www.covenant.edu. Enrollment: 850. Records go back to 1955. Alumni records maintained here; call 706-820-1560. Degrees granted: Associate; Bachelors; Masters. Attendance and degree information available by phone, fax, mail. Transcripts available by mail.

Dalton College, Registrar's Office, 213 N College Dr, Dalton, GA 30720, 706-272-4436 www.dalton.peachnet.edu (Fax: 706-272-2530) 8AM-5PM. Enrollment: 3200. Records go back to 1967. Alumni records are maintained here. Degrees granted: Associate. Attendance and degree information available by phone, fax, mail. Transcripts available by fax, mail.

Darton College, Registrar, 2400 Gillionville Rd, Albany, GA 31707-3098, 912-430-6740 (Fax: 912-430 -2926) 8AM-6PM. Enrollment: 2650. www.cavalier.dartnet.peachnet.edu. Records go back to 1966. Alumni records maintained here; call 912-430-6000. Degrees granted: Associate. Attendance and degree information available by fax, mail. Transcripts available by mail.

DeKalb College, District Admissions & Records, 555 N Indian Creek Dr, Clarkston, GA 30021, 404-299-4564 (Fax: 404-298-3830) www.dc.peachnet.edu. 8AM-5PM M-Th; 8AM-4:30PM F. Enrollment: 16000. Records go back to 1964. Degrees granted: Associate. Attendance and degree information available by phone, fax, mail. Transcripts available by mail.

DeKalb Community College
(See DeKalb College)

DeKalb Technical Institute, Registrar, 495 N Indian Creek Dr, Clarkston, GA 30021, 404-297-9522 X3 (Fax: 404-294-4234) 8AM-8PM. www.dekalb.tec.ga.us. Enrollment: 1910. Records go back 32 years. Degrees granted: Associate. Attendance and degree information available by phone, fax, mail. Transcripts available by mail.

DeVry Institute of Technology, Atlanta, Registrar, 250 N Arcadia Ave, Decatur, GA 30030, 404-292-7900 (Fax: 404-292-8117 & 404-298-1880) www.devry.edu/atl.htm. 8:30PM 5PM M,W,F; 8:30PM-6PM T,Th. Enrollment: 3000. Records go back to 1971. Transcripts available for all years; other information for last five years only. Alumni Records: Alumni Assoc., DeVry National Offices, One Tower Lane, Oakbrook Terrace, IL 60181-4624. Degrees granted: Associate; Bachelors. Attendance and degree information available by phone, fax, mail. Transcripts available by fax, mail.

East Georgia College, Registrar, 131 College Circle, Swainsboro, GA 30401, 912-237-7831 (Fax: 912-237-5161) 8AM-5PM. www.ega.peachnet.edu. Enrollment: 950. Records go back to 1973. Alumni records are maintained here. Degrees granted: Associate. Attendance and degree information available by phone, fax, mail. Transcripts available by mail.

Emanuel County Junior College
(See East Gerogia College)

Emmanuel College, Registrar, 181 Spring St, PO Box 129, Franklin Springs, GA 30639, 706-245-7226, 706-245-3136 (Fax: 706-245-4424) www.emmanuel-college.edu. 8-11:30AM, 12:30-4PM. Enrollment: 600. Records go back to 1919. Alumni records are maintained here. Degrees granted: Associate; Bachelors. Attendance and degree information available by phone, fax, mail. Transcripts available by fax, mail.

Emory University, Registrar, 100 Boisfeuillet Jones Center, Atlanta, GA 30322-1970, www.cc.emory.edu/REGISTRAR/. 404-727-6042 8AM - 4:30PM. Enrollment: 11109. Records go back to 1836. Alumni records maintained here; call 404-727-6400. Degrees granted: Associate; Bachelors; Masters; Doctorate. Attendance and degree information available by phone, mail. Transcripts available by mail.

Floyd College, Registrar, PO Box 1864, Rome, GA 30162-1864, 706-802-5000, 800-332-2406 (Fax: 706-295-6341) 8:30AM-5PM. www.fc.peachnet.edu. Enrollment: 3000. Records go back to 1970. Alumni records are maintained here. Degrees granted: Associate. Attendance and degree information available by phone, fax, mail. Transcripts available by fax, mail.

Fort Valley State University, Registrar, 1005 State College Dr, Fort Valley, GA 31030-3298, 912-825-6282, 912-825-6307 (Fax: 912-825-6155). 8AM - 5PM. Enrollment: 3100. Records go back to 1895. Alumni records maintained here; call 912-825-6315. Degrees granted: Associate; Bachelors; Masters; Ed.S. Attendance and degree information available by phone, fax, mail. Transcripts available by mail.

Gainesville College, Registrar, PO Box 1358, Gainesville, GA 30503-1358, 770-718-3641, 770-718-3644 (Fax: 770-718-3643) 8AM-5PM. www.gc.peachnet.edu. Enrollment: 2900. Records go back to 1964. Alumni records maintained here; call 770-718-3648. Degrees granted: Associate. Attendance and degree information available by phone, fax, mail. Transcripts available by fax, mail.

Georgia College, Registrar, CPO Box 23, Milledgeville, GA 31061, 912-454-2772, 912-453-6293 (Fax: 912-445-1914) 8AM - 6PM M-Th, 8AM - 5PM F. www.gcsu.peachnet.edu. Enrollment: 5710. Records go back to 1889. Alumni Records: CPO 98, Milledgeville, GA 31061. Degrees granted: Bachelors; Masters. Attendance and degree information available by phone, fax, mail. Transcripts available by fax, mail.

Georgia Institute of Technology, Registrar, 225 North Ave NW, Atlanta, GA 30332-0315, 404-894-4151, 404-894-4150 (Fax: 404-894-0167) www.gatech.edu. 8AM-4:30PM. Enrollment: 14000. Records go back to 1888. Alumni records maintained here; call 404-894-2391. Degrees granted: Bachelors; Masters; Doctorate. Attendance and degree information available by phone, fax, mail. Transcripts available by fax, mail.

Georgia Military College, Registrar, 201 E Greene St, Milledgeville, GA 31061, 912-445-2684 (Fax: 912-445-2688) 8AM-5PM. www.gmc.cc.ga.us. Enrollment: 650. Records go back to 1940. Alumni records maintained here; call 912-454-2695. Degrees granted: Associate. Special programs- Pre-Nursing Degree: Criminal Justice: Behavioral Science: Business Admin: Education. Attendance and degree information available by phone, fax, mail. Transcripts available by fax, mail.

Georgia Southern University, Registrar, PO Box 8092, Statesboro, GA 30460-8092, 912-681-0070, 912-681-5421 (Fax: 912-681-0081) www.gasou.edu. 8AM-5PM. Enrollment: 14000. Records go back to 1924. Alumni records maintained here; call 912-681-5691. Degrees granted: Bachelors; Masters; Doctorate; Education Specialist. Attendance and degree information available by phone, fax, mail. Transcripts available by fax, mail.

Georgia Southwestern State University, Registrar, 800 Wheatley St, Americus, GA 31709-4693, 912-928-1331 (Fax: 912-931-2021) www.gswrs6kl.gsw.peachnet.edu. 8AM-5PM. Enrollment: 2500. Records go back to 1926. Alumni records maintained here; call 912-928-1373. Degrees granted: Associate; Bachelors; Masters. Attendance and degree information available by phone, fax, mail. Transcripts available by fax, mail.

Georgia State University, Office of the Registrar, Student Services, PO Box 4017, Atlanta, GA 30302-4017, 404-651-2383, 404-651-3208 (Fax: 404-651-1419) www.gsu.edu. 9AM-8PM M; 8:30AM-5:15PM T-Th; 9AM-5:15PM F. Enrollment: 19200. Records go back to 1920. Alumni Records: GSU Alumni Office, University Plaza, Atlanta, GA 30303. Degrees granted: Bachelors; Masters; Doctorate. Attendance and degree information available by phone, fax, mail. Transcripts available by fax, mail.

Gordon College, Registrar, 419 College Dr, Barnesville, GA 30204, 770-358-5022, 770-358-5025 / 800-282-6504 (Fax: 770-358-3031) www.gdn.peachnet.edu. 8AM-8PM M; 8AM-5PM T-F. Enrollment: 2200. Records go back to 1955. Degrees granted: Associate. Certification: Associate of Applied Science Cooperative Degree Program. Attendance and degree information available by phone, fax, mail. Transcripts available by fax, mail.

Gupton — Jones College of Funeral Service, Registrar, 5141 Snapfinger Woods Dr, Decatur, GA 30035-4022, 770-593-2257 (Fax: 770-593-1891) 7:30AM-4PM. Enrollment: 350. Records go back to 1970. Alumni records are maintained here. Degrees granted: Associate. Attendance and degree information available by phone, mail. Transcripts available by mail.

Gwinnett Technical Institute, Registrar, 1250 Atkinson Rd, PO Box 1505, Lawrenceville, GA 30246-1505, 770-962-7580 X121 (Fax: 770-962-7985) www.gwinnett-tec.org. 8AM-6:30PM M-Th; 8AM-5PM F. Enrollment: 3448. Records go back to 1986. Alumni records maintained here; call 770-962-7580 X205. Degrees

granted: Associate. Attendance and degree information available by phone, fax, mail. Transcripts available by fax, mail. Only student may request transcript copy.

Herzing College of Business & Technology, Registrar, 3355 Lenox Rd Ste 100, Atlanta, GA 30326, 404-816-4533 (Fax: 404-816-5576) www.herzing-atlanta.edu. 8AM-6PM M-Th;8AM-3PM F. Enrollment: 300. Records go back to 1980. Degrees granted: Associate; Bachelors. Special programs- Before 1979: Atlanta Art Institute, 404-266-2662. Attendance and degree information available by phone, fax, mail. Transcripts available by fax, mail.

Institute of Paper Science and Technology, Registrar, 500 10th St NW, Atlanta, GA 30318, 404-894-7764, 404-894-7870 (switchboard) (Fax: 404-894-4778) www.ipst.edu. 8AM-5PM. Enrollment: 80. Records go back to 1929. Alumni records maintained here; call 404-894-7764. Degrees granted: Masters; PhD. Attendance and degree information available by phone, fax, mail. Transcripts available by fax, mail.

Interdenominational Theological Center, Registrar, 700 Martin Luther King JR Dr, Atlanta, GA 30314, 404-527-7708, 404-527-7707 (Fax: 706-614-6375). 9AM-5PM. Enrollment: 400. Records go back to 1958. Alumni records maintained here; call 404-527-7784. Degrees granted: Masters; Doctorate. Attendance and degree information available by phone, fax, mail. Transcripts available by fax, mail.

Kennesaw State University, Registrar, 1000 Chastain Rd, Kennesaw, GA 30144, 770-423-6200 (Fax: 770-423-6541) 8AM-7PM M-Th; 8AM-5PM F. www.kennesaw.edu. Enrollment: 13000. Records go back to 1964. Alumni records maintained here; call 770-423-6333. Degrees granted: Associate; Bachelors; Masters. Special programs- Continuing Education, 770-423-6765. Attendance and degree information available by phone, fax, mail. Transcripts available by fax, mail.

LaGrange College, Registrar, 601 Broad St, Lagrange, GA 30240-2999, 706-812-7237, 706-812-7238 (Fax: 706-884-7358) 8:15AM-5PM. www.lgc.peachnet.edu. Enrollment: 1000. Records go back to 1896. Alumni records maintained here; call 706-812-7244. Degrees granted: Associate; Bachelors; Masters. Attendance and degree information available by phone, fax, mail. Transcripts available by fax, mail.

Life Chiropractic College
(See Life College)

Life University, Registrar, 1269 Barclay Cir, Marietta, GA 30060, 770-426-2780 (Fax: 770-429-1512) www.life.edu. 8AM-5PM. Enrollment: 4000. Records go back to 1977. Alumni records maintained here; call 770-426-2925. Degrees granted: Bachelors; Masters; Doctorate. Attendance, degree and transcript information available by mail.

Macon State College, Registrar, 100 College Station Dr, Macon, GA 31206-5144, 912-471-2855, 912-471-2033 (Fax: 912-471-5343) www.mc.peachnet.edu. 8AM-6PM M-Th; 8AM-4:30PM F. Enrollment: 3600. Records go back to 1968. Alumni records maintained here; call 912-471-2710. Degrees granted: Associate; Bachelors. Special programs- Dental Hygiene, 912-471-2735: Health Information Technology, 921-471-2844: Nursing, 912-471-2761: Respiratory Therapy, 912-471-5386: Health Information Management, 912-471-2844: Health Services

Administration, 912-471-2882: Information Technology, 912-471-2808. Attendance and degree information available by phone, fax, mail. Transcripts available by fax, mail.

Medical College of Georgia, Registrar, 1120 15th St, Augusta, GA 30912, 706-721-2201 (Fax: 706-721-0186) www.mcg.edu. 8AM-5PM. Enrollment: 2500. Records go back to 1828. Alumni records are maintained here. Degrees granted: Associate; Bachelors; Masters; Doctorate. Attendance and degree information available by phone, fax, mail. Transcripts available by fax, mail.

Mercer University, Registrar, 1400 Coleman Ave, Macon, GA 31207, 912-752-2680 (Fax: 912-752-2455) www.mercer.edu. 8:30AM-5PM. Enrollment: 6800. Records go back to 1833. Alumni records maintained here; call 912-752-2715. Degrees granted: Bachelors; Masters. Special programs- Law, 912-752-2621: Medicine, 912-752-2524. Attendance and degree information available by phone, fax, mail. Transcripts available by fax, mail. Transcript request form available on web site.

Mercer University Southern School of Pharmacy, Registrar, 3001 Mercer University Dr, Atlanta, GA 30341, 770-986-3134 (Fax: 770-986-3135) www.mercer.edu. 8:30AM-5PM M-Th; 8:30AM-4:30PM F. Enrollment: 520. Records go back to 1930. Alumni Records: University Advancement, Koger Ctr, Oxford Bldg Ste 217, Atlanta, GA 30341. Degrees granted: Bachelors; Masters; Doctorate. Special programs- Pharmacy Administration, 770-986-3254: Pharmacy Practice, 770-986-3209: Pharmacy Sciences, 770-986-3237. Attendance and degree information available by phone, fax, mail. Transcripts available by mail.

Middle Georgia College, Registrar, 1100 Second St SE, Cochran, GA 31014, 912-934-3036 www.warrior.mgc.peachnet.edu. (Fax: 912-934-3049) 8AM-5PM. Enrollment: 2000. Records go back to 1884. Alumni records maintained here; call 912-934-3301. Degrees granted: Associate. Attendance and degree information available by phone, fax, mail. Transcripts available by fax, mail.

Morehouse College, Registrar, 830 Westview Dr SW, Atlanta, GA 30314, 404-215-2641 (Fax: 404-215-2600) www.morehouse.edu. 9AM-5PM. Enrollment: 2900. Records go back to 1870. Alumni records maintained here; call 404-215-2707. Degrees granted: Bachelors. Special programs- School of Medicine, 404-752-1652. Attendance and degree information available by phone, fax, mail. Transcripts available by fax, mail.

Morehouse School of Medicine, Office of Admissions, 720 Westview Dr SW, Atlanta, GA 30310-1495, 404-752-1652 (Fax: 404-752-1512) www.msm.edu. 9AM - 5PM. Enrollment: 157. Records go back to 1978. Alumni records maintained here; call 404-752-1733. Degrees granted: Doctorate. Attendance and degree information available by phone, fax, mail.

Morris Brown College, Registrar, 643 Martin Luther King, Jr. Dr NW, Atlanta, GA 30314, 404-220-0145 (Fax: 404-818-9801) 9AM-5PM. Enrollment: 2000. Records go back to 1885. Alumni records maintained here; call 404-220-0124. Degrees granted: Bachelors. Attendance and degree information available by phone, fax, mail. Transcripts available by mail.

North Georgia College & State University, Registrar, College Ave, Dahlonega, GA 30597, 706-864-1760 www.ngc.peachnet.edu. 8AM-5PM. Enrollment: 3200. Records go back to 1873. Alumni records are maintained here also. Call 706-864-1649. Degrees granted: Associate; Bachelors; Masters. Attendance and degree information available by phone, fax, mail. Transcripts available by fax, mail.

Oglethorpe University, Registrar, 4484 Peachtree Rd NE, Atlanta, GA 30319-2797, 404-364-8315, 404-364-8316 www.oglethorpe.edu. (Fax: 404-364-8500) 8:30AM - 5PM. Enrollment: 1300. Records go back to 1916. Alumni records maintained here; call 404-364-8326. Degrees granted: Bachelors; Masters. Certification: Teacher Certificate. Attendance and degree information available by phone, fax, mail. Transcripts available by mail.

Paine College, Registrar, 1235 15th St, Augusta, GA 30901-3182, 706-821-8311 (Fax: 706-774-1676). 9AM-5PM. Enrollment: 857. Records go back to 1920. Alumni records maintained here; call 706-821-8247. Degrees granted: Bachelors. Attendance and degree information available by phone, fax, mail. Transcripts available by fax, mail.

Piedmont College, Registrar, PO Box 10, Demorest, GA 30535, 706-778-3000, 706-776-0112 (Fax: 706-776-2811) 8AM-5PM. www.gateway.piedmont.edu. Enrollment: 1100. Records go back to 1897. Alumni records are maintained here. Degrees granted: Bachelors; Masters. Attendance and degree information available by phone, fax, mail. Transcripts available by fax, mail.

Reinhardt College, Registrar, 7300 Reinhardt College Parkway, Waleska, GA 30183, 770-720-5534 (Fax: 770-720-5602). 8:30AM-5PM. Enrollment: 1000. Records go back to 1960's. Alumni records maintained here; call 770-720-5545. Degrees granted: Associate; Bachelors. Attendance and degree information available by phone, fax, mail. Transcripts available by mail.

Savannah College of Art and Design, Registrar, 15 Drayton St, PO Box 3146, Savannah, GA 31402-3146, 912-238-2400; 912-644-6103 (Records Spec.), 912-644-6107/8 (Admiss. Specialist) (Fax: 912-644-6200) www.scad.edu. 8:30AM-5:30PM. Enrollment: 2800. Records go back to 1979. Alumni records maintained here; call 912-238-2400. Degrees granted: Bachelors; M.F.A., MA. Attendance, degree and transcript information available by fax, mail.

Savannah State University, Registrar, PO Box 20479, Savannah, GA 31404, 912-356-2212 (Registrar), 912-356-2181 (switchboard) (Fax: 912-356-2296). 8AM-7PM M-Th; 8AM-5PM F. Enrollment: 2725. Records go back to 1931. Alumni records maintained here; call 912-356-2427. Degrees granted: Bachelors; Masters. Special programs-Marine Biology. Attendance and degree information available by phone, fax, mail. Transcripts available by mail.

Savannah Technical Institute, Registrar, 5717 White Bluff Rd, Savannah, GA 31405-5594, www.dtae.tec.ga.us/teched/schools/savannah.html. 912-351-6362 (Fax: 912-352-4362) 8AM-5PM M-Th, 8AM-4PM F. Enrollment: 1350. Records go back to 1960. Alumni records maintained here; call 912-351-4450. Degrees granted: Associate. Attendance and degree information available by phone, fax, mail. Transcripts available by fax, mail.

Shorter College, Registrar, 315 Shorter Ave, Rome, GA 30165-4298, 706-291-2121, 706-233-7206 (Fax: 706-236-1515) www.shorter.edu. 8AM-5PM. Enrollment: 1390. Records go back to 1911. Alumni records maintained here; call 706-233-7242. Degrees granted: Bachelors; Masters. Special programs- School of Prof. Programs, Marietta, GA, 706-989-5671: Davis Center for Ministry Ed, Rome, GA, 706-233-7293. Attendance and degree information available by phone, fax, mail. Transcripts available by fax, mail.

South College, Registrar's Office, 709 Mall Blvd, Savannah, GA 31406, 912-691-6000 (switchboard), 912-691-6021 (Registrar) (Fax: 912-691-6082) www.southcollege.edu. 8:30AM-5PM. Enrollment: 600. Records go back to 1977. Alumni records are maintained here. Degrees granted: Associate; BBA. Attendance and degree information available by phone, fax, mail. Transcripts available by fax, mail.

South Georgia College, Registrar, 100 W College Park Dr, Douglas, GA 31533-5098, 912-383-4200 (Fax: 912-383-4392) 8AM-5PM. www.sgc.peachnet.edu. Enrollment: 1100. Records go back to 1906. Alumni records are maintained here. Degrees granted: Associate. Attendance and degree information available by phone, fax, mail. Transcripts available by fax, mail.

Southern Polytechnic State University, Registrar, 1100 S Marietta Pkwy, Marietta, GA 30060-2896, 770-528-7267 (Fax: 770-528-7292) www.sct.edu. 9AM-7PM M-Th; 9AM-4PM F. Enrollment: 4000. Records go back to 1948. Formerly **Southern College of Technology**. Alumni records are maintained here. Degrees granted: Associate; Bachelors; Masters. Special programs- Technical & Professional Communications: Architecture, 770-528-5483. Attendance, degree and transcript information available by fax, mail.

Spelman College, Registrar, 350 Spelman Lane SW, Atlanta, GA 30314-4399, 404-223-2127, 404-681-3643 (Fax: 404-223-1449) http://spelman.auc.edu. 9AM-5PM. Enrollment: 1900. Records go back to 1881. Alumni records maintained here; call 404-223-1427. Degrees granted: Bachelors. Attendance and degree information available by phone, fax, mail. Transcripts available by mail.

State University of West Georgia, Registrar, Carrollton, GA 30118-0001, 770-836-6438, 770-836-4521 (Fax: 770-836-4692) www.westga.edu. 8AM - 5PM. Enrollment: 8560. Records go back to 1933. Alumni records maintained here; call 770-836-6582. Degrees granted: Associate; Bachelors; Masters; Ed S. Attendance and degree information available by phone, fax, mail. Transcripts available by mail.

Thomas College, Student Services, 1501 Millpond Rd, Thomasville, GA 31792, 912-226-1621 (Fax: 912-226-1653). 8AM-5PM. Enrollment: 706. Records go back to 1950. Alumni records are maintained here. Degrees granted: Associate; Bachelors. Attendance and degree information available by phone, fax, mail. Transcripts available by fax, mail.

Thomas Technical Institute, 15689 US Highway 19N, Thomasville, GA 31792, 912-225-4096 (Fax: 912-225-4330) www.thomas-tech.com. 8AM-5PM. Enrollment: 1085. Records go back to 1948. Alumni records are maintained here. Degrees granted: Associate. Special programs- Technical. Attendance and degree information available by phone, fax, mail. Transcripts available by fax, mail.

Toccoa Falls College, Registrar's Office, PO Box 800896, Toccoa Falls, GA 30598, 706-886-6831 X5396 (Fax: 706-886-6412) 8:30AM-5PM. www.toccoafalls.edu. Enrollment: 1000. Records go back to 1912. Alumni Records: PO Box 800809, Toccoa Falls, GA 30598 (Fax: 706-886-0262). Degrees granted: Associate; Bachelors; Masters. Attendance and degree information available by phone, fax, mail. Transcripts available by fax, mail.

Truett-McConnell College, Registrar, 100 Alumni Dr, Cleveland, GA 30528, 706-865-2134 (Fax: 706-865-5135). 8AM - 4:30PM Enrollment: 2100. Records go back to 1947. Alumni records are maintained here. Degrees granted: Associate. Attendance and degree information available by phone, fax, mail. Transcripts available by mail.

University of Georgia, Registrar's Office, 105 Academic Bldg, Athens, GA 30602-6113, 706-542-4040 (Fax: 706-542-6578) www.uga.edu. 8AM-5PM. Enrollment: 29500. Records go back to 1785. Limited records available back to 1785. Alumni records are maintained here. Degrees granted: Associate; Bachelors; Masters; Doctorate; Specialist. Attendance and degree information available by phone, fax, mail. Transcripts available by fax, mail.

University of West Georgia, Registrar, 1600 Maple St, Carollton, GA 30118-0001, 770-836-6500 (Fax: 770-836-4659) www.westga.edu. Enrollment: 7947. Records go back to 1963. Degrees granted: Associate; Bachelors. Attendance and degree information available by phone, fax, mail. Transcripts available by mail.

Valdosta State University, Registrar, 1500 N Patterson St, Valdosta, GA 31698, 912-333-5727, 912-333-5729 (Fax: 912-333-5475) 8AM-5:30PM M-Th, 8AM-3PM F. www.valdosta.peachnet.edu Enrollment: 9600. Records go back to 1919. Alumni records maintained here; call 912-333-5797. Degrees granted: Associate; Bachelors; Masters; Doctorate. Attendance and degree information available by phone, fax, mail. Transcripts available by fax, mail.

Walker Technical Institute, Registrar, 265 Bicentennial Trail, Rock Springs, GA 30739, 706-764-3570 (Fax: 706-764-3707) 8AM-5PM. www.walker.tec.ga.us. Enrollment: 1100. Records go back to 1968. Alumni records are maintained here. Degrees granted: Associate. Certification: Technical. Other: Diplomas. Special programs- Medical: Accounting. Attendance and degree information available by phone, mail. Transcripts available by mail.

Waycross College, Registrar, 2001 South Georgia Parkway, Waycross, GA 31503, 912-285-6133 (Fax: 912-287-4909) 8AM-5PM. www.way.peacnet.edu Enrollment: 900. Records go back to 1976. Alumni records maintained here; call 912-285-6130. Degrees granted: Associate. Special programs- P.S.O. Program (Public School Option): "Hope" Program - State Grant providing Freshman Tuition. Attendance and degree information available by phone, fax, mail. Transcripts available by fax, mail.

Wesleyan College, Registrar, 4760 Forsyth Rd, Macon, GA 31297-4299, 912-477-1110, 912-757-5217 www.wesleyan-college.edu. (Fax: 912-757-4030) 8:30AM-5PM. Enrollment: 450. Records go back to 1836. Alumni records are maintained here. Degrees granted: Bachelors; Masters. Attendance and degree information available by phone, fax, mail. Transcripts available by fax, mail.

Young Harris College, Registrar, PO Box 96, Young Harris, GA 30582, 706-379-3111 (Ext. 5699), 706-379-3111 (Ext. 5125) (Fax: 706-379-4320) www.yhc.edu. 8:30AM-4:30PM. Enrollment: 524. Records go back to 1911. Alumni Records: Alumni Assoc., PO Box 145, Young Harris, GA 30582. Degrees granted: Associate. Attendance and degree

Hawaii

Brigham Young University (Hawaii), Registrar, Snow Administration Bldg, 55-220 Kulanui St, Laie, HI 96762, 808-293-3736, 808-293-3746 (Fax: 808-293-3745) www.byuh.edu. 8AM-5PM. Enrollment: 2000. Records go back to 1955. Alumni records maintained here; call 808-293-3648. Degrees granted: Associate; Bachelors; Professional Diploma. Attendance and degree information available by phone, fax, mail. Transcripts available by fax, mail.

Chaminade University of Honolulu, Registrar, 3140 Waialae Ave, Honolulu, HI 96816-1578, 808-735-4773, 808-735-4722 (Fax: 808-735-4777) www.chaminade.edu. 8AM-4PM. Enrollment: 1280. Records go back to 1956. Alumni Records: CUH-Alumni Assoc., 2636 Pamao Rd, Honolulu, HI 96822. Degrees granted: Associate; Bachelors; Masters. Attendance and degree information available by phone, fax, mail. Transcripts available by fax, mail.

Commonwealth International University (Honolulu Campus), Registrar, 419 South St #174, Honolulu, HI 96813, 808-942-1000 (Fax: 808-533-3064) www.dbc.edu. 8AM-5PM. Formerly **Denver Business College - Honolulu Campus**. Enrollment: 350. Records go back to 1910. Alumni records are maintained here. Degrees granted: Associate. Special programs- Medical Office Administration: International Business: Corrections Operations: Criminal Justice: Computer Graphics. Attendance and degree information available by phone, fax, mail. Transcripts available by fax, mail.

Denver Business College — Honolulu Campus
(See Commonwealth International University-Honolulu Campus)

Hawaii Community College, Registrar, 200 W Kauili, Hilo, HI 96720-4091, 808-974-7661 (Fax: 808-974-7692) 8AM-4:30PM. www.hawcc.hawaii.edu. Enrollment: 2700. Records go back to 1992. Degrees granted: Associate. Attendance and degree information available by phone, fax, mail. Transcripts available by fax, mail.

Hawaii Loa College
(See Hawaii Pacific University; merged in 1992)

Hawaii Pacific University, Registrar's Office, 1164 Bishop St #200, Honolulu, HI 96813, 808-544-0239, 800-544-0200 (Fax: 808-544-1136) www.hpe.edu. 8AM-5PM. Enrollment: 8390. Records go back to 1965. Alumni Records: 1154 Fort St Mall #216, Honolulu, HI 96813. Degrees granted: Associate; Bachelors; Masters. Certification: T.E.S.L.Q.M. Special programs- Travel

Industry Management, 808-544-0229. Attendance and degree information available by phone, fax, mail. Transcripts available by fax, mail.

Honolulu Community College, Registrar, 874 Dillingham Blvd, Honolulu, HI 96817, 808-845-9120 www.hcc.hawaii.edu. (Fax: 808-847-9872) 7:45AM-4:30PM. Enrollment: 4500. Records go back to 1966. Alumni records maintained here; call 808-956-7547. Degrees granted: Associate. Adverse incident record source- Dean of Student Services, 808-845-9236. Attendance and degree information available by fax, mail. Transcripts available by mail.

Kapiolani Community College, Registrar, 4303 Diamond Head Rd, Honolulu, HI 96816, 808-734-9532 8AM-4:30PM. www.leahi.kcc.hawaii.edu. Enrollment: 6500. Records go back to 1960. Degrees granted: Associate. Special programs- Liberal Arts: Health Education: Legal Education: Business Education: Food Service & Hotel Operations. Attendance and degree information available by phone, mail. Transcripts available by mail.

Kauai Community College, Registrar, 3-1901 Kaumualii Hwy, Lihue, HI 96766, 808-245-8226, 808-245-8225 (Fax: 808-245-8297). 8AM-4:30PM. Enrollment: 1272. Records go back to 1952. Alumni records maintained here; call 808-245-8234. Degrees granted: Associate. Attendance and degree information available by phone, mail. Transcripts available by mail.

Leeward Community College, Registrar, 96-045 Ala Ike, Pearl City, HI 96782, 808-455-0217, 808-455-0011 (Fax: 808-455-0471) http://lccada.lcc.hawaii.edu. 7:45AM-4:30PM. Enrollment: 6400. Records go back to 1968. Alumni records are maintained here. Degrees granted: Associate. Attendance and degree information available by phone, fax, mail. Transcripts available by mail.

Maui Community College
(See University of Hawaii Maui Community College)

Maui Community College, Registrar, 310 Kaahumanu Ave, Kahului, HI 96732, 808-984-3267 (Fax: 808-242-9618) 8AM-4:30PM. www.mauicc.hawaii.edu. Enrollment: 1915. Records go back to 1931. Degrees granted: Associate. Attendance and degree information available by phone, fax, mail. Transcripts available by fax, mail.

Tai Hsuan Foundation College of Acupuncture and Herbal Medicine, Registrar, 2600 S King St #206, Honolulu, HI 96826, 808-947-4788, 808-949-1050 (Fax: 808-947-1152). 9AM-5PM. Enrollment: 35. Records go back to 1970. Degrees granted:

Masters; Doctorate. Special programs- Acupuncture, Oriental Medicine. Attendance and degree information available by phone, fax, mail. Transcripts available by fax, mail.

Trans Pacific Hawaii College, Registrar, 5257 Kalanianaole Hwy, Honolulu, HI 96821, 808-377-5402 (Fax: 808-373-4754). Formerly **Kansai Gaidai Hawaii College**. 8AM-5PM. Enrollment: 200. Records go back to 1980. Alumni records are maintained here. Degrees granted: Associate. Attendance and degree information available by phone, fax, mail. Transcripts available by fax, mail.

University of Hawaii at Hilo, Records Office, 200 W Kawili St, Hilo, HI 96720-4091, 808-974-7385, 808-974-7322 http://ww2.hawaii.edu/~uhhilo. (Fax: 808-974-7691) 8AM-4:30PM. Enrollment: 2736. Records go back to 1941. Alumni records maintained here; call 808-974-7567. Degrees granted: Bachelors. Special programs- Call 808-974-7385. Attendance and degree information available by phone, mail. Transcripts available by mail.

University of Hawaii at Manoa, Registrar, 2600 Campus Rd Rm 101, Honolulu, HI 96822, www2.hawaii.edu/admrec. 808-956-8010, 808-956-8975 8AM-4:30PM. Enrollment: 17500. Records go back to 1907. Alumni records maintained here; call 808-956-7547. Degrees granted: Bachelors; Masters; Doctorate. Attendance and degree information available by phone, mail. Transcripts available by mail.

University of Hawaii — West Oahu, Student Services Office, 96-129 Ala Ike, Pearl City, HI 96782, www.uhwo.hawaii.edu. 808-454-4700 (Fax: 808-453-6075) 8AM-6PM. Enrollment: 700. Records go back to 1976. Alumni records are maintained here. Degrees granted: Bachelors. Attendance information available by phone, mail. Degree information available by phone, mail. Transcripts available by mail.

Windward Community College, Registrar, 45-720 Keaahala Rd, Kaneohe, HI 96744, 808-235-7432, 808-235-7413. 8:30AM - 4:30PM. Records go back to 1972. Degrees granted: Associate. Attendance and degree information available by phone, mail. Transcripts available by mail.

Idaho

Albertson College, Registrar, 2112 Cleveland Blvd, Caldwell, ID 83605, 208-459-5201, 208-459-5202 (Fax: 208-459-5415) www.acofi.edu/acihome.htm/. 9AM-4PM. Enrollment: 650. Records go back to 1891. Alumni records maintained here; call 208-459-5300. Degrees granted: Bachelors. Attendance and degree information available

by phone, fax, mail. Transcripts available by fax, mail.

Boise Bible College, Registrar, 8695 Marigold St, Boise, ID 83714, 208-376-7731, 800-893-7755 (Fax: 208-376-7743) 8:30AM-4:30PM. www.netnow.micron.net/~boibible. Enrollment: 140. Records go back to 1945. Alumni records are maintained here. Degrees

granted: Associate; Bachelors. Certification: One Year Bible. Attendance, degree and transcript information available by fax, mail.

Boise State University, Registrars Office, 1910 University Dr, Boise, ID 83725, 208-385-3486 (Fax: 208-385-3169) 8AM-5PM. www.idbsu.edu. Enrollment: 15000. Records go back to 1930. Alumni records maintained here; call 208-385-1959. Degrees granted: Associate; Bachelors; Masters; Doctorate. Attendance and degree information available by phone, fax, mail. Transcripts available by fax, mail.

College of Idaho
(See Albertson College)

College of Southern Idaho, Registrar, 315 Falls Ave, PO Box 1238, Twin Falls, ID 83303-1238, www.csi.cc.id.us. 208-733-9554 (Fax: 208-736-3014) 8AM-7PM M-Th; 8AM-4:30PM F. Enrollment: 4950. Records go back to 1965. Degrees granted: Associate. Attendance, degree and transcript information available by fax, mail.

Eastern Idaho Technical College, Registrar, 1600 S 2500 E, Idaho Falls, ID 83404, 208-524-3000 (Fax: 208-524-3007) www.eitc.edu. 8AM - 5PM. Enrollment: 540. Records go back to 1971. Degrees granted: Associate. Attendance and degree information available by phone, fax, mail. Transcripts available by fax, mail.

ITT Technical Institute, Registrar, 12302 W Explorer Dr, Boise, ID 83713-1529, 208-322-8844 (Fax: 208-322-0173). 8AM-7PM. Enrollment: 400. Records go back to 1968. Alumni Records: Alumni Assoc., ITT Technical Institute, 5975 Castle Creek Pkwy N Dr, Indianapolis, IN 46250. Degrees granted: Associate; Bachelors. Attendance and degree information available by phone, fax, mail. Transcripts available by fax, mail.

Idaho State University, Registration & Records, PO Box 8196, Pocatello, ID 83209, 208-236-2661 (Fax: 208-236-4231) www.isu.edu. 8AM-5PM; Summer Hours May 18th-Aug 17th: 7:30AM-4PM. Enrollment: 12000. Records go back to 1901. Alumni Records: PO Box 8033, Pocatello, ID 83209 (Fax: 208-236-2541). Degrees granted: Associate; Bachelors; Masters; Doctorate. Attendance and degree information available by phone, fax, mail. Transcripts available by mail.

Lewis - Clark State College, Registrar, 500 8th Ave, Lewiston, ID 83501, 208-799-2223, 208-799-2379 (Fax: 208-799-2429) www.lcsc.edu. 8AM-5PM. Enrollment: 3500. Records go back to 1893. Alumni records maintained here; call 208-799-2458. Degrees granted: Associate; Bachelors. Attendance and degree information available by fax, mail. Transcripts available by mail.

North Idaho College, Registrar, Coeur D' Alene, ID 83814, 208-769-3320, 208-769-3321 (Fax: 208-769-3431) www.nids.edu. 7:30AM-5PM M-Th; 7:30AM-2:30PM F. Enrollment: 3500. Records go back to 1933. Alumni records maintained here; call 208-769-7806. Degrees granted: Associate. Attendance and degree information available by phone, fax, mail. Transcripts available by fax, mail.

Northwest Nazarene College, Office of the Registrar, 623 Holly St, Nampa, ID 83686, 208-467-8541, 208-467-8011 (Fax:

208-467-8603) www.nnc.edu. 8AM - 5PM. Enrollment: 1200. Records go back to 1913. Alumni records maintained here; call 208-407-8841. Degrees granted: Bachelors; Masters. Attendance and degree information available by phone, fax, mail. Transcripts available by fax, mail.

Ricks College, Transcripts, Rexburg, ID 83460-4125, 208-356-1011, 208-356-1007 (Fax: 208-356-1035) www.ricks.edu. 8AM-5PM. Enrollment: 8300. Records go back to 1888. Alumni records maintained here; call 208-356-2234. Degrees granted: Associate. Special programs- Nursing, 208-356-1325: Interior Design, 208-356-1340: Drafting, 208-356-1362: Elementary Ed, 208-356-1348. Attendance and degree information available by phone, fax, mail. Transcripts available by fax, mail.

University of Idaho, Registrar, Moscow, ID 83844, 208-885-6731, 208-885-2020 (Fax: 208-885-9061) www.uidaho.edu/registrar. 8AM-5PM. Enrollment: 12000. Records go back to 1889. Alumni records maintained here; call 208-885-6154. Degrees granted: Bachelors; Masters; Doctorate. Attendance and degree information available by phone, fax, mail. Transcripts available by fax, mail.

Illinois

Adler School of Professional Psychology, Registrar, 65 E Wacker Pl Ste 2100, Chicago, IL 60601-7203, 312-201-5900 (Fax: 312-201-5917) www.adler.edu. 9AM-5PM. Enrollment: 413. Records go back to 1970. Alumni records maintained here; call 312-201-5900. Degrees granted: Masters; Doctorate. Attendance, degree and transcript information available by mail.

Alfred Adler Institute of Chicago
(See Adler School of Professional Psychology)

American Academy of Art, Registrar, 332 S Michigan Ave #300, Chicago, IL 60604-4301, www.aaart.edu. 312-461-0600 (Fax: 312-294-9570) 8AM-3:30PM. Enrollment: 400. Records go back to 1923. Degrees granted: Associate; Bachelors. Attendance and degree information available by phone, fax, mail. Transcripts available by mail.

American Conservatory of Music, Registrar, 36 S Wabash Ave 800, Chicago, IL 60603-2901, 312-263-4161 (Fax: 312-263-5832) 9AM-6PM. Records go back to 1886. www.members.aol.com.amerconsmu/index.. Alumni records are maintained here. Degrees granted: Associate; Bachelors; Masters; Doctorate. Attendance and degree information available by phone, fax, mail. Transcripts available by mail.

American Islamic College, Registrar, 640 W Irving Park Rd, Chicago, IL 60613, 773-281-4700. Enrollment: 500 Attendance, degree and transcript information available by mail.

American Schools of Professional Psychology, Registrar, 20 S Clark St 3rd Fl, Chicago, IL 60603, 312-201-0200 X533 (Fax: 312-201-1907). 8:30AM-5PM. Enrollment: 1250. Records go back to 1976. Alumni records maintained here; call 312-201-0200 X610. Degrees granted: Masters; Doctorate. Attendance and degree information available by phone, fax, mail. Transcripts available by mail.

Augustana College, Registrar, 639 38th St, Rock Island, IL 61201-2296, www.augustana.edu. 309-794-7277, 309-794-7211 (Fax: 309-794-7422) 8AM-4:30PM. Enrollment: 2150. Records go back to 1900. Alumni records maintained here; call 309-794-7336. Degrees granted: Bachelors. Attendance and degree information available by phone, fax, mail. Transcripts available by fax, mail.

Aurora University, Registrar, 347 S Gladstone Ave, Aurora, IL 60506-4892, 630-844-5464, 630-844-5462 www.aurora.edu. (Fax: 630-844-5463) 8AM-7PM M-Th; 8AM-6PM F; 9AM-1PM S. Enrollment: 2200. Records go back to 1893. Alumni records maintained here; call 630-844-5486. Degrees granted: Bachelors; Masters. Attendance and degree information available by phone, fax, mail. Transcripts available by fax, mail.

Barat College, Registrar, 700 E Westleigh Rd, Lake Forest, IL 60045, 847-234-3000 (Fax: 847-604-6300). 8:30AM - 4:30PM. Enrollment: 720. Records go back to 1922. Alumni records are maintained here. Degrees granted: Bachelors. Attendance and degree information available by fax, mail. Transcripts available by mail.

Belleville Area College, Registrar, 2500 Carlyle Ave, Belleville, IL 62221, 618-235-2700, 618-235-2700 (Fax: 618-235-1578). 8AM-8PM M-Th; 8AM-4PM F. Enrollment: 14000. Records go back to 1946. Alumni records are maintained here. Degrees granted: Associate. Attendance and degree information available by fax, mail. Transcripts available by fax, mail.

Benedictine University, Benedictine Central, 5700 College Rd, Lisle, IL 60532, 630-829-6000, 630-829-6500 (Fax: 630-960-1126) www.ben.edu. 8AM-6:30PM M-F; 10AM-1PM Sat. Enrollment: 2842. Records go back to 1901. Alumni records are maintained here. Degrees granted: Bachelors; Masters; Doctorate. Certification: IFM. Attendance and degree information available by phone, fax, mail. Transcripts available by fax, mail.

Black Hawk College, Registrar, 6600 34th Ave, Moline, IL 61265, 309-796-1311 (Fax: 309-792-5976). 7:30AM-6PM M-T, 7:30AM-5PM W-F. Enrollment: 7000. Records go back to 1966. Alumni records maintained here; call 309-796-1311. Degrees granted: Associate. Attendance and transcript information available by fax, mail. Degree information available by mail.

Black Hawk College East Campus, Records and Admissions Office, Box 489, Kewanee, IL 61443, 309-852-5671 X220 (Fax: 309-856-6005). Enrollment: 750. Records go back to 1967. Alumni records are maintained here. Degrees granted: Associate. Attendance and degree information available by phone, fax, mail. Transcripts available by fax, mail.

Blackburn College, Registrar, 700 College Ave, Carlinville, IL 62626, 217-854-3231 X4210 (Fax: 217-854-3713) 8AM-5PM. www.blackburn.edu. Enrollment: 575. Alumni records maintained here; call 217-854-3231 X4322. Degrees granted: Bachelors. Attendance and degree information available by phone, fax, mail. Transcripts available by mail.

Blessing-Rieman College of Nursing, Registrar, Broadway at 11th St, PO Box 7005, Quincy, IL 62305-7005, 217-228-5520 (Ext. 6992), 217-223-8400 (Ext. 6992) (Fax: 217-223-1781) www.rsa.lib.il.us/~bles/homepg. 8:30AM-5PM. Enrollment: 180. Records go back to 1908. Alumni records maintained here; call 217-223-5520 X6991. Degrees granted: Bachelors. Attendance and degree information available by phone, fax, mail. Transcripts available by fax, mail.

Bradley University, Registrar, 1501 W Bradley Ave, Peoria, IL 61625, 309-677-3101 (Fax: 309-677-2715) www.bradley.edu. 8AM-5PM. Records go back to 1897. Alumni records maintained here; call 309-677-2245. Degrees granted: Bachelors; Masters. Attendance and degree information available by phone, fax, mail. Transcripts available by fax, mail.

Brisk Rabbinical College, Registrar, 3000 W Devon, Chicago, IL 60659, 773-274-1177 (Fax: 773-274-6559) Enrollment: 40. Records go back to 1984. Degrees granted: Bachelors. Special programs- Hebrew Religious Studies. Attendance and degree information available by phone, fax, mail. Transcripts available by fax, mail.

Carl Sandburg College, Registrar, 2232 S Lake Storey Rd, Galesburg, IL 61401, 309-344-2518 (Fax: 309-344-3291) 8AM-5PM. www.csc.cc.il.us/. Records go back to 1967. Degrees granted: Associate. Attendance and degree information available by phone, fax, mail. Transcripts available by fax, mail.

Catholic Theological Union, Registrar, 5401 S Cornell Ave, Chicago, IL 60615-5698, 773-753-5320, 773-324-8000 (Fax: 773-324-3414/4360) www.ctu.edu. 8:30AM-4PM. Enrollment: 360. Records go back to 1969. Alumni records maintained here; call 312-753-7471. Degrees granted: Masters; Doctorate. Certification: Israel Study Program. Attendance and degree information available by fax, mail. Transcripts available by fax, mail.

Centralia Junior College
(See Kaskaskia College)

Chicago City-Wide College
(See City Colleges of Chicago - Chicago City-Wide College)

Chicago College of Commerce, Registrar, 11 E Adams St, Chicago, IL 60603, 312-236-3312 (Fax: 312-236-0014) 9AM - 5PM. Enrollment: 200. Records go back to 1956. Degrees granted: Associate. Certification: Machine Shorthand, Legal Transcription, Medical Transcription, Court Reporting. Attendance and degree information available by phone. Transcripts available by written request only.

Chicago Col. of Osteopathic Medicine
(See Midwestern University)

Chicago Medical School (The)
(See Finch University of Health Sciences)

Chicago School of Professional Psychology, Registrar, 806 S Plymouth Ct, Chicago, IL 60605, 312-786-9443 (Fax: 312-332-3273) www.csopp.edu. 9AM-5PM. Enrollment: 265. Records go back to 1979. Degrees granted: Doctorate. Attendance and degree information available by phone, fax, mail. Transcripts available by fax, mail.

Chicago State University, Registrar, 9501 S King Dr, Chicago, IL 60628, 773-995-2517, 773-995-2263 (Fax: 773-995-3618). 8:30AM-5PM M,T,W,F; 8:30AM-7PM Th. Enrollment: 9000. Records go back to 1905. Alumni records maintained here; call 312-995-2050. Degrees granted: Bachelors; Masters. Attendance information available by fax, mail. Degree information available by phone, fax, mail. Transcripts available by mail.

Chicago Theological Seminary, Registrar, 5757 S University Ave, Chicago, IL 60637, 312-752-5757 X227 (Fax: 312-752-0905). 8:30AM-4:30PM. Enrollment: 210. Records go back to 1971. Alumni records maintained here; call 312-752-5757 X264. Degrees granted: Masters; Doctorate. Special programs- Call 773-752-5757 X227. Attendance and degree information available by phone, fax, mail. Transcripts available by mail.

College of DuPage, Records Office, 425 22nd St, Glen Ellyn, IL 60137, www.cod.edu. 630-942-2377 (Fax: 630-858-9390) 8:30AM-5PM. Records go back to 1967. Alumni records maintained here; call 630-858-2800. Degrees granted: Associate. Attendance, degree and transcript information available by mail.

College of Lake County, Admissions Office, 19351 W Washington St, Grayslake, IL 60030, www.clc.cc.il.us. 847-543-2061 (Fax: 847-543-3061) 8AM-8PM M-Th; 8AM-4PM F. Enrollment: 14994. Records go back to 1969. Alumni records are maintained here. Degrees granted: Associate. Attendance and degree information available by phone, fax, mail. Transcripts available by fax, mail.

College of St. Francis
(See University of St. Francis)

Columbia College, Registrar, 600 S Michigan Ave, Chicago, IL 60605, 312-663-1600 (Fax: 312-663-5543). 9AM-5PM. Enrollment: 8000. Records go back to 1894. Alumni Records: 600 S Michigan, Rm 400, Chicago, IL 60605. Degrees granted: Bachelors; Masters. Attendance and degree information available by phone, fax, mail. Transcripts available by mail.

Commonwealth Business College (Branch), Registrar, 1527 47th Ave, Moline, IL 61265, 309-762-2100 (Fax: 309-762-2374). 8AM-9:30PM. Enrollment: 120. Records go back to 1986. Degrees granted: Associate; Certificates. Attendance and transcript information available by fax, mail. School will not confirm degree information. Transcripts available by fax, mail.

Concordia University, Registrar, 7400 Augusta St, River Forest, IL 60305, 708-209-3165 (Fax: 708-209-3167) www.curf.edu. 8AM-4:30PM. Enrollment: 2400. Records go back to 1913. Alumni records are maintained here. Degrees granted: Bachelors; Masters. Certification: CAS. Attendance and degree information available by phone, fax, mail. Transcripts available by written request only.

Danville Area Community College, Registrar, 2000 E Main St, Danville, IL 61832, 217-443-8800, 217-443-3222 (Fax: 217-443-8560) www.daccil.us. 8AM - 5PM Winter; 7:30AM - 4PM Summer. Enrollment: 3000. Records go back to 1946. Degrees granted: Associate. Attendance and degree information available by phone, fax, mail. Transcripts available by mail.

DePaul University, Registrar, 1 E Jackson Blvd, Chicago, IL 60604, 312-362-8610, 312-362-2077 (Fax: 312-362-5143) www.depaul.edu. 8AM-6PM. Enrollment: 17294. Records go back to 1898. Alumni Records: 25 East Jackson Blvd, Chicago, IL 60604. Degrees granted: Bachelors; Masters; Doctorate. Attendance and degree information available by phone, fax, mail. Transcripts available by fax, mail.

DeVry Institute of Technology, Chicago, Registrar, 3300 N Campbell Ave, Chicago, IL 60618, 312-929-8500 X2060 (Fax: 312-348-1780) www.devry.edu/chi.htm. 7:30AM-4:30PM M,T,F; 7:30AM-7:30PM W,Th. Records go back to 1948. Alumni Records: Alumni Assoc., DeVry Institute, One Tower Ln, Oakbrook Terrace, IL 60181. Degrees granted: Associate; Bachelors. Attendance and degree information available by phone, fax, mail. Transcripts available by fax, mail.

DeVry Institute of Technology, DuPage, Registrar, 1221 N Swift Rd, Addison, IL 60101-6106, 630-953-1300 (Fax: 630-953-1236) www.devry.edu. 8:30AM-10PM M-Th, 8:30AM-5PM F. Enrollment: 3500. Records go back to 1980. Alumni Records: Alumni Assoc., DeVry Institute, One Tower Ln, Oakbrook Terrace, IL 60181. Degrees granted: Associate; Bachelors. Attendance and degree information available by phone, fax, mail. Transcripts available by fax, mail.

DeVry Institutes, Registrar, One Tower Lane, Oak Brook Terrace, IL 60181, 630-571-7700 (Fax: 630-574-1969). 8:30AM-5PM. Enrollment: 1965. Records go back to 1948. Alumni records are maintained. Degrees granted: Associate; Bachelors. Attendance and degree information available by phone, mail. Transcripts available by mail.

Dominican University, Registrar, 7900 W Division St, River Forest, IL 60305, 708-366-2490, 708-524-6803 www.dom.edu. (Fax: 708-524-6943) Enrollment: 1800. Records go back to 1920. Alumni records are maintained here. Degrees granted: Bachelors; Masters. Attendance and degree information available by phone, mail. Transcripts available by mail.

Dr. William M. Scholl College of Podiatric Medicine, Registrar, 1001 N Dearborn St, Chicago, IL 60610, 312-280-2943, 312-280-2944 (Fax: 312-280-2495). 8:30AM-5PM. Enrollment: 400. Records go back to 1916. Alumni records are maintained here also. Call 312-280-2880. Degrees granted: Bachelors; Doctorate. Special programs- Podiatric Medicine. Attendance and degree information available by phone, fax, mail. Transcripts available by mail.

East - West University, Registrar, 816 S Michigan Ave, Chicago, IL 60605, 312-939-0111 X16 (Fax: 312-939-0083). 9AM - 6PM. Records go back to 1980. Alumni records are maintained here. Degrees granted: Associate. Attendance and degree information available by phone, fax, mail. Transcripts available by fax, mail.

Eastern Illinois University, Registrar, 600 Lincoln Ave, Charleston, IL 61920, 217-581-3511 (Fax: 217-581-3412) www.eiu.edu. 8AM-4:30PM. Enrollment: 10500. Records go back to 1895. Alumni records maintained here; call 217-581-6616. Degrees granted: Bachelors; Masters. Attendance and degree information available by phone, fax, mail. Transcripts available by fax, mail.

Elgin Community College, Registrar, 1700 Spartan Dr, Elgin, IL 60123, 847-888-7386 (Fax: 847-697-9209) www.elgin.cc.il.us. 8AM-7PM. Enrollment: 9000. Records go back to 1949. Alumni records maintained here; call 847-697-1000 X7423. Degrees granted: Associate. Attendance, degree and transcript information available by fax, mail.

Elmhurst College, Registration & Records, 190 Prospect Ave, Elmhurst, IL 60126-3296, 630-617-3052, 630-617-3200 (Fax: 630-617-3245) www.elmhurst.edu. 8AM - 8PM M-Th; 8AM- 4PM F; 8:30 - 11:30AM Sat. Enrollment: 2700. Records go back to 1871. Alumni records maintained here; call 630-617-3600. Degrees granted: Bachelors. Attendance and degree information available by phone, fax, mail. Transcripts available by fax, mail.

Eureka College, Registrar, 300 E College Ave, Eureka, IL 61530, 309-467-3721, 309-467-6303 (Fax: 309-467-6304). 8AM-5PM. Enrollment: 500. Records go back to 1855. Alumni records maintained here; call 309-467-6317. Degrees granted: Bachelors. Attendance and degree information available by phone, fax, mail. Transcripts available by fax, mail.

Finch University of Health Sciences (The Chicago Medical School), Registrar, 3333 Green Bay Rd, North Chicago, IL 60064, 847-578-3228, 847-578-3229 (Fax: 847-578-3284). 8:30AM - 4:30PM. Enrollment: 1400. Records go back to 1932. Formerly **The University of Health Sciences/Chicago Medical School**. Alumni Records: AMOCCO Bldg, North Chicago, IL 60064. Degrees granted: Bachelors; Masters; Doctorate. Special programs- Medical. Attendance and degree information available by phone, fax, mail. Transcripts available by mail.

Frontier Community College, Registrar, #2 Frontier Dr, Fairfield, IL 62837, 618-842-3111 (Fax: 618-842-4425) Enrollment: 3500. www.iecc.cc.il.us/fcc/. Records go back to 1973. Degrees granted: Associate; 2-year Associate in Applied Science, 1-year Certificates. Attendance, degree and transcript information available by written request only.

Garrett — Evangelical Theological Seminary, Registrar, 2121 Sheridan Rd, Evanston, IL 60201, 847-866-3905, 847-866-3905 (Fax: 847-866-3957) 8:30AM-4:30PM. www.garrett.nwu.edu. Enrollment: 520. Records go back to 1892. Alumni records are maintained here. Degrees granted: Masters; Doctorate. School will not confirm attendance information. Degree information available by phone, fax, mail. Transcripts available by fax, mail. Requestors must have written permission from student.

Gem City College, Registrar, PO Box 179, 700 State St, Quincy, IL 62306, 217-222-0391 (Fax: 217-222-1559). 8AM - 4:40PM. Records go back to 1871. Attendance, degree and transcript information available by written request only.

Governors State University, Registrar, University Park, IL 60466, 708-534-4500, 708-534-5000 X4490 (Fax: 708-235-3960). 8:30AM-7PM M-Th, 8:30AM-5PM F. Enrollment: 5900. Records go back to 1971. Alumni records maintained here; call 708-534-4128. Degrees granted: Bachelors; Masters. Attendance and degree information available by phone, fax, mail. Transcripts available by mail.

Greenville College, Registrar, 315 E College Ave, Greenville, IL 62246, 618-664-1840 X4222 (Fax: 618-664-9775). 8AM - 4:30PM. Enrollment: 960. Records go back to 1892. Alumni records are maintained here. Degrees granted: Bachelors. Attendance and degree information available by phone, fax, mail. Transcripts available by fax, mail.

Harold Washington College, Registrar, 30 E Lake St, Chicago, IL 60601, 312-553-6060, 312-553-6065 (Fax: 312-553-6077) 9AM - 6PM. Enrollment: 6602. Records go back to 1962. Alumni Records: 30 E Lake St, Room 1144, Chicago, IL 60601. Degrees granted: Associate. Attendance and degree information available by phone, fax, mail. Transcripts available by fax, mail.

Harrington Institute of Interior Design, Registrar, 410 S Michigan Ave, Chicago, IL 60605-1496, 312-939-4975 (Fax: 312-939-8005) www.interiordesign.edu. 8:30AM-5:00PM. Enrollment: 350. Records go back to 1961. Degrees granted: Associate; Bachelors Attendance, degree and transcript information available by fax, mail.

Harry S. Truman College, Registrar, 1145 W Wilson Ave, Chicago, IL 60640, 773-907-6814, 773-907-4700 (Fax: 773-907-4464). 8:30AM - 7PM M-Th, 8:30AM - 3PM. Enrollment: 4900. Records go back to 1958. Alumni records maintained here; call 773-907-4755. Degrees granted: Associate. Attendance and degree information available by phone, mail. Transcripts available by mail.

Heartland Community College, Registrar, 1226 Towanda Ave, Bloomington, IL 61701, 309-827-0500 (Fax: 309-827-8505) 8AM-5PM. www.heartland.edu. Enrollment: 2779. Records go back to 1994. Attendance and degree information available by phone, mail. Transcripts available by mail.

Hebrew Theological College, Registrar, 7135 N Carpenter Rd, Skokie, IL 60077, 847-982-2500 (Fax: 847-674-6381) www.htcnet.edu. Enrollment: 250. Records go back to 1922. Alumni records are maintained here. Degrees granted: Bachelors. Attendance, degree and transcript information available by fax, mail.

Highland Community College, Registrar, 2998 Pearl City Rd, Freeport, IL 61032, 815-235-6121, 815-234-6121 X285 (Fax: 815-235-6130). 8AM-5PM. Enrollment: 2682. Records go back to 1962. Alumni records maintained here; call 815-235-6121 X205. Degrees granted: Associate. Attendance and degree information available by phone, fax, mail. Transcripts available by fax, mail.

ITT Technical Institute (Branch of Indianapolis, IN), Director of Education, 375 W Higgins Rd, Hoffman Estates, IL 60195, 847-519-9300 X20 (Fax: 847-519-0153). 8AM-5PM. Enrollment: 500. Records go back to 1986. Alumni records are maintained here. Degrees granted: Associate; Bachelors. Special programs- Electrical Engineering. Attendance, degree and transcript information available by fax, mail. Need ITT student number.

Illinois Central College, Registrar L-211, One College Dr, East Peoria, IL 61635, 309-694-5354 (Fax: 309-694-8461) www.icc.cc.il.us. 8AM-4:30PM. Enrollment: 12000. Records go back to 1967. Alumni records maintained here; call 309-694-5530. Degrees granted: Associate. Attendance and degree information available by phone, fax, mail. Transcripts available by fax, mail.

Illinois College, Registrar, 1101 W College Ave, Jacksonville, IL 62650, 217-245-3013 (Fax: 217-245-3034) www.ic.edu. 8:30AM-4:30PM. Enrollment: 950. Records go back to 1829. Alumni records maintained here; call 217-245-3047. Degrees granted: Bachelors. Attendance and degree information available by phone, fax, mail. Transcripts available by fax, mail. Signature required for transcript.

Illinois College of Optometry, Registrar, 3241 S Michigan Ave, Chicago, IL 60616, 312-949-7425, 312-949-7426 (Fax: 312-949-7680) www.ico.edu. 8:30AM - 4:30PM. Enrollment: 621. Records go back to 1920. Alumni records maintained here; call 312-949-7655. Degrees granted: Bachelors; Doctorate. Attendance and degree information available by phone, fax, mail. Transcripts available by fax, mail.

Illinois Institute of Art, Registrar, 350 N Orleans St #136, Chicago, IL 60654-3532, 312-280-3500, 800-351-3450 (Fax: 312-280-3528). 9AM - 4PM. Enrollment: 600. Records go back to 1960's. Degrees granted: Associate; Bachelors; Diploma. Attendance, degree and transcript information available by mail. Must state whether attended Ray College of Design or Illinois Institute of Art.

Illinois Institute of Art (The) (Branch), Registrar, 1000 Plaza Dr, Schaumburg, IL 60173-5070, 847-619-3450 (Fax: 847-619-3064) www.ilia.aii.edu. 8AM-5PM. Enrollment: 364. Records go back to 1984. Records go back 12 years for branch campus. Alumni records are maintained here. Degrees granted: Associate; Bachelors. Attendance and degree information available by phone, fax, mail. Transcripts available by fax, mail.

Illinois Institute of Technology, Registrar, 3300 S Federal St, Chicago, IL 60616, 312-567-3784, 312-567-3024 (Graduate College) (Fax: 312-567-3313) www.iit.edu. 8:30AM-5PM. Enrollment: 7158. Records go back to 1890. Alumni Records: Alumni Assoc., 10 W 33rd St Rm 203, Chicago, IL 60606. Degrees granted: Bachelors; Masters; Doctorate. Attendance and degree information available by phone, fax, mail. Transcripts available by fax, mail.

Illinois Institute of Technology — Rice Campus, Registrar, MCE, 201 E Loop Rd, Wheaton, IL 60187, 630-682-6000, 630-682-6040 (Fax: 630-682-6010). Records go back to 1967. Formerly **Midwest College of Engineering**. Alumni records are maintained here. Degrees granted: Bachelors; Masters. Attendance and degree information available by phone, fax, mail. Transcripts available by fax, mail.

Illinois School of Professional Psychology, Registrar, 20 S Clark St, Chicago, IL 60603, 312-201-0200 X0 (Fax: 312-201-1907). 9AM - 5PM. Enrollment: 700. Records go back to 1976. Alumni records are maintained here. Degrees granted: Masters; Doctorate. Attendance and degree information available by phone, fax, mail. Transcripts available by written request only.

Illinois State University, Registrar, Normal, IL 61761-1000, 309-438-3408, 309-438-2341 (Fax: 309-438-7324) 8AM-4:30PM. www.ilstu.edu. Enrollment: 20045. Records go back to 1857. Alumni Records: Campus Box 3100, Normal, IL 61790-3100 (Fax: 309-438-8057). Degrees granted: Bachelors; Masters; Doctorate. Special programs- Criminal Justice: Teacher Education: Business Fields. Attendance and degree information available by phone, mail. Transcripts available by mail.

Illinois Valley Community College, Registrar, 815 N Orlando Smith Ave, Oglesby, IL 61348-9691, 815-224-2720 (Fax: 815-224-3033) www.ivcc.edu. Alumni records also maintained here. Call 815-224-2720 X551. Degrees granted: Associate. Attendance and degree information available by phone, fax, mail. Transcripts available by fax, mail.

Illinois Wesleyan University, Registrar, PO Box 2900, Bloomington, IL 61702, 309-556-3161, 309-556-3031 (Fax: 309-556-3411) 8AM-5PM. www.wu.edu. Enrollment: 1800. Records go back to 1850. Alumni records maintained here; call 309-556-3091. Degrees granted: Bachelors. Attendance and degree information available by phone, fax, mail. Transcripts available by fax, mail.

International Academy of Merchandising and Design, Registrar, One N State St #400, Chicago, IL 60602, 312-541-3910 (Fax: 312-541-3929) www.iamd.edu. 8AM-5PM. Enrollment: 650. Records go back to 1979. Degrees granted: Associate; Bachelors. Attendance and degree information available by phone, fax, mail. Transcripts available by fax, mail.

John A. Logan College, Registrar, Carterville, IL 62918, 618-985-3741 (Fax: 618-985-4433) www.jal.cc.il.us. 8AM-8PM M-Th; 8AM-4:30PM F. Enrollment: 5042. Records go back to 1967. Alumni records are maintained here. Degrees granted: Associate. Attendance and degree information available by phone, fax, mail. Transcripts available by fax, mail.

John Marshall Law School, Registrar, 315 S Plymouth Ct, Chicago, IL 60604, 312-427-2737 X775, 312-427-2737 X772 (Fax: 312-427-2922) www.jmls.edu. 9AM - 5:30PM. Enrollment: 1300. Records go back to 1898. Alumni records maintained here; call 312-427-2737 X411. Degrees granted: Masters; JD. Special programs- Contact Carol Belshaw, 312-427-2737 X396. Attendance and degree information available by phone, mail. Transcripts available by mail.

John Wood Community College, Registrar, 150 S 48th St, Quincy, IL 62301, 217-224-6500, 217-224-6500 X4336 (Fax: 217-224-4208). 8AM-5PM. Enrollment: 2000. Records go back to 1976. Degrees granted: Associate; Vocational. Attendance and transcript information available by fax, mail. Degree information available by phone, fax, mail.

Joliet Junior College, JJC-Transcript Request, 1215 Houbolt Ave, Joliet, IL 60431-8938, 815-729-9020 X2242, 815-729-9020 X2290 (Fax: 815-773-6675) 7:30AM - 4PM. www.jjc.cc.il.us. Enrollment: 10500. Records go back to 1910. Alumni records maintained here; call 815-729-6620. Degrees granted: Associate. Special programs- Nursing Dept holds limited records for 5 years. Attendance and degree information available by phone, mail. Transcripts available by mail.

Judson College, Registrar, 1151 N State St, Elgin, IL 60123, 847-695-2500 X2210 (Fax: 847-695-4410) www.judson-il.edu. 8AM-4PM. Enrollment: 1000. Records go back to 1963. Alumni records maintained here; call 708-695-2500. Degrees granted: Bachelors. Attendance and degree information available by phone, fax, mail. Transcripts available by mail. Only students can request transcripts.

Kankakee Community College, Registrar, PO Box 888, Kankakee, IL 60901, 815-933-0246, 815-933-0345 (Fax: 815-933-0217). 8AM-5PM. Enrollment: 4000. Records go back to 1968. Alumni records maintained here; call 815-933-0345. Degrees granted: Associate. Attendance and degree information available by phone, fax, mail. Transcripts available by mail.

Kaskaskia College, Registrar, 27210 College Rd, Centralia, IL 62801, www.kc.edu. 618-532-1981 (Ext. 241) (Fax: 618-532-1135) 7:30AM-4PM. Records go back to 1940. Formerly **Centralia Junior College**. Alumni records maintained here; call 618-532-1981. Degrees granted: Associate. Attendance and degree information available by fax, mail. Transcripts available by mail.

Keller Graduate School of Management Registrar, 225 W Washington St #100, Chicago, IL 60606-3418, 312-454-0880 (Fax: 312-454-6103). 9AM-4:30PM M-Th, 9AM-5PM F. Enrollment: 3800. Records go back to 1973. Alumni records are maintained here. Degrees granted: Masters. Attendance and degree information available by phone, mail. Transcripts available by mail. Must call corporate office (630-574-1960/2063) for any information.

Keller Graduate School of Management (West Suburban Center), Registrar, 1101 31st St, **Downers Grove**, IL 60515-5515, 630-969-6624. Records located at Keller Graduate School of Management, Registrar, 225 W Washington St #100, Chicago, IL 60606-3418.

Keller Graduate School of Management (North Suburban Center), Registrar, Tri State Intl Office Ctr, Bldg 25 Ste 13, **Lincolnshire**, IL 60069-4460, 847-940-7768. Records are located at Keller Graduate School of Management, Registrar, 225 W Washington St #100, Chicago, IL 60606-3418.

Keller Graduate School of Management (South Suburban Center), Registrar, 15255 S 94th Ave, **Orland Park**, IL 60462-3823, 708-460-9580 (Fax: 708-460-0827). Records are located at Keller Graduate School of Management, Registrar, 225 W Washington St #100, Chicago, IL 60606-3418.

Keller Graduate School of Management (Northwest Suburban Center), Registrar, 1051 Perimeter Dr, **Schaumburg**, IL 60173-5009, 847-330-0040. Records are located at Keller Graduate School of Management, Registrar, 225 W Washington St #100, Chicago, IL 60606-3418.

Kendall College, Registrar, 2408 Orrington Ave, Evanston, IL 60201, 847-866-1325, 847-866-1300 (Fax: 847-866-9346) www.kendall.edu. 8AM-4:30PM. Enrollment: 500. Records go back to 1900. Alumni records are maintained here. Degrees granted: Associate; Bachelors. Special programs- Continuing Education. Attendance and degree information available by phone, fax, mail. Transcripts available by fax, mail.

Kennedy-King College, Registrar, 6800 S Wentworth Ave, Chicago, IL 60621, 312-602-5062, 312-602-5049 (Fax: 312-602-5247). 8:30AM-7PM M-Th, 8:30AM-5PM F. Enrollment: 2502. Records go back to 1900. Alumni records are maintained here. Degrees granted: Associate. Attendance, degree and transcript information available by fax, mail. Transcript requests must be from the student.

Kishwaukee College, Admissions, Registration & Records, 21193 Malta Rd, Malta, IL 60150-9699, 815-825-2086 X218 (Fax: 815-825-2306) www.kish.cc.il.us. 7:30AM-7PM M-Th; 7:30AM-5PM F. Enrollment: 3800. Records go back to 1969. Alumni records maintained here; call 815-825-2086 X266. Degrees granted: Associate; GED. Attendance and degree information available by phone, fax, mail. Transcripts available by fax, mail.

Knowledge Systems Institute, Registrar, 3420 Main St, Skokie, IL 60076, 847-679-3135, 847-679-3145 (Fax: 847-679-3166) www.ksi.edu. 10:30AM - 6:30PM. Enrollment: 110. Records go back to 1989. Alumni records are maintained here. Degrees granted: Masters. Special programs- Computer Science Attendance, degree and transcript information available by fax, mail.

Knox College, Registrar, Galesburg, IL 61401, www.knox.edu. 309-341-7205 (Fax: 309-341-7708) 8AM-Noon, 1-4:30PM Sept-May; 8AM-Noon, 1-4PM June-Aug. Enrollment: 1100. Records go back to 1837. Alumni records maintained here; call 309-341-7337. Degrees granted: Bachelors. Special programs- Studies Abroad. Attendance and degree information available by phone, fax, mail. Transcripts available by mail.

Lake Forest College, Registrar, 555 N Sheridan Rd, Lake Forest, IL 60045, 847-735-5025, 847-735-5026 (Fax: 847-735-6276) www.lfc.edu. 8:30AM - 5PM. Enrollment: 1000. Records go back to 1860. Alumni records maintained here; call 847-735-6016. Degrees granted: Bachelors; Masters. Attendance and degree information available by phone, fax, mail. Transcripts available by fax, mail.

Lake Forest Graduate School of Management, Registrar, 280 N Sheridan Rd, Lake Forest, IL 60045, www.lfgsm.edu. 847-234-5005 (Fax: 847-295-3656) 8:30AM-4:30PM. Enrollment: 750. Records go back to 1960. Alumni records maintained here. Degrees granted: Masters. Attendance and degree information available by phone, fax, mail. Transcripts available by fax, mail.

Lake Land College, Registrar, 5001 Lake Land Blvd, Mattoon, IL 61938, 217-234-5252 (Fax: 217-234-5390) www.lakeland.cc.il.us. 7:30AM - 6:30PM M-Th, 7:30AM-5PM F. Enrollment: 5500. Records go back to 1967. Alumni records maintained here; call 217-234-5253. Degrees granted: Associate. Special programs- AG Technology, John Deere, 217-234-5308: Associate Degree Nursing, 217-234-5204: LPN, 217-234-5204: Dental Hygiene, 217-234-5203: Physical Therapist Assistant, 217-342-0955: John Deere AG Marketing, 217-234-5226. Attendance and degree information available by phone, mail. Transcripts available by fax, mail.

Lewis University, Registrar, Route 53, Romeoville, IL 60446, 815-838-0500 X5217, 815-836-5217 (Fax: 815-838-9456) www.lewisu.edu. 8:30AM-6PM M-Th; 8:30AM-4PM F. Enrollment: 4144. Records go back to 1932. Alumni records maintained here; call 815-838-0500 X244. Degrees granted: Associate; Bachelors; Masters; Nursing, Business, Arts & Sciences. Special programs- Associate Degrees in all Phases of Aviation-FAA Approved: Flight Certification by the State of Illinois. Attendance and degree information available by phone, fax, mail. Transcripts available by mail.

Lewis and Clark Community College, Registrar, 5800 Godfrey Rd, Godfrey, IL 62035, www.lc.cc.il.us. 618-466-3411 X5112 (Fax: 618-467-2310) 8AM-4PM M,Th,F; 8AM-7PM T,W. Enrollment: 6000. Records go back to 1970. Degrees granted: Associate. Attendance and degree information available by phone, fax, mail. Transcripts available by fax, mail.

Lexington College, Registrar, 10840 S Western Ave, Chicago, IL 60643, 773-779-3800 (Fax: 773-779-7450). 8:45AM - 4PM. Enrollment: 50. Records go back to 1977. Formerly **Lexington Institute of Hospitality Careers**. Alumni records are maintained here. Degrees granted: Associate Attendance, degree and transcript information available by mail.

Lincoln Christian College and Seminary, Registrar, 100 Campus View Dr, Lincoln, IL 62656, 217-732-3168 (Ext. 2244), 217-732-3168 (Ext. 2288) (Fax: 217-732-5914) www.lccs.edu. 7:30AM-4:30PM. Enrollment: 800. Records go back to 1946. Alumni records are maintained. Degrees granted: Associate; Bachelors; Masters. Attendance and degree information available by phone, fax, mail. Transcripts available by fax, mail.

Lincoln College, Registrar, 300 Keokuk St, Lincoln, IL 62656, 217-732-3155, 217-735-5050 (Fax: 217-732-2992) 8AM-5PM. www.lincolncollege.com. Enrollment: 850. Records go back to 1800's. Alumni records maintained here; call 217-732-3155 X204. Degrees granted: Associate. Attendance and degree information available by fax, mail. Transcripts available by mail.

Lincoln Land Community College, Admissions and Records, Shepherd Rd, Springfield, IL 62794-9256, 217-786-2298, 217-786-2243 (Fax: 217-786-2492) www.llcc.cc.il.us. 8AM-5PM. Enrollment: 11000. Records go back to 1969. Alumni records maintained here; call 217-786-2784. Degrees granted: Associate. Attendance and degree information available by phone, fax, mail. Transcripts available by fax, mail.

Lincoln Trail College, Registrar, 11220 State Hwy 1, Robinson, IL 62454-5707, 618-544-8657 X1137, 618-544-8657 (Fax: 618-544-9384 and 618-544-4705). 8AM - 5PM. Enrollment: 650. Records go back to 1971. Degrees granted: Associate. Special programs- Telecommunications: Nursing. Attendance and degree information available by phone, fax, mail. Transcripts available by mail. Must have written letter of request from student.

Loop College (The)
(See Harold Washington College)

Loyola University of Chicago, Registrar, 820 N Michigan Ave, Rm 504, Chicago, IL 60611, 312-915-7221, 312-915-6000 (Fax: 312-915-6448) www.luc.edu. 8:30AM-5PM. Enrollment: 13806. Records go back to 1870. Alumni Records: 6525 N Sheridan Rd, Chicago, IL 60626. Degrees granted: Bachelors; Masters; Doctorate. Special programs- Stritch School of Medicine, 708-216-3222. Attendance and degree information available by phone, fax, mail. Transcripts available by fax, mail.

Lutheran School of Theology, Registrar, 1100 E 55 St, Chicago, IL 60615, 773-753-0700, 312-256-0717 (Fax: 773-256-0782). Enrollment: 384. Alumni records are maintained here also. Call 773-256-0712. Degrees granted: Masters; Doctorate. Attendance and degree information available by phone, fax, mail. Transcripts available by mail.

Lutheran School of Theology at Chicago, Registrar, 1100 E 55th St, Chicago, IL 60615-5199, 773-256-0700, 773-256-0717 (Fax: 773-256-0782) www.stc.edu. 8:30AM-4:30PM. Enrollment: 367. Records go back to 1940. Alumni records maintained here; call 773-256-0785. Degrees granted: Masters; Doctorate. Certification: Theology. Attendance information available by phone, mail. Degree information available by phone, fax, mail. Transcripts available by mail.

MacCormac Junior College, Registrar, 506 S Wabash Ave, Chicago, IL 60605-1667, 312-922-1884 (Fax: 312-922-3196) 8AM-5PM. www.maccormac.edu. Enrollment: 415. Records go back to 1904. Degrees granted: Associate. Attendance and degree information available by phone, fax, mail. Transcripts available by mail.

MacMurray College, Records and Registration, 447 E College Ave, Jacksonville, IL 62650, 217-479-7012 (Fax: 217-245-0405) www.mac.edu. 8AM - 4:30PM. Enrollment: 700. Alumni records are maintained here also. Call 217-479-7024. Degrees granted: Associate; Bachelors. Attendance information available by phone, fax, mail. Degree information available by phone, mail. Transcripts available by mail.

Malcolm X College, Registrar, 1900 W Van Buren St, Chicago, IL 60612, 312-850-7055, 312-850-7125 (Fax: 312-850-7092). 8:30AM-6PM. Enrollment: 5000. Records go back to 1966. Alumni records are maintained here. Degrees granted: Associate. Attendance and degree information available by phone, fax, mail. Transcripts available by fax, mail.

McCormick Theological Seminary, Registrar, 5555 S Woodlawn Ave, Chicago, IL 60637, 773-947-6285, 773-947-6300 (Fax: 773-947-0376) www.mccormick.edu. 8:30AM-4:30PM. Enrollment: 450. Records go back to 1918. Alumni records maintained here; call 773-947-9821. Degrees granted: Masters; Doctorate. Attendance and degree information available by phone, fax, mail. Transcripts available by fax, mail.

McHenry County College, Registrar, 8900 US Hwy 14, Crystal Lake, IL 60012-2794, 815-455-3700, 815-455-8716 (Fax: 815-455-3766) www.mchenry.cc.il.us. 8AM-7:30PM M-Th; 8AM-4PM F. Enrollment: 4810. Records go back to 1967. Degrees granted: Associate. Attendance and degree information available by phone, fax, mail. Transcripts available by fax, mail.

McKendree College, Registrar, 701 College Rd, Lebanon, IL 62254, 618-537-6818, 618-537-6819 (Fax: 618-537-4730). 8AM-5PM. Enrollment: 1632. Records go back to 1928. Alumni records maintained here; call 618-537-4481. Degrees granted: Associate; Bachelors. Attendance and degree information available by phone, fax, mail. Transcripts available by fax, mail.

Meadville/Lombard Theological School, Registrar, 5701 S Woodlawn Ave, Chicago, IL 60637, 773-753-3195, 312-753-3195 (Fax: 773-753-1323). 9AM - 5PM. Enrollment: 83. Records go back to 1935. Alumni records maintained here; call 773-753-3195. Degrees granted: Masters; Doctorate. Attendance, degree and transcript information available by mail. $5.00.

Mennonite College of Nursing, Registrar, 804 N East St, Bloomington, IL 61701, 309-829-0715 X3594 (Fax: 309-829-0765). 8AM-4:30PM. Enrollment: 210. Records go back to 1919. Alumni records are maintained here. Degrees granted: Bachelors. Attendance and degree information available by phone, fax, mail. Transcripts available by mail.

Midstate College, Registrar, 411 W Northmoor Rd, Peoria, IL 61614, 309-692-4092, 309-692-4547 (Fax: 309-692-3893). 8AM-4:30PM. Enrollment: 350. Records go back to 1950's. Degrees granted: Associate. Attendance and degree information available by phone, fax, mail. Transcripts available by mail.

Midwest College of Engineering
(See Illinois Institute of Technology)

Midwestern University, Registrar, 555 31st St, Downers Grove, IL 60515, 630-515-6074 (Fax: 630-515-7140). 8AM-5PM. Enrollment: 1400. Records go back to 1921. Formerly **Chicago College of Osteopathic Medicine.** Alumni records are maintained here. Degrees granted: Bachelors; Masters; Doctorate. Special programs- Medical: Pharmacy: Allied Health. Attendance and degree information available by phone, fax, mail. Transcripts available by fax, mail.

Millikin University, Registrar, 1184 W Main St, Decatur, IL 62522, 217-424-6217 (Fax: 217-424-3993 & 217-425-4669) www.millikin.edu/. 8AM-5PM. Enrollment: 1850. Records go back to 1903. Alumni records maintained here; call 217-424-6384. Degrees granted: Bachelors. Attendance and degree information available by phone, fax, mail. Transcripts available by written request only.

Monmouth College, Registrar, 700 E Broadway, Monmouth, IL 61462, 309-457-2326 (Fax: 309-457-2152) www.monm.edu. 8AM-Noon, 1-4:30PM. Enrollment: 1000. Records go back to 1920's. Alumni records maintained here; call 309-457-2336. Degrees granted: Bachelors. Attendance and degree information available by phone, fax, mail. Transcripts available by mail.

Montay College
(Closed July 1995; no records available)

Moody Bible Institute, Registrar, 820 N La Salle Blvd, Chicago, IL 60610, www.moody.edu. 312-329-4261, 312-329-4000 (Fax: 312-329-8987) 8AM-4:30PM. Enrollment: 5697. Records go back to 1885. Alumni records maintained here; call 312-329-4412. Degrees granted: Masters. Attendance and degree information available by phone, fax, mail. Transcripts available by fax, mail. Only students can request transcripts.

Moraine Valley Community College, Registrar, 10900 S 88th Ave, Palos Hills, IL 60465, 708-974-5346, 708-974-2110 (Fax: 708-974-0974) www.moraine.cc.il.us. 8:30AM-7:30PM M,T; 8:30AM-5PM W-F. Enrollment: 16000. Records go back to 1969. Alumni records maintained here; call 708-974-5353. Degrees granted: Associate. Attendance and degree information available by phone, mail. Transcripts available by mail.

Morrison Institute of Technology, Registrar, 701 Portland Ave, Morrison, IL 61270-0410, 815-772-7218, 815-772-7218 (Fax: 815-772-7584) www.morrison.tec.il.us. 8AM-5PM. Enrollment: 175. Records go back to 1976. Alumni records are maintained here. Degrees granted: Associate. Attendance and degree information available by phone, mail. Transcripts available by mail.

Morton College, Registrar, 3801 S Central Ave, Cicero, IL 60650, 708-656-8000 (Fax: 708-656-9592) www.morton.cc.il.us. 9AM-8PM M-Th, 9AM-4PM F. Enrollment: 4200. Records go back to 1925. Degrees granted: Associate. Attendance and degree information available by phone, fax, mail. Transcripts available by mail.

NAES College, Registrar, 2838 W Peterson Ave, Chicago, IL 60659, 773-761-5000 (Fax: 773-761-3808) www.naes.indian.com. 9AM-5PM. Enrollment: 118. Records go back to 1977. Alumni records maintained here; call 773-761-5000. Degrees granted: Bachelors. Attendance and degree information available by phone, fax, mail. Transcripts available by fax, mail.

National College of Chiropractic, Registrar, 200 E Roosevelt Rd, Lombard, IL 60148, 630-629-2000 (Fax: 630-889-6554). 8:30AM-5PM. Enrollment: 900. Records go back to 1945. Alumni records maintained here; call 630-629-9664. Degrees granted: Bachelors; Doctorate. Attendance, degree and transcript information available by mail. Name of college necessary to accommodate records held for several schools no longer existing.

National College of Education
(See Louis University)

National-Louis University, Transcript Department, 1000 Capitol Dr, Wheeling, IL 60090, 847-465-0575 (X 5294), 847-465-0575 (X 5312) (Fax: 847-465-0594) www.nlu.nl.edu. 8:30AM - 4:30PM. Enrollment: 7500. Records go back to 1886. Alumni Records: 2840 Sheridan Rd, Evanston, IL 60201. Degrees granted: Bachelors; Masters; Doctorate; CAS Professional Certificates. Attendance and degree information available by phone, fax, mail. Transcripts available by fax, mail.

North Central College, Registrar, 30 N Brainard St, PO Box 3063, Naperville, IL 60566-7063, 630-637-5252, 630-637-5255 8:30AM - 4:30PM. Enrollment: 2500. Records go back to 1880. Alumni records are maintained here. Degrees granted: Bachelors; Masters. Attendance and degree information available by phone, mail. Transcripts available by mail.

North Park College and Theological Seminary, Registrar, 3225 W Foster Ave, Chicago, IL 60625-4895, 773-244-5560, 773-244-5564 (Fax: 773-244-4954) www.northpark.edu. 8AM-4:30PM M,Th,F; 8AM-7PM T.W. Enrollment: 2100. Records go back to 1886. Alumni records maintained here; call 708-244-5754. Degrees granted: Bachelors; Masters. Certification: Teacher. Attendance and degree information available by phone, fax, mail. Transcripts available by fax, mail.

Northeastern Illinois University, Admissions and Records, 5500 N St Louis Ave, Chicago, IL 60625, www.neiu.edu. 773-583-4050 X3650, 773-583-4050 X3647 (Fax: 773-794-6246) 8:30AM-4:30PM. Enrollment: 10000. Records go back to 1962. Alumni Records: 5350 St Louis Ave, Chicago, IL 60625. Degrees granted: Bachelors; Masters. Attendance and degree information available by phone, fax, mail. Transcripts available by fax, mail.

Northern Baptist Theological Seminary, Registrar, 660 E Butterfield Rd, Lombard, IL 60148, 630-620-2105, 630-620-2100 (Fax: 630-620-2194) www.seminary.edu. 8:30AM - 4:30PM. Enrollment: 450. Alumni records are maintained here. Degrees granted: Masters; Doctorate Attendance, degree and transcript information available by written request only. Can only release transcripts to student.

Northern Illinois University, Office of Registration & Records, Altgeld Hall Rm 212, De Kalb, IL 60115, 815-753-0689, 815-753-0680 (Fax: 815-743-0149) www.niu.edu. 8AM-4:30PM. Enrollment: 22558. Records go back to 1899. Alumni records maintained here; call 815-753-1452. Degrees granted: Bachelors; Masters; Doctorate. Special programs- J D Law, 815-753-1067. Attendance and degree information available by phone, fax, mail. Transcripts available by fax, mail.

Northwestern Business College, Registrar, 4829 N Lipps Ave, Chicago, IL 60630, 773-777-4220 (Fax: 773-777-2861). 8AM-4PM. Enrollment: 990. Alumni records are maintained here. Degrees granted: Associate. Attendance and degree information available by fax, mail. Transcripts available by mail.

Northwestern Business College (Southwestern), Registrar, 8020 W 87th St, Hickory Hills, IL 60457, 708-430-0990 (Fax: 708-430-0995). 8AM-8PM. Records go back to 1988. Degrees granted: Associate. Attendance and degree information available by phone, mail. Transcripts available by fax, mail. Call for request form.

Northwestern University, Registrar, 633 Clark St, Evanston, IL 60208, 847-491-5234 (Fax: 847-491-8458) www.nwu.edu. 8:30AM-5PM. Enrollment: 17000. Records go back to 1882. Alumni Records: Alumni Affairs, 1800 Sheridan Rd, Evanston, IL 60208. Degrees granted: Bachelors; Masters; Doctorate. Attendance and degree information available by phone, fax, mail. Transcripts available by fax, mail.

Oakton Community College, Registrar, 1600 E Golf Rd, Des Plaines, IL 60016, www.oakton.edu. 847-635-1991 (Fax: 847-635-1706) 8:30AM-8PM M-Th, 8:30AM-5PM F, 9AM-Noon Sat Fall;8:30AM-8PM M-Th Summer. Records go back to 1970. Alumni records are maintained here. Degrees granted: Associate. Attendance and degree information available by phone, fax, mail. Transcripts available by fax, mail.

Olive-Harvey College, Registrar, 10001 S Woodlawn Ave, Chicago, IL 60628, 312-291-6342, 312-291-6349 (Fax: 312-291-6185). 8AM-7PM M-Th, 8AM-5PM F. Enrollment: 3306. Records go back to 1961. Alumni records are maintained here. Degrees granted: Associate. Attendance information available by phone, fax, mail. Degree information available by fax, mail. Transcripts available by written request only.

Olivet Nazarene University, Registrar, Kankakee, IL 60901, 815-939-5201, 815-939-5011 (Fax: 815-935-4992). 8AM-4:30PM. Enrollment: 2000. Records go back to 1907. Alumni records maintained here; call 815-939-5258. Degrees granted: Associate; Bachelors; Masters. Attendance and degree information available by phone, fax, mail. Transcripts available by mail.

Olney Central College, Registrar, 305 N West St, Olney, IL 62450, 618-395-7777 (Fax: 618-392-3293). 7:30AM-4:30PM Fall, 7:30AM-4PM Summer. Enrollment: 1500. Records go back to 1963. Alumni records are maintained here. Degrees granted: Associate; Vocational. Attendance and degree information available by phone, fax, mail. Transcripts available by fax, mail.

Parkland College, Registrar, 2400 W Bradley Ave, Champaign, IL 61821, www.parkland.cc.il.us. 217-353-2625 (Fax: 217-353-2640) 7:30AM-8PM M-Th; 7:30AM-5PM F; 9AM-Noon S. Enrollment: 9500. Records go back to 1966. Alumni records are maintained here. Degrees granted: Associate. Attendance and degree information available by phone, fax, mail. Transcripts available by fax, mail.

Prairie State College, Registrar, 202 S Halsted St, Chicago Heights, IL 60411, 708-709-3514, 708-709-3516 (Fax: 708-709-3951) www.prairie.cc.il.us. 8AM-4:30PM. Enrollment: 5000. Records go back to 1958. Alumni records maintained here; call 708-709-3734. Degrees granted: Associate. Special programs- Nursing, 708-709-3517; Dental Hygiene, 708-709-3515. Attendance and degree information available by phone, fax, mail. Transcripts available by fax, mail.

Principia College, Registrar, Elsah, IL 62028, 618-374-5100, 618-374-5106 (Fax: 618-374-5105) www.prin.edu. 8AM - 5PM. Enrollment: 540. Records go back to 1934. Alumni Records: 13202 Clayton Rd, St Louis, MO 63131-1099. Degrees granted: Bachelors. Attendance and degree information available by phone, fax, mail. Transcripts available by fax, mail.

Quincy College
(See Quincy University)

Quincy University, Registrar, 1800 College Ave, Quincy, IL 62301, 217-228-5280 8AM-5PM. www.quincy.edu. Enrollment: 1000. Records go back to 1860. Formerly Quincy College. Alumni records are maintained here. Degrees granted: Bachelors; Masters. Attendance and degree information available by phone, mail. Transcripts available by mail.

Ray College of Design
(See Illinois Institute of Art)

Rend Lake College, Registrar, 468 N Ken Gray Pkwy, Ina, IL 62846, 618-437-5321 (Fax: 618-437-5677) www.rlc.cc.il.us. 8AM-4:30PM M-Th; 8AM-4PM F. Enrollment: 8500. Records go back to 1956. Alumni records are maintained here. Degrees granted: Associate. School will not confirm attendance information. Degree information available by phone, fax, mail. Transcripts available by fax, mail.

Richard J. Daley College, Registrar, 7500 S PUlaski Rd, Chicago, IL 60652, 773-838-7600 (Fax: 773-838-7605). 8AM-7PM. Records go back to 1960. Alumni records are maintained here. Degrees granted: Associate. Attendance and degree information available by phone, fax, mail. Transcripts available by mail.

Richland Community College, Registrar, One College Park, Decatur, IL 62521, 217-875-7200 (Fax: 217-875-6965) www.richland.cc.il.us. 8AM-8PM M-Th; 8AM-5PM F. Enrollment: 4000. Records go back to 1972. Alumni records are maintained here. Degrees granted: Associate. Attendance and degree information available by phone, fax, mail. Transcripts available by mail.

Robert Morris College, Registrar, 180 N LaSalle St, Chicago, IL 60601, 312-836-4888 (Fax: 312-836-4853) www.rmcil.edu. 8:30AM-5PM. Enrollment: 3500. Records go back to 1950. Alumni records maintained here; call 312-836-5469. Degrees granted: Associate; Bachelors. Attendance and degree information available by phone, fax, mail. Transcripts available by fax, mail.

Rock Valley College, Registrar, 3301 N Mulford Rd, Rockford, IL 61114-5699, 815-654-4306, 815-654-4311 (Fax: 815-654-5568) 8AM-5PM. www.rvc.cc.il.us. Enrollment: 8910. Records go back to 1965. Alumni records maintained here; call 815-654-4277. Degrees granted: Associate. Attendance and degree information available by phone, fax, mail. Transcripts available by mail.

Rockford Business College, Registrar, 730 N Church St, Rockford, IL 61103, 815-965-8616 (Fax: 815-965-0360). 8AM-9PM. Enrollment: 350. Records go back to 1950's. Alumni records are maintained here. Degrees granted: Associate. Attendance, degree and transcript information available by fax, mail.

Rockford College, Registrar, 5050 E State St, Rockford, IL 61108, 815-226-4070, 815-226-4064 (Fax: 815-226-4119) 8AM-5PM. www.rockford.edu. Enrollment: 1500. Records go back to 1925. Alumni records maintained here; call 815-226-4080. Degrees granted: Bachelors; Masters. Special programs- Regents' College (London Campus), 815-226-3376. Attendance and degree information available by phone, fax, mail. Transcripts available by mail.

Roosevelt University, Registrar, 430 S Michigan Ave, Chicago, IL 60605, 312-341-3526, 312-341-3530 (Fax: 312-341-3660) 9AM-6PM M,T; 9AM-5PM W,Th; 9AM-5PM F. www.roosevelt.edu. Enrollment: 6000. Records go back to 1945. Alumni records maintained here; call 312-341-3624. Degrees granted: Bachelors; Masters; Doctorate. Special programs- Lawyers Assistance: Continuing Ed. Attendance and degree information available by phone, fax, mail. Transcripts available by fax, mail.

Rosary College
(See Dominican University)

Rosary College, Registrar, 7900 W Division St, River Forest, IL 60305, 708-366-2490 (Fax: 708-524-5037) 8AM-5PM. www.rosarycollege.edu. Enrollment: 851. Records go back to 1919. Degrees granted: Bachelors; Masters. Attendance and degree information available by phone, mail. Transcripts available by mail.

Rush University, Registrar, 1653 W Congress Pkwy, Chicago, IL 60612, 312-942-5681 (Fax: 312-942-2219) www.rush.edu. 8AM-5PM. Records go back to 1973. Alumni records maintained here; call 312-942-7165. Degrees granted: Bachelors; Masters; Doctorate; PhD. Attendance and degree information available by phone, fax, mail. Transcripts available by fax, mail.

Saint Mary of the Lake Seminary
(See University of Saint Mary of the Lake)

Sauk Valley Community College, Registrar, 173 Illinois Rte 2, Dixon, IL 61021, 815-288-5511 (Fax: 815-288-3190) 8AM-4:30PM. www.svcc.cc.il.us/. Enrollment: 3000. Records go back to 1965. Alumni records are maintained here. Degrees granted: Associate. Attendance and degree information available by phone, fax, mail. Transcripts available by mail.

School of the Art Institute of Chicago, Registrar, 37 S Wabash Ave, Chicago, IL 60603, 312-899-5117, 312-899-5118 (Fax: 312-263-0141) www.artic.edu. 8:30AM-4:30PM. Enrollment: 3000. Records go back to 1890. Alumni records maintained here; call 312-899-5217. Degrees granted: Bachelors; Masters; Post Graduate. Attendance and degree information available by phone, fax, mail. Transcripts available by fax, mail.

Seabury-Western Theological Seminary Registrar, 2122 Sheridan Rd, Evanston, IL 60201, www.swts.nwu.edu. 847-328-9300 (Fax: 847-328-9624) 8:30AM-5PM; 9AM-4PM Jun-Aug. Enrollment: 115. Records go back to 1931. Alumni records are maintained here. Degrees granted: Masters; Doctorate. Attendance and degree information available by phone, fax, mail. Transcripts available by mail.

Shawnee Community College, Registrar, Rural Rte 1 Box 53, Ullin, IL 62992-9725, 618-634-2242 (Fax: 618-634-9028) 8AM-4PM. www.shawnee.cc.il.us. Enrollment: 2233. Records go back to 1969. Alumni records are maintained here. Degrees granted: Associate. Attendance and degree information available by phone, fax, mail. Transcripts available by fax, mail.

Sherwood Conservatory of Music, Registrar, Box A500, Chicago, IL 60605, 312-427-6267 (Fax: 312-427-6677). Enrollment: 1000. Records go back to 1920 Attendance, degree and transcript information available by mail.

Shimer College, Registrar, PO Box A500, 438 N Sheridan Rd, Waukegan, IL 60079, 847-249-7183 (Fax: 847-249-7171) www.shimer.edu. 9AM-5PM. Enrollment: 125. Records go back to 1853. Alumni records maintained here; call 708-249-7191. Degrees granted: Bachelors. Special programs- Academic, 708-623-8400. Attendance and degree information available by phone, fax, mail. Transcripts available by mail.

South Suburban College of Cook County, Registrar, 15800 S State St, South Holland, IL 60473, 708-596-2000 X5814 (Fax: 708-225-5806) www.ssc.cc.il.us. 8AM-4:30PM. Enrollment: 8677. Records go back to 1986. Alumni records maintained here; call 708-596-2000 X2456. Degrees granted: Associate. Attendance, degree and transcript information available by fax, mail.

Southeastern Illinois College, Registrar, 3575 College Rd, Harrisburg, IL 62946, 618-252-6376, 618-252-5400 (Fax: 618-252-6376) 8AM-4:30PM. www.sic.cc.il.us. Enrollment: 3382. Records go back to 1960. Degrees granted: Associate. Special programs- Incarcerated Students: Vienna Corrections Center, 618-658-2211. Attendance and degree information available by phone, fax, mail. Transcripts available by fax, mail.

Southern Illinois University at Carbondale, Admissions & Records, Carbondale, IL 62901, 618-453-4381 (Fax: 618-453-3250) www.siu.edu/noar/. 8AM-4:30PM. Enrollment: 23000. Records go back to 1869. Alumni Records: Alumni Assoc., Stone Center 6809, Carbondale, IL 62901. Degrees granted: Associate; Bachelors; Masters; Doctorate; Juris. Doctorate. Special programs- Law, 618-536-7711: Medicine, 217-782-3625. Attendance and degree information available by phone, fax, mail. Transcripts available by fax, mail. Transcripts are only released in response to requests if student authorization is contained including student's signature.

Southern Illinois University at Edwardsville, Admissions & Records, Campus Box 1047, Edwardsville, IL 62026, 618-692-2080 (Fax: 618-692-2081) www.siue.edu. 8AM-8PM M-Th, 8AM-4:30PM F, 8AM-2PM Sat. Enrollment: 11047. Records go back to 1957. Alumni records are maintained here. Degrees granted: Bachelors; Masters. Attendance and degree information available by phone, fax, mail. Transcripts available by fax, mail.

Spertus Institute of Jewish Studies, Registrar, 618 S Michigan Ave, Chicago, IL 60605, 312-922-9012, 312-322-1769 (Fax: 312-922-6406). 9AM - 5PM. Enrollment: 300. Records go back to 1924. Formerly **Spertus College of Judaica**. Degrees granted: Masters; Doctorate. Attendance and degree information available by phone, fax, mail. Transcripts available by fax, mail.

Spoon River College, Records Dept, 23235 N Co 22, Canton, IL 61520, 309-647-4645, 309-649-6205 (Fax: 309-649-6235). 8AM-5PM. Enrollment: 2000. Records go back to 1959. Alumni records are maintained here. Degrees granted: Associate. Attendance and degree information available by phone, fax, mail. Transcripts available by fax, mail.

Springfield College in Illinois, Registrar, 1500 N Fifth St, Springfield, IL 62702, 217-525-1420 X238 (Fax: 217-525-1497). 8AM-4:30PM Fall; 7:30AM-4PM M-Th Summer. Records go back to 1929. Alumni records maintained here; call 217-525-1420 X228. Degrees granted: Associate. Attendance, degree and transcript information available by mail.

St. Augustine College, Registrar, 1333 W Argyle St, Chicago, IL 60640, 312-878-8756 (Fax: 312-878-9032) www.staugustine.edu. 9AM-6:30PM. Enrollment: 1450. Records go back to 1981. Degrees granted: Associate. Attendance and degree information available by phone, fax, mail. Transcripts available by fax, mail.

St. Francis College of Nursing
(See University of St. Francis)

St. Francis Medical Center College of Nursing, Registrar, 511 NE Greenleaf St, Peoria, IL www.iaonline.com/sfmc/home 61603, 309-655-2596, 309-655-2245 (Fax: 309-655-3648) 7AM - 3:30PM. Enrollment: 150. Records go back to 1956. School of Nursing records from 1956; College of Nursing records from 1986. Alumni records maintained here; call 309-655-4125. Degrees granted: Bachelors. Attendance and degree information available by phone, mail. Transcripts available by mail.

St. Xavier University, Office of the Registrar, 3700 W 103rd St, Chicago, IL 60655, 773-298-3501, 773-298-3502 (Fax: 773-298-3508) www.sxu.edu. 8:30AM-7PM M-F; 8AM-2PM Sat. Enrollment: 4400. Records go back to 1925. Alumni records maintained here; call 773-298-3317. Degrees granted: Bachelors; Masters. Special programs- Field Based Masters of Education, 312-298-3155. Attendance and degree information available by phone, mail. Transcripts available by mail.

State Community College of East St. Louis, Registrar, 601 James R Thompson Blvd, East St Louis, IL 62201, 618-583-2500 (Fax: 618-583-2661). 8:30AM - 5PM. Enrollment: 1100. Records go back to 1969. Alumni records maintained here; call 618-583-2575. Degrees granted: Associate Attendance, degree and transcript information available by fax, mail.

Taylor Business Institute, Registrar, 200 N Michigan Ave Ste 301, Chicago, IL 60601-5908, 312-236-6400 X33 (Fax: 312-658-0867). 8:30AM-6PM. Records go back to 1975. Degrees granted: Associate. Attendance information available by phone, fax, mail. Degree and transcript information available by fax, mail.

Telshe Yeshiva-Chicago, Registrar, 3535 W Foster Ave, Chicago, IL 60625, 773-463-7738 (Fax: 773-463-2849) 8AM-5PM. Enrollment: 70. Records go back to 1960. Degrees granted: Masters. Attendance, degree and transcript information available by mail.

Trinity Christian College, Registrar, 6601 W College Dr, Palos Heights, IL 60463, 708-239-4758, 708-239-4759 (Fax: 708-239-3986) www.trnty.edu. 8AM-4:30PM. Enrollment: 600. Records go back to 1960. Alumni records are maintained here. Degrees granted: Bachelors. Attendance and degree information available by phone, fax, mail. Transcripts available by fax, mail.

Trinity Evangelical Divinity School, Director of Records, 2065 Half Day Rd, Deerfield, IL 60015, 847-317-8050 (Fax: 847-317-8097) www.tiv.edu. 8:30AM-4:30PM. Enrollment: 2049. Records go back to 1897. Alumni records are maintained here. Degrees granted: Masters; Doctorate. Attendance, degree and transcript information available by mail. Phone number required.

Trinity International University (College of Arts & Sciences), Records Office, 2065 Half Day Rd, Deerfield, IL 60015, 847-317-7050 (Fax: 847-317-7081) www.tiu.edu. 9AM-4PM. Enrollment: 800. Records go back to 1890. Alumni records maintained here; call 847-317-8145. Degrees granted: Bachelors. Special programs- Division of Open Studies, 847-317-6550. Attendance and degree information available by phone, fax, mail. Transcripts available by fax, mail. Prefer to use their form.

Triton College, Registrar, 2000 Fifth Ave, River Grove, IL 60171, 708-456-0300 (Ext. 3130) (Fax: 708-583-3180) 8:30AM-7:30PM M-Th, 8:30AM-4PM F. Enrollment: 20000. www.triton.cc.il.us. Records go back to 1969. Alumni records maintained here; call 708-456-0300 X3730. Degrees granted: Associate. Attendance and degree information available by phone, fax, mail. Transcripts available by mail.

University of Chicago, Registrar, 5801 S Ellis Ave, Chicago, IL 60637, 773-702-7880, 773-702-7879 (Fax: 773-702-3562) 9AM-4PM. www.regis.uchicago.edu. Enrollment: 11226. Records go back to 1892. Alumni records maintained here; call 773-702-2150. Degrees granted: Bachelors; Masters; Doctorate. Attendance and degree information available by phone, fax, mail. Transcripts available by fax, mail.

University of Health Sciences-Chicago Medical
(See Herman M. Finch University of Health Sciences)

University of Illinois at Chicago, Registrar, PO Box 5220, Chicago, IL 60680, 312-996-4350 www.uic.edu. 8:30AM-4:45PM. Records go back to 1936. Alumni records are maintained here. Degrees granted: Bachelors; Masters; Doctorate; MD,DDS,PharmD. Attendance and degree information available by phone, mail. Transcripts available by mail.

University of Illinois at Springfield, Registrar, PO Box 19243, Springfield, IL 62794-9243, 217-786-6709 (Fax: 217-786-6620) www.uis.edu. 8:30AM - 5PM. Enrollment: 4700. Records go back to 1970. Formerly **Sangamon State University**. Alumni records maintained here; call 217-786-7395. Degrees granted: Bachelors; Masters. Attendance and degree information available by phone, fax, mail. Transcripts available by fax, mail.

University of Illinois at Urbana—Champaign, Transcript Dept., Rm 10 Henry Admin. Bldg, 506 S Wright St, Urbana, IL 61801, 217-333-0210 (Fax: 217-333-3100) www.uiuc.edu/providers/oar/trnscrpt 8:30AM-5PM. Enrollment: 36000. Records go back to 1867. Alumni Records: 227 Illini Union, 1401 W Green St, Urbana, IL 61801. Degrees granted: Bachelors; Masters; Doctorate. Attendance information available by mail. Degree information available by phone, fax, mail. Transcripts available by fax, mail.

University of St. Francis, Registrar, 500 N Wilcox St, Joliet, IL 60435, 815-740-3391 (Fax: 815-740-4285) www.stfrancis.edu. 8AM-4:30PM. Enrollment: 4300. Records go back to 1936. Formerly **College of St. Francis**. Alumni records are maintained. Degrees granted: Bachelors; Masters. Attendance and degree information available by phone, fax, mail. Transcripts available by fax, mail.

University of St. Mary of the Lake Mundelein Seminary, Registrar, 1000 E Maple Ave, Mundelein, IL 60060, 847-566-6401 (Fax: 847-566-7330) 8AM-4PM. www.vocations.org. Enrollment: 180. Records go back to 1929. Alumni records are maintained here. Degrees granted: Bachelors; Masters; Doctorate; Licentiate of Sacred Theology. Attendance and degree information available by mail. Transcripts available by fax, mail.

VanderCook College of Music, Registrar, 3140 S Federal St, Chicago, IL 60616, 312-225-6288 (Fax: 312-225-5211) 9AM-5PM. www.mcs.com/~vcmusic. Enrollment: 810. Records go back to 1928. Alumni records are maintained here. Degrees granted: Bachelors; Masters. Special programs- Masters with Certification. Attendance and degree information available by phone, fax, mail. Transcripts available by mail.

Wabash Valley College, Admissions and Records, 2200 College Dr, Mount Carmel, IL 62863, 618-262-8641 (Fax: 618-262-8641) www.iecc.cc.il.us. 8AM-5PM. Enrollment: 1200. Records go back to 1967. Degrees granted: Associate. Attendance and degree information available by phone, fax, mail. Transcripts available by fax, mail.

Waubonsee Community College, Registrar, Illinois Rte 47 at Harter Rd, Sugar Grove, IL 60554-9799, 630-466-7900 X2370, 630-466-4811 (Fax: 630-466-4964) www.wcc.cc.il.us. 8AM-8PM M-Th; 8AM-4PM F. Enrollment: 8022. Records go back to 1967. Alumni records are maintained here. Degrees granted: Associate. Attendance and degree information available by phone, fax, mail. Transcripts available by fax, mail. Request from student only.

West Suburban College of Nursing, Registrar, Erie at Austin Blvd, Oak Park, IL 60302, 708-763-6530 (Fax: 708-763-1531) www.curf.edu. 8:30AM - 5PM. Enrollment: 240. Records go back to 1915. Alumni records are maintained here. Degrees granted: Bachelors. Special programs- Nursing. Attendance and degree information available by phone, mail. Transcripts available by mail.

Western Illinois University, Office of Registrar, 1 University Circle, Macomb, IL 61455-1390, 309-298-1891 (Fax: 309-298-2787) www.wiu.edu. 8AM - 4:30PM. Enrollment: 12700. Records go back to 1899. Alumni records maintained here; call 309-298-1914. Degrees granted: Bachelors; Masters; Education Specialist. Attendance and degree information available by phone, fax, mail. Transcripts available by fax, mail.

Wheaton College, Registrar, 501 E College Ave, Wheaton, IL 60187, 630-752-5045, 630-752-5046 (Fax: 630-752-5245) 9AM-4:30PM. www.wheaton.edu. Enrollment: 2600. Records go back to 1860. Alumni records maintained here; call 630-752-5047. Degrees granted: Bachelors; Masters; Doctorate. Attendance and degree information available by phone, fax, mail. Transcripts available by fax, mail.

Wilbur Wright College, Registrar, 4300 N Narragansett Ave, Chicago, IL 60634, 773-481-8060 (Fax: 773-481-8053) www.ccc.edu. 9AM-8PM M-Th; 9AM-4PM F. Enrollment: 7500. Records go back to 1936. Alumni records are maintained here. Degrees granted: Associate. Attendance and degree information available by phone, fax, mail. Transcripts available by fax, mail.

William Rainey Harper College, Registrar, 1200 W Algonquin Rd, Palatine, IL 60067-7398, 847-925-6501, 847-925-6600 (Fax: 847-925-6032) www.harper.cc.il.us. 8AM-8PM M-Th, 8AM-4:30PM F, 9AM-Noon Sat. Enrollment: 16212. Records go back to 1969. Alumni records maintained here; call 847-925-6490. Degrees granted: Associate. Attendance and degree information available by phone, fax, mail. Transcripts available by fax, mail.

Wright College, Records Office, 4300 North Narragansett, Chicago, IL 60634, 773-777-7900 (Fax: 773-481-8053) Enrollment: 7000. Records go back to 1936. Alumni records are maintained here. Degrees granted: Associate. Special programs- 2 Year Arts & Science Programs. Attendance and degree information available by fax, mail. Transcripts available by fax, mail.

Indiana

Ancilla College, Registrar, PO Box 1, Donaldson, IN 46513, 219-936-8898 (Fax: 219-935-1773). 8AM-4:30PM. Enrollment: 610. Records go back to 1937. Alumni records are maintained here. Degrees granted: Associate. Attendance and degree information available by phone, fax, mail. Transcripts available by fax, mail. Student's written request & signature required.

Anderson University, Registrar, 1100 E Fifth St, Anderson, IN 46012-3462, 765-641-4160, 765-641-4169 (Fax: 765-641-3015) 8AM-Noon, 1-4:30PM. www.anderson.edu. Enrollment: 2200. Records go back to 1917. Alumni records maintained here; call 765-641-4100. Degrees granted: Associate; Bachelors; Masters; Doctorate. Attendance and degree information available by phone, fax, mail. Transcripts available by mail.

Associated Mennonite Biblical Seminary, Registrar, 3003 Benham Ave, Elkhart, IN 46517-1999, 219-295-3726, 219-296-6213 (Fax: 219-295-0092) www.ambs.edu. 8AM-4PM. Enrollment: 217. Records go back to 1958. Degrees granted: Masters. Special programs- Peace Studies, 219-295-3726. Attendance, degree and transcript information available by phone, fax, mail.

Ball State University, Registrar, 2000 University Ave, Muncie, IN 47306, 317-285-1722 (Fax: 317-285-8765) www.bsu.edu. 8AM-5PM. Enrollment: 19500. Records go back to 1919. Alumni records maintained here; call 317-285-1413. Degrees granted: Associate; Bachelors; Masters; Doctorate. Attendance and degree information available by phone, mail. Transcripts available by fax, mail.

Baptist Bible College of Indiana, Registrar, N Shortridge Rd, Indianapolis, IN 46219, 317-352-8736, 800-273-2224 (Fax: 317-352-9145) www.bbci.edu. 8AM-5PM. Enrollment: 183. Records go back to 1981. Alumni records are maintained here. Degrees granted: Associate; Bachelors. Special programs- Religion. Attendance and degree information available by phone, mail. Transcripts available by mail.

Bethany Theological Seminary, Coordinator of Academic Services, 615 National Road W, Richmond, IN 47374-4019, 317-983-1816 (Fax: 317-983-1840). 8AM-5PM. Enrollment: 80. Records go back to 1905. Alumni records maintained here; call 317-983-1806. Degrees granted: Masters. Certification: Theological Studies. Special programs- Bethany Academy for Ministry Training, 317-983-1820. Attendance and degree information available by phone, fax, mail. Transcripts available by fax, mail.

Bethel College, Registrar, 1001 W McKinley Ave, Mishawaka, IN 46545, 219-257-3302 (Fax: 219-257-3277). 8AM - 5PM. Enrollment: 1526. Records go back to 1947. Alumni records maintained here; call 219-257-3310. Degrees granted: Associate; Bachelors; Masters. Attendance and degree information available by phone, fax, mail. Transcripts available by written request only.

Butler University, Registrar, 4600 Sunset Ave, Indianapolis, IN 46208, 317-940-9203 (Fax: 317-940-6539) www.butler.edu. 8:30AM-5PM. Enrollment: 4457. Records go back to 1900. Alumni records maintained here; call 317-940-9900. Degrees granted: Bachelors; Masters. Attendance and degree information available by phone, mail. Transcripts available by mail with student permission.

Calumet College of St. Joseph, Registrar's Office, 2400 New York Ave, Whiting, IN 46394, 219-473-4211 (Fax: 219-473-4259) www.ccsj.edu. 9AM - 5PM. Enrollment: 1100. Records go back to 1951. Alumni records maintained here; call 219-473-4325. Degrees granted: Associate; Bachelors. Special programs- Railroad Program. Attendance and degree information available by phone, fax, mail. Transcripts available by fax, mail.

CareerCom Junior College
(See Franklin College)

Christian Theological Seminary, Registrar, 1000 W 42nd St, Indianapolis, IN 46208-3301, 317-931-2382, 317-924-1331 (Fax: 317-923-1961) www.cts.edu. 8AM-4:30PM. Enrollment: 376. Records go back to 1958. Alumni records maintained here; call 317-931-2310. Degrees granted: Masters; Doctorate. Special programs- Advanced Studies, 317-931-2440. Attendance and degree information available by phone, fax, mail. Transcripts available by fax, mail.

Columbus IVY Tech, Records, 4475 Central Ave, Columbus, IN 47203, 812-372-9925 X130, 812-372-9925 X170 (Fax: 812-372-0311). Enrollment: 1500. Records go back to 1967. Alumni records are maintained. Degrees granted: Associate; Technical. Attendance and degree information available by phone, fax, mail. Transcripts available by fax, mail.

Commonwealth Business College, Registrar, 4200 W 81st Ave, Merrillville, IN 46410, 219-769-3321 (Fax: 219-738-1076) 8AM-5PM. Enrollment: 200. Records go back to 1976. Degrees granted: Associate. Attendance and degree information available by phone, fax, mail. Transcripts available by fax, mail.

Commonwealth Business College (LaPorte), Registrar, 325 E US Highway 20, Michigan City, IN 46360-7362, 219-877-3100, 800-519-2416 (Fax: 219-877-3110) 7:30AM-9:30PM M,T,Th; 8AM-5PM W,F. Enrollment: 130. Records go back to 1890. Alumni records are maintained here. Degrees granted: Associate. Special programs- Medical: Computer: Paralegal: Business. Attendance, degree and transcript information available by fax, mail.

Concordia Theological Seminary, Registrar, 6600 N Clinton St, Fort Wayne, IN 46825-4996, 219-452-2153, 219-452-2154 (Fax: 219-452-2121) www.ctsfw.edu. 8AM-4:30PM. Enrollment: 350. Records go back to 1900. Alumni records maintained here; call 219-452-2150. Degrees granted: Masters; Doctorate; First Professional, M.Div. Special programs- Theology, 219-452-2153. Attendance and degree information available by phone, fax, mail. Transcripts available by fax, mail.

Davenport College of Business (Branch), Registrar, 7121 Grape Rd, **Granger**, IN 46530, 219-277-8447, 800-277-8477 (Fax: 219-272-2967) 8AM-5PM; evening hours vary. www.davenport.edu. Enrollment: 400. Records go back to 1985. Alumni records are maintained here. Degrees granted: Associate. Attendance and degree information available by phone, fax, mail. Transcripts available by fax, mail.

Davenport College of Business (Branch), Registrar, 8200 Georgia St, **Merrillville**, IN 46410, www.davenport.edu 219-769-5556, 800-748-7880 (Fax: 219-756-8911) 9AM-5PM M-Th, 8AM-4PM F. Enrollment: 550. Records go back to 1987. Degrees granted: Associate. Attendance information available by phone, fax, mail. Degree information available by phone, fax, mail. Transcripts available by fax, mail.

DePauw University, Registrar, Greencastle, IN 46135, 765-658-4000, 765-658-4147 (Fax: 765-658-4139) www.depauw.edu. 8AM-4:30PM. Enrollment: 2300. Records go back to 1837. Alumni records maintained here; call 765-658-4208. Degrees granted: Bachelors. Special programs- Honor Scholar, 765-658-4684: Management Fellows, 765-658-4024: Media Fellows, 765-658-4467: Science Research Fellows, 765-658-4777. Attendance and degree information available by phone, fax, mail. Transcripts available by fax, mail.

Earlham College, Registrar, 801 National Rd W, Drawer 34, Richmond, IN 47374-4095, 765-983-1515 (Fax: 765-983-1374) 8AM-4PM. www.EARLHAM.EDU/. Enrollment: 1017. Records go back to 1847. Alumni Records: Drawer 193, Richmond, IN 47374-4095 (Fax: 765-983-1300). Degrees granted: Bachelors; Masters. Attendance and degree information available by phone, fax, mail. Transcripts available by fax, mail.

Fort Wayne Bible College
(See Taylor University-Fort Wayne)

Franklin College of Indiana, Registrar, 501 E Monroe St, Franklin, IN 46131, 317-738-8018 (Fax: 317-736-6030) 8AM-5PM M-Th; 8AM - 4PM F. Enrollment: 917. www.franklincoll.edu/recweb/. Records go back to 1844. Alumni records maintained here; call 317-738-8050. Degrees granted: Bachelors. Special programs- Journalism: Accounting: Business. Attendance and degree information available by phone, mail. Transcripts available by mail.

Goshen College, Registrar, 1700 S Main St, Goshen, IN 46526, 219-535-7517 (Fax: 219-535-7660) www.goshen.edu. 8AM-5PM. Enrollment: 1000. Records go back to 1894. Alumni records maintained here; call 219-535-7566. Degrees granted: Bachelors. Attendance and degree information available by phone, fax, mail. Transcripts available by fax, mail.

Grace College, Registrar, 200 Seminary Dr, Winona Lake, IN 46590, 219-372-5110, 219-372-5111 (Fax: 219-372-5114) www.grace.edu. 8AM-4:30PM. Enrollment: 641. Records go back to 1948. Alumni records are maintained here also. Call 219-372-5289. Degrees granted: Associate; Bachelors; Masters. Attendance and degree information available by phone, fax. Transcripts available by mail.

Grace Theological Seminary, Registrar, 200 Seminary Dr, Winona Lake, IN 46590, 219-372-5111, 219-372-5112 (Fax: 219-372-5114) www.grace.edu. 8AM - 4:30PM. Enrollment: 79. Records go back to 1937. Alumni records maintained here; call 219-372-5289. Degrees granted: Masters; Doctorate. Attendance and degree information available by phone, fax. Transcripts available by mail.

Hanover College, Registrar, PO Box 108, Hanover, IN 47243-0108, 812-866-7051, 812-866-7052 (Fax: 812-866-7054) www.hanover.edu. 8AM-5PM. Enrollment: 1093. Records go back to 1827. Alumni records maintained here; call 812-866-7013. Degrees granted: Bachelors. Attendance and degree information available by phone, fax, mail. Transcripts available by fax, mail.

Holy Cross College, Registrar, Box 308, Notre Dame, IN 46556, 219-239-8400, 219-239-8401 (Fax: 219-233-7427). 8AM-5PM. Enrollment: 507. Records go back to 1966. Alumni records are maintained here. Degrees granted: Associate. Special programs- Call 219-239-8400. Attendance and degree information available by phone, fax, mail. Transcripts available by fax, mail.

Huntington College, Registrar, 2303 College Ave, Huntington, IN 46750, 219-356-6000 (Fax: 219-356-9448) www.huntcol.edu. 8AM-5PM. Enrollment: 700. Records go back to 1897. Alumni records are maintained here. Degrees granted: Associate; Bachelors; Masters. Attendance and degree information available by phone, fax, mail. Transcripts available by fax, mail.

ITT Technical Institute, Registrar, 4919 Coldwater Rd, **Fort Wayne**, IN 46825-5532, 219-484-4107 X209, 800-866-4488 (Fax: 219-484-0860). 8AM-5PM. Enrollment: 700. Records go back to 1968. Degrees granted: Associate; Bachelors. Attendance and degree information available by phone, fax, mail. Transcripts available by mail.

ITT Technical Institute, Registrar, 9511 Angola Ct, **Indianapolis**, IN 46268-1119, 317-875-8640 X223, 800-937-4488 (Fax: 317-875-8641). 8AM-5PM. Enrollment: 900. Records go back to 1968. Degrees granted: Associate. Attendance and degree information available by phone, fax, mail. Transcripts available by fax, mail.

ITT Technical Institute, Registrar, 10999 Stahl Rd, **Newburgh**, IN 47630, 812-858-1600 (Fax: 812-858-0646). 8AM-10PM. Enrollment: 314. Records go back to 1965. Alumni Records: 5975 Castle Creek Pkwy N Dr, PO Box 50466, Indianapolis, IN 46250-0466. Degrees granted: Associate; Bachelors. Attendance and degree information available by phone, fax, mail. Transcripts available by phone, fax, mail.

Indian Vocational Technical College
(See IVY Tech State College)

Indiana Business College (Branch), Registrar, 140 E 53rd St, **Anderson**, IN 46013, www.indianabusinesscollege.com. 765-644-7514 (Fax: 765-644-5724) 7:30AM-5PM. Enrollment: 200. Records go back to 1902. Degrees granted: Associate. Special programs- Business: Accounting: Secretarial: Medical Records. Attendance information available by mail. Degree information available by phone, fax, mail. Transcripts available by fax, mail.

Indiana Business College (Branch), Registrar, 2222 Positard Dr, PO Box 1906, **Columbus**, IN 47203, 812-379-9000 www.indianabusinesscollege.com (Fax: 812-375-0414) 7:30AM-9PM M-Th; 7:30AM-4:30PM Fri. Enrollment: 150. Records go back to 1985. Degrees granted: Associate. Attendance and degree information available by phone, fax, mail. Transcripts available by mail.

Indiana Business College (Branch), Registrar, 4601 Theater Dr, **Evansville**, IN 47715, 812-476-6000 (Fax: 812-471-8576). 7:30AM - 7:30PM. Enrollment: 250. Records go back to 1993. Degrees granted: Associate; Medical Assisting, Medical Records. Special programs- Business: Medical Assisting: Medical Records. Attendance and degree information available by phone, fax, mail. Transcripts available by mail.

Indiana Business College (Branch), Registrar, 5460 Victory Dr Ste 100, **Indianapolis**, IN 46203, 317-783-5100, 317-783-5210 (Fax: 317-783-4898) 8AM-6PM. www.indianabusinesscollege.com. Enrollment: 200. Records go back to 1993. Alumni records are maintained here. Degrees granted: Associate; Medical Assisting, Medical Records, Medical Transcription. Special programs- Call 317-783-5100. Attendance, degree and transcript information available by fax, mail.

Indiana Business College, Registrar, 802 N Meridian St, **Indianapolis**, IN 46204, 317-264-5656, 800-999-9229 (Fax: 317-634-0471) www.indianabusinesscollege.com. 7:30AM -7:30PM. Enrollment: 600. Records go back to 1920. Degrees granted: Associate. Attendance and degree information available by phone, fax, mail. Transcripts available by written request only.

Indiana Business College (Branch), Registrar, 2 Executive Dr, **Lafayette**, IN 47905, 765-447-9550, 800-999-9229 (Fax: 765-447-0868) www.indianabusinesscollege. 8AM-10PM. Enrollment: 105. Records go back to 1907. Degrees granted: Associate. Special programs- Fashion: Travel: Hotel: Accounting: Business Administration: Secretarial: Medical Programs. Attendance and transcript information available by fax, mail. Degree information available by phone, fax, mail.

Indiana Business College (Branch), Registrar, 830 N Miller Ave, **Marion**, IN 46952, 765-662-7497, 800-999-9229 (Fax: 765-651-9421). 8AM-5PM. Enrollment: 188. Records go back to 1902. Degrees granted: Associate. Special programs- Call 765-662-7497. Attendance, degree and transcript information available by fax, mail.

Indiana Business College (Branch), Registrar, 1809 N Walnut St, **Muncie**, IN 47303, 765-288-8681, 765-288-8780 (Fax: 765-288-8797) 8AM-5PM. Enrollment: 250. www.indianabusinesscollege.com Records go back to 1902. Degrees granted: Associate. Attendance, degree and transcript information available by mail.

Indiana Business College (Branch), Registrar, 3175 S Third Pl, **Terre Haute**, IN 47802, www.indianabusinesscollege.com. 812-232-4458 (Fax: 812-234-2361) 7:30AM-8PM M-Th; 7:30AM-5PM. Enrollment: 282. Records go back to 1981. Degrees granted: Associate. Attendance and degree information available by phone, fax, mail. Transcripts available by fax, mail.

Indiana Business College (Branch), Registrar, 1431 Willow St, **Vincennes**, IN 47591, 812-882-2550, 800-999-9229 (Fax: 812-882-2270). 8AM-4PM. Enrollment: 85. Records go back to 1922. Degrees granted: Associate. Attendance, degree and transcript information available by phone, fax, mail.

Indiana Central University
(See University of Indianapolis)

Indiana Institute of Technology, Registrar, 1600 E Washington Blvd, Fort Wayne, IN 46803, 219-422-5561, 800-937-2448 (Fax: 219-422-7696) 8:30AM-5PM. www.INDTCH.EDU. Enrollment: 1400. Records go back to 1930. Degrees granted: Associate; Bachelors. Attendance and degree information available by phone, fax, mail. Transcripts available by fax, mail. Fax request for transcript to be followed by written request.

Indiana State University, Registrar, 200 N 7th St, Terre Haute, IN 47809, 812-237-2020 (Fax: 812-237-8039) www.isu.indstate.edu. 8AM - 4:30PM. Enrollment: 10000. Records go back to 1865. Alumni records maintained here; call 812-237-3707. Degrees granted: Bachelors; Masters. Attendance and degree information available by phone, fax, mail. Transcripts available by fax, mail.

Indiana University East, Student Records, 116 Whitewater Hall, Richmond, IN 47374, 765-973-8270, 800-959-EAST (Fax: 765-973-8288) www.iue.indiana.edu. 8AM-7PM M-Th; 8AM-5PM F. Enrollment: 2400. Records go back to 1969. Alumni records are maintained here. Degrees granted: Associate; Bachelors. Attendance and degree information available by phone, fax, mail. Transcripts available by fax, mail.

Indiana University Northwest, Registrar, 3400 Broadway, Gary, IN 46408-1197, 219-980-6815 (Fax: 219-981-4200) 8AM-6PM M,Th; 8AM-5PM TWF. Enrollment: 5300. www.indiana.edu/~iues/reghp/nw/northwesth p.htm/. Records go back to 1966. Alumni records maintained here. Call 219-980-6768. Degrees granted: Associate; Bachelors; Masters; PBC. Attendance and degree information available by phone, fax, mail. Transcripts available by fax, mail.

Indiana University Southeast, LB100, Registrar, 4201 Grant Line Rd, New Albany, IN 47150, 812-941-2240, 812-941-2454 (Fax: 812-941-2493) www.ius.indiana.edu. 8AM-5PM. Enrollment: 5400. Records go back to 1941. Alumni records are maintained here. Degrees granted: Associate; Bachelors; Masters; Doctorate. Attendance and degree information available by phone, mail. Transcripts available by mail.

Indiana University at Bloomington, Registrar, Franklin Hall Room 100, Bloomington, IN 47405, 812-855-0121 (Fax: 812-855-3311) www.indiana.edu. 9AM-4PM. Enrollment: 32300. Records go back to 1820. Alumni Records: Alumni Assoc., Indiana University, Fountain Square Ste 219, Bloomington, IN 47404. Degrees granted: Bachelors; Masters; Doctorate. Attendance and degree information available by phone, fax, mail. Transcripts available by fax, mail.

Indiana University at Kokomo, Registrar, PO Box 9003, Kokomo, IN 46904-9003, 765-455-9514 (Fax: 765-455-9475) www.iuk.edu. 8AM-5PM. Enrollment: 3065. Records go back to 1965. Alumni records maintained here; call 765-455-9411. Degrees granted: Bachelors; Masters. Attendance and degree information available by phone, fax, mail. Transcripts available by mail.

Indiana University at South Bend, Registrar, 1700 Mishawaka Ave, Rm 165, PO Box 7111, South Bend, IN 46634, 219-237-4451, 219-237-4532 (Fax: 219-237-4834) www.iusb.edu. 8AM-5PM M,Th,F; 8AM-6PM T,W. Enrollment: 8000. Records go back to 1965. Alumni records maintained here; call 219-237-4381. Degrees granted: Bachelors; Masters. Attendance and degree information available by phone, fax, mail. Transcripts available by fax, mail.

Indiana University - Purdue University at Fort Wayne, Registrar, 2101 Coliseum Blvd E, Fort Wayne, IN 46805, 219-481-6815, 219-481-6123 (Fax: 219-481-6880) www.ipfw.edu. 8AM-5PM. Enrollment: 10000. Records go back to 1960. Alumni records are maintained here. Degrees granted: Associate; Bachelors; Masters. Attendance and degree information available by phone, fax, mail. Transcripts available by fax, mail.

Indiana University - Purdue University at Indianapolis, Registrar, 425 University Blvd, Indianapolis, IN 46202, 317-274-1501 (Fax: 317-278-2240) www.iupui.edu. 8AM-7PM M-Th, 8AM-5PM. Enrollment: 27000. Records go back to 1965. Alumni records maintained here; call 317-274-8828. Degrees granted: Associate; Bachelors; Masters; Doctorate. Attendance information available by phone, fax, mail. Degree information available by phone, mail. Transcripts available by fax, mail.

Indiana Wesleyan University, Registrar, 4201 S Washington St, Marion, IN 46953, 765-677-2131, 800-332-6901 (Fax: 765-677-2809) www.indwes.edu. 8AM-5PM. Enrollment: 6000. Records go back to 1920. Alumni records maintained here; call 765-677-2110. Degrees granted: Associate; Bachelors; Masters. Attendance and degree information available by phone, fax, mail. Transcripts available by phone, fax, mail.

International Business College, Registrar, 3811 Illinois Rd, **Fort Wayne**, IN 46804, 219-459-4500, 219-459-4550 (Fax: 219-436-1896) 8:30AM-5PM. Enrollment: 500. Records go back to 1918. Degrees granted: Associate; Bachelors. Attendance and degree information available by phone, fax, mail. Transcripts available by mail.

International Business College, Registrar, 7205 Shadeland Station, **Indianapolis**, IN 46256, 317-841-6400, 800-589-6500 (Fax: 317-841-6419). 8AM-4:30PM. Enrollment: 220. Records go back to 1984. Degrees granted: Associate. Special programs- Call 317-841-6400. Attendance and degree information available by phone, fax, mail. Transcripts available by fax, mail.

Ivy Tech State College, Registrar, One W 26th St, PO Box 1763, **Indianapolis**, IN 46206-1763, 317-921-4745 (Fax: 317-921-4753). 8AM - 6PM M-Th, 9AM - 5PM F. Enrollment: 6000. Records go back to 1968. Alumni records maintained here; call 317-921-4882. Degrees granted: Associate. Attendance and degree information available by phone, fax, mail. Transcripts available by fax, mail.

Ivy Tech State College, Registrar, 8204 Hwy 311 W, **Sellersburg**, IN 47172, 812-246-3301 X4139 (Fax: 812-246-9905) www.ivy.tec.in.us. 9AM-6PM M-Th; 8AM-5PM F. Enrollment: 1800. Records go back to 1968. Alumni records maintained here; call 812-246-3301 X4129. Degrees granted: Associate. Certification: Technical Certificate. Attendance and transcript information available by mail. Degree information available by phone, fax, mail.

Ivy Tech State College — Columbus/Bloomington Tech. Inst., Registrar, 4475 Central Ave, Columbus, IN 47203, 812-372-9925 X130, 800-922-4838 (Fax: 812-372-0311). 8AM - 6PM M-Th, 8AM - 5PM F. Enrollment: 1600. Records go back to 1968. Alumni records are maintained. Degrees granted: Associate. Certification: Technical. Attendance and degree information available by phone, fax, mail. Transcripts available by fax, mail.

Ivy Tech State College — Eastcentral Technical Institute, Registrar, 4301 S Cowan Rd, PO Box 3100, Muncie, IN 47307, 765-289-2291, 800-589-8324 (Fax: 765-289-2291 X502) www.ivy.tech.inus. 8AM-5PM. Enrollment: 2200. Records go back to 1969. Alumni records maintained here; call 765-289-2291 X317. Degrees granted: Associate. Certification: Technical. Attendance and transcript information available by fax, mail. Degree information available by phone, fax, mail. Must have release form for transcript.

Ivy Tech State College — Kokomo Technical Institute, Registrar, PO Box 1373, Kokomo, IN 46903-1373, 765-459-0561 www.ivy.tec.in.uskoko/kokomo.html/. (Fax: 765-454-5111) 8AM-5PM. Enrollment: 2100. Records go back to 1967. Alumni records maintained here; call 765-454-5113 X700. Degrees granted: Associate. Certification: Technical. Attendance and degree information available by phone, fax, mail. Transcripts available by fax, mail.

Ivy Tech State College — Lafayette, Registrar, 3101 S Creasy Ln, PO Box 6299, Lafayette, IN 47903, 765-772-9118, 765-772-9119 (Fax: 765-772-9214). 8AM-5PM. Enrollment: 2800. Records go back to 1971. Alumni records maintained here; call 765-772-9193. Degrees granted: Associate. Attendance and degree information available by phone, fax, mail. Transcripts available by fax, mail.

Ivy Tech State College - Northcentral, Registrar, 1534 W Sample St, South Bend, IN 46619, 219-289-7001 X326, 219-289-7001 X322 (Fax: 219-236-7177) www.ivy.tec.in.us 8AM-6PM M-Th; 8AM-5PM F; 8AM-Noon S. Enrollment: 2815. Records go back to 1968. Alumni records are maintained here. Degrees granted: Associate. Certification: Technical. Special programs- Technical Certificates, 219-289-7001 X326: Career Development Certificates, 219-289-7001 X326. Attendance and degree information available by phone, fax, mail. Transcripts available by fax, mail.

Ivy Tech State College — Northeast Technical Inst., Registrar, 3800 N Anthony Blvd, Fort Wayne, IN 46805, 219-480-4255, 219-480-4209 (Fax: 219-480-4252). 8AM-5PM. Enrollment: 3500. Records go back to 1970. Alumni records maintained here; call 219-480-4223. Degrees granted: Associate. Attendance and degree information available by phone, fax, mail. Transcripts available by written request only.

Ivy Tech State College — Northwest Technical Inst. (Branch), Registrar, 1440 E 35th Ave, Gary, IN 46409, 219-981-1111 X418 (Fax: 219-981-4415) www.ivytech.edu. 8AM-5PM. Enrollment: 3337. Records go back to 1969. Alumni records maintained here; call 219-981-111 X444. Degrees granted: Associate. Attendance and degree information available by phone, mail. Transcripts available by mail. Mail transcript requests only accepted from student.

Ivy Tech State College — Southeast Tech. Inst., Registrar, 590 Ivy Tech Dr, Madison, IN 47250, 812-265-2580 X4130 (Fax: 812-265-4028) www.ivy.tec.in.us. 8AM-5PM. Enrollment: 1500. Records go back to 1971. Alumni records maintained here; call 812-265-2580 X4113. Degrees granted: Associate. Certification: Technical. Attendance and degree information available by phone, fax, mail. Transcripts available by fax, mail.

Ivy Tech State College — Southwest Tech. Inst., Registrar, 3501 First Ave, Evansville, IN 47710, 812-429-1433, 812-429-1434 (Fax: 812-429-9834). 8AM-6PM. Enrollment: 3500. Records go back to 1965. Alumni records are maintained here. Degrees granted: Associate. Certification: Technical. Special programs- Paramedic, 812-428-0850. Attendance and degree information available by phone, fax, mail. Transcripts available by fax, mail.

Ivy Tech State College — Wabash Valley Tech. Inst., Registrar, 7999 US Hwy 41 South, Terre Haute, IN 47802, 812-299-1121, 800-377-4882 www.ivy.tech.in.us. (Fax: 812-299-5723) 8AM-8PM M-Th; 8AM-4:45PM F. Enrollment: 2750. Records go back to 1969. Alumni records maintained here; call 812-299-1121 X206. Degrees granted: Associate. Certification: Technical. Attendance and degree information available by phone, fax, mail. Transcripts available by fax, mail.

Ivy Tech State College — Whitewater Tech. Inst., Registrar, 2325 Chester Blvd, Richmond, IN 47374, 765-966-2656, 800-659-4562 (Fax: 765-962-8741). 8AM-5PM. Enrollment: 1300. Records go back to 1968. Degrees granted: Associate. Certification: Technical. Attendance, degree and transcript information available by fax, mail.

Lutheran College of Health Professions, Registrar, 3024 Fairfield Ave, Fort Wayne, IN 46807, 219-458-2453, 219-458-2451 (Fax: 219-458-2557) 8AM-4:30PM. www.lutherancollege.edu. Enrollment: 650. Records go back to 1904. Alumni records are maintained here. Degrees granted: Associate; Bachelors. Attendance and degree information available by fax, mail. Transcripts available by fax, mail.

Manchester College, Registrar, 604 College Ave, North Manchester, IN 46962, 219-982-5234, 219-982-5284 (Fax: 219-982-5043) www.manchester.edu. 8AM-Noon,1-5PM. Enrollment: 1080. Records go back to 1800's. Alumni Records: Alumni Assoc., Manchester College, Box 175, North Manchester, IN 46962. Degrees granted: Associate; Bachelors; MACCTY. Attendance and degree information available by phone, fax, mail. Transcripts available by fax, mail.

Marian College, Registrar, 3200 Cold Spring Rd, Indianapolis, IN 46222, 317-955-6050, 800-772-7264 (Fax: 317-955-6575) www.marian.edu. 8AM-4:30PM. Enrollment: 1300. Records go back to 1851. Alumni records maintained here; call 317-955-6210. Degrees granted: Bachelors. Attendance and degree information available by phone, fax, mail. Transcripts available by fax, mail.

Martin University, Registrar, 2171 Avondale Pl, PO Box 18567, Indianapolis, IN 46218, 317-543-3249 (Fax: 317-543-4790). 8:30AM-5:30PM. Enrollment: 950. Records go back to 1977. Alumni records maintained here; call 317-543-4822. Degrees granted: Bachelors; Masters. Attendance and degree information available by phone, mail. Transcripts available by mail.

Mennonite Biblical Seminary
(See Associated Mennonite Biblical Seminary)

Michiana College (Branch), Registrar, 4422 E State Blvd, Fort Wayne, IN 46815, 219-436-2738 (Fax: 219-484-2678). Records are located at Michiana College, Registrar, South Bend, IN.

Michiana College, Registrar, 1030 E Jefferson Blvd, South Bend, IN 46617, www.michianacollege.com. 219-237-0774 (Fax: 219-237-3585) Enrollment: 390. Records go back to 1882. Degrees granted: Associate. Attendance, degree and transcript information available by mail.

Mid-America College of Funeral Service, Registrar, 3111 Hamburg Pike, Jeffersonville, IN 47130, 812-288-8878, 800-221-6158 (Fax: 812-288-5942). 7:30AM-4PM. Enrollment: 120. Records go back to 1920. Degrees granted: Associate. Attendance and degree information available by phone, fax, mail. Transcripts available by mail.

Oakland City University, Registrar, 143 N Lucretia St, Oakland City, IN 47660, 812-749-1238 (Fax: 812-749-1233) www.oak.edu. 8AM-Noon, 1-4:30PM. Enrollment: 1157. Records go back to 1885. Formerly **Oakland City College**. Alumni records maintained here; call 812-749-1223. Degrees granted: Associate; Bachelors; Masters. Attendance and degree information available by phone, fax, mail. Transcripts available by fax, mail.

Purdue University, Office of the Registrar, 1095 Hovde Hall Rm55, West Lafayette, IN 47907-1095, 765-494-6153, 765-494-6308 www.purdue.edu/registrar (Fax: 765-494-0570) 8:30AM-5PM. Enrollment: 36172. Records go back to 1875. Alumni records maintained here; call 765-494-5189. Degrees granted: Associate; Bachelors; Masters; Doctorate. Attendance and degree information available by phone, fax, mail. Transcripts available by fax, mail. Student release needed for transcript request.

Purdue University Calumet, Registrar, 2200 169th St, Hammond, IN 46323, Tele: 219-989-2993, 219-989-2976 (Fax: 219-989-2771) www.calumet.purdue.edu. Records are located at Purdue University, Registrar, West Lafayette, IN.

Purdue University North Central, Registrar, 1401 S US Hwy 421, Westville, IN 46391, www.purduenc.edu. 219-785-5342, 219-785-5200 (switchboard) (Fax: 219-785-5538) 8AM-4:30PM. Enrollment: 3400. Records go back to 1993. Alumni records maintained here; call 219-785-5268. Degrees granted: Associate; Bachelors; Masters. Attendance and degree information available by phone, fax, mail. Official transcripts may only be obtained from the West Lafayette campus.

Rose-Hulman Institute of Technology, Registrar, 5500 Wabash Ave, Terre Haute, IN 47803, 812-877-1511 X8298, 812-877-8028 (Fax: 812-877-8141) www.rose-hulman.edu. 8AM-5PM. Enrollment: 1400. Records go back to 1874. Alumni records maintained here; call 812-877-8359. Degrees granted: Bachelors; Masters. Attendance and degree information available by phone, fax, mail. Transcripts available by fax, mail.

Saint Joseph's College, Registrar's Office, PO Box 929, Rensselaer, IN 47978, 219-866-6161, 219-866-6160 (Fax: 219-866-6100) 8AM-Noon, 1 - 4:30PM. www.saintjoe.edu. Enrollment: 927. Records go back to 1891. Alumni Records: Alumni Assoc., PO Box 870, Rensselaer, IN 47978. Degrees granted: Associate; Bachelors; Masters. Certification: Music. Attendance and degree information available by phone, fax, mail. Transcripts available by fax, mail.

Saint Mary's College, Registrar, Notre Dame, IN 46556, 219-284-4560 (Fax: 219-284-4716) www.saintmarys.edu. 8AM-Noon, 1-4:30PM. Enrollment: 1550. Records go back to 1900. Alumni Records: Alumnae Relations, LeMans Hall, Notre Dame, IN 46556. Degrees granted: Bachelors. Attendance and degree information available by phone, fax, mail. Transcripts available by fax, mail.

Sawyer College, Inc., Registrar, 6040 Hohman Ave, Hammond, IN 46320, 219-931-0436 (Fax: 219-933-1239) 8AM-5PM. Enrollment: 250. Records go back to 1990. Alumni records are maintained here. Degrees granted: Associate; Certificates. Attendance and degree information available by phone, fax, mail. Transcripts available by mail.

Sawyer College, Inc. (Branch), Registrar, 3803 E Lincoln Hwy, Merrillville, IN 46410, 219-736-0436, 800-964-0218 (Fax: 219-942-3762) 8AM-5PM. Enrollment: 230. Records go back to 1985. Degrees granted: Associate. Attendance, degree and transcript information available by fax, mail.

St. Francis College, Registrar, 2701 Spring St, Fort Wayne, IN 46808, 219-434-3252, 800-729-4732 (Fax: 219-434-3183). 8:30AM-Noon, 12:30-5PM. Enrollment: 1000. Records go back to 1890. Alumni records are maintained here. Degrees granted: Associate; Bachelors; Masters. Special programs-Weekend College, 219-434-3294. Attendance and degree information available by phone, fax, mail. Transcripts available by fax, mail.

St. Mary—Of—The—Woods College, Registrar, St. Mary-of-the-Woods, IN 47876, 812-535-5269, 800-926-SMWC (Fax: 812-535-4613) www.woods.smwc.edu. 8:30AM-Noon, 1-4:30PM. Enrollment: 1250. Records go back to 1898. Alumni records maintained here; call 812-535-5211. Degrees granted: Associate; Bachelors; Masters. Certification: Gerontology. Special programs- Music: Therapy: Education: Equine Studies. Attendance and degree information available by phone, fax, mail. Transcripts available by mail.

St. Meinrad College, Registrar, St Meinrad, IN 47577, 812-357-6561, 812-357-6611 (Fax: 812-357-6816) www.saintmeinrad.edu. 8AM-4:30PM. Enrollment: 100. Records go back to 1880. College closed down as of May 1998. Alumni records maintained here; call 812-357-6501. Degrees granted: Bachelors. Attendance and degree information available by phone, fax, mail. Transcripts available by fax, mail.

St. Meinrad School of Theology, Registrar, St Meinrad, IN 47577, 812-357-6561, 812-357-6611 (Fax: 812-357-6816) 8AM-4:30PM. www.saintmeinrad.edu. Enrollment: 145. Records go back to 1880. Alumni records maintained here; call 812-357-6501. Degrees granted: Masters. Attendance and degree information available by phone, fax, mail. Transcripts available by fax, mail.

Taylor University, Registrar, 1025 W Rudisill Blvd, **Fort Wayne**, IN 46807, 219-456-2111 (Fax: 219-456-2119). 8AM-5PM. Enrollment: 410. Records go back to 1890. Alumni records maintained here; call 219-456-2211 X33331. Degrees granted: Associate; Bachelors. Attendance and degree information available by phone, fax, mail. Transcripts available by fax, mail.

Taylor University, Registrar's Office, 236 W Reade Ave, **Upland**, IN 46989, 765-998-5193, 765-998-5330 www.tayloru.edu. (Fax: 765-998-4910) 8AM-5PM. Enrollment: 1880. Records go back to 1846. Alumni records maintained here; call 765-998-5115. Degrees granted: Associate; Bachelors. Attendance and degree information available by phone, fax, mail. Transcripts available by fax, mail.

Tri-State University, Registrar, 1 University Ave, Angola, IN 46703, 219-665-4240, 219-665-4239 (Fax: 219-665-4500) www.tristate.edu. 8AM-5PM. Enrollment: 1200. Records go back to 1900. Alumni records maintained here; call 219-665-4122. Degrees granted: Associate; Bachelors. Attendance and degree information available by phone, fax, mail. Transcripts available by fax, mail.

University of Evansville, Registrar, 1800 Lincoln Ave, Evansville, IN 47722, 812-479-2267 (Fax: 812-479-2248) 8AM-5PM. www.evansville.edu Enrollment: 3162. Records go back to 1854. Alumni records maintained here; call 812-479-2000. Degrees granted: Bachelors; Masters. Attendance and degree information available by phone, fax, mail. Transcripts available by fax, mail.

University of Indianapolis, Registrar's Office, 1400 E Hanna Ave, Indianapolis, IN 46227, 317-788-3219 (Fax: 317-788-3300) www.uindy.edu. 7:30AM-9PM M-Th; 7:30AM-4:30PM F. Enrollment: 4000. Records go back to 1908. Alumni records maintained here; call 317-788-3295. Degrees granted: Associate; Bachelors; Masters; PsyD. Attendance and degree information available by phone, fax, mail. Transcripts available by fax, mail.

University of Notre Dame, Registrar, 215 Grace Hall, Notre Dame, IN 46556, 219-631-7043, 219-631-5000 (Fax: 219-631-5872) www.nd.edu. 8AM-5PM. Enrollment: 10300. Records go back to 1842. Alumni Records: 201 Main Bldg, Notre Dame, IN 46556. Degrees granted: Bachelors; Masters; Doctorate; J.D. (Law). Special programs-Law School, 219-631-5990. Attendance and degree information available by phone, fax, mail. Transcripts available by fax, mail.

University of Southern Indiana, Registrar, 8600 University Blvd, Evansville, IN 47712, 812-464-1763 (Fax: 812-464-1960) www.usi.edu. 8AM-6PM M-Th; 8AM-4:30PM F. Enrollment: 8300. Records go back to 1965. Alumni records maintained here; call 812-464-1924. Degrees granted: Associate; Bachelors; Masters. Attendance and degree information available by phone, mail. Transcripts available by mail.

Valparaiso University, Registrar, Valparaiso, IN 46383, 219-464-5212 (Fax: 219-464-5381) www.valpo.edu. 8AM-5PM. Enrollment: 3600. Records go back to 1859. Alumni records maintained here; call 219-464-5110. Degrees granted: Bachelors; Masters. Special programs- Business: Law: Nursing: Arts & Sciences. Attendance and degree information available by phone, fax, mail. Transcripts available by fax, mail.

Vincennes University, Registrar, 1002 N First St, Vincennes, IN 47591, 812-888-4220 (Fax: 812-888-5868). 8AM-4:30PM. Enrollment: 8000. Records go back to 1806. Alumni records maintained here; call 812-888-4354. Degrees granted: Associate. Attendance and degree information available by phone, fax, mail. Transcripts available by fax, mail.

Wabash College, Registrar, 301 W Wabash Ave, Crawfordsville, IN 47933, 765-361-6245, 765-361-6416 (Fax: 765-364-4432) 8AM-4:30PM. http://ruby.wabash.edu. Enrollment: 800. Records go back to 1900. Alumni records maintained here; call 765-361-6371. Degrees granted: Bachelors. Attendance and degree information available by phone, fax, mail. Transcripts available by fax, mail.

Whitewater Technical Institute
(See Ivy Tech State College - Whitewater Technical Institute)

Iowa

American Institute of Business, Registrar, 2500 Fleur Dr, Des Moines, IA 50321, 515-244-4221, 515-244-4222 (Fax: 515-244-6773) www.aib.edu. 7AM-4:30PM. Enrollment: 764. Records go back to 1930's. Alumni records are maintained here. Degrees granted: Associate. Special programs-Business. Attendance and degree information available by phone, mail. Transcripts available by fax, mail.

American Institute of Commerce (Branch), Registrar, 2302 W First St, Cedar Falls, IA 50613, 319-277-0220 (Fax: 319-268-0978) 8AM-5PM. www.aic.edu. Enrollment: 200. Records go back to 1987. Alumni records are maintained here. Degrees granted: Associate. Special programs- Legal Assistant: Paralegal. Attendance, degree and transcript information available by written request only.

American Institute of Commerce, Registrar, 1801 E Kimberly Rd, Davenport, IA 52807, 319-355-3500 (Fax: 319-355-1320) www.iowacollege.com. 8AM-5PM. Enrollment: 370. Records go back to 1946. Degrees granted: Associate. Attendance and degree information available by phone, fax, mail. Transcripts available by mail.

Briar Cliff College, Registrar, 3033 Rebecca St, Sioux City, IA 51104, 712-279-5448, 712-279-5447 (Fax: 712-279-5410) www.briar-cliff.edu. 8AM-4:30PM. Enrollment: 1150. Records go back to 1932. Alumni records maintained here; call 712-279-5396. Degrees granted: Associate; Bachelors. Attendance and degree information available by phone, fax, mail. Transcripts available by fax, mail.

Buena Vista University, Registrar, 610 W Fourth St, Storm Lake, IA 50588, 712-749-2234 (Fax: 712-749-1466) www.bvu.edu. 8AM-5PM. Enrollment: 1150. Records go back to 1891. Formerly **Buena Vista College**. Alumni records are maintained here. Degrees granted: Bachelors; Masters. Adverse incident record source- Dean of Students, 712-749-2123. Attendance and degree information available by phone, mail. Transcripts available by mail.

Central College, Registrar, 812 University, Pella, IA 50219, 515-628-5267, 515-628-5343 (Fax: 515-628-5316) www.central.edu. 8AM-5PM. Enrollment: 1300. Records go back to 1853. Alumni records maintained here; call 515-628-5281. Degrees granted: Bachelors. Attendance and degree information available by phone, fax, mail. Transcripts available by fax, mail.

Central University of Iowa, Registrar, 812 University, Pella, IA 50219, 515-628-5267, 800-458-5503 (Fax: 515-628-5316) www.central.edu. 8AM-5PM. Enrollment: 1538. Records go back to 1925. Alumni records are maintained here. Degrees granted: Bachelors. Special programs- Arts. Attendance and degree information available by phone, fax, mail. Transcripts available by fax, mail.

Clarke College, Registrar, 1550 Clarke Dr, Dubuque, IA 52001, 319-588-6314, 319-588-6300 (Fax: 319-588-6789) www.clarke.edu. 8AM-4:30PM. Enrollment: 1160. Records go back to 1904. Alumni records maintained here; call 319-588-6405. Degrees granted: Associate; Bachelors; Masters. Attendance and degree information available by phone, fax, mail. Transcripts available by fax, mail.

Clinton Community College, Registrar, 1000 Lincoln Blvd, Clinton, IA 52732, 319-244-7001, 319-244-7006 (Fax: 319-244-7107). 7:30AM-5PM. Enrollment: 1100. Records go back to 1948. Alumni records maintained here. Degrees granted: Associate. School will not confirm attendance information. Degree information available by phone, fax, mail. Transcripts available by fax, mail.

Coe College, Registrar, Cedar Rapids, IA 52402, 319-399-8526 (Fax: 319-399-8748) www.coe.edu. 8AM - 4:30PM. Enrollment: 1343. Records go back to 1885. Alumni records maintained here; call 319-399-8608. Degrees granted: Bachelors; Masters. Attendance and degree information available by phone, fax, mail. Transcripts available by written request only.

Cornell College, Registrar, 600 First St W, Mount Vernon, IA 52314, 319-895-4372 (Fax: 319-895-5672) www.cornell-iowa.edu. 8AM-4:30PM. Enrollment: 1100. Records go back to 1853. Alumni records maintained here; call 319-895-4204. Degrees granted: Bachelors. Attendance and degree information available by phone, fax, mail. Transcripts available by fax, mail.

Des Moines Area Community College, Student Records Bldg 1, 2006 S Ankeny Blvd, Ankeny, IA 50021, 515-964-6224, 515-964-6200 (Fax: 515-964-6391) www.dmacc.cc.ia.us. 8AM-5PM Fall, Spring; 7:30AM-4PM Summer. Enrollment: 11000. Records go back to 1920. Alumni records maintained here; call 515-964-6376. Degrees granted: Associate. Degree information available by phone, fax, mail. Transcripts available by fax, mail. Confirm attendance if currently enrolled. Requests for multiple term enrollment verifications must be made in writing.

Divine Word College, Registrar, S Center Ave, Epworth, IA 52045, 319-876-3353 X205 (Fax: 319-876-3407) www.svd.org. 9AM-5PM. Enrollment: 110. Records go back to 1964. Alumni records maintained here; call 319-876-3353. Degrees granted: Bachelors. Attendance and degree information available by phone, mail. Transcripts available by mail.

Dordt College, Registrar, Sioux Center, IA 51250, 712-722-6030 (Fax: 712-722-4496) www.dordt.edu. 8AM-Noon, 1-5PM. Enrollment: 1200. Records go back to 1955. Alumni records are maintained here also. Call 712-722-6022. Degrees granted: Associate; Bachelors; Masters. Attendance and degree information available by phone, fax, mail. Transcripts available by fax, mail.

Drake University, Registrar, 25th St and University Ave, Des Moines, IA 50311, 515-271-3901, 515-271-3091 (transcripts) (Fax: 515-271-3977) www.drake.edu. 8AM-4:30PM. Enrollment: 5500. Records go back to 1881. Alumni Records: Alumni Development, Drake University, 2507 University, Des Moines, IA 50311. Degrees granted: Bachelors; Masters; Doctorate; JD (Doctor of Jurisprudence). Attendance and degree information available by phone, fax, mail. Transcripts available by phone, fax, mail.

Eastern Iowa Com. College District
(See Scott Community College)

Ellsworth Community College, Registrar, 1100 College Ave, Iowa Falls, IA 50126, 800-322-9235 X436, 515-648-4611 (Fax: 515-648-3128) www.iavalley.cc.ic.us/ecc. 8AM - 5PM. Enrollment: 800. Records go back to 1940's. Alumni records maintained here; call 800-322-9235 X247. Degrees granted: Associate. Attendance and degree information available by phone, fax, mail. Transcripts available by written request only.

Emmaus Bible College, Registrar, 2570 Asbury Rd, Dubuque, IA 52001, 319-588-8000, 800-397-2425 (Fax: 319-588-1216) 8AM-4:30PM. www.emmaus.edu. Enrollment: 260. Records go back to 1945. Alumni records maintained here; call 319-588-8000. Degrees granted: Associate; Bachelors. Attendance and degree information available by phone, fax, mail. Transcripts available by fax, mail.

Faith Baptist Bible College and Theological Seminary, Registrar, 1900 NW Fourth St, Ankeny, IA 50021, 515-964-0601 X208 (Fax: 515-964-1638) www.faith.edu. 8AM-4:30PM. Enrollment: 378. Records go back to 1921. Alumni records are maintained here. Degrees granted: Associate; Bachelors; Masters. Attendance and degree information available by phone, fax, mail. Transcripts available by fax, mail.

Graceland College, Registrar, Lamoni, IA 50140, 515-784-5220, 515-784-5221 (Fax: 515-784-5474) www.graceland.edu. 8AM-5PM. Enrollment: 3892. Records go back to 1900's. Alumni records maintained here; call 515-784-5187. Degrees granted: Bachelors; Masters. Special programs- Outreach Program for BSN completion, 800-833-0524: Addiction Studies, 800-833-0524. Attendance and degree information available by phone, fax, mail. Transcripts available by fax, mail.

Grand View College, Registrar, 1200 Grandview Ave, Des Moines, IA 50316, www.gvc.edu.com 515-263-2960 (Fax: 515-263-6190) 8:15AM-4PM. Enrollment: 1480. Records go back to 1895. Alumni records maintained here; call 515-263-2957. Degrees granted: Associate; Bachelors. Attendance and degree information available by phone, fax, mail. Transcripts available by fax, mail.

Grinnell College, Registrar, PO Box 805, Grinnell, IA 50112, 515-269-3450 (Fax: 515-269-4415) www.grin.edu. 8AM-5PM. Enrollment: 1270. Records go back to 1846. Alumni records maintained here; call 515-269-4801. Degrees granted: Bachelors. Attendance and degree information available by phone, mail. Transcripts available by mail.

Hamilton College, Registrar, 1924 D Street SW, Cedar Rapids, IA 52404, 319-363-0481 (Fax: 319-363-3812) www.hamilton.edu. 8AM-5PM. Records go back to 1957. Degrees granted: Associate. Attendance and degree information available by phone, mail. Transcripts available by mail.

Hamilton Technical College, Registrar, 1011 E 53rd St, Davenport, IA 52807-2616, 319-386-3570 (Fax: 319-386-6756) 8AM-6PM M-Th; 8AM-Noon F. Enrollment: 350. Records go back to 1969. Alumni records are maintained here. Degrees granted: Associate; Bachelors. Special programs- Technical. Attendance and degree information available by phone, fax, mail. Transcripts available by fax, mail.

Hawkeye Community College, Registrar, 1501 E Orange Rd, Waterloo, IA 50704, 319-296-2320, 800-670-4769 (Fax: 319-296-2874) www.hawkeye.cc.ia.us Enrollment: 3944. Records go back to 1966. Degrees granted: Associate. Adverse incident record source- Registrar's Office, 319-296-2320. Attendance and degree information available by phone, fax, mail. Transcripts available by fax, mail.

Hawkeye Institute of Technology
(See Hawkeye Community College)

Indian Hills Community College, Registrar, 721 N 1st St, Centerville, IA 52544, 515-856-2143 (Fax: 515-856-5527) www.ihcc.cc.ia.us. 8AM-4PM. Enrollment: 490. Records go back to 1930. Alumni records are maintained here. Degrees granted: Associate. Attendance and degree information available by phone, fax, mail. Transcripts available by fax, mail.

Indian Hills Community College, Registrar, 525 Grandview Ave, Ottumwa, IA 52501, 515-683-5151, 800-726-2585 (Fax: 515-683-5184) www.ihcc.cc.ia.us. 7:15AM-4:45PM M-Th; 8:30AM-4:30PM F. Enrollment: 3500. Records go back to 1966. Alumni records are maintained here. Degrees granted: Associate. Attendance and degree information available by phone, fax, mail. Transcripts available by fax, mail.

Iowa Central Community College, Registrar, 330 Ave M, Fort Dodge, IA 50501, 515-576-7201 X2419 (Fax: 515-576-7724) www.iccia.us:8000/. 8AM-5PM M-Th, 8AM-4:30PM F. Enrollment: 3003. Records go back to 1966. Degrees granted: Associate. Attendance, degree and transcript information available by phone, fax, mail.

Iowa Lakes Community College (Emmetsburg Campus), Registrar, 3200 College Dr, Emmetsburg, IA 50536, 712-852-3554 X265, 712-362-7922 (Fax: 712-852-2152) www.ilcca.us. 8AM-5PM. Enrollment: 2050. Records go back to 1928. Alumni Records: 300 S 18th St, Estherville, IA 51334. Degrees granted: Associate. Attendance and degree information available by phone, fax, mail. Transcripts available by fax, mail.

Iowa Lakes Community College (Estherville Campus), Registrar, 300 S 18th St, Estherville, IA 51334, 712-362-7922, 712-852-5265 (Fax: 712-362-8363) 8AM-5PM. www.ilcc.ia.us. Enrollment: 2500. Records go back to 1928. Alumni records maintained here; call 712-362-7923. Degrees granted: Associate. Attendance and degree information available by phone, fax, mail. Transcripts available by fax, mail.

Iowa Lakes Community College, Registrar, 1900 N Grand Ave, Suite 8, Spencer, IA 51301, 712-262-7141 (Fax: 712-262-7141) www.ilccia.us/. Degrees granted: Associate. Attendance, degree and transcript information available by mail.

Iowa State University, Office of the Registrar, 214 Alumni Hall, Ames, IA 50011, 515-294-1840 (Fax: 515-294-1088) www.iastate.edu. 8AM-5PM. Enrollment: 25400. Records go back to 1858. Alumni Records: Alumni Suite, Memorial Union, Ames, IA 50011 (Fax: 515-294-9402). Degrees granted: Bachelors; Masters; Doctorate; Doctor Veterinary Medicine, Specialist. Attendance and degree information available by phone, fax, mail. Transcripts available by phone, fax, mail. Fax request must be signed.

Iowa Wesleyan College, Registrar, 601 N Main St, Mount Pleasant, IA 52641, 319-385-6225 (Fax: 319-385-6296). 8AM-Noon, 1-5PM. Enrollment: 820. Records go back to 1842. Alumni records maintained here; call 319-385-6215. Degrees granted: Bachelors. Attendance and degree information available by phone, fax, mail. Transcripts available by fax, mail.

Iowa Western Community College, Registrar, 2700 College Rd, PO Box 4C, Council Bluffs, IA 51502, 712-325-3200 (Fax: 712-325-3720) www.iwccia.us. Enrollment: 3600. Records go back to 1967. Alumni records are maintained here. Degrees granted: Associate. Attendance and degree information available by phone, fax, mail. Transcripts available by written request only.

Kirkwood Community College, Office of the Registrar, 6301 Kirkwood Blvd SW, PO Box 2068, Cedar Rapids, IA 52406-2068, 319-398-5603 (Fax: 319-398-4928) 8AM - 6PM M-Th; 8AM - 5PM F. www.kirkwood.cc.ia.us/. Enrollment: 11000. Records go back to 1966. Alumni records are maintained here. Degrees granted: Associate. Special programs- Community Relation (non-credit), 319-398-5412: Attendance and degree information available by phone, fax, mail. Transcripts available by fax, mail. Student only may phone for transcript.

Loras College, Registrar, 1450 Alta Vista, Dubuque, IA 52004, 319-588-7106 (Fax: 319-588-7964) www.loras.edu. 8AM - 4:30PM. Enrollment: 1809. Records go back to 1839. Alumni records maintained here; call 319-588-7170. Degrees granted: Bachelors; Masters. Attendance and degree information available by phone, fax, mail. Transcripts available by mail.

Luther College, Registrar's Office, 700 College Dr, Decorah, IA 52101-1045, 319-387-1167 (Fax: 319-387-2158) 8AM-5PM. www.luther.edu. Enrollment: 2350. Records go back to 1859. Alumni records maintained here; call 319-387-1861. Degrees granted: Bachelors. Attendance and degree information available by phone, fax, mail. Transcripts available by fax, mail.

Maharishi University of Management, Registrar, Fairfield, IA 52557, 515-472-1144 (Fax: 515-472-1133) www.mum.edu. 10AM-4PM. Enrollment: 500. Records go back to 1971. Formerly **Maharishi International University**. Alumni records maintained here; call 515-472-1190. Degrees granted: Associate; Bachelors; Masters; Doctorate. Attendance and degree information available by phone, fax, mail. Transcripts available by fax, mail.

Marshalltown Community College, Registrar's Office, 3700 S Center, Marshalltown, IA 50158, 515-752-7106 (Fax: 515-752-8149) www.iavalley.cc.ia.us. 8AM-4:30PM. Enrollment: 1200. Records go back to 1950's. Alumni records are maintained here. Degrees granted: Associate. Attendance and degree information available by phone, fax, mail. Transcripts available by fax, mail.

Marycrest International University, Registrar, 1607 W 12th St, Davenport, IA 52804, 319-326-9216, 319-326-9217 (Fax: 319-327-9606). 8AM-5PM. Enrollment: 1000. Records go back to 1939. Formerly **Teikyo Marycrest University**. Alumni records maintained here; call 319-326-9492. Degrees granted: Associate; Bachelors; Masters. Attendance and degree information available by phone, fax, mail. Transcripts available by fax, mail.

Mercy College of Health Sciences, Registrar, 928 6th Ave, Des Moines, IA 50309-1239, 515-247-3180 (Fax: 515-643-6698). 8AM-4:30PM M,T,Th. Enrollment: 378. Records go back to 1942. Alumni records are maintained here. Degrees granted: Associate. Special programs- Science: Nursing. Attendance and degree information available by phone, mail. Transcripts available by mail.

Morningside College, Registrar, 1501 Morningside Ave, Sioux City, IA 51106, 712-274-5110 (Fax: 712-274-5101) 8AM-5PM. www.morningside.edu Enrollment: 1214. Records go back to 1894. Alumni records maintained here; call 712-274-5107. Degrees granted: Bachelors; Masters. Attendance and degree information available by phone, fax, mail. Transcripts available by fax, mail.

Mount Mercy College, Registrar, 1330 Elmhurst Dr NE, Cedar Rapids, IA 52402, 319-363-8213 (Fax: 319-363-5270) 8AM-5PM M-Th; 8AM - 4:30AM F. www.mtmercy.edu. Enrollment: 1200. Records go back to 1928. Alumni records maintained here; call 319-363-8213. Degrees granted: Bachelors. Attendance and degree information available by phone, fax, mail. Transcripts available by fax, mail.

Mount St. Clare College, Registrar, 400 N Bluff Blvd, Clinton, IA 52732, 319-242-4023 (Fax: 319-242-2003). 7:30AM - 4:30PM. Enrollment: 525. Alumni records are maintained here. Degrees granted: Associate; Bachelors. Attendance and degree information available by phone, fax, mail. Transcripts available by fax, mail.

Muscatine Community College, Registrar, 152 Colorado St, Muscatine, IA 52761, 319-288-6001 (Fax: 319-288-6104). 8AM-5PM. Enrollment: 1200. Records go back to 1929. Alumni records are maintained here. Degrees granted: Associate. Attendance and degree information available by fax, mail. Transcripts available by fax, mail.

North Iowa Area Community College, Registrar, 500 College Dr, Mason City, IA 50401, 515-422-4205, 515-422-4229 www.niacc.cc.ia.us. (Fax: 515-422-1711) 7:45AM-4:15PM. Enrollment: 2700. Records go back to 1918. Alumni records maintained here; call 515-422-4397. Degrees granted: Associate. Attendance and degree information available by phone, fax, mail. Transcripts available by fax, mail.

Northeast Iowa Community College, Registrar, Box 400 Hwy 150, Calmar, IA 52132, 319-562-3263 X233 (Fax: 319-562-3719) 7:30AM-4PM. www.niccia.us. Enrollment: 4000. Records go back to 1967. Alumni records maintained here; call 319-562-3263 X300. Degrees granted: Associate. Attendance and degree information available by phone, fax, mail. Transcripts available by mail.

Northwest Iowa Community College, Registrar, 603 W Park St, Sheldon, IA 51201, 712-324-5061 X141 www.nwicc.cc.ia.us. (Fax: 712-324-4136) 8AM-4:30PM. Enrollment: 988. Records go back to 1967. Alumni records maintained here; call 712-324-5061 X220. Degrees granted: Associate. Attendance information available by phone, fax, mail. Degree and transcript information available by fax, mail.

Northwestern College, Registrar, 101 7th St SW, Orange City, IA 51041-1996, 712-737-7145 (Fax: 712-737-7117) www.nwciowa.edu. 8AM-5PM. Enrollment: 1200. Records go back to 1888. Alumni records maintained here; call 712-737-7106. Degrees granted: Associate; Bachelors. Attendance and degree information available by phone, fax, mail. Transcripts available by fax, mail.

Palmer College of Chiropractic, Registrar, 1000 Brady St, Davenport, IA 52803, 319-326-9862, 319-326-9647 (Fax: 319-327-0181) www.palmer.edu. 8AM-4:30PM. Enrollment: 1800. Records go back to 1900. Alumni records are maintained here. Degrees granted: Associate; Bachelors; Masters; Doctorate; CT. Attendance and degree information available by mail. Transcripts available by mail.

Scott Community College, Registrar, 500 Belmont Rd, Bettendorf, IA 52722, 319-441-4001, 319-441-4130 & 319-441-4181 (Fax: 319-441-4101). 8AM-5:30PM M-Th; 7:30AM-4:30PM F. Enrollment: 4000. Records go back to 1960's. Degrees granted: Associate. Attendance information available by phone, fax, mail. Degree information available by mail. Transcripts available by fax, mail.

Simpson College, Registrar, 701 N C St, Indianola, IA 50125, 515-961-1642, 515-961-1644 (Fax: 515-961-1498) www.simpson.edu. 8AM-4:30PM. Enrollment: 1900. Records go back to 1880's; on computer from 1983. Alumni records maintained here; call 515-961-1547. Degrees granted: Bachelors. Attendance and degree information available by phone, fax, mail. Transcripts available by fax, mail.

Southeastern Community College, Registrar, Drawer F, West Burlington, IA 52655, 319-752-2731 X8231, 319-524-3221 X8415 (Fax: 319-752-4957) 8AM-4:30PM. www.secc.cc.ia.us Enrollment: 2400. Records go back to 1920. Alumni records maintained here; call 319-752-2731 X8142. Degrees granted: Associate. Attendance, degree and transcript information available by phone, fax, mail.. Only authorized persons may make requests.

Southwestern Community College, Registrar, 1501 Townline St, Creston, IA 50801, 515-782-7081 (Fax: 515-782-3312) 8AM-4:30PM. www.swcc.cc.ia.us. Enrollment: 1100. Records go back to 1932. Degrees granted: Associate. Attendance and degree information available by phone, fax, mail. Transcripts available by fax, mail.

St. Ambrose University, Registrar, 518 W Locust St, Davenport, IA 52803-2898, 319-333-6202 (Fax: 319-333-6243) www.saunix.sau.edu. 9AM-4PM. Enrollment: 2640. Records go back to 1908. Alumni records maintained here; call 319-333-6290. Degrees granted: Bachelors; Masters. Special programs- ACCEL, 319-386-2225. Degree and attendance information available by phone, fax, mail. Transcripts available by mail.

St. Luke's College of Nursing & Health, Registrar, 2720 Stone Park Blvd, Sioux City, IA 51104, 712-279-3149 (Fax: 712-279-3155). 8AM-5PM. Enrollment: 100. Records go back to 1920. Alumni records are maintained here. Degrees granted: Associate. Special programs- Nursing. Attendance and degree information available by phone, fax, mail. Transcripts available by fax, mail.

University of Dubuque, Registrar, 2000 University Ave, Dubuque, IA 52001, 319-589-3270 (Fax: 319-589-3690) www.dbq.edu. 8AM-5PM. Enrollment: 1000. Computerized records are from 1989 to present. Alumni records maintained here; call 319-589-3351. Degrees granted: Associate; Bachelors; Masters; Doctorate. Attendance and degree information available by fax, mail. Transcripts available by fax, mail.

University of Iowa, Registrar, 1 Jessup Hall, Iowa City, IA 52242-1316, 319-335-0229 (Fax: 319-335-1999) www.uiowa.edu. 8:30AM-4:30PM. Enrollment: 26932. Records go back to 1965. Phone for transcripts is 319-335-0230. Records go back to 1965. Alumni records are maintained here. Degrees granted: Bachelors; Masters; Doctorate. Attendance and degree information available by phone, fax, mail. Transcripts available by mail. Phone for transcript by student only.

University of Northern Iowa, Registrar, Cedar Falls, IA 50614, 319-273-2241, 319-273-2283 (Fax: 319-273-6792) 8AM-5PM. www.uni.edu/. Enrollment: 13200. Records go back to 1876. Alumni records maintained here; call 319-273-2355. Degrees granted: Bachelors; Masters; Doctorate Attendance, degree and transcript information available by phone, fax, mail.

University of Osteopathic Medicine and Health Sciences, Registrar, 3200 Grand Ave, Des Moines, IA 50313, 515-271-1460, 515-271-1461 (Fax: 515-271-1578). 8AM-4:30PM. Enrollment: 1200. Records go back to 1900. Alumni records maintained here; call 515-271-1573. Degrees granted: Bachelors; Masters; DO, DPM. Special programs-Administrative Services, 515-271-1504. Attendance and degree information available by phone, fax, mail. Transcripts available by fax, mail.

Upper Iowa University, Registrar, Box 1857, College and Washington Sts, Fayette, IA 52142, 319-425-5268 (Fax: 319-425-5287) www.uiu.edu. 8AM-5PM. Enrollment: 3804. Records go back to 1968. Alumni records are maintained here. Degrees granted: Associate; Bachelors; Masters. Attendance and degree information available by phone, fax, mail. Transcripts available by fax, mail.

Vennard College, Registrar, Eighth Ave E, PO Box 29, University Park, IA 52595, www.kdsi.net/vennardcollege 515-673-8391 X107 (Fax: 515-673-8365) 8AM-5PM. Enrollment: 69. Records go back to 1910. Alumni records are maintained here. Degrees granted: Associate; Bachelors. Attendance and degree information available by phone, fax, mail. Transcripts available by fax, mail.

Waldorf College, Registrar, 106 South 6th St, Forest City, IA 50436, 515-582-8139, 515-582-8138 (Fax: 515-582-8194) www.waldorf.edu. 8AM-5PM. Enrollment: 678. Records go back to 1903. Alumni records are maintained here. Degrees granted: Associate; Bachelors. Attendance and degree information available by phone, fax, mail. Transcripts available by fax, mail.

Wartburg College, Registrar, 222 9th St NW, Waverly, IA 50677, 319-352-8272, 319-352-8281 (Fax: 319-352-8279). 8AM-4:30PM. Enrollment: 1530. Records go back to 1852. Alumni records maintained here; call 319-352-8491. Degrees granted: Bachelors. Attendance and degree information available by phone, fax, mail. Transcripts available by fax, mail.

Wartburg Theological Seminary, Registrar, 333 Wartburg Pl, PO Box 5004, Dubuque, IA 52004-5004, 319-589-0211, 319-589-0200 (Fax: 319-589-0333). 8AM-4:30PM. Enrollment: 190. Alumni records maintained here; call 319-589-0221. Degrees granted: Masters. Special programs- Lutheran Seminary Program in the SW, 512-477-2666. Attendance and degree information available by phone, fax, mail. Transcripts available by mail.

Western Iowa Tech Community College, Registrar, 4647 Stone Ave, PO Box 265, Sioux City, IA 51102, 712-274-6400 (Fax: 712-274-6412) www.witcc.cc.ia.us. 8AM-5PM. Enrollment: 3500. Records go back to 1968. Alumni records are maintained here. Degrees granted: Associate; GED. Special programs- GED's, 712-255-7632. Attendance and degree information available by phone, fax, mail. Transcripts available by mail.

Westmar University, Registrar, 1002 Third Ave SE, Le Mars, IA 51031, 712-546-2006, 712-546-2008 (Fax: 712-546-2020) www.westmar.edu. 8AM-5PM. Enrollment: 500. Formerly **Teikyo Westmar University**. Alumni records maintained here; call 712-546-2030. Degrees granted: Bachelors. Attendance and degree information available by phone, fax, mail. Transcripts available by mail.

William Penn College, Registrar, 201 Trueblood Ave, Oskaloosa, IA 52577, 515-673-1082 (Fax: 515-673-1396) 8AM-5PM. www.wmpenn.edu Enrollment: 730. Records go back to 1873. Alumni records maintained here; call 515-673-1044. Degrees granted: Bachelors. Special programs- College for Working Adults, 515-673-1380. Attendance and degree information available by phone, fax, mail. Transcripts available by mail.

Kansas

Allen County Community College, Registrar, 1801 N Cottonwood, Iola, KS 66749, 316-365-5116 (Fax: 316-365-3284) 8AM-5PM. www.allen.cc.ks.uf/. Enrollment: 1700. Records go back to 1923. Alumni records are maintained here. Degrees granted: Associate. Attendance and degree information available by phone, fax, mail. Transcripts available by mail.

Baker University, Registrar, 618 W 8th St, PO Box 65, Baldwin City, KS 66006-0065, 785-594-6451 X530 (Fax: 785-594-4521) 9AM-5PM. www.bakeru.edu. Enrollment: 800. Records go back to 1859. Alumni records maintained here; call 785-594-6451 X526. Degrees granted: Bachelors; Masters. Special programs- School/Professional & Graduate Studies, 785-491-4432. Attendance and degree information available by phone, fax, mail. Transcripts available by fax, mail.

Barclay College, Registrar, 607 N Kingman, PO Box 288, Haviland, KS 67059, 316-862-5252, 800-862-0226 (Fax: 316-862-5403). 8AM-5PM. Enrollment: 100. Records go back to 1917. Alumni records maintained here; call 316-862-5252. Degrees granted: Associate; Bachelors. Certification: Bible. Special programs- Barclay Advantage, 316-862-5252. Attendance and degree information available by phone, fax, mail. Transcripts available by fax, mail.

Barton County Community College, Registrar, 245 NE 30th Rd, Great Bend, KS 67530, 316-792-2701, 316-792-9216 (Fax: 316-792-3056) www.barton.cc.ks.us. 7:30AM-4:30PM. Enrollment: 7000. Records go back to 1971. Degrees granted: Associate. Attendance and degree information available by phone, fax, mail. Transcripts available by fax, mail.

Benedictine College, Registrar, 1020 N Second St, Atchison, KS 66002, 913-367-5340 X2550 (Fax: 913-367-3673) 8AM-Noon, 1-5PM. www.benedictine.edu. Enrollment: 800. Records go back to 1858. Records are hard copy before 1980. Alumni records maintained here; call 913-367-5340 X2414. Degrees granted: Associate; Bachelors; Masters. Special programs-Executive MBA. Attendance and degree information available by phone, fax, mail. Transcripts available by fax, mail.

Bethany College, Registrar, 421 N First St, Lindsborg, KS 67456, 785-227-3311 (Fax: 785-227-2004) www.bethanylb.edu. 8AM-5PM. Enrollment: 725. Records go back to 1888. Alumni records are maintained. Call 785-227-3380 X8272. Degrees granted: Bachelors. Attendance and degree information available by phone, fax, mail. Transcripts available by fax, mail.

Bethel College, Registrar, 300 E 27th St, North Newton, KS 67117, 316-283-2500 (Fax: 316-284-5286) www.bethelks.edu. 8AM-Noon, 1-5PM. Enrollment: 620. Records go back to 1893. Alumni records are maintained here. Degrees granted: Bachelors. Attendance and degree information available by phone, fax, mail. Transcripts available by fax.

Brown Mackie College, Registrar, 126 S Santa Fe Ave, Salina, KS 67401, 785-825-5422, 800-365-0433 (Fax: 785-827-7623) 8AM - 5PM. Enrollment: 350. Records go back to 1950. Alumni records are maintained here. Degrees granted: Associate. Special programs- Call 785-825-5422. Attendance and degree information available by phone, fax, mail. Transcripts available by mail.

Butler County Community College, Registrar, 901 S Haverhill Rd, El Dorado, KS 67042, 316-322-3124, 316-322-3102 (Fax: 316-322-0891) www.buccc.cc.ks.us. 8AM-5PM. Enrollment: 8000. Records go back to 1926. Alumni records maintained here; call 316-322-3228. Degrees granted: Associate. Attendance and degree information available by phone, fax, mail. Transcripts available by fax, mail.

Central Baptist Theological Seminary, Registrar, 741 N 31st St, Kansas City, KS 66102-3964, 913-371-5313, 800-677-2287 (Fax: 913-371-8110) www.cbts.edu. 8AM-4:30PM. Enrollment: 100. Records go back to 1901. Alumni Records: 741 N 31st St, Kansas City, MO 66102. Degrees granted: Masters. Attendance, degree and transcript information available by fax, mail.

Central College, Registrar, 1200 S Main St, McPherson, KS 67460, 316-241-0723 (Fax: 316-241-6032) www.centralcollege.edu. 8AM-5PM. Enrollment: 300. Records go back to 1914. Alumni records are maintained here. Degrees granted: Associate; Bachelors. Attendance and degree information available by phone, fax, mail. Transcripts available by fax, mail.

Cloud County Community College, Office of Student Records, 2221 Campus Dr, PO Box 1002, Concordia, KS 66901-1002, 913-243-1435, 800-729-5101 (Fax: 913-243-1043) www.cloudcc.cc.ks.us. 8AM-5PM. Enrollment: 3500. Records go back to 1965. Alumni records maintained here; call 913-243-1435. Degrees granted: Associate. Attendance and degree information available by phone, fax, mail. Transcripts available by mail.

Coffeyville Community College, Registrar, 400 W 11th, Coffeyville, KS 67337, 316-251-7700 X2021, 316-251-7700 X2166 (Fax: 316-252-7040). 8AM-5PM. Enrollment: 2195. Records go back to 1971. Alumni records maintained here; call 316-251-7700 X2069. Degrees granted: Associate. Attendance and degree information available by phone, mail. Transcripts available by mail.

Colby Community College, Registrar, 1255 S Range, Colby, KS 67701, 785-462-4675, 785-462-3984 (Fax: 785-462-4600). 8AM-5PM. Enrollment: 2400. Records go back to 1965. Alumni records maintained here; call 785-462-3984. Degrees granted: Associate. Attendance, degree and transcript information available by mail.

Cowley County Community College, Registrar, 125 S Second St, PO Box 1147, Arkansas City, KS 67005, 316-442-0430 (Fax: 316-441-5350) www.cowley.cc.ks.us. 8AM-4:30PM. Enrollment: 2930. Records go back to 1922. Alumni records are maintained here. Degrees granted: Associate. Attendance and degree information available by phone, fax, mail. Transcripts available by fax, mail.

Dodge City Community College, Registrar, 2501 N 14th Ave, Dodge City, KS 67801, 316-225-1321, 800-742-9519 www.dccc.dodge-city.cc.ks.us. (Fax: 316-227-9277) 8AM-5PM. Enrollment: 2277. Records go back to 1934. Alumni records are maintained here. Degrees granted: Associate. Certification: Vocational. Attendance and degree information available by phone, fax, mail. Transcripts available by fax, mail.

Donnelly College, Registrar, 608 N 18th St, Kansas City, KS 66102, 913-621-6070 X33 (Fax: 913-621-0354). 8:30AM-4:30PM. Enrollment: 750. Records go back to 1949. Alumni records are maintained here. Degrees granted: Associate. Attendance and degree information available by phone, mail. Transcripts available by mail.

Emporia State University, Registrar, 1200 Commercial St, Emporia, KS 66801, www.emporia.edu. 316-341-5154 (Fax: 316-341-5517) 8AM - 5PM; 7:30AM - 4PM Summer. Enrollment: 6000. Records go back to 1900. Alumni Records: PO Box 4047, Emporia, KS 66801. Degrees granted: Bachelors; Masters; Doctorate. Attendance and degree information available by phone, fax, mail. Transcripts available by mail.

Fort Hays State University, Registrar, 600 Park St, Hays, KS 67601, 785-628-4222 (Fax: 785-628-4085) fhsuvm.fhsu.edu. 8AM-4:30PM. Enrollment: 5800. Records go back to 1902. Alumni records maintained here; call 785-628-4430. Degrees granted: Associate; Bachelors; Masters. Attendance and degree information available by phone, fax, mail. Transcripts available by fax, mail.

Fort Scott Community College, Registrar, 2108 S Horton St, Fort Scott, KS 66701, 316-223-2700 (Fax: 316-223-6530) 7:30AM-5PM. www.ftscott.cc.ks.us. Enrollment: 1555. Records go back to 1919. Alumni records are maintained here. Degrees granted: Associate. Special programs- Call 316-223-2700. Attendance and degree information available by phone, fax, mail. Transcripts available by mail.

Friends University, Registrar, 2100 W University St, Wichita, KS 67213, 316-295-5400 (Fax: 316-269-3538) www.friends.edu. 8AM-6PM M-Th; 8AM-5PM F. Enrollment: 2700. Records go back to 1900. Alumni records maintained here; call 316-295-5900. Degrees granted: Associate; Bachelors; Masters. Attendance and degree information available by phone, fax, mail. Transcripts available by fax, mail.

Garden City Community College, Registrar, 801 Campus Dr, Garden City, KS 67846, 316-276-7611, 316-276-9530 (Fax: 316-276-9573) www.gcnet.com/gccc/. 8AM-4:30PM. Enrollment: 2400. Records go back to 1919. Degrees granted: Associate. Attendance and degree information available by phone, fax, mail. Transcripts available by fax, mail.

Haskell Indian Junior College
(See Haskell Indian Nations University)

Haskell Indian Nations University, Registrar, 155 Indian Ave #1305, PO Box 5031, Lawrence, KS 66046-4800, 785-749-8454 (Fax: 785-749-8429) www.haskell.edu. 9AM-4PM. Enrollment: 900. Alumni records maintained here; call 785-749-8481. Degrees granted: Associate; Bachelors. Attendance and degree information available by phone, fax, mail. Transcripts available by mail.

Hesston College, Registrar, PO Box 3000, Hesston, KS 67062, 316-327-8231, 316-327-8204 (Fax: 316-327-8300) www.hesston.edu. 8AM-5PM. Enrollment: 450. Records go back to 1909. Alumni records are maintained here also. Call 316-327-8110. Degrees granted: Associate. Attendance and degree information available by phone, fax, mail. Transcripts available by fax, mail.

Highland Community College, Registrar, 606 W Main St, Highland, KS 66035, 785-442-6025 (Fax: 785-442-6100) 8AM-5PM. www.highland.cc.ks.us. Enrollment: 2600. Records go back to 1930's. Alumni records maintained here; call 785-442-6109. Degrees granted: Associate. Attendance and degree information available by phone, fax, mail. Transcripts available by mail.

Hutchinson Community College, Registrar, 1300 N Plum St, Hutchinson, KS 67501, 316-665-3520, 316-665-3500 (Fax: 316-665-3301) www.hutchcc.edu. 8AM-5PM. Enrollment: 5000. Records go back to 1928. Alumni records maintained here; call 316-665-3527. Degrees granted: Associate. Attendance and degree information available by phone, fax, mail. Transcripts available by fax, mail.

Independence Community College, Registrar, College Ave and Brookside Dr, Independence, KS 67301, 316-331-4100, 800-842-6063 (Fax: 316-331-0946) www.indy.cc.ks.us. 8AM-5PM. Enrollment: 2000. Records go back to 1925. Alumni records are maintained here. Degrees granted: Associate. Attendance and degree information available by fax, mail. Transcripts available by mail.

Johnson County Community College, Records Office, 12345 College Blvd, Overland Park, KS 66210-1299, 913-469-8500, 913-469-8500 X3434 8AM-5PM. www.johnco.cc.ks.us. Enrollment: 16000. Records go back to 1971. Alumni records are maintained here. Degrees granted: Associate. Attendance and degree information available by phone, mail. Transcripts available by mail.

Kansas City College and Bible School, Registrar, 7401 Metcalf, Overland Park, KS 66204, 913-722-0272 X126 (Fax: 913-722-2135) www.wonderlink.net/~kccbslib. Enrollment: 55. Records go back to 1938. Alumni records are maintained here. Degrees granted: Associate; Bachelors. Special programs- Ministerial: Missions: Teacher Education: General Business: Secretarial Science: Music Ministry: General Studies, 913-722-0272. Attendance and degree information available by phone, fax, mail. Transcripts available by fax, mail.

Kansas City Kansas Community College, Registrar, 7250 State Ave, Kansas City, KS 66112, 913-334-1100 (Fax: 913-596-9609) www.kckcc.cc.ks.us. 7:30AM - 4:30PM. Enrollment: 6000. Records go back to 1923. Alumni records maintained here; call 913-334-1100 X632. Degrees granted: Associate. Special programs- Call 913-334-1100. Attendance and degree information available by phone, fax, mail. Transcripts available by mail.

Kansas College of Technology
(See Kansas State University - Salina, College of Technology)

Kansas Newman College, Registrar, 3100 McCormick Ave, Wichita, KS 67213, 316-942-4291 X121 www.ksnewman.edu. (Fax: 316-942-4483) 8AM-6PM M-Th; 8AM-5PM F. Enrollment: 2000. Records go back to 1933. Alumni records are maintained here. Degrees granted: Associate; Bachelors; Masters. Attendance and degree information available by phone, fax, mail. Transcripts available by fax, mail.

Kansas State University, Registrar's Office, 118 Anderson Hall, Manhattan, KS 66506-0114, 785-532-6254 (Fax: 785-532-6393; 785-532-5599 (Transcripts)) www.ksu.edu/registrar/. 8AM-Noon, 1-5PM. Enrollment: 20000. Records go back to 1863. Alumni Records: 2323 Anderson Ave, Manhattan, KS 66502. Degrees granted: Associate; Bachelors; Masters; Doctorate. Attendance and degree information available by phone, fax, mail. Transcripts available by fax, mail.

Kansas State University (Salina College of Technology), Assistant Registrar, 2409 Scanlan Ave, Salina, KS 67401-8196, 785-826-2607, 785-826-2639 (Fax: 785-826-2936) www.sal.ksu.edu. 8AM-5PM. Records go back to 1965. Alumni records maintained here; call 785-826-2642. Degrees granted: Associate; Bachelors. Special programs- Aviation: Engineering Technology. Attendance and degree information available by phone, fax, mail. Transcripts available by fax, mail.

Kansas Wesleyan University, Registrar, 100 E Clafin, Salina, KS 67401, 785-827-5541 X1260, 800-874-1154 (Fax: 785-827-0927). 8:15AM-Noon, 1-5PM. Enrollment: 720. Records go back to 1890's. Alumni records are maintained here. Degrees granted: Associate; Bachelors; Masters. Certification: Education. Adverse incident record source-Registrar's Office, 785-827-5541. Attendance and degree information available by phone, fax, mail. Transcripts available by fax, mail.

Labette Community College, Registrar, 200 S 14th St, Parsons, KS 67357, 316-421-6700 X68 (Fax: 316-421-0180). 8AM-8PM M-Th, 8AM-4:30PM F. Enrollment: 2023. Records go back to 1923. Alumni records maintained here; call 316-421-0180 X64. Degrees granted: Associate. Attendance and degree information available by phone, fax, mail. Transcripts available by fax, mail.

Manhattan Christian College, Registrar, 1415 Anderson Ave, Manhattan, KS 66502, 785-539-3571 (Fax: 785-539-0832) www.mccks.edu. 8AM-5PM. Enrollment: 300. Records go back to 1927. Alumni records are maintained here. Degrees granted: Associate; Bachelors. Attendance and degree information available by phone, fax, mail. Transcripts available by fax, mail.

Marymount College of Kansas
(See Ft. Hays State University)

McPherson College, Registrar, 1600 E Euclid, PO Box 1402, McPherson, KS 67460, 316-241-0731 (Fax: 316-241-8443). 8AM-5PM. Enrollment: 500. Records go back to 1934. Alumni records are maintained here. Degrees granted: Bachelors. Certification: Education. Attendance and degree information available by phone, fax, mail. Transcripts available by mail.

MidAmerica Nazarene University, Registrar, 2030 E College Way, Olathe, KS 66062-1899, 913-782-3750 (Fax: 913-791-3290) www.mnu.edu. 8AM - 5PM. Enrollment: 1400. Records go back to 1968. Alumni records are maintained here. Degrees granted: Associate; Bachelors; Masters; MD, MBA. Attendance and degree information available by phone, fax, mail. Transcripts available by fax, mail.

Neosho County Community College, Registrar, 800 W 14th St, Chanute, KS 66720, 316-431-2820, 316-431-6222 (Fax: 316-431-0082) www.neosho.cc.ks.us. 8AM-5PM. Enrollment: 1500. Records go back to 1981. Degrees granted: Associate. Special programs- Nursing, 316-431-2820 X254. Attendance and degree information available by phone, fax, mail. Transcripts available by written request only.

Ottawa University, Registrar, 1001 S Cedar #43, Ottawa, KS 66067-3399, 913-242-5200 X5581, 913-242-5200 X5508 (Fax: 913-242-4625) www.ott.edu. 8AM-Noon, 1-5PM. Enrollment: 8115. Records go back to 1860's. Alumni Records: 1001 S Cedar #16, Ottawa, KS 66067-3399. Degrees granted: Bachelors; Masters. Attendance and degree information available by phone, fax, mail. Transcripts available by fax, mail.

Pittsburg State University, Registrar, 1701 S Broadway, Pittsburg, KS 66762, 316-235-4200, 316-235-4206 (Fax: 316-235-4015) 8AM-4:30PM. www.pittstate.edu. Enrollment: 6500. Records go back to 1903. Alumni records maintained here; call 316-235-4759. Degrees granted: Associate; Bachelors; Masters; Specialist in Education. Attendance and degree information available by phone, fax, mail. Transcripts available by fax, mail.

Pratt Community College, Registrar, 348 NE SR61, Pratt, KS 67124, 316-672-5641 (Fax: 316-672-5288) www.pcc.cc.ks.us. 8AM-5PM. Enrollment: 1291. Alumni records are maintained here. Degrees granted: Associate. Attendance and degree information available by phone, fax, mail. Transcripts available by mail.

Seward County Community College, Registrar, 1801 N Kansas St, Box 1137, Liberal, KS 67901, www.sccc.cc.ks.us. 316-629-2616, 316-624-1951 (Fax: 316-629-2715) 7:45AM - 4:45PM. Enrollment: 1631. Records go back to 1969. Alumni records maintained here; call 316-629-2664. Degrees granted: Associate. Attendance and degree information available by phone, fax, mail. Transcripts available by mail.

Southwestern College, Registrar, 100 College St, Winfield, KS 67156, 316-221-8268 (Fax: 316-221-8384) www.sckans.edu. 8AM-Noon, 1-5PM. Enrollment: 750. Records go back to 1886. Alumni records maintained here; call 316-221-8372. Degrees granted: Bachelors; Masters. Attendance and degree information available by phone, fax, mail. Transcripts available by fax, mail.

St. Mary College, Registrar, 4100 S 4th St Trafficway, Leavenworth, KS 66048-5082, 913-682-5151, 913-758-6121 (Fax: 913-758-6140) www.smcks.edu. 8AM-4:30PM. Enrollment: 700. Records go back to 1928. Alumni records maintained here; call 913-682-5151 X6119. Degrees granted: Associate; Bachelors; Masters. Attendance and degree information available by phone, fax, mail. Transcripts available by mail.

Sterling College, Registrar, PO Box 98, Sterling, KS 67579, 316-278-4280 (Fax: 316-278-3690) www.sterling.edu. 8AM-5PM. Enrollment: 475. Records go back to 1887. Alumni records maintained here; call 316-278-4329. Degrees granted: Bachelors. Attendance and degree information available by phone, fax, mail. Transcripts available by fax, mail.

Tabor College, Registrar, 400 S Jefferson St, Hillsboro, KS 67063, 316-947-3121, 316-947-3120 X1044 (Fax: 316-947-2607) www.tabor.edu. 8AM-5PM. Enrollment: 500. Records go back to 1920. Alumni records are maintained here. Degrees granted: Associate; Bachelors. Special programs- Adult Degree Completion, 316-681-8616. Attendance and degree information available by phone, fax, mail. Transcripts available by fax, mail.

United States Army Command and General Staff College, Registrar, Reynolds Ave, Fort Leavenworth, KS 66027-1352, 913-684-2311 (Fax: 913-684-2049) 7PM-4:30PM. www.cgsc.army.com. Records go back to 1881. Degrees granted: Masters. Attendance and degree information available by phone, fax, mail. Transcripts available by fax, mail.

University of Kansas, Registrar, Lawrence, KS 66045, 785-864-4422 (Fax: 785-864-5230) www.urc.ukans.edu. 8AM-5PM. Enrollment: 26000. Records go back to 1866. Alumni records maintained here; call 785-864-4760. Degrees granted: Bachelors; Masters; PhD. Attendance and degree information available by phone, fax, mail. Transcripts available by mail.

University of Kansas Medical Center, Registrar, 3901 St & Rainbow Blvd, Kansas City, KS 66160-7190, www.kumc.edu. 913-588-4698, 913-588-7055 (Fax: 913-588-4697) 8AM-4:30PM. Records go back to 1902. Alumni records maintained here; call 913-588-1255. Degrees granted: Bachelors; Masters; Doctorate. Attendance and degree information available by phone, fax, mail. Transcripts available by mail.

Washburn University of Topeka, Registrar, 17th and College Sts, Topeka, KS 66621, 785-231-1010 X1074, 785-231-1010 X1078 www.wuacc.edu. 8AM-5PM. Enrollment: 6300. Records go back to 1865. Alumni records maintained here; call 785-231-1010 X1641. Degrees granted: Associate; Bachelors; Masters; JD. Attendance and degree information available by phone, fax, mail. Transcripts available by mail.

Wichita State University, Registrar, 1845 Fairmount, Wichita, KS 67260-0058, 316-978-3092, 316-978-3672 (Fax: 316-978-3795) 8AM-7PM M,T; 8AM-5PM W-F. Enrollment: 14568. Records go back to 1892. Alumni records maintained here; call 316-978-3827. Degrees granted: Associate; Bachelors; Masters; Doctorate. Attendance and degree information available by phone, fax, mail. Transcripts available by fax, mail.

Kentucky

Alice Lloyd College, Registrar, Purpose Rd, Pippa Passes, KY 41844, 606-368-2101 X4502 (Fax: 606-368-2125) 8AM-4:30PM. Enrollment: 500. Records go back to 1923. Alumni records maintained here; call 606-368-2101 X4601. Degrees granted:

Bachelors. Attendance and degree information available by phone, fax, mail. Transcripts available by fax, mail.

Asbury College, Registrar, One Macklem Dr, Wilmore, KY 40390-1198, 606-858-3511 X2325 (Fax: 606-858-3511 X3921)

www.asbury.edu. 8AM-5PM. Records go back to 1890. Alumni records maintained here; call 606-858-3511 X2167. Degrees granted: Bachelors. Attendance and degree information available by phone, fax, mail. Transcripts available by mail.

Asbury Theological Seminary, Registrar, 204 N Lexington Ave, Wilmore, KY 40390-1199, 606-858-3581 (Fax: 606-858-2248). 8AM-4:30PM. Enrollment: 1000. Records go back to 1923. Alumni records maintained here; call 606-858-2305. Degrees granted: Masters; Doctorate. Attendance and degree information available by phone, mail. Transcripts available by mail.

Ashland Community College, Registrar, 1400 College Dr, Ashland, KY 41101-3683, 606-329-2999 (Fax: 606-325-9403) 8AM-5PM. www.ashcc.uky.edu. Enrollment: 2300. Records go back to 1940. Alumni records are maintained here. Degrees granted: Associate. Attendance information available by phone, fax, mail. Degree and transcript information available by fax, mail.

Bellarmine College, Registrar, 2001 Newburg Rd, Louisville, KY 40205, 502-452-8133, 502-452-8131 (Fax: 502-452-8002) www.bellarmine.edu. 8AM-5PM. Enrollment: 2400. Records go back to 1938. Alumni records maintained here; call 502-452-8333. Degrees granted: Associate; Bachelors; Masters. Attendance and degree information available by phone, fax, mail. Transcripts available by mail.

Berea College, Associate to the Provost, Berea, KY 40404, 606-986-9341 X5185 (Fax: 606-985-0355) www.berea.edu. 8AM-Noon, 1-5PM. Records go back to 1855. Alumni records maintained here; call 606-986-9341 X5105. Degrees granted: Bachelors. Attendance and degree information available by phone, fax, mail. Transcripts available by fax, mail.

Bowling Green Junior College of Business
(See Western Kentucky University)

Brescia University, Registrar, 717 Frederica St, Owensboro, KY 42301-3023, 502-685-3131, 800-264-1234 (Fax: 502-686-4266). Enrollment: 700. Records go back to 1925. Alumni records are maintained here. Degrees granted: Associate; Bachelors; Masters. Special programs- Weekend College, 502-686-4252. Attendance and degree information available by mail. Transcripts available by written request only. Mail requests only with copy of student consent.

Campbellsville University, Director of Student Records, 1 University Dr, Campbellsville, KY 42718-2799, 502-789-5233, 502-789-5019 (Fax: 502-789-5020) www.campbellsvil.edu. 8AM-5PM. Enrollment: 1630. Records go back to 1950. Formerly **Campbellsville College**. Alumni records maintained here; call 502-789-5211. Degrees granted: Associate; Bachelors; Masters. Attendance and degree information available by phone, fax, mail. Transcripts available by mail.

CareerCom Junior College of Business
(See RETS Medical & Business Institute)

Centre College, Registrar's Office, 600 W Walnut St, Danville, KY 40422, 606-238-5360 (Fax: 606-238-6226) www.centre.edu. 8:30AM-4:30PM. Enrollment: 1000. Records go back to 1900. Alumni records maintained here; call 606-238-5500. Degrees granted: Bachelors. Attendance and degree information available by phone, fax, mail. Transcripts available by mail.

Clear Creek Baptist Bible College, Registrar's Office, 300 Clear Creek Rd, Pineville, KY 40977, 606-377-3196 (Fax: 606-337-2372) www.ccbbc.edu. 8AM-4:30PM. Enrollment: 170. Records go back to 1926. Alumni records are maintained here. Degrees granted: Associate; Bachelors. Attendance and degree information available by fax, mail. Transcripts available by mail.

Cumberland College, Registrar, 6174 College Station Dr, Williamsburg, KY 40769, 606-539-4316, 606-539-4217 (Fax: 606-539-4490) 8:30AM - 5PM. www.cc.cumber.edu. Enrollment: 1500. Records go back to 1889. Alumni records maintained here; call 606-539-4277. Degrees granted: Bachelors; Masters. Attendance and degree information available by phone, fax, mail. Transcripts available by mail.

Draughons College of Business
(See Franklin College Truck Driving School)

Draughons Junior College (Branch Campus), Registrar, 2424 Airway Dr and Lovers Lane, Bowling Green, KY 42103, 502-843-6750 (Fax: 502-843-6976) 8AM-5:30PM. Enrollment: 175. Records go back to 1989. Alumni records are maintained here. Degrees granted: Associate. Special programs- Business. Attendance and degree information available by phone, mail. Transcripts available by mail.

Eastern Kentucky University, Records Office, Coates Box 28-A, Richmond, KY 40457-3101, 606-622-1102, 606-622-3876 (Fax: 606-622-6207) www.eku.edu. 8:30AM-4PM. Enrollment: 16500. Records go back to 1906. Alumni records maintained here; call 606-622-1260. Degrees granted: Associate; Bachelors; Masters. Attendance, degree and transcript information available by fax, mail.

Elizabethtown Community College, Registrar, 600 College Street Rd, Elizabethtown, KY 42701, 502-769-1632, 502-769-2371 (Fax: 502-769-0736) www.uky.edu/CommunityColleges/Eli 8AM-5PM M-Th, 8AM-3PM F. Enrollment: 3131. Records go back to 1965. Alumni records are maintained here. Degrees granted: Associate. Attendance and degree information available by phone, mail. Transcripts available by mail.

Franklin College Truck Driving School, Transcript Department, 3360 Park Ave, Paducah, KY 42001, 502-443-8478 (Fax: 502-442-5329) Records go back to 1993. Formerly **CareerCom Junior College & Draughons College of Business**. Degrees granted: CDL. Attendance and degree information available by phone, fax, mail. Transcripts available by fax, mail.

Fugazzi College, Registrar, 407 Marquis Ave, Lexington, KY 40502, 606-266-0401 (Fax: 606-268-2118). 9AM - 5PM. Enrollment: 150. Records go back to 1993. Degrees granted: Associate. Special programs- Broadcasting and Operations Radio and TV: Medical Assisting: Travel and Tourism: Computer Applications: Business Management: Business Administration: Medical Transcription. Attendance, degree and transcript information available by fax, mail.

Georgetown College, Registrar, 400 E College St, Georgetown, KY 40324, 502-863-8024 www.georgetowncollege.edu. 8AM-5PM. Enrollment: 1400. Records go back to 1900. Alumni records maintained here; call 502-863-8041. Degrees granted: Bachelors; Masters. Attendance and degree information available by phone, mail. Transcripts available by mail.

Hazard Community College, Registrar, One Community College Dr, Hazard, KY 41701, 606-436-5721, 606-666-7521 (Fax: 606-439-2988). 8AM-4:30PM. Enrollment: 2300. Records go back to 1989. Alumni Records: Alumni Assoc., 400 Rd St, Lexington, KY 40505. Degrees granted: Associate. Attendance and degree information available by phone, fax, mail. Transcripts available by fax, mail.

Henderson Community College, Registrar, 2660 S Green St, Henderson, KY 42420, 502-827-1867 (Fax: 502-826-8391). 8AM-6:30PM M-Th; 8AM-5PM F. Enrollment: 1200. Records go back to 1960. Alumni records maintained here; call 502-827-1867 X236. Degrees granted: Associate. Attendance and degree information available by phone, mail. Transcripts available by written request only.

Hopkinsville Community College, Registrar, PO Box 2100, Hopkinsville, KY 42241-2100, 502-886-3921 (Fax: 502-886-0237) www.hopntsvl.hopcc.uky.edu. 8AM-4:30PM. Enrollment: 3000. Records go back to 1966. Alumni records are maintained here. Degrees granted: Associate. Attendance and degree information available by phone, mail. Transcripts available by written request only.

ITT Technical Institute (Branch of Evansville, IN), Registrar, 10509 Timberwood Cir, Louisville, KY 40223, 502-327-7424 (Fax: 502-327-7624) 8AM-9PM. Enrollment: 280. Records go back to 1993. Started in June 1993. Alumni Records: PO Box 50466, Indianapolis, IN 46250-0466. Degrees granted: Associate. Attendance and degree information available by phone, fax, mail. Transcripts available by mail.

Institute of Electronic Technology
(See Spencerian College)

Institute of Electronic Technology, Registrar, PO Box 8252, 509 s ·30th St, Paducah, KY 42002-8252, 502-444-9676, 502-444-9677 (Fax: 502-441-7202) www.iet.ky.com. 8:30AM-5PM. Enrollment: 159. Records go back to 1976. Alumni records are maintained here. Degrees granted: Associate. Special programs- Electronic Engineering Technology. Attendance and degree information available by phone, fax, mail.. Transcripts available by fax, mail.

Jefferson Community College, Registrar, 109 E Broadway, Louisville, KY 40202, 502-584-0181 X2128, X2148, X2123 (Fax: 502-584-0181 X2115) www.jcc.uky.edu. 8AM-5PM M-Th, 8AM-4:30PM. Enrollment: 8735. Records go back to 1968. Alumni records maintained here; call 502-584-0181 X2413. Degrees granted: Associate. Attendance and degree information available by phone, mail. Transcripts available by mail.

Kentucky Christian College, Registrar, 100 Academic Pkwy, Grayson, KY 41143-2205, 606-474-3212 (Fax: 606-474-3154). 8:30AM-4:30PM. Enrollment: 515. Records go back to 1919. Alumni records maintained here; call 606-474-3277. Degrees granted: Associate; Bachelors. Attendance and degree information available by phone, fax, mail. Transcripts available by fax, mail.

Kentucky College of Business (Branch), Registrar, 115 E Lexington Ave, **Danville**, KY 40422, 606-236-6991, 606-236-6992 (Fax: 606-236-1063). Records are located at National Business College, Registrar, Roanoke, VA.

Kentucky College of Business (Branch), Registrar, 7627 Ewing Blvd, **Florence**, KY 41042, 606-525-6510 (Fax: 606-525-2815). Records are located at National Business College, Registrar, Roanoke, VA.

Kentucky College of Business, Registrar, 628 E Main St, **Lexington**, KY 40508, 606-253-0621 (Fax: 606-233-3054) 8AM-4:30PM. Enrollment: 700. Records go back to 1941. Degrees granted: Associate. Special programs- Call 606-253-0621. Attendance and degree information available by fax, mail. Transcripts available by mail.

Kentucky College of Business (Branch), Registrar, 3950 Dixie Hwy, **Louisville**, KY 40216, 502-447-7634. Records are located at National Business College, Registrar, Roanoke, VA.

Kentucky College of Business (Branch), Registrar, 198 S Mayo Trail, **Pikeville**, KY 41501, 606-432-5477 (Fax: 606-437-4952) Records are located at National Business College, Registrar, Roanoke, VA.

Kentucky College of Business (Branch), Registrar, 139 Killarney Lane, **Richmond**, KY 40475, 606-623-8956 (Fax: 606-624-5544) Records are located at National Business College, Registrar, Roanoke, VA.

Kentucky Mountain Bible College, Registrar, 855 Hwy 541, PO Box 10, Vancleve, KY 41385, 606-666-5000 (Fax: 606-666-7744). 8AM-5PM. Enrollment: 57. Records go back to 1994. Degrees granted: Associate; Bachelors. Attendance and degree information available by phone, mail. Transcripts available by mail.

Kentucky State University, Registrar, 400 E Main St, Frankfort, KY 40601, 502-227-6340, 502-227-6795 (Fax: 502-227-6239) 8AM-4:30PM. www.kysu.edu. Enrollment: 2292. Records go back to 1880. Alumni records maintained here; call 502-227-6507. Degrees granted: Associate; Bachelors; Masters. Special programs- Masters of Public Administration, 502-227-6117. Attendance and degree information available by phone, fax, mail. Transcripts available by fax, mail.

Kentucky Wesleyan College, Registrar, 3000 Frederica St, PO Box 1039, Owensboro, KY 42302-1039, 502-926-3111 (Fax: 502-926-3196) www.kwc.edu. 8AM-5PM. Enrollment: 800. Records go back to 1900. Alumni records are maintained here. Degrees granted: Associate; Bachelors. Attendance and degree information available by phone, fax, mail. Transcripts available by mail.

Lees College at Hazard
(See Hazard Community College)

Lees College, Registrar, 601 Jefferson Ave, Jackson, KY 41339, 606-666-7521 (Fax: 606-666-8910). 8AM-5PM. Records go back to 1900's. Formerly **Lees College**. Degrees granted: Associate. Attendance, degree and transcript information available by mail.

Lexington Community College, Registrar Oswald Bldg, Cooper Dr, Lexington, KY 40506-0235, 606-257-4460, 606-257-4872 (Fax: 606-257-2634) www.uky.edu/LCC. 8AM-7:30PM M-Th, 8AM-4:30PM F. Enrollment: 5225. Records go back to 1965. Alumni records are maintained here. Degrees granted: Associate. Attendance and degree information available by phone, fax, mail. Transcripts available by mail.

Lexington Theological Seminary, Registrar, 631 S Limestone St, Lexington, KY 40508, 606-252-0361 (Fax: 606-253-6789). 8AM-4:45PM. Enrollment: 190. Records go back to 1865. Alumni records maintained here; call 606-252-0361. Degrees granted: Masters; Doctorate. Attendance, degree and transcript information available by fax, mail.

Lindsey Wilson College, Registrar, 210 Lindsey Wilson St, Columbia, KY 42728, 502-384-2126 X8024, 502-384-2126 X8025 (Fax: 502-384-8200) www.occ.uky.edu/occ 7:30AM-4:30PM. Enrollment: 1425. Records go back to 1923. Alumni records maintained here; call 502-384-8400. Degrees granted: Associate; Bachelors; Masters. Attendance and degree information available by phone, fax, mail. Transcripts available by mail.

Louisville Presbyterian Theological Seminary, Registrar, 1044 Alta Vista Rd, Louisville, KY 40205, 502-895-3411 (Fax: 502-895-1096) 8:30AM-5PM. Enrollment: 250. Records go back to 1920. Alumni records are maintained here. Degrees granted: Masters; Doctorate. Attendance and degree information available by phone, fax, mail. Transcripts available by written request only.

Louisville Technical Institute, Registrar, 3901 Atkinson Dr, Louisville, KY 40218, 502-456-6509 (Fax: 502-456-2341). Enrollment: 500. Records go back to 1970. Degrees granted: Associate. Special programs- Marine Mechanics Technician: Architectural Computer Ad Design Drafting: Mechanical Engineer: Electrical Engineer: Computer Graphics: Interior Design. Attendance, degree and transcript information available by mail.

Madisonville Community College, Registrar, 2000 College Dr, Madisonville, KY 42431, 502-821-2250 (Fax: 502-821-1555). 8AM-4:30PM. Enrollment: 2500. Alumni records are maintained here. Degrees granted: Associate. Attendance and degree information available by phone, fax, mail. Transcripts available by mail.

Maysville Community College, Registrar, 1755 US 68, Maysville, KY 41056, 606-759-7141 X225, 606-759-5818 X224 (Fax: 606-759-7176). 8AM-4:30PM. Enrollment: 1300. Records go back to 1968. Alumni records are maintained here. Degrees granted: Associate. Special programs- Business, 606-759-7141: IET, 606-759-7141: Nursing, 606-759-7141: Environmental Science, 606-759-7141. Attendance and degree information available by phone, fax, mail. Transcripts available by fax, mail.

Midway College, Starks Hall/101, Registrar, 512 E Stephens St, Midway, KY 40347-1120, 606-846-5340, 606-846-5341 & 606-846-5728 (Fax: 606-846-5774) www.midway.edu. 8AM-5PM. Enrollment: 975. Records go back to 1848. Alumni Records: Institutional Advancement, Marrs Hall, 512 E Stephens St, Midway, KY 40347-1120. Degrees granted: Associate; Bachelors. Attendance and degree information available by fax, mail. Transcripts available by mail.

Morehead State University, Registrar, University Blvd, Morehead, KY 40351, 606-783-2221 (Fax: 606-783-5038) 8AM-4:30PM. www.atmoreheadst.edu. Enrollment: 8300. Records go back to 1922. Alumni records maintained here; call 606-783-2221. Degrees granted: Associate; Bachelors; Masters. Attendance and degree information available by phone, fax, mail. Transcripts available by fax (in emergency), mail.

Murray State University, Assistant Registrar, PO Box 9, Murray, KY 42071-0009, 502-762-3778, 502-762-3741 (Fax: 502-762-3050) www.mursuky.edu. 8:30AM - 4:30PM. Enrollment: 8800. Records go back to 1923. Alumni records maintained here; call 502-762-3011. Degrees granted: Associate; Bachelors; Masters; Specialists. Attendance and degree information available by phone, fax, mail. Transcripts available by fax, mail.

Northern Kentucky University, Office of Registrar, Service Center LAC 301, Highland Heights, KY 41099-7011, 606-572-5556 (Fax: 606-572-6094) www.nku.edu. 8:15AM-6:15PM M-Th; 8:15AM - 4:30PM F. Enrollment: 11000. Records go back to 1970. Alumni records maintained here; call 606-572-5486. Degrees granted: Associate; Bachelors; Masters. Attendance and degree information available by phone, mail. Transcripts available by mail.

Owensboro Community College, Registrar, 4800 New Hartford Rd, Owensboro, KY 42303, 502-686-4400, 502-686-4408 (Fax: 502-686-4648) 8AM-4:30PM. Enrollment: 2300. Records go back to 1986. Alumni records are maintained here. Degrees granted: Associate. Attendance, degree and transcript information available by fax, mail.

Owensboro Junior College of Business, Registrar, 1515 E 18th St, Owensboro, KY 42303, 502-926-4040 X25, 800-960-4090 (Fax: 502-685-4090) 7:30AM-8PM. Enrollment: 200. Records go back to 1963. Degrees granted: Associate. Special programs- Call 502-926-4040 X25 Attendance, degree and transcript information available by fax, mail.

Paducah Community College, Registrar, PO Box 7380, Paducah, KY 42002-7380, 502-554-9200 X6124 (Fax: 502-554-6203) www.uky.edu/communitycolleges/pad 8AM-5PM. Enrollment: 1983. Records go back to 1968. Alumni records are maintained here. Degrees granted: Associate. Attendance and degree information available by written request only. Transcripts available by mail. Fax requests are acceptable if accompanied by a signed release.

Pikeville College, Registrar, 214 Sycamore St, Pikeville, KY 41501, 606-432-9369 (Fax: 606-432-9328) www.pc.edu. 8:30AM-5PM. Enrollment: 750. Records go back to 1936. Alumni records maintained here; call 606-432-9326. Degrees granted: Associate; Bachelors. Special programs- Osteopathic Medicine. Attendance and degree information available by phone, fax, mail. Transcripts available by mail.

Prestonsburg Community College, Registrar, One Bert T. Combs Dr, Prestonsburg, KY 41653, 606-886-3863 X396 (Fax: 606-886-6943) www.uky.edu. 8AM - 4:30PM. Enrollment: 2573. Records go back to 1964. Degrees granted: Associate. Attendance and degree information available by phone, fax, mail. Transcripts available by fax, mail.

RETS Electronic Institute, Registrar, 3000 High Rise Dr, Louisville, KY 40213, 502-968-7191 X412 (Fax: 502-968-1727) Enrollment: 400. Records go back to 1971. Degrees granted: Associate. Special programs- Micro Computer, 502-968-7191 X412. Attendance and degree information available by phone, fax, mail. Transcripts available by mail.

RETS Medical & Business Institute, Registrar, 1102 S Virginia St, Hopkinsville, KY 42240, 502-886-1302 (Fax: 502-886-3544) 8AM-10PM M-Th; 8AM-4PM F. Enrollment: 180. Records go back to 1984. Formerly **CareerCom Junior College of Business**. Alumni records are maintained here. Degrees granted: Associate. Special programs– Call 502-886-1302. Attendance and degree information available by phone, fax, mail. Transcripts available by fax, mail.

Somerset Community College, Registrar, 808 Monticello Rd, Somerset, KY 42501, 606-679-8501 (Fax: 606-677-9658) 8AM-5PM. www.uky.edu/communitycollege/som. Enrollment: 2600. Records go back to 1965. Alumni records are maintained here. Degrees granted: Associate. Special programs– Business Technology: Registered Nurse: Clinical Lab Technician: Physical Therapy Assistant. Attendance and degree information available by phone, fax, mail. Transcripts available by fax, mail.

Southeast Community College, Registrar, 700 College Rd, Cumberland, KY 40823, 606-589-2145 X2033 (Fax: 606-589-5423) www.uky.edu/community colleges/sou. 8:30AM-4:30PM. Enrollment: 2500. Records go back to 1961. Formerly **Southeastern Nebraska Technical Community College**. Alumni records are maintained here. Degrees granted: Associate. Attendance and degree information available by phone, mail. Transcripts available by mail.

Southern Baptist Theological Seminary, Registrar, 2825 Lexington Rd, Louisville, KY 40280, 502-897-4209 (Fax: 502-899-1781). 8AM-4:30PM. Enrollment: 1770. Records go back to 1859. Alumni records are maintained here. Degrees granted: Associate; Masters; Doctorate. Attendance and degree information available by phone, mail. Transcripts available by mail.

Southern Ohio College (Northern Kentucky), Registrar, 309 Buttermilk Pike, Fort Mitchell, KY 41017, 606-341-5627 (Fax: 606-341-6483). 9AM-6PM. Enrollment: 210. Records go back to 1983. Degrees granted: Associate; Diplomas. Special programs– Computer Science: Medical Assisting: Administrative Office Technician: Business Management: Accounting. Attendance, degree and transcript information available by fax, mail.

Southwestern College of Business, Registrar, 2929 S Dixie Hwy, Crestview Hills, KY 41017, 606-341-6633 9AM-7PM M-Th; 9AM-1PM F. Enrollment: 140. Records go back to 1987. Degrees granted: Associate. Attendance, degree and transcript information available by fax, mail.

Spalding University, Registrar's Office, 851 S Fourth St, Louisville, KY 40203-2188, 502-585-7110, 502-585-9911 (Fax: 502-583-1112) www.spalding.edu. 8AM-5PM. Enrollment: 1564. Records go back to 1920. Alumni records are maintained here. Degrees granted: Associate; Bachelors; Masters; Doctorate; Specialist. Attendance and degree information available by phone, fax, mail. Transcripts available by fax, mail, with signature required on fax.

Spencerian College (Branch), Registrar, 3330 Partner Pl, Lexington, KY 40503, 606-223-9608, 606-223-2899 (Fax: 606-224-7744) 8AM-5PM. Enrollment: 200. Records go back to 1997. Formerly **Institute of Electronic Technology**. Degrees granted: Associate. Special programs– Computer Repair: Occupational Science: Applied Science: Drafting: Computer Graphics: Electronic Engineering Technology: Mechanical Computer Aided Drafting: Architectural Computer Aided Grafting. Attendance, degree and transcript information available by fax, mail.

Spencerian College, Registrar, 4627 Dixie Hwy, PO Box 16418, Louisville, KY 40216, 502-447-1000 (Fax: 502-447-4574) 8AM-5PM. www.spencerian.edu. Enrollment: 2100. Records go back to 1954. Degrees granted: Associate. Attendance and degree information available by phone, mail. Transcripts available by mail.

St. Catharine College, Registrar, 2735 Bardstown Rd, St Catharine, KY 40061, 606-336-5082 (Fax: 606-336-5031). 8AM-5PM. Enrollment: 386. Alumni records are maintained here. Degrees granted: Associate. Attendance and transcript information available by fax, mail. Degree information available by phone, fax, mail. Faxed transcript requests must be followed up with original by mail.

Sue Bennett College, Registrar, 151 College St, London, KY 40741, 606-864-2238. 8AM-4:30PM. Records go back to 1900. College is permanently closed. Alumni records maintained here; call 606-864-2238 X1125. Degrees granted: Associate; Bachelors. Attendance, degree and transcript information available by fax, mail.

Sullivan College (Branch), Registrar, 2659 Regency Rd, Lexington, KY 40503, 606-276-4357. Records are located at Sullivan College, Registrar, Louisville, KY.

Sullivan College, Registrar, 3101 Bardstown Rd, Louisville, KY 40205, 502-456-6504 (Fax: 502-454-4880) 7:30AM-8PM M-Th; 7:30AM-4:30PM F; 8AM-2PM S. Enrollment: 2200. Records go back to 1960's. Alumni records are maintained here. Degrees granted: Associate; Bachelors; Masters. Attendance and degree information available by phone, fax, mail. Transcripts available by mail.

Thomas More College, Registrar, 333 Thomas More Pkwy, Crestview Hills, KY 41017, 606-344-3380 (Fax: 606-344-3345) 8:30AM-5PM. www.thomasmore.edu. Enrollment: 1500. Records go back to 1921. Formerly **Villa Madonna College**. Alumni records maintained here; call 606-344-3346. Degrees granted: Associate; Bachelors; Masters. Special programs– TAP Program 606-341-4554. Attendance, degree and transcript information available by fax, mail. Inquiry policy may change.

Transylvania University, Registrar, 300 N Broadway, Lexington, KY 40508, 606-233-8116 (Fax: 606-233-8797) www.transy.edu. 8:30AM-5PM. Records go back to 1900. Alumni records maintained here; call 606-233-8275. Degrees granted: Bachelors. Attendance and degree information available by phone, mail. Transcripts available by fax, mail.

Union College, Registrar, 310 College St, Barbourville, KY 40906, 606-546-1208 (Fax: 606-546-1663). 8AM - 4:30PM. Enrollment: 1000. Records go back to 1870. Alumni records maintained here; call 606-546-1218. Degrees granted: Associate; Bachelors; Masters. Attendance and degree information available by phone, fax, mail. Transcripts available by mail.

University of Kentucky, Registrar's Office, 10 Funkhouser Bldg, Lexington, KY 40506-0054, 606-257-3671, 606-257-1826 (Fax: 606-257-7160) www.uky.edu. 8AM-4:30PM. Enrollment: 26000. Records go back to 1900. Alumni Records: Alumni Assoc., 125 King, Lexington, KY 40506-0119. Degrees granted: Bachelors; Masters; Doctorate: Juris Doctor, MD, DD. Special programs– Dental School, 606-323-6071: Medical School, 606-323-5261. Attendance and degree information available by phone, fax, mail. Transcripts available by fax, mail.

University of Louisville, Registrar, 2211 S Third St, Louisville, KY 40292, 502-852-6522 (Fax: 502-852-7088) 9AM-5PM M,Th,F; 9AM-6PM T & W. Enrollment: 22000. Records go back to 1900. Alumni records maintained here; call 502-852-6186. Degrees granted: Associate; Bachelors; Masters; Doctorate. Attendance and degree information available by phone, fax, mail. Transcripts available by fax, mail.

Western Kentucky University, Office of the Registrar, Potter Hall, #1 Big Red Way, Bowling Green, KY 42101-3576, 502-745-3351, 502-745-5432 www.wku.edu. (Fax: 502-745-4830) 8AM-4:30PM. Enrollment: 15000. Records go back to 1906. Alumni records maintained here; call 502-745-4395. Degrees granted: Associate; Bachelors; Masters. Attendance and degree information available by phone, fax, mail. Transcripts available by fax, mail.

Louisiana

Bossier Parish Community College, Registrar, 2719 Airline Dr at I-220, Bossier City, LA 71111, 318-746-9851 (Fax: 318-742-8664) www.hpcc.cc.la.us. 8AM - 7PM M-Th, 8AM - 4PM F. Enrollment: 4700.

Records go back to 1967. Alumni records are maintained here. Degrees granted: Associate. Attendance and degree information available by phone, fax, mail. Transcripts available by fax, mail.

Centenary College of Louisiana, Registrar, PO Box 41188, Shreveport, LA 71134-1188, 318-869-5146, 318-869-5117 (Fax: 318-869-5026) www.centenary.edu. 8AM-4:30PM. Enrollment: 1000. Records go back to 1920's. Alumni records maintained here; call 318-869-5028. Degrees granted: Bachelors; Masters. Attendance and degree information available by phone, mail. Transcripts available by mail.

Delgado Community College, Registrar, 501 City Park Ave, New Orleans, LA 70119, 504-483-4492, 504-483-4490 (Fax: 504-483-4090) www.dcc.edu. 8:30AM-4:30PM. Enrollment: 10952. Records go back to 1924. Alumni records maintained here; call 504-483-4400. Degrees granted: Associate. Attendance and degree information available by phone, fax, mail. Transcripts available by fax, mail.

Delta College (Branch), Registrar, 100 Covington Center, Ste 30, Covington, LA 70433, 504-892-6651 (Fax: 504-892-5332) Enrollment: 50. Records go back to 1989. Alumni records are maintained here. Special programs- Call 504-892-6651. Attendance, degree and transcript information available by fax, mail.

Delta School of Business and Technology, Registrar, 517 Broad St, Lake Charles, LA 70601, 318-439-5765 (Fax: 318-436-5151). 8AM-5PM. Enrollment: 250. Records go back to 1974. Degrees granted: Associate. Attendance and degree information available by phone, fax, mail. Transcripts available by fax, mail.

Dillard University, Registrar, 2601 Gentilly Blvd, New Orleans, LA 70122, 504-286-4688, 504-286-4684 www.dillard.edu. 8AM-5PM. Enrollment: 1562. Records go back to 1898. Alumni records maintained here; call 504-286-4666. Degrees granted: Bachelors. Special programs- Call 504-286-4688. Attendance and degree information available by phone, mail. Transcripts available by mail.

Elaine P. Nunez Community College (See Nunez Community College)

Grambling State University, Registrar's Office, PO Box 589, Grambling, LA 71245, 318-274-2385, 318-274-2435 (Fax: 318-274-2777) 8AM-5PM. Enrollment: 7400. Records go back to 1930's. Alumni records maintained here; call 318-247-6706. Degrees granted: Associate; Bachelors; Masters; Doctorate. Attendance, degree and transcript information available by fax, mail.

Grantham College of Engineering, Registrar, 34641 Grantham College Rd, PO Box 5700, Slidell, LA 70469, 504-649-4191, 800-955-2527 (Fax: 504-649-4183) www.grantham.edu. 9AM-5PM. Enrollment: 2100. Records go back to 1951. Degrees granted: Associate; Bachelors. Attendance and degree information available by phone, fax, mail. Transcripts available by mail.

Louisiana College, Registrar, 1140 College Dr, Pineville, LA 71359, 318-487-7222 (Fax: 318-487-7191) www.lacollege.edu. 8AM-4:30PM. Enrollment: 1024. Records go back to 1910. Alumni records maintained here; call 318-487-7301. Degrees granted: Associate; Bachelors; Masters. Attendance, degree and transcript information available by fax, mail.

Louisiana State University Medical Center, Registrar, 433 Bolivar St, New Orleans, LA 70117, 504-568-4829 (Fax: 504-568-5545) www.lsumc.edu. 8AM-4:30PM. Enrollment: 3074. Records go back to 1979. Alumni records maintained here; call 504-568-4894. Degrees granted: Associate; Bachelors; Masters; Doctorate; PhD. Special programs- Call 504-568-4829. Attendance and degree information available by phone, mail. Transcripts available by mail.

Louisiana State University and Agricultural & Mechanical College, Office of Records & Registration, 112 Thomas Boyd Hall, Baton Rouge, LA 70803, 504-388-2065 (Main), 504-388-1686 (Fax: 504-388-5991) www.lsu.edu. 7:30AM - 5PM. Enrollment: 22950. Records go back to 1960's. Alumni records maintained here; call 504-388-3838 X3. Degrees granted: Bachelors; Masters; Doctorate. Attendance and degree information available by phone, fax, mail. Transcripts available by fax, mail.

Louisiana State University at Alexandria, Registrar, 8100 Hwy 71 S, Alexandria, LA 71302, 318-473-6412, 318-473-6411 (Fax: 318-473-6418). 8AM-4:30PM. Enrollment: 2580. Records go back to 1960. Degrees granted: Associate. Attendance and degree information available by phone, fax, mail. Transcripts available by fax, mail.

Louisiana State University at Eunice, Registrar, PO Box 1129, Eunice, LA 70535, 318-457-7311 (Fax: 318-546-6620) www.lsue.edu. 8AM-4:30PM. Enrollment: 2800. Records go back to 1967. Alumni records are maintained here. Degrees granted: Associate. Attendance, degree and transcript information available by fax, mail.

Louisiana State University at Shreveport, Registrar, One University Pl, Shreveport, LA 71115, 318-797-5249, 318-797-5061 (Fax: 318-797-5286) 8AM-4:30PM. www.lsus.edu. Enrollment: 4500. Records go back to 1957. Alumni records maintained here; call 318-797-5202. Degrees granted: Bachelors; Masters; Specialist. Attendance and degree information available by phone, mail. Transcripts available by mail.

Louisiana Tech University, Registrar, PO Box 3155, Ruston, LA 71272, 318-257-2176 (Fax: 318-257-4041) http://aurora.latech.edu. 8AM-5PM. Enrollment: 10000. Records go back to 1894. Alumni records are maintained here. Degrees granted: Associate; Bachelors; Masters; Doctorate. Attendance and degree information available by phone, fax, mail. Transcripts available by fax, mail. Attendance and degree information can be requested through the Internet site.

Louisiana Technical College (Sowela), Registrar, 3820 Legion St, PO Box 16950, Lake Charles, LA 70616, 318-491-2698 (Fax: 318-491-2135) 8AM-5PM. Enrollment: 907. Records go back to 1971. Alumni records are maintained here. Degrees granted: Associate. Attendance and degree information available by phone, mail. Transcripts available by mail.

Loyola University, Registrar, 6363 St. Charles Ave, New Orleans, LA 70118, www.loyno.edu. 504-865-3237 (Fax: 504-865-2110) 8:30AM - 4:45PM. Enrollment: 4485. Records go back to 1920. Alumni records are maintained here. Degrees granted: Bachelors; Masters; Law School. Attendance and degree information available by phone, fax, mail. Transcripts available by fax, mail.

McNeese State University, Registrar, 4205 Ryan St, Lake Charles, LA 70605, 318-475-5356, 318-475-5149 www.mcneese.edu. (Fax: 318-475-5189) 7:45AM-4:30PM Fall-Spring; 7:30-4:15PM Summer. Enrollment: 8137. Records go back to 1939. Alumni Records: 600 E McNeese, Lake Charles, LA 70607 (Fax: 318-475-5233). Degrees granted: Associate; Bachelors; Masters. Special programs- 318-474-5148. Attendance and degree information available by phone, fax, mail. Transcripts available by fax, mail.

New Orleans Baptist Theological Seminary, Registrar, 3939 Gentilly Blvd, New Orleans, LA 70126, 504-282-4455 X3337 (Fax: 504-286-8453) www.nobts.edu. 8AM-5PM. Enrollment: 2300. Records go back to 1919. Alumni records maintained here; call 504-282-4455 X3291. Degrees granted: Associate; Bachelors; Masters; Doctorate. Special programs- Call 504-282-4455. Attendance and degree information available by phone, fax, mail. Transcripts available by mail.

Nicholls State University, Office of Records, PO Box 2059, Thibodaux, LA 70310, 504-448-4153, 504-448-4227 www.nich.edu. 8AM-4:30PM. Enrollment: 7300. Records go back to 1948. Alumni Records: PO Box 2158, Thibodaux, LA 70310. Degrees granted: Associate; Bachelors; Masters. Attendance and degree information available by phone, fax, mail. Transcripts available by mail.

Northeast Louisiana University, University Registrar, 700 University Ave, Monroe, LA 71209, 318-342-5262 (Fax: 318-342-5274) www.nlu.edu. 8AM - 4:30PM. Enrollment: 10975. Records go back to 1932. Alumni records maintained here; call 318-342-5420. Degrees granted: Associate; Bachelors; Masters; Doctorate. Attendance and degree information available by phone, fax, mail. Transcripts available by fax, mail.

Northwestern State University, Registrar, College Ave, Natchitoches, LA 71497, 318-357-6171 (Fax: 318-357-5823) www.nsula.edu. 8AM-4:30PM. Enrollment: 8280. Records go back to 1885. Alumni records are maintained here. Degrees granted: Associate; Bachelors; Masters. Certification: Teacher. Special programs- Louisiana Scholar's College, 318-357-4577. Attendance and degree information available by fax, mail. Transcripts available by mail.

Notre Dame Seminary Graduate School of Theology, Registrar, 2901 S Carrollton Ave, New Orleans, LA 70118-4391, 504-866-7426 (Fax: 504-861-1301). 8AM-4PM. Enrollment: 125. Records go back to 1950. Alumni records are maintained here. Degrees granted: Masters. Attendance, degree and transcript information available by mail with signed release.

Nunez Community College, Registrar, 3710 Paris Rd, Chalmette, LA 70043, 504-278-7440, 504-278-7367 (Student Affairs Dept) (Fax: 504-278-7353) 8AM-7PM M-W 8AM-4:30PM Th,F. www.nunez.cc.la.us. Enrollment: 2107. Records go back to 1966. Formerly **Elaine P. Nunez CC** and **St. Bernard CC** - combined in 1992 Degrees granted: Associate. Special programs- Environmental Technology, 504-278-7440. Attendance and degree information available by phone, fax, mail. Transcripts available by fax, mail.

Our Lady of Holy Cross College, Registrar, 4123 Woodland Dr, New Orleans, LA 70131, 504-394-7744 (Fax: 504-391-2421). 8:30AM-5PM. Enrollment: 1350. Records go back to 1916. Alumni records are maintained here. Degrees granted: Associate; Bachelors; Masters. Attendance information available by phone, fax, mail. Degree and transcript information available by written request only.

Remington College, Registrar, 303 Rue Louis XIV, Lafayette, LA 70508, 318-981-4010 (Fax: 318-983-7130) 7:30AM - 9PM. Enrollment: 450. Records go back to 1991. Formerly **Southern Technical College**. Degrees granted: Associate. Special programs- Call 318-981-4010. Attendance and degree information available by phone, fax, mail. Transcripts available by fax, mail.

Southeastern Louisiana University, Registrar, ATTN: Enrollment Services, PO Box 752, Hammond, LA 70402, 504-549-2062, 504-549-2066 (Fax: 504-549-5632) www.selu.edu. 7:45AM - 4:30PM. Enrollment: 15312. Records go back to 1925. Alumni records maintained here; call 504-549-2150. Degrees granted: Associate; Bachelors; Masters. Attendance and degree information available by phone, fax, mail. Transcripts available by fax, mail.

Southern University and Agricultural & Mechanical College at Baton Rouge Registrar, Southern Branch PO Box 9454, Baton Rouge, LA 70813, 504-771-5050 (Fax: 504-771-5064). 8AM-5PM. Enrollment: 10359. Records go back to 1920's. Alumni records maintained here; call 504-771-4200. Degrees granted: Associate; Bachelors; Masters; Doctorate. Attendance and degree information available by phone, fax, mail. Transcripts available by fax, mail.

Southern University at New Orleans, Registrar, 6400 Press Dr, New Orleans, LA 70126, 504-286-5175 (Fax: 504-286-5131). 8AM-5PM. Enrollment: 4200. Records go back to 1967. Alumni records maintained here; call 504-286-5341. Degrees granted: Masters. Attendance and degree information available by phone, fax, mail. Transcripts available by mail.

Southern University / Shreveport Bossier, Registrar, 3050 Martin Luther King, Jr. Dr, Shreveport, LA 71107, 318-674-3343, 318-674-3342 (Fax: 318-674-3338). 8AM-5PM. Enrollment: 1500. Records go back to 1967. Degrees granted: Associate. Special programs- Call 800-458-1472 X342. Attendance information available by phone, mail. Transcripts available by mail.

St. Bernard Community College
(See Nunez Community College)

St. Joseph Seminary College, Registrar, St Benedict, LA 70457, 504-867-2248 (Fax: 504-867-2270). 8AM-5PM. Enrollment: 54. Records go back to 1891. Alumni records are maintained here. Degrees granted: Bachelors. Attendance and degree information available by phone, fax, mail. Transcripts available by fax, mail.

Tulane University, Office of the Registrar, 110 Gibson Hall, New Orleans, LA 70118, 504-865-5231 (Fax: 504-865-6760) www.tulane.edu. 8:30AM-5PM. Enrollment: 11000. Records go back to 1980's. Alumni Records: Alumni Assoc., 6319 Willow St, New Orleans, LA 70118. Degrees granted: Associate; Bachelors; Masters; Doctorate. Special programs- School of Medicine, 504-588-5497; School of Public Health & Tropical Medicine, 504-588-5387. Attendance, degree and transcript information available by fax, mail.

University of New Orleans, Registrar, Lakefront, New Orleans, LA 70148, 504-280-6000 (switchboard), 504-286-6216 (records) 8AM - 4:30PM. www.uno.edu. Enrollment: 14000. Records go back to 1959. Alumni records maintained here; call 504-280-2586. Degrees granted: Bachelors; Masters; Doctorate. Special programs- Call 504-280-6000. Attendance information available by fax, mail. Degree information available by phone, fax, mail. Transcripts available by mail.

University of Southwestern Louisiana, Registrar, 200 E University Ave, Lafayette, LA 70504, 318-482-1000 (Fax: 318-482-6286). 8AM - 4:30PM. Enrollment: 16902. Records go back to 1901. Alumni records maintained here; call 318-482-1000. Degrees granted: Bachelors; Masters; Doctorate. Attendance and degree information available by phone, mail. Transcripts available by mail.

Xavier University of Louisiana, Registrar, 7325 Palmetto St, New Orleans, LA 70125, 504-483-7583, 504-486-7411 (Fax: 504-455-7922) www.xula.edu.com. 8AM-5PM. Enrollment: 3500. Records go back to 1925. Alumni records maintained here; call 504-483-7575. Degrees granted: Bachelors; Masters; Pharm D. Attendance and degree information available by phone, fax, mail. Transcripts available by fax, mail.

Maine

Andover College, Registrar, 901 Washington Ave, Portland, ME 04103, 207-774-6126 (Fax: 207-774-1715) 9AM-5PM. www.andovercollege.com. Enrollment: 600. Records go back to 1969. Degrees granted: Associate. Attendance and degree information available by phone, fax, mail. Transcripts available by mail.

Bangor Theological Seminary, Registrar, 300 Union St, Bangor, ME 04401, 207-942-6781 X136, 207-990-1268 (Fax: 207-990-1267) www.BTS.edu. 8AM-4:30PM. Enrollment: 159. Records go back to 1814. Alumni records maintained here; call 207-774-5212. Degrees granted: Masters; Doctorate. Special programs- Bangor Plan, 5-year M.Div track for undergraduates, 800-287-6781 X129. Attendance and degree information available by phone, fax, mail. Transcripts available by fax, mail.

Bates College, Registrar, 2 Andrews Rd, Lewiston, ME 04240, 207-786-6097 (Fax: 207-786-8350) www.bates.edu. 8AM-4:30PM. Enrollment: 1600. Records go back to 1900. Alumni records maintained here; call 207-786-6127. Degrees granted: Bachelors. Attendance and degree information available by phone, fax, mail. Transcripts by fax, mail.

Beal College, Registrar, 629 Main St, Bangor, ME 04401, 207-947-4591, 800-660-7351 (w/in Maine) Fax: 207-947-0208). Records go back to 1960's. Degrees granted: Associate. Attendance, degree and transcript information available by fax, mail.

Bowdoin College, Office of Student Records, 4500 College Station, Brunswick, ME 04011, 207-725-3226, 207-725-3521 (Fax: 207-725-3338) www.bowdoin.edu. 8:30AM-5PM. Enrollment: 1450. Records go back to 1954. Earlier records in archives. Alumni records maintained here; call 207-725-3266. Degrees granted: Bachelors. Attendance and degree information available by phone, fax, mail. Transcripts by fax, mail..

Casco Bay College, Registrar, 477 Congress St, Portland, ME 04101-3483, 207-772-0196 (Fax: 207-772-0636) www.cascobaycollege.com. 8AM-5PM. Enrollment: 300. Records go back to 1960's. Alumni records are maintained here. Degrees granted: Associate. Attendance and degree information available by phone, fax, mail. Transcripts available by mail.

Central Maine Medical Center School of Nursing, Registrar, Lewiston, ME 04240, 207-795-2858, 207-795-2843 (Fax: 207-795-2849) 8:30AM-5PM. Enrollment: 88. Records go back to 1891. Alumni records maintained here; call 207-795-2884. Degrees granted: Associate. Attendance and degree information available by phone, fax, mail. Transcripts available by written request only.

Central Maine Technical College, Registrar, 1250 Turner St, Auburn, ME 04210, 207-784-2385 (Fax: 207-777-7353) 8AM-4:30PM. www.cmtc.net. Enrollment: 1200. Records go back to 1965. Alumni records are maintained here. Degrees granted: Associate. School will not confirm attendance information. Degree information available by phone. Transcripts available by mail.

Colby College, Office of the Registrar, 4620 Mayflower Hill, Waterville, ME 04901-8846, 207-872-3197, 207-872-3199 (Fax: 207-872-3076) www.colby.edu. 8:30AM-4:30PM. Enrollment: 1700. Records go back to 1911. Alumni records maintained here; call 207-872-3190. Degrees granted: Bachelors. Attendance and degree information available by phone, fax, mail. Transcripts available by fax, mail.

College of the Atlantic, Registrar, 105 Eden St, Bar Harbor, ME 04609, 207-288-5015 (Fax: 207-288-4126) www.coa.edu. 9AM-5PM. Enrollment: 230. Records go back to 1972. Alumni records are maintained. Degrees granted: Bachelors; Masters. Attendance and degree information available by phone, fax, mail. Transcripts available by mail. Transcripts by student request only.

Eastern Maine Technical College, Registrar, 354 Hogan Rd, Bangor, ME 04401, 207-941-4625 (Fax: 207-941-4666). 9AM-4PM. Enrollment: 2000. Records go back to 1971. Alumni records are maintained here. Degrees granted: Associate. Attendance and degree information available by phone, fax, mail. Transcripts by written request only.

Eastern Maine Vo-Tech Institute
(See Eastern Maine Technical College)

Husson College, Registrar, One College Circle, Bangor, ME 04401, 207-941-7000, 207-941-7149 (Fax: 207-941-7988) 9AM-3PM. www.husson.edu/depts/registrar/. Enrollment: 2100. Records go back to 1920's. Alumni records maintained here; call 207-941-7073. Degrees granted: Associate; Bachelors; Masters. Attendance and degree information available by phone, mail. Transcripts available by written request only. Internet site contains request form for transcripts.

Kennebec Valley Technical College, Registrar's Office, 92 Western Ave, Fairfield, ME 04937-1367, 207-453-5000, 207-453-5128 www.kvtc.mtcs.tc.me.us/. (Fax: 207-453-5010) 9AM-Noon, 1-4PM. Enrollment: 1200. Records go back to 1979. Records to 1957 for ME State School of Practical Nursing. Alumni records are maintained here. Degrees granted: Associate. Certification: Allied Health, Nursing, Business, Trades. Attendance, degree and transcript information available by phone, fax, mail.

Kennebec Valley Vo-Tech Institute
(See Kennebec Balley Technical College)

Maine College of Art, Registrar, 97 Spring St, Portland, ME 04101, 207-775-3052 (Fax: 207-772-5069) www.meca.edu/gdmeca. 8:30AM-5PM. Enrollment: 300. Records go back to 1882. Alumni records are maintained here also. Call 207-775-5095. Degrees granted: Bachelors. Special programs- Only Independent College of Art & Design in New England. Attendance, degree and transcript information available by mail. Fax requests from current or previous students only.

Maine Maritime Academy, Registrar, Castine, ME 04420, 207-326-2441, 207-326-2426 (Fax: 207-326-2510). 7:30AM-4PM. Enrollment: 650. Records go back to 1941. Alumni records maintained here; call 207-326-2337. Degrees granted: Associate; Bachelors; Masters. Attendance and degree information available by phone, mail. Transcripts available by mail.

Mid-State College Registrar, 88 Hardscrabble Rd, Auburn, ME 04210, 207-783-1478 (Fax: 207-783-1477). 8AM-4PM. Enrollment: 350. Records go back to 1986. Alumni records are maintained. Degrees granted: Associate. Attendance, degree and transcript information by written request only.

Mid-State College (Branch), Registrar, 218 Water St, Augusta, ME 04430, 207-623-3962 (Fax: 207-623-3844). 8AM-8PM M-Th, 8AM-4PM. Enrollment: 350. Records go back to 1950. Alumni records are maintained here. Degrees granted: Associate. Attendance, degree and transcript information available by mail.

Northern Maine Technical College, Registrar, 33 Edgemont Dr, Presque Isle, ME 04769, 207-768-2791 (Fax: 207-768-2831). www.nmtc.mtcs.tec.me.us. 8AM-5PM. Enrollment: 558. Records go back to 1963. Graduate and Withdrawal files - 5 years. Alumni records maintained here; call 207-768-2808. Degrees granted: Associate. Attendance and degree information available by phone, fax, mail. Transcripts available by fax, mail.

Portland School of Art
(See Maine College of Art)

Southern Maine Technical College, Registrar, Fort Road, South Portland, ME 04106, 207-767-9538, 207-767-9665 http://ctech.smtc.mtcs.tec.me.us. (Fax: 207-767-9671) 8AM-5PM. Enrollment: 2500. Records go back to 1948. Alumni records maintained here; call 207-767-9574. Degrees granted: Associate. Attendance and degree information available by phone, fax, mail. Transcripts available by fax, mail.

St. Joseph's College, Registrar, 278 Whites Bridge Rd, Standish, ME 04084-5263, 207-892-6766 (Fax: 207-893-7861) 8:30AM-4:30PM. www.sjcme.edu Enrollment: 2500. Records go back to 1912. Alumni records are maintained here. Degrees granted: Associate; Bachelors; Masters. Attendance and degree information available by phone, fax, mail. Transcripts available by fax, mail.

Thomas College, Registrar, 180 W River Rd, Waterville, ME 04901, 207-873-0771 (Fax: 207-877-0114) www.thomas.edu. 8AM-4:30PM. Enrollment: 900. Records go back to 1920's. Alumni records are maintained here. Degrees granted: Associate; Bachelors; Masters. Attendance and degree information available by phone, fax, mail. Transcripts available by fax, mail.

Unity College, Registrar's Office, HC78 Box 1, Unity, ME 04988, 207-948-3131 X244 (Fax: 207-948-6277) www.unity.edu. 8:30AM-5PM. Enrollment: 500. Records go back to 1966. Alumni records are maintained here. Degrees granted: Associate; Bachelors. Attendance and degree information available by phone, fax, mail. Transcripts by fax, mail.

University of Maine, Registrar, Orono, ME 04469, 207-581-1290, 207-581-1298 (Fax: 207-581-1314) www.maine.edu. 8AM-4:30PM. Enrollment: 10000. Records go back to 1865. Alumni records maintained here; call 207-581-1138. Degrees granted: Bachelors; Masters; Doctorate. Attendance and degree information available by phone, fax, mail. Transcripts available by fax, mail.

University of Maine at Augusta, Admission & Records, 46 University Dr, Augusta, ME 04330, www.uma.maine.edu. 207-621-3185, 207-621-3465 (Fax: 207-621-3116) Enrollment: 5300. Records go back to 1968. Alumni records are maintained here. Degrees granted: Associate; Bachelors. Attendance and degree information available by phone, fax, mail. Transcripts available by fax, mail.

University of Maine at Farmington, Registrar, 86 Main St, Farmington, ME 04938, 207-778-7000, 207-778-7240 (Fax: 207-778-7247) www.umf.maine.edu. 8AM-4:30PM. Enrollment: 2000. Records go back to 1864. Alumni records maintained here; call 207-778-7090. Degrees granted: Bachelors. Attendance and degree information available by phone, fax, mail. Transcripts by mail.

University of Maine at Fort Kent, Registrar, Pleasant St, Fort Kent, ME 04743, 207-834-7521, 207-834-7520 (Fax: 207-834-7503) www.umfk.maine.edu. 8AM-4:30PM. Enrollment: 600. Records go back to 1878. Alumni records maintained here; call 207-834-7557. Degrees granted: Associate; Bachelors. Special programs- 207-834-7652. Attendance, degree and transcript information available by fax, mail.

University of Maine at Machias, Registrar, Machias, ME 04654, 207-255-1223 (Fax: 207-255-4864). 8AM-5PM. Enrollment: 950. Records go back to 1912. Alumni records maintained here; call 207-255-1210. Degrees granted: Associate; Bachelors. Attendance and degree information available by phone, mail. Transcripts available by fax, mail.

University of Maine at Presque Isle, Registrar, 181 Main St, Presque Isle, ME 04769, 207-768-9540 (Fax: 207-768-9458) 8AM-5PM. www.umpi.maine.edu. Enrollment: 1350. Records go back to 1903. Alumni records maintained here; call 207-768-9525. Degrees granted: Bachelors. Attendance and degree information available by phone, mail. Transcripts available by mail. Will accept fax requests for transcripts, will not fax back.

University of New England, Registrar, 11 Hills Beach Rd, Biddeford, ME 04005-9599, 207-283-0171 X2473 (Fax: 207-282-6379) 9AM-4PM. www.une.edu/. Enrollment: 180. Records go back to 1940's. Alumni records are maintained here also. Call 207-283-0171 X2161. Degrees granted: Associate; Bachelors; Masters; Doctorate. Attendance and degree information available by phone, fax, mail. Transcripts available by fax, mail.

University of Southern Maine, Registrar, 96 Falmouth St, Portland, ME 04103, 207-780-5230 (Fax: 207-780-5517) 8AM-4:30PM. www.usm.maine.edu/ Enrollment: 9500. Records go back to 1896. Alumni records maintained here; call 207-780-4110. Degrees granted: Associate; Bachelors; Masters; L.L.D. Attendance and degree information available by phone, mail. Transcripts available by fax, mail.

Washington County Technical College Registrar, RR1 Box 22C, Calais, ME 04619, 207-454-1000, 207-454-1032 (Fax: 207-454-1026). 8AM - 4:30PM. Enrollment: 380. Records go back to 1969. Alumni records maintained here; call 207-454-1000. Degrees granted: Associate. Attendance and degree information available by phone, fax, mail. Transcripts available by fax, mail.

Westbrook College
(See University of New England)

Maryland

Allegany Community College, Registrar, 12401 Willowbrook Rd SE, Cumberland, MD 21502, 301-724-7700 X212 (Fax: 301-724-6892) www.ac.md.us. 8:30AM-4:30PM. Enrollment: 2800. Records go back to 1961. Alumni records are maintained here. Degrees granted: Associate. Attendance and degree information available by phone, mail. Transcripts available by mail.

Americare School of Allied Health,
Registrar, 8605 Cameron St, Suite 303, Silver Springs, MD 20910, 301-585-2074 (Fax: 301-588-6489) 8AM-5PM. Enrollment: 890. Records go back to 1974. Degrees granted: Associate. Special programs- Science: Nursing. Attendance and degree information available by phone, mail. Transcripts available by mail.

Anne Arundel Community College,
Registrar, 101 College Pkwy, Arnold, MD 21012, 410-541-2243 (Fax: 410-541-2489) sun.aacc.cc.md.us. 8:30AM-8PM M-Th, 8:30-4:30PM F, 9AM-1PM Sat. Enrollment: 11800. Records go back to 1961. Alumni records maintained here; call 410-541-2515. Degrees granted: Associate. Special programs- Architecture, 410-541-2433: Business, 410-541-2390: Computer Technologies, 410-541-2442: Criminal Justice/Paralegal, 410-315-7390: Education, 410-541-2430: Engineering Technologies, 410-541-2433. Attendance and degree information available by phone, mail. Transcripts available by mail.

Antioch University (George Meany Center
for Labor Studies), Registrar, 10000 New Hampshire Ave, Silver Spring, MD 20903, 301-431-5410 (Fax: 301-434-0371) www.antioch.edu. 9AM-4:30PM. Records go back to 1974. Alumni records are maintained here. Degrees granted: Bachelors. Attendance and degree information available by phone, mail. Transcripts available by mail from Yellow Springs location.

Baltimore City Community College
(Harbor Campus), Registrar, 600 E Lombard St, Baltimore, MD 21202, 410-986-5599 (Fax: 410-986-5577). 8AM-5PM. Degrees granted: Associate. Attendance and degree information available by phone, fax, mail. Transcripts available by mail.

Baltimore City Community College,
Registrar, 2901 Liberth Heights Ave, Baltimore, MD 21215, 410-462-7777 (Fax: 410-462-7677) www.bcc.edu. 8AM-5PM M,Th,F; 8AM-7PM T & W. Enrollment: 6500. Records go back to 1947. Alumni Records: 600 E Lombard St, Baltimore, MD 21201. Degrees granted: Associate. Attendance and degree information available by phone, fax, mail. Transcripts available by mail.

Baltimore Hebrew University, Registrar,
5800 Park Heights Ave, Baltimore, MD 21209, 410-578-6918 (Fax: 410-578-6940). 9AM-5PM. Enrollment: 340. Records go back to 1920's. Alumni records maintained here; call 410-578-6915. Degrees granted: Associate; Bachelors; Masters; Doctorate Attendance, degree and transcript information available by written request only.

Baltimore International College,
Registrar, 17 S Commerce St, Baltimore, MD 21202, 410-752-4710 X101, 410-752-1446 www.bic.baltimore.md.us (Fax: 410-752-3730) 8:30AM-5PM. Enrollment: 800. Records go back to 1972. Alumni records maintained here; call 410-752-8813. Degrees granted: Associate. Special programs- Hotel Management: Food & Beverage Management: Institutional Food Service. Attendance and degree information available by phone, fax, mail. Transcripts available by fax, mail.

Bowie State University, Admissions
Records & Reg., 14000 Jericho Park Rd, Bowie, MD 20715, 301-464-6570 (Fax: 301-464-7521) www.bowiestate.edu. 10AM-7PM M,W; 8AM-6PM T,Th; 10AM-6PM F. Enrollment: 5200. Records go back to 1930's. Alumni records maintained here; call 301-464-6584. Degrees granted: Bachelors; Masters. Attendance and transcript information available by mail. Degree information available by phone, mail.

Capitol College, Registrar, 11301
Springfield Rd, Laurel, MD 20708, 301-369-2800, 800-950-1192 (Fax: 301-953-3876) www.capitol-college.edu. 9AM-5PM M, 9AM-7PM T,W,Th, 9AM-3PM F. Enrollment: 800. Records go back to 1964. Alumni records are maintained here. Degrees granted: Associate; Bachelors; Masters. Attendance and degree information available by phone, fax, mail. Transcripts available by mail.

Catonsville Community College,
Registrar, 800 S Rolling Rd, Baltimore, MD 21228, 410-455-4380 (Fax: 410-455-4504) www.cat.cc.md.us. 8AM-8PM M-Th; 8AM-4PM F. Enrollment: 10000. Records go back to 1961. Alumni records maintained here; call 410-455-4400. Degrees granted: Associate. Attendance information available by phone, fax, mail. Degree and transcript information available by mail.

Cecil Community College, Registrar, 1000
North East Rd, North East, MD 21901, 410-287-1004 (Fax: 410-287-1001) 8:30AM-4:30PM. www.cecil.cc.md.us. Enrollment: 1348. Records go back to 1969. Alumni records maintained here; call 410-287-1000. Degrees granted: Associate. Attendance and degree information available by phone, fax, mail. Transcripts available by fax, mail.

Charles County Community College,
Registrar, Mitchell Rd, PO Box 910, La Plata, MD 20646, 301-870-3008 X7006 (Fax: 301-934-5255) www.charles.cc.md.us. 8:30AM-4:30PM. Records go back to 1974. Degrees granted: Associate. Attendance and degree information available by phone, mail. Transcripts available by mail.

Chesapeake College, Registrar, PO Box 8,
Wye Mills, MD 21679, 410-822-5400, 410-827-5846 (Fax: 410-827-9466) 8AM-4PM. www.chesapeake.edu. Enrollment: 2000. Records go back to 1965. Alumni records maintained here; call 410-827-5808. Degrees granted: Associate. Attendance and degree information available by phone, mail. Transcripts available by mail.

College of Notre Dame of Maryland,
Registrar, 4701 N Charles St, Baltimore, MD 21210, 410-532-5320, 410-532-5323 (Fax: 410-532-5789). 8AM-5PM. Enrollment: 3200. Records go back to 1895. Alumni records maintained here; call 410-435-0100. Degrees granted: Bachelors; Masters. Attendance and degree information available by phone, mail. Transcripts available by mail.

Columbia Union College, Registrar, 7600
Flower Ave, Takoma Park, MD 20912, 301-891-4119 (Fax: 301-891-4121) www.cuc.edu. 9AM-Noon, 1-4PM M,T,Th; 9-11AM,1-4PM W; 9AM-Noon F. Enrollment: 1200. Records go back to 1904. Alumni records maintained here; call 301-891-4132. Degrees granted: Associate; Bachelors. Attendance and degree information available by phone, fax, mail. Transcripts available by fax, mail.

Community College of Baltimore
(See Baltimore City Community College)

Coppin State College, Registrar, 500 W
North Ave, Baltimore, MD 21216, 410-383-5550 (Fax: 410-523-7238) 8AM-5PM. www.coppin.umd.edu. Enrollment: 3380. Records go back to 1960's. Alumni records maintained here; call 410-383-5960. Degrees granted: Bachelors; Masters. Attendance and degree information available by phone, fax, mail. Transcripts available by fax, mail.

Dundalk Community College, Registrar,
7200 Sollers Point Rd, Dundalk, MD 21222, 410-282-6700, 410-285-9823 (Fax: 410-285-9903) www.dundalk.cc.md.us. Enrollment: 3200. Records go back to 1971. Alumni records maintained here; call 410-285-9935. Degrees granted: Associate. Special programs- Call 410-285-9800. Attendance and degree information available by phone, mail. Transcripts available by written request only.

Essex Community College, Registrar,
7201 Rossville Blvd, Baltimore, MD 21237, 410-780-6363 (Fax: 410-780-6211). 8:30AM-8:30PM M-Th; 8:30AM-3:30PM F. Enrollment: 9653. Records go back to 1957. Alumni records maintained here; call 410-780-6208. Degrees granted: Associate. Attendance information available by phone, fax, mail. Degree and transcript information available by mail.

Frederick Community College,
Admissions / Registration Office, 7932 Oppossumtown Pike, Frederick, MD 21702, www.co.frederick.md.us/scchp.html. 301-846-2430 (Fax: 301-624-2799) 8:30AM-8PM M-Th; 8:30AM-4:30PM F. Enrollment: 4000. Records go back to 1957. Degrees granted: Associate. Attendance and degree information available by phone, fax, mail. Transcripts available by fax, mail.

Frostburg State University, Registrar, 101
Braddock Rd, Frostburg, MD 21532-1099, 301-687-4346, 301-682-4000 (Switchboard) (Fax: 301-687-4597) www.fsu.umd.edu. 8:30AM-4:30PM. Enrollment: 5050. Records go back to 1902. Alumni records are maintained here. Degrees granted: Bachelors; Masters. Attendance and degree information available by phone, fax, mail. Transcripts available by fax, mail.

Garrett Community College, Registrar,
PO Box 151, 687 Mosser Rd, McHenry, MD 21541, 301-387-3040, 301-387-3047 (Fax: 301-387-3055). 8:30AM-4:30PM. Enrollment: 725. Records go back to 1971. Alumni records maintained here; call 301-387-3056. Degrees granted: Associate. Special programs- Arts & Sciences: Liberal Arts: Teacher Ed: Business: Secretarial Science: Agricultural Technology: Adventure Sports. Attendance and degree information available by phone, fax, mail. Transcripts available by fax, mail.

Goucher College, Registrar, 1021 Dulaney
Valley Rd, Baltimore, MD 21204, 410-337-6500 (Fax: 410-337-6504) www.goucher.edu. 8:45AM-5PM. Enrollment: 1130. Records go back to 1885. Alumni records maintained here; call 410-337-6180. Degrees granted: Bachelors; Masters. Special programs- Master Historic Preservatory, 440-337-6200: Master Education & Arts in Teaching, 410-337-6047: Post Bac Pre-Med, 410-337-6085. Attendance and degree information available by phone, fax, mail. Transcripts available by mail.

Hagerstown Business College, Registrar, 18618 Crestwood Dr, Hagerstown, MD 21742, 301-739-2670 (Fax: 301-791-7661) 8AM-6PM. www.fred.net/hbc1/home.htm. Enrollment: 500. Records go back to 1938. Alumni records are maintained here. Degrees granted: Associate. Attendance and degree information available by phone, fax, mail. Transcripts available by fax, mail.

Hagerstown Junior College, Registrar, 11400 Robinwood Dr, Hagerstown, MD 21742, 301-790-2800 X239 (Fax: 301-791-9165). 8AM-4PM. Enrollment: 3000. Records go back to 1946. Planning purge back 5-10 years. Alumni records maintained here; call 301-790-2800 X346. Degrees granted: Associate. Attendance and degree information available by phone, fax, mail. Transcripts available by fax, mail.

Harford Community College, Records & Registration, 401 Thomas Run Rd, Bel Air, MD 21015, 410-836-4222 (Fax: 410-836-4169). 8AM-7:30PM M-Th; 8AM-4:30PM F; 9AM-1PM S. Enrollment: 5304. Records go back to 1957. Alumni records maintained here; call 410-836-4428. Degrees granted: Associate. Attendance and degree information available by phone, fax, mail. Transcripts available by fax, mail.

Home Study International / Griggs University, Registrar, 12501 Old Columbia Pike, PO Box 4437, Silver Spring, MD 20914, 301-680-6570, 301-680-6579 (Fax: 301-680-6526). 8:30AM-4:30PM M-Th, 8:30-11:30AM F. Records go back to 1909. Degrees granted: Associate; Bachelors. Attendance and degree information available by phone, fax, mail. Transcripts available by mail.

Hood College, Registrar, 401 Rosemont Ave, Frederick, MD 21701, 301-696-3616 (Fax: 301-696-3894). www.hood.edu. 8:30AM-5PM. Enrollment: 2000. Records go back to 1893. Alumni records maintained here; call 301-696-3900. Degrees granted: Bachelors; Masters. Attendance and degree information available by phone, fax, mail. Transcripts available by fax, mail.

Howard Community College, Registrar, 10901 Little Patuxent Pkwy, Columbia, MD 21044, 410-992-4800 (Fax: 410-715-2426) www.howardcc.edu. 8:30AM - 5PM. Enrollment: 5000. Records go back to 1970. Alumni records are maintained here. Degrees granted: Associate. Attendance and degree information available by phone, fax, mail. Transcripts available by fax, mail.

Johns Hopkins University, Registrar, 75 Garland Hall, 3400 N Charles St, Baltimore, MD 21218-2688, 410-516-8600 (Fax: 410-516-6477) www.jhu.edu/. 8:30AM-5PM. Enrollment: 12000. Records go back to 1879. Alumni Records: Alumni Relations, Johns Hopkins University, 3211 N Charles St, Baltimore, MD 21218. Degrees granted: Associate; Bachelors; Masters; Doctorate. Attendance and degree information available by phone, fax, mail. Transcripts available by mail.

Johns Hopkins University (Peabody Institute), Registrar, One E Mount Vernon Pl, Baltimore, MD 21202, 410-659-8266 (Fax: 410-659-8129) www.peabody.jhu.edu. 8:30AM-5PM. Enrollment: 625. Records go back to 1932. Alumni records maintained here; call 410-659-8176. Degrees granted: Bachelors; Masters; Doctorate; Artist Diploma, Graduate Performance Diploma. Attendance and degree information available by phone, fax, mail. Transcripts available by mail.

Johns Hopkins University (Columbia Center), Registrar, 3400 N Charles St, Baltimore, MD 21218, 410-516-7088 (Fax: 410-516-6477) wwww.jhu.edu. 8:30AM-4:30PM. Enrollment: 16120. Records go back to 1880. All transcripts and records are located at the home office in Baltimore. Alumni Records: Alumni Assoc., Johns Hopkins University (Columbia Centre), 3400 N Charles St, Baltimore, MD 21218. Degrees granted: Associate; Bachelors; Masters; Doctorate. Special programs- Medicine, 410-955-3080; Hygiene, 410-955-3552; Nursing, 410-955-9840. Attendance and degree information available by phone, fax, mail. Transcripts available by fax, mail. The university prefers requests be written.

Lincoln Christian College East Coast, Registrar, PO Box 629, Bel Air, MD 21014, 410-836-2000 (Fax: 410-734-4271). Enrollment: 40. Records go back to 1946. Formerly **Eastern Christian College**. Alumni records are maintained here. Degrees granted: Associate; Bachelors. Attendance, degree and transcript information available by mail. For transcript, send letter to Lincoln Christian College, 100 Campus View Dr, Lincoln, IL 62656.

Loyola College in Maryland, Registrar, Records Office MH 121, 4501 N Charles St, Baltimore, MD 21210-2699, 410-617-2504, 410-617-2659 (Fax: 410-617-5031) www.loyola.edu. 7AM-7:45PM M-Th; 7AM-3PM F. Enrollment: 6000. Records go back to 1900. Alumni records maintained here; call 410-617-2475. Degrees granted: Bachelors; Masters; Doctorate. Certification: 30 credits beyond the Masters. Attendance and degree information available by phone, mail. Transcripts available by mail. Fax available only in emergency.

Maryland College of Art and Design, Registrar, 10500 Georgia Ave, Silver Spring, MD 20902, 301-649-4454 (Fax: 301-649-2940) www.intr.net. 8AM-5PM. Enrollment: 80. Records go back to 1986. Alumni records are maintained here. Degrees granted: Associate. Attendance, degree and transcript information available by mail.

Maryland Institute College of Art, Registrar, 1300 W Mt Royal Ave, Baltimore, MD 21217, 410-225-2234, 410-225-2235 (Fax: 410-869-9206) www.mica.edu. 8:30AM-4:30PM. Enrollment: 1143. Records go back to 1930's. Alumni records are maintained here also. Call 410-225-2339. Degrees granted: Bachelors; Masters. Attendance and degree information available by phone, fax, mail. Transcripts available by written request only.

Montgomery College (Rockville Campus), Registrar, 51 Mannakee St, Rockville, MD 20850, 301-279-5046, 301-279-5034 (Registrar) (Fax: 301-279-5037) www.mc.cc.md.us. 8:30AM-6:30PM M-Th; 8:30AM-4:30PM F. Enrollment: 13624. Records go back to 1966. Transcript requests go to Germantown. Alumni records maintained here; call 301-251-7951. Degrees granted: Associate. Attendance, degree and transcript information available by mail.

Montgomery College — Germantown Campus, Registrar, ATTN: Transcripts, 20200 Observation Dr, Germantown, MD 20876, 301-353-7821, 301-353-7823 (Fax: 301-353-7815) www.mc.cc.md.us. 8:30AM-6:30PM M-Th; 8:30AM-5PM F. Enrollment: 3730. Records go back to 1947. Alumni records are maintained here. Degrees granted: Associate. Attendance, degree and transcript information available by mail.

Montgomery College — Takoma Park Campus, Registrar, Takoma Ave and Fenton St, Takoma Park, MD 20912, 301-650-1500, 301-650-1501 (Fax: 301-650-1497). 8:30AM-7PM M-Th; 8:30AM-5PM F. Enrollment: 4050. Records go back to 1945. Alumni records are maintained here. Degrees granted: Associate. Attendance, degree and transcript information available by mail.

Morgan State University, Registrar, 1700 E Cold Spring Lane, Baltimore, MD 21251, 410-319-3301, 410-319-3300 (Fax: 410-319-3259) www.morgan.edu. 8AM-5PM. Enrollment: 5800. Records go back to 1916. Alumni Records: Alumni Assoc., McKeldin Center Rm 206, Baltimore, MD 21239. Degrees granted: Bachelors; Masters; Doctorate. Attendance and degree information available by phone, fax, mail. Transcripts available by fax, mail.

Mount St. Mary's College and Seminary, Registrar, Emmitsburg, MD 21727, 301-447-5215 (Fax: 301-447-5755). 9AM-Noon, 1-5PM. Enrollment: 1500. Records go back to 1808. Alumni records maintained here; call 301-447-5362. Degrees granted: Bachelors; Masters. Attendance and degree information available by phone, fax, mail. Transcripts available by mail.

Ner Israel Rabbinical College, Registrar, 400 Mount Wilson Lane, Baltimore, MD 21208, 410-484-7200 X234 (Fax: 410-484-3060). 1-6PM. Enrollment: 400. Records go back to 1933. Alumni records are maintained here. Degrees granted: Bachelors; Masters; Doctorate. Attendance and degree information available by phone, fax, mail. Transcripts available by fax, mail.

Prince George's Community College (Branch), Registrar, Andrews AFB Degree Center, Bldg 1413 Arkansas Rd, Andrews Air Force Base, MD 20762, 301-322-0778 www.pg.cc.md.us. Records are located at Prince George's Community College, Registrar, Largo, MD.

Prince George's Community College, Registrar, 301 Largo Rd, Largo, MD 20774, 301-322-0801, 301-322-0819 (Fax: 301-322-0119) www.pg.cc.md.us. 8:30AM-7:30PM. Enrollment: 12000. Records go back to 1958. Alumni records maintained here; call 301-322-0854. Degrees granted: Associate. Attendance and degree information available by phone, fax, mail. Transcripts available by fax, mail.

Salisbury State University, Registrar, 1101 Camden Ave, Salisbury, MD 21801, 410-543-6150 (Fax: 410-548-5979) www.ssu.edu. 8AM-5PM. Enrollment: 6048. Records go back to 1926. Alumni records maintained here; call 410-543-6042. Degrees granted: Bachelors; Masters. Attendance and degree information available by phone, fax, mail. Transcripts available by fax, mail.

Sojourner-Douglass College, Registrar, 500 N Caroline St, Baltimore, MD 21205, 410-276-0306 (Fax: 410-675-1810) 8AM-4:30PM. www.host.sdc.edu. Enrollment: 258. Records go back to 1980. Alumni records are maintained here. Degrees granted: Bachelors. Attendance, degree and transcript information available by mail.

Massachusetts

St. John's College, Registrar, 60 College Ave, PO Box 2800, Annapolis, MD 21404, 410-626-2513 (Fax: 410-295-6937) www.sjca.edu. 8:30AM-Noon; 1PM-4:30PM. Enrollment: 530. Records go back to 1700's. Alumni records maintained here; call 410-626-2531. Degrees granted: Bachelors; Masters. Attendance, degree and transcript information available by fax, mail.

St. Mary's College of Maryland, Registrar, St. Mary's City, MD 20686, 301-862-0336 (Fax: 301-862-0449) www.smcm.edu. 8AM-5PM. Enrollment: 1500. Records go back to 1924. Alumni records maintained here; call 301-862-0280. Degrees granted: Bachelors. Attendance and degree information available by phone, fax, mail. Transcripts available by mail.

St. Mary's Seminary and University, Registrar, 5400 Roland Ave, Baltimore, MD 21210, 410-864-4000, 410-864-3605 (Fax: 410-864-3680). 8:30AM-4:30PM. Enrollment: 296. Alumni records maintained here; call 410-864-4264. Degrees granted: Bachelors; Masters. Attendance and degree information available by phone, fax, mail. Transcripts available by fax, mail.

Towson State University, Records Office, 8000 York Rd, Towson, MD 21252, 410-830-3240 (Fax: 410-830-3443) www.towson.edu. 8AM-5PM. Enrollment: 13700. Records go back to 1920. Alumni Records: Alumni Assoc., Arburn Dr, Arburn House, Towson, MD 21204. Degrees granted: Bachelors; Masters. Attendance and degree information available by phone, fax, mail. Transcripts available by fax, mail.

Traditional Acupuncture Institute, Registrar, American City Bldg, 10227 Wincopin Cir, Suite 100, Columbia, MD 21044, 410-997-4888, 410-596-6006 (Fax: 410-964-3544) 9AM-5PM. Enrollment: 160. Records go back to 1981. Alumni records are maintained here. Degrees granted: Masters. Attendance, degree and transcript information available by mail.

Uniformed Services University of the Health Sciences, Registrar, 4301 Jones Bridge Rd, Bethesda, MD 20814, 301-295-3197 (Fax: 301-295-3545) www.usuhs.mil/. 7:30AM-4PM. Enrollment: 165. Records go back to 1976. Alumni records maintained here; call 301-295-3578. Degrees granted: Masters; Doctorate; Graduate Nursing. Special programs- Graduate School of Nursing, 301-295-1989. Attendance and degree information available by phone, fax, mail. Transcripts available by fax, mail.

United States Naval Academy, Registrar, 589 McNair Rd, Annapolis, MD 21402, 410-293-6389 (Fax: 410-293-2327) 8AM-4:30PM. www.nadn.navy.mil. Enrollment: 4000. Records go back to 1845. Alumni records maintained here; call 410-293-1000. Degrees granted: Bachelors. Attendance and degree information available by phone, fax, mail. Transcripts available by fax, mail.

University of Baltimore, Registrar, 1420 N Charles St, Baltimore, MD 21201, 410-837-4825 (Fax: 410-837-4820) www.ubalt.edu. 8:30AM-7PM M-Th, 8:30AM-4:30PM F. Enrollment: 5000. Records go back to 1925. Alumni records maintained here; call 410-837-6131. Degrees granted: Bachelors; Masters. Special programs- Law. Attendance and degree information available by phone, fax, mail. Transcripts available by fax, mail.

University of Maryland Baltimore County, Registrar, 1000 Hilltop Circle, Baltimore, MD 21250, 410-455-3727 (Fax: 410-455-1141) www.umbc.edu. 8:30AM-4:30PM. Enrollment: 10000. Records go back to 1966. Alumni records maintained here; call 410-455-2904. Degrees granted: Bachelors; Masters; Doctorate. Attendance and degree information available by phone, fax, mail. Transcripts available by fax, mail.

University of Maryland College Park, Registrar, 1101 Mitchell Blvd, College Park, MD 20742, 301-314-8240 (Fax: 301-314-9568) www.testudo.umd.edu. 8:30AM-4:30PM. Enrollment: 33000. Records go back to 1900. Alumni records are maintained here. Degrees granted: Bachelors; Masters; Doctorate. Special programs- Adult Ed Center, U of M, College Park, MD 20742. Attendance and degree information available by phone, fax, mail. Transcripts available by fax, mail.

University of Maryland Eastern Shore, Registrar, Princess Anne, MD 21853, 410-651-2200 X6410 (Fax: 410-651-7922) 8:30AM-4:30PM. www.umes.umd.edu. Enrollment: 2925. Records go back to 1886. Alumni records maintained here; call 410-651-2200. Degrees granted: Bachelors; Masters; Doctorate. Attendance and degree information available by phone, fax, mail. Transcripts available by mail.

University of Maryland at Baltimore, Registrar, 621 W Lombard St Room 326, Baltimore, MD 21201, 410-706-7480 (Fax: 410-706-4053) www.ab.umd.edu. 8AM-4:30PM. Enrollment: 5800. Records go back to 1886. Alumni Records: 666 W Baltimore St, Baltimore, MD 21201. Degrees granted: Bachelors; Masters; Doctorate; Professional. Special programs- Dental Hygiene: Medical Technologist: Physical Therapy. Attendance and degree information available by phone, fax, mail. Transcripts available by fax, mail.

University of Maryland, University College (The), Records Office, University Blvd at Adelphi Rd, College Park, MD 20742, 301-985-7268 (Fax: 301-985-7364) 8AM-5PM M,Th; 10AM-7PM T,W; 8AM-4PM F. www.umuc.edu. Enrollment: 32000. Records go back to 1947. Alumni records are maintained here. Degrees granted: Associate; Bachelors; Masters. Attendance and degree information available by phone, mail. Transcripts available by mail.

Villa Julie College, Registrar, 1525 Green Spring Valley Rd, Stevenson, MD 21153, 410-486-7000 (Fax: 410-486-3552) www.vjc.edu. 8:30AM-4:30PM. Enrollment: 2000. Records go back to 1947. Alumni records are maintained here Degrees granted: Associate; Bachelors; Masters. Attendance and degree information available by fax, mail. Transcripts available by mail.

Washington Bible College, Registrar, 6511 Princess Garden Pkwy, Lanham, MD 20706, 301-552-1400, 800-787-0256 (Fax: 301-552-2775) www.bible.edu. 8AM-4:30PM. Enrollment: 325. Records go back to 1938. Alumni records are maintained here. Degrees granted: Associate; Bachelors. Attendance and degree information available by phone, fax, mail. Transcripts available by fax, mail.

Washington College, Registrar, 300 Washington Ave, Chestertown, MD 21620, 410-778-7299 (Fax: 410-778-7850) 8:30AM-4:30PM. www.washcoll.edu. Records go back to 1930. Alumni records maintained here; call 410-778-7812. Degrees granted: Bachelors; Masters. Attendance and degree information available by phone, fax, mail. Transcripts available by mail.

Western Maryland College, Registrar, 2 College Hill, Westminster, MD 21157, 410-857-2215, 410-857-2216 (Fax: 410-857-2752) www.wmc.car.md.us. 8:30AM-4:30PM. Enrollment: 2400. Alumni records maintained here; call 410-857-2296. Degrees granted: Bachelors; Masters. Attendance and degree information available by phone, fax, mail. Transcripts available by fax, mail.

Wor-Wic Community College, Registrar's Office Rm 109, 32000 Campus Dr, Salisbury, MD 21801, 410-334-2907, 410-334-2800 (Fax: 410-334-2954). 8:30PM-5PM Winter; 8AM-4:30PM Summer. Enrollment: 2050. Records go back to 1975. Degrees granted: Associate. Certification: Proficiency. Special programs- Continuing Education, 410-334-2815. Attendance and degree information available by phone, fax, mail. Transcripts available by fax, mail.

Massachusetts

American International College, Registrar, 1000 State St, Springfield, MA 01109, 413-737-6212 (Fax: 413-737-2803) www.aic.edu. 8:30AM-4:30PM. Enrollment: 1200. Records go back to 1885. Alumni records maintained here; call 413-737-7000. Degrees granted: Associate; Bachelors; Masters; Doctorate. Attendance and degree information available by phone, fax, mail. Transcripts available by fax, mail.

Amherst College, Registrar, Amherst, MA 01002, 413-542-2225 (Fax: 413-542-2327) www.amherst.edu. 8:30AM - 4:30PM. Enrollment: 1600. Records go back to 1800's. Alumni records maintained here; call 413-542-5900. Degrees granted: Bachelors. Attendance and degree information available by phone, fax, mail. Transcripts available by fax, mail.

Andover Newton Theological School, Registrar, 210 Herrick Rd, Newton Centre, MA 02159, 617-964-1100 X212 (Fax: 617-965-9756) www.ants.edu. 8:30AM-4:30PM. Enrollment: 500. Records go back to 1919. Alumni records maintained here; call 617-964-1100 X202. Degrees granted: Masters; Doctorate. Attendance and degree information available by phone, fax, mail. Transcripts available by mail.

Anna Maria College, Registrar, Sunset Lane, Paxton, MA 01612-1198, 508-849-3400, 508-849-3428 (Fax: 508-849-3334) www.anna-maria.edu. 8:30AM - 4:30PM. Enrollment: 1073. Records go back to 1946. Alumni records maintained here; call 508-849-3342. Degrees granted: Associate; Bachelors; Masters. Attendance and degree information available by phone, mail. Transcripts available by mail.

Aquinas College at Milton, Registrar, 303 Adams St, Milton, MA 02186, 617-696-3100 (Fax: 617-696-8706). Enrollment: 255. Records go back to 1957. Alumni records are maintained here. Degrees granted: Associate; One Year Certificates. Attendance and degree information available by phone, fax, mail. Transcripts available by fax, mail.

Aquinas College at Newton, Registrar, 15 Walnut Park, Newton, MA 02158, 617-969-4400 (Fax: 617-965-6393) 8AM-4PM. Enrollment: 210. Records go back to 1961. Alumni records maintained here; call 617-969-4400 X25. Degrees granted: Associate. Attendance and degree information available by phone, fax, mail. Transcripts available by mail.

Aquinas Junior College at Milton
(See Aquinas College at Milton)

Art Institute of Boston (The), Registrar, 700 Beacon St, Boston, MA 02215, 617-262-1223, 617-262-1223 X382 (transcript info) (Fax: 617-437-1226) 8AM-5PM. Records go back to 1950. Alumni records are maintained here. Degrees granted: Bachelors. Attendance and degree information available by phone, fax, mail. Transcripts available by written request only.

Arthur D. Little School of Management Registrar, 194 Beacon St, Chestnut Hill, MA 02167-3853, 617-552-2871, 617-552-2877 (Fax: 617-552-2051) www.arthurlittle.com. 8:30AM-5PM. Enrollment: 60. Records go back to 1965. Alumni records are maintained here. Degrees granted: Masters. Attendance, degree and transcript information available by fax, mail.

Assumption College, Registrar, 500 Salisbury St, Worcester, MA 01609, 508-767-7355, 508-767-7407 (Fax: 508-799-5411) 8:30AM-4:30PM. www.assumption.edu. Enrollment: 2150. Records go back to 1904. Alumni records maintained here; call 508-767-7223. Degrees granted: Bachelors; Masters. Attendance and degree information available by phone, fax, mail. Transcripts available by fax, mail.

Atlantic Union College, Registrar, PO Box 1000, South Lancaster, MA 01561, 978-368-2215, 978-368-2216 (Fax: 978-368-2018). 9AM-Noon,1-4PM M-Th; 9-11AM F. Enrollment: 886. Records go back to 1884. Alumni records are maintained here. Degrees granted: Associate; Bachelors; Masters. Special programs- Adult Degree, 978-368-2300: Continuing Education, 978-368-2490. Attendance and degree information available by phone, fax, mail. Transcripts available by fax, mail.

Babson College, Registrar, Babson Park, Wellesley, MA 02157, 781-239-4023, www.babson.edu. 781-239-4519 (Fax: 781-239-5618) 8:30AM-4:30PM. Enrollment: 3200. Records go back to 1921. Alumni records maintained here; call 781-239-4562. Degrees granted: Bachelors; Masters. Attendance and degree information available by phone, fax, mail. Transcripts available by fax, mail.

Barrington College

(See Gordon College)

Bay Path College, Registrar, 588 Longmeadow St, Longmeadow, MA 01106, 413-567-0621 (Fax: 413-567-0501). 8:30AM-5PM. Enrollment: 600. Records go back to 1897. Alumni records maintained here; call 413-567-0621 X421. Degrees granted: Associate; Bachelors. Attendance and degree information available by phone, fax, mail. Transcripts available by fax, mail.

Bay State College, Registrar, 122 Commonwealth Ave, Boston, MA 02116, 617-236-8034, 617-236-8000 (Fax: 617-236-4103). 8AM-5PM. Enrollment: 655. Records go back to 1970's. Degrees granted: Associate. Attendance and degree information available by phone, fax, mail. Transcripts available by mail.

Becker College (Branch), Registrar, 3 Paxton St, Leicester, MA 01524, 508-791-9241 X434 (Fax: 508-892-1435) www.becker.edu. 8:30AM-5PM. Enrollment: 400. Records go back to 1897. Alumni Records: 61 Sever St, Worcester, MA 01615-0071. Degrees granted: Bachelors. Attendance and degree information available by phone, fax, mail. Transcripts available by written request only.

Becker College, Registrar, 61 Sever St, Worcester, MA 01609, 508-791-9241 (Fax: 508-890-1511) www.beckercollege.edu. 8:30AM-5PM. Enrollment: 1500. Records go back to 1930's. Alumni records maintained here; call 508-791-9241. Degrees granted: Associate; Bachelors. Attendance and degree information available by phone, mail. Transcripts available by mail.

Bentley College, Registrar, 175 Forest St, Waltham, MA 02154-4705, 781-891-2146, 781-891-2158 (Fax: 781-891-3428) www.bentley.edu. 8:30AM-6:30PM M-Th; 8:30AM-4:30PM F; Summer: 8AM-5:30PM M-Th; Closed Fri. Enrollment: 5785. Records go back to 1917. Alumni records maintained here; call 781-891-3444. Degrees granted: Associate; Bachelors; Masters; Certificates. Special programs- BA/MBA; BA/MSA; BS/MSA. Attendance and degree information available by phone, fax, mail. Transcripts available by fax, mail.

Berklee College of Music, Registrar, 1140 Boylston St, Boston, MA 02215, 617-266-1400 X2240 (Fax: 617-247-8278) www.berklee.edu. 9AM-5PM. Enrollment: 2950. Records go back to 1945. Alumni records are maintained here. Degrees granted: Bachelors; Four Year Professional Diploma. Attendance and degree information available by phone, fax, mail. Transcripts available by fax, mail.

Berkshire Christian College, Registrar, PO Box 826, Haverhill, MA 01831, 508-372-8122. Enrollment: 35. Records go back to 1897. Alumni records are maintained here. Certification: Religion. Special programs- Bible Theology. Attendance and degree information available by phone, mail. Transcripts available by mail.

Berkshire Community College, Registrar, 1350 West St, Pittsfield, MA 01201, 413-499-4660 X236 (Fax: 413-496-9511) www.berkshire.edu. 8AM-8PM M-Th; 8AM-4PM F. Enrollment: 2300. Records go back to 1960. Alumni records are maintained here. Degrees granted: Associate. Attendance and degree information available by phone, fax, mail. Transcripts available by fax, mail.

Blue Hills Regional Technical Institute
(See Massasoit Community College)

Boston Architectural Center, Registrar, 320 Newbury St, Boston, MA 02115, 617-536-3170 (Fax: 617-536-5829) www.the-bac.edu. 9AM - 5PM. Enrollment: 850. Records go back to 1950. Alumni records are maintained here. Degrees granted: Bachelors. Special programs- Liberal Arts: Architecture. Attendance and degree information available by phone, fax, mail. Transcripts available by mail.

Boston College, Registrar, Chestnut Hill, MA 02167-3934, 617-552-3300 (Fax: 617-552-4975) www.bc.edu. 8:45AM-4:45PM. Enrollment: 12855. Records go back to 1863. Alumni records maintained here; call 617-552-3440. Degrees granted: Bachelors; Masters; Doctorate; Graduate Law School. Attendance and degree information available by phone, fax, mail. Transcripts available by fax, mail.

Boston Conservatory, Registrar, 8 The Fenway, Boston, MA 02215, 617-536-6340 X146 (Fax: 617-536-3176) 9AM-5PM. www.bostonconservatory.edu. Enrollment: 520. Records go back to 1920. Alumni records maintained here; call 617-536-6340 X128. Degrees granted: Bachelors; Masters. Attendance and degree information available by phone, fax, mail. Transcripts available by fax, mail.

Boston University, Registrar, 881 Commonwealth Ave, Boston, MA 02215, 617-353-3616 web.bu.edu. 9AM-5PM. Enrollment: 12855. Records go back to 1800's. Alumni records maintained here; call 617-353-2233. Degrees granted: Bachelors; Masters; Doctorate. Attendance and degree information available by phone, fax, mail. Transcripts available by fax, mail.

Bradford College, Office of the Registrar, 320 S Main St, Haverhill, MA 01835, 978-372-7161 X5262, 978-372-7161 X5261 (Fax: 978-521-0480) www.bradford.edu. 8:30AM-4:30PM. Enrollment: 600. Records go back to 1920. Alumni records maintained here; call 978-372-7161 X5212. Degrees granted: Associate; Bachelors. Special programs- English as Second Language. Attendance and degree information available by phone, fax, mail. Transcripts available by mail.

Brandeis University, Registrar, PO Box 9110, MS 068, Waltham, MA 02254-9110, 781-736-2010 (Fax: 781-736-3485) www.brandeis.edu. 9AM-5PM. Enrollment: 3897. Records go back to 1936. Alumni records maintained here; call 617-736-4100. Degrees granted: Bachelors. Attendance and degree information available by phone, fax, mail. Transcripts available by mail.

Bridgewater State College, Registrar, 131 Summer St, Bridgewater, MA 02325, 508-697-1200 (Fax: 508-279-6101) www.bridgew.edu. 8AM-5PM. Enrollment: 8000. Records go back to 1840. Alumni records maintained here; call 508-697-1200. Degrees granted: Bachelors; Masters. Attendance and degree information available by phone, mail. Transcripts available by mail.

Bristol Community College, Registrar, 777 Elsbree St, Fall River, MA 02720-7395, 508-678-2811 X240 (Fax: 508-676-0334) 8AM-4:30PM. www.bristol.mass.edu. Enrollment: 3120. Records go back to 1965. Alumni records maintained here; call 508-678-2811 X2169. Degrees granted: Associate. Attendance and degree information available by phone, mail. Transcripts available by mail.

Bunker Hill Community College, Registrar, 250 New Rutherford Ave, Boston, MA 02129, 617-228-2000, 617-228-2316 (Fax: 617-228-2082) www.bunkerhill.edu. 7AM-7PM. Enrollment: 6008. Records go back to 1973. Alumni records maintained here; call 617-228-2000. Degrees granted: Associate. Attendance and degree information available by phone, fax, mail. Transcripts available by fax, mail. Need signed release with fax request.

Cambridge College, Registrar, 1000 Massachusetts Ave #128, Cambridge, MA 02138, www.cambridge.edu. 617-868-1000 X101 (Fax: 617-349-3545) 9AM-7PM M-Th, 9AM-5PM F. Enrollment: 1700. Records go back to 1971. Alumni records maintained here; call 617-868-1000 X131. Degrees granted: Bachelors; Masters. Attendance and degree information available by phone, fax, mail. Transcripts available by mail.

Cape Cod Community College (Hyannis Campus), Registrar, Hyannis, MA, 508-778-2221 8:30AM - 4:30PM. Enrollment: 3700. Records go back to 1961. Alumni records maintained here; call 508-362-2131 X4011. Degrees granted: Associate. Attendance, degree and transcript information available by mail.

Cape Cod Community College, Registrar, Rte 132, West Barnstable, MA 02668, 508-362-2131 X4313, 508-362-2131 X4388 (Fax: 508-362-3988) 8:30AM - 4:30PM. Enrollment: 3700. Records go back to 1961. Alumni records maintained here; call 508-362-2131 X4011. Degrees granted: Associate. Attendance and transcript information available by mail. Degree information available by phone, mail.

Catherine College
(See Labore College)

Chamberlayne Junior College
(See Mount Ida College)

Clark University, Registrar, Worcester, MA 01610-1477, 508-793-7561 (Fax: 508-793-7548) www.clarku.edu. 9AM - 5PM. Enrollment: 2581. Records go back to 1900. Alumni records maintained here; call 508-793-7166. Degrees granted: Bachelors; Masters; Doctorate. Special programs-Professional & Continuing Education, 508-793-7217. Attendance and degree information available by phone, fax, mail. Transcripts available by mail.

College of Our Lady of the Elms. Registrar, 291 Springfield St, Chicopee, MA 01013-2839, www.elms.edu. 413-594-2761 X236, 413-594-2761 X230 (Fax: 413-592-4871) 8:30AM-4:30PM. Enrollment: 1244. Records go back to 1928. Alumni records maintained here; call 413-594-2761 X227. Degrees granted: Associate; Bachelors; Masters. Attendance and degree information available by fax, mail.

College of the Holy Cross, Registrar, College Street, Worcester, MA 01610-2395, 508-793-2511 (Fax: 508-793-3790) 8:30AM-4:30PM. www.holycross.edu. Enrollment: 2700. Records go back to 1907. Alumni records maintained here; call 508-793-2418. Degrees granted: Bachelors. Attendance and degree information available by phone, fax, mail. Transcripts available by mail.

Conway School of Landscape Design, Registrar, PO Box 179, Conway, MA 01341, 413-369-4044 (Fax: 413-369-4032) www.csld.edu. 8:30AM 4:30PM. Enrollment: 18. Records go back to 1972. Alumni records are maintained here. Degrees granted: Masters. Special programs- call 413-369-4044. Attendance and degree information available by phone, mail. Transcripts available by mail.

Curry College, Registrar, 1071 Louhill Ave, Milton, MA 02186, 617-333-2348 (Fax: 617-333-6860) www.curry.edu. 8:30AM-4:30PM. Enrollment: 1160. Records go back to 1920. Alumni records maintained here; call 617-333-2212. Degrees granted: Bachelors; Masters. Attendance and degree information available by phone, fax, mail. Transcripts available by mail.

Dean College, Registrar, Franklin, MA 02038, 508-541-1508, 800-852-7702 (Fax: 508-541-8726) www.dean.edu. 8:30AM-4:30PM. Enrollment: 1700. Records go back to 1865. Alumni records are maintained here. Degrees granted: Associate. Attendance and degree information available by phone, fax, mail. Transcripts available by fax, mail.

Dean Junior College
(See Dean College)

Eastern Nazarene College, Registrar, 23 E Elm Ave, Quincy, MA 02170-2999, 617-745-3876, 617-745-3875 (Fax: 617-745-3915) www.enc.edu. 8AM - 5PM. Enrollment: 709. Records go back to 1919. Alumni records maintained here; call 617-745-3889. Degrees granted: Bachelors; Masters. Attendance and degree information available by phone, mail. Transcripts available by mail.

Emerson College, Registrar, 100 Beacon St, Boston, MA 02116-1596, 617-824-8660 (Fax: 617-824-8619) www.emerson.edu. 9AM-5PM. Enrollment: 3800. Records go back to 1965. Some records prior to 1965 stored. Alumni records maintained here; call 617-824-8535. Degrees granted: Bachelors; Masters. Attendance and degree information available by phone, fax, mail. Transcripts available by mail.

Emmanuel College, Registrar, 400 The Fenway, Boston, MA 02115, 617-735-9960, 617-735-9961 (Fax: 617-731-9877) 8:30AM-4:30PM. www.emmanual.edu. Enrollment: 1568. Records go back to 1921. Alumni records maintained here. Call 617-735-9771. Degrees granted: Bachelors; Masters. Attendance and degree information available by phone, fax, mail. Transcripts available by mail. Fax request for transcript OK if followed by original letter.

Endicott College, Registrar, Beverly, MA 01915, 978-927-0585 X2064 (Fax: 978-927-0084). 9AM - 5PM. Enrollment: 850. Records go back to 1939. Alumni records are maintained here. Degrees granted: Associate; Bachelors; Masters. Attendance and degree information available by phone, fax, mail. Transcripts available by mail.

Episcopal Divinity School, Registrar, 99 Brattle St, Cambridge, MA 02138, 617-868-3450 (Fax: 617-864-5385). 9AM-5PM. Enrollment: 94. Records go back to 1920. Alumni records are maintained here. Degrees granted: Masters; Doctorate. Attendance and degree information available by phone, fax, mail. Transcripts available by fax, mail.

Essex Agricultural and Technical Institute, Registrar, 562 Maple St, Hathorne, MA 01937, 978-774-0050 X224 (Fax: 978-774-6530) www.agtch.org. 8AM-4PM. Enrollment: 500. Records go back to 1960. Alumni records are maintained. Degrees granted: Associate. Attendance and degree information available by phone, mail. Transcripts available by mail.

Fisher College, Registrar, 118 Beacon St, Boston, MA 02116, 617-236-8826 (Fax: 617-236-8858) www.fisher.edu. 8:30AM-4:30PM. Enrollment: 2415. Records go back to 1945. Alumni records maintained here; call 617-262-3240. Degrees granted: Associate. Attendance and degree information available by phone, mail. Transcripts available by mail.

Fitchburg State College, Registrar, 160 Pearl St, Fitchburg, MA 01420, 978-345-2151 X3138 (Fax: 978-665-3683) www.fsc.edu. 8AM-5PM. Enrollment: 3605. Records go back to 1960. Alumni records are maintained here. Degrees granted: Bachelors; Masters. Attendance and degree information available by phone, mail. Transcripts available by written request only.

Forsyth School of Dental Hygienists, 140 Fenway, Boston, MA 02115, 617-262-5200 X211 (Fax: 617-262-4021) 8AM-4:30PM. www.forsyth.orc.\\fdc\\. Enrollment: 120. Records go back to 1920. Alumni records are maintained here. Degrees granted: Associate; Bachelors. Attendance and degree information available by phone, mail. Transcripts available by mail.

Framingham State College, Registrar, 100 State St, PO Box 9101, Framingham, MA 01701-9101, 508-626-4545 (Fax: 508-626-4017) 8:30AM-4:30PM. www.frc.mass.edu. Enrollment: 3624. Records go back to 1839. Alumni records are maintained here. Degrees granted: Bachelors; Masters. Certification: Teachers Certification. Attendance and degree information available by phone, mail. Transcripts available by mail. Without release will only verify information requestor already has.

Franklin Institute of Boston, Registrar, 41 Berkley St, Boston, MA 02116, 617-423-4630 (Fax: 617-482-3706) 7:30AM-5PM. www.franklin.fib.edu. Records go back to 1908. Alumni records are maintained here. Degrees granted: Associate; Bachelors. Attendance and degree information available by phone, mail. Transcripts available by mail.

Gordon College, Registrar, 255 Grapevine Rd, Wenham, MA 01984, 978-927-2300 X 4208), 978-927-2306 (Fax: 978-524-3724) 8AM-4:30PM. www.gordonc.edu. Enrollment: 1350. Records go back to 1889. Alumni records maintained here; call 978-927-2300 X4238. Degrees granted: Bachelors; Masters. Attendance and degree information available by phone, fax, mail. Transcripts available by fax, mail.

Gordon-Conwell Theological Seminary Registrar, 130 Essex St, South Hamilton, MA 01982, 508-468-5111 X380 (Fax: 508-468-6691) www.gcts.edu. 9AM-4:30PM. Enrollment: 1015. Records go back to 1969. Degrees granted: Masters; Doctorate. Attendance and degree information available by phone, fax, mail. Transcripts available by fax, mail.

Greenfield Community College, Registrar, One College Dr, Greenfield, MA 01301, www.gcc.mass.edu. 413-774-3131 (Fax: 413-773-5129) 8:30AM-5PM. Enrollment: 1810. Records go back to 1968. Alumni records maintained here; call 413-774-3131 X523. Degrees granted: Associate. Attendance and degree information available by phone, fax, mail. Transcripts available by fax, mail.

Hampshire College, Central Records, Amherst, MA 01002, 413-582-5421 (Fax: 413-582-5584) www.hampshire.edu. 8:30AM-Noon, 1-4:30PM. Records go back to 1970. Alumni records maintained here; call 413-582-5516. Degrees granted: Bachelors. Attendance and degree information available by phone, fax, mail. Transcripts available by fax, mail.

Harvard Radcliffe College, Registrar, 20 Garden St, Cambridge, MA 02138, 617-495-1544 (Fax: 617-495-0815) www.harvard.edu. 9AM-5PM. Enrollment: 10000. Records go back to 1700's. Alumni Records: 124 Mt Auburn St, Cambridge, MA 2138. Degrees granted: Bachelors; Masters. Attendance and degree information available by phone, fax, mail. Transcripts available by mail.

Harvard University Graduate School of Arts & Sciences, Office of the Registrar, 20 Garden St, Cambridge, MA 02138, 617-495-1543 (Fax: 617-495-0815) www.harvard.edu. 9AM-5PM. Enrollment: 6000. Records go back to 1872. Earlier doctorals are at Archives. Records for graduate schools other than arts and sciences are held separately. Call for information. Alumni Records, 124 Mt Auburn St, Cambridge, MA 02138. Degrees granted: Masters; Doctorate. Attendance and degree information available by phone, fax, mail. Transcripts available by mail.

Harvard University, Registrar, Massachusetts Hall, Cambridge, MA 02138, 617-495-1000 www.harvard.edu. 8AM-5PM. Enrollment: 17760. Records go back to 1940. Alumni records are maintained here. Degrees granted: Associate; Bachelors; Masters; Doctorate. Attendance and degree information available by phone, mail. Transcripts available by mail.

Harvard University - Business School, Registrar, Baker Library 5, Soldiers Field, Boston, MA 02163, 617-495-6247, 617-496-4405 (Fax: 617-496-3955) www.harvard.edu. Enrollment: 1500. Records go back to 1920. Alumni records maintained here; call 617-495-6438. Degrees granted: Masters. Special programs- Executive Education, 617-495-6555. Attendance and degree information available by phone, mail. Transcripts available by mail.

Harvard University - Divinity School, Registrar, 45 Francis Ave, Cambridge, MA 02138, 617-495-5760, 617-495-4783 (Fax: 617-495-9489) www.harvard.edu. Enrollment: 550. Records go back to 1900. Alumni records maintained here; call 617-495-1778. Degrees granted: Masters; Doctorate. Attendance and degree information available by phone, fax, mail. Transcripts available by mail.

Harvard University - Extension School Registrar, 51 Brattle St, Cambridge, MA 02138, www.harvard.edu. 617-495-9522 (Fax: 617-495-2921) 8AM-5PM. Enrollment: 5000. Records go back to 1909. Alumni records are maintained here. Attendance and degree information available by phone, mail. Transcripts available by mail.

Harvard University - JFK School of Government, Registrar, 79 JFK St, Cambridge, MA 02138, 617-495-1150 (Fax: 617-496-3182) www.ksgwww.harvard.edu. Enrollment: 800. Alumni records are maintained. Degrees granted: Masters; Doctorate. Attendance and degree information available by phone, fax, mail. Transcripts available by written request only.

Harvard University - Medical School, Registrar, 25 Shatteck St, Boston, MA 02115, 617-432-1515 (Fax: 617-432-0275) www.harvard.edu. 8AM-5PM. Enrollment: 900. Records go back to 1782. Alumni records are maintained here. Attendance and degree information available by phone, mail. Transcripts available by mail.

Harvard University — School of Dentistry, Registrar, 188 Longwood Ave, Boston, MA 02115, 617-432-1447 (Fax: 617-432-3881) www.hsdm.med.harvard.edu. 8AM-5PM. Enrollment: 270. Records go back to 1947. Alumni records maintained here; call 617-432-1533. Degrees granted: Masters; Doctorate. Certification: Specialty. Special programs- Postdoctoral Education, 617-432-1376. Attendance information available by mail. Degree information available by phone, fax. Transcripts available by written request only.

Harvard University - School of Design, Registrar, 48 Quincy St, Cambridge, MA 02138, www.harvard.edu. 617-496-1237 (Fax: 617-495-8449) 8AM-5PM. Enrollment: 530. Records go back to 1946. Alumni records are maintained here. Degrees granted: Masters; Doctorate. Special programs- Arts Design. Attendance and degree information available by phone, mail. Transcripts available by mail.

Harvard University - School of Education, Registrar, 13 Appian Way, Cambridge, MA 02138, www.harvard.edu. 617-495-3419, 617-496-7972 (Fax: 617-495-7626) Enrollment: 1200. Records go back to 1920. Alumni records maintained here; call 617-495-4340. Degrees granted: Masters; Doctorate. Attendance and degree information available by phone. Transcripts available by mail.

Harvard University - School of Law, Registrar, 1525 Mass Ave, Cambridge, MA 02138, 617-495-4612, 617-495-4604 (Fax: 617-495-1110). Enrollment: 4000. Records go back to 1900. Alumni Records: Alumni Assoc., 1587 Mass. Ave, Baker House, Cambridge, MA 02138. Degrees granted: Masters; Doctorate; JD, Master of Laws. Special programs- LLM, 617-495-2855: ITP, 617-495-4406. Attendance and degree information available by phone, fax, mail. Transcripts available by mail.

Harvard University — School of Public Health, Registrar, 677 Huntington Ave, Boston, MA 02115, 617-432-1032 (Fax: 617-432-2009) www.hsphharvard.edu. Enrollment: 800. Records go back to 1920. Alumni records are maintained here. Degrees granted: Masters; Doctorate. Special programs- Science: Health. Attendance and degree information available by fax, mail. Transcripts available by mail.

Harvard University - Summer School, Registrar, 51 Brattle St, Cambridge, MA 02138, www.harvard.edu. 617-495-9522 (Fax: 617-495-2921) Enrollment: 5000. Records go back to 1909. Alumni records are maintained here. Degrees granted: Associate; Bachelors; Masters. Special programs- Liberal Arts. Attendance and degree information available by phone, mail. Transcripts available by mail.

Hebrew College, Registrar, 43 Hawes St, Brookline, MA 02156, 617-278-4944 (Fax: 617-264-9264) www.shamash.org/hc/. 9AM-5PM. Enrollment: 38. Alumni records are maintained here. Degrees granted: Bachelors; Masters. Attendance and degree information available by phone, mail. Transcripts available by mail.

Hellenic College / Holy Cross Greek Orthodox School of Theology, Registrar, 50 Goddard Ave, Brookline, MA 02146, 617-731-3500 (Fax: 617-232-7819) 9AM-5PM. www.hchc.edu. Enrollment: 173. Records go back to 1937. Alumni records are maintained here. Degrees granted: Bachelors; Masters. Attendance and degree information available by phone, mail. Transcripts available by fax, mail.

Holyoke Community College, Registrar, 303 Homestead Ave, Holyoke, MA 01040, 413-552-2751, 413-552-2750 (Fax: 413-534-8975) www.hcc.mass.edu/home.html. 9AM-4:30PM. Enrollment: 3500. Records go back to 1946. Alumni records maintained here; call 413-552-2253. Degrees granted: Associate. Attendance and degree information available by phone, fax, mail. Transcripts available by fax, mail. Fax requests require student release.

ITT Technical Institute, Registrar, 1671 Worcester Rd, Framingham, MA 01701-9465, 508-879-6266 (Fax: 508-879-9745) www.itt.com. 8AM-5PM. Enrollment: 270. Records go back to 1991. Alumni Records: Alumni Assoc., ITT Technical Institute, 5975 Castle Creek Pkwy N Dr, Indianapolis, IN 46250. Degrees granted: Associate. Special programs- Electronics Technology: Computer-Aided Drafting Technology. Attendance and degree information available by phone, fax, mail. Transcripts available by fax, mail.

Katharine Gibbs School, Registrar, 126 Newbury St, Boston, MA 02116, 617-578-7100 (Fax: 617-262-6210) 8AM-5PM. www.katherinegibbs.com. Enrollment: 400. Records go back to 1918. Alumni records maintained here; call 617-578-7125. Degrees granted: Associate. Attendance and degree information available by fax, mail. Transcripts available by mail.

Laboure College, Registrar, 2120 Dorchester Ave, Boston, MA 02124, 617-296-8300 X4025, 617-296-8300 X4024 (Fax: 617-296-7947) www.labourecollegeorg.com. 8AM-4:30PM. Enrollment: 400. Records go back to 1895. Alumni records maintained here; call 617-296-8300 X4030. Degrees granted: Associate. Special programs- Nutrition & Food Management, X4042: Electoneuro-diagnostic Technology, X4043: Health Information Technology, X4063: Nursing, X4040: Radiation Therapy Technology, X4039. Attendance and degree information available by phone, mail. Transcripts available by mail.

Lasell College
Lasell College, Registrar, Newton, MA 02166, 617-243-2133, 617-243-2134 (Fax: 617-243-2326). 8:30PM - 4:30PM. Enrollment: 665. Records go back to 1851. Alumni records maintained here; call 617-243-2141. Degrees granted: Associate; Bachelors. Attendance and degree information available by phone, fax, mail. Transcripts available by written request only.

Lesley College
Lesley College, Registrar, 29 Everett St, Cambridge, MA 02138-2790, 617-349-8740 (Fax: 617-349-8717) www.lesley.edu. 9AM-7PM M-Th; 9AM-5PM F. Enrollment: 6600. Records go back to 1909. Alumni records maintained here; call 617-349-8622. Degrees granted: Bachelors; Masters. Attendance and transcript information available by mail. Degree information available by phone, fax, mail.

MGH Institute of Health Professions
Registrar, 101 Merrimac St, Boston, MA 02114-4719, 617-726-3140, 617-726-3136 www.mgh.harvard.edu/depts/ihp/mgh (Fax: 617-726-8010) 8:30AM-5PM. Enrollment: 544. Records go back to 1916. Alumni records are maintained here. Degrees granted: Masters. Certification: NP, PT. Attendance and degree information available by phone, fax, mail. Transcripts available by fax, mail.

Marian Court College
Marian Court College, Registrar, 35 Little's Point Rd, Swampscott, MA 01907, 617-595-6768 (Fax: 617-595-3560). 9AM-5PM. Enrollment: 203. Records go back to 1966. Degrees granted: Associate. Attendance and degree information available by phone, fax, mail. Transcripts available by mail.

Massachusetts Bay Community College
Registrar, 50 Oakland St, Wellesley Hills, MA 02181-5399, 617-239-2500 (Fax: 617-239-2525) www.mbcc.mass.edu. 8AM-5PM. Enrollment: 3336. Records go back to 1961. Alumni records are maintained here. Degrees granted: Associate. Attendance and degree information available by phone, mail. Transcripts available by mail.

Massachusetts College of Art
Registrar, 621 Huntington Ave, Boston, MA 02115, 617-232-1555 X243, 617-232-1555 X331 (Fax: 617-566-4034) www.massart.edu. 9AM-5PM. Enrollment: 1430. Records go back to 1890's. Alumni records maintained here; call 617-232-1555 X258. Degrees granted: Bachelors; Masters. Certification: Design Teaching. Attendance, degree and transcript information available by fax, mail.

Massachusetts College of Liberal Arts
Registrar, 375 Church St, North Adams, MA 01247, 413-662-4611 (Fax: 413-662-5580) www.nasc.mass.edu. 8:30AM - 4:45PM. Enrollment: 1500. Records go back to 1908. Alumni records maintained here; call 413-662-5224. Degrees granted: Bachelors; Masters. Special programs- Life Long Learning, 413-662-5543. Attendance and degree information available by phone, fax, mail. Transcripts available by fax, mail.

Massachusetts College of Pharmacy and Allied Health Services
Registrar, 179 Longwood Ave, Boston, MA 02115, 617-732-2855 (Fax: 617-732-2801) www.mcp/ahs.edu. 8:30AM - 4:30PM. Enrollment: 1450. Records go back to 1915. Alumni records are maintained here. Degrees granted: Associate; Bachelors; Masters; Doctorate. Special programs- Continuing Education, 617-732-2961. Attendance and degree information available by phone, mail. Transcripts available by mail.

Massachusetts Community College
Registrar, 142 Berkeley St, Boston, MA 02116, www.communications.org. 617-267-7910 (Fax: 617-236-7883) 8AM-5PM. Enrollment: 450. Records go back to 1958. Alumni records are maintained here. Degrees granted: Associate. Special programs- Liberal Arts. Attendance and degree information available by phone, mail. Transcripts available by mail.

Massachusetts Institute of Technology
Registrar's Office, E19-335, 77 Massachusetts Ave, Cambridge, MA 02139, 617-253-4784 (Fax: 617-253-7459) www.mit.edu/. 9AM-5PM. Enrollment: 9960. Records go back to 1800's. Alumni records are maintained. Degrees granted: Bachelors; Masters; Doctorate. Attendance and degree information available by phone, fax, mail. Transcripts available by fax, mail.

Massachusetts Maritime Academy
Registrar, 101 Academy Dr, Buzzards Bay, MA 02532, 508-830-5036, 508-830-5037 (Fax: 508-830-5018) www.mma.mass.edu. 8AM-4:30PM. Enrollment: 750. Records go back to 1896. Alumni Records: PO Box 1910, Boston, MA 02210. Degrees granted: Bachelors. Attendance and degree information available by phone, fax, mail. Transcripts available by fax, mail.

Massachusetts School of Law-Andover
Registrar, 500 Federal St, Andover, MA 01810, 978-681-0800 (Fax: 978-681-6330) www.mslaw.edu. Enrollment: 500. Records go back to 1988. Alumni records are maintained here. Special programs- Law. Attendance and degree information available by phone, mail. Transcripts available by mail.

Massachusetts School of Professional Psychology
Registrar, 221 Rivermore St, Boston, MA 02132, 617-327-6777 (Fax: 617-327-4447). 9AM-5PM. Enrollment: 180. Records go back to 1984. Degrees granted: Doctorate. Attendance and degree information available by phone, mail. Transcripts available by mail.

Massasoit Community College
Registrar, One Massasoit Blvd, Brockton, MA 02402, 508-588-9100 (Fax: 508-427-1255). 8AM-5PM. Enrollment: 3377. Records go back to 1966. Alumni records maintained here; call 508-588-9100 X1005. Degrees granted: Associate. Attendance and degree information available by phone, fax, mail. Transcripts available by mail.

Merrimack College
Registrar, 315 Turnpike St, North Andover, MA 01845, 978-837-5000 (Fax: 978-837-5222) www.merrimack.edu. 8:30AM - 4:30PM. Enrollment: 2900. Records go back to 1947. Alumni records maintained here; call 508-837-5000 X5440. Degrees granted: Associate; Bachelors. Attendance and degree information available by phone, mail. Transcripts available by mail.

Middlesex Community College
Registrar, Springs Rd, Bedford, MA 01730, 781-280-3614 www.middlesex.cc.ma.us. (Fax: 781-280-3603) 8:30AM-9:30PM M-Th, 8:30AM-5PM F, 8:30-11:30AM Sat. Enrollment: 7000. Records go back to 1970. Alumni records maintained here; call 617-280-3523. Degrees granted: Associate. Attendance and degree information available by phone, mail. Transcripts available by mail.

Middlesex Community College
Middlesex Community College (Lowell Campus), Registrar, Kearney Square, Lowell, MA 01852, 781-280-3539. Records are located at Middlesex Community College, Registrar, Bedford, MA.

Montserrat College of Art
Montserrat College of Art, Registrar, 23 Exxex St, Beverly, MA 01915, 508-922-8222, 508-921-4242 (Fax: 508-922-4268) 9AM-4PM. www.montserrat.edu. Enrollment: 250. Records go back to 1971. Alumni records are maintained here. Degrees granted: Bachelors. Attendance, degree and transcript information available by fax, mail.

Mount Holyoke College
Mount Holyoke College, Registrar, South Hadley, MA 01075, 413-538-2025 (Fax: 413-538-3003) www.mtholyoke.edu. 8:30AM-5PM Winter; 8:30AM-4PM Summer. Enrollment: 1920. Records go back to 1898. Alumni records maintained here; call 413-538-2303. Degrees granted: Bachelors; Masters. Attendance and degree information available by phone, fax, mail. Transcripts available by mail.

Mount Ida College
Mount Ida College, Registrar, 777 Dedham St, Newton Centre, MA 02159, 617-928-4500 (Fax: 617-928-4760) www.mountida.edu. 8AM-4:30PM. Enrollment: 1640. Records go back to 1899. Alumni records are maintained here. Degrees granted: Associate; Bachelors. Attendance and degree information available by phone, fax, mail. Transcripts available by fax, mail. Grahm Junior College - Bryant & Stratton records require a one time fee.

Mount Wachusett Community College
Registrar, 444 Green St, Gardner, MA 01440, 978-632-6600, 978-632-6600 X271 (Fax: 978-632-6155) www.mwcc.mass.edu/. 8AM-5PM. Enrollment: 2800. Records go back to 1980. Alumni records are maintained here. Degrees granted: Associate. Attendance, degree and transcript information available by written request only.

New England Banking Institute
(See New England College of Finance)

New England College of Finance
Registrar, One Lincoln Plaza, 89 South St, Boston, MA 02111, 617-951-2350, 800-245-NECF (Fax: 617-951-2533) 8:30AM-4:30PM. www.finance.edu. Enrollment: 439. Records go back to 1970. Alumni records maintained here. Degrees granted: Associate. Special programs- Call 617-951-2350. Attendance and degree information available by phone, fax, mail. Transcripts available by mail.

New England College of Optometry
Registrar, 424 Beacon St, Boston, MA 02115, 617-236-6272. 9AM-4PM. Enrollment: 414. Records go back to 1900. Alumni records maintained here; call 617-236-6285. Degrees granted: Bachelors; Doctorate. Special programs- Continuing Education, 617-369-0163. Attendance, degree and transcript information available by mail.

New England Conservatory of Music
Registrar, 290 Huntington Ave, Boston, MA 02115, 617-262-1120 (Fax: 617-369-5646) www.newenglandconservatory.edu. 9AM-5PM. Enrollment: 800. Records go back to 1900. Alumni records are maintained. Degrees granted: Bachelors; Masters; Doctorate; Graduate Diploma, Artist Diploma. Attendance and degree information available by phone, fax, mail. Transcripts available by fax, mail.

New England School of Law, Registrar, 154 Stuart St, Boston, MA 02116, 617-422-7215 (Fax: 617-422-7200) www.nesl.edu. 9AM-5PM. Enrollment: 950. Records go back to 1908. Alumni records are maintained here also. Call 617-422-7203. Attendance and degree information available by phone, fax, mail. Transcripts available by mail.

Newbury College, Registrar, 129 Fisher Ave, Brookline, MA 02146, 617-730-7112 (Fax: 617-730-7095) www.newbury.edu. 9AM-5PM. Enrollment: 2425. Records go back to 1962. Alumni records maintained here; call 617-730-7210. Degrees granted: Associate; Bachelors. Attendance and degree information available by phone, fax, mail. Transcripts available by mail.

Nichols College, Office of the Registrar, PO Box 5000, Dudley, MA 01571-5000, www.nichols.edu. 508-213-2290 (Fax: 508-213-2490) 8:30AM - 4:30PM. Enrollment: 1700. Records go back to 1930's. Alumni records are maintained here. Degrees granted: Associate; Bachelors; Masters. Attendance and degree information available by phone, fax, mail. Transcripts available by mail.

North Adams State College
(See Massachusetts Col. of Liberal Arts)

North Shore Community College, Registrar, One Ferncroft Rd, Danvers, MA 01923-4093, 978-762-4000 (Fax: 978-762-4021). 8AM-4PM. Enrollment: 3090. Records go back to 1965. Alumni records are maintained here. Degrees granted: Associate. Attendance and degree information available by phone, mail. Transcripts available by mail.

Northeastern University, Transcripts Office, 117 Hayden Hall, 360 Huntington Ave, Boston, MA 02115, 617-373-2302 (Fax: 617-373-5351) www.registrar/neu.edu. 8:30AM-4:30PM. Enrollment: 18459. Records go back to 1902. Alumni Records: Alumni Assoc, Northeastern University, 346 Richards Hall, Boston, MA 02115. Degrees granted: Associate; Bachelors; Masters; Doctorate. Attendance and degree information available by phone, fax, mail. Transcripts available by mail.

Northern Essex Community College, Registrar, 100 Elliott Way, Haverhill, MA 01830, 978-556-3700, 978-556-3000 (Fax: 978-556-3729) www.necc.mass.edu. 8AM-8PM M-Th; 8AM-4PM F. Enrollment: 3588. Records go back to 1965. Alumni records maintained here; call 978-556-3862. Degrees granted: Associate. Attendance and degree information available by phone, fax, mail. Transcripts available by written request only.

Pine Manor College, Registrar, 400 Heath St, Chestnut Hill, MA 02167, 617-731-7135, 617-731-7175 (Fax: 617-731-7638) www.pmc.edu. 9AM - 5PM. Enrollment: 400. Records go back to 1917. Alumni records maintained here; call 617-731-7132. Degrees granted: Associate; Bachelors; Masters; MED. Attendance and degree information available by phone, fax, mail. Transcripts available by mail.

Pittsfield Vocational School, Registrar, 980 Valentine Rd, Pittsfield, MA 01201, 413-448-9601 (Fax: 413-499-4835) Enrollment: 1000. Records go back to 1968. Attendance and degree information available by phone, mail. Transcripts available by mail.

Pope John XXIII National Seminary, Registrar, 558 South Ave, Weston, MA 02193-2699, 781-899-5500 (Fax: 781-899-9057). 9AM-4:30PM. Enrollment: 74. Records go back to 1962. Alumni records are maintained here. Degrees granted: Masters. Attendance and transcript information available by mail. Degree information available by phone, mail.

Quincy College, Enrollment Services, 34 Coddington St, Quincy, MA 02169, 617-984-1601 (Fax: 617-984-1784) 8AM-5PM. www.ci.quincy.ma.us/quincycollege. Enrollment: 5000. Records go back to 1958. Alumni records are maintained here. Degrees granted: Associate. Attendance information available by phone, fax. Degree and transcript information available by mail.

Quincy Junior College
(See Quincy College)

Quinsigamond Community College, Registrar, 670 W Boylston St, Worcester, MA 01606, 508-854-4249, 508-854-4257 (Fax: 508-854-4357). 8AM - 4:30PM. Enrollment: 4500. Records go back to 1965. Alumni records maintained here; call 508-854-4281 X4281. Degrees granted: Associate. Attendance and degree information available by phone, fax, mail. Transcripts available by mail.

Regis College, Registrar, Weston, MA 02193, 781-768-7280, 781-768-7000 (Fax: 781-768-8339) 9AM-4:30PM Winter; 8AM-5PM Summer. www.regiscollege.edu. Enrollment: 1200. Records go back to 1927. Alumni records maintained here; call 617-768-7243. Degrees granted: Bachelors; Masters. Attendance and degree information available by phone, fax, mail. Transcripts available by fax, mail.

Roxbury Community College, Registrar, 1234 Columbus Ave, Roxbury Crossing, MA 02120, 617-427-0060 (Fax: 617-541-5351) 8:30AM-5PM. Enrollment: 1898. Records go back to 1981. Alumni records are maintained here. Degrees granted: Associate. Attendance and degree information available by phone, fax, mail. Transcripts available by fax, mail.

Salem State College, Registrar, 352 Lafayette St, Salem, MA 01970-4589, 978-741-6081, 978-741-6090 (Fax: 978-741-6336) 8:30AM - 5PM. www.salem-ma.edu. Enrollment: 10000. Records go back to 1915. Alumni records maintained here; call 978-741-6605. Degrees granted: Bachelors; Masters. Attendance and degree information available by phone, fax, mail. Transcripts available by fax, mail.

School of the Museum of Fine Arts, Boston, Registrar, 230 The Fenway, Boston, MA 02115-9975, 617-369-3621, 617-369-3616 (Fax: 617-424-6271) www.smfa.edu/. 9AM-5PM. Enrollment: 700. Records go back to 1930. Alumni records maintained here; call 617-369-3897. Degrees granted: Bachelors; Masters. Attendance, degree and transcript information available by mail. Waiver required for inquires on former students.

Simmons College, Registrar, 300 The Fenway, Boston, MA 02115, 617-521-2111 (Fax: 617-521-3144) www.simmons.edu. 8:30AM - 4:30PM. Enrollment: 4000. Records go back to 1905. Alumni records maintained here; call 617-521-2321. Degrees granted: Bachelors; Masters; Doctorate. Attendance and degree information available by phone, fax, mail. Transcripts available by fax, mail.

Simon's Rock College of Bard, Registrar, Great Barrington, MA 01230-9702, 413-528-7201 (Fax: 413-528-7248) www.simons-rock 8:30AM-4:30PM. Enrollment: 315. Records go back to 1966. Alumni records are maintained here. Degrees granted: Associate; Bachelors. Attendance and degree information available by phone, fax, mail. Transcripts available by fax, mail.

Smith College, Registrar, Northampton, MA 01063, 413-585-2550 (Fax: 413-585-2557) www.smithcollege.edu. 8AM - 4:30PM. Enrollment: 2600. Records go back to 1800's. Alumni records maintained here; call 413-585-2700. Degrees granted: Bachelors; Masters. Attendance and degree information available by phone, fax, mail. Transcripts available by fax, mail.

Southeastern Massachusetts University
(See Univ. of Massachusetts Dartmouth)

Springfield College, Registrar's Office, 263 Alden St, Springfield, MA 01109, 413-748-3149 (Fax: 413-748-3764) www.spfldcol.edu. 8:30AM - 4:15PM. Enrollment: 3159. Records go back to 1885. Alumni records maintained here; call 413-748-3163. Degrees granted: Bachelors; Masters; Doctorate. Attendance and degree information available by phone, mail. Transcripts available by mail. Fax only accepted from students.

Springfield Technical Community College, Registrar, One Armory Square, Springfield, MA 01105, 413-781-7822 X3879 (Fax: 413-739-5066) www.stcc.mass.edu. 8AM-4PM. Enrollment: 3686. Records go back to 1967. Alumni records maintained here; call 413-781-7822 X3873. Degrees granted: Associate. Attendance and degree information available by phone, fax, mail. Transcripts available by fax, mail.

St. Hyacinth College and Seminary, Registrar, 66 School St, Granby, MA 01033, 413-467-7191 X509 (Fax: 413-467-9609) 8:30AM-4:30PM. www.burks.org. Enrollment: 23. Records go back to 1957. Alumni records are maintained here. Degrees granted: Associate; Bachelors. Attendance and degree information available by phone, mail. Transcripts available by mail.

St. John's Seminary, Registrar, 127 Lake St, Brighton, MA 02135, 617-254-2610 (Fax: 617-787-2336) 9-11:30AM, 1-3PM. Enrollment: 100. Records go back to 1900. Alumni records are maintained here. Degrees granted: Masters. Attendance, degree and transcript information available by mail.

Stonehill College, Registrar, 320 Washington St, North Easton, MA 02357, www.stonehill.edu 508-565-1315 (Fax: 508-565-1434) 8AM-4:30PM. Enrollment: 2000. Records go back to 1952. Alumni records maintained here; call 508-565-1343. Degrees granted: Bachelors. Attendance and degree information available by phone, fax, mail. Transcripts available by fax, mail.

Suffolk University, Registrar, 8 Ashburton Pl, Beacon Hill, Boston, MA 02108, 617-573-8430 (Fax: 617-573-8703) www.suffolk.edu. 8AM-7PM M-Th, 8AM-4:45PM F. Enrollment: 9703. Records go back to 1985. Alumni records maintained here; call 617-573-8443. Degrees granted: Associate; Bachelors; Masters; PhD. Attendance and degree information available by phone, fax, mail. Transcripts available by fax, mail.

Swain School of Design
(See Univ. of Massachusetts at Dartmouth)

Tufts University, Registrar, Ballou Hall, Medford, MA 02155, 617-627-3267 9AM-5PM. www.tufts.edu. Enrollment: 7905. Records go back to 1856. Alumni records are maintained here. Degrees granted: Bachelors; Masters; Doctorate. Attendance and degree information available by phone, mail.

University of Massachusetts Amherst, Graduate School, 534 Goodell Bldg, Box 33292, Amherst, MA 01003-3292, 413-545-0024, 413-545-0025 (Fax: 413-577-0010) www.umass.edu/gradschool/ 8:30AM - 5PM. Enrollment: 6000. Records go back to 1896. Alumni records maintained here; call 413-545-4721. Degrees granted: Masters; Doctorate. Attendance and degree information available by phone, fax, mail. Transcripts available by fax, mail.

University of Massachusetts Boston, Registrar, 100 Morrisey Blvd, Boston, MA 02125-3393, 617-287-6200 (Fax: 617-287-6242) www.umb.edu. 8:30AM-5PM. Enrollment: 12000. Records go back to 1965. Alumni records are maintained here. Degrees granted: Bachelors; Masters; Doctorate. Attendance and degree information available by phone, fax, mail. Transcripts available by fax, mail.

University of Massachusetts Dartmouth Registrar, 285 Old Westport Rd, North Dartmouth, MA 02747-2300, 508-999-8615, 508-999-8029 (Fax: 508-999-8183) www.umassd.edu. 8AM-5PM. Enrollment: 5500. Records go back to 1950's. Alumni records maintained here; call 508-999-8031. Degrees granted: Bachelors; Masters. Attendance, degree and transcript information available by fax, mail.

University of Massachusetts Lowell, Registrar, One University Ave, Lowell, MA 01854, 978-934-2550, 978-934-2542 8:30AM-5PM. www.uml.edu. Records go back to 1890's. Alumni records maintained here; call 978-934-2223. Degrees granted: Associate; Bachelors; Masters; Doctorate. Certification: C.E.. Attendance and degree information available by phone, mail. Transcripts available by mail.

University of Massachusetts Medical Center at Worcester, Registrar, 55 Lake Ave N, Worcester, MA 01655, 508-856-2267 (Fax: 508-856-1899) www.ummed.edu. 9AM-5PM. Enrollment: 640. Records go back to 1974. Alumni records maintained here; call 508-856-2129. Degrees granted: Doctorate; PhD. Attendance and degree information available by phone, fax, mail. Transcripts available by fax, mail.

University of Massachusetts Public Services School, Transcript Department, 100 Morrissey Blvd, Boston, MA 02125, 617-287-6200 (Fax: 617-265-7173) 9AM-5PM. www.umass.edu. Enrollment: 12000. Records go back to 1965. Alumni records are maintained here Degrees granted: Bachelors; Masters; Doctorate. Special programs-Business. Attendance and degree information available by phone, mail. Transcripts available by mail.

Wellesley College, Registrar, Wellesley, MA 02181, 781-283-2307, 781-283-3312 (Fax: 781-283-3680) www.wellesley.edu. 8:30AM-4:30PM. Enrollment: 2225. Records go back to 1920. Alumni records maintained here; call 781-283-3331. Degrees granted: Bachelors. Attendance and degree information available by phone, fax, mail. Transcripts available by fax, mail.

Wentworth Institute of Technology, Office of the Registrar, 550 Huntington Ave, Boston, MA 02115, 617-989-4200, 617-989-4000 (Fax: 617-989-4591) www.wit.edu. 8:15AM-5:30PM M-Th; 8:15AM-4:45PM F; 9AM-1PM 1st Sat of month. Enrollment: 2272. Records go back to 1920. Alumni records maintained here; call 617-989-4156. Degrees granted: Associate; Bachelors. Attendance and degree information available by phone, fax, mail. Transcripts available by mail.

Western New England College, Director, Student Administrative Services, Springfield, MA 01119, 413-796-2080 (Fax: 413-796-2081) www.wnec.edu. 8AM-6:30PM M-Th, 8:30AM-4:30PM F. Enrollment: 4700. Records go back to 1970. Alumni records maintained here; call 413-782-1539. Degrees granted: Bachelors; Masters. Special programs- Weekend MBA, 413-782-1231. Attendance and degree information available by phone, fax, mail. Transcripts available by mail.

Westfield State College, Registrar, Western Ave, Westfield, MA 01086, 413-572-5240 (Fax: 413-562-3613) www.wsc.mass.edu. 8AM-5PM. Enrollment: 3710. Records go back to 1957. Alumni records maintained here; call 413-572-5236. Degrees granted: Bachelors. Attendance and degree information available by phone, fax, mail. Transcripts available by mail.

Weston School of Theology, Registrar, 3 Phillips Pl, Cambridge, MA 02138, 617-492-1960 (Fax: 617-492-5833). 8:30AM-4:30PM. Enrollment: 209. Records go back to 1922. Degrees granted: Masters; Doctorate. Attendance and degree information available by phone, fax, mail. Transcripts available by mail.

Wheaton College, Registrar, Norton, MA 02766, www.wheatonma.edu. 508-285-8247 (Fax: 508-285-8276) 8:30AM-12:30PM, 1:30-4:30PM. Enrollment: 1549. Records go back to 1890's. Alumni records are maintained here. Degrees granted: Bachelors. Special programs- Center for Work and Learning, 508-286-3798. Attendance and degree information available by phone, fax, mail. Transcripts available by fax (follow-up letter required), mail.

Wheelock College, Registrar, 200 The Riverway, Boston, MA 02215-4176, 617-734-5200 X135 (Fax: 617-566-7369). 9AM-5PM. Enrollment: 1077. Records go back to 1900. Degrees granted: Associate; Bachelors; Masters; CAGS. Attendance and degree information available by phone, fax, mail. Transcripts available by mail.

Williams College, Registrar, Williamstown, MA 01267, 413-597-4286 (Fax: 413-597-4010) www.williams.edu. 8:30AM - 4:30PM. Enrollment: 2000. Records go back to 1795. Alumni records maintained here; call 413-597-4151. Degrees granted: Bachelors; Masters. Attendance and transcript information available by fax, mail. Degree information available by phone, fax, mail.

Worcester Polytechnic Institute, Registrar, 100 Institute Rd, Worcester, MA 01609-2280, 508-831-5211 (Fax: 508-831-5931) www.wpi.edu. 9AM - 4PM. Enrollment: 3800. Records go back to 1868. Alumni records maintained here; call 508-831-5600. Degrees granted: Bachelors; Masters; PhD. Attendance and degree information available by phone, fax, mail. Transcripts available by fax, mail.

Worcester State College, Registrar, 486 Chandler St, Worcester, MA 01602-2597, 508-793-8035, 508-793-8036 (Fax: 508-793-8196). 8:15AM-5PM. Enrollment: 3750. Records go back to 1874. Alumni records are maintained here. Degrees granted: Bachelors; Masters. Attendance and degree information available by phone, fax, mail. Transcripts available by mail.

Michigan

Academy of Court Reporting (Branch), Registrar, 26111 Evergreen Rd Ste 101, Southfield, MI 48076, 248-353-4880, 216-861-3222 (Corp Office Cleveland) (Fax: 248-353-1670). 8:30AM-7PM M-Th; 8:30AM-5PM F. Enrollment: 250. Records go back to 1991. Attendance and degree information available by phone, fax, mail. Transcripts available by mail.

Adrian College, Registrar, 110 S Madison St, Adrian, MI 49221, 517-265-5161, 517-264-3180 (Fax: 517-264-3331) 8:30AM-5PM. www.adrian.edu. Enrollment: 1000. Records go back to 1859. Alumni records maintained here; call 517-265-5161. Degrees granted: Associate; Bachelors. Attendance and degree information available by phone, fax, mail. Transcripts available by fax, mail.

Albion College, Registrar, 611 E Porter St, Albion, MI 49224, 517-629-0477, 517-629-0216 (Fax: 517-629-0581) www.albion.edu. 8AM-5PM. Enrollment: 1500. Records go back to 1835. Alumni records maintained here; call 517-629-0284. Degrees granted: Bachelors. Attendance and degree information available by phone, fax, mail. Transcripts available by fax, mail.

Don't Hire a Crook!

Alma College, Registrar, Alma, MI 48801, 517-463-7348 (Fax: 517-463-7993) 8AM-Noon, 1-5PM. www.alma.edu. Enrollment: 1407. Records go back to 1886. Alumni records maintained here; call 517-463-7245. Degrees granted: Bachelors. Attendance and degree information available by phone, fax, mail. Transcripts available by fax, mail.

Alpena Community College, Registrar, 666 Johnson St, Alpena, MI 49707, 517-356-9021, 517-356-9021 X353 (Records) (Fax: 517-356-0980). 8AM-4:30PM. Enrollment: 1800. Records go back to 1952. Alumni records are maintained here. Degrees granted: Associate. Attendance and degree information available by phone, fax, mail. Transcripts available by fax, mail.

Andrews University, Registrar, Berrien Springs, MI 49104, 616-471-3399, 616-471-3375 (Fax: 616-471-6001) www.andrews.edu. 8AM-Noon, 1-5PM. Enrollment: 3000. Records go back to 1874. Alumni records maintained here; call 616-471-3591. Degrees granted: Associate; Bachelors; Masters; Doctorate. Attendance and degree information available by phone, fax, mail. Transcripts available by fax, mail.

Aquinas College, Registrar, 1607 Robinson Rd SE, Grand Rapids, MI 49506, 616-459-8281, 800-678-9593 (Fax: 616-732-4431) 8AM-6PM M-Th; 8AM-4:30PM. www.aquinas.edu. Enrollment: 2422. Records go back to 1931. Alumni records are maintained here. Degrees granted: Associate; Bachelors; Masters. Certification: Teaching. Attendance and degree information available by phone, fax, mail. Transcripts available by fax, mail.

Aquinas Junior College
(See Aquinas College)

Baker College of Auburn Hills, Registrar, 1500 University Dr, Auburn Hills, MI 48326, 248-340-0600 (Fax: 248-340-0608) www.baker.edu. Enrollment: 1081. Records go back to 1990. Alumni records are maintained here. Degrees granted: Associate; Bachelors; Masters. Special programs- Allied Health Technicians: Business. Attendance and degree information available by phone, fax, mail. Transcripts available by fax, mail.

Baker College of Flint, Registrar, G-1050 W Bristol Rd, Flint, MI 48507, 810-766-7600, 810-766-4117 (Fax: 810-766-4049) www.baker.edu. 8AM-6PM. Enrollment: 10185. Records go back to 1950. Degrees granted: Associate; Bachelors; Masters. Attendance and degree information available by phone, fax, mail. Transcripts available by mail.

Baker College of Mt. Clemens, Registrar, 34950 Little Mack, Clinton Township, MI 48035, www.baker.edu. 810-791-6610 (Fax: 810-791-6611) Admissions 9AM-6PM M-Th; 8AM-5PM F; Registrar Office 8AM-1PM. Enrollment: 1100. Records go back to 1888. Degrees granted: Associate; Bachelors; Masters. Special programs- Business Arts; Sciences. Attendance and degree information available by fax, mail. Transcripts available by mail. Transcript request form required.

Baker College of Muskegon, Registrar's Office, 1903 Marquette Ave, Muskegon, MI 49442, 616-777-5239 (Registrar); 800-937-0337, 616-777-8800 (Fax: 616-777-5265) www.baker.edu. Enrollment: 1600. Records go back to 1960. Formerly **Muskegon Business College**. Degrees granted: Associate; Bachelors; Masters; Diplomas; Certificate. Attendance and degree information available by phone, fax, mail. Transcripts available by written request only.

THIS ENTRY HAS NEW CORRECTIONS ADDED

Baker College of Owosso, Registrar's Office, 1020 S Washington St, Owosso, MI 48867, 517-723-5251 (Fax: 517-723-3355). 8AM-6PM. Enrollment: 1800. Records go back to 1983. Degrees granted: Associate; Bachelors; Masters. School will not confirm attendance information. Degree information available by phone, fax, mail. Transcripts available by fax, mail. Need student waiver for businesses to make requests.

Baker College of Port Huron, Registrar, 3403 Lapeer Rd, Port Huron, MI 48060, www.baker.edu. 810-985-7000 (Fax: 810-985-7066) Enrollment: 935. Records go back to 1990. Degrees granted: Associate; Bachelors; Masters. Special programs- Call 810-985-7000. Attendance and degree information available by phone, fax, mail. Transcripts available by fax, mail.

Bay de Noc Community College, Registrar, 2001 N Lincoln Rd, Escanaba, MI 49829, 906-786-5802 (Fax: 906-786-8515). 8AM-4:30PM. Enrollment: 2248. Records go back to 1962. Degrees granted: Associate. Attendance and degree information available by phone, fax, mail. Transcripts available by fax, mail.

Calvin College, Registrar, 3201 Burton St SE, Grand Rapids, MI 49546, 616-957-6155 (Fax: 616-957-8513) www.calvin.edu. 8AM-5PM. Enrollment: 4085. Records go back to 1898. Alumni records are maintained here. Degrees granted: Bachelors; Masters. Special programs- Accounting, 616-957-7191: Engineering, 616-957-6071: Nursing, 616-957-7076. Attendance and degree information available by phone, fax, mail. Transcripts available by fax, mail.

Calvin Theological Seminary, Registrar, 3233 Burton St SE, Grand Rapids, MI 49546, 616-957-6027, 616-957-6028 (Fax: 616-957-8621) www.Calvin.EDU. 8AM-5PM. Enrollment: 250. Records go back to 1895. Alumni records maintained here; call 616-957-8602. Degrees granted: Masters. Attendance and degree information available by phone, fax, mail. Transcripts available by fax, mail.

Center for Creative Studies-College of Art and Design, Registrar, 201 E Kirby St, Detroit, MI 48202-4034, 313-872-3118 X227 (Fax: 313-872-1521). 8:30AM-4:30PM. Enrollment: 975. Records go back to 1906. Alumni records maintained here; call 313-872-3118 X278. Degrees granted: Bachelors. Attendance and degree information available by phone, fax, mail. Transcripts available by mail.

Center for Humanistic Studies, Registrar, 40 E Ferry Ave, Detroit, MI 48202, 313-875-7440 (Fax: 313-875-2610). 8:30AM-4PM. Enrollment: 70. Records go back to 1981. Alumni Records: Dr Robert Shaw, 71 Walnut St, Suite 109, Rochester, MI 48307. Degrees granted: Masters; Specialist. Attendance and degree information available by fax, mail. Transcripts available by mail.

Central Michigan University, Registrar, Warriner Hall 106, Mount Pleasant, MI 48859, 517-774-3261 (Fax: 517-774-3783) 8AM-5PM. www.cmich.edu. Enrollment: 16500. Records go back to 1920. Alumni records maintained here; call 517-774-3312. Degrees granted: Bachelors; Masters; Doctorate. Attendance and degree information available by phone, fax, mail. Transcripts available by fax, mail.

Charles Stewart Mott Community College, Registrar, 1401 E Court St, Flint, MI 48503, 810-762-0221, 810-762-0530 (Fax: 810-762-5611) www.mcc.edu. 7:30AM-7PM M-Th; 8AM-4:30PM F. Enrollment: 11000. Records go back to 1945. Record on microfiche from 1945. Alumni records are maintained here. Degrees granted: Associate. Attendance and degree information available by phone, fax, mail. Transcripts available by fax, mail.

Cleary College, Registrar, 2170 Washtenaw Ave, Ypsilanti, MI 48197, 734-483-4400 X2244, 800-686-1883 (Fax: 734-483-0090) 8AM-5PM. www.cleary.edu. Enrollment: 800. Records go back to 1884. Alumni records maintained here; call 734-483-4400 X3373. Degrees granted: Associate; Bachelors. Attendance and degree information available by phone, fax, mail. Transcripts available by fax, mail.

Concordia College, Registrar, 4090 Geddes Rd, Ann Arbor, MI 48105, 734-995-7324, 734-995-7325 (Fax: 734-995-4610) www.ccaa.edu. 8AM-4:30PM. Enrollment: 600. Records go back to 1963. Alumni records maintained here; call 734-995-7317. Degrees granted: Associate; Bachelors. Certification: Teacher. Attendance and degree information available by phone, fax, mail. Transcripts available by fax, mail.

Cornerstone College and Grand Rapids Baptist Seminary, Registrar, 1001 E Beltline Ave NE, Grand Rapids, MI 49505, 616-222-1431, 616-949-5300 (Fax: 616-222-1540) www.cornerstone.edu. 8AM-4PM. Enrollment: 1150. Records go back to 1941. Alumni records maintained here; call 616-222--1439. Degrees granted: Associate; Bachelors; Masters; Doctorate. Attendance and degree information available by phone, fax, mail. Transcripts available by fax, mail.

Cranbrook Academy of Art, Registrar, 1221 Woodward Ave, PO Box 801, Bloomfield Hills, MI 48303-0801, 248-645-3300 (Fax: 248-646-0046) 8:30AM-5PM. www.cranbrook.edu Enrollment: 140. Records go back to 1932. Degrees granted: Masters. Attendance and degree information available by phone, fax, mail. Transcripts available by fax, mail.

Davenport College
(See Davenport College - Grand Rapids Campus)

Davenport College (Branch), Registrar, 220 E Kalamazoo St, **Lansing**, MI 48933, 517-484-2600, 800-686-1600 (Fax: 517-484-9719) www.daveport.edu. 8AM - 7PM. Enrollment: 1200. Records go back to 1966. Alumni records are maintained here. Degrees granted: Associate; Bachelors. Attendance information available by phone, fax, mail. Degree information available by fax, mail. Transcripts available by mail.

Davenport College of Business. Registrar, 415 E Fulton St, **Grand Rapids**, MI 49503, 616-732-1210 (Fax: 616-732-1178) www.d-carowit.davenport.edu. 8AM-6:30PM M-Th; 8AM-5PM F. Enrollment: 3000. Records go back to 1920. Alumni records maintained here; call 616-451-3511. Degrees granted: Associate; Bachelors. Attendance and degree information available by phone, fax, mail. Transcripts available by fax, mail.

Davenport College of Business (Branch), Registrar, 643 Waverly Rd, **Holland**, MI 49423, 616-395-4610 (Fax: 616-395-4698) www.davenport.edu. 7:30AM-6:30PM M-Th; 8AM-5PM F. Enrollment: 2700. Records go back to 1945. Alumni Records: 415 E Fulton, Grand Rapids, MI 49503. Degrees granted: Associate; Bachelors; Masters. Attendance and degree information available by phone, fax, mail. Transcripts available by fax, mail.

Davenport College of Business (Branch), Registrar, 4123 N Main St, **Kalamazoo**, MI 49006, 616-382-2835 (Fax: 616-382-3541). 8AM-6PM. Records go back to 1981. Alumni records are maintained here. Degrees granted: Associate; Bachelors. Attendance and degree information available by phone, fax, mail. Transcripts available by fax, mail.

Delta College, Registrar, 1961 Delta Rd, University Center, MI 48710, 517-686-9539, 517-686-9305 (Fax: 517-686-8736) www.delta.edu. 8AM-7PM M,Th; 8AM-4:30PM T,W,F; Summer: close at 4PM T,W and 3:30PM F. Enrollment: 10000. Records go back to 1961. Alumni records are maintained here. Degrees granted: Associate. Attendance and degree information available by phone, fax, mail. Transcripts available by fax, mail.

Delta Junior College
(See Delta College)

Detroit College of Business, Registrar, 4801 Oakman Blvd, Dearborn, MI 48126, 313-581-4400 (Fax: 313-581-6822). 8AM-8PM M-Th; 8AM-4PM F. Enrollment: 6000. Records go back to 1962. Alumni records are maintained here. Degrees granted: Associate; Bachelors. Attendance and degree information available by phone, fax, mail. Transcripts available by mail.

Detroit College of Law, Registrar, Law College Bldg-Rm 301, East Lansing, MI 48824-1300, 517-432-6823, 517-432-6820 (Fax: 517-432-6821). 9AM-6PM M,T; 9AM-4:30PM W,T. Enrollment: 750. Files older than 3 years housed at Leonard Archives, 810-477-7007. Alumni records maintained here; call 517-432-6840. Attendance and degree information available by phone, fax. Transcripts available by fax, mail.

Eastern Michigan University, Registrar, Ypsilanti, MI 48197, 734-487-4202, 734-487-2128 (Fax: 734-487-6808) www.emich.edu. Enrollment: 23000. Records go back to 1849. Alumni Records: Alumni Assoc., 013 Welch Hall, Ypsilanti, MI 48197. Degrees granted: Bachelors; Masters; Doctorate. Attendance and degree information available by phone, fax, mail. Transcripts available by mail.

Ferris State University, Registrar's Office, 420 Oak St, Big Rapids, MI 49307, 616-592-2790, 616-592-2792 (Fax: 616-592-2242) 8AM-5PM. www.ferris.edu. Enrollment: 9468. Records go back to 1895. Alumni Records: Alumni Office, Ferris State Univ., 330 Oak St, 108 West Bldg, Big Rapids, MI 49307. Degrees granted: Associate; Bachelors; Masters; Doctorate. Attendance and degree information available by phone, fax, mail. Transcripts available by fax, mail.

GMI Engineering and Management Institute
(See Kettering University)

Glen Oaks Community College, Registrar, 62249 Shimmel Rd, Centreville, MI 49032, 616-467-9945 X243, 800-994-7818 (Fax: 616-467-9068) 8AM-4PM. www.glenoaks.cc.mius. Enrollment: 1100. Records go back to 1967. Alumni records are maintained here. Degrees granted: Associate. Attendance and degree information available by phone, fax, mail. Transcripts available by fax, mail.

Gogebic Community College, Registrar, E-4946 Jackson Rd, Ironwood, MI 49938, 906-932-4231 X212 (Fax: 906-932-0868) 7:30AM-4:30PM. www.gogebic.cc.mi.us/. Enrollment: 875. Records go back to 1932. Alumni records maintained here; call 906-932-4231 X216. Degrees granted: Associate. Attendance and degree information available by phone, fax, mail. Transcripts available by mail.

Grace Bible College, Registrar, 1011 Aldon St SW, PO Box 910, Grand Rapids, MI 49509-9990, 616-538-2330, 616-261-8558 (Fax: 616-538-0599) www.gcbol.edu. 8AM-4:30PM. Enrollment: 160. Records go back to 1939. Alumni records are maintained here. Degrees granted: Associate; Bachelors. Attendance and degree information available by phone, fax, mail. Transcripts available by mail.

Grand Rapids Baptist College and Seminary
(See Cornerstone College & Grand Rapids Baptist)

Grand Rapids Community College, Registrar, 143 Bostwick St NE, Grand Rapids, MI 49503, 616-771-4120 (Fax: 616-771-4204) www.grcc.cc.mi.us. 7:30AM-7PM M-Th; 7:30AM-5PM Fri. Enrollment: 13000. Records go back to 1914. Alumni records maintained here; call 616-771-3971. Degrees granted: Associate. Special programs- Call 616-771-4100. Attendance and degree information available by fax, mail. Transcripts available by mail.

Grand Valley State University, Registrar, One Campus Dr, Allendale, MI 49401, www.gvsu.edu. 616-895-3327 (Fax: 616-895-2000) 8AM - PM M-Th; 8AM - PM F. Enrollment: 16000. Records go back to 1963. Alumni records maintained here; call 616-895-3590. Degrees granted: Bachelors; Masters. Attendance and degree information available by phone, fax, mail. Transcripts available by fax, mail.

Great Lakes Christian College, Registrar, 6211 W Willow Hwy, Lansing, MI 48917, 517-321-0242 (Fax: 517-321-5902). 8AM-5PM. Enrollment: 175. Records go back to 1949. Alumni records are maintained here. Degrees granted: Associate; Bachelors. Attendance, degree and transcript information available by fax, mail.

Great Lakes College, Registrar, 310 S Washington Ave, Saginaw, MI 48607, 517-755-3457 (Fax: 517-752-3453). 8AM-5PM. Enrollment: 1600. Records go back to 1957. Requests handled at last campus of attendance. Alumni records are maintained here. Degrees granted: Associate. Attendance and degree information available by phone, fax, mail. Transcripts available by written request only; request form required.

Henry Ford Community College, Registrar, 5101 Evergreen Rd, Dearborn, MI 48128, 313-845-6403 (Fax: 313-845-6464) www.henryford.cc.mi.us. 8AM - 7:30PM M-Th; 8AM - 4:30PM F. Enrollment: 13500. Records go back to 1936. Alumni records are maintained here. Degrees granted: Associate. Attendance and degree information available by phone, fax, mail. Transcripts available by mail.

Highland Park Community College, Records Office, Glendale Ave at Third St, Highland Park, MI 48203, 313-252-2093, 313-252-2094 (Fax: 313-865-3770) 8AM-4:30PM. Records go back to 1920. College is no longer accredited or offering any courses. Attendance, degree and transcript information available by fax, mail.

Hillsdale College, Registrar, 33 E College Ave, Hillsdale, MI 49242, 517-437-7341 (Fax: 517-437-0190) www.hillsdale.edu/. 8:30AM-5PM Fall; 8AM-4PM Summer. Enrollment: 1100. Records go back to 1877. Alumni records maintained here; call 517-437-7341 X2461. Degrees granted: Bachelors. Attendance and degree information available by phone, fax, mail. Transcripts available by fax, mail.

Hope College, Registrar, 141 E 12th St, PO Box 9000, Holland, MI 49422-9000, 616-395-7760, 800-968-7850 (Fax: 616-395-7680) www.hope.edu. 8AM - 5PM. Enrollment: 2900. Records go back to 1866. Alumni records maintained here; call 616-395-7860. Degrees granted: Bachelors. Attendance and degree information available by phone, fax, mail. Transcripts available by fax, mail.

ITT Technical Institute (Branch of Fort Wayne, IN), Registrar, 1522 E Big Beaver Rd, Troy, MI 48083-1905, 248-524-1800, 800-832-6817 (Fax: 248-528-2218) 8AM-5PM. Enrollment: 550. Records go back to 1963. Alumni Records: ITT Technical Institute, 9511 Angola Ct, Indianapolis, IN 46268. Degrees granted: Associate. Special programs- Electronics: Computer Aided Drafting. Attendance and degree information available by phone, fax, mail. Transcripts available by mail.

Jackson Community College, Registrar, 2111 Emmons Rd, Jackson, MI 49201, 517-787-0800, 517-796-8400 X517 (Fax: 517-796-8631) www.jackson.cc.mi.us. 7:30AM-6PM M-Th; 8AM-5PM F. Enrollment: 7000. Records go back to 1928. Alumni records maintained here; call 517-787-0244. Degrees granted: Associate. Attendance and degree information available by phone, fax, mail. Transcripts available by fax, mail.

Kalamazoo College, Registrar, 1200 Academy St, Kalamazoo, MI 49006, 616-337-7204 (Fax: 616-337-7251 (ATTN: Registrar)) www.kzoo.edu. 8AM-5PM. Enrollment: 1200. Records go back to 1833. Alumni records maintained here; call 616-337-7282. Degrees granted: Bachelors. Attendance and degree information available by phone, fax, mail. Transcripts available by fax, mail.

Kalamazoo Valley Community College, Registrar, PO Box 4070, Kalamazoo, MI 49003-4070, 616-372-5281 (Fax: 616-372-5161) www.kvcc.edu. 8AM-7PM M,T; 8AM-5PM W-F. Enrollment: 12000. Records go back to 1969. Alumni records are maintained here. Degrees granted: Associate. Attendance and degree information available by phone, fax, mail. Transcripts available by fax, mail.

Kellogg Community College, Registrar, 450 North Ave, Battle Creek, MI 49017-3397, 616-965-3931 X2612, 800-955-4522 (Fax: 616-965-8850) www.kellogg.cc.mi.us. 9AM-7PM M-Th, 9AM-4:30PM F. Enrollment: 8000. Records go back to 1956. Degrees granted: Associate. Attendance and degree information available by phone, fax, mail. Transcripts available by mail.

Kendall College of Art and Design, Registrar, 111 Division Ave N, Grand Rapids, MI 49503, 616-451-2787 (Fax: 616-451-9867). 8AM-5PM. Enrollment: 560. Records go back to 1928. Alumni records are maintained here. Degrees granted: Bachelors. Attendance, degree and transcript information available by written request only.

Kettering University, Registrar, 1700 W Third Ave, Flint, MI 48504, 810-762-7862, 810-762-7476 (Fax: 810-762-9836). 8AM-5PM. Enrollment: 2600. Records go back to 1919. Alumni records maintained here; call 810-762-9883. Degrees granted: Bachelors; Masters. Attendance and degree information available by phone, fax, mail. Transcripts available by fax, mail.

Kirtland Community College, Registrar, 10775 N St Helen Rd, Roscommon, MI 48653, 517-275-5121 X248 (Fax: 517-275-6789) www.kirtland.cc.mi.us. 8AM - 4:30PM. Enrollment: 1600. Records go back to 1968. Alumni records maintained here; call 517-275-5121 X284. Degrees granted: Associate. Attendance and degree information available by phone, fax, mail. Transcripts available by fax, mail.

Lake Michigan College, Registrar, 2755 E Napier St, Benton Harbor, MI 49022, 616-927-8614, 616-927-8119 (Fax: 616-927-6874). 8AM-5PM. Enrollment: 3400. Records go back to 1946. Alumni records are maintained here. Degrees granted: Associate. Attendance and degree information available by phone, fax, mail. Transcripts available by fax, mail.

Lake Superior State University, Registrar, 650 W Easterday Ave, Sault Ste. Marie, MI 49783, 906-635-2613, 906-635-2683 (Fax: 906-635-6669) www.lssu.edu. 8AM - 5PM; Summer 8AM - 4:30PM. Enrollment: 3400. Records go back to 1946. Alumni records maintained here; call 906-635-2831. Degrees granted: Associate; Bachelors; Masters. Attendance and degree information available by phone, fax, mail. Transcripts available by fax, mail.

Lansing Community College, 1110 Office of Registrar, PO Box 40010, Lansing, MI 48901-7210, 517-483-1266 (Fax: 517-483-9795) www.lansing.cc.mi.us. 8AM-5PM M-F; 8AM-8AM Th. Enrollment: 17000. Records go back to 1957. Alumni records maintained here; call 517-483-1985. Degrees granted: Associate. Attendance, degree and transcript information available by fax, mail.

Lawrence Technological University, Registrar, 21000 W Ten Mile Rd, Southfield, MI 48075, 248-204-3100, 800-CALL LTU (Fax: 248-204-3108) www.ltu.edu. 7:30AM-8PM M-Th; 7:30AM-4:30PM F. Enrollment: 4200. Records go back to 1932. Alumni records maintained here; call 248-204-2200. Degrees granted: Associate; Bachelors; Masters. Attendance and degree information available by phone, fax, mail. Transcripts available by fax, mail.

Lewis College of Business, Registrar, 17370 Meyers Rd, Detroit, MI 48235, 313-862-6300 X233 (Fax: 313-862-1027). 9AM-6PM Fall, 8AM - 5:15PM Summer. Enrollment: 250. Records go back to 1939. Alumni records maintained here; call 313-862-6300 X217. Degrees granted: Associate. Attendance and degree information available by phone, fax, mail. Transcripts available by fax, mail.

Macomb Community College, Registrar, 14500 E Twelve Mile Rd, Warren, MI 48093, 810-445-7225 www.macomb.cc.mi.us. (Fax: 810-445-7140) 8AM-7:15PM M,T; 8AM-4:30PM W,Th,F. Enrollment: 25185. Records go back to 1956. Alumni records are maintained here also. Call 810-445-7302. Degrees granted: Associate. Attendance and degree information available by phone, fax, mail. Transcripts available by written request only.

Madonna University, Registrar, 36600 Schoolcraft Rd, Livonia, MI 48150, 734-432-5400 (Fax: 734-432-5405) www.munet.edu. 8AM-5PM. Enrollment: 3500. Records go back to 1947. Alumni records maintained here; call 734-432-5601. Degrees granted: Associate; Bachelors; Masters. Attendance information available by fax, mail. Degree information available by phone, fax, mail. Transcripts available by mail.

Marygrove College, Registrar, 8425 W McNichols Rd, Detroit, MI 48221, 313-927-1200 X1260 (Fax: 313-927-1262) www.marygrove.edu. 9AM-5PM M,Th,F; 9AM-6PM T & W. Enrollment: 1800. Records go back to 1950. Alumni records maintained here; call 313-927-1441. Degrees granted: Associate; Bachelors; Masters. Attendance and degree information available by phone, fax, mail. Transcripts available by mail.

Mercy College of Detroit
(See Univ. of Detroit Mercy-Outer Drive)

Michigan Christian College
(See Rochester College (Name change 7/97))

Michigan State University, Registrar, 150 Administration Bldg, East Lansing, MI 48824, 517-355-3300 (Fax: 517-432-3347) 8AM-6PM M-Th; 8AM-5PM F. www.msu.edu/. Enrollment: 42000. Records go back to 1855. Alumni records maintained here; call 517-355-8314. Degrees granted: Bachelors; Masters; Doctorate. Certification: Two Year Agricultural Tech; Other: DVM, MD, DO. Attendance, degree and transcript information available by phone, fax, mail.

Michigan Technological University, Registrar, 1400 Townsend Dr, Houghton, MI 49931, 906-487-2319, 906-487-2317 (Fax: 906-487-3343) www.mtu.edu. 8AM-5PM. Enrollment: 6300. Records go back to 1887. Alumni records maintained here; call 906-487-2400. Degrees granted: Associate; Bachelors; Masters; Doctorate. Attendance and degree information available by phone, fax, mail. Transcripts available by fax, mail.

Mid Michigan Community College, Registrar, 1375 S Clare Ave, Harrison, MI 48625, 517-386-6658, 517-386-6657 (Fax: 517-386-9088) www.midmich.cc.mi.us. 8AM-6:30PM M-Th; 8AM-4:30PM F. Enrollment: 3500. Records go back to 1968. Alumni records are maintained here. Degrees granted: Associate. Special programs-Nursing, 517-386-6645. Attendance and degree information available by phone, fax, mail. Transcripts available by fax, mail.

Monroe County Community College, Registrar, 1555 S Raisinville Rd, Monroe, MI 48161, www.monroe.lib.mi.us/mccc. 734-384-4230 (Fax: 734-242-9711) 8AM-4:30PM. Enrollment: 3800. Records go back to 1964. Alumni records maintained here; call 734-242-7300 X4111. Degrees granted: Associate. Attendance and degree information available by phone, fax, mail. Transcripts available by mail.

Montcalm Community College, Registrar, 2800 College Dr SW, Sidney, MI 48885, 517-328-1230 www.montcalm.cc.mi.us. Fax: 517-328-2950) 8AM-4:30PM. Enrollment: 2200. Records go back to 1965. Degrees granted: Associate. Attendance and degree information available by phone, fax, mail. Transcripts available by written request only.

Muskegon Business College
(See Baker College of Muskegon)

Muskegon Community College, Registrar, 221 S Quarterline Rd, Muskegon, MI 49442, www.muskegon.cc.mi.us 616-777-0364, 616-777-0310 (Fax: 616-777-0209) 8AM-4:30PM. Enrollment: 5000. Records go back to 1936. Alumni records maintained here; call 616-777-0341. Degrees granted: Associate. Attendance information available by phone, fax, mail. Degree and transcript information available by written request only.

North Central Michigan College, Registrar, 1515 Howard St, Petoskey, MI 49770, 616-348-6605, 616-348-6618 (Fax: 616-348-6672) www.ncmc.cc.mi.us:443. 8:30AM - 5PM. Enrollment: 2000. Records go back to 1958. Alumni records maintained here; call 616-348-6621. Degrees granted: Associate; One Year Certificate. Attendance and degree information available by phone, fax, mail. Transcripts available by fax, mail.

Northern Michigan University, Records Office, 301 Cohodas Bldg, 1401 Presque Isle Ave, Marquette, MI 49855-5323, 906-227-2278 (Fax: 906-227-2231) www.nmu.edu. 8AM-5PM. Enrollment: 7898. Records go back to 1899. Alumni records maintained here; call 906-227-2610. Degrees granted: Associate; Bachelors; Masters. Attendance and degree information available by phone, mail. Transcripts available by fax, mail. Fax requests must contain picture ID and signature.

Northwestern Michigan College, Records Office, 1701 E Front St, Traverse City, MI 49686-3061, 616-922-1047, 616-922-1000 (Fax: 616-922-1570) www.nmc.edu. 8AM-5PM. Enrollment: 3900. Records go back to 1951. Alumni records maintained here; call 616-922-1019. Degrees granted: Associate. Special programs- Maritime, 616-922-1202. Attendance and degree information available by phone, fax, mail. Transcripts available by fax, mail.

Northwood University, Registrar, 3225 Cook Rd, Midland, MI 48640, 517-837-4215 (Fax: 517-837-4111) www.northwood.edu. 8:30AM-5PM. Enrollment: 1200. Records go back to 1959. Alumni records maintained here; call 517-837-4350. Degrees granted: Associate; Bachelors; Masters. Attendance and degree information available by phone, fax, mail. Transcripts available by mail.

Oakland Community College, Registrar, 2480 Opdyke Rd, Bloomfield Hills, MI 48304-2266, 248-540-1548, 248-540-1589 (Fax: 248-540-1841). 8AM-8PM M-Th, 8AM-5PM F. Enrollment: 27130. Records go back to 1965. Alumni records maintained here; call 248-540-1803. Degrees granted: Associate. Attendance and degree information available by phone, fax, mail. Transcripts available by mail.

Oakland Community College (Orchard Ridge), Registrar, 27055 Orchard Lake Rd, Farmington Hills, MI 48334, 248-471-7535. Records are not housed here. They are located at Oakland Community College, Registrar, 2480 Opdyke Rd, Bloomfield Hills, MI 48304-2266.

Oakland Community College (Highland Lakes), Registrar, 7350 Cooley Lake Rd, Waterford, MI 48327-4187, 248-540-1500 www.occ.cc.mi.us. (Info. for transcripts: 248-540-1535; attendance and degrees: 248-540-1548). Degrees granted: Associate. Attendance and degree information available phone, fax, mail. Transcripts available mail.

Oakland University, Academic Records Office, 102 O'Dowd Hall, Rochester, MI 48309-4490, 248-370-3452, 248-370-4055 (Fax: 248-370-3461) www.oakland.edu. 8AM-5PM M,T,Th,F; 8AM-6:30PM W. Enrollment: 14400. Records go back to 1959. Alumni Records: John Dodge House, Rochester, MI 48309-4490 (Fax: 248-370-4249). Degrees granted: Bachelors; Masters; Doctorate. Special programs- Continuing Education, 248-370-3120. Attendance and degree information available by phone, fax, mail. Transcripts available by fax, mail.

Olivet College, Registrar, Olivet, MI 49076, 616-749-7637, 616-749-7638 (Fax: 616-749-7178) www.olivetnet.edu. 8:30AM - Noon, 1-5PM. Enrollment: 850. Records go back to 1844. Alumni records maintained here; call 616-749-7644. Degrees granted: Bachelors; Masters. Attendance and degree information available by phone, fax, mail. Transcripts available by mail.

Reformed Bible College, Registrar, 3333 E Beltline Ave NE, Grand Rapids, MI 49505, 616-222-3000 (Fax: 616-222-3045). 8AM-5PM. Enrollment: 250. Records go back to 1940. Alumni records are maintained here. Degrees granted: Associate; Bachelors; EXCEL Degree Completion, Bachelor of Religious Education. Attendance and degree information available by phone, fax, mail. Transcripts available by fax, mail.

Rochester College, Registrar, 800 W Avon Rd, Rochester Hills, MI 48307, 248-218-2092, 248-651-5800 (Fax: 248-218-2095) www.rc.edu. 8:30AM-5PM. Enrollment: 440. Records go back to 1959. Alumni records maintained here; call 248-218-2023. Degrees granted: Associate; Bachelors. Attendance and degree information available by phone, fax, mail. Transcripts available by fax, mail.

Sacred Heart Major Seminary, Registrar, 2701 Chicago Blvd, Detroit, MI 48206, 313-883-8500, 313-883-8512 (Fax: 313-868-6440). 8:30AM - 4:30PM. Enrollment: 300. Records go back to 1926. Alumni records are maintained here. Degrees granted: Associate; Bachelors; Masters. Attendance and degree information available by phone, fax, mail. Transcripts available by fax, mail.

Saginaw Business School
(See Great Lakes Junior College)

Saginaw Valley State University, Registrar, 7400 Bay Rd, University Center, MI 48710, 517-790-4347, 517-790-4088 (Fax: 517-790-0180) www.svsu.edu. 8AM-4:30PM. Enrollment: 7500. Records go back to 1964. Alumni records maintained here; call 517-790-7075. Degrees granted: Bachelors; Masters. Attendance, degree and transcript information available by mail.

Schoolcraft College, Registrar, 18600 Haggerty Rd, Livonia, MI 48152, 734-462-4430 www.schoolcraft.cc.mi.us (Fax: 734-462-4506) 8AM - 7:30PM M, Th; 8AM - 4:30PM T,W,F. Enrollment: 8672. Records go back to 1964. Alumni records maintained here. Degrees granted: Associate. Attendance and degree information available by phone, fax, mail. Transcripts available by fax, mail.

Siena Heights College, Registrar, 1247 E Siena Heights Dr, Adrian, MI 49221, 517-264-7120, 517-264-7122 (Fax: 517-264-7744) www.sienahts.edu. 8AM-5PM; Summer 7:30AM-4:30PM M-Th; 7:30AM-1PM F. Enrollment: 1900. Records go back to 1919. Alumni records maintained here; call 517-264-7140. Degrees granted: Associate; Bachelors; Masters. Attendance and degree information available by phone, fax, mail. Transcripts available by fax, mail.

Southwestern Michigan College, Registrar, 58900 Cherry Grove Rd, Dowagiac, MI 49047-9793, 616-782-5113, 800-456-8675 (Fax: 616-782-8414) www.smc.cc.mi.us. 8AM-8PM M-Th; 8AM-5PM F. Enrollment: 3500. Records go back to 1966. Alumni records maintained here; call 616-782-5113. Degrees granted: Associate. Attendance and degree information available by phone, fax, mail. Transcripts available by fax, mail.

Spring Arbor College, Registrar, Spring Arbor, MI 49283, 517-750-6520, 517-750-6515 (Fax: 517-750-6534). 8AM-5PM. Enrollment: 2300. Records go back to 1938. Alumni records maintained here; call 517-750-6398. Degrees granted: Associate; Bachelors; Masters. Attendance and degree information available by phone, fax, mail. Transcripts available by mail.

St. Clair County Community College, Registrar, 323 Erie St, PO Box 5015, Port Huron, MI 48061-5015, 810-984-3881 (Fax: 810-984-4730). 8AM-4:30PM. Enrollment: 4500. Records go back to 1923. Alumni records maintained here; call 810-984-3881. Degrees granted: Associate. Attendance, degree and transcript information available by fax, mail.

St. Mary's College, Registrar, 3535 Indian Trail, Orchard Lake, MI 48324, 248-683-0522 (Fax: 248-683-0433). 9AM-5PM. Enrollment: 280. Records go back to 1920's. Alumni records maintained here; call 248-683-0405. Degrees granted: Bachelors. Attendance and degree information available by phone, fax, mail. Transcripts available by fax, mail.

Suomi College, Registrar, 601 Quincy St, Hancock, MI 49930, 906-487-7272, 906-487-7345 (Fax: 906-487-7509) www.suomi.edu. 8AM-4:30PM. Enrollment: 400. Records go back to 1896. Alumni records maintained here; call 906-487-7345. Degrees granted: Associate; Bachelors. Attendance and degree information available by phone, fax, mail. Transcripts available by fax, mail.

Thomas M. Cooley Law School, Registrar, 507 Grand Ave, PO Box 13038, Lansing, MI 48901-3038, 517-371-5140 X403-405 (Fax: 517-334-5716). 9AM-5PM. Enrollment: 1536. Records go back to 1976. Alumni records maintained here; call 517-371-5140 X584. Attendance and degree information available by phone, fax, mail. Transcripts available by mail.

University of Detroit Mercy, Registrar, 4001 W McNichols Rd, PO Box 19900, Detroit, MI 48219-0900, 313-993-3313 (Fax: 313-993-3317) www.udmercy.edu. 8:30AM-5PM. Enrollment: 7000. Records go back to 1877. Alumni records maintained here; call 313-993-1250. Degrees granted: Associate; Bachelors; Masters; Doctorate Attendance, degree and transcript information available by phone, fax, mail.

University of Michigan, Transcript Department, 555 LSA Building, Ann Arbor, MI 48109-1382, 734-763-9066, 313-764-1575 (Fax: 734-764-5556) 8AM-5PM. waccess.umich.edu. Enrollment: 36545. Records go back to 1817. Alumni Records: 200 Fletcher St, Ann Arbor, MI 48109-1007. Degrees granted: Bachelors; Masters; Doctorate. Special programs- Medical School, 313-764-0219: Dental School, 313-764-1512: Law, 313-764-6499. Attendance and degree information available by phone, fax, mail. Transcripts available by fax, mail.

University of Michigan - Dearborn, 240 SSC, Transcripts, 4901 Evergreen Rd, Dearborn, MI 48128-1591, 313-593-5210, 313-593-5200 (Registrar) (Fax: 313-593-5697) www.umd.umich.edu 8AM-6:30PM M,Th; 8AM-5PM T,W,F. Enrollment: 8300. Records go back to 1959. Alumni records are maintained here, 313-593-5131. Degrees granted: Bachelors; Masters. Special programs- Graduate/Master degrees, Ann Arbor, 313-763-9066. Attendance and degree information available by phone, fax, mail. Transcripts available by mail.

University of Michigan - Flint, Registrar, Flint, MI 48502, 810-762-3344 (Fax: 810-762-3346) www.flint.umich.edu. 8AM-6:30PM M-Th; 8AM-5PM F. Enrollment: 6312. Records go back to 1956. Alumni records are maintained here. Degrees granted: Bachelors; Masters. Attendance and degree information available by phone, fax, mail. Transcripts available by mail.

Walsh College of Accountancy and Business Administration, Registrar, 3838 Livernois Rd, PO Box 7006, Troy, MI 48007-7006, 248-689-8282 (Fax: 248-524-2520). 8:30AM-7PM. Enrollment: 3300. Records go back to 1922. Alumni records are maintained here umber. Degrees granted: Bachelors; Masters. Attendance and degree information available by phone, fax, mail. Transcripts available by written request only.

Washtenaw Community College, Registrar, 4800 E Huron River Dr, PO Box D-1, Ann Arbor, MI 48106, 734-973-3548 www.washtenaw.cc.mi.us/ (Fax: 734-677-5408) 8AM-7PM M-Th, 8AM-5PM F. Enrollment: 10000. Records go back to 1966. Alumni records are maintained here. Degrees granted: Associate. Attendance and degree information available by phone, fax, mail. Transcripts available by fax, mail.

Wayne County Community College District, Registrar, 801 W Fort St, Detroit, MI 48226-3010, 313-496-2862 (Fax: 313-962-1643). 8:30AM-4:30PM. Enrollment: 11500. Records go back to 1969. Alumni records maintained here; call 313-496-2727. Degrees granted: Associate. Attendance and degree information available by fax, mail. Transcripts available by mail.

Wayne State University, Student Records, 2 W Helen Newberry Joy, SSC, Detroit, MI 48202, 313-577-3531, 313-577-3550 (Fax: 313-577-3769) www.wayne.edu. 8:30AM-5PM M-Th; 8:30AM-5PM F. Enrollment: 30000. Degrees granted: Bachelors; Masters; Doctorate. Attendance and degree information available by phone, fax, mail. Transcripts available by written request only. To verify attendance and degree call 313-577-8222 or 7963. Transcript phone requests call 313-577-8218.

West Shore Community College, Student Records Office, 3000 N Stiles Rd, Scottville, MI 49454, 616-845-6211 (Fax: 616-845-0207) www.westshore.cc.mi.us. 8AM-4:30PM. Enrollment: 1500. Records go back to 1967. Alumni records are maintained here also. Call 616-845-6211 X3103. Degrees granted: Associate. School will not confirm attendance information. Degree and transcript information available by written request only. Requests for transcripts may be done by fax as long as a signature is on the request.

Western Michigan University, Registrar, Kalamazoo, MI 49008, www.wmich.edu/. 616-387-4300 8AM-5PM. Enrollment: 26500. Records go back to 1904. Alumni records are maintained here also. Call 616-387-8777. Degrees granted: Bachelors; Masters; PhD. Attendance and transcript information available by mail. Degree information available by phone, mail.

Western Theological Seminary, Registrar, 101 E 13th St, Holland, MI 49423, 616-392-8555 (Fax: 616-392-7717) www.western.org. 8AM-5PM. Enrollment: 150. Records go back to 1900. Alumni records are maintained here. Degrees granted: Masters; Doctorate. Attendance and degree information available by phone, fax, mail. Transcripts available by mail.

William Tyndale College, Registrar, 35700 W Twelve Mile Rd, Farmington Hills, MI 48331, 248-553-7200, 800-483-0707 (Fax: 248-553-5963). 8AM-5PM. Enrollment: 625. Records go back to 1945. Degrees granted: Associate; Bachelors. Attendance, degree and transcript information available by fax, mail.

Yeshiva Beth Yehuda — Yeshiva Gedolah of Greater Detroit, Registrar, 24600 Greenfield Rd, Oak Park, MI 48237, 248-968-3360 (Fax: 248-968-8613) 9:30AM-5:30PM M-Th; 9:30AM-1PM F. Enrollment: 45. Records go back to 1985. Degrees granted: Bachelors; Masters; Doctorate. Attendance and degree information available by phone, fax, mail. Transcripts available by fax, mail.

Minnesota

Alexandria Technical College, Registrar, 1601 Jefferson St, Alexandria, MN 56308, 320-762-4470, 320-762-4542 (Fax: 320-762-4430) www.alx.tec.mn.us. 8AM-4:30PM. Enrollment: 1800. Records go back to 1965. Alumni records maintained here; call 320-762-4439. Degrees granted: Associate. Attendance and degree information available by phone, fax, mail. Transcripts available by fax, mail.

Alfred Adler Institute of Minnesota, Registrar, 1001 Hwy 7 Ste 311, Hopkins, MN 55305, www.alfredadler.edu. 612-988-4170 (Fax: 612-988-4171) 9AM - 4:30pm. Enrollment: 190. Records go back to 1984. Alumni records are maintained here. Degrees granted: Masters. Attendance and degree information available by phone, fax, mail. Transcripts available by fax, mail.

American Schools of Professional Psychology (Minnesota School of Professional Psychology), Registrar, 3103 E 80th St Ste 290, Bloomington, MN 55420, 612-858-8800 (Fax: 612-858-8515). 8:30AM-4PM. Enrollment: 310. Records go back to 1987. Degrees granted: Masters; Doctorate. Special programs- Respecialization Program, 612-858-8800. Attendance and degree information available by phone, fax, mail. Transcripts available by fax, mail.

Anoka Hennepin Technical College, Registrar, 1355 W Hwy 10, Anoka, MN 55303, 612-576-4700, 612-576-4770 (Fax: 612-576-4771) www.ank.tec.mn.us. 7AM-4:30PM M-Th, 9AM-4PM F. Enrollment: 4000. Records go back to 1967. Degrees granted: Associate. Attendance and degree information available by phone, fax, mail. Transcripts available by fax, mail.

Anoka Technical College
(See Anoka Hennepin Technical College)

Anoka Ramsey Community College, Records Office, 11200 Mississippi Blvd, Coon Rapids, MN 55433, www.an.cc.mn.us 612-422-3424, 612-422-3420 (Fax: 612-422-3636) 8AM-4:30PM T,W,F; 8AM-6:30PM M,Th. Enrollment: 4500. Records go back to 1965. Degrees granted: Associate. Attendance and degree information available by phone, fax, mail. Transcripts available by fax, mail.

Arrowhead Community College — Hibbing Campus
(See Hibbing Community Campus)

Art Institute of Minnesota, Registrar, 15 South 9th St, Minneapolis, MN 55402, 612-332-3361 (Fax: 612-332-3934) www.aii.edu. 8AM-5PM. Enrollment: 269. Records go back to 1965. Alumni records maintained here; call 612-332-3361. Degrees granted: Associate. Attendance and degree information available by phone, mail. Transcripts available by mail.

Augsburg College, Registrar, 2211 Riverside Ave, Minneapolis, MN 55454, 612-330-1036, 612-330-1000 (Fax: 612-330-1425) 8AM-4:30PM. www.augsburg.edu. Enrollment: 2549. Records go back to 1869. Records for past five years other than transcripts. Alumni Records: 2124 S 7th St, Minneapolis, MN 55454. Degrees granted: Bachelors; Masters. Special programs-Studies Abroad. Attendance and degree information available by phone, fax, mail. Transcripts available by mail.

Bemidji State University, Registrar, 1500 Birchmont Dr NE, Bemidji, MN 56601-2699, 218-755-4409, 218-755-2020 (Fax: 218-744-4048) bsuweb.bemidji.msus.edu. 8AM - 4PM; Window 8AM - 3PM. Enrollment: 4700. Records go back to 1919. Alumni records maintained here; call 218-755-3989. Degrees granted: Associate; Bachelors; Masters. Attendance and degree information available by phone, fax, mail. Transcripts available by mail.

Bethany Lutheran College, Registrar, 734 Marsh St, Mankato, MN 56001, 507-386-5310, 507-386-5300 (Fax: 507-386-5376) www.blc.edu. 8AM-5PM. Enrollment: 400. Records go back to 1911. Alumni records maintained here; call 507-386-5314. Degrees granted: Associate. Attendance and degree information available by phone, fax, mail. Transcripts available by fax, mail.

Bethel College, Registrar, 3900 Bethel Dr, St Paul, MN 55112, 612-638-6250 (Fax: 612-638-6001) www.bethel.edu. 8AM-4:30PM. Enrollment: 2400. Records go back to 1905. Alumni records are maintained here. Degrees granted: Associate; Bachelors; Masters. Attendance and degree information available by phone, fax, mail. Transcripts available by fax, mail.

Bethel Theological Seminary, Registrar, 3949 Bethel Dr, St Paul, MN 55112, 612-638-6181, 612-638-6112 (Fax: 612-638-6002). 8AM-4:30PM. Enrollment: 584. Records go back to 1930. Alumni Records: Alumni Assoc., Bethel Theological Seminary, 3900 Bethel Dr, St Paul, MN 55112. Degrees granted: Masters; Doctorate. Attendance and degree information available by phone, fax, mail. Transcripts available by fax, mail.

Brainerd Community College
(See Central Lakes College)

Carleton College, Registrar, One N College St, Northfield, MN 55057, 507-646-4289, 507-646-4288 (Fax: 507-646-5419) www.carleton.edu. 8AM-5PM. Enrollment: 1800. Records go back to 1870. Pre-1953 are at school archives, 507-646-4270. Alumni records maintained here; call 507-646-4205. Degrees granted: Bachelors. Attendance and degree information available by phone, fax, mail. Transcripts available by fax, mail.

Central Lakes College, Registrar, 501 W College Dr, Brainerd, MN 56401, 218-825-2036, 218-828-2525 (Fax: 218-828-2710). 8AM-4:30PM. Enrollment: 3400. Records go back to 1958. Alumni records maintained here; call 218-828-2525. Degrees granted: Associate. Special programs- 218-825-2024. Attendance and degree information available by phone, fax, mail. Transcripts available by mail.

Century College, Registrar, 3300 Century Ave, White Bear Lake, MN 55110, 612-779-3299, 612-779-3295 (Fax: 612-773-1708). 8AM-4PM. www.century.cc.mn.us. Enrollment: 7000. Records go back to 1970. Formerly **Lakewood Community College / Northeast Metro Technical**. Alumni records maintained here; call 612-779-3338. Degrees granted: Associate. Attendance information available by phone, mail. Degree information available by phone, fax, mail. Transcripts available by fax, mail.

College of Associated Arts, Registrar, 344 Summit Ave, St Paul, MN 55102-2199, 612-224-3416 (Fax: 612-224-8854). Enrollment: 225. Records go back to 1954. Alumni records are maintained here. Degrees granted: Bachelors. Adverse incident record source- Business Manager. Attendance and degree information available by phone, fax, mail. Transcripts available by mail.

College of St. Benedict, Registrar, 37 S College Ave, St Joseph, MN 56374, 320-363-3396, 320-363-3395 (Fax: 330-363-2714). Records are located at St. John's University, Registrar, Collegeville, MN 56321.

College of St. Catherine, Registrar, 2004 Randolph Ave, St Paul, MN 55105, 612-690-6531 (Fax: 612-690-6024). 9AM-3:30PM. Enrollment: 4035. Records go back to 1905. Alumni records maintained here; call 612-690-6000. Degrees granted: Bachelors. Attendance and degree information available by phone, mail. Transcripts available by mail.

College of St. Catherine - Minneapolis, Records & Accounts, 601 25th Ave S, Minneapolis, MN 55454, 612-690-7777 (Fax: 612-690-7849). www.stkate.edu. 9AM-6:30PM. Enrollment: 1200. Alumni records maintained here; call 612-690-7759. Degrees granted: Associate; Masters. Attendance and degree information available by phone, fax, mail. Transcripts available by mail.

College of St. Scholastica, Registrar, 1200 Kenwood Ave, Duluth, MN 55811, 218-723-6039, 218-723-6039 (Fax: 218-723-6290). www.css.edu. 8AM-4:30PM. Enrollment: 2000. Records go back to 1945. Alumni records maintained here; call 218-723-6033 X6658. Degrees granted: Bachelors; Masters. Attendance and degree information available by phone, fax, mail. Transcripts available by fax, mail.

Concordia College, Registrar, 901 S 8th St, Moorhead, MN 56562, 218-299-3250 (Fax: 218-299-3224) www.cord.edu. 8AM-4:30PM. Enrollment: 2958. Alumni records maintained here; call 218-299-3743. Degrees granted: Bachelors. Attendance and degree information available by fax, mail. Transcripts available by mail.

Concordia University — St. Paul, Registrar, 275 N Syndicate St, St Paul, MN 55104, 612-641-8498, 612-641-8223 (Fax: 612-659-0207) www.csp.edu. 8AM - 4:30PM. Enrollment: 1200. Records go back to 1894. Alumni records are maintained here. Degrees granted: Associate; Bachelors; Masters. Attendance, degree and transcript information available by phone, fax, mail.

Crown College, Registrar, 6425 County Rd 30, St Bonifacius, MN 55375, 612-446-4100, 612-446-4172 (Fax: 612-446-4149) www.crown.edu. 8AM-4:30PM. Enrollment: 670. Records go back to 1916. Alumni records are maintained here. Degrees granted: Associate; Bachelors; Masters. Special programs- Graduate Studies, 800-910-GRAD; Excel Degree Completion, 612-446-4300. Attendance and degree information available by phone, fax, mail. Transcripts available by fax, mail.

Dakota County Technical College, Registrar, 1300 145th St E, Rosemount, MN 55068, 612-423-8301 (Fax: 612-423-8775). 7AM-4PM. Enrollment: 5500. Records go back to 1972. Alumni records are maintained here. Degrees granted: Associate. Attendance and degree information available by phone, fax, mail. Transcripts available by fax, mail. Request must be from subject of information.

Duluth Technical School
(See Lake Superior College)

Fergus Falls Community College, Registrar, 1414 College Way, Fergus Falls, MN 56537, 218-739-7500 (Fax: 218-739-7475) www.ff.cc.mn.us. 8AM-5PM. Records go back to 1960. Alumni records are maintained here. Degrees granted: Associate. Attendance and degree information available by phone, fax, mail. Transcripts available by fax, mail.

Fond Du Lac Tribal And Community College, Registrar, 2101 14th St, Cloquet, MN 55720, 218-879-0800 www.fdl.cc.mn.us. 8:30AM-4:30PM. Alumni records are maintained here. Degrees granted: Associate. Special programs- Liberal Arts. Attendance and degree information available by phone, mail. Transcripts available by mail.

Globe College, Registrar, 7166 N Tenth St, Oakdale, MN 55128, 612-730-5100 (Fax: 612-730-5151). 8AM-7:30PM M-Th; 8AM-4:30PM F. Enrollment: 400. Records go back to 1885. Degrees granted: Associate. Attendance and degree information available by fax, mail. Transcripts available by mail.

Golden Valley Lutheran College, Registrar, 3718 Macalaster Dr NE, Minneapolis, MN 55421, 612-788-7616 (Fax: 612-789-1549). Records go back to 1919. This school closed 5/24/85. Degrees granted: Associate. Attendance and degree information available by phone, fax, mail. Transcripts available by fax, mail.

Graduate School of America, Registrar, 330 Second Ave South, Suite 550, Minneapolis, MN 55401, 612-339-8650, 800-987-2282 X218 (Fax: 612-339-8022) www.tgsa.edu. 8:30AM - :30PM. Enrollment: 400. Records go back to 1993. Alumni records are maintained here. Degrees granted: Masters; PhD.

Gustavus Adolphus College, Registrar, 800 W College Ave, St Peter, MN 56082, 507-933-7495 (Fax: 507-933-6258) www.gac.edu. 8AM-4PM. Enrollment: 2362. Records go back to 1860. Alumni records maintained here; call 507-933-7552. Degrees granted: Bachelors. Attendance and degree information available by phone, fax, mail. Transcripts available by fax, mail.

Hamline University, Registrar, 1536 Hewitt Ave, St Paul, MN 55104, 612-523-2209, 612-523-2221 (Fax: 612-523-3043) www.hamline.edu. 8AM-5PM. Enrollment: 2562. Records go back to 1864. Alumni records maintained here; call 612-523-2272. Degrees granted: Bachelors; Masters; JD, DPA. Special programs- Law School Registrar, 612-523-2468. Attendance and degree information available by phone, fax, mail. Transcripts available by mail.

Hennepin Technical College, Registrar, 9000 Brooklyn Blvd, Brooklyn Park, MN 55445-2399, 612-425-3800 (Fax: 612-550-2197) www.htc.mnscu.edu. 8AM-5PM. Enrollment: 1650. Records go back to 1972. Degrees granted: Associate. Attendance and degree information available by phone, fax, mail. Transcripts available by fax, mail.

Hibbing Community College, Records Office, 1515 E 25th St, Hibbing, MN 55746, 218-262-6700, 800-224-4422 (Fax: 218-262-6717) www.hibcc.mn.us. 8AM-4:30PM. Enrollment: 1400. Records go back to 1916. Alumni records are maintained here. Degrees granted: Associate. Special programs- A.D. Nursing, 218-262-6700; Computer Drafting, 218-262-6700. Attendance and degree information available by phone, fax, mail. Transcripts available by fax, mail.

Inver Hills Community College, Registrar, 2500 E 80th St, Inver Grove Heights, MN 55076, 612-450-8505, 612-450-8500 (switchboard) (Fax: 612-450-8677) 8AM-6PM M-Th; 8AM-4PM F. www.ih.cc.mn.us. Enrollment: 5500. Records go back to 1970. Degrees granted: Associate. Certification: Vocational. Special programs- Nursing, 612-450-8505; EMT, 612-450-8505. Attendance and degree information available by phone, fax, mail. Transcripts available by fax, mail.

Itasca Community College, Registrar, 1851 E Hwy 169, Grand Rapids, MN 55744, 218-327-4468 (Fax: 218-327-4350) www.it.cc.mn.us. 8AM-4:30PM. Enrollment: 1200. Records go back to 1926. Degrees granted: Associate; Vocational Certificates. Attendance and degree information available by phone, fax, mail. Transcripts available by fax, mail.

Lake Superior College, Office of Student Records, 2101 Trinity Rd, Duluth, MN 55811-3399, 218-733-7600 (Fax: 218-733-5945). 8AM-4PM. Enrollment: 2800. Records go back to 1956. Known as Duluth Technical College before July 1995. Degrees granted: Associate. Attendance and degree information available by phone, fax, mail. Transcripts available by mail.

Lowthian College
(See Art Institute of Minnesota)

Luther Northwestern Theological Seminary
(See Luther Seminary)

Luther Seminary, Registrar, 2481 Como Ave, St Paul, MN 55108, www.luthersem.edu 612-641-3473, 612-641-3456 (Fax: 612-641-3425) 8:30-10AM, 10:40-Noon, 1-3:30PM Closed for Chapel. Enrollment: 819. Records go back to 1869. Alumni records maintained here; call 612-641-3451. Degrees granted: Masters; Th.D. Attendance and degree information available by phone, mail. Transcripts available by mail.

Macalester College, Registrar, 1600 Grand Ave, St Paul, MN 55105-1899, 612-696-6200 (Fax: 612-696-6600) www.macalester.edu. 8AM-4:30PM. Enrollment: 1774. Records go back to 1885. Alumni records maintained here; call 612-696-6295. Degrees granted: Bachelors. Attendance and degree information available by phone, fax, mail. Transcripts available by fax, mail.

Mankato State University, Registrar's Office, MSU 15, PO Box 8400, Mankato, MN 56002-8400, 507-389-6266, 507-389-6269 (Fax: 507-389-5917) 8AM-5PM. www.mankato.msus.edu. Enrollment: 12000. Records go back to 1876. Alumni records are maintained here also. Call 507-389-1515. Degrees granted: Associate; Bachelors; Masters. Attendance and degree information available by phone, fax, mail. Transcripts available by mail.

Martin Luther College, Registrar, 1995 Luther Ct, New Ulm, MN 56073, 507-354-8221 (Fax: 507-354-8225). 8AM - 4:30PM. Enrollment: 793. Records go back to 1884. Degrees granted: Bachelors. Attendance and degree information available by phone, fax, mail. Transcripts available by mail.

Mayo Graduate School, Registrar, 200 First St SW, Rochester, MN 55905, 507-284-3163 (Fax: 507-284-0999) www.mayo.edu. 8AM-5PM. Enrollment: 185. Records go back to 1940. Alumni records maintained here; call 507-284-2317. Degrees granted: Masters; Doctorate. Special programs- Mayo Graduate School of Medicine, 507-284-2220. Attendance and degree information available by phone, fax, mail. Transcripts available by mail.

Mesabi Range Community and Technical College (Virginia Campus), Registrar, 1001 Chestnut West, Virginia, MN 55792, 218-749-7762 (Fax: 218-749-0318) 8AM - 4:30PM. Enrollment: 1200. Records go back to 1900. Alumni records maintained here; call 800-657-3860. Degrees granted: Associate. Attendance and degree information available by fax, mail. Transcripts available by fax, mail.

Metropolitan State University, Registrar, 700 E 7th St, St Paul, MN 55106-5000, 612-772-7772 (Fax: 612-772-7738) 8AM-5PM. www.metro.msus.edu Enrollment: 5510. Records go back to 1970. Alumni records maintained here; call 612-772-7800. Degrees granted: Bachelors; Masters. Attendance and degree information available by phone, fax, mail. Transcripts available by fax, mail.

Minneapolis College of Art and Design, Registrar, 2501 Stevens Ave S, Minneapolis, MN 55404, 612-874-3727, 612-874-3700 (Fax: 612-874-3703) www.mcad.edu. 8:30AM-4PM. Enrollment: 600. Records go back to 1912. Alumni records maintained here; call 612-874-3792. Degrees granted: Bachelors; Masters. Special programs- Bachelor of Science-Visualization, 612-874-3760. Attendance and degree information available by phone, fax, mail. Transcripts available by mail.

Minneapolis Community & Technical College, Records Office, 1501 Hennepin Ave, Minneapolis, MN 55403, 612-341-7006 (Fax: 612-341-7350) www.mctc.tec.mn.us. 9AM-6PM M; 9AM-7:30PM T; 9AM-4PM W,Th; 9AM-Noon F. Enrollment: 5880. Records go back to 1968. Alumni records maintained here; call 612-341-7564. Degrees granted: Associate. Attendance, degree and transcript information available by fax, mail.

Minnesota Bible College, Registrar, 920 Mayowood Rd SW, Rochester, MN 55902, 507-288-4563 (Fax: 507-288-9046) www.mnbc.edu. 8AM-4:30PM. Enrollment: 120. Records go back to 1917. Alumni records are maintained here. Degrees granted: Associate; Bachelors. Attendance and degree information available by phone, fax, mail. Transcripts available by mail.

Minnesota West Community and Technical College, Registrar, 1593 11th Ave, Granite Falls, MN 56241, 320-564-4511 (Fax: 320-564-4582) 8AM-4:30PM. www.mnwest.mnscu.edu Enrollment: 400. Records go back to 1965. Degrees granted: Associate. Attendance, degree and transcript information available by fax, mail.

Minnesota West Community and Technical College (Worthington Campus), Registrar, 1450 Collegeway, Worthington, MN 56187, 507-372-3451 (Fax: 507-372-5801) www.wr.cc.mn.us. 8AM-4:30PM. Enrollment: 900. Records go back to 1937. Alumni records are maintained here. Degrees granted: Associate. Attendance and degree information available by phone, fax, mail. Transcripts available by fax, mail.

Moorhead State University, Registrar, 1104 7th Ave S, Moorhead, MN 56563, 218-236-2565 (Fax: 218-236-3854) 8AM-4:30PM. www.moorhead.msus.edu. Enrollment: 6464. Records go back to 1889. Alumni records maintained here; call 218-236-3265. Degrees granted: Associate; Bachelors; Masters; Specialist. Attendance and degree information available by phone, fax, mail. Transcripts available by fax, mail.

Normandale Community College, Registrar, 9700 France Ave S, Bloomington, MN 55431, 612-832-6314 (Fax: 612-832-6571). 8AM-9PM. Enrollment: 7300. Records go back to 1968. Degrees granted: Associate. Attendance and degree information available by phone, fax, mail. Transcripts available by fax, mail.

North Central Bible College, Registrar, 910 Elliot Ave S, Minneapolis, MN 55404, 612-343-4409, 612-343-4408 (Fax: 612-343-4778) www.ncbc.edu. 8AM-4:30PM. Enrollment: 1100. Records go back to 1930. Alumni records are maintained here. Degrees granted: Associate; Bachelors. Special programs- Carlson Institute Correspondence Course Dept, 612-343-4430. Attendance and degree information available by phone, fax, mail. Transcripts available by fax, mail.

North Hennepin Community College, Registrar, 7411 85th Ave N, Brooklyn Park, MN 55445, 612-424-0719 (Fax: 612-424-0929) www.nh.cc.mn.us.edu. 8AM - 4:30PM M,Th,F; 8AM - 7PM T,W. Enrollment: 5500. Records go back to 1966. Alumni records maintained here; call 612-424-0916. Degrees granted: Associate. Attendance and degree information available by phone, fax, mail. Transcripts available by fax, mail.

Northeast Metro Technical College
(See Century College)

Northland Community College, Registrar, Hwy 1 E, Thief River Falls, MN 56701, 218-681-0701, 218-681-0858 (Fax: 218-681-0724). 8AM-4:30PM. Enrollment: 1200. Records go back to 1965. Degrees granted: Associate. Attendance and degree information available by phone, fax, mail. Transcripts available by fax, mail.

Northwest Technical College — East Grand Forks, Registrar, 2022 Central Ave NE, East Grand Forks, MN 56721-2702, 218-773-3441, 218-773-4506 (Fax: 218-773-4502) www.ntc.mnsu.edu. 8AM-5PM. Enrollment: 1400. Records go back to 1972. Degrees granted: Associate. Attendance and degree information available by phone, fax, mail. Transcripts available by fax, mail.

Northwest Technical College — Moorhead, Registrar, 1900 28th Ave S, Moorhead, MN 56560, 218-299-6593, 218-299-6503 (Fax: 218-236-0342). 9AM-4PM. Enrollment: 1250. Records go back to 1967. Degrees granted: Associate. Attendance and degree information available by phone, fax, mail. Transcripts available by fax, mail.

Northwest Technical Institute, Registrar, 11995 Singletree Lane, Eden Prairie, MN 55344-5351, 612-944-0080, 800-443-4223 (Fax: 612-944-9274) www.nw-ti.com. 8AM-5PM. Enrollment: 160. Records go back to 1957. Alumni records are maintained here. Degrees granted: Associate. Special programs- Engineering Drafting & Design: Architectural Drafting & Design. Attendance and degree information available by phone, fax, mail. Transcripts available by fax, mail.

Northwestern College, Registrar, 3003 N Snelling Ave, St Paul, MN 55113, 612-631-5248 (Fax: 612-631-5124) www.nwc.edu. 8:15AM-4PM. Enrollment: 1269. Records go back to 1900. Degrees granted: Associate; Bachelors. Certification: Biblical Arts. Special programs- Distance Education, 612-631-5494; Focus 15, 612-631-5200. Attendance and degree information available by phone, fax, mail. Transcripts available by fax, mail.

Northwestern College
(See Martin Luther College)

Northwestern College of Chiropractic, Registrar, 2501 W 84th St, Bloomington, MN 55431-1599, 612-888-4777, 612-885-5440 (Fax: 612-888-6713). 8AM-4:30PM. Enrollment: 700. Records go back to 1941. Alumni records are maintained here. Degrees granted: Bachelors; First Professional. Attendance and degree information available by phone, fax, mail. Transcripts available by fax, mail.

Oak Hills Bible College
(See Oak Hills Christian College)

Oak Hills Christian College, Registrar, 1600 Oak Hills Rd SW, Bemidji, MN 56601, 218-751-8670 (Fax: 218-751-8825). 8AM-5PM. Enrollment: 150. Records go back to 1940's. Alumni records are maintained here. Degrees granted: Associate; Bachelors. Certification: One Year Bible. Attendance and degree information available by fax, mail. Transcripts available by mail.

Pillsbury Baptist Bible College, Registrar, 315 S Grove, Owatonna, MN 55060, www.pilsbury.edu 507-451-2710 X275, 507-451-2710 X276 (Fax: 507-451-6459) Enrollment: 200. Records go back to 1957. Alumni records are maintained here. Degrees granted: Associate; Bachelors; Practical Christian Workers Diploma. Attendance and degree information available by phone, fax, mail. Transcripts available by written request only.

Rainy River Community College, Registrar, 1501 Hwy 71, International Falls, MN 56649, www.lsc.cc.mn.us/rrcc/home 218-285-2207, 218-285-7722 (switchboard) (Fax: 218-285-2239) 8AM-4:30PM. Enrollment: 400. Records go back to 1967. Alumni records maintained here; call 218-285-2207. Degrees granted: Associate. Attendance and degree information available by phone, fax, mail. Transcripts available by fax, mail.

Range Technical College
(See Hibbing Community College)

Rasmussen Business College, Registrar, 12450 Wayzata Blvd Ste 315, Minnetonka, MN 55305-9845, 612-545-2000 (Fax: 612-545-7038). 8AM-9PM. Enrollment: 300. Records go back to 1966. Degrees granted: Associate. Special programs- Court Reporting. Attendance, degree and transcript information available by fax, mail.

Rasmussen College at Mankato, Registrar, 501 Holly Ln, Mankato, MN 56001, www.rasmussen.edu. 507-625-6556 (Fax: 507-625-6557) 7:30AM - 9:30PM M-Th; 7:30AM - 4:30PM F. Enrollment: 260. Records go back to 1983. Degrees granted: Associate. Attendance and degree information available by phone, fax, mail. Transcripts available by fax, mail.

Rasmussen College - Eagan, Registrar, 3500 Federal Dr, Eagan, MN 55122, 612-687-9000 (Fax: 612-687-0507) 7AM-10PM. www.rasmussen.edu Enrollment: 400. Records go back to 1975. Degrees granted: Associate. Attendance and degree information available by phone, fax, mail. Transcripts available by fax, mail.

Ridgewater College, Registrar, PO Box 1097, Willmar, MN 56201, 320-235-5114, 320-231-2974 (Fax: 320-231-7677) 8AM-4:30PM. www.ridgewater.mnscu.edu. Enrollment: 3000. Records go back to 1961. Formerly **Hutchinson Willmar Regional Technical College** Alumni records maintained here; call 320-231-2935. Degrees granted: Associate. Special programs- Student Services, 320-231-2915. Attendance, degree and transcript information available by fax, mail with student release.

Riverland Community College, Registrar, 1900 8th Ave NW, Austin, MN 55912, 507-433-0610 (Fax: 507-433-0524). 8AM-4:30PM. Enrollment: 2100. Records go back to 1940. Formerly **Austin Community College.** Degrees granted: Associate. Attendance and degree information available by phone, fax, mail. Transcripts available by fax, mail.

Rochester Community And Technical College, Admissions & Records, 851 30th Ave SE, Rochester, MN 55904-4999, www.ROCH.EDU 507-285-7265 (Fax: 507-280-3529) 8AM-4:30PM. Enrollment: 4500. Records go back to 1915. Formerly **Rochester Community College/Riverland Tech College**. Degrees granted: Associate; Diplomas and Certificates. Attendance and degree information available by phone, fax, mail. Transcripts available by fax, mail.

Saint Mary's Campus
(See College of St. Catherine Minneapolis)

Saint Paul Bible College
(See Crown College)

School of the Associated Arts
(See College of Associated Arts)

Southwest State University, Registrar, 1501 State St, Marshall, MN 56258, 507-537-6206 (Fax: 507-537-7154) 8:30AM - 4:30PM. www.southwest.msus.edu Enrollment: 2575. Records go back to 1967. Alumni records are maintained here. Degrees granted: Associate; Bachelors; Masters. Attendance and degree information available by phone, fax, mail. Transcripts available by fax, mail.

St Paul Seminary School of Divinity, St Thomas, Registrar, 2260 Summit Ave, Saint Paul, MN 55105, www.stthomas.edu 612-962-5770, 612-962-5050 (Fax: 612-962-5790) Enrollment: 200. Records go back to 1850. Formerly **Saint Paul Seminary, School of Divinity**. Alumni Records: Alumni Assoc., 2115 Summit Ave, Saint Paul, MN 55105. Degrees granted: Masters; Doctorate; Professional. Attendance, degree and transcript information available by written request only.

St. Cloud State University, Registrar, 720 Fourth Ave S, St Cloud, MN 56301-4498, 320-255-2111, 320-255-3988 (Fax: 320-255-2059) www.stcloud.msus.edu. 8AM - 4:30PM. Enrollment: 15000. Records go back to 1869. Alumni Records: 720 4th Ave South, St Cloud, MN 56301-4498. Degrees granted: Associate; Bachelors; Masters. Attendance and transcript information available by mail. Degree information available by phone, fax, mail.

St. Cloud Technical College, Registrar, 1540 Northway Dr, St Cloud, MN 56303, 320-654-5075 www.sctcweb.tec.mn.us. (Fax: 320-654-5981) 7:30AM-5PM M-Th; 7:30AM-4PM F. Enrollment: 4000. Records go back to 1960. Alumni records are maintained here. Degrees granted: Associate. Attendance and degree information available by phone, fax, mail. Transcripts by fax, mail.

St. John's University, Registrar, Collegeville, MN 56321, 320-363-3395, 320-363-3395 (Fax: 320-363-2714). 8AM-4:30PM. Enrollment: 1800. Records go back to 1857. Alumni records maintained here; call 320-363-5050 (CSB); 320-363-2778 (SJU). Degrees granted: Bachelors; Masters. Attendance and degree information available by phone, fax, mail. Transcripts available by fax, mail.

St. Mary's University of Minnesota, Registrar, 700 Terrace Heights, Winona, MN 55987-1399, 507-457-1428 (Fax: 507-457-6698). 7:30AM-4PM Summer, 7:30AM-4:30PM Fall. Records go back to 1912. Alumni records maintained here; call 507-457-1499. Degrees granted: Bachelors; Masters. Attendance and degree information available by phone, mail. Transcripts available by mail.

St. Olaf College, Registrar, 1520 St Olaf Ave, Northfield, MN 55057, 507-646-3014, 507-646-3434 (Fax: 507-646-3210) www.stolaf.edu. 8AM-5PM. Enrollment: 2900. Records go back to 1874. Alumni records maintained here; call 507-646-3028. Degrees granted: Bachelors. Special programs- Continuing Education, 507-646-3066. Attendance and degree information available by phone, fax, mail. Transcripts available by fax, mail.

St. Paul Technical College, Registrar, 235 Marshall Ave, St Paul, MN 55102, 612-221-1300, 612-221-1434 (Fax: 612-221-1416) 7:30AM-4PM. www.sptc.tec.mn.us. Enrollment: 7234. Records go back to 1919. Alumni records are maintained. Degrees granted: Associate. Special programs- Customized Training (Center for Training And Assessment) 612-228-7246. Attendance and degree information available by phone, fax, mail. Transcripts available by mail.

United Theological Seminary of the Twin Cities, Registrar, 3000 Fifth St NW, New Brighton, MN 55112, 612-633-4311 www.unitedseminary.mn.org (Fax: 612-633-4315) 8AM-5PM. Enrollment: 275. Records go back to 1864. Alumni records maintained here; call 612-633-4311 X110. Degrees granted: Masters; Doctorate. Attendance and degree information available by phone, fax, mail. Transcripts available by fax, mail.

University of Minnesota — Crookston, Registrar, Hwys 2 and 75 N, Crookston, MN 56716, 218-281-8548, 218-281-8547 (Fax: 218-281-8050) www.crk.umn.edu. 8AM-4:30PM. Enrollment: 1750. Records go back to 1966. Alumni records are maintained here. Degrees granted: Associate; Bachelors. Attendance and degree information available by phone, fax, mail. Transcripts by mail.

University of Minnesota — Duluth, Registrar's Office, Attn: Transcripts, 10 University Dr, Duluth, MN 55812, 218-726-8805, 218-726-8000 (Fax: 218-726-6389) www.d.umn.edu. 8AM-4:30PM. Enrollment: 7000. Records go back to 1950. Alumni Records: 315 D Admin. Bldg, Duluth, MN 55812. Degrees granted: Bachelors; Masters. Special programs- Call 218-726-7849. Attendance and degree information available by phone, fax, mail. Transcripts available by mail.

University of Minnesota — Morris, Registrar, 600 E Fourth St, Morris, MN 56267, www.mrs.umn.edu/services/registrar/ 320-589-6030, 320-589-6027 (Fax: 320-589-6025) 8AM-4:30PM. Enrollment: 1900. Records go back to 1960. Alumni records maintained here; call 320-589-6066. Degrees granted: Bachelors. Special programs- 320-589-6450. Attendance and degree information available by phone, mail. Transcripts available by fax, mail.

University of Minnesota - Twin Cities, Office of the Registrar, 150 Williamson Hall, 231 Pillsbury Dr SE, Minneapolis, MN 55455, www.umn.edu/registrar/webinfo.htm 612-625-5333 (Fax: 612-625-4351) 8AM-4:30PM. Enrollment: 48000. Records go back to 1880's. Alumni Records: 615 2nd Ave S, Minneapolis, MN 55402. Degrees granted: Associate; Bachelors; Masters; Doctorate. Attendance and degree information available by phone, fax, mail. Transcripts available by fax, mail.

University of St. Thomas, Registrar, 2115 Summit Ave, St Paul, MN 55105, 612-962-6707 (Fax: 612-962-6710) 8AM-4:30PM. www.stthomas.edu. Enrollment: 10160. Records go back to 1910. Alumni records maintained here; call 612-962-6430. Degrees granted: Bachelors; Masters; Doctorate. Attendance and degree information available by phone, fax, mail. Transcripts available by mail.

Vermilion Community College, Registrar, 1900 E Camp St, Ely, MN 55731, 218-365-7223 www.vr.cc.mn.us. (Fax: 218-365-7217 & 218-365-7218) 8AM-4:30PM. Enrollment: 1000. Records go back to 1922. Degrees granted: Associate. Attendance, degree and transcript information available by phone, fax, mail. Transcripts other than to colleges require signature.

Walden University, Registrar, 155 S Fifth Ave, Minneapolis, MN 55401, 612-338-7224, 800-925-3368 (Fax: 612-338-5092) www.waldenu.edu. 8AM-5PM. Enrollment: 1100. Records go back to 1970. Degrees granted: Doctorate. Attendance and degree information available by phone, fax, mail. Transcripts available by mail.

William Mitchell College of Law, Registrar, 875 Summit Ave, St Paul, MN 55105, 612-290-6363, 612-290-6328 (Fax: 612-290-6414) www.wmitchell.edu/. 8:30AM-7:30PM M-Th; 8:30AM-6PM F. Enrollment: 1100. Records go back to 1900. Alumni records maintained here; call 612-290-6371. Degrees granted: Masters; JD. Attendance and degree information available by phone, fax, mail. Transcripts available by mail.

Winona State University, Registrar, Winona, MN 55987, 507-457-5030, 507-457-5035 (Fax: 507-457-5578) 7:30AM - 4:30PM. www.winona.msos.edu. Enrollment: 7000. Records go back to 1880. Alumni records maintained here; call 507-457-5027. Degrees granted: Bachelors; Masters. Special programs- 507-457-5080. Attendance and degree information available by phone, fax, mail. Transcripts available by fax, mail.

Mississippi

Alcorn State University, Registrar's Office, 1000 ASU Drive #420, Lorman, MS 39096-9402, 601-877-6170 (Fax: 601-877-6688) 8AM-5PM M-Th; 8AM-4PM F. academic.alcorn.edu. Enrollment: 3000. Records go back to 1871. Alumni Records: 1000 ASU Dr #809, Lorman, MS 39096. Degrees granted: Associate; Bachelors; Masters; Specialists. Special programs- School of Nursing, Natchez Branch, 601-877-6550. Attendance and degree information available by phone, fax, mail. Transcripts available by mail.

Belhaven College, Registrar, 1500 Peachtree St, Jackson, MS 39202, 601-968-5922, 601-968-5921 (Fax: 601-968-9998) www.belhaven.edu. 8AM-5PM. Enrollment: 1310. Records go back to 1900. Alumni records maintained here; call 601-968-5930. Degrees granted: Bachelors; Masters. Special programs- Adult Edge Excel, 601-968-8800. Attendance and degree information available by mail. Transcripts available by fax, mail.

Blue Mountain College, Registrar's Office, PO Box 188, Blue Mountain, MS 38610, 601-685-4771 X2 (Fax: 601-685-4776). 8AM-5PM. Enrollment: 382. Records go back to 1910. Alumni Records: PO Box 111, Blue Mountain, MS 38610. Degrees granted: Bachelors. Attendance and degree information available by phone, mail. Transcripts available by mail.

Coahoma Community College, Registrar, 3240 Friars Point Rd, Clarksdale, MS 38614, 601-627-2571 (Fax: 601-627-9451) 8:30AM-4PM. Enrollment: 915. Records go back to 1949. Alumni records are maintained here. Degrees granted: Associate. Attendance and degree information available by phone, fax, mail. Transcripts available by fax, mail.

Condie Junior College
(See Phillips Junior College - Condie Campus)

Copiah-Lincoln Community College, Registrar, PO Box 457, Wesson, MS 39191, 601-643-8307 (Fax: 601-643-8212) 8AM-4:30PM. Enrollment: 2230. Records go back to 1928. Alumni records are maintained here. Degrees granted: Associate. Attendance and degree information available by phone, fax, mail. Transcripts available by mail.

Delta State University, Registrar, Cleveland, MS 38733, 601-846-4040 (Fax: 601-846-4016) www.deltast.edu. 8AM-5PM. Enrollment: 3357. Records go back to 1924. Alumni records maintained here; call 601-846-4705. Degrees granted: Bachelors; Masters; Doctorate. Attendance and degree information available by phone, fax, mail. Transcripts available by fax, mail.

East Central Community College, Registrar, PO Box 129, Decatur, MS 39327, 601-635-2111 X206 (Fax: 601-635-4060). 8AM-4:30PM. Enrollment: 2052. Records go back to 1928. Alumni records maintained here; call 601-635-2111 X323. Degrees granted: Associate. Attendance and degree information available by phone, fax, mail. Transcripts available by fax, mail.

East Mississippi Community College, Registrar, PO Box 158, Scooba, MS 39358, 601-476-8442 X219, 601-476-8442 X220 (Fax: 601-476-5618) www.emcc.cc.ms.us. 8AM-4:30PM. Enrollment: 1484. Records go back to 1927. Alumni records are maintained here. Degrees granted: Associate. Attendance and degree information available by phone, fax, mail. Transcripts available by fax, mail.

Hinds Community College, Admissions & Records, Raymond, MS 39154, 601-857-3211, 601-857-3212 (Fax: 601-857-3539) 8AM-4:30PM. www.hinds.cc.ms.us. Enrollment: 14000. Records go back to 1940's. Alumni records maintained here; call 601-857-3350. Degrees granted: Associate. Special programs- Call 601-857-3211. Attendance and degree information available by phone, fax, mail. Transcripts available by written request only.

Holmes Community College, Registrar, PO Box 369, Goodman, MS 39079, 601-472-2312 X23 (Fax: 601-472-9852). 8AM-3PM. Enrollment: 2800. Records go back to 1925. Alumni records maintained here; call 601-472-2312 X53. Degrees granted: Associate. Attendance and degree information available by phone, fax, mail. Transcripts available by fax, mail.

Itawamba Community College, Registrar, 602 W Hill St, Fulton, MS 38843, 601-862-3101 X234 (Fax: 601-862-9540) www.icc.cc.ms.us. 8AM-4PM. Enrollment: 2702. Records go back to 1948. Alumni records maintained here; call 601-862-3101 X225. Degrees granted: Associate. Attendance and degree information available by phone, fax, mail. Transcripts available by fax, mail.

Jackson State University, Registrar, 1400 J R Lynch St, Jackson, MS 39217, 601-968-2300, 601-968-2803 (Fax: 601-968-2399) www.jsums.edu. 8AM-5PM. Enrollment: 6500. Records go back to 1900's. Alumni records maintained here; call 601-968-2281. Degrees granted: Bachelors; Masters; Doctorate. Attendance, degree and transcript information available by phone, fax, mail.

Jones County Junior College, Registrar, 900 S Court St, Ellisville, MS 39437, 601-477-4036 (Fax: 601-477-4212) 8AM-4:30PM. www.jcjc.cc.ms.us. Enrollment: 4500. Records go back to 1911. Alumni records maintained here; call 601-477-4145. Degrees granted: Associate. Attendance and degree information available by phone, fax, mail. Transcripts available by mail.

Magnolia Bible College, Registrar, PO Box 1109, Kosciusko, MS 39090, 601-289-2896, 601-289-2951 (Fax: 601-289-1850) www.mbc.org. 8AM-4:30PM. Enrollment: 30. Records go back to 1976. Alumni records maintained here; call 601-289-2896. Degrees granted: Bachelors. Attendance and degree information available by phone, fax, mail. Transcripts available by mail.

Mary Holmes College, Registrar, PO Box 1257, Hwy 50 W, West Point, MS 39773, 601-494-6820 (Fax: 601-494-1881 or 601-494-6625). 8AM-5PM. Enrollment: 375. Records go back to 1946. Alumni records are maintained here. Degrees granted: Associate. Attendance and degree information available by phone, fax, mail. Transcripts available by fax, mail.

Meridian Community College, Registrar, 910 Hwy 19 N, Meridian, MS 39307, 601-484-8636, 601-484-8626 (Fax: 601-484-8607). 8AM-4:30PM M-Th; 8AM-3:30PM F. Enrollment: 3000. Records go back to 1937. Degrees granted: Associate. Special programs- Call 601-484-8621. Attendance and degree information available by phone, fax, mail. Transcripts available by fax, mail.

Meridian Junior College
(See Meridian Community College)

Millsaps College, Office of Records, 1701 N State, PO Box 150110, Jackson, MS 39210, 601-974-1120 (Fax: 601-974-1114) www.millsaps.edu. 8AM-4:30PM. Enrollment: 1240. Records go back to 1890. Alumni Records: PO Box 150552, Jackson, MS 39210. Degrees granted: Bachelors; Masters. Attendance and degree information available by phone, fax, mail. Transcripts available by mail.

Mississippi College, Registrar, PO Box 4028, Clinton, MS 39058, 601-925-3210 (Fax: 601-925-3481) www.mc.edu. 8AM-4:30PM. Enrollment: 2857. Records go back to 1826. Alumni records maintained here; call 601-925-3200. Degrees granted: Bachelors; Masters. Attendance and degree information available by phone, fax, mail. Transcripts available by mail.

Mississippi Delta Community College, Registrar, PO Box 668, Moorhead, MS 38761, 601-246-6306 (Fax: 601-246-6321). 8AM-4PM Summer, 8AM-4:30PM Fall. Enrollment: 3490. Records go back to 1940. Alumni records maintained here; call 601-246-6457. Degrees granted: Associate. Certification: Vocational. Attendance information available by phone, fax, mail. Degree information available by fax, mail. Transcripts available by mail.

Mississippi Gulf Coast Community College (Jackson City), Registrar, PO Box 100, Gautier, MS 39553, 601-497-9602 (Fax: 601-497-7696) www.mgccc.cc.ms.us. Enrollment: 7500. Records go back to 1967. Alumni records are maintained here. Degrees granted: Associate. Attendance, degree and transcript information available by phone, mail.

Mississippi Gulf Coast Community College (Jefferson Davis), Registrar, 2226 Switzer Rd, Gulfport, MS 39507, www.mgccc.cc.ms.us. 601-896-3355 (Fax: 228-896-2520) Enrollment: 4000. Records go back to 1965. Alumni records are maintained here. Degrees granted: Associate. Attendance, degree and transcript information available by phone, mail.

Mississippi Gulf Coast Community College, Registrar, PO Box 67, Perkinston, MS 39573, 601-928-5211, 601-928-6206 (Fax: 601-928-6345) www.mgccc.ms.us. 8AM-4:30PM. Enrollment: 953. Records go back to 1912. Alumni records maintained here; call 601-928-6288. Degrees granted: Associate. Attendance and degree information available by phone, fax, mail. Transcripts available by fax, mail.

Mississippi State University, Registrar's Office, 112 Allen Hall, PO Box 5268, Mississippi State, MS 39762, 601-325-2663 www.msstate.edu/dept/registrar (Fax: 601-325-1846) 8AM-5PM. Enrollment: 14788. Records go back to 1878. Alumni records maintained here; call 601-325-2434. Degrees granted: Bachelors; Masters; Doctorate. Attendance and degree information available by phone, fax, mail. Transcripts available by fax, mail.

Mississippi University for Women, Registrar, PO Box W-1605, Columbus, MS 39701, 601-329-7131, 601-329-7133 (Fax: 601-241-7481) www.muw.edu. 8AM-5PM. Enrollment: 3000. Records go back to 1884. Alumni Records: PO Box W-10, Columbus, MS 39701 (Fax: 601-329-7123). Degrees granted: Associate; Bachelors; Masters. Attendance and degree information available by phone, fax, mail. Transcripts available by fax, mail.

Mississippi Valley State University, Registrar, 14000 Hwy 82 W, Box 7264, Itta Bena, MS 38941, 601-254-3325, 601-254-3321 (Fax: 601-254-3325) www.mvsu.edu. 8AM-5PM M,T,W,Th; 8AM-4PM F. Enrollment: 2219. Records go back to 1950. Alumni records maintained here; call 601-254-3576. Degrees granted: Bachelors; Masters. Attendance and degree information available by phone, fax, mail. Transcripts available by mail.

Northeast Mississippi Community College, Registrar, Cunningham Blvd, Booneville, MS 38829, 601-728-7751, 601-720-7290 (Fax: 601-728-1165). 8AM-4:30PM. Enrollment: 3000. Records go back to 1948. Alumni records maintained here; call 601-720-7300. Degrees granted: Associate. Attendance and degree information available by phone, fax, mail. Transcripts available by mail.

Northwest Mississippi Community College (Natchez Campus), Registrar, 11 Co-Lin Circle, Natchez, MS 39120, www.172.17.204.100/co/lin.htm. 601-442-9111 (Fax: 601-446-1296) Enrollment: 600. Records go back to 1953. Alumni records are maintained here. Degrees granted: Associate. Attendance information available by phone, mail. Degree and transcript information available by mail.

Northwest Mississippi Community College, Registrar, 510 N Panola St, Senatobia, MS 38668, 601-562-3219 (Fax: 601-562-3221). 8AM-4:30PM. Enrollment: 3425. Records go back to 1900. Alumni records maintained here; call 520-562-3222. Degrees granted: Associate. Attendance and degree information available by phone, fax, mail. Transcripts available by fax, mail.

Northwest Mississippi Community College (Wesson Campus), Registrar, PO Box 649, Wesson, MS 39191, 601-643-5101 (Fax: 601-643-8213) www.colin.tislink.com. Records are located at Northwest Mississippi Com. College, (Natchez Campus), Registrar, Natchez, MS.

Pearl River Community College, Registrar, 101 Hwy 11 N, Box 5559, Poplarville, MS 39470-2298, 601-795-6801, 601-795-1213 (Fax: 601-795-1339). 8AM-4PM. Enrollment: 2670. Records go back to 1909. Alumni records maintained here; call 601-795-1183. Degrees granted: Associate. Attendance and degree information available by phone, fax, mail. Transcripts available by fax, mail.

Phillips College Inland Empire Campus, Registrar, c/o CCI, PO Box 1840, Gulfport, MS 39502, No phone-school closed. 9AM-5PM. Records go back to 1975. Degrees granted: Associate. Attendance and degree information available by fax, mail. Transcripts available by mail.

Phillips Junior College (Branch), Registrar, c/o CCI, PO Box 1840, **Gulfport**, MS 39502, No phone. School closed. Records go back to 1988. Degrees granted: Associate. Special programs- Paralegal: Electronics: Computer Info Systems. Attendance, degree and transcript information available by written request only.

Phillips Junior College, Registrar, 2680 Insurance Center Dr, **Jackson**, MS 39216, 601-362-6341 (Fax: 601-366-9407). 8AM-4:30PM. Records go back to 1973. Degrees granted: Associate. Attendance, degree and transcript information available by fax, mail.

Phillips Junior College - Springfield
(See Springfield College)

Phillips Junior College-Condie Campus
(See Phillips Junior College Gulfport)

Reformed Theological Seminary, Registrar, 5422 Clinton Blvd, Jackson, MS 39209, 601-922-4988 X236 (Fax: 601-922-1153) www.rts.edu. 8AM-5PM. Enrollment: 507. Records go back to 1966. Alumni records are maintained here. Degrees granted: Masters; Doctorate. Attendance and degree information available by phone, fax, mail. Transcripts available by mail.

Rust College, Registrar, 150 E Rust Ave, Holly Springs, MS 38635, 601-252-8000 X4057 (Fax: 601-252-6107). 8AM-5PM. Enrollment: 1180. Records go back to 1957. Alumni records maintained here; call 601-252-8000 X4015. Degrees granted: Associate; Bachelors. Attendance and degree information available by phone, fax, mail. Transcripts available by fax, mail.

Rutledge College
(See Phillips Junior College)

Southeastern Baptist College, Registrar, 4229 Hwy 15 N, Laurel, MS 39440, 601-426-6346 (Fax: 601-426-6347). 8AM-4:30PM. Enrollment: 100. Records go back to 1948. Alumni records are maintained. Degrees granted: Associate; Bachelors. Attendance and degree information available by phone, fax, mail. Transcripts available by fax.

Southwest Mississippi Community College, Registrar, Summit, MS 39666, 601-276-2001 (Fax: 601-276-3888) 8AM-4:30PM. www.smec.cc.ms.us. Enrollment: 1492. Records go back to 1932. Alumni records are maintained here. Degrees granted: Associate. Attendance and degree information available by phone, fax, mail. Transcripts available by mail.

Springfield College, Registrar, 1010 W Sunshine St, Springfield, MS 65807, 417-864-7220 (Fax: 417-864-5697) 8AM-5PM. Formerly **Phillips Junior College**. Records go back to 1981. Degrees granted: Associate. Attendance and degree information available by phone, mail. Transcripts available by mail.

Tougaloo College, Registrar, 500 W County Line Rd, Tougaloo, MS 39174, 601-977-7700, 601-977-7770 (Fax: 601-977-6185). 8AM-5PM. Enrollment: 980. Records go back to 1869. Alumni records maintained here; call 601-977-7836. Degrees granted: Associate; Bachelors. Special programs-Adult Program, 601-977-7745. Attendance information available by phone, fax, mail. Degree information available by phone, mail. Transcripts available by written request only.

University of Mississippi, Registrar, University, MS 38677, 601-232-7226 (Fax: 601-232-5869) www.olemiss.edu. 8AM-5PM. Enrollment: 10500. Records go back to 1848. Alumni records are maintained here also. Call 601-232-7375. Degrees granted: Bachelors; Masters; Doctorate; PhD. Attendance and degree information available by phone, fax, mail. Transcripts available by mail.

University of Mississippi Medical Center, Registrar, 2500 N State St, Jackson, MS 39216-4505, 601-984-1080 (Fax: 601-984-1079). 8AM-4:30PM. Enrollment: 1800. Records go back to 1955. Alumni records are maintained here. Degrees granted: Bachelors; Doctorate. Attendance and degree information available by phone, mail. Transcripts available by mail.

University of Southern Mississippi, Registrar, Box 5006, Hattiesburg, MS 39406-5001, 601-266-5006, 601-266-4814 (verify) (4818 transcripts) (Fax: 601-266-5816) www.usm.edu. 8AM-5PM. Enrollment: 14000. Records go back to 1946. Alumni Records: Box 5013, Hattiesburg, MS 39406-5001. Degrees granted: Bachelors; Masters; Doctorate. Attendance and degree information available by phone, fax, mail. Transcripts available by fax, mail.

University of Southern Mississippi (Gulf Park), Registrar, 730 E Beach Blvd, Long Beach, MS 39560, 601-865-4503, 601-865-4568 (Fax: 601-867-2657) www.usm.edu. 8AM-4:30PM. Enrollment: 1700. Records go back to 1984. Alumni Records: PO Box 5013, Hattiesburg, MS 39406. Degrees granted: Bachelors; Masters. Certification: Education. Attendance and degree information available by phone, mail. Transcripts available by mail.

Wesley Biblical Seminary, Registrar, 5980 Floral Dr, Jackson, MS 39206, 601-957-1314 (Fax: 601-991-2100) www.gowesley.com. 8AM-5PM. Enrollment: 100. Records go back to 1974. Alumni records maintained here; call 601-957-1314. Degrees granted: Masters. Attendance and degree information available by phone, fax, mail. Transcripts available by fax, mail.

Wesley College, Registrar, 111 Wesley Cir, PO Box 1070, Florence, MS 39073, 601-845-2265 (Fax: 601-845-2266) Enrollment: 110. Records go back to 1946. Alumni records are maintained here. Degrees granted: Bachelors. Attendance and degree information available by phone, fax, mail. Transcripts available by mail.

William Carey College, Registrar, 498 Tuscan Ave, Hattiesburg, MS 39401-5499, 601-582-6195, 601-582-6197 (Fax: 601-582-6196). 8AM-5PM. Enrollment: 2139. Records go back to 1911. Alumni records maintained here; call 601-582-6107. Degrees granted: Bachelors; Masters. Attendance and degree information available by phone, fax, mail. Transcripts available by fax, mail.

Wood College, Registrar, PO Box 289, Mathiston, MS 39752, 601-263-5352 (Fax: 601-263-4964). 8AM-5PM. Enrollment: 250. Records go back to 1886. Formerly **Wood Junior College**. Alumni records are maintained here. Degrees granted: Associate. Attendance and degree information available by phone, fax, mail. Transcripts available by fax, mail.

Missouri

Aquinas Institute of Theology, Registrar, 3642 Lindell Blvd, St Louis, MO 63108-3396, 314-977-3883, 314-977-3882 (Fax: 314-977-7225) www.op.org/aquinas. 8:30AM-5PM. Enrollment: 200. Records go back to 1925. Degrees granted: Masters; Doctorate. Attendance and degree information available by phone, fax, mail. Transcripts available by written request only.

Assemblies of God Theological Seminary, Registrar, 1435 N Glenstone Ave, Springfield, MO 65802, 417-268-1000 (Fax: 417-268-1001) www.hets.edu. 8AM-5PM. Enrollment: 250. Records go back to 1973. Alumni records are maintained here. Degrees granted: Masters; Doctorate. Attendance and degree information available by phone, fax, mail. Transcripts available by fax, mail. Transcript requests must be in writing from student.

Avila College, Registrar, 11901 Wornall Rd, Kansas City, MO 64145, 816-942-8400 X2210 (Fax: 816-942-3362) www.avila.edu. 8AM-5PM. Enrollment: 1300. Records go back to 1916. Alumni records maintained here; call 816-942-8400 X2236. Degrees granted: Bachelors; Masters. Attendance and degree information available by phone, fax, mail. Transcripts available by fax, mail.

Baptist Bible College, Registrar, 628 E Kearney St, Springfield, MO 65803, 417-268-6060 (Fax: 417-268-6694) www.seebbc.edu. 9AM-5PM. Enrollment: 858. Records go back to 1950. Alumni records maintained here; call 417-268-6070. Degrees granted: Associate; Bachelors; Masters. Attendance and degree information available by phone, fax, mail. Transcripts available by fax, mail.

Barnes College, Registrar, 416 S Kings Hwy Blvd, St Louis, MO 63110, 314-362-5225 www.barnes.edu. Enrollment: 443. Records go back to 1994. Attendance and degree information available by phone, mail. Transcripts available by mail.

Calvary Bible College, Registrar, 15800 Calvary Rd, Kansas City, MO 64147-1341, 816-322-0110, 816-322-5152 X1306 (Fax: 816-331-4474) www.calvary.edu. 8AM-4:30PM. Enrollment: 320. Records go back to 1931. Alumni records are maintained here. Degrees granted: Associate; Bachelors; Masters. Special programs- Christian Ministry. Attendance and degree information available by phone, fax, mail. Transcripts available by fax, mail.

Central Bible College, Registrar, 3000 N Grant Ave, Springfield, MO 65803, 417-833-2551 (Fax: 417-833-5478) www.cbcag.edu. 8:30AM-4:30PM. Enrollment: 900. Records go back to 1922. Alumni records are maintained here. Degrees granted: Associate; Bachelors. Attendance and degree information available by phone, fax, mail. Transcripts available by fax, mail.

Central Christian College of the Bible, Registrar, 911 Urbandale Dr E, Moberly, MO 65270, 660-263-3900 (Fax: 660-263-3936) www.cccb.edu. 8AM-Noon, 1-5PM. Enrollment: 140. Records go back to 1957. Alumni records are maintained here. Degrees granted: Associate; Bachelors. Attendance information available by phone, fax, mail. Degree and transcripts available by fax, mail.

Central Methodist College, Registrar, 411 CMC Square, Fayette, MO 65248, 660-248-3391 X208 (Fax: 660-248-2622) www.cmc.edu. 8AM-5PM. Enrollment: 899. Records go back to 1900. Alumni records maintained here; call 660-248-3391 X230. Degrees granted: Bachelors. Attendance and degree information available by phone, fax, mail. Transcripts available by fax, mail.

Central Missouri State University, Registrar, Warrensburg, MO 64093, 660-543-4900 (Fax: 660-543-8400) www.cmsu.edu. 8AM-5PM. Enrollment: 10805. Records go back to 1871. Alumni records are maintained here also. Call 660-543-4025. Degrees granted: Associate; Bachelors; Masters; Education Specialist. Attendance and degree information available by phone, fax, mail. Transcripts available by fax, mail.

Cleveland Chiropractic College, Registrar, 6401 Rockhill Rd, Kansas City, MO 64131, 816-333-8230 X232 (Fax: 816-523-3628) www.clevelandchiropractic.edu. 8AM-5PM. Enrollment: 615. Records go back to 1940. Alumni records maintained here; call 816-333-8230. Degrees granted: Doctorate. Attendance, degree and transcript information available by fax, mail.

College of the Ozarks, Office of the Registrar, Point Lookout, MO 65726, www.cofo.edu. 417-334-6411 (Fax: 417-335-2618) 8AM-Noon, 1-5PM, 4PM in summer. Enrollment: 1500. Records go back to 1960. Alumni records maintained here; call 417-334-6411. Degrees granted: Bachelors. Attendance and degree information available by phone, fax, mail. Transcripts available by written request only.

Columbia College, Registration, 1001 Rogers St, Columbia, MO 65216, 573-875-7507, 573-875-7504 (Fax: 573-875-7506) www.columbia.edu. 8AM-5PM. Enrollment: 6335. Records go back to 1851. Alumni records maintained here; call 573-875-7210. Degrees granted: Associate; Bachelors. Attendance and degree information available by phone, fax, mail. Transcripts available by mail.

Conception Seminary College, Registrar, PO Box 502, Conception, MO 64433, 660-944-2218 (Fax: 660-944-2800) www.msc.net/cabbey. 8:30AM-3:30PM. Enrollment: 65. Records go back to 1886. Alumni records maintained here; call 660-944-2218. Degrees granted: Bachelors. Attendance and degree information available by phone, fax, mail. Transcripts available by fax, mail.

Concordia Seminary, Registrar, 801 De Mun Ave, St Louis, MO 63105, 314-505-7107 (Fax: 314-505-7001). 8AM-Noon, 1-4:30PM. Enrollment: 500. Records go back to 1926. Alumni records maintained here; call 314-505-7371. Degrees granted: Masters; Doctorate. Attendance and degree information available by phone, fax, mail. Transcripts available by fax, mail.

Cottey College, Registrar, 1000 W Austin St, Nevada, MO 64772, 417-667-8181 (Fax: 417-667-8103) www.cottey.edu. 8AM-Noon, 1-5PM. Enrollment: 350. Records go back to 1884. Alumni records are maintained here. Degrees granted: Associate. Attendance and degree information available by phone, fax, mail. Transcripts available by fax, mail.

Covenant Theological Seminary, Registrar, 12330 Conway Rd, St Louis, MO 63141, 314-434-4044 (Fax: 314-434-4819) www.inlink.com/~covenant. 8AM-4:30PM. Enrollment: 800. Records go back to 1956. Alumni records are maintained here. Degrees granted: Masters; Doctorate. Special programs- Extension Office, 314-434-4044. Attendance and degree information available by phone, fax, mail. Transcripts available by mail. Fax request only if followed by mail request.

Crowder College, Registrar, 6601 Laclede, Neosho, MO 64850, 417-451-3223 (Fax: 417-451-4280) www.crowder.cc.mo.us. 7:30AM-4:30PM. Records go back to 1966. Alumni Records: President's Office Attn: Gale Lynch, 601 LaClede, Neosho, MO 64850. Degrees granted: Associate. Attendance and degree information available by phone, fax, mail. Transcripts available by mail.

Culver-Stockton College, Registrar, #1 College Hill, Canton, MO 63435, 217-231-6339, 217-231-6330 (Fax: 217-231-6616) 8AM-Noon, 1-5PM. www.culver.edu. Enrollment: 1000. Records go back to 1853. Alumni records are maintained. Degrees granted: Bachelors. Attendance and degree information available by phone, fax, mail. Transcripts available by mail.

DeVry Institute of Technology, Kansas City, Registrar, 11224 Holmes Rd, Kansas City, MO 64131, 816-941-0430 (Fax: 816-941-0896) www.kc.devry.edu. 8AM-5PM. Records go back to 1940. Alumni records are maintained here also. Call 816-941-0430 X570. Degrees granted: Associate; Bachelors. Attendance and degree information available by phone, fax, mail. Transcripts available by mail.

Deaconess College of Nursing, Registrar, 6150 Oakland Ave, St Louis, MO 63139, 314-768-3044, 314-768-3039 (Fax: 314-768-5673) 8:30AM-4:30PM. Enrollment: 425. Records go back to 1922. Alumni records maintained here; call 314-768-3039 or 768-3862. Degrees granted: Associate; Bachelors. Attendance and degree information available by phone, fax, mail. Transcripts available by fax, mail.

Drury College, Registrar, 900 N Benton Ave, Springfield, MO 65802, 417-873-7211, 417-873-7879 (Fax: 417-873-7529) www.drury.edu. 8AM-8:30PM M-Th; 8AM-5PM F. Enrollment: 1200. Records go back to 1874. Alumni records maintained here; call 417-873-7217. Degrees granted: Associate; Bachelors; Masters. Attendance, degree and transcript information available by fax, mail.

East Central College, Registrar, PO Box 529, Union, MO 63084, 314-583-5193, 314-583-5195 X2220 (Fax: 314-583-1897) 7:30AM-8PM. www.ecc.cc.mo.us. Enrollment: 3000. Records go back to 1969. Alumni records are maintained here. Degrees granted: Associate. Attendance and degree information available by phone, fax, mail. Transcripts available by fax, mail.

Eden Theological Seminary, Registrar, 475 E Lockwood Ave, St Louis, MO 63119-3192, 314-961-3627 X339 (Fax: 314-961-5738). Enrollment: 200. Records go back to 1920's. Alumni records are maintained here. Degrees granted: Masters; Doctorate. Attendance and degree information available by phone, fax, mail. Transcripts available by mail. Written and mail requests must be from student.

Evangel College, Registrar, 1111 N Glenstone Ave, Springfield, MO 65802, 417-865-2811 X7202 (Fax: 417-865-9599) 8AM-4:30PM. www.evangel.edu/. Enrollment: 1600. Records go back to 1955. Alumni records maintained here; call 417-865-2811 X7333. Degrees granted: Associate; Bachelors. Attendance and degree information available by phone, fax, mail. Transcripts available by fax, mail.

Fontbonne College, Registrar, 6800 Wydown Blvd, St Louis, MO 63105, 314-889-1421 (Fax: 314-889-1451) 8AM-4:30PM. www.fontbonne.edu Enrollment: 1801. Records go back to 1920. Alumni records maintained here; call 314-889-1447. Degrees granted: Bachelors; Masters. Special programs- Adult (Options) Program, 314-863-2220; Weekend MBA, 314-889-4518. Attendance and degree information available by phone, fax, mail. Transcripts available by mail.

Forest Institute of Professional Psychology, Registrar, 1322 S Campbell Ave, Springfield, MO 65807, 417-823-3477, 417-823-3414 (Fax: 417-823-3442). 8AM-5PM. Enrollment: 180. Records go back to 1979. Alumni records maintained here; call 417-823-3416. Degrees granted: Masters; Doctorate. Attendance, degree and transcript information available by fax, mail. Fax or mail requests must have release with signature of student.

Hannibal - LaGrange College, Registrar, 2800 Palmyra Rd, Hannibal, MO 63401, 573-221-3675 X207 (Fax: 573-221-6594). 8AM-5PM. Enrollment: 950. Records go back to 1921. Alumni records are maintained. Call 573-221-3675 X208. Degrees granted: Associate; Bachelors. Attendance and degree information available by phone, fax, mail. Transcripts available by fax, mail.

Harris - Stowe State College, Registrar, 3026 Laclede Ave, St Louis, MO 63103, 314-340-3600, 314-340-3601 (Fax: 314-340-3322) www.hssc.edu. 8AM-10PM M-Th, 8AM-4PM F,Sat. Enrollment: 1900. Records go back to 1919. Alumni records maintained here; call 314-340-3375. Degrees granted: Bachelors. Attendance and degree information available by phone, fax, mail. Transcripts available by fax, mail.

Hickey School, Registrar, 940 W Port Plaza, St Louis, MO 63146, 314-434-2212 (Fax: 314-434-1974) 7:30AM-5PM. Enrollment: 200. Records go back to 1933. Degrees granted: Associate. Attendance and degree information available by phone, fax, mail. Transcripts available by fax, mail.

ITT Technical Institute, Director of Education (DOE), 13505 Lakefront Dr, Earth City, MO 63045-1416, 314-298-7800 (Fax: 314-298-7800) 9AM-5PM. Enrollment: 500. Records go back to 1967. Alumni Records: 5975 Castle Creek Pkwy N Dr, PO Box 50466, Indianapolis, IN 46250-0466. Degrees granted: Associate; Bachelors. Special programs- Elec. Engineering Technology; Computer Aided Drafting Tech. Attendance, degree and transcript information available by written request only.

Jefferson College, Registrar, 1000 Viking Dr, Hillsboro, MO 63050-2441, 314-789-3951, 314-942-3000 (Fax: 314-789-3535). 8AM-4:30PM. Enrollment: 3900. Records go back to 1964. Alumni records maintained here; call 314-942-3000 X104. Degrees granted: Associate. Attendance and degree information available by phone, fax, mail. Transcripts available by fax, mail.

Kansas City Art Institute, Registrar, 4415 Warwick Blvd, Kansas City, MO 64111-1874, 816-561-4852 X244 (Fax: 816-561-6404) www.kcai.edu. 8:30AM-5PM. Enrollment: 607. Records go back to 1930. Alumni records maintained here; call 816-561-4852. Degrees granted: Bachelors. Attendance and degree information available by phone, fax, mail. Transcripts available by written request only.

Keller Graduate School of Management (Kansas City South), Registrar, 11224 Holmes Rd, Kansas City, MO 64131, 816-941-0367 (Fax: 816-941-2224) www.keller.edu. Records are located at Keller Graduate School of Management, Registrar, 225 W Washington St #100, Chicago, IL 60606-3418.

Keller Graduate School of Management (Kansas City Downtown), Registrar, City Center Square, 1100 Main St, Kansas City, MO 64105-2112, 816-221-1300 (Fax: 816-474-0318). Records are located at Keller Graduate School of Management, Registrar, 225 W Washington St #100, Chicago, IL 60606-3418.

Kemper Military School and College, Registrar, 701 Third St, Boonville, MO 65233, www.kemper.org\~welcome. 660-882-5623 (Fax: 660-882-3332) 7:30AM-5PM. Enrollment: 490. Records go back to 1926. Alumni records maintained here; call 660-882-5623 X3159. Degrees granted: Associate. Special programs- ESL: Aviation: Early Commission Program for Army. Attendance and degree information available by phone, fax, mail. Transcripts available by mail.

Kenrick - Glennon Seminary, Registrar, 5200 Glennon Dr, St Louis, MO 63119-4399, 314-644-0266 (Fax: 314-644-3079). 8AM-3:30PM. Enrollment: 60. Alumni records are maintained here. Degrees granted: Masters. Attendance and degree information available by phone, fax, mail. Transcripts available by fax, mail.

Kirksville College of Osteopathic Medicine, Registrar, 800 W Jefferson Ave, Kirksville, MO 63501, 660-626-2356 (Fax: 660-626-2926) www.kcom.edu. 8AM-5PM. Enrollment: 900. Records go back to 1892. Alumni records maintained here; call 660-626-2307. Degrees granted: Doctorate. Special programs- Master of Science in Physical Therapy, 602-841-4077: Occupational Therapy, 602-841-4077: Physician Assistant, 602-841-4077: Sports Health Care, 602-841-4077. Attendance and degree information available by phone, fax, mail. Transcripts available by fax, mail.

Lincoln University, Registrar, 820 Chestnut St, Jefferson City, MO 65102-0029, 573-681-5011 (Fax: 573-681-5013). 8AM-5PM. Enrollment: 3512. Records go back to 1912. Alumni records maintained here; call 573-681-5570. Degrees granted: Associate; Bachelors; Masters. Attendance and degree information available by phone, fax, mail. Transcripts available by mail.

Lindenwood College
(See Lindenwood University)

Lindenwood University, Registrar, 209 S Kingshighway Blvd, St Charles, MO 63301, 314-949-4954 (Fax: 314-949-4910) 8AM-6PM M-Th, 8AM-5PM F. www.lindenwood.edu. Enrollment: 4293. Records go back to 1827. Alumni records maintained here; call 314-949-4906. Degrees granted: Bachelors; Masters. Attendance, degree and transcript information available by mail.

Logan College of Chiropractic, Registrar, 1851 Schoettler Rd, PO Box 1065, Chesterfield, MO 63006-1065, 314-227-2100, 800-782-3344 (Fax: 314-207-2431) www.logan.edu. 7AM-4:30PM. Enrollment: 1116. Records go back to 1939. Alumni records are maintained here. Degrees granted: Bachelors; Doctorate. Attendance information available by phone, fax, mail. Degree and transcript information available by fax, mail.

Longview Community College, Registrar, 500 Longview Rd, Lee's Summit, MO 64081, 816-672-2244 (Fax: 816-672-2040) 8AM-6PM. www.longview.cc.mo.us. Enrollment: 6500. Records go back to 1969. Degrees granted: Associate. Attendance and degree information available by phone, fax, mail. Transcripts available by mail.

Maple Woods Community College, Registrar, 2601 NE Barry Rd, Kansas City, MO 64156, 816-437-3100 (Fax: 816-437-3351). 8AM-7PM M-Th; 8AM-4:30PM F. Enrollment: 4600. Records go back to 1969. Alumni Records: Alumni Assoc., 3200 Broadway, Kansas City, MO 64110. Degrees granted: Associate. Attendance and degree information available by phone, fax, mail. Transcripts available by mail.

Maryville University of St. Louis, Registrar, 13550 Conway Rd, St Louis, MO 63141, 314-529-9370 (Fax: 314-529-9925). 8AM-5PM. Records go back to 1926. Alumni records maintained here; call 315-529-9338. Degrees granted: Bachelors; Masters. Attendance, degree and transcript information available by fax, mail.

Midwestern Baptist Theological Seminary, Registrar, 5001 N Oak St Trafficway, Kansas City, MO 64118, www.mbts.edu 816-453-4600 (Fax: 816-453-3836) 8AM-4:30PM. Enrollment: 700. Records go back to 1958. Alumni records are maintained here. Degrees granted: Masters; Doctorate. Attendance and degree information available by phone, fax, mail. Transcripts available by fax, mail.

Mineral Area College, Registrar, PO Box 1000, Hwy 67 and 32, Park Hills, MO 63601-1000, 573-431-4593 (Fax: 573-431-2321) www.mac.cc.mo.us. 8AM-4PM. Enrollment: 2648. Records go back to 1922. Alumni records are maintained here. Degrees granted: Associate. Attendance and degree information available by phone, mail. Transcripts available by mail.

Missouri Baptist College, Records Office, One College Park Dr, St Louis, MO 63141, 314-434-1115 X2233 (Fax: 314-434-7596) www.mobap.edu. 8AM-4:30PM. Enrollment: 2000. Records go back to 1968. Alumni records maintained here; call 314-434-1115 X2302. Degrees granted: Associate; Bachelors. Special programs- Sports Medicine: Sports Management. Attendance and degree information available by phone, fax, mail. Transcripts available by fax, mail.

Missouri Southern State College, Registrar, 3950 Newman Rd, Joplin, MO 64801, 417-625-9340 (Fax: 417-625-3117). 8AM-5PM. Enrollment: 5500. Records go back to 1938. Alumni records are maintained here. Degrees granted: Associate; Bachelors. Attendance and degree information available by phone, fax, mail. Transcripts available by fax, mail.

Missouri Valley College, Registrar, 500 E College Dr, Marshall, MO 65340, 660-831-4000 www.merlin.com/tildawedfx/. (Fax: 660-831-4037) 8AM-5PM. Enrollment: 1300. Records go back to 1890. Alumni records are maintained here. Degrees granted: Associate; Bachelors. Attendance and degree information available by phone, fax, mail. Transcripts available by mail.

Missouri Western State College, Registrar, 4525 Downs Dr, St Joseph, MO 64507, 816-271-4228, 816-271-4221 (Fax: 816-271-5879) www.mwsc.edu. 8AM-4:30PM. Enrollment: 5100. Records go back to 1915. Alumni records are maintained here also. Call 816-271-4253. Degrees granted: Associate; Bachelors. Attendance and degree information available by phone, mail. Transcripts available by mail.

Moberly Area Community College, Student Services, 101 College Ave, Moberly, MO 65270, 660-263-4110 (Fax: 660-263-6448) www.moberly.cc.edu. 8AM-10PM M-Th; 8AM-8PM F. Records go back to 1927. Alumni records are maintained here. Degrees granted: Associate. Certification: LPN. Attendance and degree information available by phone, fax, mail. Transcripts available by fax, mail.

Nazarene Theological Seminary, Registrar, 1700 E Meyer Blvd, Kansas City, MO 64131, 816-333-6254 (Fax: 816-333-6271) www.nts.edu. 8AM-4:30PM. Enrollment: 277. Records go back to 1945. Alumni records maintained here; call 816-333-6254. Degrees granted: Masters; Doctorate. Attendance and degree information available by phone, fax, mail. Transcripts available by fax, mail.

North Central Missouri College, Registrar, 1301 Main St, Trenton, MO 64683, 660-359-3948. 8AM-4PM. Enrollment: 1100. Records go back to 1925. Degrees granted: Associate. School will not confirm attendance information. Degree and transcript information available by written request only.

Northwest Missouri State University, Registrar, 800 University Dr, Maryville, MO 64468-6001, 660-562-1151, 660-562-1596 (Fax: 660-562-1993) www.nwmissouri.edu. 8AM-5PM. Enrollment: 6000. Records go back to 1906. Alumni records maintained here; call 660-562-1248. Degrees granted: Bachelors; Masters; Specialist in Education. Attendance and degree information available by phone, fax, mail. Transcripts available by fax, mail.

Ozark Christian College, Registrar's Office, 1111 N Main St, Joplin, MO 64801, 417-624-2518 (Fax: 417-624-0090). 8AM-5PM. Enrollment: 663. Records go back to 1942. Alumni records are maintained here. Degrees granted: Associate; Bachelors. Attendance and degree information available by phone, fax, mail. Transcripts available by fax, mail.

Ozarks Technical Community College, Registrar, 1417 N Jefferson Ave, Springfield, MO 65802, 417-895-7195 (Fax: 417-895-7161). 8AM-4:30PM. Enrollment: 5100. Records go back to 1966. Alumni records are maintained here. Degrees granted: Associate Attendance, degree and transcript information available by mail.

Park College, Registrar, 8700 River Park Dr, Parkville, MO 64152, 816-741-6270 www.uol.com/park/index.html. (Fax: 816-587-5585) 8AM-4:30PM. Enrollment: 8494. Records go back to 1936. Alumni records maintained here; call 816-714-2000 X211. Degrees granted: Bachelors; Masters. Special programs- School of Extended Learning, 816-741-6242. Attendance and degree information available by phone, fax, mail. Transcripts available by mail.

Penn Valley Community College, Registrar, 3201 SW Trafficway, Kansas City, MO 64111, 816-759-4000, 816-759-4101 (Fax: 816-759-4478) www.kcmetro.cc.mo.u. 8AM-4:30PM Fall; 7AM-5:30PM M-Th Summer. Enrollment: 4100. Records go back to 1919. Alumni records are maintained here. Degrees granted: Associate. Special programs- Allied Health Fields, 816-759-4234. Attendance and degree information available by phone, fax, mail. Transcripts available by fax, mail.

Pioneer Community College (See Penn Valley Community College)

Platt Junior College (See Northwest Missouri Com. College)

Professional Psychology (See Forest Institute)

Ranken Technical College, Registrar, 4431 Finney Ave, St Louis, MO 63113, 314-371-0236 X1180 (Fax: 314-371-0241). 7:30AM-6:30PM M,T,Th; 7:30AM-4PM W,F. Enrollment: 1500. Records go back to 1909. Alumni records maintained here; call 314-371-0236 X1650. Degrees granted: Associate. Attendance and degree information available by phone, fax, mail. Transcripts available by mail.

Research College of Nursing (See Rockhurst College of Nursing)

Rockhurst College, Registrar, 1100 Rockhurst Rd, Kansas City, MO 64110, 816-501-4057, 816-501-4835 (Fax: 816-501-4588) www.rockhurst.edu. 8AM-6PM M-Th, 8AM-4:30PM F. Enrollment: 3000. Records go back to 1910. Alumni records maintained here; call 816-501-4581. Degrees granted: Bachelors; Masters. Attendance and degree information available by phone, fax, mail. Transcripts available by fax, mail.

Saint Mary's College of O'Fallon (See St. Charles County Com. College)

Saint Mary's Seminary, Registrar, 1701 W St Joseph, Perryville, MO 63775, 573-547-6533 X261 (Fax: 573-547-2204) Records go back to 1818. This school closed in May 1985. Attendance and degree information available by phone, fax, mail. Transcripts available by fax, mail.

Sanford-Brown Business College (Branch), Registrar, 520 E 19th Ave, **North Kansas City**, MO 64116, 816-472-7400 (Fax: 816-472-0688) www.sanford-brown.edu. 7AM-7PM M-Th, 7AM-4PM F. Enrollment: 1600. Records go back to 1985. Alumni records are maintained here. Degrees granted: Associate. Attendance and degree information available by phone, mail. Transcripts available by mail.

Sanford-Brown Business College (Branch), Registrar, 3555 Franks Dr, **St Charles**, MO 63301, 314-949-2620 (Fax: 314-949-5081). 8AM-4PM. Enrollment: 1410. Records go back to 1989. Degrees granted: Associate. Attendance and degree information available by phone, fax, mail. Transcripts available by fax, mail.

Sanford-Brown Business College, Registrar, 12006 Manchester Rd, **St Louis**, MO 63131, 314-822-7100 (Fax: 314-822-4017). www.sanford.brown.edu. 9AM-6PM. Enrollment: 1410. Records go back to 1987. Alumni records are maintained here. Degrees granted: Associate. Attendance, degree and transcript information available by fax, mail.

School of the Ozarks, Registrar, Point Lookout, MO 65726, 417-334-6411 X4223 (Fax: 417-335-2618) www.cofo.edu. Enrollment: 1550. Records go back to 1960. Alumni records are maintained here. Degrees granted: Bachelors. Attendance and degree information available by phone, mail. Transcripts available by mail.

Southeast Missouri State University, Registrar, One University Plaza, Cape Girardeau, MO 63701, 573-651-2250, 573-651-2474 (Fax: 573-651-5155) 8AM-5PM. www.semo.edu. Enrollment: 8000. Records go back to 1921. Alumni records maintained here; call 573-651-2259. Degrees granted: Associate; Bachelors; Masters; Specialist. Attendance and degree information available by phone, fax, mail. Transcripts available by fax, mail.

Southwest Baptist University, Registrar, 1601 S Springfield St, Bolivar, MO 65613, 417-326-1605, 417-326-1606 (Fax: 417-326-1514) www.sbuniv.edu. 8AM-5PM. Enrollment: 3000. Records go back to 1920's. Alumni records maintained here; call 417-326-1837. Degrees granted: Associate; Bachelors; Masters. Attendance and degree information available by phone, fax, mail. Transcripts available by mail.

Southwest Missouri State University, Registrar, 901 S National Ave, Springfield, MO 65804, 417-836-5519 (Fax: 417-836-6334) www.smsu.edu. 8AM-5PM. Enrollment: 15000. Records go back to 1908. Alumni records maintained here; call 417-836-5654. Degrees granted: Bachelors; Masters; Specialist. Attendance and degree information available by phone, fax, mail. Transcripts available by mail.

Springfield College, Registrar, 1010 W Sunshine St, Springfield, MO 65807, 417-864-7220 (Fax: 417-864-5697). 8AM-6PM. Enrollment: 400. Records go back to 1989. Degrees granted: Associate. Attendance and degree information available by phone, fax, mail. Transcripts available by mail.

St. Charles County Community College, Registrar, 4601 Mid Rivers Mall Dr, Saint Peters, MO 63376, 314-922-8000 (Fax: 314-922-8236) www.stchas.edu. Enrollment: 5500. Records go back to 1987. Degrees granted: Associate. Special programs- Arts: Science. Attendance and degree information available by phone, mail. Transcripts available by fax, mail.

St. Charles County Community College, Attn: Records, 4601 Mid Rivers Mall Dr, St Peters, MO 63376, 314-922-8237, 314-922-8000 (Fax: 314-922-8236) www.stchase.edu. 8AM-7PM M-Th; 8AM-4:30PM F. Enrollment: 5100. Records go back to 1989. Alumni records maintained here; call 314-922-8473. Degrees granted: Associate. Special programs- Art: Applied Science: LPN: Clerical. Attendance and degree information available by phone, fax, mail. Transcripts available by fax, mail.

St. Louis Christian College, Registrar, 1360 Grandview Dr, Florissant, MO 63033, 314-837-6777, 314-837-6777 X1500 (Fax: 314-837-8291). 8AM-5PM. Enrollment: 170. Records go back to 1956. Alumni records are maintained here. Degrees granted: Associate; Bachelors. Attendance and degree information available by phone, fax, mail. Transcripts available by fax, mail.

St. Louis College of Pharmacy, Registrar, 4588 Parkview Pl, St Louis, MO 63110, 314-367-8700 X1067, 314-367-8700 X1064 (Fax: 314-367-2784) www.stlcop.edu. 8:30AM-5PM. Enrollment: 860. Records go back to 1926. Alumni records maintained here; call 314-367-1046. Degrees granted: Bachelors; Masters; Pharm. D. Attendance and degree information available by phone, fax, mail. Transcripts available by mail.

St. Louis Community College, Central Student Records, 5600 Oakland Ave Rm B-013, St Louis, MO 63110, 314-644-9670 (Fax: 314-644-9752). Enrollment: 25000. Records go back to 1962. Alumni Records: Alumni Assoc., SLCC, 5600 Oakland Ave, St Louis, MO 63110. Degrees granted: Associate. Attendance and degree information available by phone, fax, mail. Transcripts available by mail.

St. Louis Community College at Florissant Valley, Registrar, 3400 Pershall Rd, St Louis, MO 63135, 314-595-4244 (Fax: 314-595-2224) www.stlcc.cc.mo.us/fv/admin. 8AM-8PM M-Th, 8AM-4:30PM F. Enrollment: 11400. Records go back to 1962. Alumni records maintained here; call 314-595-4556. Degrees granted: Associate. Attendance and degree information available by phone, mail. Transcripts available by mail.

St. Louis Community College at Meramec, Registrar, 11333 Big Bend Blvd, Kirkwood, MO 63122, www.stlcc.cc.mo.us 314-984-7601, 314-984-7500 (Fax: 314-984-7117) 7:30AM-9PM M-Th, 7:30AM-5PM F. Enrollment: 13000. Records go back to 1973. Alumni records maintained here; call 314-984-7641. Degrees granted: Associate. Special programs- AAS: Horticulture: OTA: PTA: Interior Design: Court & Conference Reporting. Attendance and degree information available by phone, fax, mail. Transcripts available by mail.

St. Louis Conservatory of Music, Registrar, 560 Trinity, St. Louis, MO 63130, 314-863-3033 (Fax: 314-286-4421) 8:30AM-5PM. Enrollment: 1200. Records go back to 1947. Alumni records are maintained here. Degrees granted. Attendance and degree information available by phone, fax, mail. Transcripts available by mail.

St. Louis University, Registrar, 221 N Grand Blvd, St Louis, MO 63103, 314-977-2269 (Fax: 314-977-3447) www.slu.edu. 8:30AM-5PM. Enrollment: 11038. Records go back to 1911. Alumni records maintained here; call 314-977-2308. Degrees granted: Associate; Bachelors; Masters; Doctorate. Attendance and degree information available by phone, fax, mail. Transcripts available by fax, mail.

St. Paul School of Theology, Registrar, 5123 Truman Rd, Kansas City, MO 64127, 816-483-9600 (Fax: 816-483-9605) www.spft.edu. 8AM-4:30PM. Enrollment: 298. Records go back to 1962. Alumni records maintained here; call 816-483-9600. Degrees granted: Doctorate; M Dir, MTS. Attendance and degree information available by phone, fax, mail. School does not provide transcripts.

State Fair Community College, Registrar, 3201 W 16th St, Sedalia, MO 65301, 660-530-5800 X296, 660-530-5800 X291 (Fax: 660-530-5546) www.sfc.cc.mo.us. 8AM-7PM M-Th, 8AM-4PM F. Enrollment: 2700. Records go back to 1968. Alumni records maintained here; call 660-530-5800 X250. Degrees granted: Associate. Attendance and degree information available by phone, fax, mail. Transcripts available by fax, mail.

Stephens College, Registrar, Columbia, MO 65215, 573-876-7277 (Fax: 573-876-7248) www.stephens.edu. 8AM-Noon, 1-5PM. Enrollment: 889. Records go back to 1900. Alumni records are maintained here. Degrees granted: Associate; Bachelors; Masters. Attendance and degree information available by phone, fax, mail. Transcripts available by mail.

TAD Technical Institute, Registrar, 7910 Troost Ave, Kansas City, MO 64131, 816-361-5640 (Fax: 816-361-2140). 9AM-5PM. Enrollment: 300. Records go back to 1980's. Formerly **ITT Technical Institute**. This school is closing down as of June 1998. Attendance, degree and transcript information available by fax, mail.

Three Rivers Community College, Registrar, 2080 Three Rivers Blvd, Poplar Bluff, MO 63901, 573-840-9665, 573-840-9666 (Fax: 573-840-9604). 8AM-4PM. Enrollment: 2405. Records go back to 1967. Alumni records maintained here; call 573-840-9695. Degrees granted: Associate. Attendance information available by phone, fax, mail. Degree and transcript information available by fax, mail.

Trenton Junior College
(See North Central Missouri College)

Truman State University, Registrar, Kirksville, MO 63501, 660-785-4143 (Fax: 660-785-7396) www.truman.edu. 8AM-5PM. Enrollment: 6000. Records go back to 1867. Formerly **Northeast Missouri State University**. Alumni records maintained here; call 660-785-4133. Degrees granted: Bachelors; Masters. Attendance and degree information available by phone, fax, mail. Transcripts available by fax, mail.

University of Health Sciences, Registrar, 2105 Independence Blvd, Kansas City, MO 64124, 816-283-2332, 816-283-2342 (Fax: 816-283-2349) www.univ.healthscience.edu. 8AM-4:30PM. Enrollment: 757. Records go back to 1916. Alumni records maintained here; call 816-283-2360. Degrees granted: Doctorate. Special programs- Doctor of Osteopathy, 816-283-2332. Attendance and degree information available by phone, fax, mail. Transcripts available by mail.

University of Missouri - Columbia, Registrar, 130 Jessie Hall, Columbia, MO 65211, 573-882-7881 (Fax: 573-884-4530) 8AM-4:30PM. www.missouri.edu/nregwww. Enrollment: 23000. Records go back to 1800's. Alumni records maintained here; call 573-882-6611. Degrees granted: Doctorate. Attendance and degree information available by phone, fax, mail. Transcripts available by fax, mail.

University of Missouri - Kansas City, Records Office, 111 SSB, 4825 Troost, Kansas City, MO 64110, 816-235-1122 (Fax: 816-235-5513) www.umkc.edu. 8AM-5PM. Records go back to 1933. Degrees granted: Bachelors; Masters; Doctorate. Attendance and transcript information available by fax, mail. Degree information available by phone, fax, mail.

University of Missouri - Rolla, Registrar, 103 Parker Hall, Rolla, MO 65401, 573-341-4181 (Fax: 573-341-4362) www.umr.edu. 8AM-4:30PM. Records go back to 1930's. Alumni records maintained here; call 314-341-4145. Degrees granted: Bachelors; Masters; Doctorate. Attendance and degree information available by phone, fax, mail. Transcripts available by fax, mail.

University of Missouri - St. Louis, Registrar, 8001 Natural Bridge Rd, St Louis, MO 63121, 314-516-5676 (Fax: 314-516-5310) www.umsl.edu. 8AM-7PM M-Th; 8AM-5PM F. Enrollment: 12650. Records go back to 1963. Alumni records are maintained here. Degrees granted: Bachelors; Masters; Doctorate. Attendance and degree information available by phone, fax, mail. Transcripts available by fax, mail.

Washington University, Registrar, One Brookings Dr, Box 1143, St Louis, MO 63130, 314-935-5919 (Fax: 314-935-4268) 8:30AM-5PM. www.wustl.edu. Enrollment: 11606. Records go back to 1978. Alumni Records: Alumni Development, Box 1210, 1 Brookings, St Louis, MO 63130. Degrees granted: Bachelors; Masters; Doctorate. Attendance and degree information available by fax, mail. Transcripts available by mail.

Webster University, Registrar, 470 E Lockwood Ave, St Louis, MO 63119-3194, www.websteruniv.edu. 314-968-7450 (Fax: 314-968-7112) 8:30AM-5:30PM M-Th, 8:30AM-4:30PM F. Enrollment: 14843. Records go back to 1915. Alumni records maintained here; call 314-968-6955. Degrees granted: Bachelors; Masters; Doctorate. Special programs- Women's Studies: Media Studies: Paralegal Studies. Attendance, degree and transcript information available by fax, mail. A third party request for a transcript requires a notarized release.

Wentworth Military Academy and Junior College, Registrar, 1880 Washington Ave, Lexington, MO 64067, 660-259-2221 X272, 660-259-2954 (Fax: 660-259-3780) 9AM-5PM. www.wma1880.org. Enrollment: 827. Records go back to 1890. Alumni records maintained here; call 660-259-2221 X234. Degrees granted: Associate. Special programs- Military Science. Attendance and degree information available by phone, fax, mail. Transcripts available by fax, mail.

Westminster College, Registrar, 501 Westminster Ave, Fulton, MO 65251-1299, 573-592-5213, 573-592-1363 (Fax: 573-592-5217) www.westminister-mo.edu. 8AM-4:30PM. Enrollment: 613. Records go back to 1800's. Alumni records maintained here; call 573-592-5319. Degrees granted: Bachelors. Attendance and degree information available by phone, fax, mail. Transcripts available by fax, mail.

William Jewell College, Registrar's Office, 500 College Hill, Liberty, MO 64068, 816-781-7700 (Fax: 816-415-5027) 8AM-5PM. www.jewell.edu. Enrollment: 1200. Alumni records are maintained. Degrees granted: Bachelors. Attendance and degree information available by phone, fax, mail. Transcripts available by fax, mail.

William Woods University, Registrar, 200 West 12th St, Fulton, MO 65251, 573-592-4248, 573-592-4251 (Fax: 573-592-1146) 8AM-4:30PM. www.wmwoods.edu. Enrollment: 1100. Records go back to 1900's. Alumni records maintained here; call 573-592-4219. Degrees granted: Associate; Bachelors; Masters. Special programs- Equestrian: Intreping: Paralegal. Attendance and degree information available by phone, fax, mail. Transcripts available by fax, mail.

Montana

Blackfeet Community College, Registrar, Browning, MT 59417, 406-338-3197 (Fax: 406-338-7808). 8AM - 4PM. Enrollment: 385. Records go back to 1980. Degrees granted: Associate. Attendance and degree information available by phone, fax, mail. Transcripts available by written request only.

Carroll College, Registrar, N Benton Ave, Helena, MT 59625, 406-447-5435, 406-447-5436 (Fax: 406-447-4533) www.carroll.edu. 9AM-4PM. Enrollment: 1412. Records go back to 1910. Alumni records maintained here; call 406-447-5413. Degrees granted: Associate; Bachelors. Attendance and degree information available by fax. Transcripts available by fax, mail.

Dawson Community College, Registrar, Glendive, MT 59330, 406-365-3396 (Fax: 406-365-8132) 198.168.48.7. 7:30AM-4:30PM. Enrollment: 700. Records go back to 1940. Alumni records are maintained here. Degrees granted: Associate. Attendance and degree information available by phone, fax, mail. Transcripts available by fax, mail.

Dull Knife Memorial College, Registrar, PO Box 98, Lame Deer, MT 59043, 406-477-6215 X305 (Fax: 406-477-6219). 8AM-4:30PM. Enrollment: 425. Records go back to 1976. Degrees granted: Associate. Special programs- Business Office Management. Attendance and degree information available by phone, mail. Transcripts available by mail.

Flathead Valley Community College, Registrar, 777 Grandview Dr, Kalispell, MT 59901, 406-756-3822, 406-756-3845 (Fax: 406-756-3965) www.FVCCMT.US. 8AM-5PM. Enrollment: 2000. Records go back to 1967. Alumni records maintained here; call 406-756-3962. Degrees granted: Associate. Certification: Office Technology, Business Management, Accounting Technology, LAN Management. Attendance, degree and transcript information available by fax, mail.

Fort Belknap College, Registrar, PO Box 159, Harlem, MT 59526-0159, 406-353-2607 X219 (Fax: 406-353-2898) 8AM-5PM. www.montana.edu/~wwvse/fbc/fbc.html. Enrollment: 385. Records go back to 1988. Degrees granted: Associate. Certification: Computer Applications. Special programs- Native American Languages, Cultural Courses. Attendance and degree information available by phone, fax, mail. Transcripts available by fax, mail.

Fort Peck Community College, Registrar, PO Box 398, Poplar, MT 59255, 406-768-5551 (Fax: 406-768-5552) 8AM-4:30PM. Enrollment: 450. Records go back to 1986. Also has records for Dawson Community College and Mile City Community College for the years 1878-1985. Alumni records maintained here; call 406-768-3155. Degrees granted: Associate. Attendance and degree information available by phone, fax, mail. Transcripts available by fax, mail.

Helena College of Technology of the University of Montana, Registrar, 115 N Roberts St, Helena, MT 59620, 406-444-6800 (Fax: 406-444-6892). 8AM-5PM. Records go back to 1939. Degrees granted: Associate. Attendance and degree information available by phone, mail. Transcripts available by mail.

Little Big Horn College, Registrar, PO Box 370, Crow Agency, MT 59022, 406-638-7212 (Fax: 406-638-7213/2229) 8AM-5PM. www.main.lbhc.cc.mt.us. Enrollment: 250. Records go back to 1984. Degrees granted: Associate. Special programs- Pre Nursing & Pre Medical. Attendance, degree and transcript information available by fax, mail.

Miles Community College, Registrar, 2715 Dickinson St, Miles City, MT 59301, 406-232-3031 (Fax: 406-232-5705) www.mcc.cc.mt.us. 7:30AM-5PM M-Th; 7:30AM-4PM F. Enrollment: 625. Records go back to 1939. Alumni records maintained here; call 406-232-3516. Degrees granted: Associate. Special programs- Nursing Dept, 406-233-3544. Attendance and degree information available by phone, fax, mail. Transcripts available by fax, mail.

Montana State University College of Technology-Great Falls, Registrar, 2100 16th Ave S, Great Falls, MT 59405, 406-771-4300 (Fax: 406-771-4317) 8AM-5PM. www.msucotgf.montana.edu. Enrollment: 1100. Records go back to 1969. Degrees granted: Associate. Attendance, degree and transcript information available by mail.

Montana State University - Billings, Registrar, 1500 N 30th, Billings, MT 59101, 406-657-2880 (Fax: 406-657-2302) 8AM-5PM. www.msubillings.edu. Enrollment: 3700. Records go back to 1927. Alumni records maintained here; call 406-657-2244. Degrees granted: Associate; Bachelors; Masters. Special programs- Vocational, 406-656-4445 X120. Attendance and degree information available by phone, fax, mail. Transcripts available by fax, mail.

Montana State University - Bozeman, Registrar, Bozeman, MT 59717, 406-994-0211, 406-994-6650 (Fax: 406-994-1972) 8AM-5PM. www.montana.edu. Enrollment: 11000. Records go back to 1893. Alumni Records: Alumni Assoc., 1501 S 11th, Bozeman, MT 59717. Degrees granted: Bachelors; Masters; Doctorate. Special programs- Architecture & Ag. Attendance and degree information available by phone, fax, mail. Transcripts available by mail.

Montana Tech of the University of Montana, Registrar, 1300 W Park St, Butte, MT 59701-8997, 406-496-4256 (Fax: 406-496-4710) www.mtech.edu. 8AM-4:30PM. Enrollment: 1800. Records go back to 1900. Alumni records maintained here; call 406-496-4278. Degrees granted: Associate; Bachelors; Masters. Special programs- Minerals, Energy & Environ. Engineer., 800-445-TECH; 406-496-4178. Attendance and degree information available by phone, fax, mail. Transcripts available by fax, mail.

Montana Tech of the University of Montana — College of Technology, Registrar, 25 Basin Creek Rd, Butte, MT 59701, 406-496-3732, 406-496-3701 (Fax: 406-496-3710). 7:30AM-5PM. Enrollment: 400. Records go back to 1969. Degrees granted: Associate. Special programs- Call 406-496-3732. Attendance and degree

information available by phone, fax, mail. Transcripts available by fax, mail.

Rocky Mountain College, Registrar, 1511 Poly Dr, Billings, MT 59102, 406-657-1030 (Fax: 406-259-9251) www.rocky.edu. 8AM-4:30PM. Enrollment: 800. Records go back to 1900. Alumni records maintained here; call 406-657-1009. Degrees granted: Associate; Bachelors. Attendance and degree information available by phone, fax, mail. Transcripts available by fax, mail.

Salish Kootenai College, Registrar, PO Box 117, Pablo, MT 59855, 406-675-4800 (Fax: 406-675-2427) www.sku.edu. 8AM-4:30PM. Enrollment: 1000. Records go back to 1977. Alumni records are maintained here. Degrees granted: Associate; Bachelors. Special programs- Native American Studies: Nursing: Dental: Truck Driving: Computer Science: Dental Technician: Business Management. Attendance and degree information available by phone, fax, mail. Transcripts available by mail.

Stone Child Community College, Registrar, RR 1 Box 1082, Box Elder, MT 59521-9796, 406-395-4313, 406-395-4269 (Fax: 406-395-4836). 8AM - 4:30PM. Enrollment: 250. Records go back to 1990. Degrees granted: Associate. Attendance and degree information available by phone, fax, mail. Transcripts available by fax, mail.

University of Great Falls, Registrar, 1301 20th St S, Great Falls, MT 59405, 406-791-5200 (Fax: 406-791-5209) www.ugf.edu. 8AM-4:30PM. Enrollment: 1200. Records go back to 1932. Formerly College of Great Falls. Alumni records maintained here; call 406-791-5291. Degrees granted: Associate; Bachelors; Masters. Attendance and degree information available by phone, fax, mail. Transcripts available by fax.

University of Montana, Registrar, Missoula, MT 59812, 406-243-2995 (Fax: 406-243-4087) www.umt.edu. 9AM - 4PM. Enrollment: 12000. Records go back to 1893. Alumni records are maintained here also. Call 406-243-5211. Degrees granted: Associate; Bachelors; Masters; Doctorate. Certification: Elementary & Secondary Education. Attendance and degree information available by phone, fax, mail. Transcripts by fax, mail.

University of Montana — Missoula /College of Technology, Registrar, 909 South Ave W, Missoula, MT 59801, www.umt.edu/. 406-243-7887 (Registrar), 406-243-7882 (Admissions) (Fax: 406-243-7899) Enrollment: 850. Records go back to 1969. Alumni Records: Alumni Assoc., University of Montana-Missoula, Brantley Hall Rm 115, Missoula, MT 59812. Degrees granted: Associate; Certificates of Completion (programs under 2 years). Special programs- Continuing Education, 406-243-7875. Attendance and degree information available by phone, fax, mail. Transcripts available by fax, mail (require specific written permission).

Western Montana College of the University of Montana, Registrar's Office, 710 S Atlantic St, Dillon, MT 59725-3598, 406-683-7371 (Fax: 406-683-7493) www.wmc.edu. 8AM-5PM. Enrollment: 1150. Records go back to 1897. Alumni records are maintained here. Degrees granted: Associate; Bachelors. Attendance, degree and transcript information available by written request only.

Nebraska

Bellevue University, Registrar, Galvin Rd at Harvell Dr, Bellevue, NE 68005, 402-293-3780 (Fax: 402-293-2020). 8AM-5PM. Enrollment: 2400. Records go back to 1966. Alumni records maintained here; call 402-293-3707. Degrees granted: Bachelors; Masters. Attendance and degree information available by phone, fax, mail. Transcripts available by mail.

Bishop Clarkson College, Registrar, 333 S 44th St, Omaha, NE 68131, 402-552-3033, 402-552-2543 www.clarksoncollege.edu. (Fax: 402-552-6057) Enrollment: 600. Records go back to 1880. Alumni records are maintained here. Degrees granted: Associate; Bachelors; Masters. Special programs- Nursing: Administrative Health Services. Attendance and degree information available by phone, mail. Transcripts available by mail.

Central Community College, Registrar, PO Box 4903, Grand Island, NE 68802-4903, 308-384-5220, 308-389-6412 (Fax: 308-389-6398) www.ccneb.edu. 8AM - 4:30PM. Enrollment: 1500. Records go back to 1976. Alumni Records: 2727 W 2nd #211, Hastings, NE 68101. Degrees granted: Associate. Attendance and degree information available by mail. Transcripts available by written request only.

Central Technical Community College, Registrar, PO Box 1024, Hastings, NE 68902-1024, 402-463-9811, 402-461-2415 (Fax: 402-461-2454) www.cccins.ccneb.edu. 9AM-5PM. Enrollment: 1700. Records go back to 1966. Alumni Records: Alumni Assoc., Central Technical Community College, 2727

W 2nd, Hastings, NE 68901. Degrees granted: Associate. Attendance and degree information available by phone, fax, mail. Transcripts available by written request only.

Chadron State College, Registrar, 1000 Main St, Chadron, NE 69337, 308-432-6221 (Fax: 308-432-6229) www.csc.edu. 7:30AM-4:30PM. Enrollment: 3206. Records go back to 1911. Alumni records maintained here; call 308-432-6362. Degrees granted: Bachelors; Masters; Specialist. Special programs- Health Opportunities Program, 888-298-2293. Attendance and degree information available by phone, fax, mail. Transcripts available by fax, mail.

Clarkson College, Registrar, 101 S 42nd St, Omaha, NE 68131, 402-552-3041, 402-552-2543 (Fax: 402-552-6057) 8AM-5PM. www.clrkcol.crksnet.edu. Enrollment: 600. Records go back to 1869. Alumni records maintained here; call 402-552-3439. Degrees granted: Associate; Bachelors; Masters. Certification: Nurse Practitioner. Attendance and degree information available by phone, fax, mail. Transcripts available by mail.

College of St. Mary, Registrar, 1901 S 72nd St, Omaha, NE 68124, 402-399-2443, 402-399-2442 (Fax: 402-399-2341) www.csm.edu. 8AM-6:30PM. Enrollment: 1100. Records go back to 1923. Alumni records maintained here; call 402-399-2456. Degrees granted: Associate; Bachelors. Attendance and degree information available by phone, mail. Transcripts available by phone, mail.

Concordia University, Registrar, 800 N Columbia Ave, Seward, NE 68434, 402-643-

7230, 402-643-7228 (Fax: 402-643-4073) 8AM-5PM. www.ccsn.edu. Enrollment: 1150. Records go back to 1894. Formerly **Concordia College**. Alumni records maintained here; call 402-643-7276. Degrees granted: Bachelors; Masters. Certification: Lutheran Teacher Diploma. Attendance and degree information available by phone, fax, mail. Transcripts available by fax, mail.

Creighton University, Registrar, 2500 California Plaza, Omaha, NE 68178, 402-280-2701 (Fax: 402-280-2527) 8:30AM - 4:30PM. www.creighton.edu. Enrollment: 6300. Records go back to 1878. Alumni records maintained here; call 402-280-2222. Degrees granted: Associate; Bachelors; Masters; Doctorate. Attendance, degree and transcript information available by fax, mail.

Dana College, Registrar, 2848 College Dr, Blair, NE 68008, 402-426-7209 (Fax: 402-426-7386) www.dana.edu. 8AM-5PM. Enrollment: 575. Records go back to 1930. Alumni records maintained here; call 402-426-7235. Degrees granted: Bachelors. Attendance and degree information available by phone, fax, mail. Transcripts available by fax, mail.

Doane College, Registrar, 1014 Boswell Ave, Crete, NE 68333, 402-826-8251 (Fax: 402-826-8600) www.doane.edu. 8AM-Noon, 12:30-4:30PM. Enrollment: 1700. Records go back to 1975. Alumni records maintained here; call 402-826-8258. Degrees granted: Bachelors; Masters. Attendance and degree information available by phone, fax, mail. Transcripts available by fax, mail.

Grace University, Registrar, 1311 South 9th St, Omaha, NE 68108, www.graceu.edu. 402-449-2838, 402-449-2830 X2811 (Fax: 402-341-9587) 8AM-Noon, 1-5PM. Enrollment: 500. Records go back to 1943. Alumni records maintained here; call 402-449-2815. Degrees granted: Associate; Bachelors; Masters. Attendance and degree information available by phone, fax, mail. Transcripts available by fax, mail.

Grand Island College, Registrar, PO Box 399, 410 W Second St, Grand Island, NE 68802, 308-382-8044, 308-382-8047 (Fax: 308-382-5072). 7:30AM-5PM. Enrollment: 125. Records go back to 1983. Degrees granted: Associate. Attendance and degree information available by phone, fax, mail. Transcripts available by fax, mail.

Hastings College, Registrar, 800 N Turner Ave, PO Box 269, Hastings, NE 68902-0269, 402-461-7306, 402-461-7303 (Fax: 402-461-7490) www.hastings.edu/. 8AM-Noon, 1-5PM. Enrollment: 1095. Records go back to 1883. Alumni records maintained here; call 402-461-7363. Degrees granted: Bachelors. Special programs- MAT Graduate Program, 402-461-7388. Attendance and degree information available by phone, fax, mail. Transcripts available by mail.

ITT Technical Institute (Branch of Earth City, MO), Registrar, 9814 M St, Omaha, NE 68127-2056, 402-331-2900 (Fax: 402-331-9495). 7:30AM-5PM. Enrollment: 150. Records go back to 1990. Alumni records maintained here. Degrees granted: Associate. Attendance information available by phone. Degree information and transcripts available by fax, mail.

Lincoln School of Commerce, Registrar, PO Box 82826, 1821 K St, Lincoln, NE 68501-2826, 402-474-5315 (Fax: 402-474-5302) www.lscadvantage.com. 8AM - 10PM. Records go back to 1885. Alumni records are maintained here. Degrees granted: Associate; Diplomas; Certificates. Attendance and degree information available by phone, fax, mail. Transcripts available by mail.

McCook Community College, Registrar, 1205 E Third St, McCook, NE 69001, 800-658-4348, 308-345-6303 www.mpccane.us. (Fax: 308-345-3305) 8AM-5:30PM M-Th, 8AM-4PM F. Enrollment: 980. Records go back to 1926. Alumni records are maintained here. Degrees granted: Associate. Attendance and degree information available by phone, fax, mail. Transcripts available by fax, mail.

Metropolitan Community College, Registrar, PO Box 3777, Omaha, NE 68103, www.kcmetro.cc.mo.us. 402-449-8400 (Fax: 402-457-2244) Attendance and degree information available by phone, fax, mail. Transcripts available by mail.

Mid-Plains Community College Registrar Office, 1101 Halligan Dr, North Platte, NE 69101, 308-532-8740, 308-534-9265 (Fax: 308-532-8494) www.mpccane.us. 8AM-5PM. Enrollment: 2000. Records go back to 1965. Degrees granted: Associate. Attendance and degree information available by phone, fax, mail. Transcripts available by fax, mail.

Midland Lutheran College, Registrar, 900 Clarkson St, Fremont, NE 68025, 402-721-5480 X6220, 402-721-5480 X6223 (Fax: 402-721-0250) www.mlc.edu. 8AM - :30PM. Enrollment: 1060. Records go back to 1883. Alumni records are maintained here. Degrees granted: Associate; Bachelors. Attendance and degree information available by phone, fax, mail.

Nebraska Christian College, Registrar, 1800 Syracuse St, Norfolk, NE 68701, 402-371-5960 (Fax: 402-371-5967) 8AM-5PM. www.nechristian.edu Enrollment: 150. Records go back to 1944. Alumni records are maintained here. Degrees granted: Bachelors. Attendance and degree information available by phone, mail. Transcripts available by written request only.

Nebraska College of Business, Registrar, 3350 N 90th St, Omaha, NE 68134-4710, 402-572-8500 (Fax: 402-573-1341). 9AM-6PM. Enrollment: 300. Records go back to 1940's. Alumni records are maintained. Degrees granted: Associate. Special programs- Medical Program, 402-572-8500. Attendance and degree information available by phone, fax, mail. Transcripts available by fax, mail.

Nebraska College of Technical Agriculture, Registrar, Curtis, NE 69025, 308-367-4124 (Fax: 308-367-5203). 8AM-5PM. Enrollment: 325. Records go back to 1967. Alumni records maintained here; call 308-367-4124. Degrees granted: Associate. Attendance and degree information available by phone, mail. Transcripts available by mail.

Nebraska Indian Community College, Registrar, PO Box 428, Macy, NE 68039, 402-837-5078 (Fax: 402-837-4183). 8AM-5PM. Enrollment: 100. Records go back to 1980. Alumni records are maintained here. Degrees granted: Associate. School will not confirm attendance or degree information. Transcripts available by fax, mail.

Nebraska Methodist College of Nursing and Allied Health, Registrar, 8501 W Dodge Rd, Omaha, NE 68114, 402-390-4879. Enrollment: 453. Alumni records maintained here; call 402-354-4952. Degrees granted: Associate; Bachelors. Attendance, degree and transcript information available by fax, mail.

Nebraska Wesleyan University Registrar, 5000 St Paul Ave, Lincoln, NE 68504, 402-465-2242 (Fax: 402-465-2179) 8AM-5PM. www.nebrwesleyan.edu. Enrollment: 1700. Records go back to 1887. Alumni records are maintained. Call 402-465-2316. Degrees granted: Bachelors. Attendance and degree information available by phone, fax, mail. Transcripts available by mail.

Northeast Community College, Dir, Enrollment Management, 801 E Benjamin Ave, PO Box 469, Norfolk, NE 68702-0469, www.neccne.us. 402-644-0415, 402-644-0524 (Fax: 402-644-0650) 8AM-5PM. Enrollment: 5000. Records go back to 1928. Alumni records maintained here; call 402-644-0463. Degrees granted: Associate. Attendance and degree information available by phone, fax, mail. Transcripts available by fax, mail.

Peru State College, Registrar, Peru, NE 68421, 402-872-2239 (Fax: 402-872-2375) www.peru.edu. 8:30AM-4:30PM. Enrollment: 1900. Records go back to 1867. Alumni Records: PO Box 10, Peru, NE 68421. Degrees granted: Associate; Bachelors; Masters. Attendance and degree information available by phone, mail. Transcripts available by written request only.

Platte Valley Bible College, Registrar, Box 1227, Scottsbluff, NE 69363, 308-632-6933 (Fax: 308-632-8599) www.pvbc.edu. Enrollment: 67. Records go back to 1951. Alumni records are maintained here. Degrees granted: Associate; Bachelors. Special programs- Arts: Science. Attendance and degree information available by phone, fax, mail. Transcripts available by mail.

Southeast Community College, Registrar, 8800 O St, Lincoln, NE 68520, 402-437-2609, 800-642-4075 (Fax: 402-437-2404) www.southeastedu. 8AM-8PM M-Th; 8AM-5PM F. Enrollment: 4600. Records go back to 1970. Alumni records are maintained here. Degrees granted: Associate. Special programs- Motorcycle/Small Engines: Health Trades: Fire Protection. Attendance and degree information available by phone, fax, mail. Transcripts available by fax, mail.

Southeastern Nebraska Technical Community College
(See Southeast Community College)

Spencer School of Business
(See Grand Island College)

Union College, Records, 3800 S 48th St, Lincoln, NE 68506, 402-486-2509 (Fax: 402-486-2895) www.ucollege.edu. 8:30AM-Noon, 1-5PM. Enrollment: 600. Records go back to 1933. Alumni records are maintained here. Degrees granted: Associate; Bachelors. Attendance and degree information available by phone, fax, mail. Transcripts available by mail.

University of Nebraska Medical Center, Registrar, 984230 Nebraska Medical Center, Omaha, NE 68198-4230, 402-559-7391 (Fax: 402-559-6796) www.unmc.edu. 8AM-4:30PM. Enrollment: 2765. Records go back to 1902. Alumni records maintained here; call 402-559-4354. Degrees granted: Bachelors; Masters; Doctorate. Attendance and degree information available by phone, fax, mail. Transcripts available by mail.

University of Nebraska at Kearney, Registrar, Founders Hall, 905 W 25th St, Kearney, NE 68849, 308-865-8527 (Fax: 308-865-8484) www.betty-boop.unk.edu. 8AM-5PM. Enrollment: 8500. Records go back to 1903. Alumni Records: 2222 9th Ave, Kearney, NE 68849. Degrees granted: Bachelors; Masters. Attendance and degree information available by phone, fax, mail. Transcripts available by fax, mail.

University of Nebraska at Omaha, Registrar, 60th and Dodge Sts, Omaha, NE 68182, www.unomaha.edu/registrar/. 402-554-2314 (Fax: 402-554-3472) 8AM - 5PM. Enrollment: 16000. Records go back to 1906. Alumni records maintained here; call 402-554-3367. Degrees granted: Associate; Bachelors; Masters; Doctorate. Attendance and degree information available by phone, fax, mail. Transcripts available by mail.

University of Nebraska at Lincoln, Registration & Records, PO Box 880416, Lincoln, NE 68588-0416, 402-472-3684, 402-472-3649 (Fax: 402-472-8220) www.unl.edu. 8AM-5PM. Enrollment: 25000. Records go back to 1869. Alumni records maintained here; call 402-472-2841. Degrees granted: Bachelors; Masters; Doctorate; Juris Doctor. Attendance and degree information available by phone, mail. Transcripts available by fax, mail.

Wayne State College, Registrar, 1111 Main St, Wayne, NE 68787, 402-375-7241, 402-375-7239 (Fax: 402-375-7204) www.wsc.edu. 8AM-5PM. Enrollment: 4000. Records go back to 1891. Alumni records maintained here; call 402-375-7209. Degrees granted: Bachelors; Masters; Ed Specialist. Attendance and degree information available by phone, mail. Transcripts available by mail.

Western Nebraska Community College, Registrar, 1601 E 27th St, Scottsbluff, NE 69361, 308-635-6012 (Fax: 308-635-6100) 8AM-5PM. www.wnccne.us. Enrollment: 3300. Records go back to 1926. Alumni records maintained here; call 308-635-6080. Degrees granted: Associate. Special programs- Nursing, 308-635-6060: Aviation Maintenance, 308-254-5450: Railroad Operations, 308-762-2333: Cosmetology, 308-254-5450. Attendance and degree information available by phone, fax, mail. Transcripts available by fax, mail.

Western Technical Community College Area
(See Western Nebraska Com. College)

York College, Registrar, 1125 E 8th St, York, NE 68467-2699, 402-363-5678, 402-363-5677 (Fax: 402-363-5699) 8AM-5PM. www.yc.ne.edu. Enrollment: 525. Records go

back to 1890. Alumni records maintained here; call 402-363-5678. Degrees granted: Bachelors. Attendance and degree information available by phone, fax, mail. Transcripts available by fax, mail.

Nevada

Clark County Community College
(See Community College of Southern Nevada)

Community College of Southern Nevada, Registrar, 3200 E Cheyenne Ave, North Las Vegas, NV 89030, 702-651-4060, 702-651-4536 (Fax: 702-643-1474) www.ccsn.nevada.edu. 8AM - 6PM. Enrollment: 26000. Records go back to 1971. Degrees granted: Associate. Special programs- Limited Entry, 702-651-5633. Attendance information available by phone, mail. Degree information and transcripts available by written request only.

Deep Springs College, Dean of Students, HC 72, Box 45001, Dyer, NV 89010-9803, 760-872-2000, 760-872-4465 (Fax: 760-872-4466) www.dpsprngs.edu. 8AM-5PM. Enrollment: 26. Records go back to 1917. Alumni records are maintained here. Special programs- Call 760-872-2000. Attendance and degree information available by phone, fax, mail. Transcripts available by phone, fax, mail.

Great Basin College, Registrar, 1500 College Pkwy, Elko, NV 89801, 702-753-2102, 702-753-2273 (Fax: 702-753-2311). 8AM-5PM. Enrollment: 3000. Records go back to 1969. Formerly **Northern Nevada Community College**. Degrees granted: Associate. Attendance and degree information available by phone, fax, mail. Transcripts available by fax, mail.

Las Vegas College, Registrar, 3320 E Flamingo Rd Ste 30, Las Vegas, NV 89121-4306, 702-434-0486 (Fax: 702-434-8601).

7AM-4PM. Records go back to 1970's. Alumni records are maintained here. Degrees granted: Associate. Special programs- Call 702-434-0486 Attendance, degree and transcript information available by fax, mail.

Morrison College - Reno, Records Dept, 140 Washington St, Reno, NV 89503, 702-323-4145 (Fax: 702-323-8495). 8:30AM-7:30PM M-Th; 8AM-5PM F. Enrollment: 225. Records go back to 1960. Alumni records are maintained here. Degrees granted: Associate; Bachelors. Attendance, degree and transcript information available by fax, mail.

Old College
(See Turkey Meadows Com. College)

Phillips Junior College of Las Vegas
(See Las Vegas College)

Sierra Nevada College, Registrar, PO Box 4269, Incline Village, NV 89450-4269, 702-831-1314, 702-831-7799 (Fax: 702-831-1347) 8AM-5PM. www.sierranevada.edu. Enrollment: 700. Records go back to 1969. Degrees granted: Bachelors. Attendance and degree information available by phone, fax, mail. Transcripts available by fax, mail.

Truckee Meadows Community College
Registrar, 7000 Dandini Blvd, Reno, NV 89512, 702-673-7042 (Fax: 702-673-7028) 8AM-5PM M,Th,F; 8AM-7PM T,W. www.tmcc.edu. Enrollment: 10214. Records go back to 1972. Degrees granted: Associate. Special programs- Call 702-973-7042. Attendance, degree and transcript information available by mail.

University of Nevada, Las Vegas, Registrar, 4505 Maryland Pkwy, Las Vegas, NV 89154, 702-895-3771 (Fax: 702-895-4046) www.nscee.edu/univ. 8AM-5PM. Enrollment: 20272. Records go back to 1955. Alumni records maintained here; call 702-895-3621. Degrees granted: Bachelors; Masters; Doctorate. Special programs- Continuing Education. Attendance and degree information available by phone, mail. Transcripts available by mail.

University of Nevada, Reno, Admissions & Records, MS 120, Reno, NV 89557, 702-784-6865 (Fax: 702-784-4283) www.unr.edu. 8AM - 4:30PM. Enrollment: 12350. Records go back to 1904. Alumni records maintained here; call 702-784-6620. Degrees granted: Bachelors; Masters; Doctorate. Attendance and degree information available by fax, mail. Transcripts available by written request only.

Western Nevada Community College, Registrar, 2201 W College Pkwy, Carson City, NV 89703, 702-887-3000 (Fax: 702-887-3141) www.scs.unr.edu/wncc. Enrollment: 5000. Records go back to 1970's. Alumni records maintained here; call 702-887-3164. Degrees granted: Associate. Special programs- Call 702-887-3000. Attendance and degree information available by phone, mail. Transcripts available by mail.

New Hampshire

Antioch University (Antioch New England Graduate School), Registrar, 40 Avon St, Keene, NH 03431, 603-357-3122 (Fax: 603-357-0718) www.antioch.negs.edu. Records are located at College at Antioch University, Registrar, 795 Livermore St, Yellow Springs, OH 45387.

Castle College, Registrar, 23 Searles Rd, Windham, NH 03087, 603-893-6111 (Fax: 603-898-0547) www.castlecollege.org. 8AM-5PM. Records go back to 1965. Alumni records are maintained here. Degrees granted: Associate. Attendance and degree information available by phone, fax, mail. Transcripts available by mail.

Colby-Sawyer College, Registrar, 100 Main St, New London, NH 03257, 603-526-3673, 603-526-3674 (Fax: 603-526-2135). 8AM-5PM. Enrollment: 780. Records go back to 1940. Alumni records maintained here; call 603-526-3727. Degrees granted: Associate; Bachelors. Attendance and degree information available by phone, fax, mail. Transcripts available by mail.

College for Lifelong Learning, Registrar, 125 N State St, Concord, NH 03301-6438, 603-228-3000 www.usnh.unh.edu. (Fax: 603-

229-0964) Enrollment: 2400. Records go back to 1972. Alumni records are maintained here also. Call 603-228-3000 X329. Degrees granted: Associate; Bachelors. Attendance and degree information available by phone, mail. Transcripts available by written request only.

Daniel Webster College, Registrar, Nashua, NH 03063, 603-577-6510, 603-577-6000 (Fax: 603-577-6001) www.dwc.edu. 8:30AM-5PM. Enrollment: 1000. Records go back to 1965. Alumni records maintained here; call 603-577-6620. Degrees granted: Associate; Bachelors. Attendance and degree information available by phone, fax, mail. Transcripts available by fax, mail. Telephone inquiries are accepted at present, but may be discontinued.

Dartmouth College, Registrar, 6014 McNutt, Hanover, NH 03755, 603-646-2246 (Fax: 603-646-2247) www.dartmouth.edu. 8AM-4PM. Enrollment: 4400. Records go back to 1769. Alumni records maintained here; call 603-646-3643. Degrees granted: Bachelors; Masters; Doctorate. Attendance and degree information available by phone, fax, mail. Transcripts available by written request only.

Franklin Pierce College, Registrar, PO Box 60, Rindge, NH 03461, 603-899-4100, 603-899-4094 (Fax: 603-899-4308) www.fpc.edu. 8AM-4:30PM. Enrollment: 2700. Records go back to 1962. Alumni records maintained here; call 603-899-4100. Degrees granted: Associate; Bachelors; Masters. Attendance and degree information available by phone, fax, mail. Transcripts available by written request only.

Franklin Pierce Law Center, Registrar, 2 White St, Concord, NH 03301, 603-228-1541 X1103, 603-228-1963 X 1103 or X1119 (Fax: 603-228-1074) www.fplc.edu. 8AM-4:30PM. Enrollment: 400. Records go back indefinitely. Alumni records maintained here; call 603-228-1541 X1181. Degrees granted: Masters; Doctorate. Attendance and degree information available by phone, fax, mail. Transcripts available by fax, mail.

Hesser College, Registrar, 3 Sundial Ave, Manchester, NH 03103, 603-668-6660 (Fax: 603-666-4722) www.hesser.edu. 8AM-4:30PM. Enrollment: 2500. Records go back to 1915. Alumni records are maintained here. Degrees granted: Associate. Attendance and degree information available by phone, fax, mail. Transcripts available by fax, mail.

Keene State College, Records Retrieval, 229 Main St, Box 2607, Keene, NH 03435-2607, 603-358-2321 www.keene.edu. 9AM-4:30PM. Enrollment: 4800. Records go back to 1909. Alumni records maintained here; call 603-358-2369. Degrees granted: Associate; Bachelors; Masters. Attendance and degree information available by phone, mail. Transcripts available by mail.

Magdalen College, Registrar, 511 Kearsarge Mtn Rd, Warner, NH 03102, www.magdalen.edu 603-456-2656 (Fax: 603-456-2660) Enrollment: 70. Records go back to 1978. Alumni records are maintained here. Degrees granted: Associate; Bachelors. Attendance, degree and transcript information available by phone, mail.

McIntosh College, Registrar, 23 Cataract Ave, Dover, NH 03820, 603-742-1234, 603-742-3536 (Fax: 603-742-7292) 7:30AM-10:30PM. www.mcintosh.driver.nh.us. Records go back to 1920. Degrees granted: Associate. Attendance and degree information available by phone, fax, mail. Transcripts available by written request only.

Merrimack Valley College
(See University of New Hampshire at Manchester)

New England College, Registrar, Henniker, NH 03242-0788, 603-428-2203, 603-428-2235 (Fax: 603-428-2266) www.nec.edu. 8:30AM - 4:30PM. Enrollment: 1100. Records go back to 1947. Alumni records maintained here; call 603-428-2300. Degrees granted: Bachelors; Masters. Attendance and degree information available by phone, fax, mail. Transcripts available by fax, mail.

New Hampshire College, Registrar, 2500 N River Rd, Manchester, NH 03106-1045, 603-668-2211 (Fax: 603-645-9665) www.nhc.edu. 8AM-4:30PM. Enrollment: 6100. Alumni records maintained here; call 603-645-9799. Degrees granted: Associate; Bachelors; Masters. Attendance and degree information available by phone, fax, mail. Transcripts available by mail.

New Hampshire Community Technical College, Registrar, 505 Amerst St, PO Box 2052, Nashua, NH 03061-2052, 603-882-6923, 603-882-7022 (Fax: 603-882-8690) 8AM-4:30PM. www.tec.nh.us. Enrollment: 1060. Records go back to 1969. Formerly **New Hampshire Technical College at Nashua.** Alumni records are maintained here. Degrees granted: Associate. Attendance and degree information available by phone, mail. Transcripts available by mail.

New Hampshire Community Technical College at Laconia, Registrar, 379 Prescott Hill Rd, Laconia, NH 03246, 603-524-3207 (Fax: 603-524-8084) www.laco.tec.nh.us. 8AM-4PM. Enrollment: 1000. Records go back to 1969. Alumni records are maintained here. Degrees granted: Associate. Attendance and degree information available by phone, fax, mail. Transcripts available by fax, mail.

New Hampshire Community Technical College at Manchester, Registrar, 1066 Front St, Manchester, NH 03102, 603-668-6706 (Fax: 603-668-5354) 8AM - 4PM. www.manchester.tec.nh.us. Enrollment: 1800.

Records go back to 1945. Alumni records are maintained here. Degrees granted: Associate. Attendance and transcript information available by fax, mail. Degree information available by phone, fax, mail.

New Hampshire Community Technical College at Stratham, Registrar, 277 Portsmouth Ave., Stratham, NH 03885, 603-772-1194 (Fax: 603-772-1198) www.stra.tec.nh.us. 8AM-8PM M-Th, 8AM-4PM F. Enrollment: 1300. Records go back to 1945. Alumni records are maintained here. Degrees granted: Associate. Attendance and degree information available by phone, fax, mail. Transcripts available by written request only.

New Hampshire Technical College, Registrar, One College Dr, **Claremont**, NH 03743-9707, www.tec.nh.us. 603-542-7744 (Fax: 603-543-1844) 8AM-4:30PM. Records go back to 1968. Alumni records are maintained. Degrees granted: Associate. Attendance and degree information available by fax, mail. Transcripts available by fax, mail.

New Hampshire Technical College at Berlin, Registrar, 2020 Riverside Dr, Berlin, NH 03570, 603-572-1113, 8AM - 4:30PM. www.berlin.tec.nh.us. Enrollment: 590. Records go back to 1965. Alumni records are maintained here. Degrees granted: Associate. Attendance and degree information available by phone, mail. Transcripts available by mail.

New Hampshire Technical Institute, Registrar, 11 Institute Dr, Concord, NH 03301-7412, 603-271-NHTI, 603-225-1804 (Fax: 603-271-7139) www.tec.NH.us. 8AM-4:30PM. Enrollment: 3500. Records go back to 1965. Alumni records are maintained. Degrees granted: Associate. Special programs- Certificate Programs, 603-225-1877. Attendance and degree information available by phone, mail. Transcripts available by fax.

Notre Dame College, Registrar, 2321 Elm St, Manchester, NH 03104, 603-669-4298 (Fax: 603-644-8316) www.notredame.edu. 8AM-5PM. Enrollment: 1350. Records go back to 1950. Alumni records maintained here; call 603-669-4298. Degrees granted: Associate; Bachelors; Masters. Certification: Early Childhood Paralegal. Attendance, degree and transcript information available by fax, mail.

Plymouth State College, Registrar, 17 High St, MSC #7, Plymouth, NH 03264, www.plymouth.edu/ 603-535-2345 (Fax: 603-535-2724) 8AM-4:30PM. Enrollment: 4300. Records go back to 1870's. Alumni records maintained here; call 603-535-2218. Degrees granted: Associate; Bachelors; Masters. Special programs- Meteorology. Attendance and degree information available by phone, fax, mail. Transcripts available by fax, mail.

Rivier College, Registrar, 420 S Main St, Nashua, NH 03060-5086, 603-888-1311 (Fax: 603-888-6447) www.river.edu. 8AM-5PM. Enrollment: 2700. Records go back to 1937. Alumni records maintained here; call 603-888-1311 X8522. Degrees granted: Associate; Bachelors; Masters. Attendance and degree

information available by phone, mail. Transcripts available by fax, mail.

School for Lifelong Learning
(See College for Lifelong Learning)

St. Anselm College, Registrar, 100 St Anselm Dr, Manchester, NH 03102-1310, 603-641-7000, 603-641-7400 (Fax: 603-641-7116) www.anselm.edu. 8:30AM - 4:30PM. Enrollment: 2500. Records go back to 1800's. Alumni records maintained here; call 603-641-7220. Degrees granted: Associate; Bachelors. Attendance and degree information available by phone, fax, mail. Transcripts available by written request only.

University of New Hampshire, Registrar's Office, 11 Garrison Ave, Durham, NH 03824-3511, 603-862-1500, 603-862-1587 (transcripts & degrees) (Fax: 603-862-1817) 8AM-4:30PM. http://unhinfo.unh.edu. Records go back to 1866. Alumni Records: Alumni Assoc., Edgewood Rd, Durham, NH 03824. Degrees granted: Associate; Bachelors; Masters; Doctorate. Attendance and degree information available by phone, fax, mail. Transcripts available by fax, mail.

University of New Hampshire at Manchester, Registrar, 220 Hackett Hill Rd, Manchester, NH 03102, 603-668-0700 www.unh.edu/unhm/index.html. (Fax: 603-623-2745) 8AM-6:30PM M-Th, 8AM-4:30PM F. Enrollment: 2000. Records go back to 1988. All transcript information is kept in Durham. Records can be accessed as Transcript Office, 7 Garrison Ave, Durham, NH 3824 Alumni records are maintained here also. Call 603-862-2040. Degrees granted: Associate; Bachelors. Attendance and degree information available by phone, mail. Transcripts available by written request only.

University of New Hampshire, Keene State College, Registrar, 17 High St, MSC #44, Plymouth, NH 03264-1595, 603-535-2336 (Fax: 603-535-2528) www.unh.ksc.edu. 8AM-4:30PM. Enrollment: 4000. Records go back to 1871. Alumni records are maintained here. Degrees granted: Associate; Bachelors; Masters. Special programs- Science: Education. Attendance and degree information available by phone, mail. Transcripts available by mail.

White Pines College, Registrar, Chester, NH 03036, 603-887-4401, 800-974-6372 (Fax: 603-887-1777). 8:30AM-4:30PM. Records go back to 1965. Alumni records are maintained here. Degrees granted: Associate. Attendance and degree information available by phone, fax, mail. Transcripts available by fax, mail.

New Jersey

Assumption College for Sisters, Registrar, 350 Bernardsville Rd, Mallinckrodt Convent, Mendham, NJ 07945-0800, 973-

543-6528 (Fax: 973-543-9459). 9AM-4PM. Enrollment: 321. Records go back to 1953. Degrees granted: Associate. Attendance,

degree and transcript information available by mail.

Atlantic Community College, Registrar, 5100 Black Horse Pike, Mays Landing, NJ 08330-2699, 609-343-5092 (Fax: 609-343-4914) www.atlantic.edu. 9AM-4:30PM. Enrollment: 5900. Records go back to 1969. Alumni records are maintained here. Degrees granted: Associate. Attendance, degree and transcript information available by fax, mail.

Bergen Community College, Registrar, 400 Paramus Rd, Paramus, NJ 07652, www.bergen.cc.nj.us. 201-447-7857 (Fax: 201-670-7973) 9AM-5PM. Records go back to 1968. Degrees granted: Associate. Attendance, degree and transcript information available by fax, mail.

Berkeley College (Waldwick Campus), Registrar, 100 W Prospect St, Waldwick, NJ 07463, 201-652-1346, 201-652-1346 Ext. 126 (Fax: 201-670-7737) www.berkeley.org. 7:30AM-4:30PM. Records go back to 1961. Alumni records are maintained here. Degrees granted: Associate. Attendance and degree information available by fax, mail. Transcripts available by mail.

Berkeley College (West Paterson Campus), Office of the Registrar, 44 Rifle Camp Rd, West Paterson, NJ 07424, 973-278-5400, 973-652-1346 (Fax: 973-278-2242) www.berkeley.org. 8:30AM-4:30PM. Enrollment: 1900. Records go back to 1945. Alumni records are maintained here. Degrees granted: Associate. Attendance information available by phone, fax, mail. Degree information available by fax, mail. Transcripts available by written request only.

Berkeley College of Business (Woodbridge Campus), Registrar, 430 Rahway Ave, Woodbridge, NJ 07095, 732-750-1800 (Fax: 732-750-0652). 7:30AM-4:30PM. Alumni records are maintained here. Degrees granted: Associate. Attendance and degree information available by phone, fax, mail. Transcripts available by mail.

Beth Medrash Govoha, Registrar, 617 Sixth St, Lakewood, NJ 08701, 732-367-1060 (Fax: 732-367-7487). 9AM-1:40PM. Enrollment: 2200. Records go back to 1970. Alumni records are maintained here. Degrees granted: Bachelors; Masters; Advanced Talmudic, Rabbinic Ordination, Advanced Rabbinic, Graduate Talmudic Diploma, Advanced Graduate Talmudic Diploma. Attendance, degree and transcript information available by fax.

Bloomfield College, Registrar, 467 Franklin St, Bloomfield, NJ 07003, 973-748-9000 (Fax: 973-743-3998). 7:30AM-5PM. Records go back to 1950's. Alumni records are maintained here. Degrees granted: Associate; Bachelors. Attendance and degree information available by phone, fax, mail. Transcripts available by mail.

Brookdale Community College (Fort Monmouth Learning Center), Registrar, 918 Murphy Dr, Fort Monmouth, NJ 07703, 732-224-2933 (registrar), 732-224-2595 (switchboard). Records are located at Brookdale Community College, Registrar, Lincroft, NJ.

Brookdale Community College, (Freehold Learning Center) Registrar, 47 Throckmorton St, Freehold, NJ 07728, 732-224-2268 soho.ios.com/~andrewjr. 9AM-7PM M-Th; 9AM-5PM F; 9AM-1PM S. Records go back to 1970. Degrees granted: Associate. Attendance, degree and transcript information available by mail.

Brookdale Community College, Registrar, 765 Newman Springs Road, **Lincroft**, NJ 07738, 732-224-2000 (Fax: 732-224-2242). 9AM-7PM M-Th; 9AM-5PM F; 9AM-Noon S. Enrollment: 13000. Records go back to 1969. Alumni records are maintained here. Degrees granted: Associate Attendance, degree and transcript information available by mail.

Brookdale Community College (Long Branch Learning Center), Registrar, Third Ave and Broadway, Long Branch, NJ 07740, 908-842-1900. Records are located at Brookdale Community College, Registrar, Lincroft, NJ.

Brookdale Community College (Bayshore Learning Center), Registrar, 311 Laurel Ave, West Keansburg, NJ 07734, 732-842-1900. Records are located at Brookdale Community College, Registrar, Lincroft, NJ.

Burlington County College, Registrar, County Rte 530, Pemberton, NJ 08068-1599, 609-894-4900 (Fax: 609-894-0764). Alumni records maintained here; call 609-894-9311 Ext. 7331. Degrees granted: Associate. Attendance and degree information available by fax, mail. Transcripts available by mail.

Caldwell College, Registrar, 9 Ryerson Ave, Caldwell, NJ 07006-6195, 973-228-4424 (Fax: 973-403-1784). 9AM-4:30PM. Enrollment: 1800. Records go back to 1939. Alumni records maintained here; call 973-228-4424 Ext. 411. Degrees granted: Bachelors; Masters. Certification: EED, SNC. Attendance, degree and transcript information available by fax, mail.

Camden County College, Registrar, PO Box 200, Blackwood, NJ 08012, 609-227-7200 Ext. 4200 (Fax: 609-374-4917) 8:30AM-8:30PM. www.camdencc.edu. Enrollment: 13500. Records go back to 1968. Alumni records are maintained here. Degrees granted: Associate. Attendance and degree information available by phone, fax, mail. Transcripts available by fax, mail.

Camden County College (Branch Campus), Registrar, 200 N Broadway, Camden, NJ 08102-1102, 609-338-1817 (Fax: 609-756-0497). Records are located at Camden County College, Registrar, Blackwood, NJ.

Centenary College, Registrar, 400 Jefferson St, Hackettstown, NJ 07840, 908-852-1400 Ext. 2213 (Fax: 908-852-3454) www.centenary.edu. 8:30AM-6:45PM M-Th; 8:30AM-4:30PM F. Enrollment: 800. Records go back to 1800's. Alumni records are maintained here also. Call 908-852-1400. Degrees granted: Associate; Bachelors. Attendance and degree information available by phone, fax, mail. Transcripts available by written request only.

College of New Jersey (The), Registrar, PO Box 7718, Ewing, NJ 08628-0718, 609-771-1855, 609-771-2141 (Fax: 609-771-5180) www.trenton.edu. 8:30AM-4:30PM. Enrollment: 7000. Records go back to 1900. Formerly **Trenton State College**. Alumni records maintained here; call 609-771-2393. Degrees granted: Bachelors; Masters. Attendance and degree information available by phone, mail. Transcripts available by mail.

College of St. Elizabeth, Registrar, 2 Convent Rd, Morristown, NJ 07960-7989, 973-290-4000 Ext. 8 (Fax: 973-290-4499). 8AM-4:30PM. Enrollment: 1800. Alumni records maintained here; call 973-292-6300. Degrees granted: Associate; Bachelors; Masters. Attendance and degree information available by phone, fax, mail. Transcripts available by mail.

County College of Morris, Registrar, Rte 10 and Center Grove Rd, Randolph, NJ 07869, 973-328-5200 (Fax: 973-328-5209) 8:30AM-4:30PM. www.ccm.edu. Records go back to 1965. Alumni records maintained here; call 973-328-5059. Degrees granted: Associate. Attendance and degree information available by phone, fax, mail. Transcripts available by fax, mail.

Cumberland County College, Registrar, College Dr, PO Box 517, Vineland, NJ 08360, 609-691-8600 (Fax: 609-691-9157) 8AM-5:30PM. www.cccnj.net. Enrollment: 2700. Records go back to 1966. Alumni records are maintained here. Degrees granted: Associate. Special programs- Aquaculture: Aviation: Horticulture: Radiography: Quality Assurance. Attendance information available by phone. Degree information available by phone, fax, mail. Transcripts available by mail.

Drew University, Office of the Registrar, 36 Madison Ave, Madison, NJ 07940, 201-408-3025 (Fax: 201-408-3044) www.drew.edu. 9AM-5PM. Enrollment: 2000. Records go back to 1917. Alumni Records: 120 Madison Ave, Madison, NJ 07940. Degrees granted: Bachelors; Masters; Doctorate. Certification: Medical Humanities. Attendance and degree information available by phone, fax, mail. Transcripts available by written request by student only.

Essex County College, Registrar, 303 University Ave, Newark, NJ 07102, 973-877-3111 (Fax: 973-623-6449). 8:30AM-7:30PM M-Th; 9AM-5PM F. Enrollment: 8500. Records go back to 1968. Alumni records maintained here; call 973-877-3039. Degrees granted: Associate. Attendance and degree information available by phone, fax, mail. Transcripts available by fax, mail.

Essex County College (West Essex Branch Campus), Registrar, 730 Bloomfield Ave, West Caldwell, NJ 07006, 973-403-2539, 973-877-3155 (Cental Campus) (Fax: 973-228-6181). 8AM-4:30PM. Alumni records maintained here; call 973-877-3039. Degrees granted: Associate. Attendance and degree information available by fax, mail. Transcripts available by mail.

Fairleigh Dickinson University (Teaneck-Hackensack Campus), Registrar, University Plaza 3, Hackensack, NJ 07840, 908-687-0420 (Fax: 908-962-2209) www.fdu.edu. Records are located at Fairleigh Dickinson University, Registrar, Teaneck, NJ.

Fairleigh Dickinson University (Florham-Madison Campus), Office of Enrollment Services, 285 Madison Ave, Madison, NJ 07940, 201-593-8600, 973-443-8500 (Fax: 201-593-8604) www.fdu.edu. 9AM-5PM. Records go back to 1958. Alumni records maintained here; call 201-443-7013. Degrees granted: Associate; Bachelors; Masters. Attendance and transcript information available by fax, mail. Degree information available by phone, fax, mail.

Fairleigh Dickinson University (Rutherford Campus), Registrar, 223 Montrose Ave, Rutherford, NJ 07070, www.fdu.edu. Records are located at Fairleigh Dickinson University, (Teaneck-Hackensack Campus), Registrar, Hackensack, NJ 07840.

Fairleigh Dickinson University, Registrar, 1000 River Rd, Teaneck, NJ 07666, 201-692-2218, 201-692-2213 (Fax: 201-692-2209) www.fdu.edu. 9AM-5PM. Enrollment: 9500. Records go back to 1952. Alumni records maintained here; call 201-692-7013. Degrees granted: Bachelors; Masters. Special programs- Continuing Education, 201-692-6500. Attendance and transcript information available by mail. Degree information available by phone, fax, mail.

Felician College, Registrar, 262 S Main St, Lodi, NJ 07644, 973-778-1190 Ext. 6038, 973-778-1029 (Fax: 973-778-4111) www.felician.edu. 8:30AM-4:30PM M,T,F; 8:30AM-8PM W,Th. Enrollment: 1150. Records go back to 1942. Alumni records are maintained here. Degrees granted: Associate; Bachelors; Masters. Attendance and degree information available by phone, fax, mail. Transcripts available by fax, mail.

Georgian Court College, Registrar's Office, Kingscote, Admin Bldg, 900 Lakewood Ave, Lakewood, NJ 08701-2697, 732-364-2200 Ext. 228 (Fax: 732-367-3920) www.georgian.edu. 8:30AM-4:30PM. Enrollment: 2400. Records go back to 1908. Alumni records maintained here; call 732-364-2200 Ext. 232. Degrees granted: Bachelors; Masters. Attendance and degree information available by phone, mail. Transcripts available by mail.

Glassboro State College
(See Rowan University)

Gloucester County College, Registrar, 1400 Tanyard Rd, Sewell, NJ 08080, 609-468-5000 Ext. 282, 609-468-5000 Ext. 238 (Fax: 609-848-8498) www.gcc.cc.nj.us. 8:30AM-5PM. Enrollment: 5000. Records go back to 1968. Alumni records maintained here; call 609-468-5000 Ext. 273. Degrees granted: Associate. Attendance and degree information available by phone, mail. Transcripts available by written request only.

Hudson County Community College, Registrar, 168 Sip Ave, Jersey City, NJ 07306, 201-714-2138 (Fax: 201-714-2136) 9AM-6PM M-Th; 9AM-5PM F. www.hudson.cc.nj.us. Enrollment: 3950. Records go back to 1974. Alumni records maintained here; call 201-714-2228. Degrees granted: Associate. Attendance and degree information available by fax, mail. Transcripts available by mail.

Immaculate Conception Seminary, Registrar, 400 S Orange Ave, South Orange, NJ 07079, 973-761-9374 (Fax: 973) www.iwu.edu. 9AM-5PM. Enrollment: 170. Records go back to 1945. Degrees granted: Masters. Attendance and degree information available by fax, mail. Transcripts available by fax, mail.

Jersey City State College, Registrar, 2039 Kennedy Blvd, Jersey City, NJ 07305, 201-200-3336 (Fax: 201-200-2044). 8:30AM-5PM. Enrollment: 10000. Records go back to 1930. Alumni records maintained here; call 201-200-3196. Degrees granted: Bachelors; Masters. Attendance and degree information available by phone, fax, mail. Transcripts available by mail.

Katharine Gibbs School (Branch Campus), Registrar, 80 Kingsbridge Rd, Piscataway, NJ 08854, 732-885-1580 (Fax: 732-885-1235). Enrollment: 300. Records go back to 1984. Alumni records are maintained here. Degrees granted: Associate. Attendance and degree information available by phone, fax, mail. Transcripts available by fax, mail.

Katherine Gibbs School, Registrar, 33 Plymouth St, Montclair, NJ 07042, 973-744-2010 (Fax: 973-744-2298). 8AM-10PM. Enrollment: 400. Records go back to 1960. Alumni Records: 52 Vanderbilt Avenue, New York, NY 10017. Degrees granted: Associate. Special programs- Applied Sciences.

Attendance, degree and transcript information available by fax, mail.

Kean College of New Jersey, Registrar, 1000 Morris Ave, Union, NJ 07083, 908-527-2445 (Fax: 908-527-0423). 8:30AM-4:30PM. Enrollment: 12000. Records go back to 1960. Alumni records maintained here; call 908-527-2526. Degrees granted: Bachelors; Masters. Attendance and degree information available by phone, fax, mail. Transcripts available by mail.

Mercer County Community College (James Kerney Campus), Registrar, N Broad and Academy Sts, Trenton, NJ 08690, 609-586-4800 (Fax: 609-586-6944) www.mccc.edu. Records are located at Mercer County Community College, Registrar, Trenton, NJ.

Mercer County Community College, Registrar, 1200 Old Trenton Rd, Box B, Trenton, NJ 08690-0182, 609-586-4800 (Fax: 609-586-6944) www.mccc.edu. 8AM-7PM M-Th; 8AM-5PM F. Enrollment: 8500. Records go back to 1966. Alumni records are maintained here. Degrees granted: Associate Attendance, degree and transcript information available by fax, mail.

Middlesex County College, Registrar's Office, 155 Mill Rd, PO Box 3050, Edison, NJ 08818-3050, 732-906-2523 (Fax: 732-906-7785). Enrollment: 10500. Records go back to 1966. Alumni records maintained here; call 732-906-2564. Degrees granted: Associate. Special programs- Liberal Arts, 732-906-2528: Business Tech, 732-906-2502: Engineering & Science, 732-906-2501: Health Tech, 732-906-2533: Open College, 732-906-2533. Attendance and degree information available by phone, mail. Transcripts available by mail.

Monmouth University, Registrar, Norwood and Cedar Aves, West Long Branch, NJ 07764-1898, 732-571-3477 (Fax: 732-263-5141) www.monmouth.edu. 9AM-5PM. Enrollment: 4500. Records go back to 1933. Alumni records maintained here; call 732-571-3489. Degrees granted: Associate; Bachelors; Masters. Attendance and degree information available by fax, mail. Transcripts available by mail.

Montclair State College, Registrar, Valley Rd and Normal Ave, Upper Montclair, NJ 07043-1624, 973-655-4376 (Fax: 973-655-7371) www.montclair.edu. 8:30AM-4:30PM. Enrollment: 12800. Records go back to 1908. Alumni records maintained here; call 973-655-4141. Degrees granted: Bachelors; Masters. Attendance and degree information available by phone, fax, mail. Transcripts available by fax, mail.

New Brunswick Theological Seminary, Registrar, 17 Seminary Pl, New Brusnwick, NJ 08901-1196, 732-246-5593 (Fax: 732-249-5412) www.rutgers,edu. 8:30AM-4PM. Enrollment: 185. Records go back to 1920's. Alumni records maintained here; call 732-246-5600. Degrees granted: Masters; M. Div. Attendance and degree information available by phone, fax, mail. Transcripts available by fax, mail.

New Jersey Institute of Technology, Registrar, University Heights, Newark, NJ 07102-9938, 973-596-3236, 973-596-3241 (Fax: 973-802-1854) www.njit.edu. 8:30AM-4:30PM. Enrollment: 8000. Records go back to 1919. Alumni records are maintained here. Degrees granted: Bachelors; Masters; Doctorate. Attendance and degree information available by phone, fax, mail. Transcripts available by mail.

Northeastern Bible Institute, Registrar, PO Box 676, Essex Fells, NJ 07021, 973-992-0730 (Fax: 973-992-1085). Records go back to 1950. Formerly **Northeastern Bible College** Closed as a degree-granting college 6/30/90, currently operating as a bible institute offering non-credit courses. Alumni Records: Alumni Assoc., PO Box 141, Essex Falls, NJ 07021. 1950-1990 attendance and degree information available by phone, fax, mail. Transcripts available by mail.

Ocean County College, Admissions & Records, College Dr/PO Box 2001, Toms River, NJ 08754-2001, 732-255-0304, 732-255-0444 (Mary) www.ocean.cc.nj.us. 8AM-8PM M-Th; 8AM-5PM F. Records go back to 1966. Alumni records maintained here; call 732-255-0400. Degrees granted: Associate. Attendance and degree information available by fax, mail. Transcripts available by mail.

Passaic County Community College, Registrar, One College Blvd, Paterson, NJ 07505-1179, 973-684-6400 (Fax: 973-684-6778) 9AM-7PM M,Th; 9AM-5PM T,W,F. Enrollment: 3700. Records go back to 1971. Alumni records maintained here; call 201-684-5656. Degrees granted: Associate. Attendance and degree information available by phone, fax, mail. Transcripts available by fax, mail.

Princeton Theological Seminary, Registrar, 64 Mercer St CN 821, Princeton, NJ 08542-0803, 609-497-7820 (Fax: 609-683-0741). 8:30AM-4:30PM. Enrollment: 800. Records go back to 1920. Alumni records are maintained here. Degrees granted: Masters; Ph.D. Attendance and degree information available by phone, fax, mail. Transcripts available by mail.

Princeton University, Office of the Registrar, Box 70, Princeton, NJ 08542, 609-258-3361 (Fax: 609-258-6328) 8:45AM-5PM. www.princeton.edu Enrollment: 6424. Records go back to 1909. Alumni records maintained here; call 609-258-1900. Degrees granted: Bachelors; Masters; Doctorate. Attendance and degree information available by phone, fax, mail. Transcripts available by fax, mail.

Rabbinical College of America, Registrar, 226 Sussex Ave, Morristown, NJ 07960, 973-267-9404 (Fax: 973-267-5208) www.rca.edu. 9AM-5PM. Enrollment: 190. Records go back to 1965. Alumni records are maintained here. Degrees granted: Bachelors. Attendance, degree and transcript information available by mail.

Ramapo College of New Jersey, Registrar, 505 Ramapo Valley Rd, Mahwah, NJ 07430-1680, 201-529-7700, 201-529-7695 (Fax: 201-529-6448) www.ramapo.edu. 8:30AM-4:30PM. Enrollment: 4600. Records go back to 1971. Alumni records maintained here; call 201-529-7612. Degrees granted: Bachelors; Masters. Special programs- MALS (Graduate), 201-529-7423. Science in Edu. Technology (Masters); 201-529-7721; Undergraduate Study Abroad, 201-529-7463. Attendance and degree information available by phone, fax, mail. Transcripts available by mail; student signature required.

Raritan Valley Community College, Registrar's Office, PO Box 3300, Somerville, NJ 08876, 908-526-1200 Ext. 8371, 908-526-8260 (Fax: 908-231-8811) 8:30AM-4:30PM. www.raraitan.edu\. Enrollment: 12000. Records go back to 1970. Alumni records are maintained here. Degrees granted: Associate. Attendance, degree and transcript information available by fax, mail.

Rider College, Registrar, 2083 Lawrenceville Rd, Lawrenceville, NJ 08648-3099, 609-896-5065 (Fax: 609-895-5447) www.rider.edu. 8:30AM-5PM. Records go back to 1925. Alumni records maintained here; call 609-895-5340. Degrees granted: Bachelors; Masters. Attendance and degree information available by phone, fax, mail. Transcripts available by fax, mail.

Rider College (Westminster Choir College), Registrar, 101 Walnut Lane, Princeton, NJ 08540, 609-921-7100 Ext. 207 (Fax: 609-921-8829). 8:30AM-5PM. Enrollment: 375. Records go back to 1920. Alumni records are maintained here. Degrees granted: Bachelors; Masters. Attendance and degree information available by phone, fax, mail. Transcripts available by mail.

Rowan College of New Jersey
(See Rowan University)

Rowan University (Camden Campus), Registrar, 200 N Broadway, Camden, NJ 08102, www.rowan.edu. 609-756-5400 (Fax: 609-756-5430) Records are located at Rowan University, Registrar, Glassboro, NJ.

Rowan University, Registrar, 201 Mullica Hill Rd, Glassboro, NJ 08028-1701, 609-256-4350 (Fax: 609-256-4424) www.rowan.edu. 8AM-4:30PM. Enrollment: 9000. Records go back to 1980. Alumni records maintained here; call 609-256-4131. Degrees granted: Bachelors; Masters. Attendance and degree information available by phone, fax, mail. Transcripts available by mail.

Rutgers, The State University of New Jersey Camden Campus, Registrar, 311 N Fifth St, Camden, NJ 08102, 609-225-6054 (Fax: 609-225-6453) http://www.rutgers.edu. 8:30AM-4:30PM. Enrollment: 5000. Records go back to 1934. Alumni Records: Capehart Bldg, Camden, NJ 08102 (Fax: 609-225-6113). Degrees granted: Bachelors; Masters; JD. Attendance and degree information available by phone, fax, mail. Transcripts available by fax, mail.

Rutgers, The State University of New Jersey New Brunswick Campus, Registrar, PO Box 1360, Piscataway, NJ 08903, www.rutgers.edu. 732-445-2757 (Fax: 732-445-5948) Degrees granted: Bachelors; Masters; Doctorate. Attendance and degree information available by phone, fax, mail. Transcripts available by fax, mail.

Rutgers, The State University of New Jersey Newark Campus, Registrar, 249 University Ave, Rm 309, Newark, NJ 07102, 973-353-5324 (Fax: 973-353-1357) 8:30AM-4:30PM. Enrollment: 10000. Records go back to 1940. Alumni records maintained here; call 201-648-5242. Degrees granted: Bachelors; Masters. Attendance and degree information available by phone, fax, mail. Transcripts available by fax, mail.

Salem Community College, Director of Enrollment Services, 460 Hollywood Ave, Carneys Point, NJ 08069, 609-299-2100, 609-351-2707 (Fax: 609-299-9193). 8:30AM-7:30PM M-Th; 8:30AM-4:30PM F. Enrollment: 1150. Records go back to 1972. Alumni records are maintained here. Degrees granted: Associate. Attendance and degree information available by phone, fax, mail. Transcripts available by mail.

Seton Hall University (School of Law), Registrar, One Newark Ctr, Newark, NJ 07102-5210, 973-642-8162 (Fax: 973-642-8734). 8:30AM-6PM. Enrollment: 1250. Records go back to 1930. Alumni records maintained here; call 973-642-8711. Degrees

granted: Doctorate. Attendance and degree information available by phone, fax, mail. Transcripts available by mail.

Seton Hall University, Registrar, 400 S Orange Ave, South Orange, NJ 07079, 973-761-9374, 973-761-9372 (Fax: 973-275-2040) www.shu.edu. 8:45AM-6PM. Enrollment: 10000. Records go back to 1800's. Alumni records maintained here; call 973-761-9822. Degrees granted: Bachelors; Masters; Doctorate. Attendance and degree information available by phone, fax, mail. Transcripts available by mail.

Somerset County College
(See Raritan Valley Community College)

St. Peter's College (Englewood Cliffs Campus), Registrar, Hudson Terrace, Englewood Cliffs, NJ 07632, 201-568-7730 (Fax: 201-568-6614) www.spc.edu. Degrees granted: Associate; Bachelors; Masters. Attendance and degree information available by mail. For transcripts, go to the Jersey City Campus Registrar.

St. Peter's College, Registrar, 2641 Kennedy Blvd, Jersey City, NJ 07306, 201-915-9035 (Fax: 201-915-9038) www.spc.edu. 9AM-8PM M-Th; 9AM-5PM F. Records go back to 1916. Alumni records maintained here; call 201-915-9204. Degrees granted: Associate; Bachelors; Masters. Attendance and degree information available by phone, fax, mail. Transcripts available by fax, mail.

Stevens Institute of Technology, Registrar, Castle Point on the Hudson, Hoboken, NJ 07030, 201-216-5210 (Fax: 201-216-8030) www.stevens-tech.edu. 8AM-5PM. Records go back to 1870. Alumni records maintained here; call 201-216-5163. Degrees granted: Bachelors; Masters; Doctorate. Attendance and degree information available by phone, fax, mail. Transcripts available by mail.

Stockton College of New Jersey, Registrar, Jimmy Leeds Rd, Pomona, NJ 80240, www.stockton.edu. 609-652-1776 (Fax: 609-748-5547) Enrollment: 5000. Records go back to 1972. Alumni records are maintained here. Degrees granted: Bachelors. Special programs- Arts: Science. Attendance, degree and transcript information available by mail.

Stockton State College, Registrar, Jimmy Leeds Rd, Pomona, NJ 08240, 609-652-4235 (Fax: 609-652-4598) www.stockton.edu. 8:30AM-4:30PM. Records go back to 1975. Alumni records maintained here; call 609-652-4468. Attendance and degree information available by phone, fax, mail. Transcripts available by mail.

Sussex County Community College, Registrar, College Hill, Newton, NJ 07860, 973-300-2215 (Fax: 973-579-5226). 8AM-8PM M-Th; 8AM-5PM F. Enrollment: 2300. Records go back to 1982. Degrees granted: Associate. Attendance and degree information available by phone, fax, mail. Transcripts available by fax, mail.

Talmudical Academy of New Jersey, Registrar, Rte 524, PO Box 7, Adelphia, NJ 07710, 732-431-1600 (Fax: 732-431-3951) 9AM-5PM. Enrollment: 450. Records go back to 1971. Alumni records are maintained here. Degrees granted: Bachelors. Attendance, degree and transcript information available by mail.

Thomas A. Edison State College, Registrar, 101 W State St, Trenton, NJ 08608-1176, 609-984-1180 (Fax: 609-777-0477) www.tesc.edu. 8AM-4:30PM. Enrollment:

8000. Records go back to 1972. Alumni records maintained here; call 201-877-1458. Degrees granted: Associate; Bachelors. Attendance and degree information available by phone, fax, mail. Transcripts available by fax, mail.

Union County College, Registrar, 1033 Springfield Ave, Cranford, NJ 07016, 908-709-7132 (Fax: 908-709-1392) www.ucc.edu. 8:30AM-4:30PM. Enrollment: 9000. Records go back to 1933. Alumni records maintained here; call 908-709-7113. Degrees granted: Associate. Attendance and degree information available by fax, mail. Transcripts available by written request only plus signed release.

Union County College (Elizabeth Campus), Registrar, 12 W Jersey St, Elizabeth, NJ 07206, 908-965-6050, 908-709-7500 (Fax: 908-709-1392). Records are located at Union County College, Registrar, Cranford, NJ.

Union County College (Plainfield Campus), Registrar, 232 E Second St, Plainfield, NJ 07060, 908-889-8500. Records are located at Union County College, Registrar, Cranford, NJ.

University of Medicine and Dentistry ((New Jersey Dental School)), Registrar, 110 Bergen St, Newark, NJ 07103, 973-982-4728 (Fax: 973-982-3689) www.umdni.edu. 8AM-4PM. Enrollment: 350. Records go back to 1956. Alumni records maintained here; call 973-982-6883. Degrees granted: Doctorate. Attendance and degree information available by phone, fax, mail. Transcripts available by written request only.

University of Medicine and Dentistry of New Jersey, Registrar, 215 S Orange, Rm B640, Newark, NJ 07103-2714, 973-972-7300 (Fax: 973-972-6930). 8:30AM-4:30PM. Enrollment: 750. Records go back to 1960. Alumni records maintained here; call 973-972-6864. Degrees granted: Doctorate. Attendance and degree information available by phone, fax, mail. Transcripts available by mail.

University of Medicine and Dentistry of New Jersey (Graduate School of Biomedical Sciences), Registrar, 185 S Orange Ave, Newark, NJ 07103, 973-972-4300 Ext. 5 www.umdnj.edu. Records located at University of Medicine & Dentistry of New Jersey, Registrar, Newark, NJ.

University of Medicine and Dentistry of New Jersey (School of Health-Related Professions), Registrar, 65 Bergen St, Newark, NJ 07107, 973-972-4211 (Fax: 973-972-5591) www.umdnj.edu. Records are located at University of Medicine & Dentistry of New Jersey, Registrar, Newark, NJ.

University of Medicine and Dentistry of New Jersey (Robert Wood Johnson Medical School), Registrar, 675 Hoes Lane, Piscataway, NJ 08854-5635, 732-235-4565 (Fax: 732-235-5078) www.umdnj.edu. 8:30AM-5PM. Enrollment: 900. Records go back to 1974. Alumni records maintained here; call 732-235-4565. Degrees granted: Masters; Doctorate. Attendance and degree information available by phone, fax, mail. Transcripts available by mail.

University of Medicine and Dentistry of New Jersey (School of Osteopathic Medicine), Registrar, Academic Ctr, One Medical Center Dr #210, Stratford, NJ 08084, 609-566-7055 (Fax: 609-566-6895) www.umdnj.edu. Records are located at University of Medicine & Dentistry of New Jersey, Registrar, Newark, NJ.

Warren County Community College, Registrar, 475 Rte 57 W, Washington, NJ 07882, 908-835-9222, 908-689-9222 (Fax: 908-689-5824) www.warren.cc.nj.us. 9AM-5PM. Enrollment: 2200. Records go back to 1981. Degrees granted: Associate.

Attendance, degree and transcript information available by mail.

William Paterson College of New Jersey, Office of the Registrar, College Hall 358 Hamburg Tpk, PO Box 913, Wayne, NJ 07470-0913, 973-720-2000 (Fax: 973-720-3075) www.willpaterson.edu. 8:30AM-4:30PM. Alumni Records: Alumni Office, 300 Pompton Rd, Wayne, NJ 07470. Degrees granted: Bachelors; Masters. Certification: Education. Attendance and degree information available by phone, fax, mail. Transcripts available by mail.

New Mexico

Albuquerque Technical — Vocational Institute, Records Office, 525 Buena Vista Dr SE, Albuquerque, NM 87108, 505-224-3202, 505-224-3232 (Fax: 505-224-3237) www.tri.cc.nm.us. 8AM-7PM M-Th; 8AM-5PM F. Enrollment: 15000. Records go back to 1965. Degrees granted: Associate. Attendance and degree information available by phone, mail. Transcripts available by mail.

Clovis Community College, Registrar, 417 Schepps Blvd, Clovis, NM 88101, 505-769-4025, 505-769-4199 (Fax: 505-769-4190) 8AM-4:30PM. www.clovis.cc.nm.us. Enrollment: 4000. Records go back to 1970. Degrees granted: Associate. Attendance and degree information available by phone, mail. Transcripts available by mail.

College of Santa Fe, Registrar, 1600 St Michael's Dr, Santa Fe, NM 87505, 505-473-6317 (Fax: 505-473-6127) 8AM-5PM. www.state.nm.vs/csf/. Enrollment: 1450. Records go back to 1947. Alumni records maintained here; call 505-473-6312. Degrees granted: Associate; Bachelors; Masters. Attendance and degree information available by phone, fax, mail. Transcripts available by fax, mail.

College of the Southwest, Registrar, 6610 Lovington Hwy, Hobbs, NM 88240, 505-392-6561, 800-530-4400 (Fax: 505-392-6006). 8AM-5PM. Enrollment: 500. Records go back to 1956. Alumni records are maintained here. Degrees granted: Bachelors; Masters. Attendance and degree information available by phone, fax, mail. Transcripts available by fax, mail.

Dona Ana Branch Community College (See New Mexico State University)

Eastern New Mexico University, Registrar, Portales, NM 88130, 505-562-2175 (Fax: 505-562-2566) www.enmu.edu. 8AM-4PM. Enrollment: 4000. Records go back to 1950's. Degrees granted: Associate; Bachelors; Masters. Attendance and degree information available by phone, fax, mail. Transcripts available by fax, mail.

Eastern New Mexico University-Roswell, Registrar, PO Box 6000, Roswell, NM 88202, 505-624-7145, 505-624-7149 (Fax: 505-624-7119). 8AM-5PM. Records go back to 1958. Degrees granted: Associate. Attendance and degree information available by phone, fax, mail. Transcripts available by fax, mail.

ITT Technical Institute (Branch of Tucson, AZ), Registrar, 5100 Masthead NE, Albuquerque, NM 87109-4366, 505-828-1114, 800-636-1114 (Fax: 505-828-1849). 8AM-5PM. Enrollment: 300. Records go back to 1907. Alumni records are maintained. Degrees granted: Associate; Bachelors. Attendance and degree information available by phone, fax, mail. Transcripts available by fax, mail.

Institute of American Indian and Alaskan Native Culture and Arts, Registrar, St. Michael's Dr, Box 20007, Santa Fe, NM 87504, 505-986-5512, 505-988-6495 (Fax: 505-988-6446). Enrollment: 128. Records go back to 1962. Degrees granted: Associate. Attendance and degree information available by phone, fax, mail. Transcripts available by fax, mail.

International Institute of Chinese Medicine, Registrar, PO Box 4991, Santa Fe, NM 87502-4991, 505-473-5233 (Fax: 505-473-9279) www.thuntek.net/IICM. 9AM-5PM. Records go back to 1985. Degrees granted: Masters. Attendance and degree information available by phone, fax, mail. Transcripts available by fax, mail.

Luna Vocational Technical Institute, Registrar, PO Box 1510, Las Vegas, NM 87701, 505-454-2548 (Fax: 505-454-2518) 8AM-4:30PM. www.lvti.cc.nm.us. Enrollment: 1700. Records go back to 1970. Degrees granted: Associate. Attendance and degree information available by phone, fax, mail. Transcripts available by fax, mail.

Mesa Technical College, Registrar, 911 South 10th St, Tucumcari, NM 88401, 505-461-4413 (Fax: 505-461-1901) 8:30AM-4:30PM. www.mesatech.cc.nm.us. Enrollment: 350. Records go back to 1958. Alumni records are maintained here. Degrees granted: Associate. Attendance, degree and transcript information available by phone, mail.

Nazarene Bible College (Nazarene Indian Bible College), Registrar, 2315 Markham Rd SW, Albuquerque, NM 87105, 505-877-0240, 888-877-6422 (Fax: 505-877-6214). 8AM-5PM Fall; 9AM-4:30PM Summer. Enrollment: 50. Records go back to 1955. Degrees granted: Associate; Bachelors. Attendance and degree information available by phone, fax, mail. Transcripts available by mail.

New Mexico Highlands University, Registrar, National Ave, Las Vegas, NM 87701, 505-454-3424 (Fax: 505-454-3552) 8AM-5PM. www.nmhu.edu. Enrollment: 2800. Records go back to 1893. Alumni records are maintained here. Degrees granted: Associate; Bachelors; Masters. Attendance and degree information available by phone, fax, mail. Transcripts available by fax, mail.

New Mexico Institute of Mining and Technology, Registrar, Socorro, NM 87801, 505-835-5133 (Fax: 505-835-6511) www.nmt.edu. 8AM-5PM. Enrollment: 1350. Records go back to 1889. Alumni records are maintained here. Degrees granted: Associate; Bachelors; Masters; Doctorate. Attendance and degree information available by phone, fax, mail. Transcripts available by fax, mail.

New Mexico Junior College, Registrar, 5317 Lovington Hwy, Hobbs, NM 88240, 505-392-5113 (Fax: 505-392-0322). 8AM-5PM. Enrollment: 2000. Records go back to 1967. Alumni records are maintained here. Degrees granted: Associate. Attendance and degree information available by phone, fax, mail. Transcripts available by fax, mail.

New Mexico Military Institute, Registrar, 100 W College Blvd, Roswell, NM 88201, 505-624-8070 (Fax: 505-624-8058) 7:30AM-4:30PM. www.NMMINM.US. Enrollment: 850. Records go back to 1885. Alumni records are maintained here. Degrees granted: Associate. Attendance and degree information available by phone, fax, mail. Transcripts available by mail.

New Mexico State University, Registrar, Box 30001, Dept 3AR, Las Cruces, NM 88003, 505-646-3411 (Fax: 505-646-6330) 8AM-5PM. www.nmsu.edu. Records go back to 1960. Alumni records are maintained here. Degrees granted: Associate; Bachelors; Masters; Doctorate. Attendance and degree information available by phone, fax, mail. Transcripts available by mail.

New Mexico State University at Alamogordo, Registrar, 2400 N Scenic Dr, PO Box 477, Alamogordo, NM 88310, http://abcc.nmsu.edu. 505-439-3600 (Fax: 505-439-3760) Records are located at New Mexico State University, Registrar, Las Cruces, NM.

New Mexico State University at Carlsbad, Registrar, 1500 University Dr, Carlsbad, NM 88220, 505-885-8831, 505-234-9222 (Fax: 505-885-4951). 8AM-5PM. Records go back to 1950. Alumni records maintained here; call 505-646-3616. Degrees granted: Associate. Attendance and degree information available by phone, fax, mail. Transcripts available by fax, mail.

New Mexico State University at Grants, Registrar, 1500 3rd St, Grants, NM 87020, www.nmsu.edu. 505-287-7981 (Fax: 505-287-2329) Records are located at New Mexico State University, Registrar, Las Cruces, NM.

Northern New Mexico Community College, Registrar, 1002 N Onate St, Espanola, NM 87532, 505-747-2193 (Fax: 505-747-2180). 8AM-5PM M,Th,F; 8AM-6PM T,Th. Enrollment: 2200. Records go back to 1970. Alumni records maintained here; call 505-747-2130. Degrees granted: Associate. Attendance and degree information available by fax, mail. Transcripts available by mail.

Parks College, Registrar, 1023 Tijeras Ave NW, Albuquerque, NM 87102, 505-843-7500, 505-843-7500 (Fax: 505-242-1986). 8AM-9:30PM. Enrollment: 250. Records go back to 1978. Degrees granted: Associate. Attendance and degree information available by phone, mail. Transcripts available by written request only.

Pima Medical Institute (Branch), Registrar, 2201 San Pedro Dr NE Bldg 3 Ste 100, Albuquerque, NM 87110, 505-881-1234 (Fax: 505-884-8371). Records go back to 1985. Attendance and degree information available by phone, mail. Transcripts available by mail.

San Juan College, Records Office, 4601 College Blvd, Farmington, NM 87402, 505-599-0320, 505-599-0510 (Fax: 505-599-0500) 8AM-5PM. www.sjc.cc.nm.us. Enrollment: 4700. Records go back to 1972.

Degrees granted: Associate. Attendance, degree and transcript information available by mail.

Santa Fe Community College, Registrar, PO Box 4187, Santa Fe, NM 87502-4187, 505-428-1000 (Fax: 505-438-1237). 8AM-5PM. Enrollment: 5500. Records go back to 1983. Degrees granted: Associate. Attendance, degree and transcript information available by mail.

Southwest Acupuncture College (Branch Campus), Registrar, 4308 Carlisle Blvd NE Ste 205, Albuquerque, NM 87107, 505-888-8898 www.swacupuncture.com. (Fax: 505-888-1380) Records are located at Southwest Acupuncture College, Registrar, Santa Fe, NM.

Southwest Acupuncture College, Registrar, 325 Paseo De Peralta #500, Santa Fe, NM 87501, 505-438-8884 (Fax: 505-438-8885) www.swacupuncture.com. 9AM - 5PM. Enrollment: 190. Records go back to 1981. Degrees granted: Masters. Attendance and degree information available by phone, fax, mail. Transcripts available by fax, mail.

Southwestern Indian Polytechnic Institute, Registrar, 9169 Coors Rd NW, Box 10146, Albuquerque, NM 87184, http://kafka.sipi.tec.nm.us/homepage.html. 505-897-5346 (Fax: 505-897-5320) 8AM - 4:30PM. Enrollment: 600. Records go back to 1971. Degrees granted: Associate. Attendance information available by phone, fax, mail. Degree information available by phone, fax. Transcripts available by mail.

St. John's College, Registrar, Santa Fe, NM 87501-4599, 505-984-6075, 505-984-6000 (Fax: 505-984-6003) www.sjca.edu.

9AM-5PM. Enrollment: 470. Records go back to 1964. Alumni records maintained here; call 505-984-6103. Degrees granted: Bachelors; Masters. Attendance and degree information available by phone, fax, mail. Transcripts available by mail.

University of Albuquerque, Records Office, Student Service Center, Room 250, Albuquerque, NM 87131, 505-277-2916, 505-277-6820 (Fax: 505-277-6809) 8AM-5PM. www.http://www/unm/edu. Enrollment: 24000. Records go back to 1889. Alumni Records: Hodgin Hall 1st Flr, Albuquerque, NM 87131. Degrees granted: Bachelors; Masters; Doctorate. Attendance and degree information available by phone, fax, mail. Transcripts available by fax, mail.

University of New Mexico, Records Office, Student Services Ctr Rm 250, Albuquerque, NM 87131-2039, 505-277-2917 (Fax: 505-277-6809) www.unm.edu. 8AM - 5PM. Enrollment: 25000. Records go back to 1889. Alumni records maintained here; call 505-277-5808. Degrees granted: Associate; Bachelors; Masters; Doctorate. Special programs- Law School: Medical School. Attendance and degree information available by phone, fax, mail. Transcripts available by fax, mail.

University of New Mexico (Gallup Branch), Registrar, 200 College Rd, Gallup, NM 87301, 505-863-7623, 505-863-7623 (Fax: 505-863-7610). Records are located at University of New Mexico, Records Office, Albuquerque, NM.

University of New Mexico (Los Alamos Branch), Registrar, 4000 University Dr, Los Alamos, NM 87544, 505-662-5919. Records

are located at University of New Mexico, Records Office, Albuquerque, NM.

University of New Mexico (Valencia Branch), Registrar, 280 La Entrada, Los Lunas, NM 87031, 505-925-8500, 505-925-8580 (Fax: 505-925-8501). Records are located at University of New Mexico, Records Office, Albuquerque, NM.

University of Phoenix (Albuquerque Main), Registrar, 7471 Pan American Fwy NE, Albuquerque, NM 87109, 505-927-0099, 505-821-4800 (Fax: 505-894-1758). 8AM-6PM. Enrollment: 1550. Records go back to 1986. Alumni Records: 4615 E Elwood St, Phoenix, AZ 85040. Degrees granted: Associate; Bachelors; Masters. Attendance and degree information available by phone, fax, mail. Transcript records are housed at University of Phoenix, Registrar, PO Box 52069, Phoenix, AZ 85072.

Western New Mexico University, Registrar, PO Box 680, 1000 W College Ave, Silver City, NM 88062, 505-538-6118 (Fax: 505-538-6155) www.wnmu.edu. 8AM-4:30PM. Enrollment: 2500. Records go back to 1910. Alumni records maintained here; call 505-538-6336. Degrees granted: Associate; Bachelors; Masters. Attendance and degree information available by phone, fax, mail. Transcripts available by fax, mail.

New York

Academy of Aeronautics
(See College of Aeronautics)

Adelphi University, Registrar, South Ave, Garden City, NY 11530, 516-877-3300 (Fax: 516-877-3326) www.adelphi.edu. 8:30AM-7PM M-Th; 8:30AM-4:30PM F. Records go back to 1898. Degrees granted: Associate; Bachelors; Masters; Doctorate. Attendance and degree information available by phone, mail. Transcripts available by mail.

Adirondack Community College, Registrar, Bay Road, Queensbury, NY 12804, 518-743-2280 (Fax: 518-745-1433). 8AM-5PM. Enrollment: 3600. Records go back to 1962. Alumni records are maintained. Degrees granted: Associate. Special programs- OTA: PTA: Nursing. Attendance and degree information available by phone, fax, mail. Transcripts available by mail.

Albany Business College
(See Bryant and Stratton)

Albany College of Pharmacy of Union University, Registrar, 106 New Scotland Ave, Albany, NY 12208, panther.acp.edu 518-445-7200, 518-445-7221 (Fax: 518-445-7202) 8:30AM - 4:30PM. Enrollment: 700. Records go back to 1881. Alumni records maintained here; call 518-445-7305. Degrees granted: Bachelors; PharmD. Attendance and degree information available by phone, fax, mail. Transcripts available by written request only.

Albany Law School, Registrar, 80 New Scotland Ave, Albany, NY 12208, 518-445-2330 (Fax: 518-445-2320). 8:30AM - 4:30PM. Enrollment: 710. Records go back to

1930. Alumni records maintained here; call 518-462-5516. Degrees granted: Doctorate. Attendance and degree information available by phone, fax, mail. Transcripts available by mail.

Albany Medical College of Union University, Registrar, 47 New Scotland Ave, Albany, NY 12208, 518-262-4970 (Fax: 518-262-6515). 8AM-4PM. Enrollment: 169. Records go back to 1839. Alumni records maintained here; call 518-262-5970 Ext. 5033. Degrees granted: Masters; Doctorate. Attendance, degree and transcript information available by mail.

Alfred University, Registrar, Saxon Dr, Alfred, NY 14802, 607-871-2122 (Fax: 607-871-2347) www.alfred.edu. 8:30AM-4:30PM. Enrollment: 2300. Records go back to 1925. Alumni records maintained here; call 607-871-2144. Degrees granted: Masters; Doctorate; Ph.D. Attendance and degree information available by phone, fax, mail. Transcripts available by fax, mail.

American Academy McAllister Institute of Funeral Service, Inc., Registrar, 450 W 56th St, New York, NY 10019, 212-757-1190 (Fax: 212-765-5923) 9AM-3:30PM. Enrollment: 135. Records go back to 1930. Degrees granted: Associate. Attendance and degree information available by mail. Transcripts available by fax, mail.

American Academy of Dramatic Arts, Registrar, 120 Madison Ave, New York, NY 10016, 212-686-0250, 212-686-9244 (Fax: 212-545-7934). 9AM-2PM, 3-5PM. Records go back to 1885. Degrees granted: Associate.

Attendance, degree and transcript information available by fax, mail.

Associated Beth Rivkah Schools, Registrar, 310 Crown St, Brooklyn, NY 11225, 718-735-0414 (Fax: 718-735-0422) 8:30AM-4:30PM. Enrollment: 100. Records go back to 1964. Alumni records are maintained here. Degrees granted: Judaic Teacher Training. Attendance, degree and transcript information available by mail.

Audrey Cohen College, Registrar, 345 Hudston St, New York, NY 10014-4598, 212-343-1234, 212-343-1234 Ext. 3702 (Fax: 212-343-7399) www.audrey-cohen.edu. 9AM-6PM M,W; 9AM-7PM T,Th; 9AM-5PM F. Enrollment: 1200. Records go back to 1964. Alumni records maintained here; call 212-343-1234 Ext. 3202. Degrees granted: Bachelors; Masters. Attendance and degree information available by fax, mail. Transcripts available by mail. Authorization needed.

Bank Street College of Education, Registrar, 610 W 112th St, New York, NY 10025, 212-875-4407, 212-875-4406 (Fax: 212-875-4677) www.bnkst.edu. 9AM - 5PM. Enrollment: 900. Records go back to 1919. Alumni records maintained here; call 212-875-4606. Degrees granted: Masters. Attendance and degree information available by fax, mail. Transcripts available by mail. Transcripts released only at request of person whose record is requested.

Bard College, Registrar, Annandale-On-Hudson, NY 12504, 914-758-7458 (Fax: 914-758-7036) www.bard.edu. 9AM-5PM. Enrollment: 1000. Records go back to 1940.

Alumni records maintained here; call 914-758-7407. Degrees granted: Bachelors; MA, MFA. Attendance and degree information available by phone, fax, mail. Transcripts available by fax, mail.

Barnard College, Registrar, 3009 Broadway, New York, NY 10027-6598, www.barnard.columbia.edu 212-854-2011 (Fax: 212-854-9470) 9:30AM - 4:30PM. Enrollment: 2200. Records go back to 1892. Alumni records maintained here; call 212-854-2005. Degrees granted: Bachelors. Attendance and degree information available by phone, fax, mail. Transcripts available by mail.

Berkeley College, Registrar, W Red Oak Lane, White Plains, NY 10604, 201-652-1346 (Fax: 201-670-7737) www.berkeley.org. Records are located at Berkeley College, (Waldwick Campus), Registrar, 100 W Prospect St, Waldwick, NJ 07463.

Berkeley College of New York, Registrar, 3 E 43rd St, New York, NY 10017, 212-986-4343 (Fax: 212-697-3371) www.berkeley.org. Records are located at Berkeley College, (Waldwick Campus), Registrar, 100 W Prospect St, Waldwick, NJ 07463.

Berkeley School — Hicksville
(See Berkeley Colleges)

Bernard M. Baruch College, Registrar, 17 Lexington Ave, New York, NY 10010, 212-802-2182, 212-802-2185 (Fax: 212-802-2190). 9:15AM-7PM M-Th; 9:15AM-4:45PM F. Records go back to 1920. Alumni records maintained here; call 212-8002-2900. Degrees granted: Bachelors; Masters. Attendance, degree and transcript information available by fax, mail.

Beth HaTalmud Rabbinical College, Registrar, 2127 82nd St, Brooklyn, NY 11214, 718-259-2525. 9AM - 2PM. Records go back to 1990. Attendance and degree information available by phone, fax, mail. Transcripts available by mail.

Beth Hamedrash Shaarei Yosher, Registrar, 4102 16th Ave, Brooklyn, NY 11204, 718-854-2290. 8AM-5PM. Records go back to 1957. Alumni records are maintained here. Degrees granted: Bachelors; Masters; Doctorate; Talmudic 1st and 2nd. Attendance and degree information available by phone, mail. Transcripts available by mail.

Beth Israel School of Nursing
(See Phillips Beth Israel School of Nursing)

Beth Jacob Hebrew Teachers College, Registrar, 1213 Elm Ave, Brooklyn, NY 11230, 718-339-4747 (Fax: 718-998-5766). 9AM-5PM. Alumni records are maintained here. Degrees granted: Bachelors. Attendance and degree information available by phone, fax, mail. Transcripts available by fax, mail.

Beth Medrash Eeyun Hatalmud, Registrar, 14 Fred Eller Dr, Monsey, NY 10952, 914-356-0477 (Fax: 914-356-7867). Enrollment: 120. Attendance and degree information available by fax, mail. Transcripts available by mail.

Boricua College, Registrar, 3755 Broadway, New York, NY 10032, 212-694-1000 (Fax: 212-694-1015). 9:30AM-8PM. Records go back to 1976. Degrees granted: Associate; Bachelors. Attendance and degree information available by fax, mail. Transcripts available by mail.

Borough of Manhattan Community College, Registrar, 199 Chambers St, New York, NY 10007, 212-346-8201 (Fax: 212-346-8110) www.bmcc.cuny.edu. 8:30AM-7PM M-Th; 8:30AM-Noon F. Enrollment: 16500. Records go back to 1964. Alumni records maintained here; call 212-346-8807. Degrees granted: Associate. Attendance, degree and transcript information available by mail.

Bramson Ort Technical Institute, Registrar, 69-30 Austin St, Forest Hills, NY 11375, 718-261-5800 (Fax: 718-575-5120). Degrees granted. Attendance, degree and transcript information available by fax, mail.

Briarcliffe College, Registrar, 1055 Stewart Ave, Beta Page, NY 11714, 516-470-6000 Ext. 435 (Fax: 516-470-6020) www.bcl.edu. 9AM - 8PM M-Th; 9AM - 5PM F. Enrollment: 1243. Records go back to 1966. Formerly **Briarcliffe School, Inc.** Degrees granted: Associate. Attendance and degree information available by phone, fax, mail. Transcripts available by written request only.

Briarcliffe School, Inc. (Branch Campus), Registrar, 10 Lake St, Patchogue, NY 11772, 516-654-5300 (Fax: 516-654-5082). Records are located at Briarcliffe College, Registrar, Beta Page, NY.

Briarcliffe Secretarial School
(See The College for Business)

Bronx Community College, Registrar, W 181st St and University Ave, Bronx, NY 10453, 718-289-5712 (Fax: 718-289-6308). 9AM-5PM. Records go back to 1960. Degrees granted: Associate. Attendance and degree information available by phone, mail. Transcripts available by mail.

Brooklyn College, Registrar, 2900 Bedford Ave, Brooklyn, NY 11210-2889, 718-951-5693 146.245.2.151. 10AM-4:30PM. Records go back to 1931. Alumni records maintained here; call 718-951-5000 Ext. 5065. Degrees granted: Bachelors; Masters. Attendance, degree and transcript information available by mail.

Brooklyn Law School, Registrar, 250 Joralemon St, Brooklyn, NY 11201, 718-780-7913 (Fax: 718-780-7548). 9AM-5PM M,W-F; 8AM-6PM T. Records go back to 1901. Alumni records maintained here; call 718-780-7966. Attendance and degree information available by phone, fax, mail. Transcripts available by mail.

Broome Community College, Registrar, Upper Front St, PO Box 1017, Binghamton, NY 13902, 607-778-5527 (Fax: 607-778-5294) www.sunybroome.edu. 9AM-5PM. Enrollment: 5800. Records go back to 1947. Alumni records are maintained here. Degrees granted: Associate. Attendance and degree information available by phone, fax, mail. Transcripts available by mail.

Bryant & Stratton Business Institute, Registrar, 1259 Central Ave, **Albany**, NY 12205, 518-437-1802, 716-884-8000 (Fax: 518-437-1048). 7:30AM-8PM. Enrollment: 500. Records go back to 1800's. Alumni records maintained here; call 518-437-1802. Degrees granted: Associate. Attendance and degree information available by phone, fax, mail. Transcripts available by fax, mail.

Bryant & Stratton Business Institute, Registrar, 1028 Main St, **Buffalo**, NY 14202, 716-884-9120 (Fax: 716-884-0091) 7:30AM-9PM. www.bryantstratton.edu. Records go back to 1932. Alumni records are maintained here. Degrees granted: Associate. Attendance and degree information available by phone, fax, mail. Transcripts available by fax, mail.

Bryant & Stratton Business Institute, Registrar, 1214 Abbott Rd, **Lackawanna**, NY 14218-1989, 716-821-9331, 716-884-8000 www.bryantstratton.edu. (Fax: 716-821-9343) 8AM-6PM M-Th; 9AM-5PM F. Enrollment: 381. Records go back to 1988. Alumni records maintained here; call 716-821-9331. Degrees granted: Associate. Attendance and degree information available by phone, fax, mail. Transcripts available by mail.

Bryant & Stratton Business Institute (North Campus), Registrar, 8687 Carling Rd, Liverpool, NY 13090, 315-652-6500 (Fax: 315-652-5500) www.bryantstratton.edu. 8AM-8PM M-Th; 8AM-5PM F. Enrollment: 369. Records go back to 1983. Alumni records are maintained here. Degrees granted: Associate. Attendance and degree information available by phone, fax, mail. Transcripts available by mail.

Bryant & Stratton Business Institute (Henrietta Campus), Registrar, 1225 Jefferson Rd, **Rochester**, NY 14623, www.bryantstratton.edu. 716-292-5627, 716-884-8000 (Fax: 716-292-6015) 7:30AM-8PM M-Th; 7:30AM-5PM F, 9AM-1PM S. Enrollment: 628. Records go back to 1985. Alumni records are maintained here. Degrees granted: Associate. Attendance and degree information available by phone, fax, mail. Transcripts available by mail.

Bryant & Stratton Business Institute, Registrar, 82 St Paul St, **Rochester**, NY 14604-1381, 716-325-6010 (Fax: 716-325-6805). 7:30AM-7PM. Enrollment: 265. Records go back to 1973. Alumni records maintained here; call 716-325-6010 Ext. 232. Degrees granted: Associate. Attendance and degree information available by phone, fax, mail. Transcripts available by mail.

Bryant & Stratton Business Institute, Registrar, 953 James St, **Syracuse**, NY 13203, 315-472-6603, 716-884-8000 (Fax: 315-474-4383) www.bryantstratton.edu. 8AM - 7PM. Enrollment: 537. Records go back to 1950. Alumni records are maintained here. Degrees granted: Associate. Attendance and degree information available by phone, fax, mail. Transcripts available by mail.

Bryant & Stratton Business Institute, Registrar, 200 Bryant and Stratton Way, **Williamsville**, NY 14221, 716-631-0260 Ext. 308 (Fax: 716-631-0273) 8AM-8:30PM. www.bryantstratton.edu. Records go back to 1988. Alumni records are maintained here. Degrees granted: Associate. Attendance, degree and transcript information available by fax, mail.

Canisius College, Registrar, 2001 Main St, Buffalo, NY 14208, 716-888-2990 (Fax: 716-888-2996) www.canisius.edu. 8:30AM-7PM M-Th; 8:30AM-5PM F. Enrollment: 4900. Records go back to 1940. Alumni records maintained here; call 716-888-2700. Degrees granted: Associate; Bachelors; Masters. Attendance and degree information available by phone, mail. Transcripts available by fax, mail.

Cayuga County Community College, Registrar, 197 Franklin St, Auburn, NY 13021, 315-255-1743 (Fax: 315-255-2117). 7:30AM-5PM. Enrollment: 2800. Records go back to 1954. Alumni records maintained here; call 315-255-1743 Ext. 224. Degrees granted: Associate. Attendance and degree information available by phone, fax, mail. Transcripts available by fax, mail.

Cazenovia College, Registrar, Seminary St, Cazenovia, NY 13035, 315-655-7225 (Fax: 315-655-2157) www.cazcollege.edu. 8:30AM-5PM. Enrollment: 850. Records go back to 1900. Alumni records maintained here; call 315-655-7367. Degrees granted:

Associate; Bachelors. Attendance and degree information available by phone, fax, mail. Transcripts available by mail.

Central Yeshiva Tomchei Tmimim-Lubavitch, Registrar, 841-853 Ocean Pkwy, Brooklyn, NY 11230, 718-774-3430. 9:30AM-5:30PM. Records go back to 1985. Alumni records maintained here; call 718-859-2277. Degrees granted: Associate. Attendance and degree information available by phone, mail. Transcripts available by mail.

Christ the King Seminary, Registrar, 711 Knox Rd, PO Box 607, East Aurora, NY 14052-0607, 716-652-8900 (Fax: 716-652-8903). 9AM-4PM. Enrollment: 110. Records go back to 1950, some destroyed. Alumni records are maintained here. Degrees granted: Masters. Attendance and degree information available by phone, fax, mail. Transcripts available by written request only.

City College, Registrar, Convent Ave at 138th St, New York, NY 10031, 212-650-7850 www.ccnyu.cuny.edu (Fax: 212-650-6108) 9AM-5PM M,Th,F; 9AM-6:30PM T,W. Enrollment: 14000. Records go back to 1910. Alumni records are maintained here. Degrees granted: Bachelors; Masters. Special programs- BBA Degrees at **Baruch College**, 212-447-3000. Attendance and degree information available by phone, fax, mail. Transcripts available by mail.

City University of Burough-Manhattan College,
(See Burough of Manhattan Com. College.)

City University of New York College, Registrar, 94-20 Guy R Brewer Blvd, Jamaica, NY 11451, 718-262-2145, 718-262-2146 (Fax: 718-262-2631) www.cuny.edu. Alumni records maintained here; call 718-262-2420. Degrees granted: Bachelors; Education Certifications. Attendance and degree information available by fax, mail. Transcripts available by mail.

City University of New York - John Jay College, Registrar, 445 W 59th St, New York, NY 10019, 212-237-8000 (Fax: 212-237-8777). Enrollment: 12000. Records go back to 1964. Alumni records maintained here; call 212-237-8547. Degrees granted: Masters. Attendance and degree information available by phone, fax, mail. Transcripts available by fax, mail.

Clarkson University, Student Admin. Services, Box 5575, Potsdam, NY 13699-5575, 315-268-6451 (Fax: 315-268-6452) 8AM-4:30PM. www.clarkson.edu. Enrollment: 2500. Records go back to 1900. Alumni Records: Box 5525, Potsdam, NY 13699-5525. Degrees granted: Bachelors; Masters; Doctorate. Attendance and degree information available by phone, fax, mail. Transcripts available by fax, mail.

Clinton Community College, Registrar, 136 Clifton Pt Dr, Plattsburgh, NY 12901, 518-562-4124 (Fax: 518-561-8621). 8AM-4PM. Enrollment: 1600. Records go back to 1976. Alumni records maintained here; call 518-562-4195. Degrees granted: Associate. Attendance and degree information available by phone, fax, mail. Transcripts available by mail.

Cochran School of Nursing-St Johns, Registrar, 967 N Broadway, Yonkers, NY 10701, 914-964-4283 (Fax: 914-964-4971). Enrollment: 110. Records go back to 1894. Alumni records are maintained here. Degrees granted: Associate. Attendance and degree information available by phone, fax, mail. Transcripts available by fax, mail.

Colgate Rochester Divinity School/ Bexley Hall / Crozer Theo. Sem., Registrar, 1100 S Goodman St, Rochester, NY 14620, 716-271-1320 Ext. 243 (Fax: 716-271-2166) www.crds.edu. 8AM-5PM. Records go back to 1817. Alumni records are maintained here. Degrees granted: Masters; Doctorate. Attendance and degree information available by phone, fax, mail. Transcripts available by mail.

Colgate University, Registrar, 13 Oak Dr, Hamilton, NY 13346, 315-228-7406, 315-228-7676 (Fax: 315-824-7125) www.colgate.edu. 8AM-4:30PM. Enrollment: 2800. Records go back to 1822. Alumni Records: Alumni Assoc., Colgate University, Merrill House, Hamilton, NY 13346. Degrees granted: Bachelors; Masters. Attendance and degree information available by phone, fax, mail. Transcripts available by fax, mail.

College for Human Services
(See Audrey Cohen College)

College of Aeronautics, Registrar, La Guardia Airport, 8601 23rd Ave, E Elmhurst, Flushing, NY 11369, 718-429-6600 (Fax: 718-429-0256) www.mordor.com/coa/coa. 9AM-5PM. Records go back to 1932. Alumni records maintained here; call 718-429-6600 Ext. 189. Degrees granted: Associate; Bachelors. Attendance and degree information available by phone, fax, mail. Transcripts available by fax, mail.

College of Insurance, Registrar, 101 Murray St, New York, NY 10007, 212-962-4111, 212-346-9366 (Fax: 212-732-5669). 9:30AM-5:30PM M-Th; 9AM-5PM F. Enrollment: 2500. Records go back to 1901. Alumni records maintained here; call 212-962-4111 Ext. 344. Degrees granted: Associate; Bachelors; Masters. Attendance, degree and transcript information available by fax, mail.

College of Mount St. Vincent, Registrar, 6301 Riverdale Ave, Riverdale, NY 10471, www.cmsv.edu. 718-405-3267 (Fax: 718-405-3448) 8:30AM - 4:30PM. Enrollment: 1500. Records go back to 1913. Alumni records maintained here; call 718-405-3334. Degrees granted: Associate; Bachelors; Masters. Special programs- Contact Vice Pres., 718-405-3252. Attendance and degree information available by phone, fax, mail. Transcripts available by mail.

College of New Rochelle (Co-op City Campus), Registrar, 950 Baychester Ave, Bronx, NY 10457, 718-320-0300 (Fax: 718-379-8633) www.cnr.edu. Records are located at College of New Rochelle, Registrar, New Rochelle, NY.

College of New Rochelle (South Bronx Campus), Registrar, 332 E 149th St, Bronx, NY 10451, 718-665-1310 www.cnr.edu Records are located at College of New Rochelle, Registrar, New Rochelle, NY.

College of New Rochelle (Brooklyn Campus), Registrar, 1368 Fulton St, Brooklyn, NY 11216, www.cnr.edu. 718-638-2500 (Fax: 718-230-4523) Records are located at College of New Rochelle, Registrar, New Rochelle, NY.

College of New Rochelle, Registrar, 29 Castle Pl, New Rochelle, NY 10805, 914-654-5214 (Fax: 914-654-5554) www.cnr.edu. 9AM-6PM. Enrollment: 7000. Records go back to 1904. Alumni records maintained here; call 914-654-5294. Degrees granted: Bachelors; Masters. Attendance and degree information available by phone, fax, mail. Transcripts available by mail.

College of New Rochelle (DC 37 Campus), Registrar, 125 Barclay St, New York, NY 10007, 212-815-1710 (Fax: 212-349-4089) www.cnr.edu. Records are located at College of New Rochelle, Registrar, New Rochelle, NY.

College of New Rochelle (New York Theological Seminary Campus), Registrar, 5 W 29th St, New York, NY 10001, 212-689-6208 www.cnr.edu. Records are located at College of New Rochelle, Registrar, New Rochelle, NY.

College of New Rochelle (Rosa Parks Campus), Registrar, 144 W 125th St, New York, NY 10024, www.cnr.edu 212-662-7500 Records are located at College of New Rochelle, Registrar, New Rochelle, NY.

College of St. Rose, Registrar, 432 Western Ave, Albany, NY 12203, 518-454-5213, 518-454-5211 (Fax: 518-454-2100). 9:30AM-2:30PM, 3:30-6PM M-Th; 9:30AM-4:30PM F. Enrollment: 4000. Records go back to 1920. Alumni records maintained here; call 518-454-5105. Degrees granted: Bachelors; Masters. Attendance and degree information available by phone, fax, mail. Transcripts available by mail.

College of Staten Island, Registrar, 2800 Victory Blvd, Staten Island, NY 10314, 718-982-2121 www.csi.cuny.edu. 9AM - 5PM. Enrollment: 12512. Records go back to 1955. Alumni records maintained here; call 718-982-2290. Degrees granted: Associate; Bachelors; Masters. Attendance, degree and transcript information available by mail.

Columbia University, Registrar, 1150 Amsterdam Ave, New York, NY 10027, 212-854-1458 www.columia.edu. 9AM - 5PM. Records go back to 1754. Alumni records maintained here; call 212-870-2535. Degrees granted: Associate; Bachelors; Masters; Doctorate. Attendance, degree and transcript information available by mail.

Columbia University Teachers College, Registrar, 525 W 120th St, New York, NY 10027, 212-678-4065 (Fax: 212-678-4048). 8AM-5PM. Records go back to 1898. Alumni records are maintained here. Degrees granted: Masters; Doctorate. Attendance and degree information available by phone, fax, mail. Transcripts available by mail.

Columbia-Greene Community College, Registrar, 4400 Route 23, Hudson, NY 12534, 518-828-4181 (Fax: 518-828-8543) 8AM-5PM. www.sunyegcc.edu. Enrollment: 1660. Records go back to 1969. Degrees granted: Associate. Attendance and degree information available by phone, fax, mail. Transcripts available by fax, mail.

Concordia College, Registrar, 171 White Plains Rd, Bronxville, NY 10708-1998, 914-337-9300 Ext. 2103 (Fax: 914-395-4500). 9AM-5PM. Enrollment: 600. Records go back to 1881. Alumni records maintained here; call 914-337-9300 Ext. 2167. Degrees granted: Associate; Bachelors. Special programs- Accelerated Degree Program, 914-337-9300 Ext. 2142: Attendance and degree information available by phone, fax, mail. Transcripts available by fax, mail.

Cooper Union for the Advancement of Science and Art, Registrar, 30 Cooper Square, New York, NY 10003, 212-353-4124, 212-353-4120 (Fax: 212-353-4343) 9AM-4:30PM. www.cooper.edu. Enrollment: 883. Records go back to 1859. Alumni records maintained here; call 212-3534175. Degrees granted: Bachelors; Masters. Attendance and degree information available

by phone, fax, mail. Transcripts available by fax, mail.

Cornell University, Registrar, 222 Day Hall, Ithaca, NY 14853, www.cornell.edu/ 607-255-4232 (Fax: 607-255-6262) Enrollment: 19000. Records go back to 1800. Alumni records are maintained here. Degrees granted: Bachelors; Masters; PhD. Attendance and degree information available by phone, fax, mail. Transcripts available by fax, mail.

Cornell University Medical College, Registrar, 1300 York Ave Rm C-118, New York, NY 10021, 212-746-1056 (Fax: 212-746-5981) Enrollment: 400. Records go back to 1895. Alumni records are maintained here r. Degrees granted: Doctorate; PhD. Attendance, degree and transcript information available by fax, mail.

Cornell University School of Medical Sciences, Registrar, 445 E 69th St, Room 412, New York, NY 10021, 212-746-6565 (Fax: 212-746-8906). Enrollment: 230. Records go back to 1912. Alumni records are maintained here. Degrees granted: Doctorate. Special programs- Medical Science PhD. Attendance and degree information available by phone, fax, mail. Transcripts available by fax, mail.

Corning Community College, Registrar, 1 Academic Dr, Corning, NY 14830-3297, 607-962-9230 (Fax: 607-962-9456). 8AM-5PM M-Th; 8AM - 4PM F. Enrollment: 5100. Records go back to 1956. Alumni records maintained here; call 607-962-9320. Degrees granted: Associate. Attendance and degree information available by phone, fax, mail. Transcripts available by mail.

Culinary Institute of America, Registrar, PO Box 53 N Rd, Hyde Park, NY 12538, www.culinary.edu. 914-452-9600 Ext. 1347, 914-452-9600 Ext. 1267 (Fax: 914-451-1058) Enrollment: 2065. Alumni records maintained here; call 914-452-9600 Ext. 1401. Degrees granted: Associate; Bachelors. Attendance and degree information available by phone, fax, mail. Transcripts available by mail.

D'Youville College, Registrar, 320 Porter Ave, Buffalo, NY 14201, 716-881-7626 (Fax: 716-881-7790). 8:30AM - 4:30PM. Enrollment: 1900. Records go back to 1908. Alumni Records: 631 Niagara St, Buffalo, NY 14201. Degrees granted: Bachelors; Masters. Attendance and degree information available by phone, fax, mail. Transcripts available by fax, mail.

Daemen College, Registrar, 4380 Main St, Amherst, NY 14226-3592, 716-839-8214 (Fax: 716-839-8343) www.daemen.edu. 8:30AM - 4:30PM. Enrollment: 2150. Records go back to 1947. Alumni records maintained here; call 716-839-8555. Degrees granted: Bachelors; Masters. Attendance and degree information available by phone, fax, mail. Transcripts available by fax, mail.

Darkei No'am Rabbinical College, Registrar, 2822 Ave J, Brooklyn, NY 11210, 718-338-6464 (Fax: 718-338-0622). 9AM-4PM. Enrollment: 50. Records go back to 1978. Degrees granted: Bachelors. Attendance, degree and transcript information available by fax, mail.

Derech Ayson Rabbinical Seminary, Registrar, 802 Hicksville Rd, Far Rockaway, NY 11691, 718-327-7600 (Fax: 718-327-1430). Enrollment: 150. Records go back to 1975. Attendance and degree information available by phone, fax, mail. Transcripts available by fax, mail.

Dominican College of Blauvelt, Registrar, 470 Western Hwy, Orangeburg, NY 10962, 914-359-7800, 201-476-0600 (Fax: 914-359-2313) www.dc.edu. 8:30AM-5PM. Enrollment: 1720. Records go back to 1964. Alumni records are maintained here. Degrees granted: Associate; Bachelors; Masters. Special programs- Call 914-359-7800. Attendance and degree information available by phone, fax, mail. Transcripts available by written request only.

Dover Technical School, Registrar, 3075 Veterans Memorial Highway, Ronkonkoma, NY 11779, 516-471-9100 (Fax: 516-471-9144). 8AM-5PM. Enrollment: 400. Records go back to 1997. Certification: Technical; Other: Diploma. Attendance and degree information available by phone, mail. Transcripts available by mail.

Dowling College, Registrar, Idle Hour Blvd, Oakdale, NY 11769-1999, 516-244-3250 (Fax: 516-563-4754) www.dowling.edu. 8AM-8PM M-Th; 9AM-5PM F; 9AM-2PM Sat. Enrollment: 6000. Records go back to 1970. Alumni records maintained here; call 516-244-3106. Degrees granted: Bachelors; Masters. Attendance and degree information available by fax, mail. Transcripts available by fax, mail.

Dutchess Community College (Branch Campus), Registrar, 53 Pendell Rd, Poughkeepsie, NY 12601-1595, 914-431-8000 www.sunydutchess.edu (Fax: 914-431-8983) 8AM-9PM M-Th; 8AM-5PM F. Enrollment: 7025. Records go back to 1957. Degrees granted: Associate. Attendance, degree and transcript information available by fax, mail.

Dutchess Community College, Registrar, 53 Pendell Rd, Poughkeepsie, NY 12601-1595, www.sunydutchess.edu. 914-431-8000 (Fax: 914-431-8983) 8AM-9PM. Records go back to 1957. Alumni records maintained here; call 914-471-4500. Degrees granted: Associate. Attendance and degree information available by fax, mail. Transcripts available by mail.

Dutchess Community College (South Campus), Registrar, Hollowbrook Park, Wappingers Falls, NY 12590, 914-298-0755 www.sunydutchess.edu. Records are located at Dutchess Community College, Registrar Poughkeepsie, NY.

Elmira College, Registrar, 1 Park Place, Elmira, NY 14901, 607-735-1895, 607-735-4895 (Fax: 607-735-1759) www.elmira.edu. 8AM-5PM. Enrollment: 2000. Records go back to 1855. Alumni records maintained here; call 607-735-1855. Degrees granted: Associate; Bachelors; Masters. Special programs- JVA Washington Semester, 607-735-1703. Attendance and degree information available by phone, fax, mail. Transcripts available by fax, mail.

Erie Community College City Campus, Registrar, 121 Ellicott St, Buffalo, NY 14203, davey.sunyerie.edu. 716-851-1166 (Fax: 716-851-1129) 8AM-6PM M,T; 8AM-4PM W-F. Enrollment: 3200. Records go back to 1971. Alumni Records: 4041 Southwestern Blvd, Orchard Park, NY 14127-2155. Degrees granted: Associate. Special programs-Alcohol Counseling Technician. Attendance and degree information available by phone, fax, mail. Transcripts available by mail.

Erie Community College North Campus (Amherst), Registrar, 6205 Main St, Williamsville, NY 14221, 716-851-1467, 716-851-1468 www.sunyerie.edu (Fax: 716-851-1429) 8AM-4PM M,Th,F; 8AM-6PM T,W. Enrollment: 6000. Records go back to 1950. Alumni records maintained here; call 716-851-1002. Degrees granted: Associate. Attendance and degree information available by phone, fax, mail. Transcripts available by mail.

Erie Community College South Campus, Registrar, 4041 Southwestern Blvd, Orchard Park, NY 14127-2199, 716-851-1668, 716-851-1667 (Fax: 716-851-1670). 8AM-4PM; 4-8PM W. Enrollment: 3500. Records go back to 1985. Alumni records maintained here; call 716-851-1663. Degrees granted: Associate. Attendance information available by phone, fax, mail. Transcripts available by fax, mail.

Farmingdale State University (See State University of New York-College of Tech at Farmingdale)

Fashion Institute of Technology, Registrar, Seventh Ave at 27th St, New York, NY 10001-5992, 212-217-7676 (Fax: 212-217-7481). 10AM - 4PM. Records go back to 1945. Alumni records maintained here; call 212-217-7158. Degrees granted: Associate; Bachelors; Masters. Attendance and degree information available by phone, fax, mail. Transcripts available by mail.

Finger Lakes Community College, Registrar, 4355 Lakeshore Dr, Canandaigua, NY 14424, 716-394-3500 Ext. 290 (Fax: 716-394-5005). 8:30AM-5PM. Records go back to 1968. Alumni records are maintained here. Degrees granted: Associate. Attendance and degree information available by phone, fax, mail. Transcripts available by mail.

Five Towns College, Registrar, 305 N Service Rd, Dix Hills, NY 11746-6055, 516-424-7000 (Fax: 516-424-7006). 8AM-6PM M-Th, 8AM-4PM F. Enrollment: 600. Records go back to 1974. Alumni records are maintained here. Degrees granted: Associate; Bachelors. Attendance and degree information available by phone, mail. Transcripts available by written request only.

Fordham University, Registrar, E Fordham Rd, Bronx, NY 10458, 718-817-3901 (Fax: 718-817-3921) www.fordham.edu. 9AM-4:45PM. Enrollment: 14000. Records go back to 1918. Alumni Records: 113 W 60th, New York, NY 10023. Degrees granted: Bachelors; Masters. Attendance and degree information available by phone, fax, mail. Transcripts available by fax, mail.

Friends World at Long Island University, Registrar, 239 Montauk Hwy, South Hampton, NY 11968, 516-287-8329 (Fax: 516-287-8463) www.livnet.edu. Records go back to 1965. Alumni records are maintained here. Degrees granted: Bachelors. Attendance and degree information available by phone, fax, mail. Transcripts available by written request only.

Fulton-Montgomery Community College, Registrar, Rte 67, Johnstown, NY 12095, 518-762-4651 Ext. 222 (Fax: 518-762-4334). 8AM-4PM. Enrollment: 1750. Records go back to 1964. Alumni records are maintained here. Degrees granted: Associate. Attendance and degree information available by phone, fax, mail. Transcripts available by written request only.

General Theological Seminary, Registrar, 175 Ninth Ave, New York, NY 10011-4977, 212-243-5150, 212-243-5150 Ext. 235 (Fax: 212-727-3907). 8:30AM-5PM. Enrollment: 120. Records go back to 1920. Alumni records are maintained here. Degrees granted: Masters; Ph.D. Attendance and degree information available by phone, fax, mail. Transcripts available by mail.

Genesee Community College, Registrar, One College Rd, Batavia, NY 14020, www.sunygenesee.cc.ny.us 716-343-0055 Ext. 6218, 716-343-0055 Ext. 6486 (Fax: 716-343-6810) 8AM-6:30PM M-Th; 8AM-4:30PM F; 8:30-10:30AM S. Records go back to 1967. Alumni records maintained here; call 716-343-0055-X6262. Degrees granted: Associate. Attendance and degree information available by mail. Transcripts available by fax, mail.

Graduate School and University Center, Registrar, 33 W 42nd St, New York, NY 10036, 212-642-1600 (Fax: 212-642-2779). 9AM-5PM. Records go back to 1961. Alumni records maintained here; call 212-642-2850. Degrees granted: Masters; Ph.D. Attendance and degree information available by phone, fax, mail. Transcripts available by fax, mail.

Hadar Hatorah Rabbinical Seminary, Registrar, 824 Eastern Pkwy, Brooklyn, NY 11213, 718-735-0250 (Fax: 718-735-4455). Enrollment: 300. Records go back to 1964. Alumni records are maintained here. Degrees granted: Bachelors. Attendance, degree and transcript information available by mail.

Hamilton College, Registrar, 198 College Hill Rd, Clinton, NY 13323, 315-859-4637 (Fax: 315-859-4632) www.hamilton.edu. 8:30AM-4:30PM. Enrollment: 1650. Records go back to 1810. Alumni records maintained here; call 315-859-4412. Degrees granted: Bachelors. Attendance and degree information available by phone, fax, mail. Transcripts available by fax, mail. Transcript request must include signature.

Hartwick College, Registrar, Oneonta, NY 13820, 607-431-4460 (Fax: 607-431-4006) 9AM-5PM. www.hartwick.edu. Enrollment: 1500. Records go back to 1928. Alumni records maintained here; call 607-431-4010. Degrees granted: Bachelors. Attendance and degree information available by phone, fax, mail. Transcripts available by fax, mail.

Health Science Center at Brooklyn
(See State University of New York)

Hebrew Union College — Jewish Institute of Religion, Registrar, One W Fourth St, New York, NY 10012, 212-674-5300, 212-674-5300 Ext. 220 (Fax: 212-388-1720). 8:30AM-5:30PM. Enrollment: 150. Records go back to 1883. Alumni Records: 3101 Clifton Ave, Cincinnati, OH 45220. Degrees granted: Masters; Doctorate. Special programs- Hebrew Union College, Cincinnati, 513-221-1875. Attendance and degree information available by phone, fax, mail. Transcripts available by mail.

Helene Fuld School of Nursing, Registrar, 1879 Madison Ave, New York, NY 10035, 212-423-1000 Ext. 238 (Fax: 212-427-2453). 8AM-4PM. Records go back to 1946. Alumni records maintained here; call 212-423-1000 Ext. 216. Degrees granted: Associate. Attendance and degree information available by phone, fax, mail. Transcripts available by mail.

Herkimer County Community College, Registrar, Reservoir Rd, Herkimer, NY 13350, 315-866-0300 Ext. 280 (Fax: 315-866-7253) www.hccc.ntenet.com. 8AM-4PM. Enrollment: 2300. Records go back to 1968. Alumni records maintained here; call 315-866-0300 Ext. 259. Degrees granted: Associate. Attendance and degree information available by phone, fax, mail. Transcripts available by fax, mail.

Hilbert College, Director of Student Services, 5200 S Park Ave, Hamburg, NY 14075-1597, 716-649-7900 (Fax: 716-649-0702) www.hilbert.edu. 8:30AM-5PM. Enrollment: 800. Records go back to 1957. Alumni records are maintained here. Degrees granted: Associate; Bachelors. Attendance and degree information available by phone, fax, mail. Transcripts available by fax, mail.

Hobart & William Smith College, Registrar, Geneva, NY 14456, 315-781-3651 (Fax: 315-781-3920) http://hws3.hws.edu. 9AM-4PM. Enrollment: 1740. Records go back to 1908. Alumni records maintained here; call 315-781-3700. Degrees granted: Bachelors. Attendance and degree information available by phone, fax, mail. Transcripts available by fax, mail.

Hofstra University, Office of Financial and Academic Records, Room 126, Hempstead, NY 1149-1260, 516-463-6680 (Fax: 516-463-4936) www.hofstra.edu. 9AM-8PM M-Th; 9AM-5PM F. Enrollment: 12056. Records go back to 1936. Alumni records maintained here; call 516-463-6636. Degrees granted: Bachelors; Masters; Doctorate; Professional Diplomas. Attendance and degree information available by phone, fax, mail. Transcripts available by fax, mail.

Holy Trinity Orthodox Seminary, Registrar, PO Box 36, Jordanville, NY 13361, 315-858-0945 (Fax: 315-858-0945). Enrollment: 40. Records go back to 1948. Alumni records are maintained here. Degrees granted: Bachelors. Special programs-Theological Studies Conducted in Russian Language. Attendance and degree information available by phone, mail. Transcripts available by mail.

Hostos Community College, Registrar, 475 Grand Concourse, Bronx, NY 10451, 718-518-6771 (Fax: 718-518-4260). 11AM-7PM. Records go back to 1970. Alumni records maintained here; call 718-518-4306. Degrees granted: Associate. Attendance and degree information available by phone, fax, mail. Transcripts available by mail.

Houghton College, Registrar, Houghton, NY 14744, 716-567-9350 (Fax: 716-567-9572) www.houghton.edu. 8AM-5PM. Records go back to 1883. Alumni records maintained here; call 716-567-9456. Degrees granted: Bachelors. Attendance and degree information available by phone, fax, mail. Transcripts available by mail.

Houghton College (Buffalo Suburban Campus), Registrar, 910 Union Rd, West Seneca, NY 14224, 716-674-6363 (Fax: 716-674-6363 Ext. 764). Records are located at Houghton College, Registrar, Houghton, NY.

Hudson Valley Community College, Registrar, 80 Vandenburgh Ave, Troy, NY 12180, 518-270-1569, 518-283-1100 (Fax: 999-999-9999) www.hvcc.edu. 8AM-5PM. Enrollment: 10000. Records go back to 1988. Alumni records maintained here; call 518-270-7556. Degrees granted: Associate. Attendance and degree information available by phone, mail. Transcripts available by mail.

Hunter College, Registrar, 695 Park Ave, New York, NY 10021, 212-772-4500. 10AM-6PM. Records go back to 1906. Alumni records are maintained here also. Call 212-772-4087. Degrees granted: Bachelors; Masters. Attendance, degree and transcript information available by mail.

Interboro Institute, Registrar, 450 W 56th St, New York, NY 10019, 212-399-0091 (Fax: 212-765-5772) www.Interboro.com. 9AM-5PM. Enrollment: 900. Records go back to 1945. Degrees granted: Associate.

Attendance and degree information available by fax, mail. Transcripts available by mail.

Iona College, Registrar, 715 North Ave, New Rochelle, NY 10801-1890, 914-633-2508, 914-633-2000 (Fax: 914-633-2182) www.iona.edu. 9AM-5PM. Enrollment: 5588. Records go back to 1941. Alumni Records: 115 Beechmont Dr, New Rochelle, NY 10801. Degrees granted: Associate; Bachelors; Masters. Attendance and degree information available by phone, mail. Transcripts available by written request only.

Iona College (Manhattan Campus), Registrar, 425 W 33rd St, New York, NY 10001, 212-630-0270 (Fax: 212-630-0275) www.iona.edu. Records are located at Iona College, Registrar, New Rochelle, NY.

Iona College (Rockland Campus), Registrar, One Dutch Hill Rd, Orangeburg, NY 10962, 914-359-2252 (Fax: 914-359-2261). Records are located at Iona College, Registrar, New Rochelle, NY.

Iona College (Yonkers Campus), Registrar, 1061 N Broadway, Yonkers, NY 10701,. Records are located at Iona College, Registrar, New Rochelle, NY.

Ithaca College, Office of the Registrar, 228 Job Hall, Ithaca, NY 14850-7014, 607-274-3127, 607-274-3123 (Fax: 607-274-1366) 9AM-4PM. www.ithaca.edu. Enrollment: 5700. Records go back to 1892. Alumni Records: 210 Alumni Hall, Ithaca, NY 14850-7014. Degrees granted: Bachelors; Masters. Attendance and degree information available by phone, fax, mail. Transcripts available by fax, mail.

Jamestown Business College, Registrar, PO Box 429, Fairmount Ave, Jamestown, NY 14702-0429, 716-664-5100 (Fax: 716-664-3144) www.jbcny.org. 8AM - 5PM. Enrollment: 350. Records go back to 1920. Degrees granted: Associate. Attendance and degree information available by phone, fax, mail. Transcripts available by fax, mail.

Jamestown Community College, Academic Transcripts, 525 Falconer St, Jamestown, NY 14701, 716-665-5220 Ext. 332 (Fax: 716-665-4115) www.sunyjcc.edu. 8:30AM-5PM. Enrollment: 3500. Records go back to 1950. Alumni records are maintained here. Degrees granted: Associate. Financial Aid Transcripts: Financial Aids Office, 716-665-5220. Attendance and degree information available by phone, fax, mail. Transcripts available by fax, mail; requires signature.

Jamestown Community College (Cattaraugus County Campus), Registrar, 525 Falconer Jamestown St, Olean, NY 14760, 716-665-5220 Ext. 332 (Fax: 716-665-4115). 8:30AM - 4:30PM. Enrollment: 3800. Records go back to 1950. Alumni records are maintained here. Degrees granted: Associate. Attendance and degree information available by phone, fax, mail. Transcripts available by fax, mail.

Jefferson Community College, Registrar, Coffeen St, Watertown, NY 13601, 315-786-2417, 315-786-2436 (Fax: 315-786-2459) 9AM-4PM. www.sunyjefferson.edu. Enrollment: 3500. Records go back to 1961. Alumni records maintained here; call 315-786-2327. Degrees granted: Associate. Attendance and degree information available by phone, fax, mail. Transcripts available by fax, mail.

Jewish Theological Seminary of America, Registrar, 3080 Broadway, New York, NY 10027, 212-678-8007 (registrar), 212-678-8000 (switchboard) (Fax: 212-678-

8002) 9AM-5PM. Records go back to 1885. Alumni records are maintained here. Degrees granted: Bachelors; Masters; Doctorate; Rabbamic Ordination. Attendance, degree and transcript information available by fax, mail.

John Jay College of Criminal Justice, Registrar, 445 W 59th St Room 4113, New York, NY 10019, 212-237-8986, 212-237-8020 (Fax: 212-237-8777) 9AM-5PM. www.jjay.cuny.edu. Enrollment: 10313. Records go back to 1965. Alumni records maintained here; call 212-237-8550. Degrees granted: Associate; Bachelors; Masters. Attendance and degree information available by phone, fax, mail. Transcripts available by mail.

Julliard School, Registrar, 60 Lincoln Center Plaza, New York, NY 10023, 212-799-5000 (Fax: 212-724-0263) 9AM-5PM. www.julliard.eud. Records go back to 1905. Alumni records maintained here; call 212-799-5000 Ext. 344. Degrees granted: Bachelors; Masters; Doctorate. Attendance and degree information available by phone, fax, mail. Transcripts available by fax, mail. Only a student can request a transcript.

Katherine Gibbs School, Registrar, 320 S. Service Rd, **Melville**, NY 11747, 516-293-2460 (Fax: 516-293-1276). 9AM-10PM. Enrollment: 350. Records go back to 1915. Alumni records maintained here; call 516-293-1024. Degrees granted: Associate. Attendance and degree information available by phone, fax, mail. Transcripts available by fax, mail.

Katherine Gibbs School, Registrar, 200 Park Ave, **New York**, NY 10166, 212-973-4954, 212-973-4950 (Fax: 212-338-9606) 8:30AM-8PM. www.katherinegibbs.com. Records go back to 1918. Alumni records maintained here; call 212-745-9480. Degrees granted: Associate. Attendance and degree information available by phone, fax, mail. Transcripts available by fax, mail.

Kehilath Yakov Rabbinical Seminary, Registrar, 206 Wilson St, Brooklyn, NY 11211, 718-963-3940 (Fax: 718-387-8586). 9AM-5:30PM. Attendance, degree and transcript information available by fax, mail.

Keuka College, Registrar, Keuka Park, NY 14478, 315-536-4411 Ext. 5204 (Fax: 315-536-5216). 8:30AM-4:30PM. Enrollment: 920. Records go back to 1900. Alumni records maintained here; call 315-536-5238. Degrees granted: Bachelors. Attendance and degree information available by phone, fax, mail. Transcripts available by mail.

King's College, Registrar, Lodge Rd, Briarcliff Manor, NY 10510, 914-941-7200 (Fax: 914-941-9460) http://137.229.123.226. 8:30AM-5PM. Records go back to 1976. Alumni records are maintained here. Degrees granted: Associate; Bachelors. Certification: Teacher. Attendance and degree information available by phone, fax, mail. Transcripts available by mail.

Kingsborough Community College, Registrar, 2001 Oriental Blvd, Manhattan Beach, Brooklyn, NY 11235, 718-368-5000, 718-368-5090 (Fax: 718-368-5692) www.kbcc.cuny.edu/ 9AM - 7:15PM Tues, Wed. Enrollment: 15460. Records go back to 1963. Alumni records are maintained here. Degrees granted: Associate. Special programs- Marine Technology. Attendance, degree and transcript information available by mail.

La Guardia Community College, Registrar, 31-10 Thomson Ave, Long Island City, NY 11101, 718-482-7232 (Fax: 718-482-5008) www.lagcc.cuny.edu. 9:30AM-5PM M,T; 2-8PM W; 9:30AM-8PM Th; Closed F. Enrollment: 11000. Records go back to 1971. Alumni records maintained here; call 718-482-5054. Degrees granted: Associate. Attendance, degree and transcript information available by written request only.

Laboratory Institute of Merchandising, Registrar, 12 E 53rd St, New York, NY 10022, www.katherinegibbs.com. 212-752-1530 (Fax: 212-832-6708) 8:30AM-4:30PM. Enrollment: 215. Records go back to 1939. Alumni records are maintained here. Degrees granted: Associate; Bachelors. Attendance and degree information available by phone, fax, mail. Transcripts available by mail.

LeMoyne College, Registrar, Le Moyne Heights, Syracuse, NY 13214, 315-445-4100 (Fax: 315-445-4540) www.lemoyne.edu. Records go back to 1946. Alumni records maintained here; call 315-445-4545. Degrees granted: Bachelors; Masters. Attendance and degree information available by phone, fax, mail. Transcripts available by mail.

Lehman College, Registrar, 250 Bedford Park Blvd W, Bronx, NY 10468, 718-960-8613. 9AM-5PM. Records go back to 1970. Alumni records maintained here; call 718-960-8044. Degrees granted: Bachelors; Masters. Attendance, degree and transcript information available by mail.

Long Island University (Brentwood Campus), Registrar, Second Ave, Brentwood, NY 11717, 516-273-5112 www.liunet.edu. Records are located at Long Island University, (C.W. Post Campus), Registrar, Brookville, NY.

Long Island University (Brooklyn Campus), Registrar, University Plaza, Brooklyn, NY 11201, 718-488-1000, 718-488-1013 (Registrar) www.liunet.edu. Enrollment: 11000. Records go back to 1926. Alumni records are maintained here. Degrees granted: Associate; Bachelors; Masters; Doctorate. Attendance, degree and transcript information available by mail.

Long Island University (C.W. Post Campus), Registrar, 720 Northern Blvd., Brookville, NY 11548, 516-299-2755, 516-299-2000 (Fax: 516-299-2721) www.liu.edu. 9AM-5PM M,W,Th,F; 9AM-8PM T. Enrollment: 8100. Records go back to 1954. Alumni records maintained here; call 516-299-2263. Degrees granted: Associate; Bachelors; Masters; Doctorate. Attendance and degree information available by phone, fax, mail. Transcripts available by fax, mail.

Long Island University, Registrar, 555 Broadway, Dobbs Ferry, NY 10522, 914-674-7269 (Fax: 914-674-7269) www.liunet.edu. 9:30AM-7PM. Enrollment: 1000. Records go back to 1975. Alumni records are maintained here. Degrees granted: Masters. Special programs- Psychology, 914-674-7231; MBA, 914-674-7231; Education, 914-674-7231; Health, 914-674-7231. Attendance and degree information available by fax, mail. Transcripts available by mail.

Long Island University (Rockland Campus), Registrar, Rte 340, Orangeburg, NY 10962, 914-359-7200 (Fax: 914-359-7248) www.liunet.edu/. 9AM-8PM M-Th; 9AM-5PM F. Enrollment: 400. Records go back to 1990. Alumni Records: University Center, 700 Northern Blvd, Brookville, NY 11548. Degrees granted: Masters. Certification: Adv. Business. Special programs- Graduate Records at C W Post, 516-299-2755. Attendance and degree information available by phone, fax, mail. Transcripts available by mail.

Manhattan College, Registrar, 4513 Manhattan College Pkwy, Riverdale, NY 10471, 718-862-7312, 718-862-7313 (Fax: 718-862-7457) www.mancol.edu. 8:30AM-4PM. Enrollment: 3200. Records go back to 1800. Alumni records maintained here; call 718-862-7431. Degrees granted: Bachelors; Masters. Attendance and degree information available by phone, fax, mail. Transcripts available by mail.

Manhattan School of Music, Registrar, 120 Claremont Ave, New York, NY 10027, 212-749-2802 Ext. 480, 212-749-2802 Ext. 478 (Fax: 212-749-5471) www.msmnyc.edu. 9AM-5PM. Records go back to 1918. Alumni records maintained here; call 212-749-2802 Ext. 502. Degrees granted: Bachelors; Masters; Doctorate. Attendance, degree and transcript information available by fax, mail.

Manhattanville College, Registrar, 2900 Purchase St, Purchase, NY 10577, 914-694-2200, 914-323-5337 (Fax: 914-323-5211). 9AM-4PM. Records go back to 1914. Alumni records maintained here; call 914-323-5173. Degrees granted: Bachelors; Masters. Attendance and degree information available by phone, fax, mail. Transcripts available by mail.

Maria College of Albany, Registrar, Rm 100, 700 New Scotland Ave, Albany, NY 12208-1798, 518-438-3111 Ext. 24, 518-438-1368 (Fax: 518-438-7170). 8:30AM - 4PM. Enrollment: 900. Records go back to 1963. Alumni records maintained here; call 518-489-7436. Degrees granted: Associate. Attendance and degree information available by phone, fax, mail. Transcripts available by fax, mail.

Marist College, Registrar, 290 North Rd, Poughkeepsie, NY 12601, 914-575-3250, 914-575-3000 www.marist.edu. 8AM-5PM. Enrollment: 4500. Records go back to 1945. Alumni records maintained here; call 914-575-3283. Degrees granted: Bachelors; Masters. Attendance and degree information available by phone, mail. Transcripts available by mail.

Maryknoll School of Theology, Archive Dept, Maryknoll, NY 10545, 914-941-7590 Ext. 2500, 914-941-7636 Ext. 2500 (Fax: 914-941-5753) www.maryknoll.org. School closed in May, 1995. Degrees granted: Masters. Attendance, degree and transcript information available by written request only.

Marymount College, Registrar, 100 Marymount Ave, Tarrytown, NY 10591-3796, 914-332-8211, 914-332-8316 (Fax: 914-631-8586) www.marymt.edu. 9AM - 5PM. Enrollment: 900. Records go back to 1908. Alumni records maintained here; call 914-332-8353. Degrees granted: Bachelors. Attendance and degree information available by phone, fax, mail. Transcripts available by mail.

Marymount Manhattan College, Registrar, 221 E 71st St, New York, NY 10021, 212-517-0400, 212-517-0513 (Fax: 212-517-0413). 8AM-4:30PM. Enrollment: 2000. Records go back to 1936. Alumni records maintained here; call 212-517-0530. Degrees granted: Bachelors. Special programs- Continuing Education, 212-517-0564. Attendance and degree information available by phone, fax, mail. Transcripts available by mail.

Mater Dei College, Registrar, 5428 State Hwy 37, Ogdensburg, NY 13669, 315-393-5930 (Fax: 315-393-5930 Ext. 440). 8AM-5PM. Enrollment: 350. Records go back to 1960. Alumni records are maintained here. Degrees granted: Associate. Attendance, degree and transcript information available by mail.

Medaille College, Registrar, 18 Agassiz Circle, Buffalo, NY 14214, 716-884-3281 (Fax: 716-884-0291) www.medaille.edu. 8AM-8:15PM M,T; 8AM-6PM W,Th; 8AM-4PM F. Enrollment: 900. Records go back to 1937. Alumni records maintained here; call 716-884-3281 Ext. 208. Degrees granted: Associate; Bachelors. Attendance, degree and transcript information available by fax, mail.

Medgar Evers College, Registrar's Office, 1150 Carroll St RC-101, Brooklyn, NY 11225, 718-270-6079, 718-270-4900 (Fax: 718-270-6239) www.mec.cuny.edu. 9AM-7PM M,Th; 9AM-3PM F. Enrollment: 8000. Records go back to 1975. Degrees 'granted: Associate; Bachelors. Attendance, degree and transcript information available by fax, mail.

Mercy College (**Bronx Campus**), Registrar, 50 Antin Place, Bronx, NY 10462, 718-798-8952. Records are located at Mercy College, Registrar, Dobbs Ferry, NY.

Mercy College, Registrar, 555 Broadway, Dobbs Ferry, NY 10522, 914-674-7265 (Fax: 914-693-9455). 9AM-7PM M-Th; 9AM-5PM F; 9AM-12:30PM S. Records go back to 1950's. Alumni records maintained here; call 914-674-7314. Degrees granted: Associate; Bachelors; Masters. Attendance and degree information available by phone, fax, mail. Transcripts available by mail.

Mercy College (**White Plains Campus**), Registrar, Martine Ave and S Broadway, White Plains, NY 10601, 914-948-3666 (Fax: 914-948-6732). Records are located at Mercy College, Registrar, Dobbs Ferry, NY.

Mercy College (**Yorktown Campus**), Registrar, 2651 Strang Blvd, Yorktown Heights, NY 10598, 914-245-6100, 914-693-4500 (registrar). Records are located at Mercy College, Registrar, Dobbs Ferry, NY.

Mesivta Tifereth Jerusalem of America, Registrar, 141 E Broadway, New York, NY 10002, 212-964-2830 (Fax: 212-349-5213) 9AM-5PM. Enrollment: 87. Records go back to 1937. Alumni records are maintained here. Attendance and degree information available by fax, mail. Transcripts available by mail.

Mesivta Torah Vodaath Rabbinical Seminary, Registrar, 425 E 9th St, Brooklyn, NY 11218, 718-941-8000 (Fax: 718-941-8032). 8AM-4PM. Attendance, degree and transcript information available by mail.

Mirrer Yeshiva Central Institute, Registrar, 1791 Ocean Pkwy, Brooklyn, NY 11223, www.oberen32.com. 718-645-0536 (Fax: 718-645-9251) 9AM - 4:30PM. Alumni records are maintained here. Attendance and degree information available by fax, mail. Transcripts available by mail.

Mohawk Valley Community College (Branch Campus), Registrar, Floyd Ave, Rome, NY 13440, 315-792-5494, 315-792-5336 (Fax: 315-792-5698). 8:M-7PM M-Th; 8AM-4:30PM F. Enrollment: 4800. Records go back to 1900's. Alumni records maintained here; call 315-792-5340. Degrees 'granted: Associate. Attendance and degree information available by phone, fax, mail. Transcripts available by fax, mail.

Mohawk Valley Community College, Registrar, 1101 Sherman Dr, Rm 162, Utica, NY 13501-5394, 315-792-5336, 315-792-5400 (Fax: 315-792-5698) www.mvcc.edu. 8AM-7PM M-Th; 8AM-4:30PM F. Enrollment: 5300. Records go back to 1988.

Alumni records maintained here; call 315-792-5340. Degrees granted: Associate. Attendance and degree information available by phone, fax, mail. Transcripts available by mail.

Molloy College, Registrar, PO Box 5002, Rockville Centre, NY 11571-5002, 516-678-5000 Ext. 226, 516-678-5000 Ext. 229 (Fax: 516-256-2232). Enrollment: 2300. Records go back to 1955. Alumni records maintained here; call 516-678-5000 Ext. 218. Degrees granted: Associate; Bachelors; Masters. Special programs- Nursing. Attendance and degree information available by phone, mail. Transcripts available by mail.

Monroe College, Registrar, 29 E Fordham Rd, Bronx, NY 10468, www.monroecol.edu 718-933-6700 Ext. 317 (Fax: 718-220-3032) 8:30AM-7:30PM M-Th; 8:30AM-2PM F. Enrollment: 2000. Records go back to 1960. Alumni records maintained here; call 718-933-6700 Ext. 310. Degrees granted: Associate. Attendance and degree information available by phone, fax, mail. Transcripts available by fax, mail. Fax inquiry requires ID verification.

Monroe College (**New Rochelle Campus**), Registrar, 434 Main St, New Rochelle, NY 10801, 914-632-5400, 718-933-6700 Ext. 317 (Fax: 914-632-5462) www.monroecol.edu. 8:30AM-7:30PM M-Th; 8:30AM-2PM. Enrollment: 600. Records go back to 1983. Degrees granted: Associate. Attendance and degree information available by mail. Transcripts available by fax, mail. Fax inquiry requires ID verification.

Monroe Community College, Registrar, 1000 E Henrietta Rd, Rochester, NY 14623, 716-292-2300, 716-292-2243 (Fax: 716-292-3850). 8AM-4:30PM. Records go back to 1961. Alumni records maintained here; call 716-292-2000. Degrees granted: Associate. Attendance and degree information available by phone, fax, mail. Transcripts available by fax, mail.

Mount Sinai School of Medicine, Registrar, One Gustave L Levy Pl, New York, NY 10029, 212-241-6691, 212-241-6500 (Fax: 212-369-6013) www.mssm.esu. 9AM-5PM. Enrollment: 485. Records go back to 1972. Alumni records maintained here; call 212-241-6565. Degrees granted: Bachelors; Masters; First Professional Degree. Attendance and degree information available by phone, fax, mail. Transcripts available by fax, mail.

Mount St. Mary College, Registrar, 330 Powell Ave, Newburgh, NY 12550, 914-569-3258, 914-569-3237 (Fax: 914-562-6762) 8AM-5PM. www.msmc.edu. Enrollment: 1900. Records go back to 1935. Alumni records maintained here; call 914-569-3217. Degrees granted: Bachelors; Masters. Attendance and degree information available by phone, fax, mail. Transcripts available by fax, mail.

Nassau Community College, Registrar, One Education Dr, Garden City, NY 11530-6793, 800-613-2592, 516-572-7357 (A-K) 516-572-7360 (L-Z) (Fax: 516-572-7130) www.sunynassau.edu. 8AM-7:30PM M-Th; 8AM-4:30PM F. Enrollment: 20000. Records go back to 1959. Alumni records maintained here; call 519-572-7484. Degrees granted: Associate. Attendance, degree and transcript information available by fax, mail. Transcripts released only to students.

Nazareth College of Rochester, Registrar, 4245 East Ave, Rochester, NY 14618-3790, www.naz.edu. 716-389-2800 (Fax: 716-586-2452) 8:30AM-4:30PM.

Enrollment: 2800. Records go back to 1924. Alumni records maintained here; call 716-389-2470. Degrees granted: Bachelors; Masters. Attendance and degree information available by phone, fax, mail. Transcripts available by mail.

New School University (Parsons School of Design), Registrar, 66 Fifth Ave, New York, NY 10003, 212-229-5762 (registrar), 212-229-5720 (records) (Fax: 212-229-5470; 229-8582 (registrar's fax)) www.newschool.edu. 9AM-6PM. Enrollment: 10000. Records go back to 1800's. Alumni records maintained here; call 212-229-5662. Degrees granted: Associate; Bachelors; Masters; Doctorate; BPA, MSSC, MS, MPS, DSSC, MPA. Attendance and degree information available by phone, fax, mail. Transcripts available by fax, mail.

New School for Social Research, Registrar, 66 W 12th St, New York, NY 10011, 212-229-5720 (Fax: 212-229-5470). 10AM-6PM. Enrollment: 6500. Records go back to 1919. Alumni records maintained here; call 212-229-5662. Degrees granted: Bachelors; Masters; Doctorate. Attendance and degree information available by phone, fax, mail. Transcripts available by fax, mail.

New York Chiropractic College, Registrar, 2360 State Rte 89, Seneca Falls, NY 13148-0800, 315-568-3000, 315-568-3058 (Fax: 315-568-3056) www.nycc.net. Enrollment: 936. Records go back to 1919. Alumni records are maintained here. Degrees granted: Doctorate. Attendance and degree information available by fax, mail. Transcripts available by mail.

New York City Technical College, Registrar, 300 Jay St, Brooklyn, NY 11201, www.nyctc.cuny.edu. 718-260-5800 (Fax: 718-254-8532) 9:30AM-8PM M,Th; 9:30AM-4PM T,W; 9:30AM-3PM F. Enrollment: 1102. Records go back to 1940. Alumni records maintained here; call 718-260-5402. Degrees granted: Associate; Bachelors. Special programs- Dental. Attendance and degree information available by phone, fax, mail. Transcripts available by fax, mail.

New York College of Podiatric Medicine, Registrar, 1800 Park Avenue, New York, NY 10035, 212-410-8054 (registrar), 212-410-8000 (switchboard) (Fax: 212-722-4918) www.nycpm.edu. 9AM - 5PM. Enrollment: 485. Records go back to 1911. Alumni records maintained here; call 212-410-8013. Degrees granted: Doctorate. Attendance and degree information available by fax, mail. Transcripts available by mail. General information will be given over the phone.

New York Institute of Technology (**Central Islip Campus**), Registrar, 211 Carleton Ave, Central Islip, NY 11722, 516-348-3210 (registrar), 516-686-7580 (switchboard) (Fax: 516-348-0912) www.nyit.edu. Records are located at New York Institute of Technology, (Old Westbury), Registrar, Old Westbury, NY.

New York Institute of Technology (**Manhattan Campus**), Registrar, 1855 Broadway, New York, NY 10023, 212-261-1600, 212-261-1603 (Fax: 212-261-1646) www.nyit.edu. Records are located at New York Institute of Technology, (Old Westbury), Registrar, Old Westbury, NY.

New York Institute of Technology (Old Westbury), Registrar, 268 Wheatley Rd, Old Westbury, NY 11568-1036, 516-686-7580 (registrar), 516-686-7906 (switchboard) (Fax: 516-626-0673) www.nyit.edu. 9AM-7PM M-

Th; 9AM-5PM F. Enrollment: 10,000. Records go back to 1955. Alumni records maintained here; call 516-626-7632. Degrees granted: Associate; Bachelors; Masters; DO. Attendance and degree information available by phone, fax, mail. Transcripts available by fax, mail.

New York Law School, Registrar, 57 Worth St, New York, NY 10013, 212-431-2100 (Fax: 212-343-2137). 10AM-7PM M-Th; 10AM-5PM F. Enrollment: 1400. Records go back to 1895. Alumni records maintained here; call 212-431-2800. Degrees granted: Doctorate; Juris Doctor. Attendance and degree information available by phone, fax, mail. Transcripts available by mail.

New York Medical College, Registrar, Sunshine Cottage, Admin Bldg, Valhalla, NY 10595, 914-993-4495 (Fax: 914-993-4613). 9AM-5PM. Records go back to 1920. Alumni records maintained here; call 914-993-4555. Degrees granted: Masters; Doctorate; Ph.D. Attendance and degree information available by phone, mail. Transcripts available by mail.

New York School of Interior Design, Registrar, 170 E 70th St, New York, NY 10021-5110, 212-472-1500 Ext. 207 (Fax: 212-472-3800) www.nysid.edu. 9AM-5PM M-F; Summer 9AM-5PM M-Th. Enrollment: 750. Records go back to 1923. Alumni records maintained here; call 212-472-1500 Ext. 404. Degrees granted: Associate; Bachelors. Attendance, degree and transcript information available by fax, mail.

New York Theological Seminary, Registrar, 5 W 29th St, New York, NY 10001-4599, 212-532-4012 (Fax: 212-684-0757) www.nyts.edu. 9AM - 5PM. Enrollment: 500. Records go back to 1906. Alumni records are maintained here. Degrees granted: Masters; Doctorate. Attendance and degree information available by fax. Transcripts available by written request only.

New York University, Registrar, PO Box 910, New York, NY 10276-0910, 212-998-4250 (Fax: 212-995-4587) www.nyu.edu. 9AM-5PM. Records go back to 1913. Alumni records maintained here; call 212-998-6965. Degrees granted: Bachelors; Masters; Doctorate; Ph.D. Attendance and degree information available by phone, fax, mail. Transcripts available by mail. To access records prior to 1990, send a written request with student authorization.

Niagara County Community College, Registrar, 3111 Saunders Settlement Rd, Sanborn, NY 14132, 716-731-3271 Ext. 130 www.sunyniagara.cc.ny.us (Fax: 716-731-4053) 8AM-5PM. Enrollment: 2500. Records go back to 1968. Alumni records are maintained here. Degrees granted: Associate. Attendance and degree information available by phone, fax, mail. Transcripts available by fax, mail.

Niagara University, Registrar, Niagara University, NY 14109, 716-286-8730 (Fax: 716-286-8733) www.niagara.edu. 9AM-5PM. Records go back to 1856. Alumni Records: Butler Bldg, Niagara University, NY 14109. Degrees granted: Associate; Bachelors; Masters. Attendance and degree information available by phone, fax, mail. Transcripts available by fax, mail.

North Country Community College, Registrar, 20 Winona Ave, PO Box 89, Saranac Lake, NY 12983, 518-891-2915 (Fax: 518-891-2915 Ext. 214) www.nccc.edu. Enrollment: 1550. Records go back to 1967. Alumni records maintained here; call 518-891-2915 Ext. 224. Degrees granted: Associate. Attendance and degree information

available by phone, fax, mail. Transcripts available by fax, mail.

Nyack College, Registrar, One South Blvd, Nyack, NY 10960-3698, 914-358-1710 Ext. 121 www.nyackcollege.edu (Fax: 914-353-6429) 8:30AM - 4:30PM M,T,Th,F; 8AM - Noon W. Enrollment: 1000. Records go back to 1910. Alumni records maintained here; call 914-358-1710 Ext. 361. Degrees granted: Associate; Bachelors. Special programs-Adult Degree Completion, 914-358-1710 Ext. 572. Attendance and degree information available by phone, fax, mail. Transcripts available by fax, mail.

Ohr Hameir Theological Seminary, Registrar, Furnace Woods Rd, PO Box 2130, Peekskill, NY 10566, 914-736-1500 (Fax: 914-736-1055) 8AM-4:30PM. Enrollment: 100. Alumni records are maintained here. Attendance and degree information available by phone, mail. Transcripts available by mail.

Ohr Somayach Institutions, Registrar, 244 Route 306, PO Box 334, Monsey, NY 10952, 914-425-1370 (Fax: 914-425-8865). 9:30AM-3:30PM. Records go back to 1985. Alumni Records: 115 S Gate Dr, Spring Valley, NY 10977. Degrees granted: Associate; Bachelors. Attendance and degree information available by phone, mail. Transcripts available by mail.

Olean Business Institute, Registrar, 301 N Union St, Olean, NY 14760, 716-372-7978 (Fax: 716-372-2120). 8AM - 5PM. Enrollment: 200. Records go back to 1960. Degrees granted: Associate. Special programs- Business, 716-372-7978: Paralegal, 716-372-7978: Secretarial Science, 716-372-7978. Attendance and degree information available by phone, fax, mail. Transcripts available by fax, mail.

Onondaga Community College, Registration Office, 4941 Onondaga Rd, Syracuse, NY 13215, www.sunayce.edu. 315-469-2357, 315-469-7741 (Fax: 315-469-6775) 8:30AM -4:30PM; Fall-Spring Open until 7PM W. Enrollment: 7100. Records go back to 1962. Alumni records maintained here; call 315-498-6058. Degrees granted: Associate. Special programs- Nursing. Attendance and degree information available by phone, fax, mail. Transcripts available by mail.

Orange County Community College, Registrar, 115 South St, Middletown, NY 10940, 914-341-4140, 914-341-4150 (Fax: 914-342-8662) www.orange.cc.ny.us. 9AM - 8PM M-Th;9AM - 4:30PM F. Enrollment: 5500. Records go back to 1950. Alumni records maintained here; call 914-341-4751. Degrees granted: Associate. Attendance and degree information available by phone, fax, mail. Transcripts available by fax, mail.

Pace University, Registrar, One Pace Plaza, New York, NY 10038, 212-346-1315, 212-346-1200 www.pace.edu. (Fax: 212-346-1643) 9AM - 6PM M-Th; 9AM - 5PM F. Enrollment: 30000. Records go back to 1905. Alumni records maintained here; call 212-346-1764. Degrees granted: Associate; Bachelors; Masters; Doctorate. Attendance and degree information available by phone, mail. Transcripts available by mail. Phone inquiry available for records from 1985 to present.

Pace University (Pleasantville/Briarcliff), Registrar, 861 Bedford Rd, Pleasantville, NY 10570, www.pace.edu 914-773-3200, 914-773-3431 (Registraqr) (Fax: 914-773-3862) 9AM-5PM. Enrollment: 4000. Records go back to 1960's. Alumni records maintained here; call 914-923-2701. Degrees granted:

Associate; Bachelors; Masters. Certification: Teaching. Attendance and degree information available by phone, fax, mail. Transcripts available by mail.

Pace University (White Plains), Registrar, 78 N Broadway, White Plains, NY 10603, 914-422-4213, 914-422-4200 www.pace.edu. (Fax: 914-422-4248) Records are located at Pace University, (Pleasantville/ Briarcliff), Pleasantville, NY.

Pacific College of Oriental Medicine (Branch), Registrar, 915 Broadway 3rd Fl, New York, NY 10010, 212-982-3456 (switchboard) (Fax: 212-982-6514) www.ormed.edu. 8:30AM-5:30PM M-Th, 8:30AM-5PM F. Records go back to 1993. Alumni records are maintained here. Degrees granted: Masters. Attendance and degree information available by phone, fax, mail. Transcripts available by fax, mail.

Parsons School of Design, Registrar, 66 W 12th St, New York, NY 10011, 212-229-5720 (records), 212-229-5792 (registrar) (Fax: 212-229-5470; 229-8582 (registrar's fax)). Records go back to 1964. Degrees granted: Associate; Bachelors; Masters. Attendance and degree information available by phone, fax, mail. Transcripts available by fax, mail.

Paul Smith's College, Registrar, PO Box 265, Paul Smiths, NY 12970-0265, 518-327-6231 www.paulsmiths.edu (Fax: 518-327-6951) 8AM-5PM. Enrollment: 750. Records go back to 1946. Alumni records maintained here; call 518-327-6161. Degrees granted: Associate; Bachelors. Certification: Baking. Special programs- Hotel Restaurant Management. Attendance and degree information available by phone, fax, mail. Transcripts available by fax, mail.

Phillips Beth Israel School of Nursing, Registrar, 310 E 22nd St, New York, NY 10010, 212-614-6108, 212-614-6176 (Fax: 212-614-6109). 8AM-4:30PM. Enrollment: 140. Records go back to 1904. Alumni records are maintained here. Degrees granted: Associate. Attendance, degree and transcript information available by fax, mail. Transcripts available by fax, mail.

Plaza Business Institute, Registrar, 74-09 37th Ave, Jackson Heights, NY 11372, 718-779-1430, 718-779-1548 (Fax: 718-779-7423). 8AM-8:30PM M,T,Th;8AM-5PM W,F. Records go back to 1970's. Alumni records are maintained here. Degrees granted: Associate. Attendance, degree and transcript information available by fax, mail.

Polytechnic University, Office of the Registrar, 6 MetroTech Ctr, Brooklyn, NY 11201, 718-260-3486 (Fax: 718-260-3052). 9AM - 6PM M,Th; 9AM - 5PM T,W,F. Current Enroll-ent: 3253. Records go back to 1986. Alumni records maintained here; call 718-260-3486 Ext. 3188. Degrees granted: Bachelors; Masters; Doctorate. Attendance and degree information available by phone, fax, mail. Transcripts available by fax, mail.

Polytechnic University (Long Island Center), Office of the Registrar, Rte 100, Farmingdale, NY 11735, 516-755-4400. Records are located at Polytechnic University, Registrar, Brooklyn, NY.

Polytechnic University (Westchester Graduate Center), Registrar, 36 Saw Mill River Rd, Hawthorne, NY 10532, 718-260-3900, 718-260-3486 (Fax: 718-260-3136) www.poly.edu. Records are located at Polytechnic Univ., Registrar, Brooklyn, NY.

Pratt Institute, Registrar, 200 Willoughby Ave, Brooklyn, NY 11205, 718-636-3534,

718-636-3500 (switchboard) (Fax: 718-636-3548) www.pratt.edu. 9AM-5PM Winter; 9AM-4PM Summer. Enrollment: 3400. Records go back to 1887. Alumni records maintained here; call 718-636-2531. Degrees granted: Associate; Bachelors; Masters. Attendance and degree information available by phone, fax, mail. Transcripts available by fax, mail.

Queens College, Transcript Division, Jefferson Hall Rm 100, 65-30 Kissena Blvd, Flushing, NY 11367, 718-997-4400, 718-997-5000 (switchboard) (Fax: 718-997-4439) www.qc.edu. 8AM-5PM M-F; Summer 8AM-5PM M-Th. Enrollment: 17500. Records go back to 1946. Alumni records maintained here; call 718-997-3930. Degrees granted: Bachelors; Masters. Attendance and degree information available by phone, fax, mail. Transcripts available by fax, mail.

Queensborough Community College, Registrar, 222-05 56th Ave, Bayside, NY 11364-1497, 718-631-6212, 718-631-6262 (Fax: 718-281-5041) www.cuny.edu. 9AM-5PM M,Th,F; 9AM-6:30PM T,W. Enrollment: 20000. Records go back to 1962. Alumni records maintained here; call 718-631-6391. Degrees granted: Associate. Attendance and degree information available by fax, mail. Transcripts available by mail.

Rabbinical Academy Mesivta Rabbi Chaim Berlin, Registrar, 1605 Coney Island Ave, Brooklyn, NY 11230, 718-377-0777 (Fax: 718-338-5578). Alumni records are maintained here. Attendance, degree and transcript information available by mail.

Rabbinical College Beth Shraga, Registrar, 28 Saddle River Rd, Monsey, NY 10952, 914-356-1980 (Fax: 914-425-2604). Alumni records are maintained here. Degrees granted: Bachelors. Attendance and degree information available by phone, mail. Transcripts available by mail.

Rabbinical College Bobover Yeshiva B'nei Zion, Registrar, 1577 48th St, Brooklyn, NY 11219, 718-438-2018 (Fax: 718-871-9031). 9AM - 5PM. Enrollment: 387. Records go back to 1976. Alumni records are maintained here. Attendance, degree and transcript information available by mail.

Rabbinical College Ch'san Sofer, Registrar, 1876 50th St, Brooklyn, NY 11204, 718-236-1171 (Fax: 718-236-1119) Alumni records are maintained here. Attendance, degree and transcript information available by mail.

Rabbinical College of Long Island, Registrar, 201 Magnolia Blvd, Long Beach, NY 11561, 516-431-7304 (Fax: 516-431-8662). 9AM-5PM. Records go back to 1970's. Alumni records are maintained here. Attendance, degree and transcript information available by phone, fax, mail.

Rabbinical Seminary Adas Yereim, Registrar, 185 Wilson St, Brooklyn, NY 11211, 718-388-1751 (Fax: 718-388-3531) 9:30AM-5:30PM. Enrollment: 90. Records go back to 1990. Alumni records are maintained here. Attendance and degree information available by phone, fax, mail. Transcripts available by fax, mail. If a signed release is on file, party may call or Fax to obtain information.

Rabbinical Seminary M'kor Chaim, Registrar, 1571 55th St, Brooklyn, NY 11219, 718-851-0183 (Fax: 718-853-2967). Alumni records are maintained here. Attendance and degree information available by phone, mail. Transcripts available by mail.

Rabbinical Seminary of America, Registrar, 92-15 69th Ave, Forest Hills, NY 11375, 718-268-4700 (Fax: 718-268-4684). Attendance, degree and transcript information available by mail.

Regents College of the University of the State of New York, Registrar, 7 Columbia Circle, Albany, NY 12203-5159, www.regents.edu. 518-464-8500 Ext. 141 (Fax: 518-464-8646) 9AM-5PM T,Th,F; 9AM-8PM M,W. Enrollment: 17270. Records go back to 1970's. Alumni records maintained here; call 518-464-8500 Ext. 145. Degrees granted: Bachelors. Attendance and degree information available by phone, fax, mail. Transcripts available by fax, mail.

Rensselaer Polytechnic Institute, Student Records, 110 Eighth St, Troy, NY 12180-3590, 518-276-6231, 518-276-6610 (Fax: 518-276-6180) www.rpi.edu. 8:30AM-5PM Fall & Spring. Enrollment: 6400. Records go back to 1900's. Alumni records maintained here; call 518-276-6205. Degrees granted: Bachelors; Masters; Doctorate. Special programs- Hartford Graduate Center, 275 Windsor St, Hartford, CT 06120. Attendance and degree information available by phone, fax, mail. Transcripts available by fax, mail.

Roberts Wesleyan College, Registrar, 2301 Westside Dr, Rochester, NY 14624-1997, 716-594-6220, 716-594-6219 (Fax: 716-594-6371) www.roberts.edu. 8AM-5PM. Enrollment: 1411. Records go back to 1800's. Alumni records maintained here; call 716-594-6404. Degrees granted: Associate; Bachelors; Masters. Special programs- MSM, OM, M.Ed, M.S.W., 716-594-6600. Attendance and degree information available by phone, fax, mail. Transcripts available by fax, mail.

Rochester Business Institute, Registrar, 1850 Ridge Rd E, Rochester, NY 14622, 716-266-0430 (Fax: 716-266-8243) 8AM - 7PM M-Th, 8AM - 5PM F. Enrollment: 410. Records go back to 1920. Alumni records maintained here; call 716-266-0430 Ext. 41. Degrees granted: Associate. Attendance and degree information available by phone, fax, mail. Transcripts available by fax, mail. Written permission needed unless sponsoring agency or student.

Rochester Institute of Technology, Office of the Registrar, George Eastman Bldg, 27 Lomb Memorial Dr, Rochester, NY 14623-5603, 716-475-2825, 716-475-2827 (Fax: 716-475-7005) www.rit.edu. 8:30AM - 6PM M-Th; 8:30AM - 4:30PM F. Enrollment: 13500. Records go back to 1800's. Alumni Records: Alumni Assoc., 41 Lomb Memorial Dr, Rochester, NY 14623-5603. Degrees granted: Associate; Bachelors; Masters; Doctorate. Special programs-Industrial Design, 716-475-2668: Imaging Science, 716-475-5944: Packaging Science, 716-475-2278. Attendance and degree information available by phone, fax, mail. Transcripts available by fax, mail.

Rockefeller University, Office of Graduate Studies, 1230 York Ave, Box 177, New York, NY 10021, 212-327-8000, 212-327-8886 (Fax: 212-327-8505) www.rockefeller.edu. Enrollment: 400. Records go back to 1960. Alumni records are maintained here. Degrees granted: Doctorate. Special programs- PhD Program in Science. Attendance and degree information available by phone, fax, mail. Transcript statements available by fax, mail.

Rockland Community College (Haverstraw Learning Center), Registrar, 15 W Broad St, Haverstraw, NY 10927, 914-942-0624. Records are located at Rockland Community College, Registrar, Suffern, NY.

Rockland Community College (Nyack Learning Center), Registrar, 92-94 Main St, Nyack, NY 10960, 914-358-9392. Records are located at Rockland Community College, Registrar, Suffern, NY.

Rockland Community College (Spring Valley Learning Center), Registrar, 185 N Main St, Spring Valley, NY 10977, 914-574-4700. Records are located at Rockland Community College, Registrar, Suffern, NY.

Rockland Community College, Registrar, 145 College Rd, Suffern, NY 10901, 914-574-4328 (Fax: 914-574-4493). 8AM-8PM M-Th, 9AM-5PM F. Enrollment: 6500. Records go back to 1959. Alumni Records: Rockland Community College, 145 College Rd, Rm 6206, Suffern, NY 10901. Degrees granted: Associate. Attendance, degree and transcript information available by fax, mail.

Russell Sage College Main Campus, Director of Records & Registration, 45 Ferry St, Troy, NY 12180, 518-244-2205 (Fax: 518-244-2460) www.sage.edu. Enrollment: 1021. Records go back to 1917. Alumni records are maintained here. Degrees granted: Associate; Bachelors; Masters. Attendance and degree information available by phone, fax, mail. Transcripts available by fax, mail.

Sage Colleges (Sage Junior College of Albany), Director of Admissions & Registration, 140 New Scotland Ave, Albany, NY 12208, 518-292-1715 (Fax: 518-292-1964) www.sage.edu. 8:30AM-5PM; 8:30AM-4:30PM Summer. Enrollment: 800. Records go back to 1957. Alumni records maintained here; call 518-292-1725. Degrees granted: Associate. Certification: Legal Studies, Computer Science. Attendance and degree information available by phone, fax, mail. Transcripts available by fax, mail.

Sage Colleges, Director of Records & Registration, 45 Ferry St, Troy, NY 12180, 518-244-2205 (Fax: 518-244-2460) www.sage.edu. 8:30AM-5PM. Enrollment: 3620. Records go back to 1917. Alumni records are maintained here also. Call 518-244-2242. Degrees granted: Associate; Bachelors; Masters. Special programs-Associate Level, 518-244-2000. Attendance and degree information available by phone, fax, mail. Transcripts available by fax, mail.

Sara Schenirer Teacher Seminary, Registrar, 4622 14th Ave, Brooklyn, NY 11219, 718-633-8557 (Fax: 718-435-0115). Records go back to 1941. Alumni records are maintained here. Degrees granted. Attendance, degree and transcript information available by mail.

Sarah Lawrence College, Registrar, One Meadway, Bronxville, NY 10708, 914-395-2301, 914-395-2301 Ext. 2302 (Fax: 914-395-2666) www.slc.edu. 9AM - 5PM. Enrollment: 1306. Records go back to 1928. Alumni records maintained here; call 914-395-2530. Degrees granted: Bachelors; Masters. Special programs- Center for Continuing Education, 914-395-2205. Attendance and degree information available by phone, mail. Transcripts available by mail. Transcripts only available with written permission from the student.

Schenectady County Community College, Registrar, 78 Washington Ave, Schenectady, NY 12305, 518-381-1200, 518-381-1348 www.crisny.org/education/capreg/sccc/index.htm. (Fax: 518-346-0379) 8:30AM-7:30PM M-Th, 8:30AM-4:30PM F. Records go back to 1970's. Alumni records maintained here;

call 518-381-1200. Degrees granted: Associate. Attendance and degree information available by phone, fax, mail. Transcripts available by fax, mail.

School of Visual Arts, Registrar, 209 E 23rd St, New York, NY 10010, 212-592-2200, 212-592-2000 (Fax: 212-592-2069) 8AM-5:45PM. www.schoolofvisualarts.edu. Enrollment: 5100. Records go back to 1940's. Alumni records maintained here; call 212-592-2300. Degrees granted: Bachelors; Masters. Attendance and degree information available by phone, fax, mail. Transcripts available by fax, mail.

Seminary of the Immaculate Conception, Registrar, 440 W Neck Rd, Huntington, NY 11743, 516-423-0483 (Fax: 516-423-2346). 8:30AM-4:30PM. Enrollment: 155. Records go back to 1936. Alumni records are maintained here. Degrees granted: Masters; Doctorate. Attendance, degree and transcript information available by written request only.

Sh'or Yoshuv Rabbinical College, Registrar, 1526 Central Ave, Far Rockaway, NY 11691, 718-327-7444 (Fax: 718-327-6303). 9AM-5PM. Enrollment: 110. Records go back to 1991. Alumni records are maintained here. Degrees granted: Bachelors. Attendance and degree information available by phone, fax, mail. Transcripts available by fax, mail.

Siena College, Registrar, 515 Loudon Rd, Loudonville, NY 12211-1462, 518-783-2310 (Fax: 518-786-5060) www.siena.edu. 8:30AM-4:30PM. Enrollment: 2942. Records go back to 1940's. Alumni records maintained here; call 518-783-2430. Degrees granted: Bachelors; Masters. Attendance and degree information available by phone, fax, mail. Transcripts available by mail.

Simmons Institute of Funeral Service, Registrar, 1828 South Ave, Syracuse, NY 13207, 315-475-5142 (Fax: 315-475-3817). 8AM-3PM M-F, 8AM-Noon Sat. Enrollment: 70. Records go back to 1950's. Alumni records are maintained here. Degrees granted: Associate; NAOS. Attendance and degree information available by phone, fax, mail. Transcripts available by mail.

Skidmore College, Registrar, 815 N Broadway, Saratoga Springs, NY 12866-1632, 518-580-5710 (Fax: 518-584-7963) 8AM-4:30PM. www.skidmore.edu. Enrollment: 2100. Records go back to 1912. Alumni records maintained here; call 518-580-5610. Degrees granted: Bachelors; Masters. Special programs- UWW, 518-580-5450: MALS, 518-580-5480. Attendance and degree information available by phone, mail. Transcripts available by fax, mail.

Southampton College of Long Island University, Registrar Office, 239 Montauk Hwy, Southampton, NY 11968, 516-283-4000 Ext. 8325 (Fax: 516-287-8125) 8AM-5PM. www.southampton.liunet.edu. Enrollment: 1400. Records go back to 1963. Alumni records maintained here; call 516-283-4000 Ext. 8347. Degrees granted: Bachelors; Masters. Attendance and degree information available by phone, fax, mail. Transcripts available by fax, mail.

St Anthony On Hudson, Registrar, 517 Washington Ave, Rensselaer, NY 12144, 518-463-2261, 518-472-1000 (Fax: 518-472-1013). Degrees granted, Priest. Attendance and degree information available by phone, mail. Transcripts available by mail.

St. Bernard's Institute, Registrar, 1100 S Goodman St, Rochester, NY 14620, 716-271-

3657 (Fax: 716-271-2045). 8:30AM - 4:30PM. Enrollment: 150. Records go back to 1893. Alumni records are maintained here. Degrees granted: Bachelors; Masters. Attendance and degree information available by phone, fax, mail. Transcripts available by fax, mail.

St. Bonaventure University, Registrar, Rte 417, St Bonaventure, NY 14778, 716-375-2020, 716-375-2000 (Fax: 716-375-2135) www.sbu.edu. 8:30AM - 4:30PM. Enrollment: 2822. Records go back to 1920's. Alumni records maintained here; call 716-375-2375. Degrees granted: Masters. Attendance and degree information available by phone, fax, mail. Transcripts available by fax, mail.

St. Francis College, Registrar, 180 Remsen St, Brooklyn, NY 11201, 718-522-2300 Ext. 242, 718-489-5242 (Fax: 718-624-6677) 9AM-5PM. www.stfranciscollege.edu. Enrollment: 2100. Records go back to 1930. Alumni records maintained here; call 718-522-2300 Ext. 362. Degrees granted: Associate; Bachelors. Attendance and degree information available by fax, mail. Transcripts available by mail.

St. John Fisher College, Registrar, 3690 East Ave, Rochester, NY 14618, 716-385-8015 (Fax: 716-385-7303). 8:30AM - 4:30PM. Enrollment: 1900. Records go back to 1951. Alumni records maintained here; call 716-385-8001. Degrees granted: Bachelors; Masters. Certification: ACCT. Special programs- Academic Dean, 716-385-8116. Attendance and degree information available by phone, fax, mail. Transcripts available by fax, mail.

St. John's University, Registrar, 8000 Utopia Pkwy, Jamaica, NY 11439, 718-990-1487 (Fax: 718-990-1677). 8:30AM-7:30PM M, 8:30AM-4:30PM T-Th, 8:30AM-3PM. Alumni records maintained here; call 718-990-6232. Degrees granted: Associate; Bachelors; Masters; Doctorate. Attendance and degree information available by phone, mail. Transcripts available by mail.

St. John's University (Branch), Registrar, 300 Howard Ave, **Staten Island**, NY 10301, 718-390-4545 (Fax: 718-390-4590) www.stjohns.edu. Records are located at St. John's University, Registrar, Jamaica, NY.

St. Joseph's College, Registrar, 245 Clinton Ave, Brooklyn, NY 11205-3688, 718-636-6800 (Fax: 718-636-6075). 9AM-5PM. Enrollment: 1300. Records go back to 1921. Alumni records are maintained. Degrees granted: Bachelors. Attendance and degree information available by phone, fax, mail. Transcripts available by fax, mail.

St. Joseph's College (Suffolk), Registrar, 155 Roe Blvd, Patchogue, NY 11772, 516-447-3239 (Fax: 516-654-1782). 8:30AM-5PM. Records go back to 1920's. Alumni records maintained here; call 516-447-3215. Degrees granted: Bachelors; Masters. Special programs- Graduate Files, 718-636-6800. Attendance and degree information available by phone, fax, mail. Transcripts available by mail.

St. Joseph's Seminary, Registrar, 201 Seminary Ave, Yonkers, NY 10704, 914-968-6200 Ext. 8208 (Fax: 914-968-7912). 9AM-5PM. Records go back to 1896. Alumni records are maintained here. Degrees granted: Masters; M.Div. Attendance and degree information available by phone, fax, mail. Transcripts available by fax, mail.

St. Lawrence University, Registrar, 23 Ramoda Dr, Canton, NY 13617, 315-229-

5267 (Fax: 315-229-7424) www.stlawu.edu. 8AM-4:30PM. Enrollment: 1920. Records go back to 1856. Alumni records maintained here; call 315-229-5513. Degrees granted: Bachelors; Masters. Attendance and degree information available by phone, fax, mail. Transcripts available by mail.

St. Thomas Aquinas College, Records Office, 125 Rte 340, Sparkill, NY 10976, 914-398-4300 www.stac.edu. 8:30AM - 5PM. Enrollment: 2500. Records go back to 1958. Alumni records maintained here; call 914-398-4017. Degrees granted: Associate; Bachelors; Masters. Special programs-Continuing Education (HS), 914-398-4200. Attendance and degree information available by phone, mail. Transcripts available by mail.

St. Vladimir's Orthodox Theological Seminary, Registrar, 575 Scarsdale Rd, Crestwood, NY 10707, 914-961-8313 (Fax: 914-961-4507). 9AM-3PM. Degrees granted: Masters; Doctorate. Attendance and degree information available by phone, mail. Transcripts available by mail.

State University College at Brockport, Registrar, 350 New Campus Dr, Brockport, NY 14420, www.brockport.edu 716-395-2531 8AM-5PM. Enrollment: 9148. Records go back to 1940's. Alumni records maintained here; call 716-395-5124. Degrees granted: Bachelors; Masters. Certification: ADV Study. Attendance and degree information available by phone, fax, mail. Transcripts available by fax, mail.

State University College at Cortland, Registrar, PO Box 2000, Cortland, NY 13045, 607-753-4701 (Fax: 607-753-5989) 8:30AM-4PM. www.cortland.edu. Enrollment: 5700. Records go back to 1867. Alumni records maintained here; call 607-753-2516. Degrees granted: Bachelors; Masters. Certification: CAS. Attendance and degree information available by phone, fax, mail. Transcripts available by fax, mail.

State University College at Fredonia, Registrar, Fredonia, NY 14063, 716-673-3323, 716-673-3171 www.fredonia.edu. 9AM-5PM. Enrollment: 4500. Records go back to 1900's. Alumni records maintained here; call 716-673-3553. Degrees granted: Bachelors; Masters. Attendance and degree information available by phone, mail. Transcripts available by mail.

State University College at Geneseo, Records Office, Erwin 102, 1 College Circle, Geneseo, NY 14454, 716-245-5566, 716-245-5567 (Fax: 716-245-5005) 8AM - 4:15PM. http://mosaic.cc.geneseo.edu/geneseo.html. Enrollment: 5200. Records go back to 1800's. Alumni Records: Alumni Assoc., Schrader Bldg, Geneseo, NY 14454. Degrees granted: Bachelors; Masters. Attendance and degree information available by phone, fax, mail. Transcripts available by mail.

State University College at Old Westbury, Registrar, PO Box 210, Old Westbury, NY 11568, 516-876-3055, 516-876-3092 (Fax: 516-876-3209) 9AM-4:45PM. www.westbury.edu. Enrollment: 4000. Records go back to 1976. Alumni records maintained here; call 516-876-3140. Degrees granted: Bachelors. Attendance and degree information available by phone, mail. Transcripts available by mail.

State University College at Oneonta, Registrar, Oneonta, NY 13820-4015, 607-436-2531 (Fax: 607-436-2164) 8AM-4:30PM. www.oneonta.edu. Enrollment: 5200. Records go back to 1889. Alumni records maintained here; call 607-536-2526. Degrees granted: Bachelors; Masters.

Attendance and degree information available by phone, fax, mail. Transcripts available by fax, mail.

State University College at Oswego,
Registrar, Oswego, NY 13126, 315-341-2234, 315-341-2237 (Fax: 315-341-3167) 8AM-5PM. www.oswego.edu. Enrollment: 8500. Records go back to 1940. Alumni Records: Alumni Assoc., King Alumni Hall, Oswego, NY 13126. Degrees granted: Bachelors; Masters. Attendance and degree information available by phone, fax, mail. Transcripts available by fax, mail.

State University College at Plattsburgh,
Registrar, 101 Broad St, Plattsburgh, NY 12901, 518-564-2100 (Fax: 518-564-4900) www.plattsburgh.edu. 9AM-4PM. Enrollment: 6182. Records go back to 1890's. Alumni records maintained here; call 518-564-2090. Degrees granted: Bachelors; Masters. Attendance and degree information available by phone, fax, mail. Transcripts available by mail.

State University College at Potsdam,
Registrar, Pierrepont Ave, Potsdam, NY 13676, 315-267-2154 (Fax: 315-267-2157) 8AM-4:30PM. www.potsdam.edu. Enrollment: 4294. Records go back to 1880's. Alumni records maintained here; call 315-267-2120. Degrees granted: Bachelors; Masters. Attendance and degree information available by phone, mail. Transcripts available by mail.

State University College at Purchase,
Registrar, 735 Anderson Hill Rd, Purchase, NY 10577-1400, 914-251-6360 (Fax: 914-251-6373) www.purchase.edu. 8:30AM-5PM. Enrollment: 2500. Records go back to 1970. Alumni records maintained here; call 914-251-6054. Degrees granted: Bachelors; Masters. Special programs- Performing Arts (Theater and Film). Attendance and degree information available by phone, mail. Transcripts available by mail.

State University of New York (College of Optometry at New York City), Registrar, 100 E 24th St, Manhattan, NY 10010, 212-780-4900, 212-780-5100 (Fax: 212-780-5104) 8AM-5PM. www.sunyopt.edu. Enrollment: 296. Records go back to 1972. Alumni records are maintained here. Degrees granted: Masters; Doctorate; OD. Attendance, degree and transcript information available by mail.

State University of New York (College of Environmental Science and Forestry), Registrar, Syracuse, NY 13210, 315-470-6655 (Fax: 315-470-6933) www.esf.edu. 8AM-4:30PM. Enrollment: 1566. Records go back to 1912. Alumni records maintained here; call 315-470-6632. Degrees granted: Associate; Bachelors; Masters; Doctorate. Attendance and degree information available by phone, fax, mail. Transcripts available by mail.

State University of New York College at Buffalo, Registrar, 1300 Elmwood Ave, Buffalo, NY 14222, 716-878-4905 (Fax: 716-878-3159) www.buffalostate.edu. 8:15AM-5PM. Enrollment: 11528. Records go back to 1920's. Alumni records maintained here; call 716-878-6001. Degrees granted: Bachelors; Masters. Attendance and degree information available by phone, fax, mail. Transcripts available by mail.

State University of New York College at Farmingdale, Office of the Registrar, Greenley Hall, Melville Rd, Farmingdale, NY 11735-1021, www.farmingdale.edu. 516-420-2776, 516-420-2000 (switchboard) (Fax: 516-420-2275) 8:30AM - 8PM M-Th; 8:30AM-

4:30PM F. Enrollment: 6718. Records go back to 1965. Alumni records maintained here; call 516-420-2288. Degrees granted: Associate; Bachelors. Attendance and degree information available by phone, fax, mail. Transcripts available by fax, mail.

State University of New York College of Ag and Tech at Cobleskill, Registrar, Cobleskill, NY 12043, 518-234-5521 (Fax: 518-234-5333). 8AM - 4:15PM. Enrollment: 2400. Records go back to 1930's. Alumni records maintained here; call 518-234-5628. Degrees granted: Associate; Bachelor of Technology. Special programs- Call 518-234-5525. Attendance and degree information available by phone, fax, mail. Transcripts available by fax, mail.

State University of New York College of Ag and Tech / Morrisville, Registrar, Morrisville, NY 13408, 315-684-6066 (Fax: 315-684-6421) www.morrisville.edu. 8AM-5PM. Enrollment: 3151. Records go back to 1920's. Alumni records maintained here; call 315-684-6030. Degrees granted: Associate. Special programs- 315-684-6066. Attendance and degree information available by phone, fax, mail. Transcripts available by mail.

State University of New York College of Technology at Alfred, Registrar, Engineering Tecnology Bldg, Alfred, NY 14802, 607-587-4795, 607-587-4796 (Fax: 607-587-3294) www.alfredtech.edu/. 8:30AM - 4:30PM. Enrollment: 3000. Records go back to 1911. Alumni records maintained here; call 607-587-4260. Degrees granted: Associate; Bachelors. Attendance and degree information available by phone, fax, mail. Transcripts available by fax, mail.

State University of New York College of Technology at Canton, Registrar, Cornell Dr, Canton, NY 13617-1098, 315-386-7042, 315-386-7647 www.canton.edu (Fax: 315-386-7929) 8AM-5PM Winter; 8AM-4PM Summer. Enrollment: 2000. Records go back to 1906. Alumni records maintained here; call 315-386-7127. Degrees granted: Associate. Attendance and degree information available by phone, mail. Transcripts available by mail.

State University of New York College of Technology at Delhi, Office of Records & Registration, 124 Bush Hall, Delhi, NY 13753, 607-746-4560, 607-746-4561 (Fax: 607-746-4569). 8AM-5PM. Enrollment: 1891. Records go back to 1948. Alumni records maintained here; call 607-746-4603. Degrees granted: Associate. Attendance, degree and transcript information available by fax, mail.

State University of New York Empire State College (Northeast Center), Registrar, 845 Central Ave, Albany, NY 12206, 518-485-5964 (Fax: 518-485-5985) www.esc.edu. Records are located at State University of New York Empire State College, Saratoga Springs, NY.

State University of New York Empire State College (Niagara Frontier Regional Center), Registrar, 617 Main St Market Arcade, Buffalo, NY 14203-1498, 716-853-7700 (Fax: 716-853-7713) www.esc.edu. Records are located at State University of New York Empire State College, Saratoga Springs, NY.

State University of New York Empire State College (Hudson Valley Regional Center), Registrar, 200 N Central Ave, Hartsdale, NY 10530, 914-948-6206. Records are located at State University of New York Empire State College, Saratoga Springs, NY.

State University of New York Empire State College (Metropolitan Regional Center), Registrar, 225 Varick St, New York, NY 10014, 212-647-7800 (Fax: 212-647-7829) www.esc.edu. Records are located at State University of New York Empire State College, Saratoga Springs, NY.

State University of New York Empire State College (Long Island Regional Center), Registrar, Trainor House, PO Box 130, Old Westbury, NY 11568, 516-997-4700. Records are not housed here. Records are located at State University of New York Empire State College, Saratoga Springs, NY.

State University of New York Empire State College (Genessee Valley Regional Center), Registrar, 8 Prince St, Rochester, NY 14607, 716-244-3641 (Fax: 716-473-1949) www.esc.edu. Records are located at State University of New York Empire State College, Saratoga Springs, NY.

State University of New York Empire State College, Registrar, Two Union Ave, Saratoga Springs, NY 12866, 518-587-2100 Ext. 209 (Fax: 518-587-5404) www.esc.edu. 8:30AM-4:30PM. Alumni records are maintained here. Degrees granted: Associate; Bachelors; Masters. Attendance and degree information available by phone, mail. Transcripts available by mail.

State University of New York Health Sciences - Buffalo
(See State University of New York at Buffalo, Main Campus)

State University of New York Health Science Center at Brooklyn, Registrar, 450 Clarkson Ave, Brooklyn, NY 11203, 718-270-1875 (Fax: 718-270-7592) www.hscbklyn.edu. 10AM - 6PM. Enrollment: 1672. Alumni records are maintained here. Degrees granted: Bachelors; Masters; Doctorate. Attendance and degree information available by phone, mail. Transcripts available by mail.

State University of New York Health Science Center at Syracuse, Registrar, 155 Elizabeth Blackwell St, Syracuse, NY 13210, www.hscsyr.edu. 315-464-4604 (Fax: 315-464-8867) 8:30AM - 4:30PM. Enrollment: 1200. Records go back to 1902. Alumni records maintained here; call 315-464-4361. Degrees granted: Associate; Bachelors; Masters; Doctorate. Special programs- College of Medicine Alumni, 315-464-4361: Health Related Professions Alumni, 315-464-4416. Attendance and degree information available by phone, fax, mail. Transcripts available by fax, mail.

State University of New York Institute of Technology / Utica/Rome, Registrar, PO Box 3050, Utica, NY 13504-3050, 315-792-7265, 315-792-7262 (Fax: 315-792-7804) www.sunyit.edu. 8AM - 5PM. Enrollment: 2500. Records go back to 1966. Alumni records maintained here; call 315-792-7266. Degrees granted: Bachelors; Masters. Attendance and degree information available by phone, fax, mail. Transcripts available by fax, mail.

State University of New York Maritime College, Registrar, Fort Schuyler, Throggs Neck, NY 10465, 718-409-7265 (Fax: 718-409-7264) www.sunymaritime.edu. 8:30AM-4:30PM. Enrollment: 810. Records go back to 1878. Alumni Records: Alumni Assoc., SUNY Maritime College, 6 Pennyfield Ave, Bronx, NY 10465. Degrees granted: Bachelors; Masters. Attendance and degree

information available by phone, fax, mail. Transcripts available by fax, mail.

State University of New York at Albany, Registrar, 1400 Washington Ave, Albany, NY 12222, 518-442-3070 (Fax: 518-442-2560) www.albany.edu. 9AM-5PM M-Th; 9AM-4PM F. Enrollment: 16616. Alumni records are maintained here. Degrees granted: Bachelors; Masters; Doctorate. Attendance, degree and transcript information available by mail.

State University of New York at Binghamton, Registrar, PO Box 6002, Binghamton, NY 13902-6002, 607-777-6568, 607-777-6569 (Fax: 607-777-6515) 9:30AM-4PM. www.binghamton.edu. Enrollment: 12089. Records go back to 1950's. Alumni records maintained here; call 607-777-2431. Degrees granted: Bachelors; Masters; Doctorate. Attendance and degree information available by phone, fax, mail. Transcripts available by fax, mail.

State University of New York at New Paltz, Records & Registration, 75 S Manheim Blvd, New Paltz, NY 12561, 914-257-3100 (Fax: 914-257-3009) www.newpaltz.edu. 8:30AM - 4:30PM. Enrollment: 7852. Records go back to 1961. Alumni records maintained here; call 914-257-3230. Degrees granted: Bachelors; Masters. Attendance and transcript information available by fax, mail. Degree information available by phone, fax, mail.

State University of New York at Stony Brook, Registrar Office, Stony Brook, NY 11794-1101, 516-632-6885 (Fax: 516-632-9685) www.sunysb.edu. 8:40AM-4PM. Enrollment: 17500. Records go back to 1961. Alumni records maintained here; call 516-632-6330. Degrees granted: Bachelors; Masters; Doctorate. Attendance and degree information available by phone, fax, mail. Transcripts available by fax, mail.

Stenotype Academy, Registrar, 15 Park Row, New York, NY 10038, 212-962-0002 (Fax: 212-608-8210) 8AM-7PM M-Th, 8AM-3PM F. Enrollment: 700. Records go back to 1970's. Alumni records are maintained here Degrees granted: Associate. Attendance and degree information available by phone, fax, mail. Transcripts available by fax, mail.

Suffolk Community College (Western), Registrar, Crooked Hill Rd, Brentwood, NY 11717, 516-434-6750 www.li.net/~scc/. Records are located at Suffolk Community College, (Ammerman), Selden, NY.

Suffolk Community College (Eastern), Registrar, Speonk-Riverhead Rd, Riverhead, NY 11901, www.sunysuffolk.edu. 516-548-2500 (Fax: 516-548-3613) Records are located at Suffolk Community College, (Ammerman), Selden, NY.

Suffolk Community College (Ammerman), Registrar, 533 College Rd, NFL Bldg, Rm 30, Selden, NY 11784, 516-451-4008, 516-451-4110 (switchboard) (Fax: 516-451-4015; 451-4216 (attend & grades)) www.li.net/~scc/. 9AM-8PM M-Th, 9AM-5PM F. Enrollment: 19500. Records go back to 1985. Alumni records maintained here; call 516-732-7979. Degrees granted: Associate. Attendance information available by phone, fax, mail. Degree and transcript information available by fax, mail.

Sullivan County Community College, Registrar, PO Box 4002, Loch Sheldrake, NY 12759, 914-434-5750 (Fax: 914-434-4806). Enrollment: 2000. Records go back to 1964. Alumni records are maintained here. Degrees granted: Associate. Attendance and degree

information available by phone, fax, mail. Transcripts available by fax, mail.

Syracuse University, Registrar, Syracuse, NY 13244, 315-443-1870, 315-443-2187 http://sumweb.syr.edu/registrar/index.htm. 8AM - 4:30PM. Enrollment: 18970. Records go back to 1873. Alumni records maintained here; call 315-443-3514. Degrees granted: Associate; Bachelors; Masters; Doctorate. Certification: Advanced Study. Attendance and degree information available by phone, mail. Transcripts available by mail.

Talmudical Institute of Upstate New York, Registrar, 769 Park Ave, Rochester, NY 14607, 716-473-2810. Records go back to 1952. Attendance and degree information available by phone, fax, mail. Transcripts available by fax, mail.

Talmudical Seminary Oholei Torah, Registrar, 667 Eastern Pkwy, Brooklyn, NY 11213, 718-774-5050 (Fax: 718-778-0784) 9:30AM - 5PM. Enrollment: 232. Records go back to 1985. Alumni records are maintained here. Attendance, degree and transcript information available by mail.

Taylor Business Institute, Registrar, 120 W 30th St, New York, NY 10001, 212-279-0510 (Fax: 212-947-9793) www.tbi.edu. 9AM-5PM. Enrollment: 500. Records go back to 1970. Degrees granted: Associate. Attendance, degree and transcript information available by mail.

Technical Career Institute, Registrar, 320 W 31st St, New York, NY 10001, 212-594-4000 Ext. 270 (Fax: 212-629-3937) www.jci.edu. 8:45AM-6:45PM M, 8:45AM-4:45PM W-F. Enrollment: 3500. Records go back to 1940. Degrees granted: Associate. Attendance, degree and transcript information available by fax, mail.

Tompkins Cortland Community College, Registrar, PO Box 139, 170 North St, Dryden, NY 13053, 607-844-3211 Ext. 4301, 607-844-6582 (Fax: 607-844-9665) www.ithaca.ny.us/Education/TC3. 8:30AM-4PM. Enrollment: 2925. Records go back to 1968. Alumni records maintained here; call 607-844-8211 Ext. 4366. Degrees granted: Associate. Attendance and transcript information available by mail. Degree information available by phone, mail.

Torah Temimah Talmudical Seminary, Registrar, 555 Ocean Pkwy, Brooklyn, NY 11218, 718-438-5779 (Fax: 999-999-9999). Enrollment: 248. Alumni records are maintained here. Degrees granted: Bachelors. Attendance, degree and transcript information available by mail.

Touro College (Huntington Branch), Registrar, 300 Nassau Rd, Huntington, NY 11743, 516-421-2244 (Fax: 516-421-2675). 9AM-7PM M-Th, 9AM-3PM F. Enrollment: 896. Records go back to 1980. Alumni records maintained here; call 516-421-2244 Ext. 315. Degrees granted: Masters; Doctorate. Attendance, degree and transcript information available by fax, mail. Proper letterhead required when confirming degree.

Touro College, Registrar, Empire State Bldg Ste 5122, 350 Fifth Ave, New York, NY 10118, 212-463-0400 Ext. 636 (Fax: 212-627-9542). Records are located at Touro College, Registrar, 844 6th Ave, New York, NY 10001.

Touro College, Registrar, 844 6th Ave, New York, NY 10001, 212-463-0400 Ext. 634 (Fax: 212-627-9542) www.touro.edu. 8AM-5PM. Records go back to 1971. Alumni Records: Touro College, 350 Fifth Ave,

Empire State Bldg Ste 5122, New York, NY 10118. Degrees granted: Bachelors. Attendance and degree information available by phone, fax, mail. Transcripts available by fax, mail.

Trocaire College, Registrar-Student Services, 360 Choate Ave, Buffalo, NY 14220-2094, 716-826-1200 (Ext. 1225), 716-826-1200 (Ext. 1224) (Fax: 716-828-6117) www.trocaire.edu. 8AM - 6PM M-Th, 8AM - 4PM F. Enrollment: 1000. Records go back to 1960. Alumni records maintained here; call 716-826-1200 Ext. 1212. Degrees granted: Associate. Attendance and degree information available by phone, fax, mail. Transcripts available by fax, mail.

Ulster County Community College, Registrar, Stone Ridge, NY 12484, www.ulster.cc.ny.us/. 914-687-5075 (Fax: 914-687-5126) 8:30AM - 7:30PM M-Th, 8:30AM - 4:30PM F. Enrollment: 2500. Records go back to 1963. Alumni records maintained here; call 914-687-5261. Degrees granted: Associate. Attendance and degree information available by phone, mail. Transcripts available by fax, mail.

Union College, Registrar, Whitaker House, Schenectady, NY 12308, 518-388-6109 (Fax: 518-388-6173) www.union.edu. 8:30AM-5PM. Enrollment: 2100. Records go back to 1938. Alumni records maintained here; call 518-388-6168. Degrees granted: Bachelors; Masters; Doctorate. Special programs-Graduate, 518-388-6288. Attendance and degree information available by phone, fax, mail. Transcripts available by fax (followed by letter), mail.

Union Theological Seminary, Registrar, 3041 Broadway, New York, NY 10027-5710, 212-280-1555, 212-662-7100 (Fax: 212-280-1539) www.uts.columbia.edu. 9AM - 5PM. Enrollment: 310. Records go back to 1935. Alumni records maintained here; call 212-280-1511. Degrees granted: Masters; Doctorate. Attendance and degree information available by phone, fax, mail. Transcripts available by mail.

United States Merchant Marine Academy, Registrar, Steamboat Rd, Kings Point, NY 11024, 516-773-5000, 516-773-5485 (Fax: 516-773-5241) www.usmma.edu. 8AM-4:30PM. Enrollment: 900. Records go back to 1939. Alumni records maintained here; call 516-773-5658. Degrees granted: Bachelors. Attendance and degree information available by phone, fax, mail. Transcripts available by fax, mail.

United States Military Academy, Graduate Records Branch, Office of the Dean, West Point, NY 10996-5000, 914-938-3708, 914-938-2050 (Fax: 914-938-3018) www.usma.edu. 7:45AM - 4:30PM. Enrollment: 4000. Records go back to 1920. Alumni records are maintained here. Degrees granted: Bachelors. Attendance and degree information available by phone, fax, mail. Transcripts available by mail.

United Talmudical Academy, Registrar, 82 Lee Ave, Brooklyn, NY 11211, 718-963-9260 (Fax: 718-963-9775). 9AM-5PM. Records go back to 1985. Alumni records are maintained here. Attendance, degree and transcript information available by mail.

University of Rochester, Registrar, 225 Lattimore Hall, Rochester, NY 14627-0038, 716-275-5131 (Fax: 716-275-2190) 8AM-5PM. www.rochester.edu. Enrollment: 9200. Records go back to 1850's. Alumni records maintained here; call 716-273-5888. Degrees granted: Bachelors; Masters; Doctorate. Special programs- Simon Business School:

Eastman School of Music. Attendance and degree information available by phone, fax, mail. Transcripts available by fax, mail.

Utica College of Syracuse University, Registrar, 1600 Burrstone Rd, Utica, NY 13502-4892, 315-792-3195 (Fax: 315-792-3292) 8:30AM-5PM. www.ucsu.edu. Enrollment: 2000. Records go back to 1947. Alumni records maintained here; call 315-792-3025. Degrees granted: Bachelors. Attendance and degree information available by phone, mail. Transcripts available by mail.

Utica Junior College
(See Hinds Com. College, Utica Campus)

Utica School of Commerce (Branch), Registrar, PO Box 462, **Canastota**, NY 13032, 315-697-8200 (Fax: 315-697-2805). Records are located at Utica School of Commerce, Utica, NY.

Utica School of Commerce (Branch), Registrar, 17-19 Elm St, **Oneonta**, NY 13820, 607-432-7003 (Fax: 607-432-7004). Records are located at Utica School of Commerce, Utica, NY.

Utica School of Commerce, Registrar, 201 Bleecker St, **Utica**, NY 13501, 315-733-2307 (Fax: 315-733-9281). 7:30AM - 4:30PM. Enrollment: 600. Records go back to 1896. Alumni records are maintained here. Degrees granted: Associate. Attendance, degree and transcript information available by fax, mail.

Vassar College, Registrar, 124 Raymond Ave, Box 11, Poughkeepsie, NY 12604-0011, www.ucsu.edu. 914-437-5270, 914-437-5271 (Fax: 914-437-7060) www.ucsu.edu. 8:30AM-5PM. Enrollment: 2350. Records go back to 1865. Alumni records maintained here; call 914-437-5445. Degrees granted: Bachelors; Masters. Attendance and degree information available by phone, fax, mail. Transcripts available by fax, mail.

Villa Maria College of Buffalo, Registrar, 240 Pine Ridge Rd, Buffalo, NY 14225-3999, 716-896-0700 Ext. 337 (Fax: 716-896-0705) 8AM-4PM. www.villa.edu. Records go back to 1964. Alumni records maintained here; call 716-896-0700 Ext. 327. Degrees granted: Associate. Attendance information available by fax, mail. Degree information available by phone, fax, mail. Transcripts available by mail.

Wadhams Hall Seminary/College, Registrar, 6866 State Highway 37, Ogdensburg, NY 13669, 315-393-4231 (Fax: 315-393-4249). 8AM - 4PM. Enrollment: 24. Records go back to 1924. Alumni records are maintained here. Degrees granted: Bachelors. Certification: Pre-Theologate. Attendance information available by phone. Degree and transcript information available by written request only.

Wagner College, Registrar, Howard Ave and Campus Rd, Staten Island, NY 10301, 718-390-3173, 718-390-3207 (Fax: 718-390-3344) www.wagner.edu. 10AM-4PM.

Enrollment: 1800. Alumni records maintained here; call 718-390-3240. Degrees granted: Bachelors; Masters. Certification: Nursing. Attendance, degree and transcript information available by fax, mail.

Webb Institute, Registrar, Crescent Beach Rd, Glen Cove, NY 11542, 516-671-2213 www.webb-institute.edu (Fax: 516-674-9838) Enrollment: 80. Records go back to 1900. Alumni records are maintained here. Degrees granted: Bachelors. Attendance and degree information available by phone, fax, mail. Transcripts available by fax, mail.

Wells College, Registrar, Aurora, NY 13026-0500, 315-364-3215 (Fax: 315-364-3383) www.wells.edu. 8:30AM-Noon, 1-4:30PM. Enrollment: 320. Records go back to 1900. Alumni records maintained here; call 315-364-3200. Degrees granted: Bachelors. Attendance and degree information available by phone, fax, mail. Transcripts available by fax, mail; student signature required for written transcript requests.

Westchester Business Institute, Registrar, PO Box 710, 325 Central Ave, White Plains, NY 10606, 914-948-4442 (Fax: 914-948-8216) 8AM-11PM. Enrollment: 1000. Records go back to 1960. Alumni records are maintained here. Degrees granted: Associate. Attendance, degree and transcript information available by fax, mail.

Westchester Community College, Registrar, 75 Grasslands Rd, Valhalla, NY 10595, 914-785-6810 (Fax: 914-785-6277). 9AM-8PM M-Th, 9AM-5PM F. Enrollment: 11211. Records go back to 1950. Alumni records maintained here; call 914-785-6670. Degrees granted: Associate. Attendance and degree information available by phone, mail. Transcripts available by mail.

Wood School (The)
(See Wood Tobe-Coburn School)

Wood Tobe Coburn School, Registrar, 8 E 40th St, New York, NY 10016, 212-686-9040 Ext. 36 (Fax: 212-686-9171). 8AM-5PM. Records go back to 1954. Alumni records are maintained here. Degrees granted: Associate. Attendance and degree information available by phone, fax, mail. Transcripts available by mail.

Yeshiva Derech Chaim, Registrar, 1573 39th St, Brooklyn, NY 11218, 718-438-3070 (Fax: 718-435-9285) Enrollment: 165. Attendance, degree and transcript information available by mail.

Yeshiva Karlin Stolin Beth Aaron V'Israel Rabbinical Institute, Registrar, 1818 54th St, Brooklyn, NY 11204, 718-232-7800 (Fax: 718-331-4833). 9AM-5PM. Enrollment: 50. Records go back to 1981. Alumni records are maintained here. Degrees granted: Bachelors; 1st Professional Degree Attendance, degree and transcript information available by mail.

Yeshiva Mikdash Melech, Registrar, 1326 Ocean Pkwy, Brooklyn, NY 11230-5655,

718-339-1090 (Fax: 718-998-9321). Enrollment: 80. Alumni records are maintained here umber. Attendance and degree information available by phone, mail. Transcripts available by mail.

Yeshiva Shaar HaTorah Talmudic Research Institute, Registrar, 83-96 117th St, Kew Gardens, NY 11415, 718-846-1940 (Fax: 718-846-1942) 9AM-5PM. Enrollment: 142. Records go back to 1977. Alumni records are maintained. Degrees granted: Bachelors; Masters; Rabbinic 1st and 2nd. Attendance and degree information available by phone, mail. Transcripts available by mail.

Yeshiva University, Registrar, 500 W 185th St, New York, NY 10033-3299, 212-960-5400 Ext. 274 (Fax: 212-960-0004) www.yu.edu. 9AM-5PM M,W; 1-5PM T,Th. Enrollment: 5279. Records go back to 1950. Alumni records are maintained here. Degrees granted: Associate; Bachelors; Masters; Doctorate. Attendance and degree information available by phone, fax, mail. Transcripts available by mail.

Yeshiva of Nitra - Rabbinical College Yeshiva Farm Settlement, Registrar, Pines Bridge Rd, Mount Kisco, NY 10549, 718-387-0422 (Fax: 718-387-9400) 9AM-5PM. Enrollment: 190. Records go back to 1948. Alumni records are maintained here. Degrees granted: Bachelors; Rabbinic Degree. Attendance, degree and transcript information available by mail.

Yeshivas Novominsk, Registrar, 1569 47th St, Brooklyn, NY 11219, 718-438-2727 (Fax: 718-438-2472) 9AM-5PM. Enrollment: 113. Records go back to 1932. Alumni records are maintained here. Degrees granted: Bachelors; Talmudic 1st. Attendance and transcript information available by mail. Degree information available by fax, mail.

Yeshivath Viznitz, Registrar, PO Box 446, Monsey, NY 10952, 914-356-1010 (Fax: 914-356-7359). 9AM-5PM. Enrollment: 345. Alumni records are maintained here. Degrees granted: Bachelors; Rabbinic 1st and 2nd. Attendance, degree and transcript information available by mail.

Yesivath Zichron Moshe, Registrar, Laurel Park Rd, PO Box 580, South Fallsburg, NY 12779, 914-434-5240 (Fax: 914-434-1009). Enrollment: 120. Records go back to 1931. Alumni records are maintained here. Attendance, degree and transcript information available by mail.

North Carolina

Alamance Community College, Registrars Office, Student Services, PO Box 8000, Graham, NC 27253-8000, 336-578-2002 www.netpath.net/lrc/index (Fax: 336-578-1987) 8AM-8PM M-Th; 8AM-5PM F. Enrollment: 3500. Records go back to 1959. Alumni records are maintained here. Degrees granted: Associate. Attendance and degree

information available by phone, fax, mail. Transcripts available by fax, mail.

Anson Community College, Registrar, PO Box 126, Polkton, NC 28135, 704-272-7635 www.co.anson.nc-us/anson/anson5htm. (Fax: 704-272-8904) 8AM-5PM. Enrollment: 590. Records go back to 1950's. Alumni records are maintained here. Degrees granted:

Associate. Attendance and degree information available by phone, fax, mail. Transcripts available by fax, mail.

Appalachian State University, Registrar, Boone, NC 28608, 828-262-2050 (Fax: 828-262-3136) www.acs.appstate.edu. 8AM-5PM. Enrollment: 12000. Records go back to 1929. Alumni records maintained here; call 828-

262-2038. Degrees granted: Bachelors; Masters; Doctorate; EDS. Attendance and degree information available by phone, fax, mail. Transcripts available by fax, mail.

Asheville - Buncombe Technical Community College, Registrar, 340 Victoria Rd, Asheville, NC 28801, 828-254-1921 X147 (Fax: 828-251-6718) www.ashevile.cc.nc.us. 8:30AM-8PM M,W; 8:30AM-4:30PM T,Th,F. Enrollment: 4300. Records go back to 1959. Degrees granted: Associate. Special programs- Radiography. Attendance, degree and transcript information available by fax, mail.

Atlantic Christian College
(See Barton College)

Barber-Scotia College, Registrar, 145 Cabarrus Ave W, Concord, NC 28025, 704-789-2900, 704-789-2902 (Fax: 704-793-4950). 8AM-5PM. Alumni records are maintained here. Degrees granted: Bachelors. Attendance, degree and transcript information available by mail.

Barton College, Office of Registrar, College Station, Wilson, NC 27893, 919-399-6327 (Fax: 919-237-1620) www.barton.edu. 8:30AM-5PM. Enrollment: 1338. Records go back to 1902. Alumni records maintained here; call 919-399-6360. Degrees granted: Bachelors. Attendance and degree information available by phone, fax, mail. Transcripts available by fax, mail.

Beaufort County Community College, Registrar, PO Box 1069, Washington, NC 27889, 919-946-6194 (Fax: 919-946-0271). 8:15AM-5PM M-Th; 8:15AM-4PM F. Enrollment: 1250. Records go back to 1970. Degrees granted: Associate. Attendance and degree information available by phone, fax, mail. Transcripts available by mail.

Belmont Abbey College, Registrar, 100 Belmont-Mount Holly Rd, Belmont, NC 28012-2795, 704-825-6732, 704-825-6733 (Fax: 704-825-6727) www.bac.edu. 8:30AM-4:30PM. Enrollment: 900. Alumni records maintained here; call 704-825-6889. Degrees granted: Bachelors; Masters. Attendance and degree information available by phone, mail. Transcripts available by mail.

Bennett College, Records Office, 900 E Washington St, Greensboro, NC 27401-3239, 336-370-8620 (Fax: 336-272-7143) 8AM-5PM. Enrollment: 600. Records go back to 1928. Alumni records are maintained here. Degrees granted: Bachelors. Attendance and degree information available by phone, fax, mail. Transcripts available by fax, mail.

Bladen Community College, Registrar, PO Box 266, Dublin, NC 28332-0266, www.bcc.cc.nc.us.html 910-862-2164 (Fax: 910-862-7424) 8AM-4:30PM M-Th; 8AM-3PM F. Enrollment: 600. Records go back to 1967. Degrees granted: Associate. Attendance and degree information available by phone, fax, mail. Transcripts available by fax, mail.

Bladen Technical Institute
(See Bladen Community College)

Blanton's College, Registrar, 126 College St, Asheville, NC 28801, 828-687-6883. Alumni records are maintained here. Degrees granted: Associate. Attendance, degree and transcript information available by mail.

Blue Ridge Community College, Registrar, College Dr, Flat Rock, NC 28731-9624, www.blueridge.cc.nc.us/ 828-692-3572 X217, 704-692-3572 X300 (Fax: 828-692-2441) 8AM - 8PM M-Th; 8AM - 4:30PM F. Enrollment: 1606. Records go back to 1969. Degrees granted: Associate. Attendance and

degree information available by phone, fax, mail. Transcripts available by mail.

Blue Ridge Technical College
(See Blue Ridge Community College)

Brevard College, Registrar, 400 N Broad St, Brevard, NC 28712-3306, 828-883-8292 www.lightnin.brevard.edu (Fax: 828-884-3790) 8AM-4:30PM. Enrollment: 650. Records go back to 1934. Alumni records are maintained here. Degrees granted: Associate. Attendance and degree information available by phone. Transcripts available by fax, mail.

Brookstone College of Business, Registrar, 7815 National Service Rd, Greensboro, NC 27409, 336-668-2627. Degrees granted: Associate. Attendance and degree information available by phone, mail. Transcripts available by mail.

Brunswick Community College, Registrar, PO Box 30, Supply, NC 28462-0030, www.brunswick.cc.nc.us/brunswick. 910-754-6900 X325, 910-754-6900 X320 (Fax: 910-754-9609) 8AM-5PM. Enrollment: 900. Records go back to 1979. Alumni records are maintained here. Degrees granted: Associate. Attendance and degree information available by phone, fax, mail. Transcripts available by mail.

Caldwell Community College And Technical Institute, Registrar, 2855 Hickory Blvd, Hudson, NC 28638, 828-726-2200, 704-726-2273 (Fax: 828-726-2216) 8AM - 8PM M-Th, 8AM - 5PM F. www.caldwell.cc.tech.edu. Enrollment: 3000. Records go back to 1960's. Alumni records are maintained here. Degrees granted: Associate. Attendance and degree information available by phone, fax, mail. Transcripts available by fax, mail.

Campbell University, Registrar's Office, PO Box 367, Buies Creek, NC 27506, 910-893-1200 (Fax: 910-893-1424) 8:30AM-5PM. www.campbell.edu. Enrollment: 5800. Records go back to 1836. Alumni Records: Alumni Assoc., PO Box 158, Buies Creek, NC 27506. Degrees granted: Bachelors; Masters; Doctorate. Attendance and degree information available by phone, fax, mail. Transcripts available by fax, mail.

Cape Fear Community College, Registrar, 411 N Front St, Wilmington, NC 28401-3993, 910-343-0481 (Fax: 910-763-2279) www.cfcc.wilmington.net/. 8AM-6PM M-Th, 8AM-5PM F. Enrollment: 2730. Records go back to 1967. Alumni records are maintained here. Degrees granted: Associate. Attendance and degree information available by phone, fax, mail. Transcripts available by fax, mail.

Catawba College, Registrar, 2300 W Innes St, Salisbury, NC 28144, 704-637-4111 (Fax: 704-637-4777) www.catawba.edu. 8:30AM-5PM. Enrollment: 1300. Records go back to 1851. Alumni records maintained here; call 704-637-4394. Degrees granted: Bachelors; Masters. Attendance and degree information available by phone, fax, mail. Transcripts available by fax, mail.

Catawba Valley Community College, Student Records, 2550 Hwy 70 SE, Hickory, NC 28602, www.cvcc.cc.nc.us 828-327-7009, 704-327-7000 (Fax: 828-327-7276 X224) 8AM-8PM M-Th; 8AM-5PM F. Enrollment: 3300. Records go back to 1960. Alumni records are maintained here. Degrees granted: Associate. Attendance and degree information available by phone, fax, mail. Transcripts available by fax, mail.

Carteret Community College, Student Services, 3505 Arendell St, Morehead City, NC 28557, www.gofish.CARTERETnc.us 919-247-4142, 919-247-6000 (Fax: 919-247-2514) 8AM-8PM M-Th; 8AM-3:30PM F. Enrollment: 1400. Records go back to 1963. Degrees granted: Associate. Attendance and degree information available by phone, fax, mail. Transcripts available by fax, mail.

Cecil's College, Registrar, 1567 Patton Ave, Asheville, NC 28806, 828-252-2486 (Fax: 828-252-8558) 9AM-6PM. Enrollment: 175. Records go back to 1930's. Degrees granted: Associate. Attendance and degree information available by phone, fax, mail. Transcripts available by fax, mail.

Central Carolina Community College, Registrar, 1105 Kelly Dr, Sanford, NC 27330, 919-775-5401 (Fax: 919-774-1500). 7:30AM-6PM M-Th; 7:30AM-3:30PM F. Enrollment: 3200. Records go back to 1962. Alumni records are maintained here. Degrees granted: Associate. Attendance and degree information available by phone, mail. Transcripts available by mail.

Central Piedmont Community College, Registrar, PO Box 35009, Charlotte, NC 28235, 704-330-6566 (Fax: 704-330-6568) 8AM-5PM. www.cpcc.cc.nc.us/home.htm. Enrollment: 10916. Records go back to 1965. Alumni records maintained here; call 704-342-6666. Degrees granted: Associate. Attendance and degree information available by phone, fax, mail. Transcripts available by fax, mail.

Chowan College, Registrar, PO Box 1848, Murfreesboro, NC 27855, 919-398-6280, 919-398-6281 (Fax: 919-398-1190). 8:30AM-5PM. Enrollment: 800. Records go back to 1846. Alumni records are maintained here. Degrees granted: Associate; Bachelors. Attendance and degree information available by phone, fax, mail. Transcripts available by mail.

Cleveland Community College, Registrar, 137 S Post Rd, Shelby, NC 28152, www.cleveland.cc.nc.us 704-484-4099 (Fax: 704-484-4036) 8AM-8 PM M-Th, 8AM - 4PM F. Enrollment: 2040. Records go back to 1965. Degrees granted: Associate. Attendance and degree information available by phone, fax, mail. Transcripts available by mail.

Cleveland Technical College
(See Cleveland Community College)

Coastal Carolina Community College, Registrar, 444 Western Blvd, Jacksonville, NC 28546-6877, 910-938-6251, 910-938-6252 (Fax: 910-455-2767). 8AM - 5PM. Enrollment: 3500. Records go back to 1967. Degrees granted: Associate. Attendance and degree information available by phone, fax, mail. Transcripts available by fax, mail.

College of the Albemarle, Registrar, PO Box 2327, Elizabeth City, NC 27906-2327, 919-335-0821 X252 (Fax: 919-335-2011). 8AM-4:30PM. Enrollment: 1900. Records go back to 1960. Degrees granted: Associate. Attendance and degree information available by phone, fax, mail. Transcripts available by mail.

Craven Community College, Dean of Records, 800 College Ct, New Bern, NC 28562, 919-638-7223, 919-638-4131 (Fax: 919-638-4232). 8AM-10PM M-Th, 8AM-5PM F. Enrollment: 2200. Records go back to 1968. Alumni records maintained here; call 919-638-4131. Degrees granted: Associate. Attendance, degree and transcript information available by fax, mail.

Davidson College, Registrar, PO Box 1719, Davidson, NC 28036, 704-892-2227 (Fax: 704-892-2732) www.davidson.edu. 8:30AM-5PM. Enrollment: 1700. Records go back to 1837. Alumni records maintained here; call 704-892-2111. Degrees granted: Bachelors. Attendance and degree information available by phone, fax, mail. Transcripts available by fax, mail.

Davidson County Community College, Student Records Office, PO Box 1287, Lexington, NC 27293-1287, 336-249-8186 (Fax: 336-249-0379). 8:30AM-5PM. Enrollment: 2500. Records go back to 1964. Degrees granted: Associate. Attendance and degree information available by phone, fax, mail. Transcripts available by fax, mail.

Duke University, Registrar, PO Box 90054, Durham, NC 27708-0001, 919-684-2813 www.registrar.duke.edu/registrar/ (Fax: 919-684-4500) 8AM-5PM. Enrollment: 11000. Records go back to 1938. Alumni Records: 614 Chapel Dr, Box 90573, Durham, NC 27708-0570. Degrees granted: Bachelors; Masters; Doctorate. Attendance and degree information available by phone, fax, mail. Transcripts available by fax, mail.

Durham Technical Community College Registrar, 1637 Lawson St, Durham, NC 27703, www.dtcc.cc.nc.us. 919-686-3315 (Fax: 919-686-3669) 8AM-6PM M-Th; 8AM-5PM F. Enrollment: 3183. Records go back to 1960's. Practical Nursing records available from 1940's. Alumni records are maintained here. Degrees granted: Associate. Attendance and degree information available by phone, fax, mail. Transcripts available by fax, mail.

East Carolina University, Registrar, E. Fifth St, Greenville, NC 27858-4353, 919-328-6524 (Fax: 919-328-4232). 8AM-5PM. Enrollment: 16176. Records go back to 1907. Alumni records are maintained here also. Call 919-328-6072. Degrees granted: Bachelors; Masters; Doctorate; Special programs-Medical School, 919-816-2201. Attendance and degree information available by phone, fax, mail. Transcripts available by fax, mail.

East Coast Bible College, Registrar, 6900 Wilkinson Blvd, Charlotte, NC 28214, 704-394-2307 (Fax: 704-393-3689). Enrollment: 200. Records go back to 1976. Alumni records are maintained here. Degrees granted: Associate; Bachelors Attendance, degree and transcript information available by written request only.

Edgecombe Community College, Registrar, 2009 W Wilson St, Tarboro, NC 27886, 919-823-5166 (Fax: 919-823-6817) 8AM-5PM. www.edgecombe.cc.us. Enrollment: 2000. Records go back to 1960's. Formerly **Edgecombe Technical College**. Alumni records are maintained here. Degrees granted: Associate. Attendance and degree information available by phone, fax, mail. Transcripts available by fax, mail.

Elizabeth City State University, Registrar, 1704 Wicksville Rd, ECSU Box 953, Elizabeth City, NC 27909, 252-335-3300, 252-335-3301 (Fax: 252-335-3729) www.ecsu.edu. 8AM-5PM. Enrollment: 2000. Records go back to 1894. Alumni Records: Alumni Assoc., Campus Box 977, Elizabeth City, NC 27909. Degrees granted: Bachelors. Attendance and degree information available by phone, fax, mail. Transcripts available by fax.

Elon College, Registrar, Campus Box 2106, Elon College, NC 27244, www.elon.edu 336-584-2376, 336-584-9711 (Fax: 336-538-2735) Enrollment: 3500. Records go back to 1889. Alumni Records: Alumni Relations,

Campus Box 2600, Elon College, NC 27244. Degrees granted: Bachelors; Masters. Special programs- General Studies, Honors Programs, 336-584-2121: International & Special, 336-584-2224: Accounting, Business Admin, Economics, MBA, 336-584-2566: Fine Arts, Music, Performing Arts, Visual Arts, Theatre, 336-584-2440: Public Admin., Sociology, 336-584-2396: English, Languages, Philosophy, Religious Studies, 336-584-2211: Education, Teaching Fellows, Writing Program, 336-584-2201: Health, Phys Education, Leisure/Sports Management, 336-584-2682: Biology, Chemistry, Computing Sci, Mathematics, Physics, 336-584-2701: Education, Teacher Education, M Ed, 336-584-2353. Attendance and degree information available by phone, mail. Transcripts available by mail.

Fayetteville State University, Registrar, 1200 Murchison Rd, Fayetteville, NC 28302, 910-486-1185 (Fax: 910-486-1599) 8:30AM-4:30PM. www.uncfsu.edu. Enrollment: 3719. Records go back to 1900. Alumni records are maintained here. Degrees granted: Associate; Bachelors; Masters; Doctorate. Attendance and degree information available by phone, mail. Transcripts available by written request only.

Fayetteville Technical Community College, Registrar, PO Box 35236, 2201 Hull Rd, Fayetteville, NC 28303, 910-678-8252, 910-678-8474 www.faytech.cc.nc.us. (Fax: 910-678-8407) Enrollment: 7112. Records go back to 1961. Alumni records maintained here; call 910-678-8268. Attendance and degree information available by phone, fax, mail. Transcripts available by mail.

Forsyth Technical Community College, Registrar, 2100 Silas Creek Pkwy, Winston-Salem, NC 27103, 336-723-0371 X7314 (Fax: 336-761-2098). 8AM-7PM M-Th; 8AM-3PM F. Enrollment: 4900. Records go back to 1960. Alumni records are maintained here. Degrees granted: Associate; Arts & Science, Applied Science. Attendance, degree and transcript information available by fax, mail.

Gardner-Webb University, Registrar, PO Box 997, Boiling Springs, NC 28017, 704-434-2361 X222 www.gardnerweb.edu. (Fax: 704-434-4329) Enrollment: 1970. Records go back to 1947. Alumni records are maintained here. Degrees granted: Associate; Bachelors; Masters. Attendance and degree information available by phone, mail. Transcripts available by mail.

Gaston College, Registrar, 201 Hwy 321 S, Dallas, NC 28034, 704-922-6200, 704-922-6232 (Fax: 704-922-6233). Enrollment: 4000. Records go back to 1960. Degrees granted: Associate. Attendance and degree information available by fax, mail. Transcripts available by mail.

Greensboro College, Registrar, 815 W Market St, Greensboro, NC 27401, 336-373-7474 www.greensboro.edu (Fax: 336-271-2237) 8AM-4PM. Enrollment: 784. Records go back to 1960's. Alumni records are maintained here. Degrees granted: Bachelors. Attendance and degree information available by phone, mail. Transcripts available by mail.

Guilford College, Registrar, 5800 W Friendly Ave, Greensboro, NC 27410-4171, 336-316-2000 (Fax: 336-316-2948) 8:30PM-5PM. www.guilford.edu. Enrollment: 1558. Records go back to 1837. Alumni records are maintained here. Degrees granted: Bachelors. Attendance and degree information available

by phone, fax, mail. Transcripts available by fax, mail.

Guilford Technical Community College, Registrar, PO Box 309, Jamestown, NC 27282, www.technet.gtcc.cc.nc.us 336-454-1126 X2235, 910-334-4822 X2235 (Fax: 336-454-2510) 8AM - 7PM M-Th, 8AM - 5PM F. Enrollment: 5900. Records go back to 1966. Alumni records are maintained here. Degrees granted: Associate. Attendance and degree information available by phone, fax, mail. Transcripts available by fax, mail.

Halifax Community College, Registrar, PO Drawer 809, Weldon, NC 27890, 919-536-7221, 919-536-2551 (Fax: 919-536-4144) www.mail.hcc.cc.nc.us. Enrollment: 993. Alumni records maintained here; call 919-536-7289. Degrees granted: Associate. Attendance and degree information available by phone, mail. Transcripts available by mail.

Haywood Community College, Registrar, Freedlander Dr, Clyde, NC 28721, 828-627-4507, 704-627-4500 (Fax: 828-627-4513) 8AM-7PM. www.haywoodnc.us/sac.htm. Enrollment: 1500. Records go back to 1964. Degrees granted: Associate. Attendance and transcript information available by mail. Degree information available by phone, fax, mail.

High Point University, Registrar, University Station, Montlieu Ave, High Point, NC 27262-3598, www.highpoint.edu 336-841-9131, 910-841-9021 (Fax: 336-841-4599) 8:30AM-5PM; 4:30 in Summer. Enrollment: 2500. Records go back to 1924. Alumni records maintained here; call 336-841-9135. Degrees granted: Bachelors; Masters. Special programs- Home Furnishings Marketing, 910-841-9110. Attendance and degree information available by phone, fax, mail. Transcripts available by fax, mail.

Isothermal Community College, Registrar, PO Box 804, Spindale, NC 28160, www.isothermal.cc.nc.us. 828-286-3636 X240, 704-286-3636 X267 (Fax: 828-286-8109) 8AM-8PM M-Th; 8AM-4:30PM F. Enrollment: 1800. Records go back to 1964. Alumni records maintained here; call 828-286-3636 X261. Degrees granted: Associate. Attendance and degree information available by phone, fax, mail. Transcripts available by written request only.

James Sprunt Community College, Registrar, PO Box 398, Kenansville, NC 28349-0398, 910-296-2500, 910-296-2501 (Fax: 910-296-1222). Enrollment: 1000. Records go back to 1962. Alumni records are maintained here. Degrees granted: Associate. Attendance and degree information available by phone, fax, mail. Transcripts available by fax, mail.

John Wesley College, Registrar, 2314 N Centennial St, High Point, NC 27265, 336-889-2262 (Fax: 336-889-2261) 8AM-5PM. Enrollment: 176. Alumni records maintained here; call 336-889-2262. Degrees granted: Associate; Bachelors. Certification: Christian Workers. Attendance and degree information available by phone, fax, mail. Transcripts available by mail.

Johnson C. Smith University, Registrar, 100 Beatties Ford Rd, Charlotte, NC 28216, 704-378-1013, 704-378-1108 (Fax: 704-330-1302) www.jcsu.edu. 8:15AM-5:15PM. Enrollment: 1400. Records go back to 1867. Alumni records maintained here; call 704-378-1026. Degrees granted: Bachelors. Special programs- Honors College, 704-378-1253: International Studies, 704-378-1097. Attendance and degree information available by phone, fax, mail. Transcripts available by mail.

Johnston Community College, Registrar, PO Box 2350, Smithfield, NC 27577, www.johnston.cc.nc.us. 919-934-3051 (Fax: 919-989-7862) 8AM-9PM M-Th; 8AM-5PM F. Enrollment: 2700. Records go back to 1969. Degrees granted: Associate. Attendance and degree information available by phone, fax, mail. Transcripts available by fax, mail.

Lees-McRae College, Registrar, PO Box 128, Banner Elk, NC 28604, 828-898-8738 (Fax: 828-898-8814) www.lees-mcrae.edu. 8:30AM - 4:30PM. Enrollment: 657. Records go back to 1932. Alumni records are maintained here. Degrees granted: Bachelors. Special programs- Performing Arts. Attendance and degree information available by phone, fax, mail. Transcripts available by fax, mail.

Lenoir Community College, Registrar, PO Box 188, Kinston, NC 28501, 919-527-6223 X306 (Fax: 919-527-1199). 8AM-5PM M-Th, 8AM-4PM F. Enrollment: 1545. Records go back to 1960's. Alumni records are maintained here. Degrees granted: Associate. Attendance and degree information available by phone, fax, mail. Transcripts available by fax, mail.

Lenoir-Rhyne College, Registrar, Seventh Ave and Eighth St NE, PO Box 7291, Hickory, NC 28603, 828-328-7278, 704-328-7277 (Fax: 828-328-7368) www.lrc.edu. 8:30AM-5PM. Enrollment: 1500. Records go back to 1940's. Alumni records are maintained here. Degrees granted: Bachelors; Masters. Attendance and degree information available by phone, mail. Transcripts available by mail.

Louisburg College, Registrar Office, 501 N Main St, Louisburg, NC 27549, 919-496-2521 X236, 919-496-2521 X327 (Fax: 919-496-1788) www.louisburg.edu. 8:30AM - 5PM. Enrollment: 568. Records go back to 1900's. Alumni records are maintained here. Degrees granted: Associate. Attendance and degree information available by phone, fax, mail. Transcripts available by fax, mail.

Mars Hill College, Registrar, Marshall St, Mars Hill, NC 28754, 828-689-1151 (Fax: 828-689-1437). 8AM - 4:30PM. Enrollment: 1184. Records go back to 1910. Alumni records maintained here; call 828-689-1102. Degrees granted: Bachelors. Attendance and degree information available by phone, fax, mail. Transcripts available by mail.

Martin Community College, Registrar, 1161 Kuhukee Park Rd, Williamston, NC 27892-9988, 919-792-1521 (Fax: 919-792-0826) 8AM - 4:30PM. Enrollment: 650. Records go back to 1968. Degrees granted: Associate. Attendance and degree information available by phone, fax, mail. Transcripts available by fax, mail, in-person.

Mayland Community College, Registrar, PO Box 547, Spruce Pine, NC 28777, 828-765-7351 (Fax: 828-765-0728) 8AM-5PM. www.mayland.cc.nc.us. Enrollment: 750. Records go back to 1972. Degrees granted: Associate. Attendance, degree and transcript information available by fax, mail.

McDowell Technical Community College, Registrar, Rte 1 Box 170, Marion, NC 28752, 828-652-6021 X402 (Fax: 828-652-1014). 9AM-8:30PM T,Th; 8AM-4PM M,W,F. Enrollment: 1000. Records go back to 1964. Degrees granted: Associate. Attendance and degree information available by phone, fax, mail. Transcripts available by fax, mail.

Meredith College, Registrar, 3800 Hillsborough St, Raleigh, NC 27607-5298, 919-829-8593, 919-829-2867 (Fax: 919-829-2878) www.meredith.edu. 8AM-5PM. Enrollment: 2500. Records go back to 1900's. Alumni records maintained here; call 919-829-8391. Degrees granted: Bachelors; Masters. Special programs- Graduate Dept., 919-829-8353. Attendance, degree and transcript information available by fax, mail. To confirm attendance or degree, make request on letterhead and provide explanation.

Methodist College, Registrar, 5400 Ramsey St, Fayetteville, NC 28311-1420, 910-630-7036, 910-630-7035 (Fax: 910-630-2123) 8AM-5PM. www.methodist.edu. Enrollment: 1600. Records go back to 1963. Alumni records maintained here; call 910-630-7170. Degrees granted: Associate; Bachelors. Attendance and degree information available by phone, fax, mail. Transcripts available by fax, mail.

Mitchell Community College, Registrar, 500 W Broad St, Statesville, NC 28677, 704-878-3246, 704-878-3200 (Fax: 704-878-0872). 8AM-5PM. Enrollment: 1450. Records go back to 1930. Alumni records are maintained here, 704-878-3356. Degrees granted: Associate. Attendance and degree information available by phone, fax, mail. Transcripts available by mail.

Montgomery Community College. Registrar, PO Box 787, Troy, NC 27371, 910-576-6222 X225 (Fax: 910-576-2176). 8AM-5PM M-Th; 8AM-3PM F. Enrollment: 600. Records go back to 1967. Alumni records are maintained here. Degrees granted: Associate. Attendance, degree and transcript information available by mail.

Montgomery Technical College
(See Montgomery Community College)

Montreat - Anderson College. Registrar, PO Box 1267, Montreat, NC 28757, 828-669-8011 X3731, 704-669-8012 X3733 (Fax: 828-669-0120) www.montreat.edu. 8AM-4:30PM. Enrollment: 1000. Records go back to 1916. Alumni records maintained here; call 828-669-8011 X3703. Degrees granted: Associate; Bachelors. Attendance and degree information available by phone, fax, mail. Transcripts available by fax, mail.

Mount Olive College. Registrar, 634 Henderson St, Mount Olive, NC 28365, 919-658-7165 X3019, 919-658-2502 (Fax: 919-658-7179) 8AM-5PM. Enrollment: 1800. Records go back to 1951. Alumni records maintained here; call 919-658-2502. Degrees granted: Associate; Bachelors. Special programs- Modular Programs, 800-653-0854. Attendance and degree information available by phone, fax, mail. Transcripts available by fax, mail.

Nash Community College. Registrar, PO Box 7488, Rocky Mount, NC 27804-0488, 919-443-4011 (Fax: 919-443-0828). 8AM-5PM M-Th; 8AM-4PM F. Enrollment: 1800. Records go back to 1968. Degrees granted: Associate. Attendance and degree information available by phone, fax, mail. Transcripts available by mail.

North Carolina Agricultural and Technical State University, Office of the Registrar, Dowdy Bldg, 1601 E Market St, Greensboro, NC 27411, 336-334-7595, 336-334-7596 (Fax: 910-334-7466) www.ncat.edu. 8AM-5PM M,Th,F; 8AM-7PM T,W. Enrollment: 7300. Records go back to 1930. Alumni records maintained here; call 910-334-7583. Degrees granted: Bachelors; Masters; Doctorate. Attendance

and degree information available by phone, fax, mail. Transcripts available by mail.

North Carolina Central University, Registrar, 1801 Fayetteville St, Durham, NC 27707, 919-560-6262 (Fax: 919-560-5012) www.nccu.edu. 8AM-5PM. Enrollment: 5000. Records go back to 1950. Alumni records maintained here; call 919-560-6363. Degrees granted: Bachelors; Masters. School will not confirm attendance information. Degree information available by phone, mail. Transcripts available by written request only.

North Carolina School of the Arts, Registrar, 200 Waughtown St, PO Box 12189, Winston-Salem, NC 27117-2189, 336-770-3294. 8:30AM-5PM. Enrollment: 735. Records go back to 1965. Alumni records maintained here; call 910-770-3332. Degrees granted: Bachelors; Masters. Attendance and degree information available by mail. Transcripts available by mail.

North Carolina State University, Registrar, PO Box 7313, Raleigh, NC 27695-7313, 919-515-2572 (Fax: 919-515-2376) 8AM-5PM. www.ncsu.edu. Enrollment: 27500. Records go back to 1887. Alumni Records: Alumni Assoc., PO Box 7503, Raleigh, NC 27695-7503. Degrees granted: Bachelors; Masters; Doctorate. Attendance and degree information available by phone, fax, mail. Transcripts available by fax, mail.

North Carolina Weselyan College, Registrar, 3400 N Wesleyan Blvd, Rocky Mount, NC 27804, 919-985-5124 (Fax: 919-977-3701) www.ncwc.edu. 8AM-5PM. Enrollment: 1800. Records go back to 1960. Alumni records maintained here; call 919-985-5145. Degrees granted: Bachelors. Attendance and degree information available by phone, fax, mail. Transcripts available by fax, mail.

Pamlico Community College, Registrar, PO Box 185, Hwy 306 S, Grantsboro, NC 28529, 919-249-1851 (Fax: 919-249-2377). 7:30AM-10PM. Enrollment: 205. Records go back to 1962. Alumni records are maintained here. Degrees granted: Associate. Special programs- 919-249-1851. Attendance, degree and transcript information available by mail.

Peace College, Registrar, 15 E Peace St, Raleigh, NC 27604, 919-508-2250 (Fax: 919-508-2326) www.peace.edu. 8:15AM-4:45PM. Enrollment: 450. Records go back to 1900. Alumni records maintained here; call 919-508-2000. Degrees granted: Associate; Bachelors. Attendance information available by phone, mail. Degree information available by phone. Transcripts available by mail.

Pfeiffer University, Registrar, PO Box 960, Misenheimer, NC 28109-0960, 704-463-1360 X2056, 704-463-1360 X2057 (Fax: 704-463-1363) www.pfeifferunv.edu. 8AM-Noon, 1-5PM. Enrollment: 1800. Records go back to 1955. Alumni records are maintained here. Degrees granted: Bachelors; Masters. Attendance and degree information available by phone, fax, mail. Transcripts available by written request only.

Phillips Junior Colleges Phillips Junior Colleges were closed 1997. They are either closed, reorganizing, or have new names. Not available at time of printing.

Piedmont Baptist College, Registrar, 716 Franklin St, Winston-Salem, NC 27101, 336-725-8344 (Fax: 336-725-5522) 8AM-5PM. www.ibnet.org/pbc.htm. Enrollment: 300. Records go back to 1947. Alumni records are maintained here. Degrees granted: Associate; Bachelors; Masters. Attendance and degree information available by phone, fax, mail. Transcripts available by phone, fax, mail.

Piedmont Community College, Registrar, PO Box 1197, Roxboro, NC 27573, 336-599-1181 (Fax: 336-597-3817) 8AM-5PM. Enrollment: 1200. Records go back to 1970. Alumni records are maintained here. Degrees granted: Associate. Attendance and degree information available by phone, fax, mail. Transcripts available by fax, mail.

Pitt Community College, Registrar, PO Drawer 7007, Greenville, NC 27835-7007, 919-321-4232 (Fax: 919-321-4209) www.pit.cc.edu. 8AM-5PM. Enrollment: 4700. Records go back to 1963. Alumni records maintained here; call 919-321-4322. Degrees granted: Associate. Attendance, degree and transcript information available by fax, mail.

Queens College, Registrar, 1900 Selwyn Ave, Charlotte, NC 28274, 704-337-2211 (Fax: 704-337-2218). 8:30AM - 6PM M-Th, 8:30AM - 3PM F. Enrollment: 1600. Records go back to 1900. Alumni records maintained here; call 704-337-2214. Degrees granted: Bachelors; MBA, MED, MAT. Attendance and degree information available by phone, fax, mail. Transcripts available by fax, mail.

Randolph Community College, Registrar, PO Box 1009, Asheboro, NC 27204-1009, 336-633-0200, 336-633-0224 (Fax: 336-629-4695) www.randolph.cc.nc.uc/randolph/. 8AM-5PM. Enrollment: 1400. Records go back to 1963. Degrees granted: Associate. Attendance and degree information available by phone, fax, mail. Transcripts available by mail.

Richmond Community College, Registrar, PO Box 1189, Hamlet, NC 28345, 910-582-7113, 910-582-7000 (Fax: 910-582-7102). 8AM-5PM. Enrollment: 1600. Records go back to 1966. Alumni records maintained here; call 910-582-7122. Degrees granted: Associate. Attendance and degree information available by phone, fax, mail. Transcripts available by mail.

Roanoke Bible College, Registrar, 714 First St, Elizabeth City, NC 27909, www.icwnet.com/nc/edu/roanoke/. 252-334-2070 (Fax: 252-334-2071) 9AM-5PM. Enrollment: 170. Records go back to 1948. Alumni records are maintained here. Degrees granted: Associate; Bachelors. Attendance and degree information available by phone, fax, mail. Transcripts available by fax, mail.

Roanoke-Chowan Community College, Registrar, Rte 2 Box 46-A, Ahoskie, NC 27910, 919-332-5921, 919-332-3211 (Fax: 919-332-2210) www.roanoke.cc.nc.us. 8:15AM - 5PM. Enrollment: 800. Records go back to 1967. Alumni records are maintained here. Degrees granted: Associate. Attendance and degree information available by phone, fax, mail. Transcripts available by mail.

Robeson Community College, Registrar, PO Box 1420, Lumberton, NC 28359, 910-738-7101 (Fax: 910-738-8917). Enrollment: 1450. Records go back to 1966. Degrees granted: Associate; Vocational Diploma. Attendance and degree information available by fax, mail. Transcripts available by mail.

Rockingham Community College, Registrar, PO Box 38, Wentworth, NC 27375-0038, 336-342-4261 X118 (Fax: 336-349-9986) www.rockingham.edu. 8AM-5PM. Enrollment: 2000. Records go back to 1966. Alumni records are maintained here. Degrees granted: Associate. Attendance and degree

information available by phone, fax, mail. Transcripts available by fax, mail.

Rowan-Cabarrus Community College, Registrar, PO Box 1595, Salisbury, NC 28145, 704-637-0760 X270, 704-637-0760 X221 (Fax: 704-633-6804). Enrollment: 3500. Records go back to 1963. Alumni records maintained here; call 704-637-0760 X216. Degrees granted: Associate. Attendance and degree information available by phone, fax, mail. Transcripts available by mail with original pen and ink signature.

Rutledge Colleges
(See Phillips Junior Colleges)

Salem College, Registrar, Salem Station, PO Box 10548, Winston-Salem, NC 27108, www.salem.edu. 336-721-2618 (Fax: 336-917-5432) 8:30AM-5PM. Enrollment: 900. Records go back to 1925. Alumni records maintained here; call 336-721-2608. Degrees granted: Bachelors; Masters. Attendance and degree information available by phone, fax, mail. Transcripts available by mail.

Sampson Community College, Registrar, PO Drawer 318, Clinton, NC 28329-0318, 910-592-8081, 910-592-8084 (Fax: 910-592-8048) www.sampson.edu. Enrollment: 995. Records go back to 1965. Alumni records are maintained here. Degrees granted: Associate. Attendance and degree information available by phone, fax, mail. Transcripts available by fax, mail.

Sampson Technical Institute
(See Sampson Community College)

Sandhills Community College, Registrar, 2200 Airport Rd, Pinehurst, NC 28374, www.normandy.sandhills.cc.nc. 910-695-3739, 910-695-3740 (Fax: 910-695-1823) 8AM - 4:30PM. Enrollment: 2300. Records go back to 1963. Degrees granted: Associate. Attendance and degree information available by phone, fax, mail. Transcripts available by fax, mail. Fax available for confirmation only.

Shaw University, Registrar, 118 E South St, Raleigh, NC 27601, 919-546-8415, 919-546-8416 (Fax: 919-546-8553). 8AM-5PM. Enrollment: 2432. Records go back to 1930. Alumni records maintained here; call 919-546-8270. Degrees granted: Bachelors. Attendance, degree and transcript information available by fax, mail.

Southeastern Baptist Theological Seminary, Registrar, PO Box 1889, Wake Forest, NC 27588-1889, 919-556-3101 X215 (Fax: 919-556-0998) www.sebts.edu. 8AM-5PM M-Th; 8AM-4PM F. Enrollment: 1700. Records go back to 1954. Alumni records are maintained here. Degrees granted: Associate; Bachelors; Masters; Doctorate. Attendance and degree information available by phone, fax, mail. Transcripts available by fax, mail.

Southeastern Community College, Registrar, PO Box 151, Whiteville, NC 28472, 910-642-7141 (Fax: 910-642-5658) www.scc.edu. 8:30AM-5PM. Enrollment: 1500. Records go back to 1965. Alumni records are maintained here. Degrees granted: Associate. Attendance, degree and transcript information available by fax, mail.

Southwestern Community College, Registrar, 447 College Drive, Sylva, NC 28779, www.southwest.cc.nc.us. 828-586-4091 X219, 704-586-4091 X273 (Fax: 828-586-3129) 8AM-5PM. Enrollment: 1140. Records go back to 1964. Alumni records are maintained here. Degrees granted: Associate. Special programs- Diploma-Electro-Neuro Diagnostics Technology. Attendance, degree

and transcript information available by fax, mail.

St. Andrews Presbyterian College, Registrar, 1700 Dogwood Mile, Laurinburg, NC 28352, 910-277-5221, 910-277-5219 (Fax: 910-277-5020) www.sapc.edu. 8:30AM-5PM. Enrollment: 750. Records go back to 1961. Alumni records maintained here; call 910-277-5668. Degrees granted: Bachelors. Attendance, degree and transcript information available by mail.

St. Augustine's College, Registrar, 1315 Oakwood Ave, Raleigh, NC 27610-2298, 919-516-4199 (Fax: 919-516-4415) 8AM-6PM. www.augustine.edu. Enrollment: 1700. Records go back to 1920. Alumni records maintained here; call 919-516-4023. Degrees granted: Bachelors. Attendance and degree information available by phone, fax, mail. Transcripts available by mail.

Stanly Community College, Registrar, 141 College Dr, Albemarle, NC 28001, 704-982-0121 X237 (Fax: 704-982-0819). 8AM-5PM. Enrollment: 1800. Records go back to 1972. Degrees granted: Associate. Attendance and degree information available by phone, fax, mail. Transcripts available by mail.

Surry Community College, Dept of Student Services, PO Box 304, Dobson, NC 27017, 336-386-8121 (Fax: 336-386-8951) www.surry.cc.edu. 8AM-8PM. Enrollment: 3200. Records go back to 1965. Alumni records are maintained here. Degrees granted: Associate. Attendance and degree information available by phone, fax, mail. Transcripts available by written request only.

Technical College of Alamance
(See Alamance Community College)

Tri-County Community College, Registrar, 4600 East US 64, Murphy, NC 28906, 828-837-6810, 704-837-2412 (Fax: 828-837-3266). 8AM-6:30PM. Enrollment: 1000. Records go back to 1991. Degrees granted: Associate. School will not confirm attendance information. Degree information available by phone, fax, mail. Transcripts available by fax, mail.

University of North Carolina at Asheville, Registrar, One University Heights, Asheville, NC 28804, 828-251-6575 (Fax: 828-251-6841) www.unca.edu. 8AM-5PM. Enrollment: 3300. Records go back to 1930's. Alumni records maintained here; call 828-251-6512. Degrees granted: Bachelors; Masters. Attendance and degree information available by phone, fax, mail. Transcripts available by mail.

University of North Carolina at Chapel Hill, Registrar, CB # 2100, 105 Hanes Hall, Chapel Hill, NC 27599-2100, 919-962-3954, 919-962-8291 (Fax: 919-962-3349) www.unc.edu. 8AM-4:30PM. Enrollment: 24468. Records go back to 1902. Alumni Records: Geo. Watts Hill Alumni Center, CB 9180, Chapel Hill, NC 27599-2100. Degrees granted: Bachelors; Masters; Doctorate. Attendance and degree information available by phone, fax, mail. Transcripts available by fax, mail.

University of North Carolina at Charlotte, Registrar, 9201 University City Blvd, Charlotte, NC 28223-0001, 704-547-3487 (Fax: 704-547-3340) www.uncc.edu. 8AM-5PM. Enrollment: 16370. Records go back to 1960. Alumni records maintained here; call 704-547-2273. Degrees granted: Bachelors; Masters; Doctorate. Attendance and degree information available by phone, fax, mail. Transcripts available by fax, mail.

University of North Carolina at Greensboro, Registrar, PO Box 26179, Greensboro, NC 27402-6179, 336-334-5946 (Fax: 336-334-3649) www.uncg.edu. 8AM-5PM. Enrollment: 12600. Records go back to 1891. Alumni records maintained here; call 336-334-5696. Degrees granted: Bachelors; Masters; Doctorate. Attendance and degree information available by phone, fax, mail. Transcripts available by fax, mail.

University of North Carolina at Pembroke, Registrar, One University Dr, PO Box 1510, Pembroke, NC 28372, 910-521-6303 (Fax: 910-521-6548) 8AM-5PM. www.uncp.edu/registrar/. Enrollment: 3000. Records go back to 1900's. Formerly **Pembroke State University**. Alumni records are maintained here. Degrees granted: Masters. Attendance and degree information available by phone, fax, mail. Transcripts available by fax, mail.

University of North Carolina at Wilmington, Registrar, 601 S College Rd, Wilmington, NC 28403-3297, 910-962-3125 (Fax: 910-962-3887) www.uncwil.edu. 8AM-5PM. Enrollment: 7463. Records go back to 1947. Degrees granted: Bachelors; Masters. Attendance information available by mail. Degree and transcript information available by fax, mail.

Vance - Granville Community College, Registrar, PO Box 917, Poplar Creek Rd, Henderson, NC 27536, 919-492-2061 (Fax: 919-430-0460). Enrollment: 2500. Records go back to 1970. Alumni records are maintained here. Degrees granted: Associate. Attendance and degree information available by phone, fax, mail. Transcripts available by mail.

Wake Forest University, Registrar, PO Box 7207 Reynolda Station, Winston-Salem, NC 27109, 336-758-5206 (Fax: 336-758-6056) www.wfu.edu. 8:30AM-5PM. Enrollment: 3860. Records go back to 1834. For Medical School records call 910-716-4271. Alumni records maintained here; call 336-758-5264. Degrees granted: Bachelors; Masters; Doctorate. Attendance and degree

information available by phone, fax, mail. Transcripts available by fax, mail.

Wake Technical Community College, Registrar, 9191 Fayetteville Rd, Raleigh, NC 27603-5696, www.wake.tech.cc.edu. 919-662-3253 Enrollment: 7000. Records go back to 1963. Alumni records are maintained here. Degrees granted: Associate. Attendance, degree and transcript information available by written request only.

Warren Wilson College, Registrar, PO Box 9000, Asheville, NC 28815-9000, 828-298-3325 (Fax: 828-299-3326) www.warren-wilson.edu. 8AM-5PM. Enrollment: 620. Records go back to 1894. Alumni records are maintained here. Degrees granted: Bachelors; Masters. Attendance and degree information available by phone, fax, mail. Transcripts available by fax, mail.

Wayne Community College, Admissions & Records, Caller Box 8002, Goldsboro, NC 27533-8002, 919-735-5151 (Fax: 919-736-3204) www.wayne.cc.nc.us. 8AM-5PM. Enrollment: 2650. Records go back to 1957. Alumni records are maintained here. Degrees granted: Associate. Attendance and degree information available by phone, fax, mail. Transcripts available by fax, mail.

Western Carolina University, Registrar, Cullowhee, NC 28723, 828-227-7232 (Fax: 828-227-7217) www.wcu.edu. 8AM-5PM. Enrollment: 6500. Records go back to 1920. Alumni records maintained here; call 828-227-7335. Degrees granted: Bachelors; Masters. Attendance and degree information available by phone, fax, mail. Transcripts available by fax, mail.

Western Piedmont Community College, Registrar, 1001 Burkemont Ave, Morganton, NC 28655-9978, 828-438-6041, 704-428-6052 (Fax: 828-438-6065). 8AM-5PM. Enrollment: 2500. Records go back to 1963. Degrees granted: Associate. Attendance and degree information available by phone, fax, mail. Transcripts available by fax, mail.

Wilkes Community College, Registrar, PO Box 120, Collegiate Dr, Wilkesboro, NC 28697-0120, 336-838-6140, 336-838-6135 (Fax: 336-838-6277) www.wilkes.cc.nc.us. 8AM-5PM. Enrollment: 1800. Records go back to 1966. Alumni records are maintained here. Degrees granted: Associate. Attendance and degree information available by phone, fax, mail. Transcripts available by fax, mail.

Wilson Technical Community College, Registrar, 902 Herring Ave, PO Box 4305, Wilson, NC 27893, 919-291-1195 X277 (Fax: 919-243-7148) www.wilsontech.cc.nc.us. 8AM-5PM. Enrollment: 1300. Records go back to 1956. Alumni records maintained here; call 919-291-1195 X276. Degrees granted: Associate. Attendance and degree information available by phone, fax, mail. Transcripts available by fax, mail.

Wingate College, Registrar, Wingate, NC 28174-0157, 704-233-8126, 704-233-8128 (Fax: 704-233-8125) www.wingate.edu. 8:30 AM-5PM. Enrollment: 1250. Records go back to 1896. Alumni records maintained here; call 704-233-8114. Degrees granted: Bachelors; Masters. Special programs- W' International (Study Foreign Country/Visit): Wingate in London. Attendance and degree information available by phone, fax, mail. Transcripts available by mail.

Winston—Salem State University, Registrar, 601 Martin Luther King, Jr. Dr, Winston-Salem, NC 27110, 336-750-3330, 336-750-3331 (Fax: 336-750-3332). Enrollment: 2800. Records go back to 1892. Alumni records maintained here; call 336-750-2125. Degrees granted: Bachelors. Attendance and degree information available by phone, fax, mail. Transcripts available by mail.

North Dakota

Aaker's Business College, Registrar, 201 N Third St, Grand Forks, ND 58203-5876, 701-772-6646 (Fax: 701-772-1087) 8AM-5PM. Records go back to 1966. Degrees granted: Associate. Attendance and degree information available by phone, mail. Transcripts available by mail.

Bismarck State College, Registrar, PO Box 5587, Bismarck, ND 58506-5587, www.bsc.nodak.edu. 701-224-5429 (Fax: 701-224-5643) 8AM - 5PM M-Th, 8AM - 4PM F. Enrollment: 2481. Alumni records maintained here; call 701-224-5431. Degrees granted: Associate. Attendance and degree information available by phone, fax, mail. Transcripts available by fax, mail.

Dickinson State University, Registrar, 291 Campus Dr, Dickinson, ND 58601, 701-277-2331, 800-279-4295 (Fax: 701-227-2006) www.dsu.nodak.edu. 7:45AM - 4:30PM. Enrollment: 1600. Records go back to 1918. Alumni records maintained here; call 701-227-2082. Degrees granted: Associate; Masters. Certification: Truck Driving. Attendance and degree information available by phone, fax, mail. Transcripts available by fax, mail.

Fort Berthold Community College, Registrar, PO Box 490, New Town, ND

58763, 701-627-3665 (Fax: 701-627-3609) 8AM-5PM. www.fort-berthold.cc.nd.us. Enrollment: 210. Records go back to 1978. Alumni records are maintained here at. Degrees granted: Associate. Attendance and degree information available by phone, fax, mail. Transcripts available by fax, mail.

Jamestown College, Registrar, 600 College Ln, Jamestown, ND 58405, 701-252-3467 (Fax: 701-253-4318) www.jc.edu. 8AM-5PM. Enrollment: 1080. Records go back to 1920. Alumni records maintained here; call 701-252-3467 X2557. Degrees granted: Bachelors. Attendance and degree information available by phone, fax, mail. Transcripts available by mail.

Lake Region Community College
(See Univ. of North Dakota Lake Region)

Little Hoop Community College, Registrar, PO Box 269, Fort Totten, ND 58335, 701-766-4415 (Fax: 701-766-4077) 8AM-4:30PM. www.littlehoop.cc.edu. Enrollment: 150. Records go back to 1974. Alumni records are maintained here. Degrees granted: Associate; Vocational. Attendance, degree and transcript information available by fax, mail.

Mayville State University, Registrar, 330 Third St NE, Mayville, ND 58257, 701-786-

4774, 701-786-4773 www.masu.nodak.edu (Fax: 701-786-4748) 8AM-Noon, 12:30 - 4:30PM. Enrollment: 780. Records go back to 1889. Alumni records maintained here; call 701-786-4754. Degrees granted: Associate; Bachelors. Attendance and degree information available by phone, fax, mail. Transcripts available by fax, mail.

Medcenter One College of Nursing, Registrar, 512 N Seventh St, Bismarck, ND 58501, 701-323-6270 (Fax: 701-323-6967) 8AM-4:30PM. www.medcenterone.com. Enrollment: 90. Records go back to 1909. Alumni records maintained here; call 701-323-6283. Degrees granted: Bachelors. Attendance and degree information available by phone, fax, mail. Transcripts available by fax, mail.

Minot State University, Registrar, Minot, ND 58707, www.warp6.cs.misu.nodak.edu/ 701-858-3340 (Fax: 701-839-6933 & 701-858-3386) 7:30AM - 4:30PM. Enrollment: 3000. Records go back to 1913. Alumni records maintained here; call 701-858-3234. Degrees granted: Associate; Bachelors; Masters; Specialist. Attendance and degree information available by phone, fax, mail. Transcripts available by fax, mail.

North Dakota State College of Science, Registrar, 800 N Sixth St, Wahpeton, ND 58076, 800-342-4325 X2203, 701-671-2236 (Fax: 701-671-2332) www.ndscs.nodak.edu/. 7:45AM - 4:45PM. Enrollment: 2542. Records go back to 1903. Alumni records maintained here; call 701-671-2247. Degrees granted: Associate. Attendance and degree information available by phone, fax, mail. Transcripts available by fax, mail.

North Dakota State University, Office of the Registrar, PO Box 5196, Fargo, ND 58105, 701-231-8295, 701-231-7981 (Fax: 701-231-8959) www.ndsu.nodak.edu. 8AM-5PM Sep-May; 7:30AM-4PM Jun-Aug. Enrollment: 9600. Records go back to 1896. Alumni Records: PO Box 5144, Fargo, ND 58105. Degrees granted: Bachelors; Masters; Doctorate. Attendance and degree information available by phone, fax, mail. Transcripts available by fax, mail.

North Dakota State University (Bottineau), Registrar, First St and Simrall Blvd, Bottineau, ND 58318, 701-228-5487 www.165.234.172.78.homepage.htm/. (Fax: 701-228-5499) 8AM-5PM. Enrollment: 370. Records go back to 1906. Alumni records maintained here; call 701-228-5435. Degrees granted: Associate. Attendance and degree information available by phone, fax, mail. Transcripts available by fax, mail.

Sitting Bull College, Registrar, HC1 Box 4, Fort Yates, ND 58538, 701-854-3861 (Fax: 701-854-3403). 8AM - 4:30PM. Enrollment: 229. Records go back to 1971. Formerly **Standing Rock College** Alumni records are maintained here. Degrees granted: Associate. Attendance and degree information available by phone, fax, mail. Transcripts available by fax, mail.

Tri-College University, Registrar, 209 Engineering Technology Bldg, North Dakota State University, Fargo, ND 58105, 701-231-8170 (Fax: 701-231-7205). Records located at

North Dakota State College of Science, Registrar, Wahpeton, ND.

Trinity Bible College, Academic Records Office, 50 S Sixth St, Ellendale, ND 58436, 701-349-3621 X2034 (Fax: 701-349-5443). 8:30AM-5PM. Enrollment: 322. Records go back to 1948. Alumni records maintained here; call 701-349-5621 X2036. Degrees granted: Associate; Bachelors. Attendance and degree information available by phone, fax, mail. Transcripts available by fax, mail.

Turtle Mountain Community College, Registrar, PO Box 340, Belcourt, ND 58316-0340, 701-477-5605 (Fax: 701-477-5028). 8AM-4:30PM. Enrollment: 600. Records go back to 1973. Degrees granted: Associate. Attendance and degree information available by phone, fax, mail. Transcripts available by fax, mail.

United Tribes Technical College, Registrar, 3315 University Dr, Bismarck, ND 58504, 701-255-3285 X216 (Fax: 701-255-7718) www.uttc.edu. 8AM-5PM. Enrollment: 265. Records go back to 1969. Alumni records are maintained here. Degrees granted: Associate. Attendance and degree information available by phone, fax, mail. Transcripts available by fax, mail.

University of Mary, Registrar's Office, 7500 University Dr, Bismarck, ND 58504-9652, 701-255-7500 X410, 701-255-7500 X512 (Fax: 701-255-7687). 8AM - 4:30PM. Enrollment: 2100. Records go back to 1959. Alumni records are maintained here. Degrees granted: Associate; Bachelors; Masters. Attendance and degree information available by phone, fax, mail. Transcripts available by fax, mail.

University of North Dakota, Admissions & Records, Box 8382, University Station, Grand Forks, ND 58202-8232, 701-777-2711 (Fax: 701-777-2696) www.und.nodak.edu. 8AM-4:30PM. Enrollment: 10500. Records go back to 1883. Alumni records maintained

here; call 701-777-2611. Degrees granted: Bachelors; Masters; Doctorate. Attendance and degree information available by phone, fax, mail. Transcripts available by fax, mail.

University of North Dakota (Lake Region), Registrar, N College Dr, Devils Lake, ND 58301, 701-662-1515, 701-662-1556 (Fax: 701-662-1570) 8AM-4:30PM. www.und.lr.nodak.edu. Enrollment: 700. Records go back to 1941. Alumni records maintained here; call 701-662-1520. Degrees granted: Associate. Attendance and degree information available by phone, fax, mail. Transcripts available by fax, mail.

University of North Dakota (Williston), Registrar, PO Box 1326, Williston, ND 58801, 701-774-4212, 701-774-4210 (Fax: 701-774-4211) www.und-w.nodak.edu. 8AM - 5PM. Enrollment: 700. Records go back to 1961. Alumni records are maintained here. Degrees granted: Associate. School will not confirm attendance information. Degree information available by phone, fax, mail. Transcripts available by written request only.

Valley City State University, Registrar, College St, Valley City, ND 58072, 701-845-7295 (Fax: 701-845-7245) 7:45AM - 4:30PM. www.vcsu.nodak.edu. Enrollment: 1000. Records go back to 1892. Alumni records maintained here; call 701-845-7411. Degrees granted: Bachelors. Attendance and degree information available by phone, fax, mail. Transcripts available by fax, mail

Ohio

A T E S Technical Institute
(See E T I Technical College of Niles)

Academy of Court Reporting (Branch), Registrar, 614 Superior NW, **Cleveland**, OH 44113, 216-861-3222 (Fax: 216-861-4517). 8AM-5PM. Records go back to 1970. Degrees granted: Associate. Attendance, degree and transcript information available by mail.

Academy of Court Reporting (Branch), Registrar, 630 E Broad St, **Columbus**, OH 43215, 614-221-7770 (Fax: 614-221-8429). 8AM-5PM. Records go back to 1975. Degrees granted: Associate. Attendance, degree and transcript information available by mail.

Air Force Institute of Technology, Registrar, 2950 P St, Wright-Patterson AFB, OH 45433-7765, 937-255-5100, 937-255-3094 (Fax: 937-255-2791) 7:30AM-5PM. www.afit.af.mil/AFITHome.html Enrollment: 650. Records go back to 1951. Alumni records maintained here; call 513-255-9623. Degrees granted: Masters; Doctorate. Attendance and degree information available by phone, fax, mail. Transcripts available by fax, mail.

Antonelli Institute of Art and Photography, Registrar, 124 E Seventh St, Cincinnati, OH 45202-2592, 513-241-4338 (Fax: 513-241-9396) www.antonellic.com.

8AM-5PM. Enrollment: 223. Records go back to 1988. Degrees granted: Associate. Attendance and degree information available by phone, fax, mail. Transcripts available by fax, mail.

Art Academy of Cincinnati, Registrar, 1125 St. Gregory St, Cincinnati, OH 45202, 513-562-8749, 513-721-5205 (Fax: 513-562-8778) www2.eos.net/artacady. 8:30AM - 5PM M,W,Th. Enrollment: 187. Alumni records maintained here; call 513-562-8746. Degrees granted: Associate; Bachelors; Masters. Attendance and degree information available by phone, fax, mail. Transcripts available by fax, mail.

Ashland University, Registrar, 401 College Ave, Ashland, OH 44805, 419-289-5028, 419-289-4142 (Fax: 419-289-5333) 7:30AM-5PM. www.ashland.edu. Enrollment: 5700. Records go back to 1921. Alumni records maintained here; call 419-289-5040. Degrees granted: Associate; Bachelors; Masters. Special programs- Seminary, 419-289-5907. Attendance and degree information available by phone, fax, mail. Transcripts available by mail.

Athenaeum of Ohio, Registrar, 6616 Beechmont Ave, Cincinnati, OH 45230-2091, 513-231-2223 (Fax: 513-231-3254). 8:30AM-5PM. Enrollment: 248. Alumni records are maintained here. Degrees granted: Masters. Attendance and degree information available

by phone, fax, mail. Transcripts available by mail.

Baldwin—Wallace College, Registrar, 275 Eastland Rd, Berea, OH 44017, 440-826-2126, 440-826-2127 (Fax: 440-826-6522) 8:30AM - 4:30PM. www.baldwinw.edu. Enrollment: 4400. Records go back to 1956. Alumni records are maintained here. Degrees granted: Bachelors; Masters. Attendance and degree information available by phone, fax, mail. Transcripts available by mail.

Belmont Technical College, Registrar, 120 Fox-Shannon Pl, St. Clairsville, OH 43950, 740-695-9500 (Fax: 740-695-2247). 8AM-4:30PM. Enrollment: 1790. Records go back to 1971. Degrees granted: Associate. Attendance and degree information available by phone, fax, mail. Transcripts available by mail.

Bluffton College, Registrar, 280 W College Ave, Bluffton, OH 45817-1196, 419-358-3322 (Fax: 419-358-3323) www.bluffton.edu. 8AM-Noon, 1-5PM. Enrollment: 1000. Records go back to 1900. Alumni records maintained here; call 419-358-3245. Degrees granted: Bachelors; Masters. Attendance and degree information available by phone, fax, mail. Transcripts available by fax, mail.

Bohecker's Business College, Registrar, 326 E Main St, Ravenna, OH 44266, www.home/aol.bohecker.com. 330-297-7319,

330-297-7373 (Fax: 330-296-2159) 8AM-5:30PM M-Th, 8AM-2PM F. Enrollment: 150. Records go back to 1922. Degrees granted: Associate. Attendance, degree and transcript information available by mail.

Borromeo College of Ohio
(See Center for Pastoral Leadership)

Bowling Green State University, Office of Registration & Records, 110 Admin. Bldg, Bowling Green, OH 43403, 419-372-7973, 419-372-7960 (Fax: 419-372-7977) 8AM-5PM. www.bgsu.edu/. Enrollment: 16450. Records go back to 1914. Alumni records are maintained here. Degrees granted: Associate; Bachelors; Masters; Doctorate. Attendance and degree information available by phone, fax, mail. Transcripts available by fax, mail.

Bowling Green State University (Firelands College), Registrar, 901 Rye Beach Rd, Huron, OH 44839, 419-433-5560 (Fax: 419-433-9696). Records are located at Bowling Green State University, Office of Registration & Records, Bowling Green, OH.

Bradford School, Registrar, 6170 Busch Blvd, Columbus, OH 43229, 614-846-9410, 800-678-7981 (Fax: 614-846-9656). 8AM-5PM. Records go back to 1940's. Formerly **Office Training School & Columbus Business University**. Degrees granted: Associate. Attendance and degree information available by phone, fax, mail. Transcripts available by written request only.

Bryant & Stratton Business Institute (Branch), Registrar, Sears Bldg 3rd Fl, 691 Richmond Rd, **Richmond Heights**, OH 44143, 216-461-3151 (Fax: 216-461-2827). Records are located at Bryant & Stratton College, Registrar, Parma, OH.

Bryant & Stratton College, Registrar, 1700 E 13th St, **Cleveland**, OH 44114, 216-265-3151 (Fax: 216-771-7787). 8AM-9PM. Enrollment: 300. Records go back to 1940's. Degrees granted: Associate; Bachelors. Attendance and degree information available by phone, fax, mail. Transcripts available by fax, mail.

Bryant & Stratton College, Registrar, 12955 Snow Rd, **Parma**, OH 44130-1013, 216-265-3151 (Fax: 216-265-0325). 8AM-10PM M-Th; 8AM-5PM Fri. Records go back to 1852. Degrees granted: Associate. Attendance and degree information available by mail. Transcripts available by fax, mail.

Capital University, Registrar, 2199 E Main St, Columbus, OH 43209, 614-236-6150 (Fax: 614-236-6820) www.capital.edu. 8AM-4:30PM. Enrollment: 3988. Records go back to 1850. Alumni records maintained here; call 614-236-6701. Degrees granted: Bachelors; Masters; JD. Attendance and degree information available by phone, fax, mail. Transcripts available by mail.

Case Western Reserve University, Registrar's Office, 10900 Euclid Ave, 223 Pardee Hall, Cleveland, OH 44106-7042, 216-368-4337, 216-368-4310 (Fax: 216-368-8711) 9AM-4PM. www.cwru.edu. Enrollment: 9000. Records go back to 1896. For M.D. Degrees prior to 5/92, call 216-368-6621. Alumni Records: Alumni Assoc., 10900 Euclid Ave, Baker Bldg 316, Cleveland, OH 44106-7035. Degrees granted: Bachelors; Masters; Doctorate. Attendance and degree information available by mail. Transcripts available by mail.

Cedarville College, Academic Records, N Main St, Box 601, Cedarville, OH 45314-0601, 937-766-2211, 937-766-7710 (Fax: 937-766-7663) www.cedarville.edu. 8AM-5PM. Enrollment: 2297. Records go back to

1800's. Alumni records maintained here; call 513-766-7858. Degrees granted: Associate; Bachelors. Attendance and degree information available by phone, fax, mail. Transcripts available by fax, mail. Telephone number required.

Center for Pastoral Leadership Cleveland Diocese, Records Office, 28700 Euclid Ave, Wickliffe, OH 44092, 440-943-7600 (Fax: 440-943-7577). Enrollment: 90. Records go back to 1957. Formerly **Borromeo College of Ohio**. Degrees granted: Bachelors. Special programs- Arts: Theological Studies. Attendance, degree and transcript information available by mail.

Central Ohio Technical College, Registrar, 1179 University Dr, Newark, OH 43055-1767, 740-366-9208 (Fax: 740-364-9508) www.cotc.tcc.oh.us. 8AM-5PM. Enrollment: 1712. Records go back to 1971. Alumni records are maintained here. Degrees granted: Associate. Attendance and degree information available by phone, fax, mail. Transcripts available by fax, mail.

Central State University, Registrar, 1400 Brush Row Rd, Wilberforce, OH 45384, 513-376-6231 (Fax: 513-376-6188). 9AM - 4PM. Enrollment: 2700. Records go back to 1947. Degrees granted: Associate; Bachelors; Masters. Attendance, degree and transcript information available by mail.

Chatfield College, Registrar, 20918 State Rte 251, St Martin, OH 45118, 513-875-3344 (Fax: 513-875-3912) 8AM-5PM. Enrollment: 300. Records go back to 1968. Degrees granted: Associate. Attendance and degree information available by phone, fax, mail. Transcripts available by mail.

Cincinnati Bible College and Seminary, Registrar, 2700 Glenway Ave, Cincinnati, OH 45204, 513-244-8170, 513-244-8162 (Fax: 513-244-8140). 8:30AM-4:30PM. Enrollment: 900. Records go back to 1924. Alumni records maintained here; call 513-244-8113. Degrees granted: Associate; Bachelors; Masters. Attendance and degree information available by phone, fax, mail. Transcripts available by fax, mail.

Cincinnati College of Mortuary Science, Registrar, 6455 W North Bend Rd, Cincinnati, OH 45224, 513-761-2020 (Fax: 513-761-3333) www.ccms.edu. 8AM - 4PM. Records go back to 1989. Alumni records are maintained here. Degrees granted: Associate; Bachelors. Attendance information available by written request only. Degree information available by phone, fax, mail. Transcripts available by fax, mail.

Cincinnati State Technical & Community College. Registrar, 3520 Central Pkwy, Cincinnati, OH 45223, 513-569-1500 (Fax: 513-569-1883). 8AM-7PM M-Th, 8AM-5PM F. Enrollment: 5500. Records go back to 1968. Alumni records are maintained here. Degrees granted: Associate. Attendance and degree information available by phone, fax, mail. Transcripts available by mail.

Circleville Bible College, Registrar, 1476 Lancaster Pike, PO Box 458, Circleville, OH 43113, www.biblecollege.edu. 740-477-7740, 740-474-8896 (Fax: 740-477-7755) 8:30AM - 4:30PM. Enrollment: 180. Records go back to 1948. Alumni records maintained here; call 740-477-7760. Degrees granted: Associate; Bachelors. Attendance information available by phone, fax, mail. Degree information available by phone, mail. Transcripts available by mail.

Clark State Community College, Registrar, 570 E Leffels Lane, PO Box 570, Springfield, OH 45505, 937-328-6014 (Fax: 937-328-3853). 8AM-5PM. Enrollment: 2200. Records go back to 1962. Alumni records maintained here. Degrees granted: Associate. Attendance and degree information available by phone, fax, mail. Transcripts available by written request only.

Cleveland College of Jewish Studies, Registrar, 26500 Shaker Blvd, Beachwood, OH 44122, 216-464-4050 (Fax: 216-464-5827). 8:30AM-4PM. Enrollment: 1000. Alumni records are maintained here. Degrees granted: Bachelors; Masters. Attendance and degree information available by phone, fax, mail. Transcripts available by fax, mail.

Cleveland Institute of Art, Registrar, 11411 East Blvd, Cleveland, OH 44106, 216-421-7321, 216-421-7320 (Fax: 216-421-7333). 8:30AM-5PM. Enrollment: 481. Records go back to 1882. Alumni records maintained here; call 216-421-7412. Degrees granted: Bachelors. Attendance and degree information available by phone, fax, mail. Transcripts available by fax, mail.

Cleveland Institute of Electronics, Inc., Registrar, 1776 E 17th St, Cleveland, OH 44114, 216-781-9400, 800-243-6446 (Fax: 216-781-0331) www.cie-wc.edu. 8:30AM-4:45PM. Enrollment: 5600. Records go back to 1934. Degrees granted: Associate. Attendance and degree information available by phone, fax, mail. Transcripts available by mail.

Cleveland Institute of Music, Registrar, 11021 East Blvd, Cleveland, OH 44106, www.cwru.edu/cim/cimhome/html. 216-795-3203 (Fax: 216-791-1530) 9AM-5PM. Enrollment: 350. Records go back to 1920. Alumni records are maintained here. Degrees granted: Bachelors; Masters; Doctorate. Attendance information available by fax, mail. Degree information available by phone, fax, mail. Transcripts available by mail.

Cleveland State University, Registrar, Euclid Ave at 24th St, Cleveland, OH 44115, 216-687-3700 (Fax: 216-687-5501) www.csuohio.edu. 8AM-6PM M-Th; 8AM-5PM F. Degrees granted: Bachelors; Masters; Doctorate. Attendance and degree information available by phone, fax, mail. Transcripts available by fax, mail.

College at Antioch University, Registrar, 795 Livermore St, Yellow Springs, OH 45387, www.antioch-college.edu. 937-767-6328 (Fax: 937-767-6452) 10AM - 4:30PM. Enrollment: 625. Records go back to 1860. Formerly **Antioch University**. Alumni records maintained here; call 937-767-6381. Degrees granted: Bachelors; Masters; Doctorate. Special programs- Antioch Education Abroad, 937-767-6366. Attendance and degree information available by phone, mail. Transcripts available by fax, mail.

College of Mount St. Joseph, Registrar's Office, 5701 Delhi Rd, Cincinnati, OH 45233, 513-244-4621 (Fax: 513-244-4201) www.msj.edu. 8:30AM-6:30PM M-Th; 8:30AM-4:30PM F. Records go back to 1920. Alumni records maintained here; call 513-244-4425. Degrees granted: Associate; Bachelors; Masters. Attendance and degree information available by phone, fax, mail. Transcripts available by fax, mail.

College of Wooster, Registrar, Wooster, OH 44691, www.wooster.edu/registrar/ 330-263-2366, 330-263-2000 (Fax: 330-263-2260) 8AM-Noon, 1-4:30PM. Enrollment: 1700. Records go back to 1866. Alumni records maintained here; call 330-263-2324.

Degrees granted: Bachelors. Attendance and degree information available by phone, fax, mail. Transcripts available by fax, mail.

Columbus College of Art and Design,
Registrar, 107 N Ninth St, Columbus, OH 43215, www.ccad.edu. 614-224-9101 (Fax: 614-222-4040) 8:30AM-5PM. Enrollment: 1760. Records go back to 1960. Alumni records are maintained here. Degrees granted: Bachelors. Attendance, degree and transcript information available by mail.

Columbus Para-Professional Institute,
Registrar, 1900 E Dublin-Granville, Columbus, OH 43229, 614-891-5030 (Fax: 614-891-5130) 8:30AM-6PM. Records go back to 1975. Attendance and degree information available by fax, mail. Transcripts available by fax, mail.

Columbus State Community College,
Registrar, 550 E Spring St, PO Box 1609, Columbus, OH 43216-1609, 614-227-2643 (Fax: 614-227-5117) www.cscc.edu. 8AM-7:30PM M-Th; 9:30AM-4:30PM F. Enrollment: 1700. Records go back to 1963. Alumni records are maintained here. Degrees granted: Associate. Attendance and degree information available by mail. Transcripts available by fax, mail.

Cuyahoga Community College
(Metropolitan), Registrar, 2900 Community College Ave, Cleveland, OH 44115, 216-987-4030 (Fax: 216-696-2567) www.tri-c.cc.oh.us. 8:30AM-8PM. Enrollment: 9000. Records go back to 1969. Alumni Records: Cuyahoga Community College, 700 Carnegie Ave, Cleveland, OH 44115. Degrees granted: Associate. Attendance and degree information available by phone, fax, mail. Transcripts available by mail.

Cuyahoga Community College
(Eastern), Registrar, 4250 Richmond Rd, Highland Hills, OH 44122, www.tri-c.cc.oh.us. 216-987-2021 (Fax: 216-987-2214) 8:30AM-8PM M-Th; 8:30AM-5PM F; 11AM-1PM S. Records go back to 1963. Degrees granted: Associate. Attendance and degree information available by phone, mail. Transcripts available by mail.

Cuyahoga Community College
(Western), Admissions & Records, 11000 W Pleasant Valley Rd, Parma, OH 44130, 216-987-5150 (Fax: 216-987-5071). 8AM-8:30PM M-Th; 8AM-5PM F. Alumni Records: 700 Carnegie Ave, Cleveland, OH 44115. Degrees granted: Associate. Attendance and degree information available by phone, fax, mail. Transcripts available by mail.

David N. Myers College, Office of
Registrar, 112 Prospect Ave SE, Cleveland, OH 44115, 216-523-3823, 216-523-3873 (Fax: 216-696-6430). 8:30AM - 5PM. Enrollment: 1362. Records go back to 1848. Formerly Dyke College. Alumni records maintained here; call 216-523-3861. Degrees granted: Associate; Bachelors. Attendance and degree information available by phone, fax, mail. Transcripts available by mail.

Davis College, Registrar, 4747 Monroe St,
Toledo, OH 43623, 419-473-2700 (Fax: 419-473-2472) www.daviscollege.com. 9AM-6PM. Enrollment: 462. Records go back to 1945. Degrees granted: Associate. Attendance and degree information available by phone, fax, mail. Transcripts available by mail.

DeVry Institute of Technology,
Columbus, Registrar, 1350 Alum Creek Dr, Columbus, OH 43209, 614-253-7291, 800-733-3879 Ext. 1982 (Fax: 614-252-4108). 8:30AM-5PM. Enrollment: 2700. Alumni

records are maintained here. Degrees granted: Bachelors. Attendance and degree information available by phone, mail. Transcripts available by fax, mail.

Defiance College, Registrar, 701 N Clinton
St, Defiance, OH 43512, 419-783-2358 (Fax: 419-784-2468). 8AM-5PM. Enrollment: 884. Records go back to 1906. Alumni records maintained here. Call 419-783-2306. Degrees granted: Associate; Bachelors; Masters. Attendance and degree information available by phone, fax, mail. Transcripts available by written request only.

Denison University, Registrar, PO Box B,
Granville, OH 43023, 740-587-6530, 740-587-6296 (Fax: 740-587-8388) www.denison.edu. 8:30AM - 4:30PM. Enrollment: 2013. Records go back to 1960. Alumni records maintained here; call 740-587-6576. Degrees granted: Bachelors. Special programs- Prior to 1960- Archives, 740-587-6399. Attendance and degree information available by phone, fax, mail. Transcripts available by fax, mail.

ETI Technical College (Niles Campus),
Registrar, 2076-86 Youngstown-Warren Rd, Niles, OH 44446-4398, 330-652-9919 (Fax: 330-652-4399) www.eti-college.com. 9AM-6PM. Enrollment: 240. Records go back to 1989. Degrees granted: Associate. Attendance and degree information available by phone, fax, mail. Transcripts available by phone, fax, mail.

ETI Technical College, Registrar, 1320 W
Maple St NW, North Canton, OH 44720, 330-494-1214 (Fax: 330-494-8112) 9AM-5PM. Enrollment: 350. Records go back to 1983. Degrees granted: Associate. Attendance and degree information available by phone, fax, mail. Transcripts available by fax, mail.

Edison State Community College,
Registrar, 1973 Edison Dr, Piqua, OH 45356, www.edison.cc.oh.us. 937-778-8600 (Fax: 937-778-1920) 8AM-5PM. Enrollment: 2755. Records go back to 1973. Degrees granted: Associate. Attendance and transcript information available by fax, mail. Degree information available by phone, fax, mail.

Findlay College
(See University of Findlay)

Franciscan University of Steubenville,
Registrar, University Blvd, Steubenville, OH 43952, www.franuniv.edu. 740-283-6207 (Fax: 740-283-6472) 8:30AM - 4:30PM. Enrollment: 2000. Records go back to 1946. Alumni records maintained here; call 740-283-3771 Ext. 6414. Degrees granted: Associate; Bachelors; Masters. Special programs- MBA 4+1, 740-283-6270: Pre-Theology, 740-283-6226. Attendance information available by mail. Transcripts available by mail.

Franklin University, Registrar, 201 S Grant
Ave, Columbus, OH 43215-5399, 614-341-6242 (Fax: 614-224-0434) www.franklin.edu. 8AM - 6PM M-Th; 8AM - 5PM F. Enrollment: 5000. Records go back to 1950. Alumni records maintained here; call 614-341-6409. Degrees granted: Associate; Bachelors; Masters. Attendance and degree information available by phone, fax, mail. Transcripts available by fax, mail.

God's Bible College, Registrar, 1810
Young St, Cincinnati, OH 45210, 513-721-7944 Ext. 210 (Fax: 513-721-3971) www.gbs.edu. 8AM-5PM. Enrollment: 183. Records go back to 1900. Alumni records maintained here; call 513-721-7944 Ext. 267. Degrees granted: Bachelors. Attendance information available by written request only.

Degree information available by phone, fax, mail. Transcripts available by fax, mail.

Hebrew Union College — Jewish Institute of Religion, Registrar, 3101
Clifton Ave, Cincinnati, OH 45220, 513-221-1875 (Fax: 513-221-0321). Enrollment: 130. Records go back to 1906. Alumni records are maintained here. Degrees granted: Masters; Doctorate; M.Phil. Attendance and degree information available by phone, fax, mail. Transcripts available by mail.

Heidelberg College, Registrar, 310 E
Market St, Tiffin, OH 44883, 419-448-2090, 419-448-2257 (Fax: 419-448-2124) www.heidelberg.edu/. 8AM-5PM. Enrollment: 1300. Records go back to 1900. Alumni records maintained here; call 419-448-2383. Degrees granted: Bachelors; Masters. Attendance and degree information available by phone, fax, mail. Transcripts available by fax, mail.

Hiram College, Registrar, Hiram, OH
44234, 330-569-5210, 330-569-5255 (Fax: 330-569-5211) www.hiram.edu. 8:30AM-5PM. Enrollment: 1000. Records go back to 1930. Alumni records maintained here; call 330-569-5283. Degrees granted: Bachelors. Attendance and degree information available by phone, fax, mail. Transcripts available by fax, mail if requested by the student.

Hocking Technical College, Registrar,
3301 Hocking Pkwy, Nelsonville, OH 45764, 614-753-3591 (Fax: 614-753-2586). 8AM-5:30PM M-Th, 8AM - 4:30PM F. Enrollment: 5995. Records go back to 1968. Alumni records are maintained here. Degrees granted: Associate; LPN. Attendance and degree information available by phone, fax, mail. Transcripts available by fax, mail. Phone number required.

ITT Technical Institute, Registrar, 3325
Stop Eight Rd, Dayton, OH 45414-9915, www.ittesi.com 937-454-2267 (Fax: 937-454-2278) 8AM-5PM. Records go back to 1948. Degrees granted: Associate. Attendance and degree information available by phone, mail. Transcripts available by fax, mail.

ITT Technical Institute, Registrar, 1030 N
Meridian Rd, Youngstown, OH 44509-4017, www.ittesi.com 330-270-1600 (Fax: 330-270-8333) 8AM-10PM. Enrollment: 380. Records go back to 1968. Degrees granted: Associate. Attendance, degree and transcript information available by fax, mail.

International College of Broadcasting,
Registrar, 6 S Smithville Rd, Dayton, OH 45431-1833, 937-258-8251, 937-258-8252 (Fax: 937-258-8714). 8AM - 8PM. Enrollment: 125. Records go back to 1933. Degrees granted: Associate. Attendance and degree information available by phone, fax, mail. Transcripts available by fax, mail.

Jefferson Community College, Registrar,
4000 Sunset Blvd, Steubenville, OH 43952, 740-264-5591 (Fax: 740-264-2991). 8AM-7:30PM. Enrollment: 1550. Records go back to 1969. Formerly Jefferson Technical College Alumni records are maintained here. Degrees granted: Associate. Attendance and degree information available by phone, fax, mail. Transcripts available by fax, mail.

John Carroll University, Registrar, 20700
N Park Blvd, University Heights, OH 44118, 216-397-4291 (Fax: 216-397-3049) www.jcu.edu. 8:30AM-5PM. Enrollment: 3482. Records go back to 1886. Alumni records maintained here; call 216-397-4322. Degrees granted: Bachelors; Masters. Attendance and degree information available

by phone, fax, mail. Transcripts available by fax, mail.

Kent State University (Ashtabula), Registrar, Ms. Bates, 3325 W 13th St, Ashtabula, OH 44004, 440-964-4216 (Fax: 440-964-4269) www.kent.edu. 8AM-5PM. Records go back to 1921. Degrees granted: Associate; Bachelors. Attendance, degree and transcript information available by fax, mail.

Kent State University (Geuaga), Registrar, 14111 Claridon-Troy Rd, Burton Township, OH 44021, 440-834-4187 (Fax: 440-834-8846) www.kent.edu. 8AM-8PM M-Th, 8AM-5PM F, 8AM-2PM Sat. Enrollment: 26800. Records go back to 1960. Degrees granted: Associate. Attendance, degree and transcript information available by fax, mail.

Kent State University (Stark), Registrar, 6000 Frank Ave NW, Canton, OH 44720, 330-499-9600, 330-535-3377 (Fax: 330-494-6121). 8AM-7:30PM M-Th, 8AM-5PM F. Enrollment: 2700. Records go back to 1960. Alumni records are maintained here. Degrees granted: Associate; Bachelors. Attendance and degree information available by phone, fax, mail. Transcripts available by fax, mail.

Kent State University (East Liverpool), Registrar, 400 E Fourth St, East Liverpool, OH 43920, 330-385-3805 (Fax: 330-385-6348) www.kenteliv.kent.edu. 8AM-8PM M-Th, 8AM-5PM F. Enrollment: 750. Records go back to 1963. Alumni records are maintained here. Degrees granted: Associate. Attendance and degree information available by phone, fax, mail. Transcripts available by fax, mail.

Kent State University, Registrar, PO Box 5190, Kent, OH 44242, 330-672-3131 (Fax: 330-672-4836) www.kent.edu. 8AM-5PM. Enrollment: 26796. Records go back to 1921. Alumni records maintained here; call 216-672-5368. Degrees granted: Associate; Bachelors; Masters; Doctorate. Attendance and degree information available by phone, fax, mail. Transcripts available by fax, mail.

Kent State University (Tuscarawas), Registrar, 330 University Dr NE, New Philadelphia, OH 44663-9403, 330-339-3391 (Fax: 330-339-3321) www.kent.edu. 8AM-8PM M-Th; 8AM-5PM F and when not in session. Enrollment: 1482. Records go back to 1962. Alumni Records: Alumni Assoc., Williamson Alumni Center, Kent, OH 44242. Degrees granted: Associate. Attendance and degree information available by phone, fax, mail. Transcripts available by fax, mail.

Kent State University (Salem), Registrar, 2491 State Rte 45 S, Salem, OH 44460, www.kent.edu. 330-332-0361 (Fax: 330-332-9256) 9AM-8PM M, 9AM-6PM T-Th, 9AM-4:30PM F. Records go back to 1965. Degrees granted: Associate; Bachelors. Attendance and degree information available by phone, fax, mail. Transcripts available by fax, mail.

Kent State University (Trumbull), Registrar, 4314 Mahoning Ave NW, Warren, OH 44483, www.kent.edu. 330-847-0571 (Fax: 330-847-6571) 8AM-6PM M-Th, 8AM-5PM F, 9AM-1PM Sat. Records go back to 1960. Degrees granted: Associate. Attendance information available by fax, mail. Degree information available by phone, fax, mail. Transcripts available by mail.

Kenyon College, Registrar, Gambier, OH 43022-9623, 740-427-5121 (Fax: 740-427-5615) www.kenyon.edu. 8:30AM - 4:30PM. Enrollment: 1500. Records go back to 1930. Alumni records maintained here; call 740-427-5121. Degrees granted: Bachelors. Attendance and degree information available

Kettering College of Medical Arts, Registrar, 3737 Southern Blvd, Kettering, OH 45429, 937-296-7201, 513-296-7874 (Fax: 937-296-4238) www.ketthealth.com. 8:30AM-5PM M-Th; 8:30AM-2PM F. Enrollment: 619. Records go back to 1967. Alumni Records: Alumni Assoc., 3535 Southern Blvd, Kettering, OH 45429. Degrees granted: Associate. Attendance and degree information available by phone, fax, mail. Transcripts available by fax, mail.

Lake Erie College, Registrar, 391 W Washington St, Painesville, OH 44077, www.lakeerie.edu 440-639-7823 (Fax: 440-352-3533) 8AM-5PM M-F; 8AM-7PM F. Enrollment: 708. Records go back to 1856. Alumni records maintained here; call 440-639-7831. Degrees granted: Bachelors; Masters. Attendance and degree information available by phone, fax, mail. Transcripts available by mail.

Lakeland Community College, Registrar, 7700 Clocktower Dr, Kirtland, OH 44094, 440-953-7100, 440-953-7230 (Fax: 440-975-4330) www.lakeland.cc.oh.us. 8AM - 8:30PM M-Th, 7:30AM-5PM F, 8:30AM-12:30PM Sat. Enrollment: 8200. Records go back to 1967. Degrees granted: Associate. Attendance and degree information available by phone, fax, mail. Transcripts available by mail. Request form required.

Lima Technical College, Registrar, 4240 Campus Dr, Lima, OH 45804, 419-221-1112 Ext. 8070 (Fax: 419-995-8098) www.ltc.tec.oh.us. 8AM-5PM. Enrollment: 2583. Records go back to 1974. Alumni records are maintained here. Degrees granted: Associate. Attendance and degree information available by phone, fax, mail. Transcripts available by fax, mail.

Lorain County Community College, Admissions & Records, 1005 N Abbe Rd, Elyria, OH 44035, 800-995-5222 Ext. 4032, 440-365-5222 (Fax: 440-366-4167) www.lorainccc.edu. 8:30AM-7:30PM M-Th; 8:30AM-4:30PM F. Enrollment: 7000. Records go back to 1965. Alumni records are maintained here. Degrees granted: Associate. Attendance and degree information available by phone, fax, mail. Transcripts available by mail.

Lourdes College, Registrar, 6832 Convent Blvd, Sylvania, OH 43560, 419-885-3211 Ext. 207, 419-885-3211 Ext. 323 (Fax: 419-882-3987) www.lourdes.edu. 8:30AM-6PM M-Th, 8:30AM-4:30PM, 9AM-1PM Sat. Enrollment: 1500. Records go back to 1958. Alumni records are maintained here. Degrees granted: Bachelors. Attendance and transcript information available by fax, mail. Degree information available by phone, fax, mail.

MTI Business College
(See Westside Institute of Technology)

Malone College, Registrar, 515 25th St NW, Canton, OH 44709, 330-471-8129 (Fax: 330-471-8478) www.malone.edu. 8AM-5PM. Enrollment: 2239. Records go back to 1892. Alumni records maintained here; call 330-471-8237. Degrees granted: Bachelors; Masters. Attendance and degree information available by phone, fax, mail. Transcripts available by fax, mail.

Marietta College, Registrar, Marietta, OH 45750, 740-376-4728, 740-376-4723 (Fax: 740-376-4896) www.marietta.edu. 8:30AM-5PM. Enrollment: 1100. Records go back to 1835. Alumni records are maintained here. Degrees granted: Associate; Bachelors;

Masters. Attendance and degree information available by phone, fax, mail. Transcripts available by fax, mail.

Marion Technical College, Student Records, 1467 Mt Vernon Ave, Marion, OH 43302-5694, 614-389-4636 (Fax: 614-389-6136) www.mtc.tec.oh.us. 8AM-6PM. Enrollment: 1800. Records go back to 1971. Degrees granted: Associate. Attendance and transcript information available by fax, mail. Degree information available by phone, fax, mail.

McGregor School of Antioch University (The), Registrar, 800 Livermore St, Yellow Springs, OH 45387-1609, 513-767-6321 (Fax: 513-767-6461). 8:30AM-5PM M-F, 7AM-3PM Sat. Enrollment: 781. Records go back to 1987. Formerly **Antioch University** (School for Adult and Experiential Learning) Degrees granted: Bachelors; Masters. Attendance and degree information available by phone, fax, mail. Transcripts available by written request only.

Medical College of Ohio at Toledo, Registrar, 3045 Arlington Ave, Toledo, OH 43614-5805, 419-383-4198 (Fax: 419-383-4005). 8:30AM-5PM. Enrollment: 1029. Records go back to 1955. Alumni records are maintained here. Degrees granted: Masters; Doctorate. Attendance and degree information available by phone, fax, mail. Transcripts available by fax, mail.

Methodist Theological School in Ohio, Registrar, PO Box 1204, 3081 Columbus Pike, Delaware, OH 43015-0931, 614-362-3344 (Fax: 614-362-3381) www.mtso.edu. 8:30AM-4:30PM. Enrollment: 270. Records go back to 1960. Alumni records maintained here; call 614-363-1146. Degrees granted: Masters. Special programs- M Div: MACE: MTS: MASM: MALA: MA-ADAM. Attendance, degree and transcript information available by fax, mail.

Miami University (Hamilton Campus), Registrar, 1601 Peck Blvd, Hamilton, OH 45011, www.ham.muohio.edu. 513-785-3202 (Fax: 513-785-3148) 8AM-7:30PM M-Th; 8AM-5PM F. Records go back to 1968. Alumni records maintained here; call 513-529-5957. Degrees granted: Associate; Masters. Attendance and degree information available by phone, fax, mail. Transcripts available by written request only.

Miami University (Middletown Campus), Records & Registration, 4200 E University Blvd, Middletown, OH 45042, 513-727-3217, 513-529-8726 (Fax: 513-727-3220) www.mid.muohio.edu. 9AM-5PM. Enrollment: 2444. Records go back to 1976. Alumni records maintained here; call 513-529-5957. Degrees granted: Associate. Attendance, degree and transcript information available by mail.

Miami University, Office of the Registrar, Oxford, OH 45056, 513-529-1809 (Fax: 513-529-7255). 8AM-5PM. Enrollment: 17900. Records go back to 1826. Alumni Records: Murstein Alumni Center, 725 E Chestnut, Oxford, OH 45056-2480. Degrees granted: Associate; Bachelors; Masters; Doctorate. Attendance and degree information available by phone, mail. Transcripts available by mail.

Miami-Jacobs College, Registrar, PO Box 1433, 400 E Second St, Dayton, OH 45402, 937-461-5174, 937-449-8282 (Fax: 937-461-3384) www.mjweb.miamijacobs.edu. 8AM-4:30PM. Enrollment: 300. Records go back to 1960. Degrees granted: Associate. Attendance and transcript information available by fax, mail. Degree information available by phone, fax, mail.

Mount Union College, Registrar, 1972 Clark Ave, Alliance, OH 44601, 330-823-6018 (Fax: 330-823-5097) www.muc.edu. 8AM-5PM. Enrollment: 1900. Records go back to 1800's. Alumni records maintained here; call 330-823-2030. Degrees granted: Bachelors. Attendance, degree and transcript information available by phone, fax, mail. Transcript request applies to student only.

Mount Vernon Nazarene College, Registrar, 800 Martinsburg Rd, Mount Vernon, OH 43050, 614-397-1244 Ext. 4530, 614-397-6862 Ext. 4530 (Fax: 614-397-2769) 8AM-4:30PM. www.mvnc.edu. Enrollment: 1450. Records go back to 1968. Alumni records are maintained here. Degrees granted: Associate; Bachelors; Masters. Attendance and degree information available by fax. Transcripts available by written request only.

Muskingum Area Technical College, Registrar, 1555 Newark Rd, Zanesville, OH 43701, 740-454-2501 (Fax: 740-454-0035). 8AM-5PM. Enrollment: 2280. Records go back to 1971. Alumni records are maintained here. Degrees granted: Associate. Attendance and transcript information available by fax, mail. Degree information available by phone, fax, mail.

Muskingum College, Registrar, New Concord, OH 43762, 614-826-8164 (Fax: 614-826-8404) www.muskingum.edu. 8AM-Noon, 1-5PM. Enrollment: 1100. Records go back to 1904. Alumni records are maintained here. Degrees granted: Bachelors; Masters. Attendance and degree information available by phone, mail. Transcripts available by fax, mail.

North Central Technical College, Registrar, PO Box 698, 2411 Kenwood Circle, Mansfield, OH 44901-0698, www.nctc.tec.oh.us. 419-755-4837, 419-755-4857 (Fax: 419-755-4729) 8:30AM-7:45PM M-Th; 8:30AM-4:30PM F; 9AM-1PM Sat. Enrollment: 2857. Records go back to 1966. Degrees granted: Associate. Attendance, degree and transcript information available by fax, mail. Signatures on faxed requests for transcripts will be verified.

Northeastern Ohio Universities College of Medicine, Registrar, 4209 State Rte 44, PO Box 95, Rootstown, OH 44272-0095, www.neoucom.edu. 330-325-2511 (Fax: 330-325-2159) 7:30AM-5PM. Enrollment: 425. Records go back to 1977. Alumni records are maintained here. Attendance and degree information available by phone, fax, mail. Transcripts available by fax, mail.

Northwest State Community College, Registrar, 22-600 State Rte 34, Archbold, OH 43502, 419-267-5511 Ext. 317 (Fax: 419-267-2688). 8AM-4PM. Enrollment: 2000. Records go back to 1965. Formerly **Northwest Technical College**. Degrees granted: Associate. Attendance information available by phone, fax, mail. Degree and transcript information available by mail.

Northwestern College, Registrar, 1441 N Cable Rd, Lima, OH 45805, 419-998-3141 (Fax: 419-229-6926) www.nc.edu. 7:30AM-4:30PM. Enrollment: 1700. Records go back to 1925. Degrees granted: Associate. Attendance and degree information available by phone, fax, mail. Transcripts available by fax, mail.

Notre Dame College, Registrar, 4545 College Rd, South Euclid, OH 44121, 216-381-1680 Ext. 285 (Fax: 216-381-3802) www.ndc.edu. 8:30AM-4:30PM. Enrollment: 640. Records go back to 1922. Alumni records are maintained here. Degrees granted:

Associate; Bachelors; Masters. Attendance and degree information available by phone, fax, mail. Transcripts available by mail.

Oberlin College, Registrar, Oberlin, OH 44074, 440-775-8450 (Fax: 440-775-8800) www.oberlin.edu. 8AM-4:30PM. Enrollment: 2745. Records go back to 1985. Alumni records maintained here; call 440-775-8692. Degrees granted: Bachelors; Masters. Attendance, degree and transcript information available by mail.

Ohio College of Podiatric Medicine, Student Records, 10515 Carnegie Ave, Cleveland, OH 44106, 216-231-3300 Ext. 348 (Fax: 216-231-3300 Ext. 350) www.ocpm.edu. 9AM-4:30PM. Enrollment: 500. Records go back to 1917. Alumni records maintained here; call 216-231-3300 Ext. 228. Degrees granted: Doctorate. Attendance and degree information available by phone, fax, mail. Transcripts available by fax, mail.

Ohio Dominican College, Registrar's Office, 1216 Sunbury Rd, Columbus, OH 43219, 614-251-4650, 614-251-4652 (Fax: 614-252-0776) www.odc.edu/. 8AM - 4:30PM. Enrollment: 1949. Records go back to 1911. Alumni records maintained here; call 614-251-4617. Degrees granted: Associate; Bachelors. School will not confirm attendance information. Degree information available by phone, fax, mail. Transcripts available by written request only.

Ohio Northern University, Registrar, 525 S Main St, Ada, OH 45810, 419-772-2024 www.onu.edu. 8AM - 5PM. Enrollment: 2900. Records go back to 1871. Alumni records maintained here; call 419-772-2038. Degrees granted: Bachelors; PharmD, JD. Attendance and degree information available by phone, mail. Transcripts available by mail.

Ohio State University, Registrar, 205 Bricker Hall, 190 N Oval Drive, Columbus, OH 43210, 614-292-8500 (Fax: 614-292-2363) www.ohio-state.edu. 9:30AM - 5PM. Enrollment: 41818. Records go back to 1873. Alumni Records: Alumni House, 567 Fawcett Center, 2400 Olintangy Rd, Columbus, OH 43201. Degrees granted: Bachelors; Masters; Doctorate; Medical. Attendance and degree information available by phone, fax, mail. Transcripts available by fax, mail. For transcript requests write: OSU Transcripts Division, 202 Lincoln Tower, 1800 Cannon Dr, Columbus, OH, 43210-1233 Phone number required.

Ohio State University (Lima Campus), Registrar, 4240 Campus Dr, Lima, OH 45804, 419-221-1641 www.ohio-state.edu. Records are located at Ohio State University, Registrar, Columbus, OH.

Ohio State University (Mansfield Campus), Registrar, 1680 University Dr, Mansfield, OH 44906, Tele: 419-755-4011 www.ohio-state.edu. Records are located at Ohio State University, Registrar, Columbus, OH.

Ohio State University (Marion Campus), Registrar, 1465 Mount Vernon Ave, Marion, OH 43302, 614-292-8500, 614-292-9133 (Fax: 614-292-5817) www.ohio-state.edu. Records are located at Ohio State University, Registrar, Columbus, OH.

Ohio State University (Newark Campus), Registrar, University Dr, Newark, OH 43055, 740-366-3321 www.ohio-state.edu. Records located at Ohio State University, Registrar, Columbus, OH.

Ohio State University (Agricultural Technical Institute), Registrar, 1328 Dover Rd, Wooster, OH 44691, 330-264-3911 (Fax: 330-262-7634) www.ohio-state.edu. Records are located at Ohio State University, Registrar, Columbus, OH.

Ohio University, Registrar, Chubb Hall, Athens, OH 45701-2979, www.ohiou.edu/ & www.cats.ohiou.edu/~regoff 740-593-4180, 740-593-4191 (Fax: 740-593-4184) 8AM-5PM. Enrollment: 24309. Records go back to 1893. Alumni records maintained here; call 740-593-4300. Degrees granted: Associate; Bachelors; Masters; PhD; DO. Attendance and degree information available by phone, fax, mail. Transcripts available by mail.

Ohio University (Chillicothe Campus), Student Records, Chillicothe, OH 45601, 740-774-7240, 740-774-7241 (Fax: 740-774-7214) www.ohiou.edu. Records located at Ohio University, Registrar, Athens, OH.

Ohio University (Southern), Registrar, 1804 Liberty Ave, Ironton, OH 45638, 740-533-4600 (Fax: 740-533-4632). Records located at Ohio University, Registrar, Athens, OH.

Ohio University (Lancaster Campus), Registrar, 1570 Granville Pike, Lancaster, OH 43130, 740-654-6711 (Fax: 740-687-9497). Records are located at Ohio University, Registrar, Athens, OH.

Ohio University (Eastern), Registrar, St Clairsville, OH 43950, 740-695-1720 (Fax: 740-695-7079) www.eastern.ohiou.edu. Records are located at Ohio University, Registrar, Athens, OH.

Ohio University (Zanesville Campus), www.cats.ohiou.edu. Registrar, Zanesville, OH 43701, 740-453-0762 (Fax: 740-453-6161) Records are located at Ohio University, Registrar, Athens, OH.

Ohio University Belmont
(See Ohio University Eastern)

Ohio Valley Business College, Registrar, 16808 St Clare Ave, PO Box 7000, East Liverpool, OH 43920, 330-385-1070 (Fax: 330-385-4606). 8AM - 4PM. Enrollment: 130. Records go back to 1921. Degrees granted: Associate. Special programs-Administration, 216-385-1070. Attendance and degree information available by phone, fax, mail. Transcripts available by fax, mail.

Ohio Wesleyan University, Registrar, 61 S Sandusky St, Delaware, OH 43015, 740-368-3201, 740-368-3200 (Fax: 740-368-3210) 8:30AM-Noon, 1-5PM. www.owu.edu. Enrollment: 1800. Records go back to 1946. Alumni records maintained here; call 740-368-3318. Degrees granted: Bachelors. Attendance and degree information available by phone, fax, mail. Transcripts available by fax, mail.

Otterbein College, Registrar, Westerville, OH 43081, 614-823-1350 (Fax: 614-823-1009) www.otterbein.edu/registrar. 8:30AM-5PM. Enrollment: 2600. Records go back to 1847. Alumni records maintained here; call 614-823-1400. Degrees granted: Bachelors; Masters. Attendance and degree information available by phone, fax, mail. Transcripts available by mail.

Owens Community College (Branch), Registrar, 300 Davis St, Findlay, OH 45840, 419-423-6827 (Fax: 419-423-0246). 8AM-5PM. Records go back to 1989. Alumni records maintained here; call 419-661-7220. Degrees granted: Associate. Special programs- Toledo Campus, 419-661-7220.

Attendance and degree information available by phone, fax, mail. Transcripts available by fax, mail.

Owens Community College, Registrar, PO Box 10000, 30335 Oregon Rd, Toledo, OH 43699, www.http://www.owens.cc.oh.us. 419-661-7323 (Fax: 419-661-7418) 8AM-7:30PM M,Th; 8AM-5PM T,W; 8AM-4:30PM F. Enrollment: 11000. Records go back to 1965. Alumni records maintained here; call 419-661-7114. Degrees granted: Associate. Attendance and degree information available by phone, fax, mail. Transcripts available by fax, mail.

Owens Technical College
(See Owens Community College)

Pontifical College Josephinum, Registrar, 7625 N High St, Columbus, OH 43235, 614-885-5585 (Fax: 614-885-2307) www.pcj.edu. 8:30AM-4:30PM. Enrollment: 53. Alumni records are maintained here. Degrees granted: Bachelors; Masters. Attendance and degree information available by phone, fax, mail. Transcripts available by fax, mail.

RETS Technical Center, Registrar, 116 Westpark Rd, Centerville, OH 45459, 937-433-3410 (Fax: 937-435-6516). 8AM-7PM M-Th; 8AM-5PM F. Enrollment: 380. Records go back to 1953. Degrees granted: Associate. Attendance and degree information available by phone, mail. Transcripts available by mail.

Rabbinical College of Telshe, Registrar, 28400 Euclid Ave, Wickliffe, OH 44092-2523, 440-943-5300 (Fax: 440-943-5303). 8AM-5PM. Enrollment: 150. Degrees granted: Masters; Doctorate. Attendance, degree and transcript information available by mail.

Rio Grande College
(See University of Rio Grande)

Sawyer College of Business, Registrar, 3150 Mayfield Rd, Cleveland Heights, OH 44118, 216-932-0911 (Fax: 216-932-1654) Records go back to 1973. Degrees granted: Associate. Attendance and degree information available by phone, mail. Transcripts available by mail.

Shawnee State University, Registrar, 940 Second St, Portsmouth, OH 45662, www.shawnee.edu 740-355-2262 (Fax: 740-355-2593) 7AM-6PM M-Th, 7AM-5PM F. Enrollment: 3185. Records go back to 1970. Alumni records maintained here; call 740-355-2257. Degrees granted: Associate; Bachelors. Attendance and degree information available by phone, fax, mail. Transcripts available by mail.

Sinclair Community College, Registrar, 444 W Third St, Dayton, OH 45402-1460, 937-512-2736 (Fax: 937-512-3456) www.sinclair.edu. 8AM-7PM M-Th; 8AM-5PM F. Enrollment: 19800. Records go back to 1887. Alumni records maintained here; call 937-512-3030. Degrees granted: Associate. Attendance and degree information available by phone, fax, mail. Transcripts available by mail.

Southeastern Business College, Registrar, 1855 Western Ave, **Chillicothe**,. OH 45601, 740-774-6300 (Fax: 740-774-6317). 8:30AM-10PM. Enrollment: 130. Records go back to 1985. Degrees granted: Associate. Attendance and degree information available by phone, fax, mail. Transcripts available by fax, mail.

Southeastern Business College, Registrar, 1176 Jackson Pike Ste 312,

Gallipolis, OH 45631, 740-446-4367 (Fax: 740-446-1424) Records are located at Southeastern Business College, Registrar, Chillicothe, OH.

Southeastern Business College, Registrar, 420 E Main St, **Jackson**, OH 45640, 740-286-1554, 740-286-2458 (Fax: 740-286-4476) Enrollment: 102. Records older than 1997 are located at Chillicothe, OH. Degrees granted: Associate. Attendance and degree information available by phone, fax, mail. Transcripts available by fax, mail.

Southeastern Business College, Registrar, 1522 Sheridan Dr, **Lancaster**, OH 43130, 740-687-6126. Records located at Southeastern Business College, Registrar, Chillicothe, OH.

Southeastern Business College, Registrar, 1907 N Ridge Rd, **Lorain**, OH 44055, 440-277-0021 (Fax: 440-277-7989) 8:30AM-5PM. Enrollment: 120. Records go back to 1971. Degrees granted: Associate. Attendance and degree information available by phone, fax, mail. Transcripts available by fax, mail.

Southeastern Business College, Registrar, 3879 Rhodes Ave, **New Boston**, OH 45662, 740-456-4124 (Fax: 740-456-5163). 8:30AM-5PM. Enrollment: 200. Records go back to 1981. Also have some (not all) records from **Portsmouth Interstate Business College** from 1940's. Degrees granted: Associate. Attendance and degree information available by phone, fax, mail. Transcripts available by mail.

Southeastern Business College, Registrar, 4020 Milan Rd, **Sandusky**, OH 44870, 419-627-8345 (Fax: 419-627-1958) Enrollment: 130. Degrees granted: Associate. Attendance and degree information available by phone, fax, mail. Transcripts available by fax, mail.

Southern Ohio College (Branch), Registrar, 2791 Mogadore Rd, Akron, OH 44312, 330-733-8766 Ext. 51 (Fax: 330-733-5853). 8AM-6:30PM M,T,Th; 8AM-5PM W,F. Enrollment: 200. Records go back to 1975. Formerly **Buckeye College**. Degrees granted: Associate. Attendance and degree information available by phone, fax, mail. Transcripts available by mail.

Southern Ohio College, Registrar, 1011 Glendale Milford Rd, Cincinnati, OH 45237, 513-771-2424 (Fax: 513-771-3413). 8AM-6:30PM. Enrollment: 1035. Degrees granted: Associate. Attendance, degree and transcript information available by fax, mail.

Southern State Community College, Registrar, 200 Hobart Dr, Hillsboro, OH 45133, 937-393-3431 (Fax: 937-393-9831). 8AM-5PM. Enrollment: 1600. Records go back to 1976. Alumni records are maintained here. Degrees granted: Associate. Attendance and degree information available by phone, fax, mail. Transcripts available by fax, mail.

Southwestern College of Business (Branch), Registrar, 632 Vine St, Suite 200, **Cincinnati**, OH 45202, 513-421-3212 (Fax: 513-421-8325) 8AM-7PM. Enrollment: 180. Records go back to 1977. Degrees granted: Associate. Attendance, degree and transcript information available by mail.

Southwestern College of Business, Registrar, 9910 Princeton-Glendale Rd, **Cincinnati**, OH 45246, 513-874-0432 (Fax: 513-874-0123). 9AM-7PM. Enrollment: 160. Records go back to 1977. Degrees granted: Associate. Attendance and degree information available by phone, fax, mail. Transcripts available by fax, mail.

Southwestern College of Business, Registrar, 225 W First St, **Dayton**, OH 45402, 937-224-0061. 9AM-7PM M-Th, 9AM-1PM F. Records go back to 1976. Degrees granted: Associate. Special programs- Corporate Office, 513-874-0432. Attendance, degree and transcript information available by phone, mail.

Southwestern College of Business, Registrar, 631 S Briel Blvd, **Middletown**, OH 45044, 513-423-3346 (Fax: 513-423-8462) 9AM-7PM M-Th, 9AM-1PM F. Records go back to 1979. Degrees granted: Associate. Attendance and degree information available by phone, fax, mail. Transcripts available by fax, mail.

St. Mary Seminary, Registrar, 28700 Euclid Ave, Wickliffe, OH 44092-2585, 440-943-7667 (Fax: 440-943-7577). 8AM-4PM. Enrollment: 73. Records go back to 1976. Degrees granted: Masters. Attendance, degree and transcript information available by mail.

Stark State College of Technology, Registrar, 6200 Frank Ave NW, Canton, OH 44720, 330-966-5460 Ext. 211 (Fax: 330-966-6594) www.stark.cc.oh.us.. 8AM - 8PM. Enrollment: 4400. Records go back to 1960. Formerly **Stark Technical College**. Alumni records maintained here; call 330-966-5460 Ext. 211. Degrees granted: Associate. Attendance, degree and transcript information available by fax, mail.

Stautzenberger College, Registrar, 5355 Southwyck Blvd, Toledo, OH 43614, 419-866-0261 (Fax: 419-867-9821). 8AM-10PM M-Th, 9AM-5PM F, 9AM-1PM Sat. Enrollment: 348. Records go back to 1968. Degrees granted: Associate. Special programs- Medical Assisting: Dental Assisting: Veterinary Assisting: Novell Network. Attendance, degree and transcript information available by fax, mail.

Stautzenberger College (Findlay), Registrar, 1637 Tiffin Ave, Findlay, OH 45840, 419-423-2211, 800-842-3687 (Fax: 419-423-0725). 8AM-5PM. Enrollment: 150. Records go back to 1988. Degrees granted: Associate. Attendance and transcript information available by mail. Degree information available by phone, fax, mail.

Terra State Community College, Registrar, 2830 Napoleon Rd, Fremont, OH 43420, 419-334-8400 Ext. 333 (Fax: 419-334-9035) www.terra.cc.oh.us. 8AM-5:30PM M-Th, 8AM-4:30PM F. Enrollment: 2500. Records go back to 1970. Alumni records maintained here; call 419-334-8400 Ext. 345. Degrees granted: Associate. Attendance and degree information available by phone, fax, mail. Transcripts available by fax, mail.

Tiffin University, Registrar, 155 Miami St, Tiffin, OH 44883, 419-447-6442 Ext. 216 (Fax: 419-443-5006) www.tiffin.edu. 8AM-5PM. Enrollment: 1023. Records go back to 1924. Degrees granted: Associate; Bachelors; Masters. Attendance and degree information available by phone, fax, mail. Transcripts available by fax, mail.

Trinity Lutheran Seminary, Registrar, 2199 E Main St, Columbus, OH 43209-2334, 614-235-4136 (Fax: 614-238-0263). 8AM-4:30PM. Enrollment: 261. Records go back to 1920. Degrees granted: Masters. Attendance and degree information available by phone, fax, mail. Transcripts available by fax, mail.

Trumbull Business College, Registrar, 3200 Ridge Rd, Warren, OH 44484, 330-369-3200 (Fax: 330-369-6792). 7:30AM - 5PM. Enrollment: 200. Records go back to 1972. Degrees granted: Associate. Attendance, degree and transcript information available by fax, mail.

Union Institute, Registrar, 440 E McMillan St, Cincinnati, OH 45206-1925, 513-861-6400 (Fax: 513-861-3218) www.tui.edu. 9AM-5PM. Enrollment: 2100. Records go back to 1969. Alumni records are maintained here. Degrees granted: Bachelors; PhD. Attendance and degree information available by phone, fax, mail. Transcripts available by mail.

Union for Experimenting College and Universities
(See The Union Institute)

United Theological Seminary, Registrar, 1810 Harvard Blvd, Dayton, OH 45406, 513-278-5817 (Fax: 513-278-1218) 8:30AM-4:30PM. www.united.edu. Enrollment: 560. Records go back to 1874. Alumni records are maintained here. Degrees granted: Masters; Doctorate. Attendance and degree information available by phone, fax, mail. Transcripts available by written request only.

University of Akron, Office of Registrar, Transcript Clerk, Akron, OH 44325, 330-972-8300 (Fax: 330-972-8632) www.uakron.edu. 8AM-5PM. Enrollment: 24000. Records go back to 1800's. Alumni Records: 138 Fir Hill, Akron, OH 44325. Degrees granted: Associate; Bachelors; Masters; Doctorate. Attendance and degree information available by phone, fax, mail. School does not provide transcripts.

University of Cincinnati, Registrar, 2624 Clifton Ave, Cincinnati, OH 45221-0060, 513-556-9900 www.uc.edu. 8AM-5PM. Enrollment: 36000. Records go back to 1900. Alumni records maintained here; call 513-556-4641 or 4344. Degrees granted: Associate; Bachelors; Masters; Doctorate; PhD. Attendance and degree information available by phone, mail. Transcripts available by mail.

University of Cincinnati — Clermont College, Registrar, 4200 Clermont College Dr, Batavia, OH 45103, 513-732-5200 (Fax: 513-732-5303). 9AM-6PM M-Th, 9AM-5PM F. Records go back to 1973. Alumni Records: Alumni Assoc., Univ. of Cincinnati, Alumni Center, PO Box 210024, Cincinnati, OH 45221-0024. Degrees granted: Associate. Attendance and degree information available by phone, fax, mail. Transcripts available by mail.

University of Cincinnati — Raymond Walters College, Registrar, 9555 Plainfield Rd, Cincinnati, OH 45236-1096, 513-745-5600 (Fax: 513-745-5768) www.uc.edu. 8AM-7PM M-Th, 8AM-5PM F. Enrollment: 3850. Records go back to 1992. Alumni Records: Alumni Assoc., Univ. of Cincinnati, PO Box 210024, Cincinnati, OH 45221-0024. Degrees granted: Associate. Attendance and degree information available by phone, fax, mail. Transcripts available by fax, mail.

University of Dayton, Registrar, 300 College Park Ave, Dayton, OH 45469, 513-229-4141, 800-259-8864 www.udayton.edu. 8:30AM-4:30PM. Enrollment: 6435. Records go back to 1989. Alumni Records: Alumni Impaired Relations, Alumni House, Dayton, OH 45469-2710. Degrees granted: Bachelors; Masters; Doctorate. Attendance and degree information available by phone, mail. Transcripts available by mail.

University of Findlay, Registrar, 1000 N Main St, Findlay, OH 45840, 419-424-4556 www.findlay.edu/start.html. (Fax: 419-424-4822) 8:30AM-5PM. Enrollment: 3300. Records go back to 1983. Alumni records

maintained here; call 419-424-4516. Degrees granted: Associate; Bachelors; Masters. Attendance and degree information available by phone, fax, mail. Transcripts available by fax, mail.

University of Rio Grande, Registrar, E College Ave, Rio Grande, OH 45674, 614-245-7368 (Fax: 614-245-7445) 8AM-5PM. www.urgrcc.edu. Enrollment: 2032. Records go back to 1920. Alumni records maintained here; call 614-245-7527. Degrees granted: Associate; Bachelors; Masters. Attendance and degree information available by phone, fax, mail. Transcripts available by fax, mail.

University of Steubenville
(See Franciscan University of Steubenville)

University of Toledo, Registrar, 2801 W Bancroft St, Toledo, OH 43606, 419-530-2701 (Fax: 419-530-7251) www.utoledo.edu. 9AM-5PM M,Th,F; 9AM-7PM T,W; Summer 9AM-5PM. Enrollment: 21353. Records go back to 1800's. Alumni records maintained here; call 419-527-2601. Degrees granted: Associate; Bachelors; Masters; Doctorate; PhD. Attendance and degree information available by phone, fax, mail. Transcripts available by fax, mail.

Urbana University, Registrar, One College Wy, Urbana, OH 43078, 937-484-1353 (Fax: 937-484-1322) www.urbana.edu. 8AM-4:30PM. Enrollment: 1073. Records go back to 1950. Alumni records maintained here; call 937-484-1323. Degrees granted: Associate; Bachelors. Attendance and degree information available by phone, mail. Transcripts available by mail.

Ursuline College, Registrar, 2550 Lander Rd, Pepper Pike, OH 44124, 440-646-8131 (Fax: 440-646-8129) 8:30AM-5PM. http://home.earthlink.net/~ursuline. Records go back to 1950. Alumni records maintained here; call 440-646-8375. Degrees granted: Bachelors; Masters. Attendance and degree information available by phone, fax, mail. Transcripts available by mail.

Virginia Marti College of Fashion and Art, Registrar, 11724 Detroit Ave, Lakewood, OH 44107, 216-221-8584 (Fax: 216-221-2311). Degrees granted: Associate. Attendance and degree information available by phone, mail. Transcripts available by mail.

Walsh College
(See Walsh University)

Walsh University, Registrar, 2020 Easton St NW, Canton, OH 44720, 330-490-7194 (Fax: 330-490-6175). 8AM-5PM. Enrollment: 1241. Records go back to 1960. Alumni records maintained here; call 330-490-7111. Degrees granted: Associate; Bachelors; Masters. Certification: Teacher Prep. Attendance and degree information available by phone, fax, mail. Transcripts available by mail.

Washington State Community College Records Office, 710 Colegate Dr, Marietta, OH 45750, www.wscc.edu. 740-374-8716 (Fax: 740-373-7496) 7:30AM - 4:30PM. Enrollment: 2100. Records go back to 1972. Degrees granted: Associate. Attendance and degree information available by phone, fax, mail. Transcripts available by fax, mail.

West Side Institute of Technology, Registrar, 1140 Euclid Ave, Cleveland, OH 44115, 216-621-8228 (Fax: 216-651-4077). 7:30AM - 5:30PM. Enrollment: 255. Records go back to 1961. Alumni records are maintained here. Degrees granted: Associate. Special programs- Heat/Refrigeration

Program. Attendance and degree information available by phone, fax, mail. Transcripts available by phone, fax, mail.

West Side Institute of Technology, Registrar, 9801 Walford Ave, Cleveland, OH 44102, 216-651-1656 (Fax: 216-651-4077). Enrollment: 300. Records go back to 1957. Alumni records are maintained here. Degrees granted: Associate. Attendance and degree information available by phone, mail. Transcripts available by fax, mail.

Wilberforce University, Registrar, Wilberforce, OH 45384, 937-376-2911 (Fax: 937-376-2627) www.wilberforce.edu. 8AM-4:30PM. Enrollment: 958. Records go back to 1900. Alumni records maintained here; call 937-376-2911 Ext. 707. Degrees granted: Bachelors. Attendance and degree information available by phone, fax, mail. Transcripts available by fax, mail.

Wilmington College, Registrar, Pyle Center Box 1286, Wilmington, OH 45177, 937-382-6661 Ext. 213, 937-382-6661 Ext. 464 (Fax: 937-382-7077) www.wilmington.edu. 8AM-5PM. Enrollment: 1000. Records go back to 1900. Alumni Records: Alumni Assoc., Pyle Center Box 1307, Wilmington, OH 45177. Degrees granted: Bachelors. Attendance and degree information available by phone, fax, mail. Transcripts available by fax, mail.

Winebrenner Theological Seminary, Registrar, 701 E Melrose Ave, PO Box 478, Findlay, OH 45839, 419-422-4824, 800-992-4987 (Fax: 419-422-3999). 8AM-5PM. Enrollment: 100. Records go back to 1842. Alumni records are maintained here. Degrees granted: Masters. Attendance and degree information available by phone, fax, mail. Transcripts available by mail.

Wittenberg University, Registrar, PO Box 720, Springfield, OH 45501, 937-327-6132 (Fax: 937-327-6340) www.wittenberg.edu. 8AM-5PM. Enrollment: 2180. Records go back to 1900. Alumni Records: Alumni Assoc., PO Box 720, Springfield, OH 45501. Degrees granted: Bachelors. Attendance and degree information available by phone, fax, mail. Transcripts available by fax, mail.

Wright State University (Lake), Registrar, 7600 State Rte 703, **Celina**, OH 45822, www.wright.edu 419-586-0324 (Fax: 419-586-0358) Records are located at Wright State University, Registrar, Dayton, OH.

Wright State University, Registrar, 3640 Colonel Glenn Hwy, **Dayton**, OH 45435, 513-873-5588 (Fax: 513-873-5795) www.wright.edu. 8:30AM-7PM M-Th, 8:30AM-5PM F. Enrollment: 15900. Records go back to 1964. Alumni records maintained here; call 513-873-2251. Degrees granted: Associate; Bachelors; Masters; Doctorate; Medicine, Psy D. Special programs- School Medicine, 513-873-3013. Attendance and degree information available by phone, fax, mail. Transcripts available by fax, mail.

Xavier University, Registrar, 3800 Victory Pkwy, Cincinnati, OH 45207-3131, 513-745-3941, 513-745-2966 (Fax: 513-745-2969) www.xu.edu. 8AM-7PM M-Th; 8AM-5PM F. Enrollment: 6200. Records go back to 1920's. Alumni records maintained here; call 513-745-3337. Degrees granted: Associate; Bachelors; Masters; Doctorate. Attendance and degree information available by phone, fax, mail. Transcripts available by written request only.

Youngstown College of Business and Prof Drafting
(See ITT Technical Institute)

Youngstown State University, Records Office, 410 Wick Ave, Youngstown, OH 44555, www.ysu.edu. 330-742-3182, 330-742-3184 (Fax: 330-742-1408) 8AM-5PM.

Enrollment: 13000. Records go back to 1908. Alumni records maintained here; call 330-742-3497. Degrees granted: Associate; Bachelors; Masters; Doctorate. Attendance

and degree information available by phone, fax, mail. Transcripts available by fax, mail.

Oklahoma

Bacone College, Registrar, 2299 Old Bacone Rd, Muskogee, OK 74403-1597, 580-683-4581 Ext. 275-277 (Fax: 580-687-5913). 8AM-4:30PM. Enrollment: 500. Records go back to 1880. Alumni records are maintained here. Degrees granted: Associate. Attendance and degree information available by phone, fax, mail. Transcripts available by fax, mail.

Bartlesville Wesleyan College, Registrar, 2201 Silver Lake Rd, Bartlesville, OK 74006, 918-335-6358, 918-335-6200 (Fax: 918-335-6229) www.bwc.edu. 8AM-Noon, 1-5PM. Enrollment: 550. Records go back to 1909. Alumni records are maintained here. Degrees granted: Associate; Bachelors. Special programs- Nursing, 918-333-6151. Attendance and degree information available by phone, fax, mail. Transcripts available by fax, mail.

Bethany Nazarene College
(See Southern Nazarene University)

Cameron University, Registrar, 2800 Gore Blvd, Lawton, OK 73505, 580-581-2238 (Fax: 580-581-5514) www.cameron.edu. 8AM-Noon, 1-5PM. Enrollment: 5600. Records go back to 1920. Alumni records maintained here; call 580-581-2988. Degrees granted: Associate; Bachelors; Masters. Special programs- Teacher Certification, 580-581-2339. Attendance and degree information available by phone, fax, mail. Transcripts available by fax, mail.

Carl Albert State College, Registrar, 1507 S McKenna, Poteau, OK 74953-5208, 405-647-1300, 918-647-1200 (Fax: 405-647-1306) 8AM-4:30PM. www.casc.cc.ok.us. Enrollment: 2000. Records go back to 1934. Alumni records maintained here. Call 405-647-1373. Degrees granted: Associate. Special programs- Nursing-RN, 918-647-1350; Physical Therapist Assistant, 918-647-1357. Attendance and degree information available by phone, fax, mail. Transcripts available by fax, mail.

Connors State College, Registrar, Rte 1 Box 1000, Warner, OK 74469, 918-463-6241, 918-463-6300 (Fax: 918-463-6272). 8AM-4:30PM. Enrollment: 2200. Records go back to 1927. Alumni Records: Alumni Assoc., 2501 N 41st St E, Muskogee, OK 74403. Degrees granted: Associate. Attendance and degree information available by phone, fax, mail. Transcripts available by written request only.

East Central University, Registrar, Ada, OK 74820, 580-332-8000 (Fax: 580-436-5495) www.ecok.edu. 8AM-5PM. Enrollment: 4500. Records go back to 1900. Alumni records maintained here; call 580-332-8000 Ext. 611. Degrees granted: Bachelors; Masters. Attendance and degree information available by phone, fax, mail. Transcripts available by fax, mail.

Eastern Oklahoma State College, Registrar, 1301 W Main St, Wilburton, OK 74578, 580-465-2361 Ext. 346 (Fax: 580-465-2431). 8AM - 5PM. Enrollment: 2400. Records go back to 1911. Alumni records maintained here; call 580-465-2361 Ext. 215. Degrees granted: Associate. Special programs- Nursing, 918-465-2361 Ext. 346. Attendance, degree and transcript information available by fax, mail.

El Reno Junior College
(See Redlands Community College)

Hillsdale Free Will Baptist College, Registrar, PO Box 7208, Moore, OK 73153, 405-912-9000 (Fax: 405-912-9050). Enrollment: 150. Records go back to 1959. Alumni records maintained here; call 405-912-9008. Degrees granted: Associate; Bachelors; Bible Certificate. Attendance and degree information available by phone, fax, mail. Transcripts available by fax, mail.

Langston University, Registrar, PO Box 907, Langston, OK 73050-0907, 405-466-3225, 405-466-3226 (Fax: 405-466-3381). 8AM-5PM. Enrollment: 4070. Records go back to 1910. Alumni records maintained here; call 405-466-3201 Ext. 2999. Degrees granted: Associate; Bachelors; Masters. Attendance and degree information available by phone, fax, mail. Transcripts available by mail.

Mid-America Bible College, Registrar, 3500 SW 119th St, Oklahoma City, OK 73170-9797, 405-691-3800 (Fax: 405-692-3165). 8:30AM-4PM. Enrollment: 450. Records go back to 1956. Alumni records are maintained here. Degrees granted: Associate; Bachelors. Attendance and degree information available by phone, fax, mail. Transcripts available by fax, mail.

Murray State College, Registrar, 1100 S Murray, Tishomingo, OK 73460, 580-371-2371 Ext. 108 (Fax: 580-371-9844) www.msc.cc.ok.us. 8AM-4:30PM. Enrollment: 1700. Records go back to 1950's. Alumni records are maintained here. Degrees granted: Associate. Attendance information available by phone, fax, mail. Degree and transcript information available by fax, mail.

Northeastern Oklahoma A&M College, Registrar, 200 I St NE, Miami, OK 74354, www.neoam.cc ok.us. 405-542-8441, 800-234-3409 (Fax: 405-540-6474) 8AM-4:30PM. Enrollment: 2381. Records go back to 1940's. Alumni records maintained here; call 405-540-6372. Degrees granted: Associate. Attendance and degree information available by phone, fax, mail. Transcripts available by fax, mail.

Northeastern State University, Registrar, Tahlequah, OK 74464, 918-456-5511 Ext. 2200 (Fax: 918-456-2342) www.nsuok.edu. 8AM-Noon, 1-5PM. Enrollment: 9300. Records go back to 1900. Alumni records maintained here; call 405-456-5511 Ext. 4200. Degrees granted: Bachelors; Masters. Special programs- Doctor of Optometry, 918-456-5511 Ext. 4000. Attendance, degree and transcript information available by mail.

Northern Oklahoma College, Registrar, PO Box 310, 1220 E Grand Ave, Tonkawa, OK 74653-0310, 580-628-6200 (Fax: 580-628-5260) www.north-ok.edu. 8AM-5PM. Enrollment: 2300. Records go back to 1901. Alumni records maintained here; call 508-628-6200. Degrees granted: Associate. Attendance and degree information available by phone, fax, mail. Transcripts available by fax, mail.

Northwestern Oklahoma State University, Registrar, 709 Oklahoma Blvd, Alva, OK 73717, www.nwalva.edu. 580-327-8553 (Fax: 580-327-1881) 8AM-5PM. Enrollment: 2000. Records go back to 1897. Alumni records maintained here; call 580-327-8593. Degrees granted: Bachelors; Masters. Attendance and degree information available by phone, fax, mail. Transcripts available by fax, mail.

Oklahoma Baptist University, Registrar, OBU Box 61173, Shawnee, OK 74801, 405-878-2023, 405-878-2025 (Fax: 405-878-2046) 8AM-5PM. www.okbu.edu. Enrollment: 2400. Records go back to 1910. Alumni Records: OBU Box 61275, Shawnee, OK 74801. Degrees granted: Associate; Bachelors; Masters. Attendance and degree information available by phone, fax, mail. Transcripts available by fax, mail.

Oklahoma Christian University, Registrar, PO Box 11000, Oklahoma City, OK 73136-1100, 405-425-5200 (Fax: 405-425-5208) www.oc.edu. 8AM - 5PM. Enrollment: 1445. Records go back to 1951. Alumni records maintained here; call 405-425-5120. Degrees granted: Bachelors; Masters. Attendance and degree information available by phone, fax, mail. Transcripts available by fax, mail.

Oklahoma City Community College, Registrar, 7777 S May Ave, Oklahoma City, OK 73159, 405-682-7512 (Fax: 405-682-7521) www.okc.cc.ok.us. 8AM-8PM M; 8AM-6PM T,W; 11:30AM-6PM Th; 8AM-5PM F. Enrollment: 10000. Records go back to 1990. Alumni records maintained here; call 405-682-7523. Degrees granted: Associate. Attendance and degree information available by phone, fax, mail. Transcripts available by fax, mail.

Oklahoma City University, Registrar, 2501 N Blackwelder Ave, Oklahoma City, OK 73106, 405-521-5296, 405-521-5298 (Fax: 405-521-5264) www.okcu.edu. 8AM-6PM M, 8AM-5PM T-F. Enrollment: 4680. Records go back to 1904. Alumni records are maintained here. Degrees granted: Bachelors; Masters; JD. Attendance and degree information available by fax, mail. Transcripts available by mail.

Oklahoma Panhandle State University, Registrar, Box 430, Goodwell, OK 73939, 580-349-2611 Ext. 296 (Fax: 580-349-2302). 8AM-4:30PM. Enrollment: 1150. Records go back to 1921. Alumni records maintained here; call 580-349-2611. Degrees granted: Associate; Bachelors. Attendance and degree information available by phone, fax, mail. Transcripts available by fax, mail.

Oklahoma State University, Registrar's Office, 103 Whitehurst, **Stillwater**, OK 74078, 405-744-6888 (Fax: 405-744-8426) 8AM-5PM. www.pio.okstate.edu. Enrollment: 18000. Records go back to 1900. Alumni Records: 212 Student Union, Stillwater, OK 74078. Degrees granted: Bachelors; Masters; Doctorate. Attendance and degree information available by phone, fax, mail. Transcripts available by fax, mail.

Oklahoma State University (Oklahoma City), Registrar, 900 N Portland Ave, Oklahoma City, OK 73107, 405-945-3254 (Fax: 405-945-3325) www.pio.okstate.edu. 8AM-6PM. Enrollment: 4100. Records go back to 1961. Alumni records maintained here; call 405-945-8618. Degrees granted: Associate. Attendance and degree information available by phone, fax, mail. Transcripts available by mail.

Oklahoma State University (Okmulgee)

Registrar, 1801 E Fourth St, Okmulgee, OK 74447, 405-756-6211 (Fax: 405-756-4157) www.osu-okmulgee.edu. 7:30AM-4:30PM. Enrollment: 2188. Records go back to 1946. Alumni records maintained here; call 405-756-6211. Degrees granted: Associate. Attendance and degree information available by phone, fax, mail. Transcripts available by fax, mail.

Oklahoma State University College of Osteopathic Medicine, Registrar, 1111 W 17th St, Tulsa, OK 74107, 580-582-1972 www.osu.com.okstate.edu (Fax: 580-561-8243) 8AM-5PM. Enrollment: 348. Records go back to 1977. Alumni records maintained here; call 580-561-8250. Attendance and degree information available by phone, fax, mail. Transcripts available by fax, mail.

Oral Roberts University, Registrar, 7777 S Lewis Ave, Tulsa, OK 74171, 918-495-6549 (Fax: 918-495-6607) www.oru.edu. 8AM-4:30PM. Enrollment: 5000. Records go back to 1960. Alumni records are maintained here also. Call 918-495-6627. Degrees granted: Bachelors; Masters; Doctorate. Attendance and degree information available by phone, mail. Transcripts available by mail.

Phillips Theological Seminary, Registrar, 102 University Dr, PO Box 2335 University Station, Enid, OK 73702, Campus closed. 918-610-8303 for information. Records are located at Phillips Univ., Registrar, Enid, OK.

Phillips University, Registrar, 100 S University Ave, Enid, OK 73701, Campus closed. 918-610-8303 for information. 8:30AM-4PM. www.phillips.edu. Enrollment: 700. Records go back to 1906. Alumni records maintained here; call 580-548-2293. Degrees granted: Bachelors; Masters.

Redlands Community College, Registrar, 1300 S Country Club Rd, El Reno, OK 73036, 405-262-2552 (Fax: 405-422-1200) 8AM-5PM. www.redlands.cc.ok.us. Enrollment: 2100. Records go back to 1938. Alumni records maintained here. Call 405-262-2552 Ext. 2339. Degrees granted: Associate. Attendance and degree information available by phone, fax, mail. Transcripts available by fax, mail.

Rogers State College, Registrar, Will Rogers and College Hill, Claremore, OK 74017, 918-343-7541 (Fax: 918-343-7595). 8AM-5PM. Enrollment: 3000. Records go back to 1908. Alumni records maintained here; call 918-343-7769. Degrees granted: Associate. Attendance and degree information available by phone, fax, mail. Transcripts available by written request only.

Rose State College, Registrar, 6420 SE 15th St, Midwest City, OK 73110, 405-733-7308 (Fax: 405-733-7440). 8AM-8PM M-Th, 8AM-6PM Fri. Records go back to 1971. Alumni records maintained here; call 405-736-0313. Degrees granted: Associate. Attendance and degree information available by phone, mail. Transcripts available by mail.

Sayre Junior College
(See Southwestern Oklahoma State University at Sayre)

Seminole State College, Registrar, PO Box 351, Seminole, OK 74818-0351, 405-382-9950 Ext. 248, 405-382-9950 Ext. 230 (Fax: 405-382-9524) www.ssc.cc.ok.us. 8AM - 5PM. Enrollment: 1600. Records go back to 1970. Formerly Seminole Junior College. Alumni records maintained here; call 405-382-9218. Degrees granted: Associate. Attendance and degree information available by phone, fax, mail. Transcripts available by fax, mail.

Southeastern Oklahoma State University, Registrar, PO Box 4139, Durant, OK 74701-0609, 580-924-0121, 580-924-0121 Ext. 2240 (Fax: 580-920-7472). 8AM-5PM. Enrollment: 4000. Records go back to 1909. Alumni records are maintained here. Degrees granted: Bachelors; Masters. Attendance and degree information available by phone, fax, mail. Transcripts available by fax, mail.

Southern Nazarene University, Registrar's Office, 6729 NW 39th Expwy, Bethany, OK 73008, 405-491-6386 (Fax: 405-491-6320) www.snu.edu. 8AM-5PM. Enrollment: 1834. Records go back to 1900's. Alumni records maintained here; call 405-491-6312. Degrees granted: Bachelors; Masters. Attendance and degree information available by phone, fax, mail. Transcripts available by fax, mail.

Southwestern College of Christian Ministries, Registrar, PO Box 340, Bethany, OK 73008, 405-789-7661 Ext. 3423 (Fax: 405-789-7669 Ext. 3432) www.sccm.edu. 8:30AM - 4:30PM. Enrollment: 210. Records go back to 1946. Alumni records maintained here; call 405-789-7661 Ext. 3422. Degrees granted: Associate; Bachelors; Masters. Attendance and degree information available by phone, fax, mail. Transcripts available by fax, mail.

Southwestern Oklahoma State University (Sayre Campus), Registrar, 409 E Mississippi, Sayre, OK 73662, 580-928-5533 (Fax: 580-928-5533). 8AM-5PM. Enrollment: 531. Records go back to 1938. Degrees granted: Associate. Attendance and degree information available by phone, fax, mail. Transcripts available by fax, mail.

Southwestern Oklahoma State University Registrar, 100 Campus Dr, Weatherford, OK 73096, 580-772-6611, 580-774-3778 (Fax: 580-774-3795) 8AM-5PM. www.swosu.edu. Enrollment: 5000. Records go back to 1918. Alumni records maintained here; call 580-774-3267. Degrees granted: Associate; Bachelors; Masters. Special programs- Associate, 405-928-5533. Attendance and degree information available by phone, fax, mail. Transcripts available by fax, mail.

St. Gregory's University, Registrar, 1900 W MacArthur St, Shawnee, OK 74801, 405-878-5433 (Fax: 405-878-5198) www.sgc.edu. 8AM-4:30PM. Enrollment: 500. Records go back to 1920. Alumni records maintained here; call 405-878-5171. Degrees granted: Associate. Attendance information available by phone, fax, mail. Degree and transcript information available by fax, mail.

Tulsa Community College (Metro), Registrar's Office, 909 S Boston Ave, Tulsa, OK 74119, 580-595-7226 (Fax: 580-595-7347) www.tulsa.cc.ok.us. 8AM-7PM M-Th, 8AM-5PM F. Enrollment: 21500. Records go back to 1970. Formerly Tulsa Junior College (Metro). Alumni records maintained here; call 580-595-7927. Degrees granted: Associate. Attendance and degree information available by mail. Transcripts available by fax, mail.

University of Central Oklahoma, Registrar, 100 N University Dr, Box 151, Edmond, OK 73034, 405-341-2980 Ext. 2331 (Fax: 405-341-4964) www.ucok.edu. 8AM-7:30PM M; 8AM-5PM T-F. Enrollment: 15000. Records go back to 1891. Alumni records maintained here; call 405-341-2980 Ext. 2421. Degrees granted: Bachelors; Masters. Attendance and degree information available by phone, fax, mail. Transcripts available by fax, mail.

University of Oklahoma, Registrar's Office, 1000 Asp Ave, Norman, OK 73019, 405-325-2012 (Fax: 405-325-7047) www.ou.edu. 8AM-5PM. Enrollment: 16455. Records go back to 1940. Alumni records: Alumni Assoc., Univ. of Oklahoma, 900 Asp Ave, Norman, OK 73019. Degrees granted: Bachelors; Masters; Doctorate. Special programs- Health Sciences, 405-271-1537. Attendance and degree information available by phone, fax, mail. Transcripts available by fax, mail.

University of Oklahoma Health Sciences Center, Registrar, PO Box 26901, Oklahoma City, OK 73190, 405-271-1537, 405-271-2359 (Fax: 405-271-2480) www.ouhsc.edu. 8AM-5PM. Enrollment: 3000. Records go back to 1900's. Alumni records maintained here; call 405-325-1710. Degrees granted: Bachelors; Masters; Doctorate. Attendance and degree information available by phone, fax, mail. Transcripts available by fax, mail.

University of Science and Arts of Oklahoma, Registrar, PO Box 82345, Chickasha, OK 73018, 405-224-3140 Ext. 204 (Fax: 405-521-6244) 8AM-5PM. www.mercur.usao.edu. Enrollment: 1600. Records go back to 1911. Alumni records maintained here; call 405-224-3140 Ext. 290. Degrees granted: Bachelors. Attendance and degree information available by phone, mail. Transcripts available by mail.

University of Tulsa, Registrar, 600 S College Ave, Tulsa, OK 74104, 405-631-2253 (Fax: 405-631-2622) www.utulsa.edu. 8AM - 6PM M-Th; 8AM - 5PM F. Enrollment: 3168. Records go back to 1912. Alumni records maintained here; call 405-631-2555. Degrees granted: Bachelors; Masters; Doctorate; JD. Special programs-Law School, 918-631-3523. Attendance, degree and transcript information available by fax, mail.

Western Oklahoma State College, Admissions and Registrar, 2801 N Main St, Altus, OK 73521, 580-477-2000, 580-477-7722 (Fax: 580-521-6154) 7:30AM-4:30PM. www.western.cc.ok.us. Enrollment: 1703. Records go back to 1926. Alumni records are maintained here. Degrees granted: Associate. Attendance and degree information available by phone, fax, mail. Transcripts available by fax, mail.

Oregon

Bassist College, Registrar, 2000 SW Fifth Ave, Portland, OR 97201, 503-228-6528, 888-228-6528 (Fax: 503-228-4227) www.bassist.edu. 7:30AM-5PM. Enrollment: 160. Records go back to 1981. Alumni records are maintained here. Degrees granted: Associate; Bachelors. Attendance and degree information available by phone, fax, mail. Transcripts available by mail.

Blue Mountain Community College, Registrar, PO Box 100, Pendleton, OR 97801, www.bmcc.cc.or.us. 541-276-1260 (Fax: 541-278-5818) 8AM-5PM. Enrollment: 1000. Records go back to 1916. Degrees granted: Associate. Attendance and degree information available by mail. Transcripts available by fax, mail.

Central Oregon Community College, Registrar, 2600 NW College Way, Bend, OR 97701, www.cocc.edu. 541-383-7250 (Fax: 541-383-7506) 8AM-5PM. Enrollment: 3200. Records go back to 1949. Alumni records are maintained here. Degrees granted: Associate. Attendance and degree information available by phone, fax, mail. Transcripts available by fax, mail.

Chemeketa Community College, Registrar, PO Box 14007, Salem, OR 97309, www.chemek.cc.or.us. 503-399-5001 (Fax: 503-399-3918) 8AM - 4:30PM. Enrollment: 40000. Records go back to 1955's. Transcripts available from 1970 on. Alumni records are maintained here. Degrees granted: Associate. Attendance and degree information available by phone, fax, mail. Transcripts available by fax, mail.

Clackamas Community College, Registrar, 19600 S Molalla Ave, Oregon City, OR 97045, 503-657-6958 (Fax: 503-650-6654) www.clackamas.cc.or.us. 8AM - 5PM. Enrollment: 27000. Records go back to 1966. Degrees granted: Associate. Special programs- Nursing, 503-657-6958 Ext. 2214: Accelerated Degree, 503-657-6958 Ext. 2214. Attendance and transcript information available by fax, mail. Degree information available by phone, fax, mail.

Clatsop Community College, Registrar, 1653 Jerome Ave, Astoria, OR 97103, 503-325-0910, 503-338-2437 (Record Dept) (Fax: 503-325-5738) www.clatsop.cc.or.us. 8AM-5PM. Enrollment: 2500. Records go back to 1958. Degrees granted: Associate. Attendance and degree information available by phone, fax, mail. Transcripts available by fax, mail.

Concordia University, Registrar, 2811 NE Holman St, Portland, OR 97211, 503-280-8510, 503-288-9371 (Fax: 503-280-8661) www.cu-portland.edu. 8AM-6PM M-Th, 8AM-4:30PM F. Enrollment: 1000. Records go back to 1905. Formerly **Concordia College**. Alumni records maintained here; call 503-280-8505. Degrees granted: Associate; Bachelors; Masters of Education. Attendance and degree information available by phone, fax, mail. Transcripts available by fax, mail.

Eastern Oregon State College, Registrar, La Grande, OR 97850, 541-962-3519 (Fax: 541-962-3799) www.eou.edu/. 8AM-5PM. Enrollment: 1850. Records go back to 1929. Alumni records are maintained here also. Call 541-962-3844. Degrees granted: Associate; Bachelors; MTE. Attendance and degree information available by phone, fax, mail. Transcripts available by fax, mail.

Eugene Bible College, Registrar, 2155 Bailey Hill Rd, Eugene, OR 97405, 541-485-1780 (Fax: 541-485-5801) www.ebc.edu. 8AM-5PM. Enrollment: 250. Records go back to 1925. Alumni records are maintained here. Degrees granted: Bachelors. Certification: Bible. Attendance and degree information available by phone, fax, mail. Transcripts available by fax, mail.

George Fox College
(See George Fox University)

George Fox University, Registrar, Newberg, OR 97132, 503-538-8383, 503-554-2218 (Fax: 503-554-3880). 8AM-5PM. Enrollment: 2250. Records go back to 1891. Alumni records maintained here; call 503-538-8383. Degrees granted: Bachelors; Masters; Doctorate. Attendance and degree information available by phone, fax, mail. Transcripts available by fax, mail.

ITT Technical Institute, Registrar, 6035 NE 78th Ct, Portland, OR 97218-2854, 503-255-6500 (Fax: 503-255-6135) Enrollment: 600. Records go back to 1979. Alumni records are maintained here. Degrees granted: Bachelors. Attendance and degree information available by phone, fax, mail. Transcripts available by fax, mail.

Lane Community College, Registrar, 4000 E 30th Ave, Eugene, OR 97405, www.lanecc.edu. 541-726-2213, 541-726-2207 (Fax: 541-744-3995) 8AM-4:45PM M,T,W,F; 9AM-4:45PM Th. Enrollment: 9917. Records go back to 1964. Degrees granted: Associate. Attendance and degree information available by phone, fax, mail. Transcripts available by mail.

Lewis and Clark College, College of Arts & Sciences, 0615 SW Palatine Hill Rd, Portland, OR 97219, 503-768-7334 (Fax: 503-768-7333) www.lclark.edu. 8AM-4:30PM. Enrollment: 1700. Alumni records maintained here; call 503-768-7950. Degrees granted: Bachelors; Masters. Attendance and degree information available by phone, fax, mail. Transcripts available by fax, mail.

Linfield College, Office of the Registrar, Unit D - 900 SE Baker, McMinnville, OR 97128-6894, www.linfield.edu. 503-434-2200 (Fax: 503-434-2215) 8AM-5PM. Enrollment: 1500. Records go back to 1847. Alumni records maintained here; call 503-434-2200. Degrees granted: Bachelors; Masters. Attendance and degree information available by phone, fax, mail. Transcripts available by mail.

Linn-Benton Community College, Registrar, 6500 SW Pacific Blvd, Albany, OR 97321, 541-917-4812 (Fax: 541-917-4811). 8:30AM-4:30PM. Enrollment: 25000. Records go back to 1967. Degrees granted: Associate. Attendance and degree information available by phone, fax, mail. Transcripts available by fax, mail.

Marylhurst College, Registrar, PO Box 261, Marylhurst, OR 97036, www.marylhurst.edu/. 503-699-6267 Ext. 3316 (Fax: 503-636-9526) 8AM-5PM. Enrollment: 1660. Records go back to 1893. Alumni records are maintained here. Degrees granted: Bachelors; Masters. Special programs- Masters Art Therapy, 503-699-6244: Early Scholars Program. Attendance and degree information available by phone, fax, mail. Transcripts available by fax, mail.

Mount Angel Seminary, Records & Registration, St. Benedict, OR 97373, 503-845-3951 (Fax: 503-845-3126). 8AM-5PM. Enrollment: 150. Records go back to 1900's. Alumni records are maintained here. Degrees granted: Bachelors; Masters. Attendance and degree information available by phone, fax, mail. Transcripts available by fax, mail.

Mount Hood Community College, Admissions Office, 26000 SE Stark St, Gresham, OR 97030, 503-667-6422, 503-667-7392 (Fax: 503-667-7388) www.mhccna:8080. 8AM-7:30PM M-Th, 8AM - 4:30PM F. Enrollment: 12000. Records go back to 1965. Alumni records are maintained here. Degrees granted: Associate. Attendance, degree and transcript information available by mail.

Multnomah Bible College, Registrar, 8435 NE Glisan St, Portland, OR 97220, 503-255-0332 Ext. 372 (Fax: 503-254-1268). 8AM-5PM. Enrollment: 725. Records go back to 1936. Alumni records are maintained here. Degrees granted: Bachelors; Masters. Attendance and degree information available by phone, fax, mail. Transcripts available by fax, mail.

Northwest Christian College, Registrar, 828 E 11th Ave, Eugene, OR 97401, 541-343-1641 Ext. 15 (Fax: 541-343-9159) www.nwcc.edu. 8AM - 5PM. Enrollment: 400. Records go back to 1895. Alumni records maintained here; call 541-343-1641. Degrees granted: Associate; Bachelors; Masters. Attendance and degree information available by phone, fax, mail. Transcripts available by fax, mail.

Oregon College of Oriental Medicine, Registrar, 10525 SE Cherry Blossom Dr, Portland, OR 97216, 503-253-3443 www.infinite.org/oregon.acupuncture. (Fax: 503-253-2701) 9AM-5PM. Enrollment: 170. Records go back to 1983. Alumni records are maintained here. Degrees granted: Masters. Special programs- Acupuncture & Oriental Medicine. Attendance and degree information available by phone, mail. Transcripts available by mail.

Oregon Graduate Institute
(See Oregon Graduate Institute of Science & Technology)

Oregon Graduate Institute of Science and Technology, Registrar, PO Box 91000, Portland, OR 97291-1000, 503-690-1382, 503-690-1028 (Fax: 503-690-1285) www.ogi.edu. 8AM-5PM. Enrollment: 350. Records go back to 1965. Alumni records maintained here; call 503-690-1144. Degrees granted: Masters; Doctorate. Certification: Computahonal Finance. Attendance and degree information available by phone, mail. Transcripts available by fax, mail.

Oregon Health Sciences University, Registrar's Office L109A, 3181 SW Sam Jackson Park Rd, Portland, OR 97201, 503-494-7800 (Fax: 503-494-4629). 7:30AM - 4PM. Degrees granted: Bachelors; Masters; Ph.D.,DMD,MD. Special programs- School of Dentistry, 503-494-8825. Attendance and degree information available by phone, fax, mail. Transcripts available by mail.

Oregon Institute of Technology, Registrar, Klamath Falls, OR 97601-8801, 541-885-1300, 541-885-1141 (Fax: 541-885-1274) www.ohsu.edu. 8AM-5PM.

Enrollment: 2400. Records go back to 1947. Alumni records maintained here; call 503-885-1130. Degrees granted: Associate; Bachelors; Masters. Attendance and degree information available by phone, fax, mail. Transcripts available by fax, mail.

Oregon State University, Registrar, Corvallis, OR 97331, 541-737-4331, 541-737-4048 www.orst.edu/regist.htm OR www.osu.orst.edu. (Fax: 541-737-2482) 8AM-5PM. Enrollment: 14000. Records go back to 1868. Alumni records maintained here; call 541-737-2351. Degrees granted: Bachelors; Masters; Doctorate. Attendance and degree information available by phone, fax, mail. Transcripts available by fax, mail.

Pacific Northwest College of Art, Registrar, 1219 SW Park Ave, Portland, OR 97205, 503-226-4391 (Fax: 503-226-4842) www.fta.com/~pnca. 9AM-5PM. Enrollment: 269. Records go back to 1911. Alumni records are maintained here. Degrees granted: Bachelors. Attendance and degree information available by phone, fax, mail. Transcripts available by mail.

Pacific University, Registrar, 2043 College Way, Forest Grove, OR 97116, 503-359-2234 (Fax: 503-359-2950) http://nclic.pacificu.edu. 8AM-5PM. Records go back to 1900's. Alumni records maintained here; call 503-359-6151 Ext. 2206. Degrees granted: Bachelors; Masters; Doctorate. Attendance and degree information available by phone, fax, mail. Transcripts available by fax, mail.

Portland Community College, Student Records, PO Box 19000, Portland, OR 97280, 503-614-7100 (Fax: 503-645-0894) www.pcc.edu. 8AM-5PM. Enrollment: 38000. Records go back to 1961. Degrees granted: Associate. Attendance and degree information available by fax, mail. Transcripts available by mail.

Portland State University, Registrar, PO Box 751, Portland, OR 97207-0751, 503-725-3435 (Fax: 503-725-5525) www.pdx.edu. 8AM-6:30PM. Enrollment: 17200. Records go back to 1907. Alumni Records: Alumni Assoc., PO Box 751, Portland, OR 97207. Degrees granted: Bachelors; Masters; Doctorate. Attendance and transcript information available by fax, mail. Degree information available by phone, fax, mail.

Reed College, Registrar, 3203 SE Woodstock Blvd, Portland, OR 97202, 503-771-1112 Ext. 7793 (Fax: 503-777-7795) www.reed.edu. 10AM-5PM. Enrollment: 1320. Records go back to 1930. Second phone number is 503-777-7293. Alumni records are maintained here Call 503-771-7589. Degrees granted: Bachelors; Masters. Attendance and degree information available by phone, fax, mail. Transcripts available by mail.

Rogue Community College, Student Records, 3345 Redwood Hwy, Grants Pass, OR 97527, 541-471-3501 (Fax: 541-471-3576) www.roguecom.col.or.us. 9AM - 4PM. Records go back to 1971. Degrees granted: Associate. Attendance information available by phone, fax, mail. Degree and transcript information available by fax, mail.

Southern Oregon State College, Registrar, 1250 Siskiyou Blvd, Ashland, OR 97520-5005, 541-552-6600, 541-552-6000 Ext. 6605(Verification Officer) (Fax: 541-552-6614) www.sou.edu/. 8AM-5PM. Enrollment: 4500. Records go back to 1920. Alumni records maintained here; call 541-552-6361. Degrees granted: Associate; Bachelors; Masters. Certification: Education, Accounting, Anthropology. Attendance and degree information available by phone, fax, mail. Transcripts available by mail.

Southwestern Oregon Community College, Registrar, 1988 Newmark Ave, Coos Bay, OR 97420, 541-888-7339 (Fax: 541-888-7247). 8AM-5PM. Enrollment: 4700. Records go back to 1962. Alumni records maintained here; call 541-888-7210. Degrees granted: Associate. Attendance and degree information available by phone, fax, mail. Transcripts available by fax, mail.

Treasure Valley Community College, Registrar, 650 College Blvd, Ontario, OR 97914, 541-889-6493 Ext. 235 (Fax: 541-881-2721) www.tvcc.cc.org.us. 8AM-5PM. Enrollment: 3000. Records go back to 1962. Degrees granted: Associate. Attendance and degree information available by phone, fax, mail. Transcripts available by fax, mail.

Umpqua Community College, Registrar, Roseburg, OR 97470, 541-440-4616 (Fax: 541-440-4612). 8AM-4PM. Enrollment: 6885. Records go back to 1964. Degrees granted: Associate. Attendance, degree and transcript information available by mail.

University of Oregon, Office of Registrar, Eugene, OR 97403-5257, 541-346-3243, 541-346-2937 (Fax: 541-346-5815) www.uoregon.edu. 8AM-5PM. Enrollment: 17500. Records go back to 1875. Alumni records maintained here; call 541-346-3178. Degrees granted: Bachelors; Masters; Doctorate; JD, Certificates. Special programs-Law, 541-346-3852. Attendance and degree information available by phone, fax, mail. Transcripts available by fax, mail.

University of Portland, Registrar, 5000 N Willamette Blvd, Portland, OR 97203, 503-283-7321 (Fax: 503-283-7508) 8:30AM - 4:30PM. www.uofport.edu. Enrollment: 2535. Records go back to 1901. Alumni records are maintained. Call 520-283-7328. Degrees granted: Bachelors; Masters. Attendance and degree information available by phone, fax, mail. Transcripts available by fax, mail.

Warner Pacific College, Registrar, 2219 SE 68th Ave, Portland, OR 97215, 503-775-4366 Ext. 611, 503-788-7489 (Fax: 503-788-7425) 8AM - 5PM. www.warnerpacific.edu. Enrollment: 700. Records go back to 1937. Alumni records maintained here; call 503-788-7492. Degrees granted: Associate; Bachelors; Masters. Attendance and degree information available by phone, fax, mail. Transcripts available by fax, mail.

Western Baptist College, Registrar, 5000 Deer Park Dr SE, Salem, OR 97301-9891, 503-375-7014, 503-851-8600 (Fax: 503-585-4316) www.wbc.edu. 8AM-5PM. Records go back to 1935. Alumni records are maintained here. Degrees granted: Associate; Bachelors. Special programs- Call 503-375-7014. Attendance and degree information available by phone, fax, mail. Transcripts available by fax, mail.

Western Business College, Registrar, 425 SW Washington, Portland, OR 97204, 503-222-3225 (Fax: 503-228-6926) Enrollment: 500. Records go back to 1955. Degrees granted: Associate. Attendance and degree information available by phone, fax, mail. Transcripts available by mail.

Western Conservative Baptist Seminary (See Western Seminary)

Western Culinary Institute, Registrar, 1316 S W 13th Ave, Portland, OR 97201, 503-294-9770 (Fax: 503-223-0126). Enrollment: 430. Records go back to 1984. Alumni records are maintained here. Attendance and degree information available by phone, fax, mail. Transcripts available by fax, mail.

Western Evangelical Seminary, Registrar, 12753 SW 68th Ave, Tigard, OR 97223, 503-538-8383 (Fax: 503-598-4338). 8:30AM - 4:30PM. Enrollment: 250. Records go back to 1949. Alumni records are maintained here. Degrees granted: Masters. Attendance and degree information available by phone, fax, mail. Transcripts available by fax, mail.

Western Oregon State College, Registrar's Office, Monmouth, OR 97361, 503-838-8415, 503-838-8327 (Fax: 503-838-8923) www.wosc.osshe.edu. 8AM-5PM. Enrollment: 3848. Records go back to 1890. Alumni records maintained here; call 503-838-8153. Degrees granted: Associate; Bachelors; Masters. Attendance and degree information available by phone, fax, mail. Transcripts available by fax, mail.

Western Seminary, Registrar, 5511 SE Hawthorne Blvd, Portland, OR 97215, 503-233-8561 (Fax: 503-239-4216). 8:30AM-4PM. Records go back to 1926. Degrees granted: Masters; Doctorate. Attendance and degree information available by phone, fax, mail. Transcripts available by fax, mail.

Western States Chiropractic College, Registrar, 2900 NE 132nd Ave, Portland, OR 97230, 503-251-5710 (Fax: 503-251-5723). 8AM-4:30PM. Enrollment: 460. Records go back to 1904. Alumni records maintained here; call 503-251-5713. Degrees granted: Bachelors; Doctor of Chiropractic. Attendance and degree information available by phone, fax, mail. Transcripts available by written request only.

Willamette University, Registrar, 900 State St, Salem, OR 97301, 503-370-6206 (Fax: 503-375-5395) www.willamette.edu. 8AM-Noon, 1-5PM. Enrollment: 2525. Records go back to 1900's. Alumni records maintained here; call 503-370-6340. Degrees granted: Bachelors; Masters; Doctorate. Attendance and degree information available by phone, fax, mail. Transcripts available by fax, mail.

Pennsylvania

Academy of the New Church College
(See Bryn Athyn College of the New Church)

Albright College, Registrar, PO Box 15234, Reading, PA 19612-5234, 610-921-2381, 610-921-7256 (Fax: 610-921-7530). 8AM-5PM. Enrollment: 1130. Records go back to 1930. Alumni records maintained here; call 610-921-2381. Degrees granted: Bachelors. Attendance and degree information available by phone, fax, mail. Transcripts available by fax, mail.

Allegheny College, Registrar, 520 N Main St, Meadville, PA 16335, 814-332-2357 (Fax: 814-337-0988) www.alleg.edu. 8AM-5PM. Enrollment: 1800. Records go back to 1821. Alumni Records: Alumni Assoc., 400 N Main St, Meadville, PA 16335. Degrees granted: Bachelors. Special programs- Studies Abroad. Attendance and degree information available by phone, fax, mail. Transcripts available by mail.

Allentown College of St. Francis de Sales, Registrar, 2755 Station Ave, Center Valley, PA 18034, 610-282-1100 Ext. 1223 (Fax: 610-282-2206) www.allencol.edu. 8:30AM-4:45PM. Enrollment: 2220. Records go back to 1965. Alumni records maintained here; call 610-282-1100 Ext. 1245. Degrees granted: Bachelors; Masters. Attendance and degree information available by phone, fax, mail. Transcripts available by mail.

Altoona School of Commerce, Registrar, 508 58th St, Altoona, PA 16602, 814-944-6134 (Fax: 814-944-4684). 8AM-4PM. Enrollment: 108. Records go back to 1960. Alumni records maintained here; call 814-944-6134. Degrees granted: Associate. Attendance and degree information available by phone, fax, mail. Transcripts available by fax, mail.

Alvernia College, Registrar, 400 St Bernadine St, Reading, PA 19607, 610-796-8201 (Fax: 610-777-6632) www.alvernia.edu. 8AM-4:30PM. Enrollment: 1250. Records go back to 1962. Alumni records are maintained here also. Call 610-796-8212. Degrees granted: Associate; Bachelors. Attendance and degree information available by phone, fax, mail. Transcripts available by fax, mail.

American College, Registrar, 270 Bryn Mawr Ave, Bryn Mawr, PA 19010, www.amercoll.edu 610-526-1462 (Fax: 610-526-1486) 8:30AM-5PM M-Th, 8:30AM-4PM F. Enrollment: 35000. Records go back to 1927. Degrees granted: Masters. Attendance and degree information available by phone, fax, mail. Transcripts available by fax, mail.

American Institute of Design, Registrar, 1616 Orthodox St, Philadelphia, PA 19124-3706, 215-288-8200 Ext. 23 (Fax: 215-288-0466). 8AM-5PM. Records go back to 1967. School is out of business. Degrees granted: Associate. Attendance and degree information available by phone, fax, mail. Transcripts available by fax, mail.

Antonelli Institute, Registrar, 300 Montgomery Ave, Erdenheim, PA 19038, www.antonelli.org 215-836-2222 (Fax: 215-836-2794) 8:30AM-5PM. Enrollment: 160. Records go back to 1938. Degrees granted: Associate. Attendance, degree and transcript information available by fax, mail.

Art Institute of Philadelphia, Records Office, 1622 Chestnut St, Philadelphia, PA 19103-5198, 215-567-7080 (Fax: 215-246-3339). 8AM-5PM. Enrollment: 2200. Records go back to 1976. Alumni records are maintained here. Degrees granted: Associate. Attendance and degree information available by phone, fax, mail. Transcripts available by fax, mail.

Art Institute of Pittsburgh, Registrar, 526 Penn Ave, Pittsburgh, PA 15222-3269, 412-263-6600 (Fax: 412-263-3715) www.aii.edu. 7:30AM-5PM M,W,F; 7:30AM-7PM T,Th. Enrollment: 2100. Records go back to 1966. Alumni records maintained here; call 412-263-6600 Ext. 271. Degrees granted: Associate. Attendance and degree information available by fax, mail. Transcripts available by fax, mail.

Baptist Bible College and Seminary, Registrar, PO Box 800, 538 Venard Rd, Clarks Summit, PA 18411, 717-586-2400 Ext. 217 (Fax: 717-586-1753). 8AM-5PM. Records go back to 1932. Alumni records are maintained here. Degrees granted: Associate; Bachelors; Masters; Doctorate. Attendance and degree information available by phone, fax, mail. Transcripts available by fax, mail.

Beaver College, Registrar, 450 S Easton Rd, Glenside, PA 19038-3295, 215-572-2100 (Fax: 215-572-2126) www.beaver.edu. 8:30AM-7:30PM M-Th; 8:30AM-5PM F. Enrollment: 2600. Records go back to 1949. Alumni records maintained here; call 215-572-2160. Degrees granted: Associate; Bachelors; Masters; Post Bachelor. Attendance and degree information available by phone, fax, mail. Transcripts available by mail.

Berean Institute, Registrar, 1901 W Girard Ave, Philadelphia, PA 19130-1599, 215-763-4833 (Fax: 215-236-6011). 9AM-5PM. Enrollment: 500. Records go back to 1940. Alumni records are maintained here. Degrees granted: Associate. Attendance and degree information available by phone, fax, mail. Transcripts available by fax, mail.

Berks Technical Institute, Registrar, 2205 Ridgewood Rd, Wyomissing, PA 19610, 610-372-1722 (Fax: 610-376-4684) 8AM-5PM. www.berkstech.com. Records go back to 1984. Degrees granted: Associate. Attendance and degree information available by phone, mail. Transcripts available by mail.

Biblical Theological Seminary, Registrar, 200 N Main St, Hatfield, PA 19440, 215-368-5000 (Fax: 215-368-6907) www.biblical.edu. 8:30AM-4:30PM. Enrollment: 300. Records go back to 1972. Alumni records are maintained here. Degrees granted: Masters; Doctorate. Attendance and degree information available by phone, mail. Transcripts available by mail.

Bloomsburg University of Pennsylvania Registrar, 400 E Second St, Bloomsburg, PA 17815, 717-389-4263 (Fax: 717-389-2507) www.bloomu.edu. 8AM-4:30PM. Enrollment: 7000. Records go back to 1888. Alumni records maintained here; call 717-389-4058. Degrees granted: Associate; Bachelors; Masters. Attendance and degree information available by phone, fax, mail. Transcripts available by written request only.

Bradford School, Registrar, 707 Grant St, Gulf Tower, Pittsburgh, PA 15219, 412-391-6710 (Fax: 412-471-6714) 8AM-4:30PM.

www.bradfordschools.com. Records go back to 1957. Degrees granted: Associate. Attendance and degree information available by phone, mail. Transcripts available by mail.

Bradley Academy for the Visual Arts, Registrar, 1409 Williams Rd, York, PA 17402-9012, 717-755-2300 (Fax: 717-840-1951) www.bradley-acad.com. 7:30AM-5:30PM. Enrollment: 300. Records go back to 1988. Alumni records maintained here; call 717-848-1447. Degrees granted: Associate. Attendance and degree information available by phone, fax, mail. Transcripts available by mail.

Bryn Athyn College of the New Church, Registration, PO Box 717, Bryn Athyn, PA 19009, 215-947-4200 8AM-4:30PM. www.newchurch.edu/college. Enrollment: 160. Alumni records are maintained here. Degrees granted: Associate; Bachelors. Attendance and degree information available by phone, mail. Transcripts available by mail.

Bryn Mawr College, Registrar's Office, 101 N Merion Ave, Bryn Mawr, PA 19010, www.brynmawr.edu 610-526-5141 (Fax: 610-526-5133) 9AM-5PM. Enrollment: 1850. Records go back to 1885. Alumni records maintained here; call 610-526-5227. Degrees granted: Bachelors; Masters; Doctorate. Attendance and degree information available by phone, fax, mail. Transcripts available by mail.

Bucknell University, Office of the Registrar, 102 Marts Hall, Lewisburg, PA 17837-2086, 717-524-1201, 717-524-1244 (Fax: 717-524-3922) www.bucknell.edu. 8:30AM-4:30PM. Enrollment: 3600. Records go back to 1846. Alumni records maintained here; call 717-524-3223. Degrees granted: Bachelors; Masters. Attendance and degree information available by phone, mail. Transcripts available by mail.

Bucks County Community College, Registrar, Swamp Rd, Newtown, PA 18940, 215-968-8100 (Fax: 215-968-8110) www.bucks.edu. 7:45AM-4:30PM M-Th, 7:45AM-4PM F. Records go back to 1965. Alumni records maintained here; call 215-968-8461. Degrees granted: Associate. Attendance and degree information available by phone, fax, mail. Transcripts available by fax, mail.

Business Institute of Pennsylvania (Branch), Registrar, 628 Arch St, **Meadville**, PA 16335, 814-724-0700 (Fax: 814-724-2777) www.biop.com. 8AM-4PM. Records go back to 1955. Alumni records are maintained here. Degrees granted: Associate. Attendance and degree information available by phone, mail. Transcripts available by mail.

Business Institute of Pennsylvania (Branch), Registrar, RD 1 Schoolhouse Rd, **Pulaski**, PA 16143, 724-964-0700 (Fax: 724-964-8128) www.biop.com. 8AM-4PM. Enrollment: 75. Records go back to 1977. Alumni records are maintained here. Degrees granted: Associate. Attendance and degree information available by phone, mail. Transcripts available by mail.

Business Institute of Pennsylvania, Registrar, 335 Boyd Dr, **Sharon**, PA 16146, 724-983-0700 (Fax: 724-983-8355) www.biop.com. 8:30AM-4:30PM. Enrollment: 300. Records go back to 1985. Degrees granted: Associate. Attendance, degree and transcript information available by written request only. Phone number required.

Butler County Community College, Registrar, College Dr, Oak Hills, PO Box 1203, Butler, PA 16003-1203, 724-287-8711 Ext. 331 (Fax: 724-285-6047). 8AM-6:30PM M-Th; 8AM-4PM F. Enrollment: 3000. Records go back to 1965. Degrees granted: Associate. Attendance and degree information available by phone, fax, mail. Transcripts available by mail.

Cabrini College, Registrar's Office, 610 King of Prussia Rd, Radnor, PA 19087-3699, 610-902-8545 (Fax: 610-902-8309). 8AM-7PM M-Th; 8AM-5PM F. Enrollment: 2000. Records go back to 1957. Alumni records are maintained here. Degrees granted: Bachelors; Masters. Attendance and degree information available by fax, mail. Transcripts available by mail.

California University of Pennsylvania, Academic Records, 250 University Ave, California, PA 15419, 724-938-4434 (Fax: 724-938-4340) www.cup.edu. Enrollment: 6200. Records go back to 1852. Alumni records are maintained here. Degrees granted: Associate; Bachelors; Masters. Special programs- Arts: Science. Attendance and degree information available by phone, mail. Transcripts available by fax, mail.

Cambria—Rowe Business College (Indiana Campus), Registrar, 422 S 13th St, Indiana, PA 15701, 724-463-0222 (Fax: 724-463-7246). 8AM-5PM. Enrollment: 140. Records go back to 1993. Degrees granted: Associate. Attendance, degree and transcript information available by phone, fax, mail.

Cambria—Rowe Business College, Registrar, 221 Central Ave, Johnstown, PA 15902, 814-536-5168 (Fax: 814-536-5160) www.crbc.net. 8AM-5PM. Records go back to 1897. Degrees granted: Associate. Attendance and degree information available by phone, fax, mail. Transcripts available by fax, mail.

Carlow College, Registrar's Office, 3333 Fifth Ave, Pittsburgh, PA 15213-3165, 412-578-6084 www.carlow.edu. 8AM-4PM. Records go back to 1929. Alumni records maintained here; call 412-578-6087. Degrees granted: Bachelors; Masters. Attendance and degree information available by phone, mail. Transcripts available by mail.

Carnegie Mellon University, Enrollment Services, 5000 Forbes Ave, Pittsburgh, PA 15213, 412-268-2000 Ext. 2004 (Fax: 412-268-6651) www.cmu.edu. 8:30AM-5PM. Enrollment: 2575. Records go back to 1920. Alumni records maintained here; call 412-268-2063. Degrees granted: Bachelors; Masters; Doctorate. Attendance and degree information available by phone, fax, mail. Transcripts available by fax, mail.

Cedar Crest College, Registrar, 100 College Dr, Allentown, PA 18104, 610-740-3765, 610-437-4471 www.cedarcrest.edu (Fax: 610-740-3766) 8:30AM-4:30PM. Enrollment: 1700. Records go back to 1900's. Alumni records maintained here; call 610-606-4609. Degrees granted: Bachelors. Attendance and degree information available by phone, fax, mail. Transcripts available by fax, mail.

Center For Degree Studies
(See ICS Learing Systems)

Central Pennsylvania Business School, Registrar, College Hill Rd, Summerdale, PA 17093-0309, www.centralpenn.edu. 717-728-2205, 717-728-2229 (Fax: 717-732-5254)

8AM-5PM. Enrollment: 535. Records go back to 1960. Alumni records are maintained here. Degrees granted: Associate. Attendance and degree information available by phone, fax, mail. Transcripts available by fax, mail.

Chatham College, The Hub, Woodland Rd, Pittsburgh, PA 15232, 412-365-1777 (Fax: 412-365-1643) www.chatham.edu. 9AM-5PM. Enrollment: 1000. Records go back to 1920. Alumni records maintained here; call 412-365-1255. Degrees granted: Bachelors; Masters. Attendance and degree information available by phone, fax, mail. Transcripts available by fax, mail.

Chestnut Hill College, Registrar's Office, 9601 Germantown Ave, Philadelphia, PA 19118-2693, 215-248-7005, 215-248-7117 (Fax: 215-248-7155) www.chc.edu. 8:30AM-4:30PM. Enrollment: 1100. Records go back to 1953. Alumni records maintained here; call 215-248-7144. Degrees granted: Associate; Bachelors; Masters. Attendance and degree information available by phone, fax, mail. Transcripts available by fax, mail.

Cheyney University of Pennsylvania, Registrar's Office, Cheyney and Creek Rds, Cheyney, PA 19319, 610-399-2225 (Fax: 610-399-2385). 9AM-4PM M,T,Th,F; 10AM-4PM W. Enrollment: 1357. Records go back to 1837. Alumni records maintained here; call 610-399-2000. Degrees granted: Bachelors; Masters. Attendance and degree information available by phone, fax, mail. Transcripts available by mail.

Chubb Institute-Keystone School, Registrar, 965 Baltimore Pike, Springfield, PA 19064, 610-543-1747 (Fax: 610-543-7479) ccs.chubb.com. 9AM-5PM. Enrollment: 500. Records go back to 1950. Alumni records maintained here; call 610-543-1747. Degrees granted: Associate. Attendance and degree information available by phone, fax, mail. Transcripts available by fax, mail.

Churchman Business School, Registrar, 355 Spring Garden St, Easton, PA 18042, 610-258-5345, 610-258-5346 (Fax: 610-258-8086). 7:30AM-4PM. Enrollment: 180. Records go back to 1911. Alumni records are maintained here. Degrees granted: Associate. Attendance and degree information available by phone, fax, mail. Transcripts available by fax, mail.

Clarion University of Pennsylvania, Registrar's Office, 122 Carrier Hall, Clarion, PA 16214, 814-226-2229 (Fax: 814-226-2039) www.clarion.edu. 8:30AM-4:30PM. Enrollment: 5470. Records go back to 1870. Alumni Records: Alumni Assoc., Clarion Univ. of Pennsylvania, Alumni House, Clarion, PA 16214. Degrees granted: Associate; Bachelors; Masters. Attendance and degree information available by phone, fax, mail. Transcripts available by mail.

Clarion University of Pennsylvania (Venango), Registrar, W First St, Oil City, PA 16301, 814-676-6591 www.clarion.edu. Records are located at Clarion Univ. of Pennsylvania, Registrar's Office, Clarion, PA.

College Misericordia, Registrar, 301 Lake St, Dallas, PA 18612-1098, 717-674-6756, 717-674-6308 www.miseri.edu (Fax: 717-675-2441) 8:30AM-4:30PM. Enrollment: 1800. Records go back to 1920's. Alumni records maintained here; call 717-674-6248. Degrees granted: Associate; Bachelors; Masters. Attendance and transcript information available by written request only. Degree information available by phone, fax, mail.

Community College of Allegheny County (Boyce), Registrar, 595 Beatty Rd, Monroeville, PA 15146, 724-325-6674 (Fax: 724-325-6797) www.ccac.edu. 9AM-4PM. Enrollment: 13000. Records go back to 1966. Alumni records maintained here; call 412-371-8651. Degrees granted: Associate. Attendance and degree information available by phone, fax, mail. Transcripts available by mail.

Community College of Allegheny County (Allegheny), Registrar, 808 Ridge Ave, SSC 120, Pittsburgh, PA 15212, 412-237-2525 (Fax: 412-237-4581) www.ccac.edu. 8AM-5PM. Enrollment: 20000. Records go back to 1966. Alumni Records: Alumni Assoc., 800 Alumni Affairs, Pittsburgh, PA 15212. Degrees granted: Associate. Attendance, degree and transcript information available by fax, mail.

Community College of Allegheny County (North), Registrar, 8701 Perry Hwy, Pittsburgh, PA 15237, 412-369-3700 (Fax: 412-369-3635) www.ccac.edu. 8AM-4PM. Enrollment: 38000. Records go back to 1966. Alumni records maintained here; call 412-366-7000. Degrees granted: Associate. Attendance and degree information available by phone, fax, mail. Transcripts available by fax, mail.

Community College of Allegheny County (South), Registrar, 1750 Clairton Rd Rte 885, West Mifflin, PA 15122, 412-469-6202, 412-469-6203 (Fax: 412-469-6371). 8AM-4PM. Enrollment: 4000. Records go back to 1960. Alumni records maintained here; call 412-469-6243. Degrees granted: Associate. Attendance, degree and transcript information available by mail.

Community College of Beaver County, Registrar, One Campus Dr, Monaca, PA 15061-2588, 724-775-8561 Ext. 106 (Fax: 724-728-7599) www.ccbc.cc.pa.us. 8AM-4:30PM. Enrollment: 2500. Records go back to 1969. Alumni records maintained here; call 724-775-8561. Degrees granted: Associate. Attendance, degree and transcript information available by fax, mail.

Community College of Philadelphia, Registrar, 1700 Spring Garden St, Philadelphia, PA 19130-3991, 215-751-8261 (Fax: 215-751-8001) www.ccp.cc.pa.us. 9AM-6:45PM M,T;9AM-4:45PM W,Th;9AM -3:45 PM F; Summer 9-4:45 M-W;9-3:45 Th. Enrollment: 18305. Records go back to 1964 Degrees granted: Associate. Attendance and degree information available by phone, fax, mail. Transcripts available by mail. Call 215-751-8259 to confirm attendance and degree.

Computer Tech, Registrar, 107 Sixth St, Pittsburgh, PA 15222, 412-391-4197, 800-447-8324 (Fax: 412-391-4224) 8:30AM-5PM. www.computer.tech.com/. Enrollment: 600. Records go back to 1967. Degrees granted: Associate. Attendance and degree information available by phone, fax, mail. Transcripts available by mail.

Consolidated School of Business, Registrar, 2124 Ambassador Circle, **Lancaster**, PA 17601, 717-394-6211 (Fax: 717-394-6213). 8AM-5PM. Enrollment: 180. Records go back to 1986. Degrees granted: Associate. Attendance and degree information available by phone, fax, mail. Transcripts available by fax, mail.

Consolidated School of Business, Registrar, 1605 Clugston Rd, **York**, PA 17404, 717-764-9550 (Fax: 717-764-9469) 9AM-5:30PM. Enrollment: 175. Records go back to 1976. Alumni records are maintained here. Degrees granted: Associate. Attendance and degree information available by fax, mail. Transcripts available by mail.

Curtis Institute of Music, Registrar, 1726 Locust St, Philadelphia, PA 19103, 215-893-5252 (Fax: 215-893-9065). 9AM-5PM. Enrollment: 161. Records go back to 1926. Alumni records are maintained here. Degrees granted: Bachelors; Masters. Attendance and degree information available by phone, fax, mail. Transcripts available by fax, mail.

Dean Institute of Technology, Registrar, 1501 W Liberty Ave, Pittsburgh, PA 15226, 412-531-4433 (Fax: 412-531-4435). 7:45AM-4PM M-Th, 7:45AM-3PM F. Enrollment: 230. Records go back to 1974. Degrees granted: Associate. Special programs-Construction Engineering. Attendance and degree information available by phone, fax, mail. Transcripts available by fax, mail.

Delaware County Community College, Registrar, 901 S Media Line Rd, Media, PA 19063, 610-359-5000 (Fax: 610-359-5343) www.dccc.edu. 9AM-9PM. Enrollment: 9800. Records go back to 1967. Alumni records maintained here; call 610-359-7399. Degrees granted: Associate. Attendance and degree information available by phone, fax, mail. Transcripts available by fax, mail.

Delaware Valley College of Science and Agriculture, Registrar's Office, 700 E Butler Ave, Doylestown, PA 18901, 215-345-1500 Ext. 2378, 215-489-2378 (Fax: 215-230-2962) www.devalcol.edu. 8:30AM-7PM M; 8:30AM-4:30PM T-F. Enrollment: 2200. Records go back to 1896. Alumni records maintained here; call 215-345-1500 Ext. 2424. Degrees granted: Associate; Bachelors. Attendance and degree information available by phone, mail. Transcripts available by mail.

Dickinson College, Registrar, Carlisle, PA 17013, 717-245-1315, 717-245-1680 (Fax: 717-245-1534) www.dickinson.edu. 8AM-4:30PM; Summer 8AM-Noon, 1-4PM. Enrollment: 1850. Records go back to 1783. Alumni Records: Alumni Assoc., 249 W Loother St, Carlisle, PA 17013. Degrees granted: Bachelors. Attendance and degree information available by phone, fax, mail. Transcripts available by fax, mail.

Dickinson School of Law (Pennsylvania State University), Registrar, 150 S College St, Carlisle, PA 17013, 717-240-5210, 717-240-5276 (Fax: 717-243-4366). 8AM-5PM. Records go back to 1925. Alumni records maintained here; call 717-240-5250. Degrees granted: Doctorate. Attendance and degree information available by phone, mail. Transcripts available by mail.

Douglas School of Business, Registrar, 130 Seventh St, Monessen, PA 15062, 724-684-7644, 724-684-3684 (Fax: 724-684-7463) www.mvid.com/douglas.htm. 8AM-5PM. Records go back to 1904. Degrees granted: Associate. Attendance and degree information available by phone, fax, mail. Transcripts available by mail.

Drexel University - OSIR, Registrar, 3141 Chestnut St, Philadelphia, PA 19104, www.drexel.edu 215-895-2300 (Fax: 215-895-1692) 9AM-5PM M,T,Th,F; 9:30AM-5PM W. Enrollment: 11000. Records go back to 1891. Alumni records maintained here; call 215-895-2586. Degrees granted: Bachelors; Masters; Doctorate. Attendance and degree information available by phone, fax, mail. Transcripts available by mail.

DuBois Business College, Registrar, One Beaver Dr, Du Bois, PA 15801, 814-371-6920 (Fax: 814-371-3974). 8:30AM-5PM.

www.dbcollege.com Enrollment 165. Records go back to 1960. Alumni records maintained here; call 814-371-6920. Degrees granted: Associate. Attendance and degree information available by phone, fax, mail. Transcripts available by fax, mail.

Duff's Business Institute, Registrar, 110 Ninth St, Pittsburgh, PA 15222, 412-261-4530 (Fax: 412-261-4546). 8AM-4PM. Enrollment: 450. Records go back to 1925. Degrees granted: Associate. Attendance and degree information available by phone, fax, mail. Transcripts available by mail.

Duquesne University, Registrar, 600 Forbes Ave, Pittsburgh, PA 15282, 412-396-6212 (Fax: 412-396-5622) www.duq.edu. 8:30AM-5PM. Records go back to 1846. Alumni records are maintained here also. Call 412-396-6209. Degrees granted: Bachelors; Masters; Doctorate. Attendance and degree information available by phone, fax, mail. Transcripts available by fax, mail.

East Stroudsburg University of Pennsylvania, Registrar, 200 Prospect St, East Stroudsburg, PA 18301, 717-422-3148 (Fax: 717-422-3842) www.esu.edu. 8AM-4:30PM. Enrollment: 5500. Records go back to 1890's. Alumni records maintained here; call 717-424-3533. Degrees granted: Associate; Bachelors; Masters. Special programs- Graduate School, 717-422-3536. Attendance and degree information available by phone, fax, mail. Transcripts available by mail.

Eastern Baptist Theological Seminary, Registrar, 6 Lancaster Ave, Wynnewood, PA 19096-3494, 610-645-9329, 610-645-9330 (Fax: 610-649-3834) www.ebts.edu. 8:30AM-6:30PM. Enrollment: 413. Records go back to 1925. Alumni records maintained here; call 610-896-5000. Degrees granted: Masters; Doctorate. Attendance and degree information available by phone, fax, mail. Transcripts available by mail.

Eastern College, Registrar, 10 Fairview Dr, St Davids, PA 19087-3696, 610-341-5854 (Fax: 610-341-1707) www.eastern.edu. 8AM-8PM. Enrollment: 2300. Records go back to 1952. Alumni records maintained here; call 610-341-5936. Degrees granted: Associate; Bachelors; Masters. Attendance and degree information available by phone, fax, mail. Transcripts available by fax, mail.

Edinboro University of Pennsylvania, Records & Registration, Edinboro, PA 16444, 814-732-2100 Ext. 300, 814-732-5555 Ext. 300 (Fax: 814-732-2680) www.edinboro.edu. 8AM-4:30PM. Enrollment: 7300. Records go back to 1900. Alumni records maintained here; call 814-732-2715. Degrees granted: Associate; Bachelors; Masters. Attendance and degree information available by phone, mail. Transcripts available by mail.

Electronic Institutes, Registrar, 19 Jamesway Plaza, Middletown, PA 17057-4851, 717-944-2731, 800-884-2731 (Fax: 717-944-2734) www.ei.tec.pa.us. 8AM-3PM. Enrollment: 180. Records go back to 1959. Degrees granted: Associate. Attendance and degree information available by phone, fax, mail. Transcripts available by fax, mail.

Electronic Institutes, Registrar, 4634 Browns Hill Rd, Pittsburgh, PA 15217-2919, 412-521-8686 (Fax: 412-521-9277) 8AM-3:30PM. Enrollment: 40. Records go back to 1966. Degrees granted: Associate. Attendance and degree information available by phone, fax, mail. Transcripts available by fax, mail.

Elizabethtown College, Director of Records, One Alpha Dr, Elizabethtown, PA

17022-2298, 717-361-1409, 717-361-1422 (Fax: 717-361-1485). 8:30AM-5PM. Enrollment: 1500. Records go back to 1899. Alumni records maintained here; call 717-361-1403. Degrees granted: Bachelors. Attendance and degree information available by phone, fax, mail. Transcripts available by mail.

Erie Business Center, Registrar, 246 W Ninth St, Erie, PA 16501, 814-456-7504 (Fax: 814-456-4882) www.eriebc.com. 8AM-5PM. Enrollment: 300. Records go back to 1955. Alumni records maintained here; call 814-456-7504. Attendance and degree information available by phone, fax, mail. Transcripts available by fax, mail.

Erie Business Center (Erie Business Center South), Registrar, 170 Cascade Galleria, New Castle, PA 16101, 724-658-3595, 724-658-9066 (Fax: 724-658-3083) www.eriebc.com. 8AM-5PM. Enrollment: 85. Records go back to 1970. Degrees granted: Associate. Attendance and degree information available by phone, fax, mail. Transcripts available by mail.

Evangelical School of Theology, Registrar, 121 S College St, Myerstown, PA 17067, 717-866-5775 (Fax: 717-866-4667) www.evangelical.edu. 8AM-4PM. Enrollment: 125. Records go back to 1953. Alumni records maintained here; call 717-866-5775. Degrees granted: Bachelors; Masters. Attendance and degree information available by phone, mail. Transcripts available by mail.

Franklin & Marshall College, Registrar, PO Box 3003, Lancaster, PA 17604-3003, 717-291-4168 (Fax: 717-399-4413) www.fandm.edu. 8:30AM-4:30PM. Records go back to 1853. Alumni records maintained here; call 717-291-3955. Degrees granted: Bachelors. Attendance and degree information available by phone, fax, mail. Transcripts available by fax, mail.

Gannon University, Registrar's Office, University Square, Erie, PA 16541, 814-871-7243 (Fax: 814-871-5870) www.gannon.edu. 8AM-4:30PM. Records go back to 1930. Alumni records maintained here; call 814-871-7473. Degrees granted: Associate; Bachelors; Masters. Attendance and degree information available by phone, fax, mail. Transcripts available by fax, mail.

Geneva College, Registrar, 3200 College Ave, Beaver Falls, PA 15010, 724-847-6600 (Fax: 724-847-6696) www.geneva.edu. 8AM-4:30PM. Enrollment: 1600. Records go back to 1900. Alumni records maintained here; call 724-847-6525. Degrees granted: Associate; Bachelors; Masters. Attendance and degree information available by phone, fax, mail. Transcripts available by mail.

Gettysburg College, Registrar, 300 N Washington St, Gettysburg, PA 17325-1486, 717-337-6240 (Fax: 717-337-6245) 8AM-5PM. www.gettysburg.edu. Enrollment: 2200. Records go back to 1832. Alumni records maintained here; call 717-337-6518. Degrees granted: Bachelors. Attendance and degree information available by phone, fax, mail. Transcripts available by fax, mail.

Gratz College, Registrar, Old York Rd and Melrose Ave, Melrose Park, PA 19027, 215-635-7300 (Fax: 215-635-7320) www.gratzcollege.edu. 9AM-5PM M-Th, 9AM-3PM F. Enrollment: 125. Records go back to 1940. Alumni records are maintained here. Degrees granted: Bachelors; Masters. Attendance and degree information available by phone, fax, mail. Transcripts available by fax, mail.

Grove City College, Registrar, 100 Campus Dr, Grove City, PA 16127-2104, 724-458-2172 (Fax: 724-458-2980) www.gcc.edu. 8:30AM-Noon, 1-5PM. Enrollment: 2300. Records go back to 1896. Alumni records maintained here; call 412-458-2300. Degrees granted: Bachelors; Masters. Attendance and degree information available by phone, fax, mail. Transcripts available by fax, mail.

Gwynedd—Mercy College, Registrar, Gwynedd Valley, PA 19437, 215-646-7300 (Fax: 215-641-5573) www.gmc.edu. 8AM-6PM M-Th; 8AM-4PM F. Enrollment: 1900. Records go back to 1949. Alumni records maintained here; call 215-646-7300 Ext. 178. Degrees granted: Associate; Bachelors; Masters. Attendance and degree information available by phone, fax, mail. Transcripts available by fax, mail.

Harcum College, Registrar, 750 Montgomery Ave, Bryn Mawr, PA 19010-3476, 610-526-6007 (Fax: 610-526-1640) 9AM-5PM. www.harcum.edu. Enrollment: 650. Records go back to 1921. Alumni records maintained here; call 610-526-6006. Degrees granted: Associate. Attendance and degree information available by phone, fax, mail. Transcripts available by mail.

Harrisburg Area Community College, Registrar, One HACC Dr, Harrisburg, PA 17110-2999, 717-780-2370, 717-780-2689 (Fax: 717-231-7674) www.hacc.edu. 8AM-8PM M-Th; 8AM-5PM F; 9AM-1PM S. Enrollment: 11000. Records go back to 1964. Alumni records maintained here; call 717-780-2583. Degrees granted: Associate. Attendance and degree information available by phone, fax, mail. Transcripts available by written request only.

Harrisburg Area Community College (Lancaster Campus), Registrar, 1008 New Holland Ave, Lancaster, PA 17604, 717-293-5000 (Fax: 717-293-8967). 9AM-7:30PM M,T; 9AM-5PM W,Th; 9AM-4:30PM F. Enrollment: 1281. Records go back to 1989. Alumni records maintained here; call 717-780-2400. Degrees granted: Associate. Attendance, degree and transcript available by mail.

Harrisburg Area Community College (Lebanon Campus), Registrar, 735 Cumberland St, Lebanon, PA 17042, www.hacc.edu 717-270-4222 (Fax: 717-270-6385) 8:30AM-7:30PM M,T; 8:30AM-6PM W,Th; 8:30AM-5PM; 8AM-1PM Sat. Enrollment: 750. Records go back to 1980. Alumni records maintained here; call 717-780-2400. Degrees granted: Associate. Attendance and degree information available by phone, fax, mail.

Haverford College, Registrar, 370 Lancaster Ave, Haverford, PA 19041-1392, 610-896-1022 (Fax: 610-896-4960). 9AM-5PM Academic year; 8:30AM-4:30PM Summer. Enrollment: 1120. Records go back to 1883. Alumni records maintained here; call 610-896-1001. Degrees granted: Bachelors. Attendance and degree information available by phone, fax, mail. Transcripts available by fax, mail.

Holy Family College, Registrar's Office, Grant and Frankford Aves, Philadelphia, PA 19114-2094, 215-637-4851, 215-637-7700 (Fax: 215-281-9067) www.hfc.edu. 8AM-7:30PM M-Th, 8AM-4PM F, 8:30AM-12:30PM Sat. Enrollment: 2800. Records go back to 1950. Alumni records maintained here; call 215-637-7700. Degrees granted: Associate; Bachelors; Masters. Special programs- Business: Health: Education:

Humanities: Nursing: Graduate Education/ Nursing/Psychology 215-637-7203. Degree and attendance information available by phone, fax, mail. Transcripts available by fax, mail.

Hussian School of Art, Registrar, 1118 Market St, Philadelphia, PA 19107-3679, 215-981-0900 (Fax: 215-864-9115) www.hussianart.edu. 9AM-3PM. Enrollment: 140. Records go back to 1946. Alumni records are maintained here at the same phone number. Degrees granted: Associate; AST. Special programs- Commercial Art. Attendance, degree and transcript information available by fax, mail.

ICM School of Business, Registrar, 10 Wood St, Pittsburgh, PA 15222, 412-261-2647 (Fax: 412-261-6491) 8AM-4:30PM. www.icmschool.com. Enrollment: 500. Records go back to 1960. Degrees granted: Associate. Attendance and degree information available by phone, fax, mail. Transcripts available by fax, mail.

ICS Learning Systems, Registrar, 225 Oak St, Scranton, PA 18515, 717-342-7701, 800-233-4191 (Fax: 717-961-4871) 8AM-5:15PM. www.icslearn.com Records go back to 1980. Degrees granted: Associate. Attendance and degree information available by phone, fax, mail. Transcripts available by fax, mail.

ITT Technical Institute (Branch of Youngstown, OH), Registrar, 8 Parkway Ctr, Pittsburgh, PA 15220, 412-937-9150 www.ittesi.com. 8AM-6PM. Enrollment: 400. Records go back to 1992. Degrees granted: Associate. Attendance, degree and transcript information available by mail.

Immaculata College, Registrar, Immaculata, PA 19345, 610-647-4400 Ext. 3009 (Fax: 610-251-1668) 8:30AM-4:30PM. www.immaculata.edu. Enrollment: 2000. Records go back to 1925. Alumni records maintained here; call 610-647-4400 Ext. 3135. Degrees granted: Associate; Bachelors; Masters; Doctorate. Special programs- Accelerated Degree, 800-37-ACEL. Attendance and degree information available by phone, fax, mail. Transcripts available by fax, mail.

Indiana University of Pennsylvania, Registrar's Office, 68 Sutton Hall, Indiana, PA 15705, 724-357-2217, 412-357-5731 (Fax: 724-357-4858) www.iup.edu/cwis. 8AM-4:30PM. Records go back to 1940. Alumni records maintained here; call 724-357-7942. Degrees granted: Bachelors; Masters; Doctorate. Attendance and degree information available by phone, fax, mail. Transcripts available by fax, mail.

Indiana University of Pennsylvania (Armstrong County), Registrar, Kittanning, PA 16201, 724-543-1078. Records are located at Indiana University of Pennsylvania, Registrar's Office, Indiana, PA.

Indiana University of Pennsylvania (Punxsutawney Campus), Registrar, Punxsutawney, PA 15767, 814-938-6711. Records are located at Indiana University of Pennsylvania, Registrar's Office, Indiana, PA.

Jefferson Medical College, Registrar, 1015 Walnut St G22, Philadelphia, PA 19107, 215-955-6748 (Fax: 215-923-6974) Enrollment: 915. Records go back to 1900's. Formerly **Thomas Jefferson University.** Alumni records are maintained here. Degrees granted: Masters; Doctorate. Special programs- Graduate, 215-955-8982: Allied Health Sciences, 215-955-8893. Attendance

and degree information available by phone, mail. Transcripts available by fax, mail.

Johnson Technical Institute, Registrar, 3427 N Main Ave, Scranton, PA 18508-1495, 717-342-6404, 800-2-WEWORK (Fax: 717-348-2181) www.jti.org. 8AM-5PM. Enrollment: 383. Records go back to 1920. Alumni records maintained here; call 717-342-6404 Ext. 127. Degrees granted: Associate. Attendance and degree information available by phone, fax, mail. Transcripts available by fax, mail.

Juniata College, Registrar, 1700 Moore St, Huntingdon, PA 16652, 814-643-4310 Ext. 270 (Fax: 814-641-3199). 8AM-5PM. Records go back to 1932. Alumni records maintained here; call 814-643-4310. Degrees granted: Bachelors. Attendance and degree information available by phone, fax, mail. Transcripts available by fax, mail. Phone number required.

Keystone Junior College, Registrar, PO Box 50, La Plume, PA 18440-0200, 717-945-5141 Ext. 2301, 717-945-6956 (Fax: 717-945-6961). 9AM-5PM. Records go back to 1868. Alumni records maintained here; call 717-945-5141. Degrees granted: Associate. Attendance and degree information available by phone, mail. Transcripts available by fax, mail.

King's College, Registrar, 133 N River St, Wilkes-Barre, PA 18711, 717-208-5870 (Fax: 717-208-9049) www.kings.edu. 8:30AM-4:30PM. Enrollment: 2300. Records go back to 1946. Alumni records maintained here; call 717-826-5900. Degrees granted: Bachelors; Masters. Attendance and degree information available by phone, mail. Transcripts available by mail.

Kutztown University, Registrar's Office, PO Box 730, Kutztown, PA 19530, 610-683-4485 www.kutztown.edu (Fax: 610-683-1586) 8AM-4:30PM M,W-F; 8AM-6:30PM T. Records go back to 1867. Alumni records maintained here; call 610-683-4110. Degrees granted: Bachelors; Masters. Attendance and degree information available by phone, fax, mail. Transcripts available by mail.

La Roche College, Registrar, 9000 Babcock Blvd, Pittsburgh, PA 15237, 412-536-1076, 412-367-4300 Ext. 118 (Fax: 412-367-9368) www.laroche.edu. 8:30AM-6:30PM M, 8:30AM-4:30PM T-Th. Enrollment: 1630. Records go back to 1963. Alumni records maintained here; call 412-367-9300 Ext. 140. Degrees granted: Bachelors; Masters. Special programs- Accelerated B.S., 412-367-9360 Ext. 359. Attendance and degree information available by phone, mail. Transcripts available by mail.

La Salle University, Registrar, 1900 W Olney Ave, Philadelphia, PA 19141, 215-951-1020 www.lasalle.edu. 8:30AM-4:30PM. Enrollment: 5228. Records go back to 1863. Alumni records maintained here; call 215-951-1535. Degrees granted: Associate; Bachelors; Masters. Attendance and degree information available by phone, mail. Transcripts available by mail.

Lackawanna Junior College, Registrar's Office, 501 Vine St, Scranton, PA 18509, 717-961-7840 (Fax: 717-961-7858). 9AM-6PM M,Th; 9AM-5PM T,W; 9AM-4:30PM F. Enrollment: 850. Records go back to 1900's. Alumni records maintained here; call 717-961-7829. Degrees granted: Associate. Attendance, degree and transcript information available by fax, mail.

Lafayette College, Registrar, High St, Easton, PA 18042, 610-250-5090 (Fax: 610-

250-1975) www.lafayette.edu. 8:45AM-5PM Fall-Spring hours; 8:15AM-4:30PM Summer hours. Enrollment: 2000. Records go back to 1800. Alumni records maintained here; call 610-250-5040. Degrees granted: Bachelors. Attendance and degree information available by phone, fax, mail. Transcripts available by fax, mail.

Lake Erie College of Osteopathic Medicine, Registrar, 1858 W Grandview Blvd, Erie, PA 16509, 814-866-8115, 814-866-6641 (Fax: 814-864-8699) www.lecom.edu. 8AM-4:30PM. Enrollment: 409. Records go back to 1993. Degrees granted: Doctorate. Attendance and degree information available by phone, fax, mail. Transcripts available by mail.

Lancaster Bible College, Registrar, 901 Eden Rd, Lancaster, PA 17601, 717-569-7071 (Fax: 717-560-8211). 8AM-4PM. Enrollment: 650. Records go back to 1930. Alumni records are maintained here. Degrees granted: Associate; Bachelors; Masters. Attendance and degree information available by phone, mail. Transcripts available by phone, mail.

Lancaster Theological Seminary, Registrar, 555 W James St, Lancaster, PA 17603-2897, 717-290-8718 (Fax: 717-393-4254) www.lts.org. 8:30AM-5PM. Records go back to 1900's. Alumni records maintained here; call 717-290-8729. Degrees granted: Masters; Doctorate. Attendance, degree and transcript information available by fax, mail.

Lansdale School of Business, Registrar, 201 Church Rd, North Wales, PA 19454, 215-699-5700 (Fax: 215-699-8770) . 8AM-10PM. www.lsbonline.com   Records go back to 1950. Degrees granted: Associate. Attendance and degree information available by phone, fax, mail. Transcripts available by fax, mail.

Laurel Business Institute, Registrar, 11-15 Penn St, PO Box 877, Uniontown, PA 15401, 724-439-4900. 8AM-5PM. Degrees granted: Associate. Attendance and degree information available by written request only. Transcripts available by fax.

Lebanon Valley College, Registrar, 101 N College Ave, Annville, PA 17003-0501, 717-867-6215 (Fax: 717-867-6018) www.lvc.edu. 8AM-4:30PM. Enrollment: 1875. Records go back to 1883. Alumni records maintained here; call 717-867-6320. Degrees granted: Associate; Bachelors; Masters. Special programs- MBA, 717-867-6335: MSE, 717-867-6190. Attendance and degree information available by phone, fax, mail. Transcripts available by fax, mail.

Lehigh Carbon Community College, Registrar, 4525 Education Park Dr, Schnecksville, PA 18078-2598, 610-799-1174 (Fax: 610-799-1173) www.lccc.edu. 8AM-9PM. Enrollment: 5000. Records go back to 1968. Alumni records maintained here; call 610-799-2121. Degrees granted: Associate. Attendance and degree information available by phone, mail. Transcripts available by mail.

Lehigh County Community College
   (See Lehigh Carbon Community College)

Lehigh University, Registrar, 27 Memorial Dr W, Bethlehem, PA 18015, 610-758-3200 (Fax: 610-758-3198)   www.lehigh.edu. 8:15AM-4:45PM. Enrollment: 6300. Records go back to 1860. Alumni records maintained here; call 610-758-3200. Degrees granted: Bachelors; Masters; PhD. Attendance and degree information available by phone, fax, mail. Transcripts available by fax, mail.

Lincoln Technical Institute, Registrar, 5151 Tilghman St, Allentown, PA 18104-3298, 610-398-5301 (Fax: 610-395-2706) 8AM-5PM. www.lincolntech.com. Records go back to 1967. Degrees granted: Associate. Attendance and degree information available by phone, mail. Transcripts available by mail.

Lincoln University, Registrar, Lincoln University, PA 19352-0999, 610-932-1087 www.lincoln.edu/pages/registrar (Fax: 610-932-7659) 8AM-5PM. Enrollment: 1500. Records go back to 1930. Alumni records are maintained here. Degrees granted: Bachelors; Masters. Attendance and degree information available by phone, fax, mail. Transcripts available by mail.

Lock Haven University, Student Records, Sullivan Hall 207, Lock Haven, PA 17745, 717-893-2006, 717-893-2008 (Fax: 717-893-2734)   www.lhup.edu.   8AM-4PM. Enrollment: 3300. Records go back to 1935. Alumni records maintained here; call 717-893-2021. Degrees granted: Associate; Bachelors; Masters. Certification: Teacher Education. Attendance and degree information available by phone, fax, mail. Transcripts available by written request only.

Lutheran Theological Seminary at Gettysburg, Registrar, 61 NW Confederate Ave, Gettysburg, PA 17325-1795, 717-334-6286 Ext. 201 (Fax: 717-334-3469) 8:30AM-4:30PM.   www.ela.org/dmltsg/index.html. Enrollment: 200. Records go back to 1930. Alumni records maintained here; call 717-334-3469 Ext. 210. Degrees granted: Masters; STM. Attendance and degree information available by fax, mail. Transcripts available by mail.

Lutheran Theological Seminary at Philadelphia, Registrar, 7301 Germantown Ave, Philadelphia, PA 19119, 215-248-4616 (Fax: 215-248-4577). 9AM-4:30PM; Summer hours 8:30AM-4PM. Records go back to 1864. Alumni records maintained here; call 215-248-4616. Degrees granted: Masters; Doctorate; Doctor of Ministry, Academic Master. Attendance and degree information available by phone, fax, mail. Transcripts available by mail.

Luzerne County Community College, Registrar, 1333 S Prospect St, Nanticoke, PA 18634, 717-740-0338, 717-740-0339 (Fax: 717-740-0238) www.luzerne.edu. 8AM-5PM. Enrollment: 6000. Records go back to 1968. Alumni records maintained here; call 717-740-0387. Degrees granted: Associate. Attendance information available by phone, fax, mail. Degree information available by phone, mail. Transcripts available by fax, mail.

Lycoming College, Registrar's Office, 700 College Pl, Williamsport, PA 17701, 717-321-4045, 717-321-4000 (Fax: 717-321-4337) www.lycoming.edu. 8AM - 4:30PM. Enrollment: 1450. Records go back to 1812. Alumni records maintained here; call 717-321-4134. Degrees granted: Bachelors. Attendance and degree information available by phone, fax, mail. Transcripts available by fax, mail.

Manor Junior College, Registrar, 700 Fox Chase Rd, Jenkintown, PA 19046, 215-885-2360 Ext. 51 (Fax: 215-576-6564). 9AM-5PM. Enrollment: 659. Records go back to 1948. Alumni records maintained here; call 215-885-2360 Ext. 214. Degrees granted: Associate. Attendance and degree information available by phone, fax, mail. Transcripts available by mail.

Mansfield University of Pennsylvania, Registrar's Office, 112 S Hall, Mansfield, PA

16933, 717-662-4202, 717-662-4877 (Fax: 717-662-4122)   www.mnsfld.edu.   8AM-4:15PM. Enrollment: 2800. Records go back to 1950. Alumni records maintained here; call 717-662-4292. Degrees granted: Bachelors; Masters. Attendance and degree information available by phone, fax, mail. Transcripts available by mail.

Marywood University, Registrar, 2300 Adams Ave, Scranton, PA 18509, www.marywwood.edu. 717-348-6280 Ext. 482 (Fax: 717-961-4758) 8:30AM-6PM M-Th, 8:30AM-4:30PM F. Enrollment: 3000. Records go back to 1915. Alumni records maintained here; call 717-348-6206. Degrees granted: Bachelors; Masters. Attendance and degree information available by fax, mail. Transcripts available by mail.

McCann School of Business, Registrar, Main and Pine Sts, Mahanoy City, PA 17948, 717-773-1820 (Fax: 717-773-0483) 8AM-5PM. www.mccannschool.com. Enrollment: 150. Records go back to 1897. Alumni records are maintained here. Degrees granted: Associate; Paralegal. Attendance and degree information available by phone, fax, mail. Transcripts available by fax, mail.

McCann School of Business (Branch), Registrar, 47 S Main St, Mahonoy City, PA 17948, 717-773-1820 (Fax: 717-773-0483). 8:30AM-4:30PM. Records go back to 1932. Alumni records are maintained here. Degrees granted: Associate. Attendance, degree and transcript information available by fax, mail.

Median School of Allied Health Careers, Registrar, 125 Seventh St, Pittsburgh, PA 15222-3400, 412-391-7021, 412-391-0422 (Fax: 412-232-4348) www.medianschool.com. 8AM-4:30PM. Enrollment: 320. Records go back to 1970. Degrees granted: Associate. Attendance and degree information available by phone, fax, mail. Transcripts available by written request only.

Medical College of Pennsylvania and Hahnemann University, Registrar's Office, 2900 Queen Lane, Philadelphia, PA 19129, 215-991-8206, 215-991-8207 (Fax: 215-843-5243). 8:30AM-4:30PM. Enrollment: 800. Records go back to 1940. Alumni records are maintained here. Degrees granted: Doctorate. Attendance and degree information available by phone, mail. Transcripts available by mail.

Mercyhurst College, Registrar, 501 E 38th St, Erie, PA 16546, 814-824-2250 (Fax: 814-824-2172) www.hamlet.com. 8AM-4:30PM. Enrollment: 320. Records go back to 1926. Alumni records maintained here; call 814-824-2538. Degrees granted: Bachelors; Masters. Attendance and degree information available by phone, mail. Transcripts available by fax, mail.

Messiah College, Registrar, Grantham, PA 17027, 717-691-6074 (Fax: 717-796-5373). 8AM-Noon, 1-5PM. Enrollment: 2400. Records go back to 1900. Alumni records maintained here; call 717-691-6019. Degrees granted: Bachelors. Attendance and degree information available by phone, fax. School does not provide transcripts.

Messiah College (Philadelphia Campus), Registrar, 2026 N Broad St, Philadelphia, PA 19121, 717-691-6074 (Fax: 717-796-5373) www.messiah.edu. Records are located at Messiah College, Registrar, Grantham, PA.

Millersville University, Registrar, PO Box 1002, Millersville, PA 17551-1002, 717-872-3035 (Fax: 717-872-3016) www.millersv.edu. 8AM-5PM. Alumni records maintained here; call   717-872-3352.   Degrees   granted:

Associate; Bachelors; Masters. Attendance and degree information available by phone, fax, mail. Transcripts available by fax, mail.

Montgomery County Community College, Office of Admissions, PO Box 400, Blue Bell, PA 19422-0796, 215-641-6551, 215-619-7333 (Fax: 215-641-6681) www.mc3.edu. 8:30AM-7PM M-Th; 8:30AM-5PM F. Enrollment: 8500. Records go back to 1966. Alumni records maintained here; call 215-641-6359. Degrees granted: Associate. Special programs- Nursing, 215-641-6671: Medical Lab Technician, 215-641-6671: Dental Hygiene, 215-641-6671. Attendance and degree information available by fax, mail. Transcripts available by mail.

Moore College of Art and Design, Registrar, The Parkway at 20th St, Philadelphia, PA 19103, 215-568-4515 (Fax: 215-568-8017). 9AM-5PM. Records go back to 1844. Alumni records are maintained here. Degrees granted: Bachelors. Attendance and degree information available by phone, fax, mail. Transcripts available by fax, mail.

Moravian College, Registrar, 1200 Main St, Bethlehem, PA 18018, 610-861-1350, 610-861-1351 (Fax: 610-861-3919) 8AM-4:30PM. www.moravian.edu. Enrollment: 1800. Records go back to 1742. Alumni records maintained here; call 610-861-1366. Degrees granted: Bachelors; Masters. Attendance and degree information available by phone, fax, mail. Search requires name plus social security number. Transcripts available by mail.

Mount Aloysius College, Registration & Records, 7373 Admiral Peary Hwy, Cresson, PA 16630, 814-886-6343, 814-886-6356 (Fax: 814-886-2978) www.mtaloy.edu. 8:30AM-4:30PM. Enrollment: 1160. Records go back to 1939. Alumni records maintained here; call 814-886-6408. Degrees granted: Associate; Bachelors. Attendance and degree information available by phone, fax, mail. Transcripts available by fax, mail.

Muhlenberg College, Registrar, 2400 Chew St, Allentown, PA 18104, 610-821-3190 (Fax: 610-821-3234) . 8AM-5PM. www.muhlberg.edu. Enrollment: 1785. Records go back to 1900's. Alumni records maintained here; call 610-821-3305. Degrees granted: Bachelors. Attendance and degree information available by phone, fax, mail. Transcripts available by fax, mail.

National Education Center - Thompson Campus
(See Thompson Institute)

Neumann College, Registrar, One Neumann Dr, Aston, PA 19014, 610-558-5523, 610-558-5524 (Fax: 610-459-1370) www.neuman.edu. 8:30AM-5:30PM M-Th; 9AM-5PM F. Enrollment: 1300. Records go back to 1965. Alumni records maintained here; call 610-558-5544. Degrees granted: Associate; Bachelors; Masters. Attendance and degree information available by phone, mail. Transcripts available by mail.

Newport Business Institute, Registrar, 945 Greensburg Rd, Lower Burrell, PA 15068, 724-339-7542, 800-752-7695 (Fax: 724-339-2950) www.akvalley.com/newport. 8AM-5PM. Enrollment: 200. Records go back to 1946. Formerly **New Kensington Commercial School**. Alumni records are maintained here Degrees granted: Associate. Attendance and degree information available by phone, fax, mail. Transcripts available by fax, mail.

Newport Business Institute, Registrar, 941 W Third St, Williamsport, PA 17701, 717-326-2869 (Fax: 717-326-2136). 8AM-5PM. Enrollment: 100. Records go back to 1955. Degrees granted: Associate. Attendance and degree information available by phone, mail. Transcripts available by mail.

Northampton County Area Community College, Records Office, 3835 Green Pond Rd, Bethlehem, PA 18020, 610-861-5494 (Fax: 610-861-5551) www.nrhm.cc.pa.us. 8AM-7PM M-Th, 8AM-4PM F. Enrollment: 6000. Records go back to 1967. Alumni records maintained here; call 610-861-5453. Degrees granted: Associate. Attendance and degree information available by phone, fax, mail. Transcripts available by fax, mail. Phone number required.

Northeast Institute of Education, Registrar, 314 Adams Ave, Scranton, PA 18501-0470, 717-346-6666. 8AM-5PM. Records go back to 1936. Alumni records are maintained here. Degrees granted: Bachelors; Masters. Attendance and degree information available by phone, mail. Transcripts available by mail.

Northumberland County Area Business School, Registrar, 600 Park Ave, Marion Heights, PA 17832, 717-373-1680 (Fax: 717-373-1689) www.ncal.org. 8AM-5PM. Enrollment: 40. Records go back to 1994. Degrees granted: Associate. Special programs- Business. Attendance and degree information available by phone, mail. Transcripts available by mail.

Pace Institute, Registrar, 606 Court St, Reading, PA 19601, 610-375-1212 (Fax: 610-375-1924). 8AM-5PM. Records go back to 1977. Degrees granted: Associate. Attendance and degree information available by phone, fax, mail. Transcripts available by fax, mail.

Penn Technical Institute, Registrar, 110 Ninth St, Pittsburgh, PA 15222-3618, 412-232-3940 Ext. 247 (1998 transcripts), 412-232-3547 (transcripts prior to 1998) www.pti-tec.com. 8AM-5PM. Enrollment: 1700. Records go back to 1949. Degrees granted: Associate. Attendance information available by phone, mail. Degree information available by phone, fax, mail. Transcripts available by fax, mail.

Pennco Tech, Registrar, 3815 Otter St, Bristol, PA 19007-3696, 215-824-3200 Ext. 42 (Fax: 215-785-1945) 8AM-4:30PM. www.penncotech.com Enrollment: 350. Records go back to 1970. Degrees granted: Associate. Attendance, degree and transcript information available by fax, mail.

Pennsylvania Academy of the Fine Arts
Registrar, 118 N Broad St, Philadelphia, PA 19102, 215-972-7600 Ext. 3501 (Fax: 215-569-0153) www.pond.com/~pafa. 9AM-5PM. Enrollment: 280. Records go back to 1806. Alumni records are maintained here. Degrees granted: Masters. Attendance and degree information available by phone, fax, mail. Transcripts available by mail.

Pennsylvania Business Institute
(Closed fall 1995)

Pennsylvania College of Optometry, Registrar, 1200 W Godfrey Ave, Philadelphia, PA 19141, 215-276-6260. 8:30AM-4:30PM. Enrollment: 650. Records go back to 1919. Alumni records maintained here; call 215-276-6230. Degrees granted: Bachelors; Masters; Doctorate. Attendance, degree and transcript information available by mail.

Pennsylvania College of Podiatric Medicine, Registrar, 8th and Race Sts, Philadelphia, PA 19107, 215-625-5444 (Fax: 215-627-2815). 8:30AM-5PM. Enrollment: 400. Records go back to 1967. Alumni records maintained here; call 215-625-5411. Degrees granted: Doctorate. Attendance and degree information available by phone, fax, mail. Transcripts available by fax, mail.

Pennsylvania College of Technology, Registrar, 1 College Ave, Williamsport, PA 17701, 717-327-4772, 717-326-3761 (Fax: 717-321-5536) www.pct.edu. 8AM-4:30PM Summer hours 7:30AM-5:30PM M-W, 7:30AM-5PM Th. Enrollment: 4750. Records go back to 1963. Alumni records are maintained here. Degrees granted: Associate; Bachelors. Special programs- Aviation Technology, 717-327-4775. Attendance and degree information available by phone, fax, mail. Transcripts available by fax, mail.

Pennsylvania College of Technology, Registrar, One College Ave, Williamsport, PA 17701, 717-326-3761 (Fax: 717-321-5536) www.pct.edu. Enrollment: 4700. Records go back to 1965. Alumni records are maintained here. Degrees granted: Bachelors. Attendance and degree information available by phone, fax, mail. Transcripts available by fax, mail.

Pennsylvania Institute of Culinary Arts, Registrar, 717 Liberty Ave, Pittsburgh, PA 15222-3500, 412-566-2433 (Fax: 412-566-2434) www.paculinary.edu. 8AM-5PM. Records go back to 1990. Degrees granted: Associate. Attendance and degree information available by phone, mail. Transcripts available by mail.

Pennsylvania Institute of Technology, Registrar, 800 Manchester Ave, Media, PA 19063, 610-892-1525 (Fax: 610-892-1522). 8AM-8PM. Enrollment: 500. Records go back to 1950. Alumni records maintained here; call 610-892-1554. Degrees granted: Associate. Special programs- Continuing Education, 610-892-1562. Attendance and degree information available by phone, mail. Transcripts available by fax, mail.

Pennsylvania State University (Ogontz Campus), Registrar, 1600 Woodland Rd, Abington, PA 19001-3990, 215-881-7332 (Fax: 215-881-7317) www.psu.edu/registrar/. 8AM-5PM. Records go back to 1983. Alumni Records: Pennsylvania State University, 105 Old Main, University Park, PA 16802. Degrees granted: Associate; Bachelors. Attendance and degree information available by phone, fax, mail. Transcript records are located at the main campus, 112 Shields Bldg, University Park, PA 16802 (814-863-8500).

Pennsylvania State University (Altoona Campus), Registrar, Ivyside Park, Altoona, PA 16001-3760, 814-949-5000 (Fax: 814-949-5702) www.psu.edu/registrar/. Enrollment: 3500. Records go back to 1984. Alumni records maintained here; call 814-949-5105. Degrees granted: Associate; Bachelors; Masters; Doctorate. Attendance and degree information available by phone, fax, mail. Transcript records are located at the main campus, 112 Shields Bldg, University Park, PA 16802 (814-863-8500).

Pennsylvania State University (Du Bois Campus), Registrar, College Pl, Du Bois, PA 15801, 814-375-4700, 814-375-4722. Alumni records are maintained here. Degrees granted: Associate; Bachelors. Attendance and degree information available by phone, fax, mail. Transcript records are located at the main campus, 112 Shields Bldg, University Park, PA 16802.

Pennsylvania State University (Worthington-Scranton), Registrar, 120 Ridge View Dr, Dunmore, PA 18512, 717-963-2500 (Fax: 814-865-6359) www.psu.edu/registrar/. Alumni records are maintained here. Degrees granted: Associate; Bachelors; Masters; Doctorate. Attendance and degree information available by phone, fax, mail. Transcript records are located at the main campus, 112 Shields Bldg, University Park, PA 16802 (814-863-8500).

Pennsylvania State University (Erie-Behrend College), Registrar, 5091 Station Rd, Erie, PA 16563, www.psu.edu/registrar/ 814-898-6000, 814-898-6104 (Fax: 814-898-6382) Enrollment: 3200. Alumni records maintained here; call 814-898-6159. Degrees granted: Associate; Bachelors; Masters. Attendance and degree information available by phone, fax, mail. Transcript records are located at the main campus, 112 Shields Bldg, University Park, PA 16802 (814-863-8500).

Pennsylvania State University (Lehigh Valley), Registrar, 8380 Mohr Lane, Fogelsville, PA 18051, www.an.psu.edu 610-285-5000, 610-285-5060 (Fax: 610-285-5220) Enrollment: 600. Records go back to 1980. Alumni Records: Alumni Assoc., 105 Old Main, University Park, PA 16802. Degrees granted: Associate. Attendance and degree information available by phone, fax, mail. Transcript records are located at the main campus, 112 Shields Bldg, University Park, PA 16802.

Pennsylvania State University (Hazleton Campus), Registrar, Hazleton, PA 18201, www.psu.edu/registrar/. 717-450-3000 (Fax: 814-865-6359) Records go back to 1986. Alumni records are maintained here. Degrees granted: Associate; Bachelors; Masters; Doctorate. Attendance and degree information available by phone, fax, mail. Transcript records are located at the main campus, 112 Shields Bldg, University Park, PA 16802 (814-863-8500).

Pennsylvania State University (Hershey Medical Center), Registrar, 500 University Dr, Hershey, PA 17033, 717-531-4103 (Fax: 717-531-6225). Records go back to 1967. Alumni records maintained here; call 717-531-7063. Degrees granted: Associate; Bachelors; Masters; Doctorate; MD. Special programs- Medicine, 717-531-4103. Attendance and degree information available by phone, fax, mail. Transcript records are located at the main campus, 112 Shields Bldg, University Park, PA 16802.

Pennsylvania State University (Wilkes-Barre Campus), Registrar, PO Box PSU, Lehman, PA 18627, 717-675-2171, 717-675-9233 (Fax: 717-675-1339) www.psu.edu. Enrollment: 800. Records go back to 1900. Alumni records are maintained here. Degrees granted: Associate; Bachelors; Masters; Doctorate. Attendance and degree information available by phone, fax, mail. Transcript records are located at the main campus, 112 Shields Bldg, University Park, PA 16802.

Pennsylvania State University (Great Valley Graduate Center), Registrar, 30 E Swedesford Rd, Malvern, PA 19355, www.gv.psu.edu 610-648-3275 (Fax: 610-889-1334) Enrollment: 1600. Alumni records maintained here; call 610-648-3208. Degrees granted: Associate; Bachelors; Masters; Doctorate. Attendance and degree information available by phone, mail. Transcript records are located at the main campus, 112 Shields Bldg, University Park, PA 16802.

Pennsylvania State University (Delaware Campus), Registrar, 25 Yearsley Mill Rd, Media, PA 19063, 610-892-1350 (Fax: 814-865-6359). Degrees granted: Associate; Bachelors; Masters; Doctorate. Attendance and degree information available by phone, fax, mail. Transcript records are located at the main campus, 112 Shields Bldg, University Park, PA 16802 (814-863-8500).

Pennsylvania State University (Harrisburg-Capital College), Registrar, Rte 230, Middletown, PA 17057, 717-948-6020, 717-948-6022 (Fax: 717-948-6325) www.hbg.psu.edu. 8AM-6PM M,Th; 8AM-5PM T,W,F. Enrollment: 3500. Records go back to 1969. Degrees granted: Associate; Bachelors; Masters; Doctorate. Attendance and degree information available by phone, fax, mail. Transcript records are located at the main campus, 112 Shields Bldg, University Park, PA 16802.

Pennsylvania State University (Beaver), Campus Registrar, 100 University Dr, Monaca, PA 15061-2799, 724-773-3500, 724-773-3786 (Fax: 724-773-3557) www.psu.edu. Enrollment: 900. Records go back to 1965. Alumni records maintained here; call 724-773-3815. Degrees granted: Associate. Attendance and degree information available by phone, fax, mail. Transcript records are located at the main campus, 112 Shields Bldg, University Park, PA 16802.

Pennsylvania State University (Mont Alto Campus), Registrar, Campus Dr, Mont Alto, PA 17237, 717-749-6000 (Fax: 814-865-6359). Degrees granted: Associate; Bachelors; Masters; Doctorate. Attendance and degree information available by phone, fax, mail. Transcript records are located at the main campus, 112 Shields Bldg, University Park, PA 16802 (814-863-8500).

Pennsylvania State University (New Kensington Campus), Registrar, Rt 780, 3550 Seventh Street Rd, New Kensington, PA 15068, 724-339-5466 (Fax: 724-339-5434) 8AM-5PM. www.psu.edu/registrar/. Records go back to 1800's. Alumni records are maintained here. Degrees granted: Bachelors; Masters; Doctorate. Attendance and degree information available by phone, fax, mail. Transcript records are located at the main campus, 112 Shields Bldg, University Park, PA 16802 (814-863-8500).

Pennsylvania State University (Berks), Registrar, Tulpehocken Rd, PO Box 7009, Reading, PA 19610-7009, 610-396-6085 (Fax: 610-865-6359) www.psu.edu/registrar/. Records go back to 1988. Alumni records maintained here; call 610-320-4890. Degrees granted: Bachelors. Attendance and degree information available by phone, fax, mail. Transcript records are located at the main campus, 112 Shields Bldg, University Park, PA 16802 (814-863-8500).

Pennsylvania State University (Schuylkill Campus), Registrar, 200 University Dr, Schuylkill Haven, PA 17972, 717-385-6000, 717-385-6125 (Fax: 717-385-3672). Enrollment: 1100. Records go back to 1983. Alumni records are maintained here. Degrees granted: Associate. Attendance and degree information available by phone, fax, mail. Transcript records are located at the main campus, 112 Shields Bldg, University Park, PA 16802.

Pennsylvania State University (Shenango Campus), Registrar, 147 Shenango Ave, Sharon, PA 16146, www.psu.edu/registrar/. 724-983-2861 (Fax: 724-865-6359) Degrees granted: Associate; Bachelors; Masters; Doctorate. Attendance

and degree information available by phone, fax, mail. Transcript records are located at the main campus, 112 Shields Bldg, University Park, PA 16802 (814-863-8500).

Pennsylvania State University (Fayette), Registrar, PO Box 519, Rte 119 N, Uniontown, PA 15401, 724-430-4100 (Fax: 724-430-4184) www.psu.edu/registrar/. Records go back to 1982. Alumni records are maintained here. Degrees granted: Associate; Bachelors; Masters; Doctorate. Attendance and degree information available by phone, fax, mail. Transcript records are located at the main campus, 112 Shields Bldg, University Park, PA 16802 (814-863-8500).

Pennsylvania State University, Registrar, 112 Shields Bldg, **University Park,** PA 16802, 814-865-6357 (Fax: 814-865-6359). 8AM-5PM. Records go back to 1800's. Alumni Records: Alumni Assoc., The Pennsylvania State University, 101 Old Main, University Park, PA 16802. Degrees granted: Associate; Bachelors; Masters; Doctorate. Attendance and degree information available by phone, fax, mail. Transcripts available by fax, mail.

Pennsylvania State University, Registrar's Office, 112 Shields Bldg, University Park, PA 16802-1271, 814-863-8500 www.psu.edu/registrar/ (Fax: 814-865-6359) Enrollment: 70000. Records go back to 1865. Formerly **Pennsylvania State University (McKeesport Campus)** Alumni Records: 105 Old Main, University Park, PA 16802-1271. Degrees granted: Associate; Bachelors; Masters; Doctorate. Attendance and degree information available by phone, fax, mail. Transcript records are located at the main campus, 112 Shields Bldg, University Park, PA 16802.

Pennsylvania State University (York Campus), Registrar, 1031 Edgecomb Ave, York, PA 17403, 717-771-4057 (Fax: 717-771-4062) www.psu.edu/registrar/. 8AM-5PM. Enrollment: 2100. Records go back to 1984. Alumni records maintained here; call 717-771-4127. Degrees granted: Associate. Attendance and degree information available by phone, fax, mail. Transcript records are located at the main campus, 112 Shields Bldg, University Park, PA 16802 (814-863-8500).

Philadelphia College of Art
(See The University of the Arts)

Philadelphia College of Bible, Records Office, 200 Manor Ave, Langhorne, PA 19047-2990, 215-752-5800, 215-702-4293 (Fax: 215-702-4341) www.PCB.EDU. 8AM-7:30PM. Records go back to 1913. Alumni records are maintained here. Degrees granted: Associate; Bachelors; Masters. Attendance information available by phone, fax, mail. Degree and transcript information available by fax, mail.

Philadelphia College of Osteopathic Medicine, Registrar, 4170 City Ave, Philadelphia, PA 19131, 215-871-6700 (Fax: 215-871-6719) www.pcom.edu. Enrollment: 975. Alumni records maintained here; call 215-871-6120. Degrees granted: Masters; Doctorate; First Professional Degree. Attendance and degree information available by phone, fax, mail. Transcripts available by fax, mail.

Philadelphia College of Pharmacy and Science, Registrar, 600 S 43rd St, Philadelphia, PA 19104-4495, 215-596-8813 (Fax: 215-895-1177). Records go back to 1821. Alumni records maintained here; call 215-596-8856. Degrees granted: Bachelors; Masters; Doctorate. Attendance and degree

Pennsylvania

Philadelphia College of Textiles and Science, Registrar, Schoolhouse Lane & Henry Ave, Philadelphia, PA 19144, 215-951-2990 (Fax: 215-951-2112). 9AM-5PM. Records go back to 1884. Alumni records are maintained here. Degrees granted: Bachelors; Masters. Attendance, degree and transcript information available by mail.

Pierce College, Registrar, 1420 Pine St, Philadelphia, PA 19102, 215-545-6400, 215-893-4330 (Fax: 215-546-5996). 8:30AM-5PM. Enrollment: 2500. Records go back to 1940's. Alumni records maintained here; call 215-545-6400. Degrees granted: Associate; Bachelors. Certification: Proficiency. Attendance and degree information available by phone, fax, mail. Transcripts available by written request only.

Pittsburgh Institute of Aeronautics, Registrar, PO Box 10897, Pittsburgh, PA 15236-0897, 412-462-9011 (Fax: 412-466-0513). 8AM-4:30PM. Records go back to 1930's. Degrees granted: Associate. Attendance and degree information available by phone, fax, mail. Transcripts available by fax, mail.

Pittsburgh Institute of Mortuary Science, Registrar, 5808 Baum Blvd, Pittsburgh, PA 15206, 412-362-8500 (Fax: 412-362-1684). 8AM-4PM. Records go back to 1939. Alumni records are maintained here. Degrees granted: Associate; Bachelors. Attendance information available by phone, mail. Degree information available by phone, fax, mail. Transcripts available by mail.

Pittsburgh Technical Institute, Registrar, 635 Smithfield St, Pittsburgh, PA 15222-2560, 412-471-1011 (Fax: 412-471-9014). 7AM-6PM. Enrollment: 1034. Records go back to 1970's. Degrees granted: Associate. Attendance and degree information available by fax, mail. Transcripts available by phone, fax, mail.

Pittsburgh Theological Seminary, Registrar, 616 N Highland Ave, Pittsburgh, PA 15206, 412-362-5610 (Fax: 412-363-3260) 8:30AM-4:30PM. Enrollment: 302. Records go back to 1910. Alumni records are maintained here. Degrees granted: Masters; Doctorate. Attendance and degree information available by phone, fax, mail. Transcripts available by mail.

Point Park College, Registrar, 201 Wood St, Pittsburgh, PA 15222, 412-392-3861 (Fax: 412-391-1980) 8:30AM-4:30PM. Enrollment: 2300. www.lm.com/~markv20/ppc.html. Records go back to 1960. Alumni records maintained here; call 412-392-3816. Degrees granted: Associate; Bachelors; Masters. Attendance and degree information available by phone, fax, mail. Transcripts available by mail.

Reading Area Community College, Registrar, PO Box 1706, 10 S 2nd St, Reading, PA 19603-1706, 610-372-4721 Ext. 224, 610-607-6243 (Fax: 610-607-6290) 8AM-5PM. www.readingpa.com/racc. Records go back to 1971. Alumni records maintained here; call 610-372-4721 Ext. 5018. Degrees granted: Associate. Attendance and degree information available by phone, fax, mail. Transcripts available by fax, mail.

Reconstructionist Rabbinical College, Registrar, 1299 Church Rd, Wyncote, PA 19095, 215-576-0800 (Fax: 215-576-6143) 9AM-5PM. www.RRC.EDU. Enrollment: 75. Records go back to 1970. Alumni records

maintained here; call 215-576-5210. Degrees granted: Masters; Doctorate; Rabbi. Attendance and degree information available by phone, fax, mail. Transcripts available by mail.

Robert Morris College (Pittsburgh College), Registrar, Narrows Run Rd, Coraopolis, PA 15108, 412-262-8256 (Fax: 412-262-8696). 8AM-5PM. Enrollment: 5000. Records go back to 1962. Alumni records are maintained here. Degrees granted: Associate; Bachelors; Masters. Attendance and degree information available by phone, mail. Transcripts available by mail.

Rosemont College, Registrar, 1400 Montgomery Ave, Rosemont, PA 19010-1699, 610-527-0200 Ext. 2305, 610-527-0220 Ext. 2307 (Fax: 610-526-2984). 9AM-5PM. Enrollment: 950. Records go back to 1922. Alumni records are maintained here. Degrees granted: Bachelors; Masters. Attendance and degree information available by phone, fax, mail. Transcripts available by fax, mail.

Saint Francis College, Office of the Registrar, PO Box 600, Loretto, PA 15940, 814-472-3009 (Fax: 814-472-3354). 9AM-Noon, 12:30-4:30PM. Enrollment: 1700. Records go back to 1895. Alumni records maintained here; call 814-472-3015. Degrees granted: Associate; Bachelors; Masters. Attendance and degree information available by phone, fax, mail. Transcripts available by mail.

Sawyer School, Registrar, 717 Liberty Ave, Pittsburgh, PA 15222, 412-261-5700 (Fax: 412-281-7269) www.sawyer.edu. 8AM-5PM. Enrollment: 400. Records go back to 1970. Alumni records are maintained here. Degrees granted: Associate. Special programs- Health Information Technology, 412-261-5700. Attendance and degree information available by fax, mail. Transcripts available by mail.

Schuylkill Business Institute, Registrar, 2400 W End Ave, Pottsville, PA 17901, 717-622-4835 (Fax: 717-622-6563). 8AM-5PM. Records go back to 1977. Alumni records are maintained here. Degrees granted: Associate. Attendance and degree information available by phone, mail. Transcripts available by mail.

Seton Hill College, Registrar, Greensburg, PA 15601, 724-838-4218, 724-838-4255 (Fax: 724-830-1294) www.setonhill.edu. 8AM-6PM M-Th; 8AM-4PM F. Enrollment: 1100. Records go back to 1920. Alumni records maintained here; call 724-838-4226. Degrees granted: Bachelors; Masters. Special programs- Physician Assistant, 724-838-4255; Art, 724-838-4255: Education, 724-838-4255. Attendance and degree information available by phone, fax, mail. Transcripts available by mail.

Shenango Valley School of Business (See Business Institute of Pennsylvania)

Shippensburg University of Pennsylvania, Registrar, Shippensburg, PA 17257, 717-532-1381 (Fax: 717-532-1388) www.ship.edu. 8AM-4:30PM. Records go back to 1930's. Alumni records maintained here; call 717-532-1218. Degrees granted: Bachelors; Masters. Attendance and degree information available by phone, mail. Transcripts available by fax, mail.

Slippery Rock University of Pennsylvania, Academic Records, Slippery Rock, PA 16057, 724-738-2010 (Fax: 724-738-2936) www.sru.edu. 8AM-4:30PM. Enrollment: 7000. Records go back to 1890's. Alumni records maintained here; call 724-738-2018. Degrees granted: Bachelors;

Masters. Special programs- Doctorate in Physical Therapy. Attendance and degree information available by phone, fax, mail. Transcripts available by fax, mail.

South Hills Business School, Registrar, 480 Waupelani Dr, State College, PA 16801-4516, 814-234-7755 (Fax: 814-234-0926) 8AM-5PM. www.southhills.edu. Enrollment: 350. Records go back to 1966. Degrees granted: Associate. Attendance and degree information available by mail. Transcripts available by fax, mail.

St. Charles Borromeo Seminary, Registrar, 100 E Wynnewood Rd, Wynnewood, PA 19096, 610-667-3394 Ext. 235 (Fax: 610-667-1422) 8:30AM-4:30PM. Enrollment: 500. Records go back to 1920. Alumni records are maintained here. Degrees granted: Bachelors; Masters. Attendance and degree information available by phone, fax, mail. Transcripts available by mail.

St. Joseph's University, Registrar, 5600 City Line Ave, Philadelphia, PA 19131, 610-660-1010 (Fax: 610-660-1019) www.sju.edu. 8:30AM-7PM. Enrollment: 7000. Records go back to 1851. Alumni records are maintained here. Degrees granted: Bachelors; Masters. Attendance and degree information available by phone, fax, mail. Transcripts available by mail.

St. Vincent College and Seminary, Registrar, Frazier Purchase Rd, Latrobe, PA 15650, 724-537-4559 (Fax: 724-537-4554). 9AM-4PM. Records go back to 1871. Alumni records are maintained here. Degrees granted: Bachelors; Masters. Attendance and degree information available by phone, fax, mail. Transcripts available by mail.

Susquehanna University, Office of the Registrar, Selinsgrove, PA 17870, 717-372-4109, 717-374-0101 (Fax: 717-372-2753) 8:15AM-Noon, 1-4:30PM. www.susqu.edu. Enrollment: 1550. Records go back to 1950. Alumni records maintained here; call 717-372-4115. Degrees granted: Bachelors. Attendance and degree information available by phone, fax, mail. Transcripts available by fax, mail.

Swarthmore College, Registrar, 500 College Ave, Swarthmore, PA 19081, 610-328-8000 www.swarthmore.edu. 8:30AM-Noon, 1-4:30PM. Enrollment: 1350. Records go back to 1864. Alumni records are maintained here. Degrees granted: Bachelors; Masters. Attendance and degree information available by phone, mail. Transcripts available by mail.

Talmudical Yeshiva of Philadelphia, Registrar, 6063 Drexel Rd, Philadelphia, PA 19131, 215-477-1000, 215-473-1212 (Fax: 215-477-5065). 8AM-5PM. Enrollment: 115. Records go back to 1975. Alumni records are maintained here. Attendance and degree information available by phone, mail. Transcripts available by mail.

Temple University, Registrar, Broad and Montgomery Sts, Conwell Hall 2nd Flr, Philadelphia, PA 19122, 215-204-7517 www.temple.edu. 8:30AM - 4:30PM. Enrollment: 30040. Records go back to 1890's. Alumni records maintained here; call 215-204-7521. Degrees granted: Bachelors; Masters; Doctorate. Attendance and degree information available by phone, mail. Transcripts available by mail. Graduation date required.

Thaddeus Stevens State School of Technology, Registrar, 750 E King St, Lancaster, PA 17602, 717-299-7796. 8AM-4PM. Records go back to 1913. Alumni

421

records maintained here; call 717-295-9666. Degrees granted: Associate. Attendance and degree information available by phone, fax, mail. Transcripts available by fax, mail.

Thiel College, Registrar, 75 College Ave, Greenville, PA 16125, 724-589-2110, 412-589-2007 (Fax: 724-589-2850). 8AM-4:30PM. Enrollment: 1000. Records go back to 1866. Alumni records maintained here; call 724-589-2140. Degrees granted: Associate; Bachelors. Special programs- Respiratory Care Certificate Program, 412-589-2186. Attendance and degree information available by phone, fax, mail. Transcripts available by fax, mail.

Thomas Jefferson University, Registrar, 11th & Walnut St, Philadelphia, PA 19107, 215-955-6000 (Fax: 215-503-7241) www.tju.edu. 8AM-5PM. Enrollment: 2599. Records go back to 1976. Alumni records are maintained here. Degrees granted: Associate; Bachelors; Masters; Doctorate. Attendance and degree information available by phone, mail. Transcripts available by mail.

Thompson Institute, Registrar, 5650 Derry St, Harrisburg, PA 17111-4112, 717-564-4112 (Fax: 717-564-3779) 8:30AM-4:30PM. www.thompsoninstitute.org. Enrollment: 400. Records go back to 1918. Alumni records are maintained here. Degrees granted: Associate. Attendance, degree and transcript information available by mail.

Thompson Institute (Branch), Registrar, University City Science Ctr, 3440 Market St, Philadelphia, PA 19104, 215-387-1530 (Fax: 215-387-0106) www.libertynet.com. Enrollment: 500. Records go back to 1987. Formerly **National Education Center Thompson Campus**. Degrees granted: Associate. Special programs- Medical Assisting: Medical Office Management. Attendance and degree information available by phone, fax, mail. Transcripts available by fax, mail.

Tri-State Business Institute, Registrar, 5757 W 26th St, Erie, PA 16506, 814-838-7673. 8AM-5PM. Enrollment: 325. Records go back to 1984. Alumni records are maintained here. Degrees granted: Associate. Attendance and degree information available by phone, mail. Transcripts available by mail.

Triangle Tech, Registrar, PO Box 551, **Du Bois**, PA 15801-0551, 814-371-2090 (Fax: 814-371-9227) www.triangle-tech.com. 9AM-8PM. Records go back to 1944. Alumni records are maintained here. Degrees granted: Associate. Attendance and degree information available by phone, fax, mail. Transcripts available by fax, mail. Phone number required.

Triangle Tech, Registrar, 2000 Liberty St, **Erie**, PA 16502-9987, 814-453-6016 (Fax: 814-454-2818) www.triangle-tech.com. 8AM-5PM. Enrollment: 200. Records go back to 1944. Alumni Records: 1940 Perrysville Ave, Pittsburgh, PA 15214-3897. Degrees granted: Associate. Attendance and degree information available by phone, fax, mail. Transcripts available by fax, mail. Phone number required.

Triangle Tech, Registrar, 222 E Pittsburgh St, **Greensburg**, PA 15601-9944, 724-832-1050 (Fax: 724-834-0325) www.triangle-tech.com. 7:30AM-4PM. Enrollment: 250. Records go back to 1978. Degrees granted: Associate. Attendance and degree information available by phone, fax, mail. Transcripts available by fax, mail. Phone number required.

Triangle Tech (Main), Registrar, 1940 Perrysville Ave, Pittsburgh, PA 15214-3897, 412-359-1000 Ext. 197, 412-359-7221 (Fax: 412-359-1012) www.triangle-tech.com. 8AM-5PM. Enrollment: 387. Records go back to 1947. Alumni records are maintained here. Degrees granted: Associate. Attendance and degree information available by phone, fax, mail. Transcripts available by fax, mail.

Triangle Tech - Monroeville School of Business, Registrar, 1940 Perrysville Ave, Pittsburgh, PA 15214-3897, 412-359-1000, 800-TRI-TECH (Fax: 412-359-1000) www.triangle-tech.com. 8AM-6PM M-Th, 8AM-4PM F. Enrollment: 261. Records go back to 1989. Alumni records are maintained here. Degrees granted: Associate. Attendance and degree information available by phone, mail. Transcripts available by fax, mail.

Trinity Episcopal School for Ministry, Registrar, 311 Eleventh St, Ambridge, PA 15003, 724-266-3838, 800-874-8754 (Fax: 724-266-4617). 8:30AM-5PM. Enrollment: 150. Records go back to 1976. Alumni records are maintained here. Degrees granted: Masters; Basic Christian Studies, Anglican Studies. Attendance and degree information available by phone, fax, mail. Transcripts available by fax, mail.

University of Pennsylvania, Registrar, 3451 Walnut St, Franklin Bldg Room 221, Philadelphia, PA 19104, 215-898-1561 www.upenn.edu. 9AM-5PM. Enrollment: 22700. Records go back to 1740. Alumni records maintained here; call 215-898-7811. Degrees granted: Bachelors; Masters; Doctorate. Attendance and degree information available by phone, mail. Transcripts available by mail.

University of Pittsburgh (Bradford Campus), Registrar, 300 Campus Dr, Bradford, PA 16701, 814-362-7600 (Fax: 814-362-7578) www.pitt.edu. 8AM-5PM. Enrollment: 1200. Records go back to 1963. Alumni records maintained here; call 814-362-7655. Degrees granted: Bachelors. Attendance and degree information available by phone, mail. Transcripts available by mail.

University of Pittsburgh (Greensburg Campus), Registrar, 1150 Mount Pleasant Rd, Greensburg, PA 15601, 724-836-9900, 724-836-9899 (Fax: 724-836-7176) www.pitt.edu. 8:30AM-6PM M-Th; 8:30AM-5PM F. Enrollment: 1300. Records go back to 1963. Alumni records maintained here; call 724-836-9905. Degrees granted: Bachelors. Attendance, degree and transcript information available by fax, mail.

University of Pittsburgh (Johnstown Campus), Registrar, 6PJ, 132 Biddle Hall, Johnstown, PA 15956, 814-269-7060 (Fax: 814-269-7068) www.pitt.edu/~upjweb. 8AM-4PM. Records go back to 1927. Alumni records are maintained here. Degrees granted: Associate; Bachelors. Attendance and degree information available by phone, mail. Transcripts available by fax, mail.

University of Pittsburgh, Registrar, G-3 Thackeray Hall, Pittsburgh, PA 15260, 412-624-7660 www.pitt.edu. 8:30AM-4:45PM. Enrollment: 26328. Records go back to 1787. Alumni records maintained here; call 412-624-8222. Degrees granted: Bachelors; Masters; Doctorate. Attendance and degree information available by phone, mail. Transcripts available by mail.

University of Pittsburgh (Titusville Campus), Registrar, 504 E Main St, Titusville, PA 16354, 814-827-4482, 814-827-4470 (Fax: 814-827-4448) www.pitt.edu. 8:30AM-5PM. Enrollment: 323. Records go

back to 1969. Degrees granted: Associate. Attendance and degree information available by phone, fax, mail. Transcripts available by mail.

University of Scranton, Registrar, 800 Linden St, Scranton, PA 18510-4501, 717-941-7720, 717-941-7721 (Fax: 717-941-4148) www.UofS.EDU. 8:30AM-4:30PM. Enrollment: 5000. Records go back to 1930. Alumni records maintained here; call 717-941-7720. Degrees granted: Associate; Bachelors; Masters. Attendance and degree information available by phone, fax, mail. Transcripts available by fax, mail.

University of the Arts, Registrar, 320 S Broad St, Philadelphia, PA 19102, 215-875-4848 www.uarts.edu. 9AM-5PM. Enrollment: 1300. Alumni records maintained here; call 215-875-4826. Degrees granted: Associate; Bachelors; Masters. Special programs- New Studies Center (now PIE), 215-875-3350. Attendance and degree information available by phone, mail. Transcripts available by written request only.

Ursinus College, Registrar, Box 1000, Main Street, Collegeville, PA 19426-1000, 610-409-3000 Ext. 2225, 610-409-3605 (Fax: 610-489-0627) www.ursinus.edu. 8:30AM-5PM. Enrollment: 1250. Records go back to 1869. Alumni records maintained here; call 610-409-3585. Degrees granted: Bachelors. Attendance and degree information available by phone, mail. Transcripts available by mail.

Valley Forge Christian College, Registrar, 1401 Charlestown Rd, VFCC Box 51, Phoenixville, PA 19460, 610-935-0450 (Fax: 610-935-9353) www.vfcc.edu. 8AM-4:30PM. Enrollment: 500. Records go back to 1938. Alumni records are maintained here. Degrees granted: Associate; Bachelors. Attendance and degree information available by phone. Transcripts available by mail.

Valley Forge Military College, Registrar, 1001 Eagle Rd, Wayne, PA 19087-3695, 610-989-1455, 610-989-1200 (Fax: 610-989-1550) www.vfmac.edu. 8:30AM-4:30PM. Enrollment: 225. Alumni records are maintained here. Attendance and degree information available by phone, fax, mail. Transcripts available by written request only.

Villa Maria College
(See Gannon University)

Villanova University, Registrar, 800 Lancaster Ave, Villanova, PA 19085, 610-519-4032 (Fax: 610-519-4033) www.vill.edu. 9AM-5PM. Enrollment: 10000. Records go back to 1855. Degrees granted: Associate; Bachelors; Masters; Doctorate. Attendance and degree information available by phone, fax, mail. Transcripts available by fax, mail.

Washington and Jefferson College, Registrar, 45 S Lincoln St, Washington, PA 15301, 724-223-6017. 9AM-Noon, 1-5PM. Enrollment: 1100. Records go back to 1901. Alumni records maintained here; call 724-223-6079. Degrees granted: Associate; Bachelors. Attendance and degree information available by phone, mail. Transcripts available by mail.

Waynesburg College, Registrar, 51 W College St, Waynesburg, PA 15370, 724-852-3252 www.waynesburg.edu. 8AM-4:30PM. Records go back to 1849. Alumni records maintained here; call 724-852-3300. Degrees granted: Bachelors; Masters. Attendance and degree information available by phone, mail. Transcripts available by mail.

West Chester University of Pennsylvania, Registrar, EO Bull Center Room 154, West Chester, PA 19383, 610-436-3541 (Fax: 610-436-2370) www.wcupa.edu. 8AM-4:15PM M,T,Th,F; 9AM-4:15PM W. Records go back to 1971. Alumni records maintained here; call 610-436-2813. Degrees granted: Bachelors; Masters. Attendance and degree information available by phone, fax, mail. Transcripts available by mail. Phone number required.

West Virginia Career College (Branch Campus), Registrar, PO Box 278, Mount Braddock, PA 15465, 724-437-4600 (Fax: 724-437-6053). Records are located at West Virginia Career College, Registrar, 148 Willey St, Morgantown, WV 26505.

Westminster College, Registrar's Office, South Market St, New Wilmington, PA 16172, 724-946-7136, 724-946-6336 (Fax: 724-946-7171). 8AM-4:30PM. Enrollment: 1500. Records go back to 1800's. Alumni records maintained here; call 724-946-7008. Degrees granted: Bachelors; Masters. Attendance and degree information available by phone, mail. Transcripts available by mail.

Westminster Theological Seminary, Registrar, Church Rd and Willow Grove Ave, Glenside, PA 19038, 215-572-3809, 215-887-5511 (Fax: 215-887-5404) www.wts.edu. 8:30AM-4:30PM. Enrollment: 610. Records go back to 1930's. Alumni records are maintained here. Degrees granted: Masters; Doctorate. Attendance and degree information available by phone, fax, mail. Transcripts available by mail.

Westmoreland County Community College, Registrar, Armbrust Rd, Youngwood, PA 15697-1895, 724-925-4069, 412-925-4182 (Fax: 724-925-4292). 8AM-5PM. Enrollment: 6000. Records go back to 1970. Degrees granted: Associate. Attendance and degree information available by phone, fax, mail. Transcripts available by fax, mail.

Widener University, Registrar, One University Pl, Chester, PA 19013-5792, 610-499-4140 (Fax: 610-499-4576) 8:30AM-5PM. www.widener.edu. Enrollment: 7500. Records go back to 1876. Alumni records maintained here; call 610-499-1154. Degrees granted: Bachelors; Masters; Doctorate. Attendance and degree information available by phone, fax, mail. Transcripts available by fax, mail.

Widener University at Harrisburg (School of Law), Registrar, 3800 Vartan Way, PO Box 69381, Harrisburg, PA 17106-9381, 717-541-3904 (Fax: 717-541-1923) www.widener.edu. 8:45AM-5PM M,W-F; 8:45AM-6PM T. Enrollment: 500. Records go back to 1989. Alumni Records: Alumni Office, Widener University, One University Place, Chester, PA 19013. Attendance, degree and transcript information available by mail.

Wilkes University, Registrar, 267 S Franklin St, Wilkes-Barre, PA 18766, 717-408-4855, 717-408-4856 (Fax: 717-408-7885) www.wilkes.edu. 8:30AM-4:30PM. Records go back to 1933. Alumni Records: Evans Alumni House, Wilkes Univ., 110 S River St, Wilkes-Barre, PA 18766. Degrees granted: Bachelors; Masters; PharmD. Attendance and degree information available by phone, fax, mail. Transcripts available by fax, mail.

Williamson Free School of Mechanical Trades, Registrar, 106 S Middletown Road Rt 352, Media, PA 19063, 610-566-1776 (Fax: 610-566-6502). Enrollment: 254. Records go back to 1911. Alumni records are maintained here. Degrees granted: Associate; Diplomas in Brickmasonry, Carpentry, Painting/Wallcovering. Special programs-Power Plant Tech: Machine Tool Tech: Horticulture/Landscaping/Turf Management. Attendance and degree information available by phone, fax, mail. Transcripts available by mail.

Williamsport Area Community College

(See Pennsylvania College of Technology)

Williamsport School of Commerce
(See Newport Business Institute)

Wilson College, Registrar, 1015 Philadelphia Ave, Chambersburg, PA 17201-1285, 717-264-4141 Ext. 3355, 717-262-2007 (Fax: 717-264-1578). 8AM-4:30PM. Enrollment: 821. Records go back to 1869. Alumni records maintained here; call 717-264-3182. Degrees granted: Associate; Bachelors. Attendance and degree information available by phone, fax, mail. Transcripts available by mail.

Yeshiva Beth Moshe, Registrar, 930 Hickory St, Scranton, PA 18505, 717-346-1747 9AM-5PM. Enrollment: 60. Records go back to 1965. Attendance, degree and transcript information available by mail.

York College of Pennsylvania, Records Office, Country Club Rd, York, PA 17405-7199, 717-846-7788, 717-815-1232 (Fax: 717-849-1607) www.yorkcol.edu. 8:30AM-5PM; Summer Hours:8AM-5PM M-Th, 8-11:30AM F. Records go back to 1788. Alumni records maintained here; call 717-846-7788 Ext. 1500. Degrees granted: Associate; Bachelors; Masters. Attendance and degree information available by phone, fax, mail. Transcripts available by mail.

York Technical Institute, Registrar, 1405 Williams Rd, York, PA 17404, 717-757-1100 (Fax: 717-757-4964) www.yorktech.edu. 8AM-5PM. Records go back to 1979. Degrees granted: Associate. Attendance and degree information available by phone, mail. Transcripts available by mail.

Yorktowne Business Institute, Registrar, W Seventh Ave, York, PA 17404, 717-846-5000 (Fax: 717-848-4584) www.ybi.edu. 8AM-5PM. Enrollment: 220. Records go back to 1977. Degrees granted: Associate. Attendance and degree information available by phone, fax, mail. Transcripts available by fax, mail.

Rhode Island

Brown University, Registrar, Box K, Providence, RI 02912, 401-863-1851 www.brown.edu/Administration/Registrar/. 8AM-4PM. Enrollment: 7000. Records go back to 1764. Alumni records maintained here; call 401-863-3307. Degrees granted: Bachelors; Masters; Doctorate. Attendance and degree information available by phone, mail. Transcripts available by mail.

Bryant College, Academic Records Office, 1150 Douglas Pike, Smithfield, RI 02917-1284, 401-232-6080, 401-232-6083 (Fax: 401-232-6065) www.bryant.edu. 8AM-8PM M-Th; 8AM-4:30PM F. Alumni records maintained here; call 401-232-6040. Degrees granted: Associate; Bachelors; Masters. Attendance and degree information available by phone, fax, mail. Transcripts available by written request only.

Bryant Col. of Business Administration
(See Bryant College)

Community College of Rhode Island, Registrar, 400 East Ave, Warwick, RI 02886-1805, 401-825-2125, 401-333-7097 (Fax: 401-825-2394 Ext. 401). 8AM-7PM M-Th; 8AM-4PM F (when in session); 8AM-4PM (otherwise). Enrollment: 15000. Records go back to 1964. Alumni records maintained here; call 401-825-2181. Degrees granted: Associate. Attendance and degree information

available by phone, fax, mail. Transcripts available by mail.

Johnson & Wales University (Branch Campus), Registrar, 8 Abbott Park Pl, Providence, RI 02903, 401-598-1000 (Fax: 401-598-2837) www.jwu.wdu. 8:30AM-4:30PM. Enrollment: 10000. Records go back to 1952. Inactive records: "Dept of Inactive Records," same address. Alumni records maintained here; call 401-598-1072. Degrees granted: Associate; Bachelors; Masters; Doctorate. Attendance and degree information available by fax, mail. Transcripts available by mail.

Johnson and Wales College
(See Johnson & Wales University)

Katharine Gibbs School, Registrar, 178 Butler Ave, Providence, RI 02906, 401-861-1420 (Fax: 401-421-6230). 9AM-5PM. Enrollment: 300. Records go back to 1911. Alumni records maintained here; call 212-885-6964 (Corporate Office). Degrees granted. Special programs- Executive Assistant Program: Legal Executive Program: Medical Executive Program. Attendance and degree information available by phone, fax, mail. Transcripts available by mail.

Naval War College, Registrar, 686 Cushing Rd, Newport, RI 02841-5010, 401-841-6597, 401-841-3373 (Fax: 401-841-2460) 7:30AM-

4PM. www.usnwc.edu/nwc/. Enrollment: 500. Records go back to 1884. Alumni records are maintained here. Degrees granted: Masters. Special programs- CCE, 401-841-2134. Attendance and degree information available by phone, fax, mail. Transcripts available by mail.

New England Institute of Technology, Registrar, 2500 Post Rd, Warwick, RI 02886-2251, 401-739-5000 (Fax: 401-738-5122). 8:30AM-5:30PM. Enrollment: 2000. Records go back to 1985. Degrees granted: Associate; Bachelors. Attendance and degree information available by phone, fax, mail. Transcripts available by fax, mail.

Providence College, Academic Records Office, Providence, RI 02918, 401-865-2366, 401-865-2854 (Fax: 401-865-2826) 8AM-5PM. www.providence.edu. Enrollment: 5481. Records go back to 1919. Alumni records maintained here; call 401-865-2414. Degrees granted: Associate; Bachelors; Masters; Doctorate. Attendance and degree information available by phone, mail. Transcripts available by mail.

Rhode Island College, Registrar, Providence, RI 02908, 401-456-8212 (Fax: 401-456-8379) www.ric.edu. 8AM-4:30PM. Enrollment: 9000. Records go back to 1854. Alumni records maintained here; call 401-456-8000. Degrees granted: Bachelors;

Masters; Doctorate; CAGS. Attendance, degree and transcript information available by fax, mail.

Rhode Island School of Design, Registrar, 2 College St, Providence, RI 02903, 401-454-6151, 401-454-6153 (Fax: 401-454-6598) www.risd.edu. 8:30AM-4:30PM. Enrollment: 1987. Records go back to 1930's. Alumni records maintained here; call 401-454-6620. Degrees granted: Bachelors; Masters. Attendance and degree information available by phone, fax, mail. Transcripts available by mail.

Roger Williams College Providence Branch, Registrar, 150 Washington St, Providence, RI 02903-3300, 401-253-1040 (Fax: 401-276-4848) www.rwu.edu/.

Enrollment: 3400. Records go back to 1919. Degrees granted: Associate; Bachelors. Special programs- Arts: Science. Attendance and degree information available by phone, fax, mail. Transcripts available by mail.

Roger Williams University, Registrar, One Old Ferry Rd, Bristol, RI 02809-2921, 401-254-3033 (Fax: 401-254-3363) 8AM-5PM. Records go back to 1948. Alumni records maintained here; call 401-254-3005. Degrees granted: Associate; Bachelors. Attendance and degree information available by phone, fax, mail. Transcripts available by mail.

Salve Regina University, Registrar, 100 Ochre Point Ave, Newport, RI 02840-4192, 401-847-6650 (Fax: 401-847-6650 Ext. 2996) www.terryj.salves.salve.edu. 8AM-5PM. Enrollment: 2200. Records go back to 1947.

Alumni records maintained here; call 401-847-6650. Degrees granted: Associate; Bachelors; Masters; Doctorate. Attendance and degree information available by phone, mail. Transcripts available by mail.

University of Rhode Island, Registrar, Administration Bldg, Kingston, RI 02881-0806, 401-874-2835, 401-874-2816 (Fax: 401-874-2910). 8:30AM-4:30PM. Enrollment: 13500. Records go back to 1892. Alumni records maintained here; call 401-792-2242. Degrees granted: Bachelors; Masters; Doctorate. Attendance and degree information available by phone, mail. Transcripts available by mail.

South Carolina

Aiken Technical College, Registrar, PO Box 696, Aiken, SC 29802-0696, 803-593-9231 (Fax: 803-593-6641) www.aik.tec.sc. 7:30AM-7PM. Enrollment: 2200. Records go back to 1972. Alumni records maintained here; call 803-593-9231 Ext. 1263. Degrees granted: Associate. Attendance and degree information available by phone, fax, mail. Transcripts available by fax, mail.

Allen University, Registrar, 1530 Harden St, Columbia, SC 29204, 803-376-5737 (Fax: 803-376-5729) 9AM-5PM. Records go back to 1906. Degrees granted: Associate; Bachelors. Attendance and degree information available by phone, fax, mail. Transcripts available by fax, mail.

Anderson College, Registrar, 316 Blvd, Anderson, SC 29621, 864-231-2120 www.icusc.org/anderson/achome.htm (Fax: 864-231-5605) 8:30AM-4:30PM. Enrollment: 800. Records go back to 1945. Alumni records maintained here; call 864-231-2064. Degrees granted: Associate; Bachelors. Attendance and degree information available by phone, fax, mail. Transcripts available by fax, mail.

Baptist College at Charleston
(See Charleston Southern University)

Beaufort Technical College
(See Technical Col. of the Low Country)

Benedict College, Registrar, 1600 Harden St, Columbia, SC 29204, 803-253-5143 www.icusc.org/benedict/bchome.htm. (Fax: 803-253-5146) Records go back to 1870. Alumni records are maintained here. Degrees granted: Bachelors. Attendance and degree information available by phone, fax, mail. Transcripts available by fax, mail.

Bob Jones University, Registrar, Greenville, SC 29614, 864-242-5100 Ext. 2010, 800-BJANDME (Fax: 1-800-2-faxBJU) www.bju.edu. Enrollment: 4400. Records go back to 1927. Alumni records are maintained here. Degrees granted: Associate; Bachelors; Masters; Doctorate. Attendance and degree information available by phone, fax, mail. Transcripts available by fax, mail.

Central Carolina Technical College, Registrar, 506 N Guignard Dr, Sumter, SC 29150-2499, www.sum.tec.sc.us. 803-778-1961 Ext. 430, 803-778-7830 (Records) (Fax: 803-773-4859) Enrollment: 2200. Records go back to 1963. Alumni records are maintained here. Degrees granted: Associate. Attendance and degree information available by phone, mail. Transcripts available by mail. Phone requests require proper ID and verification.

Charleston Southern University, Registrar, PO Box 118087, Charleston, SC 29423, 843-863-8060 (Fax: 843-863-8023). Enrollment: 2600. Records go back to 1969. Alumni records are maintained here. Degrees granted: Bachelors; Masters. Special programs- Air Force ROTC, 843-863-7149. Attendance and degree information available by phone, fax, mail. Transcripts available by fax, mail.

Chesterfield-Marlboro Technical College Registrar, 1201 Chesterfield Hwy #9 W, PO Drawer 1007, Cheraw, SC 29520-1007, 803-921-6900, 803-921-6934 (Fax: 803-537-6148). 8AM-7PM M-Th; 8AM-1:30PM F. Enrollment: 1025. Records go back to 1969. Degrees granted: Associate. Attendance and degree information available by phone, fax, mail. Transcripts available by fax, mail.

Citadel Military College of South Carolina, Registrar, Citadel Station 171 Moultrie St, Charleston, SC 29409, 803-953-6969, 803-953-6976 (Fax: 803-953-7630) 8AM-5PM. www.citadel.edu. Enrollment: 4300. Records go back to 1842. Alumni records maintained here; call 803-953-7697. Degrees granted: Bachelors; Masters. Attendance and degree information available by phone, fax, mail. Transcripts available by phone, fax, mail.

Claflin College, Registrar, 700 College Ave NE, Orangeburg, SC 29115, 803-534-2710 www.icusc.org/claflin/cchome.htm. (Fax: 803-535-5387) Degrees granted: Bachelors. Attendance and degree information available by phone, fax, mail. Transcripts available by fax, mail.

Clemson University, Transcripts, 104 Sikes Hall, Clemson, SC 29634, 864-656-2174, 864-656-0199 (Fax: 864-656-0622) www.clemson.edu. 8AM-4:30PM. Enrollment: 17000. Records go back to 1900's. Alumni Records: Box 345603, Clemson, SC 29634. Degrees granted: Bachelors; Masters; Doctorate. Attendance and degree information available by phone, fax, mail. Transcripts available by fax, mail.

Coastal Carolina University, Registrar, PO Box 261954, Conway, SC 29528-6054, 843-349-2025 (Fax: 843-349-2909) www.coastal.edu. 8AM-5PM. Alumni records are maintained here also. Enrollment: 4500. Records go back to 1993. Records prior to July 1, 1993 are housed at University of South Carolina. Call 843-349-2006. Degrees granted: Bachelors; Masters. Certification: Gerontology. Attendance and degree

information available by phone, fax, mail. Transcripts available by fax, mail.

Coker College, Registrar, 300 E College Ave, Hartsville, SC 29550, 803-383-8022 (Fax: 803-383-8095) www.coker.edu. Enrollment: 800. Degrees granted: Bachelors. Attendance and degree information available by phone, fax, mail. Transcripts available by mail.

College of Charleston, Registrar's Office, 66 George St, Charleston, SC 29424, 803-953-5668 (Fax: 803-953-6560) 8:30AM-5PM. www.cofc.edu Enrollment: 10000. Alumni records maintained here; call 803-953-5630. Degrees granted: Bachelors; Masters. Attendance and degree information available by phone, fax, mail. Transcripts available by fax, mail.

Columbia Bible College & Seminary
(See Columbia International University)

Columbia College, Registrar, 1301 Columbia College Dr, Columbia, SC 29203, 803-786-3672 (Fax: 803-786-3771). 8:30AM-5PM. Degrees granted: Bachelors; Masters. Attendance and degree information available by phone, fax, mail. Transcripts available by fax, mail.

Columbia International University, Registrar, PO Box 3122, Columbia, SC 29203-3122, 803-754-4100 (Fax: 803-786-4209). 8AM-5PM. Records go back to 1927. Alumni records maintained here; call 803-754-4100 Ext. 3004. Degrees granted: Associate; Bachelors; Masters; Doctorate. Attendance and degree information available by phone, mail. Transcripts available by fax, mail.

Columbia Junior College of Business, Registrar, PO Box 1196, 3810 Main St, Columbia, SC 29202, 803-799-9082 (Fax: 803-799-9005). 8AM-5:30PM. Enrollment: 300. Records go back to 1935. Degrees granted: Associate. Attendance and degree information available by phone, fax, mail. Transcripts available by fax, mail.

Converse College, Registrar, 580 E Main St, Spartanburg, SC 29302-0006, 864-596-9094 www.icusc.org/converse/cchome.htm. (Fax: 864-596-9202) 8:30AM - 5PM. Enrollment: 1200. Records go back to 1800's. Alumni records are maintained here. Degrees granted: Bachelors; Masters; EDS. Attendance and degree information available by fax, mail. Transcripts available by mail.

Denmark Technical College, Registrar, PO Box 327, Denmark, SC 29042, 803-793-5182 (Fax: 803-793-5942). 8:30AM-5PM.

Degrees granted: Associate. Attendance, degree and transcript information available by fax, mail.

Erskine College Seminary, Registrar, 2 Washington St, Due West, SC 29639, 864-379-8872 (Fax: 864-379-2167) www.erskine.edu. 8AM-5PM. Enrollment: 750. Records go back to 1890's. Alumni records maintained here; call 803-379-8881. Degrees granted: Bachelors; Masters; Doctorate. Certification: Theology. Attendance and degree information available by phone, fax, mail. Transcripts available by mail.

Florence-Darlington Technical College, Registrar, PO Box 100548, Florence, SC 29501-0548, 803-661-8090, 803-661-8095 (Fax: 803-661-8041) www.flo.tec.sc.us. 8:30AM-8PM M-Th, 8:30AM-5PM F. Enrollment: 3000. Records go back to 1963. Alumni records maintained here; call 803-661-8002. Degrees granted: Associate. Special programs- Continuing Education, 803-661-8126. Attendance and degree information available by phone, fax, mail. Transcripts available by fax, mail.

Forrest Junior College, Registrar, 601 E River St, Anderson, SC 29624, 864-225-7653 (Fax: 864-261-7471). 8AM-9PM. Enrollment: 110. Records go back to 1960. Degrees granted: Associate. Attendance and degree information available by phone, fax, mail. Transcripts available by mail.

Francis Marion College, Registrar, PO Box 100547, Florence, SC 29501-0547, 803-661-1175 (Fax: 803-661-1219) www.fmarion.edu. Enrollment: 4000. Records go back to 1970. Alumni records maintained here; call 803-661-1228. Degrees granted: Bachelors; Masters. Attendance, degree and transcript information available by mail.

Furman University, Registrar, 3300 Poinsett Hwy, Greenville, SC 29613, www.furman.edu. 864-294-2031 (Fax: 864-294-3551) Enrollment: 2500. Records go back to 1826. Alumni records maintained here; call 864-294-3464. Degrees granted: Bachelors; Masters. Attendance and degree information available by phone, fax, mail. Transcripts available by fax, mail.

Greenville Technical College, Registrar, PO Box 5616, Greenville, SC 29606-5616, 864-250-8117, 864-250-8114 (Fax: 864-250-8535) www.gvltec.edu. 8AM-7PM M-Th; 8AM-1PM F. Enrollment: 8000. Records go back to 1963. Alumni Records: Alumni Assoc., Greenville Technical College, PO Box 5616, Greenville, SC 29606-5161. Degrees granted: Associate. Attendance and degree information available by phone, fax, mail. Transcripts available by fax, mail.

Horry-Georgetown Technical College, Registrar, PO Box 1966, Conway, SC 29526, 803-347-3186, 803-349-5224 (Fax: 803-347-2962) www.hgtc. 8AM-8:30PM M-Th; 8AM-4:30PM F. Enrollment: 3200. Records go back to 1966. Alumni records are maintained here at the same phone number. Degrees granted: Associate. Attendance and degree information available by phone, fax, mail. Transcripts available by mail.

ITT Technical Institute, Education Department, One Marcus Dr Ste 402, Greenville, SC 29615, 864-288-0777, 800-932-4488 (Fax: 864-297-0930). 8AM-5PM. Enrollment: 285. Records go back to 1992. Alumni records are maintained here. Degrees granted: Associate. Attendance, degree and transcript information available by mail.

Johnson & Wales University (Branch Campus), Registrar, 701 E Bay St, Charleston, SC 29403, 803-727-3063, 803-727-3006 (Fax: 803-727-3094) www.sims.net/organizations/jwu-sc/jwu.html. 8:30AM-4:30PM. Enrollment: 1100. Records go back to 1984. Alumni Records: 8 Abbott Park Pl, Providence, RI 02903. Degrees granted: Associate; Bachelors. Special programs- Culinary Arts: Pastry Arts: Hotel Management. Attendance and degree information available by phone, fax, mail. Transcripts available by mail.

Lander University, Registrar, 320 Stanley Ave, Greenwood, SC 29649-2099, 864-388-8398 (Fax: 864-388-8890). 8AM-5PM. Records go back to 1872. Alumni records maintained here; call 864-388-8351. Degrees granted: Bachelors; Masters. Attendance and degree information available by phone, fax, mail. Transcripts available by fax, mail.

Limestone College, Registrar, 1115 College Dr, Gaffney, SC 29340, 864-489-7151 (Fax: 864-487-8706) 8:30AM-5PM. www.limestone.edu Enrollment: 1600. Records go back to 1895. Alumni records maintained here; call 803-489-7151 Ext. 604. Degrees granted: Associate; Bachelors. Attendance and degree information available by phone, fax, mail. Transcripts available by fax, mail.

Lutheran Theological Southern Seminary, Registrar, 4201 N Main St, Columbia, SC 29203, 803-786-5150 Ext. 210 (Fax: 803-786-6499). 8:30AM-4:30PM. Records go back to 1880's. Alumni records are maintained here. Degrees granted: Bachelors; Masters. Attendance and degree information available by phone, fax, mail. Transcripts available by fax, mail.

Medical University of South Carolina, Registrar, 171 Ashley Ave, Charleston, SC 29425, 803-792-3281 (Fax: 803-792-3764) www.musc.edu. 8AM-5PM. Enrollment: 2276. Records go back to 1946. Alumni records maintained here; call 803-792-7979. Degrees granted: Bachelors; Masters; Doctorate. Attendance information available by phone, fax, mail. Degree and transcript information available by fax, mail.

Midlands Technical College, Registrar, PO Box 2408, Columbia, SC 29202, 803-738-7703 (Fax: 803-738-7880). 8AM-6:30PM M-Th; 8AM-4:30PM F. Enrollment: 9300. Records go back to 1905. Alumni records maintained here; call 803-822-3064. Degrees granted: Associate. Attendance and degree information available by phone, fax, mail. Transcripts available by fax, mail.

Morris College, Registrar, 100 W College St, Sumter, SC 29150-3599, 803-775-9371, 803-775-9371 Ext. 239 (Fax: 803-773-3687) www.icusc.org/morris/mchome.htm. 8AM-5PM. Enrollment: 900. Records go back to 1912. Alumni records maintained here; call 803-775-9371 Ext. 226. Degrees granted: Bachelors. Attendance and degree information available by fax, mail. Transcripts available by mail.

Newberry College, Registrar, 2100 College St, Newberry, SC 29108, 803-321-5124 (Fax: 803-321-5627) www.newberry.edu. 8AM-4:30PM. Enrollment: 700. Records go back to 1900. Alumni records maintained here; call 803-321-5143. Degrees granted: Bachelors. Attendance and degree information available by phone, fax, mail. Transcripts available by fax, mail.

North Greenville College, Records Office, PO Box 1892, Tigerville, SC 29688, 864-977-7009 www.icusc.org/n_greenv/nghome.htm (Fax: 864-977-7021) 8:30AM-5PM M-Th; 8:30AM-Noon F. Alumni records maintained here; call 864-977-7015. Degrees granted: Associate; Bachelors. Attendance information available by phone. School will not confirm degree information. Transcripts available by written request only.

Orangeburg-Calhoun Technical College, Registrar, 3250 St Matthews Rd, Orangeburg, SC 29115, 803-536-0311 (Fax: 803-535-1388) www.octech.org. 8:30AM-5PM. Enrollment: 1780. Records go back to 1968. Degrees granted: Associate. Attendance and degree information available by phone, fax, mail. Transcripts available by fax, mail.

Phillips Junior College Charleston, School closed and may have been purchased and re-opened under another name. No further information is available at press time.

Phillips Junior College Greenville, School closed and may have been purchased and re-opened under another name. No further information is available at press time.

Piedmont Technical College, Student Records, Emerald Rd, PO Box 1467, Greenwood, SC 29648, 864-941-8364, 864-941-8363 (Fax: 864-941-8566) www.piedmont.tec.sc.us. 8AM-8:30PM M-Th; 8AM-5PM F. Enrollment: 3300. Records go back to 1966. Alumni records maintained here; call 864-941-8304. Degrees granted: Associate. Attendance and degree information available by phone, fax, mail. Transcripts available by fax, mail.

Presbyterian College, Registrar, S Broad St, PO Box 975, Clinton, SC 29325, 864-833-8224 (Fax: 864-833-8481) www.presby.edu. 9AM-5PM. Alumni records maintained here; call 864-833-8211. Degrees granted: Bachelors. Attendance and degree information available by phone, fax, mail. Transcripts available by mail.

Rutledge College-Charleston
(See Phillips Junior College Charleston)

Rutledge College-Greenville
(See Phillips Junior College Greenville)

Sherman College of Straight Chiropractic, Registrar, 2020 Springfield Rd, PO Box 1452, Spartanburg, SC 29304, www.shermancsc.edu. 864-578-8770 (Fax: 864-599-4860) 8AM-4:30PM. Enrollment: 288. Records go back to 1976. Alumni records are maintained here. Degrees granted: Doctorate. Attendance and degree information available by phone, fax, mail. Transcripts available by mail.

South Carolina State University, Registrar, 300 College Ave NE, PO Box 1627, Orangeburg, SC 29117, 803-536-7185 (Fax: 803-536-8990) www.scsu.edu. 8AM-5PM. Records go back to 1896. Alumni records maintained here; call 803-536-8946. Degrees granted: Bachelors; Masters; Doctorate. Attendance and degree information available by phone, mail. Transcripts available by mail.

Southern Wesleyan University, Registrar, PO Box 1020, Central, SC 29630-1020, 864-639-2453 Ext. 325 (Fax: 864-639-1956) www.icusc.org/s_wesley/swhome.htm. 8AM-4:30PM. Enrollment: 1271. Records go back to 1906. Formerly **Central Wesleyan College**. Alumni records maintained here; call 864-639-2453 Ext. 368. Degrees granted: Bachelors; Masters. Attendance, degree and transcript information available by fax, mail. Need to provide ID number.

Spartanburg Methodist College, Registrar, 1200 Textile Rd, Spartanburg, SC 29301-0009, 864-587-4232 (Fax: 864-587-4355) www/s,csc/edi. 8AM-5PM. Records go back to 1911. Alumni records maintained here; call 864-587-4220. Degrees granted: Associate. Attendance and degree information available by phone, fax, mail. Transcripts available by fax, mail.

Spartanburg Technical College, Registrar, PO Drawer 4386, Spartanburg, SC 29305-4386, 864-591-3680, 864-591-3685 (Fax: 864-591-3689) www.tec.sc.us. 8AM-6:30PM M,T; 8AM-5PM W,Th; 8AM-1:30PM F. Enrollment: 2476. Records go back to 1962. Degrees granted: Associate. Attendance and degree information available by phone, fax, mail. Transcripts available by fax, mail.

Sumter Area Technical College
(See Central Carolina Technical College)

Technical College of the Lowcountry, Registrar, 921 S Ribaut Rd, PO Box 1288, Beaufort, SC 29902, 803-525-8210, 803-525-8209 (Fax: 803-525-8285) www.tcl.tec.sc.us. 8:30AM-5PM. Enrollment: 1356. Records go back to 1988. Alumni records are maintained here. Degrees granted: Associate. Attendance information available by phone, fax, mail. Degree information available by fax. Transcripts available by written request only.

Tri-County Technical College, Student Records, PO Box 587, Pendleton, SC 29670, 864-646-8361 Ext. 2194 (Fax: 864-646-8256). 8AM-9PM. Records go back to 1962. Alumni records are maintained here Degrees granted: Associate. Attendance and degree information available by phone, fax, mail. Transcripts available by fax, mail.

Trident Technical College, Admissions & Records, AM-M, PO Box 118067, Charleston, SC 29423-8067, 803-574-6321 (Fax: 803-569-6483). 8AM-6:30PM M-Th; 8AM-1PM F. Records go back to 1970's. TTC from 1970's; **Berkeley, Charleston, Dorchester Tech** to 1950's; **Palmer College** from 1970's. Degrees granted: Associate. Attendance and degree information available by phone, fax, mail. Transcripts available by fax, mail..

University of South Carolina-Aiken, Registrar, 171 University Pkwy, Aiken, SC 29801, 803-648-6851 (Fax: 803-641-3494) 8AM-5PM. www.usca.sc.edu. Enrollment: 3100. Alumni records maintained here; call 803-641-3480. Degrees granted: Associate; Bachelors. Attendance and degree information available by phone, fax, mail. Transcript records are housed at University of South Carolina, Registrar, Columbia, SC, 29208.

University of South Carolina-Beaufort, Registrar, 801 Carteret St, Beaufort, SC 29902, 803-521-4100, 803-521-4102 (Fax: 803-521-4198). 8:30AM-5PM. Enrollment: 1350. Alumni records are maintained here.

Degrees granted: Associate. Attendance and degree information available by phone, fax, mail. Transcript records are housed at University of South Carolina, Registrar, Columbia, SC, 29208.

University of South Carolina-Coastal College
(See Coastal Carolina University)

University of South Carolina-Columbia University Registrar, Columbia, SC 29208-0001, 803-777-5555 (Fax: 803-777-6349) www.argo.regs.sc.edu. Enrollment: 38000. Records go back to 1801. Alumni records maintained here; call 803-777-4111. Degrees granted: Associate; Bachelors; Doctorate; MD, JD. Attendance and degree information available by phone, fax, mail. Transcripts available by mail.

University of South Carolina — Lancaster, Registrar, PO Box 889, Lancaster, SC 29721, 803-285-7471 (Fax: 803-289-7116). 8:30AM-5PM. Enrollment: 1200. Alumni records are maintained here. Degrees granted: Associate; Nursing, Criminal Justice, Business. Attendance information available by phone, fax, mail. Degree information available by written request only. Transcript records are housed at University of South Carolina, Registrar, Columbia, SC, 29208.

University of South Carolina — Salkehatchie, Registrar, PO Box 617, Allendale, SC 29810, 803-584-3446. Records are located at University of South Carolina-Columbia, University Registrar, Columbia, SC 29208-0001.

University of South Carolina — Spartanburg, Registrar, 800 University Way, Spartanburg, SC 29303, 864-503-5220 (Fax: 864-503-5727) www.uscs.edu. Enrollment: 3300. Records go back to 1967. Alumni records maintained here; call 864-503-5235. Degrees granted: Associate; Bachelors; Masters. Attendance and degree information available by phone, fax, mail. Transcript records are housed at University of South Carolina, Registrar, Columbia, SC, 29208.

University of South Carolina - Sumter, Registrar, 200 Miller Rd, Sumter, SC 29150, 803-775-6341 (Fax: 803-775-3319) 8:30AM-5PM. www.uscsu.sc.edu/. Enrollment: 1200. Alumni records maintained here; call 803-775-6341. Degrees granted: Associate. Attendance and degree information available by phone, fax, mail. Transcript records are housed at University of South Carolina, Registrar, Columbia, SC, 29208.

University of South Carolina - Union, Registrar, PO Drawer 729, Union, SC 29379, 864-429-8728 (Fax: 864-427-3682) Enrollment: 400. Records go back to 1965. Alumni records are maintained here. Degrees granted: Associate. Attendance and degree information available by phone, fax, mail.

Transcript records are housed at University of South Carolina, Registrar, Columbia, SC, 29208.

Voorhees College, Registrar, 1411 Voorhees Rd, PO Box 678, Denmark, SC 29042, www.icusc.org/voorhees/vchome.htm. 803-793-3351 Ext. 7309 (Fax: 803-793-1117) 8AM-5PM. Enrollment: 715. Records go back to 1897. Alumni records maintained here; call 803-793-3351. Degrees granted: Bachelors. Attendance and degree information available by phone, fax, mail. Transcripts available by mail.

Williamsburg Technical College, Registrar, 601 Martin Luther King Jr. Ave, Kingstree, SC 29556-4197, 803-354-2021 Ext. 165 (Fax: 803-354-7269) Noon-8PM M,W,Th,F. www.wil.tec.sc.us Enrollment: 622. Records go back to 1969. Alumni records are maintained here. Degrees granted: Associate. Attendance and degree information available by phone, fax, mail. Transcripts available by written request only.

Winthrop University, Records & Registration, 101 Tillman Hall, Rock Hill, SC 29733, 803-323-2194 (Fax: 803-323-4600) www./LURCH.WINTHROP.EDU. 8:30AM-5PM. Enrollment: 5000. Records go back to 1886. Alumni Records: 304 Tillman Hall, Rock Hill, SC 29733 (Fax: 803-323-2584). Degrees granted: Bachelors; Masters. Attendance and degree information available by phone, fax, mail. Transcripts available by fax, mail. SS# is needed.

Wofford College, Registrar, 429 N Church St, Spartanburg, SC 29303-3663, 864-597-4030, 864-597-4031 (Fax: 864-597-4019) www.wofford.edu. 8:30AM-5PM. Enrollment: 1100. Records go back to 1854. Alumni records maintained here; call 864-597-4202. Degrees granted: Bachelors. Attendance and degree information available by phone, fax, mail. Transcripts available by fax, mail.

York Technical College, Student Records, 452 S Anderson Rd, Rock Hill, SC 29730, 803-327-8002, 803-981-7083 (Fax: 803-327-8059) www.yorktech.com. 8AM-7PM M-Th; 8AM-5PM F. Enrollment: 3600. Records go back to 1964. Degrees granted: Associate. Attendance, degree and transcript information available by fax, mail.

South Dakota

Augustana College, Registrar, 29th St and Summit Ave, Sioux Falls, SD 57197, 605-336-4121 (Fax: 605-336-4450) 8AM-5PM. www.augie.edu Enrollment: 1700. Records go back to 1889. Alumni records maintained here; call 605-336-5230. Degrees granted: Associate; Bachelors; Masters. Attendance and degree information available by phone, fax, mail. Transcripts available by fax, mail.

Black Hills State University, Admissions & Records, 1200 University Ave, USB 9502, Spearfish, SD 57799-9502, 605-642-6011, 605-642-6343 (Fax: 605-642-6214) www.bhsu.edu. 7AM - 4PM. Enrollment: 2700. Records go back to 1885. Alumni records maintained here; call 605-642-6228. Degrees granted: Associate; Bachelors; Masters. Attendance, degree and transcript information available by fax, mail.

Dakota State University, Registrar, 820 N Washington St, Madison, SD 57042, 605-256-5145 (Fax: 605-256-5020) www.dsu.edu. 8AM-5PM. Enrollment: 1300. Records go back to 1881. Alumni records maintained here; call 605-256-5122. Degrees granted: Associate; Bachelors. Attendance and degree information available by phone, fax, mail. Transcripts available by fax, mail.

Dakota Wesleyan University, Registrar, 1200 W University, Campus Box 903, Mitchell, SD 57301, 605-995-2642, 605-995-2647 (Fax: 605-995-2643). 8AM-Noon, 1-5PM. Enrollment: 700. Records go back to 1896. Also have records from **Methodist School of Nursing.** Alumni Records: PO Box 908, Mitchell, SD 57301. Degrees granted: Associate; Bachelors; Masters. Attendance and degree information available by phone, fax, mail. Transcripts available by fax, mail.

Huron University, Coordinator, Academic Services, 333 Ninth St SW, Huron, SD 57350, 605-352-8721 (Fax: 605-352-7421) 8AM-5PM. www.huron.edu. Enrollment: 600. Records go back to 1883. Alumni records are maintained here. Degrees granted: Associate; Bachelors; Masters. Attendance, degree and transcript information available by fax, mail.

Kilian Community College, Registrar, 224 N Phillips Ave, Sioux Falls, SD 57102, 605-336-1711 (Fax: 605-336-2606) 8AM-5PM. Enrollment: 180. Records go back to 1977. Alumni records are maintained here. Degrees granted: Associate. Attendance and degree information available by phone, fax, mail. Transcripts available by mail.

Lake Area Vocational — Technical Institute, Registrar, 230 11th St NE, PO Box 730, Watertown, SD 57201, 605-882-5284 (Fax: 605-882-6299) www.lati.tec.sd.us. 8AM-5PM. Enrollment: 1200. Records go back to 1965. Alumni records are maintained here. Degrees granted: Associate. Attendance and degree information available by phone, fax, mail. Transcripts available by mail.

Mitchell Technical Institute, Registrar, 821 N Capital St, Mitchell, SD 57301, 605-995-3024, 605-995-3023 (Fax: 605-996-3299) 8AM-5PM. www.mti.tec.sd.us. Enrollment: 700. Records go back to 1968. Degrees granted: Associate. Attendance and degree information available by phone, mail. Transcripts available by mail.

Mount Marty College, Registrar, 1105 W Eighth St, Yankton, SD 57078, 605-668-1515 (Fax: 605-668-1607) www.mtmc.edu. 8AM-5PM. Enrollment: 1000. Records go back to 1936. Alumni records maintained here; call 605-668-1526. Degrees granted: Associate; Bachelors; Masters. Certification: Secretarial, Computer Management. Attendance and degree information available by phone, fax, mail. Transcripts available by fax, mail.

National College, Registrar's Office, PO Box 1780, Rapid City, SD 57709, 605-394-4907, 605-394-4925 (Fax: 605-394-4869) www.national.edu. 8AM-5PM. Enrollment: 2000. Records go back to 1950's. Degrees granted: Associate; Bachelors. Attendance and degree information available by phone, fax, mail. Transcripts available by mail.

Nettleton Junior College, Registrar, 100 S Spring Ave, Sioux Falls, SD 57104,. 8AM-9:30PM. Enrollment: 150. Records go back to 1919. Apparently this school is no longer in existence. Degrees granted: Associate.

North American Baptist Seminary, Registrar, 1525 S Grange Ave, Sioux Falls, SD 57105-1599, 605-336-6588 (Fax: 605-335-9090). 8AM-4:30PM. Degrees granted: Masters; Doctorate. Attendance and degree information available by phone, fax, mail. Transcripts available by mail.

Northern State University, Registrar, 1200 S Jay St, Aberdeen, SD 57401, 605-626-2012 (Fax: 605-626-2587) www.northern.edu. 8AM-5PM; 7:30AM-4:30PM Summer. Enrollment: 2700. Records go back to 1902. Alumni records are maintained here. Degrees granted: Associate; Bachelors; Masters. Attendance and degree information available by phone, fax, mail. Transcripts available by fax, mail.

Oglala Lakota College, Registrar, PO Box 490, Kyle, SD 57752, 605-455-2321 Ext. 236 (Fax: 605-455-2787) www.olc.com. 8:30AM-5PM. Enrollment: 1000. Records go back to 1978. Alumni records are maintained here. Degrees granted: Associate; Bachelors; Masters. Special programs- Lakota Studies, 605-455-2321 Ext. 236. Attendance information available by phone, fax, mail. Degree information available by phone, mail. Transcripts available by fax, mail.

Presentation College, Registrar, 1500 N Main St, Aberdeen, SD 57401, 605-229-8426 Ext. 424 (Fax: 605-229-8332) 8AM-4:30PM. www.presentation.edu. Enrollment: 380. Records go back to 1950. Alumni records maintained here; call 605-229-8442. Degrees granted: Associate; Bachelors. Attendance and degree information available by phone, fax, mail. Transcripts available by mail.

Sinte Gleska University, Registrar, PO Box 490, Rosebud, SD 57570, 605-747-2263 (Fax: 605-747-2098). 9AM - 5PM. Enrollment: 780. Records go back to 1972. Degrees granted: Associate; Bachelors; Masters. Attendance and degree information available by phone, fax, mail. Transcripts available by mail. Student request needed for all applications.

Sioux Falls College, Registrar, 1501 S Prairie, Sioux Falls, SD 57105, 605-331-5000 (Fax: 605-361-6615) www.thecoo.edu. Enrollment: 1000. Records go back to 1883. Alumni records are maintained here. Degrees granted: Bachelors. Attendance and degree information available by phone, mail. Transcripts available by mail.

Sisseton-Wahpeton Community College Registrar, PO Box 689 Old Agency, Agency Village, SD 57262, 605-698-3966 (Fax: 605-698-3132) www.swcc.cc.sd.us/cc.htm. 8AM-5PM. Enrollment: 200. Records go back to 1979. Alumni records are maintained here. Degrees granted: Associate. Attendance and degree information available by phone, mail. Transcripts available by mail.

South Dakota School of Mines and Technology, Registrar, 501 E St. Joseph St, Rapid City, SD 57701, 605-394-2400 (Fax: 605-394-1924) www.sdsmt.edu. 7:30AM-4:30PM. Enrollment: 2500. Records go back to 1800's. Alumni records maintained here; call 605-394-2347. Degrees granted: Bachelors; Masters; Doctorate. Attendance and degree information available by phone, fax, mail. Transcripts available by fax, mail.

South Dakota State University, Registrar, Box 2201 University Station, Brookings, SD 57007, 605-688-4121, 605-688-6637 (Fax: 605-688-6384) www.sdstate.edu. 8AM-5PM. Enrollment: 8600. Records go back to 1881. Alumni Records: Thompkins Alumni Assoc., TAC 101, Brookings, SD 57006. Degrees granted: Associate; Bachelors; Masters; Doctorate. Attendance and degree information available by phone, fax, mail. Transcripts available by mail.

Southeast Technical Institute, Registrar, 2301 Career Pl, Sioux Falls, SD 57107, 605-367-7624 (Fax: 605-367-8305). Enrollment: 2600. Records go back to 1968. Degrees granted: Associate. Attendance, degree and transcript information available by fax, mail.

University of Sioux Falls, Registrar, 1101 W 22nd St, Sioux Falls, SD 57105, 605-331-6650 (Fax: 605-331-6615) www.usf.edu. 8AM-5PM. Enrollment: 950. Records go back to 1883. Alumni records maintained here; call 605-331-6608. Degrees granted: Associate; Bachelors; Masters. Attendance and degree information available by phone, fax, mail. Transcripts available by mail.

University of South Dakota, Registrar, 414 E Clark St, Vermillion, SD 57069-2390, 605-677-5301 (Fax: 605-677-6753). 8AM-5PM. Enrollment: 7500. Records go back to 1882. Alumni records maintained here; call 605-677-6715. Degrees granted: Bachelors; Masters; Doctorate. Attendance and degree information available by phone, fax, mail. Transcripts available by fax, mail. Call before sending fax.

Western Dakota Technical Institute, Registrar, 800 Mickelson Dr, Rapid City, SD 57701-4178, www.wdti.tec.sd.us. 605-394-4034, 800-544-8765 (Fax: 605-394-1789) 7:30AM-4PM. Enrollment: 850. Records go back to 1968. Degrees granted: Associate. Special programs- Agriculture: Business: Health: Human Services: Electronics: Mechanics: Construction Trades. Attendance and degree information available by phone, fax, mail. Transcripts available by mail.

Tennessee

Aguinas College, Registrar, 4210 Harding Rd, Nashville, TN 37205, 615-297-7545 (Fax: 615-297-7970) www.aquinas.edu. 8AM-3:40PM. Enrollment: 400. Records go back to 1961. Alumni records are maintained here. Degrees granted: Associate; Bachelors. Attendance and degree information available by phone, fax, mail. Transcripts available by fax, mail.

American Baptist College, Registrar, 1800 Baptist World Ctr, Nashville, TN 37207, 615-228-7877. 8AM-4:30PM. Records go back to 1924. Alumni records are maintained here also. Call 615-228-7877. Degrees granted: Bachelors. Attendance and degree information available by phone, mail. Transcripts available by mail.

Austin Peay State University, Registrar, 601 College St, Clarksville, TN 37044-4448, 931-648-7121, 931-648-7123 (Fax: 931-648-6264) www.apsu.edu. 8AM - 4:30PM. Enrollment: 8000. Records go back to 1927. Alumni records maintained here; call 931-648-7979. Degrees granted: Associate; Bachelors; Masters. Attendance and degree information available by phone, fax, mail. Transcripts available by fax, mail.

Baptist Memorial College of Health Science, Registrar, 1003 Monroe Ave, Memphis, TN 38104, 901-227-4585 (Fax: 901-227-4311) 8AM-5PM. Enrollment: 350. Records go back to 1995. Degrees granted: Associate. Special programs- Nursing: Radiology: Respiratory Therapy. Attendance and degree information available by phone, mail. Transcripts available by mail.

Belmont College
(See Belmont University)

Belmont University, Registrar, 1900 Belmont Blvd, Nashville, TN 37212-3757, 615-460-6619 (Fax: 615-460-5415) 8AM-4:30PM. www.belmont.edu Enrollment: 3000. Records go back to 1955. Alumni records maintained here; call 615-460-5723. Degrees granted: Associate; Bachelors; Masters. Attendance and degree information available by phone, fax, mail. Transcripts available by fax, mail.

Bethel College, Registrar, 325 Cherry Ave, McKenzie, TN 38201, 901-352-4000 (Fax: 901-352-4069) www.bethel-college.edu. 8AM-4:30PM. Enrollment: 550. Records go back to 1842. Alumni records maintained here; call 901-352-4044. Degrees granted: Bachelors; Masters. Attendance and degree information available by phone, fax, mail. Transcripts available by fax, mail.

Bryan College, Registrar, Box 7000, Dayton, TN 37321-7000, 423-775-7237, 423-775-2041 (switchboard) (Fax: 423-775-7330) 8AM-5PM. www.bryan.edu. Enrollment: 450. Records go back to 1930's. Alumni records maintained here; call 423-775-7312. Degrees granted: Associate; Bachelors. Attendance and degree information available by phone, fax, mail. Transcripts available by fax, mail.

Carson-Newman College, Registrar, Box 71985, Jefferson City, TN 37760, 423-471-3240 (Fax: 423-471-3502) 8:30AM - 5PM. www.cn.edu. Enrollment: 2100. Records go back to 1930's. Alumni Records: Box 71988, Jefferson City, TN 37760. Degrees granted: Associate; Bachelors; Masters. Attendance and degree information available by phone, fax, mail. Transcripts available by fax, mail.

Chattanooga State Technical Community College, Registrar, 4501 Amnicola Hwy, Chattanooga, TN 37406, 423-697-4401 (Fax: 423-697-4709) www.CSTCCTN.US. 7:30AM-5:30PM M-Th; 7:30AM-4:30PM F. Enrollment: 8676. Records go back to 1965. Alumni records are maintained here. Degrees granted: Associate. Attendance and degree information available by phone, fax, mail. Transcripts available by fax, mail.

Christian Brothers University, Registrar, 650 East Pkwy S, Memphis, TN 38104, 901-321-3239 (Fax: 901-321-3257) www.cbu.edu. 8AM-4:30PM. Enrollment: 1800. Records go back to 1950's. Alumni records are maintained here. Degrees granted: Bachelors; Masters. Attendance and degree information available by phone, fax, mail. Transcripts available by fax, mail.

Church of God Theological Seminary, Registrar, PO Box 3330, 900 Walker St NE, Cleveland, TN 37311, 423-478-1131 Ext. 7725 www.wingnet.net/~cogseminary/. (Fax: 423-478-7711) 8AM-5PM. Enrollment: 275. Records go back to 1975. Alumni records maintained here; call 423-478-1132 Ext. 7707. Degrees granted: Masters. Attendance and degree information available by phone, fax, mail. Transcripts available by fax, mail..

Cleveland State Community College, Registrar, PO Box 3570, Cleveland, TN 37320-3570, 423-472-7141 Ext. 268 (Fax: 423-478-6255) www.clscc.cc.tn.us. 8AM - 6PM M-Th, 8AM - 4:30PM F. Enrollment: 3600. Records go back to 1967. Alumni records are maintained here. Degrees granted: Associate. Attendance and degree information available by phone, mail. Transcripts available by mail.

Columbia State Community College, Registrar, PO Box 1315, Hwy 412 W, Columbia, TN 38402-1315, 931-540-2545 (Fax: 931-540-2535) www.COSCCTN.US. 7:45PM-4:15PM. Enrollment: 3600. Records go back to 1966. Alumni records maintained here; call 615-540-2514. Degrees granted: Associate. Attendance and degree information available by phone, mail. Transcripts available by mail.

Crichton College, Registrar, PO Box 757830, Memphis, TN 38157-7830, 901-367-9800 (Fax: 901-367-3866). 8AM-5PM. Enrollment: 700. Records go back to 1945. Alumni records are maintained here. Degrees granted: Bachelors. Special programs-Continuing Education. Attendance and degree information available by phone, fax, mail. Transcripts available by mail.

Cumberland University, Registrar, S Greenwood St, Lebanon, TN 37087-3554, 615-444-2562 (Fax: 615-444-2569) 8AM-4:30PM. www.cumberland.edu. Enrollment: 1000. Records go back to 1900. Alumni records maintained here; call 615-444-2562 Ext. 238. Degrees granted: Associate; Bachelors; Masters. Attendance and degree information available by phone, fax, mail. Transcripts available by mail.

David Lipscomb University, Registrar, 3901 Granny White Pike, Nashville, TN 37204-3951, 615-269-1000 (Fax: 615-269-1808) 7:45AM-4:30PM. www.dlu.edu. Degrees granted: Bachelors; Masters. Attendance and degree information available by phone, fax, mail. Transcripts available by fax, mail. Student must sign prior form agreeing to allow 3rd party to receive enrollment info.

Draughons Junior College (Branch Campus), Registrar, 1860 Wilma Rudolph Blvd, Clarksville, TN 37040, 931-552-7600 (Fax: 931-552-3624). 7:30AM - 4:30PM. Enrollment: 400. Records go back to 1954. Degrees granted: Associate. Attendance and degree information available by phone, fax, mail. Transcripts available by fax, mail.

Draughons Junior College, Registrar, Plus Park at Pavilion Blvd, Nashville, TN 37217, 615-361-7555 (Fax: 615-367-2736) 8AM-6PM M-Th; 8AM-2PM F. Enrollment: 300. Records go back to 1940's. Degrees granted: Associate. Attendance and degree information available by phone, fax, mail. Transcripts available by mail.

Dyersburg State Community College, Admissions & Records, 1510 Lake Rd, Dyersburg, TN 38024, 901-286-3330 (Fax: 901-286-3325) www.dscc.cc.tn.us. 8AM-4:30PM. Enrollment: 2000. Records go back to 1969. Alumni records maintained here; call 901-286-3247. Degrees granted: Associate. Attendance and degree information available by phone, fax, mail. Transcripts available by fax, mail.

East Tennessee State University, Registrar, PO Box 70561, Johnson City, TN 37614-0561, 423-439-4230 (Fax:' 423-439-6604) www.etsu.edu. 8AM - 4:30PM. Enrollment: 11500. Records go back to 1911. Alumni Records: ETSU Alumni Assoc., Box 70709, Johnson City, TN 37614. Degrees granted: Associate; Bachelors; Masters; Doctorate. Certification: Respiratory Therapy, Surgical Technician, Dental Assistant. Attendance and degree information available by phone, fax, mail. Transcripts available by fax, mail.

Emmanuel School of Religion, Registrar, One Walker Dr, Johnson City, TN 37601, 423-461-1520 (Fax: 423-926-6198)

www.esr.educ. 8AM-5PM Winter; 8AM-4PM Summer. Records go back to 1965. Alumni records are maintained here. Degrees granted: Masters; Doctorate. Attendance and degree information available by phone, fax, mail. Transcripts available by fax, mail.

Fisk University, Registrar, 1000 17th Ave N, Nashville, TN 37208-3051, 615-329-8587 (Fax: 615-329-8802) www.fisk.edu. 9AM-5PM. Degrees granted: Bachelors; Masters. Attendance and degree information available by phone, fax, mail. Transcripts available by fax, mail.

Free Will Baptist Bible College, Registrar, PO Box 50117, Nashville, TN 37205, 615-383-1340, 615-383-1346 Ext. 5233 (Fax: 615-269-6028). 8AM-4:30PM. Records go back to 1942. Alumni Records: 3606 West End Ave, Nashville, TN 37205. Degrees granted: Associate. Certification: Teacher Education. Special programs- Sports Medicine. Attendance and degree information available by phone, fax, mail. Transcripts available by fax, mail.

Freed—Hardeman University, Registrar, 158 E Main St, Henderson, TN 38340-2399, 901-989-6648, 901-989-6649 (Fax: 901-989-6650) www.fhu.edu. 8AM-5PM. Enrollment: 1500. Records go back to 1900's. Alumni records maintained here; call 901-989-6022. Degrees granted: Bachelors; Masters. Attendance and degree information available by phone, fax, mail. Transcripts available by fax, mail.

Fugazzi College (Branch), Registrar, 5042 Lindbar Dr, Nashville, TN 37211, 615-333-3344 (Fax: 615-333-3429). 8AM-5PM. Enrollment: 160. Records go back to 1989. Degrees granted: Associate. Attendance and degree information available by phone, fax, mail. Transcripts available by fax, mail.

Harding University Graduate School of Religion, Registrar, 1000 Cherry Rd, Memphis, TN 38117, 901-761-1353 (Fax: 901-761-1358) www.harding.edu. 8AM-5PM. Enrollment: 200. Records go back to 1958. Alumni records are maintained here. Degrees granted: Masters; Doctorate. Attendance and degree information available by phone, fax, mail. Transcripts available by fax, mail.

Hiwassee College, Registrar, HC Box 646, 225 Hiwassee College Dr, Madisonville, TN 37354, 423-442-2001 Ext. 215 (Fax: 423-442-3520) www.hiwassee.edu. 8AM-5PM. Records go back to 1849. Alumni records maintained here; call 423-442-2091. Degrees granted: Associate. Attendance and degree information available by phone, fax, mail. Transcripts available by fax, mail.

ITT Technical Institute, Registrar, 10208 Technology Dr, Knoxville, TN 37932, 423-671-2800 (Fax: 423-671-2811). 8AM-5PM. Records go back to 1988. Alumni Records: ITT Technical Institute, 9511 Angola Ct, Indianapolis, IN 46268. Degrees granted: Associate; Bachelors. Attendance and degree information available by phone, fax, mail. Transcripts available by fax, mail.

ITT Technical Institute, Registrar, 441 Donelson Pike, Nashville, TN 37214-8029, 615-889-8700 (Fax: 615-872-7209) 8AM-5PM. Enrollment: 350. Records go back to 1985. Alumni records maintained here; call 317-594-4274. Degrees granted: Associate; Bachelors. Attendance and degree information available by phone, fax, mail. Transcripts available by fax, mail.

Jackson State Community College, Records Office, 2046 North Pkwy, Jackson, TN 38301-3797, 901-425-2654 (Fax: 901-

425-2653) www.jscc.cc.tn.us. 8AM-4:30PM. Enrollment: 3500. Records go back to 1967. Degrees granted: Associate. Attendance and degree information available by phone, fax, mail. Transcripts available by mail.

John A. Gupton College, Registrar, 1616 Church St, Nashville, TN 37203, 615-327-3927 (Fax: 615-321-4518) 8:30AM-4:30PM. www.guptoncollege.com. Enrollment: 75. Records go back to 1946. Degrees granted: Associate. Attendance and degree information available by phone, fax, mail. Transcripts available by mail.

Johnson Bible College, Registrar, 7900 Johnson Dr, Knoxville, TN 37998, 423-579-2302, 423-579-2230 (Fax: 423-579-2337) www.jbc.edu. 8AM-5PM. Enrollment: 450. Records go back to 1893. Alumni records maintained here; call 423-579-2353. Degrees granted: Associate; Bachelors; Masters. Attendance and degree information available by phone, mail. Transcripts available by mail.

King College, Registrar, 1350 King College Rd, Bristol, TN 37620, 423-652-4739 (Fax: 423-968-4456) www.king.edu. 8AM-5PM. Enrollment: 600. Records go back to 1800's. Alumni records are maintained here also. Call 423-652-4717. Degrees granted: Bachelors. Attendance and degree information available by phone, fax, mail. Transcripts available by mail.

Knoxville Business College, Registrar, 720 N Fifth Ave, Knoxville, TN 37917, 423-524-3043 Ext. 45 (Fax: 423-637-1027). 8AM-9:30PM. Records go back to 1882. Degrees granted: Associate. Attendance and degree information available by phone, fax, mail. Transcripts available by mail.

Lambuth College
(See Lambuth University)

Lambuth University, Registrar, 705 Lambuth Blvd, Jackson, TN 38301, 901-425-3207, 901-425-3208 (Fax: 901-988-4600) www.lambuth.edu. 8:30AM - 4:30PM. Enrollment: 1000. Records go back to 1920's. Alumni records maintained here; call 901-425-3465. Degrees granted: Bachelors. Attendance and degree information available by phone, fax, mail. Transcripts available by fax, mail.

Lane College, Registrar, 545 Lane Ave, Jackson, TN 38301-4598, 901-426-7600 (Fax: 901-426-7594) www.lane-college.edu. 8AM-5PM. Enrollment: 626. Records go back to 1882. Alumni records maintained here; call 901-426-7523. Degrees granted: Bachelors. Attendance and degree information available by phone, mail. Transcripts available by mail.

LeMoyne - Owen College, Registrar, 807 Walker Ave, Memphis, TN 38126, 901-942-7321 (Fax: 901-942-6209) www.lemoyne-owen.edu. 8:30AM - 4:30PM. Enrollment: 1500. Records go back to 1915. Alumni records are maintained here. Degrees granted: Bachelors; Masters. Attendance and degree information available by phone, fax, mail. Transcripts available by fax, mail.

Lee University, Registrar, PO Box 3450, Cleveland, TN 37320-3450, 423-614-8200 (Fax: 423-614-8016) www.chattanooga.net. 9AM-Noon; 1-5PM. Enrollment: 2800. Records go back to 1947. Alumni records are maintained here. Degrees granted: Bachelors; Masters. Attendance and degree information available by phone, fax, mail. Transcripts available by fax, mail.

Lincoln Memorial University, Registrar, Cumberland Gap Pkwy, Harrogate, TN 37752-0901, 423-869-6212, 423-869-3611 (Fax: 423-869-6387). 8AM - 4PM. Enrollment: 2000. Records go back to 1915. Alumni records are maintained here. Degrees granted: Associate; Bachelors; Masters; Ed.S. Attendance and degree information available by phone, fax, mail. Transcripts available by mail.

Martin Methodist College, Registrar, 433 W Madison St, Pulaski, TN 38478, 931-363-9809 (Fax: 931-363-9818) www.usit.net. 8AM-4:30PM. Enrollment: 500. Records go back to 1870. Alumni records maintained here; call 931-363-7456. Degrees granted: Bachelors. Attendance and degree information available by phone, mail. Transcripts available by mail.

Maryville College, Registrar, 502 E Lamar Alexander Pkwy, Maryville, TN 37804, 423-981-8212, 423-981-8211 (Fax: 423-981-8010 or 423-981-8070). 8AM-5PM. Enrollment: 900. Records go back to 1819. Alumni records maintained here; call 423-981-8199. Degrees granted: Bachelors. Attendance and degree information available by phone, fax, mail. Transcripts available by fax, mail.

Meharry Medical College, Admissions & Records, 1005 D.B. Todd Blvd, Nashville, TN 37208, 615-327-6223, 615-327-6520 (Fax: 615-327-6228) 8:30AM-5PM. Enrollment: 867. Records go back to 1897. Alumni records are maintained. Call 615-327-6266. Special programs- School of Dentistry, 615-327-6182. Attendance and degree information available by phone, fax, mail. Transcripts available by mail.

Memphis College of Art, Registrar, 1930 Poplar Ave, Overton Park, Memphis, TN 38104, 901-726-4085 Ext. 29 (Fax: 901-726-9371). 8AM - 5PM. Enrollment: 250. Records go back to 1936. Alumni records are maintained here. Degrees granted: Bachelors; Masters. Attendance, degree and transcript information available by fax, mail.

Memphis Theological Seminary, Registrar, 168 East Pkwy S, Memphis, TN 38104, 901-458-8232 (Fax: 901-452-4051). Enrollment: 282. Records go back to 1970. Alumni records are maintained here. Degrees granted: Masters; Doctorate. Attendance and degree information available by phone, fax, mail. Transcripts available by fax, mail.

Mid-America Baptist Theological Seminary, Registrar's Office, 2216 Germantown Rd South, Germantown, TN 38138, 901-751-8453 (Fax: 901-751-8454). 8AM - 4:30PM. Records go back to 1971. Alumni records are maintained here. Degrees granted: Associate; Masters; Doctorate. Attendance and degree information available by phone, fax, mail. Transcripts available by fax, mail.

Mid-South Bible College
(See Crichton College)

Middle Tennessee State University, Registrar, Murfreesboro, TN 37132, 615-898-2600 (Fax: 615-898-5538) www.mtsu.edu. 8AM -4:30PM. Enrollment: 18400. Records go back to 1911. Alumni records maintained here; call 615-898-2922. Degrees granted: Bachelors; Masters; Doctorate. Attendance and degree information available by phone, mail. Transcripts available by mail.

Milligan College, Registrar, PO Box 52, Milligan College, TN 37682, 423-461-8788, 423-461-8729 www.milligan.milligan-college.tn.us. (Fax: 423-461-8716) 8AM-Noon, 1-5PM. Enrollment: 866. Records go back to 1913. Alumni records maintained here; call 423-461-8718. Degrees granted:

Associate; Bachelors; Masters. Attendance and degree information available by phone, fax, mail. Transcripts available by fax, mail.

Mississippi Industrial College
(See Lane College)

Motlow State Community College, Admissions & Records, PO Box 88100, Tullahoma, TN 37388-8100, 931-393-1500, 931-393-1520 (Fax: 931-393-1681) 8AM-4:30PM. www.mscc.cc.tn.us. Enrollment: 3200. Records go back to 1969. Alumni records maintained here; call 931-393-1690. Degrees granted: Associate. Attendance and degree information available by phone, fax, mail. Transcripts available by fax, mail.

Nashville State Technical Institute, Registrar, 120 White Bridge Rd, Nashville, TN 37209-4515, 615-353-3216 (Fax: 615-353-3202) www.nsti.tec.tn.us. 8AM-4:30PM. Enrollment: 7400. Records go back to 1970. Alumni records are maintained here. Degrees granted: Associate. Attendance and degree information available by phone, fax, mail. Transcripts available by fax, mail.

Northeast State Technical Community College, Registrar, PO Box 246, 2425 Hwy 75, Blountville, TN 37617-0246, 423-323-3191 www.nstcctn.us (Fax: 423-323-3083/0215) Degrees granted: Associate. Attendance and degree information available by phone, fax, mail. Transcripts available by mail.

O'More College of Design, Registrar, 423 S Margin St, PO Box 908, Franklin, TN 37065, 615-794-4254 (Fax: 615-790-1662). 8AM-4:30PM. Records go back to 1970. Alumni records are maintained here. Degrees granted: Bachelors. Attendance and degree information available by phone, mail. Transcripts available by mail.

Pellissippi State Technical Community College, Registrar, 10915 Hardin Valley Rd, PO Box 22990, Knoxville, TN 37933-0990, www.pstccctn.us. 423-694-6632, 423-694-6564 (Fax: 423-539-7016) Enrollment: 8000. Records go back to 1974. Alumni records are maintained here. Degrees granted: Associate. Special programs- Continuing Education, 423-694-6587. Attendance and degree information available by phone, fax, mail. Transcripts available by fax, mail. Fax inquiry available to other colleges only.

Rhodes College, Registrar, 2000 North Pkwy, Memphis, TN 38112, 901-843-3885 (Fax: 901-843-3576) www.rhodes.edu. 8:30AM-3:30PM. Enrollment: 1430. Records go back to 1848. Alumni records maintained here; call 901-843-3845. Degrees granted: Bachelors; Masters. Attendance and degree information available by phone, fax, mail. Transcripts available by fax, mail.

Roane State Community College, Registrar, Rte 8 Box 69, Patton Lane, Harriman, TN 37748, 423-882-4523 (Fax: 423-882-4562). 8:30AM-5PM. Records go back to 1971. Alumni records are maintained here. Degrees granted: Associate. Attendance and degree information available by phone, fax, mail. Transcripts available by fax, mail.

Scarritt Bennett Center, Alumni/AE Dept, 1008 19 Ave S, Nashville, TN 37212, 615-340-7500, 615-340-7486 (Fax: 615-340-7463). Records go back to 1900. **Scarritt College** and **Scarritt Graduate School** closed in 1988; transcripts available here. Alumni records are maintained here. Degrees granted: Bachelors; Masters; Diploma. School will not confirm attendance or degree information. Transcripts available by fax, mail.

Shelby State Community College, Registrar, PO Box 40568, Memphis, TN 38174-0568, 901-544-5931, 901-544-5681 (Fax: 901-544-5630) www.sscctn.us. 8AM-7PM M-Th; 8AM-4:30PM F. Enrollment: 6361. Records go back to 1992. Alumni Records: Alumni Assoc., 1256 Union Ave, Memphis, TN 38104. Degrees granted: Associate. Attendance and degree information available by phone, fax, mail. Transcripts available by mail.

Southern Adventist University, Registrar, PO Box 370, Collegedale, TN 37315-0370, 423-238-2111, 423-238-2897 (Fax: 423-238-3003) www.southern.edu. 8AM-Noon, 1-5PM. Enrollment: 1695. Records go back to 1892. Formerly **Southern College of Seventh Day Adventists**. Alumni records are maintained here. Degrees granted: Associate; Bachelors; Masters. Certification: Auto Body and Auto Mechanics, M.S. Ed. Attendance and degree information available by phone, fax, mail. Transcripts available by fax, mail.

Southern College of Optometry, Registrar, 1245 Madison Ave, Memphis, TN 38104, 901-722-3228, 901-722-3200 (Fax: 901-722-3279) www.sco.edu. 8:30AM-4:30PM. Enrollment: 480. Records go back to 1932. Alumni records maintained here; call 901-722-3217. Degrees granted: Doctorate. Special programs- Optometry. Attendance and degree information available by phone, fax, mail. Transcripts available by fax, mail.

State Technical Institute at Knoxville
(See Pellissippi State Technical Com. College)

State Technical Institute at Memphis, Records Office, 5983 Macon Cove, Memphis, TN 38134-7693, www.stim.tec.tn.us 901-383-4190, 901-383-4194 (Fax: 901-383-4473) 8AM-7PM M-Th; 8AM-4:30PM F. Enrollment: 10000. Records go back to 1976. Alumni records are maintained here. Degrees granted: Associate. Attendance and degree information available by phone, fax, mail. Transcripts available by fax, mail.

Tennessee Institute of Electronics, Registrar, 3203 Tazewell Pike, Knoxville, TN 37918, 423-688-9422 (Fax: 423-688-2419) www.tie1.com. Enrollment: 200. Records go back to 1947. Degrees granted: Associate. Attendance and degree information available by phone, fax, mail. Transcripts available by fax, mail.

Tennessee State University, Registrar's Office, 3500 John Merritt Blvd, Nashville, TN 37209-1561, 615-963-5131 (Fax: 615-963-5108) www.tnstate.edu. 8AM-4:30pm. Records go back to 1912. Alumni records maintained here; call 615-963-5880. Degrees granted: Associate; Bachelors; Masters; Doctorate. Attendance and degree information available by phone, fax, mail. Transcripts available by mail.

Tennessee Technological University, Registrar, Office of Records, Box 5097, Cookeville, TN 38505, 931-372-3317, 931-372-3505 (Fax: 615-372-6111) www.tntech.edu. 8AM-4:30PM. Enrollment: 8000. Records go back to 1915. Alumni Records: Box 5157, Cookeville, TN 38505 (Fax: 615-372-6365). Degrees granted: Associate; Bachelors; Masters; Doctorate.

Attendance and degree information available by phone, fax, mail. Transcripts available by fax, mail.

Tennessee Temple University, Registrar, 1815 Union Ave, Chattanooga, TN 37404, 423-493-4100 Ext. 4215 (Fax: 423-493-4497) www.tntemple.edu. Enrollment: 600. Records go back to 1946. Alumni records maintained here; call 423-493-4464. Degrees granted: Associate; Bachelors; Masters. Attendance and degree information available by phone, fax, mail. Transcripts available by fax, mail.

Tennessee Wesleyan College, Registrar, PO Box 40, Athens, TN 37371, 423-745-7504 Ext. 5214 (Fax: 423-744-9968). 8:30AM-4:30PM. Enrollment: 756. Records go back to 1857. Alumni records maintained here; call 423-745-7504 Ext. 5202. Degrees granted: Bachelors. Attendance and degree information available by phone, fax, mail. Transcripts available by fax, mail.

Trevecca Nazarene University, Registrar, 333 Murfreesboro Rd, Nashville, TN 37210, 615-248-1267, 615-248-1268 (Fax: 615-248-7799) www.trevecca.edu. 8AM-4:30PM. Enrollment:1516. Alumni records maintained here; call 615-248-1320. Degrees granted: Associate; Bachelors; Masters. Attendance information available by phone. Degree information available by phone, fax, mail. Transcripts available by fax, mail.

Tri-Cities State Technical Institute
(See Northeast State Technical Community College)

Tusculum College, Registrar, PO Box 5050, Greeneville, TN 37743, 423-636-7300 (Fax: 423-638-5181). 8AM - 5PM. Enrollment: 1500. Records go back to 1900. Alumni records are maintained here. Degrees granted: Bachelors; Masters. Attendance and degree information available by phone, fax, mail. Transcripts available by fax, mail.

Union University, Academic Center, 10 Union University Dr, Jackson, TN 38305, 901-661-5040 (Fax: 901-661-5187) www.uu.edu. 8AM-5PM. Enrollment: 2200. Records go back to 1925. Alumni records maintained here; call 901-661-5208. Degrees granted: Associate; Bachelors; Masters. Attendance and degree information available by phone, fax, mail. Transcripts available by fax, mail.

University of Memphis, Office of the Registrar, Campus Box 526615, Memphis, TN 38152-6615, www.memphis.edu 901-678-3927, 901-678-2671 (Fax: 901-678-3249) Enrollment: 19000. Records go back to 1912. Alumni Records: Alumni Assoc., Alumni Center, Memphis, TN 38152. Degrees granted: Bachelors; Masters; Doctorate; JD. Attendance and degree information available by phone, fax, mail. Transcripts available by fax, mail.

University of Tennessee at Chattanooga Registrar, 615 McCallie Ave, Chattanooga, TN 37403-2598, 423-755-4416 (Fax: 423-785-2172) www.admin.utc.edu. 8AM-5PM. Enrollment: 8300. Alumni records are maintained here. Degrees granted: Bachelors; Masters. Attendance information available by phone, fax, mail. Degree information available by phone, fax, mail. Transcripts available by mail.

University of Tennessee at Martin, Registrar, University St, Martin, TN 38238, 901-587-7049, 901-587-7050 (Fax: 901-587-7048) www.utm.edu. 8AM - 5PM. Enrollment: 5800. Records go back to 1927. Alumni records maintained here; call 901-587-7610. Degrees granted: Bachelors; Masters. Attendance and degree information available by phone, fax, mail. Transcripts available by fax, mail.

University of Tennessee, Knoxville, Registrar, 209 Student Services Bldg, Knoxville, TN 37796-0200, 423-974-2101 (Fax: 423-974-6341) www.getgrades.com. 8AM-5PM. Records go back to 1880. Alumni records are maintained here. Degrees granted: Bachelors; Masters; Doctorate. Attendance and degree information available by phone, fax, mail. Transcripts available by mail.

University of Tennessee, Memphis, Office of Enrollment Services, 119 Randolph Hall, Memphis, TN 38163, 901-448-5560, 901-448-5562 (Fax: 901-448-7772) 8AM-5PM. http://utmgopher.utmem.edu/utm.html. Enrollment: 2080. Records go back to 1912. Alumni records are maintained here. Degrees granted: Bachelors; Masters; Doctorate. Attendance and degree information available by phone, fax, mail. Transcripts available by fax, mail.

University of the South, Registrar, 735 University Ave, Sewanee, TN 37375-1000, 931-598-1314, 931-598-1731 (Fax: 931-598-1145). 8AM-4:30PM. Records go back to 1858. Alumni records maintained here; call 931-598-1402. Degrees granted: Bachelors; Masters; Doctorate. Attendance, degree and transcript information available by mail. Transcripts available by mail.

Vanderbilt University, Registrar, 242 Alexander Hall, Nashville, TN 37240, 615-322-7701 (Fax: 615-343-7709) 8AM-5PM. www.vanderbilt.edu Enrollment: 10000. Records go back to 1875. Alumni records maintained here; call 615-322-4219. Degrees granted: Bachelors; Masters; Doctorate. Attendance and degree information available by phone, fax, mail. Transcripts available by fax, mail.

Volunteer State Community College, Registrar, 1480 Nashville Pike, Gallatin, TN 37066, 615-452-8600 Ext. 3461 (Fax: 615-230-3645). Enrollment: 6000. Records go back to 1971. Alumni records are maintained here. Degrees granted: Associate. Attendance and degree information available by phone, fax, mail. Transcripts available by fax, mail.

Walters State Community College, Registrar, 500 S Davy Crockett Pkwy, Morristown, TN 37813-6899, 423-585-0828, 423-585-2600 (Fax: 423-585-2631) 8AM-4:30PM. www.wscc.cc.tn.us. Enrollment: 5800. Records go back to 1970. Alumni records are maintained here. Degrees granted: Associate. Attendance and degree information available by phone, fax, mail. Transcripts available by fax, mail.

Texas

Abilene Christian University, Registrar, ACU Station Box 7940, Abilene, TX 79699, 915-674-2235, 915-674-2236 (Fax: 915-674-2238) www.acu.edu/. 8AM - Noon, 1-5PM. Enrollment: 4500. Records go back to 1906. Alumni Records: ACU Box 29131, Abilene, TX 79699 (Fax: 915-674-6789). Degrees granted: Bachelors; Masters; Doctorate. Attendance and degree information available by phone, fax, mail. Transcripts available by fax, mail.

Abilene Intercollegiate School of Nursing, Registrar, 2149 Hickory, Abilene, TX 79601, 915-672-2441 (Fax: 915-672-5026) www.inthenet.com/aisn.htm. 8AM-5PM. Enrollment: 150. Records go back to 1975. Alumni records maintained here; call 915-672-2441. Degrees granted: Bachelors; Masters. Attendance and degree information available by phone, fax, mail. Transcripts available by mail.

Alvin Community College, Director, A&R, 3110 Mustang Rd, Alvin, TX 77511-4898, 281-388-4616, 281-388-4615 (Fax: 281-388-4929) www.alvin.cc.tx.us. 8AM-5PM. Enrollment: 3800. Records go back to 1949. Alumni records maintained here; call 281-388-4615. Degrees granted: Associate. Attendance, degree and transcript information available by phone, fax, mail. Phone request accepted when from another institution.

Amarillo College, Registrar, PO Box 447, Amarillo, TX 79178, 806-371-5030 (Fax: 806-371-5066) www.actx.edu. 8AM-4:30PM. Enrollment: 6000. Records go back to 1929. Alumni records maintained here; call 806-371-5000. Degrees granted: Associate. Attendance and degree information available by phone, fax, mail. Transcripts available by fax, mail.

Amber University, Registrar, 1700 Eastgate Dr, Garland, TX 75041, 972-279-6511 (Fax: 972-279-9773). 8AM-5PM. Enrollment: 1300. Records go back to 1982. Alumni records are maintained here. Degrees granted: Bachelors; Masters. Attendance and degree information available by mail. Transcripts available by mail.

American Technological University
(See University of Central Texas)

Angelina College, Registrar, PO Box 1768, Lufkin, TX 75902, 409-639-1301 (Fax: 409-639-4299). 8AM - 9PM M-Th. Enrollment: 4000. Records go back to 1968. Alumni records are maintained here. Degrees granted: Associate. Attendance and degree information available by phone, fax, mail. Transcripts available by fax, mail.

Angelo State University, Registrar, 2601 West Ave N, San Angelo, TX 76909, 915-942-2043 (Fax: 915-942-2078) 8AM - 5PM. www.angelo.edu Enrollment: 6200. Records go back to 1928. Alumni records maintained here; call 915-942-2122. Degrees granted: Associate; Bachelors; Masters. Certification: Teaching. Attendance and degree information available by phone, mail. Transcripts available by mail.

Arlington Baptist College, Registrar, 3001 W Division St, Arlington, TX 76012-3425, 817-461-8741 (Fax: 817-274-1138). 8AM-4PM. Enrollment: 200. Records go back to 1939. Alumni records are maintained here. Degrees granted: Bachelors. Certification: Bible. Special programs- Distance Education. Attendance and degree information available

by phone, fax, mail. Transcripts available by fax, mail.

Art Institute of Dallas, Registrar, 2 N Park E, 8080 Park Ln, Dallas, TX 75231, 214-692-8080, 800-275-4243 (Fax: 214-692-6541). Enrollment: 1200. Records go back to 1986. Alumni records are maintained here. Degrees granted: Associate. Attendance and degree information available by phone, fax, mail. Transcripts available by fax, mail.

Art Institute of Houston, Registrar, 1900 Yorktown, Houston, TX 77056, 713-623-2040 X750, 800-275-4244 (Fax: 713-966-2701) www.aii.edu. Enrollment: 1427. Records go back to 1978. Alumni records are maintained here. Degrees granted: Associate. Attendance and degree information available by phone, mail. Transcripts available by mail.

Austin College, Registrar, 900 N Grand Ave, Sherman, TX 75090-4440, 903-813-2371 (Fax: 903-813-2378) www.austinc.edu. 8:30AM-5PM. Enrollment: 1100. Records go back to 1919. Alumni records are maintained here. Degrees granted: Bachelors; Masters. Attendance and degree information available by phone, fax, mail. Transcripts available by fax, mail.

Austin Community College, Registrar, 5930 Middle Fiskville Rd, Austin, TX 78752-4390, www.austin.cc.tx.us. 512-223-7000 (Fax: 512-483-7791) 8AM - 4:30PM. Enrollment: 15,000. Records go back to 1900. Alumni records are maintained here. Degrees granted: Associate. Attendance and degree information available by phone, fax, mail. Transcripts available by fax, mail.

Austin Presbyterian Theological Seminary Registrar, 100 E 27th St, Austin, TX 78705-5797, 512-472-6736, 800-777-6127 (Fax: 512-479-0738). 8:30AM - 5PM. Enrollment: 330. Records go back to 1902. Alumni records are maintained here. Degrees granted: Masters; Doctorate. Attendance and degree information available by phone, fax, mail. Transcripts available by mail.

Baptist Missionary Association Theological Seminary, Registrar, 1530 E Pine St, Jacksonville, TX 75766, 903-586-2501 (Fax: 903-586-0378) 9AM - 4PM. www.geocities.com/athens/acropolis/3386. Enrollment: 60. Records go back to 1965. Degrees granted: Associate; Bachelors; Masters. Attendance and degree information available by phone, fax, mail. Transcripts available by fax, mail.

Baylor College of Dentistry, Registrar, PO Box 660677, Dallas, TX 75246-0677, 214-828-8230 (Fax: 214-828-8346) www.tambcd.edu. 8AM-4:30PM. Records go back to 1905. Alumni records are maintained here. Degrees granted: Doctorate. Attendance and degree information available by phone, mail. Transcripts available by mail.

Baylor College of Medicine, Registrar, One Baylor Plaza, Houston, TX 77030, 713-798-7766, 713-798-4600 (Fax: 713-798-7951) 8AM-5PM. www.bcm.tmc.edu. Enrollment: 1145. Records go back to 1900. Alumni records maintained here; call 713-798-4054. Degrees granted: Masters; Doctorate. Attendance and degree information available by phone, fax, mail. Transcripts available by mail.

Baylor University, Registrar, PO Box 97068, Waco, TX 76798, 254-755-1181 (Fax:

254-755-2233) www.baylor.edu. 8AM - 5PM. Enrollment: 12800. Records go back to 1900. Alumni records maintained here; call 254-755-1121. Degrees granted: Bachelors; Masters; Doctorate. Attendance and degree information available by phone, fax, mail. Transcripts available by fax, mail.

Bee County College
(See Coastal Bend College)

Bishop College
(See Paul Quinn College)

Blinn College, Admissions & Records, 902 College Ave, Brenham, TX 77833, 409-830-4140, 409-830-4152 (Fax: 409-830-4110) 8AM-5PM. www.blinncol.edu. Enrollment: 9700. Records go back to 1899. Alumni records maintained here; call 409-830-4180. Degrees granted: Associate. Adverse incident record source- 409-830-4190. Attendance and degree information available by phone, fax, mail. Transcripts available by mail.

Brazosport College, Registrar, 500 College Dr, Lake Jackson, TX 77566, 409-265-6131 X221 www.brazosport.edu. 8AM-5PM. Enrollment: 1860. Records go back to 1947. Alumni records are maintained here. Degrees granted: Associate. Attendance and degree information available by phone, mail. Transcripts available by mail.

Brookhaven College, Registrar, 3939 Valley View Lane, Farmers Branch, TX 75244-4997, 972-860-4700 (Fax: 972-860-4897) 8AM-4:30PM. www.dcccd.edu/bhc. Enrollment: 7000. Records go back to 1977. Alumni records are maintained here. Degrees granted: Associate. Attendance and degree information available by phone, fax, mail. Transcripts available by fax, mail.

Cedar Valley College, Registrar, 3030 N Dallas Ave, Lancaster, TX 75134, 972-860-8201 (Fax: 972-860-8001). 8AM - 4:30PM. Records go back to 1966. Degrees granted: Associate. Attendance and degree information available by phone, mail. Transcripts available by mail.

Central Texas College, Registrar, PO Box 1800, Killeen, TX 76540-9990, 254-526-1308 (Fax: 254-526-1481). 8AM-5PM. Records go back to 1968. Alumni records are maintained here also. Call 254-526-1306. Degrees granted: Associate. Special programs- Hanau, German, 011-49-6181-95060: Camp Market, Korea, 011-82-32-523-5110. Attendance and degree information available by phone, fax, mail. Transcripts available by fax, mail.

Cisco Junior College, Registrar, Rte 3 Box 3, Cisco, TX 76437, 254-442-2567 (Fax: 254-442-2546) www.cisco.cc.tx.us. 8AM - 4PM. Enrollment: 2550. Records go back to 1920's. Alumni records are maintained here. Degrees granted: Associate. Attendance and degree information available by phone, fax, mail. Transcripts available by fax, mail.

Clarendon College, Registrar, PO Box 968, Clarendon, TX 79226, 806-874-3571 (Fax: 806-874-3201). 8AM - 4:30PM. Enrollment: 850. Records go back to 1925. Alumni records are maintained here. Degrees granted: Associate. Attendance and degree information available by phone, fax, mail. Transcripts available by written request only.

Coastal Bend College, Registrar, 3800 Charco Rd, Beeville, TX 78102, 512-358-3130 (Fax: 512-358-3130) www.bcc.cc.px.us. 8AM-4:30PM. Enrollment: 5500. Records go back to 1967. Alumni records are maintained here. Degrees granted: Associate. Attendance, degree and transcript information available by mail.

College of the Mainland, Admissions Office, 1200 Amburn Rd, Texas City, TX 77591, www.mainland.cc.tx..us/ 409-938-1211 X263, 888-258-8859 (Fax: 409-938-1306) 8AM-5PM. Records go back to 1968. Alumni records are maintained here. Degrees granted: Associate. Attendance and degree information available by phone, fax, mail. Transcripts available by mail.

Collin County Community College, Registrar, 2200 W University Dr, PO Box 8001, McKinney, TX 75070, 972-377-1722, 972-377-1790 (Fax: 972-377-1723). 8AM-5PM M,T,Th,F; 8AM-8PM W. Records go back to 1985. Alumni records are maintained here. Degrees granted: Associate. Attendance and degree information available by phone, fax. Transcripts available by fax, mail.

Commonwealth Institute of Funeral Service, Registrar, 415 Barren Springs Dr, Houston, TX 77090, 713-873-0262 (Fax: 713-873-5232). 8AM - 4PM. Enrollment: 150. Records go back to 1945. Degrees granted: Associate. Attendance and degree information available by phone, mail. Transcripts available by written request only.

Community College of the Air Force (Affiliate), 882 TRSS/TSOE, 939 Missile Rd #1003, Sheppard AFB, TX 76311-2260, 940-676-6640 (Fax: 940-676-4025). 7AM-4PM. Enrollment: 9000. Records go back to 1967. Alumni records are maintained here. Degrees granted: Associate. Certification: Certificate of Training. Attendance and transcript information available by mail. School will not confirm degree information. Degree confirmation obtained from CCAF/RR 130 West Maxwell Blvd, Suite 130 Maxwell AFB AL, 36112-6613.

Concordia Lutheran College, Registrar, 3400 I H 35 N, Austin, TX 78705, 512-452-7661 www.concordia.edu (Fax: 512-459-8517) 8AM-5PM M,T,Th,F; 8AM-6PM W. Enrollment: 700. Records go back to 1926. Alumni records are maintained here. Degrees granted: Associate; Bachelors. Attendance and degree information available by phone, fax, mail. Transcripts available by written request only.

Corpus Christi State University
(See Texas A & M-Corpus Christi)

Criswell College, Enrollment Services, 4010 Gaston Ave, Dallas, TX 75246, www.criswell.edu 214-821-5433 (Fax: 214-818-1310) 8AM-4:30PM. Enrollment: 450. Records go back to 1970. Alumni records are maintained here. Degrees granted: Associate; Bachelors; Masters. Attendance, degree and transcript information available by fax, mail.

Dallas Baptist University, Registrar, 3000 Mountain Creek Pkwy, Dallas, TX 75211-9299, 214-333-5334 (Fax: 214-333-5142) www.dbu.edu. 8AM-6PM M-T; 8AM-5PM W-F; 9AM-1PM 2nd Sat of each month. Enrollment: 3500. Records go back to 1965. Alumni records maintained here; call 214-333-5166. Degrees granted: Associate; Bachelors; Masters; Police Academy. Attendance and degree information available by phone, fax, mail. Transcripts available by mail.

Dallas Christian College, Registrar, 2700 Christian Pkwy, Dallas, TX 75234, 214-241-3371 (Fax: 214-241-8021) www.popi.net/dcc. 8AM-5PM. Enrollment: 282. Records go back to 1950. Alumni records are maintained

here. Degrees granted: Associate; Bachelors. Attendance and degree information available by phone, fax, mail. Transcripts available by mail.

Dallas County Community — Brook Haven College
(See Brook Haven College)

Dallas County Community - El Centro College
(See El Centro College)

Dallas Theological Seminary, Registrar, 3909 Swiss Ave, Dallas, TX 75204, 214-841-3608 (Fax: 214-841-3664) www.dts.edu. 8AM-4:30PM. Enrollment: 1531. Records go back to 1924. Alumni records maintained here; call 214-841-3606. Degrees granted: Masters; Doctorate. Attendance and degree information available by phone, fax, mail. Transcripts available by fax, mail.

DeVry Institute of Technology, Dallas, Registrar, 4801 Regent Blvd, Irving, TX 75063-2440, 214-929-6777 (Fax: 214-929-6778) www.devry-dal.com. 8AM-7PM M,T; 8AM-5PM W-F. Enrollment: 2300. Records go back to 1969. Alumni Records: Alumni Assoc., DeVry Institute of Technology, One Tower Lane, Oakbrook Terrace, IL 60181-4624. Degrees granted: Associate; Bachelors. Attendance and degree information available by phone, mail. Transcripts available by mail.

Del Mar College, Registrar, 101 Baldwin Blvd, Corpus Christi, TX 78404-3897, www.delmar.edu 512-886-1248 (Fax: 512-886-1595) 7:30AM-7:30PM M-Th; 7:30AM-Noon F. Records go back to 1935. Alumni records maintained here; call 512-886-1317. Degrees granted: Associate. Attendance and degree information available by phone, fax, mail. Transcripts available by fax, mail.

East Texas Baptist University, Registrar, 1209 N Grove Ave, Marshall, TX 75670-1498, 903-935-7963 (Fax: 903-938-1705) 8AM-4:30PM. www.etbu.edu/. Enrollment: 1300. Records go back to 1917. Alumni records are maintained here. Degrees granted: Associate; Bachelors; Masters. Attendance and degree information available by phone, fax, mail. Transcripts available by fax, mail.

East Texas State University at Texarkana, Admissions, ETSU-T, 2600 N Robison Rd, PO Box 5518, Texarkana, TX 75505, 903-838-6514 (Fax: 903-832-8890) 8AM-5PM. www.tsu.texarkana.edu. Enrollment: 1184. Records go back to 1971. Alumni records are maintained here. Degrees granted: Bachelors; Masters. Attendance and degree information available by phone, fax, mail. Transcripts available by mail.

Eastfield College, Registrar, 3737 Motley Dr, Mesquite, TX 75150-2099, 972-860-7002, 972-860-7100 www.efc.dccd.edu/. 8AM-7PM M-Th; 8AM-4:30PM F. Enrollment: 8458. Records go back to 1970. Degrees granted: Associate. Attendance, degree and transcript information available by mail.

El Centro College, Registrar, Main and Lamar Sts, Dallas, TX 75202-3604, 214-860-2311 www.BCB5310.DCCCD.ED (Fax: 214-860-2335)- 8AM-7PM. Enrollment: 4800. Records go back to 1966. Alumni records are maintained here. Degrees granted: Associate. Attendance and degree information available by phone, fax, mail. Transcripts available by fax, mail.

El Paso Community College, Registrar, PO Box 20500, El Paso, TX 79998, 915-831-2300 (Fax: 915-931-2161) www.epcc.edu. 8AM-5PM M-F; 8AM-Noon S. Enrollment:

20000. Records go back to 1970. Degrees granted: Associate. Attendance and degree information available by phone, fax, mail. Transcripts available by fax, mail.

Episcopal Theological Seminary of the Southwest, Registrar, PO Box 2247, Austin, TX 78768-2247, 512-472-4133 (Fax: 512-472-3098) www.etss.simplenet.com. 8:15AM-2PM. Enrollment: 65. Records go back to 1955. Alumni records are maintained here. Degrees granted: Masters. Certification: Individual Theological Study; Other: Diploma in Sacred Theology. Attendance and degree information available by phone, fax, mail. Transcripts available by mail.

Fashion and Art Institute of Dallas
(See Art Institute of Dallas)

Frank Phillips College, Registrar, PO Box 5118, Borger, TX 79008-5118, 806-274-5311 (Fax: 806-274-6835). 8AM-5PM. Records go back to 1948. Degrees granted: Associate. Attendance and degree information available by written request only. Transcripts available by fax, mail.

Galveston College, Registrar, 4015 Ave Q, Galveston, TX 77550, 409-763-6551 X234 (Fax: 409-762-9367) www.gc.edu. 8:30AM-7PM. Records go back to 1967. Alumni records are maintained here. Degrees granted: Associate. Attendance and degree information available by phone, fax, mail. Transcripts available by fax, mail.

Grayson County College, Registrar, 6161 Grayson Dr, Denison, TX 75020, 903-463-8650 (Fax: 903-463-5284) www.grayson.edu. 8AM-4PM. Enrollment: 3200. Records go back to 1965. Degrees granted: Associate. Attendance and degree information available by phone, fax, mail. Transcripts available by fax, mail.

Hardin-Simmons University, Registrar, Sandefer Memorial Bldg, Box 16190, Abilene, TX 79698, 915-670-1200, 915-670-1201 (Fax: 915-670-1261) www.hsutx.edu/. 9AM-5PM. Enrollment: 2400. Records go back to 1891. Alumni Records: Box 16102, Abilene, TX 79698 (Fax: 915-670-1574). Degrees granted: Associate; Bachelors; Masters. Attendance and degree information available by phone, fax, mail. Transcripts available by fax, mail.

Henderson County Junior College
(See Trinity Community College)

Hill College, Registrar, PO Box 619, Hillsboro, TX 76645, 254-582-2555 (Fax: 254-582-7591) www.hill-college.cc.tx.us. 8AM - 4PM. Enrollment: 2600. Records go back to 1923. Alumni records are maintained here. Degrees granted: Associate. Attendance and degree information available by phone, fax, mail. Transcripts available by written request only.

Houston Baptist University, Registrar, 7502 Fondren Rd, Houston, TX 77074-3298, 281-649-3000. Alumni records are maintained here. Degrees granted: Bachelors; Masters. Attendance, degree and transcript information available by mail.

Houston Community College (Central College), Registrar, 1300 Holman Ave, PO Box 7849, Houston, TX 77004, 713-523-6000 (Fax: 713-718-6112) www.hccs.cc.tx.us. 8AM-5PM. Enrollment: 23330. Records go back to 1968. Alumni records are maintained here. Degrees granted: Associate. Attendance, degree and transcript information available by mail.

Houston Community College (College Without Walls), Registrar, 4310 Dunlavy St,

Houston, TX 77270, 713-868-0795. Records are located at Houston Community College, (Central College), Registrar, Houston, TX.

Houston Community College (Northeast College), Registrar, 4638 Airline Dr, PO Box 7849, Houston, TX 77270-7849, 713-694-5384. Records are located at Houston Community College, (Central College), Registrar, Houston, TX.

Houston Community College (Southeast College), Registrar, 6815 Rustic St, Houston, TX 77012, 713-641-2725. Records are located at Houston Community College, (Central College), Registrar, Houston, TX.

Houston Community College (Southwest College), Registrar, 5407 Gulfton St, Houston, TX 77081, 713-661-4589. Records are located at Houston Community College, (Central College), Registrar, Houston, TX.

Houston Community College, Registrar, PO Box 7849, Houston, TX 77270-7849, 713-718-5041 (Fax: 713-869-5743) 8AM-4:30PM. www.hccs.cc.tx.us Enrollment: 23330. Records go back to 1971. Alumni records are maintained here. Degrees granted: Associate. Attendance, degree and transcript information available by mail.

Houston Community College System, Registrar, PO Box 7849, Houston, TX 77270, 713-718-2000, 713-718-8500 (Fax: 713-869-5743) www.hccs.cc.tx.us. 8AM-4:30PM. Enrollment: 42000. Records go back to 1971. Alumni records maintained here; call 713-718-8530. Degrees granted: Associate. Attendance, degree and transcript information available by fax, mail.

Houston Graduate School of Theology Registrar, 1311 Holman St., Suite 200, Houston, TX 77004, 713-942-9505 (Fax: 713-942-9506) www.flash.net/~hgst. 8AM-5PM. Enrollment: 100. Records go back to 1986. Alumni records are maintained here. Degrees granted: Masters; Doctorate. Attendance and degree information available by phone, fax, mail. Transcripts available by mail.

Howard College, Admissions Office, 1001 Birdwell Lane, Big Spring, TX 79720, www.hc.cc.tx.us 915-264-5000, 915-264-5105 (Fax: 915-264-5082) 8AM-6PM M-Th; 8AM-3PM F. Enrollment: 2100. Records go back to 1945. Alumni records maintained here; call 915-264-5000. Degrees granted: Associate. Attendance, degree and transcript information available by mail.

Howard Payne University, Registrar, 1000 Fisk Ave, Brownwood, TX 76801, 915-649-8011 (Fax: 915-649-8909). 8AM-5PM. Enrollment: 1480. Records go back to 1889. Alumni records are maintained here. Degrees granted: Bachelors. Attendance and degree information available by phone, fax, mail. Transcripts available by fax, mail.

Huston—Tillotson College, Registrar, 900 Chicon St, Austin, TX 78702, 512-505-3082 (Fax: 512-505-3190). 8:30AM-5:30PM. Enrollment: 620. Records go back to 1800's. Alumni records are maintained here. Degrees granted: Bachelors. Attendance and degree information available by phone, fax, mail. Transcripts available by written request only.

ICI University, Registrar, 6300 N Belt Line Rd, Irving, TX 75063, 972-751-1111 (Fax: 972-714-8185) www.ici.edu. 8AM-4:30PM. Enrollment: 8500. Records go back to 1973. Degrees granted: Associate; Bachelors; Masters. Attendance, degree and transcript information available by written request only.

ITT Technical Institute, Registrar, 2201 Arlington Downs Rd, **Arlington**, TX 76011-6319, 817-640-7100 (Fax: 817-649-8078) www.itt.track-star.com. 8AM-5PM. Enrollment: 400. Records go back to 1963. Alumni Records: 9511 Angola Ct, Indianapolis, IN 46268. Degrees granted: Associate. Attendance, degree and transcript information available by mail.

ITT Technical Institute (Branch of Indianapolis, IN), Registrar, 6330 Hwy 290E #150, **Austin**, TX 78723-9975, 512-467-6800 (Fax: 512-467-6677). 8AM-6PM. Enrollment: 500. Records go back to 1985. Alumni Records: 6330 Hwy 290E, S150, Austin, TX 78723-9975. Degrees granted: Associate. Attendance and degree information available by phone, fax, mail. Transcripts available by fax, mail.

ITT Technical Institute, Registrar, 1640 Eastgate Dr, Suite 100, **Garland**, TX 75041, 972-279-0500 (Fax: 972-613-4523) 8AM-5PM. www.itt.track-star.com Enrollment: 350. Records go back to 1990. Alumni records are maintained here. Degrees granted: Associate. Attendance and degree information available by phone, fax, mail. Transcripts available by fax, mail.

ITT Technical Institute (Branch of Indianapolis, IN), Registrar, 15621 Blue Ash Dr Ste 160, **Houston**, TX 77090-5818, 713-873-0512, 800-879-6486 (Fax: 713-873-0518). 8AM-4:30PM. Enrollment: 400. Records go back to 1970. Alumni Records: ITT Technical Institute, 9511 Angola Ct, Indianapolis, IN 46268. Degrees granted: Associate. Attendance and degree information available by phone, fax, mail. Transcripts available by mail.

ITT Technical Institute, Registrar, 2950 S. Gessner, **Houston**, TX 77063, 713-952-2294 (Fax: 713-952-2393). 8AM-10PM. Enrollment: 550. Records go back to 1986. Alumni Records: 9511 Angola Ct, Indianapolis, IN 46268. Degrees granted: Associate. Attendance and degree information available by phone, fax, mail. Transcripts available by fax, mail.

ITT Technical Institute, Registrar, 4242 Piedras Dr E Ste 100, **San Antonio**, TX 78228-1414, 210-737-1881, 800-880-0570 (Fax: 210-737-0731). 8AM-5PM. Records go back to 1970's. Alumni Records: 9511 Angola Ct, Indianapolis, IN 46268. Degrees granted: Associate. Attendance and degree information available by phone, mail. Transcripts available by mail.

Institute for Christian Studies, Registrar, 1909 University Ave at 20th St, Austin, TX 78705, 512-476-2772 (Fax: 512-476-3919) www/ics/edu. 8AM-5PM. Enrollment: 121. Records go back to 1977. Alumni records maintained here. Degrees granted: Bachelors; Masters; Off-campus graduate degree program through Abilene Christian University. Attendance and degree information available by phone, fax, mail. Transcripts available by mail.

Jacksonville College, Registrar, 105 B.J. Albritton Dr, Jacksonville, TX 75766-4759, 903-586-2518, 903-586-2802 (Fax: 903-586-0743) 8AM-5PM. Enrollment: 350. Records go back to 1899. Alumni records are maintained here. Degrees granted: Associate. Attendance and degree information available by phone, fax, mail. Transcripts available by fax, mail.

Jarvis Christian College, Registrar, PO Box 1470, Hawkins, TX 75765, 903-769-5700 (Fax: 903-769-4842) www.jarvis.edu. 8AM-5PM. Enrollment: 500. Records go back to 1912. Alumni records maintained here; call 903-769-5711. Degrees granted: Bachelors. Attendance and degree information available by phone, fax, mail. Transcripts available by mail.

KD Studio, Registrar, 2600 Stemmons Fwy, Suite 117, Dallas, TX 75207, 214-638-0484 (Fax: 214-630-5140) www.kdstudio.edu. 8AM-6PM. Enrollment: 140. Records go back to 1979. Alumni records are maintained here. Degrees granted: Associate. Attendance and degree information available by mail. Transcripts available by written request only.

Kilgore College, Registrar, 1100 Broadway, Kilgore, TX 75662-3299, 903-984-8531 (Fax: 903-983-8607) www.kilgore.cc.tx.us. 8AM-4:30PM. Enrollment: 4300. Records go back to 1935. Alumni records maintained here; call 903-983-8187. Degrees granted: Associate. Attendance and degree information available by phone, fax, mail. Transcripts available by fax, mail.

Kingwood College, Registrar, 20000 Kingwood Dr, Kingwood, TX 77339, www.nhmccd.cc.tx.us\colleges\kc\. 713-359-1600, 713-359-1614 (Fax: 713-359-0477) 8AM-9:30 PM M-Th;8AM-4:30PM F. Enrollment: 3400. Records go back to 1974. Alumni records are maintained here. Degrees granted: Associate. Attendance and degree information available by phone, fax, mail. Transcripts available by written request only. Telephone queries regarding transcripts are accepted from other learning institutions.

Lamar University at Beaumont, Registrar, 4400 Martin Luther King, Jr. Pkwy Blvd, Beaumont, TX 77710, 409-880-8365, 409-880-8358 (Fax: 409-880-8463) www.lamar.edu. 8AM-5PM. Enrollment: 8414. Records go back to 1923. Alumni records are maintained here. Degrees granted: Bachelors; Masters; Doctorate. Attendance and degree information available by phone, fax, mail. Transcripts available by mail.

Lamar University at Orange, Registrar, 410 W Front St, Orange, TX 77630, 409-883-7750 (Fax: 409-882-3374) 8AM-5PM. www.hal.lamar.edu/orange/. Enrollment: 1500. Records go back to 1984. Alumni records are maintained here. Degrees granted: Associate. Attendance and degree information available by phone, mail. Transcripts available by written request only.

Lamar University at Port Arthur, Registrar, PO Box 310, Port Arthur, TX 77641-0310, www.hal.lamar.edu/portarthur/ 409-983-4921, 800-477-5872 (Fax: 409-984-6000) 8AM-5PM M,T,Th,F, 8AM-6PM W. Enrollment: 2500. Records go back to 1975. Alumni records are maintained here. Degrees granted: Associate. Attendance and degree information available by phone, fax, mail. Transcripts available by written request only.

Laredo Community College, Registrar, W End Washington St, Laredo, TX 78040-4395, 956-721-5109 (Fax: 956-721-5493). 8AM-5PM. Enrollment: 7000. Records go back to 1947. Alumni records maintained here; call 956-721-5461. Degrees granted: Associate. Attendance, degree and transcript information available by phone, fax, mail.

Laredo State University
(See Texas A & M International Univ.)

LeTourneau University, Registrar, PO Box 7001, Longview, TX 75607, 903-233-3450, 903-233-3451 (Fax: 903-233-3411) www.letu.edu. 8AM-5PM. Enrollment: 3900. Records go back to 1946. Alumni records

Don't Hire a Crook!

maintained here; call 903-233-3670. Degrees granted: Associate; Bachelors; Masters. Attendance and degree information available by phone, fax, mail. Transcripts available by mail.

Lee College, Admissions & Records, PO Box 818, Baytown, TX 77522, 713-427-5611 (Fax: 713-425-6831) www.lee.edu. 7:30AM-5:15PM M-Th; 7:30AM - Noon F. Enrollment: 5700. Records go back to 1934. Alumni records are maintained here. Degrees granted: Associate. Attendance and degree information available by phone, mail. Transcripts available by mail. All transcripts must be requested by the student.

Lon Morris College, Registrar, 800 College Ave, Jacksonville, TX 75766, 903-589-4005 (Fax: 903-586-8562) www.lonmorris.edu. 8:30AM-5PM. Enrollment: 350. Records go back to 1900. Alumni records are maintained here. Degrees granted: Associate. Attendance and degree information available by mail.

Lubbock Christian University, Registrar, 5601 19th St, Lubbock, TX 79407-2099, 806-796-8800 X225 (Fax: 806-796-8917) www.lcu.edu. Enrollment: 1200. Records go back to 1957. Alumni records are maintained here also. Call 806-796-8800 X378. Degrees granted: Bachelors; Masters. Attendance and degree information available by phone, fax, mail. Transcripts available by fax, mail.

McLennan Community College, Registrar, 1400 College Dr, Waco, TX 76708, 254-299-8507 (Fax: 254-299-8653) 8AM-7PM M-Th; 8AM-5PM F. www.mcc.cc.tx.us. Enrollment: 5500. Records go back to 1966. Degrees granted: Associate. Attendance, degree and transcript information available by fax, mail.

McMurry University, Registrar, PO Box 338, McMurry Station, Abilene, TX 79697, 915-691-6401 (Fax: 915-691-6599) www.mcm.acu.edu/. 8AM-5PM. Enrollment: 1500. Records go back to 1923. Alumni Records: PO Box 938, Abilene, TX 79697. Degrees granted: Associate; Bachelors. Attendance and degree information available by phone, mail. Transcripts available by written request only from students.

Midland College, Registrar, 3600 N Garfield St, Midland, TX 79705, 915-685-4508 (Fax: 915-685-4714) www.midland.edu. 8AM-4:30PM. Records go back to 1962. Alumni records are maintained here. Degrees granted: Associate. Attendance and degree information available by phone, fax, mail. Transcripts available by mail.

Midwestern State University, Registrar & Admissions, 3410 Taft Blvd, Wichita Falls, TX 76308-2099, 940-397-4321 (Fax: 940-397-4672) www.mwsu.edu. 8AM - 5PM. Enrollment: 5833. Records go back to 1922. Alumni records maintained here; call 940-397-4121. Degrees granted: Associate; Bachelors; Masters. Certification: Teacher Cert. Attendance and degree information available by phone, mail. Transcripts available by fax, mail.

Miss Wade's Fashion Merchandising College, Registrar, PO Box 586343, Dallas Apparel Mart Ste M5120, Dallas, TX 75258, 214-637-3520 (Fax: 214-637-0827). 8AM-4:30PM. Enrollment: 280. Degrees granted: Associate. Attendance and degree information available by phone, fax, mail. Transcripts available by fax, mail.

Mountain View College, Registrar, 4849 W Illinois Ave, Dallas, TX 75211-6599, www.mvc.dccdd.edu · 214-860-8600 (Fax: 214-333-8570) 8AM-8PM M-Th; 8AM-5PM

F. Enrollment: 5500. Records go back to 1965. Degrees granted: Associate. Attendance, degree and transcript information available by fax, mail.

Navarro College, Registrar, 3200 W Seventh Ave, Corsicana, TX 75110, 903-874-6501 (Fax: 903-874-4636) www.nav.cc.tx.us. 8AM-7PM M-Th; 8AM-5PM F. Enrollment: 320. Records go back to 1946. Alumni records are maintained here. Degrees granted: Associate. Attendance and degree information available by phone, fax, mail. Transcripts available by fax.

North Central Texas College, Registrar, 1525 W California St, Gainesville, TX 76240, www.nctc.cc.tx.us. 940-668-4222 (Fax: 940-668-6049) 8AM - 8PM in session. Enrollment: 4000. Records go back to 1924. Alumni records maintained here; call 940-668-4213. Degrees granted: Associate. Attendance and degree information available by phone, fax, mail. Transcripts available by fax, mail.

North Harris College, Registrar, 2700 W. Thorne, Houston, TX 77073, 281-618-5420, 281-618-5788 (Fax: 281-618-7141) www.nhc.ccd.edu. Enrollment: 9500. Records go back to 1981. Degrees granted: Associate. Attendance and degree information available by phone, fax, mail. Transcripts available by mail.

North Harris Montgomery Community College, Registrar, 250 N Sam Houston Pkwy E, Houston, TX 77060, 281-260-3573 (Fax: 281-260-3513) www.nhmccd.edu. 8AM-5PM. Enrollment: 20000. Records go back to 1975. Degrees granted: Associate. Attendance and degree information available by phone, fax, mail. Transcripts available by fax, mail.

North Lake College, Registrar, 5001 N MacArthur Blvd, Irving, TX 75038-3899, 214-273-3310. 8AM-8PM M-Th; 8AM-4:30PM F. Enrollment: 3252. Records go back to 1977. Degrees granted: Associate. Attendance, degree and transcript information available by mail.

North Texas State University
(See University of North Texas)

Northeast Texas Community College, Registrar, PO Drawer 1307, Mount Pleasant, TX 75456-1307, 903-572-1911 (Fax: 903-572-6712) www.ntcctx.us. 8AM-6PM M-Th; 8AM-Noon F. Enrollment: 1935. Records go back to 1985. Alumni records are maintained here. Degrees granted: Associate. Attendance and degree information available by phone, fax, mail. Transcripts available by fax, mail.

Northwood University (Branch), Registrar, 1114 W FM 1382, PO Box 58, Cedar Hill, TX 75104, 972-291-1541, 800-927-9663 (Fax: 972-291-3824) www.northwood.edu. 8AM-5PM. Enrollment: 1050. Records go back to 1946. Alumni records are maintained here. Degrees granted: Associate; Bachelors. Attendance and degree information available by phone, mail. Transcripts available by mail.

Oblate School of Theology, Registrar, 285 Oblate Dr, San Antonio, TX 78216-6693, 210-341-1366 X212 (Fax: 210-341-4519) www.oblate-sch-theology.edu. 8AM-Noon, 1-4PM. Enrollment: 140. Records go back to 1930's. Degrees granted: Masters; Doctorate. Attendance, degree and transcript information available by mail.

Odessa College, Registrar, 201 W University Blvd, Odessa, TX 79764, 915-335-6404 (Fax: 915-335-6303) www.odessa.edu 8AM-6PM. Enrollment: 5039. Records go

back to 1946. Degrees granted: Associate. Attendance, degree and transcript information available by fax, mail.

Our Lady of the Lake University, Registrar, 411 SW 24th St, San Antonio, TX 78207-4689, www.ollusa.edu 210-434-6711 X316, 210-434-6711 X317 (Fax: 210-436-2314) Enrollment: 3300. Records go back to 1920's. Alumni records maintained here; call 210-434-6711 X469. Degrees granted: Bachelors; Masters; Doctorate. Attendance and degree information available by phone, fax, mail. Transcripts available by fax, mail.

Palo Alto College, Registrar, 1400 W Villaret Blvd, San Antonio, TX 78224-2499, 210-921-5000 (Fax: 210-921-5310) www.accd.edu. 8AM-5PM. Enrollment: 7400. Records go back to 1983. Alumni records are maintained here. Degrees granted: Associate. Attendance and degree information available by phone, fax, mail. Transcripts available by fax, mail.

Pan American University, Admissions Office, 1201 W University Dr, Edinburg, TX 78539, 210-381-2206 (Fax: 210-381-2212) www.panam.edu. Enrollment: 13366. Records go back to 1952. Alumni records maintained here; call 210-381-2326. Degrees granted: Associate; Bachelors; Masters; Doctorate. Attendance and degree information available by phone, mail. Transcripts available by mail.

Panola College, Registrar, 1109 W Panola St, Carthage, TX 75633, 903-693-2038, 903-693-2037 (Fax: 903-693-5588) 8AM-4:30PM. www.panola.cc.tx.us. Enrollment: 1725. Records go back to 1947. Alumni records maintained here; call 903-693-2044. Degrees granted: Associate. Special programs- Forest Technology, 903-693-2034; Associate Degree Nursing, 903-693-2034. Attendance and degree information available by fax, mail. Transcripts available by mail.

Paris Junior College, Records Office, 2400 Clarksville St, Paris, TX 75460, 903-782-0212, 903-782-0302 (Fax: 903-784-0309) 8AM-5PM. www.paris.cc.tx.us. Enrollment: 2400. Records go back to 1924. Alumni records maintained here; call 903-785-9574. Degrees granted: Associate. Attendance and degree information available by phone, fax, mail. Transcripts available by fax, mail.

Parker College of Chiropractic, Registrar, 2500 Walnut Hill Lane, Dallas, TX 75229-5668, 972-438-6932 (Fax: 972-352-8425) www.parker.cc.edu. 8AM-5PM. Enrollment: 193. Records go back to 1982. Alumni records are maintained here. Degrees granted: Bachelors; Masters; Doctorate; First Professional Degree. Attendance and degree information available by phone, fax, mail. Transcripts available by fax, mail.

Paul Quinn College, Registrar, 3837 Simpson Stuart Rd, PO Box 411238, Dallas, TX 75241, 214-302-3540, 214-302-3543 (Fax: 214-302-3613) www.pqc.edu. 8AM - 6PM. Enrollment: 800. Records go back to 1880. Alumni records maintained here; call 214-302-3571. Degrees granted: Bachelors. Attendance and degree information available by phone, fax, mail. Transcripts available by mail.

Prairie View A & M University, Registrar, PO Box 2610, Prairie View, TX 77446, 409-857-2690, 409-587-2618 (Fax: 409-857-2699). 8AM-5PM. Enrollment: 6000. Records go back to 1930's. Alumni records are maintained here also. Call 409-857-4516. Degrees granted: Bachelors; Masters. Attendance and degree information available

by phone, fax, mail. Transcripts available by fax, mail.

Ranger College, Registrar, College Cir, Ranger, TX 76470-3298, 254-647-3234 (Fax: 254-647-1656) www.ranger.edu. 8AM-5PM. Enrollment: 875. Records go back to 1926. Alumni records are maintained here. Degrees granted: Associate. Attendance and degree information available by phone, fax, mail. Transcripts available by fax, mail.

Rice University, Office of the Registrar, 6100 Main St, Houston, TX 77005-1892, 713-527-4999 (Fax: 713-285-5323) www.ruf.rice.edu/~reg/. 8:30PM-5PM. Enrollment: 4200. Records go back to 1916. Alumni records are maintained here. Degrees granted: Bachelors; Masters; Doctorate. Attendance and degree information available by phone, fax, mail. Transcripts available by fax, mail.

Richland College, Registrar, 12800 Abrams Rd, Dallas, TX 75243-2199, 214-238-6051, 214-238-6104 (Fax: 214-238-6149) 8:30AM-7PM M-Th; 8:30AM-5PM F. www.rlc.dcccd.edu. Records go back to 1972. Alumni records are maintained here. Degrees granted: Associate. Attendance, degree and transcript information available by mail. Transcript requests must be made by student; from one college to another can be requested by phone.

Sam Houston State University, Registrar, PO Box 2029, Huntsville, TX 77341, 409-294-1035 (Fax: 409-294-1097) www.shsu.edu. 8AM-5PM. Enrollment: 12400. Records go back to 1800's. Alumni records maintained here; call 409-294-1841. Degrees granted: Bachelors; Masters; Doctorate. Certification: Teacher. Attendance and degree information available by phone, fax, mail. Transcripts available by mail.

San Antonio College, Registrar, 1300 San Pedro Ave, San Antonio, TX 78212-4299, 210-733-2000, 210-733-2581 (Fax: 210-733-2579). 7:45AM-7PM M-Th; 7:45AM-5PM F. Records go back to 1960's. Degrees granted: Associate. Attendance and degree information available by phone, mail. Transcripts available by mail; phone and fax if going to another educational institution.

San Jacinto College, Registrar, 8060 Spencer Hwy, Pasadena, TX 77505, 281-476-1844 (Fax: 281-476-1892) www.sjcd.cc.tx.us. 8AM - 4:30PM. Enrollment: 10000. Records go back to 1961. Alumni records are maintained here. Degrees granted: Associate. Attendance and degree information available by phone, mail. Transcripts available by mail.

San Jacinto College North Campus, Registrar, 5800 Uvalde Rd, Houston, TX 77049, 281-459-7102, 281-458-4050 X7206 (Fax: 281-459-7125). Enrollment: 4080. Records go back to 1974. Degrees granted: Associate. Certification: Technology. Attendance and degree information available by fax, mail. Transcripts available by mail.

Schreiner College, Registrar, 2100 Memorial Blvd, Kerrville, TX 78028, 830-896-5411 X351 (Fax: 830-896-3232). 8AM-5PM. Records go back to 1923. Alumni records maintained here; call 830-896-5411 X201. Degrees granted: Associate; Bachelors; Masters. Certification: Voc. Nursing. Attendance and degree information available by phone, fax, mail. Transcripts available by written request only.

South Plains College, Registrar, 1401 College Ave, Levelland, TX 79336, 806-894-9611 X2370 (Fax: 806-897-3167) www.spc.cc.tx.us. 8AM - 4PM. Enrollment:

5800. Alumni records maintained here; call 806-894-9611 X2217. Degrees granted: Associate. Attendance and degree information available by phone, fax, mail. Transcripts available by written request only.

South Texas College of Law, Registrar, 1303 San Jacinto St, Houston, TX 77002-7000, 713-659-8040 (Fax: 713-646-2939) www.stcl.edu. 9AM-5PM. Enrollment: 1250. Records go back to 1920's. Alumni records are maintained here. Degrees granted: Doctorate; First Professional Degree. Attendance, degree and transcript information available by mail.

Southern Methodist University, Registrar, PO Box 750276, Dallas, TX 75275-0276, 214-768-2045, 214-768-2038 (Fax: 214-768-2507) www.smu.edu. 8:30AM-5PM. Enrollment: 9172. Records go back to 1913. Alumni Records: Alumni Relations, PO Box 750173, Dallas, TX 75275. Degrees granted: Bachelors; Masters; Doctorate. Attendance and degree information available by phone, fax, mail. Transcripts available by phone, fax, mail.

Southwest Texas Junior College, Registrar, 2401 Garner Field Rd, Uvalde, TX 78801-6297, 210-591-7276 (Fax: 210-591-7396) www.swtjc.cc.tx.us. 8AM-6PM M-Th; 8AM-5PM F. Enrollment: 3250. Records go back to 1945. Degrees granted: Associate. Attendance and degree information available by phone, fax, mail. Transcripts available by fax, mail.

Southwest Texas State University, Registrar, 601 University Dr, San Marcos, TX 78666-4606, 512-245-2728 (Fax: 512-245-8126) www.swt.edu. 8AM - 5PM. Enrollment: 20000. Records go back to 1900's. Alumni records maintained here; call 512-245-2371. Degrees granted: Associate; Bachelors; Masters; Doctorate. Attendance and degree information available by phone, fax, mail. Transcripts available by fax, mail.

Southwestern Adventist College, Registrar, PO Box 567, Keene, TX 76059, 817-645-3921 X221 (Fax: 817-556-4744) 8AM-4:30PM. www.swac.edu. Enrollment: 1000. Records go back to 1893. Alumni records are maintained here at the same phone number. Degrees granted: Bachelors; Masters. Attendance and degree information available by phone, fax, mail. Transcripts available by fax, mail.

Southwestern Assemblies of God University, Registrar, 1200 Sycamore St, Waxahachie, TX 75165, 972-937-4010 X142 (Fax: 972-923-0488) www.sagu.edu. 8AM-5PM. Enrollment: 1150. Records go back to 1930's. Alumni records are maintained here. Degrees granted: Associate; Bachelors. Attendance and degree information available by phone, fax, mail. Transcripts available by mail.

Southwestern Baptist Theological Seminary, Registrar, PO Box 22600, Fort Worth, TX 76122, 817-923-1921 X2000 (Fax: 817-921-8759) www.swbts.edu. 8AM-Noon, 1-5PM. Enrollment: 3500. Records go back to 1908. Alumni records maintained here; call 817-923-1921 X2380. Degrees granted: Masters; Doctorate. Attendance and degree information available by phone, fax, mail. Transcripts available by fax, mail.

Southwestern Christian College, Registrar, PO Box 10, Terrell, TX 75160, 972-524-3341 X128 (Fax: 972-563-7133). 8AM-5PM. Enrollment: 205. Records go back to 1950. Alumni records are maintained here. Degrees granted: Associate; Bachelors.

Attendance and degree information available by phone, fax, mail. Transcripts available by fax, mail.

Southwestern University, Registrar, University Ave at Maple St, Georgetown, TX 78626, 512-863-1952, 512-863-1951 (Fax: 512-863-5788) www.southwestern.edu. 8AM-Noon, 1-5PM. Enrollment: 1200. Records go back to 1880's. Alumni records are maintained here. Degrees granted: Bachelors. Attendance and degree information available by phone, fax, mail. Transcripts available by fax, mail.

St. Edward's University, Registrar, 3001 S Congress Ave, Austin, TX 78704, 512-448-8750, 512-448-8400 (Fax: 512-448-8492) 8AM-5PM. VEnrollment: 2410. Records go back to 1885. Alumni records maintained here; call 512-448-8512. Degrees granted: Bachelors; Masters. Attendance and degree information available by phone, fax, mail. Transcripts available by fax, mail.

St. Mary's University, Registrar, One Camino Santa Maria, San Antonio, TX 78228-8576, www.stmarytx.edu. 210-436-3701 (Fax: 210-431-2217) 8AM-5PM Winter; 8AM-4PM Summer. Enrollment: 4000. Records go back to 1930. Alumni records maintained here; call 210-436-3325. Degrees granted: Bachelors; Masters; Doctorate; JD. Special programs- Continuing Studies, 210-436-3321. Attendance and degree information available by phone, fax, mail. Transcripts available by fax, mail.

St. Philip's College, Registrar, 1801 Martin Luther King, San Antonio, TX 78203, www.stphillips.edu 210-531-3290 (Fax: 210-531-3235) 7:30AM-7PM M-Th; 7:30AM-5PM F. Enrollment: 7250. Records go back to 1940's. Alumni records are maintained here. Degrees granted: Associate. Attendance and degree information available by phone, fax, mail. Transcripts available by fax, mail. Fax requests from other institutions only.

Stephen F. Austin State University, Office of the Registrar, SFA PO Box 13050, Nacogdoches, TX 75962, 409-468-2501, 409-468-2161 (Fax: 409-468-2261) 8AM-5PM. www.sfasu.edu/registrar. Enrollment: 11800. Records go back to 1923. Alumni Records: SFA PO Box 6096, Nacogdoches, TX 75962 (Fax: 409-468-1007). Degrees granted: Bachelors; Masters; Doctorate. Certification: Forestry, Teaching. Attendance and degree information available by phone, mail. Transcripts available by mail.

Sul Ross State University, Admissions & Records, Box C-2, Alpine, TX 79832, 915-837-8050, 915-837-8075 (Fax: 915-837-8431) www.SULROSS.EDU. 8AM-5PM. Enrollment: 3100. Records go back to 1924. Alumni Records: Box C-187, Alpine, TX 79832. Degrees granted: Associate; Bachelors; Masters. Attendance and degree information available by phone, fax, mail. Transcripts available by mail.

Sul Ross State University (Rio Grande College), Registrar, Rt 3 Box 1200, Eagle Pass, TX 78852, 830-773-8974, 830-278-3339 (Fax: 830-773-8996) www.sulross.edu. 9AM-6PM. Enrollment: 900. Alumni records are maintained here. Degrees granted: Bachelors; Masters. Attendance and degree information available by phone, mail. Transcripts available by written request only.

Tarleton State University, Registrar, 1297 W Washington St, Tarleton Station, Stephenville, TX 76402, 254-968-9121 (Fax: 254-968-9389) www.tarleton.edu. 8AM-5PM. Enrollment: 6600. Alumni Records: Alumni Assoc., Box T-0060, Stephenville, TX 76402.

Degrees granted: Associate; Bachelors; Masters. Attendance and degree information available by phone, fax, mail. Transcripts available by mail.

Tarrant County Junior College (Northwest Campus), Registrar, 4801 Marine Creek Pkwy, Fort Worth, TX 76179, 817-515-7100 (Fax: 817-515-7732) 8AM-5PM. www.tcjc.cc.tx.us. Enrollment: 26000. Records go back to 1976. Degrees granted: Associate. Special programs- Criminal Justice: Fire Tech: Aviation Maintenance. Attendance and degree information available by phone, fax, mail. Transcripts available by written request only.

Tarrant County Junior College, Director, Admissions & Records, 1500 Houston St, **Fort Worth,** TX 76102-6599, 817-515-5291, 817-515-5231 (Fax: 817-882-5278) www.tcjc.cc.tx.us. 8AM-5PM. Records go back to 1967. Degrees granted: Associate. Attendance and degree information available by phone, fax, mail. Transcripts available by fax, mail.

Tarrant County Junior College (South Campus), Registrar, 5301 Campus Dr, Fort Worth, TX 76119, 817-515-4590 (Fax: 817-515-5278) www.tcjc.cc.tx.us. 8AM - 5PM. Enrollment: 24000. Records go back to 1967. Alumni records are maintained here. Degrees granted: Associate. Attendance and degree information available by phone, fax, mail. Transcripts available by written request only.

Tarrant County Junior College (Northeast campus) Registrar, 828 Harwood Rd, Hurst, TX 76054, 817-515-6100 (Fax: 817-575-6988) www.tcjc.cc.tx.us. 8AM-7PM M-Th; 8AM-5PM F (Aug-May); 7:30AM-7PM M-Th (Jun-Jul). Enrollment: 11500. Records go back to 1967. Degrees granted: Associate. Attendance and degree information available by phone, fax, mail. Transcripts available by mail.

Temple Junior College, Registrar, 2600 S First St, Temple, TX 76504-7435, 254-298-8300 www.templejc.edu. 8AM-4:30PM. Enrollment: 2544. Records go back to 1926. Alumni records are maintained here. Degrees granted: Associate. Attendance and degree information available by phone, mail. Transcripts available by mail.

Texarkana College, Registrar, 2500 N Robinson Rd, Texarkana, TX 75599, 903-838-4541 (Fax: 903-832-5030) 8AM-5PM. www.is.tc.cc.tx.us Enrollment: 4500. Records go back to 1927. Alumni records are maintained here. Degrees granted: Associate. Attendance, degree and transcript information available by fax, mail.

Texas A & M International University, Registrar, 5201 University Blvd, Laredo, TX 78041-1999, 956-326-2001, 956-326-2250 (Fax: 956-326-2199) www.tamiu.edu. 8AM-5PM. Enrollment: 2500. Records go back to 1970. Alumni records are maintained here. Degrees granted: Bachelors; Masters. Attendance and degree information available by phone, fax, mail. Transcripts available by fax, mail.

Texas A & M University, Registrar, College Station, TX 77843, 409-845-1003, 409-845-1030 (Fax: 409-845-0727) www.tamu.edu. 8AM-5PM. Enrollment: 42000. Records go back to 1876. Alumni records maintained here; call 409-845-7514. Degrees granted: Bachelors; Masters; Doctorate. Attendance, degree and transcript information available by phone, fax, mail.

Texas A & M University — Corpus Christi, Registrar, 6300 Ocean Dr, Corpus Christi, TX 78412, 512-991-6810, 512-994-2632 (Fax: 512-994-5887) www.tamcc.edu. 8AM-7PM M-Th; 8AM-3PM F. Enrollment: 5800. Records go back to 1947. Alumni records maintained here; call 512-994-2420. Degrees granted: Bachelors; Masters; Doctorate. Attendance and degree information available by phone, fax, mail. Transcripts available by mail.

Texas A & M University — Galveston, Registrar, PO Box 1675, Galveston, TX 77553, 409-740-4414, 800-850-6376 (Fax: 409-740-4731) www.tamug.tamu.edu. 8AM-5PM. Enrollment: 1250. Records go back to 1983. Degrees granted: Bachelors. Special programs- Corps of Cadets, 409-740-4588. Attendance and degree information available by phone, fax, mail. Official transcripts requested and produced from main campus at College Station.

Texas A & M University — Kingsville, Registrar, Campus Box 105, Kingsville, TX 78363, 512-593-2811 (Fax: 512-593-2195) www.tamuk.edu. 8AM-5PM. Enrollment: 6000. Records go back to 1925. Alumni records are maintained here. Degrees granted: Bachelors; Masters; Doctorate. Attendance and degree information available by phone, fax, mail. Transcripts available by fax, mail.

Texas A & M University — Commerce, Records & Reports, PO Box 32011, Commerce, TX 75429-3011, 903-886-5448, 903-886-5102 (Fax: 903-886-5888) www.tamu-commerce.edu/. 8AM-5PM. Enrollment: 7700. Records go back to 1929. Alumni records maintained here; call 903-886-5765. Degrees granted: Bachelors; Masters; Doctorate. Attendance and degree information available by phone, fax, mail. Transcripts available by fax, mail.

Texas Arts and Industry University
(See Texas A&M University-Kingsville)

Texas Chiropractic College, Registrar, 5912 Spencer Hwy, Pasadena, TX 77505, 713-487-1170 (Fax: 713-487-2009) www.tcc.edu. 8AM-5PM. Enrollment: 525. Records go back to 1930. Alumni records are maintained here. Degrees granted: Bachelors; Doctorate. Attendance and degree information available by fax, mail. Transcripts available by mail.

Texas Christian University, Registrar, PO Box 297004, Fort Worth, TX 76129, 817-921-7828, 817-921-7818 (Fax: 817-921-7333) www.tcu.edu/. 8AM - 5PM. Enrollment: 6900. Records go back to 1890. Alumni Records: Alumni Assoc., 2901 Princeton St, Fort Worth, TX 76129. Degrees granted: Doctorate. Attendance and degree information available by phone, fax, mail. Transcripts available by fax, mail.

Texas College, Registrar, 2404 N Grand Ave, Tyler, TX 75712, 903-593-8311 X215 (Fax: 903-593-0588) www.texascollege.edu. 8AM-5PM. Enrollment: 324. Records go back to 1900's. Alumni records are maintained here. Degrees granted: Bachelors. Attendance, degree and transcript information available by written request only.

Texas College of Osteopathic Medicine
(See University of North Texas Health Science Center at Fort Worth)

Texas Lutheran University, Registrar, 1000 W Court St, Seguin, TX 78155-5999, 830-372-8040 (Fax: 830-372-8179) 8AM-5PM. www.txlutheran.edu. Enrollment: 1350. Records go back to 1925. Alumni records maintained here; call 830-372-8025. Degrees granted: Associate; Bachelors. Attendance and degree information available by phone,

fax, mail. Search requires name plus social security number, Transcripts available by fax, mail.

Texas Southern University, Registrar, 3100 Cleburne St, Houston, TX 77004, 713-313-7080, 713-313-7857 (Fax: 713-313-1878) www.tsu.edu. 8AM-5PM. Enrollment: 7500. Records go back to 1947. Alumni records are maintained here. Degrees granted: Bachelors; Masters; Doctorate. Attendance and degree information available by phone, fax, mail. Transcripts available by mail.

Texas Southmost College
(See University of Texas at Brownsville Texas Southmost College)

Texas State Technical College-Amarillo, Registrar, PO Box 11197, Amarillo, TX 79111, 806-335-2316 X268 (Fax: 806-335-4262) www.tstc.edu. 8AM-5PM. Enrollment: 1200. Records go back to 1970. Alumni records are maintained here. Degrees granted: Associate. Attendance and degree information available by mail. Transcripts available by mail.

Texas State Technical College — Harlingen, Registrar, 2424 Boxwood, Harlingen, TX 78550-3697, 956-425-0644, 956-425-0663 (Fax: 956-430-3124) www.tstc.edu. 8AM-6PM. Enrollment: 3056. Records go back to 1974. Alumni records are maintained here. Degrees granted: Associate. Attendance information available by phone, fax, mail. Degree information available by phone, mail. Transcripts available by written request only.

Texas State Technical College — Sweetwater, Registrar, 300 College Dr, Sweetwater, TX 79556, 915-235-7377, 915-235-7361 (Fax: 915-235-7416) www.ts.tech.us.edu. 9AM - 5PM. Enrollment: 900. Records go back to 1970. Alumni records are maintained here. Degrees granted: Associate. Attendance and degree information available by phone, fax, mail. Transcripts available by fax, mail.

Texas State Technical College - Waco, Registrar, 3801 Campus Dr, Waco, TX 76705, 817-867-2366, 817-867-2361 (Fax: 817-867-2250). 8AM-5PM. Enrollment: 3700. Records go back to 1965. Alumni records are maintained here. Degrees granted: Associate. Attendance and transcript information available by mail. Degree information available by phone, fax, mail.

Texas Tech University, Registrar, PO Box 45015, Lubbock, TX 79409-5015, 806-742-3652, 806-742-3661 (Fax: 806-742-0355) www.ttu.edu. 8AM-5PM. Enrollment: 24000. Records go back to 1925. Alumni Records: Alumni Assoc., Texas Tech University, PO Box 45001, Lubbock, TX 79409-5001. Degrees granted: Bachelors; Masters; Doctorate. Attendance and degree information available by phone, mail. Transcripts available by mail.

Texas Tech University Health Sciences Center, Registrar, 3601 Fourth St, Lubbock, TX 79430, 806-743-2300 (Fax: 806-743-3027) www.ttunsc.com. 8AM-5PM. Enrollment: 1800. Records go back to 1972. Alumni records are maintained here. Degrees granted: Bachelors; Masters; Doctorate. Certification: EMT. Attendance and degree information available by phone, fax, mail. Transcripts available by mail.

Texas Wesleyan University, Registrar, 1201 Wesleyan St, Fort Worth, TX 76105-1536, 817-531-4414, 817-531-4245 (Fax: 817-531-4464) www.txwesleyan.edu. 8AM-5PM. Enrollment: 2800. Records go back to

1890's. Alumni records maintained here; call 817-531-4414. Degrees granted: Bachelors; Masters; Doctorate. Special programs- TX Wesleyan School of Law, 214-579-1071. Attendance and degree information available by phone, fax, mail. Transcripts available by fax, mail.

Texas Women's University, Registrar, PO Box 425559, Denton, TX 76204, 940-898-3033, 940-898-3036 (Fax: 940-898-3072). 8AM-5PM. Enrollment: 10000. Records go back to 1901. Alumni Records: PO Box 425795, Denton, TX 76204 (Fax: 940-898-2497). Degrees granted: Bachelors; Masters; Doctorate. Attendance and degree information available by phone, fax, mail. Transcripts available by mail.

Tomball College, Registrar, 30555 Tomball Pkwy, Tomball, TX 77375-4036, 713-351-3310, 800-96-STARS www.nhmccd.cc.tx.us. (Fax: 713-351-3384) 8AM-9:30PM M-Th; 8AM-4:30PM F. Enrollment: 3500. Records go back to 1988. Alumni records are maintained here. Degrees granted: Associate. Attendance and degree information available by phone, fax, mail. Transcripts available by fax, mail.

Trinity University, Registrar, 715 Stadium Dr, San Antonio, TX 78212-7200, 210-736-7201 (Fax: 210-736-7202) www.trinity.edu. 8AM-5PM. Records go back to 1895. Alumni records maintained here; call 210-736-8404. Degrees granted: Bachelors; Masters. Attendance and degree information available by phone, fax, mail. Transcripts available by written request only.

Trinity Valley Community College, Registrar, 500 S Prairieville, Athens, TX 75751, 903-677-8822 (Fax: 903-675-6316) 8AM-5PM. www.tvcc.cc.tx.us. Enrollment: 3143. Records go back to 1946. Alumni records maintained here; call 903-675-6386. Degrees granted: Associate. Attendance and degree information available by phone, fax, mail. Transcripts available by fax, mail.

Tyler Junior College, Registrar, PO Box 9020, Tyler, TX 75711, 903-510-2397, 903-510-2404 (Fax: 903-510-2634) www.TYLERTX.US. 8AM-8PM M-Th; 8AM-5PM F. Enrollment: 7800. Records go back to 1926. Alumni records maintained here; call 903-510-2497. Degrees granted: Associate. Attendance, degree and transcript information available by fax, mail.

University of Central Texas, Records Office, PO Box 1416, Killeen, TX 76540, 254-526-8262 X253 (Fax: 254-526-8403) 8AM-7PM. www.vvm.com/uct. Enrollment: 2200. Records go back to 1973. Alumni records are maintained here. Degrees granted: Bachelors; Masters. Attendance and degree information available by phone, fax, mail. Transcripts available by mail.

University of Dallas, Registrar, 1845 E Northgate Dr, Irving, TX 75061-4799, 214-721-5221 (Fax: 214-721-5132) www.ud.edu. 8AM-4:30PM. Enrollment: 2700. Records go back to 1956. Alumni records maintained here; call 214-721-5066. Degrees granted: Bachelors; Masters; Doctorate. Attendance and degree information available by phone, mail. Transcripts available by mail.

University of Houston, Transcript Office, 4800 Calhoun Blvd, Houston, TX 77204-2161, 713-743-1010 (Fax: 713-743-9050) www.uh.edu. 8AM-7PM M,T; 8AM-5PM W-F. Enrollment: 30000. Records go back to 1927. Alumni records maintained here; call 713-743-9550. Degrees granted: Bachelors; Masters; Doctorate. Attendance and degree

information available by phone, fax, mail. Transcripts available by fax, mail.

University of Houston — Clear Lake, Office of Enrollment Services, 2700 Bay Area Blvd, Box 13, Houston, TX 77058-1098, www.cl.uh.edu\admissions. 281-283-2534, 281-283-2536 (Fax: 281-283-2530) 10AM-7PM M-Th; 8AM-5PM F. Enrollment: 7000. Records go back to 1974. Alumni Records: 2700 Bay Area Blvd Box 318, Houston, TX 77059-1098. Degrees granted: Bachelors; Masters. Attendance and degree information available by phone, fax, mail. Transcripts available by fax, mail.

University of Houston — Downtown, Registrar, One Main St, Houston, TX 77002, 713-221-8999, 713-221-8000 (Fax: 713-221-8157) www.dt.uh.edu. 8AM-6PM M-Th; 8AM-5PM F. Enrollment: 8000. Records go back to 1956. Alumni records are maintained here. Degrees granted: Bachelors. Special programs- Urban Education: Criminal Justice. Attendance and degree information available by phone, fax, mail. Transcripts available by mail.

University of Houston — Victoria, Registrar, 2506 E Red River, Victoria, TX 77901-4450, 512-788-6222, 512-576-3151 (Fax: 512-572-9377). 8AM - 5PM. Enrollment: 1500. Records go back to 1973. Alumni records are maintained here. Degrees granted: Bachelors; Masters. Attendance and degree information available by phone, fax, mail. Transcripts available by mail.

University of Mary Hardin — Baylor, Registrar, Box 8425, Belton, TX 76513, 817-939-4510, 817-939-4509 (Fax: 817-933-5052) www.umhb.edu. 8AM - 5PM. Enrollment: 2200. Records go back to 1845. Alumni Records: Box 8427, Belton, TX 76513 (Fax: 817-939-4535). Degrees granted: Bachelors; Masters. Attendance and degree information available by phone, fax, mail. Transcripts available by fax, mail.

University of North Texas, Registrar's Office, PO Box 311400, Denton, TX 76203-1400, 940-565-2111 (Fax: 940-565-3878) www.unt.edu. 8AM-5PM. Enrollment: 26000. Alumni Records: Alumni Assoc., PO Box 311250, Denton, TX 76203-1250. Degrees granted: Bachelors; Masters; Doctorate. Attendance and degree information available by phone, fax, mail. Transcripts available by mail.

University of North Texas Health Science Center at Fort Worth, Registrar, 3500 Camp Bowie Blvd, Fort Worth, TX 76107-2970, 817-735-2201, 817-735-2241 (Fax: 817-735-2568). 8AM - 5PM. Enrollment: 628. Records go back to 1974. Alumni records maintained here; call 817-735-2559. Degrees granted: Bachelors; Masters; Doctorate. Attendance and degree information available by phone, fax, mail. Transcripts available by fax, mail.

University of St. Thomas, Registrar, 3800 Montrose Blvd, Houston, TX 77006-4696, http://basil.stthom.edu. 713-522-7911 (Fax: 713-525-2125) 8:30AM-5:30PM M-Th; 8:30AM-5PM F. Records go back to 1946. Alumni records maintained here; call 713-525-3115. Degrees granted: Bachelors; Masters; Doctorate. Attendance and degree information available by phone, fax, mail. Transcripts available by mail.

University of Texas Health Science Center at San Antonio, Registrar, 7703 Floyd Curl Dr, San Antonio, TX 78284-7702, 210-567-2621, 210-567-2661 (Fax: 210-567-2685) www.uthscsa.edu. 8AM-4:30PM.

Enrollment: 426. Records go back to 1965. Alumni records are maintained here. Degrees granted: Bachelors; Masters; Doctorate. Attendance and degree information available by phone, fax, mail. Transcripts available by fax, mail.

University of Texas Medical Branch at Galveston, Registrar, 301 University Blvd, Galveston, TX 77555-1305, 409-772-1215 (Fax: 409-772-5056) www.utmb.edu. 8AM-5PM. Enrollment: 2300. Records go back to 1891. Alumni records maintained here; call 409-772-1215. Degrees granted: Bachelors; Masters; Doctorate. Attendance and degree information available by phone, fax, mail. Transcripts available by fax, mail.

University of Texas Southwestern Medical Center at Dallas, Registrar, 5323 Harry Hines Blvd, Dallas, TX 75235, 214-648-3606, 214-648-2670 (Fax: 214-648-3289) 8AM-4:30PM. www.swmed.edu. Enrollment: 1700. Records go back to 1944. Alumni records are maintained here. Degrees granted: Doctorate. Attendance and degree information available by phone, fax, mail. Transcripts available by fax, mail.

University of Texas at Arlington, Registrar, PO Box 19088, Arlington, TX 76019, 817-272-3372 (Fax: 817-272-3223) www.uta.edu. 8AM-7PM M-Th; 8AM-5PM F. Enrollment: 22000. Records go back to 1917. Alumni records maintained here; call 817-272-2594. Degrees granted: Bachelors; Masters; Doctorate. Attendance and degree information available by phone, fax, mail. Transcripts available by mail.

University of Texas at Austin, Registrar, Main Bldg Room 1, Austin, TX 78712, 512-475-7575, 512-475-7689 (Fax: 512-475-7515) 8AM-5PM. www.texas.edu/. Enrollment: 48000. Records go back to 1883. Alumni records maintained here; call 512-471-3812. Degrees granted: Bachelors; Masters; Doctorate. Attendance and degree information available by phone, fax, mail. Transcripts available by fax, mail. Student may request transcript by phone.

University of Texas at Brownsville, Registrar, 80 Fort Brown, Brownsville, TX 78520, 956-544-8254 (Fax: 956-544-8832). 7:30AM-7PM M-Th; 7:30AM-1:30PM F. Enrollment: 8000. Records go back to 1991. Alumni records are maintained here. Degrees granted: Bachelors; Masters. Attendance, degree and transcript information available by fax, mail.

University of Texas at Dallas, Records & Registration, PO Box 830688 MCII, Richardson, TX 75083-0688, 972-883-2111, 972-883-2342 (Fax: 972-883-6335) www.utdallas.edu. 8AM-7PM M-Th; 9AM-5PM F. Enrollment: 9000. Records go back to 1969. Alumni records are maintained here. Degrees granted: Bachelors; Masters; Doctorate. Certification: Teacher Education. Attendance and degree information available by phone, fax, mail. Transcripts available by fax, mail.

University of Texas at El Paso, Registrar, 500 W University Ave, El Paso, TX 79968, 915-747-5550 (Fax: 915-747-5012) www.utep.edu. 8AM-5PM M-F. Records go back to 1915. Alumni records are maintained here. Degrees granted: Bachelors; Masters; Doctorate. Attendance and degree information available by phone, fax, mail. Transcripts available by fax, mail.

University of Texas at San Antonio, Registrar, 6900 N Loop 1604 W, San Antonio, TX 78249-0616, 210-691-4530,

210-458-4545 www.utsa.edu. 8AM-5:00PM. Records go back to 1973. Alumni records are maintained here. Degrees granted: Bachelors; Masters; Doctorate. Attendance and degree information available by phone, mail. Transcripts available by mail.

University of Texas at Tyler, Registrar, 3900 University Blvd, Tyler, TX 75799, 903-566-7000 (Fax: 903-566-7068). 8AM-5PM. Enrollment: 4477. Records go back to 1971. Alumni records maintained here; call 903-566-7411. Degrees granted: Bachelors; Masters. Attendance and degree information available by phone, fax, mail. Transcripts available by fax, mail.

University of Texas of the Permian Basin, Registrar, 4901 E University Blvd, Odessa, TX 79762, 915-552-2635 (Fax: 915-552-2621) www.utpb.edu. 8AM-6PM M-Th; 8AM-5PM F. Enrollment: 2400. Records go back to 1972. Alumni Records: Alumni Assoc., Development Office, Odessa, TX 79762. Degrees granted: Bachelors; Masters. Attendance and degree information available by phone, fax, mail. Transcripts available by fax, mail.

University of Texas — Houston Health Science Center, Registrar, PO Box 20036, 7000 Fannin Ste 2250, Houston, TX 77225, 713-792-7444 (Fax: 713-794-5701) www.uth.tmc.edu. 8AM-5PM. Enrollment: 3097. Records go back to 1948. Alumni records are maintained here. Degrees granted: Bachelors; Masters; Doctorate. Attendance and degree information available by phone, fax, mail. Transcripts available by mail.

University of Texas — Pan American, Registrar, 1201 W University Dr, Edinburg, TX 78539-2999, 956-381-2201 (registrar), 956-381-2011 (switchboard) (Registrar Fax: 956-381-2212) 8AM - 5PM. www.panam.edu. Enrollment: 14000. Records go back to 1927. Alumni records maintained here; call 956-381-3667. Degrees granted: Associate; Bachelors; Masters; Doctorate. Attendance and degree

information available by phone, mail. Transcripts available by mail.

University of the Incarnate Word, Registrar, 4301 Broadway, San Antonio, TX 78209, 210-829-6006 (Fax: 210-829-3922). 8AM-5PM. Records go back to 1910. Formerly **Incarnate Word College**. Alumni records maintained here; call 210-829-6014. Degrees granted: Bachelors; Masters. Attendance and degree information available by phone, fax, mail. Transcripts available by fax, mail.

Vernon Regional Junior College, Registrar, 4400 College Dr, Vernon, TX 76384, 940-552-6291 X2204, 940-552-6291 X2205 (Fax: 940-553-1753) 8AM-5PM. http://sol.wf.net:80/~vrjc. Enrollment: 1800. Records go back to 1972. Degrees granted: Associate. Attendance and degree information available by phone, fax, mail. Transcripts available by mail.

Victoria College, Registrar, 2200 E Red River St, Victoria, TX 77901-4494, 512-572-6411 (Fax: 512-572-3850). Enrollment: 3700. Alumni records maintained here; call 512-573-3291 X440. Degrees granted: Associate. Attendance and degree information available by phone, fax, mail. Transcripts available by fax, mail.

Wayland Baptist University, Office of the Registrar, WBU #735, Plainview, TX 79072, 806-296-4706, 806-296-5521 (Fax: 806-296-4580). 8:30AM-5PM. Enrollment: 3500. Records go back to 1910. Alumni records maintained here; call 806-296-4844. Degrees granted: Associate; Bachelors; Masters. Certification: Secretarial. Attendance and degree information available by phone, fax, mail. Transcripts available by mail.

Weatherford College, Registrar, 308 E Park Ave, Weatherford, TX 76086, 817-594-5471, 817-598-6353 (Fax: 817-594-9435) www.wc.edu. 8AM-5PM M-Th; 8AM-4PM F. Records go back to 1920's. Alumni records are maintained here. Degrees granted: Associate. Attendance and degree information

available by phone, fax, mail. Transcripts available by written request only.

West Texas A & M University, Registrar, 2501 Fourth Ave, WTAMU Bos 60877, Canyon, TX 79016, 806-651-2022 (Fax: 806-651-2936) www.wtamu.edu. 8AM-5PM. Enrollment: 6500. Records go back to 1911. Alumni records are maintained here. Degrees granted: Bachelors; Masters. Certification Education/Teacher. Attendance and degree information available by phone, fax, mail. Transcripts available by fax, mail.

West Texas State University
(See West Texas A & M University)

Western Texas College, Registrar, 6200 S College Ave, Snyder, TX 79549, 915-573-8511 (Fax: 915-573-9321). 8AM-Noon, 1-5PM. Enrollment: 1100. Records go back to 1970. Alumni records are maintained here. Degrees granted: Associate. Attendance and degree information available by phone, fax, mail. Transcripts available by mail.

Wharton County Junior College, Registrar, 911 Boling Hwy, Wharton, TX 77488, 409-532-6382, 409-532-6381 (Fax: 409-532-6494). 8AM - 5PM. Enrollment: 3700. Records go back to 1946. Alumni records maintained here; call 409-532-6322. Degrees granted: Associate. Attendance and degree information available by phone, fax, mail. Transcripts available by fax, mail.

Wiley College, Registrar, 711 Wiley Ave, Marshall, TX 75670, 903-927-3221 (Fax: 903-938-8100) www.wiley.edu. 8AM-5PM. Enrollment: 600. Records go back to 1900's. Alumni records maintained here; call 903-927-3225. Degrees granted: Bachelors. Attendance, degree and transcript information available by mail. Inquiries by phone or fax will be accepted only in special circumstances.

Utah

Brigham Young University, Records Dept B150 ASB, Provo, UT 84602, 801-378-2631, 801-378-4470 (Fax: 801-378-6583) www.byu.edu. Enrollment: 30000. Records go back to 1875. Alumni Records: Alumni Services, 146 Alum, Provo, UT 84602. Degrees granted: Bachelors; Masters; Doctorate. Attendance and degree information available by phone, fax, mail. Transcripts available by fax. Written requests by fax or mail for transcripts must have student's signature.

College of Eastern Utah, Registrar, 451 E 400 N, Price, UT 84501, 801-637-2120 X5205, 801-637-2120 X5200 (Fax: 801-637-4102) www.ceu.edu. 8AM - 5PM. Enrollment: 3000. Records go back to 1938. Alumni records maintained here; call 801-637-2120 X5246. Degrees granted: Associate. Attendance and degree information available by phone, fax, mail. Transcripts available by fax, mail.

Dixie College, Registrar, 225 S 700 E, St George, UT 84770, 435-652-7700 (Fax: 435-656-4005) www.dixie.edu. 9AM - 4:30PM. Enrollment: 5000. Records go back to 1911. Alumni records maintained here; call 801-435-7538. Degrees granted: Associate. Attendance and degree information available by phone, fax, mail. Transcripts available by fax, mail.

ITT Technical Institute, Registrar, 920 W LeVoy Dr, Murray, UT 84123, 801-263-3313 (Fax: 801-263-3497). 8AM-8PM. Enrollment: 530. Records go back to 1970's. Alumni Records: 9511 Angola Ct, Indianapolis, IN 46286. Degrees granted: Associate; Bachelors. Attendance and degree information available by phone, fax, mail. Transcripts available by written request only.

LDS Business College, Registrar, 411 E S Temple St, Salt Lake City, UT 84111, 801-524-8140, 801-524-8141 (Fax: 801-524-1900) www.ldsbc.edu. 8AM-5PM. Records go back to 1930. Prior records in archives. Alumni records are maintained here. Degrees granted: Associate. Attendance and degree information available by phone, fax, mail. Transcripts available by fax, mail.

Mountain West College, Registrar, 3098 Highland Dr, Salt Lake City, UT 84106, 801-485-0221 (Fax: 801-485-0057). 8:30AM-8PM. Records go back to 1982. Formerly **Phillips Junior College**. Degrees granted: Associate. Attendance and degree information available by phone, fax, mail. Transcripts available by fax, mail.

Salt Lake Community College, Registrar's Office, PO Box 30808, Salt Lake City, UT 84130, 801-957-4298, 801-957-4085 (Fax: 801-957-4958) www.slcc.edu.

8AM-8PM M-Th; 8AM-4:30PM F. Enrollment: 20000. Records go back to 1948. Alumni records maintained here; call 801-957-4838. Degrees granted: Associate. Attendance and degree information available by phone, fax, mail. Transcripts available by mail.

Snow College, Registrar, Ephraim, UT 84627, 435-283-7000 (Fax: 435-283-7149) 9AM-4PM. www.inst.snow.edu. Records go back to 1888. Alumni records are maintained here. Degrees granted: Associate. Attendance and degree information available by phone, fax, mail. Transcripts available by fax. Fax request requires student permission.

Southern Utah University, Registrar, 351 W Center, Cedar City, UT 84720, 435-586-7715 (Fax: 435-865-8223) www.suu.edu. 8AM-5PM. Enrollment: 5500. Records go back to 1896. Alumni records are maintained here. Degrees granted: Bachelors; Masters. Attendance and degree information available by phone, mail. Transcripts available by mail.

Stevens College of Business, Registrar, 2168 Washington Blvd, Ogden, UT 84401-1467, 801-394-7791 (Fax: 801-393-1748). 8AM-5PM. Enrollment: 250. Records go back to 1950. Degrees granted: Associate. Attendance and degree information available by phone, fax, mail. Transcripts available by written request only.

Stevens-Henager College of Business (Branch Campus), Registrar, 25 E 1700 S, Provo, UT 84606-6157, 801-375-5455 (Fax: 801-375-9836) 8AM-5PM. Enrollment: 150. Records go back to 1980. Transcripts for Provo students prior to 1992 at Ogden Campus of Stevens College of Business. Degrees granted: Associate. Attendance and degree information available by phone, fax, mail. Transcripts available by phone, fax, mail.

University of Phoenix (Salt Lake City Main), Registrar, 5251 Green St, Salt Lake City, UT 84123, 801-263-1444, 800-224-2844 (Fax: 801-269-9766) www.uophx.edu. Records are located at University of Phoenix, Registrar, 4615 E Elwood St 3rd Flr, Phoenix, AZ 85072-2069.

University of Utah, Registrar, 201S 1460 E, Rm 250N, Salt Lake City, UT 84112-9056, 801-581-8965, 801-581-7197 (Fax: 801-585-7860) www.utah.edu. 7:30AM - 5PM. Enrollment: 27000. Records go back to 1850. Alumni records maintained here; call 801-581-6995. Degrees granted: Bachelors; Masters; Doctorate. Attendance and degree information available by phone, fax, mail. Transcripts available by mail.

Utah State University, Registrar, Logan, UT 84322-1400, 801-797-3988 (Fax: 801-797-4077) www.usu.edu. Enrollment: 20000. Alumni records maintained here; call 801-797-2055. Degrees granted: Bachelors; Masters; Doctorate. Attendance and degree information available by phone, fax, mail. Transcripts available by fax, mail.

Utah Technical College at Provo (See Utah Valley Community College)

Utah Technical College Salt Lake City (See Salt Lake Community College)

Utah Valley Community College (See Utah Valley State College)

Utah Valley State College, Registrar, 800 W 1200 S, Orem, UT 84058, 801-222-8468, 801-222-8472 (Fax: 801-225-4677) www.uvsc.edu. 8AM-5PM. Enrollment: 14000. Records go back to 1963. Alumni records maintained here; call 801-222-8205.

Degrees granted: Bachelors. Attendance and degree information available by phone, fax, mail. Transcripts available by fax, mail.

Weber State University, Registrar, 1102 University Circle, Ogden, UT 84408-1102, 801-626-6757, 801-626-6757 (Fax: 801-626-6679). 8AM-7:30PM. Records go back to 1913. Alumni records maintained here; call 801-626-6564. Degrees granted: Associate; Bachelors; Masters. Attendance and degree information available by phone, fax, mail. Transcripts available by fax, mail.

Westminster College of Salt Lake City, Registrar, 1840 S 1300 E, Salt Lake City, UT 84105, www.wcslc.edu. 801-488-4100 (Fax: 801-484-6450) 8AM-6PM M,W,F; 8AM-6PM T,Th. Enrollment: 2067. Records go back to 1985. Alumni records are maintained here. Degrees granted: Bachelors; Masters. Certification: Teaching. Attendance and degree information available by phone, fax, mail. Transcripts available by fax, mail.

Vermont

Bennington College, Registrar, Bennington, VT 05201, 802-442-5401 X4404, 802-442-5401 X4405 (Fax: 802-447-4269). 9AM-5PM. Enrollment: 380. Records go back to 1932. Alumni records are maintained here. Degrees granted: Bachelors; Masters. Attendance, degree and transcript information available by fax, mail.

Burlington College, Registrar, 95 North Ave, Burlington, VT 05401-8477, 802-862-9616 (Fax: 802-658-0071) www.burlcol.edu. 9AM-5PM. Enrollment: 170. Records go back to 1972. Alumni records maintained here; call 802-862-9616. Degrees granted: Associate; Bachelors. Special programs-Independent Degree Program (IDP), 802-862-9616: Cinema Studies & Film Production Program, 802-862-9616. Attendance and degree information available by phone, fax, mail. Transcripts available by mail.

Castleton State College, Registrar, Castleton, VT 05735, 802-468-1211, www.csc.vsc.edu/ 802-468-1209 (Fax: 802-468-5237) 8AM-4:30PM. Enrollment: 2000. Records go back to 1787. Alumni records are maintained here. Degrees granted: Bachelors; Masters; CAGS, Associate. Attendance and degree information available by phone, fax, mail. Transcripts available by mail.

Champlain College, Registrar's Office, 163 S Willard St, PO Box 670, Burlington, VT 05402-0670, 802-860-2715 (Fax: 802-860-2761) 8:30AM - 5PM. www.champlain.edu. Enrollment: 1300. Records go back to 1965. Alumni records maintained here; call 802-860-2747. Degrees granted: Associate; Bachelors. Certification: Secretarial and Concentrated Study. Attendance and degree information available by phone, fax, mail. Transcripts available by fax, mail.

College of St. Joseph, Registrar, Rutland, VT 05701, 802-773-5900 X241 (Fax: 802-773-5900 X258). 8:30AM - 7:30PM. Enrollment: 500. Records go back to 1964. Alumni records are maintained here. Degrees granted: Associate; Bachelors; Masters. Attendance and degree information available by phone, mail. Transcripts available by mail. Phone requests for transcripts must be signed later.

Community College of Vermont, Registrar, Waterbury, VT 05676, 802-241-3535, 802-241-1191 (Fax: 802-241-3526) 8:30AM-4:30PM. www.ccv.vse.edu. Enrollment: 4800. Records go back to 1975. Alumni Records: CCV Alumni Assoc., Battell Block Bldg, Middlebury, VT 05753. Degrees granted: Associate. Attendance information available by phone, fax, mail. Degree information available by mail. Transcripts available by written request only.

Goddard College, Registrar, Plainfield, VT 05667, 802-454-8311 X288, 802-454-8311 X213 (Fax: 802-454-1451) 9AM-4:30PM. www.goddard.edu. Enrollment: 500. Records go back to 1938. Alumni records are maintained here. Degrees granted: Bachelors; Masters. Attendance and degree information available by phone, fax, mail. Transcripts available by mail.

Green Mountain College, Registrar, 16 College St, Poultney, VT 05764, 802-287-8215, 802-287-8216 (Fax: 802-287-8099) www.clanpresott.com/greenenglish 8AM-4:30PM. Enrollment: 600. Records go back to 1834. Alumni records maintained here; call 802-287-9308. Degrees granted: Bachelors. Attendance and degree information available by phone, fax, mail. Transcripts available by mail.

Johnson State College, Registrar, Johnson, VT 05656, 802-635-2356 X229 (Fax: 802-635-1248) www.jsc.vse.edu. 8AM-5PM. Enrollment: 1400. Records go back to 1828. Alumni records are maintained here. Degrees granted: Bachelors; Masters. Attendance and degree information available by phone, fax, mail. Transcripts available by mail.

Landmark College, Registrar, Putney, VT 05346, 802-387-4767, 802-387-6707 (Fax: 802-387-6703) www.landmarkcollege.org. 8AM-4:30PM. Alumni records are maintained here. Degrees granted: Associate. Attendance, degree and transcript information available by phone, fax, mail.

Lyndon State College, Registrar, Vail Hill, Lyndonville, VT 05851, 802-626-9371 X6494 (Fax: 802-626-9770). 9AM-4PM.

Enrollment: 1200. Records go back to 1911. Alumni records maintained here. Degrees granted: Bachelors; Masters. Attendance and degree information available by phone, mail. Transcripts available by mail.

Marlboro College, Registrar, Marlboro, VT 05344, www.marlboro.edu. 802-257-4333 X233, 802-258-9233 (Fax: 802-257-4154) 8:30AM-4:30PM. Enrollment: 275. Records go back to 1946. Alumni records are maintained here. Degrees granted: Bachelors. Attendance and degree information available by phone, fax, mail. Transcripts available by mail.

Middlebury College, Registrar, Old Chapel Bldg, Middlebury, VT 05753, 802-443-5382 (Fax: 802-443-2063) www.middlebury.edu. 8AM-5PM. Records go back to 1800. Alumni records are maintained here. Degrees granted: Bachelors; Masters; Doctorate. Attendance and degree information available by phone, fax, mail. Transcripts available by fax, mail.

Norwich University, Registrar, Northfield, VT 05663, 802-485-2035 (Fax: 802-485-2042) www.norwich.edu. 8AM-4:30PM. Alumni records are maintained here. Degrees granted: Associate; Bachelors; Masters. Special programs- Graduate Programs & Adult Degree BA, 802-828-8725. Attendance and degree information available by phone, fax, mail. Transcripts available by fax, mail.

School for International Training, Registrar, PO Box 676, Brattleboro, VT 05301, 802-257-7751, 802-258-3283 (Fax: 802-258-3233) www.sit.edu. 8:30AM-4:30PM. Enrollment: 1600. Records go back to 1964. Alumni records are maintained here. Degrees granted: Bachelors; Masters. Attendance and degree information available by phone, fax, mail. Transcripts available by fax, mail.

Southern Vermont College, Registrar, Monument View Rd, Bennington, VT 05201, 802-442-5427 X228 (Fax: 802-447-4695) 8AM-4:30PM. www.svc.edu. Enrollment: 600. Records go back to 1926. Alumni records are maintained here. Degrees granted: Bachelors. Attendance and degree information available by phone, fax, mail. Transcripts available by mail.

St. Michael's College, Registrar, Winooski Park, Colchester, VT 05439, 802-654-2571 (Fax: 802-654-2690) www.smcvt.edu. 8AM-4:30PM. Enrollment: 2600. Records go back to 1901. Alumni records maintained here; call 802-654-2527. Degrees granted: Bachelors; Masters. Special programs- School of International Studies, 802-654-2300. Attendance and degree information available by phone, fax, mail. Transcripts available by fax, mail.

Sterling College, Registrar, Craftsbury Common, VT 05827, 802-586-7711 (Fax: 802-586-2596) www.sterlingcollege.org. 9AM-5PM. Enrollment: 80. Records go back to 1958. Degrees granted: Associate. Special programs- Resource Management (Experimental). Attendance, degree and transcript information available by phone, fax, mail.

Trinity College of Vermont, Registrar, 208 Colchester Ave, Burlington, VT 05401, 802-658-0337 X247 (Fax: 802-658-5446) 8AM-4:30PM. www.trinityvt.edu. Records go back to 1925. Alumni records are maintained here. Degrees granted: Bachelors; Masters. Attendance and degree information available

by phone, fax, mail. Transcripts available by fax, mail.

University of Vermont, Academic Transcript, Burlington, VT 05405-0160, 802-656-2045 (Fax: 802-656-8230) . 8AM-5PM. www.uvm.edu Enrollment: 9000. Records go back to 1791. Alumni records maintained here; call 802-656-2010. Degrees granted: Bachelors; Masters; Doctorate. Attendance and degree information available by phone, fax, mail. Transcripts available by fax, mail.

Vermont College of Norwich University Registrar, College St, Montpelier, VT 05602, 802-828-8727, 802-828-8726 (Fax: 802-828-8585). 8AM - 4:30PM. Enrollment: 1000. Records go back to 1934. Alumni records maintained here; call 802-485-2100. Degrees granted: Bachelors; Masters. Attendance and degree information available by phone, mail. Transcripts available by mail.

Vermont Law School, Asst Registrar, PO Box 96, South Royalton, VT 05068, 802-763-8303 (Fax: 802-763-7071) 8:30AM - 5PM. www.vermontlaw.edu. Enrollment: 500. Records go back to 1973. Alumni records are maintained here. Degrees granted: Masters; JD. Attendance and degree information

available by phone, fax, mail. Transcripts available by fax, mail.

Vermont Technical College, Registrar, PO Box 500, Randolph Center, VT 05061, 802-728-1303 (Fax: 802-728-1390) www.vts.vsc.edu. 8AM - 4:30PM; 8AM - 4PM Summers. Enrollment: 750. Records go back to 1900. Alumni records maintained here; call 802-728-1261. Degrees granted: Associate; Bachelors. Attendance and degree information available by phone, fax, mail. Transcripts available by fax, mail.

Woodbury College, Registrar, 660 Elm St, Montpelier, VT 05602, 802-229-0516 (Fax: 802-229-2141) www.woodbury-college.edu. 8AM-5PM. Alumni records are maintained here. Degrees granted: Associate. Attendance and degree information available by phone, fax, mail. Transcripts available by mail..

Virginia

Averett College, Registrar, 420 W Main St, Danville, VA 24541, 804-791-5600 (Fax: 804-799-0658) www.averett.edu. 8AM-5PM. Enrollment: 2500. Records go back to 1859. Alumni records maintained here. Call 804-791-5600. Degrees granted: Bachelors Masters. Attendance and degree information available by phone, mail. Transcripts available by mail.

Blue Ridge Community College, Coordinator, Admissions & Records, PO Box 80, Weyers Cave, VA 24486, 540-234-9261 (Fax: 540-234-9598) www.br.cc.cr.us. 8:15AM-5PM. Enrollment: 2500. Records go back to 1967. Alumni records are maintained here. Degrees granted: Associate. Special programs- Veterinary Technology, 540-234-9261 X283. Attendance and degree information available by phone, fax, mail. Transcripts available by mail.

Bluefield College, Registrar, 3000 College Dr, Bluefield, VA 24605, 540-326-3682, 540-326-4348 (Fax: 540-326-4288) 8:30AM-Noon, 1-5PM. www.bluefield.edu. Enrollment: 818. Records go back to 1922. Alumni records are maintained here. Degrees granted: Associate; Bachelors. Attendance and degree information available by phone, fax, mail. Transcripts available by fax, mail.

Bridgewater College, Registrar, Bridge-water, VA 22812, 540-828-8000 (Fax: 540-828-5479) www.bridgewater.edu. 8AM-5PM. Enrollment: 1069. Records go back to 1920. Degrees granted: Bachelors. Attendance and degree information available by phone, fax, mail. Transcripts available by fax, mail.

Bryant & Stratton College, (Branch) Registrar, 1120 W Mercury Blvd, **Hampton**, VA 23666-3309, 757-838-2122 (Fax: 757-838-4708) www.bryantstratton.edu. 9AM-6PM. Enrollment: 300. Records go back to 1981. Alumni records are maintained here. Degrees granted: Associate. Attendance and degree information available by fax, mail. Transcripts available by written request only.

Bryant & Stratton College, Registrar, 301 Centre Pointe Drive, **Virginia Beach**, VA 23462, 757-499-7900 (Fax: 757-499-9977) 8AM-5PM. www.bryantstratton.edu.

Enrollment: 261. Records go back to 1960's. Degrees granted: Associate. Attendance and degree information available by phone, fax, mail. Transcripts available by mail.

Central Virginia Community College. Registrar, 3506 Wards Rd, Lynchburg, VA 24502-2498, 804-832-7630 (Fax: 804-386-4681) www.cv.cc.va.us. 8:30AM - 4:30PM. Enrollment: 4000. Records go back to 1967. Alumni records maintained here; call 804-832-7619. Degrees granted: Associate. Attendance and degree information available by phone, fax, mail. Transcripts available by fax, mail.

Christendom College, Registrar, 134 Christendon Dr, Front Royal, VA 22630, 540-636-2900 (Fax: 540-636-1655) 9AM - 5PM. www.christendom.edu. Enrollment: 230. Records go back to 1977. Alumni records are maintained here. Degrees granted: Associate; Bachelors. Attendance and degree information available by phone, fax, mail. Transcripts available by mail.

Christopher Newport College, Registrar, 50 Shoe Lane, Newport News, VA 23606-2998, 757-594-7155 (Fax: 757-594-7711) www.cnu.edu. 8AM-5PM. Enrollment: 4800. Records go back to 1971. Alumni records maintained here; call 757-594-7712. Degrees granted: Bachelors. Attendance and degree information available by phone, fax, mail. Transcripts available by fax, mail.

Clinch Valley College of the University of Virginia, Registrar, #1 College Ave, Wise, VA 24293, 540-328-0116, 540-328-0118 (Fax: 540-328-0115) www.clinch.edu. 8AM-5PM. Enrollment: 1500. Records go back to 1954. Alumni records are maintained here. Degrees granted: Bachelors. Attendance and degree information available by phone, fax, mail. Transcripts available by fax, mail.

College of William and Mary, Registrar, PO Box 8795, Williamsburg, VA 23187-8795, 757-221-2800 (Fax: 757-221-2799) www.wm.edu. 8AM - 4:30PM. Enrollment: 7700. Records go back to 1693. Alumni records maintained here; call 804-221-1842. Degrees granted: Bachelors; Masters; Doctorate. Attendance and degree

information available by phone, mail. Transcripts available by mail.

Commonwealth College (Branch Campus), Registrar, 8141 Hull St Rd, Richmond, VA 23235-6411, 804-745-2444, 800-735-2420 (Fax: 804-745-6884) 8AM-5PM. www.bryantstratton.edu Enrollment: 320. Records go back to 1980's. Alumni records are maintained here. Degrees granted: Associate. Attendance and degree information available by fax, mail. Transcripts available by written request only.

Community Hospital of Roanoke Valley College of Health Sciences, Registrar, PO Box 13186, Roanoke, VA 24016, 540-985-8483, 888-985-8483 (Fax: 540-985-9773) www.health.chs.edu. 8AM-5PM. Enrollment: 600. Records go back to 1982. Alumni records maintained here; call 540-985-9031. Degrees granted: Associate. Attendance and degree information available by phone, mail. Transcripts available by mail.

Dabney S. Lancaster Community College, Registrar, PO Box 1000, Clifton Forge, VA 24422-1000, 540-862-4246 (Fax: 540-862-2398) 8AM - 5PM. www.dl.cc.va.us. Enrollment: 1800. Records go back to 1967. Alumni records are maintained here. Degrees granted: Associate. Attendance and degree information available by phone. Transcripts available by mail.

Danville Community College, Registrar, 1008 S Main St, Danville, VA 24541, 804-797-3553 (Fax: 804-797-8541). 8AM-5PM. Enrollment: 4000. Records go back to 1968. Alumni records are maintained here. Degrees granted: Associate. Attendance and degree information available by phone, mail. Transcripts available by mail.

ECPI College of Technology, Registrar, 5555 Greenwich Rd, Virginia Beach, VA 23462-6542, 757-671-7171 (Fax: 757-671-8661) www.ecpi.edu. 8AM - 5PM. Enrollment: 800. Records go back to 1966. Alumni records are maintained here. Degrees granted: Associate; Technical Diploma. Attendance and degree information available by phone, mail. Transcripts available by mail.

Eastern Mennonite University, Registrar, 1200 Park Rd, Harrisonburg, VA 22801-2462, 540-432-4110, 540-432-4085 (Fax: 540-432-4444) www.emu.edu/. 8AM - 5PM. Enrollment: 1200. Records go back to 1917. Alumni records maintained here; call 540-432-4206. Degrees granted: Associate; Bachelors; Masters; First Professional Degree. Special programs- Adult Degree Completion Program, 540-432-4983. Attendance and degree information available by phone, mail. Transcripts available by fax, mail.

Eastern Shore Community College, Registrar, 29300 Lankford Hwy, Melfa, VA 23410, 757-787-5900 X15, 757-787-5915 (Fax: 757-787-5919) www.es.cc.va.us. 8AM-5PM. Enrollment: 700. Records go back to 1971. Alumni records are maintained here. Degrees granted: Associate. Attendance and degree information available by phone, fax, mail. Transcripts available by fax, mail.

Eastern Virginia Medical School, Office of the Registrar, 700 Olney Rd, Room 1007, PO Box 1980, Norfolk, VA 23501-1980, 757-446-5813, 757-446-5244 (Fax: 757-446-5817) 8AM-4:30PM. www.evms.edu. Enrollment: 595. Records go back to 1972. Alumni records maintained here; call 757-446-5805. Degrees granted: Masters; Doctorate. Attendance and degree information available by phone, mail. Transcripts available by mail.

Emory and Henry College, Registrar, PO Box 947, Emory, VA 24327, 540-944-6128, 540-944-6116 (Fax: 540-944-6884) www.ehc.edu. 8AM - 4PM. Enrollment: 885. Records go back to 1902. Alumni records are maintained here. Degrees granted: Bachelors. Attendance and degree information available by phone, fax, mail. Transcripts available by fax, mail.

Ferrum College, Registrar, Ferrum, VA 24088, 540-365-4275 (Fax: 540-365-4278) 8AM-5PM. www.ferrum.edu. Enrollment: 1100. Records go back to 1913. Alumni records maintained here; call 540-365-4216. Degrees granted: Bachelors. Attendance and degree information available by phone, fax, mail. Transcripts available by mail.

George Mason University, Registrar, 4400 University Dr, Fairfax, VA 22030-4444, 703-993-2448, 703-993-2441 (Fax: 703-993-2467) 9AM-5PM. www.gmu.edu. Enrollment: 24000. Records go back to 1972. Alumni records maintained here; call 703-993-8696. Degrees granted: Bachelors; Masters; Doctorate. Attendance and degree information available by phone, mail. Transcripts available by fax, mail.

Germanna Community College, Registrar, PO Box 339, Locust Grove, VA 22508, 540-727-3000, 540-727-3030 (Fax: 540-423-1009) www.gc.cc.va.us. 8AM - 5PM. Enrollment: 3500. Records go back to 1970. Alumni records are maintained here. Degrees granted: Associate. Attendance and degree information available by phone, fax, mail. Transcripts available by mail.

Hampden—Sydney College, Registrar's Office, Hampden-Sydney, VA 23943, 804-223-6274, 804-223-6203 (Fax: 804-223-6860) 8:30AM - 5PM. www.hsc.edu. Enrollment: 970. Degrees granted: Bachelors. Attendance and degree information available by phone, mail. Transcripts available by mail.

Hampton University, Registrar, East Queen St, Hampton, VA 23668, 757-727-5324, 757-727-5325 (Fax: 757-727-5095) 8AM-5PM. www.hampton.edu Enrollment: 6000. Records go back to 1868. Alumni records

maintained here; call 804-727-5485. Degrees granted: Bachelors; Masters; Doctorate. Attendance, degree and transcript information available by mail.

Hollins College, Registrar, PO Box 9708, Roanoke, VA 24020, 540-362-6311, 540-362-6312 (Fax: 540-362-6642). 8:30AM-4:30PM. Enrollment: 871. Records go back to 1800's. Alumni Records: Alumni Affairs, PO Box 9626, Roanoke, VA 24020. Degrees granted: Bachelors; Masters. Attendance and degree information available by phone, fax, mail. Transcripts available by mail.

ITT Technical Institute (Branch of Evansville, IN), Registrar, 863 Glenrock Rd, Norfolk, VA 23502, 757-466-1260 (Fax: 757-466-7630) www.itt.nors. 8AM-5PM. Enrollment: 21467. Records go back to 1988. Alumni Records: ITT Technical Institute, 9511 Angola Ct, Indianapolis, IN 46268. Degrees granted: Associate; Bachelors. Attendance and degree information available by phone, mail. Transcripts available by mail.

Institute of Textile Technology, Registrar, 2551 Ivy Rd, Charlottesville, VA 22903, 804-296-5511 (Fax: 804-296-2957) www.itt.edu. 8AM - 4:30PM. Enrollment: 27. Records go back to 1971. Alumni records are maintained here. Degrees granted: Masters. Attendance and degree information available by phone, mail. Transcripts available by written request only.

J. Sargeant Reynolds Community College, Registrar, PO Box 85622, Richmond, VA 23285-5622, 804-371-3029 (Fax: 804-371-3631) www.jsr.cc.va.us. 8:15AM - 5PM. Enrollment: 9000. Records go back to 1972. Degrees granted: Associate. Attendance and degree information available by phone, fax, mail. Transcripts available by fax, mail.

James Madison University, Registrar, Harrisonburg, VA 22807, 540-568-6281 (Fax: 540-568-7954) www.jmu.edu/registrar. 8AM-5PM. Enrollment: 13000. Records go back to 1908. Alumni records maintained here; call 540-568-3628. Degrees granted: Bachelors; Masters. Attendance and degree information available by phone, mail. Transcripts available by mail.

John Tyler Community College, Admissions & Records, 13101 Jefferson Davis Hwy, Chester, VA 23831-5399, 804-796-4151 (Fax: 804-796-4163). 7:40AM-7PM M-Th; 7:45AM-5PM F. Enrollment: 5000. Records go back to 1967. Alumni records are maintained here. Degrees granted: Associate. Attendance and degree information available by phone, fax, mail. Transcripts available by fax, mail.

Johnson & Wales University (Branch Campus), Registrar, 2428 Alameda Ave Stes 316-318, Norfolk, VA 23513, 757-853-3508, 800-277-CHEF (Fax: 757-857-4869). 8:30AM-4:30PM. Enrollment: 550. Records go back to 1987. Alumni Records: 8 Abbott Park Pl, Providence, RI 02903. Degrees granted: Associate. Special programs- Culinary Arts. Attendance and degree information available by fax, mail. Transcripts available by mail.

Judge Advocate General's School, Registrar, 600 Massie Rd, Charlottesville, VA 22903-1781, 804-972-6303, 804-972-6304 (Fax: 804-972-6338). 8AM - 4:30PM. Enrollment: 84. Records go back to 1950. Alumni records are maintained here. Degrees granted: Masters. Attendance and degree information available by phone, mail. Transcripts available by mail.

Liberty University, Registrar, 1971 University Blvd, Lynchburg, VA 24502-2269, 804-582-2397, 800-522-6225 (Fax: 804-582-2187) www.liberty.edu. 8:30AM-4PM. Enrollment: 8000. Records go back to 1971. Alumni records maintained here; call 804-582-2834. Degrees granted: Associate; Bachelors; Masters; Doctorate. Attendance and degree information available by phone, fax, mail. Transcripts available by fax, mail.

Longwood College, Registrar, 201 High St, Farmville, VA 23909, 804-395-2095, 804-395-2728 (Fax: 804-395-2252) www.lwc.edu. 8:15AM-5PM. Enrollment: 3200. Records go back to 1884. Alumni records maintained here; call 804-395-2044. Degrees granted: Bachelors; Masters. Attendance and degree information available by phone, fax, mail. Transcripts available by mail.

Lord Fairfax Community College, Registrar, PO Box 47, Middletown, VA 22645, 540-869-1120 X114 (Fax: 540-869-7881; 540-868-7007 (Admissions)) 8AM-5PM. www.lf.cc.va.us. Enrollment: 3500. Records go back to 1970. Alumni records are maintained here. Degrees granted: Associate. Attendance, degree and transcript information available by mail.

Lynchburg College, Registrar, 1501 Lakeside Dr, Lynchburg, VA 24501-3199, 804-544-8300 X8218 (Fax: 804-544-8658) 8AM-5PM. www.lynchburg.edu. Enrollment: 1600. Records go back to 1903. Alumni records are maintained here. Degrees granted: Bachelors; Masters. Attendance and degree information available by phone, mail. Transcripts available by mail.

Mary Baldwin College, Registrar, Frederick and New St, Staunton, VA 24401, 540-887-7071, 800-468-2262 (Fax: 540-886-5561) 8AM-5PM. www.mbc.edu. Enrollment: 2140. Records go back to 1842. Alumni records maintained here; call 540-887-7007. Degrees granted: Bachelors; Masters. Attendance and degree information available by phone, fax, mail. Transcripts available by mail.

Mary Washington College, Registrar, 1301 College Ave, Fredericksburg, VA 22401-5358, www.mwc.edu. 540-654-1063 (Fax: 540-654-2145) 8:30AM-4PM. Enrollment: 4000. Records go back to 1911. Alumni records maintained here; call 540-654-1011. Degrees granted: Bachelors; Masters. Certification: Education. Attendance and degree information available by phone, fax, mail. Transcripts available by mail.

Marymount University, Registrar, 2807 N Glebe Rd, Arlington, VA 22207, 703-284-1520 (Fax: 703-516-4505) 8AM - 6PM M-Th; 8AM - 5PM F. www.marymount.edu. Enrollment: 4000. Records go back to 1950. Alumni records maintained here; call 703-284-1541. Degrees granted: Associate; Bachelors; Masters. Attendance and degree information available by phone, fax, mail. Transcripts available by fax, mail.

Mountain Empire Community College, Registrar, PO Drawer 700, Big Stone Gap, VA 24219, 540-523-2400 X209 (Fax: 540-523-2400) www.me.cc.ba.us. 8AM-4:30PM. Enrollment: 3000. Records go back to 1972. Alumni records are maintained here. Degrees granted: Associate. Attendance and degree information available by phone, fax, mail. Transcripts available by fax, mail.

National Business College (Branch Campus), Registrar, 100 Logan St, **Bluefield**, VA 24605, 540-326-3621. Records are located at National Business College, (Corporate Office), Registrar, Salem, VA.

National Business College (Branch Campus), Registrar, 300A Piedmont Ave, **Bristol**, VA 24201, 540-669-5333. Records are located at National Business College, (Corporate Office), Registrar, Salem, VA.

National Business College (Branch Campus), Registrar, 1819 Emmet St, **Charlottesville**, VA 22903, 804-295-0136 (Fax: 804-979-8061). Records are located at National Business College, (Corporate Office), Registrar, Salem, VA.

National Business College (Branch Campus), Registrar, 734 Main St, **Danville**, VA 24541, 804-793-6822. Records are located at National Business College, (Corporate Office), Registrar, Salem, VA.

National Business College (Branch Campus), Registrar, 51-B Burgess Rd, **Harrisonburg**, VA 22801, 540-432-0943 (Fax: 540-432-1133). Records are located at National Business College, (Corporate Office), Registrar, Salem, VA.

National Business College (Branch Campus), Registrar, 104 Candlewood Ct, **Lynchburg**, VA 24502, 804-239-3500. Records are located at National Business College, (Corporate Office), Registrar, Salem, VA.

National Business College, Registrar, PO Box 6400, **Roanoke**, VA 24017, 800-666-6221 (Fax: 504-389-5239). Records are located at National Business College, (Corporate Office), Registrar, Salem, VA.

National Business College (Corporate Office), Registrar, Transcripts, 1813 E Main St, Salem, VA 24153, 800-666-6221 (Fax: 540-986-4608) 7:30AM-9PM M-Th; 7:30AM-5PM F. Enrollment: 400. Records go back to 1886. Alumni records are maintained here. Degrees granted: Associate. Attendance and degree information available by phone, fax, mail. Transcripts available by written request only.

New River Community College, Registrar, PO Drawer 1127, Dublin, VA 24084, www.nr.cc.va.us. 540-674-3603 (Fax: 540-674-3644) 8AM-5PM. Enrollment: 3435. Records go back to 1969. Alumni records maintained here; call 540-674-3600. Degrees granted: Associate. Attendance and degree information available by phone, fax, mail. Transcripts available by mail.

Norfolk State University, Registrar, 2401 Corprew Ave, Norfolk, VA 23504, 757-683-8229, 757-683-8124 (Fax: 757-683-8907) 8AM-4:30PM. www.cyclops.nsu.edu/. Enrollment: 8000. Records go back to 1935. Alumni records maintained here; call 804-683-8135. Degrees granted: Bachelors; Masters; Doctorate. Attendance and degree information available by phone, mail. Transcripts available by fax, mail.

Northern Virginia Community College (Alexandria Campus), Registrar, 3001 N Beauregard St, Alexandria, VA 22311, 703-845-6333 www.nv.cc.va.us. 8:30AM - 5PM. Enrollment: 60000. Records go back to 1970's. Alumni records maintained here; call 703-323-2364. Degrees granted: Associate. Attendance and degree information available by phone, mail. Transcripts available by mail.

Northern Virginia Community College (Annandale Campus), Registrar, 8333 Little River Tpke, Annandale, VA 22003, 703-323-3328 (Fax: 703-323-3367) www.nv.cc.va.us. 9AM-6PM M-Th, 9AM-4PM F. Enrollment: 15000. Records go back to 1965. Alumni records maintained here; call 703-323-3747. Degrees granted: Associate. Attendance and

degree information available by phone, mail. Transcripts available by fax, mail.

Northern Virginia Community College (Manassas Campus), Registrar, 6901 Sudley Rd, Manassas, VA 22110, 703-257-6600 (Fax: 703-257-9296) www.nv.cc.va.us. 8AM-5:30PM Enrollment: 3800. Records go back to 1970's. Alumni records are maintained here. Degrees granted: Associate. Attendance and degree information available by phone, mail. Transcripts available by fax, mail.

Northern Virginia Community College (Loudon Campus), Registrar, 1000 Harry Flood Byrd Hwy, Sterling, VA 20164, www.nv.cc.va.us 703-450-2500 (Fax: 703-451-2536) 8AM-5:30PM. Enrollment: 4200. Records go back to 1974. Alumni records maintained here; call 703-323-2364. Degrees granted: Associate. Attendance and degree information available by phone, mail. Transcripts available by fax, mail.

Northern Virginia Community College (Woodbridge Campus), Registrar, 15200 Neabsco Mills Rd, Woodbridge, VA 22191, www.nv.cc.va.us 703-878-5700 (Fax: 703-670-8433) 8AM-7:30PM M-Th; 8AM-5PM F. Enrollment: 5500. Records go back to 1970's. Alumni records are maintained here. Degrees granted: Associate. Attendance and degree information available by phone, fax, mail. Transcripts available by fax, mail.

Old Dominion University, Registrar, 5215 Hampton Blvd, Norfolk, VA 23529-0053, 757-683-4425 (Fax: 757-683-5357). 8AM-5PM. Enrollment: 17000. Records go back to 1930. Alumni records maintained here; call 757-683-3097. Degrees granted: Bachelors; Masters; Doctorate. Attendance and degree information available by phone, mail. Transcripts available by mail.

Patrick Henry Community College, Registrar, PO Drawer 5311, Martinsville, VA 24115, 540-638-8777, 800-232-7997 (VA) (Fax: 540-656-0320) www.ph.cc.va.us. Enrollment: 2000. Records go back to 1971. Degrees granted: Associate. Attendance and degree information available by phone, fax, mail. Transcripts available by fax, mail.

Paul D. Camp Community College, Registrar, 100 N College Dr, PO Box 737, Franklin, VA 23851-0737, 757-569-6700 (Fax: 757-569-6795) www.pcva.us. 8AM-4:30PM. Enrollment: 1500. Records go back to 1970. Degrees granted: Associate. Attendance and degree information available by written request only. Transcripts available by written request only.

Piedmont Virginia Community College Registrar, 501 College Dr, Charlottesville, VA 22902, www.pvcc.cc.va..us. 804-977-3900, 804-961-5411 (Fax: 804-971-8232) Enrollment: 4300. Records go back to 1972. Degrees granted: Associate. Attendance and degree information available by phone, fax, mail. Transcripts available by mail.

Presbyterian School of Christian Education
(See Union Theological Seminary (Richmond))

Protestant Episcopal Theological Seminary in Virginia
(See Virginia Theological Seminary)

Radford University, Registrar, PO Box 6904, Radford, VA 24142, 540-831-5271 (Fax: 540-831-6642) www.runet.edu/. 8AM-5PM. Enrollment: 8500. Records go back to 1910. Alumni records maintained here; call 540-831-5248. Degrees granted: Bachelors; Masters. Attendance and degree information

available by phone, fax, mail. Transcripts available by mail.

Randolph - Macon College, Registrar, PO Box 5005, Ashland, VA 23005-5505, www.rmc.edu 804-752-7227 (Fax: 804-752-7231) 8:30AM-5PM. Enrollment: 1080. Records go back to 1834. Alumni records maintained here; call 804-752-7222. Degrees granted: Bachelors. Attendance and degree information available by phone, fax, mail. Transcripts available by fax, mail.

Randolph - Macon Woman's College, Registrar, 2500 Rivermont Ave, Lynchburg, VA 24503-1526, 804-947-8143, 804-947-8131 (Fax: 804-947-8999) www.rmwc.edu. 8:30AM-4:30PM. Enrollment: 730. Records go back to 1891. Alumni records maintained here; call 804-947-8102. Degrees granted: Bachelors. Attendance and degree information available by phone, mail. Transcripts available by mail.

Rappahannock Community College, Registrar, 12745 College Dr, Glenns, VA 23149, 804-758-6700 (Fax: 804-758-3852) 8AM-4:30PM. www.rcc.va.us. Enrollment: 2000. Records go back to 1970. Alumni records are maintained here. Degrees granted: Associate. Attendance and degree information available by phone, fax, mail. Transcripts available by mail.

Regent University, Registrar, 1000 Regent University Dr, Virginia Beach, VA 23464, 757-579-4094 (Fax: 757-575-5317) www.regent.edu. 8:30AM - 5:30PM. Enrollment: 1500. Records go back to 1977. Alumni records maintained here; call 804-579-4461. Degrees granted: Bachelors; Masters; Doctorate. Attendance and degree information available by phone, fax, mail. Transcripts available by fax, mail.

Richard Bland College, Registrar, 11301 Johnson Rd, Petersburg, VA 23805, 804-862-6206 (Fax: 804-862-6189). 8AM-5PM. Enrollment: 1200. Records go back to 1961. Alumni records maintained here; call 804-862-6215. Degrees granted: Associate. Attendance and degree information available by phone, fax, mail. Transcripts available by fax, mail.

Roanoke College, Registrar, 221 College Lane, Salem, VA 24153-3794, 540-375-2210 (Fax: 540-375-2213) www.roanoke.edu. 8AM-4:30PM. Enrollment: 1700. Records go back to 1982. Alumni records are maintained here. Degrees granted: Bachelors. Attendance and degree information available by phone, fax, mail. Transcripts available by fax, mail.

Shenandoah University, Registrar, 1460 University Dr, Winchester, VA 22601, 540-665-5585, 540-665-3499 (Fax: 540-665-5446) 9AM-5PM. www.su.edu. Enrollment: 2300. Records go back to 1930. Alumni records maintained here; call 540-665-4511. Degrees granted: Associate; Bachelors; Masters; Doctorate. Attendance and degree information available by phone, fax, mail. Transcripts available by fax, mail.

Southern Virginia College, Registrar, One College Hill Dr, Buena Vista, VA 24416, 540-261-8400 (Fax: 540-261-8451) 8:30AM-5PM. www.southernvirginia.edu. Enrollment: 210. Records go back to 1950's. Alumni records are maintained here. Degrees granted: Associate; Bachelors. Attendance and degree information available by phone, fax, mail. Transcripts available by written request only.

Southside Virginia Community College, Admissions & Records, 109 Campus Dr, Alberta, VA 23821, 804-949-1014, 804-949-1013 (Fax: 804-949-7863) www.sv.cc.va.us.

8AM-4:30PM. Enrollment: 3600. Records go back to 1970. Degrees granted: Associate. Attendance and degree information available by phone, fax, mail. Transcripts available by fax, mail.

Southwest Virginia Community College, Registrar, PO Box SVCC, Richlands, VA 24641, 540-964-2555 X294 (Fax: 540-964-9307) www.sw.cc.va.us. 8AM-4:30PM. Enrollment: 4235. Records go back to 1968. Alumni records are maintained here. Degrees granted: Associate. Attendance and degree information available by phone, mail. Transcripts available by mail.

St. Paul's College, Registrar, 115 College Dr, Lawrenceville, VA 23868, 804-848-4356 (Fax: 804-848-0303) 8AM-5PM. Enrollment: 700. Records go back to 1888. Alumni records are maintained here. Degrees granted: Bachelors. Attendance and degree information available by phone, mail. Transcripts available by mail.

Strayer College
(See Strayer University)

Strayer University, Registrar, 3045 Columbia Pike, Arlington, VA 22204, 703-892-5100 (Fax: 703-679-2640) 9AM-6PM. www.strayer.edu. Enrollment: 9500. Records go back to 1920's. Alumni records maintained here; call 703-769-2676. Degrees granted: Associate; Bachelors; Masters. Attendance and degree information available by phone, fax, mail. Transcripts available by mail. To confirm attendance or degree call 703-339-1000.

Sweet Briar College, Registrar, Sweet Briar, VA 24595, 804-381-6179 (Fax: 804-381-6484) www.registrar.sbc.edu. 8:30AM - 5PM. Enrollment: 634. Records go back to 1901. Alumni records maintained here; call 804-381-6131. Degrees granted: Bachelors. Attendance and degree information available by phone, mail. Transcripts available by mail.

Thomas Nelson Community College, Records Office, PO Box 9407, Hampton, VA 23670, 757-825-2843 (Fax: 757-825-2763) www.tncc.cc.va.us/. 8AM-6PM M-Th; 8AM-5PM F; 8AM-12:30PM Summer. Enrollment: 7500. Records go back to 1968. Alumni records maintained here; call 757-825-2719. Degrees granted: Associate. Attendance information available by phone, fax, mail. Degree and transcript information available by fax, mail.

Tidewater Community College, Registrar, 7000 College Dr, Portsmouth, VA 23703, 757-822-2150 (Fax: 757-686-5022) www.tc.cc.va.us. 9AM - 5PM. Enrollment: 3500. Records go back to 1968. Alumni records are maintained here. Degrees granted: Associate. Attendance, degree and transcript information available by mail.

Union Theological Seminary, Registrar, 3401 Brook Rd, Richmond, VA 23227, 804-254-8054 (Fax: 804-254-8060) www.utsva.edu. 9AM-5PM. Enrollment: 130. Records go back to 1915. Alumni records are maintained here. Degrees granted: Masters; Doctorate; Ed. S. Attendance information available by phone, fax. Degree information available by phone, fax, mail. Transcripts available by fax, mail.

University of Richmond, Registrar, Richmond, VA 23173, 804-289-8639 (Fax: 804-287-6578) www.urich.edu. 8AM-5PM. Enrollment: 2700. Records go back to 1830. Alumni records maintained here; call 804-289-8473. Degrees granted: Bachelors;

Masters. Attendance and degree information available by phone, mail. Transcripts available by fax, mail.

University of Virginia, Registrar, PO Box 9009, Charlottesville, VA 22906, 804-924-4122, 804-924-4124 (Fax: 804-924-4156) 8AM-5PM. www.virginia.edu. Enrollment: 18000. Records go back to 1819. Alumni records maintained here; call 804-971-9721. Degrees granted: Bachelors; Masters; Doctorate. Attendance and degree information available by phone, fax, mail. Transcripts available by fax, mail.

University of Virginia Clinch Valley College, Registrar, Wise, VA 24293, 540-328-0116 (Fax: 540-328-0115) www.clinch.edu. Enrollment: 1300. Records go back to 1954. Alumni records are maintained here. Degrees granted: Bachelors. Special programs- Arts: Science. Attendance and degree information available by phone. Transcripts available by mail.

Virginia Commonwealth University, Registrar, 827 W Franklin St, PO Box 2520, Richmond, VA 23284-2520, 804-828-1349 (Fax: 804-828-8121) 8AM-5PM M,W,F; 8AM-7PM T,Th. www.vcu.edu/safweb. Enrollment: 23722. Records go back to 1838. Alumni records maintained here; call 804-828-2586. Degrees granted: Bachelors; Masters; Doctorate. Attendance and degree information available by phone, mail. Transcripts available by mail.

Virginia Highlands Community College, Admissions Office, PO Box 828, Abingdon, VA 24210, 540-628-6094 (Fax: 540-628-7576) 8AM-5PM. www.vh.cc.va.us. Enrollment: 1800. Records go back to 1969. Alumni records are maintained here. Degrees granted: AAS, AA&S. Attendance and degree information available by phone, fax, mail. Transcripts available by fax, mail.

Virginia Intermont College, Registrar, 1013 Moore St, Bristol, VA 24201, www.vic 540-669-6101, 800-451-1842 (Fax: 540-669-5763) 8:30AM-Noon, 1-4:30PM. Enrollment: 751. Records go back to 1800's. Alumni records are maintained here. Degrees granted: Associate; Bachelors. Attendance and degree information available by phone, fax, mail. Transcripts available by mail.

Virginia Military Institute, Registrar, Lexington, VA 24450, www.vmi.edu 540-464-7213, 540-464-7000 (Fax: 540-464-7726) Enrollment: 1200. Records go back to 1842. Alumni records maintained here; call 540-464-7221. Degrees granted: Bachelors. Attendance and degree information available by phone, fax, mail. Transcripts available by mail.

Virginia Polytechnic Institute and State University, Office of Registrar, Enrollment Services, 248 Burruss Hall, Blacksburg, VA 24061-0134, 540-231-5611, 540-231-6252 (Fax: 540-231-5527) www.vt.edu. 8AM-5PM. Enrollment: 25000. Records go back to 1896. Alumni records are maintained here. Degrees granted: Bachelors; Masters; Doctorate. Attendance information available by phone. Degree information available by phone, fax, mail. Transcripts available by fax, mail.

Virginia State University, Registrar, PO Box 9217, One Hayden Dr, Petersburg, VA 23806, 804-524-5275, 804-524-5269 (Fax: 804-524-6758) www.vsu.edu. 8AM - 5PM. Enrollment: 4000. Records go back to 1882. Alumni records maintained here; call 804-524-5906. Degrees granted: Bachelors;

Masters. Attendance and degree information available by phone, fax, mail. Transcripts available by mail.

Virginia Theological Seminary, Registrar, 3737 Seminary Rd, Alexandria, VA 22304, 703-370-6600 (Fax: 703-370-6234) www.vts.edu. 8:45AM-4:45PM. Enrollment: 150. Records go back to 1985. Alumni records maintained here; call 703-370-6600 X1712. Degrees granted: Masters; Doctorate. Attendance and degree information available by phone, fax, mail. Transcripts available by fax, mail.

Virginia Union University, Registrar, 1500 N Lombardy St, Richmond, VA 23220-1711, 804-257-5845, 804-257-5846 (Fax: 804-257-5797). 8:30AM - 4:30PM. Enrollment: 1400. Records go back to 1800's. Alumni records maintained here; call 804-329-7403. Degrees granted: Bachelors; Masters; Doctorate. Attendance and degree information available by phone, mail. Transcripts available by mail.

Virginia Wesleyan College, Office of the Registrar, 1584 Wesleyan Dr, Norfolk, VA 23502-5599, 757-455-3200, 757-455-3358 (Fax: 757-461-0370) 8:30AM - 4:30PM. Enrollment: 1450. Records go back to 1966. Alumni records maintained here; call 757-455-3298. Degrees granted: Bachelors. Attendance and degree information available by phone, fax, mail. Transcripts available by mail.

Virginia Western Community College, Registrar, 3095 Colonial Ave SW, PO Box 14007, Roanoke, VA 24038, 540-857-7236 (Fax: 540-857-7544) www.vw.cc.va.us. 7:30AM-5PM. Enrollment: 1850. Records go back to 1966. Alumni records are maintained here. Degrees granted: Associate; Career Studies. Attendance and degree information available by mail. Search requires name plus social security number, signed release. No fee for transcripts. Attendance and degree confirmed only to employers or schools.

Washington and Lee University, University Registrar's Office, Reid Hall, Lexington, VA 24450-0303, 540-463-8455 (Fax: 540-463-8045) www.wlu.edu. 8:30AM-4:30PM. Enrollment: 2000. Records go back to 1845. Alumni records maintained here; call 540-463-8464. Degrees granted: Bachelors; BA, BS, JD. Former degrees: MA, MS (to 1948); PhD (to 1908); LLB (to 1968). Attendance and degree information available by phone, fax, mail. Transcripts available by mail.

Wytheville Community College, Registrar, 1000 E Main St, Wytheville, VA 24382, 540-223-4700, 800-468-1195 (Fax: 540-228-6506) www.wc.cc.va.us. 8AM - 5PM. Enrollment: 1800. Records go back to 1968. Alumni records are maintained here. Degrees granted: Associate. Attendance and degree information available by phone, fax, mail. Transcripts available by fax, mail.

Washington

Antioch University (Seattle Campus), Registrar, 2326 6th Ave, Seattle, WA 98121, www.SEATTLE.ANTIOCH.EDU. 206-441-5352 X771 (Fax: 206-441-3307) 9AM-5PM. Enrollment: 800. Records go back to 1985. Pre-1985 records housed at Antioch University, 795 Livermore St., Yellow Springs, OH 45387, 513-767-6401. Alumni records maintained here; call 206-441-5352 X5110. Degrees granted: Bachelors; Masters. Certification: Education. Attendance and degree information available by phone, fax, mail. Transcripts available by fax, mail.

Art Institute of Seattle, Registrar, 2323 Elliott Ave, Seattle, WA 98121-1633, 206-448-0900 X884, 206-448-0900 X870 (Fax: 206-448-2501) www.ais.edu. 7AM-8PM. Enrollment: 2500. Records go back to 1982. Records to 1982 for AIS, to 1955 for **Burnley School of Professional Art**. Alumni records are maintained here. Degrees granted: Associate. Attendance and degree information available by phone, mail. Transcripts available by mail.

Bastyr College of Naturopathic Medicine
(See Bastyr University)

Bastyr University, Registrar, 14500 Juanita Dr NE, Bothell, WA 98011, 425-823-1300 (Fax: 425-823-6222) www.bastyr.edu. 8AM-4:30PM. Enrollment: 860. Records go back to 1978. Alumni records are maintained here. Degrees granted: Bachelors; Masters; 1st Professional Degree(ND). Attendance and degree information available by phone, mail. Transcripts available by mail.

Bellevue Community College, Enrollment Services, 3000 Landerholm Cir SE, Mainstop B125, Bellevue, WA 98007-6484, 425-641-2222, 425-641-2205 (Fax: 425-603-4065) 8AM-5PM. www.bcc.ctc.edu. Enrollment: 18000. Records go back to 1966. Alumni records maintained here; call 425-641-2386. Degrees granted: Associate. Attendance and degree information available by phone, fax, mail. Transcripts available by fax, mail.

Big Bend Community College, Registrar, 7662 Chanute St, Moses Lake, WA 98837-3299, www.bbcc.ctc.edu. 509-762-5351 X226 (Fax: 509-762-6243) 8AM - 4:30PM. Enrollment: 3000. Records go back to 1962. Degrees granted: Associate. Special programs- Commercial Pilot, 509-762-5361 X256. Attendance and degree information available by phone, fax, mail. Transcripts available by fax, mail.

Central Washington University, Registrar, Academic Services, 400 E 8th Ave, Ellensburg, WA 98926-7463, 509-963-3001 (Fax: 509-963-3022) www.cwu.edu. 8AM-5PM. Enrollment: 8500. Records go back to 1890. Alumni records maintained here; call 509-963-2752. Degrees granted: Bachelors; Masters. Attendance and degree information available by phone, fax, mail. Transcripts available by fax, mail.

Centralia College, Registrar, 600 W Locust St, Centralia, WA 98531, 360-736-9391 X221 (Fax: 360-330-7503) 8AM-4:30PM. Enrollment: 3300. Records go back to 1925. Alumni records are maintained here. Degrees granted: Associate. Special programs-Nursing Program: Air/Engineering Program. Attendance and degree information available by phone, fax, mail. Transcripts available by mail.

City University, Registrar, 335 116th Ave SE, Bellevue, WA 98004, 800-426-5596, 425-637-1010 (Fax: 425-450-4665) www.cityu.edu. 8AM-4:30PM. Enrollment: 13159. Records go back to 1973. Alumni Records: Alumni Assoc., 919 SW Grady Way 2nd Flr, Renton, WA 98055. Degrees granted: Associate; Bachelors; Masters. Attendance and degree information available by phone, fax, mail. Transcripts available by mail.

Clark College, Registrar, 1800 E McLoughlin Blvd, Vancouver, WA 98663, 360-992-2136 (Fax: 360-992-2876) www.clark.edu. 8AM-4:30PM. Enrollment: 11000. Records go back to 1935. Alumni records are maintained here. Degrees granted: Associate. Attendance and degree information available by phone, fax, mail. Transcripts available by fax, mail.

Columbia Basin College, Registrar, 2600 N 20th Ave, Pasco, WA 99302, 509-547-0511 (Fax: 509-546-0401) 7:30AM - 4:30PM. www.ctc.edu/~cbcwww/. Enrollment: 6000. Records go back to 1955. Degrees granted: Associate. Attendance and degree information available by phone, fax, mail. Transcripts available by fax, mail. Can only confirm by phone, cannot give out info.

Cornish College of the Arts, Registrar, 710 E Roy St, Seattle, WA 98102, 206-323-1400 (Fax: 206-720-1011). 9AM-4PM. Enrollment: 642. Records go back to 1914. Alumni records are maintained here. Degrees granted: Bachelors. Certification: Acting. School will not confirm attendance information. Degree information available by phone, fax, mail. Transcripts available by fax, mail.

Court Reporting Institute, Registrar, 929 N 130th St, Seattle, WA 98133, 206-363-8300 (Fax: 206-363-8306) Enrollment: 75. Records go back to 1991. Degrees granted: Associate. Attendance and degree information available by phone, mail. Transcripts available by mail.

Eastern Washington University, Registrar, 526 5th St MS 150, Cheney, WA 99004, 509-359-6202, 509-359-2321 (Fax: 509-359-6153) www.ewu.edu/. 8AM - 5PM. Enrollment: 7600. Records go back to 1912. Alumni records maintained here; call 509-359-6303. Degrees granted: Bachelors; Masters. Certification: Educ. School will not confirm attendance information. Degree information available by phone. Transcripts available by mail.

Edmonds Community College, Registrar, 20000 68th Ave W, Lynnwood, WA 98036, 425-640-1456 (Fax: 425-640-1159) www.edcc.edu. 8AM-5PM. Enrollment: 18800. Records go back to 1967. Degrees granted: Associate. Attendance and degree information available by fax, mail. Transcripts available by mail.

Everett Community College, Registrar, 801 Wetmore Ave, Everett, WA 98201, 425-388-9206 (Fax: 425-388-9173 (ATTN: Paula Mayo) www.evcc.ctc.edu. 9AM-5PM. Records go back to 1954. Alumni records are maintained here. Degrees granted: Associate. Attendance and degree information available by phone, fax, mail. Transcripts available by fax, mail.

Evergreen State College, Registration & Records, Library 1100, Olympia, WA 98505, 360-866-6000 X6180, 360-866-6000 X6091 (Fax: 360-866-6680) www.evergreen.edu. 9AM-4PM. Enrollment: 3600. Records go back to 1970. Personal files are kept for 7 years after student leaves. Alumni records maintained here; call 360-866-6000 X6551. Attendance and degree information available by phone, fax, mail. Transcripts available by written request only.

Gonzaga University, Registrar, Spokane, WA 99258, 509-328-4220 X3192, 509-324-5592 (Fax: 509-324-5828) www.gonzaga.edu. 8AM-5PM. Enrollment: 5000. Records go back to 1887. Alumni records maintained here; call 509-328-4220 X5999. Degrees granted: Bachelors; Masters; Doctorate; JD. Attendance and degree information available by phone, fax, mail. Transcripts available by fax, mail.

Grays Harbor College, Records Office, 1620 Edward P. Smith Dr, Aberdeen, WA 98520, 360-538-4028, 360-538-4027 (Fax: 360-538-4299) 8AM-5PM M,W,Th,F; 8AM-7PM T. www.ghc.library.ctc.edu. Enrollment: 2700. Records go back to 1930. Degrees granted: Associate. Special programs- Natural Fisheries Tech. Attendance and degree information available by phone, fax, mail. Transcripts available by fax, mail.

Green River Community College, Registrar, 12401 SE 320th St, Auburn, WA 98002, 253-833-9111 X2511 (Fax: 253-288-3454) www.ctc.edu. 7:30AM-4:30PM. Enrollment: 9500. Records go back to 1965. Degrees granted: Associate. Special programs- Arts: Pre-Professional: Applied Arts: Applied Science. Attendance, degree and transcript information available by fax, mail.

Henry Cogswell College, Registrar, 2802 Wetmore Ave, Everett, WA 98201, 425-258-3351 (Fax: 425-822-1006). 9AM-6PM. Enrollment: 200. Records go back to 1979. Formerly **Cogswell College North**. Alumni records are maintained here. Degrees granted: Bachelors. Attendance and transcript information available by fax, mail. Degree information available by phone, fax, mail. Transcripts available by fax, mail.

Heritage College, Registrar, 3240 Fort Rd, Toppenish, WA 98948, 509-865-2244 X1605, 509-865-8506 (Fax: 509-865-4469). 8AM-5PM. Enrollment: 1100. Records go back to 1982. Alumni records are maintained here. Degrees granted: Bachelors; Masters. Attendance and degree information available by phone, fax, mail. Transcripts available by fax, mail.

Highline Community College, Registrar, PO Box 98000, Des Moines, WA 98198-9800, 206-878-3710 X3244, 206-878-3710 X3228 (Fax: 206-870-3782). 8AM - 4:30PM. Enrollment: 10000. Records go back to 1961. Alumni records are maintained here. Degrees granted: Associate. Attendance and degree information available by phone, fax, mail. Transcripts available by fax, mail.

ITT Technical Institute, Registrar, 12720 Gateway Dr Ste 100, Seattle, WA 98168, 206-244-3300 (Fax: 206-246-7635). 8AM-8PM. Enrollment: 400. Records go back to 1969. Alumni Records: Alumni Assoc., PO Box 50472, Indianapolis, IN 46250. Degrees granted: Associate; Bachelors. Attendance and degree information available by phone, fax, mail. Transcripts available by mail.

ITT Technical Institute, Education Dept, N 1050 Argonne Rd, **Spokane**, WA 99212-2610, 509-926-2900 (Fax: 509-926-2908). 8AM-5PM. Enrollment: 250. Records go back to 1985. Alumni Records: 9511 Angola Ct, Indianapolis, IN 46268. Degrees granted: Associate. Attendance and degree information available by phone, fax, mail. Transcripts available by mail.

John Bastyr College of Naturopathic Medicine
(See Bastyr University)

Lake Washington Technical College, Registrar, 11605 132nd Ave NE, Kirkland, WA 98034, 425-739-8100 (Fax: 425-828-5648). 9AM-7PM. Enrollment: 8500. Records go back to 1949. Alumni records are maintained here. Degrees granted: Associate. Attendance, degree and transcript information available by mail.

Lower Columbia College, Admissions Office, PO Box 3010, 1600 Maple St, Longview, WA 98632-0310, 360-577-2303 (Fax: 360-578-5470). 9AM-5PM. Enrollment: 4000. Records go back to 1934. Alumni records are maintained here. Degrees granted: Associate. Attendance and degree information available by phone, fax, mail. Transcripts available by fax, mail.

Lutheran Bible Institute of Seattle, Registrar, 4221 228th Ave SE, Issaquah, WA 98029, www.lbi.edu. 425-392-0400 (Fax: 425-392-0404) 8AM-5PM. Enrollment: 180. Records go back to 1945. Alumni records are maintained here. Degrees granted: Associate; Bachelors. Attendance and degree information available by phone, fax, mail. Transcripts available by fax, mail.

North Seattle Community College, Registrar, 9600 College Way N, Seattle, WA 98103, 206-527-3669 (Fax: 206-527-3635) http://nsccux.sccd.ctc.edu. 8AM-4:30PM. Enrollment: 8500. Records go back to 1970. Alumni records maintained here; call 206-527-3604. Degrees granted: Associate. Attendance and degree information available by phone, fax, mail. Transcripts available by fax, mail.

Northwest College of Art, Registrar, 16464 State Hwy 305, Poulsbo, WA 98370-0932, 360-779-9993 www.nwca.edu. 8AM - 5PM. Enrollment: 260. Records go back to 1989. Degrees granted: Associate; Bachelors. Attendance and degree information available by phone, mail. Transcripts available by mail.

Northwest College of the Assemblies of God, Registrar, PO Box 579, Kirkland, WA 98083, 425-822-8266 X5230 (Fax: 425-827-0148). 8AM-5PM. Enrollment: 850. Records go back to 1934. Alumni records maintained here; call 425-889-5206. Degrees granted: Bachelors. Attendance and degree information available by fax, mail. Transcripts available by mail.

Northwest Indian College, Registrar, 2522 Kwina Rd, Bellingham, WA 98226, 360-676-2772 (Fax: 360-738-0136). 8AM-5PM. Enrollment: 600. Records go back to 1983. Alumni records are maintained here. Degrees granted: Associate. Attendance and degree information available by phone, fax, mail. Transcripts available by fax, mail.

Northwest Institute of Acupuncture and Oriental Medicine, Registrar, 1307 N 45th St, Seattle, WA 98103, 206-633-2419 (Fax: 206-633-5578). 9AM-6PM M-Th. Enrollment: 150. Records go back to 1981. Degrees granted: Masters. Special programs- Acupuncture Masters. Attendance and degree

information available by phone, fax, mail. Transcripts available by mail.

Olympic College, Registrar, 1600 Chester Ave, Bremerton, WA 98337, 360-478-4542, 800-259-6718 X4504 (Fax: 360-792-2135). 8AM-6PM. Enrollment: 8000. Records go back to 1946. Degrees granted: Associate. Attendance, degree and transcript information available by fax, mail.

Pacific Lutheran University, Registrar's Office, Tacoma, WA 98447, 253-535-7136, 253-535-7133 (Transcripts) (Fax: 253-535-8320) www.plu.edu/. 8AM-6PM M-Th; 8AM-5PM F. Alumni records maintained here; call 253-535-7415. Degrees granted: Masters. Certification: Teaching. Attendance and degree information available by phone, fax, mail. Transcripts available by fax, mail.

Peninsula College, Registrar, 1502 E Lauridsen Blvd, Port Angeles, WA 98362, 360-452-9277 (Fax: 360-457-8100). 8AM-5PM. Degrees granted: Associate. Attendance and degree information available by phone, fax, mail. Transcripts available by mail.

Pierce College, Transcripts/Records, 9401 Farwest Dr SW, Lakewood, WA 98498, www.pierce.ctc.edu. 253-964-6622, 253-964-6501 (Fax: 253-964-6427) Enrollment: 13000. Records go back to 1967. Degrees granted: Associate. Attendance and degree information available by phone, fax, mail. Transcripts available by fax, mail.

Pima Medical Institute, Registrar, 1627 Eastlake Ave E, Seattle, WA 98102, 206-322-6100 (Fax: 206-324-1985) 7:30AM-6PM. www.pimamed.com. Enrollment: 250. Records go back to 1990. Degrees granted: Associate. Special programs- Workforce Training & Education Coordinating Board 360-586-8683. Attendance and degree information available by phone, fax, mail. Transcripts available by fax, mail.

Puget Sound Christian College, Registrar, 410 Fourth Ave N, Edmonds, WA 98020, 425-775-8686 (Fax: 425-775-8688). 7:30AM - 4:30PM. Enrollment: 200. Records go back to 1950. Alumni records are maintained here. Degrees granted: Associate; Bachelors. Special programs- Degree Completion Program, 425-775-8686. Attendance and degree information available by phone, fax, mail. Transcripts available by mail.

Renton Technical College, Registrar, 3000 Fourth St NE, Renton, WA 98056, 206-235-2352 (Fax: 206-235-2372) www.ctc.edu/~renton. Enrollment: 14000. Records go back to 1942. Degrees granted: Associate; Associates & Applied Science. Attendance, degree and transcript information available by fax, mail.

Seattle Central Community College, Registrar, 1701 Broadway, Seattle, WA 98122, http://edison.sccd.ctc.edu. 206-587-6918 (Fax: 206-344-4390) 8AM-4:30PM M,W-F; 8AM-6:30PM T. Enrollment: 10,000. Records go back to 1966. Degrees granted: Associate. Attendance and degree information available by phone, fax, mail. Transcripts available by mail.

Seattle Pacific University, Registrations & Records, 3307 Third Ave W, Seattle, WA 98119, 206-281-2031, 206-281-2034 (Fax: 206-281-2669) www.spu.edu. 8:30AM-4:30PM M,T,W,F; 9:30AM-4:30PM Th. Enrollment: 3400. Records go back to 1891. Alumni records maintained here; call 206-281-2586. Degrees granted: Bachelors; Masters; Doctorate. Attendance and degree

information available by phone, fax, mail. Transcripts available by fax, mail.

Seattle University, Registrar, 12th Ave and E Columbia St, Seattle, WA 98122, 206-296-5850, 206-296-5851 (Fax: 206-296-2443) 8AM-6PM. www.seattleu.edu. Records go back to 1897. Alumni records maintained here; call 206-296-6127. Degrees granted: Bachelors; Masters; Doctorate. Attendance and degree information available by phone, mail. Transcripts available by fax, mail.

Shoreline Community College, Records Office, 16101 Greenwood Ave N, Seattle, WA 98133, www.ctc.edu/~welcome 206-546-4101, 206-546-4523 (Fax: 206-546-5835) 8AM-4:30PM. Enrollment: 7500. Records go back to 1964. Call 206-546-4614 for transcripts. Degrees granted: Associate. Attendance and degree information available by phone, fax, mail. Transcripts available by mail.

Skagit Valley College, Registrar, 2405 E College Way, Mount Vernon, WA 98273, 360-416-7600, 360-416-7689 (Fax: 360-416-7890) www.svc.ctc.edu. 8AM - 5PM. Enrollment: 6496. Records go back to 1926. Degrees granted: Associate. Special programs- Nursing; Firefighter Training: Paralegal. Attendance and degree information available by phone, fax, mail. Transcripts available by fax, mail.

South Puget Sound Community College, Registrar, 2011 Mottman Rd SW, Olympia, WA 98512, 360-754-7711 X243, 360-754-7711 X240 (Fax: 360-586-4336) 8AM-5PM. www.spscc.ctc.edu. Enrollment: 500. Records go back to 1965. Alumni records are maintained here. Degrees granted: Associate. Attendance and degree information available by phone, fax, mail. Transcripts available by fax, mail.

South Seattle Community College, Records, 6000 16th Ave SW, Seattle, WA 98106, www.sccd.ctc.edu/south. 206-764-5399 (Fax: 206-764-7947) 7:30AM-5PM. Records go back to 1975. Degrees granted: Associate. Attendance and degree information available by phone, fax, mail. Transcripts available by written request only.

Spokane Community College, Registrar, 1810 N Greene St MS2150, Spokane, WA 99207-5399, www.scc.spokane.cc.wa.us 509-533-8005, 509-533-7011 (Fax: 509-533-8839) 7:30AM-4:30PM. Records go back to 1970. Degrees granted: Associate; AAS. Attendance and degree information available by phone, fax, mail. Transcripts available by fax, mail.

Spokane Falls Community College, Registrar, W 3410 Fort George Wright Dr, Spokane, WA 99224-5288, 509-533-3518 (Fax: 509-533-3237). 8AM - 4:30PM. Enrollment: 6000. Records go back to 1971. Degrees granted: Associate. Attendance and degree information available by phone, fax, mail. Transcripts available by fax, mail.

St. Martin's College, Registrar, Lacey, WA 98503, 360-438-4356 (Fax: 360-438-4514) 8AM-5PM. Enrollment: 1100. Records go back to 1920. Alumni records maintained here; call 360-438-4366. Degrees granted: Associate; Bachelors; Masters. Attendance and degree information available by phone, fax, mail. Transcripts available by fax, mail.

Tacoma Community College, Registrar, 6501 S 19th St, Tacoma, WA 98466, 206-566-5036, 206-566-5037 (Fax: 206-566-6011) www.tacoma.ctc.edu. 8AM - 4:30PM. Enrollment: 800. Records go back to 1965. Alumni records are maintained here. Degrees granted: Associate. Attendance and degree information available by phone, fax, mail. Transcripts available by fax, mail.

University of Puget Sound, Office of the Registrar, Records Unit, 1500 N Warner, Tacoma, WA 98416, 253-756-3160, 253-756-3119 (Fax: 253-756-3108) www.ups.edu. 8:30AM-4:30PM. Records go back to 1888. Alumni records maintained here; call 253-756-3245. Degrees granted: Bachelors; Masters. Special programs- Continuing Education, 253-756-3306. Attendance and degree information available by phone, fax, mail. Transcripts available by fax, mail.

University of Washington, Registrar, 1400 NE Campus Park Way, Box 355850, Seattle, WA 98195-5850, www.washington.edu. 206-543-8580, 206-543-5378 (Fax: 206-685-3660) 8AM-4:30PM. Enrollment: 34000. Records go back to 1869. Alumni records maintained here; call 206-543-0540. Degrees granted: Bachelors; Masters; Doctorate. Attendance and degree information available by phone, mail. Transcripts available by fax, mail.

Walla Walla College, Registrar, 204 S College Ave, College Place, WA 99324, www.wwc.edu 509-527-2811 (Fax: 509-527-2574) 8:30AM-Noon, 1-4:30PM M-Th; 8:30AM-Noon F. Enrollment: 1700. Records go back to 1905. Alumni records maintained here; call 509-527-2093. Degrees granted: Associate; Bachelors; Masters. Attendance and degree information available by phone, fax, mail. Transcripts available by fax, mail.

Walla Walla Community College, Registrar, 500 Tausick Way, Walla Walla, WA 99362, 509-527-4283, 509-522-2500 (Fax: 509-527-3661) www.ww.cc.wa.us. 8AM-5PM. Enrollment: 3000. Records go back to 1967. Degrees granted: Associate. Attendance and degree information available by phone, fax, mail. Transcripts available by fax, mail.

Washington State Community College District 17, Transcript Office, 1810 N Green St, Spokane, WA 99217, www.scc.ctc.edu. 509-533-7012, 800-248-5644 X8005 (Fax: 509-533-8839) Enrollment: 4000. Records go back to 1964. Alumni records are maintained

here. Degrees granted: Associate. Attendance and degree information available by phone, fax, mail. Transcripts available by mail.

Washington State University, (Richland) 2710 University Dr, Richland, WA 99352,. Records are located at Washington State University, Registrar, Pullman, WA.

Washington State University, Registrar, PO Box 641035, Pullman, WA 99164-1035, 509-335-5330, 509-335-5511 (Fax: 509-335-7823) www.wsu.edu. 8AM - 5PM. Enrollment: 17,500. Records go back to 1890. Alumni Records: Alumni Assoc., PO Box 646150, Pullman, WA 99164-6150. Degrees granted: Bachelors; Masters; Doctorate; Vet Med. Attendance and degree information available by phone, fax, mail. Transcripts available by fax, mail.

Washington State University, (Vancouver) 14204 NE Salmon Creek Ave, Vancouver, WA 98686,. Records are located at Washington State University, Registrar, Pullman, WA.

Wenatchee Valley College, Registrar, 1300 Fifth St, Wenatchee, WA 98801, 509-662-1651 X2136, 509-664-2563 (Fax: 509-664-2511) www.wvc.ctc.edu. Enrollment: 4000. Records go back to 1939. Alumni records maintained here; call 509-662-1651 X2151. Degrees granted: Associate. Attendance and degree information available by phone, fax, mail. Transcripts available by fax, mail.

Western Business College, (Branch) Registrar, 6625 East Mill Plain Blvd, Vancouver, WA 98661, 360-694-3225 (Fax: 360-737-7719) Enrollment: 85. Records go back to 1956. Degrees granted: Associate. Attendance and degree information available by phone, fax, mail. Transcripts available by fax, mail.

Western Washington University, Registrar, 516 High St, Bellingham, WA 98225, 360-650-3430 (Fax: 360-650-7327) 8AM-5PM. www.wwu.edu.. Enrollment: 10708. Records go back to 1899. Alumni records maintained here. Degrees granted: Bachelors; Masters. Special programs- Hixley College of Environmental Studies, Center for Small Business. Attendance and degree

information available by phone, fax, mail. Transcripts available by fax, mail.

Whatcom Community College, Registrar, 237 W Kellogg Rd, Bellingham, WA 98226, 360-676-2170 (Fax: 360-676-2171). 8AM-5PM. Enrollment: 5000. Records go back to 1970. Degrees granted: Associate. Attendance and degree information available by phone, fax, mail. Transcripts available by written request only.

Whitman College, Registrar, Walla Walla, WA 99362, 509-527-5983 (Fax: 509-527-4967) www.whitman.edu. 8:30AM-Noon, 1-4:30PM. Enrollment: 1300. Records go back to 1859. Alumni records maintained here; call 509-527-5167. Degrees granted: Bachelors. Attendance and degree information available by phone, fax, mail. Transcripts available by fax, mail.

Whitworth College, Academic Records, W 300 Hawthorne, Spokane, WA 99251, 509-777-3201, .509-466-1000 (Fax: 509-777-3722) 9AM-4PM. www.whitworth.edu. Enrollment: 1568. Records go back to 1896. Alumni records maintained here; call 509-466-3799. Degrees granted: Bachelors; Masters. Certification: Educ. Attendance and degree information available by phone, fax, mail. Transcripts available by mail.

Yakima Valley Community College, Registrar, PO Box 1647, Yakima, WA 98907, 509-574-4700, 509-574-4600 (Fax: 509-574-6860) www.rfttc.org/~yvcc. 7:30AM - 5PM. Enrollment: 5995. Records go back to 1928. Alumni records are maintained here. Degrees granted: Associate. Attendance and degree information available by phone, fax, mail. Transcripts available by fax, mail.

West Virginia

Alderson - Broaddus College, Registrar, Philippi, WV 26416, 304-457-6278, 304-457-6227 (Fax: 304-457-6239) 8AM - 4:30PM. www.mountain.net/ab. Enrollment: 850. Records go back to 1895. Alumni records maintained here; call 304-457-6202. Degrees granted: Associate; Bachelors; Masters. Attendance and degree information available by phone, fax, mail. Transcripts available by fax, mail.

Appalachian Bible College, Registrar, PO Box ABC, Bradley, WV 25818, 304-877-6428 (Fax: 304-877-5082) 8-Noon, 1-5PM. ourworld.compuserve.com:80/homepages/Alan_Roberts. Enrollment: 250. Records go back to 1950. Alumni records are maintained here. Degrees granted: Associate; Bachelors. Attendance and degree information available by phone, fax, mail. Transcripts available by fax, mail.

Beckley College
(See The College of West Virginia)

Bethany College, Registrar, Bethany, WV 26032, 304-829-7831, 304-829-7832 (Fax: 304-829-7788) www.bethany.wvnet.edu.

8AM-4:30PM. Enrollment: 750. Records go back to 1900. Alumni records maintained here; call 304-829-7411. Degrees granted: Bachelors. Attendance, degree and transcript information available by fax, mail.

Bluefield State College, Registrar, 219 Rock St, Bluefield, WV 24701, 304-327-4060 (Fax: 304-325-7747) www.bscvax.wvnet.edu. 8AM - 4PM. Enrollment: 2500. Records go back to 1930's. Alumni records are maintained here. Degrees granted: Associate; Bachelors. Attendance and degree information available by phone, fax, mail. Transcripts available by fax, mail.

College of West Virginia (The), Registrar, 609 S Kanawha St, Beckley, WV 25802, 304-253-7351 X448, 800-766-6067 (Fax: 304-253-5072). Enrollment: 2000. Formerly **Beckley College**. Alumni records are maintained here. Degrees granted: Associate; Bachelors; Certificate. Special programs- Medical, Criminal Justice. Attendance and degree information available by phone, fax, mail. Transcripts available by fax, mail.

Computer Tech (Branch), Registrar, Country Club Rd Ext, Fairmont, WV 26554,

304-363-5100 (Fax: 304-366-9948). 8:30AM - 6PM. Records go back to 1988. Degrees granted: Associate. Attendance, degree and transcript information available by fax, mail. Signed request from student required

Concord College, Registrar, PO Box 1000, Athens, WV 24712, 304-384-5237 (Fax: 304-384-9044) www.concord.wvnet.edu. Records go back to 1920's. Alumni records are maintained here. Degrees granted: Bachelors. Attendance and degree information available by phone, fax, mail. Transcripts available by mail.

Davis & Elkins College, Registrar, 100 Campus Dr, Elkins, WV 26241, 304-637-1900 (Fax: 304-637-1982) 8:30AM-5PM. www.dne.wvnet.edu. Records go back to 1904. Alumni records are maintained here. Degrees granted: Associate; Bachelors. Special programs- Nursing, 304-636-3300. Attendance and degree information available by phone, fax, mail. Transcripts available by fax.

Fairmont State College, Registrar, 1201 Locust Ave, Fairmont, WV 26554, 304-367-4141, 304-367-4142 (Fax: 304-367-4789)

8AM-4PM. www.fairmont.wvnet.edu. Enrollment: 6300. Records go back to 1900. Alumni records maintained here; call 304-367-0932. Degrees granted: Associate; Bachelors; Certificate. Attendance, degree and transcript information available by mail.

Glenville State College, Registrar, 200 High St, Glenville, WV 26351, 304-462-4117, 304-462-7361 (Fax: 304-462-8619) 8AM - 4PM. www.glenville.wvnet.edu. Enrollment: 2400. Records go back to 1880. Alumni records maintained here; call 304-462-7361 X122. Degrees granted: Associate; Bachelors. Attendance and degree information available by phone, fax, mail. Transcripts available by fax, mail.

Huntington Junior College, Registrar, 900 Fifth Ave, Huntington, WV 25701, 304-697-7550 (Fax: 304-697-7554). Records go back to 1936. Degrees granted: Associate. Special programs- Court Reporting, 304-697-7550. Attendance and degree information available by phone, fax, mail. Transcripts available by fax, mail.

Huntington Junior College of Business, Registrar, 900 Fifth Ave, Huntington, WV 25701, 304-697-7550 (Fax: 304-697-7554) 8AM-5PM. Enrollment: 550. Records go back to 1936. Alumni records are maintained here. Degrees granted: Associate; Diploma. Special programs- Business. Attendance and degree information available by phone, mail. Transcripts available by mail.

Marshall University, Registrar, Huntington, WV 25701, 304-696-6410 (Fax: 304-696-2252) www.marshall.edu. 8AM-4:30PM. Records go back to 1920's. Alumni records are maintained here. Degrees granted: Bachelors; Masters; First Professional Degree. Attendance and degree information available by phone, fax, mail. Transcripts available by fax, mail.

Mountain State College, Registrar, Spring at 16th St, Parkersburg, WV 26101, 304-485-5487 (Fax: 304-485-3524) 8AM-5PM. www.mountainstate.org. Records go back to 1888. Degrees granted: Associate. Attendance and degree information available by phone, fax, mail. Transcripts available by mail.

National Institute of Technology (Cross Lanes Campus), Registrar, 5514 Big Tyler Rd, Cross Lanes, WV 25313-9998, 304-776-6290 (Fax: 304-776-6262) www.ni.tech.edu. 8AM-5PM. Records go back to 1971. Enrollment: 308. Alumni records are maintained here. Degrees granted: Associate. Attendance and transcript information available by written request only. Degree information available by phone, fax, mail.

Northeastern Christian Junior College (See Ohio Valley College)

Ohio Valley College, Registrar, 4501 College Pkwy, Parkersburg, WV 26101, 304-485-7384 (Fax: 304-485-3106) 8AM-5PM. www.ovcollege.edu. Enrollment: 409. Records go back to 1960. Alumni records maintained here; call 304-485-7384. Degrees granted: Associate; Bachelors. Special programs- NCJC records at King of Prussia, 610-337-7328. Attendance and degree information available by phone, fax, mail. Transcripts available by fax, mail.

Potomac State College of West Virginia University, Registrar, 101 Fort Ave, Keyser, WV 26726, 304-788-6800 (Fax: 304-788-6939). 8AM-4:30PM. Records go back to 1901. Alumni records are maintained here. Degrees granted: Associate. Attendance and degree information available by phone, mail. Transcripts available by mail.

Salem College at Clarksburg (See Salem Teikyo University)

Salem-Teikyo University, Registrar, 223 W Main St, Salem, WV 26426, 304-782-5297 www.salem-teikyo.wvnmet.edu. (Fax: 304-782-5297) Enrollment: 800. Records go back to 1888. Alumni records maintained here; call 304-782-5351. Degrees granted: Bachelors; Masters. Attendance and degree information available by phone, fax, mail. Transcripts available by fax, mail.

Shepherd College, Registrar, Shepherdstown, WV 25443, 304-876-5463 (Fax: 304-876-5136) www.shepherd.wvnet.edu/register/ 8AM-4:30PM. Records go back to 1871. Alumni records maintained here; call 304-876-5157. Degrees granted: Associate; Bachelors. Attendance and degree information available by phone, fax, mail. Transcripts available by fax, mail.

Southern West Virginia Community & Technical College, Registrar, PO Box 2900, Mt Gay, WV 25637, 304-792-7098 X218, 304-792-7160 X120-122 (Registrar) (Fax: 304-792-7056) www.wvnet.edu. 8AM-4:30PM. Enrollment: 3100. Records go back to 1971. Alumni records are maintained here. Degrees granted: Associate. Attendance and degree information available by phone, fax, mail. Transcripts available by fax, mail.

University of Charleston, Registrar, 2300 MacCorkle Ave SE, Charleston, WV 25304, 304-357-4740, 304-357-4737 (Fax: 304-357-4715). Records go back to 1900's. Alumni records are maintained here. Degrees granted: Associate; Bachelors; Masters. Attendance and degree information available by phone, fax, mail. Transcripts available by mail.

Webster College, Registrar, 412 Fairmont Ave, Fairmont, WV 26554, 304-363-8824 8AM-4PM. Enrollment: 2200. Records go back to 1926. Degrees granted: Associate. Attendance and degree information available by phone, mail. Transcripts available by mail.

West Liberty State College, Registrar, West Liberty, WV 26074, 304-336-8007, 304-336-8008 (Fax: 304-336-8285) 8AM-4PM. www.wlsvax.wunet.edu. Enrollment: 2400. Records go back to 1925. Alumni records maintained here; call 304-336-8124. Degrees granted: Associate; Bachelors. Attendance and degree information available by phone, fax, mail. Transcripts available by fax, mail.

West Virginia Business College, Registrar, 116 Pennsylvania Ave, Nutter Fort, WV 26301, 304-624-7695. 8AM-5PM. Records go back to 1880. Degrees granted: Associate. Attendance and degree information available by phone, mail. Transcripts available by mail.

West Virginia Business College (Branch Campus), Registrar, 1052 Main St, Wheeling, WV 26003, 304-232-0631. 8AM-5PM. Records go back to 1920. Degrees granted: Associate. Attendance and degree information available by phone, mail. Transcripts available by mail.

West Virginia Career College, Registrar, 1000 Virginia St E, Charleston, WV 25301, 304-345-2820 (Fax: 304-345-1425). 8AM-4PM. Degrees granted: Associate. Attendance and degree information available by phone, mail. Transcripts available by mail.

West Virginia Career College, Registrar, 148 Willey St, Morgantown, WV 26505, 304-296-8282 (Fax: 304-296-4327). 8AM-4PM. Enrollment: 250. Records go back to 1922. Alumni records are maintained here. Degrees

granted: Associate. Attendance and degree information available by phone, mail. Transcripts available by mail.

West Virginia Graduate College (See Marshall University (Merged 7/1/97))

West Virginia Institute of Technology, Registrar, Montgomery, WV 25136, 304-442-3151, 304-442-3167 (Fax: 304-442-3097) 8AM-4:30PM. www.wvit.wvnet.edu. Enrollment: 2300. Records go back to 1895. Alumni records maintained here; call 304-422-1005. Degrees granted: Associate; Bachelors; Masters. Attendance and degree information available by phone, fax, mail. Transcripts available by fax, mail.

West Virginia Northern Community College, Registrar, 1704 Market St, Wheeling, WV 26003, 304-233-5900 X4211, 304-233-5900 X4212 (Fax: 304-233-8132). 8:30AM-5PM. Enrollment: 2700. Records go back to 1972. Alumni records maintained here; call 304-233-5900 X4265. Degrees granted: Associate. Attendance, degree and transcript information available by mail.

West Virginia School of Osteopathic Medicine, Registrar, 400 N Lee St, Lewisburg, WV 24901, 304-647-6230 (Fax: 304-645-4859). 8AM-4:30PM. Records go back to 1974. Alumni records maintained here; call 304-647-6382. Degrees granted: Bachelors; Masters; First Professional Degree. Attendance and degree information available by phone, mail. Transcripts available by mail.

West Virginia State College, Registrar, Post Office Box 1000, Institute, WV 25112, 304-766-3144 (Fax: 304-766-4104) 8:30AM-5PM. www.wvsc.wvnet.edu/wvsc.html. Records go back to 1958. Alumni records are maintained here. Degrees granted: Bachelors. Attendance and degree information available by phone, fax, mail. Transcripts available by mail.

West Virginia University, Admissions & Records, PO Box 6009, Morgantown, WV 26506-6009, 304-293-2124 (Fax: 304-293-8991). 8:15AM-4:45PM. Alumni Records: PO Box 4269, Morgantown, WV 26506-6009 (Fax: 304-293-4733). Degrees granted: Bachelors; Masters; Doctorate. Attendance and degree information available by phone, fax, mail. Transcripts available by fax, mail.

West Virginia University Parkersburg, Registrar, 300 Campus Dr, Parkersburg, WV 26101, 304-424-8220, 304-424-8222 (Fax: 304-424-8332) www.wvup.wvnet.edu. 8AM-4:30PM. Enrollment: 3612. Records go back to 1961. Alumni records are maintained here. Degrees granted: Bachelors. Attendance and degree information available by phone, fax, mail. Transcripts available by fax, mail.

West Virginia Wesleyan College, Registrar, College Ave, Buckhannon, WV 26201, 304-473-8470 (Fax: 304-473-8531) 8AM-4PM. www.wvwc.edu. Enrollment: 1650. Records go back to 1890. Alumni records maintained here; call 304-473-8509. Degrees granted: Bachelors; Masters. Special programs- Outreach Education, 304-473-8430. Attendance and degree information available by phone, fax, mail. Transcripts available by fax, mail.

Wheeling Jesuit University, Registrar, 316 Washington Ave, Wheeling, WV 26003, 304-243-2238 (Fax: 304-243-2500) www.wjc.edu. 8:30AM-5PM. Records go back to 1955. Alumni records maintained here; call 304-243-2309. Degrees granted: Bachelors; Masters. Attendance and degree

information available by phone, fax, mail. Transcripts available by fax, mail.

Wisconsin

Alverno College, Registrar, PO Box 343922, 3401 S 39th St, Milwaukee, WI 53234-3922, 414-382-6370, 414-382-6069 (Fax: 414-382-6354). www.alverno.edu. 8AM-5PM. Enrollment: 2151. Records go back to 1950's. Alumni records maintained here; call 414-382-6090. Degrees granted: Associate; Bachelors; Masters. Attendance and degree information available by phone, fax, mail. Transcripts available by mail.

Bellin College of Nursing, Registrar, PO Box 23400, 725 S Webster Ave, Green Bay, WI 54305-3400, 920-433-3560 (Fax: 920-433-7416). 8AM-4:30PM. Records go back to 1970's. Degrees granted: Associate. Attendance and degree information available by phone, mail. Transcripts available by mail.

Beloit College, Registrar, 700 College St, Beloit, WI 53511, 608-363-2640 (Fax: 608-363-2718) stu.beloit.edu. Enrollment: 1200. Alumni records maintained here; call 608-363-2218. Degrees granted: Bachelors. Attendance and degree information available by phone, fax, mail. Transcripts available by fax, mail.

Blackhawk Technical College, Records, PO Box 5009, Janesville, WI 53547-5009, 608-757-7668, 608-757-7661 (Fax: 608-757-9407). 8AM-4:30PM. Enrollment: 2530. Records go back to 1968. Degrees granted: Associate. School will not confirm attendance information. Degree information available by phone, fax, mail. Transcripts available by fax, mail.

Cardinal Stritch University, Registrar, 6801 N Yates Rd, Milwaukee, WI 53217, 414-410-4000 acs.stritch.edu. 8AM-5PM. Enrollment: 5176. Records go back to 1937. Alumni records are maintained here. Degrees granted: Bachelors; Masters; Doctorate. Attendance and degree information available by fax, mail. Transcripts available by mail.

Carroll College, Registrar, 100 N East Ave, Waukesha, WI 53186, 414-524-7208 (Fax: 414-524-7139) www.cc.edu. 8AM-4:30PM. Enrollment: 2240. Alumni records maintained here; call 414-524-7237. Degrees granted: Bachelors; Masters. Attendance and degree information available by fax, mail. Transcripts available by written request only.

Carthage College, Registrar, 2001 Alford Dr, Kenosha, WI 53140, 414-551-6100 (Fax: 414-551-6208) www.carthage.edu. 8AM-4:30PM. Enrollment: 2200. Records go back to 1873. Alumni records maintained here; call 414-551-5700. Degrees granted: Bachelors; Masters; Paralegal. Attendance and degree information available by phone, fax, mail. Transcripts available by mail.

Chippewa Valley Technical College. Registrar, 620 W Clairemont Ave, Eau Claire, WI 54701, www.chippewa.tec.wi.us. 715-833-6269 (Fax: 715-833-6470) 7:30AM - 8:30PM. Records go back to 1940's. Alumni records are maintained here. Degrees granted: Associate. Attendance information available by phone, fax, mail. Transcripts available by mail.

Columbia College of Nursing, Registrar, 2121 E Newport Ave, Milwaukee, WI 53211, 414-961-3530 (Fax: 414-961-4121). 8AM-4PM. Enrollment: 400. Alumni records maintained here; call 414-961-3897. Certification: Diploma in Nursing.

Attendance, degree and transcript information available by written request only.

Concordia University Wisconsin, Registrar, 12800 N Lake Shore Dr, Mequon, WI 53097, 414-243-4345, 414-243-4393 (Fax: 414-243-4351) www.cuw.edu. 8AM - 4:30PM. Enrollment: 3700. Records go back to 1800's. Alumni records are maintained here. Degrees granted: Associate; Bachelors; Masters. Attendance and degree information available by phone, fax, mail. Transcripts available by fax.

Edgewood College, Registrar's Office, 855 Woodrow St, Madison, WI 53711, 608-257-4861 (Fax: 608-257-1455) 8AM-4:30PM. www.edgewood.edu. Enrollment: 2000. Records go back to 1945. Alumni records are maintained here. Degrees granted: Associate; Bachelors; Masters. Attendance and degree information available by phone, fax, mail. Transcripts available by written request only.

Fox Valley Technical Institute, Registrar, 1825 N Bluemound Dr, PO Box 2277, Appleton, WI 54913-2277, 920-735-5712 www.foxvalley.tec.wi.us (Fax: 920-735-4713) 8AM-8PM. Enrollment: 4500. Records go back to 1930's. Degrees granted: Associate; Certificates and Diplomas. Attendance and degree information available by phone, fax, mail. Transcripts available by fax, mail.

Gateway Technical College, Registrar, 3520 30th Ave, Kenosha, WI 53144-1690, 414-656-8972, 414-656-8972 (Fax: 414-656-7209) www.gateway.tec.wi.us. Enrollment: 10,000. Records go back to 1940's. Alumni records maintained here; call 414-656-7233. Degrees granted: Associate; Vocational Diplomas. Attendance and degree information available by phone, fax, mail. Transcripts available by mail.

Herzing College of Technology, Registrar, 1227 N Sherman Ave, Madison, WI 53704, 608-249-6611 (Fax: 608-249-8593) www.herzing.edu. Enrollment: 515. Records go back to 1948. Formerly **Wisconsin School of Electronics**. Alumni records are maintained here. Degrees granted: Associate; Bachelors. Attendance and degree information available by phone, fax, mail. Transcripts available by fax, mail.

ITT Technical Institute, Registrar, 6300 W Layton Ave, Greenfield, WI 53220-4612, 414-282-9494 (Fax: 414-282-9698). 8AM-4PM. Records go back to 1970's. Alumni Records: 9511 Angola Ct, Indianapolis, IN 46268. Degrees granted: Associate; Bachelors Degree-Electronics. Attendance and degree information available by phone, mail. Transcripts available by written request only.

Keller Graduate School of Management (Milwaukee Center), Registrar, 100 E Wisconsin Ave #2550, Milwaukee, WI 53202, www.keller.edu. 414-278-7677 (Fax: 414-278-0137) Records are located at Keller Graduate School of Management, 225 W Washington St #100, Chicago, IL 60606-3418.

Keller Graduate School of Management (Waukesha Center), Registrar, 20935 Swenson Dr, Waukesha, WI 53186, 414-798-9889 (Fax: 414-798-9912) www.keller.edu. Records are located at Keller Graduate School of Management, 225 W Washington St #100, Chicago, IL 60606-3418.

LacCourte Oreilles Ojibwa Community College, Registrar, Rte 2 Box 2357, Hayward, WI 54843, 715-634-4790 (Fax: 715-634-5049). 8AM-4:30PM. Enrollment: 400. Records go back to 1981. Degrees granted: Associate. Attendance, degree and transcript information available by mail.

Lakeland College, Registrar, PO Box 359, Sheboygan, WI 53082-0359, 920-565-1216 (Fax: 920-565-1206). 8AM - 4:30PM. Enrollment: 1800. Records go back to 1920. Alumni records are maintained here. Degrees granted: Bachelors; Masters. Attendance and degree information available by phone, fax, mail. Transcripts available by fax, mail.

Lakeshore Technical College, Registrar/Records, 1290 North Ave, Cleveland, WI 53015, 920-458-4183 X115, 920-684-4408 X115 (Fax: 920-693-3561) www.ltc.tec.wi.us. 7:30AM - 3:45PM. Enrollment: 3700. Records go back to 1940. Alumni records are maintained here. Degrees granted: Associate. Attendance, degree and transcript information available by fax, mail.

Lawrence University, Registrar, PO Box 599, Appleton, WI 54912, 920-832-6578, 920-832-6570 (Fax: 920-832-7025) 8AM-Noon, 1-5PM. www.lawrence.edu. Enrollment: 1200. Records go back to 1920. Alumni records maintained here; call 920-832-6521. Degrees granted: Bachelors. Attendance and degree information available by phone, fax, mail. Transcripts available by written request only.

Madison Area Technical College, Registrar, 3350 Anderson St, Madison, WI 53704, www.madison.tec.wi.us. 608-246-6210 (Fax: 608-246-6400) Records go back to 1920's. Degrees granted: Associate. Attendance and degree information available by phone, fax, mail. Transcripts available by mail.

Madison Junior College of Business, Registrar, 31 S Henry St, Madison, WI 53703, 608-251-6522 (Fax: 608-251-6590) 7AM-4PM. www.madjrcoll.org. Enrollment: 100. Records go back to 1905. Degrees granted: Associate. Attendance and degree information available by phone, fax, mail. Transcripts available by fax, mail.

Marantha Baptist Bible College, Registrar, 745 W Main St, Watertown, WI 53094, 920-261-9300 X363 (Fax: 920-261-9109) 8AM-5PM. www.mbbc.edu. Records go back to 1968. Alumni records are maintained here. Degrees granted: Associate; Bachelors; Masters. Certification: P.C.T. Attendance and degree information available by phone, fax, mail. Transcripts available by fax, mail.

Marian College of Fond du Lac, Registrar, 45 S National Ave, Fond Du Lac, WI 54935, 920-923-7618, 920-923-7619 (Fax: 920-923-7154) www.mariancoll.edu. 8AM-6PM M-Th; 8AM-4:30PM F. Enrollment: 2500. Records go back to 1938. Alumni records maintained here; call 920-923-8133. Degrees granted: Bachelors; Masters. Attendance and degree information available by phone, fax, mail. Transcripts available by fax, mail.

Marquette University, Registrar, MH 310, PO Box 1881, Milwaukee, WI 53201-1881, 414-288-7034 (Fax: 414-288-1773) www.mu.edu. 8AM-4:30PM. Enrollment: 10781. Records go back to 1881. Alumni Records: 1212 W Wisconsin Ave, Milwaukee, WI 53201-1881 (Fax: 414-288-3956). Degrees granted: Bachelors; Masters; Doctorate. Attendance and degree information available by phone, fax, mail. Transcripts available by fax, mail.

Medical College of Wisconsin, Registrar, 8701 Watertown Plank Rd, Milwaukee, WI 53226, 414-456-8733, 414-456-8296 (Fax: 414-456-6506) www.mcw.edu. 8AM - 5PM. Enrollment: 800. Records go back to 1940's. Alumni records are maintained here. Degrees granted: Bachelors; Masters; Doctorate. Attendance, degree and transcript information available by mail. Inquiries regarding medical degrees can be made at 414-456-8873. Inquiries regarding graduate degrees can be made at 414-456-8206. Inquiries regarding preventative medicine degrees can be made at 414-456-4510.

Mid-State Technical College, Registrar, 500 32nd St N, Wisconsin Rapids, WI 54494, www.midstate.tec.wi.us 715-422-5502 (Fax: 715-422-5345) 7:30AM-4:30PM. Enrollment: 15000. Records go back to 1967. Alumni records maintained here; call 715-422-5528. Degrees granted: Associate. Attendance and degree information available by phone, fax, mail. Transcripts available by fax.

Milwaukee Area Technical College, Registrar, 700 W State St, Milwaukee, WI 53233, 414-297-6470 (Fax: 414-297-6371) 7AM-4PM. www.milwaukee.tec.wi.us. Records go back to 1920. Alumni records maintained here; call 414-297-6624. Degrees granted: Associate. Attendance and degree information available by phone, fax, mail. Transcripts available by mail.

Milwaukee Institute of Art and Design, Registrar, 273 E Erie St, Milwaukee, WI 53202, 414-276-7889 X680 (Fax: 414-291-8077). 8AM-4:30PM. Enrollment: 500. Records go back to 1974. Alumni records maintained here; call 414-276-7889. Degrees granted: Bachelors. Attendance and degree information available by phone, fax, mail. Transcripts available by fax, mail.

Milwaukee School of Engineering, Registrar, 1025 N Broadway, Milwaukee, WI 3202-3109, www.msoe.edu. 414-277-6763 (X7215 Registrar) (Fax: 414-277-6914) Enrollment: 2900. Records go back to 1940's. Alumni records are maintained here. Degrees granted: Associate; Bachelors; Masters. Attendance and degree information available by phone, fax, mail. Transcripts available by fax, mail.

Moraine Park Technical College, Registrar, PO Box 1940, 235 N National Ave, Fond Du Lac, WI 54936-1940, 920-924-3193, 920-924-3215 www.mptc.tec.wi.us. (Fax: 920-924-3421) Enrollment: 12000. Records go back to 1970's. Degrees granted: Associate. Attendance and degree information available by phone, mail. Transcripts available by mail.

Mount Mary College, Registrar, 2900 N Menomonee River Pkwy, Milwaukee, WI 53222, 414-258-4810 X281 (Fax: 414-256-1224). 8AM-4:30PM. Records go back to 1915. Alumni records maintained here; call 414-258-4810. Degrees granted: Bachelors; Masters. Attendance and degree information available by phone, fax, mail. Transcripts available by written request only.

Mount Senario College, Registrar, 1500 W College Ave, Ladysmith, WI 54848, 715-532-5511 X120 (Fax: 715-532-7690) www.mscfs.edu. 8AM-4:30PM. Enrollment:

760. Records go back to 1964. Alumni records maintained here; call 715-532-5511 X107. Degrees granted: Associate; Bachelors. Special programs- Outreach Department, 715-532-5511 X189. Attendance and degree information available by phone, fax, mail. Transcripts available by fax, mail.

Nashotah House, Registrar, 2777 Mission Rd, Nashotah, WI 53058-9793, 414-646-3371 (Fax: 414-646-2215) www.nashotah.edu. 8:30AM-4:30PM. Enrollment: 40. Records go back to 1921. Alumni records are maintained here. Degrees granted: Masters; Anglican Studies. Attendance and degree information available by phone, fax. Transcripts available by mail.

Nicolet Area Technical College, Registrar, Box 518, Rhinelander, WI 54501, 715-365-4422, 715-365-4480 (Fax: 715-365-4411) 8AM - 4PM. www.nicolet.tec.wi.us/. Enrollment: 1700. Records go back to 1968. Degrees granted: Associate. Attendance and degree information available by phone, fax, mail. Transcripts available by fax, mail.

North Central Technical College, Registrar, 1000 W Campus Dr, Wausau, WI 54401, www.northcentral.tec.wi.us. 715-675-3331 (Fax: 715-675-9776) 8AM-6PM M-Th, 8AM-4:30PM F. Records go back to 1912. Alumni records are maintained here. Degrees granted: Associate. Attendance and degree information available by phone, fax, mail. Transcripts available by mail.

Northeast Wisconsin Technical College, Registrar, PO Box 19042, 2740 W Mason St, Green Bay, WI 54307, 920-498-5400 (Fax: 920-498-6242) 8AM-5PM. www.nwtc.tec.wi.us. Enrollment: 20000. Records go back to 1913. Alumni records maintained here; call 920-498-5426. Degrees granted: Associate. Attendance and degree information available by phone, fax, mail. Transcripts available by mail.

Northeast Wisconsin Technical College (Marinette Campus), 1601 University Ave, Marinette, WI 54143,. Records are located at Northeast Wisconsin Technical College, Registrar, Green Bay, WI.

Northland College, Registrar, 1411 Ellis Ave, Ashland, WI 54806, 715-682-1227 (Fax: 715-682-1308) http://bobb.northland.edu. 8AM-Noon, 1-4PM. Enrollment: 850. Records go back to 1892. Alumni records maintained here; call 715-682-1497. Degrees granted: Bachelors. Attendance and degree information available by phone, fax, mail. Transcripts available by written request only.

Ripon College, Registrar, PO Box 248, 300 Seward St, Ripon, WI 54971, www.ripon.edu 920-748-8119, 920-748-8326 (Fax: 920-748-7243) 8AM-Noon, 1-5PM. Enrollment: 750. Records go back to 1851. Alumni records maintained here; call 920-748-8126. Degrees granted: Bachelors. Attendance and degree information available by phone, fax, mail. Transcripts available by mail.

Sacred Heart School of Theology, Registrar, PO Box 429, 7335 S Hwy 100, Hales Corners, WI 53130-0429, 414-425-8300 X7228 (Fax: 414-529-6999) 8AM-5PM. Enrollment: 90. Records go back to 1968. Alumni records are maintained here. Degrees granted: Bachelors; Masters; First Professional Degree. Attendance and degree information available by phone, fax, mail. Transcripts available by fax, mail.

Saint Francis Seminary, Registrar, 3257 S Lake Dr, St Francis, WI 53235, 414-747-6450, 414-747-6400 (Fax: 414-747-6442) www.sfs.edu. 8AM-5PM. Records go back to

1845. Alumni records are maintained here. Degrees granted: Bachelors; Masters. Attendance and degree information available by phone, fax, mail. Transcripts available by fax, mail.

Silver Lake College, Registrar, 2406 S Alverno Rd, Manitowoc, WI 54220, 920-684-6691 X131 (Fax: 920-684-7082) 8AM-4:30PM. www.sl.edu/slc.html. Enrollment: 1200. Records go back to 1930's. Alumni records are maintained here. Degrees granted: Associate; Bachelors; Masters. Special programs- Business: Education. Attendance and degree information available by phone, fax, mail. Transcripts available by written request only.

Southwest Wisconsin Technical College Registrar, 1800 Bronson Blvd, Fennimore, WI 53809, 608-822-3262 (Fax: 608-822-6019) www.southwest.tec.wi.us. 7:30AM-4PM. Records go back to 1969. Degrees granted: Associate. Attendance and degree information available by phone, fax, mail. Transcripts available by written request only.

St. Norbert College, Registrar, 100 Grant St, De Pere, WI 54115-2099, 920-403-3216 (Fax: 920-403-4035) www.snc.edu. 8AM-Noon, 1-4:30PM. Enrollment: 2000. Records go back to 1902. Alumni records maintained here; call 920-403-3022. Degrees granted: Bachelors; Masters. Attendance and degree information available by phone, mail. Transcripts available by mail.

Stratton College, Registrar, 1300 N Jackson St, Milwaukee, WI 53202-2608, 414-276-5200 X6 (Fax: 414-276-3930) 8AM-5PM. Records go back to 1863. Alumni records are maintained here. Degrees granted: Associate. Attendance and degree information available by phone, fax, mail. Transcripts available by mail.

University of Wisconsin, Registrar, Room 130 Patterson Bldg., 750 University Ave., Madison, WI 53706, 608-262-3811 (Fax: 608-262-6002) www.wisc.edu. 8AM-5PM. Enrollment: 39000. Records go back to 1848. Alumni records are maintained here. Degrees granted: Bachelors; Masters; Doctorate. Attendance and degree information available by phone, fax, mail. Transcripts available by mail.

University of Wisconsin — Baraboo-Sauk County, Registrar, 1006 Connie Rd, Baraboo, WI 53913, 608-356-8351 X245 (Fax: 608-356-4074) www.uwc.edu. 8AM-5PM. Enrollment: 400. Records go back to 1968. Degrees granted: Associate. Attendance and degree information available by phone, fax, mail. Transcripts available by written request only.

University of Wisconsin — Barron County, Registrar, 1800 College Dr, Rice Lake, WI 54868, 715-234-8176, 715-234-8024. 8AM-5PM. Enrollment: 500. Records go back to 1968. Alumni records are maintained here. Degrees granted: Associate. Attendance and degree information available by phone, mail. Transcripts available by written request only.

University of Wisconsin - Eau Claire, Registrar, S 130, Eau Claire, WI 54702, 715-836-5912, 715-836-3839 (Fax: 715-836-3846) 7:45AM-4:30PM. www.uwec.edu. Enrollment: 10000. Records go back to 1916. Alumni Records: Alumni Assoc., UWEC, S2116, Eau Claire, WI 54702. Degrees granted: Associate; Bachelors; Masters. Certification: Ed. Attendance and degree

information available by phone, fax, mail. Transcripts available by fax, mail.

University of Wisconsin - Fond du Lac
Registrar, Campus Dr, Fond Du Lac, WI 54935, www.fdl.uwc.edu. 920-929-3606 (Fax: 920-929-7640) Records are located at Univ. of Wisconsin, Registrar, Madison, WI.

University of Wisconsin — Fox Valley, Registrar, PO Box 8002, Menasha, WI 54952-8002, 920-832-2620. 8AM-5PM. Enrollment: 1250. Alumni records are maintained here. Degrees granted: Associate. Attendance and degree information available by phone, mail. Transcripts available by mail.

University of Wisconsin - Green Bay, Registrar, 2420 Nicolet Dr, Green Bay, WI 54311, www.uwgb.edu. 920-465-2055 (Fax: 920-465-2765) 8AM-4:30PM. Enrollment: 5400. Records go back to 1969. Alumni records maintained here; call 920-465-2586. Degrees granted: Associate; Bachelors; Masters. Attendance and degree information available by fax, mail. Transcripts available by mail.

University of Wisconsin — La Crosse, Registrar, 1725 State St, La Crosse, WI 54601, 608-785-8576, 608-785-8951 (Fax: 608-785-6695) www.uwlax.edu/. 8AM-4:30PM. Enrollment: 8700. Records go back to 1906. Alumni records maintained here; call 608-785-8489. Degrees granted: Associate; Bachelors; Masters. Attendance and degree information available by phone, fax, mail. Transcripts available by fax, mail.

University of Wisconsin — Madison, Registrar, 750 University Ave, AW Peterson Ofc Bldg Room 60, Madison, WI 53706, 608-262-2408 (Fax: 608-262-0123) 7:45AM-4:30PM. www.registrar.wisc.edu/registrar. Enrollment: 40000. Records go back to 1848. Alumni records maintained here; call 608-262-2551. Degrees granted: Bachelors; Masters; Doctorate. Attendance and degree information available by phone, mail. Transcripts available by mail.

University of Wisconsin — Manitowoc County, Registrar, 705 Viebahn St, Manitowoc, WI 54220-6699, 920-683-4700 (Fax: 920-683-4776). 8AM-5PM. Enrollment: 500. Alumni records maintained here; call 920-683-4713. Degrees granted: Associate. Adverse incident record source- 920-683-4700. Attendance and degree information available by phone, fax, mail. Transcripts available by fax.

University of Wisconsin — Marathon County, Registrar, 518 S Seventh Ave, Wausau, WI 54401-5396, 715-261-6239, 715-261-6241 (Fax: 715-261-6333) www.uwc.edu. 8AM-5PM. Enrollment: 827. Records go back to 1960. Alumni records maintained here; call 715-261-6296. Degrees granted: Associate. Attendance and degree information available by phone, mail. Transcripts available by written request only.

University of Wisconsin — Marinette County, Registrar, 750 W Bay Shore St, Marinette, WI 54143, 715-735-4300 (Fax: 715-735-4307) www.uwc.edu/mnt. 8AM-5PM. Enrollment: 350. Records go back to 1968. Alumni records are maintained here. Degrees granted: Associate. Attendance and degree information available by phone, mail. Transcripts available by written request only.

University of Wisconsin — Marshfield-Wood County, Registrar, PO Box 150, Marshfield, WI 54449, 715-389-6530 (Fax: 715-389-6517) www.uwc.edu. 7:45AM-4:30PM. Enrollment: 550. Records go back to 1964. Degrees granted: Associate. Attendance

and degree information available by phone, fax, mail. Transcripts available by written request only.

University of Wisconsin - Milwaukee, Registrar, PO Box 729, Milwaukee, WI 53201, 414-229-5774 (Fax: 414-229-6940) 8AM-4:30PM. www.des.uwm.edu. Enrollment: 22000. Records go back to 1956. Alumni records are maintained here. Degrees granted: Bachelors; Masters; Doctorate. Attendance and degree information available by phone, fax, mail. Transcripts available by fax, mail.

University of Wisconsin — Oshkosh, Records Office, 800 Algoma Blvd, Oshkosh, WI 54901, 920-424-0325, 920-424-1199 (Fax: 920-424-1098) www.uwosh.edu. 8:30AM-3:30PM. Enrollment: 11000. Records go back to 1850's. Alumni records maintained here; call 920-424-3414. Degrees granted: Associate; Bachelors; Masters. Attendance and degree information available by phone, mail. Transcripts available by mail.

University of Wisconsin — Parkside, Registrar, Box 2000, Kenosha, WI 53141-2000, 414-595-2284, 414-595-2281 (Fax: 414-595-2283) www.uwp.edu. 7:45AM-4:30PM. Enrollment: 4851. Records go back to 1968. Alumni records maintained here; call 414-595-2414. Degrees granted: Bachelors; Masters. Attendance and degree information available by phone, fax, mail. Transcripts available by fax, mail.

University of Wisconsin — Platteville, Registrar, One University Plaza, Platteville, WI 53818-3099, 608-342-1321 (Fax: 608-342-1389) www.uwplatt.edu/registrar/. 7:45AM-4:45PM. Enrollment: 5000. Records go back to 1800's. Alumni records maintained here; call 608-342-1181. Degrees granted: Associate; Bachelors; Masters. Special programs- Masters Program Graduate Office, 608-342-1321. Attendance and degree information available by phone, mail. Transcripts available by fax, mail.

University of Wisconsin — Richland, Registrar, Hwy 14 W, Richland Center, WI 53581, 608-647-6186 (Fax: 608-647-6225) 8AM-5PM. www.richland.uwc.edu/. Enrollment: 375. Records go back to 1967. Alumni records are maintained here Degrees granted: Associate. Attendance and degree information available by phone, mail. Transcripts available by written request only.

University of Wisconsin - River Falls, Registrar, River Falls, WI 54022, 715-425-3342, 715-425-3231 (Fax: 715-425-3352) www.uwrf.edu/registrar/records.htm 8AM-4:30PM. Enrollment: 5600. Records go back to 1874. Alumni records maintained here; call 715-425-3505. Degrees granted: Bachelors; Masters. Attendance and degree information available by phone, mail. Transcripts available by mail.

University of Wisconsin - Rock County Registrar, 2909 Kellogg Ave, Janesville, WI 53546, 608-758-6522 (Fax: 608-758-6564) www.rock.uwc.edu. 8AM-5PM. Enrollment: 800. Records go back to 1968. Alumni records maintained here; call 608-758-6522. Degrees granted: Associate. Attendance and degree information available by phone, mail. Transcripts available by written request only.

University of Wisconsin - Sheboygan County, Registrar, One University Dr, Sheboygan, WI 53081, 920-459-6633 (Fax: 920-459-6602) www.bratshb.uwc.edu. 8AM-5PM. Enrollment: 550. Records go back to 1950. Degrees granted: Associate. Attendance and degree information available by phone,

fax, mail. Transcripts available by written request only.

University of Wisconsin — Stevens Point, Registrar, Stevens Point, WI 54481, 715-346-4301, 715-346-3815 (Fax: 715-346-2558) www.uwsp.edu. 7:45AM-4:30PM. Enrollment: 8400. Records go back to 1894. Alumni records maintained here; call 715-346-3811. Degrees granted: Associate; Bachelors; Masters. Attendance and degree information available by phone, fax, mail. Transcripts available by fax, mail.

University of Wisconsin — Stout, Registrar, Menomonie, WI 54751-0790, 715-232-2121, 715-232-2157 (Fax: 715-232-2436) 8AM-4:30PM. www.uwstout.edu. Enrollment: 7200. Records go back to 1893. Alumni records maintained here; call 715-232-1151. Degrees granted: Bachelors; Masters. Attendance and degree information available by phone, fax, mail. Transcripts available by mail.

University of Wisconsin — Superior, Registrar, 1800 Grand Ave, Superior, WI 54880, 715-394-8228, 715-394-8218 (Fax: 715-394-8040) www.uwsuper.edu. 8AM-5PM. Enrollment: 2000. Records go back to 1922. Alumni records maintained here; call 715-394-8101. Degrees granted: Bachelors; Masters; Specialist. Attendance and degree information available by phone, mail. Transcripts available by mail.

University of Wisconsin - Washington County, Registrar, 400 University Dr, West Bend, WI 53095, www.washington.uwc.edu 414-335-5201, 414-335-5201 (Fax: 414-335-5220) Enrollment: 634. Records go back to 1968. Degrees granted: Associate. Attendance and degree information available by phone, mail. Transcripts available by written request only.

University of Wisconsin — Waukesha County, Registrar, 1500 University Dr, Waukesha, WI 53188, 414-521-5210 (Fax: 414-521-5491) www.uwc.ecu\waukesha. 8AM-5PM. Enrollment: 1600. Records go back to 1966. Alumni records maintained here; call 414-521-5435. Degrees granted: Associate. Attendance and degree information available by phone, mail. Transcripts available by written request only.

University of Wisconsin - Whitewater, Registrar, 800 W Main St, Whitewater, WI 53190, 414-472-1580, 414-472-1211 (Fax: 414-472-1515) www.uww.edu. 7:45AM-4:30PM. Enrollment: 10500. Records go back to 1885. Alumni records maintained here; call 414-472-1105. Degrees granted: Associate; Bachelors; Masters. Attendance and degree information available by phone, fax, mail. Transcripts available by fax, mail.

Viterbo College, Registrar, 815 S Ninth St, La Crosse, WI 54601, 608-796-3180 (Fax: 608-796-3050) www.viterbo.edu. 8AM - 4:30PM. Enrollment: 1600. Alumni records maintained here; call 608-791-0471. Degrees granted: Bachelors; Masters. Attendance and transcript information available by mail. Degree information available by phone, mail.

Waukesha County Technical College, Registrar, 800 Main St, Pewaukee, WI 53072, 414-691-5266, 414-691-5283 (Fax: 414-691-5123) www.waukesha.tec.wi.us. 8AM-7:30PM. Enrollment: 35004. Records go back to 1960. Alumni records maintained here; call 414-691-5500. Degrees granted: Associate. Attendance information available by fax, mail. Transcripts available by mail.

Western Wisconsin Technical College, Registrar, 304 N Sixth St, La Crosse, WI

54601, 608-785-9149, 608-785-9190 (Fax: 608-785-9094) www.tec.wi.us. 8AM - 8PM. Enrollment: 7000. Records go back to 1917. Alumni records maintained here; call 608-785-9892. Degrees granted: Associate; Applied Sciences and Technical Diplomas. Attendance and degree information available by phone, fax, mail. Transcripts available by fax, mail.

Wisconsin Conservatory of Music, Registrar, 1584 N Prospect Ave, Milwaukee, WI 53202, 414-276-5760 (Fax: 414-276-6076) www.wcmusic.org. Enrollment: 1400. Records go back to 1899. Alumni records are maintained here. Special programs- Fine Arts. Attendance, degree and transcript information available by mail.

Wisconsin Indianhead Tech College in Superior, Educational Services, 600 N 21st St, Superior, WI 54880, 715-394-6677 (Fax: 715-394-3771). Enrollment: 500. Records go back to 1915. Alumni records are maintained here. Degrees granted: Associate. Attendance and degree information available by phone, fax, mail. Transcripts available by fax, mail.

Wisconsin Indianhead Tech Institute in Ashland, Admissions and Records Office, 2100 Beaser Ave, Ashland, WI 54806, www.witc.wi.tec.us 715-682-4591 (Fax: 715-682-8040) Enrollment: 350. Records go back to 1921. Alumni records are maintained. Degrees granted: Associate. Attendance and degree information available by phone, fax, mail. Transcripts available by fax, mail.

Wisconsin Indianhead Tech Institute in New Richmond, Registrar, 1019 S Knowles, New Richmond, WI 54017, www.witc.tec.wi.us 715-246-6561 (Fax: 715-246-2777) Enrollment: 500. Records go back to 1969. Alumni records are maintained here. Degrees granted: Associate. Attendance and degree information available by phone, fax, mail. Transcripts available by mail.

Wisconsin Indianhead Tech Institute in Rice Lake, Student Services, 1900 College Dr, Rice Lake, WI 54868, 715-234-7082 (Fax: 715-234-5172) www.witc.tec.wi.us. Enrollment: 625. Records go back to 1950's. Alumni records are maintained here. Degrees granted: Associate. Attendance and degree information available by phone, fax, mail. Transcripts available by fax, mail.

Wisconsin Indianhead Technical College Registrar, 505 Pine Ridge Drive, **Shell Lake**, WI 54871, 715-468-2815 (Fax: 715-468-2819) www.witc.tec.wi.us. 8AM-4:30PM. Enrollment: 7500. Records go back to 1972. Alumni records are maintained here.

Degrees granted: Associate. Attendance and degree information available by phone, fax, mail. Transcripts available by mail.

Wisconsin Lutheran College, Registrar, 8800 W Bluemond Rd, Milwaukee, WI 53226, www.its.mew.edu. 414-443-8817, 414-443-8800 (Fax: 414-443-8514) 7:30AM-3:30PM. Enrollment: 425. Records go back to 1973. Alumni records maintained here; call 414-443-8790. Degrees granted: Bachelors. Attendance and degree information available by phone, fax, mail. Transcripts available by written request only.

Wisconsin School of Professional Psychology, Registrar, 9120 W Hampton Ave Ste 212, Milwaukee, WI 53225, 414-464-9777 (Fax: 414-358-5590). 9AM-5PM. Enrollment: 90. Records go back to 1980. Alumni records are maintained here. Degrees granted: Doctorate. Attendance, degree and transcript information available by written request only.

Wyoming

Casper College, Registrar, 125 College Dr, Casper, WY 82601, 307-268-2211, 307-268-2499 (Fax: 307-268-2611) 8AM-5PM. www.cc.whecn.edu. Enrollment: 3800. Records go back to 1945. Alumni records maintained here; call 307-268-2218. Degrees granted: Associate. Attendance and degree information available by phone, fax, mail. Transcripts available by fax, mail.

Central Wyoming College, Registrar, 2660 Peck Ave, Riverton, WY 82501, 307-855-2000 (Fax: 307-855-2092) 8AM-5PM. Records go back to 1966. Alumni records are maintained here. Degrees granted: Associate, Attendance and degree information available by phone, fax, mail. Transcripts available by fax, mail.

Eastern Wyoming College, Registrar, 3200 W C St, Torrington, WY 82240, 307-532-8230, 307-532-8207 (Fax: 307-532-8222) www.ewc1.ewc.whecn.edu 8AM-4:30PM. Enrollment: 1800. Records go back to 1948. Alumni records maintained here; call 307-532-8304. Degrees granted: Associate. Attendance and degree information available by phone, fax, mail. Transcripts available by fax.

Laramie County Community College, Registrar, 1400 E College Dr, Cheyenne, WY 82007, 307-778-5222 (Fax: 307-778-1350) www.lcc.whecn.edu. 8AM-5PM. Enrollment: 4000. Records go back to 1968. Alumni records maintained here; call 307-778-1213. Degrees granted: Associate. Attendance, degree and transcript information available by fax, mail.

Northern Wyoming Community College District (Gillette Campus), Registrar, 720 W 8th St, Gillette, WY 82716, 307-686-0254 X403 (Fax: 307-686-0339). 8AM-5PM. Degrees granted: Associate. Attendance and degree information available by phone, fax, mail. Transcripts available by fax, mail.

Northwest College, Registrar, 231 W Sixth St, Powell, WY 82435, 307-754-3149 (Fax: 307-754-6700) www.nwc.whecn.edu. 8AM-5PM. Records go back to 1946. Alumni records maintained here; call 307-754-6034. Degrees granted: Associate. Attendance and degree information available by phone, fax, mail. Transcripts available by fax, mail.

Sheridan College
(See Northern Wyoming Community College District)

University of Wyoming, Registrar, Knight Hall, PO Box 3964, Laramie, WY 82071, 307-766-5272 (Fax: 307-766-3960) www.uwyo.edu. 8AM-5PM. Records go back to 1886. Alumni Records: PO Box 3137, Laramie, WY 82071. Degrees granted: Bachelors; Masters; Doctorate. Attendance and degree information available by phone, fax, mail. Transcripts available by mail.

Western Wyoming College, Registrar, PO Box 428, Rock Springs, WY 82901, 307-382-1641, 307-382-1639 (Fax: 307-382-1636) 8AM-5PM. www.wwcc.edu. Enrollment: 2000. Records go back to 1959. Alumni records maintained here; call 307-382-1600. Degrees granted: Associate. Attendance, degree and transcript information available by phone, fax, mail. Transcript request must come from student.

Wyoming Technical Institute, Registrar, 4373 North Third St, Laramie, WY 82072, 307-742-3776 www.wyoming.tech.us.com. 7AM-6PM. Enrollment: 850. Records go back to 1969. Degrees granted: Associate; Certificates. Attendance and degree information available by phone, mail. Transcripts available by mail.

Credit Report Designations

Notifications by Credit Reporting Agencies are coded with abbreviations. Here are the more common abbreviations and their meanings. Status Comments, Items of Public Record, Association Codes and Types of Accounts are listed separately.

Status Comment Key

Below are examples of abbreviations of credit report items, known as status comments.

Abbreviation	Explanation
BK ADJ PLN	Debt included in or completed through Bankruptcy Chapter 13
BK LIQ REO	Debt included in or discharged through Bankruptcy Chapter 7, 11 or 12
CHARGE OFF	Unpaid balance reported as a loss by credit grantor
CLOS NP AA	Credit line closed / not paying as agreed
COLL ACCT	Account seriously past due / assigned to attorney, col. agency, or credit grantor's own collection department
CO NOW PAY	Now paying / was a charge-off
CUR WASCOL	Current amount was a collection account, insurance claim or government claim
CUR WAS DL	Current account / was past due
CUR WASFOR	Current account. Foreclosure was started
CUR WAS 30	Current account / was 30 days past due date. Number 30, 60, 90, 120, 150, or 160 indicates days past due
CUR WAS 30-2	Current account / was 30 days past due date two times. Dash with number indicates times past due date
DECEASED	Consumer reported as deceased
DEEDINLIEU	Credit grantor received deed for collateral in lieu of foreclosure on a defaulted mortgage
DELINQ 60	Account delinquent 60 days past due date. Other intervals are 90, 120, 150, 180
DEL WAS 90	Account was delinquent 90 days past due date / now 30 or 60 days past due date
DEL WAS 120	Account was delinquent 120 days past due date / now 30, 60, or 90 days past due date
FORCLOSURE	Credit grantor reclaimed collateral to settle defaulted mortgage
FORE PROC	Foreclosure proceedings started
GOV CLAIM	Claim filed with government for insured portion of balance on defaulted student loan
NS CLAIM	Claim filed with government for insured portion of balance on account secured by real estate
NOT PAY AA	Account not being paid as agreed
PD BY DLER	Credit grantor paid by company who originally sold the merchandise
PD CHG OFF	Paid account / was a charge-off
PD COLL AC	Paid account / was a collection account, insurance claim or government claim
IPD FORECLO	Paid account. A foreclosure was started
PD NOT AA	Paid account. Some payments were made past the agreed due dates
PD REPO	Paid account / was a repossession
PD VOL SUR	Paid account / was a voluntary surrender
PD WAS 30	Paid account / was 30 days past due date. Dash with number indicates times past due date
PD WAS 60	Paid account / was delinquent 60 days past due date
PD WAS 90	Paid account / was delinquent 90 days past due date
PD WAS 120	Paid account / was delinquent 120 days past due date
PD WAS 150	Paid account / was delinquent 150 days past due date
PD WAS 180	Paid account / was delinquent 180 days past due date
REDMD REPC	Account was a repossession / now redeemed
REPO	Merchandise was taken back by credit grantor. Balance may be due
SCNL	Credit grantor cannot locate consumer
SCNL NWLOC	Credit grantor could not locate consumer / consumer now located
SETTLED	Account legally paid in full for less than the full balance
TERM DFALT	Early termination by default of original terms of lease or sales contract
VOLUN SURR	Voluntary surrender
30 DAY DEL	Account 30 days past due date. 30 followed by a dash with number indicates times past due
30 WAS 60	Account was delinquent 60 days past due date / now 30 days

Items of Public Record Key

Below are examples of abbreviations of credit report items that are public records.

Abbreviation	*Explanation*
BK 7-FILE	Voluntary or involuntary petition in Bankruptcy. Chapter 7 (liquidation) filed
BK 7-DISC	Voluntary or involuntary petition in Bankruptcy. Chapter 7 (liquidation) discharged
BK 7-DISM	Voluntary or involuntary petition in Bankruptcy. Chapter 7 (liquidation) dismissed
BK 11-FILE	Voluntary or involuntary petition in Bankruptcy. Chapter 11 (reorganization) filed
BK 11-DISC	Voluntary or involuntary petition in Bankruptcy. Chapter 11 (reorganization) discharged
BK 11-DISM	Voluntary or involuntary petition in Bankruptcy. Chapter 11 (reorganization) dismissed
BK 12-FILE	Voluntary or involuntary petition in Bankruptcy. Chapter 12 filed
BK 12-DISC	Voluntary or involuntary petition in Bankruptcy. Chapter 12 discharged
BK 12-DISM	Voluntary or involuntary petition in Bankruptcy. Chapter 12 dismissed
BK 13-FILE	Voluntary or involuntary petition in Bankruptcy. Chapter 13 filed
BK 13-DISC	Voluntary or involuntary petition in Bankruptcy. Chapter 13 discharged
BK 13-DISM	Voluntary or involuntary petition in Bankruptcy. Chapter 13 dismissed
CITY LN	City tax lien
CITY LN REL	City tax lien released
CO. LN	County tax lien
CO. LN REL	County tax lien released
FED TAX LN	Federal tax lien
FED TAX REL	Federal tax lien release
JUDGMENT	Judgment
JUDGMT SAT	Judgment satisfied
JUDGMTVACAT	Judgment vacated either before or after it has been satisfied
MECH LIEN	Mechanic's lien
MECH RELE	Mechanic's lien released
NT RESPON	Not responsible notice, e.g. husband/wife claims not responsible for debts incurred by the spouse
STAT TX LN	State tax lien
STA TX REL	State tax lien released
SUIT	Suit
SUIT DISMD	Suit dismissed
WAGE ASIGN	Wage assignment
WA RELEASE	Wage assignment released

Association Codes Key

An association code, under The Equal Credit Opportunity Act, describes one's legal relationship to an account.

Abbreviation	*Explanation*
0-UNDESIGNATED	Not reported by the subscriber (Code is A if association is terminated)
1-INDIVIDUAL	Individual is the only person associated with the account (Code is H if association is terminated)
2-JOINT CONTRACTUAL	Individual is expressly obligated to repay all debts on the account by reason of having signed an agreement. Other associates may or may not have contractual responsibility
3-JOINT/AUTHORIZED USER	Individual has use of this joint account for which another has contractual responsibility. (Code is C if association is terminated)
4-JOINT/UNDESIGNATED	Individual has use of this joint account. Association cannot be distinguished between 2 & 3 above. (Code is D if association is terminated)
5-CO-SIGNER	Individual has guaranteed this account and assumes responsibility should the maker default (Code is F if association is terminated)
6-ON BEHALF OF	Individual has signed an agreement for the purpose of securing credit for another individual other than spouse. (Code is F if association is terminated)
7-SIGNER	Individual is responsible for this account guaranteed by a co-maker (Code is G if association is terminated)

Types of Accounts Key

The following examples explain the type of account one may have with a credit granter

Abbreviation	Explanation	Abbreviation	Explanation
ADD	Address information for mailing	LEA	Lease
AUT	Auto	MED	Medical debt
A/M	Account monitor by credit grantor	M/H	Mobile home
BUS	Business loan personally guaranteed	NCM	Note loan with co-maker
CCP	Combined credit plan	NCS	Note loan with co-signer
CHG	Charge account	NTE	Note loan
CLS	Credit line secured	PHC	Prescreen / extract report
COL	Collection department / agency / attorney	PIA	Prescreen / invitation to apply
COM	Co-maker (not borrower)	PMI	Prescreen / extract promotion inquiry
COS	Co-signer (not borrower)	PPO	Prescreen / pre-approved offer
CPS	Consumer product service	PPI	Prescreen / post prescreen inquiry
CRC	Credit card	PSC	Solicitation
CRD	Consumer relations display	P/S	Partially secured
C/C	Check credit or line of credit	QST	Account reviewed by credit granter
DCP	Data correction profile	RCK	Returned check
DCS	Debit counseling service	REC	Recreational merchandise
D/C	Debit card	REN	Rental agreement
EDU	Educational	RVW	Account review by credit granter
FHA	FHA home improvement	R/C	Conventional real estate mortgage – terms are in years
F/C	FHA co-signer (not borrower)		
F/S	Family support	R/E	Real estate type unknown – terms are in years
GEA	Government employee advance	R/F	FHA real estate mortgage – terms are in years
GMD	Government miscellaneous debt	R/O	Real estate mortgage with/without other collateral, usually a second mortgage – terms in months
GOP	Government overpayment		
G/B	Government benefit	R/V	VA real estate mortgage – terms in years
G/F	Government fine	SCO	Secured by co-signer
G/G	Government grant	SDL	Government secured direct loan
H/E	Home equity	SEC	Secured
HHG	Secured by household goods	SGL	Government secured guaranteed loan
H/I	Home improvement	SLC	Co-maker (not borrower)
H + O	Secured by household goods and other collateral	SUM	Summary of accounts with same status
IDV	Address information for government	UDL	Government unsecured direct loan
INS	Insurance claim	UGL	Government unsecured guaranteed loan
ISC	Installment sales contract	UNK	Unknown
I/L	Installment loan	UNS	Unsecured

State Agency Public Record Restrictions Table

O	Open to Public	R	Some Access Restrictions (Requesters Screened)	N/A	Not Available to the Public
F	Special Form Needed	S	Sever Access Restrictions (Signed Authorization, et c.)	L	Available only at Local Level

State	Criminal Records	UCC Records	Worker's Comp	Driving Records[6]	Vehicle Records	Vessel Records	Voter Reg.[7]
Alabama	S	O,F	S	R	S	O	L
Alaska	R	O,F	R	S	R	N/A	L
Arizona	R	O,F	S	S	S	R	L
Arkansas	S	O,F	O	S	R	O	L
California	N/A,L	O,F	R	S	S	S	L
Colorado	O	O,F	S	R	R	O	O
Connecticut	O	O,F	S	S	S	O	L
Delaware	S	O,F	S	R	R	R	O
Dist. of Columbia	S,F	O,F	S	S	S	S	O
Florida	O	O,F	S	R	R	R	L
Georgia	S	L,F[8]	S	S	S	O	O
Hawaii	O	O,F	S	R	N/A	R	L
Idaho	S	O,F	S	R	R	S	L
Illinois	S,F	O,F	O	S	R	O	L
Indiana	R,F	O,F	S	R	R	R	L
Iowa	O	O,F	O	R	R	L	O
Kansas	O,F	O,F	R	R	R	R	L
Kentucky	R	O,F	R	R	R	O	O
Louisiana	S	L,F[1]	R	R	R	O	L
Maine	O	O,F	R	R	R	O	L
Maryland	S	O,F	O	R	R	O	L
Massachusetts	R,F	O,F	R	R	R	O	L
Michigan	O	O,F	R	R	R	R	L
Minnesota	R	O,F	S	R	R	O	L
Mississippi	N/A,L	O,F	R	R	R	O	L

---

[6] This category, Driving, indicates restriction codes based on the assumption the requester is the general public. In general, these records are open ("O") to employers and their agents.

[7] This category, Voter Registration, indicates most record searching requires going to the local county or municipality. However, many state election agencies will sell customized voter lists statewide or for multiple counties.

[8] Georgia and Louisiana UCCs are filed locally, but a state central index is available.

State	Criminal Records	UCC Records	Worker's Comp	Driving Records[6]	Vehicle Records	Vessel Records	Voter Reg.[7]
Missouri	O	O,F	R	R	R	R	L
Montana	O	O,F	R	R	R	R	O
Nebraska	O	O,F	R	R	R	L	L
Nevada	S	O,F	S	R	R	O	L
New Hampshire	S	O,F	S	R	S	S	L
New Jersey	R	O,F	O,F	S	S	S	L
New Mexico	S	O,F	S	S	S	S	L
New York	L	O,F	S	R	R	R	L
North Carolina	N/A,L	O,F	R	R	R	O	L
North Dakota	S	O,F	S	R	R,F	O	L
Ohio	S,F	O,F	O	R	R	O	O&L
Oklahoma	O	O,F	O	R	O	R	O&L
Oregon	O	O,F	S	R	R	O	L
Pennsylvania	R,F	O,F	S	S	S	N/A	L
Rhode Island	S,L	O,F	S	R	S	R	L
South Carolina	O	O,F	S	R	R	O	O
South Dakota	S,F	O,F	S	R	R	R	L
Tennessee	N/A,L	O,F	S	R	R	O	L
Texas	O	O,F	S,F	R	R	R	L
Utah	N/A,L	O,F	S	R	R	R	L
Vermont	N/A,L	O,F	S	R	R	R	L
Virginia	S,F	O,F	R	S	S	R	L
Washington	O	O,F	S	S	S	S	L
West Virginia	S,F	O,F	S	R	R	R	L
Wisconsin	O	O,F	S	R	R	O	L
Wyoming	S,F	O,F	S	R	R	O	L

O	Open to Public	R	Some Access Restrictions (Requesters Screened)
		N/A	Not Available to the Public
F	Special Form Needed	S	Sever Access Restrictions (Signed Authorization, et c.)
		L	Available only at Local Level

Recommended Resources

Books, Periodicals & Publishers

Featured Publishers

BRB Publications, Inc.

www.brbpub.com

> 4653 S Lakeshore Dr #3
> Tempe, AZ 85282
> 800-929-3811
> Fax 800-929-3811

This company provides an in-depth and comprehensive look at public records, public agencies and the retrieval firms who access these records. They publish the only series of books and CD-ROMs totally dedicated to the understanding of public records.

Facts on Demand Press

A division of BRB Publications, Facts on Demand Press provides unique "How to" titles for both the novice and professional. Their *Online Ease Series* is especially useful.

Government Records

Armed Forces Locator

By Richard S. Johnson and Debra Johnson Knox
MIE Publishing Inc. 800-937-2133
ISBN: 1-877639-50-8, Pub 2/99, Pages 320, Price $22.95

This book brings together every conceivable means to local current and former members of the military. This edition includes Internet and foreign base information.

Find Public Records Fast

By Michael Sankey, Carl R. Ernst and James R. Flowers Jr.
Facts on Demand Press, 800-929-3764
ISBN: 1-889150-07-x, Pub 7/99, Pages 520, Price 19.95

Find Public Records Fast is an examination of over 11,000 locations where public records are stored. Includes a "how to search" section.

Government Information on the Internet

By Greg R. Notess
Bernan Press 800-271-4447
ISBN: 0-89059-10901, Pub 11/98, Pages 768, Price $38.50

Government Information on the Internet includes 1,200 entries that cover a wide variety of subjects from business to health to legal information. Each site summarized in detail.

The MVR Book

By Michael Sankey
BRB Publications Inc. 800-929-3811
ISBN: 1-879792-48-6, Pub 1/99 (annual), Pages 360, Price 19.50

The MVR Book is the national reference detailing—in practical terms—the privacy, restrictions, access procedures, regulation, and database systems of all state-held driver and vehicle records.

The Sourcebook of County Court Records

By Michael Sankey, Carl R. Ernst and James R. Flowers Jr
BRB Publications Inc. 800-929-3811
ISBN: 1-879792-44-3, Pub 8/98, Pages 608, Price 35.00

County Court Records offers in-depth profiles of over 7,000 courts at the local level. Includes extensive city-county cross reference index.

The Sourcebook of State Public Records

By Michael Sankey, Carl R. Ernst and James R. Flowers Jr
BRB Publications Inc. 800-929-3811
ISBN: 1-879792-45-1, Pub 10/98, Pages 448, Price 35.00

State Public Records examines all major state public record databases, how to access, fees, what's online, etc. Includes over 5,400 record locations.

Periodicals

HR Magazine & HR News

Both of these periodicals are published monthly by SHRM (see organizations).

You And The Law – Quick And Easy Advice For Managing Employment Law Changes

The National Institute of Business Management,
1750 Old Meadow Road, Suite 302, McLean, VA 22102
ISSN 0731-1109, Published monthly
Questions and comments (800) 543-2055 or (703) 905-8000

The National Institute of Business Management's helpful monthly newsletter addresses human resource concerns, including newsworthy issues, articles, perspectives, advice, Q & A, and legal comments.

Private Sources, Retrieval & Unique Searching Aids

The Sourcebook of Local Court & County Record Retrievers

By Michael Sankey, Carl R. Ernst and James R. Flowers Jr
BRB Publications Inc. 800-929-3811
ISBN: 1-879792-50-8, Pub 1/99 (annual), Pages 624, Price 45.00

Local Court & County Record Retrievers is a national guide to information retrievers who search indexes and obtain documents from Federal, State and Local Courts, and from County Agencies. Provides over 14,000 listings, by county. Includes profiles.

The County Locator

By Carl R Ernst and Michael Sankey
BRB Publications Inc. 800-929-3811
ISBN: 1-879792-39-7, Pub 5/98, Pages 544, Price 19.50

The County Locator consists of three cross-reference indices with over 100,000 place name and zip code combinations. Shows when ZIP Codes cross county lines and indicates where ZIP Codes are not geographic.

Public Records Online

Edited by Michael L Sankey, Carl R. Ernst and James R. Flowers Jr.
Facts on Demand Press, 800-929-3764
ISBN: 1-889150-10-x, Pub 3/99, Pages 416, Price 19.95

Public Records Online is the authoritative guide to online access of public records and public information. Profiles of free and pay-for sources. Indices included.

Find It Online

By Alan M Schlein and Shirley Kwan Kisaichi
Facts on Demand Press, 800-929-3764
ISBN: 1-889150-06-1, Pub 2/99, Pages 400, Price 19.95

2 -time Pulitzer Nominee Alan Schlein, with Kwan Kisaichi, has produced a comprehensive "How To" section combined with complete profiles of best sites and databases.

Online Competitive Intelligence 1st edition

By Helen P. Burwell
Facts on Demand Press, 800-929-3764
ISBN: 1-889150-08-8, Pub 1/99, Pages 396, Price 25.95

Helen Burwell reveals inside information on where to find and how to use the best commercial and Internet sources to evaluate your competition or achieve success with a new product.

The Investigators Little Black Book 2

By Robert Scott
Crime Time Publishing, 310-840-5317
ISBN: 0-9652369-2-7, Pub 1998, Pages 260, Price 19.95

This uniquely sized 4 x 8 pocketbook contains over 2,500 sources of information including public and private databases, government sources, law enforcement contacts, criminal record sources, financial record sources, and more.

Get the Facts on Anyone

By Dennis King
MacMillan
ISBN: 0-02-862821-7, Pub 4/99, Pages 288, Price 14.95

Get the Facts on Anyone is a goldmine of a reference reveals inside investigative techniques that professionals use to find out almost anything about anyone, legally. Recommended because its practicality and is very well written.

PRRS-Print

By Michael Sankey, Carl R. Ernst and James R. Flowers Jr.
BRB Publications Inc. 800-929-3811
ISBN: 1-879792-51-6, Pub Jan & July, Pages 2,400, Price 169.00
Loose-leaf: A three volume set, updated semi-annually

PRRS-Print, which is the *Public Record Research System* in print, is an in-depth reference to over 26,000 sources of public records and public information. Extensive profiles of federal agencies, county recorder offices, state and county courts, state agencies, accredited post-secondary institutions, occupational licensing and business registration agencies, Public Record Retrieval Network members. Maps, indexes, extensive place name-county-ZIP Code cross references. Extremely thorough.

CD-Roms

The premier supplier of public record related CD-ROMs is Merlin Information Services. They carry close to 100 quality CD products including BRB Publications' Public Record Research System. Located in Kalispell, MT, Merlin can be reached at 800-367-664 or at their web site at www.merlindata.com.

Organizations

National Employee Rights Institute (NERI)

600 Harrison St #535
San Francisco, CA 94107

NERI was founded to help the employed and the unemployed understand and enforce their rights in the workplace. As such, the organization's knowledge of these rights and the implementation of them is extensive.

Society for Human Resources Management (SHRM)

www.shrm.org

1800 Duke St
Alexandria, VA 22314
703-548-3440
Fax 703-836-0367

According to their web site, SHRM "is the leading voice of the human resource profession, representing 63,000 professional and student members from around the world. SHRM provides its membership with education and information services, conferences and seminars, government and media representation, and publications that equip human resource professionals for their roles as leaders and decision makers within their organizations."

Web Sites

Drug Testing

Institute for a Drug-Free Workplace

www.drugfreeworkplace.org

The site includes the following mission statement on the main page: "The Institute for a Drug-Free Workplace is an independent, self-sustaining coalition of businesses, business organizations and individuals dedicated to preserving the rights of employers and employees in drug-abuse prevention programs and to positively influencing the national debate of these issues."

Making Your Workplace Drug Free: A Kit for Employers

www.health.org/wpkit

This site is geared towards helping employees establish a drug free work environment. Both employee and employer fact sheets are included.

Government Agencies

Bureau of Labor Statistics
http://stats.bls.gov

This web page provides various statistics and data regarding labor, employment and the economy.

Employment and Training Administration
www.doleta.gov

This site offers a large amount of links and news regarding employment and training in the US.

Department of Labor (DOL)
www.dol.gov

The Department of Labor is the primary labor-related, government agency. This is their main site, which links to many items that are of interest to employers and employees alike.

Occupational Safety & Health Administration (OSHA)
www.osha.gov

OSHA's goal is promote health and safety for employees and employers in America. They have a searchable technical manual available at www.osh-slc.gov/TechMan_toc/TechMan_sect.html. Also, rules regarding OSHA-related recordkeeping is available at www.osha-slc.gov/rkeep_toc/rkeep_toc_by_sect.html.

Human Resources

Cornell University, Office of Human Resources
www.cornell.edu/Admin/HR_manual_toc.html

This site presents an online version of the human resource policy manual used by Cornell University. Visiting this site will provide you with the opportunity to view another organization's manual that may even include policies which are adaptable to your company.

The Human Resource Professional's Gateway to the Internet
www.teleport.com/~erwilson

This site contains organized links to human resource-related sites and listservs as well as search engines and recruitment-oriented pages.

Legal Information

FindLaw

www.findlaw.com

From this site, you can search for laws and legal resources by state, branch or even on the national level. Links are also divided into categories for ease of searching.

Listservs

ADA-LAW

listserv@ndsuvml.bitnet

The human resource related list focuses on issue related to the legal aspects of ADA-LAW.

HR-L

Mail-server@bcrnet.com

The HR Mailing List is an moderated, open discussion list covering all aspects of human resources.

Index

A

Access to Information 114
ADA 86, 166-167, 176, 184, 465
ADAM Safeguard 9, 22, 234
Addresses 49, 71, 80, 84
Age 47, 50, 99
Age Discrimination in Employment Act
 of 1967 160-161
Age Discrimination in Employment Act
 of 1975 160-161
AIDS 176
Alabama 266, 274, 280, 289
Alaska.......................266, 274, 280, 292
American Driving Records.................79
American Management Association ..90
Am. with Disabilities Act........ *see* ADA
Applicant/Resume Evaluation....33, 195
Applicant Waiver 25-26, 56, 196
Application
 basic form..................21-24, 197-200
 purpose of the................................21
Arizona.....................266, 274, 280, 293
Arkansas...................266, 274, 280, 295
Availability......................... 99-100, 143

B

Background Investigation 37
Bahls, Jane Esater..............................92
Bankruptcy Courts 83
Basic Application Form ....
 ....21-24, 197-199
Behavior...143
Benefits 118, 127, 190-191
Bureau of Labor Statistics................463

C

California 40, 266, 274, 280, 297
CDL..77
CIC 9, 241
Citizenship 100
Civil Court Searches 82

Civil Record Searches 39, 44, 82-85
Civil Rights Act of 1866.......... 160, 162
Civil Rights Act of 1964.... 23, 160, 161
Civil Rights Act of 1991................... 27
Classified Ads................................... 11
COBRA 170
Coffman, Stephen 87
Colorado 266, 274, 280, 312
Common Law Limitations........ 155-156
Company Screening Policy 38
Compliance with Policy.................. 143
Confidentiality Agreement ....
 .... 121-122, 131, 200
Connecticut............. 266, 274, 280, 315
Consumer Credit & Protection Act.. 170
Consumer Reporting Agencies........ 177
Consumer Reporting Employment
 Clarification Act of 1998............. 167
Consumer Reports 167, 177
 vs. Credit reports............................ 52
Contact With Others 114
Cornell University 464
Corrective Interviews 148-150
 how to conduct............................ 149
Credit Bureaus 47, 51
Credit Header Information............... 47
Credit History Checks 39, 44, 51-52
Credit Reports.............. 37, 51, 453-455
 designations 453-455
 vs. consumer reports 52
Criminal Background Check Release ....
 .... 29, 31, 201
Criminal History Checks ....
 .... 39, 44, 60-64, 100
Criminal Records.............. 265, 457-458

D

Date of Birth ....
 .... 23, 47, 50, 80, 84, 101, 118
Davis-Bacon Act...................... 171-172
Death Claim.. 48
Delaware.................. 267, 274, 280, 317

Department of Health & Human
   Services (DDHS)..........................124
Department of Labor.............................
   ....89, 169, 172, 464
Dependability.....................................143
Dictionary of Occupational Titles....116
Disabilities 100
Discipline
   a motivational approach to ... 150-151
District of Columbia...............................
   ....267, 275, 280, 318
DMV 40, 78, 80, 274-279
Drivers' Privacy Protection Act (DPPA)
  273
Dress Codes......................................130
Drivers' License Numbers ....
   ....42, 77, 80, 84, 101
Drivers' Licenses 77, 81, 273-279
Driving Record Abstract 78-79
Driving Records ....
   ....*See* Motor Vehicle Reports
Drug Testing 89-92
   technologies used for.......................91
   when it may be administered..........91
Duerr, Douglas 90
Duties and Responsibilties 113-115

E

Economic Status...................................99
Education Amendments Act of 1972
   ....160, 163
Education Verification 67-69
Educational Background
   verification of...........................39, 44
EEOC 23, 38, 172
Employee Data Sheet...............118, 202
Employee Polygraph Protection Act......
  94
Employee Protection 170
Employee Retirement Income Security
   Act................................... 169-170
Employee Searches 174-175
Employment & Training Administration
   ....171, 464
Employment At-Will............... 153-154
Employment Eligibility Verification......
   .... *See* I-9
Employment History Verification.........
   .... 39, 44, 53-59

Equal Employment Opportunity Act of
   1972 160-161
Equal Pay Act of 1963............. 160, 163
Equifax 47, 51
Equipment, Machinery & Tools 113
Ethnic Background 109
Exit Interview 157
   report 204-205
Experian....................................... 47, 51
Extent of Authority & Responsibility
   113
Exxon Valdez Oil Spill..................... 89

F

Fair Labor Standards Act......... 169, 171
Fake IDs..42-43
Family & Medical Leave Act 171
FBI... 62
FCRA..........................52, 167, 177-181
Federal Discrimination Laws.... 159-168
Findlaw 465
Florida 63, 267, 275, 280, 319
FOIA...................................74, 164-165
Forms................... 18, 25, 117, 193
Fortune 13
FTC... 180

G

Garnishment of Wages 170
Gender 23, 109
General Release Form ..29-30, 131, 206
Georgia 267, 275, 280, 324
Government Contracts, Grants or
   Financial Aid 171
Government Records 457-459
Grievances, how to handle.............. 152

H

Hawaii..................... 267, 275, 281, 328
Handwriting Analysis...................... 94
Header Information, credit 47
Health Care Benefits........................ 190
Height 23
Hiring a Candidate........................... 109
Holidays... 128
Home Visits 189
Hours of Employment 127, 175
HR-L... 465
HR Magazine 92, 97, 460

HR News..460

I

I-9...................24, 27-28, 101, 131, 203
ID; identification..............................27
Idaho.......................267, 275, 281, 328
Illinois.....................267, 275, 281, 329
Immigration & Nationality Act........171
Immigration Reform & Control Act......
....*see* IRCA
Independence, on the job.................144
Independent Judgment, Initiative &
     Supervision....................................114
Indiana....................268, 275, 281, 337
Induction Form..........................120, 207
Initiative.................................. 143-144
Inspections.......................................174
Institute for a Drug-Free Workplace......
....93
Intake Person................................18, 42
Interaction With Others....................144
Interviews................................... 96-104
     computer-assisted............................97
     proper questioning during..............99
     questions after...................... 103-104
     what you should ask during.... 99-103
Iowa..........................268, 275, 281, 341
IRCA.....................27-28, 160, 165, 171
Interactive Voice Response, IVR.......97

J

Job Awareness..................................143
Job Descriptions....................... 113-116
     readymade.....................................116
Job Structure....................................114

K

Kansas......................268, 275, 281, 344
Kentucky..................268, 276, 281, 346
Koeb, Gary..87

L

Labor-Management Reporting &
     Disclosure Act...............................170
Lambeth Jr., Walter............................90
Level of Education............................115
Licenses & Registrations.. 39, 44, 70-73
Lie Detector Tests..............................94
Lieber, Ron...13

Lien & Judgment Searches................ 83
Local Police Record Request...............
....65-66, 208
Lost Time Claims..................... 188-189
Louisiana................. 268, 276, 281, 349

M

Maine...................... 268, 276, 281, 351
Maryland................. 269, 276, 281, 352
Massachusetts.......... 269, 276, 281, 355
McNamara-O'Hara Service Contract
     Act.. 171
Medical Providers............................ 188
Memberships in Organizations........ 100
Michigan.................. 269, 276, 281, 361
Microsoft... 13
Migrant & Seasonal Agricultural
     Worker Protection Act................. 171
Military Service Records Checks..........
........39, 44, 74-76, 100-101, 209-210
Mine Safety & Health Act of 1977.. 172
Mine Safety & Health Administration
.... 172
Minnesota............... 269, 276, 281, 366
Mississippi......... 61, 269, 276, 281, 370
Missouri............. 74, 269, 276, 281, 372
Montana................... 269, 277, 282, 376
Motor Vehicle Reports......... 20, 29, 39,
     44, 77-81, 133, 273-280, 457-458
MVRs......... *See* Motor Vehicle Reports

N

Names........................... 48, 80, 84, 101
     additional.. 48
National Academy of Sciences........ 116
National Employee Rights Institute
     (NERI)... 463
National Institute of Drug Abuse....... 89
National Labor Relations Act.. 160, 163
National Labor Relations Board...... 173
National Origin.................... 23, 99, 109
National Personnel Records Center ... 74
NCIC... 62
Nebraska.................. 269, 277, 282, 377
Nevada..................... 270, 277, 282, 379
New Employee Record Chart...............
.... 117, 211
New Hampshire....... 270, 277, 282, 379
New Hire Reporting Form....... 126, 212
New Hire Reporting Offices............ 125

New Hire Reporting Requirements ..124
New Jersey 60, 63,
    78, 80, 124, 270, 277, 282, 380
New Mexico 270, 277, 282, 384
New York 61, 72, 270, 277, 283, 385
Nike 97
Non-Compete Agreement ....
    .... 109, 121-123, 213
North Carolina....40, 270, 277, 283, 397
North Dakota............270, 278, 283, 402
Nuclear Regulatory Commission 61

O

Occupational Safety & Health Act ...169
Ohio...........................270, 278, 283, 403
Oklahoma 271, 278, 283, 410
Oregon......................271, 278, 283, 412
Organizations 463
Orientation 111
OSHA...................... 169-170, 172, 464

P

Paperwork Policies.............................17
Past Employers.......................49, 53, 56
Pay Rate 127
Pennsylvania 63, 271, 278, 283, 414
Pension & Welfare Benefits
    Administration...................... 169-170
Performance Review Form ....
    .... 142-147, 214-215
Performance Reviews............... 142-145
Personal Identifiers............................84
Personal References 59
Personal Responsibility & Work
    Opportunity Reconciliation Act of
    1996.............................124, 160, 166
Personality Traits 115
Plant Closing & Layoffs...................170
Pre-Employment Screening ....
    .... 37, 40-41, 231
    companies..................... 40, 231-263
Previous Employment Check ....
    .... 37, 49, 53-56, 216
Pregnancy Discrimination Act of 1978
    ....160, 165
Previous Employers 23
Prior Work Experience....................115
Pritchard, David 13
Privacy Questions, The 71, 169
Privacy Act Of 1974................ 164-165

Probationary Employment............... 112
Productivity 144
Professional Associations 73
Professional Licenses & Registrations
    confirmation of 39, 44, 70
PSTC... 97
Psychemedics Corporation 89-90
Psychological Testing...................86-88
Public Record Restrictions 457-458

Q

Quality 144
Questions
    after the interview 103-104
    not to include on the basic
        application 23
    to ask at the interview 99-103

R

Record Retention Requirements 174
Recruitment 10-13
Rehabilitation Act of 1973 ....
    .... 32, 160, 164
Reid Psychological Systems 86-88
Rejecting Candidates 107
Rejection Letter 108, 217
Relationships, family 101
Release Form, usage 21, 24
Religion 23, 99
Request for Education Verification ....
    ....68-69, 218
Request for Information........56-57, 219
Resumes.........................33-34, 96, 195
Retention Efforts 129
Rhode Island 271, 278, 283, 423

S

Sample Company Policy 138
Screening Options 39
Search Fees, licensing agencies 72
Secret Service 43
Security Magazine 94
SHL Aspen Tree Software................ 98
Sick Leave 127
Signature................................... 18, 22
    for driving record requests............. 29
Skills & Aptitudes Testing................ 94
SmithKline Beecham........................ 91

Social Security Numbers.......................
   21-22, 39, 42, 44, 46-50, 71, 80, 84,
   101, 118, 132, 223
   allocations 223-228
   verification of 39, 44, 46
Society for Human Resources
   Management...................................463
South Carolina..........271, 278, 283, 424
South Dakota............271, 278, 283, 426
Specialized Skills 115
Substance Abuse Test Consent ....
   ....32, 132, 220
Surveillance.....................................176

T

Taft-Hartley Act...............................172
TelServe 98
Tennessee 40, 271, 279, 283, 427
Termination......................................153
   legitimate reasons for 153
Terms of Employment......................114
Testing Methods........................... 86-95
Texas 271, 279, 283, 431
Title VII of the Civil Rights Act of
   1964.............................. 23, 160-161
Trans Union.................................47, 51

U

UCC Records 457-458
Union Membership....................99, 170
Unsatisfactory Performance.................
   .... 140-141, 148-151
USA Today 95
Utah....................40, 272, 279, 283, 438

V

Vacation 128
Vehicle Records ....
   ....See Motor Vehicle Records
Verification of Educational Background
   .... 39, 44, 67-69
Verification of Past Employment...........
   .... 39, 44, 53-59
   by mail..................................... 56-57
   by phone................................... 53-55
   problems with........................... 57-59
Vermont 40, 272, 279, 283, 439
Vessel Records 457-458

Veteran's Reemployment Rights Act.....
   170
Vietnam Era Veteran's Readjustment
   Assistance Act 164
Virginia................... 272, 279, 283, 440
Voter Registration....................457-458

W

W-4................................ 16, 122, 134
Wages & Hours 169
Walsh-Healey Public Contracts Act ......
   171
WARN.. 170
Washington.. 63, 78, 272, 279, 283, 444
Web Sites...........................93, 463-465
Weight 23
West Virginia.......... 272, 279, 284, 446
Wisconsin 272, 279, 284, 448
Wonderlic 98
Worker Adjustment & Retraining
   Notifications Act......................... 170
Workers' Compensation.......................
   ....172, 182-191, 221, 457-458
   Act 172
   release form 181-182, 221
Working Conditions 113
Working in Groups.................... 96, 109
Workplace Safety & Health............. 169
Wyoming................. 272, 279, 284, 451

Y

You and the Law 27, 90, 460

This is not the way to make headlines!

Top nurse's resume fake, charges say

Leads Forensic Hospital

POLICE REPORT

School custodian faces theft charges in Stafford

STAFFORD: A school custo-
been accused of stealing
red weed trim-
from the
chool, po-

28, of Pat-
ed Tuesday
y valued at
eiving stolen
ering with

ued at $668.
ie custodian's
aid.

ased from Ocean
oms River. yester-
ing $12,000 bail.

Stealing at work reported going up

Judo instructor charged with assaulting boys

UNION CITY: A judo instru-
accused of staging a fight-to-t
death pit bull match in his a
has been charged with assau
two of his former students, p
said.

Norcris Castaneda, 27, of I
Bergen, faces charges of cru
animals, fighting or baitin
nd maintaining a public
fter Saturday night's pol
obukan Dojo, his judo a

He is also awaiting tri
lt charges filed Apri'
— Diego Reyes, th

Teacher charged in sex attack

By CORI ANNE NATOLI
TOMS RIVER BUREAU

A JACKSON TEACHER of 32 years
has been charged with sexually as-
saulting and endangering the welfare of a female student during a
middle school science class.

Christa McAuliffe Middle School
teacher Philip C. Levbarg, 55, was
charged Monday with sexually as-
saulting a girl on two occasions between Dec. 1 and Dec. 2
Churchill

Ex-college official says she stole $1.4 million

MORRISTOWN: The former trea-
surer of Drew University admitted
yesterday that she stole $1.4 mil-
lion in school funds.

Eroilda Torrales took the money
from 1989-96 by using university
credit cards to buy "clothes, furni-
ture, computers, lighting fixtures"
for personal use, said Sgt. Stephen
P. Foley of the Morris County
prosecutor's office.

Torrales, 42, is paying back
about $400,000 by liquidating all of
her and her family's assets, including a house, condominium,
two Mercedes-Benz cars and one
BMW, said her lawyer, Gregg D.
Trautmann.

The sum includes her $160,00
pension from Drew, which auth
ities normally would not be ab
seek, Trautmann said.

☐ *From wire services*

THURSDAY, JULY 23, 1998

BRIEFS

Juvenile officer accused of raping 16-year-old

HACKENSACK: An officer at th
Bergen County Juvenile Detention Center was charged yesterday with raping a 16-year-old
tainee.

Bruce Glaze, 29, of Hacke
was arrested yesterday on
ual assault charge, and held at
Bergen County Jail in lieu of
$25,000 bail.

Glaze, a juvenile detention
cer at the facility, performed
"various acts of sexual penetra-
tion" upon the 16-yee old girl
under his supervi   the Bergen County prosecutor's office
said in a release.

Hospital to release report on embezzlement

CAMDEN: Cooper Hospital/
rsity Medical Center said
it will make public an
detailing how top
millions of

Nanny sentenced for taped abuse

MORRISTOWN (AP) — A
nanny who was videotaped
abusing an infant in her care
was sentenced Friday to four
years in prison for child
endangerment.

Calling the case against
Siobhan Diaz of Randolph
"purely 1990s," state Superior
Court Judge Lewis Weinstein
said he agreed with an ap-

<u>Notes</u>

Send Me A Copy!